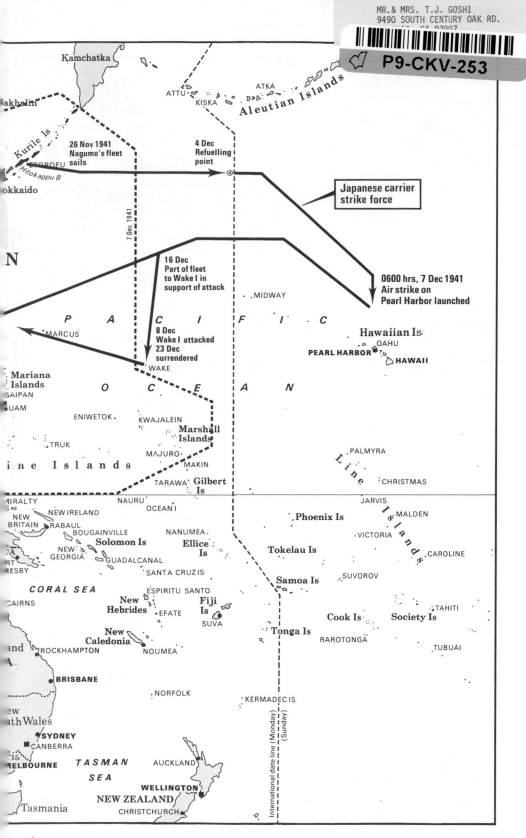

Kamchatka

ATTU ATKA
KISKA Aleutian Islands

Sakhalin

Kurile Is
ETOROFU
Hitokappu B
Hokkaido

26 Nov 1941
Nagumo's fleet
sails

4 Dec
Refuelling
point

Japanese carrier
strike force

7 Dec 1941

N

16 Dec
Part of fleet
to Wake I in
support of attack

MIDWAY

0600 hrs, 7 Dec 1941
Air strike on
Pearl Harbor launched

P   A   C   I   F   I   C

MARCUS

8 Dec
Wake I attacked
23 Dec
surrendered

Hawaiian Is
OAHU
PEARL HARBOR
HAWAII

O   C   E   A   N

Mariana
Islands
SAIPAN
GUAM

WAKE

ENIWETOK
KWAJALEIN

Marshall
Islands

TRUK
MAJURO
MAKIN

ine Islands

TARAWA Gilbert
Is

PALMYRA

Line

CHRISTMAS

MIRALTY
NEW IRELAND
NEW
BRITAIN RABAUL
BOUGAINVILLE
NEW
GEORGIA GUADALCANAL
SANTA CRUZ IS

NAURU
OCEAN I

JARVIS
MALDEN

Phoenix Is

VICTORIA

CAROLINE

Islands

NANUMEA
Solomon Is Ellice
Is

Tokelau Is

Samoa Is

SUVOROV

RESBY

CORAL SEA

CAIRNS

ESPIRITU SANTO
New
Hebrides EFATE

Fiji
Is
SUVA

TAHITI

Cook Is   Society Is

Tonga Is

RAROTONGA

New
Caledonia
ROCKHAMPTON NOUMEA

TUBUAI

and

BRISBANE

NORFOLK

KERMADEC IS

ew
th Wales

SYDNEY
CANBERRA

TASMAN
SEA

AUCKLAND

MELBOURNE

NORFOLK

International date line (Monday)
(Sunday)

Tasmania

WELLINGTON
NEW ZEALAND
CHRISTCHURCH

Books by John Costello

The Pacific War
The Battle of the Atlantic (with Terry Hughes)
Jutland 1916 (with Terry Hughes)
The Concorde Conspiracy (with Terry Hughes)
D-Day (with Warren Tute and Terry Hughes)

THE PACIFIC WAR

THE PACIFIC WAR

John Costello

Rawson, Wade Publishers, Inc.
New York

Copyright © 1981 by Atlantic Communications, Inc.

All rights reserved

Composition by American–Stratford Graphic Services, Inc.
Brattleboro, Vermont

Printed and bound by Fairfield Graphics,
Fairfield, Pennsylvania

Designed by James L. McGuire

Second Printing February 1982

Library of Congress Cataloging in Publication Data

Costello, John.
    The Pacific War.

    Bibliography: p.
    Includes index.
    1. World War, 1939–1945—Pacific Ocean. I. Title.
D767.C67   940.54'26   81-7381
ISBN 0-89256-206-4   AACR2

Grateful acknowledgment is made for permission to quote from the following works:

"Take Up the White Man's Burden" Copyright by Rudyard Kipling from
The Definitive Edition of Kipling's Verse: reprinted by permission of the
National Trust, Eyre Methuen Ltd. and Doubleday & Co., Inc. New York.

Midway: The Battle that Doomed Japan by Mitsuo Fuchida and Masatake
Okumiya, US Naval Institute Press, Annapolis, Maryland, 1955. Copyright
© 1955 the US Naval Institute Annapolis.

Photographs courtesy of the United States National Archives, unless otherwise noted.

Preface

It is now forty years since the Pacific was engulfed by the flames of World War II. The epic scale of those gigantic campaigns has been matched by the outpouring of literature about them. Yet among the many hundreds of books—from the monumental scholarship of Samuel Eliot Morison to the vivid reportage of war correspondents like *Life* magazine's Robert Sherrod and the recent moving memoir of William Manchester—no single comprehensive volume has sought to trace the origins and to chronicle the course of one of mankind's greatest struggles.

That is the objective of this book: to span in a single narrative the century and a half of history that brought the United States, Great Britain, and the other Allied powers to the fatal collision with Japan on December 7, 1941—the "day that will live in infamy." It seeks to render a concise account of the political, economic, and military action of the ensuing war, whose battles were fought across a third of the earth's surface. The fighting in China, Malaya, Burma, the East Indies, the Philippines, New Guinea, the Solomon Islands, and the Aleutians is treated as being among the diverse components of a massive military campaign that ultimately brought about the defeat of Japan despite deep divisions in the Allied command. This book reviews how, after the spectacular initial victories, the Japanese advance was held at the frontier of Australia before the "incredible victory" won at Midway enabled the growing power of the U.S. Navy to mount the largest amphibious operation in history, projecting American forces across the Pacific Island stepping stones to the very shores of Japan.

"Human history," wrote H. G. Wells in 1920, "becomes more and more a race between education and catastrophe." Nothing could better underscore the wisdom of this observation than an examination of the historical forces that caused the Pacific War, whose awesome resolution came through the sinister mushroom clouds over Hiroshima and Nagasaki. Today the world continues to live in fear of the final atomic holocaust, while the missiles of the United States and the Soviet Union threaten incomprehensible destruction. A delicate balance of overkill is justified by each of the superpowers in their determination to avert being taken by surprise by "a nuclear Pearl Harbor."

Yet even for someone of my age, who can recollect but dimly German air raids and the war ending with the radio announcement of "V-J Day," it is not hard to see why most people under forty have consigned the tragedies of Pearl Harbor, Singapore, and Corregidor to a vague period of "recent history" comfortably distanced by the more recent wars fought in Korea and Vietnam. What is important is not only that these conflicts were triggered by a still evolving historical process, but that they occurred on the rim of the world's greatest ocean—an area that cradles the greater part of the world's population and prized natural resources. For over a century this part of the globe has been a focus of international tension and rivalry as Great Britain and the United States competed with Russia, with the other European powers, and then with the rising industrial might of Japan for commercial and military supremacy over China. In the wake of Europe's waning influence, such American leaders as Theodore and Franklin Roosevelt, General Douglas MacArthur and John F. Kennedy pursued a policy of acting in concert with Britain, Australia, and the other Western powers to keep the vast marketplace of the Pacific Rim—above all, China—open to the West. Japan was and remains the key factor in the equation.

To comprehend the scope and causes of the Pacific conflict, it is essential to look back to its origins in the eighteenth century. For the purposes of this book, a review of such complex events has inevitably required the compression of a broad sweep of political, social, and economic history in order to isolate some of the forces that contributed to the war. Moreover, the very vastness of the area of operations—which found American soldiers fighting alongside those from Britain, Australia, China, and Holland —dictates an imbalance in the treatment. It is clear that the American drive across the Pacific actually brought about the downfall of Japan; yet attention has to be paid to the long campaigns of the China-Burma-India theater, which exerted a powerful and continuing influence on the overall Allied strategy. While this was admittedly a "subsidiary" theater of operations, its outcome led to a total realignment of power in Asia, which in turn gave rise to the conflicts in Korea and Indochina.

In presenting a comprehensive and readable account of both the international rivalries and the military record, I trust that my goal of a coherent narrative has not been achieved at the expense of too many omissions and compressions. *The Pacific War* has been written with the unique benefit of new material only very recently made available and released to the National Archives in Washington and the Public Records Office in London. In the final stages of assembling the manuscript, I have had access to over half a million documents, the first part of an extensive archive of the National Security Agency to be opened to research. It will take years for scholars to sift and weigh every piece of this mass of significant data. The secret record of the day-by-day victories and defeats in the intelligence war will undoubtedly change many long-held views of World War II.

While appreciating both the unique advantage and the obligation to be cautious that stem from being one of the first to dig through hitherto closed records, I have been able to include important new evidence in a revised narrative. The most startling conclusions, drawn from this fascinating wealth of material after discussions with prominent historians, I have reserved for a final "After-Action Report." This reveals how Roosevelt and Churchill lost an astonishing gamble: the belief that an American strategic bombing offensive from bases in the Philippines combined with British battleships rushed to the Far East in the late summer of 1941 would deter Japan from going to war. This calculated, yet ultimately inadequate strategy, which reversed twenty years of defensive planning in order to hold the Philippines, can now be seen as possibly the prime cause of the Pearl Harbor disaster.

The Pacific War also sets forth for the first time the steps by which the American codebreakers uncovered the secret Japanese plan to attack Midway, and how ULTRA/MAGIC intelligence made possible General MacArthur's victorious return to the Philippines and the spectacular final British reconquest of Burma. Astonishing new evidence is presented, revealing the extent to which Allied war leaders were privy to Japan's desperate military plight in the summer of 1945. Inevitably this new intelligence must raise fresh doubts about the decision to drop the two atomic bombs.

The Pacific War is intended to be read not just for the insights the new documentation may provide into the successes and blunders of military leaders, but also as a record of impressive valor by the men and women who fought, suffered, and gave "the last full measure of devotion." It recounts, too, the story of spectacular technical and organizational triumphs. Although sadly harnessed to the forces of destruction, such technology provided a new impetus to the postwar world. It is my hope that this attempt to provide a comprehensive account of these complex forces may bring about a clearer understanding of the Pacific War—both for readers who remember those days as part of the fabric of their lives and for those to whom the events are already history and legend belonging to the recent past. I hope, too, that many will be encouraged to discover for themselves some of the hundreds of excellent works that have been of inestimable value to me in preparing this broad general history.

Finally, it is my purpose in writing *The Pacific War* to suggest the terrible price extracted by the catastrophic folly of armed conflict between nations. This book can only serve as an imperfect gesture to the memory of the millions who perished when East and West collided. May their sacrifice not have been in vain, and may this account make some small contribution to our collective enlightenment. Humanity must win its race against catastrophe. The question "Why?" must never again be asked by future generations through another tragic enquiry of war.

London and
New York

John Costello
July 1981

Acknowledgments

In compiling this record of the great confrontation in the Pacific between East and West, I must first acknowledge the contribution that has been made from the works of many historians and war leaders—in addition to those by the men and women who took part, whose accounts make up the vast and still growing body of the published record on World War II. At the same time, I would like to extend my thanks to the many hundreds of Americans who responded to my request for reminiscences of the war, on the home front as well as overseas, and to the newspapers and magazines that carried my recent appeal. So great has been the flood of replies that it has not proved possible to do justice to them in this book; but I intend that many of these individual stories will appear in my next project —a revealing social history of World War II entitled *What We're Fighting For*.

In the course of gathering material for *The Pacific War*, I have benefited from the counsel of distinguished historians and specialists. I am particularly indebted to the advice kindly given by Dr. Forest C. Pogue, Director of the Marshall Foundation and Eisenhower Institute. Admiral Edwin T. Layton, Captain W. J. Holmes, Captain Edward Beach, Ronald Lewin, and other participants provided invaluable firsthand information during the course of the U.S. Naval Institute's 1977 Naval History Symposium. Dr. Dean Allard of the U.S. Navy's Operational Archives gave unfailing help in pinpointing key reports and signals. Dr. David Kahn was generous with advice on the newly released Japanese intercepts, based on his unparalleled knowledge of the history of codebreaking. Dr. William C. Corson and Robert T. Crowley illuminated from their extensive experience valuable details of the intelligence background to Pearl Harbor, which was augmented by information from Captain T. Kimmel and his son Tom Kincaid-Kimmel. Dr. Ruth Harris gave me the benefit of her findings and fresh insight into the MAGIC story, part of which was published in the February 1981 *Pacific Historical Review*.

Archival research is a formidable and often daunting task. Therefore I am particularly indebted to the guidance and assistance I received from the staffs of the National Archives in Washington and the Public Records Office in Kew. It would not have been possible to uncover and include much of the new material still being declassified by the United States National Security Agency without the guidance of John E. Taylor of the Modern Military Branch. His help, together with that of Edward Reese and their assistant Terri Hammnett, processed a small mountain of hitherto top-secret documents. Maria Loescher of the Old Army and Navy Branch was instrumental in directing my research into the voluminous records of the Pearl Harbor Liaison Office and Secretary of War's Safe File. This uncovered significant new evidence that indicates Roosevelt received advance warning of the Japanese war plan. In this context I am also extremely grateful for the interested and efficient help received from the staff of the Franklin D. Roosevelt Memorial Library at Hyde Park, especially Bob Parks and Mrs. Dernier. For allowing me to burrow through the considerable picture resources of the National Archive, my special thanks to Jim Trimble—and to Peter Harris for his exacting photographic work. I would also like to extend my gratitude to William H. Cunliffe for his expert reading of the manuscript and his helpful comments.

The considerable demands made in the course of researching and verifying information for such an extensive study has magnified my respect for the inexhaustible facilities afforded to writers by three of the world's greatest repositories of knowledge: The Library of Congress, The New York Public Library, and the Library of Columbia University. I wish to pay tribute to their inestimable resources as well as to the courteous efficiency of their staff.

Special gratitude must be reserved for my publisher and editor James O'Shea Wade. His unwavering confidence inspired, shaped, and nursed an ambitious project to what I trust will be a rewarding fruition. No small measure of the credit must be accorded to the tireless effort of his assistant editor, Charles G. McCurdy. I am also especially beholden to John Hawkins and the ever-cheerful staff of the Paul Reynolds Literary Agency, who have contributed much to sustaining an author struggling to make New York a second home.

I am particularly indebted to Lawrence Pratt. His unflagging interest and assistance, together with the support that I have received from my American friends, Gerald P. Jantzi, Chauncey W. Smith, and Gary Lazarus, provided essential encouragement—not least of which has been listening to dissertations on the finer points of Allied wartime strategy. To Kenneth Nichols, Jr., I owe a considerable debt for generous logistical support that made possible my extensive research in Washington.

Too frequently the reader is unaware of the enormous contribution given to a book by those who apply their expertise in typing and reworking the manuscript at the various stages of copy editing and proof reading. Therefore it is with special regard that I acknowledge the diligent skill of Judy McCusker, Ann Adelman, and Mary Flower. They have done much to polish my prose and eliminate errors and inconsistencies.

Jim Maguire has designed *The Pacific War* in fine style and once again Richard Natkiel has allowed me to include his definitive cartography. My thanks to them both, along with Brendan Lemon and Eddie Aguila, who put in long hours compiling the notes and the bibliography.

I would like to express my appreciation to Phillip Ziegler, my patient editor at William Collins across the Atlantic—and to Admiral Morgan Giles who, along with Graham Sergeant and David Rowley, provided unstinting support during the first decade of my writing career. Finally, I wish to say thank you to my parents for providing me with the books, education, and inspiration that has laid the foundation for whatever success I may achieve as an author.

Contents

CONTENTS

THE
PACIFIC
WAR

1

Destiny Made Manifest

Take up the White Man's Burden—
Send forth the best ye breed—
Go bind your sons to exile
To serve the captive's need

To wait in heavy harness
On fluttered folks and wild—
Your new caught sullen peoples,
Half devil and half child.

> —Rudyard Kipling's clarion call to Americans to take
> up the imperial cause, made in 1898 after the United
> States annexed the Philippines

The Mediterranean era died with the discovery of
America; the Atlantic era is now at the height of its
development and must soon exhaust the resources at
its command; the Pacific era, destined to be the greatest
of all, is just at its dawn.

> —President Theodore Roosevelt, 1903

On the afternoon of Sunday, December 7, 1941, the President of the
United States was relaxing over his luncheon tray in the White House
study. Conversation with his aide Harry Hopkins touched on matters far
removed from the war that was threatening to draw Americans into Britain's battle against the German U-boats.

Franklin Delano Roosevelt was eating an apple when the telephone
rang on his broad desk. Apologizing for the interruption, the operator
explained that the Secretary of the Navy was making an urgent call.
Hopkins glanced at his watch. It was 1:40 p.m. as he noticed Roosevelt's

stunned expression. Frank Knox's incredible news was that the Navy Department had just received the signal from Hawaii: "AIR RAID PEARL HARBOR THIS IS NOT A DRILL."

The President, out of sheer disbelief, questioned its accuracy, but the Secretary of the Navy was certain there could be no doubt. Roosevelt and Hopkin's astonishment echoed that of the Secretary of the Navy, whose first reaction to the report had been to insist, "This can't be true, this must mean the Philippines?" To American eyes it was strategic madness for a nation no bigger than the State of California to contemplate a fight with the United States. But this had been looming ever since a trade embargo had been imposed that summer to cut Japan off from her vital oil supplies after months of fruitless negotiation had failed to halt her march of aggression in China. Resort to such drastic measures had brought warnings from the U.S. Ambassador in Tokyo that the military dominated government might be prompted to commit "national hara-kiri." To guard against this possibility, twenty years of American strategic planning were reversed with the decision to send reinforcements out across the Pacific to defend the Philippines against invasion. As the build-up got under way, General Douglas MacArthur had been encouraged to believe that not only would he be able to secure the United States Far Eastern territories, but that his fleets of strategic bombers could deter Japan from launching into a Pacific war.

A final effort was being made to negotiate a temporary resolution of the crisis, when on November 26, 1941, the President received startling intelligence that Japan was preparing for war within ten days if her demands were not met. Alerts were flashed out across the Pacific to the U.S. commanders. But an attack on Hawaii was regarded as unlikely since the main Japanese strike was expected to be delivered against the Philippines five thousand miles to the east. Nor had Roosevelt given up hope that his personal plea, sent to the Emperor the previous evening, might stay the blow. That very afternoon the Secretary of State was due to meet with the envoys from Tokyo. But now, as the President observed, the decision had been made for him, and he reached for the telephone to call the heads of the Army and Navy to issue the orders that would effectively send the United States to war.

Within the hour, radio stations from coast to coast interrupted football broadcasts, concerts, and variety shows to bring Americans the electrifying report of the Pearl Harbor attack. People were at first incredulous; then, as continuing news flashes confirmed the destruction that Japanese bombers had inflicted on their Pacific Fleet, national shock turned into collective outrage. Even strident isolationists demanded revenge.

The blow that had fallen on Pearl Harbor was the United States' most shattering defeat; yet, at the same time, it had welded Americans in an extraordinary display of national unity. Across the country soldiers, sailors, and airmen on leave hastened back to their bases, young men flocked to the recruiting stations, and civilians prepared for air raids. In their determination to avenge December 7, 1941, few Americans had occasion to recall that thirty-four years earlier—almost to the week—the United States had been set on a collision course with Japan by F.D.R.'s cousin and predecessor in the White House.

THE BIG STICK

On December 16, 1907, President Theodore Roosevelt had assembled the might of the U.S. Navy for review on Hampton Roads before it sailed to enforce his expanionist policy "to see the United States as the dominant power in the Pacific." It was a blustery Chesapeake day, which set the bunting fluttering as the presidential yacht *Mayflower* steamed slowly between the flanks of sixteen great white-hulled battleships and their escorts anchored in twin columns. Saluting guns boomed and a wintry sun sparkled off gleaming brightwork. Sousa marches echoed across the choppy water over which cordite fumes mingled with clouds of gritty black smoke swirling up from a forest of buff-colored funnels.

"Did you ever see such a fleet on such a day?" Roosevelt proudly exclaimed. One presidential hand was cocked in a stiff salute while the other held onto his top hat, which was being snatched by the breeze. "By George, isn't it magnificent!" he roared. The spectacle of a battle fleet in the heady first decade of the twentieth century not only inspired national pride but proclaimed the state of a nation's industrial and military prestige. An impressive naval force was the prerequisite for any nation that sought a place in the imperial race, and the U.S. Navy's strength, while inferior to that of Great Britain and Germany, was growing steadily. That morning, as America's fleet weighed anchor to steam majestically out of the James River, the President was confident that its circumnavigation of the globe would demonstrate the United States as one of the world's great powers. This display was required by the diplomacy that he characterized as "speaking softly and carrying the 'Big Stick.'" It was to show the flag across the Pacific and underline American resolve to deter Japan, which Roosevelt feared might "get the 'Big Head' and enter into a career of insolence and aggression." He was concerned that Japan's ambitions might not coincide with his plan to prop up the crumbling Chinese empire. The Japanese Navy also represented a potential threat to the security of the Philippines, which the United States had taken over less than a decade earlier, after defeating Spain in a decisive war.

Roosevelt's assertive presidency had already brought America into a tacit alignment with Britain to ensure a balance of power in the Far East, as other European nations vied with Japan for commercial and territorial advantage. Only 120 years after the thirteen colonies had broken away from England, American expansionists, led by the President, were embracing the imperial values of their former adversary with an enthusiasm that would have shocked the founding fathers. George Washington himself had warned against "entangling foreign alliances." But by the end of the nineteenth century, his successors were invoking a doctrine of "Manifest Destiny" to pursue a policy of overseas expansion that many Americans then believed was a divinely granted Anglo-Saxon mission of global supremacy.

The "special relationship," as it was characterized on both sides of the Atlantic, had a particular appeal to the advocates of American expansion and to the British who saw that their nation's power was passing its peak. The foundations of Britain's Empire had been laid in the eighteenth-century wars that defeated France and Spain and assured British control of much of North America as well as the subcontinent of India. Over the next hundred years, the British exploited their unchallenged naval supremacy and their economic advantage as the first industrial nation to send the flag in the wake of world trade. More by accident than design, by the century's end the Union Jack flew over nearly one third of the earth. At her Diamond Jubilee in 1897, Queen Victoria ruled over almost half a billion subjects.

The Victorian notion of a supreme Pax Britannica was tested in the Sudan, South Africa, on the northwest frontier of India, and most severely in the Far East, where Russian, German, and Japanese interests were colliding with those of Britain as well as America. At stake on the Asian mainland and in the Pacific were commercial opportunities believed to be opening up in China. Western investors built railways and developed mines in China as they sought to create a huge new market among millions of Chinese for European and American products.

That the United States had joined the competition for economic advantage, taking sides in the contention between Europe's powers for influence in the western Pacific and on the Asian mainland, was inevitable given the historic attraction of the Orient. Spain had risen to dominance in the sixteenth century by exploiting the riches from the Americas discovered by Columbus, while Britain and France were to compete for control of North America and the Caribbean. The decline of the sugar trade and the loss of the thirteen American colonies resulted in even greater attention being paid by Britain to the exploration of India. By the end of the eighteenth century, the merchants of the new American Republic were also looking across the Pacific to the Orient. They sought a profitable alternative to an Atlantic trade that brought them a poor return on their exports of salt cod and barrel staves, which could not finance the growing demand for imports of the textiles and tools being turned out by England's mills.

The vast expanse of ocean that reached west beyond the largely unknown Pacific shore of the North American continent had just been systematically charted in the decade before independence by a series of Royal Navy expeditions commanded by Captain James Cook. These voyages of exploration added the empty continent of Australia to the Crown, as well as establishing the Sandwich Islands—the name originally given to the Hawaiian group—as essential mid-Pacific ports of call for water and provisioning. The extended voyages were instrumental in opening up the great ocean to practical navigation by showing how lime and citrus juice could prevent the disease of scurvy, which had hitherto made such long sea passages a hazardous undertaking.

Accompanying Cook aboard the *Discovery* on his third voyage was a corporal of Marines, a Yankee adventurer named John Ledyard who was to be mightily impressed by the extravagant prices that Chinese traders paid when they arrived at Canton for sea-otter pelts bartered from Russia. He returned to America fired by the vision of a great commercial venture. Ledyard lobbied his friend Thomas Jefferson to win support for establishing Oriental trade, conceiving of the idea that the "commerce of the east, should, if it were possible, be made common to all powers." The principle of "equal opportunity" was to become the foundation for the notion of an "open door" to China. American merchants realized that the prized furs of seal and otter—along with the sandalwood that was to be gathered free in Hawaiian forests and the "bêche-de-mer" seaslug that was a delicacy of the Mandarin palate and abundant in tropical lagoons—could become the staple of a rich trade with the Chinese. Ledyard was the inspiration, but it was New York bankers who financed the first American vessel to sail round Cape Horn. Early in 1784, the *Empress of China* arrived at the Whampoa anchorage. Lining the banks of the muddy Canton River were the warehouse "factories" through which the Chinese traded teas, silks, and porcelains—exotic luxuries for westerners. The Manchu rulers of China had long confined the contact of their 4,000-year-old Empire with the foreign "barbarians" to the one outlet at Canton. Now the Americans had staked a claim to the rich traffic which had been the preserve of the Europeans. The huge profits realized by the *Empress of China*'s cargo in New York was a powerful stimulant to the merchants and financiers of Baltimore, Philadelphia, and Boston to seek their share of what rapidly proved a new trade route between the West and the Orient.

Britain, whose Royal Navy was the ultimate arbiter of maritime endeavor, regarded the control of the Pacific as less important in securing command over India than the defeat of Napoleon's Nile campaign, which ultimately intended to march east. The leaders of the youthful American Republic foresaw the dangers of competing for England's trade. "Our commerce on the ocean and in other countries or . . . must be paid for by frequent wars," Thomas Jefferson lamented, after the Royal Navy did little to curtail the Barbary Coast pirates who attacked American vessels in the Mediterranean. The third President of the United States was convinced that the Atlantic would always be "a breeder of wars," and he initiated the transcontinental movement westward toward the Pacific shores by engineering the purchase of the Louisiana territories from Napoleon in 1803. Jefferson was even more concerned about the threat posed by large military establishments to republican liberty; he therefore kept the infant U.S. Navy restricted to building only a few squadrons of frigates. While these had proved adequate forces to crush pirates, they were insufficient to support America's assertion of her right, as a neutral, to trade with the French during the Napoleonic Wars. The resulting conflict with Britain in 1812 was a sharp lesson for the U.S. Navy in the realities of seapower. America's "handful of fir-built frigates" won a string of early victories under Stephen Decatur and Oliver H. Perry, but were ultimately to be overwhelmed by the vastly superior Royal Navy.

The final defeat of Napoleon in 1815 ensured British naval supremacy and mercantile predominance throughout the first part of the nineteenth century, when the main energies of the United States were directed to extending American control across the continent. Confident of her mastery over the seas, and with unparalleled industrial productivity, Britain moved toward free trade, which removed what had been a major cause of friction with America. Although still economically tied to England, the United States benefited as British commerce shifted emphasis from the Atlantic trade to the expanding traffic in India and the Far East that promised even larger markets for manufactured goods. The profits from rising exports brought the raw material of five continents into the flourishing factories of Manchester, Birmingham, and Sheffield, where it was manufactured into textiles, tools, and steam engines by machines and furnaces sweated over by men, women, and children. Cotton from America's Southern states played its part in the system of British trade. Confident he could rely on the Royal Navy to police the Atlantic against interference by France and Spain, President James Monroe in 1821 proclaimed the doctrine of "non-interference" by other European powers in the affairs of North and South America.

The "Monroe Doctrine" was to become a uniquely American expression of territorial imperialism and so firmly rooted an element of national policy that by 1845 it was transmuted into what the editor of the *New York Morning News* interpreted as "the fulfillment of our manifest destiny to overspread the continent." The ringing call of "Manifest Destiny" would become more than a convenient moral pretext for war with Spain's former Mexican colony to bring republican liberty to the open spaces west of the Mississippi. Once the military campaign had forced the secession of Mexican California to the United States and the British government had been persuaded to give up a large part of the Oregon Territory in that same year of 1846, Americans had their "windows on the orient" as the spiritual inertia of westward expansion was directed out across the Pacific. The incentive was the extravagant profits of the China trade, which had already made millionaires of the Derby, Delano, and Astor dynasties, feeding the myth of fortunes to be had from what one newspaper called the "harvest which ripens in Asian fields."

American traders were impressed by the ease with which their fellow English-speaking merchant adventurers were benefiting from that harvest, as Britain's commerce advanced steadily eastward from its Indian base until it seemed destined to play a dominant role in China too. The British Empire spanned the globe because more often than not it was the flag that followed to protect British traders or, as in the case of the Cape Colony, to guard a strategic port on the maritime highway to India. Except for Canada, the subcontinent was the only deliberately laid foundation in the rising imperial edifice. The reasons for its foundation were economic, and its architects were the servants of the semi-autonomous East India Company, playing the role of commercial conquistador for Britain. A typical entrepreneur was Sir Stamford Raffles, who in 1819 purchased from the Sultan of Johore an island to establish a trading center off the tip of Malaya. Less far-sighted, the British government was reluctant to accept Singapore. Only when it tapped the trade of the Dutch East Indies was the island's importance realized. By the end of the century, Singapore was one of the Empire's most flourishing commercial centers and, after Hong Kong, the bastion of the Royal Navy in the East.

Had there been a British imperial blueprint, the strategic importance of Singapore's position commanding the sea lanes from India to China and Australia might have been properly appreciated long before the Committee of Imperial Defence decided to turn it into the "Gibraltar of the Far East" in 1921. Although the Pacific and its approaches had been opened up to Britain by Captain Cook, successive governments in London regarded it as too distant, vast, and lacking opportunities for commercial exploitation. Australia was chosen for settling convicts because they could no longer be transported to the American colonies. Only after transplanted Merino sheep flourished and gold was discovered by midcentury was its economic importance to the Empire appreciated as colonization began in earnest. Even then, Australians would not be granted self-governing status until 1901, thirty-four years after Canada had been federated to become a Dominion. New Zealand too had been visited by Cook, but its settlement was left to independent companies and missionaries, who had to wage a long campaign for the British government's recognition as they struggled for control of the land with the native inhabitants. The Maoris, like the Polynesians in Fiji and Tonga to the north, were persuaded to embrace Christ's spiritual kingdom even while they petitioned the British monarch for her temporal protection. This was not granted until the appearance of German warships signaled a new scramble for the Pacific Island territories.

GUNBOAT DIPLOMACY

Even India, always regarded as the most precious jewel in Queen Victoria's crown imperial, came belatedly under direct British government in 1858, after the mutiny had shown the East India Company incapable of managing the territory it had systematically weaned from Mogul rule. For a time it seemed that China herself might be brought under the British Crown by the Empire-building of a ubiquitous company that had made a dependency of the Moslem princely states of Malaya and installed a "White Rajah" to rule in Sarawak on the north coast of Borneo. The resourceful Canton agents of the East India Company had been instrumental in expanding the import of opium that had been pioneered by the Dutch through Macao. As the number of Chinese addicts increased, demand for the narcotic burgeoned and the British obliged with a plentiful supply from Indian poppies. Banned by imperial decree, the traffic was conducted through middlemen and condoned by corrupt Cantonese officials. It brought the East India Company greatly increased trading advantages with which to meet the demands of a fashionable Regency for the import of chinoiserie. By 1835, bootleg opium had become the mainstay of the China trade. Because it was uncontrolled and untaxed, the Emperor was forced to act against the foreign abuse of his authority and the drain on the Imperial treasury.

An intemperate ultimatum was sent to Queen Victoria, promising that unless her subjects desisted in their "insults to a mighty Empire," England would be invaded and "your people pounded into mincemeat." Angered by such preposterous bluster and well aware that British trade would suffer if the opium dealers were forced out of business, Her Majesty's Foreign Secretary was determined to put the Chinese firmly in place with an exercise in "gunboat diplomacy" of the sort that Britain had used to cow the Turks in the Mediterranean. Acting with customary impulsiveness, Lord Palmerston ordered to China sixteen Royal Navy warships escorting twenty-seven troop transports. In a matter of months, Western military arms had crushed the Emperor's armies in what came to be called the First Opium War. Britain's incursions stopped with the

1842 Treaty of Nanking, which granted her extensive trading and extra-territorial rights at Hong Kong, Shanghai, and three other ports. Kow-towing by British subjects to Imperial officials was abolished as the profitable trade in opium continued. Palmerston's forceful diplomacy, by exposing China's weakness, had forced open the door to Western penetration and set an unfortunate example for other nations eager to win similar concessions.

Americans, who had been careful to maintain neutrality during the war, promptly sailed into the newly open treaty ports. Ranking behind Britain as the biggest importers of opium, they had soon taken over the lion's share of the China trade because their sleek black-hulled Yankee clippers outpaced the British sailing vessels and led the race to bring valuable cargoes around Cape Horn to the East Coast and on across the Atlantic to European markets. The 1850s became the Golden Age of U.S. maritime trading in the Pacific. Whalers from Nantucket ranged over its expanse in pursuit of the sperm whale and its precious oil, as the adventure of Pacific voyages, recounted by Richard Henry Dana and Herman Melville, made the American public conscious of the bounty awaiting them across the western ocean. This image and the even greater lure of gold, discovered in California in 1849, brought the first big migration of settlers to the Pacific coast. Trade with China was expanding, adding its powerful incentive to opening the "overland northwest passage" across the United States that promised investors in the transcontinental railroad enormous returns. Thousands of Chinese coolies were indentured as cheap labor to lay the track eastward through the Continental Divide. The symbolic gold spike was driven home in Utah in 1869, linking the Central Pacific with the Union Pacific. The railroad made the West Coast the "bridge to Asia" envisioned by Dana twenty years earlier when he predicted that San Francisco would grow to become "the sole emporium of the new world, the awakened Pacific." That dream was not to be fully realized. In the same year, the Suez Canal was opened, to provide a faster route between Europe and the Far East. This hastened the end of the American clipper trade, already suffering from competition with British steamers.

The pursuit of worldly treasure was not the sole incentive for the eastward march of the British Empire or American expansionists proclaiming their nation's manifest destiny across the Pacific. Britain and now the post-Civil War United States were in an industrial age that promised their societies rising national prosperity, apparently guaranteed by political systems which encouraged the investment of capital and the application of technology to the conversion of natural resources into products for the markets of the world. Anglo-American success in this great endeavor gave rise to a belief that the English countries were destined to impose their political and economic systems on less fortunate nations. This conviction was given added significance by the growing influence of the humanitarian and evangelical movements, which provided the British with the moral impetus for their crusade against slavery. By midcentury there was a widespread belief that Britain's mission was to bring Christianity, order, and civilization to the "lesser breeds without the law." As Lord Palmerston put it: "Our duty—our vocation—is not to enslave but to set free. We stand at the head of moral, social and political civilisation. Our task is to lead the way and direct the march of other nations."

By the second half of the nineteenth century, imperialism had been endowed with moral purpose. "Philanthropy plus 5%" was how it came to be regarded by high-minded British taxpayers, who funded their government's large Navy in the expectation that it would be employed exporting Christianity as well as furthering trade. This reflected the religious revival in Victorian England that led to a frenzy of church and chapel building as missionaries set out for Africa in emulation of Livingstone and to distant islands in the South Seas where they sought to convert the heathens to the ways of God and Western morality.

Preaching that nakedness was a sin required the natives to wear clothes, so creating more demand for the textiles that were staple British exports. On the other side of the Atlantic the New England Missionary Society was also dispatching its high-minded soldiers of Christ across the Pacific to Hawaii. In 1821, the first of the "self-exiled heralds of God" arrived in the native kingdom. Twenty years later, Melville described how they had joined expatriate planters in converting the islands into an American colony "poised between barbarism and civilisation." The moral crusade to save a "Niagara of souls passing into darkness" was a strong incentive to American donations and missions after Britain had levered open the door into China. Congress was urged to support the export of tobacco as a substitute for opium, a grandiose scheme that helped create the myth of a vast potential market for commerce and religion in China, to be shared by American businessmen and missionaries seeking earthly as well as spiritual profit.

Commerce and Christianity had a disastrous impact on China, where the humiliation of defeat by the British had already undermined Manchu authority. The missionaries, in addition to the growing numbers of westerners pursuing trade, aggravated a civil unrest that stemmed from famines and the rampant corruption of Mandarin bureaucrats. Rebellions broke out; in Canton, the nominally Christian Taiping insurrectionists rebelled, advanced north, and took control of Yangtze provinces. For over a decade they defied the Imperial Army. The struggle cost the lives of 25 million peasants, one of the greatest catastrophes that the human race ever inflicted upon itself.

The British, as they had done in India, at first encouraged the weakening of the central rulers' authority. When, in 1854, the Manchus once more attempted to halt the opium trade, Prime Minister Lord Palmerston, vowing to teach the "insolent barbarian" a lesson, predictably sent in the gunboats again. British and French troops occupied Canton and Tientsin; two years later, the Chinese were forced to sign a new treaty, to which the Russians and the United States were also parties. For the first time it established the principle of equal commercial opportunity at the nine more ports that were opened up to trade, permitted Christian missions to proselytize, and established foreign legations at Peking. When the Emperor changed his mind the following year and tried to prevent diplomats from entering Peking, British and French troops were sent to occupy the city and subsequently burned down the Imperial Summer Palace. Manchu rule was on the verge of collapse. Realizing that such an eventuality would disrupt trade, and having little desire to govern China as well as India, the British government in 1860 accepted the Emperor's agreement to legalize opium and other concessions as the price of peace. General Charles Gordon was seconded to assist in the restoration of order. He took over command of the "Ever-Victorious Army," raised by Frederick T. Ward, an American soldier of fortune. Ward had been hired to lead the campaign against the Taiping rebels, and with Gordon's assistance, they were finally crushed in 1864.

The Opium Wars had won Britain her Hong Kong colony as well as control of the rich Yangtze trade. Her dominant position was viewed with increasing unease by American trading houses with interests in China, as British steamships began to displace the Yankee clippers on the Pacific. One missionary-turned-diplomat tried to bring about the annexation of Formosa so that the United States could offset the advantages of Hong Kong by the commercial exploitation of the mainland. The Whig administration of President Millard Fillmore, preoccupied with the divisive issue of slavery that threatened to split the Union, wanted to avoid involvement in Far Eastern disputes. However, it bowed to the pressure of banking and commercial interests worried about America's declining share of the China trade. The government sent an expedition to establish relations with Japan, which had always avoided contact with the West.

The Spanish and Portuguese had made the first efforts to open the door to Japan in the sixteenth century, but these had been frustrated in 1641 when the Tokugawa family came to power and decided that foreign influence was harmful to their rule. Their hereditary leader, the Shōgun, banned firearms and all contact with the West, except for allowing an annual visit by one Dutch trading ship to the southernmost port of Nagasaki. A rigid feudal authority was imposed through the Samurai warrior caste, which was dedicated to the Shōgunate's rule in the name of the semi-divine but powerless Mikado. For two centuries industrious farming and fishing enabled the Japanese to support their medieval social and economic system in self-imposed isolation. Japanese xenophobia was reinforced by the reports of the impact of westerners on China, as well as Russia's periodic efforts to take the Kurile Islands by force and after Japan had rejected the Czar's embassy. The British, who also believed that the "Slav Menace" was the most serious threat to their position in the East, had tried, unsuccessfully, to make a treaty with Japan. The United States had failed after sending the U.S. Navy to rescue shipwrecked whalers imprisoned by the Shōgun.

FRIENDLY MEDIATION

In 1852, Commodore Matthew C. Perry, brother of the hero of the 1812 War, was selected for his forceful bearing and sent out to command the U.S. Navy's East India Squadron. He was charged with the delicate mission of establishing relations with Japan. To the astonishment of the Japanese lining the shore of Edo Bay on the morning of July 6, 1853, four black-hulled warships hove into sight. Amazement turned into panic when they saw smoke pouring from the funnels of two side-wheelers, each with a sloop in tow and their guns run out for action. The thunder of a thirteen-gun salute was Commodore Perry's way of announcing his arrival to a "weak and semi-barbarous people" as he anchored defiantly within sight of the sprawling city of Edo at the head of what would later become Tokyo Bay. President Fillmore had instructed Perry to secure "friendship, commerce, a supply of coal and provisions and protection for our shipwrecked people." Shrewdly assessing the Japanese character, the Commodore, dressed resplendently in his dress uniform, refused to treat with underlings, and made the unheard-of demand of an audience with the Mikado. He threatened to blow the Shōgun's boats from the water when they ordered him to Nagasaki.

Perry was a believer in "manifest destiny"; he saw his mission as "God's purpose," and thought it was his responsibility to "bring a singular and isolated people into the family of nations." His daughter was married into the Belmont banking family, which had invested heavily in the Far East trade, so he was well aware of the commercial importance of opening trade with Japan before "our great maritime rival England" could do so. His show of bravado impressed the Shōgun. After Shinto priests' prayers for a "Kamikaze" had failed to raise the "Divine Wind" to scatter the foreign vessels, as the great storm of 1281 had saved Japan from a Mongol invasion, the Shōgun agreed to a ceremonial acceptance of the casket containing a letter from the President to the Mikado. Perry then sailed away, promising to come back with a stronger fleet. The Japanese were left to reflect on their first lesson in gunboat diplomacy.

"Old Bruin" returned with a more awe-inspiring force of twenty-four ships bearing gifts, including guns, 100 gallons of whiskey, clocks, farm implements, a telegraph, and a small steam train. Intrigued by American technology and impressed by the Commodore's magisterial bearing and warnings about "the Cossack and the Saxon," the Shōgun's delegates agreed to open two ports and receive a consul at Shimoda. The trading treaty had still to be negotiated when the Commodore sailed triumphantly home having brought "a mighty empire into the family of nations" without bloodshed. It was two years before commercial terms were agreed to by Japan in return for Washington's promise to act as "friendly mediators" by extending American good offices "in matters of difference as may arise between the government of Japan and other European nations."

Negotiations dragged on for five more years before the Treaty of Kanagawa was signed; it gave the United States the right to trade through five Japanese ports and establish an embassy at Edo. Nor was it merely an auspicious new chapter of commercial opportunity, Americans were told by Senator William H. Seward, who maintained that the United States was destined to civilize and reform "the constitution, laws, and customs of the land that is greeted by the rising sun." Before this assignment could be taken on, America was thrown into turmoil by the outbreak of the Civil War. So it turned out that the British had the chance to move in and develop the Japanese silk trade; in 1858, Britain signed her treaty at Edo. Just two years had passed since the Crimean War had been fought to block Russian access to the Mediterranean, and British policy was primarily devoted to deterring any southern encroachment on India and China. An insecure Shōgun proved reluctant to extend the full rights of this unequal treaty until the French joined with the Royal Navy in bombarding the port of Kagoshima and fortifications on the Straits of Simonoseki in 1864. As a result, the Shōgunate suffered tremendous loss of face. This hastened the downfall of its reactionary rule as local rebellions erupted into civil war.

The British gave tacit support to a group of young Samurai aristocrats who believed their nation could escape the chaos overtaking China only by embracing Western industrial and military technology and becoming a powerful modern state. The faction's ultimate triumph in the civil war of 1867 brought a new national unity under the boy Emperor Meiji. Their far-sighted leadership continued through the "Genro" council, which restored Imperial rule and set about transforming a feudal society at a pace that would soon astonish the world by its success. A banking system was set up to attract Western investment, and the production and export of silk was made the basis of the Japanese economy. A modern navy was established with British-built warships under the supervision of Royal Navy officers. The Imperial Army was issued its first modern firearms and trained by the French—until they were defeated in the 1871 Franco-Prussian War, when they were quickly replaced by

Russian officers. American missionaries and teachers were allowed to re-form Japan's educational system. Japanese students arriving at Yale and Harvard were soon impressing their hosts by their remarkable application and eagerness to learn Western ways.

When the Americans emerged from their Civil War, they found British advisers helping to shape the policies of the Meiji government and British bankers and merchants regulating Japan's export trade. The volume of Japanese trade was only a small part of the British Empire's total. The British government was therefore not much threatened by the reawakened U.S. diplomacy in the Pacific launched by an expansionist Secretary of State, William Seward. Seward engineered the purchase of Alaska from Russia for $7.2 million despite furious congressional criticism of his "ineffable folly." He then proceeded to annex Midway Island as a coaling station for the U.S. Navy Asiatic Squadron which, in 1867, was sent to Formosa "to protect American interests."

Any temptation for American expansionists to launch a policy of gunboat diplomacy across the Pacific was curtailed by congressional reluctance to sustain a large navy during the Reconstruction immediately following the Civil War. Expansionists, who advocated a policy of for-eign trade based on reciprocal treaties, were also to get short shrift from the protectionist-minded administrations during the Gilded Age that followed. Domestic markets accelerated industrial growth, fed by the railroads, which tapped the nation's wealth of natural resources. Drawing on the labor force created by the inflow of European immigrants, American factories produced a flood of manufactured goods that were soon competing in world markets with Britain, who was now also facing the challenge of Germany, France, and Russia for global markets that had been her exclusive preserve. Japan, too, was trying to find an outlet for her manufactures, and in 1876 borrowed the favorite diplomatic tactic of Western imperialism by sending her warships across the China Sea to demand concessions from the independent kingdom of Korea.

Japan's quest for markets and influence on the mainland was watched with concern by expansionist-minded American politicians, thinkers, and military men. Their own Navy was too weak to intervene: after the Civil War, it had been allowed to shrink to a coastal defense force of fifty ironclad warships that had been rendered obsolete by the big guns and steel hulls of French and British battleships. Similar warships were being built for the Japanese in European shipyards, and the ominous implications for U.S. maritime and naval power in the Pacific were per-suasively expounded by Captain Alfred Thayer Mahan. His service with the Asiatic Squadron had provided him with first-hand evidence of the "almost incredible" state of disrepair and neglect that had overtaken the U.S. Navy. By 1880, the United States lacked both the modern war-ships and adequate coaling bases to protect its interests at a time when the competition for territory and commercial advantage among European powers was centered in the Pacific.

Distinguished for his intellectual ability rather than his seamanship, Mahan was appointed to the newly founded Naval War College in 1884. His ascetic appearance and booming "quarterdeck voice" suited his self-appointed role as prophet of American seapower. "War is not fighting but business," he told young naval officers, lecturing them on the lesson to be drawn from Britain's successful exploitation of maritime power and world trade to become the earth's greatest Empire. Mahan derived from history the principle that seapower was a necessary adjunct to national greatness, not just military but economic. He was constantly to remind the penny-pinching administrations in Washington that a strong Navy was the essential "midwife to commerce."

American expansionists were inspired by Mahan's theories of how the English-speaking people had risen to global dominance. Across the Atlantic, the Empire could be observed at its splendid zenith as Queen Victoria celebrated her Jubilees marking the century's closing decades. Yet behind the pomp and circumstance, the economic foundation of imperial power was slipping away and British political leaders were locked in debate over the future of their Empire.

"We may hold all the ground we have, or its equal, or more; yet America may be the primate nation in world trade," William Ewart Gladstone declared in 1878, two years before he was returned to power at the head of the second of four Liberal governments. He had discerned the root cause of weakness in Britain's ability to sustain her imperial posture. A debate was dividing British political parties and leaders between those Liberals who wanted future expansion through the "informal empire" of trade without control and those Conservatives and breakaway Liberals who believed that it was necessary to impose territorial rule to secure trade. Although the "formal Empire" was to increase in extent during the last two decades of the nineteenth century as Britain competed with the European powers in the race to "partition the world," as Gladstone had foreseen her share of total world trade slumped. It plummeted from over 30 percent in 1875 to less than 18 percent by the turn of the century, when it was overtaken by the soaring industrial production and exports of the United States and Germany.

The outward appearance of great imperial power was nonetheless still maintained by the Royal Navy's global supremacy. The guns of British battleships still defended the Empire's territory, strung out around the globe, connected by steamer routes and submarine telegraph cables. This was the fragile web of communications that enabled a few thousand colonial officials to exercise generally enlightened rule over a third of the earth's peoples.

The very frailty of the bonds of Empire, competing with the United

States and envious European powers out to "partition the world," worried British imperialists like Joseph Chamberlain. A successful Birmingham businessman turned radical politician, Chamberlain led the revolt of a group of Liberals in Gladstone's government, which wanted Home Rule for Ireland. Believing this would start the break-up of the Empire, the Unionists joined with the Conservatives in campaigning for a closer imperial union. Chamberlain felt that America had a unique role to play in securing the Empire's destiny, and he worked hard to achieve it during the six years to 1901 he served as Colonial Secretary.

"We are brothers in the same family," Chamberlain said in 1887 in Toronto, after he had negotiated a settlement of the long-standing dispute with the United States over the border with Canada. He suggested a link that came to be known as the "special relationship" between Anglo-American interests. It became a theme of British foreign policy as "splendid isolation" was abandoned in recognition of the Empire's inability to meet the challenge of both the European powers and the United States. London grew increasingly deferential to Washington; concessions were made in South America over the future Panama Canal and in the Alaskan fisheries dispute, and the Royal Navy was withdrawn from the western Atlantic. This was intended as an earnest of British hopes that the U.S. Navy might one day join in the establishment of a "Pax Anglo-Saxonica" across the globe.

The notion of a shared Anglo-Saxon world mission was fiercely opposed by anti-imperialists in the United States, who sought to remind their countrymen of republican ideals and charged that Mahan was the "advance agent of American imperialism." But the captain's writings were eagerly taken up by expansionist politicians like Senator Albert J. Beveridge, who believed that manifest destiny extended to making America the "trustee under God of the civilization of the world." The gospel of expansionism was preached by evangelists—the most strident was Reverend Josiah Strong, a congregational pastor from Cincinnati, who proclaimed in his 1885 tract *Our Country* that the United States was destined to become the "mighty workshop of the world and our people the hands of destiny." Public fervor was aroused by Strong's bestseller, which justified Americans' special mission because their nation was "the representative of the largest liberty, the purest Christianity and the largest civilization."

Captain Mahan's more earthly rationale was no less inspirational to the business community. "Whether they will or no, Americans must begin to look outward. The growing production of the country demands it," he was to write five years later, reflecting the current belief that the national economy had to expand its overseas markets or face stagnation. This fitted well with the grand geopolitical theories being promulgated by Charles and Brooks Adams, whose writings were attracting a large number of disciples among rising legislators responding to growing populist mood. Among them were Republican Senator Henry Cabot Lodge and the meteorically successful Theodore Roosevelt from New York. Their conception of America's new manifest destiny was colored by their belief that the careers of nations were governed by fashionable Social Darwinistic principles that favored the survival of the fittest. They feared that after a century devoted to expanding west across the continent, America risked a decline in national energy unless reinvigorated by the challenge of conquering the overseas frontier.

THE PACIFIC CHALLENGE

That "new frontier" for the expansionist Republicans lay west across the ocean. There, strategically sited but unannexed Hawaii and the remnants of the Spanish Empire, the Philippines, could provide the bases from which U.S. power could be projected to the Asian mainland. Mahan had drawn up the prospectus for establishing American maritime supremacy in the Pacific; but the incentive for establishing it was provided by the European powers, Russia, and Japan. They seemed intent on carving the "rotting Chinese watermelon" into their own spheres of economic interest.

Debilitated by intrusive British and French pressure as well as repeated rebellions, the Celestial rule of the Ch'ing Dynasty had not yet collapsed only because it was being propped up by Britain and France, who had more to lose than gain if China slid into chaos. Since 1861 the Manchu Empire had been under a septugenarian dowager, a former concubine, who ruled from the tottering Dragon Throne by exploiting xenophobia to offset civil discontent in the provinces. Intrigue, bribery, and murder were the tools of her authority. Instead of modernizing the Chinese armed forces, she spent the funds raised by extortionate levies on her subjects to embellish Imperial palaces. In 1900, the diminutive rouge-cheeked Empress still ruled nominally over the Celestial Empire whose economy was now being undercut by the railway, mining and trading concessions granted to the European powers.

Britain held the dominant share, controlling almost three quarters of the China trade through her Hong Kong colony and the port of Shanghai, from which her gunboats policed the Yangtze and her agents administered the Chinese Customs Service. From her colonial base at Weihaiwei on the tip of the Shantung Peninsula, the Royal Navy battleships kept jealous watch on the Russians across the Yellow Sea at Port Arthur and the Germans who had moved into Tsingtao. The south was the seat of French-controlled Cochin China, the former tributary kingdoms of Cambodia, Laos, and Annam, consolidated in 1887, 1893, and 1898 respectively as the Union of Indochina and now the center of her Far East empire.

Discomfited by the rivalry among European powers for "spheres of influence" on the Asian mainland, the advocates of American expansion across the Pacific were becoming concerned that the exclusionist commercial policies of France and Germany were closing the door to the China trade. This concern turned to alarm when German warships enforced the annexation of the Bismarck, New Guinea, Mariana, Marshall, and Caroline islands—all of which were declared part of the Hohenzollern empire by 1890. Kaiser Wilhelm's aggressive moves to secure a "place in the sun" were being executed by studiously following Mahan's theories. Both the Kaiser and Admiral Alfred von Tirpitz, father of the growing German Navy, were among the captain's most ardent admirers; when Mahan's seminal study *The Influence of Sea Power upon History* was published in 1890, it became required reading for every officer in the Imperial Fleet.

The growing seriousness of the challenge now developing in the Pacific was brought home to Americans when the 1888 dispute over control of the strategic island of Samoa almost erupted into a shooting match between the U.S. Navy and German warships sent to the island. War was averted when a typhoon sank the rival squadrons anchored in Apia Harbor. The Royal Navy's sole cruiser escaped because her captain put the safety of his ship before national prestige. The crisis had exposed the weakness of U.S. maritime power. The Big Navy advocates now implored Congress to fund the construction of a fleet of twenty modern battleships and to annex Hawaii as a Pacific base before the Kaiser seized it. The American planters in control of the islands effected the overthrow of the native queen, a stout, fire-breathing Polynesian nationalist named Lilluokalanni. In 1893 the self-appointed Hawaiian "president," Sanford Dole, petitioned Washington to annex the islands, but incoming Democratic President Grover Cleveland, an avowed anti-imperialist, effectively squashed the bill in Congress.

The Cleveland administration's tacit support of "informal trade imperialism" also stopped short of intervention the following year as U.S. rights under the 1882 trade treaty with Korea were threatened when Japan went to war with China in a bid to turn that tributary state into her exclusive sphere of influence on the mainland. Japan's Prussian-trained troops trounced the Chinese Army, but the intervention of Russia in the peace negotiations blocked Japan's intended annexation of Korea and allowed her control over Formosa instead.

The Japanese entry into the imperial power struggle was noted approvingly by the American press, but it alarmed Mahan. He warned that the appearance of Japan as a strong ambitious state required that the United States immediately increase its naval strength in the Pacific. His advice was not heeded until 1896, when President William McKinley brought the Republican Party back to power and Mahan's followers into office. John Hay became Secretary of State and Theodore Roosevelt Assistant Secretary of the Navy. Pragmatic expansion was the policy of the McKinley administration as these men of strong conviction serving under a weak President looked for the opportunity to take over control of Spain's vulnerable but strategically located colonial possessions in the Caribbean and Pacific. Mahan had already convinced Roosevelt of the necessity for the United States to counter Germany's Pacific ambitions to take over the Philippines as "An American Hong Kong" that could be made the military and commercial base to win a large share of the China trade.

The time was ripe in 1898 when the prospect of war with Spain threatened after the battleship *Maine* blew up in Havana Harbor on February 18. William Randolph Hearst's jingoistic "yellow press" stirred American bellicosity. Roosevelt's chance came two weeks later when the Secretary of the Navy, wearied by the crisis, took the day off. His deputy cabled the Asiatic Squadron orders to concentrate on Hong Kong for "OFFENSIVE OPERATIONS IN THE PHILIPPINES." By anticipating the official declaration of war on Spain by a full month, the Assistant Secretary of the Navy ensured that his favored commander, Commodore George Dewey, would beat the Germans into Manila Bay with his less than formidable force of five light cruisers and gunboats.

"You may fire when you are ready, Mr. Gridley," Dewey told the captain of his flagship, the U.S.S. *Olympia*, just after dawn on May 1 as he led the squadron toward the anchored enemy warships. Two hours later not a single Spanish ship remained afloat. The Philippines were America's for the taking. Theodore Roosevelt was making his personal contribution to the "splendid little war" with the Rough Riders in Cuba when McKinley reluctantly issued the order that made the United States an openly imperial power. "If only old Dewey had just sailed away when he smashed the Spanish Fleet," he was heard to complain on learning that the Filipino guerrilla leader Emilio Aquinaldo looked to the Americans as liberators, "what a lot of trouble he would have saved." The bitter truth of his words would haunt succeeding Presidents for half a century, because McKinley's republican sentiments favoring Philippine independence were overcome by news that a German force had sailed into Manila. American troops were sent to occupy the city and Congress was asked to annex the islands "to fulfill our destinies as a nation."

The Spanish-American War, in which Britain remained officially neutral while giving naval support to the United States, was ended by the 1898 Treaty of Paris, which confirmed that the Stars and Stripes would continue to fly over the Philippines, Guam, and Puerto Rico. The annexation of Hawaii marked the climax of the momentous year in which the policies of the expansionists triumphed and America appeared to have abandoned the policy of "informal empire" to join the imperial ranks. The acquisition of colonies profoundly alarmed American anti-imperialists—but it delighted the British. Joseph Chamberlain, then Colonial Secretary, believed that this new role of the United States held great significance for the Empire and proclaimed it "would help our work." In a letter to *The Times* of London the poet of Empire, Rudyard Kipling, invited America to "Take up the White Man's Burden." "Rather poor poetry, but great good sense for the expansionist point of view," Roosevelt noted approvingly. However, the weight of that burden was felt in casualties suffered by the U.S. Army in the Philippines. Crushing the Aquinaldo guerrillas was a brutal initiation in imperial responsibility that cost 40,000 lives.

The pacification of the Philippines tarnished somewhat the righteousness of U.S. declarations that China must remain a nation open to free trade and commerce. At last Americans heeded Mahan and undertook construction of a powerful fleet that could deploy from Hawaii and the Philippines to rule the western ocean. The Pacific had become "our inland sea," according to Brooks Adams; "our geographical position, our wealth, our energy permit us to enter the development of eastern Asia and reduce it to part of our economic sphere."

The grandiose vision of a potentially vast China market to be opened up across the ocean appeared to answer the prayers of American businessmen struggling out of the severe recession that had afflicted their economy during the early years of the decade when prices and profits had tumbled, labor unrest had grown alarmingly, and the financial community had been shaken by the Panic of 1893. Much of the blame was put on the high tariffs European nations were imposing to keep out America's surplus agricultural and industrial production. "American factories are producing more than the American people can use; American soil is producing more than they can consume," Senator Beveridge had warned in 1897, indicating the solution: "Fate has written our policy for us; the trade of the world shall be ours."

The cause of overseas economic expansion was already being taken up by bankers and industrialists. Led by John Pierpont Morgan and Andrew Carnegie, the America China Development Company had been formed in 1895 to provide the capital and management required to effect a rapid industrialization of that vast country by building railways, sinking coal mines, and constructing steel mills. This was the beginning of the pursuit of an illusory economic mission that would dominate U.S. foreign policy in the Far East for half a century. It took scant account of the preexisting European and Russian interests already funding mines and railways in an effort to turn China into a series of exclusive economic colonies—or of the almost insurmountable problems of investing in a state whose administrative system was crumbling into chaos. Precisely how the 400 million Chinese peasants on the brink of starvation were to be transformed into well-fed consumers of American manufactured goods was not given much consideration in the company prospectus.

It was an omission little heeded by both government and business facing an apparent economic crisis whose magnitude was summed up by the American Bankers' Association in 1898: "Our capacity to produce far exceeds our capacity to consume. The home markets can no longer keep furnaces to blast or looms in action. That capital may earn its increment and labor be employed, enterprise must contend in the markets of the world for the sale of our surplus products." The paramount market, as Brooks Adams was to remind them the following year in his influential analysis *America's Economic Supremacy*, was China. "East Asia is the prize for which all energetic nations are grasping," he contended, pointing out that Britain's Empire was "wearing down" and that America must inherit her role as guarantor of the open door to the Chinese trade in what he believed would be a showdown between Russia and the United States for control of the resources of the Asian mainland.

The British government was indeed feeling the burdens of its responsibilities in the Far East as competition with the European powers increased. That same year the German naval challenge began, and with a war in South Africa against the Dutch Boer settlers, Prime Minister Arthur Balfour's Conservative cabinet decided in 1899 it was "not prepared to undertake the responsibility for governing what is potentially one third China." Since the United States also had a powerful interest in maintaining free trade with these Yangtze provinces, secret discussions took place in London and Washington to make the "special relationship" a more formal alliance in the Far East. Yet even the anglophile U.S. Secretary of State, John Hay, realized that anything that went beyond a publicly admitted "friendly understanding" would be an "impossible dream," given the realities of American politics.

Secretary Hay therefore launched a diplomatic initiative by which he hoped the United States could win the agreement of the rival world powers to keep the principle of an open door in China, regardless of their "spheres of influence," to free trade and investment. Notes were sent out from Washington in the spring of 1899 asking for recognition of the right of free commercial access to China. Anti-expansionist Democrats immediately challenged the policy as "the imperialism of idealism," an intended cloak for the United States to establish economic rather than political hegemony. But, as *The Times* of London accurately observed, opposition was muted because "Even the anti-imperialists welcome an imperial policy which contemplates no conquests but commerce." This was precisely what the Russians feared. The first "Open Door" note was accorded a frosty reception in St. Petersburg because it was seen as part of a deep-laid Anglo-American plot to sabotage the great Manchurian railway scheme through which the Czar hoped to establish control over the mineral-rich province—a view that was confirmed by the enthusiastic welcome the U.S. initiative received from the British government. Joseph Chamberlain called Hay's plan "the noblest of causes" and proposed that now "the

Stars and Stripes and the Union Jack should wave together over an Anglo-Saxon alliance."

Informal and unrecognized though this Pax Anglo-Americana had to remain, its unspoken existence greatly assisted Hay as he pursued his diplomatic offensive. American ambassadors managed to elicit more or less favorable responses from the French and German, which were overstated in order to bluster the Russians into line. In March 1900, Hay successfully pulled off his diplomatic coup by circulating a second note indicating that all the great powers had now accepted the principles set out in the proposal, as well as China's territorial integrity, as "final and definitive." No one called the bluff of this overstatement. It was followed up by a third note confirming the Open Door doctrine, which was not disputed because it was circulated in July 1900 after the outbreak of the Boxer Rebellion, threatening all foreign interests in China.

Circumstance and diplomatic sleight of hand had enabled the United States to establish an important principle of international policy, which, if the Open Door could be upheld, American expansionists believed could secure her economic supremacy in the China markets. Brooks Adams hailed Secretary Hay for effectively "industrializing the Monroe Doctrine" as the principle appeared to have won general acceptance by 1901 when Britain, France, Russia, Germany, and Japan joined with the U.S. Army in a joint military expedition. With secret encouragement by the Empress, the Boxer rebels had laid siege to their Peking legations after sacking missions, tearing up railway track, and lynching westerners in an eruption of violence against the "foreign devils" that spread over northern China. Moving swiftly to protect their common interests, the foreign powers demonstrated a remarkable unity with U.S. policy. But when in June the rebellion had been crushed, the contest for territory and influence recommenced in earnest. The Japanese laid claim to Fukien and sent troops to the offshore island of Amoy; the Russians encroached deeper into Manchuria; and the Germans consolidated their control over the Shantung Peninsular and began moving inland toward the Yangtze.

The British government realized that it would need more than just the informal alliance with America to uphold the Open Door and protect their mutual interests. More soldiers were transferred from India to Shanghai. But by September 1901, the rising German naval challenge caused Lord Selborne, First Lord of the Admiralty, to report that there was "a sound argument for keeping our naval strength in Chinese waters as long as it is compatible with the safety of the Empire." In an attempt to secure the balance of power in the Far East, Britain in 1902 finally abandoned her "splendid isolation" to enter a naval alliance with Japan. The Royal Navy and the Imperial Japanese Navy were mutually pledged to each other's support in the event of attack by Russia, her ally France, or Germany. Confident that this treaty had restored its naval supremacy over the other powers, the British government now began to withdraw warships from the China station. Within two years there were no battleships flying the White Ensign in Far Eastern waters, even though the government of the new Dominion of Australia, moving toward its exclusion of Oriental immigrants, voiced extreme disquiet at resting the main burden of the Empire's defense in the western Pacific on the Japanese Fleet.

It was Russia and Germany, not Japan, that were discerned to be the principal threats to their mutual interests by Prime Minister Arthur Balfour and Theodore Roosevelt, who had become twenty-sixth President of the United States after the assassination in 1901 of William McKinley. The new President quickly decided that the United States would need the military power to intervene to support the Open Door; but without the fleet of forty-eight battleships that had been envisaged by Admiral Dewey's 1903 plan, there was little he could do but resort to diplomacy to try to maintain the balance of power in the Far East. His cherished hope, expressed in the paternal exhortation to the Japanese ambassador that the former protégé across the Pacific must prove herself a "great and civilized nation," was soon to be shaken. Japan was pressing to establish her own sphere of influence on the mainland, and resented Russia carving up Manchuria with extensions to the Trans-Siberian Railway. When a line was built down the Darien Peninsula, Tokyo saw this as a direct threat to Korea and decided to act swiftly.

On February 8, 1904, the Japanese Fleet attacked the Russian Far East Squadron without warning as it lay at anchor in Port Arthur. The Japanese troops that were landed took the port and rapidly established their superiority over the Czar's army by battling their way up the Darien Peninsula to capture Mukden. It was a smartly executed campaign that won the admiration of both the President and the Wall Street bankers who financed Japan's war.

The anti-Slav sentiment of Americans was reinforced by a widespread popular belief that the Japanese were acting in the best interests of the United States. The British Prime Minister, Arthur Balfour, was also pleased to see the humiliation suffered by the Russians: "Japan is never likely to have a Navy sufficient to meet the fleets of the Christian world, who could therefore always cut her off from free communications with the mainland of Asia."

However, the Japanese Navy's triumph over the Russians in the Strait of Tsushima the following May convinced Roosevelt that America's protégé might go too far in upsetting the balance of power. Admiral Heihachiro Togo's destruction of the Czar's Baltic Fleet, which had steamed halfway round the world to avenge the defeat at Port Arthur, dramatically announced Japan's arrival among the ranks of the major powers. Swiftly the President assumed the uncharacteristic role of peacemaker, but was unable to get the British to persuade their ally to come to the peace table although Roosevelt's secret communications with Tokyo revealed that Japan was approaching financial and military exhaustion.

Not until August were delegates of the warring nations on their way to Portsmouth, New Hampshire, after the Czar had been persuaded to make peace by the German Kaiser, who feared that his fellow despot might be toppled by revolution. Roosevelt had also convinced the Japanese that he would be a less than impartial chairman. Although he stayed away from the conference, the President played a role behind the scenes in the negotiations that left Japan in control of the territory she had gained but did not provide the huge indemnity she demanded. America insisted Japan should make this last concession, but it provoked riots in Tokyo, where Roosevelt's name was denounced in the streets.

The President was hailed nonetheless by the European powers for bringing the Russo-Japanese War to an end through a spectacular exercise of personal diplomacy. Yet Roosevelt had achieved this only at the expense of the Open Door policy. The United States, by recognizing Japan's claim to Port Arthur and suzerain rights over Korea, encouraged the formulation of a Japanese Monroe Doctrine toward northern China. Roosevelt had made the sacrifice only because he was anxious to check the potential Russian threat to Anglo-American interests in the rich Yangtze trading area.

THE YELLOW PERIL

For all his public protests that he had "come to love Japan and the Japanese," Roosevelt shared Mahan's fear that the emergence of a major new power in the Pacific rendered it essential to establish American naval supremacy on that ocean—particularly in view of the Royal Navy's ties with the Imperial Navy. Significantly, one of Roosevelt's first actions after the Treaty of Portsmouth had been signed was to send Congress a request for the funds to speed up construction of twenty-eight battleships to ensure that the U.S. Navy could maintain a two-to-one superiority in the Pacific. Britain, relieved that the Russian naval threat had been removed, took the opportunity to extend the term of her treaty with Japan, despite renewed Australian protest, and recalled most of her cruisers to home waters.

Although conflicts between British and American interests in the Far East were evident, the leaders of the two nations continued to see a unity of purpose. "The larger interests of our two nations is the same," President Roosevelt wrote confidentially to King Edward VII, even though U.S. Navy strategists were saying openly that, "of all the powers in the East, the United States will probably clash with none except Japan."

The first hint of that collision came the next year when the "idiots of the California legislature," as the President called them privately, reacted to a growing "yellow peril" hysteria. Resentment on the West Coast had grown steadily against Japanese who flooded in via Hawaii, where they had been earlier welcomed as cheap plantation labor. In an emotionally charged atmosphere after the 1906 earthquake and press headlines claiming: "JAPANESE MENACE AMERICAN WOMEN," the San Francisco City Council called for a halt to immigration and for segregation between Oriental and white children. The Japanese, already insulted by the "White Australia Policy" being enacted by the Canberra government, were outraged at America's attempt to exclude immigrants and again took to the streets of Tokyo protesting the "national insult." Angry diplomatic protests were sent to Washington, insisting that the "evil be removed." The President managed to soothe tempers through a "Gentleman's Agreement" whereby the Japanese government would "voluntarily" restrict emigration.

The United States' first crisis with Japan was over, but it had made the President's "love" for that nation less ardent. Heeding Mahan's repeated warnings, Roosevelt called on Congress for more funds so as to double the rate of battleship construction. To muster public support for those extra millions, he ordered a spectacular fleet review and a circumnavigation by all sixteen of the U.S. Navy's battleships.

"Your cruise is a peaceful one," Roosevelt told Admiral Robley Evans aboard the presidential yacht on that breezy December day in 1907. "But," he was quick to add with a flashing smile, "you realize your responsibilities if it should turn out otherwise." The gout-ridden admiral earnestly hoped that his guns would only fire salutes. The press called the cruise "UNCLE SAM'S GREATEST SHOW ON EARTH," noting with relish that besides magazines stocked with shells, the "Great White Fleet" carried 15,000 pounds of chocolate bonbons, sixty grand pianos and as many barber's chairs, and sufficient white paint to keep hulls in trim for "a feast, a frolic or a fight."

The *New York Times* revealed that the older battleships had been rigged out with wood and canvas "armor." Scare stories about sabotage plots against America's $100 million worth of floating national pride dogged the fleet's unspectacularly slow progress around the coast of the Americas. Rumors that Japan was about to send troops disguised as Mexican peons into Arizona were leaked by German agents. The Kaiser, who had cabled his congratulation to the White House on "the greatest enterprise in the history of any navy," generously offered the services of the High Seas Fleet to protect the East Coast in the event that Britain was dragged into a war by some incident between the Americans and the Japanese.

An underestimation of the battleships' coal consumption, rather than the machinations of the Kaiser or Tokyo's studied delay in issuing an invitation to the Great White Fleet, proved to be the main worry during the eleven-month voyage. The fleet steamed round South America and up to San Francisco before crossing the Pacific, via Hawaii, to Australia. An ecstatic welcome was given by crowds in Sydney, who paraded banners proclaiming: WHITE AUSTRALIA and MONROE DOCTRINE FOR THE PACIFIC. British newspapers expressed chagrin that the new Dominion preferred to look to the U.S. Navy for protection rather than the Royal Navy.

Japan's government, which was in the process of concluding a secret agreement with Russia to partition Manchuria into two spheres of interest, was understandably cool about welcoming the American warships. Diplomatic tension increased until an accord, worked out in Washington between Secretary of State Elihu Root and Ambassador Takahira, produced a formal invitation. On October 18, 1908, after riding out a typhoon, the line of American battleships dropped anchor in Tokyo Bay. Heavy mist shrouded the fleet's arrival, making it less dramatic than Perry's appearance sixty-five years earlier.

"Champagne festivities—in fact the very idyll of Madame Butterfly transmuted to reality," said one of the glowing newspaper reports of the welcoming banquets, balls, and ice-cream receptions complete with 10,000 children chanting "Yankee Doodle Dandy." Even the Emperor Meiji made an unprecedented appearance, and the hero of Tsushima, Admiral Togo, joined in blanket-tossing ritual with American soldiers. One of the young ensigns present, William H. Halsey, was later to write: "If we had known what the future held, we wouldn't have caught him the third time!"

The Japanese had every reason to celebrate. During the junketing in Tokyo, the Root-Takahira accord was signed in Washington. Its publication was tactfully withheld until after the fleet had visited Amoy. Although the agreement acknowledged "the independence and integrity of China and the principle of equal opportunity," it conceded Japan's "special interest" in Manchuria. The U.S. Secretary of War, who had promised that the cruise would be a "powerful force to open the door onto China," was disappointed to find that it had the opposite result.

"Never again will they dare laugh at Uncle Sam," Roosevelt pronounced when he welcomed the fleet safely home next spring. German newspapers, however, observed that America's "Big Stick" was no more coercive than a "palm twig." The cruise brought the Roosevelt presidency to a close. It had been an exercise in realpolitik that temporarily succeeded in deflecting Japanese expansion from the Philippines. Its purpose was to buy the time necessary to build the big U.S. Navy both the President and Mahan believed essential to carry out America's mission in the Pacific.

It was not without significance that in the same year Pearl Harbor in the Hawaiian Islands was chosen as the main Pacific base for the American Fleet. This was a compromise to meet the need for a mid-ocean port from which battleships could be sent to protect the Philippines and also guard the canal the United States was building in Panama. The lessons of Port Arthur weighed heavily in the admirals' calculations; they believed warships in Luzon's Subic Bay could easily be ambushed by a Japanese battle fleet.

President Roosevelt approved the U.S. Navy's decision not to station battleships in the western Pacific because he thought the Great White Fleet's cruise had shown that a fleet could be rapidly deployed to Manila in the event of a crisis. But as Britain was being forced by the German challenge to shift her concerns and her warships from the warm China Sea to the cold swells of the English Channel, the Anglo-American naval presence in the Far East was soon to prove too weak to sustain the China policy. Mahan had warned and Roosevelt foreseen that, in the final analysis, only a powerful military presence would keep the Open Door open. Their successors were to find that when it came to mines and railways, there was no Open Door at all.

2

Scraps of Paper

When Theodore Roosevelt left office in 1909, his grand design, which had been founded on expectations of continuing Anglo-Saxon global dominance, was threatened by the spectacular rise of Japanese military and industrial power in the face of Britain's declining presence in the Far East. Policing the Empire was now taking second place to guarding the British Isles against the dangers posed by the Kaiser's growing High Seas Fleet across the North Sea. The alliance with Japan conveniently allowed the Royal Navy to reduce the size of the Singapore fleet so as to concentrate its battleships in home waters. This situation continued, despite the unhappiness of the Dominions and of the Malay Federation which were providing millions to build new dreadnoughts to match Germany's accelerating naval program.

The enforced British retreat from maritime superiority in the Far East and America's lack of an adequate forward naval base in the Philippines were to give the Japanese *de facto* supremacy in the western Pacific. Roosevelt's ambitious foreign policy had anticipated the construction of a large fleet to allow the United States a two-ocean capability. But the actual building of the Big Navy was a task that his successors inherited, and they found Congress reluctant to provide funds for building the battleships that might spark off a second naval arms race in the Pacific. Yet without the strong fleet necessary to project American power across the ocean, successive administrations still persisted with the policy of trying to impose the Open Door China doctrine on Japan. The lack of the "Big Stick" of military power to back up their diplomatic posturing was to prove a factor that would lead to Pearl Harbor.

The U.S. Navy's hope for a fleet commensurate with its new Pacific commitments was to be rapidly dashed by Roosevelt's successor. As a former Governor of the Philippines, President Howard Taft believed himself an expert on Asian affairs. Declaring "the American dollar can aid suffering humanity," he decided that business rather than battleships could guarantee the U.S. destiny in China. He drafted the virile young giants of American industry—including the mighty House of Morgan, Bethlehem Steel, the Pennsylvania Railroad, and Standard Oil—into the China Consortium. Its mission, to shore up the crumbling Celestial Empire, was directed with evangelical zeal by the State Department professionals of the newly set up Far East Division. They backed the vision of American adventurers like Willard Straight who in 1906 was appointed consul general in Mukden. To him, China was the "new West," and his crusade to use U.S. policy to establish America's economic supremacy on the mainland was part and parcel of what he confessed was "The Great Game of Empire." But while the gunboats of the Far East Squadron successfully advanced the business of the Standard Oil Company up the Yangtze River, the ambitious plans of Straight and the Far Eastern Division came crashing down inland. Through the China Consortium they had tried to neutralize Japanese and Russian influence in Manchuria by bringing their railway lines under international control. Fear of a U.S. commercial monopoly had brought the scheme to nought. Efforts by American bankers to win a quarter share of the line being built by Britain, France, and Germany along the Yangtze was rendered ineffective when the Hukuang loan scheme foundered because of Chinese suspicions and British reluctance to support it.

It was Willard Straight—whose dazzling talent was to take him on to become a partner in the Morgan bank and to found the influential *New Republic* magazine—who predicted the failure of "Dollar Diplomacy" because "the American investor is not willing to buy Chinese bonds, unless the government will protect him by all diplomatic means." To the dismay of the Taft administration, Wall Street preferred to invest its money in Tokyo, thereby encouraging the Japanese efforts to further their expansion on the mainland. In 1911, when the rotten edifice of the Manchu state was finally shaken down, its death throes had already, ironically, been hastened by another young American visionary—a half-blind, hunchbacked Stanford graduate by the name of Homer Lea, who became the unlikely leader for the rebel army. The Chinese General Gordon, as his admirers called him, was one of the architects of the revolution. But he died a year after American-educated Dr. Sun Yat-sen was declared provisional president, in 1911, of a Chinese republic.

It now seemed that the American hope of establishing a republican system on the far side of the Pacific was at hand; yet reality soon dashed these hopes. The new "Republic" was little more than an empty title. Sun Yat-sen's regime in Canton faced the colossal task of establishing its authority over a score of feuding provinces and rival warlords, while the Japanese tried to exploit the breakdown of government to control Manchuria. This struggle for power had been predicted by Homer Lea in his book *The Valor of Ignorance*, which had created a sensation in 1909 by prophesying the decline of Britain's Empire and forecasting an apocalyptic war between the United States and Japan for control of the Pacific. His warnings had raised fresh outbursts of "yellow peril" fear on the West Coast. Lea's strategic evaluation of the Philippines—"Japan's dominion of Asia will be no more than tentative, and her eventual destruction will depend on who holds these islands"—was to become the basis for America's Pacific military strategy until the outbreak of World War II.

WAR PLAN ORANGE (orange was the code for Japan, red for Great Britain, and black for Germany) was finalized by the U.S. Army and Navy planners in 1911. It was based on the assumption that the troops garrisoning the Philippines could hold out against Japanese attack until relieved by the fleet, which would fight its way across the Pacific for a final showdown with the Imperial Navy. Yet from its inception, the plan suffered from a fatal flaw. It would take weeks, possibly months, for the battle fleet to sortie from its West Coast bases and perhaps fight its way across the Pacific—by which time the Japanese could be in control of the Philippines. The steady rise of German naval power was another headache for the admirals after the General Board of the U.S. Navy had failed in 1911 to convince Congress of the need to accelerate battleship construction to complete the 1903 plan for a fleet of forty-eight by 1920.

Such a "Big Navy" was considered a luxury that the penny-pinching politicians of both parties rejected. In 1912 they restricted the laying down of new battleships to one annually. That same year put an idealistic Democrat, Woodrow Wilson, in the White House, who called on Germany and Britain to halt the naval arms race that was spiraling toward war. Elevating principle above practicality, the new administration redoubled its efforts to shape the destiny of civil war–torn China with no more than a small fleet of gunboats to back up diplomacy. "If we had a fleet of battleships ploughing the Pacific; if we had a foreign policy persistent and constant in its nature and supported by the 'big stick,' " complained the U.S. Minister in Peking to the Secretary of State, "the attitude of the nations towards us might be very different. As it is we are helpless."

SPECIAL INTERESTS

Less than a year after the mayor of Tokyo's spectacular gift of cherry trees to Washington, D.C., discriminatory anti-Japanese legislation in California precipitated a new crisis. "AMERICA PREPARES FOR WAR," ran the headlines in Japan, as the U.S. Army began reinforcing the Philippines. Like the cousin who had been his predecessor as Assistant Secretary of the Navy fifteen years earlier, the young Franklin Delano Roosevelt, responding to the urging of the venerable Admiral Mahan, made plans to concentrate the battle fleet in the Pacific. It brought a storm in the cabinet as Wilson vetoed the sending of warships through the Panama Canal as inflammatory. In an attempt to alleviate national tensions, Wilson pressured the California State legislature to drop its bill barring Japanese from owning land. Yet the antagonisms between Washington and Tokyo still smoldered on into August 1914, when the Pacific crisis was overshadowed by the explosion of war in Europe.

The United States remained officially neutral, but the Wilson administration's determination that "Germany shall not be allowed to win this war" underscored the unofficial alliance of Anglo-American interests. However, the "special relationship" was to be strained by events in the Pacific when Japan, with the encouragement of her naval ally, "seized the opportunity of a thousand years" to take over the Kaiser's China base at Tsingtao and pounce on Germany's imperial possessions in the Marshall and Caroline islands. The result in a dramatic shift of the balance of power set the Imperial Navy astride America's sea route to the Philippines. The Japanese government was emboldened to issue "Twenty-One Demands," which defined a greatly expanded sphere of interest to include Shantung, Fukien, South Manchuria, and Inner Mongolia, as well as insisting on placing "advisers" with the Chinese government. The United States led the chorus of protest at this bid by Japan to take advantage of the European war to reverse the Open Door policy and turn China's northern provinces into a vassal state. Only after the strongest pressure from her British ally and President Wilson (who had declared that the United States must be the "champions of the sovereign rights of China") did Tokyo withdraw the demands.

The crisis in the Pacific along with the spreading U-boat war across the Atlantic that in 1915 brought the sinking of the *Lusitania*, finally awoke Congress to the need for American preparedness and the call for building a navy "second to none." That year the Wilson administration authorized the General Board to plan on a 156-ship program to build for the United States "incomparably the greatest navy in the world" within five years. This was cut to three years when the bill was passed in August 1916 in the aftermath of the great clash between the British and German fleets at Jutland two months earlier.

The German failure to defeat the Royal Navy's surface supremacy led to renewed emphasis on submarine warfare. The Kaiser's equivocal reaction to Wilson's attempt to restrict U-boat attacks brought the likelihood of war with Germany nearer; it was to become a reality in April 1917 after President Wilson's reelection. The lack of a two-ocean naval capability ruled out any confrontation with Japan. Wilson proclaimed the reason for America's crusade as "the world must be made safe for democracy," and sent a powerful fleet speeding across the Atlantic to join the Royal Navy at Scapa Flow. An accommodation with Tokyo in these circumstances was a necessity. Hasty diplomatic negotiations conducted in Washington between Secretary of State Robert Lansing and Japan's ambassador Count Ishii resulted in another pious accord. Announced in November 1917, it reaffirmed the "Open Door" but gave American approval to Japan's territorial acquisitions and her "special interests" in China.

This glossing over of the fundamental split between Tokyo and Washington averted a wartime crisis in the Pacific. Japanese insistence on retaining control of the former German areas, the presence of her troops in Siberia (ostensibly to rescue the White Russian army), and the resolve of America's allies to force Carthaginian terms on Germany wrecked President Wilson's hope that the 1919 Versailles Peace Conference could bring universal disarmament under the League of Nations.

Months of wrangling would shred Wilson's utopian Fourteen Point Plan. One of the most divisive issues was Japan's determined pressing of a claim to Shantung in addition to the mandate she wanted from the League to control the Caroline, Marshall, and Mariana islands taken from Germany which Britain had already agreed to support in return for the Imperial Navy's assistance in the Mediterranean during the U-boat war. U.S. opposition to this was in no way alleviated by Australia's mandate to New Guinea, the Bismarck Archipelago, and the Solomons, or the fact that New Zealand would administer the adjacent Gilbert and Ellice group.

Threatened with a walkout that would have wrecked the final stages of the conference, Wilson finally conceded the Japanese demand to remain in control of the Shantung Peninsula in return for a pledge that such occupation was to be temporary. He hoped that he had thereby saved the League, which he believed would be able to hold Japan to her withdrawal and curb what he saw as "Prussian militarism." It was a disastrous sacrifice. American opinion—Wilson had told the Allied leaders—was determined that "China should not be oppressed by Japan." The President sailed home to find that the Republican senators, led by Henry Cabot Lodge, were raising a vociferous campaign against American participation in the League, which the President had unwisely insisted on linking to the peace terms. Felled by a stroke in the middle of a nationwide tour to rally support for the treaty, the ailing President saw the end of his dream of the United States leading the world in collective security. In November 1919 the Senate voted 55 to 39 against ratification of the Versailles Peace Treaty.

The Republican landslide in the next year's elections signaled the finish of "Wilsonian internationalism," although President Warren Harding was careful to include a reminder in his inaugural address to forestall the growing clamor for isolationism. With millions of dollars due in war debts, America had become the world's creditor. Harding's determination to see her "the most eminent of nations with a navy equal to her aspirations" was a reassurance to his supporters in the business community as well as a recognition that the United States was soon to have a fleet supplanting the power of war-exhausted Britain. To the dismay of the Big Navy lobby, the isolationists and disarmers in Congress were busy cutting the huge funds allocated to the big 1916 naval building program. The Navy General Board's insistence on two sixteen-battleship fleets as the minimum needed to "protect our interests in both oceans against any possible combination against us" had already led the Japanese to reply by laying down the keels of eight superdreadnoughts to match the mighty 16-inch-gunned, 40,000-ton monsters being built in America.

Joined by the alliance with Japan, the British government viewed with rising alarm the prospect of being caught up in a naval arms race in the Pacific. The Royal Navy had emerged triumphant from the long struggle with Germany and still nominally supreme at sea. But most of the battle fleet was aging after arduous wartime steaming, and building replacement warships was placing a crippling burden on the economy of a nation financially exhausted by the Great War. "We should be up against the greatest resources in the world," Prime Minister Lloyd George cautioned the Committee of Imperial Defence at its crucial 1921 meeting in London. "No British statesman, therefore, could commit his country to what might be a disastrous rivalry except for the most imperative and convincing reasons." Colonial Secretary Winston Churchill took the view that the alliance would have to be sacrificed because "no more fatal policy could be contemplated than that of basing our naval policy on a possible combination with Japan against the United States."

The Prime Minister shared the concern voiced by other committee members that such a course would inevitably provoke Japanese hostility. He reminded Churchill tartly of "one more fatal policy" whereby Britain would have to rely entirely on the uncertain support of the U.S. Navy. The Canadian Prime Minister saw the alliance as incompatible with retaining the close relationship with the United States, but even the anti-Japanese Australian and New Zealand governments appreciated that it might prove better to antagonize Japan for an uncertain and informal relationship with America. The British government now faced having to make a painful decision about the course of strategic policy with the realization that Washington rather than Whitehall was the ultimate arbiter. Nonetheless, the committee agreed to go ahead with Admiral Sir John Jellicoe's plan for turning Singapore into the great naval bastion for stationing the Royal Navy's third battle fleet, which would stand guard over the sea route from India to Australia and uphold Britain's extensive interests in China.

The public outcry in America grew as the battle between the supporters and opponents of the two-ocean fleet raged on Capitol Hill. However, it was not Congress, the traditional enemy of the U.S. Navy, that was to sink the fleet this time. Secretary of State Charles Evans Hughes, in the spring of 1921, issued an invitation to world naval powers to assemble that fall in Washington to discuss disarmament. He was planning to bargain with the U.S. Navy's huge but still unbuilt naval might to bring about a masterstroke of international diplomacy that would halt the naval arms race and placate the pacifists in Congress. And his chances of pulling the scheme off were increased dramatically that summer as the result of an exploit by Army aviators.

EPITAPH FOR THE BATTLESHIP

At midday on July 21, 1921, eight biplane bombers rumbled at 90 miles an hour over the Virginia Capes. Above them, in a DH-4 fighter trailing a long blue pennant, flew the Assistant Chief of the Army Air Corps, Brigadier General William Mitchell. After months of trying to persuade his superiors and still more reluctant admirals of the potential of airpower, "Billy" Mitchell had been given the chance to demonstrate that the airplane had made the battleship obsolete. As they flew toward the former German dreadnought *Oestfriesland*, wallowing at anchor in the long Atlantic swells, Mitchell knew he must not fail the test: "We had to kill, lay out and bury this great ship."

Watching the bombers peel off one by one to make their attack were the top brass of the U.S. military establishment, foreign military attachés, and the press corps packing the deckrails of the battleship *Pennsylvania*— a floating grandstand anchored a safe distance from the rust-streaked dreadnought.

The tall waterspouts of near misses temporarily hid the *Oestfriesland*. Then great gouts of yellow flame flowered from her superstructure and decks, proving that the hardened steel of Mitchell's specially designed 2,000-pound bombs had penetrated the Krupp armorplate. It took less than half an hour for the hull of the veteran of the 1916 Battle of Jutland to succumb to the air attack and sink stern first. A long mournful wail of ships' sirens saluted her end as the bombers circled in triumph over the debris. Aboard the *Pennsylvania*, the Secretary of the Navy and the admirals gave the appearance of "attending a funeral, as if one of their dearest friends was being buried and they couldn't believe it," as one journalist observed—noting too that it was a general who pronounced the epitaph: "A bomb has been fired that will be heard round the world."

The release of sensational newsreels showing a handful of seemingly flimsy planes dispatching the great battlewagon turned "Billy" Mitchell into a hero overnight to the backers of disarmament in Congress, who demanded why they should go on wasting millions building battleships that could be sunk by an aircraft costing only a few thousand dollars. Captain Mahan's doctrine, however, was to prove harder to sink than the *Oestfriesland*. The sceptical "Gun Club" admirals still refused to believe that airplanes would seriously threaten fleets maneuvering at high speed and protected by antiaircraft guns. Their views were upheld by the September 1921 report of the U.S. Army Navy Joint Board, endorsed by the august signature of Chief of Staff General John "Black Jack" Pershing. "The battleship is still the backbone of the fleet and the nation's defenses," it concluded, much to the anger of Mitchell's supporters. For four more years America's flamboyant apostle of airpower waged a relentless campaign to change his superior's blinkered attitudes—a crusade he continued even after his celebrated court-martial for insubordination in 1925 and subsequent resignation.

But the Japanese military establishment took Mitchell's doctrine of airpower more seriously. The Imperial Navy immediately began intensive studies to learn how to apply the lessons their observers had noted during the *Oestfriesland* sinking. America's Secretary of State had been impressed, too—but perhaps not quite in the way that Billy Mitchell had intended. Charles Evans Hughes, a former Republican presidential candidate who had been only narrowly defeated by Woodrow Wilson in 1916, was preparing to open a new chapter of diplomatic history that would ensure the United States supremacy in the Pacific. After the great airplane versus battleship controversy that summer, it was clear that Congress would never vote the funds required to complete a Navy "second to none."

"We are seeking to establish a Pax Americana maintained not by arms but by mutual respect and good will," Hughes said in July, anticipating that the conference would achieve a far broader purpose than the Naval Limitation objective which the U.S. Senate had just approved. On November 12, with the statesmen and admirals of the world's leading powers assembled in the palm-decorated hall of the Daughters of the American Revolution, Hughes played his powerful hand with a spectacular flourish at the opening day's session. Cheers broke from the press gallery at his announcement that "competition in naval armaments must stop," followed by the breathtaking proposal that this should be achieved by the immediate scrapping of over a million tons of warships. It was a move that caught the politicians by surprise and left the admirals spluttering. Britain's First Sea Lord, the dashing war hero Earl Beatty, appeared "like a bull dog sleeping on a sunny door step who had been probed by the foot of an itinerant soap canvasser."

"Mr. Secretary Hughes sank in thirty-five minutes more ships than all the admirals of the world have destroyed in a cycle of centuries" was how Colonel Repington, the veteran reporter of *The Times* of London, described the impact of that momentous opening day. But by volunteering that America should set the example to other nations in the wholesale scrapping of her mighty fleet, Hughes had ensured the support of the British. Prime Minister Lloyd George had taken pains to reassure worried members of the House of Commons that the Royal Navy was not about to give up its century of maritime supremacy or its guardianship of the Empire's trade routes. The delegation led by former Prime Minister Arthur Balfour had been sent to Washington "to maintain our close friendship and co-operation with Japan" in order to sustain the Open Door and "preclude any competition in naval armaments between the Pacific Powers."

The survival of Britain's alliance with Japan was, however, secondary to Lloyd George's relief at being offered the chance to avoid a ruinous arms race by America's grand gesture of disarmament. Hughes had also cleverly constructed his plan to leave the Royal Navy with a face-saving superiority of twenty-two capital ships to the U.S. Navy's proposed eighteen—although these would be more modern battleships. Already in the throes of an economic crisis and in debt to the U.S. Treasury for multi-million-dollar war loans, the British government overruled the objections of its admirals to indicate willingness to go along with the American plan and also use its influence to persuade the Japanese ally to accept it.

The Tokyo delegation fiercely opposed the attempt being made to cut back its battle fleet to ten, which would leave Japan permanently at a 60 percent inferiority to the navies of the Anglo-Saxon powers because Hughes had called for a ten-year "naval holiday" in capital ship construction. For a month the Japanese held out against the limitation plan, unaware that behind the scenes the U.S. Army's most skilled codebreakers were at work in a secret "Black Chamber" located in New York busily monitoring the confidential cable exchanges with Tokyo. This gave Secretary Hughes the immense advantage of being able to stay ahead of the negotiations because he knew that the Japanese government had already decided to accept his limits if their delegates could not get an improvement on the 3:5:5 ratio demanded by the United States and Britain.

Fittingly, it was left to Britain's last Victorian Prime Minister, Arthur Balfour, to engineer the terms to which the Japanese finally agreed. Limitation was made conditional upon British and American assurances that the status quo would be maintained in the Far East by their promises not to build major bases in Hong Kong, Guam, or Manila. In return, Japan undertook not to station military planes or warships in the mandated islands under her control. Hawaii and Singapore were specifically exempted from this supplementary treaty, which was accepted by Tokyo—after Japan had been conceded the right to finish construction of one more battleship, the *Mutsu*, for which yen had allegedly been collected by Japanese schoolchildren.

The acceptance by France and Italy of a capital ship ratio half that of Japan's made it inevitable that the British government would accede to the Washington Naval Treaty, despite the disquiet of the admirals. By doing so the British signaled another major retreat from imperial power even as it became clear that continuing the Anglo-Japanese naval alliance was incompatible with Hughes's scheme of imposing a "moral" Pax Americana in the Pacific. As Lloyd George had foreseen, Britain was to be left tenuously dependent on the "special relationship" and the U.S. Navy for protecting her interests in the Far East. This became plain when the Committee of Imperial Defence warned that in the event of another European conflict tying down the Home and Mediterranean fleets, the Royal Navy would have no warships to spare from which a Third Fleet could be formed. Hence there would be no fleet to send to Singapore to defend the approaches to Australia, the vital rubber and tin supplied by Malaya, or the immense capital Britain had invested in China. There was no choice but to assume that the United States could be relied on for support.

PAPER TREATIES

Confident that the Naval Limitation and Non Fortification Treaty had established parity in the Pacific, Secretary Hughes made it the foundation on which he began the next round of negotiations to achieve his principal diplomatic goal: to secure the Open Door Policy and preserve China's integrity by restraining Japanese expansion on the mainland. He knew that a weak Britain was ready to cut her ties with the Imperial Navy in return for assurances that Anglo-American economic supremacy would remain dominant. But as the Australian Prime Minister William Hughes had already warned the Imperial Conference meeting that year in London, this economic rivalry underlay the differences with Japan. What he termed "the modern riddle of the Sphinx" had to be resolved. There were no easy solutions because, as he pointed out, Japan "feels her geographical circumstances give her a special right to the China markets. But other countries want the market too, and so comes the demand for the 'Open Door.' " An additional complication was the racial slur felt by the Japanese as a result of his government's "White Australia" policy against Oriental immigration. Conflicting demands were building up that made a clash in the western Pacific inevitable. William Hughes warned: "Talk about disarmament is useless unless the cause of naval armament is removed."

This was the very trap that Secretary Hughes was setting up for himself and his successors. The Washington Conference was not concerned with attempting to reconcile the forces behind Japan's expansionism, only with containing them. The Limitation Treaty on which future American policy in the Far East would be based could only be effective if the United States maintained its fleet to the treaty limits necessary to maintain its five-to-three superiority in the western Pacific. Economic pressures would soon force the U.S. Navy to fall behind—and the status quo shifted against America as the Japanese carefully maintained their fleet strength. After a decade of relative stability, that advantage was to be exploited. Japan's renewed aggressive thrust into China left the Western powers without the military strength or unity to enforce the Open Door.

Hughes's first step was to sever the ties between London and Tokyo, offering Japan, in exchange, a Four Power Treaty with Britain, France, and the United States in which each guaranteed to respect the others' territories and interests. A key part of that diplomatic package required the Japanese to give up their concession to the Shantung Peninsula in a quid pro quo with the British to abandon their base at Weihaiwei, both of which the Chinese government vociferously maintained since the Versailles Conference had been conceded under pressure. The worn rhetoric promising to respect "the sovereignty, the independence and the territorial and administrative integrity of China" was solemnly reiterated again and agreed to by the nations taking part. After twenty years, the Nine Power Treaty finally established Hay's "Open Door" doctrine as a binding commitment on the whole international community. But it was only made acceptable to Tokyo by the inclusion of a proviso that the signatories would ban "action inimical to the security" of national interests in China. Japan was also given confidential assurance by former Secretary of State Elihu Root (the éminence grise behind the drafting of the treaty) that this was intended to be recognition of their extensive railway and industrial interests in Manchuria.

When the Nine Power Treaty was paraded for signature on February 12, 1922, Secretary Hughes delivered a valedictory that summed up the five months of haggling, compromise, and backstairs-dealing as "the greatest step in history to secure the reign of peace." Time would prove that the Washington Treaty system, signed without a word about how it was going to be enforced was in fact worthless. "An international kiss" was how one skeptical U.S. senator unkindly but accurately dismissed Secretary of State Frank Kellogg's later attempt to shore up the paper edifice in 1928 with a treaty outlawing aggression and war.

The outcome of the Washington international conferences did not please the U.S. Navy. The limitation treaty negotiated by Secretary Hughes would have made Mahan turn in his grave. The fleet that was "second to none" had been scrapped and three decades of naval experience ignored. Roosevelt's warning that the Philippines would become America's "Achilles heel" now appeared only too true. Without sufficient warships, the ORANGE War Plan was to remain no more than a comforting fiction. The sole consolation for the admirals was that the hulls of two partly completed battlecruisers had been salvaged from the wholesale scrapping on the slipways. These were scheduled for completion as the big carriers *Lexington* and *Saratoga*, and their speed at long range would later provide practical demonstrations under the command of successive far-sighted officers to develop the tactics of independently operated fast carrier strike forces that would ultimately save the U.S. Navy in the Pacific.

Secretary Hughes promised that the Washington treaties of 1921 would usher in an "era of good feeling in the Far East." The era proved to be less than a decade, during which the U.S. Navy again declined and the economy boomed, as industry turned to producing consumer goods instead of armaments. The Washington treaty system succeeded in ensuring that the door stayed open—if not wide open—to trade and investment in China during the booming twenties as Japan carried out her promise to withdraw from Shantung, and Britain made a stage-by-stage surrender of her extraterritorial concessions in Kwantung, Hankow, and Amoy, in addition to surrendering supervisory control of Chinese trade and customs collections. This was part of continuing Anglo-American efforts to strengthen the authority of the strife-torn Republican government, which continued its struggle to reimpose strong central control over an unruly China torn by Communist factions and semi-independent provincial warlords and governors. The frequent internal upheavals and rebellions gave the Japanese the excuse to retain their Kwantung Army's garrison along the Manchurian railway and their extensive mining operations. Britain also used it as the justification for continuing the Royal Navy's gunboats on the Yangtze and the policing of the international port of Shanghai.

The endemic instability of the Chinese Republic continued to be a disincentive to American investors and bankers, who put their money into the flourishing industries of Japan while the Japanese increased their investment in mineral-rich Manchuria. By the end of the twenties, Tokyo and London shared equal control of 70 percent of all the foreign investment in China compared to the United States' 6 percent stake. After all the trumpeting about the promise of the legendary China market, by 1930 American exports to Japan were running at twice the rate, and this had doubled by mid-decade to make the Japanese their third-largest overseas customer. The United States had by now replaced Britain as the principal market for silk export as Japan became increasingly dependent on American oil and strategic raw material imports. Buoyed by the rising expectations, an increasingly urbanized population became devotees of the Western lifestyle, jazz, and Hollywood films. Massive dollar loans helped finance the rebuilding of Tokyo after the devastating 1923 earthquake, although the Japanese accusation that the interest rates were usurous would cause friction. "Everywhere I go, I hear the opinion expressed that our countries have at last understood one another," U.S. Ambassador Woods reported that year, "that we are united in ties of friendship more strongly than any paper treaty could establish."

The ties were to be strained once again the following year when Congress passed the Natural Origins Act to end mass immigration. Its total ban on immigration by Orientals, while allowing a quota of Europeans, was another reminder, like the White Australia Act, of the Anglo-Saxon nations' racialism. Japan protested about that "racial insult," and her extreme nationalist "patriotic societies," already fearing the erosion of traditional values, called for a boycott on American goods, films, and music. However, they had little impact on a public seemingly enchanted with modeling itself on the celluloid image of a United States that visiting students and Imperial Navy midshipmen found from personal visits was truly a promised land of unbounded plenty and industrial might.

Until the end of the twenties boom, Japan's imperialists were held in check by a succession of moderate governments elected from the majority party in the Diet, and by the country's growing dependence on the U.S. economy. "When Wall Street sneezes, Tokyo catches flu," was the joke often repeated by Japanese businessmen—until they were hit by the financial cataclysm that struck their economy after the American stock market crash in 1929. The value of the yen plummeted, driving Japan off the gold standard. The market for silk, the country's main export, vanished, ruining millions of small farmers who depended on the silkworms for their livelihood. The world slump deepened, while the high tariff barriers erected by the Western nations sheltered their own shrinking industries but dried up the market for Japan's manufactured goods. National discontent grew. The "zaibatsu"—the conglomerate family banking and industrial empires like Mitsui, Mitsubishi, Sumimoto, and Yashuda, which ruled the heights of the Japanese economy—were protested by left-wing groups pressing for agrarian reform and by the growing lines of unemployed. The nationalists in the armed services, chafing under the restrictions of the naval limitation treaty, blamed the Japanese government for conceding too much and becoming too dependent on the United States by failing to exploit the opportunities on the Chinese mainland.

The impact of the Depression was to turn Japan again toward an aggressive expansion of her interests on the Asian mainland, where the Imperial Kwantung Army, guarding the Japanese railways and coal mines in Manchuria, now faced a growing threat posed by Chinese nationalism. Following the death of Sun Yat-sen in 1925, the presidency of the strife-torn Republic had passed to an ambitious young general, Chiang Kai-shek. He proved both a ruthless and an effective leader, undertaking a military campaign to crush the communist faction with which the government had been in uneasy alliance. Determining to bring the provincial warlords under his Nationalist control, Chiang moved the seat of the Kuomintang government from Canton to Nanking on the lower Yangtze in 1927. He then set out with his Kuomintang Army on a "Northern Expedition," reaching Peking the following year. This brought United States recognition of the extension of the Republic's authority as well as increasing support from the Soviet Union.

Washington's open encouragement of Chiang Kai-shek's "anti-imperialist crusade" sent tempers flaring in Tokyo. The United States was charged with breaching the Four Power Treaty because the Kuomintang Army's march northward was seen as a menace to Japan's extensive economic and industrial interests in Manchuria. This roused the concern of the military bureaucracy which the Meiji Constitution had invested with inviolable and supreme control over the navy, army, and national security. The growing division between the moderate civilians in the government and the military leadership was exacerbated during the course of the 1930 London Naval Conference. The ten-year "naval holiday" on capital ship construction was ending and the Imperial Navy wanted to raise its battleship strength by 10 percent. The United States, whose own fleet had been falling behind even the 5:5:3 ratio, was not about to allow the Japanese to gain superiority in the Pacific, and not only resisted but sought to get the capital ship limit extended to cover cruiser construction. The British, who regarded cruisers as the essential warships of imperial defense, had been instrumental in excluding them at Washington and after ten years were no more enthusiastic to concede. But with the Royal Navy under the cost-cutting ax of a Labour government battling to survive the worsening Depression, the British once again sided with the Americans. Although the delegation led by Admiral Kichisaburo Nomura left London with what amounted to a de facto agreement to a 70 percent cruiser ratio, the civilian-dominated cabinet in Tokyo lost face with the armed services by capitulating over their battleship plans. Reaction to what Winston Churchill perceived as yet another example of "the spurning of an Asiatic power by the western world" was swift. A wave of indignant protest swept through the young officer cadres of the Imperial Navy, who charged the politicians with betraying the nation. On November 14 Prime Minister Yuko Hamaguchi was shot at Tokyo Station. Drastic surgery saved his life, but the assassination attempt was followed by a succession of plots hatched by the army and patriotic societies against the Diet.

Democracy in Japan was now facing a severe test. The cabinet of the ailing Hamaguchi was forced out of office in April, but the new Prime Minister, Reijiro Wakatsuki, who had been chief delegate at the recent London Conference, was given a rough passage. It was soon evident that Tokyo had lost control of the headstrong generals of the Kwantung Army as incidents escalated that summer along the Manchurian railway line their troops were guarding. Three years earlier, in pursuit of their goal of turning Manchuria into a satellite state of Japan's, they had dynamited the train of the venerable Marshal Chang Tso-lin, disposing of the Chinese warlord who appeared to be transferring his allegiance to the Nationalist cause. The final stage of their takeover plan went into operation on September 18, 1931, when another explosion on the tracks outside Mukden provided the excuse the Kwantung Army needed to send its troops marching out across Manchuria in pursuit of "Chinese Bandits." As the conquest of Manchuria got under way it was applauded by the rightists, the "Strike North" faction of the army, and influential patriotic groups led by the Cherry Blossom Society. The Wakatsuki cabinet was reduced to cabling the Kwantung generals to "GUARD AGAINST IMPETUOUS ACTS," and fielding the loud chorus of international protest. Recognizing that unless Japan honored her obligations under the Nine Power Pact the whole Washington Treaty system would collapse, Secretary of State Henry Stimson urged that America should take the lead in threatening sanctions: "If we lie down and let them treat them [the treaty system] like scraps of paper, nothing will happen and the future of the peace movement will receive a blow that it will not recover from for a very long time."

President Herbert Hoover, although an old China hand himself, and equally determined to "uphold the moral foundations of international life," feared that sanctions would lead to war. Stimson's proposed oil and trade embargo resembled "sticking pins in tigers" to the President, who was concerned that his Secretary of State was proving "more of a warrior than a diplomat." Nonetheless, Secretary of War Patrick J. Hurley argued that Japan would only respond to force, although Hoover eschewed such action because the "United States had never set out to preserve peace among nations by force," and would give no backing to Britain and France in bringing pressure to bear on the aggressor through the League of Nations. The Manchuria crisis had to be settled through the Nine Power Treaty and the Kellogg Pact, which were "solely moral instruments." Still the President recognized that America must find a way of discharging her treaty obligations through appropriate "moral reprobation" to turn on Japan. By December, Hoover and Stimson concluded that the way out of the dilemma was through the concoction of a declaration inviting the League to join the United States in refusing to recognize "the fruits of aggression." The weakness of this position was self-evident, but Hoover told his cabinet, "Nonrecognition might not prevent aggression, but recognition would give it outright approval."

On January 7, 1932, the United States took the lead with the publication of Stimson's "Nonrecognition" note announcing that no settlement in Manchuria would be recognized that did not conform strictly to terms set out for the Republic of China's territorial integrity that bound the signatories of the Nine Power Treaty. The note—which Hoover believed would be one of the most significant diplomatic papers of the century—was delivered to China and Japan, to be followed by a similar declaration from Britain. (The last, much to the State Department's annoyance, left out reference to territorial integrity and was seen in Tokyo as a tacit recognition by London of special Japanese interests in Manchuria.)

America's moral stance and diplomatic bluff was effectively called on January 28, when the Imperial Navy sent a fleet to Shanghai. Stimson wanted to send in the Asiatic Fleet "to put the situation morally in its place." But such a show of force would have been impossible without the Royal Navy's support and the British government made it clear that it was not prepared to get embroiled while the fleet base at Singapore was incomplete. In any case the President refused even to keep the Pacific Fleet at Hawaii after its mid-February maneuvers as a "Big Stick" threat to Japan. On February 23, five days after the League had formally given its support to the "Nonrecognition doctrine" only to be greeted with renewed Japanese aggression, Stimson responded by publishing an open letter to Senator William E. Borah. This merely reiterated the U.S. position and hinted at a renewal of the naval race in the Pacific in an effort, as the Secretary of State put it, "to encourage China, enlighten the American public, exhort the league, stir up the British and warn Japan."

If it achieved any of these objectives, it failed miserably to deter the Japanese. Moral reprobation, while it satisfied the high-mindedness of Americans like Hoover who wished to condemn aggression but take no risk to halt it, predictably had little effect in Tokyo. The new cabinet under Tsuyoshi Inukai that had followed the December ouster of Wakatsuki by army pressure was walking a precarious tightrope. The seventy-five-year-old Premier, with the Emperor's encouragement, hoped to appease the military by encouraging a de facto mainland state which, through diplomatic bargaining with the Chinese Nationalists, could be brought into being without an outright rupture of the Nine Power Treaty. But without waiting on Tokyo, the Kwantung Army proclaimed the puppet regime of Manchukuo independent in March 1932, and although the Japanese finally withdrew from Shanghai in May, Chiang Kai-shek—with American encouragement—broke off negotiations. The collapse of Inukai's diplomacy precipitated his assassination that same month in an attempted coup led by fanatical army officers of the Cherry Blossom Society who slew one of the leading "zaibatsu," Baron Takuma Dan, head of the Mitsui combine. The sensational trial, in which the insurrectionists appealed to the Emperor to intervene to restore the traditional national harmony of "showa" by ousting Western-style politicians and industrialists, attracted enormous public support and resulted in only light sentences. In response to the new national mood, Prince

Saionji, the last Genro, advised the Emperor to appoint a "whole nation" cabinet under Admiral Makoto Saito. Its subsequent moves to recognize Manchukuo reflected the continued demise of moderate politicians and the ascendancy of the militarists under the threat of "government by assassination."

During the summer of 1932, while Japan moved to consolidate her control over Manchuria, Stimson repeated his call for the "will of the people of the world" to rally to the cause of the Kellogg Pact. The League responded by sending a Commission of inquiry led by Lord Lytton to investigate the situation in Manchuria. The Japanese made little attempt to hide the consolidation of their control of what was now a mainland satellite state even while the League Commission under Lord Lytton was in Manchuria on its fact-finding investigation. Stimson again repeated the U.S. call for the "will of the people of the world" to rally behind the Kellogg Pact and condemn aggression. But the formal Japanese recognition of the Manchukuo regime in September exposed the "international kiss" for what it was—an inspiration to Mussolini and Hitler when they too set Italy and Germany on a course of militaristic aggression. Fascist powers might turn outward on a course of expansive conquest, but the democracies turned inward in response to the impact of the Depression.

In Britain and the United States the dole lines lengthened and the budgets of the armed forces were slashed in an effort to alleviate the deepening economic misery. As American public opinion took refuge in the creed of isolationism, British Chiefs of Staff became increasingly worried about the weakening Anglo-American presence in the Far East and began urging the government to accommodate rather than confront Japan in China. The alternative was to step up an impossibly expensive program to build British military power, based on Singapore; yet as the 1932 meeting of the Committee of Imperial Defence warned: "It would be the height of folly to perpetuate Britain's defenceless state there." Then the war plan was little more than a draft improvisation calling for the withdrawal of British troops from Shanghai and Tientsin to garrison Hong Kong before a Japanese advance. It was hoped that the Crown Colony that was the center of Britain's commercial power could be defended by submarines until a battle fleet could steam out all the way from home waters to Singapore. But even the most optimistic estimate suggested that this would take at least forty-two days—and in common with the U.S. ORANGE War Plan for sending the fleet to Manila, it took little account of the attrition that such an ocean march of battleships would suffer, or how speedily Japan might be able to mount her own offensive.

Defied by the Japanese in Manchuria and defeated by the American electorate in his bid for a second term, President Hoover hoped to leave office with the League of Nations solidly backing the U.S. position over China. The Lytton Commission's report in January 1933 was far from the total condemnation that Washington expected. However, the League's refusal to recognize Manchukuo was enough to precipitate Japan's withdrawal as her Kwantung Army marched southwest toward Peking into Jehol Province and the militarists in Tokyo believed they had now shed themselves of all restraint.

America's consistent refusal to invoke nothing more than words in support of the League and the treaty system her own diplomats had engineered had shown just how toothless and helpless the international community was when it came to upholding and enforcing the fragile framework on which peace rested. A dangerous precedent had been set. "The military themselves and the public through military propaganda are prepared to fight rather than surrender to moral or other pressures from the West," Ambassador Joseph Grew warned from Tokyo. He predicted that a continued pursuit of the nonrecognition doctrine without adequate means or will to enforce it on Japan would "mean that one side or the other would eventually have to eat crow."

It was a precipient and timely warning. But the incoming Democratic administration failed to heed this call for a realistic approach to Far Eastern policy. President-elect Franklin D. Roosevelt had announced in January 1933 that he would continue Hoover's China policy to "uphold the sanctity of international treaties." Faced with the urgent need to implement his promised New Deal so as to stave off the collapse of the American economy, Roosevelt knew he had no choice but to continue putting principle before expediency when it came to dealing with Japan's aggression. There could be no accommodation because of the "deepest sympathy" he felt for China through his Delano ancestors. Yet he was no more prepared than Hoover had been to countenance sanctions or a display of military force in the Pacific. On March 7 he warned the cabinet members at its second meeting to "avoid war with Japan."

Morality rather than reality continued to dominate and add to the dangerous contradiction inherent in America's stand in the Far East. While the British began to shift toward a policy of appeasement to accommodate Japanese expansion in the absence of any positive American move to curb it, the State Department's "old China hands," led by Stanley K. Hornbeck, were equally determined that the "Open Door" was not going to be shut by Japan's imperialist drive. They were to find that it would take more than moral pronouncements to keep it open. The hardliners, against any change in the status quo, found a willing supporter in the Secretary of State. Cordell Hull was a veteran Tennessee lawyer who owed his appointment to his standing among the Southern Democrats rather than to the President's belief that a wiser and more experienced intellect was needed to unravel the tightening knots in American Far Eastern policy.

To Hull's untutored and blinkered perception of international affairs, all problems ultimately devolved into a simplistic issue of trade barriers. This view worked against any attempt by State Department minds less rigidly locked on China than Hornbeck's to deal with the narrow range of choices facing the United States as the Far East crisis worsened in succeeding years. America could make the firm stand against Japan that Hoover had been unwilling to risk; or, as Grew suggested in his letter to the new President, she would withdraw "gracefully and gradually perhaps, but not the less effectively in the long run, permitting our treaty rights to be nullified, the Open Door to be closed, our vested economic interests to be dissolved." Since by 1930 these investments in China totaled less than $200 million while annual exports to Japan were approaching that same figure, there was sound economic justification for following this course.

A century of commitment to the Chinese market made it emotionally and politically unthinkable for Roosevelt to pull out of China. Instead, Grew's alternative, which was to "insist and continue to insist, not aggressively yet none the less firmly, on the maintenance of our legitimate rights and interests in this part of the world," was adopted as the guiding principle of the new administration's Far Eastern policy. This involved encouraging Chinese resistance as the counterforce to Japan's aggression. The course necessitated Hull's early rejection of Chiang Kai-shek's suggestion that the United States act in the role of mediator. Nor was the Secretary of State prepared to act out the role of "mentor to the League" when it was suggested that America take the lead in proposing an arms embargo. Sanctions, Roosevelt believed, would lead to war, and he was no keener to embark on this risk-strewn course than his predecessor. The President made clear to Ambassador William C. Bullitt the following year that force was not an option when he proposed following Theodore Roosevelt's "Big Navy" policy with the advice, "We should speak softly and build three ships to her one."

Japan's withdrawal from the League and the rapid increase of the Imperial Navy's shipbuilding budget heralded the end of naval limitations and with it the collapse of the Washington Treaty system for maintaining the status quo in the Pacific. Ambassador Grew had reported that the Japanese military now looked on America as their principal enemy "because the United States is standing in the way of their nation's expansion." This was a clear warning that Washington's policy of encouraging China's intransigence in refusing to recognize Manchukuo would eventually reach the point where Japan would either have to climb down or escalate an all-out war on the mainland to reach a final resolution of the dispute.

POTOMAC STRATEGY

The warning brought an intensive study in Washington of the ORANGE War Plan. It had been revised many times to take account of the cuts in naval appropriations and by now the time that would be taken for the Pacific Fleet to make its forced march across the ocean made its implementation all but impossible. The Army was way below strength, at less than 100,000, without modern aircraft and tanks. The Navy had fallen short of its treaty strength, and was in need of 30,000 men. Because of economies on maintenance, the fleet could only steam at full speed for four hours. To start construction of twenty-six new warships, Roosevelt resorted to earmarking $250,000 from the National Recovery Program—ostensibly to provide work in the shipyards. Such expenditure would not enable the United States to match the 150 new warships built by Japan in the decade, but the collapse of the 1934 Disarmament Conference (dismissed by Winston Churchill as "a solemn and protracted farce") alarmed enough congressmen to ensure passage of a bill that would lay down the hundred warships and thousand aircraft needed to bring the U.S. Navy up to full treaty limits.

The President faced a public storm stirred up by the "professional pacifists," who accused him of launching a fresh naval arms race. Yet he feared that even with the proposed increase in strength, the U.S. Navy would have to abandon the Philippines. An ominous move was made in April 1934 by the Tokyo Foreign Ministry, which issued a stiff protest against "technical and financial assistance" to China. It was followed by a SECRET AND CONFIDENTIAL report from the Commander of the Asiatic Fleet and General Commanding the Philippines, who warned that the "spectacular rise" of Japan's sea- and airpower had "combined to make the defense of Manila Bay and Corregidor futile with the forces available." This shattering admission that America's Pacific defense plan was a sham came only a month before Congress passed the Tydings-McDuffie Act to make the Philippines independent by 1946. The isolationist-inspired bid to ditch the United States' main base in the Far East undermined the State Department's China policy and destroyed any credibility in the ORANGE War Plan. Notwithstanding, ORANGE remained the cornerstone of the U.S. military strategy because, although the Navy planners were strongly advising withdrawal to Hawaii to defend the eastern Pacific, there was no acceptable alternative.

The fallacies inherent in this brand of "Potomac Strategy" were to dominate the thinking of admirals and generals in Washington until they were uprooted by the bombs falling on Pearl Harbor and the Philippines. Yet the dangers were more than evident by the autumn of 1935. Delegates of the naval powers were due to meet in Britain to discuss what was to be done when the Washington and London limitation treaties expired the following year. Facing a de facto "Pax Japonica" in the Far East unless the Imperial Navy could be held to the old restrictions, the Anglo-American delegations refused to countenance Japan's demand for parity. Since Hitler's Germany had already inveigled British support for a battleship and submarine program, the new Japanese cabinet of Admiral Keisuke Okada, under pressure from the navy, appreciated only too well that its political survival depended on Admiral Isoroku Yamamoto returning from London with an agreement to build a fleet equal in strength to Britain and America. This intransigent position brought about the breakdown of the conference after months of futile discussion. Japan's subsequent abrogation of the Washington Naval Treaty and rapid laying down of new battleships upset the military balance of the entire system of pacts on which the stability of the Pacific region was founded. A large fleet now became essential if Tokyo was to succeed in enforcing its own "Monroe Doctrine" in the Far East—an idea that was formally couched in a proposal sent to Washington for the joint partition of the Pacific so that each nation could define "a reign of law and order in the regions geographically adjacent to their respective countries." Cordell Hull quickly and publicly denounced the plan because it would give Japan what he termed "carte blanche" to deal as she pleased with China. The United States "would not go back on our treaties." But in refusing to abandon the Open Door policy, and without the determination to use force to defend it, by 1935 even the State Department hardliners saw that this would lead Japan into a continuing encroachment in China. By limiting their policy to righteous protests, Americans were simply passing the burden of sustaining their position onto the long-suffering Chinese.

The President's State of the Union message in January 1936 was full of gloom. Japan had walked out of the Naval Limitation talks; Italian troops were marching through Ethiopia and the Nazis had assassinated the Austrian Chancellor, prompting Roosevelt's warning that "many of the old jealousies are being resurrected, old passions aroused, new stirrings for armaments and power in more than one land rear their ugly heads." A month later he was asking Congress for the biggest naval appropriations in history for "prudent" self-defense. A storm of opposition was organized by the isolationists and pacifists. A million signatures were collected by the People's Mandate To End War; 50,000 veterans staged a "March for Peace" in front of the White House; and children organized a classroom strike to demand "schools not battleships." "To hell with Europe and the rest of the nations," roared one senator, summing up the tidal wave of isolationist sentiment that swept across America even as Mussolini was staging his victory parades in Rome, Hitler calling another half million Germans to arms, Japan sending reinforcements to the Kwantung Army garrison in Peking, and a ferocious civil war erupting in Spain. But isolationism dominated Capitol Hill. Senator Gerald Nye's Neutrality Bill passed in August 1936—its purpose to keep the United States in strict international purdah.

CHINESE INCIDENTS

While American pacifists and isolationists were combining to prevent the President from intervening in the growing turmoil that swept around the world, extremists of quite the opposite temper had struck in Japan. On February 26, 1936, a fanatical band of Imperial Army officers seized the War Ministry. The seventy-three-year-old Prime Minister Okada narrowly escaped assassination by hiding in a laundry closet when the rebels burst into his residence, putting two aides to the sword as part of their plot to dispose of "the evil men around the Throne." It was three days before the mutiny was put down, during which their calls on the Emperor to declare the "Showa" restoration attracted a great deal of public sympathy from the fervor whipped up by Shinto-inspired patriotic societies and rightist groups demanding a renewal of national unity.

Hirohito's Genro, Prince Saionji, was instrumental in meeting the crisis by installing Foreign Minister Hirota Koki as Premier. Increasingly hostage to the military faction, the new cabinet resorted to "red ink bonds" to finance an expanded armament program that was soon swallowing up nearly half Japan's annual budget. Deficit financing drained more funds from the small businessmen and farmers, increasing civil discontent as the "zaibatsu" barons whose combines were turning out the new warships, guns, and aircraft became richer and still more unpopular with the left. The right-wing groups continued to promote the expansionist cause and the military faction to such a degree that the threat of "government by assassination" stifled moderate politicians in the Diet. With cabinets increasingly dependent for their survival on the military bureaucracy and moving to the dictates of army policy, Japan was progressing toward a totalitarian Fascist state.

The Kwantung Army had now become the instrument for achieving the goal of national expansion in China as it tightened its grip on Jehol Province. Yet rather than force an immediate showdown with the Nationalist Chinese forces occupying Peking, Tokyo's military leaders—with one eye on the need to increase their preparedness to meet a Russian threat from Siberia—ordered the troops to be ready for operations in the north and to mount a campaign of economic subversion against Chiang

Kai-shek's regime. The German-equipped Kuomintang Army was rife with disputes and rebellions that mirrored the problems of the Nanking government as it continued the struggle to bring China's warring provinces and factions under central control. Pursuing his long vendetta against the Communists appeared to be Chiang Kai-shek's overriding objective in 1935 as Mao Tse-tung led the 8,000 survivors of his Long March north from Kiangsi to their refuge in the hills of Shensi Province. However, in the closing days of 1936, Chiang's refusal to concentrate his forces against the Japanese brought him into conflict with his own generals, who kidnapped him until he agreed to accept an uneasy alliance with Mao Tse-tung. With Russian backing and arms, the Kuomintang and Communist forces now began an all-out campaign of resistance to the Japanese that Stalin rewarded in August 1937 with a non-aggression pact. Tokyo responded by joining Hitler's Anti-Comintern Pact and redoubling the effort to bring about a final resolution of the "China Incident."

The conflict between Japan and China was already smoldering during the summer of 1937 when the effete Prince Fumimaro Konoye was called on by the Emperor for the second time to form an administration after the collapse in June of the previous cabinet. This time the popular leader of Japan's rightists accepted. He was an astute political intriguer, who had championed the cause of the army's "Imperial Way" faction because he shared the belief that it was Japan's destiny to rule the Asian mainland. Three years earlier, during a tour of the United States, he had seen how Americans were "blinded by faith in the matchless superiority of their own brand of democracy," which contributed to their antagonism of Japan's drift toward totalitarianism. But at the same time he had concluded that because business and political leaders he had talked to were disillusioned with the "demonstrated impotency of the League of Nations," the isolationists would block any direct action to uphold the Nine Power Treaty in China by U.S. military force or sanctions.

Only a month after becoming Prime Minister, Konoye was to put this hypothesis to the test when the Sino-Japanese conflict erupted. On the sultry night of July 1, 1937, the "incident" that sparked an all-out war occurred near Peking's historic Marco Polo Bridge. A jittery unit of the Kwantung Army, which had been sent in to guard Japanese interests in the city, opened fire on a nearby Nationalist troop encampment after one of its soldiers suddenly vanished into the dark. It later turned out that he was merely relieving himself, but shots rang out, and in three weeks what had started as another one of hundreds of "incidents" was escalating into a pitched battle between the rival armies south of the old Manchu capital.

"China's sovereign rights cannot be sacrificed, even at the expense of war," the Nationalist government adamantly proclaimed from Nanking, in rejection of Japan's demands for a "fundamental resolution" of the incident and recognition of Manchukuo. On August 14, Chiang Kai-shek dispatched his tiny air force to bomb the Japanese base at Shanghai. The fact that they only succeeded in killing innocent Chinese civilians in no way assuaged Japan's anger. It was an outrageous attack on an international port, Tokyo claimed, and vowed a "war of chastisement." The war minister hurried to the Imperial Palace to promise the Emperor that he would "crush the Chinese in three months." However, the Imperial General Staff were hesitant to embark on a campaign against China of Napoleonic scale—particularly when they believed that the real threat came from Russia, their old enemy. The Tokyo railroad terminals echoed to the exultant "Banzais" of troops eager to be off to join the triumphant march south of the Kwantung Army, which by the autumn had captured Peking and Tientsin while Imperial Navy cruisers and a battleship blockaded Shanghai.

Public opinion in the United States, which had been largely complacent about the savage Civil War raging in Spain, was awakened by newspaper headlines reporting that American missionaries and sailors were being killed in the crossfire in China. National concern that the Asiatic Fleet and 2,300 servicemen were helpless to protect Uncle Sam's interests and lives led to a pacifist call for their prompt evacuation; polls showed this to be the collective wish of nearly half the nation. The President was faced with major political and diplomatic problems as a chorus of international protest was directed at Japan. The United States could not desert China, any more than it could intervene, since neither the Americans nor the British could muster more than a token military or naval force. The President wanted to send aid discreetly to Chiang Kai-shek, before the isolationist press learned that ships were being loaded with bombers for China and the Senate furiously demanded the strict application of the Neutrality Act, which prohibited deliveries of arms to belligerents.

Roosevelt fumed in private frustration at pacifists, isolationists, and "bandit nations" alike. On October 5, 1937, he made an attempt to rally American and international opinion with a call for action deliberately staged in the isolationists' heartland of Chicago. But his appeal for nations to join together to "quarantine" Japan before it was too late to check what he called "the epidemic of world lawlessness" fell on deaf ears. The League of Nations issued its standard condemnations while Japanese soldiers trampled over the Chinese territory that nine nations had solemnly bound themselves to respect. Tokyo continued to insist that the whole affair was only another incident. Ambassador Grew cautioned Washington on the futility of directing "moral thunderbolts" to check the aggression of a nation that could now be stopped only by a concerted stand of the part of the Western powers. Britain, which had the most extensive Chinese interests and lacked the strength to defend them alone, looked to the United States to take the lead by summoning to Washington the nine powers who sixteen years earlier had vowed to uphold China's sovereignty. In the outburst of isolationist withdrawal that gripped Capitol Hill and the press, Roosevelt refused to give American blessing to sanctions. The conference finally assembled in Brussels in November 1937, but its disunity brought little comfort to the Chinese and further alienated the Japanese. In what proved to be the death rattle of the Washington Treaty system, a fusillade of paper bullets was fired off at Tokyo. The scraps of paper were brushed aside by Japan's military leaders, who pressed on with a conflict on the mainland that would determine whether they or the Anglo-Saxon powers were to decide the fate of China and the destiny of the Pacific.

3
Foreign Wars

"Peaceful below us lay the rich valley, the serenity broken only by the bomb-born column of smoke rising from the city of Nanking"—so Lieutenant Masatake Okumiya began the afternoon on which he nearly plunged Japan into a precipitate war with America. On December 12, 1937, his plane was leading a squadron of Imperial Navy bombers hunting for boats carrying Chinese troops fleeing up the Yangtze from besieged Nanking. The main body of Chiang Kai-shek's army had already been evacuated north toward Chunking that morning when the U.S.S. *Panay* left the ancient walled city, towing three Standard Oil barges and carrying the last U.S. Embassy personnel and a party of Western journalists on board. Her twin buff funnels and awning-rigged upperwalls were unmistakably those of the shallow-draft gunboats that plied China's river highway guarding Western commercial interests. Yet neither her appearance nor the outsize flags billowing from her bow and stern staffs would protect the *Panay* from fire from Japanese artillery.

So far, the British gunboat H.M.S. *Ladybird* had been shelled, but the luckier *Panay* had run the gauntlet unscathed and was churning 30 miles upstream when Lieutenant Commander James J. Hughes, radioing his position to Shanghai, judged it safe to anchor his ship. Hands were piped to a leisurely Sunday lunch, which was interrupted at 1:30 p.m. when aircraft were sighted. Lieutenant Okumiya, "wild with joy" that he had found the Chinese craft, was already leading the attack.

"They're letting go bombs, get under cover," yelled Chief Quartermaster Lang. Seconds after the captain reached the pilothouse, it was ripped apart by an explosion. On deck, Universal Newsman Norman Alley instinctively grabbed his movie camera and kept it turning; he was amazed that the pilots, whose faces he could easily make out, persisted in their attack when they could clearly see the American flags. Twenty minutes later two barges were ablaze and the *Panay* sinking in the muddy waters of the Yangtze when Lieutenant Arthur F. Anders, the executive officer, took over command from the injured captain. Speechless from a throat wound, Anders scribbled "Abandon Ship" on a bloody scrap of paper. The final boatload reached the shelter of the reeds as a Japanese launch sped upriver, raking the sinking vessel and the banks with machine-gun bullets. Two American seamen and an Italian journalist died. The survivors' ordeal was to continue for two more days as they struggled through to the Chinese lines, hunted by the Japanese.

The news of the *Panay*'s sinking outraged Americans and brought fears in Tokyo that it might lead to war. The Japanese foreign minister rushed a note of "full and sincere apologies" to the U.S. Embassy. Remembering how the sinking of the U.S.S. *Maine* had precipitated war with Spain, Ambassador Grew was getting ready to pack. His fears proved precipitate. The Japanese government pulled back from the brink of war by acceding to the United States' formal demand for an apology and compensation. Both Washington and Tokyo were anxious to cool the crisis. The President, after viewing the Universal News film, had ordered that it be censored before release to the cinemas, with the close-ups of the pilots removed to make Japan's explanation that her planes had mistaken the *Panay*'s identity convincing. The whole incident was considered closed by Christmas when the Japanese handed over a check for compensation of $2,214,007.36.

The day after the *Panay* was sunk, General Iwane Matsui—a squat figure mounted astride a symbolic white horse—had led his troops into Nanking proclaiming that "the Imperial Way is shining forth." He promised "the dawn of a new renaissance for Asia." But in the next four weeks his soldiers unleashed a barbarous sack of the city, which was pillaged in the misplaced hope that the Nationalists would be stunned into surrender. An estimated quarter of a million Chinese—women and children as well as men—were put to the sword in the Rape of Nanking; systematic butchery that even hardened German Army observers reported that Japan's soldiers were no more than "bestial machinery."

Far from weakening Chiang Kai-shek's resolve, the Nationalist determination to resist became implacable. First-hand accounts of the barbarity from outraged Christian missionaries roused American sympathy for China and condemnation for the inhuman soldiers of Japan. Secretary of State Hull, who had denounced the *Panay* sinking as the work of "wild half-insane army and navy officials," now exploded with moral outrage, but was stayed by his Department's cautious view about intervention. Not so the President. He had revived his quarantine plan after Chief of Naval Operations William D. Leahy brought him the Asiatic Fleet's proposal for joining with the Royal Navy for what its commander, Admiral Harry E. Yarnell, called "a naval war of strangulation against Japan." But with the House then fiercely debating Representative Louis Ludlow's bill to give Congress rather than the President the power to initiate the bill for a declaration of war, Roosevelt moved with extreme caution in making the necessary steps to sound out British support for reviving Big Stick diplomacy to check Japan.

The idea was broached at a confidential session in the White House on December 16, 1937, to the British ambassador, Sir Ronald Lindsay. He reported Roosevelt's suggestion as "the utterance of a hare-brained statesman," a view shared by the British Prime Minister, Neville Chamberlain, who had told his cabinet on October 6, 1937, that "he could not imagine anything more suicidal than to pick a quarrel with Japan at the present moment when the European situation had become so serious." The Foreign Secretary (Secretary of State), Anthony Eden, was a man of sterner fiber. He cabled Washington his interest in backing an "overwhelming display of naval force" that might include as many as nine Royal Navy battleships. To prepare the way, Admiral Leahy sent his Chief of War Plans to London. Although he had his doubts about how seriously the President intended to take the blockade plan, Captain Royal E. Ingersoll's discussions with Captain Tom Phillips, the sympathetic Admiralty Director of Plans, produced a proposal for a joint blockade. A British battle fleet would be sent out to the base at Singapore to shut off the eastern approaches to the Pacific, while the U.S. Navy closed off the western half of the ocean.

The defeat, by one vote, of the Ludlow amendment had encouraged Roosevelt's hopes that joint display of Anglo-Saxon naval might would deter Japan. At the beginning of January 1938, he sent a message to the British Prime Minister asking his support for calling an international conference on China as a preliminary move. The "Record of Conversation" between the U.S. Navy and the Royal Navy was initialed on January 13, 1938. It was rendered pointless on the very same day by a cable from Downing Street to the White House asking the President to "hold his hand for a short while." Chamberlain was about to launch his disastrous policy of appeasement with recognition of Italy's Abyssinian conquests, which required a strong Royal Navy fleet in the Mediterranean to "encourage" Mussolini to respond. There were no warships to be spared for the Far East, leaving the British government with no choice but to try to appease Japan in China after the Chief of Staff had reported in February that they would be "seriously handicapped if forced into war, either in west or east." The Anglo-American blockade scheme was never a serious possibility because the Singapore base could not accommodate a large battle fleet for another two years, and the Admiralty had now revised to over two months the time it would take to send out the warships—if a force were available. Yet that same year's meeting of the Committee of Imperial Defence promised that an "adequate fleet" would be sent east to protect the Dominions. Their most realistic estimate was that only one battleship could be on station by 1942, although the Australian High Commissioner was told there would be seven. The committee had decided too that "the security of Singapore would be the keystone on which the survival of the British Commonwealth of Nations depended." But reality was destined to fall far short of its expectation as the Far East crisis festered.

"PEACE IN OUR TIME"

The moral force of the Pax Americana without adequate naval strength was not sufficient to contain the spreading war in China, and the failure to resolve a united strategy with the British forced the U.S. Joint Board members to recognize that their whole Pacific defense strategy was "unsound in general" because the ORANGE War Plan's premise that the Army garrison could hold the Philippines until the fleet had battled its way across the Pacific was now "wholly inapplicable." The strategists began a radical reappraisal of their planning and the President authorized a billion-dollar Naval Expansion Bill that would raise the Navy's strength by 20 percent over the old treaty limit. When Congress passed the act, the U.S. Navy was set on course toward its goal of achieving a genuine two-ocean capability for the first time, although its immediate objective was to match Japan in the race that was accelerating across the Pacific. Two fast battleships and 40,000 tons of carrier construction were authorized, in addition to funding to bring the number of naval aircraft to nearly 3,000. Only one carrier was actually to be laid down in addition to the three in service and the three building. The Japanese already had six operational and were building more, but in spite of Roosevelt's impatient concern, the Bureau of Ships was still evolving the design of a new fleet of fast carriers, and the first of the *Essex* class would not be approved for two years.

The President shared with a growing number of senior admirals an appreciation of the potential of carrier task forces. Their importance was again to be underscored by the results of that year's fleet exercise, which had been shifted from the Atlantic to the Pacific as another cautionary warning to Japan. In March, the execution of Fleet Problem XIX had given the Navy's leading exponent of naval air operations, Admiral Ernest J. King, a chance to show the still skeptical "Gun Club" how to operate a carrier striking group independent of the battleships. Evading the main force of the fleet in the thick weather fronts northwest of Hawaii, his carrier *Saratoga* swept in undetected to dispatch her aircraft in a surprise mock bombing raid on Pearl Harbor.

The vulnerability to carrier strikes of the United States' base in the mid-Pacific was confirmed in a similar exercise in 1932. However, the danger to Hawaii was overshadowed in the calculations of American strategists by Hitler's march into Austria and demands on Czechoslovakia. Germany's mounting belligerency and growing fleet of battleships and U-boats killed the comfortable assumption that the Royal Navy could be relied on to defend the Atlantic, leaving the U.S. Navy to concentrate its strength on the Pacific.

"We in the Americas are no longer a far away continent, to which the eddies of controversies beyond the seas could bring no interest or harm," Roosevelt warned in August as the European crisis threatened. Congress had already been asked for an additional $300 million for 10,000 aircraft for "national defense." Now the administration looked for ways to effect the defense of the Atlantic hemisphere with the President's "good neighbor" policy in Latin America. Alarming reports of the activities of German business and political infiltration were reaching Washington, indicating that the Monroe Doctrine was under threat. So the fleet exercises were scheduled the next year for the Caribbean, and units were allocated to constitute a permanent Atlantic Squadron, which had been operated only intermittently in the years after World War I.

The turmoil of the Czechoslovakian crisis in the fall of 1938 brought Europe to the brink of war. President Roosevelt could only appeal to Hitler "for the sake of humanity" to reach a peaceful solution over his demands for the Sudetenland. Relief was as great in the United States as in Europe when Chamberlain flew back to London waving his scrap of paper after his disastrous demarche at Munich with the French Premier Édouard Daladier.

"Peace in our time" was a promise that meant little to the Führer and less to Prime Minister Konoye, whose government was committed to an escalation of the campaign in China after the military bureaucracy in November had set up Imperial General Headquarters to manage Japan's undeclared war on the mainland. Oskar Trautmann, the German ambassador to the Nationalists, made little headway in his effort to negotiate a halt to the Sino-Japanese conflict. Although Chiang Kai-shek's army was retreating up the Yangtze, Chiang stubbornly refused to embrace any part of the "Imperial Way" as set out in Tokyo's demands. By January 1938, negotiations were broken off as Japan sent more troops to China and her leaders began preparing to establish another client regime. A further 100,000 men were mobilized to be shipped across to the mainland to join the eight divisions of the "China Expeditionary Force" who were fighting a campaign that was still being officially described as "an incident."

In reality, the Sino-Japanese conflict had already blossomed into a full-scale war, and during the summer of 1938 Japan became the first nation to mobilize. Strict controls were clamped on industry and gasoline rationing was introduced along with a strict press censorship exercised by the Home Ministry's ruthless secret police force. Military drills were made a compulsory part of the school curriculum, rice became scarce, and veneration for the Emperor was encouraged. Passengers in streetcars were expected to doff their hats when passing the Imperial Palace; later, drivers would stop so that everyone could bow in solemn respect. Printed government publications exhorted the nation to "Spiritual Mobilization" and "self-sacrifice" for the coming crusade to "Liberate Asia from Imperialism."

The Japanese leaders, by the end of the year, had successfully exploited the "China Incident" to stifle democracy and turn Japan into a Far Eastern version of a Fascist state, with decrees that "conduct contrary to the interests of the nations must be eradicated." While the army and navy were agreed in rapidly arming for a war of national territorial expansion, they quarreled over which parts of Asia should be "liberated." The Japanese Navy believed that the nation's imperial destiny would be fulfilled by a southward march to take over the rich British, Dutch, and French colonies in the Far East. The Army High Command favored striking north against their traditional Russian enemy in Siberia as an alternative to dragging out the increasingly costly campaign to finish off the "China Incident."

Now it was the turn of the officers of Japan's Korean Army, who took it upon themselves to give their own impetus to the "Strike North" strategy. On July 29, they defied orders from Tokyo to overrun Soviet frontier posts at Lake Kashan, where Siberia bordered Manchuria and Korea. Fearing for the security of its Pacific port of Vladivostok less than 60 miles away, the Red Army spared no punches and counterattacked in force with tanks and aircraft. Lacking armor and planes, the Japanese were speedily sent packing back across the frontier in a bloody retreat; the fighting was brought to a halt with a border truce on September 11, 1939.

The Korean Army's humiliating defeat was offset by the victories won by the soldiers of the China Expeditionary Force, which with the autumn occupation of Wuhan and Canton controlled all the ports and the five principal cities. Britain had attempted to reopen negotiations to end the Sino-Japanese War, hoping to bring about a settlement that would ensure protection for her own threatened interests. Tokyo demanded that the fighting go on until America ceased encouraging the Chinese Nationalists and recognized Manchukuo. But the United States maintained its steadfast refusal to agree to any such infringement of the Open Door or Nine Power Treaty, and the peace moves again failed. In November, the defection of the Nationalist leader Wang Cheng-wei provided the Japanese with the leader they needed to prepare for an alternative Chinese government in Nanking. But as long as America continued to support Chiang Kai-shek and the Soviet Union sent arms to Mao Tse-tung's guerrilla army, Imperial General Headquarters in Tokyo realized that it must either accept a victorious stalemate or commit more forces to a military campaign to subdue the rest of China. To find an alternative way out of this dilemma, Prime Minister Prince Konoye on November 11 proclaimed "a new order in East Asia" to save China from her traditional fate as the "victim of the imperialistic ambitions of the occidental powers."

NEW ORDER FOR ASIA

After launching Japan on her crusade to "liberate" Asia, the Konoye cabinet resigned in January 1939, leaving the new government of Prime Minister Kiichiro Hiranuma to resolve the dispute between the army and navy over whether or not Japan should cast in her lot with Germany by joining the Axis in a Tripartite Pact. The navy minister and his deputy, Vice Admiral Isoroku Yamamoto, protested that such an alignment would bring open conflict with the United States, along with possible oil and trade sanctions. Their opposition effectively blocked the alliance Hitler wanted as he propelled Germany relentlessly toward war with his escalating demands on Poland.

Tokyo's protestation that her government intended "no territorial ambitions" had a familiar ring. It did not need this declaration to make Japan's blueprint for the "New Order" in Asia appear the same as the Führer's design for a New Order in Europe. It was dismissed by Chiang Kai-shek and by Washington with American refusal to consider any infringement of the Nine Power Treaty. Roosevelt promptly announced a $25 million loan to the Chungking government to carry on the war. Atrocity reports echoing the horrors of Nanking continued on the front pages of newspapers; Henry Luce's championship of the Nationalist cause in *Time* magazine stirred the public, already influenced by the words of Pearl S. Buck.

The President, alarmed by the clouds of war gathering across the Atlantic in the spring of 1939, sought to avoid the risk of opening up a conflict in the Pacific. In addition to isolationist pressures, the powerful if less vocal weight of the business community was against it. Big profits were being made from the oil, textile, machinery, and strategic material exports that were feeding the Japanese war machine. Only when the new, military-dominated cabinet under Prime Minister Hiranuma took office in January was the wisdom of doing nothing questioned as Imperial troops were landed on Hainan and the Spratlys. Seizing these offshore islands gave Japan a jumping-off base from which to attack the Philippines as well as Hong Kong and Indochina.

The mounting tension in Europe precluded any British attempt to confront Japan, and the British government hoped that the United States would respond by sending its fleet into the Pacific. Meanwhile the leaders in London sought to reassure Australians that they "would not abdicate our position in the Far East," and that the Foreign Office assumed "any Japanese threat to Australia and New Zealand, whether by descent upon them or indirectly in the form of an expedition to Singapore, would be a matter to which the United States could hardly remain for long indifferent." Just how indifferent and for how long was a matter of immediate concern for the Australian Prime Minister. "What Britain calls the Far East is to us the Near North," Robert Menzies told the Canberra Parliament in May, announcing that delegates had been sent to Washington to explore the American administration's attitudes "to aggressive moves by Japan in the Pacific, particularly in the event of Britain at the time being involved with Germany and Italy and unable to send the necessary naval forces to the Pacific to contain Japan."

The Australian mission, led by Richard E. (later Lord) Casey, were disturbed to find that the British Foreign Office was too optimistic in believing America could be relied on to defend the western Pacific. The isolationist tide was running strongly against standing up to Japanese aggression, and the State Department worried about the dangers that imposing sanctions would provoke. Roosevelt's limited response in January to the worsening situation in China was to call for a voluntary embargo of aircraft parts to Japan, followed the next month by the cessation of export credits. The failure of such moral efforts to control aggression was given its dramatic proof in March 1939, when German troops marched into Czechoslovakia, effectively trampling underfoot the six-month-old Munich agreement. Appalled, the governments of Britain and France stepped up their arms orders in the United States in preparation for the inevitable clash with Hitler.

The British Chiefs of Staff, by their decision that the dispatch of a fleet to Singapore "must depend on our resources and the state of war in Europe," had already signaled their virtual abandonment of the Far East. Without the resolute backing of the United States, the weakness of both Britain and France was quickly exploited by the Japanese, who engineered "incidents" in Tientsin and Shanghai to demand that control over the remaining concessions should be ceded to the Imperial Army and the puppet Chinese government in Nanking recognized. Diplomatic negotiations resulted in a "Far Eastern Munich." Observing how this policy of appeasement further undercut the U.S. position, Admiral Harry Yarnell, the peppery commander of the Asiatic Squadron, reported from Shanghai: "the British Lion has been kicked and cuffed to an incredible extent, and still he takes it."

The Admiralty planners were now thrown into a quandary. The threat of war with Germany and her Italian Axis partner looked closer daily; no battleships could be spared for Singapore to defend Malaya and so uphold the solemn promises to protect Australia. Urgent pleas went out to Washington for the U.S. Navy to send its battlecruisers to the western Pacific. The President considered such a move too provocative, though he did cancel the fleet's scheduled appearance at the New York World Fair in May to dispatch it through the Panama Canal to exercise off the West Coast. But he was "speaking too softly," and the Big Stick failed to impress the Japanese. Two months later, soldiers of the China Expeditionary Force were blockading the British Tientsin concession in a brazen attempt to acquiesce to their authority in the occupied territories. This time Roosevelt reacted more firmly. On July 26 he announced that the United States intended to abrogate the 1911 Treaty of Commerce and Navigation, which put Japan on six-month notice that the next step could be an embargo on trade and oil. Tokyo shrewdly guessed, however, that Washington would think long and hard before taking what would be a major step toward a Pacific War.

GRAND STRATEGY

Faced with the deteriorating international situation in Europe and the Far East, the American military had to consider how best to deal with the old strategic nightmare of a two-ocean war. After a six-month intensive study, the Joint Board strategists concluded that inadequate bases in Guam and Manila, together with the lack of a strong British fleet at Singapore, dictated the abandonment of the obsolete ORANGE War Plan—and with it the Philippines. Even a strategic withdrawal to defend the West Coast, Panama, and Alaska was threatened by Japan's overwhelming superiority in carriers, which their report concluded made Pearl Harbor vulnerable to air strikes that "could damage Major Fleet units without warning. . . ."

Not since World War I has there been such a drastic revision of the U.S. military strategy as that undertaken in the summer of 1939, when the U.S. Army and Navy Chiefs of Staff had to decide on either an Atlantic or a Pacific plan of defense. Their recommendation was that the immediate danger came not from Japan but from the Axis powers. Britain and France faced war with Germany; Franco's Fascist regime had triumphed in Spain with the aid of the Luftwaffe, and the danger loomed of an Axis advance down the western Atlantic seaboard to support growing German interest in South America. The Joint Board's report unanimously advised the President to concentrate the Navy in the Atlantic and the Caribbean. This, of necessity, required a defensive posture in the Pacific to hold Hawaii—at the certain cost of losing the Philippines if Japan attacked. The memorandum specifically warned the President to resist the political temptation to defend the islands as "contrary to a reasoned evaluation of the United States interest."

This far-reaching conclusion recast half a century of American grand strategy. It was unhesitatingly approved by the President, who had concluded that the threat posed by Nazi Germany was a far greater menace to American interests in Europe and South America than that posed by Japan. The dramatic switch in strategic objectives was reflected in the new RAINBOW War Plans, so called because unlike the now unrealistic traditional single-color directives, they dealt with meeting a combination of enemies and potential alliances. The new set of "Joint Army and Navy Basic War Plans" projected at the end of June 1939 encompassed five contingencies. RAINBOW 1 was limited to Hemisphere Defense, preventing "the violation of the letter and spirit of the Monroe Doctrine" out into the mid-Atlantic and the Pacific as far as Hawaii, Wake, and Samoa—but, significantly, not defending the Philippines or Guam. The others were an extension of this objective. RAINBOW 2 envisaged the British and French engaged in a war with the Axis in which the United States "does not provide maximum participation in Europe" but undertakes "to sustain the interests of the Democratic Powers in the Pacific . . . and to defeat the enemy forces." RAINBOW 3 was predicated on the need for "securing control of the Western Pacific" in a development of the old ORANGE war strategy for a fleet march to retake the Philippines. RAINBOW 4 envisaged the U.S. armed forces having to concentrate on an Atlantic war and its corollary; while RAINBOW 5 assumed that they would be in alliance with Britain and France and would play a major role in the "decisive defeat of Germany."

As the European crisis smoldered during the summer of 1939, the military planners in Washington rushed ahead with the detailed work on RAINBOW 2. It appeared increasingly likely that America would be drawn in to supply, if not support, Britain and France should they go to war to prevent Germany from devouring Poland. This would dictate a defensive posture in the Pacific, with the burden shouldered by the U.S. Navy and to a lesser extent the Army. Staff talks with Royal Navy officers were secretly reopened to revive the Ingersoll-Phillips "Record of Conversation" on how best to contain and deter Japan. It was accepted that not much could be done to prevent the invasion and occupation of Hong Kong and the Philippines, but the U.S. Navy remained reluctant to commit itself to dispatching a fleet to Singapore, which was the pivotal point in mounting a defense of Malaya, the Dutch East Indies, and the approaches to Australia. Still to be accepted in Washington was the fact that the realities of planning for coalition warfare in the Pacific would find Americans having to go to the defense of European imperial possessions.

Europe's diplomats consulted about how to counter Hitler's impatient demands on Poland while America's military planners debated how best to avoid war in the Pacific. Roosevelt, informed that Germany would be ready to strike "without further preparation" by September, sent a strong plea to Moscow urging the Soviets not to side with the Nazis. Stalin, facing the challenge of Japan in the East and fearing German invasion in the West, had embarked on a desperate search for a defensive alliance; his emissaries were simultaneously sent to London, Paris, and Berlin.

Virulently anti-Communist, Hitler nevertheless needed to secure Germany's eastern flank against Russia to cover the Wehrmacht's intended Blitzkrieg into Poland. Originally he hoped that Japan could fulfill that role by signing a military alliance that would be a check on Moscow. The Imperial Army wanted to strike north against Russia, but neither the navy nor the civilian ministers were ready to be embroiled in a war for the Europeans. After a long courtship, Tokyo turned down the Axis marriage contract early in the summer of 1939. Hitler complained that the Japanese were "cool and unreliable," and sent Foreign Minister Ribbentrop to woo Stalin instead.

When the news of a possible Nazi-Soviet pact leaked out, it caused great consternation in Tokyo. In Japan's view such an agreement would irrevocably upset the Anti-Comintern Pact whose purpose was to discourage an attack by Russian forces now massing along their Siberian frontier. Faced with the threat, the Kwantung Army generals decided to sabotage the negotiations. Since late May, the Japanese had been probing the Soviet defenses in a series of "incidents" along the frontier that marked the Manchukuo border along the Khalka River. Alarmed at the incursions into the windswept pastureland of the Mongols, Stalin had sent out Lieutenant General Georgi Zhukov. The Red Army's leading armored-warfare exponent was promised he could have all the tanks and aircraft necessary to protect Outer Mongolia from being swallowed up in Japan's new Asian order. On July 19, 1939, three Banzaiing divisions of the Imperial Army made a massive attack concentrated at Nomonhan. Their fanaticism fired by a thirst to revenge the drubbing received the previous year, the Japanese troops hurled themselves against the Russian lines as Zhukov held to his deep defense line and waited for his reserves of tanks and aircraft to arrive via the Trans-Siberian Railway.

On August 19, 1939, Ribbentrop and Stalin were sealing the Nazi-Soviet Pact. Hitler briefed his generals for the attack on Poland, dismissing the British and French as "little worms," the Japanese as "lacquered monkeys," and their Emperor as "a companion piece for the late Czars." That same day Zhukov hurled his counteroffensive at Nomonhan. In a savage precursor of the Blitzkrieg that was soon to be launched against Poland, the Red Army concentrated flamethrowers, tanks, and large numbers of aircraft into a devastating assault on the 20-by-40-mile strip of territory Japan had occupied along the Khalka River.

Lacking both heavy tanks and air support, the Japanese suffered a punishing defeat, losing 20,000 men in the ten days before they were forced back into Manchukuo to sue for another truce. The Russian victory meant a humiliating loss of prestige for the army general staff. It finally killed their "Strike North" strategy. The shockwaves toppled the Hiranuma cabinet, which had already seen its foreign policy wrecked by Hitler's pact with Stalin. Premier Hiranuma tendered his resignation to the Emperor, citing "intricate and baffling situations recently arising in Europe." According to reports from Ambassador Grew, the new cabinet formed at the end of August by General Nobuyaki Abe offered a chance of repairing relations between Tokyo and Washington. Foreign Minister Nomura ordered negotiations to begin for a new commercial treaty, while the army and navy backed the objective set out in an "Outline for Foreign Policy" to drive a wedge between the Anglo-American position by putting pressure to bear on Britain to make concessions and cease allowing the Burma Road to be used to send aid to the Nationalist Chinese. "Britain has vast interests in China, but not the power to protect them," the document noted. "The United States, on the other hand, with minimal interests there, possesses the greatest force to restrain Japan." Hopes of effecting a rapprochement were lost in the face of the skepticism of State Department hardliners, the Imperial Navy's renewed call for Japan's southward expansion, and the climactic events in Europe.

HITLER'S WAR

German troops marched into Poland on September 1, 1939. Hitler ignored the French and British ultimatum, and within forty-eight hours a general war broke out across the Atlantic. On the night of Sunday, September 3, the passenger liner *Athenia* was sunk by a U-boat as she steamed out to cross the Atlantic, packed with refugees from the war. The specter of the *Lusitania* was raised by the loss of twenty-two American lives, but Roosevelt broadcast reassuringly that the U.S. Navy would be deployed in the Atlantic to "keep war from our firesides."

The President's reminder to the isolationists that "even a neutral cannot close his mind or conscience" indicated that he was already committed to practical steps to ensure that the United States did not remain a spectator in the life-or-death struggle the democracies were now facing with the Nazi dictatorship. Britain and France were counting on a revision of the neutrality laws to receive their multi-million dollars of American arms orders that as belligerents they were automatically now denied. Roosevelt had also gone much further by offering the Royal Navy clandestine assistance. King George VI, during his July visit to Washington, had been assured by the President that the U.S. Navy would carry out a "Neutrality Patrol" in the western hemisphere to give effect to the secret agreement made in Anglo-American naval staff talks that spring that "command of the Western and Southern Atlantic, as well as the Pacific, would have to be assured by the United States." On September 23, the South American states were called together at the Pan American Conference in Panama to restate the Monroe Doctrine by declaring a Neutrality Zone reaching hundreds of miles out into the Atlantic—to be enforced by the U.S. Atlantic Squadron. Both the President and his naval staff, however, continued to resist British pressure to send their warships to Singapore. They knew that anti-Japanese though American public opinion was, it would not stand for sending the U.S. Navy to protect the colonial possessions of European powers.

The rate at which British merchant shipping was lost to mines and U-boats during the "Phony War" in the autumn of 1939 helped Roosevelt persuade Congress on October 26 to soften the strict provisions of the Neutrality Act with the "cash-and-carry" amendment, which favored the democracies. The British and French were to go on receiving arms supplies, provided they paid for them in cash and carried them in non-American freighters. At the same time Roosevelt made two moves that were to have a profound influence on the course of the war. The first was to send a letter of September 11 to Winston Churchill (restored on the outbreak of hostilities to the British cabinet as First Lord of the Admiralty), inviting him to "keep in touch with me personally." It was the beginning of a momentous partnership. The second, exactly a month later, was to set up a highly secret "Uranium Advisory Committee" to consider an alarming report from leading émigré physicists, signed by Albert Einstein, which warned that German scientists were racing to construct an atomic bomb of incalculable destructive potential.

A phony calm had also settled over the Far East as Japan's leaders awaited developments in the European war. In common with the British and French, the Japanese civilians that winter endured the first food shortages. The worsening economic crisis found the army withdrawing their support from General Abe's cabinet. In January 1940 Admiral Mitsumasa Yonai formed a new government, which because of his corpulence attracted the ironical tag of the "no rice cabinet" when even stricter rationing was introduced after poor harvests. Yet with perverse logic, considering that Japan relied on the quarter billion dollars of American imports, much of it vital strategic material and oil, her leaders and newspapers railed against President Roosevelt for his continued support of Chiang Kai-Shek. Ex-premier Konoye was rallying the Diet behind his "League for a Holy War" to win a final solution to the China Incident. Since Britain and the United States were not prepared to help in resolving a peace on the mainland, he urged an alliance with Germany and Italy to bring about the "new order" in Asia.

At the end of January 1940, the United States commercial treaties with Japan were allowed to expire without renewal. As the hardliners began pointing out, the way was now open for the President to impose mandatory rather than moral sanctions against Japan. "The tendency is a healthy one, which will continue if Uncle Sam stays tough and the Chinese remain uncooperative," advised influential republican Frank Knox, the publisher of the Chicago *Daily News*. "The only hope for a return to peace in the Far East is the continuance of this trend." It was just one of the indications that American policy was toughening against the Japanese while the skirmishing in China continued. Moreover, with the Russians fighting in Finland and the U-boat sinking of British merchantmen in the Atlantic, it was the only news in the press to remind people that a war was really going cn at all. President Roosevelt in his State of the Union address felt the need to remind the nation of the dangerous reality it was facing. After carefully restating his intention to keep out of the European conflict, he proclaimed: "there is a vast difference between keeping out of the war and pretending that the war is none of our business."

The White House set about countering the isolationists by emphasizing that Britain and France must now be regarded as the front line of America's Atlantic defenses. The spring of 1940 was to prove just how shockingly weak those defenses were as Germany carried out her lightning invasions of Norway and then Holland, Belgium, and France. Churchill became Prime Minister on a tide of defeat to rally a shattered nation with his promise of "blood, toil, tears and sweat." With the British Expeditionary Force cut off and evacuating from Dunkirk and the Panzers racing for the French capital, Roosevelt capitalized on the growing alarm of Americans to call on congressmen to "recast their thinking about national protection" by voting $1.1 billion for the U.S. Army. The Joint Board planners began detailed preparations to prepare the RAINBOW 5 strategy to meet the likely threat of a German-dominated Atlantic seaboard after Italy stabbed France in the back by joining the war.

Churchill was daily cabling Roosevelt for more aircraft and supplies so that Britain could make good his promise: "We shall never surrender." He begged for the loan of fifty old American destroyers to augment Britain's antisubmarine capability, and tried again to persuade the President to send a strong force of warships to Singapore, "to keep the Japanese dog quiet." The President knew that such aid to Britain would raise a storm of criticism. The U.S. Navy was desperately short of warships to meet either its Atlantic or Pacific commitments. Not until the shock of the fall of Paris on July 18 did Roosevelt dare to ask Congress to vote a staggering increase in appropriations to provide for a 70 percent growth in naval strength to include eleven new fast battleships to operate with the fleet of eleven *Essex* carriers in addition to nearly fifty cruisers and over one hundred destroyers. The United States was now committed to building a two-ocean navy that would completely outstrip Japan's 1939 "fourth building program" for eighty additional warships and the doubling of her naval air strength. But American admirals were only too well aware that it would take nearly four years to turn the blueprint into overwhelming naval supremacy on the Pacific.

"POSITIVE ARRANGEMENTS"

The spectacular military victory of Hitler's spring Blitzkrieg through western Europe encouraged the Japanese Army leaders to urge the Yonai cabinet to join the Axis Pact and exploit Britain's weak position in the Far East. France's Vichy government was presented with demands for air bases in Indochina and the British were pressed to close the Burma Road in preparation for a final drive against the Chinese Nationalists. Anticipating that this might trigger an American oil embargo, Tokyo stepped up the pace of its negotiations with the Dutch for the surrender of massive concessions in the East Indies as an alternative source of strategic raw materials. To the British and Dutch exile governments in London, the only hope of resisting the insistent Japanese demands appeared to be to send a powerful American naval force to Singapore.

President Roosevelt was only prepared to go as far as keeping the Pacific Fleet on station at Hawaii after completion of spring maneuvers. Even this was over the forceful protest of Admiral James O. Richardson, the Commander in Chief, who argued that his six battleships and three carriers could more efficiently and safely project its presence from the West Coast bases. His continued warnings eventually cost him the command, although Admiral Stark had explained that the fleet was to remain at Pearl Harbor "because of the deterrent effect which it is thought that your presence may have on the Jap's going into the East Indies." Keeping the main strength of the U.S. Navy in the mid-Pacific, although it was a warning to Japan, brought frequent jitters in Washington that it offered too tempting a target for a hit-and-run attack. The first of many alarms had been sent flashing out on June 21, the day before Germany and France signed their armistice: IMMEDIATELY ALERT COMPLETE DEFENSE ORGANIZATION TO DEAL WITH POSSIBLE TRANS PACIFIC RAID. The many false alerts were to encourage an illusory sense of security on Hawaii.

Through the month of July 1940, while Churchill rallied the British to a magnificent defiance of Germany, American isolationists held rallies and marches to proclaim, as one placard put it, "THE YANKS ARE NOT COMING!" Across the Pacific in Japan, in the wake of Hitler's "Victory in the West," the military bureaucrats in control of Japan's destiny decided that they too did not "want to miss the bus." They brought Prince Konoye back to power to fulfill his promise of "building of a New Order in Greater East Asia." On July 26, 1940, he unveiled his plan of action to achieve this. It was entitled "Main Principles for Coping with the Changing World Situation," and the Liaison Conference of political and military leaders warmly endorsed it. What they had approved was a policy based on the assumption that Germany would soon bring about the defeat of Britain and end Anglo-American interference in the Far East. It took for granted that the United States would accept the reality of the situation and not interfere with the priority mission to isolate Chiang Kai-shek by cutting off his supply lines prior to a final resolution of the "China Incident." A neutrality agreement was to be sought with the Soviet Union in which an alliance with Germany was expected to be helpful. As a member of the Axis, Konoye enthusiastically predicted that "Positive arrangements will be undertaken in order to include the British, French, Dutch and Portuguese islands of the Orient within the substance of the New Order."

"Positive arrangements" meant first trying diplomacy. But in the event that they might not prove "positive" enough, Konoye gave notice to the army and navy to be ready in twelve months to go to war against Britain and the United States. To carry out this national crusade, he brought two leading militarists into his new cabinet: Lieutenant General Hideki Tojo, an energetic militarist and former Chief of Staff of the Kwantung Army who had earned the nickname "The Razor," was made war minister. Yosuke Matsuoka, a firebrand nationalist politician who was known as "The Talking Machine" and had been educated in America, became foreign minister. As the new cabinet set its timetable for achieving the "New Order" in Asia, Prince Saionji, the venerated last Meiji "Genro," warned the Emperor that recalling Konoye back was "like inviting a robber back to investigate his crime because no one else could be such an authority on it."

Prime Minister Konoye's return to power was accompanied by a warning from Ambassador Grew in Tokyo to expect renewed Japanese aggression. Coinciding as it did with Congress passing legislation requiring licenses to export to Japan, this strengthened the hand of those members of Roosevelt's cabinet like Treasury Secretary Henry Morgenthau and Interior Secretary Harold L. Ickes who wanted a greater American commitment to Britain as well as a tougher policy toward the Japanese. On July 26, the President announced restrictions on the export of aviation fuel, lubricating oil, and heavy melting scrap. It was a move he felt confident about with the support of two Republican stalwarts whom he had invited to join the administration to give it the appearance of national unity before facing the autumn presidential election campaign.

Frank Knox, former Republican vice-presidential candidate, newspaperman, and Roosevelt Rough Rider, was appointed Secretary of the Navy; and Henry L. Stimson took over as Secretary of the Army. The veteran seventy-two-year-old Stimson brought a unique insight into American-Japanese affairs that reached back to his friendship with Theodore Roosevelt's Secretary of State, Elihu Root. He drew upon experience as Secretary of War, Governor of the Philippines, and as Herbert Hoover's

Secretary of State during the Manchurian crisis. Stimson backed Harold Ickes's repeated calls for "some straight acting which will show Japan that we mean business and that we are not the least bit afraid of her." The State Department, however, advised against an outright embargo on oil and scrap iron exports because, in Hull's cautious assessment, "we must not push Japan too much at this time as we might push her to take the Dutch East Indies."

Despite the Secretary of State's caution, by October the President had extended a total ban on all iron and steel scrap. This first sign that America was slipping an economic noose around Japan's neck hardened the determination of the Konoye cabinet to speed up its moves to impose a "New Order" on Asia. The British government capitulated to Japan's demand to close the Burma Road supply line to Chiang Kai-shek, and the Vichy Governor in Indochina was presented with a virtual ultimatum demanding bases for a military expedition to be launched north against the Nationalists. As the Luftwaffe began its nightly bombing to blitz Britain into submission during the first week of September 1940, Foreign Minister Matsuoka was deep in discussions with the German ambassador in Tokyo on the terms of the proposed Tripartite Pact. Hitler intended that the pact should assist his plans to invade England by encouraging the Japanese to attack Singapore, as well as providing a cover for his long-range plan to attack Russia. Matsuoka's brief was to win German support for a move south to gain control of the oil reserves of the Dutch East Indies—but he had been given strict instructions not to get Japan entangled in Germany's war.

After two weeks of horsetrading, Matsuoka was triumphantly recommending to an Imperial Conference in the presence of the Emperor that in return for recognizing "the leadership of Germany and Italy in the establishment of a new order in Europe," Hitler and Mussolini would back Japan's efforts to bring about the "New Order" in Asia and "with all political, economic and military means." This, Matsuoka jubilantly pointed out, "would force the United States to act more prudently." At the same time, Hitler was also assuring Mussolini that "it is the best way to keep America entirely out of the picture or to render her entry into the war ineffective." When the Tripartite Pact was signed on September 27 in Berlin, the biggest Tokyo paper, *Asahi Shimbun*, predicted: "It seems inevitable that a collision should occur between Japan, determined to establish a sphere of influence in East Asia, including the Southwest Pacific, and the United States, which is determined to meddle in the affairs on the other side of a vast ocean by every means short of war."

The Tripartite Pact was greeted with public rejoicing in Tokyo and enthusiastic support by the militarists who saw that it cleared the way for Japan's conquest of Southeast Asia. As Hitler intended, it caused consternation in London and Washington because the Pacific had now become inextricably locked in with the European war. In Washington the rapid fall of France caused the American military planners to assume that the invasion and submission of England was "within the realms of possibility." It was estimated that Britain might be knocked out of the war within six months as they began preparing for a RAINBOW 4 scenario in which the United States would fight an Atlantic war alone. They urged that the shipment of arms be diverted to building up America's ground and air forces as the Selective Service Bill to begin conscription was sent to Congress. The President, however, had faith in Churchill's ability to rally his country after the defiant "We shall never surrender!" speech. He overruled the Joint planners' recommendations, and guns, planes, and munitions continued to be sent across the Atlantic to the British Isles.

When it came to the Pacific, Roosevelt was more cautious in giving the Australian government the defense commitment it wanted. "The United States cannot very well complain if we decide not to fight her battles in the Far East," Prime Minister Menzies indicated in July, after his mission to Washington had failed to elicit "any specific guarantee of the status quo, even in relation to Australia, New Zealand and the Netherland East Indies." Nonetheless, the President's response to the Tripartite Pact was to promise Chiang Kai-shek fifty pursuit planes and a $100 million of financial assistance. He also provided the British with the assurances they needed to agree to reopen the Burma Road at the risk of Japanese displeasure. This marked the end of Churchill's Far Eastern policy of appeasement. His cooperation ensured by Roosevelt's agreement at last to release the fifty refurbished four-piper destroyers that the Royal Navy desperately needed in the Atlantic battle against the U-boats. A cautious President had only been moved by repeated pressure from Knox and Stimson, as well as the assurance of Republican presidential candidate Wendell Willkie that the "warships for bases" deal would have his support.

The isolationists were roused to fury. "An act of war," shrilled the St. Louis *Post Dispatch*, denouncing the move as the worst "sucker real-estate deal in history." Facing a decline in popularity in the opinion polls that was cutting into his lead in the final weeks of the campaign, Roosevelt felt obliged to enter the electoral fray to answer the charge that he was preparing to plunge the United States into war with Germany on the Atlantic.

"I give you one more assurance," he told an audience thick with Irish isolationists in Boston on October 30, 1940. "I have said this before, but I shall say it again and again and again: Your boys are not going to be sent to any foreign wars!"

4

Europe First

Many Americans, finding no candidate who openly supported the isolationist cause, nonetheless took comfort from Roosevelt's apparent "no war" pledge. Five days later, Republican Wendell Willkie went down to defeat by 5 million votes. Yet the President would later admit that his Boston speech was prompted by the need to give the nation a "sweeping reassurance" on the belligerency issue at a time when he still hoped that his naval assistance and supplies would enable Britain to defeat Germany. That hope was shattered by the icy realism of a Naval War Plans Division memorandum that arrived on his Oval Office desk less than two weeks after his unprecedented third-term reelection to the White House.

The twenty-four-page report was a brutally frank reassessment of American strategy bearing the endorsement of the Chief of Naval Operations. "I believe the United States, in addition to sending naval assistance, would also need to send air and land forces to Europe, Africa or both, and to participate in the land offensive," Admiral Harold R. Stark concluded. The reality of the Nazi domination of the western Atlantic from Norway to Spain, with the threat of the extension of Axis power through the Mediterranean down the coast of Africa, had made strategic nonsense of all the President's no-war guarantees.

If Nazi Germany was eventually to be defeated, the United States must prepare to join in the fighting as set out in the RAINBOW 5 strategy, which called for concentrating forces in the Atlantic while the minimum commitment was made in the Far East. Stark's pro-British stance had been influenced by the reports of his Assistant Chief of Naval Operations, Admiral Robert L. Ghormley, who was stationed in London as a semipermanent observer. The U.S. Army delegation, which arrived after the RAF had defeated the Luftwaffe, concluded that Britain could now survive to continue the struggle against Germany—provided America gave the massive support that Churchill was asking for. At the same time, the British Chiefs of Staff stressed their helplessness to resist attack by Japan because there were no warships that could be spared from the Mediterranean or the Atlantic to send to Singapore. "The support of the American battle fleet would obviously transform the strategical situation in the Far East," the U.S. mission was informed; but the Stark plan to concentrate on the Atlantic war meant the U.S. Navy's commitment in the Pacific would necessarily be limited.

"Plan D for Dog," as the Chief of Naval Operations had so designated it in his memorandum, quickly won the approval of the Army as the logical foundation for RAINBOW strategies. Disturbed at first by the possibility that British needs might be given too much emphasis in directing the U.S. strategy, by Christmas 1940 General George C. Marshall had agreed that the Joint Board should make it the basis of future development. The Army Chief of Staff was facing the enormous task of transforming a rundown peacetime force of under 200,000 troops into a 1½-million-strong army that would have to fight overseas—a task complicated by the fact that the recently introduced Selective Service was to last for only a year.

The President supported the "Europe First" commitment implicit in "Plan Dog" and authorized staff talks with the British to lay the groundwork for its speedy implementation. His conviction that the Germans posed a far greater menace than Japan came in part from his concern that German physicists were working to develop an atomic bomb. These fears were based on Hitler's promises that the Reich's scientists were developing a new weapon. Disturbing evidence was presented by a second letter from Einstein in March. Concern was heightened when Paris fell and the renowned French nuclear physics laboratory and its director, Pierre Joliot-Curie, were taken over by the Germans. Reports from Britain, as well as Roosevelt's own top-secret "Advisory Committee on Uranium," confirmed the practicality of constructing a fission weapon. In June 1940 this top-secret team of experts was incorporated into the President's recently established National Defense Research Committee, under the scientist Vannevar Bush. The committee now had access to the millions of dollars necessary to fund an experimental program to build the first atomic pile. American agents stealthily set out to buy up the world's supplies of uranium ore, which the Belgian Union Minière had fortunately shipped to the United States before their country was overrun.

The prospect that the Germans might be working on weapons of incalculable destructive potential was a threat that the President and his military advisers had to take into their long-term calculations, while their immediate concern as 1940 drew to a close was Churchill's warning that Britain was financially "stripped to the bone" and unable to afford the armaments to keep on fighting.

Roosevelt met the crisis by inventing the idea of Lend-Lease, to "get rid of this silly, foolish dollar sign" by loaning the British whatever arms and supplies they needed without payment. The United States must become the "Arsenal of Democracy," he told the nation in a Fireside Chat on December 29, 1940; this policy was no more than the prudent action of a neighbor who lent a garden hose to douse the fire next door before it threatened his own home. The isolationists rejected such a simplistic view and for two months put up stiff opposition to the President's Lend-Lease Bill. It might not have been passed by Congress at all if the politicians had known the extent to which the President was intending to commit America to the European war.

While the debate over Lend-Lease dragged on in Capitol Hill through February and March 1941, across Washington a high-level delegation of British and Canadian military officers, ostensibly part of the British purchasing Commission, commuted in civilian clothes between the palatial Wardman Park Hotel above Washington's Rock Creek Park and the adjoining Navy and War Department buildings on Constitution Avenue. Just sixteen days after the President had signed the Lend-Lease Bill into law, the ABCl (American, British) conversations concluded on March 27, 1941, by accepting the Joint Board strategic dictum that "since Germany is the predominant member of the Axis powers, the Atlantic and European War is considered to be the decisive theater." The decision "not willingly to engage in any war against Japan" was to have far-reaching implications. It had been taken despite British advice that an American aircraft carrier and four heavy cruisers should be sent to reinforce Singapore base which Britain admitted to being unable to defend. "The security of the Far Eastern position, including Australia and New Zealand, is essential to the cohesion of the British Commonwealth and the maintenance of its war effort."

The British Chiefs of Staff had stated in their policy memorandum that "Singapore is the key to the defense of those interests and its retention must be assured." After they had learned of the bastion's vulnerability to landward attack, the U.S. Army planners condemned such a move as "a strategic error of the first magnitude." Marshall and Stark regarded the base as a political symbol of Britain's determination to maintain her Far Eastern Empire. They were prepared to accept that its loss, along with Malaya and the Philippines, would be a "serious blow," but one that the strategic necessity dictated might have to be "absorbed without leading to final disaster." The United States, they contended, must exert "its principal military effort in the Atlantic or navally in the Mediterranean," as the U.S. Chiefs of Staff Committee report concluded, adding that while it agreed "the retention of Singapore is desirable . . . it also believes that the diversion to the Asiatic theater of sufficient forces to assure the retention of Singapore might jeopardize the success of the main effort of the Associated Powers in a non-decisive theater." Instead, it was decided that the U.S. Navy should send additional ships to the Atlantic, which in turn would enable the Royal Navy to send what large warships it could to

Singapore to retain the same level of Anglo-American naval strength in the western Pacific.

"STRAWS IN THE WIND"

RAINBOW 5 was expanded as a basis of future planning. The British, however, made another ploy the following month to provide for more adequate forces in the Far East. "Many drifting straws seem to indicate Japanese intentions to make war on us or something that would force us to make war on them in the next few weeks or months," Churchill had cabled the President on February 15. He painted a dire vision of Australia invaded by a Japanese war machine fueled by the oil of the Dutch East Indies. The April ABDA (American, British, Dutch, Australian) staff talks in Singapore reiterated the call for U.S. Navy warships to be sent to the base as a deterrent. Once again Marshall and Stark rejected the move as inconsistent with America's overall strategy.

The "drifting straws" came from the British intercepts of the radio messages from Japan's ambassador in Berlin to Tokyo, which they were reading with the aid of the recently delivered American "Purple" decoding machines. Washington's intelligence services were also following the pressure Hitler was pressing on Japan to fulfill her Tripartite Pact obligations. "Wipe out England's key position in the Far East," Foreign Minister Ribbentrop was urging Envoy Baron Hiroshi Oshima, assuring him that the German U-boats were winning the Battle of the Atlantic and an immediate attack on Singapore "would be the best way to keep America out of the conflict."

Churchill encouraged the President to prevent Japan from "taking the plunge" by issuing a formal declaration that any attack on British or Dutch possessions in the Far East would bring the United States into the war. Roosevelt knew that politically his hands were tied by the isolationists, and public opinion polls that showed that while six out of ten Americans were ready for firm action against the Japanese, only four out of ten were prepared to risk war. He believed he had already gone as far as he dared by extending Lend-Lease to the Chinese nationalists and permitting Colonel Claire Chennault to recruit American Army Air Force crews for his "First Volunteer Group." Piloting Curtiss "Warhawk" fighters with their noses painted to look like shark snouts, the "Flying Tigers"—as they became known—began shooting down Japanese planes over China for a $500 per "kill" bounty.

In the spring of 1941 Washington was able to follow, through the intercepted traffic passing between Berlin and Tokyo, the breathless pace at which Foreign Minister Matsuoka was pursuing his "Blitzkrieg Diplomacy." Yet the United States only issued stern warnings to Japan that any further "incidents" in China would not be tolerated. "It was the old question of what we should do in the Far East to slow the Japs down," Secretary of War Stimson recorded. Hull suggested sending battleships out across the Pacific, "popping up here and there to keep the Japs guessing." Britain continued calling for the U.S. Fleet to visit Singapore.

Admiral Stark rejected both schemes as dangerous divisions of forces that would invite attack. Only four aged cruisers were finally sent across the Pacific, calling briefly at Britain's Far East naval base and at Sydney as a token reassurance that Uncle Sam had not forgotten the Australians. The U.S. Navy was now hard put to maintain even a meaningful presence in both oceans. At the beginning of the year, when Admiral King had been designated Commander in Chief of the Atlantic Fleet, the intention had been to transfer a quarter of the Pacific Fleet in response to Hitler's sending U-boats westward to retaliate for Lend-Lease. Stark had explained to Admiral Husband E. Kimmel, the new Pacific Fleet Commander who had relieved Admiral Richardson, that "the question of our entry into the war now seems to be *when*, not whether."

The President had already given his preliminary approval to Admiral King to commence escorting British convoys at the beginning of April. Then intelligence intercepts revealed that the Japanese foreign minister was on his way to Berlin. Fearing this presaged some move in the Pacific, Roosevelt deemed it inadvisable to weaken Kimmel's fleet, and postponed the transfer of warships and the convoying until May.

This was a serious setback to the Royal Navy, as the U-boat compaign had been stepped up during the first months of 1941 to coincide with the Luftwaffe's blitz of the British ports, in a major effort to cut the Atlantic lifeline at both ends. The Germans had also begun a twin thrust through the Balkans and North Africa in support of the faltering campaign of their Italian allies to turn the Mediterranean into an Axis lake. "If we lose in the Atlantic we lose everywhere," General Marshall warned the President, voicing the Chief of Staff's concern that their new "Europe First" strategy was already being threatened by the enormous British shipping losses. Then Britain was forced into another military evacuation in Crete at the same time as her army in Libya was being hammered back by General Erwin Rommel's panzers. The forecasts of her chances of survival made by U.S. Army Intelligence chiefs now became so bleak that Marshall felt obliged to replace them with officers who "have a little broader vision." The isolationists were roused into furious protest by the President's decision at the end of April to relieve some of the pressure on the Royal Navy by extending the U.S. Navy's Hemisphere Defense Patrols out across the Atlantic to Greenland and the tip of Africa. "America Firsters" rallying in Manhattan were told by Charles Lindbergh, "we cannot win this war for England regardless of how much assistance we send."

The President and his military advisers had already secretly come to the same conclusion. But with the Army and Navy locked in a procurement struggle to win priority over the national industrial resources each needed to complete the Thousand Bomber Program and a two-ocean fleet, it would be nearly two years before the "Victory Program" gave the United States the strength needed to take on Germany and Japan at once. Already by the late spring it was evident that just sustaining the British was going to demand more planes, tanks, and guns than had been estimated in December. Now it became yet more imperative to prevent any escalation of tension in the Pacific.

The Americans, however, found that they were trapped in an impossible situation when it came to constructing a foreign policy to deal with Japan. The State Department resurrected Theodore Roosevelt's "speak softly" diplomacy when they advised making no compromise over China "while simultaneously giving by our acts in the Pacific new glimpses of diplomatic, economic and naval 'big sticks.'" But by 1941 these sticks would prove hardly menacing enough to cow a powerful, military Japan determined to bring about the "New Order" in Asia. The United States was equally insistent on upholding the moral sanctity of international treaties and insisted on a strict adherence to the Open Door policy that precluded any settlement of the Sino-Japanese conflict. Both wanted to avoid war, and each began the year with preparations for a round of negotiations to try to resolve the crisis. But diplomacy would be frustrated by their inflexible postures, which ultimately made it impossible for either nation to steer aside from a collision course in the Pacific.

In January, Cordell Hull delivered another sermon to the House Foreign Affairs Committee, condemning Japan's "broad and ambitious plans for establishing herself in a dominant position in the entire region of the western Pacific" by force of arms. Even as the Secretary of State was indicating that any future Japanese aggression would be countered with increasing economic reprisals, two American clerics were on their way back with an ambitious plan to act as intermediaries in opening negotiations between Washington and Tokyo.

Bishop James E. Walsh, in his capacity as Superior General of the "Catholic Foreign Mission Society of America" headquartered in Maryknoll, New York, had journeyed to Japan in November accompanied by his Vicar General, Father James M. Drought. Ostensibly they had crossed the Pacific to inspect their Japanese missions, but the trip had quite another purpose that was supported by Postmaster General Frank C. Walker, the Roosevelt cabinet's most prominent Roman Catholic member. It had also been facilitated by Taro Terasaki, the spymaster chief of the Foreign Office American Bureau, who from the U.S. Embassy in Washington ran the entire Japanese espionage network in the western hemisphere. The idea that the Maryknoll fathers should take this highly unusual diplomatic rather than spiritual initiative sprang from the mercurial Drought, whose isolationist, anti-Roosevelt convictions had already been given public expression in the "Must we dance to every rumbling of foreign drums" speech he wrote for Wendell Willkie's unsuccessful presidential bid.

Upon their arrival in Tokyo, the two priests held extensive discussions with bankers and a senior member of the Army Ministry's Military Affairs Bureau, who arranged a meeting with Foreign Minister Matsuoka—the man Hull considered as "crooked as a bundle of fishhooks." The American priests appeared to suit the Japanese purpose of conducting a private diplomacy with the United States to avoid any public admission that Japan might be seeking a compromise solution to the China Incident. This way they hoped to take advantage of the widening split between the Nationalists and the Communists to effect a solution on terms that would allow Japan to complete her scheme for establishing an economic empire in southern Asia at Britain's expense but without checking the flow of American oil.

It was to this end that former Foreign Minister Admiral Kichisaburo Nomura, who was known to Roosevelt and an admitted Americanophile, was dispatched to Washington in February to supervise and encourage the delicate process of negotiation. His arrival in the United States coincided with the return of the Maryknoll fathers, who met the President through the offices of the Postmaster General. They were encouraged to think that the President would respond favorably to their presentation of the issues to be negotiated with Tokyo, not because Roosevelt or Hull had any intention of abiding by their unofficial recommendations but because they hoped that the Japanese would choose to check their operations in China while diplomacy got under way. It was agreed that the Secretary of State should meet with Ambassador Nomura privately for a frank personal exchange of views. In deference to the need for absolute secrecy insisted on by Matsuoka's go-betweens, the series of "backstairs meetings" began with the impeccably polite admiral slipping into the Carlton Hotel's service entrance and upstairs to Hull's private suite.

The incongruous process of diplomatic negotiation between Hull and Nomura had barely got off to a faltering start when Walsh and Drought submitted their "Draft Understanding" at the beginning of April. Since it had been drawn up in consultation with agents of Japan, the "Understanding" not surprisingly conveyed Tokyo's minimum negotiating stance. This called on the United States to recognize Japanese authority over a large area of China in addition to terminating aid to Chiang Kai-shek and putting pressure on him to make peace. Hull was affronted. He at once rejected the document as "much less accommodating than we had been led to believe it would be and all that the most ardent Japanese imperialist could want."

Instead, the Secretary of State insisted that negotiations had to be conducted to satisfy a four-point American demand. This required Japan to respect the territorial integrity of other nations; to refrain from interfering in their internal affairs; to support the Open Door principle of equality of commercial opportunity; and to abide by the status quo in the Pacific except where it was altered by peaceful means. In his excessive eagerness to get talks under way, Nomura had overstressed American willingness to negotiate on the basis of the "Draft Understanding." He also failed to appreciate just how great a stumbling block the Tripartite Pact was to become, as the United States began insisting that Japan detach herself from Hitler. Weeks of intensive evening meetings in the Carlton Hotel produced no progress and Hull's patience was being tried by the sibilant politeness of the admiral, whose ability to follow the difficult discussion was affected by advancing deafness. The peculiar circumstances under which the discussions took place militated against any real progress and concealed from both parties the true extent of the differences that separated them. Hull and Nomura struggled on, obedient to their instructions from Roosevelt and Konoye, each of whom saw a virtue in playing for time. But while the Japanese were preparing to fight in less than nine months, the American military machine would need another year and a half to build up sufficient strength to take on a Pacific war in addition to facing the Germans across the Atlantic.

OPENING BIDS

When the cherry trees of Washington and Tokyo burst into bloom during the first spring weeks of 1941, it was becoming clear to Prime Minister Konoye that his grand design based on the Tripartite Pact was disintegrating. Germany had abandoned her invasion of England, and the United States had toughened its stance, stepping up more arms supplies to Britain and the Nationalist Chinese, and gradually tightening the economic noose on strategic materials exported to Japan.

The Japanese foreign minister's mission to Moscow during the second week of April to negotiate a non-aggression pact with Stalin was taken as evidence that Matsuoka, on his way back from Berlin, was now being forced into playing both his Russian and German diplomatic cards in the effort to speed up winning concessions in Washington. "Now that Japan and Russia have fixed up their problem, Japan can straighten out the Far East and Germany will handle Europe," Stalin told the diminutive envoy, as they exchanged farewell hugs at Moscow's Central Station on April 13. "Later, together all of us will deal with America," he promised. Yet he already knew how hollow this was because his master spy in Tokyo, Richard Sorge, was warning that Germany was preparing to invade the Soviet Union.

Peabody Museum, Salem

OPENING THE DOOR Commodore Perry (above left) brought Japan into the Pacific trade (below, Canton's bustling Whampoa anchorage). Captain Mahan (above right) preached how a big navy was "the midwife to commerce."

BIG STICKS AND PALM TWIGS Battlefleets like Theodore Roosevelt's Great White Fleet (left) by 1921 were under attack by aircraft (below Billy Mitchell bombs the old USS *Alabama*) and disarmers at the Washington Conference (above right, Secretary Hughes; left, Arthur Balfour).

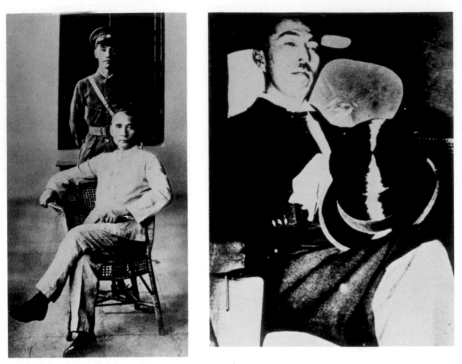

CLOSING THE DOOR The Republic of China presided over by Sun Yet Sen and his successor Chiang Kai-shek (above left, in 1924) faced civil turmoil aggravated in 1931 when the Nationalist Army (below, manning defenses in Manchuria) was attacked by Japan's Kwantung Army. In 1937 when Prince Konoye (above right) became Japanese premier

war was raging. American forces (above, U.S. Marines in Shanghai) were too weak to intervene even when the gunboat Panay was sunk (below).

DETERRENT AND DENOUEMENT General MacArthur (below) was promised a big fleet of B-17 bombers to defend the Philippines. Secretary of State Hull (above left) was to spin out diplomacy with Japan until the deterrent was in place. But General Tojo (above right) bowed to militarist pressure to order Admiral Yamamoto (above, center) to execute his

bold plan—on December 7, 1941 the Japanese carrier planes made their surprise attack on Pearl Harbor (above and below).

DIRECT SHOCKS The destruction of American airpower enabled General Homma (above) to invade Luzon on December 22, 1941—twelve days after Admiral Phillips (below) had lost his life when the *Prince of Wales* and *Repulse* were sunk by Japanese bombers (below right).

Japan's military planners were also drawing up a scheme that provided for attacking the United States if Ambassador Normura's mission in Washington failed. The Imperial Navy's senior tacticians were preparing an audacious plan to eliminate the United States' naval strength in the Pacific. It was the brainchild of Admiral Isoroku Yamamoto, who had headed his country's delegation to the 1935 London Naval Conference before becoming Vice Minister of the Navy. An outspoken advocate of naval airpower, he had made strenuous efforts to prevent a clash with the United States, whose industrial might had made a powerful impression on Yamamoto during his travels there as a young officer. His repeated warnings that Japan lacked the resources to win such a war had made him a prime target of the extreme nationalists. In July 1939, his friend and fellow admiral, Prime Minister Yonai, had sent him to sea as Commander in Chief of the Combined Fleet "as the only way to save his life." On the outbreak of the fighting in Europe, which came only two weeks after his appointment, Yamamoto instituted a rigorous program that called for his men "to reach a superhuman degree of skill and fighting efficiency"—letting it be known that he regarded "death in training as a hero's death."

While the Combined Fleet was being exercised to a new pitch of readiness for action, its Commander in Chief continued to lead the senior echelons of the Imperial Navy's resistance to forming an alliance with the Axis. It was unsuccessful. Many of the hot-blooded junior officers had switched their allegiance to Germany after what they regarded as Britain's abandonment of Japan in 1921, and had been powerfully influenced by the discipline and purpose of the Nazi state during tours of duty with the Kriegsmarine or in the embassy at Berlin. Yamamoto's two years at Washington from 1925 to 1927 and travels made earlier while on a language course at Harvard had convinced him that the German-influenced attitude that Americans were "weak willed and spoiled by luxuries" was dangerously wide of the mark. He reminded those who dismissed the fighting capacity of the U.S. Navy of the exploits of Admiral Farragut and Dewey. But above all it was the might of America's material resources that made it foolhardy for Japan to risk war with the United States. "Anyone who has seen the auto factories in Detroit and the oil fields in Texas," he cautioned the hotheads, "knows that Japan lacks the national power for a naval race with America."

When Prince Konoye backed Matsuoka's pro-Axis diplomacy to take Japan into the Tripartite Pact, the belief that Germany would soon conquer England, coupled with the threat of the cabinet resignation, speedily shuffled the last opposition on the naval staff into line. "At this stage to profess shock and indignation at American economic pressure is either childishly impetuous or suggests an extraordinary in-attentiveness to events," Yamamoto wrote to a brother officer, convinced that the economic noose would be slowly tightened until Japan was left with no choice but to go to war. Summoned to Tokyo, Yamamoto that September made no secret of his belief that Konoye's policies had made a fight with the United States inevitable. "If we are ordered to do it," he told the Prime Minister to his face, "then I can guarantee to put up a tough fight for the first six months, but I have absolutely no confidence in what would happen if it went on for one or two years. It is too late to do anything about the Tripartite Pact now, but I hope at best you'll make every effort to avoid war with America."

Confronted with Konoye's determination to press ahead with the "New Order" in Asia, which Yamamoto believed must certainly lead to open conflict with the United States, he dutifully began preparations to fight the war he had opposed for so long. The naval staff had prepared their plans to meet the American ORANGE war strategy, whose broad outlines had long been known in Tokyo. "Yōgeki Sakusen"—"interceptive operations"—was the key to the strategy that had been drawn up in 1933 to take account of the 60 percent inferiority imposed on the Japanese battle fleet by the Washington treaty system. A force of long-range submarines had been built whose mission would be to attack American warships steaming to the relief of the Philippines. Then a Pacific Fleet, its strength hopefully cut by 30 percent, would be engaged in a "decisive battle" when the odds favored Japan in home waters.

It was a strategy that looked backward to Admiral Togo's 1905 victory over a ponderous line of Russian dreadnoughts, rather than forward to take account of the way that carrier-borne airpower could revolutionize naval warfare. Through the thirties, by successively advancing east toward the area of the Pacific in which they intended to bring off the decisive confrontation—by 1940 it was set in the vicinity of the Marshalls—the Japanese planners recognized that it might prove difficult to lure the Americans into an action in hostile waters. These were the inherent weaknesses of the "Yōgeki Sakusen" surprise strategy that disturbed Yamamoto. More than anyone else, he appreciated the need for Japan to win a quick war in the Pacific. A year or so's delay in bringing about the "Jutland style"—confrontation would allow the U.S. Pacific Fleet to grow too mighty to conquer and possibly starve the Combined Fleet of the fuel it needed to carry on steaming.

Yamamoto had approvingly noted during the 1940 war games how easily the carrier strike planes had been able to knock out the fleet's battleships. "It makes me wonder if they couldn't get to Pearl Harbor," he remarked to his Chief of Staff, Fukudome, resurrecting a daring scheme that had always been dismissed by the naval staff as too risky. But Yamamoto was a shrewd gambler, who took pride in his mastery of Shōgi (Japanese chess) and poker, in both of which he relied on his finely tuned instinct for calculating odds. On the night of November 11, 1940, when the Swordfish biplanes flew from the Royal Navy carrier

Illustrious to cripple the Italian battle fleet lying in its Taranto base it became apparent that such odds could be turned in the Combined Fleet's favor. Yamamoto broached the possibility of making a similar attack on Hawaii to the naval minister and on January 7 submitted a nine-page outline entitled "Views on Preparations for War." "Success would not be easy to achieve," it admitted of a Pearl Harbor strike; "but if all officers and men concerned were united in truly selfless determination, then success might, with Heaven's help, be possible."

The destruction of the U.S. naval strength in such a preemptive strike could win the time Japan needed to take over the oilfields of the Dutch East Indies, Malaya, and the Philippines. Faced with a "fait accompli" in the western Pacific, Yamamoto reasoned that there was a good chance the United States would accept an early truce, adding: "the outcome must be decided on the first day." At the same time he submitted the proposal to the 11th Air Fleet, taking care that it went not to the cautious Admiral Chuichi Nagumo but to his Chief of Staff. Rear Admiral Takijiro Onishi quickly proposed putting the plan in the hands of Commander Minoru Genda—a resourceful thirty-six-year-old aviation tactical expert who had made his reputation in China. As naval attaché in London during the previous autumn, Genda had carefully studied the reports of the Taranto attack and was quick to conclude that the proposed scheme was risky but had a reasonable chance of success. This was enough to confirm Yamamoto's instinct that the gamble could succeed. In April 1941 he ordered plans to be worked up for "Operation Z"—named after the historic signal pendant flown by Admiral Togo's flagship at the Battle of Tsushima. As an indication of just how much was at stake, Yamamoto confided to his staff officer, Yasuji Watanabe, "If we fail, we'd better give up the war."

Absolute secrecy and accurate intelligence were the keys to the success of Operation Z. Any warning of the Japanese force's approach to Hawaii would send the American warships to sea and bring their land-based bombers in to counterattack. Ever since the tactical maneuvers of 1932, the U.S. Navy had been aware of the dangers of air strikes to its main Pacific base. This vulnerability had been again exposed just three years earlier by Admiral King. In consequence, patrols by Army and Navy aircraft had been increased. During the early months of 1941, these had been extended deeper into the Pacific in response to a spate of alerts radioed by Washington in reaction to Tokyo's diplomatic moves.

The British attack on Taranto had prompted Secretary of the Navy Stimson to order that "Highest priority must be given to getting more interceptor aircraft, AA guns and additional radar equipment," to protect Oahu against surprise attack. He also suggested in December to Admiral Kimmel that antitorpedo net barriers should be laid down around "Battleship Row"; but the new Pacific Fleet Commander rejected the idea on the ground that it "would restrict boat traffic by narrowing the channel." Additional precautions were not taken even after Ambassador Grew relayed cocktail party rumors passed on by the Peruvian envoy in February 1941 that Japan was preparing for a surprise mass attack on Pearl Harbor. The warning was not explicit. Nor were any of the similar rumors that reached Navy and Army Intelligence in Washington during the next eleven months specific enough to identify Hawaii as the focus of Japan's war plan. The Philippines, the Malay Peninsula, or the Dutch East Indies all appeared more obvious objectives to the logical military American mind than islands over five and a half thousand miles away from Japan's obvious strategic objectives in the East Indies.

Intelligence was the key to both Japan's success and America's failure over Pearl Harbor. Admiral Yamamoto set in motion the huge task of planning and coordinating the massive naval air operation that was to realize his strategic gamble for control of the western Pacific. Above his table aboard the battleship *Nagato* hung a detailed map of the U.S. Navy's base, marked with anchorages, defenses, and fuel-storage depots. In his desk drawer he kept a weighty volume, *The Habits, Strengths and Defenses of the American Fleet in the Hawaiian Area*—a bible of data on warship movements, depths of water, the patterns of air and sea patrols that were kept constantly updated by reports from agents in Hawaii, submarine surveillance, intercepted radio traffic, and the general background of intelligence gleaned from newspaper reports.

One of the key agents in a far-flung espionage net was twenty-eight-year-old Takeo Yoshikawa, a former naval ensign who had been recruited as a junior diplomat spying in Honolulu under the supervision of Nagao Kita, Japan's consul in Honolulu. Assuming the name Tadashi Monmura, the friendly official at the consulate with a penchant for taking pretty girls on sightseeing tours and flights over Pearl Harbor attracted little attention on Oahu among so many Japanese-Americans. Throughout the spring of 1941, Consul Kita's intelligence reports kept a stream of information flowing to Tokyo as Yamamoto's staff assembled the details necessary to planning Operation Z. Since absolute security was vital, only a handful of trusted key officers knew about the significance of Pearl Harbor. To guard against arousing American suspicion through increased espionage activity on the Hawaiian Islands, surveillance was stepped up by Japanese spies operating in the West Coast ports, the Canal Zone, and Manila, in addition to those reporting shipping movements from the main British and Dutch bases throughout the Far East. However, the request for assistance from the Abwehr very nearly blew the whole plan after the Yugoslav double agent Dusko Popov revealed to his British contacts that the German Navy's Tokyo attaché had visited

Taranto and that he himself had been instructed to go to the United States with the purpose of visiting Pearl Harbor with a checklist of information required on the Pacific Fleet's base. In August 1941, Popov was sent to New York to brief the FBI in person on the apparent import of his intended mission. But his sexual escapades on a trip to Miami so alienated J. Edgar Hoover, the agency's fastidious director, that the significance of his information was apparently buried.

ENTER MAGIC

Just how vital was the security enforced by Yamamoto, the Commander in Chief of the Combined Fleet, was never in fact appreciated. Neither he nor Imperial General Headquarters suspected that the Americans and the British were reading a large part of their most sensitive diplomatic radio traffic. This enabled both London and Washington to keep abreast of Foreign Minister Matsuoka's efforts to enlist the help of Berlin and Moscow in achieving Japanese aims in the Far East. The incalculable intelligence advantage came about because the U.S. Army had persisted with its code-breaking operations, which in 1921 had been spectacularly successful in securing the Washington Naval Treaty. Henry Stimson had disbanded the "Black Chamber" when he became Secretary of State in 1929 on the moral grounds that "gentlemen do not read each other's mail." In 1941 as Secretary of War he was able to take great comfort from the fact that the Army had reconstituted its code-breaking team in 1935 under the brilliant young cryptanalyst Colonel William Friedman. Through a deftly organized burglary operation at the office of the Japanese naval attaché in Washington that year, Friedman's Special Intelligence Service had been able to reconstruct an early version of the German-designed Enigma cipher machine. This was an electromechanical device based on a typewriter that transposed letters by routing electrical impulses through a changeable plugboard key and the contacts of revolving rotors.

For almost two years the Americans had been reading the so-called Red Code, until 1937 when the Japanese introduced a more sophisticated version designated "Alphabetical Typewriter 97." Unable to get hold of this new, closely guarded machine, Friedman's team tried for three years to reconstruct their own device to unravel the Purple Code. Only the chance inspiration by one of the team that the Japanese might have substituted the Enigma machine's rotors for selector step switches like those used in telephone exchanges led to the successful reconstruction of the Purple decoders. Skillful detective work by the Navy cryptanalysts revealed that the all-important plugboard key setting was changed on

ten-day cycles. So by the spring of 1941, the code-breaking teams of
Friedman's SIS unit and those under Lieutenant Commander Alwyn D.
Kramer's OP20GZ section of Naval Intelligence, who shared the task of
processing the intercepts on alternative days, were deciphering "all but
2–3% of the diplomatic Purple traffic." But so great was the volume of
this traffic, and so undermanned were the teams of American cryptanalysts
trained in the intricacies of the Japanese language, that neither the Army
nor Naval Intelligence were able to provide for proper collation and
evaluation of the vast flow of decoded messages.

"Operation Magic" was the cover name given to protect the source
and circulation of the secret intelligence provided by the Army and
Navy cryptologists who were eavesdropping in on other Japanese
codes as well as Purple. The most important information was pouched
and sent by special courier to the President, Secretaries of Navy and
War, Directors of Naval and Military Intelligence, Chief of War Plans
Directorate, and the Secretary of State. The privileged few therefore saw
only selected intercepts before the courier destroyed each copy, so for all
the brilliance of the actual codebreaking, no senior American leader was
fully aware of the overall intelligence picture given by Magic. Events
were to show that this was the major flaw in the whole operation and
that neither Army or Navy intelligence experts were assembling from
the small clues a pattern that might have pointed to Hawaii as a significant Japanese objective.

A contributory factor to this failure was the concern for security
that became almost obsessive during the spring and summer of 1941. The
intercepts revealed that the Japanese were being warned by "reliable
sources" in Berlin that their codes were being read by the Americans.
This leak almost certainly came from a lapse by the British embassy in
Washington transmitting very sensitive Magic information to London in
a low-grade cipher which was being read by the Germans. Although
Japanese confidence in the security of their most secret codes remained
unshaken, there was alarm in Washington. The rules for protecting
Magic information were tightened up to the extent that the Army refused
to continue accepting responsibility for delivering its messages to the
President after intercepts had been mislaid and one discovered crumpled
up in a White House wastebasket.

The most important result was that the practice of sending out Magic
Summaries to the Army and Navy Command at Hawaii was drastically
curtailed, and after July was only made at the express instruction of the
Chief of Naval Operations. This dried up an important source of intelligence to the Pacific Fleet, which had not been provided with its own
Purple decoding machine. Six of the complicated devices had originally
been assembled by the end of 1941, one each for the two service centers

in Washington (which also retained two spares), and one that had been sent to the naval base at Cavite in the Philippines. The machine originally intended for Pearl Harbor had been sent to London along with a spare in the exchange of technological secrets with the British made in the fall of 1940. In the package deal, negotiated by Sir Henry Tizard, the latest centimeter radar device and an Enigma machine to decipher the German codes developed by Britain's cryptanalysts were part of the trade-off for the key to enabling London to break into the Japanese codes. That the British were tardy in providing the Americans with the key to the Wehrmacht's traffic because of ostensible security considerations was to prove particularly galling later when it was claimed that the absence of a Purple machine at Pearl Harbor contributed to the catastrophe of December 1941. A special grievance was felt by Admiral Husband E. Kimmel, one of the U.S. Navy's star flag officers, who had been sent out in February 1941 to "shake up" the Pacific Fleet.

Since the previous November, when the Imperial Navy had drastically revised its operational code and cipher system, the Americans had been deprived of detailed information about the operations of the Combined Fleet. Analysis of its radio traffic from the listening posts that ringed the Pacific was now their principal source about the movements of Japanese warships. In interpreting the overall position, Magic's insight into the diplomatic traffic, as well as the espionage reports being fed to Tokyo by its consulates, could have provided many vital clues to Kimmel's intelligence staff.

Penetrating the new Combined Fleets' codes had become such a priority by May 1941 that a Combat Intelligence Unit was set up in Hawaii under the command of Lieutenant Joseph J. Rochefort, a former enlisted man whose understanding of the Japanese language, plus a natural talent for cryptography, were now applied to tackling the crucial fleet code in which most operational orders were given, as well as the flag officers' code. Months later Rochefort's team had only succeeded in breaking the codes that the Japanese Navy used for signaling routine information about the weather, fuel-supply situations, and personnel changes. This had to be assessed in conjunction with the general background level of traffic and radio direction reports in a process of traffic analysis that relied on intelligent guesswork to construct a picture of the Imperial Fleet's likely movements. As Rochefort and Kimmel knew, the method was dangerously vulnerable to the enemy's deception practice of frequently transferring the call signs of battleships and carriers to destroyers and submarines so as to camouflage the whereabouts of senior commanders and their striking groups.

The need for accurate signal intelligence to supplement traffic analysis became even more pressing for the Pacific Fleet command when in mid-

May 1941, in response to Britain's critical military situation, the President reactivated orders to dispatch three battleships, an aircraft carrier, and a force of cruisers from Pearl Harbor to reinforce the Atlantic Fleet. After a spectacular defeat by German airborne forces, the British were evacuating Crete while Rommel was pressing on with his advance through Libya to threaten the Suez Canal.

The Germans used their military triumph in Greece to prod their Far Eastern Axis partner to review her obligation to the Tripartite Pact. "It is necessary for Japan to attack Singapore," Marshal Hermann Göring stressed to Baron Oshima, Tokyo's envoy in Berlin, shortly before the foreign minister arrived at the end of March. Matsuoka's conferences with Hitler and his high command left no doubt that Germany was dissatisfied with Japanese inactivity against the British and even more disturbed to learn that negotiations were being secretly conducted with the Americans. The Tripartite Pact had been intended to ensure the tying down of the U.S. Navy in the Pacific, where it could not send reinforcements to the Royal Navy to help in the war against the U-boats on the Atlantic. So after Matsuoka returned to Tokyo, he determined to take a line with the United States that would restore Hitler's confidence. On May 12, Nomura presented Hull with a formal reply to the United States in accordance with a set of unspecified principles that would evidently lead to domination by Japan. In addition, the plan required the United States to assume normal trading relations immediately.

The Secretary of State was affronted and quickly rejected the Japanese proposals. Nor were the Germans any happier with Japan's continued reluctance to respond to their demands that Britain's Far East possessions should be attacked. Oshima cabled Tokyo from Berlin a week later that feeling was running high against the "violently anti-Axis expansion of the United States in the Atlantic," and that Hitler was strongly of the opinion that "Japan was evading her duty to enter the war." Magic intercepts enabled Roosevelt to track the souring of relations between Japan and Germany. So he decided to drive another wedge into the Tripartite Pact. On May 22, the day that the squadron heading east to reinforce the Atlantic Fleet entered the Panama Canal, he ordered that U.S. Marines be sent to relieve the British troops garrisoning Iceland. That same day came the news that the superbattleship *Bismarck*, pride of Hitler's Kriegsmarine, was making a breakout through the mists of the Arctic to join the battle against the Atlantic convoys. Americans caught their collective breaths during the six days that it took the Royal Navy to chase, hunt down, and on May 27 finally sink one of the world's most powerful warships. That night, taking advantage of the hardened national mood following the sinking of two U.S. merchantmen, President Roosevelt declared an "unlimited national emergency." To check Hitler's bid "to gain control of the seas," Roosevelt told the nation in a radio broadcast that he was extending the U.S. Navy's patrol deep into the eastern Atlantic, "to ensure the delivery of the needed supplies to Britain."

It was a significant escalation of undeclared war on the Axis power. But Hitler resisted the temptation to intensify operations in the West because he was on the verge of a momentous assault in the East.

5

"A Sinister Twilight"

The whole course of the war was to be dramatically turned during the early hours of Sunday, July 22, 1941. Under a thunderous artillery barrage spewing from the muzzles of 6,000 guns, German tank and infantry divisions rolled like a tidal wave across the Soviet border. Although Stalin had been repeatedly warned of what was coming from British and American sources drawing on Magic and Ultra intelligence, which confirmed the reports made from Tokyo by master spy Richard Sorge, the Red Army was sent reeling before "Operation Barbarossa's" three massive Blitzkrieg thrusts toward Leningrad, Moscow, and Kiev. For Winston Churchill, the launching of Hitler's campaign to the east came as the climactic turning point in Britain's struggle against Germany. It freed England from the threat of German invasion and the Prime Minister urged the nation to join with him in offering an alliance to the Soviet Union. "We are resolved to destroy Hitler and every vestige of the Nazi regime. From this nothing will turn us. Nothing!" Yet Stalin was slow to reply to this magnanimous gesture, and to Roosevelt's equally impressive defiance of American anti-Communist sentiment to offer Lend-Lease aid.

The Führer's long-planned crusade to rid the world of bolshevism, while it achieved spectacular military triumphs during its first weeks, was to prove a diplomatic disaster. It spurred a new resolve in the United States, despite Hitler's assurance to Mussolini that it would bring "a tremendous relief for Japan in East Asia and thereby a much stronger threat to American activities through Japanese intervention." He had miscalculated badly. The attack on Russia very nearly ruptured the Tripartite Pact on which Japan was depending for Germany's aid in maintaining good relations with Stalin so as to preclude any threat from Siberia while the army and navy concentrated on their southward thrust. Prime Minister Konoye felt betrayed because the Germans clearly trusted their Axis partners too little to warn them of Barbarossa—even though he had feared the worst since receiving an April report from Oshima in Berlin that "Germany is confident she can defeat Russia and she is preparing to fight at any moment."

The Japanese cabinet members were divided by the foreign minister's strident advocacy of following Hitler's dictates to launch into an attack on Vladivostok and march north against Russia. Reneging on his recent pledges to Stalin, the headstrong Matsuoka had rushed to the Imperial Palace to try to win the Emperor's backing for a Siberian adventure. But he had so lost face with his colleagues that he was now regarded as "Hitler's office boy." The army staff had no intention of taking on Soviet tanks and aircraft until they could be certain that the Germans had smashed the Red Army to the brink of defeat, and the naval staff were adamantly set against opening up any war in the north now that their planning was geared to a rapid southward thrust to secure the oil resources of the Dutch East Indies that would be needed to make Japan independent of the United States if diplomacy failed.

This indeed appeared the likely outcome by the end of June 1941. Two months of secret discussion had brought Japan and America no nearer to an accommodation; in fact, they were drifting further apart as positions hardened. The day before Operation Barbarossa moved into Russia, the United States had rejected Japan's latest proposals. The Secretary of State's June 21 reply to Nomura made it clear that Tokyo's plan for an independent China protected by Japanese troops was unacceptable. Aid to the Nationalists would be continued and Japan would be expected to withdraw from the Tripartite Pact in anticipation of any settlement.

Hull accompanied this firm restatement of America's position with an Oral Note which questioned the good faith of the Japanese government by pointedly asserting that "some Japanese leaders in influential positions are definitely committed to a course which calls for the support of Nazi Germany and its policies of conquest." Matsuoka took this as a personal insult, and used it as the excuse for severing further negotiations with the United States in anticipation that now Japan had no choice but to cast her lot in with Hitler. But the German invasion of the Soviet Union scarcely twenty-four hours later upset his machinations. The Prime Minister carried the Japanese cabinet in opposing the foreign minister's call for an immediate attack on Russia, and began to consider how best to revive the Washington talks in order to avoid being dragged into war. This did not stop Matsuoka. "Japan is preparing for all possible eventualities as regards the USSR in order to join forces with her in active crushing of the communist menace," Matsuoka radioed Oshima in Berlin on July 2. The ambassador was ordered to convey to Ribbentrop that the "Japanese government have decided to secure 'points d'appui' in French Indo-China to enable Japan further to strengthen her pressure on Great Britain and the United States of America," and to present this as a "valuable contribution to the common front" by promising: "we Japanese are not going to sit on the fence while you Germans fight the Russians."

That Tokyo was staying on the fence for the time being was evident in Washington from Magic eavesdropping on the circuit to Berlin and the conflicting messages to the American ambassador seeking clarification of Hull's latest position. Roosevelt could guess at the turmoil swirling around the Japanese leadership. He was having to deal with dissension that had broken out in his own cabinet, too.

On June 23, Interior Secretary Harold Ickes wanted an immediate oil embargo because "Japan is so occupied with what is happening in Russia and what may happen in Siberia that she won't venture a hostile move against the Dutch East Indies." As "Petroleum Co-Ordinator," Ickes was pressing every available tanker to keep Britain supplied and he advocated a hard-line policy against the Japanese because oil was the "sine qua non in order to fight against what we are fighting for." A week later, when he tried to push the embargo by threatening his resignation, the President reminded him: "I think it will interest you to know that the Japanese are having a real drag-down and knock-out fight among themselves for the past week trying to decide which way they are going to jump." Believing that sanctions might prompt Japan to jump south rather than north, Roosevelt explained the reason for his caution: "I simply have not got the Navy to go around and every little episode in the Pacific means fewer ships in the Atlantic."

Magic intercepts had revealed that the French in Indochina were being pressed for air and sea bases, and Rear-Admiral Richmond Kelly Turner, the Chief of Naval War Plans, after meeting with Nomura on June 20, had reported to Admiral Stark that any oil shutoff would send Japan into an attack on the Dutch East Indies. The Chief of Naval Operations had passed the memorandum on to the President, noting: "I concur in general."

On July 2, the Emperor presided over an Imperial Conference that took the momentous decision to carry forward a policy of southward expansion, "no matter what obstacles may be encountered." Appropriately for the occasion, Hirohito sat impassively on his dais in full dress uniform listening to Prince Konoye drone through his prepared statement, "Outline of National Policies in View of Present Developments." In it the cabinet rejected Matsuoka's advice for an immediate attack on Russia, in favor of executing Japan's advance "southward in order to establish firmly a basis for her self-existence and self-protection." A move against Siberia was only to be made if "the German-Soviet war should develop to our advantage." Konoye laid down: "our Empire is determined to follow a program which will result in the establishment of the

Greater East Asia Co-Prosperity Sphere." This would secure for Japan the markets, oil, and mineral wealth of the British, Dutch, and French Far Eastern possessions. But first and foremost was the need to "dispose of the China Incident." This necessitated cutting off the reopened Burma Road along which American supplies were reaching the Chinese Nationalists. A "joint protectorate" in Indochina was to be set up with the Vichy regime to provide the army with a base from which to launch north against the Kuomintang-held provinces, west against Thailand and Burma, as well as south to threaten Malaya. Such a move, it was hoped, would persuade the British to return to a policy of appeasement. But if diplomacy should fail, 2 million more troops were to be conscripted and arms production stepped up. "Preparations for war with Great Britain and the United States will be made," Konoye announced, indicating that Japan must be prepared to take this ultimate step to achieve her national crusade.

After a debate in which Matsuoka's alternative "Strike North" policy was again rejected, the Emperor's assent was automatic. The Japanese government was locked on the course to war. Yet since neither Konoye, nor the army or navy, was yet ready to fight, it was agreed that one final effort would be made to reach these goals by diplomacy. What slim chance remained of reaching an accord with the Americans required that the intractable Matsuoka be dropped as foreign minister. His ouster was engineered through Konoye's expedient requiring the entire cabinet to submit their resignations. It was then reappointed en bloc with the exception of its most pro-Hitler member, who was replaced by the more amenable Admiral Teijiro Toyoda.

What was intended to be a placatory gesture toward the United States was at once negated in Washington when Magic intercepts revealed that Tokyo was pressing the French government for bases at Saigon and Camranh Bay. This clear threat to the security of Thailand, Malaya, and the Philippines was confirmed by intercepts of Japan's July 24 ultimatum to Vichy President Marshal Pétain that the Imperial Army was ready to march in. After Japanese bombs fell on the American church in Nanking and alongside the gunboat *Tutuila*, Cordell Hull had sided with the hardliners in supporting the immediate embargo of oil and the freezing of Japan's assets in America. Marshall and Stark, worried that this brought the danger of a two-ocean conflict closer before the United States had completed adequate military preparations, again urged caution. But France's decision on July 24 to agree to the Japanese establishing forward bases in Indochina forced him to respond. Two days later the State Department publicly condemned the move as foreshadowing "further and more obvious movements of conquest." The President on July 26 announced that Japanese funds would be frozen and trade further restricted.

Roosevelt, however, was careful to make plain that his intention was not to goad Japan into war by imposing a total embargo on oil. The President, as Ickes noted, "was still unwilling to draw the noose tight. He thought it might be better to slip the noose around Japan's neck and give it a jerk now and then."

The "jerk" that Roosevelt intended was interpreted by Ickes to require "an export license before any goods can be shipped to Japan but the President indicated that we could still continue to ship oil and gasoline." Roosevelt himself went out of his way to explain personally to Ambassador Nomura that he was not ordering a total ban on oil exports to Japan when he put forward a proposal to solve the present crisis by neutralizing Indochina to open the door for all nations to trade there. But he cautioned that an "exceedingly serious situation would immediately result" if the Tokyo government made any move toward seizing the Dutch East Indies oilfields. This was as far as he allowed himself to go in issuing the ultimatum that the British and Dutch governments in London had wanted in response to Churchill's fear that even a limited constriction in oil supplies would prompt the Japanese to "run amok."

The President was not optimistic that his order would have much impact in checking Japan's military, but he had deliberately reserved the option of imposing a total embargo by only cutting off high-octane gasoline exports and reducing heavy oil exports to just below the previous year's level. Still, hardliners in Washington and Tokyo interpreted the restriction and freeze as total. The *New York Times* called it "the most drastic blow short of war." Facing a bellicose outburst in the Japanese press, Ambassador Grew warned that it would precipitate a "vicious circle of reprisals and counter reprisals" that could lead to open conflict. The strongest reaction came from the Imperial Navy. As Japan's biggest oil consumer, the naval staff felt direct pressure. A total shut-off would leave the fleet with less than a year's reserve of fuel before the warships literally ran out of steam. So the naval staff urged the Prime Minister to speed up preparation to implement the plan to move south in order to secure the oil supplies in the East Indies. The new militancy in Tokyo was monitored in Washington as Magic intercepts of communications to Ambassador Oshima in Berlin advised him that Japan might need to take "immediate steps to break asunder this ever strengthening chain of encirclement."

The "noose" around Japan's neck was to be jerked far tighter even than the President intended. At the beginning of August he left Washington to take a momentous "fishing trip" that began in the glare of publicity aboard the yacht *Potomac* off the New England coast. It ended cloaked in secrecy aboard the heavy cruiser *Augusta* in the remote mists of Newfoundland. On August 9, the battleship *Prince of Wales*, still bearing her scars from the *Bismarck* action, steamed into Placentia Bay and dropped anchor off the village of Argentia alongside the *Augusta*. Within hours the President and the British Prime Minister, meeting personally for the first time, quickly achieved a strong rapport on global strategy, while their military advisers met separately to agree on what Roosevelt carefully defined as "broad principles which should guide our policies along the same road."

The U.S. delegation, headed by General Marshall, Admiral Stark, and General Arnold, had decided beforehand not to make any commitments that might give the British an opportunity to march them down that road to war. So after three days of the most persuasive briefings directed by Admiral Pound and General Dill, Churchill was disappointed that his team had failed to persuade the U.S. Navy to send warships into the Mediterranean or begin convoying British shipping across the Atlantic. When it came to the Far East, however, it was apparent that there had been a significant revision of American planning toward the strong deterrent strategy in the Far East that the British had failed to achieve during the spring staff talks.

"We are now trying to build up the defense of the Philippines as a direct defense to the Indian Ocean and Singapore," Admiral Stark informed the meeting called aboard the *Prince of Wales* on August 11 which was to review Admiral Pound's position paper. The Chief of Naval Operations called for Britain's representatives to help out and "rearrange their schedules" for certain key Lease-Lend armaments so that antiaircraft guns and heavy bombers could be sent out to Manila. Without hesitation Pound and Dill agreed that "a strong defense of the Philippine Islands [would] directly strengthen the defense of Singapore and the Netherlands East Indies." This went far beyond the limited defense envisioned by the RAINBOW 5 War Plan, or even Churchill's hope in April that "modest arrangements" could be made to increase Anglo-American strength in the Far East.

Then the danger of a direct Japanese attack on either Manila or Singapore had seemed remote to the military planners in London and Washington. But not in Canberra. The Australian government had cabled that it was "gravely concerned at this most serious situation," after the Singapore Defence Committee had reported on the bastion's weakness in December 1940. Churchill had replied reassuringly: "It always being understood that if Australia is seriously threatened by invasion we shall not hesitate to compromise or sacrifice the Mediterranean position for the sake of our kith and kin." Both governments had learned with considerable unease of the secret Japanese-American discussions, anticipating that any deal struck would weaken Britain's ability to resist further appeasement in the Far East. The breakdown of the talks following the attack on Russia and Japan's move to demand bases in Indochina had thrust on the United States the burden of responsibility for curbing any further aggression. In July, the British Joint Plans Committee had concluded that "the Japanese government are unlikely to be deterred by threats or economic action." Since the First Sea Lord had confirmed that he "could not collect a fleet to proceed to the Far East," Churchill had sailed for the historic conference knowing that he must persuade Roosevelt to send out whatever reinforcements were needed in the western Pacific to deter Japan and reassure Australia.

Fortunately for the Prime Minister, he found that the President had already come to the same conclusion. Airpower, along with the recent mobilization of the Commonwealth Army, had provided the U.S. War Department planners with the rationale for reversing their twenty-year-old pessimistic assumptions to conclude that the Philippines could now be successfully defended. The U.S. Navy, however, had expressed its skepticism by refusing to send out any major units other than submarines to reinforce the Asiatic Fleet in Manila. Not for the first—or last—time the boundless foreign policy objectives of the United States were allowed to dictate a risky strategy that would fall far short of what its limited military capability could support. But now the embargo was clamped on oil, Roosevelt had to present the reinforcements sent to the Philippines—along with Churchill's promise to send a few capital ships to Singapore—as a deterrent powerful enough to block a Japanese advance southward from Formosa and Indochina to seize alternative supplies.

Nonetheless, the President was still not ready to commit the United States to joining the war if Japan attacked British or Dutch possessions in the Far East. He was to be forcefully reminded how powerful isolationist support was still running when the House passed by a single vote the bill to continue the draft and federalize the National Guard units on August 12—the day the Conference concluded with the signing of the "Atlantic Charter." This proclaimed Anglo-Saxon unity to uphold Roosevelt's Four Freedoms, but in spite of great press fanfares it was to leave unmoved the 75 percent of Americans who still opposed going to war against Germany.

Significantly, a small majority were prepared to resist Japan's aggression at the risk of war, but Roosevelt had argued against Churchill's request for a joint declaration that "any further encroachments . . . might lead to war between Japan and the United States." His scheme to "baby them along for three months" began with Secretary Hull toning down the Prime Minister's strong words into an offer of a detente if Tokyo would "re-embark on a program of peace in the Pacific"; he also floated the suggestion of a meeting between the President and Prime Minister Konoye in Alaska. The official Japanese response appeared encouraging, even if the intelligence indicated that the military build-up in Indochina was progressing rapidly.

PLANNING FOR THE ATTACK

Winston Churchill would record that "the whole of the Japanese menace lay in a sinister twilight compared with our other needs," as the autumn of 1941 saw the U-boats intensifying their attacks on Atlantic convoys, the German panzers taking Kiev, and Rommel's Afrika Corps driving the British back into Egypt. Alarm over Japan's stationing air squadrons and 30,000 troops in her new forward bases in Indochina would have been considerably greater if British and American intelligence had known the scale of the clandestine preparation for war going on throughout the Far East. From Guam to Burma, Manila to Malaya, scores of agents of the Imperial Army and Navy were gathering information on defenses, airstrips, landing beaches, and potential collaborators. All this information was filtering back to Imperial General Headquarters to be incorporated into the "Unit 82 Strike South Plan" for a massive land, sea, and air offensive. Much of the detailed army planning was worked out at a hutted encampment outside the Formosan capital of Taipeh under the camouflage of the Taiwan Army Research Section.

The driving force on the small team of staff officers planning military operations in Southeast Asia was Masanobu Tsuji. An ultra-nationalist who had once plotted to assassinate Prince Konoye, Tsuji now brought his fanatical dedication to bear on mastering the enormous task of assembling details of every country that Japan had designated for her Co-Prosperity Sphere. He investigated the best ways of equipping troops to fight in the jungle where they would have to face, besides the enemy, the threat of malaria and a steamy humidity that would rust their weapons overnight. Diet, clothing, and equipment were tested, as well as assault techniques, in closely guarded exercises at Hainan in the Gulf of Tonkin. The troops were kept confined in stifling holds along with their horses and limited water in order to test their endurance. Meanwhile agents disguised as Chinese coolies were working in the Philippines and Malaya, ferreting out information about strategic roads and bridges on the line of proposed advance.

After six months of exhaustive planning, Colonel Tsuji by the summer of 1941 was able to send the General Staff Headquarters in Tokyo a series of reports that provided the practical blueprint by which Japan could carry out the military conquest of Southeast Asia. They convinced the Imperial Army Chief, Hajime Sugiyama, that the Navy's long-advocated mission of southern expansion was not only feasible but could be achieved quickly. In answer to the general's close questioning as to how long op-

THE PACIFIC WAR

erations would take, Tsuji confidently predicted, with surprising accuracy: "If we commence on Miji Setsu [November 3] we will be able to capture Manila by the New Year, Singapore by Kigensetsu [February 11], Java on Army Commemoration Day [March 10] and Rangoon on the Emperor's Birthday [April 19]." The secret plan was designated "Operation No. 1"—the master blueprint for the takeover of Southeast Asia. Tsuji, relishing his reputation as "Colonel of Operations," was sent in August to Saigon to oversee the main army part of the plan for the invasion of Thailand and Malaya and for capturing Britain's fortress at Singapore in order to eliminate her as a power in the Far East.

While the Imperial Army planned and rehearsed for its invasion of Malaya and the Philippines, the Imperial Navy was hard at work training for its strike against Hawaii. Day after day squadrons of naval planes raced over the Honshu city of Kagoshima. The pilots who flew their Nakajima torpedo bombers dangerously low over the roof of the Yamagataya department store to make dummy runs against the target vessels anchored in the bay had no idea that their practice site, with its high peak and narrow approach, had been especially selected by Admiral Yamamoto for its topographical similarity to Pearl Harbor. From other bases on Kyushu, aircrews rehearsed the difficult techniques, pulling plummeting Aichi bombers out of steep dives 500 feet nearer the water to improve their accuracy. And off the rocky coast of Shikoku, volunteer teams practiced attack runs in temperamental "Type A" midget submarines. Naval ordinance experts experimented by attaching winglets to torpedoes to stop them diving into the mud of shallow harbors, and fins were fitted to 16-inch armor-piercing shells to turn them into bombs to be used against battleships.

By the end of the summer of 1941, the staff had solved all the technical and operational problems. In the somber setting of the Naval War College, in Tokyo's suburbs, Admiral Yamamoto unveiled his plan to attack Pearl Harbor to the September 2 Staff Conference. War games were played to rehearse the navy's role in the Imperial General Staff's grand plan for simultaneous invasions of Malaya, the Philippines, Wake, Guam, Borneo, and Java. Only when these had been successfully demonstrated did the Combined Fleet Staff get their chance to show how effectively Operation Z's audacious six-carrier strike could deal with the U.S. Pacific Fleet at Pearl Harbor.

But Navy Chief Admiral Osami Nagano was skeptical, as were many of the staff admirals. For the next two months a fierce debate would rage between them and the Combined Fleet Staff over whether Operation Z should be made part of the master plan. It was to be resolved finally late in October. "The presence of the U.S. Fleet in Hawaii is a dagger pointed at our throats," came the tersely worded memorandum from the Combined Fleet, insisting that their operation to eliminate it was "absolutely essential." "Unless it is carried out, Admiral Yamamoto has no confidence that he can fulfill his responsibility" the memorandum concluded, forcing Nagano to give his approval rather than face the implied resignation threat by his Commander in Chief.

FAR EASTERN BASTIONS

There was little in the broad outline of Operation Z—on which Yamamoto was pinning his career and the fate of his nation—that was not familiar to the Americans. That summer the Hawaiian Army Air Commander, Major General Frederick L. Martin, had sent a memorandum to the War Department in Washington asking for more aircraft to expand his patrols to guard against what he foresaw as the worst eventuality: Japan's fleet attacking with "the employment of six enemy carriers against Oahu simultaneously, each approaching on a different course." His concern echoed a Joint Board study of March 31, 1941, which read like a synopsis of the top-secret plan in the black manila folder that Admiral Yamamoto kept under lock and key: "*A declaration of war might be preceded by:* 1. A surprise submarine attack. . . . 2. A surprise attack on Oahu including ships and installations . . . launched from one or more carriers which would probably approach inside 300 miles." Yet for all this inspired guesswork, the U.S. Army Chief still considered Hawaii "the strongest fortress in the world." General Marshall was convinced from his visit to Oahu the previous year that with "adequate air defense"—as he put it in a May 1941 report to the President, "enemy carriers and escorts and transports will begin to come under air attack at a distance of 750 miles." He therefore concluded that "a major attack against Oahu is considered impractical."

If too great a confidence in their own military readiness and reliance on strategic logic blinkered America's most senior generals and admirals toward the danger to Hawaii during 1941, at the same time their concern was increasingly focused on making the Philippines the effective barrier to deter a Japanese advance south into the Netherlands East Indies. That this represented a dramatic westward shift of U.S. strategy had been spelled out before the Atlantic Charter Conference with the British that endorsed it by an August memorandum drawn up by the head of the War Plans Division. "From 1922 until later 1940 our policy with regard to the Philippines was to maintain existing strength but to undertake no further permanent improvements except as a measure of economy," Major General Leonard T. Gerow reported, in outlining the steps taken to reverse this decision since the 1939 recommendation to the Chief of Staff that "U.S. forces in the Philippines be withdrawn at the earliest opportunity."

The initial call for reinforcements to enable more than a token defense of America's sprawling island territory on Japan's doorstep came from the U.S. Army Commander in the Philippines. Major General George Grunert was informed in December 1940 that his Philippine Scouts would be doubled to 12,000 and a limited increase would be made to the strength of the U.S. Army 31st Infantry Division. But the War Department warned that he could expect no major troop or plane shipments to reinforce his command because the Atlantic-oriented RAINBOW 5 strategy precluded moves "which might result in involving us in action in a theater which we are not prepared to sustain." Marshall himself maintained that sending more forces to the Philippines was "just what Germany would like to see us undertake." In the course of the spring Anglo-American staff conferences, he would consistently reject British efforts to pressure the United States for an increased military and naval commitment to the western Pacific.

Yet already strong political pressure was being put on Roosevelt to undo one of the fundamental tenets on which the RAINBOW 5 strategy rested. In January, Philippine President Manuel Quezon expressed his concern about the course of Japanese expansion and urged the President to provide funds for mobilizing the Commonwealth Army, saying that "The project would provide the funds required for mobilizing the Filipinos to defend themselves." "The project would greatly enhance the defensive strategy of the United States in the area" was the view also pressed by Quezon's military adviser and Field Marshal of the Commonwealth Army, General Douglas MacArthur. The son of a Civil War general who had become the first military governor of the Philippines, MacArthur's acumen and drive had propelled him through a dazzling military career. From the head of his class and captain at West Point, service in Luzon had been followed by brilliant exploits in the trenches of the Western Front under Pershing, the post of Superintendent of the Military Academy, and a rapid rise to Chief of Staff. After five years at the pinnacle of the U.S. Army, in 1935 he returned to the Philippines as military adviser, retiring two years later as the world's highest paid officer.

An egotistical commander, driven by a histrionic impulse, MacArthur was soon revered by the Filipinos because he relished the theatricality of his role as field marshal, making appearances in a gold-braided uniform of his own design. He was lionized by society hostesses, but preferred to retreat to the seclusion of the penthouse that his friend Quezon had built for his wife and small son atop the palatial Manila Hotel. The regal splendor in which MacArthur lived may have had much to do with the unreality of the grandiose scheme he devised for defending the Philippines by raising a 1 million-strong Filipino army, which he intended to recruit and train along the lines of Switzerland's militia. Four years of budgetary restrictions had cut down his hopes of being able to breathe new life into the old ORANGE War Plan. As 1941 began he was a field marshal in name only, commanding a regular army less than 4,000 strong supplemented by less than 20,000 barely trained irregulars.

Yet by early 1941, as the threat began building toward the Philippines with the increase of Japanese forces in Formosa coinciding with the movement south toward Indochina, many of the generals in Washington (who had begun their careers in the islands) began softening their hard-nosed decision to abandon the Filipinos. Douglas MacArthur still exercised considerable influence amongst America's top political and military circles. By the end of May 1941, the War Department had given its blessing to MacArthur's scheme for installing 12-inch coastal batteries to protect Luzon. This had been followed by an ambitious plan to build strategic roads and air-raid shelters as well as expanding Luzon's airfields and runways to take the heavy bombers—although Grunert's air force then consisted of a few score obsolete fighters and medium bombers. Congress was presented with a $52 million bill for the burgeoning Philippine defense program, to be paid with funds from sugar excise taxes and a devaluation of the U.S.-controlled Filipino currency.

The breakdown of American-Japanese negotiations in June, which followed the submission of MacArthur's unrealistic year-end deadline for raising and equipping an army of 120,000 Filipinos, gave irreversible momentum to the political and military advocates who wanted to set the U.S. Pacific defense line more than 5,000 miles west of its original boundary at Hawaii. Now Secretary of War Stimson urged the President that "all practical steps should be taken to increase the defensive strength of the Philippines." Even Marshall had reversed his earlier stand, and on June 24 wrote confidentially to MacArthur that because of his "qualifications and vast experience," he had been picked to supersede Grunert as U.S. Army Commander in the Far East "should the situation approach a crisis."

That crisis came exactly a month later when Japan moved into advance bases in Indochina. It was no accident that Roosevelt chose July 26—the same day that he issued the order freezing Japanese assets—to announce that MacArthur had been recalled to active duty as a major general to mobilize the Philippine Army with $10 million drawn from the President's emergency fund. This unprecedented strategic U-turn by the American planners was warmly welcomed by the British two weeks later at the Atlantic Charter Conference. Delighted that a way had now been found to fulfill his pledge to defend "kith and kin" in Australia, Winston Churchill promised Roosevelt that he would send a battleship and carrier task force to Singapore as part of the Anglo-American policy for a rapid build-up of military force to deter Japan's advance south.

No sooner had the decision been taken than on August 14 the U.S. War Plans Division issued a call for more reinforcements to be sent to Mac-

Arthur: "The present attitude of Japan indicates she may consider a reduction of the Philippine Islands a prior requirement to commencement of other plans for expansion. The ability of the Philippine islands to withstand a determined attack with present means is doubtful." General Gerow called on the U.S. Navy to send more warships out to the Asiatic Fleet and advised dispatching another infantry regiment, a battalion of tanks, and another eighty-seven fighters, noting that "shipping remains a controlling factor."

The report, however, also noted that there need be no delay in getting new heavy bombers out to Luzon because they could be flown there by a circuitous route that would take them from Hawaii, Midway, Wake, New Guinea, and Darwin to avoid Japanese patrols from the Marshalls. These aircraft provided the way to bring about a quick build-up of American military power in the western Pacific without having to draw any scarce shipping from the Atlantic.

The "Flying Fortress"—as the four-engine bomber had been dubbed when the prototype Boeing 299 appeared six years earlier—had acquired a reputation as something of a wonder weapon. Originally designed to protect America from hostile enemy fleets, the U.S. Army Air Corps prophets of strategic bombing envisaged the task of what they officially designated the B-17 to be primarily offensive. Equipped with the sophisticated Norden sight and armed with guns to beat off fighters, they proclaimed that the Fortress's 1,000-mile range made daylight precision bombing from an altitude of 4 miles a practical reality. General Arnold was convinced that the four-engined bomber would revolutionize warfare, but he was unable until late 1940 to persuade an isolationist-minded Congress to provide funds to acquire the B-17 in quantity. So it was not until the British had acquired twenty Fortresses under Lend-Lease the following summer that the doctrine was first tested in battle.

The results of the RAF July and August raids against the German battlecruisers in Brest, and attacks on Berlin, and Oslo were hardly a vindication for Arnold. Eight out of the twenty Fortresses had crashed or been shot down, and only two 1,100-pound bombs were estimated to have landed on target. Goebbels's propaganda was derisorily calling the wonder bombers "Flying Coffins" and the British were condemning the B-17 for its trouble-plagued turbo-charged engines, poor oxygen system, and tendency to ice up. The American investigating team that hurried over to England to rescue the Fortresses's tarnished image blamed bad aircrews and the fact that the RAF insisted on bombing 2 miles too high —the British planes had been fitted with the less reliable Sperry bombsight because the Norden device was considered to be a national secret. Nonetheless, Boeing was already building in mechanical fixes, including more armor and a completely redesigned tail on the later model B-17s that were being rolled off the Seattle production lines ready for their long flight out across the Pacific.

The Fortress controversy with the British erupted at a critical juncture for the U.S. Army Chiefs, who were proposing to make the bombers the basis of America's deterrent against Japan in the Far East. It was a measure of the concern of General Marshall that as soon as he returned from the Atlantic Charter Conference, he took off for Seattle accompanied by the Secretary of War. The demonstrations that were laid on not only completely restored their faith in the B-17 by Boeing but convinced them that the United States had at last found the solution to defending the Philippines as well as affording the chance to take the offensive against Japan if necessary.

Marshall and Stimson returned to Washington full of confidence that the bombers would open up a whole new range of strategic options to the United States in the Far East. On August 26, the Chief of Staff issued the order to set the play in motion with the dispatch of the first nine B-17s waiting in Hawaii. By September 12, when they had all arrived safe from Japanese detection, a delighted Secretary of War concluded that this gave America the chance "to get back into the islands in a way it hadn't been able to for years." He did everything to press for an increase in the production rate. MacArthur was promised he would be given priority to receive 128 planes by February 1942, and Stimson was regularly posted with the progress in shuttling them out stealthily across the Pacific. If Japan's suspicion appeared aroused, he was ready to announce that America was merely carrying out the normal replacement of "obsolescent aircraft in the Philippines with more modern aircraft."

The widening strategic aim of the War Department was reflected by General Gerow's October 8 review of progress: "The present deterrents should be maintained and further strengthened by provision of strong offensive air forces in the Philippines, prepared to operate from bases in the British possessions to the south and from Russia." Since August soundings were being taken in London and Moscow to establish an alternative ferry route out from Alaska via Vladivostok through Malaya to Luzon. Russian airfields would place the B-17s within striking range of Tokyo, but Stalin was not eager for Japan to be given any excuse to attack in Siberia; nor was his cooperation assured by the blunt refusal that met his requests for a few of the new bombers. The British, on the other hand, along with the Dutch and Australians readily agreed to make available airfields in Borneo, New Guinea, Rabaul, and Darwin, in addition to contributing half the 6-million-gallon stockpile of gasoline MacArthur was collecting.

War Department planners used National Geographic Society maps of the Far East, marked with large blue circles radiating from Vladivostok,

Singapore, and Manila, to indicate the long striking capabilities of American bombers compared with the short red arcs of Japanese planes. This graphic presentation accompanying the Secretary of War's report convinced Stimson that the United States would soon have sufficient air strength to prevent any movement by Japanese forces across the South China Sea. Although the Asiatic Fleet was weak and the American, British, Dutch, Australian, and New Zealand naval forces could only muster a dozen cruisers and less than thirty destroyers, from the devastation wrought by German bombers in Norway and Crete, the report predicted: "Experience has shown that such a force is highly effective against naval craft operating in restricted waters." If a Japanese invasion fleet heading for the Netherlands East Indies tried to avoid being smashed up by Philippine-based airpower by taking the long route around in the Pacific, the U.S. Navy would have plenty of time to send its battleships charging west from Pearl Harbor. It was assumed that the islands were the principal "obstacle to her advance south" and would not be attacked because the "cost of the operation would be so great that Japan would hesitate to make the effort, except as a last resort." Nor did the War Plans Division believe that this would prompt an attack on Siberia, since there was the prospect that America would supply the Russians with the B-17s to make a reality of the "threat of bombardment operating against the Japanese homeland."

Each day that passed with another Fortress safely ferried to the Philippines, added to the Army's confident predictions. On October 13, a memorandum for General Marshall suggested that MacArthur's 227 aircraft were already a "tremendously strong offensive and defensive force" that made the Philippines the "key or base point" of a line to be held which passed from Hong Kong through Luzon to the Palau Islands. It recommended that the U.S. Army Commander in the Far East should be given supreme command of all land, sea, and air forces—it was a proposal that both the Chiefs of Naval Operations rejected even though MacArthur and Hart were already exchanging harsh words over each other's precise responsibilities in the event of war.

Marshall had promised that the Philippines would have "highest priority" for equipment, and MacArthur was so carried away by the prospect of all the bombers, tanks, and guns to be shipped out to him that on October 1 he reported confidently he could soon have 200,000 armed men ready for combat. So when he saw the RAINBOW 5 War Plan for the first time in September, he dismissed as "too negativistic" its requirement for him to execute the well-rehearsed ORANGE strategic retreat to hold the Bataan Peninsula in the event of hostilities. Claiming that the arrival of the bombers "has changed the whole picture in the Asiatic area," he called on the Joint Board to revise the plan in favor of his alternative, much riskier beach defense strategy. The Asiatic Fleet

Commander, hardly on the most cordial of terms with MacArthur, was pressed into supporting the change in the Philippine war plan by the brimming confidence of the Army Staff. Yet Hart, an admiral with long and distinguished service, must have entertained the gravest doubts that his three cruisers, thirteen destroyers, and twenty-nine submarines would be able to guard a coastline more extensive than the United States, even with an air force ten times the size of that envisaged by MacArthur.

The Joint Board in Washington would also overlook General Grunert's report on leaving the Philippines, which had clearly revealed the appalling state of unreadiness of the Commonwealth Army. Not only did the Board give its blessing to MacArthur's exaggerated promises that his Filipino troops stood ready to turn back any invader at the beachhead; it also promised him still more planes, tanks, and soldiers as soon as shipping became available. Major General L. Brereton, who carried approval to Manila when he arrived to take up his appointment as air commander during the first day of November, recalled how MacArthur had reacted like a small boy. "Lewis, you are as welcome as the flowers in May," exclaimed the general as he excitedly leapt up from his desk to embrace him, at the same time shouting to Richard Sutherland, his Chief of Staff, "Dick, they are going to give us everything we have asked for!"

What MacArthur had failed to grasp was that it would be nearly May of the following year before he got the forces promised—assuming that there was no Japanese attack. Marshall was already worrying that they might not wait that long once they discovered the rate at which the United States was rushing reinforcements across the Pacific. On November 15, the Army Chief of Staff took the highly unusual step of calling in Washington's senior press correspondents to brief them on the need for their newspapers to observe secrecy, particularly about the movement of the heavy bombers to the Philippines. To emphasize its importance for national security, he told them that MacArthur would be getting "the greatest concentration of heavy bomber strength anywhere in the world," and he incautiously speculated that with Russian cooperation it would soon be possible to bomb Japan. As it happened, that very morning Tokyo's concern had been aroused and a message relayed to the consulate in Manila to investigate the rate at which the bombers were arriving and along what route they flew. When the Magic intercept of that signal reached Marshall and Stark, they decided that more fighters should be shipped out by carrier to Wake and Midway so that the next flight of B-17s (scheduled for the beginning of December) could be protected as it swung south within range of air attack from the Marshalls. Four days later the Chief of Staff, reacting to MacArthur's latest plan for taking the offensive, called on his team to investigate a plan for "general incendiary attacks to burn up the wood and paper structures of the densely populated Japanese cities." Already the planning staff were racing to complete and ship out to MacArthur photographs and target maps of six hundred industrial targets.

The knowledge that the United States would soon be ready to threaten a retaliatory strategic bombing offensive against Japan led Secretary of War Stimson to record in his diary that he was praying each night for the maximum delay and urging the President and State Department to play out the diplomatic negotiations for at least six months. The balance of military power in the Far East would be transformed once the United States was in a position to threaten Japan with a strategic bombing offensive against her combustible cities. It was this possibility that prompted the Secretary of War to urge the essential need to continue diplomatic maneuvering for another six months. By April 1942 the Philippine build-up would be complete, and with the arrival of the battleships Britain had promised to send out, for the first time Anglo-American military power would be enough "to halt Japan's march south and secure the safety of Singapore."

In tandem with the dramatic westward shift that had occurred since August in the American defense posture in the Pacific, the British had also been scraping together resources to reinforce their position in Malaya. At the Atlantic Charter Conference Churchill had promised Roosevelt to send "a formidable, fast, high class squadron" of battleships and carriers out to Singapore to "exert a paralyzing effect on Japanese naval action."

It was a pledge that the Prime Minister was to fulfill, in spite of the fact that the Admiralty, like the U.S. Navy, maintained the deepest doubts about the wisdom of committing major naval forces to the Far Eastern deterrent strategy. But Churchill could marshal powerful arguments to justify the move. The pledge to Australia to defend Singapore had to be seen to be fulfilled not solely by the Americans. Even more important, the Malay States supplied nearly half the world's natural rubber and more than half the tin ore. Just as the Philippines presented an obstacle blocking Japan's route to the oil of the Netherlands East Indies, Malaya was the western obstacle barring that advance south.

Standing guard over the most economically productive and strategically important real estate in Britain's Far Eastern empire was the new Changi naval base at the tip of Singapore island. The city's broad, palm-lined avenues bespoke a gracefully tailored imperial style that was echoed in the grandeur of the government buildings. Indeed, colonialism was echoed in every aspect of an outpost that boasted no fewer than 2,000 tennis courts, along with the polo grounds, cricket pitches, and race course. Like the oak-paneled clubs and verandahed Raffles Hotel, the privileged retreat of white men seeking to ease their burden, these were manifestations of a European caste system from which the Japanese had now promised Asians liberation.

The defense of British interests was intended to be the great naval base, a vaunted "Gibraltar of the Far East," which was finally ready to receive its fleet in 1938 after the then astronomic expenditure of £60 million. It had been a source of military pride and political controversy ever since Admiral Lord Jellicoe had selected the site on the mangrove creeks of the Johore Strait during his 1921 mission in quest of imperial defense. Work had begun, halted, and begun again throughout the thirties as successive governments juggled with the relative priority of defense and budgetary cuts. In 1941, the huge dry dock had yet to hold its first battleship or the sprawling barracks their first ship's company. The vast oil-storage tanks were full and great 15-inch gun emplacements reared out from the heights, an impressive display of imperial might. Yet without the Royal Navy battle fleet, it was a fortress lacking a garrison: a British Maginot Line, whose mighty batteries pointed only out to sea, fatal testimony to the designer's folly in assuming that the 400 miles of dense jungle that lay in its defenseless rear, across the shallow Johore Strait, were "impenetrable," just like the Ardennes Forest on which the French had relied to complete their great fortress line.

Singapore might be guarded by "more guns than currants in a Christmas pudding," as one Australian newspaper colorfully reassured its readers, but the British Chiefs of Staff in London had been made aware of its vulnerability to a back-door attack from Malaya in 1937. That autumn they had received the disturbing report of the local army commander, Major General William Dobbie. After intensive study he and his Chief of Staff, General Arthur Percival, had concluded that since the Royal Navy might not be able to send out a fleet for over two months and the Malayan jungle across the Johore Strait was "in most places *not impassable*," as had been assumed, the Japanese would have plenty of time to advance south through Thailand. This meant that if Britain was going to hold on to her Far Eastern fortress, she would also have to find the means to defend the entire Malay Peninsula.

But while the British were frantically rearming to face Germany, finding the troops and equipment to garrison Malaya was an impossible task. A division or two might be spared from the Indian Army, but facing the same dilemma as the Americans trying to defend the Philippines, the solution appeared to be offered by the advocates of airpower. It was the RAF which argued that bombers and fighters were a cheaper and surer alternative for protecting Singapore than battleships. By 1940, airfields were being hurriedly constructed to protect ports and possible invasion beaches along the Malay Peninsula. But they were laid down so close to the coast that they would be quickly overrun in a successful seaborne assault. The Whitehall planners compounded their strategic error by allocating only 150 planes to the defense of the whole of Malaya and Singapore Island itself. Forced to give priority to keeping modern fighters for defending the British isles against German bombers, only obsolete types like the Brewster Buffaloes (rejected by the U.S. Navy) were available. Their performance was poor, like that of the Australian and New Zealand pilots, who made up for their lack of combat training with a bluff spirit.

"Let England have the 'Super' Spitfire and the 'Hyper' Hurricane, 'Buffaloes' are quite good enough for Malaya," Air Chief Marshal Sir Brooke-Popham, the former Governor of Kenya, had announced when he arrived to take up his appointment as Commander in Chief for the Far East in 1940. The veteran aviator complacently assumed that his four Indian Army brigades and two battalions of regular British troops evacuated from Shanghai would be more than adequate to defend Singapore and the long Malayan coastline. His folly was matched by that of his Army Commander, who told the recently arrived former attaché in Tokyo not to "discourage the chaps" when he recounted the impressive efficiency of the Imperial Army. Major General L. E. Bond subscribed to the prevalent view that the Japanese were hopeless, shortsighted fighters. "You can take it from me, we have little to fear from them."

Whitehall, by May 1941, had decided otherwise. Waking up to the Japanese menace developing in the Far East, they relieved the blimpish Bond with the uninspiring if dedicated General Percival. He rapidly came to the alarming conclusion that his command was too weak for more than a token defense—certainly not able to hold but for the six months that the Admiralty now estimated it would take before the battle-fleet arrived. The military situation in North Africa was desperate, and Percival was told there was no chance of meeting his request for the minimum reinforcement of forty-eight infantry battalions or two tank regiments which were "beyond the bounds of possibility."

THE FATAL BLUFF

Winston Churchill, who just a year before had admitted to his Chief of Staff, General Ismay, that "The idea of trying to defend the whole of the Malay Peninsula cannot be entertained," was still convinced that "the defence of Singapore must therefore be based on a strong local garrison and the general potentialities of seapower." This prompted his ready agreement during the Atlantic Charter Conference to provide the naval component of the Anglo-American Far Eastern deterrent to Japan.

"The most economical disposition would be to send *Duke of York* to the Far East. She could be joined by *Repulse* or *Renown* and one aircraft carrier capable of high speed," Churchill instructed, in a personal minute to the First Lord of the Admiralty and the First Sea Lord after a policy discussion with them the day after returning to London. Admiral Pound's response a week later was: "after considering this most carefully, I cannot recommend it." For the next two months the First Sea Lord would conduct a stubborn campaign to make the Prime Minister change his mind and not risk one of the new battleships and a carrier.

Churchill was equally determined that this was the only way that he could carry out his undertaking to the President. He rejected Admiral Pound's case that no force of battleships that the Royal Navy could muster would be powerful enough to act as a deterrent to the mighty Japanese fleet. Pound's concessionary proposal to send four old battleships as the nucleus of a fleet in the Indian Ocean was also contemptuously rejected. Describing them as "floating coffins," the Prime Minister, who prided himself on his grasp of naval strategy, insisted on one of the largest King George V class battleships and a modern carrier as a minimum. He enlisted the Foreign Secretary's aid to win the War Cabinet's agreement by arguing that a show of seapower at Singapore would not only deter Japan but reassure the Australian government. At last, on October 20, 1941, Churchill got his way.

Reluctantly, First Sea Lord Dudley Pound had to agree to send out the *Prince of Wales* to Capetown, where she would join up with the brand-new carrier *Indomitable,* then working in the West Indies. A final review would be taken of the tentative plan to send the force on to Singapore after rendezvousing in the Indian Ocean with the old battlecruiser *Repulse,* then escorting a convoy to the Middle East. They would hardly make up the mighty fleet that the prewar planners had envisaged as the bulwark of Britain's defense in the Far East. Churchill selected Admiral Sir Tom Phillips for the command, not the wisest appointment because his long staff tour at the Admiralty had deprived him of recent seagoing experience. "Tom Thumb," as the Vice-Chief of the Naval Staff was known because of his diminutive height, had fallen out with the Prime Minister. Phillips, known in the service as something of a "pocket Napoleon," was a gunnery officer who held the fierce conviction that "bombers were no match for battleships."

"There is nothing like having something that can catch and kill anything," Churchill cabled the White House on November 2, a week after the *Prince of Wales* had sailed from the Clyde. "The firmer your attitude and ours, the less chance of their taking the plunge." The next day came the news that Admiral Phillips's force would be deprived of its carrier— the *Indomitable* had run aground on a Bermuda reef. That it would be without the protection of aircover was reason enough for not sending the force on to Singapore; but when the battleship reached Capetown on November 16, there was not even the review promised to the First Sea Lord. Admiral Phillips was too wedded to his belief that aircraft posed no threat to battleships, and the Prime Minister felt bound by his commitment to the President to dispatch a force to the Far East "to serve as a deterrent to Japan." It was General Jan Christian Smuts, after a brief meeting with Phillips, who perceived the strategic blunder into which Britain and America were heading. The South African Prime Minister cabled Churchill on the day the battleship put out from Capetown, pointing out the dangers implicit in stationing battle fleets at Singapore and Hawaii, "each separately inferior to the Japanese Navy," and warning: "If the Japanese are really nippy there is an opening here for a first class disaster."

This sound advice was ignored by the Prime Minister because the British and American hopes of preventing a conflict from breaking out in the Far East were based on a policy of visible deterrence. The diplomatic and military bluff had been prompted in part by the Magic traffic passing between Berlin and Tokyo. Since before the invasion of Russia, the exchanges between Ambassador Oshima and the foreign ministry had revealed the intense diplomatic efforts that the Germans were making to get Japan to fulfill the spirit of the Tripartite Pact by attacking Siberia and Singapore. Yet at the same time it was apparent that the Konoye government was extremely hesitant to commit itself to Hitler's war, which was confirmed by the sacking of the pro-German Matsuoka in July.

Eavesdropping on Japan's diplomatic communications had played an important part in the August reversal of Anglo-American strategy in the Far East. At their August meeting, the President and Prime Minister clearly concluded that by collectively menacing the Japanese with the hastily repaired weapon of their military power in the Philippines and Malaya they could at best deter Japan from striking south to seize the oil supplies of the Netherlands East Indies and so force Tokyo to climb down to accept a dictated peace in China as economic sanctions throttled the economy. At worst they were prepared to accept the risk of provoking an attack on Russia. But neither statesman, nor any of their political or service advisers, believed that even the most bellicose Japanese militarist would be so foolhardy as to risk attacking Britain and the United States simultaneously. Yet this assumption was founded on a serious misreading of Japan's national psychology, economic predicament, and military capability. It was an astonishing error of political judgment and military intelligence that is nowhere more clearly revealed than in the smug October assessment of the U.S. Army: "Consideration of Japanese forces and her capabilities leads to the conclusion that air and ground units now available or scheduled for dispatch to the Philippine Islands in the immediate future have changed the entire picture in the Asiatic area. The action taken by the War Department may well be the determining factor in Japan's eventual decision and, consequently, have a vital bearing on the course of the war as a whole." Such wishful underestimating of their opponent's ability to call their deterrent bluff in the Far East, within two months was to defeat Anglo-American policy.

What Churchill and Roosevelt did not know when they took this fatal gamble was that the Japanese had already so minutely catalogued the military weakness of the British and American bases that the arrival of a few battleships and squadrons of bombers was a bluff that could be called. What they could not know, because it had not been communicated to any of Tokyo's diplomats and was therefore not uncovered by Magic, was that an Imperial Conference had already irrevocably resolved to launch the offensive southward, if diplomatic efforts failed to bring about Japan's "New Order" in Asia. The United States' oil embargo had by now forced on Tokyo a relentless timetable dictated by the military and industrial consumption of the nation's oil reserves at the rate of 12,000 tons every twenty-four hours.

The pressure on Prime Minister Konoye to effect a diplomatic breakthrough was therefore becoming daily more acute; Japan's lifeblood was draining away and the army and navy were demanding action before their planes, tanks, and ships were immobilized for want of fuel. The crisis came to a head when the Japanese cabinet met with the military leaders on September 3. Army Chief General Sugiyama insisted, "Things cannot be allowed to drag on," and Navy Chief Admiral Nagumo warned, "Although I feel sure we have a chance to win a war right now, I am afraid that the chance will vanish with the passage of time." Konoye wanted time to achieve his diplomatic breakthrough in a personal summit with the American President. The military wanted a deadline placed on the negotiations. After seven hours of heated argument, the military won their case as the government resolved: "For the self-defense and self-preservation of our Empire, we will complete preparations for war, with the first ten days of October as a tentative deadline, determined if necessary, to wage war against the United States, Britain and the Netherlands."

Prime Minister Konoye now had less than six weeks in which to achieve a diplomatic miracle.

6

"National Hara-Kiri"

At the stroke of ten on the morning of September 6, 1941, the Tokyo Palace ushers bowed the frock-coated ministers of the Japanese cabinet, accompanied by the Chiefs of Staff, into the Imperial Conference Chamber. As they took their places, the ritual of the meeting assumed a heavier than usual solemnity appropriate to the presence of a semi-divine. Privy Council President Yoshimi Hara took the chair to speak for the Emperor. Hirohito, a small bespectacled figure seated on an altar-like dais, appeared quite detached as he silently followed the familiar argument rehearsed again in formal flat tones by his generals and admirals. Diplomacy, they asserted, was failing to achieve Japan's aims: "The purposes of war with the United States, Great Britain and the Netherlands are to expel the influence of the three countries from East Asia, to establish a sphere for the self-defense and the self-preservation of our Empire and to build a New Order in Greater East Asia."

The military solution owed more to the expediency of striking before it was too late than sound strategic logic, as the Emperor had learned from his briefing the previous day when General Sugiyama had forecast that the "operation in the South Pacific could be disposed of in three months," but would give no categorical assurance that the Imperial forces could "absolutely win." His memorandum predicted only a "long war of endurance" and anticipated that "it will be well nigh impossible to expect a surrender from the United States." By going to war they would be gambling that a lightning takeover of Southeast Asia, the seizing of the oil and natural resources along with a defensive perimeter of Pacific Island bases, could secure for Japan an "invincible position," thereby enabling her diplomats "to influence the trend of affairs and bring the war to an end."

The military leaders' uncertainty that they could win that quick victory was the cause for hesitation which allowed Prime Minister Konoye to press his plan for winning concessions through negotiation in a personal summit with the President of the United States. Privy Council President Hara did his best to convey the Emperor's fears that the military were now determined to give belligerency precedence over diplomacy, a charge which Admiral Nagumo and General Sugiyama consistently evaded until the Emperor broke protocol with a shrill demand that they answer. The leaders of Japan were stunned speechless by this unprecedented intervention from the throne. Then they were even more astonished to hear Hirohito's piping voice reading a Haiku poem composed by his grandfather, the Emperor Meiji:

All the seas everywhere are brothers to one another
Why then do the winds and waves of strife rage so violently over the world?

Cryptic though His Majesty's dramatic plea for peace was, it embarrassed the military leaders, who could now hardly ignore the Imperial injunction to give diplomacy another chance. When Prime Minister Konoye adjourned the conference in an atmosphere of "unprecedented tenseness" at noon, he had been granted a delay until October 15 to achieve a positive result from the negotiations with the United States.

Less than six weeks remained for Konoye to overcome the huge stumbling block created by Washington's latest demand that "fundamental and essential questions" had to be settled before a summit meeting could take place. That night he summoned the American ambassador to a clandestine meeting at his mistress' house, in which he pressed for the summit with the President with "the least possible delay." The cable that Grew sent off to the State Department afterwards passed on the Japanese Premier's apparent change of heart: "we conclusively and wholeheartedly agree" to Secretary Hull's recent Oral Note setting out four principles for upholding China's sovereignty, and reinstating the "Open Door" doctrine.

Yet for all Konoye's willingness to make the concessions, his initiative was overshadowed in Washington because it appeared that America was on the brink of war with Germany. The September 4 attack on the U.S. destroyer *Greer* in the Atlantic gave President Roosevelt an opportunity to charge Hitler with "piracy" as he ordered the U.S. Navy to sink submarines on sight and to start escorting British convoys. The Führer carefully chose not to react, even though the President's Chief of Naval Operations wrote, "we are all but, if not actually in it."

Preoccupied with the danger threatening in the Atlantic and the sudden death of his mother, Roosevelt when he finally came to consider Tokyo's new initiative had grown cool to the idea of a summit that might cast him in the role of a Neville Chamberlain in a "Far East Munich." Madame Chiang Kai-shek and her influential industrialist brother T. V. Soong, the Nationalist foreign minister, had flown to Washington to lobby the White House and Congress for more aid. They were holding press conferences to remind the American people of their pledge to protect China's integrity.

Those State Department officials, led by Stanley K. Hornbeck, who had consistently supported a "no compromise" policy toward Japan were dubious of the sincerity of Konoye's change of heart and even more doubtful that he would be able to persuade the military to accept the loss of face involved in pulling out of China. Their skepticism that the militant faction of his cabinet really was prepared to abandon the Tripartite Pact was hardened when the Secretary of State resumed his private discussions with the Japanese ambassador. Nomura indicated that while his government would take an "independent" interpretation of its obligations to the Axis in return for U.S. assistance to bring the Nationalist Chinese to a peace conference, Tokyo would insist on stationing troops on the mainland.

Japanese insistence on deploying military power to protect their economic interests in China had always been considered by the United States to be a fundamental break of the Open Door principle. Although the real situation in the Far East had long since overtaken the sacred doctrine, the President and the Secretary of State believed, as they always had, that any compromise of that principle would be taken as a fundamental betrayal of their international obligations. Convinced of the moral correctness of their position, which they were now stiffening with military force, Roosevelt and Hull believed they had only to stand firm until the oil embargo bit down on Japan's economy before her leaders abandoned their principles. This was the dangerously misconceived rationale behind Roosevelt's decision to continue to "baby along" with the negotiation process, doomed to failure even before it had recommenced because Washington and Tokyo were marching to the beat of different drums.

The difference in tempo should have been apparent from Magic intercepts of Tokyo's instructions to Nomura, which set deadlines and constantly urged haste. The State Department's man on the spot, Ambassador Grew, whose over-simplistic assessments of the Japanese political scene as a battle between moderates and the military had encouraged the "all or nothing" judgments made in Washington, now proved to be right. His stream of cables repeatedly emphasized that time was short. But the warnings fell on deaf ears, for Cordell Hull was following specific presidential instructions to spin out diplomacy. Negotiations were confused by Ambassador Nomura's willingness to clutch at straws and concede far more than Tokyo would give, while at the same time making overoptimistic reports of American flexibility. All the double-talk reinforced the State Department's long-held belief in Japanese duplicity as Magic intelligence revealed the growing scale of the troop movements south into Indochina. At the same time, the detailed instructions to Nomura from Tokyo were being read in advance in translations made under extreme pressure by Army and Navy codebreakers untutored in the subtle nuances of diplomatic language. Frequently their blunt prose would appear to over- rather than understate the Japanese negotiating positions.

The pace that was being forced on delicate diplomatic exchanges was dictated by Konoye's own concern that his position as Prime Minister was being undermined. An assassination attempt on September 18 forcibly reminded him that time was running out. A week later, in a final effort to get a meeting under way with the President, he promised virtual abnegation of the Tripartite Pact, the neutralization of Indochina, and—going as far as he dared—to agree to reduce Japan's troops in China. Washington was still adamant that there must be what it termed "a meeting of minds" before a summit. This brought a warning from Ambassador Grew that the days of the Konoye cabinet were numbered and that its fall "will probably lead to unbridled acts."

Japanese foreign policy had for more than a year been subject to the decisions of the so-called Liaison Conferences at which Imperial General Headquarters now dictated the decisions of the cabinet. With the military leaders rapidly losing patience with their diplomats, it was only a matter of time before the war decision was made. The first step to that irrevocable action was taken on September 25 by the war minister, General Tojo, who refused to consider making even a token troop withdrawal from the mainland to get a summit under way. He wanted to "petition the Emperor to hold an Imperial Conference and decide on war." Konoye repeatedly tried to persuade the general to accept a token concession, only to be told the "way of diplomacy is not always a matter of concession; sometimes it is oppression." There were less than twenty-four hours to go before the October 15 deadline when Konoye sent a last desperate plea to Roosevelt through Bishop Walsh. No response was forthcoming.

When Ambassador Nomura cabled on October 16, 1941, that his plea for a summit had again been ignored, Konoye had no option but to resign. The Emperor's Jushin Council of elder statesmen after heated deliberation recommended the war minister, General Tojo, to succeed Prince Konoye. He was the only cabinet member supported with full confidence by the military. Making a second break with constitutional tradition, Hirohito, in appointing Tojo, instructed him to "go back to blank paper" for a last effort to reach a diplomatic solution. It was a final overture to the United States for a conciliatory gesture, and it went unheeded despite Ambassador Grew's warning against "any possible misunderstanding of the ability or readiness of Japan to plunge into a suicidal war." The State Department concluded that hard-line militarists were in charge in Tokyo, a view confirmed by the new government's broadcast promise to "go forward with a united nation to accomplish its bold task." That same day a virtual war

alert was flashed out to all U.S. Pacific bases: "BEST INTELLIGENCE SUG-
GESTS JAPAN MIGHT ATTACK RUSSIA OR BRITISH AND DUTCH COLONIES IN THE
EAST INDIES."

Dutifully responding to the Emperor's wishes rather than his own conviction, the new Prime Minister of Japan issued instructions for the Foreign Ministry to make a final attempt at negotiations. He at once came
under attack from the navy, which was alarmed at the rapid consumption
of oil stocks. Its minister warned: "the situation is urgent; we must have
a decision one way or the other."

Japanese impatience was met with American procrastination. On October 21, the President had to be reassured by the Secretary of War that
the U.S. bomber force in the Philippines presented him with "the possibility of great effective power" and advised that "even this imperfect
threat, if not promptly called by the Japanese, bid fair to stop Japan's
march to the south and secure the safety of Singapore." Winston Churchill also believed that the Anglo-American "stick" was now big enough
to impress the Tokyo militants. "The firmer your attitude and ours," he
cabled Roosevelt on November 2, "the less chance of their taking the
plunge."

Neither the President nor his military chiefs wanted to precipitate
Japan into war by any hasty response at a critical time for the United
States. October had brought the U.S. Navy into an "undeclared war" in
the Atlantic. American lives had been lost when U-boats torpedoed the
destroyer *Kearny* and sank the *Reuben James*. On October 9, Roosevelt
asked Congress to rescind the Neutrality Act to allow the arming of
American merchant ships. There were renewed warnings from the Army
and Navy Chiefs that Germany was "the most dangerous enemy" and that
a flare-up in the Pacific must be avoided—at least until the spring of 1942,
when the War Department reported that "U.S. air and submarine strength
in the Philippines [would] be a positive threat to any Japanese operations
south of Formosa." The President and the Secretary of State resolved to
look for a formula "to give us more time."

That time was already fast running out. On November 3, the Emperor
and the Imperial General Command finally approved Admiral Yamamoto's
Pearl Harbor attack plan and the Combined Fleet sailed for final battle
practice. All Japanese naval codes were changed, in what U.S. Navy Intelligence predicted was a sure sign of imminent war.

Then, on November 5, Magic revealed instructions from the Tokyo
Foreign Ministry to Ambassador Nomura that "a last effort" was to be
made to negotiate and that it's failure would put the Pacific situation "on
the brink of chaos." His deadline was November 15—less than three weeks
away. Ambassador Grew reminded the State Department once more that
failure in this round of negotiations could result in an "all out do-or-die

attempt actually risking national Hara-Kiri to make Japan impervious to economic embargoes rather than yield to foreign pressure."

Also on November 5, just twenty-four hours after the Supreme War Council's decision that in a month's time it would be impossible to launch military operations because of winter weather, Prime Minister Tojo managed to talk the Imperial Conference into postponing the deadline until December 1 to allow for a final attempt "to solve the problem by diplomacy." To help the struggling Nomura in this last bid for peace, it was announced that Saburo Kurusu would be sent to Washington to assist in the new round of talks. The weekly Pan Am Clipper was held at Manila to fly the former Japanese consul in Chicago and Berlin ambassador to the United States. His knowledge of the country and his American wife were expected to be valuable in presenting and explaining Tokyo's last plan for a Pacific peace. It consisted of a two-part initiative. The first—Proposal A —called for a comprehensive settlement of the Sino-Japanese conflict with a limited withdrawal of Japanese troops. The second—Proposal B—was a fallback to buy time with a "modus vivendi" in which Japan would halt further military operations in return for a U.S. agreement to supply 1 million gallons of aviation gasoline.

Anticipating what the Japanese plan would be from the intercepted Magic translations of the two proposals, the President advised Hull to "strain every nerve" and "do nothing to precipitate a crisis." Appreciating that the negotiating process now hung on a slender thread, Roosevelt wanted to spin it out as long as possible. On November 7, he therefore explained in a message to Churchill that he was moving very cautiously toward meeting Chiang Kai-shek's latest demands for more Lend-Lease supplies. He confided that he was counting on time for "continuing efforts to strengthen our defenses in the Philippine Islands, paralleled by similar efforts by you in the Singapore area, which will tend to increase Japan's distant hesitation."

Neither the President nor the Prime Minister wanted a showdown that would force Japan into a Pacific war which would interfere with the struggle they were waging in unofficial partnership against Hitler. Yet Churchill knew that by urging Roosevelt to take an uncompromising stand and handing over responsibility to the United States, any rupture of this round of negotiations might prompt Japan to attack British or Dutch territory. If the blow fell, he was confident that although there had as yet been no firm commitment, the Americans would have to intervene. Indeed, this became evident during the next four weeks as the fatal calendar of military and diplomatic maneuvering brought about the collision toward which the United States and Japan had been heading for three decades. Impact was made inevitable by the U.S. refusal to make the smallest concession to the Japanese, stemming from a mistaken faith in the

Anglo-American deterrent strategy in the Far East. The United States was to be caught off-guard by a breakdown of command and failure of intelligence. Too much focus was given to the Philippines and insufficient to Hawaii as possible objectives for Japan's all-out attack.

WAR WARNINGS

These failures were to become evident in the fatal calendar of diplomatic and military events in the final month of Pacific peace:

November 7

Pearl Harbor Strike Force: After dress rehearsal of Operation Z by the 350 aircraft flown from the 6 carriers of the Combined Fleet's "Strike Force," Admiral Yamamoto issued "Operation Order No. 2" setting December 8 as Y Day for the attack on Oahu (December 7 Hawaiian time).

November 10

Washington: Ambassador Nomura arrived at the White House to present the "A" Proposal for a comprehensive settlement. Knowing that the "modus vivendi" would be Japan's next move, Secretary of State Hull stalled. The President rejected an immediate reply by telling Nomura, "Nations must think one hundred years ahead."

November 14

Washington: Secretary of State Hull rejected Tokyo's "A" Proposal. He insisted on the evacuation of all Japanese troops from China. This was a blow to Nomura, who had already mistakenly reported to Tokyo that the United States was "not entirely unreceptive." Now he had to explain they were making a demand that would be entirely unacceptable to the military, who had fought a four-year war at the cost of 1 million lives to settle the national interest on the mainland.

November 15

Washington: Bishop Walsh's effort to mediate was dismissed by the State Department as "naive." Hull concluded after meeting Kurusu that the new envoy was "deceitful." Magic intercepted Tokyo's message to Consul Kita in Honolulu ordering him to make a "ships in harbor" report twice weekly. (But this clue was *not* passed on to Pearl Harbor.)

November 16

Pearl Harbor Strike Force: Concealed by strict radio silence, the carriers sailed individually from the Inland Sea to avert suspicion—their destination remote Tankan Bay in the Kurile Islands. To camouflage their movements, Yamamoto ordered their radio call signs transferred to destroyers.

Washington: Magic intercepted a cable from Tokyo to Ambassador Nomura advising him: "Fate of the Empire hangs by a sheer thread . . . please fight harder!"

November 20
Washington: Ambassador Nomura presented Tokyo's "B" proposal for a "modus vivendi" as "absolutely final." The preemptive Magic translation had already persuaded the Secretary of State to regard it as "an ultimatum." The President, however, told him to give it "sympathetic study."

November 21
London: The British Joint Intelligence Committee transmitted to its Far Eastern Command the assessment that if negotiations broke down, Japan would not attack Siberia or try to cut the Burma Road or invade Malaya or the Netherlands East Indies because of the danger of precipitating an all-out war; only a limited invasion of Thailand was anticipated. (The War Department, which was breaking the British codes as well as the Japanese, circulated a copy of this intelligence.

November 22
Washington: Magic intercepted Tokyo's message to Nomura that the deadline for negotiations had been extended four days, to November 29. "After that things are automatically going to happen."
Pearl Harbor Strike Force: Waiting at Tankan Bay, Admiral Nagumo received orders to sail on November 26. (The signal was intercepted but in the JN25 code that could not be broken by U.S. Naval Intelligence.)

November 24
Washington: Magic intercepts revealed Tokyo's clarification to Nomura that as a precondition to any agreement, America must cease aid to Chiang Kai-shek and lift the oil embargo. Hull, seeing this as a hardening of Japan's position, told Roosevelt that the outlook was "critical and virtually hopeless." The President informed his cabinet: "We are likely to be attacked next Monday for the Japs are notorious for attacking without warning." He then cabled Churchill: "We must all prepare for real trouble, possibly soon."
Manila and Hawaii: The Chief of Naval Operations flashed warning of "SURPRISE AND AGGRESSIVE MOVEMENTS" by Japan.

November 25
Washington: The President's War Council approved the three month "modus vivendi" despite Roosevelt's concern about how to "maneuver Japan" into firing the first shot.

November 26
Pearl Harbor Strike Force: At dawn Admiral Nagumo's fleet put to sea, his final instruction from Yamamoto being: "In case negotiations with the United States reach a successful conclusion, the task force will immediately put about and return to the homeland."
Washington: Intelligence reports that troop convoys had been sighted south of Formosa, apparently steaming for Indochina, were taken by the President as "evidence of bad faith on the part of the Japanese." Roosevelt, new evidence indicates, was actually acting on receipt of a secret

leak of Japan's war plan. Hull accordingly was told to drop the State Department's counter-proposal for a "modus vivendi" to resume oil supplies "on a monthly basis for civilian needs." That afternoon the Secretary of State formally rejected Tokyo's "B" proposal for a temporary resolution of the crisis. Instead, Hull submitted a strongly worded document tying any relaxation of the oil embargo to the Japanese government's acceptance of ten specific conditions. These were a reiteration of the Open Door doctrine, which required the "withdrawal of all military, naval, air and police forces from China and Indochina."

Tokyo: "This is an ultimatum," Prime Minister Tojo told his cabinet, having assumed the ten conditions to indicate that the American government was "unyielding and unbending." He saw "no glimmer of hope." Japanese consulates and embassies worldwide were warned that codes were to be destroyed when the war imminent signal was broadcast, hidden in the weather forecast. NIGASHI NO KESAME (East Wind Rain) would indicate hostilities with the United States.

November 27

Washington: The Secretary of State received Hornbeck's assessment: "the Japanese Government does not desire or intend or expect to have forthwith armed conflict with the United States." He put "Odds of five to one that the United States will *not* be at 'war' on or before December 15." However, Hull knew otherwise, telling the Secretary of War he had washed his hands of it, and that it was now "in the hands of you and Knox—the Army and the Navy." But in an unprecedented move, Marshall and Stark jointly submitted a memorandum to the President: "If the current negotiations end without agreement, Japan may attack the Burma Road; Thailand; Malaya; the Netherlands East Indies; the Philippines; the Russian Maritime Provinces. . . . *The most essential thing now, from the United States viewpoint, is to gain time.* Considerable Army and Navy reinforcements have been rushed to the Philippines but the desirable strength has not yet been reached." Magic monitoring of the weather warning code prompted an alert radioed to all commands: "NEGOTIATIONS WITH JAPAN APPEAR TERMINATED . . . JAPANESE FUTURE ACTION UNPREDICTABLE BUT HOSTILE ACTION POSSIBLE AT ANY MOMENT. IF HOSTILITIES CANNOT REPEAT CANNOT BE AVOIDED THE UNITED STATES DESIRES JAPAN COMMIT THE FIRST ACT."

Hawaii: Garrison Commander General Short received the alert with the additional instructions: "MEASURES SHOULD BE CARRIED OUT SO AS NOT REPEAT NOT TO ALARM CIVIL POPULATION OR DISCLOSE INTENT." He therefore interpreted the whole message as a sabotage warning. Pacific Fleet Commander in Chief Admiral Kimmel received the specific alert: "THIS DISPATCH IS TO BE CONSIDERED A WAR WARNING . . . AGGRESSIVE ACTION EXPECTED BY JAPAN IN THE NEXT FEW DAYS." He too believed that Hawaii was under no immediate threat because of the appended intelligence summary indicating that Japan's strike was expected to hit "PHILIPPINES, THAI OR KRA PENINSULA OR BORNEO."

Manila: Appended to MacArthur's order was the instruction: "SHOULD HOSTILITIES OCCUR YOU WILL CARRY OUT THE TASKS ASSIGNED IN REVISED RAINBOW 5." This called for him "to conduct air raids against enemy forces and installations within tactical operating radius of available bases. . . ."

November 28
Ceylon: H.M.S. *Prince of Wales* docked at Colombo en route to Singapore naval base.

Hawaii: The U.S.S. *Enterprise,* one of the Pacific Fleet's two carriers, sailed for Wake Island to ferry in a squadron of Marine fighters to protect the next shuttle flight of B-17 bombers.

Washington: The President made an effort to sustain negotiations by informing Ambassador Nomura that America would "continue to be patient." A crisis meeting at the White House was told of the latest intelligence estimates that Japanese invasion forces were ready to sail from Shanghai, Formosa, and Hainan to deliver "a terrific blow to all of the three powers, Britain at Singapore, the Netherlands and ourselves at the Philippines." The President accepted that, "If the British fought, we would have to fight," but he proposed to make a last-ditch personal plea to the Emperor.

November 29
Berlin: Magic revealed a report from Ambassador Oshima that German Foreign Minister Ribbentrop had pledged: "Should Japan become engaged in a war against the United States, Germany of course, would join the war immediately."

Tokyo: Prime Minister Tojo advised his cabinet and Imperial General Headquarters that there was now no alternative but war, or "we'll lose our chance to fight."

November 30
Pearl Harbor Strike Force: North of the Pacific shipping lanes, concealed by weather fronts, six carriers in three columns, flanked by battleships and cruisers, refueled from their tankers at the halfway point. More than 200 miles ahead, Japanese submarines were patrolling to give warning of approaching vessels. Yamamoto's orders were to abandon Operation Z if the force was spotted before December 6.

London: Churchill cabled Roosevelt that the only chance of averting war was for an unequivocal American declaration "that any further act of aggression by Japan will immediately lead to grave consequences."

December 1
London: The Admiralty ordered the battlecruiser *Repulse,* on passage with *Prince of Wales* to Singapore, to divert to Darwin, "to disconcert the Japanese and at the same time increase security."

Tokyo: "Matters have reached the point where Japan must begin war with the United States, Great Britain and the Netherlands to preserve her Empire," Prime Minister Tojo reluctantly advised an Imperial Conference. The Emperor did not dissent. To protect Operation Z, the Foreign Ministry agreed to present its formal rejection of America's conditions precisely half an hour before Pearl Harbor was due to be attacked. The code signals for war were flashed out: HINODE YAMAGATA to the Southern Army instructed the invasion fleets to be ready to sail on the planned schedule against Malaya and the Philippines. NIITAKA YAMA NOBORE (Climb Mount Niitaka) unleashed the Pearl Harbor Strike Force.

Washington: Roosevelt summoned the British ambassador and informed him that U.S. Intelligence anticipated Malaya and Siam would be invaded. He assured Lord Halifax that with any attack on British or Dutch possessions, "we should all be in it together."

December 2

Hawaii: The Pacific Fleet Combat Intelligence Unit discovered that all Japanese warship call signs had been changed again. A big operation appeared imminent, but radio traffic and direction analysis of the unbroken Japanese fleet codes indicated that the Combined Fleet was still in the Inland Sea with only a single carrier as far east as the Marshall Islands. "Do you mean to say they could be rounding Diamond Head and you wouldn't know about it?" Admiral Kimmel asked, after examining his fleet intelligence officer's report. "I would hope they could be sighted before that," Captain Edwin T. Layton replied.

December 3

Singapore: H.M.S. *Prince of Wales* docked at the Changi naval base and carefully censored headlines welcomed the "powerful naval force" defending Malaya.

Hainan Island: The 14 Japanese transports and escorting warships of the Malayan invasion force sailed from Samah Bay, Hainan for the four-day crossing the Gulf of Thailand.

Hawaii: Admiral Kimmel received "highly reliable information" from Naval Intelligence in Washington that Magic had intercepted messages the day before instructing all Japanese embassies to begin destruction of codes and sensitive documents. He had not, however, been forwarded two even more vital bits of evidence clearly indicating Japanese interest in Hawaii: the October 9 intercept (decoded on November 24) instructing the Japanese Consulate to make detailed reports by dividing up the Pearl Harbor into alphabetically coded areas; and the November 15 signal, decoded that very day: "As relations between Japan and the United States are most critical, make your ships in harbor report irregular, but at the rate of twice a week. Although you are already no doubt aware, please take care to maintain secrecy."

December 4
Guam: The U.S. Naval Governor was ordered to destroy all classified material.
Washington: The Navy's listening post at Cheltenham Maryland picked up what the operator reported as the EAST WIND RAIN war warning message. It was apparently passed on by Commander Safford, but no action was taken and all copies subsequently disappeared. The grim news from the Pacific was temporarily eclipsed by the sensational exposure by the isolationist Chicago *Tribune* of what purported to be a U.S. "Victory Plan" to invade Germany in 1943.
Pearl Harbor Strike Force: Less than 1,000 miles due north of Midway and shrouded by thick weather fronts, Admiral Nagumo ordered refueling before his course was set southeast for the run to Hawaii.

December 5
Hawaii: The carrier *Lexington* put to sea to ferry Marine aircraft to reinforce Midway for the bomber flight due in two days' time.
Manila: Admiral Sir Tom Phillips flew in from Singapore to ask General MacArthur and Admiral Hart for American air and warship support for his proposed foray by Force Z "against Japanese movements in the South China Sea." Next day, news that RAF patrols from Malaya had sighted a large Japanese invasion convoy heading across the Gulf of Siam sent Phillips flying back to Singapore "to be there when the war starts."
Tokyo: Newspapers crackled with belligerent headlines: "Scandalous Encirclement of Japan," "Trampling on Japan's Peaceful Intentions," "Four Nations Simultaneously Start Military Preparations."
Washington: The Japanese envoys summoned to the State Department could not explain why large convoys were moving across the South China Sea. The President and the Chiefs of Staff then accepted Army Intelligence estimates Japan would not attack the United States and that "the most probable line of action for Japan is the occupation of Thailand."

December 6
Malayan Invasion Force: South of Cape Cambodia, nineteen Japanese transports escorted by cruisers and destroyers were sighted through a cloudbreak by a Royal Australian Air Force Hudson patrolling from Kota Bharu on the northern Malayan coast. The pilot radioed that the convoy was heading east, apparently toward Thailand, before he was shot down.
London: Churchill summoned the Chiefs of Staff for a crisis meeting. From the latest intelligence on the Japanese convoys they concluded: "It is not possible to tell whether they were going to Bangkok, to the Kra Peninsula, or whether they were just cruising round as a bluff." The code "Raffles" had been radioed out to put the entire Far East Command on war alert.

Singapore: General Percival and his Commander in Chief spent most of the day debating whether to launch "Operation Matador" to send the 11th Indian Division across the border into Thailand and forestall an invasion of the strategic ports of Singora and Patani. Air Marshal Brooke-Popham hesitated after receiving the cabled advice of the British minister in Bangkok not to preemptively cross the frontier and give Japan an excuse to attack. Advance troops were therefore ordered only to begin moving up to the border, even though that evening an RAF patrol reported that the Japanese convoy was now less than 100 miles from Singora.

Pearl Harbor Strike Force: By afternoon some 600 miles northwest of Hawaii, all hands cheered Admiral Yamamoto's Nelsonian signal: "THE RISE OR FALL OF THE EMPIRE DEPENDS UPON THIS BATTLE EVERYONE WILL DO HIS DUTY WITH UTMOST EFFORTS." Pearl Harbor was confirmed as the target for the next morning's attack, after the Japanese reconnaissance submarine I72 reported that the Lahaina anchorage on the northwest of Oahu was empty. Consul Kita's latest Hawaiian intelligence report, relayed from Tokyo, was that all eight battleships of the U.S. Pacific Fleet, as well as three cruisers and sixteen destroyers, were in harbor, only the two carriers were still at sea. There was little air activity, indicating that "now would be a good opportunity to attack."

Washington: The latest intelligence at 9 P.M. indicated that the Japanese invasion convoys were on course for Thailand. Roosevelt sent off a personal telegram asking the Emperor, "FOR THE SAKE OF HUMANITY," to intervene "TO PREVENT FURTHER DEATH AND DESTRUCTION IN THE WORLD." He told Eleanor wryly, "This son of man has just sent his final message to the son of God." He was back with his stamp collection, chatting with Harry Hopkins half an hour later when Lieutenant Commander Kramer arrived with the pouch containing the latest Magic intercepts of Japan's formal rejection of the American ten-point proposals. The President handed it to his aide with the comment: "This means war." He rejected Hopkins's suggestion that America strike first. "No, we can't do that," Roosevelt reacted. "We are a democracy and a peaceful people. But we have a good record."

He tried to reach Admiral Stark by telephone, only to learn that he was at a National Theater performance of *The Student Prince*. The President realized that there was after all nothing very new in the first thirteen parts of Tokyo's final communiqué to warrant alarming the audience by paging the Chief of Naval Operations. It was the same conclusion reached by Chief of Army Intelligence, who decided there was "no reason for alerting or waking up" General Marshall.

Formosa: Late in the afternoon the twenty-seven transports put out from the Formosan port of Takao with the 48th Division of the Imperial Army, to head south for the Philippines. The pilots of the four hundred aircraft of the Imperial Navy's 11th Air Fleet were briefed for the massive air assault next day to wipe out the American B-17 bombers on Luzon.

COUNTDOWN TO WAR

Dawn was already breaking over London on Sunday, December 7, when the clock struck midnight in the White House and the President retired for the night. Ready on his desk was a thirty-page draft of a speech to be delivered to Congress with which he hoped to win its support for declaring war if the Japanese attacked British or Dutch possessions in the Far East but not the Philippines. Across Washington on Massachusetts Avenue, the radio operator was standing by in the Japanese Embassy for Tokyo to transmit the fourteenth part of the message to be delivered by Ambassador Nomura. A few blocks south on Constitution Avenue the duty watch of the OP 20 G unit of Naval Intelligence were also anxiously awaiting the same message.

By a tragic oversight, what might have proved the vital indication of the imminent air attack on Pearl Harbor was already lying in Lieutenant Commander Kramer's "Pending" tray. That very afternoon, Mrs. Dorothy Edgers, a new Japanese linguist on the OP 20 G team, had begun the task of translating a second-priority message cabled in low-grade code by the Japanese consul general in Honolulu. The contents indicated an extensive interest in shipping movements at Pearl Harbor which so roused Mrs. Edger's curiosity that she brought the intercepts to the notice of her senior officer. Overtaxed by the laborious task of decoding and translating the long diplomatic messages, they told her, "It can wait until Monday."

Midnight in Washington was the end of a bright tropical afternoon across the Pacific on Oahu, as the bars, dancehalls, and pinball parlors of the Honolulu waterfront prepared to cater to the usual boisterous Saturday night revelers chasing entertainment, beer, and women. Technically, the Army and Navy personnel were on full war alert, but alerts had by now become so frequent as to be nothing unusual. No one on the staff of Army Headquarters at Fort Shafter or on the Naval Staff of the Pacific Fleet or the 14th Naval District was expecting anything out of the ordinary. Boats were busily plying between Battleship Row, where the pride of the Pacific Fleet was secured to the dolphins south of Ford Island, and the jetties, ferrying Bluejackets ashore. For those not on liberty, the big attraction was the Fleet Band Championships, being held that evening in Block Hall. At the Army airfields of Hickam and Wheeler, guards patrolled the neatly parked rows of bombers and fighters. As a precaution against sabotage, their antiaircraft batteries ammunition was safely locked away in the central magazines.

"ALL CARRIERS AND HEAVY CRUISERS ARE AT SEA. NO SPECIAL REPORTS ON THE FLEET OAHU IS QUIET. . . ." Consul Kita had radioed to Tokyo in the day's final message. Because he had already destroyed his other cipher, he had been transmitting the information for the past few days in the low-grade code that the Americans had designated PA-K2. It was relatively easy to break, but because it was assumed only to contain diplomatic information, this clue to Japanese interest in Pearl Harbor would only be translated late the following afternoon. That Saturday, the local FBI in Honolulu had also stumbled across two more pieces of evidence that might have been seen as significant if taken together with the other intelligence. A local Japanese dentist's phone had tapped a suspicious conversation with a "Mr. Mori" in Tokyo discussing local weather and flying conditions. And in the evening an unusual quantity of smoke indicated that the Japanese Consulate was burning a large amount of paper.

One officer and a switchboard operator manned the Naval Control Center on Ford Island. The recently arrived Army mobile radar on the north coast were scheduled to operate for their usual three hours, from 4 to 7 A.M., and only seven Navy PBY flying boats had been slated to take off from the Ford Island base to make the dawn antisubmarine patrol along the south coast of Oahu. Pearl Harbor was known to be most vulnerable to carrier air strikes from the north, and the Joint Board's March 1941 assessment on the island's defenses had recommended round-the-compass air patrols 300 miles out into the Pacific. But a shortage of planes and a heavy training schedule had prevented this, "unless other intelligence indicates that a surface raid is probable." Admiral Bellinger, Kimmel's Air Defense Officer, would later testify: "The information available to me—limited and unofficial as it was—did not indicate that I should recommend to the Commander in Chief Pacific Fleet that distant patrol plane search for the security of Pearl Harbor be undertaken at this time."

Too many alerts, too much intelligence pointing the impending Japanese attacks toward the western side of the Pacific, too great a reliance on Magic information, and too logical an analysis of Japanese military intentions, with a consequent failure to accord importance to the last-minute Pearl Harbor clues, allowed Admiral Kimmel and General Short to sleep too soundly that night. The gates of "the greatest fortress in the world" were left wide open to the northwest, through which a Japanese striking force was plowing at a steady 24 knots toward Oahu.

The American commanders in the Philippines had less excuse for their low state of alert. Although the latest intelligence summaries from Washington indicated that Japan would avoid attacking the United States, Manila was less than 500 miles south of enemy forces in Formosa. The 16th Naval District possessed a Purple decoding machine, unlike Hawaii, and although MacArthur would claim that the interservice rivalry kept him from seeing Magic intercepts that night, he paced back and forth in his penthouse suite atop the Manila Hotel in deep concern, oblivious to the drifting sounds of the party being thrown by the B-17 crews of the 17th Bombardment Group for their commander. General Brereton had excused himself early from what had been billed as "the best entertainment this side of Minsky's" because he was scheduled to fly to Java early the next morning for a staff conference with the Dutch. The Asiatic Fleet Commander, Admiral Hart, spent the evening at his headquarters in the nearby Marsman Building, troubled by a deep foreboding that Japan must be about to strike at the Philippines across the 300 miles that separated Luzon from Formosa.

Packed into sweaty holds aboard the scores of transports, the soldiers of the Japanese Imperial Army who spent that night heading toward their invasion beaches read again the pamphlet specially prepared by Colonel Tsuji's team, which instructed: "READ THIS ALONE—AND THE WAR CAN BE WON." It informed them that they had embarked on a great crusade of liberation to free "a hundred million Asians tyrannized by three hundred thousand whites."

At their Formosa headquarters, General Masaharu Homma and Admiral Takahashi faced a night worrying that their carefully orchestrated sea and air offensive against the Philippines could be disrupted. Mist and low clouds threatened to keep grounded the 11th Air Fleet's bombers while the American fortresses launched a devastating counterblow against their own bases and invasion convoy.

General Yamashita, commanding the Malayan invasion force approaching the Kra Peninsula, was also preoccupied with weather as his armada divided in two, one section heading for the Siamese ports and the other for Kota Bharu's beaches. Aboard the heaving deck of the command ship *Ryujo Maru* heading for Singora, Colonel Tsuji paced in the dark, overhearing two officers saying, "What fools to think of disembarkation in such heavy seas." Apprehension was rising below decks as the soldiers looked for reassurance in the colonel's instruction manual: "Even if the waves are rough or the water deep, with your lifejackets you will be quite safe. Should you be out of your depth, the waves will wash you towards shore."

Yamashita's other worry was the British fleet at Singapore. Would they appear to smash up his invasion before he could count on the seaborne protection of Admiral Jisaburo Ozawa's battle fleet, patrolling in the South China Sea? The most immediate task of locating and destroying the Royal Navy battleships would fall to the navy's ninety-nine bombers and thirty-nine torpedo planes, waiting on the airfields in Indochina.

At Singapore it had been a routine Sunday afternoon—"curry tiffin," cricket, and pink gins served on verandahs at the "Blue Hour." The return of the battlecruiser *Repulse* that afternoon gave cause for celebration, prompting a lusty chorus of "There'll Always Be an England" at the white-domed Seaview Club. Admiral Phillips had flown back from Manila to a crisis conference with his staff, and at Army Headquarters General Percival had failed to persuade Brooke-Popham to give the go ahead for Operation Matador.

Admiral Yamamoto played game after game of Shogi with Staff Officer Watanabe as the Combined Fleet flagship *Nagato* swung peacefully round her buoy in the tranquil beauty of Hashirajima anchorage in Japan's Inland Sea. Before he turned in to snatch a few hours' rest, he composed a classic thirty-one-syllable "waka" poem:

> It is my sole wish to serve the Emperor as His shield
> I will not spare my life or honor.

West of the International Dateline, the population of Japan slumbered on through the last hours of December 7 into December 8, unaware that thousands of their countrymen were making preparations in 169 ships and over 2,000 aircraft to set the Pacific ablaze at dawn. The sequence of their attacks was carefully timed to explode across 6,000 miles of ocean like a firecracker as the sun rose westward from Hawaii to Wake to Guam to Hong Kong to the Philippines to Malaya and Siam.

The calamitous attacks, which began at midnight on December 7 in Hawaiian waters, presaged six months of defeat and humiliation for the Anglo-Saxon powers as Japan came within an ace of establishing her dominance over the Pacific.

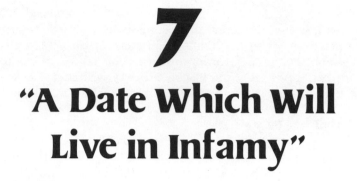

7

"A Date Which Will Live in Infamy"

Hawaiian Time
12.00 hrs.

Oahu

Under a full moon 8 miles south of the entrance to Pearl Harbor, the Japanese crews of the five I Class submarines worked busily to launch the midgets on a choppy sea. The winking lights of Waikiki Beach were plainly visible as the two-man units of Commander Nagi Iwasa's Special Attack Force squeezed through the narrow conning towers of their tiny submarines. An hour later, four of the midgets successfully reached for the booms that guarded the mile-wide mouth to the Pacific Fleet's anchorage.

Tokyo (8:45 P.M., Sunday, December 7, Tokyo Time)　**01.15 hrs.**

Ambassador Grew received the President's urgent cable for the Emperor, which had been held up by the censors for ten hours. Within the hour, Grew was on his way to the Japanese Foreign Ministry.

Washington, D.C. (7:30 A.M., Sunday, December 7, Eastern Time)
02.00 hrs.

The OP 20 G duty staff in Naval Intelligence completed the Purple decoding of the last part of Tokyo's message picked up an hour earlier. It read: "The Japanese government regrets that it is impossible to reach an agreement through further negotiations." Commander Kramer pouched the Magic transcripts and set off for the White House.

Pearl Harbor Strike Force　03.00 hrs.

Plunging through heavy seas some 230 miles north of Oahu, the warships' gun crews were closed up at action stations. Scouting out ahead were two heavy cruisers. Aboard the six carriers, aircraft were being fueled and bombed up as their aircrew were roused. After donning their "thousand-stitch" good-luck belts and leaving family letters enclosing ritual clips of hair and fingernails, the flyers ate a celebratory breakfast of rice and red snapper. Sake toasts preceded their tense final briefing. "In my flying togs I entered the operations room," Commander Mitsuo Fuchida wrote after his farewell meeting with Admiral Nagumo. As Fuchida passed down to the dimly lit briefing room, he saw that "the room was not large enough for all the men, some of whom had to stand out in the passageway. On the blackboard was written the positions of ships in Pearl Harbor as of 06.00 December 7. We were 230 miles due north of Oahu."

Pearl Harbor   03.50 hrs.

A periscope was sighted off the harbor mouth by U.S.S. *Condor*, one of two minesweepers patrolling off the harbor boom. The destroyer *Ward* joined in a two-hour abortive sweep of the area, without further contact. No report was signaled to the Control Center on Ford Island.

Washington (9:30 A.M.)   04.00 hrs.

Returning to OP 20 G after completing the Magic delivery round, Commander Kramer received another URGENT VERY IMPORTANT Purple decode. It advised Ambassador Nomura that the fourteen-part final Japanese message must be delivered precisely at 1 P.M., Washington time, followed by orders to destroy the embassy's remaining code machine. From his two years' service in Hawaii, Kramer realized that the deadline might coincide with a dawn attack on Pearl Harbor. He hurried across to Admiral Stark's office. The Chief of Naval Operations, still reading the earlier Magic bulletins, believed that the Pacific Fleet was already on full alert, so he decided against issuing another warning. Colonel Bratton, head of the Army SIS Magic unit, also concluded that it must indicate "an attack on an American installation in the Pacific." He tried to see General Marshall, but learned that he was out taking a long Sunday morning ride in the grounds of Fort Meyer.

Across Massachusetts Avenue in the Japanese Embassy, Ambassador Nomura was growing impatient with the slow progress made by the cipher clerk in decoding Tokyo's message. On reading the deadline, he put in a call to the Secretary of State's office for a 1 o'clock appointment, insisting: "It is a matter of extreme urgency."

Pearl Harbor Anchorage   04.30 hrs.

A midget submarine of the Japanese Special Attack Force crept past Keanpapuaa Point in the predawn gloom, found the harbor boom open to admit two minesweepers, and slipped in. Under strict instructions not to let loose its two torpedoes until dawn, it stealthily circled Ford Island while its commander, eyes glued to his tiny periscope, carefully logged the positions of the warships.

Washington (11:00 A.M.)   05.30 hrs.

General Marshall, on returning to his office, agreed with Colonel Bratton's concern about the 1 P.M. deadline. He drafted an urgent dispatch to be sent immediately to the Army Commanders in Panama, San Francisco, the Philippines, and Hawaii: "JUST WHAT SIGNIFICANCE THE HOUR SET MAY HAVE WE DO NOT KNOW BUT BE ON THE ALERT ACCORDINGLY."

Admiral Stark approved that the cable be headed "INFORM NAVY," but Marshall turned down the offer to send the warning by naval radio. The general had not been told that the Army cable line to Oahu was out of order. The duty officer had to route it by commercial Western Union office—without a PRIORITY stamp, it would take over six hours to reach General Short at Fort Shafter.

The final Magic delivery to the Secretary of State interrupted his conference with Frank Knox and Henry Stimson to prepare a presidential draft asking Congress to declare war in the anticipation of the attack on Siam and Malaya. The news of the 1 P.M. deadline confirmed their fears that there might be "something hanging in the air."

Pearl Harbor Strike Force   05.30 hrs.

Ahead of the main striking force, now less than 200 miles north of Oahu, the seaplanes were launched from the cruisers *Tone* and *Chikuma* on Nagumo's orders to make a predawn reconnaissance of both Pearl Harbor and Lahaina anchorage. The spray was sweeping over the lurching flight decks as the crew wrestled to hold down the rows of attack planes being ranged for takeoff while their pilots, gunners, and bombardiers scrambled aboard.

North Malayan Coast (11:45 Singapore Time)   **05.45 hrs.**

The most southerly of General Yamashita's three invasion forces, carrying the 56th Infantry Regiment, arrived on the beach at Kota Bharu at the mouth of the Kelantan River. Four escorting destroyers and a light cruiser began a bombardment of the pillboxes and defenses manned by the 9th Indian Army Division. In pouring rain and rough seas, the first of more than 5,000 Japanese troops started splashing ashore under heavy cross fire.

Singapore (midnight)   **06.00 hrs.**

"Someone's opened fire," a voice came down the telephone at RAF headquarters, requesting permission to scramble the aircraft at Kota Bharu base. "Go for the transports, you bloody fools!" he was told. Hudsons began taking off for a sporadic series of attacks that set one transport ablaze but did not halt the landing. General Percival was now at headquarters telephoning the Governor. "Well, I suppose you'll shove the little men off," a sleepy Sir Shenton Thomas retorted, before calling the chief of police to round up all local Japanese. Two hours later, the "little men" had pushed back the defenders at Kota Bharu to secure the first invasion beachhead of Japan's new empire.

Pearl Harbor Strike Force   06.00 hrs.

The Imperial Navy battle ensign was broken out above Togo's famous Z pendant signal flying at the *Akagi*'s masthead, as Commander Fuchida fastened the Hachimaki headband given him by the flagship's crew. On the pitching deck, motors burst into life and green signal lamps flashed in the murk. Chocks were pulled and the first plane roared forward. Cheers rang out as its pilot successfully coordinated his takeoff with the rearing bows. The next fifteen minutes saw aircraft peeling off the six carriers, some barely scraping the wave tops. Yet only one fighter crashed, failing to make the tricky synchronization. The 183 aircraft of the first strike wave, 49 Val bombers carrying their winged armor-piercing shells, 40 "Kates" each with a deadly oxygen-powered Long Lance torpedo beneath its belly, and the escort of 43 Zero fighters, wheeled around the warships, taking up formation. Then, led by Fuchida, they climbed up through the clouds to burst into a glorious sunrise and, with metal aglitter in the bright morning light, set course south. With the help of a tailwind, the navigator estimated that ninety minutes would bring them over Pearl Harbor.

Task Force 8—U.S. Pacific Fleet   06.15 hrs.

At dawn the U.S.S. *Enterprise* was approximately the same distance west of Oahu as the Japanese Fleet was to the north. Admiral Halsey launched a search patrol of fighters before sending off a flight of Dauntless dive bombers to Oahu.

Pearl Harbor   06.30 hrs.

Three PBY patrol flying boats armed with depth charges scouted off the waters at Ford Island to carry out the routine dawn security patrol off Oahu's southern coast.

At 06.37 the boom defenses at the harbor entrance had again been opened to admit the target-towing vessel *Antares*. The guard destroyer *Ward* surged forward at full speed to bear down on a small submarine. Roused from his bunk, Lieutenant Commander William Outerbridge ordered a gunfire and depth charge attack, simultaneously making a voice transmission to the Naval Control Center. A few minutes later, he confirmed: "WE HAVE ATTACKED FIRED UPON AND DROPPED DEPTH CHARGES UPON SUB OPERATING IN DEFENSIVE AREA" before heading off to investigate the sighting of a suspicious sampan. The lone duty officer at the Operation Center, despite two reports, failed to elicit confirmation of the attack and so gave a low priority to the attack report. It would be nearly three quarters of an hour before the harbor duty destroyer *Monaghan* was alerted. Meanwhile, just after 7 A.M., one of the PBYs on antisubmarine patrol depth-charged another contact. The pilot signaled his report in code, which took more than half an hour to clear for circulation.

By then it was clear that Pearl Harbor was under attack from enemy submarines, but it was already too late to put the eighty-six ships on alert as the Pacific Fleet awakened to the lazy routine of another Sunday. Only three quarters of the crews were aboard and many ships had watertight doors clipped open.

Kahuku Point, Oahu   07.02 hrs.

Atop the northernmost promontory of the island, the two-man crew of the mobile Army radar unit at Opana would already have switched their set off if the breakfast truck had arrived on time. Now Private George E. Elliot, the plotter, was amazed to witness "something completely out of the ordinary on the radar screen." Private Joseph Lockard's check revealed nothing malfunctioning, so they began plotting the progress of the fluttering green blips, indicating a huge flight of aircraft approaching from 37 miles to the north. Urgent telephone calls to Army headquarters at Fort Shafter resulted in the duty pilot's blunt reply: "Don't worry about it." The pilot confidently assumed that the blips must be the expected incoming flight of B-17s from the West Coast.

Washington (1:00 P.M.)   **07.30 hrs.**

As the deadline for the delivery of Tokyo's final message to the U.S. government arrived, Ambasador Nomura was still awaiting the typing of a fine copy. His aide telephoned the State Department to apologize and put back his appointment by half an hour.

Tokyo (3:00 A.M.)   **07.30 hrs.**

The Japanese foreign minister, Togo, reached the Imperial Palace and waited while the Emperor was roused to receive the appeal from President Roosevelt. Hirohito dictated a formal response, knowing that it was too late to halt the Japanese war machine.

Kra Peninsula, Thailand (1:30 A.M.)   **07.30 hrs.**

Fourteen transports carrying General Yamashita's main landing force dropped anchor off Singora Beach. Without a shot being fired, the assault waves landed easily in spite of the rough water. Colonel Tsuji's special unit arrived by rickshaw at the Japanese Consulate. Pounding on the gate finally wakened the fat official, who greeted them drunkenly: "Ah! The Japanese Army." He drove them to the local police headquarters, where they hoped with a 100,000 tical bribe to enlist support and uniforms to sneak a busload of Japanese soldiers in disguise through to the British lines across the frontier. The Thai police greeted the Japanese call: "Ally with us and attack the British Army," with bullets. Tsuji's "dream plan" had collapsed, but it made little difference to the fate of Singora and Patani. Yamashita's forces quickly overwhelmed the few Thai Army units. Within hours, resistance was "suspended for the time being" on orders from Bangkok.

Off Oahu   07.35 hrs.

The reconnaissance seaplanes from the Japanese cruisers remained undetected and radio reports signified that the Pacific Fleet was still in Pearl Harbor. A local Hawaiian radio station forecast was picked up by Fuchida's command plane, promising a warm, clear, and sunny day. Moments later he was rewarded with his first glimpse of the island's terrain, so familiar to him from maps and photographs. "All of a sudden the clouds broke, and a long line of coast appeared. We were over Kahuku Point, the northern tip of the island, and it was now time for our deployment."

The only confusion to the otherwise clockwork precision of the strike now occurred when Fuchida, convinced that one flight of torpedo bombers had not responded to his "Black Dragon" smoke flare signal to send them in first, sent off a second. This flare was mistaken by the dive bombers as the signal sending them into the attack to prevent enemy fighters taking off. They broke away, climbed up to 12,000 feet, and came racing down on the Oahu airfields.

Sweeping round the Kodakan peaks from the southwest, Fuchida studied his objective through binoculars before ordering his radio operator: "Notify all planes to launch attack."

07.49 hrs.

"TO TO TO TO TO" flashed out to all pilots (the first two letters of *Totsugeki!*—Charge!). Seconds later, as he watched the first wave of torpedo bombers sweeping in over Battleship Row, Fuchida ordered his operator to tap out "TORA TORA TORA"—the prearranged TIGER TIGER TIGER code signal that would let Admiral Nagumo know complete surprise had been achieved. Five thousand miles away aboard the *Akagi* an excited yeoman passed the message on to Admiral Yamamoto, who impassively continued the game of Shōgi he was playing with Watanabe, his staff gunnery officer.

Over Oahu's jewel-green canefields and pineapple plantations, three startled civilian fliers were suddenly caught up in the racing maelstrom of diving planes. Roy Vitousek, a Honolulu lawyer, dived for his home field. The same instinctive reaction to duck the attack saved Jimmy Duncan of the Hui Lele Flying Club as he was chased by a fiery stream of tracer bullets from the Zero. Flying instructor Cornelia Fort also managed to get her light plane and stunned pupil-pilot down through a rainstorm of bullets onto John Rogers civil airport.

07.56 hrs.

The Japanese were concentrating the main weight of their attack on the military airfields, while the torpedo planes hit the battleships. The first wave of eighteen dive bombers struck Hickam Field, the Army base south of Pearl Harbor—where row upon row of fighters and bombers were parked wingtip to wingtip on the aprons as a protection against sabotage—while bombers plastered the flying boat ramps on Ford Island. Explosions rocked the hangars, sending blazing chunks of PBY boats into the air.

07.56 hrs.

The raid erupted with such sudden fury that for the first few minutes few aboard the warships of the Pacific Fleet could grasp what was happening. The forenoon watch had just been piped to breakfast and color parties assembled on fantails, awaiting the 8 o'clock signal to hoist ensigns; the soothing chiming of church bells drifted across the harbor through a thousand open scuttles, until it was abruptly drowned by the rattle of machine-gun fire, the scream of bombs, and the crump of exploding torpedoes.

The first "Kate" raced in over the *Nevada*, the stern marker on Battleship Row, shredding the ensign with cannonfire. The astonished band continued thumping out a few more bars of the Star Spangled Banner without missing a beat. The first torpedo splashed into the water abaft the *Arizona*, where Ensign G. S. Flanningan, like thousands of others, had just heard the air-raid siren sound off in disbelief. "I was in the bunk room and everyone thought it was a joke to have an air raid on Sunday. Then I heard an explosion." Aboard the *Maryland*, Seaman First Class Short was writing Christmas cards at his machine-gun station on the battleship's towering superstructure. "Suddenly I noticed planes diving on the Naval Air Base nearby. At first I thought they were our planes just in mock diving practice attack, but when I saw smoke and flames rising from a building, I looked closer and saw that they were not American planes. I broke out the ammunition nearby, loaded my machine gun and opened fire on two torpedo planes coming in from the east which had just dropped two torpedoes."

07.58 hrs.

The first explosions roused the commander of Patrol Wing Two to broadcast the alarm from the control tower at Ford Island: "AIR RAID PEARL HARBOR, THIS IS NOT DRILL." Minutes later Admiral Kimmel's headquarters radioed the electrifying message to outlying Pacific Fleet Commands.

High over Pearl Harbor with his flight of level bombers, Fuchida's heart beat faster as he saw "waterspouts rising alongside the battleships, followed by more and more waterspouts." Four of the great battleships at the head of the row were moored in pairs, and the two outermost, *Oklahoma* and *West Virginia*, were soon being torn by torpedo explosions. The first hit the "WeeVee" at about 8 A.M., and in the opening minutes of the attack five more slammed into her armored flanks. Lieutenant C. V. Ricketts was at breakfast in the wardroom when General Quarters sounded: "As I went up the ladder to the starboard side of the quarter deck, I heard the word being passed 'The Japs are attacking.' As I reached the quarterdeck I felt the ship being hit. She was shaken some but I was not bombed off my feet. I thought then that instead of actual hits the vibration might be caused by bombs falling close aboard."

With thousands of tons of water pouring into her wounded port side, the "WeeVee" was developing a menacing list by the time the gunnery officer reached the bridge. Captain Mervyn S. Bennion ordered him below to organize the counter-flooding. Slithering on crazily slanting smoke-filled passageways past stretcher and fire parties, Ricketts managed to coordinate enough men to open the starboard seacocks and save the battleship from capsizing. She was slowly settling onto the harbor mud, with her decks awash. "During all this time extremely heavy bombing and straffing attacks occurred," recalled the battleship's navigator, Lieutenant Commander T. Beattie, who was uninjured while the captain beside him was mortally wounded by flying shrapnel. "Just about then the U.S.S. *Arizona*'s forward magazines blew up with a tremendous explosion and large sheets of flame shot skyward, and I began to wonder about our own magazines and whether they were flooded."

Ricketts's prompt action saved the *West Virginia* from the fate now overtaking the *Oklahoma*, the outboard companion of the *Maryland*, moored ahead at berth F5. The noise of gunfire sent Commander Jesse L. Kenworthy, Jr., racing back up the starboard ladder he had just descended from the wardroom, calling the crew to go to battle stations. "As I reached the upper deck, I felt a very heavy shock and heard a loud explosion and the ship immediately began to list to port. Oil and water descended on the deck and by the time I had reached the boat deck, the shock of two more explosions on the port side was felt. As I attempted to get to the Conning Tower over decks slippery with oil and water, I felt the shock of another very heavy explosion on the port side." *Oklahoma*'s captain, along with many senior officers, was ashore, and the battleship's watertight integrity was poor, with many of her below deck hatches clipped open. As water began flooding from one compartment into another, her crew made a frantic scramble to escape while she started to roll over. Kenworthy and the lucky ones managed to scramble over her starboard bilge as she turned turtle. More than four hundred hands were trapped below in the topsy-turvy blackness of a flooding tomb.

Overhead, Fuchida's group began its own bombing run as the antiaircraft gunners went into action, recovering from their initial shock. "Dark grey bursts blossomed here and there until the sky was clouded with shattering near misses which made our plane tremble. . . . Suddenly the plane bounded as if struck by a huge club. 'The fuselage is holed to port,' reported the radio man behind me, 'and the steering wire is damaged.'" In those fifteen deadly minutes after eight o'clock, the awful majesty of the *Arizona*'s end was not lost on Fuchida and his crew. He watched as the "column of dark red smoke rose 1,000 feet into the air and a stiff shock wave rocked the plane. I called our pilot's attention to the spectacle and he observed: 'Yes commander, the powder magazine must have exploded.' Terrible indeed."

The signal tower had just hoisted SAIL when a series of volcanic explosions destroyed the *Arizona* and a thousand American sailors. Across the harbor where his ship U.S.S. *Ramapo* was berthed alongside the pier, Mechanic First Class Francis T. Bean saw the fatal torpedo hit: "About two minutes later a spurt of flame came out of the guns in No. 2 turret, followed by an explosion of the forward magazines. The foremast leaned forward, and the whole forward part of the ship was enveloped in flame and smoke and continued to burn fiercely."

Aboard the doomed battleship, Ensign Jim D. Miller was in No. 3 turret: "Shortly after I had reached the booth the turret was shaken by a bomb explosion of not very great intensity. After a minute or two a much more terrific explosion shook the turret. Smoke poured in through the overhang hatch, and I could see nothing but reddish flame outside. The phones went dead, all power went off. . . ." Fighting choking gases and water pouring into the lower handling room, Miller's crew climbed up the escape hatches to witness a scene of terrifying devastation on deck: "Fuel oil was coming up from some place on the port side and catching fire. The ship was down by the bow, and the quarterdeck began to come awash. . . . The main and forecastle decks were ablaze. . . . Our life rafts were cut down and put into the water and all hands ordered to go over the side. Men found the rafts difficult to paddle, and most of them crawled aboard motor launches or started swimming toward Ford Island."

Fuchida now made his bombing run over the *Maryland*, which had so far been protected by the capsizing *Oklahoma*. Pressing the release trigger, he watched mesmerized as his four bombs "in perfect formation plummeted like the devils of doom. . . . They became small as poppy seeds and finally disappeared just as tiny white flashes of smoke appeared on and near the ship." The two hits he jubilantly reported actually had little effect on the *Maryland*'s stout armored deck. She survived the attack—the least damaged of the battleships and the first to return to active service.

Aboard the *Tennessee*, damage was also not too severe. Only two bombs had burst on board, and most of the fires that were raging in her superstructure had been started by the flaming debris that came raining down from the explosion of the *Arizona*'s magazines. At the head of the row, the *California* was the last of the battleships to be hit as two torpedoes rip into her side, below the bridge. Quick counter-flooding prevented her from capsizing, but she too was now slowly settling onto the mud as burning oil engulfed her stern. The *Nevada* meanwhile, at the stern of Battleship Row, whose gun crews were marginally faster getting into action, had beaten off all but one of the low-flying Kates. The last now succeeded in sending a single torpedo into her bows, opening up a 40- by 30-foot gash. The *Nevada*'s vitals were undamaged as her engine-room hands battled to raise steam to get under way.

After half an hour of continuous torpedo and dive-bombing attacks there was a comparative lull as the strafing and bombing continued, but at a slower pace for the next twenty minutes. During this time the destroyer *Helms*, which was the only warship actually under way in the whole harbor, managed to run down another midget submarine—whose exhausted commander later beached the craft and surrendered.

Washington (1:40 P.M.) **08.10 hrs.**

Just before the lull in the attack on Pearl Harbor, Admiral Kimmel relayed a signal: "AIR RAID PEARL HARBOR. THIS IS NOT DRILL," which reached the Secretary of the Navy. "My God!" Knox exclaimed in disbelief. "This can't be true, this must mean the Philippines." When he confirmed that there had been no error, he telephoned the White House. The President then called the State Department to break the news to Cordell Hull, advising him to receive Ambassador Nomura and Envoy Kurusu, already waiting in the anteroom. The Secretary was not to tell them of the raid, but "to receive their reply formally and coolly bow them out."

The Japanese diplomats were ushered in, formally attired, and were quite at a loss to understand Hull's ill-concealed icy anger. He pretended to study the fourteen-part message before spitting out: "In all my fifty years of public service, I have never seen such a document that was more crowded with infamous falsehoods and distortions." As they were bowing themselves out in an embarrassed fluster, a State Department official overheard Hull muttering under his breath, "Scoundrels and piss-ants!" as the door closed.

Oahu 08.30 hrs.

The pace of the Japanese air attack was now building up again as Admiral Bloch, Commandant of the 14th Naval District, "cool as a cucumber," was on the phone to Secretary of the Navy Knox delivering a damage report: "He could look through a window and see smoke and flames from the ships still burning in the harbor."

The end of the lull coincided with the arrival of the twelve B-17s flying in from the West Coast, tanks down to their last gallons of gasoline. Major Truman Langdon heard a voice shouting over his intercom warning that the wheeling planes were hostile. "Damn it, those are Japs," he shouted, ordering his pilots to land on whatever airfield they could. They all got down safely, but one pancaked on a golf course and another was shot in half as it reached the end of Hickam Field's runway.

The Pan Am *Anzac Clipper*, due to land at Ford Island slip, had already been diverted to Hilo in time to avoid the arrival of the second wave of Japanese planes. The Marine Dauntlesses that had flown off the *Enterprise* were not so fortunate. Lacking fuel reserves to divert, they landed as best they could, dodging the Zeros' cannonfire and the falling bombs. Most of them were down with their wings peppered full of holes, but a last desperate radio message was picked up by the carrier from one confused pilot, calling: "Don't shoot! This is an American plane!"

"A DATE WHICH WILL LIVE IN INFAMY"

08.40 hrs.

The "lull" ended with the resumption of high-level bombing as the second wave of eighty-six dive bombers, fifty-four level bombers, and thirty-six fighters swept round the east coast of Oahu to join in the raid. During both attacks, no U.S. Navy pilots managed to get their planes into the air before they were destroyed, but a handful of Army fighters did somehow succeed in getting off from Wheeler Field. Hopelessly outnumbered, they nevertheless accounted for eleven of the enemy. The sky over Pearl Harbor was punctuated by black columns of smoke from the burning battleships and mushrooms of antiaircraft fire growing more dense by the minute.

Another midget submarine had succeeded in penetrating to the northern end of the harbor. The destroyer *Monaghan* now raced to the spot as the Japanese skipper coolly fired a torpedo at the tender *Curtiss*—it missed—before loosing off its second at the destroyer bearing down with guns blazing away. The *Monaghan's* sharp prow sliced the midget sub with the impact of a locomotive hitting a tin can as depth charges were hurled over the stern for good measure. The moment of triumph for skipper and crew was spoiled when the destroyer's propellers, racing hard astern, failed to stop the *Monaghan* from piling into a blazing barge.

The second air attack concentrated on the battleship *Nevada*, now under way and being cheered by the men on the upturned *Oklahoma* as she crept past down the channel, her batteries blazing away at the Japanese dive bombers. The tugs that had been sent out to prevent her sinking and blocking the main channel successfully nudged her ashore at Waipo Point, their pumps helping to fight the blaze that threatened to engulf her after her fire-main had been severed by a bomb.

The *Nevada's* dash for safety had drawn the main attacks of the second wave of high-level bombers away from their original target, which was the *Pennsylvania*, dry-docked for repairs. One bomb penetrated the fleet flagship's boat deck as a spectacular explosion blew off the bows of the destroyer *Shaw* in the nearby floating dock. Flooding was ordered in an effort to quench the flames, but flaming oil spread rapidly, igniting the torpedoes and magazines aboard the two destroyers sharing the dry dock.

Seeing that all the battleships were either ablaze or sinking, the Japanese focused the final minutes of their second strike against the northern harbor, disposing of the old target ship *Utah* and a number of auxiliary vessels. They failed to hit the cruisers or to set the Navy Yard's extensive oil-storage tank farm ablaze.

08.50 hrs.

As the second wave headed north back to the carriers, less than two hours after the raid began, Commander Fuchida's lone bomber circled above Pearl Harbor, photographing his triumph and the "seemingly impossible task" his pilots had achieved. "A warm feeling came with the realization that the reward of those efforts was unfolded before my eyes," he remembered. "I counted four battleships definitely sunk and three severely damaged, and extensive damage had also been inflicted upon other types of ships. The seaplane base at Ford Island was all in flames, as were the airfields, especially Wheeler Field."

The great pall of black smoke that spiraled thousands of feet into the clear Sunday sky over Pearl Harbor was a symbol of Japan's tactical victory and the United States' tragedy. The death and destruction were not at an end. Thousands would spend the day battling the flames that threatened the battleships still afloat, as small craft dodged the pools of burning oil, snatching fuel-blackened survivors from the water. The doctors at the military hospitals on Oahu battled for the lives of the hundreds of burned and mutilated seamen. Many were to be saved through the application of the new "miracle" antibiotic sulfonamides with the hastily sterilized "flit guns" which were used to douse badly burned victims dying from infection and dehydration. For two days divers and rescue parties waged an agonizing struggle, cutting their way to reach the men who could be heard tapping desperately in the upturned hull of the *Oklahoma*. Only thirty out of more than four hundred would be got out alive.

The final American death toll climbed to 2,403 servicemen killed—1,000 of them lost in the *Arizona*. Nearly 2,000 had been wounded and 18 warships wrecked too badly to be salvaged. Only 43 planes remained operational; 188 were destroyed on the ground and another 159 damaged. All this destruction, which effectively wiped out the entire battleship strength of the Pacific Fleet, was achieved at a cost to Japan of only twenty-nine planes and their crews and the loss of the five midget submarines together with all but one crew. This was far less than Yamamoto had dared to expect. That morning, as he received the first reports, he ordered his battleship force to raise steam for a dawn sortie to go to Admiral Nagumo's aid if the American carriers appeared to launch a counterattack.

Washington (3:00 P.M.)   **09.30 hrs.**

The Pearl Harbor raid was still in progress when Stimson, Knox, Hull, Admiral Stark, and General Marshall gathered for their first war conference in the White House that afternoon. Roosevelt, firmly in command of the situation, fired out a succession of orders for guarding military installations and factories, grounding all private planes, silencing all amateur radio operators, setting up censorship, and ordering the FBI to round up Japanese aliens.

In a hectic meeting punctuated by frequent telephone reports from Pearl Harbor, they discussed the declaration of war, that he must present to Congress the next day. One of the more welcome callers was Winston

Churchill. His gruff voice came on the line after that of American Ambassador John Winant, with whom he was dining at Chequers when the BBC 9 P.M. bulletin carried the news.

"Mr. President, what's all this about Japan?" the Prime Minister began. The President interrupted, "It's quite true. They have attacked Pearl Harbor. We are all in the same boat now." Churchill told him that an attack was also under way in Malaya, and they agreed to make simultaneous declarations of war the next day.

Task Force 8   09.42 hrs.

Racing for Oahu from the west, Admiral Kimmel received a signal that there was "some indication" the Japanese were to the northwest. Halsey was accordingly ordered to intercept with the *Enterprise* and three cruisers. In the confusion following the raid, a stream of false sightings and misinterpreted radio fixes sent the Task Force chasing off first to the south, then toward the Marshalls at dusk. This undoubtedly saved Halsey and his carrier. If he had encountered the vastly superior Japanese force, he would have been annihilated. It was no comfort to "Bill" Halsey, however, whose anger and frustration exploded the following afternoon when he saw the wreckage in Pearl Harbor still smoking: "Before we're through with 'em, the Japanese language will be spoken only in hell!"

Shanghai, China (4:00 A.M.)   **10.00 hrs.**

A telephone call from the gunboat *Wake* woke Lieutenant Commander Columbus D. Smith at his town apartment with the news of Pearl Harbor. He rushed down to the harbor to carry out his orders to scuttle his command but was halted at the pier by Japanese guards, who arrested him, announcing that the Imperial Navy seized the *Wake*, renaming it *Tatara*. The British gunboat *Petrel* had resisted ignominious surrender, until her captain's defiance was silenced by heavy artillery fire.

Manila, Philippines (4:00 A.M.)   **10.00 hrs.**

Just an hour had passed since a phone call roused Admiral Hart with Admiral Kimmel's warning. General MacArthur's astonished reaction was to exclaim: "Pearl Harbor! It should be our strongest point." Brigadier Leonard T. Gerow, Chief of the Army's War Plans Division, came on the line at 3:40 A.M., as MacArthur was dressing, to confirm the news and tell the general that he "wouldn't be surprised if you get an attack there in the near future."

General Brereton was awakened minutes before 4 A.M. by MacArthur's Chief of Staff, Richard Sutherland. Immediately he put his flyers on alert—many of them having only just returned to their bases from the party in the Manila Hotel. Arriving at Manila headquarters an hour later, Brereton wanted to send his B-17s off at once to raid Formosa. But a fatal paralysis gripped MacArthur's command that morning. His Chief of Staff insisted on a preliminary reconnaissance mission because there was little information about what they were going to find to bomb on Formosa.

At 5:30 A.M. MacArthur received a cable from Washington directing him to execute RAINBOW 5 War Plan at once, although he would later insist that "my orders were explicit not to initiate hostilities against the Japanese." The shock of events seemed to have clouded his judgment, leading him to believe, according to President Quezon, "that the Philippines would remain neutral and would not be attacked by the Japanese." Others blamed MacArthur's apparent cataleptic state for his astonishing refusal to give Brereton permission to make a preemptive raid on Formosa since justification had already been provided at 6:12 A.M. with reports from Admiral Hart's Naval Headquarters that Japanese carrier planes were bombing the seaplane tender *William B. Preston*, anchored in the Gulf of Davao.

MacArthur would claim that "he had not the slightest doubt he would be attacked," denying he had ever been informed of Brereton's request—though Army records clearly show that he was. The general would blame his air commander for not carrying out his orders to evacuate the remaining B-17 bombers left on Clark Field to the relative safety of Luzon. Yet there can be little doubt that MacArthur's failure to act that morning contributed to the disaster that overtook his command.

The Philippines might not have been saved if Brereton had been allowed to make the preemptive raid, but the Japanese bombers were grounded by weather, sitting ducks for the American B-17s whose attack might have disrupted the Japanese invasion schedule.

Formosa (4:00 A.M.)   **10.00 hrs.**

Dawn fog grounded the four hundred planes of the Navy's 11th Air Fleet and Army 5th Air Group—according to the plan they should have been striking Luzon airfields to wipe out MacArthur's air force. Admiral Takahashi was certain that the news of Pearl Harbor would bring the American bombers raining destruction on his planes. There was nothing he could do but wait for the weather to clear. His aircrew waited despondently by their planes in gasmasks, anticipating a raid that never materialized.

Pearl Harbor Strike Force   10.00 hrs.

With the return of the first Japanese aircraft, the roughening seas made landing even more hazardous than their takeoff had been. Twenty-nine planes were lost, but by the time the second wave flew in an hour later, the deck crews had rearmed and refueled the first wave as their pilots stood by for another raid. The last plane to land was Fuchida's. He strongly urged launching a third strike against the so far undamaged oil farm and repair facilities, to render Pearl Harbor useless as a base for many months. At this moment of supreme decision Nagumo's instinct for caution, borne of the risk to his carriers from possible counterattacks, triumphed over his willingness to grasp a much greater strategic prize. "To remain within range of enemy land based planes was distinctly to our disadvantage," he reasoned, as he ordered a withdrawal to the Marshalls—a decision for which he was later criticized.

Tokyo (7:00 A.M.) **11.30 hrs.**

The Japanese nation first learned they were at war from the Tokyo radio, NHK, as announcer Morio Tateno opened the early morning bulletin with the urgent news: "The Army and Navy divisions of the Imperial Headquarters jointly announced at six o'clock this morning, December 8, that the Imperial Army and Navy forces have begun hostilities against the American and British forces in the Pacific at dawn today." The Prime Minister was later to make a sober broadcast telling the nation to put all their energies into defeating the Western powers: "To annihilate this enemy and to establish a stable new order in East Asia, the nation must necessarily anticipate a long war. . . ." Later that morning trumpets preceded the reading of the Imperial War Proclamation that "the task bequeathed by Our Forefathers will be carried forward, and that the source of evil will be speedily eradicated and an enduring peace immutably established in East Asia, preserving thereby the glory of our Empire."

Singapore (5:00 A.M.) **11.30 hrs.**

Just as news of Japan's attack was being broadcast to 120 million people in the United States, the air-raid sirens were wailing over Singapore. Searchlights probed the dark sky as the enemy bomber pilots homed in onto the city because the official could not be located in time to switch off the street lights. Antiaircraft fire erupted around the Changi naval base, and from the *Prince of Wales* and the *Repulse;* but most of the bombs fell on Chinatown, killing sixty-one people.

Guam Island (8:27 A.M.) **12.57 hrs.**

Japanese naval bombers were raiding the island from their base in Saipan, 100 miles away. The five hundred-odd sailors and Marines of the garrison had nothing but machine guns and pistols. The bombs destroyed the Marine barracks; the U.S.S. *Penguin* sank in Apia Harbor, leaving only two old patrol craft and an oiler in "Guam's Navy" to repel the invasion force whose four destroyers had already sailed from Hashirajima in the Inland Sea four days earlier.

Wake Island (12:00 P.M.) **13.00 hrs.**

Just before midday, thirty-six Japanese bombers setting out from Roi in the Marshalls flew in out of a rain squall to bomb and strafe the most heavily defended U.S. atoll in the Pacific. Lacking a radar set, the island garrison had only fifteen seconds warning—no time for the antiaircraft gunners or Marine fighters, recently delivered by the *Enterprise*, to scramble into action before the bombing and strafing. Explosions destroyed seven of their precious fighters as fires consumed the large gasoline-storage tank. Twelve Marines died, along with six members of the staff of the Pan Am hotel. As the Japanese turned tail for home, one Marine noticed: "The pilots in every one of the planes was grinning wildly. Every one wiggled his wings to signify Banzai." Pan Am's big flying boat *Philippine Clipper*, which escaped with only twenty-three bullet holes, took off with seventy airline personnel and the wounded from Wake. As Captain Hamilton piloted his course northeast, he radioed back that a Japanese cruiser and destroyers were over the horizon heading for Wake.

Manila, Philippines (7:15 A.M.)   **13.45 hrs.**

General Brereton unsuccessfully tried again to get MacArthur's permission to send an air reconnaissance mission to Formosa, after General Arnold phoned from Washington, telling him not to get caught in a repetition of Pearl Harbor with his bombers grounded. Then when one of the island's only two working radars at Iba airfield 85 miles north of Manila reported unidentified aircraft approaching, he scrambled thirty-six P-40 fighters and all but one of the B-17s. All the fighters were recalled after this was found to be a false alarm, but the B-17s were left to circle aimlessly. MacArthur cabled Washington, "our tails are up in the air," as his Chief of Staff telephoned Brereton to deny his request to launch an air strike against Formosa "for the present."

Hong Kong (8:00 A.M.)   **14.00 hrs.**

The Japanese attack against Britain's colony in China began with a raid by thirty-five dive bombers. One group hurtled in over Kowloon on the mainland, leaving the garrison's five planes smoking ruins, as another unit dived in over the harbor, shooting up seven civil planes, including the Pan Am *Hong Kong Clipper*, which roared up in a sheet of flame. Britain had long ago decided not to defend Hong Kong. Major General C. M. Maltby, the garrison's commander, had war orders directing him only to hold out for "as long as possible" with six battalions of Indian and Canadian infantry and twenty-eight field guns of the Singapore and Hong Kong Artillery. His naval force consisted of an ancient destroyer and eight motor torpedo boats, but Maltby hoped to be able to fight a delaying action of "a week to ten days" with his meager forces holding mainland defenses above Kowloon known as the Gedrinker's Line. Six Japanese infantry battalions were already moving into the attack from China, undeterred by the blown bridges and the small British advance force of a Bren gun carrier and a handful of armored cars.

Manila, Philippines (9:00 A.M.)   **15.00 hrs.**

Thirty-two Japanese Army bombers that had managed to take off in spite of the weather opened the bombing on the Baguio and Tuguegarao airfields in northern Luzon. The fog had by now lifted in Formosa, permitting 192 planes of the Navy's 11th Air Fleet to take off for their 300-mile flight to the Philippines.

News of the air raid allowed General Brereton to call MacArthur's Chief of Staff to again point out that the Japanese had now made an "overt act" and asking Sutherland's permission to recall the B-17s, still circling over Mount Arayat, to load them with bombs. "If Clark Field is attacked," he warned, "we won't be able to operate on it." To his amazement, he was refused. It was to be another forty-five minutes before Sutherland phoned back with permission to send out a photo-reconnaissance flight, followed by a call from MacArthur himself agreeing to a bombing raid later that afternoon if the aerial pictures identified targets.

Washington (8:30 P.M.)   **15.00 hrs.**

Roosevelt's full executive assembled that evening at the White House to find the President in a solemn mood. It was, he told them, the most serious session since Lincoln's cabinet meeting at the outbreak of the Civil War. Secretary of Labor Frances Perkins recorded: "It was obvious to me that Roosevelt was having a dreadful time just accepting the idea that the navy could be caught unaware."

At 9:30 the Democratic and Republican leaders of Congress were ushered into the meeting. Once again Roosevelt rehearsed the terrible sequence of the day's events and the futile saga of the negotiations with Japan. Outside the unfamiliarly dark White House portico, the crowd that had been gathering all afternoon beyond the railings on Pennsylvania Avenue broke into another chorus of "God Bless America."

Clark Field, Luzon (12:00 P.M.)   **17.30 hrs.**

The sixteen B-17s were back on the ground at Clark Field, three being loaded up with camera equipment and the rest with 100-pound and 300-pound bombs. Five minutes before midday, Brereton reported to MacArthur that he was ready to "send out a mission in the afternoon." Yet the sense of urgency was evaporating as the bomber pilots went off duty for lunch. The P-40 Warhawk fighters, which had been patrolling over the South China Sea, were recalled for refueling. This was to be the final blunder in a chain of errors that had paralyzed the Philippine command in the ten hours since receiving the news of Pearl Harbor.

Minutes after midday, the single radar operator at Iba Field picked up the approaching Japanese squadrons. He tapped out the alarm by teletype to Clark Field. The receiving operator had just joined the pilots at lunch. Eventually, a lieutenant at Clark Field was raised by telephone who in response to frantic messages from Iba agreed to pass on the radar report "at the earliest opportunity." He failed to do anything fast enough. Iba's own fighter squadron was now caught on the ground refueling by over a hundred Japanese fighters and bombers. Clark Field also came under attack.

"Here comes the Navy," one of the aircrew remarked, as the three photo-reconnaissance B-17s started taxiing toward the black specks racing down the far end of the airfield. One pilot wondered aloud, "Why are they dropping tinfoil?" Another grabbed a movie camera. The air-raid sirens began wailing, making the answer unnecessary. "That's not tinfoil, those are goddamned Japs!" Aircrews rushed for their machines, others dived for cover or just ducked as the first enemy planes roared over, guns blazing and bombs tearing up the earth in flames.

The three B-17s attempting to get into the air never made it, as bombs turned the aircraft into sheets of flame and set ablaze those still neatly parked in front of their hangers. Somehow four Warhawks managed to scramble aloft but could not stop the aerial bombardment that thundered across Clark Field in three well-coordinated waves. It was a repeat performance of Pearl Harbor, as Clark and the other airfields were swallowed up in exploding bombs and a holocaust of blazing aircraft.

Taking count of the charred skeletons and smoking wreckage as the Japanese rumbled off at 1:37 P.M., it was plain that a crippling blow had been struck to MacArthur's air strength. Only seventeen Flying Fortresses survived at Mindanao and more than three quarters of the fighters had been destroyed. In half an hour the Japanese had won the air superiority needed to ensure the successful invasion of the Philippines. That afternoon Brereton received a blistering phone call from General Arnold, demanding to know "how in the hell" he had been caught after all the warnings.

Singapore (12:30 P.M.)   **18.30 hrs.**

Aboard the *Prince of Wales*, the captains of the two British capital ships and Force Z's staff officers met for a conference at which an ashen-faced Sir Tom Phillips had to decide what to do in response to the Admiralty's signals of the previous afternoon: "ON ASSUMPTION THAT JAPANESE EXPEDITION IN SOUTH CHINA SEA ON COURSE INDICATING INVASION REPORT WHAT ACTION WOULD BE POSSIBLE TO TAKE WITH NAVAL OR AIR FORCES."

Confusing intelligence had been pouring in to give Admiral Phillips no clear picture of the overall situation. The Japanese landings at Singora and Patani appeared to be successful, and the Indian troops who were too late to put Operation Matador into effect were already retreating from their advance positions in pouring monsoon rain. At Kota Bharu, the Japanese beachhead was pushing inland to threaten the airfield. It was believed that the Malaya and Siam invasion convoys were only covered by two battleships.

Sweating profusely in the prickly heat and steaming humidity of the admirals' cuddy, Phillips was aware by now that his deterrent mission had failed and unhappy about letting Force Z stay inactive in the harbor to become the target for enemy bombs. He outlined his plan to sail by dusk to smash the invasion beachheads at Singora. Success must depend on achieving surprise and securing adequate fighter protection for his warships. Adjourning for lunch, he signaled the Admiralty of his intentions and requested Air Vice Marshal Pulford, the RAF commander, for:

A. Reconnaissance 100 miles north of Ford daylight 9th December.
B. Reconnaissance 100 miles midpoint Singora 10 miles from coast starting first light 10 December.
C. Fighter protection off Singora at daylight 10th December.

But the battle raging on the Japanese beachhead in northern Malay was already making this request impossible, five hours before Force Z was due to put to sea.

Kota Bharu (4 P.M.) **22.00 hrs.**

The counterattacks against the Japanese beachhead had failed, and stray bullets whistling across the Kelantan River over the airfield perimeter prompted the Australian commander to request permission from Singapore to evacuate his remaining planes 150 miles south to Kuantan. Ground personnel joined the stream of evacuees leaving the town as the surviving Indian troops were concentrated for a final stand that night.

Singapore (5:35 P.M.) **23.35 hrs.**

The sun was sinking over the great colonial city as the *Prince of Wales* and the *Repulse* slipped their moorings and steamed slowly out of the Johore Channel. For the few witnessing their departure, it was a visible manifestation of the Governor's Order of the Day, posted in English, Malay, and Chinese: "We are ready; we have plenty of warning and our preparations have been made and tested. . . . We are confident." Not nearly so confident, Admiral Layton watched Force Z sail with the foreboding that he had seen the last of the aggressive admiral who had been sent out to relieve him. Already Tom Phillips's uneasiness about his mission was showing as he told the flag captain on the bridge of the *Prince of Wales* steaming out into the open sea: "I'm not sure that Pulford realizes the importance I attach to fighter cover over Singora on the tenth." Below decks, however, none of this uneasiness had filtered through to the more than 2,000 men, glad to be leaving the stifling heat of the harbor and eager for action. That afternoon they had loudly cheered Captain Tennant of the *Repulse* when he told them, "We are off to look for trouble."

Midway Island (10:31 P.M.) **00.31 hrs. Monday, December 8**

The moonlit beauty of a tranquil ocean night was shattered by orange gunflashes and shells crashing into the sandy shores of the atoll that was America's fixed aircraft carrier in mid-Pacific. The Japanese destroyers *Ushio* and *Sazanami* had been designated the Midway Destruction Force, but that night's operation, in which they exchanged shells with the shore batteries setting a hangar ablaze and killing a Marine officer, was just a nuisance raid.

Darkness now enclosed the Pacific Ocean, which had become the world's greatest theater of war. San Francisco and Los Angeles were blacked out and that evening had seen jumpy nerves and defenses tested by an air-raid alarm following reported sightings of Japanese carriers off the coast. Across in Oahu, rescue work was feverishly going on to release the men trapped in the *Oklahoma*. At lonely Wake Island the Marine garrison was manning its artillery battery, expecting an attack. On Guam, with no heavy guns to defend them, the night was another long vigil of courageous despair. In Manila, General MacArthur and his commanders were taking stock of the day's military disaster and wondering how they could now repel an invasion on the beachheads without air support. In Hong Kong, the men of the Volunteer Defense Corps drawn from the business community were preparing for the battle.

That evening, a final blow fell on what slim hopes remained that Britain and America might be able to check the flood of Japan's rising tide of conquest in the Far East. The last two Allied battleships afloat in the western Pacific were in line ahead at a steady 17 knots on a northeasterly course. Already 100 miles from Singapore and heading out into the South China Sea, they picked up an urgent signal from the Changi radio station: "FIGHTER PROTECTION ON WEDNESDAY TENTH WILL NOT REPEAT WILL NOT BE POSSIBLE." Admiral Phillips's yeoman was soon back with another signal telling him that the only reconnaissance possible the next day would be a single PBY Catalina flying boat mission. A more experienced commander might have realized then and there that his mission was impossible. To "Napoleon" Phillips, retreat was just not in the Royal Navy tradition. "Well," he said resignedly before retiring to his quarters, "we must get on with it."

On that first night of global war, following the day's unmitigated disaster, only the British Prime Minister retired content, relieved to know that the United States was henceforth fighting alongside as a full Ally. "Being saturated and satiated with emotion and sensation, I went to bed and slept the sleep of the saved and thankful."

8

Direct Shocks

"So we had won after all," was Winston Churchill's immediate reaction to the climactic chapter of military defeat for the Anglo-Saxon powers that began on December 7, 1941. He realized that the Pearl Harbor attack had brought the United States resolutely into a global war. Within hours of the attack the White House switchboard was jammed with calls from congressmen and leading members of the America First Committee pledging support for the war.

A mood of fierce national determination swept across the United States, given expression by the President at noon the next day when he entered the House of Representatives on the arm of his Marine captain son James. Supported by steel leg braces, he stood before the lectern to deliver the historic address to the emergency session of Congress. Deliberately, he paced his words, which were being broadcast coast to coast live by the radio networks:

"Yesterday, December 7, 1941—a date which will live in infamy—the United States was deliberately attacked by the naval and air forces of the Empire of Japan." Proceeding through a solemn litany of the previous day's "unprovoked and dastardly attack," he warned: "there is no blinking at the fact that our people, our territory and our interests are in grave danger." He concluded the ten-minute speech by asking Congress to declare war on Japan, confidently predicting that "with the unbounding determination of our people we will gain the inevitable victory."

The President's final "So help us God" was greeted with an eruption of cheering and stamping by the packed chamber, leaving no doubt that this was the least controversial of the many requests his nine-year-old administration had laid before Congress. Within the hour it had been passed "nem con" by the Senate and with only one dissenting pacifist vote in the House.

At 4:10 P.M. that afternoon Roosevelt, wearing a black armband of mourning, put his signature to the declaration of war against Japan, surrounded by congressional leaders and a battery of popping flashbulbs. Outside, the winter streets were unfamiliarly dark as a nationwide black- out went into effect across the United States. Soldiers paced guard past strategic factories, ports, and shipyards. Machine-gun posts sprouted at the White House and Washington's government buildings. Treasury Sec- retary Morgenthau had tripled the President's guard, but was unable to persuade him to have tanks stationed outside in Pennsylvania Avenue.

Throughout that day, officials in cities across the country had been su- pervising frenzied precautions to prevent air raids and sabotage. New York Mayor Fiorello La Guardia, determined to protect Manhattan "from such an attack as surprised Pearl Harbor," had been mobilizing civilian defense. The police department rounded up Japanese and other aliens from Axis countries, to be dispatched across the harbor by boat to custody on Ellis Island. All day a somber crowd had been milling before the Times Square illuminated news bulletin board as uniformed sailors cheerfully told anyone who would listen, "We can whip them in no time." In cities across America young men had been crowding in to sign up and lines were long outside Army and Navy recruiting stations.

On the West Coast, where the threat from Japanese invasion appeared a possibility, antiaircraft batteries were being hurried into position on the Hollywood Hills and at Long Beach and Seattle—the great aircraft manu- facturing plants of Boeing and Douglas being thought to be obvious tar- gets for marauding enemy bombers. Farmers armed with pitchforks and shotguns patrolled the empty beaches of Puget Sound to ward off landing attempts, for that Monday night the invasion scare seemed very real. Sirens wailed out their warning shortly after six o'clock from Los Angeles to San Francisco after a policeman reported an unidentified aircraft recon- noitering the coast west of San Jose. General William Ord Ryan, in charge of Western Defense Command, was in "no doubt that they came from a carrier." Refusing to acknowledge that it had been a false alarm, he claimed his fighter planes must have frightened the Japanese off.

Spy and sabotage reports against native Japanese-Americans were jam- ming the precinct switchboards in the west, and in Washington a heavy police guard was required to protect the embassy where Ambassador Nomura and his staff were now virtual hostages. Along the Potomac that night, four of the cherry trees that had been a 1912 gift from the citizens of Tokyo were chopped down in mindless protest. Across the country many Americans of Japanese lineage chipped in together to pay for messages in newspapers and telegrams to the White House protesting their loyalty. But it was not enough to stop their store windows from be- ing smashed or to keep "patriotic" citizens from organizing a boycott of their shops along with all Japanese goods.

The administration was level-headed enough to realize that air raids and invasion threats were unlikely eventualities, but the imposition of the nightly blackout and the distribution of gasmasks continued for many months. Such measures conditioned Americans to the reality of war and the need for restrictions on personal liberty and consumption to mobilize the nation for a long, hard struggle.

In Great Britain, where the wail of the sirens and the screech of falling bombs had been part of the daily routine for more than two years, the news of Pearl Harbor brought the knowledge that America would now be fighting the war alongside. This new spirit of comradeship among the English-speaking peoples did not include the Irish Republic, which had spurned Churchill's call for unity. He also sent a message of support to "struggling China"—"The British Empire and the United States have been attacked by Japan. Always we have been friends: now we face a common enemy."

On December 8, the Prime Minister's 3 P.M. announcement in the House of Commons had actually beaten the President by two hours to make the formal declaration taking Britain into war with Japan. His intention had been to sustain the American commitment to the "Europe First" strategy, even though the United States was still not officially at war with Germany. That morning Churchill had announced to the War Cabinet his intention "to go over at once to see Roosevelt." The idea was not well received by the Foreign Secretary, Anthony Eden, who was about to leave on an arduous sea trip to Russia to confer with Stalin, nor by the British Chiefs of Staff, who feared that it might be too soon after the defeat of Pearl Harbor to put pressure on their new Ally across the Atlantic. Brushing aside their caution, the Prime Minister cheerfully observed: "Oh that's the way we talked while we were wooing her; now that she's in the harem, we can talk to her quite differently." He rejected Roosevelt's reservation, conveyed by a cable from the British ambassador, Lord Halifax, that "your coming here might be rather strong medicine," by cabling back: "It would be disastrous to wait another month before we settle common action in face of the new adverse situation in the Pacific. I hope to start tomorrow night. . . ." Forty-eight hours later, the President reconsidered and agreed.

Roosevelt was reluctant to receive the Prime Minister until the United States was formally at war with Germany. That same morning he had skated over the issue when he told reporters that Germany and Italy "consider themselves at war with the United States at this moment," and he had not referred to it in his national broadcast rallying Americans "to the most tremendous undertaking." Once again he was waiting on Hitler to make the move, since he knew he could not risk a divisive debate in Congress over whether the Atlantic or the Pacific had priority.

The German High Command was equally divided. With their Russian offensive stalled like Napoleon's in the snow before Moscow, a strong case was put to Hitler against plunging into an all-out war with the United

States. Japan had begun the conflict, so they were not obliged automatically to declare war under the Tripartite Pact. Moreover, there was little military benefit that Japan could bring except by attacking Russia in the Far East; the Führer's racial belief in the nordic superiority could hardly concede a need for Asiatic help to beat the Slavs. But his pride was finally stung into a decision following a report from his chargé d'affaires in Washington that reached Berlin on December 10, warning "within 24 hours the U.S. will declare war on Germany." The very next morning, in a vituperative attack on Roosevelt—"the man who is the main culprit in this war"—the Führer pitted the Third Reich against the United States. With considerable relief, the President's reciprocal declaration of war against Germany and Italy passed Congress twenty-four hours later without a single dissenting vote.

In those three days while British and American leaders anxiously waited for Hitler to take the plunge, Japan's "First Operational Phase" plan rolled on against Allied positions in the western Pacific. Thick weather once again closed in over Formosa, and only a token raid on Nichol's Field was made by seven Japanese bombers as a small landing force occupied Bataan and the Camiguin Islands off Luzon's north coast. Except for the capture of an outrigger canoe full of spies, there was an ominous lack of enemy activity in the Marianas, where the lone and ill-defended American outpost of Guam lay within sight of Japanese-held Tinian.

For the defenders of Hong Kong there was to be no let-up. Bombing raids continued on the harbor, and Japanese infantry began moving up to threaten the defensive strongpoints of the Gedrinker's Line above the Jubilee Reservoir, which held the colony's water supply. Fifteen hundred miles to the south the Japanese assault forces, equipped with light tanks and bicycles, were already probing through the thin defenses of the frontier with Siam to secure the neck of the Kra Peninsula and open up the strategic west coast road and rail links that ran down to Johore Province, the back gate to the fortress of Singapore. A belated attempt to send up the Operation Matador force to hold the border crossing at Kroh had failed when the Indian troops were driven back by Japanese tanks in a monsoon downpour. One bombing attack on Singora had been launched from the nearby Alor Star Airfield before heavy Japanese air raids forced its evacuation, but not before one of its six Blenheims had taken off on a suicidal mission.

The only chance of blocking the Japanese advance into Malaya depended on the 11th Indian Division, which had pulled back from the Siam border to reoccupy its waterlogged positions and defend the town of Sitra and the main road to the south. Simultaneously, a second thrust was developing down the west coast of Malaya from the invasion beachhead at Kota Bharu, as the Indian troops under Lieutenant General Sir Lewis Heath's Central Malaysian Command were steadily beaten back into the jungle by heavy air attacks. The mood was still confident at General Percival's headquarters. Although the RAF had lost nearly half its Brewster Buffaloes in the first day's fighting, he believed that the three to one superiority of British ground forces would be enough to block the Japanese advance on Singapore.

DEADLY PURSUIT

Much depended on whether the two great capital ships and four destroyers of Force Z could successfully disrupt the Japanese troop convoys. Admiral Phillips spent the second morning of the Pacific War steaming northwest on this mission, looping around the Anambas Islands up into the Gulf of Siam. Hopes of victory ran high as a thick pall of clouds, dropping frequent steamy rain squalls, shielded them from enemy aircraft. At midday, an RAF Catalina flying boat arrived to flash confirmation: "JAPANESE LANDING NORTH OF SINGORA." "Whatever we meet, I want to finish quickly and so get away to the eastward before the Japanese can mass a formidable scale of attack against us," Admiral Phillips stated in his Order of the Day. Anticipating that Force Z might run into nothing more formidable than an old battlecruiser, his crews were told, "Shoot to sink!" In less than eighteen hours he confidently expected to be pounding Japanese invasion transports into the shallows of the beachhead, unaware that by mid-afternoon his force had been sighted by patrolling submarine I-65. Its reports began a massive air and sea hunt for his ships.

Admiral Sadaichi Matsunaga's Saigon headquarters was thrown into turmoil by the news because he was about to dispatch the 22nd Air Fleet bombers to attack the British warships, which had been incorrectly reported as still at Singapore. At dusk, two surface forces of seven cruisers and two battleships were racing south as Matsunaga's pilots scoured the darkening waters of the Gulf to try for a torpedo bomber attack before nightfall. It was well into the evening before they were recalled after failing to find the British warships. Force Z had been sighted briefly at about 5 P.M. by float planes from the cruisers.

The sinister black specks hanging on the horizon were also seen by the *Prince of Wales*'s lookouts. Admiral Phillips, unaware that the float planes' radio reports had failed to reach Saigon, decided that the game was up. Aborting his mission, he nevertheless decided to hold course north until dark to fool the enemy, but he dispatched the destroyer *Tenedos*, which was running low on fuel, to steam south to radio the next morning for fighter cover.

Bitter disappointment settled on Force Z as its course was reversed south shortly after 8:15 P.M. As fate would have it, this was only minutes before a force of Japanese cruisers would have come within range of their guns. However, the wisdom of the decision was confirmed within the hour by another signal from his Chief of Staff at Singapore warning of intelligence reports of an enemy air fleet in southern Indochina: "THEY COULD ATTACK YOU IN FIVE HOURS AFTER SIGHTING AND MUCH DEPENDS ON WHETHER YOU HAVE BEEN SEEN TODAY."

Despite this clear warning, Admiral Phillips's mind was to be abruptly changed by a second signal from Admiral Palliser, which the yeoman handed to him at forty minutes past midnight—"ENEMY REPORTED LANDING KUANTAN." It was in fact an unconfirmed report, which later proved to have been a false alarm caused by water buffaloes blowing up beach-defense land mines. But Phillips took his Chief of Staff's message at face value. He believed a second major enemy invasion must have begun half-way down the Malayan coast. Urgent intervention was needed if the British troops already engaged to the north were not to be cut off. Unwilling to break radio silence to confirm the report, he decided that Palliser would anticipate his decision to attack and would have arranged aircover over Kuantan at dawn.

News that they would be going into action after all sent spirits soaring aboard the *Prince of Wales*. An hour later the captain of Imperial Navy submarine I-58 sighted the *Repulse* steaming through the cross wires of his periscope. His torpedoes missed, but his radio alarm was relayed to Saigon, where the weary air crews of the 22nd Air Flotilla were ordered to snatch a few hours' rest while their planes were rearmed and refueled for takeoff at first light.

In the remaining hours of darkness, Force Z zigzagged at high speed westward across the Gulf of Siam, throwing off the shadowing submarine. That evening in London, Churchill had met with his advisers in the underground war room beneath Whitehall's Storey's Gate. They debated for an hour about what to do with "the only key weapon in our hands" in the Far East now that its role as a deterrent had failed. The Prime Minister proposed sending the *Prince of Wales* and *Repulse* to reinforce the U.S. Pacific Fleet "as a proud gesture" to "knit the English speaking world together." Admiral Pound wanted to return to the Atlantic. No agreement had been reached, according to Churchill, when it was decided, "as the hour was late . . . to sleep on it." Before he awoke next morning catastrophe was to overtake Force Z.

Hong Kong's fate was decided that night when the Japanese launched their main force against the British defenses at Kowloon. Wearing rubber-soled shoes, the soldiers of the Imperial Army's 228th Infantry Regiment stole silently up through the barbed wire to drop grenades down the ventilation shafts of the key strongpoint of Gedrinker's Line at the Shing Mun redoubt. By the early hours of the morning Japanese troops were in control of the commanding heights above the line, cutting Hong Kong's principal water supply. General Maltby's plan to hold the mainland for a week before withdrawing to fight a last-ditch stand on the hills above Kowloon was scrapped.

The second dawn to break over the Pacific since Pearl Harbor brought the first loss of American territory to the seven hundred men of the Japanese Imperial Navy's Special Naval Landing Forces, whose role was similar to that of the U.S. Marine Corps. They came storming ashore at Dungas Beach on Guam and advanced rapidly into Agana. A fierce twenty-five-minute engagement was fought as the native chomorros of the Insular Guard Force battled alongside a handful of U.S. Marines. When Captain McMillin, the Governor, received reports that 5,000 enemy troops were landing at various points around the island, he concluded that any further resistance was suicidal. Three long blasts on a motorcar horn brought a cease-fire. Surrender negotiations were conducted in sign language, and an hour later the Governor and his men, stripped to their underpants, were forced to witness the hauling up of the Rising Sun on the Government House flagstaff. Japan had taken Guam at the cost of ten dead. Seventeen Americans had lost their lives, and the remaining five hundred, including a detachment of Navy nursing personnel, were quickly rounded up to become the first to experience the humiliating Japanese treatment of prisoners of war.

As the sun came up that morning 1,500 miles to the west, the second stage of Japan's operation against the Philippines swung into action as two "Surprise Attack" convoys headed for separate landing points on the north of Luzon. The main obstacle to carrying out the assault proved to be rough seas, rather than the short-lived defense of the beach by a single Filipino Army regiment. Landing of troops began from six transports under the covering gunfire of a light cruiser, six destroyers, and three minesweepers. A raid by five B-17s caused an interruption of operations when the American bombers sank a minesweeper and sent the invasion force out to sea for maneuvering room. By late afternoon the strategic airfield at Aparri was in Japanese hands. Rough surf had also caused the other Surprise Attack Force to call off operations that day at Vigan on the northwest coast of Luzon. The next morning, however, operations were resumed and over 4,000 troops were landed, making a shambles of General MacArthur's "beach defense" strategy and securing the landing areas for the full-scale invasion to come.

There were, unfortunately, no invasion transports within 100 miles of Kuantan on the Malayan coast when Force Z's Walrus float plane skimmed over the shoreline shortly after daybreak on December 10. "ALL'S QUIET AS A WET SUNDAY AFTERNOON," the destroyer *Express* signaled, confirming the bad news shortly before 8 A.M. when she rejoined the *Prince of Wales* after a thorough reconnaissance of the approaches to the tiny port. Admiral Phillips, however, remained convinced that an enemy force must be landing somewhere in the vicinity. Overlooking that the *Tenedos* would already have signaled Singapore for immediate aircover more than 100 miles to the south, he now ordered Force Z north in pursuit of a suspicious-looking tug towing barges that had been sighted earlier by the *Repulse*.

It was a rash decision. Force Z had lost its cloaking clouds and was plowing a zigzag furrow across a glassy calm, in horizon-to-horizon visibility from the air. Aloft were 100 Japanese pilots, eagerly scouring the waters 100 miles to the south off the Anambas, where the British warships would have been if they had stayed on the last course reported by the submarine. Just before 10 A.M. they found the *Tenedos*. For the next half an hour the old Royal Australian Navy destroyer dodged in and out of waterspouts thrown up by the scores of bombs, sending urgent signals that she was being dive-bombed.

The destroyer's alarms, picked up by *Prince of Wales*, made Phillips realize the mortal danger that loomed. Abandoning the northward pursuit of the phantom invasion, he ordered course reversed. As Force Z commenced its final dash back to Singapore, he did not break radio silence to call for aircover.

That same *Prince of Wales* Walrus spotter plane which had first been sighted by a Japanese patrol at 10:15 A.M. now lured the pilots of the 22nd Air Flotilla onto Force Z. Some had flown as far south as Singapore and their fuel gauges were way past the half-full mark when the long-awaited signal was given by Lieutenant Haruki Iki: "SIGHTED ENEMY BATTLESHIPS SEVENTY NAUTICAL MILES SE KUANTAN COURSE SOUTH EAST." The news put fresh life into the crews of the fifty torpedo planes and thirty-four bombers sent racing north. In Saigon, Admiral Matsunaga donned flying gear to lead another strike if his first wave failed to destroy the British battleships.

It was just 11:10 A.M. when the radar probing the horizon on *Repulse*'s fighting top picked up the blips of the first enemy planes heading into the attack, minutes before they became visible to the lookouts some 70 degrees off the port bow. Marine buglers blared action stations as the loudspeakers reverberated: "STAND BY FOR BARRAGE." By 11:13, when the nine twin-engined "Betty" bombers swung in for a head-on strike, the burnished sky was being peppered with puffs of exploding antiaircraft shells pumped aloft by the multiple pom-pom batteries, big brown mushrooms hurled up by the high-angle guns. The great turrets that were the battlewagon's raison d'être were useless, but every Oerlikon and machine gun blazed skywards toward the Japanese planes, which pressed on through a hail of high explosives and bullets.

"Look at those yellow bastards come!" CBS correspondent Cecil Brown, aboard the *Repulse*, heard one of the gunners yell as they thundered low overhead and nine black bombs came wobbling down. Helm hard-over, the great battlecruiser responded like a destroyer, racing at

24 knots through mountainous geysers, unscathed except for a hit on her hangar deck. "FIGHTING EFFICIENCY UNIMPAIRED," she signaled the flagship ahead. The men of her escorting destroyer *Electra* cheered.

There was a brief respite the crews of the British ships knew could not last long as they lit up cigarettes. Sure enough, at 11:30 the *Prince of Wales* radar picked up a flight of torpedo bombers heading over the starboard horizon. They first zoomed defiantly up into a convenient cloud; then, after what seemed an age to the waiting men, began swooping down in twos and threes in a well-coordinated attack. They pressed through the curtain of fire that sent one down in a fireball and visibly ripped into the wings and fuselages of others. At mast-height they loosed a shoal of torpedoes. The two great battlewagons sheared apart like ponderous skaters, heeling hard-over as they combed into the die-straight tracks closing their bows at nearly 70 knots. The deadly Long Lance oxygen powered torpedoes hissed harmlessly past the *Repulse*. But the *Prince of Wales*'s Captain Leach gave his order putting the helm over a fatal fraction of a second too late. The battleship's stern was rent by a twin detonation that jammed her rudder, shearing her port propeller shaft, and the turbines, freed of load, disintegrated, flooding the port engine room with scalding steam as water came pouring through the damaged stern.

The *Prince of Wales* had again lived up to her sad reputation as an unlucky ship. The three black "not under control" balls were run up her masthead as she lost way, circling helplessly. Captain Tennant, aboard the *Repulse,* was unable to elicit a response to his request for a damage report. When his yeoman of signals confirmed that no request for fighter cover had been transmitted by the flagship, he broke radio silence with the emergency call: ENEMY AIRCRAFT ATTACKING. The call sent pilots scrambling into cockpits of their fighters at the Singapore airfield. Only six Brewster Buffaloes could be spared, and it was to take them over an hour to fly the 150 miles to the unequal contest.

The Japanese bombers now gathered for the kill. A pilot was circling overhead relaying a running commentary, which brought cheers at Matsunaga's Saigon headquarters. The bomb and torpedo attacks were concentrating on the undamaged *Repulse,* as the battlecruiser swerved the waterspouts of near misses which sent clouds of steam up from red-hot gun barrels. Captain Tennant's fine judgment saved his ship from another low-level attack. "We have dodged 17 torpedoes so far thanks to Providence," he flashed to the crippled flagship. There was no reply, but it was apparent from the way the *Prince of Wales* barrage was now faltering that her power was dying.

With fewer modern antiaircraft guns, providence deserted the valiant *Repulse*. At twelve minutes past noon, Lieutenant Iki, whose plane had been first to sight the British, now seized his chance to lead down his flight of torpedo bombers. One cartwheeled into the sea. Another evaporated into air, but the skillfully executed attack, which had veered off from the *Prince of Wales* at the last moment, caught the battlecruiser in an "anvil," with torpedoes splashing into the water on each side of her foaming bow waves. "STAND BY FOR TORPEDOES!" the loudspeakers blared throughout the ship only seconds before a sickening crump, crump, crump rocked her first to port, then starboard, like a boxer slammed by left and right hooks.

Reports from below left no doubt the *Repulse* was doomed. Thousands of tons of seawater were pouring into her torn hull, although she was still making 15 knots. Captain Tennant made preparation to abandon ship. The Carley floats and life rafts were cut free from her listing superstructure. Men were struggling up through smoke-filled decks jammed with wounded and stretcher parties as he leaned over the bridge to bellow: "You've put up a good show, now save yourselves." Sailors began diving from the crazily listing upperworks into the water, one hurtling to his doom down the smokestack. The great hull jerked over, sending those on deck scrambling over the side. Slithering uncontrollably over the slimy flanks, their flesh was torn by the forest of barnacles, their bones smashed against the flange of the bilge keel.

Tennant stayed on the bridge, to be dragged down by the churning suction as his ship sank under him. Fighting his way to the surface with lungs bursting, he joined the survivors floundering in tepid water, soupy with the stinking black fuel oil. Destroyers were already picking their way through the flotsam to rescue those who had enough strength to reach the scrambling nets over their sides.

The Japanese pilots now turned their attention again to the *Prince of Wales*, whose stouter construction kept her afloat as more bombs burst into the powerless hull. Captain Leach and his crew were fighting a losing battle to save their ship. The destroyer *Express* had come alongside to supply electrical power and take off the wounded. Tugs had been radioed from Singapore, but the great battleship would never make port. At around 1 P.M. she began to founder. Captain Leach could be heard calling out: "Good-bye. . . . Thank you . . . Good luck . . . God bless you," over the pitiful cries of those trapped below coming up through the stern ventilators. Twenty minutes later the *Prince of Wales* rolled over, all but capsizing the *Express*, whose decks were packed with survivors.

Circling in triumph over the foaming mass of debris, a Japanese plane supposedly flashed in English: "WE HAVE FINISHED OUR TASK NOW YOU MAY CARRY ON" to the destroyers left with the grim rescue mission. The six RAF Buffaloes arrived over the scene of destruction just as the battleship took her death plunge. Too slow to catch the last of the enemy bombers, there was little they could do but fly over the survivors, waggling their wings in encouragement. It was a sight that made an indelible impression on Flight Lieutenant T. A. Vigors: "During that hour I had seen many men in dire danger, waving and cheering and joking as if they were on holiday at Brighton waving at low flying aircraft. It shook me, for here was something above human nature."

Vice admiral Sir Tom Spencer Vaughan Phillips KCB had forfeited his life by tragic miscalculations which proved how very wrong had been his belief that aircraft were "no match" for battleships. The Japanese that morning had delivered unchallengeable proof to the most skeptical of "Gun Club" officers who had scoffed at Billy Mitchell twenty years before. The attacks on Taranto and Pearl Harbor had proved that aircraft could sink static battleships. The damage inflicted on the *Bismarck* nine months earlier had shown their vulnerability while at sea. Now the ignominious speed with which the *Prince of Wales* and the *Repulse* had been dispatched was indisputable proof that the mighty battleships' reign as the final arbiters of seapower was finally at an end. Henceforth these great floating fortresses could be effective naval weapons only with massive fighter protection from aircraft carriers.

The news of Force Z's untimely end sent a shudder through the men in Singapore. That night as the destroyers docked at Changi to put ashore the 2,800 survivors, Air Vice Marshal Pulford, the RAF commander, was at the dockside. "My God!" he greeted a shocked and bedraggled Captain Tennant, "I hope you don't blame me for this. We didn't even know where you were." The sinking of the *Prince of Wales* and the *Repulse* had cost the Royal Navy 47 officers and 793 men.

That night the Japanese celebrated their triumph, won at the cost of only three planes lost. The next day they would fly over the watery battlefield to drop a wreath of flowers on the patches of drifting oil and debris.

On the morning of December 10, Winston Churchill's bedside phone had rung as he worked through his dispatches. It was the First Sea Lord, Admiral Pound, on the line. His voice choking with emotion, he reported: "The *Prince of Wales* and the *Repulse* have been sunk."

"In all the war I never received a more direct shock," the Prime Minister wrote, recalling how he "writhed and twisted in bed as the full horror of the news sank in." The enormity of the loss was summed up by the diary entry of General Sir Alan Brooke, the British Chief of the Imperial General Staff: "It means that from Africa eastwards to America, through the Indian Ocean and the Pacific, we have lost control of the sea."

9
The Somber Panorama

On the morning of December 10, 1941, while the pilots of the Imperial Navy's 22nd Air Fleet were bombing their way to a spectacular victory over the British battle squadron, the aerial armada of the 11th Air Fleet was winging toward the Philippines to deliver an equally devastating blow to U.S. sea- and airpower in the western Pacific.

The leading Japanese planes were picked up by U.S. Army radar just before midday as they approached the northern coast of Luzon after flying south from airfields on Formosa. General Brereton's command managed to send up thirty-five P-48 fighters to intercept. But the Warhawks were outmaneuvered and outnumbered, and could not stop the eighty Japanese medium bombers from rumbling on to raid the Luzon airfields. They were followed by successive waves that for two hours carried out uninterrupted target practice on the Cavite naval base from 20,000 feet—high above the reach of antiaircraft fire. General MacArthur's wife and small son watched in appalled fascination from the balcony of the Manila Hotel penthouse. From the rooftop of the Marsman Building just a quarter of a mile away, Admiral Hart too raged helplessly at the flames and pillars of smoke rising from the ruins of the docks 8 miles to the southwest of Manila.

Five hundred men were killed, but the most serious loss as far as Hart was concerned was the destruction of the Asiatic Fleet's entire stock of torpedoes and the damage inflicted on two submarines. The submarines were the only remaining hope of attacking the Japanese invasion convoys heading for the Philippines; of his fleet of twenty-eight, one third were patrolling off enemy ports in Formosa and mainland China, one third were cruising off likely landing beaches, and one third were held in reserve. With his base in ruins, Hart decided that evening to evacuate his remaining two destroyers and a handful of minesweepers and tenders, leaving the naval defense of the islands to the submarines and five patrol boats.

Far out in the Pacific, after the third day of heavy air attacks had cost Major James Devereux all but four of his remaining fighters, the defenders of Wake Island labored through the night, shifting the positions of the artillery to repel an enemy landing attempt. Admiral Sadamichi Kajioka's invasion force of four transports, escorted by two light cruisers and four destroyers, was already heading for the three low sandy islets fringing the atoll's extinct underwater crater. Aboard the flagship cruiser *Yubari* he held a last-minute briefing with his staff officers. He knew the island was protected by six 5-inch and twelve 3-inch gun batteries, so they "expected to have a rough time."

At 3 A.M. lookouts on Wake's southern tip at Peacock Point reported seeing winking lights far out on the dark horizon. Major Devereux immediately called his five hundred-strong garrison to General Quarters. Orders were to hold fire until the Japanese were inshore, when the four remaining fighters were to take off.

At 5:30 the first shells began kicking up sand and panicking the island's squawking population of gooney birds. Seventy-five minutes later the Japanese warships, led by the *Yubari,* had approached to within 1.5 miles of the Peacock Point battery. Its commander, First Lieutenant Clarence A. Barniger, had the satisfaction of recording an immediate hit on the Japanese flagship: "Both shells entered her port side just above the waterline. The ship immediately belched smoke and steam through the side and her speed diminished. At 7,000 yards two more hit her in about the same place. Her whole side was engulfed in steam."

Admiral Kajioka's flagship was already limping out to sea as the battery on the tip of Wake's tiny Peale Island landed its third salvo squarely on a destroyer that was escorting in two transports to the beach. The *Hayate* exploded instantaneously. As the smoke cleared, they could see that it had broken in two and was sinking rapidly. The Marine gunners were so astonished by their success in sinking the first Japanese warship that they ceased firing. Their jubilation was rudely broken by Platoon Sergeant Henry Bedell yelling, "Knock it off you bastards and get back to your guns. Wha' d'ya think this is, a ball game!?"

Spurred on by their success, they hit the second destroyer as well as setting one of the two transports on fire. Battery B, on the "finger" of Peale Island, had also deflected a third assault by three destroyers, hitting two before they beat a hasty retreat behind thick smoke.

Major Paul T. Putnam took off with Wake's four surviving Grumman F4F Wildcat fighters, each with a brace of bombs to pursue the fleeing warships. Shuttling back and forth to reload, they scored two hits before landing one bomb at 7:31 A.M. on the quarterdeck of the destroyer *Kisargi*, blowing her up with her own depth charges. At this point Admiral Kajioka decided to accept defeat and order his surviving ships back to Kwajalein. He reported that his retreat was due to the Americans, who "fiercely counter-attacked and we were temporarily forced to retire."

The news of Wake garrison's incredible victory was being radioed to Washington as the 4th Marine Defense Battalion at Pearl Harbor, under orders from Admiral Kimmel, was loading up the seaplane tender *Tangier* with ammunition, spare aircraft engines, and supplies to rush a relief expedition to the lonely atoll. Holding Midway, Wake, and Samoa were now the keys to the Pacific Fleet strategy, although Kimmel had received a pessimistic signal the day before from Admiral Stark, alerting him to the danger of "additional attacks in order to render Hawaii untenable" and suggesting that it was "questionable" whether Midway and Wake could now be held.

The most urgent priority for the surviving fleet units was to prevent an anticipated invasion of Hawaii or the seizure by the Japanese of the strategic islands in the southern Pacific, Samoa, Palmyra, and Johnston, which guarded the vital sea route to Australia and the lifeline through to MacArthur in the Philippines. Dismayed by the bleak forecast from Washington, Kimmel countered with a reply that he was hoping to "retrieve our initial disaster" by reorganizing the Pacific fleet around three carrier task forces. Oahu's undamaged stocks of fuel and ammunition would allow Kimmel to send one task force to make an offensive attack on forward Japanese bases in the Marshalls, while the second stood guard over the Hawaiians, and the third went to the relief of Wake.

Admiral Kimmel's plan for deploying the fast carrier task forces was to be the basis of the United States' winning naval strategy in the Pacific; but in those first shocked weeks after Pearl Harbor, confusion and discord plagued the U.S. Navy afloat and ashore in Washington. The Wake expedition had to await the arrival of the *Saratoga*, crossing from the West Coast; high winds and lack of practice prevented the *Lexington*'s task force from refueling at sea and forced Vice-Admiral Wilson Brown to bring his ships back to harbor before setting out to raid Japanese bases on Jaluit, the largest of the Marshalls. What proved to be the biggest setback to Kimmel and his soundly conceived strategy of striking back hard to relieve Wake was the arrival of the Secretary of the Navy, who acted to preempt "a nasty congressional investigation." A politician's instinct had sent Knox out to "get the actual facts" and arrange for a suitable scapegoat. The sight of so many burned and battered battleships in the Pearl Harbor mud left him visibly angered. Returning to Washington on December 14, he had already decided to tell the President that Kimmel should be replaced as Pacific Fleet Commander.

THE ARCADIA CONFERENCE

On the Sunday following the Pearl Harbor attack, Winston Churchill, accompanied by the British Chiefs of Staff, sailed for the United States aboard the Royal Navy's newest battleship, H.M.S. *Duke of York*. Leaving General Sir Alan Brooke behind to "look after the shop," their paramount concern was to persuade the Americans to hold to the declared "Europe First" strategy of defeating Hitler and not divert their resources to the Pacific. The battleship's hatches were battened down in anticipation of a stormy Atlantic crossing, as Churchill settled to the task of briefing his team for their forthcoming joint discussions, with the help of "three papers on the future course of the war as I conceived it should be steered." Entitled "The Atlantic Front," "Notes on the Pacific," and "The Campaign of 1943," the Prime Minister's presentations were masterpieces of lucid strategic analysis outlining Britain's war aims.

Adjoining the Prime Minister's cabin in the admiral's quarters of the battleship, a special traveling map room had been set up so the Prime Minister could keep track of the global war. The news from North Africa, where the 8th Army offensive had temporarily put Rommel into retreat from Tobruk, gave some comfort for the Allied cause, as did the Red Army's heroic stand before the very gates of Moscow. The Foreign Secretary, Anthony Eden, was en route by warship to Murmansk for meetings with Stalin when Churchill radioed encouraging advice that the "Russian declaration of war on Japan would be greatly to our advantage." Roosevelt had also backed the idea of getting the Soviet Union to relieve the pressure in the Far East, following MacArthur's suggestion that it would be "a masterstroke." But the President's cable suggesting a "joint planning conference to investigate possibilities" was ignored by Stalin.

The day the Prime Minister left London he had dispatched a rallying message to the Chinese colony, praising the "stubborn defense of the people and fortress of Hong Kong. Our hearts are with you in your ordeal." General Maltby was already evacuating the positions on the Kowloon peninsula. In the hills facing toward shore the surviving Canadian, Scottish, and Indian troops were now spread very thinly, along with 2,000 Hong Kong volunteers, for a last-ditch defense of the small island with its teeming townships.

Two days later they had hurled back the first Japanese invasion attempt, but incessant bombing and shelling across the quarter mile that separated Hong Kong from the mainland so weakened their positions that no reserves were available to repel the massive assault that was launched on the night of December 18. By the glow of blazing oil tanks, six enemy battalions had been ferried across the channel by dawn. The military position was now hopeless, but Maltby and the Governor rallied their men to continued resistance in a series of bitterly fought rearguard actions across the hills and peaks of the island. For the next seven days and nights, Hong Kong was yielded yard by bloody yard by its defenders.

The British Chiefs of Staff and Churchill were resigned to the eventual loss of the Crown Colony perched so indefensibly on the Chinese coast, but they were quite unprepared for the speed with which the Japanese began their march of conquest south through Malaya. After the loss of the Royal Navy's capital ships, enemy transports flooded troops into the ports of Singora and Patani. With no RAF planes to intervene, the only attempt to stem the landings came on the night of December 11, when the Dutch submarine O-XV1 attacked four Japanese transports off Patani. None of her torpedoes hit and Lieutenant Kotaener lost his boat the next day when it ran into a British minefield.

Reinforcements were already being shipped out to Malaya as four squadrons of Hurricane fighters, originally en route to the Red Army, were diverted from Persia east to Singapore. The 18th Division of the British Army, whose troopships were rounding the Cape of Good Hope en route to the desert war in Libya, were diverted to the Far East. Their voyage across the Indian Ocean would take until mid-January. Churchill feared a Japanese thrust developing north to threaten India. On December 12 he had extended the command of the British Commander in the Far East, General Sir Archibald Wavell, together with the warning "You must look east. Burma is placed under your command. You must resist the Japanese advance towards Burma and India and try to cut their communications down the Malay Peninsula."

The proposal for a united German-Japanese thrust against India was, in fact, put forward in Berlin two days later when Ambassador Oshima briefed Hitler on Tokyo's war aims. This was the strategic nightmare most feared by the British military staff in New Delhi, as alarming reports flooded in from Malaya, but Wavell's forces were already so overstretched that he could do nothing more than cable General Percival to hold out until the troop convoy crossed the Indian Ocean.

"The eyes of the Empire are upon us. Our whole position in the Far East is at stake," General Percival had already told his commanders in Malaya in a rallying order sent out from Singapore on December 10, instructing them to hold their positions along the Siamese border "to the last man." They had a three-to-one advantage in numbers, but the "long and grim" struggle he predicted would now see his British officers pitting poorly trained divisions against battle-hardened Japanese soldiers and light tanks. Most of the Indian troops had neither tanks, antitank guns, nor experience of armored warfare, because the prewar planners held these would be unnecessary in the Malay jungle. They had overlooked the arterial roads built to transport the rubber and tin down the peninsula to

Singapore; it was along these highways that the Japanese were to drive their "Bicycle Blitzkrieg."

General Yamashita's campaign down the Malayan Peninsula got off to a flying start on the night of December 11, when his tanks were sent rumbling down the asphalt road in pouring rain to probe the perimeter where the 11th Indian Division was supposedly barring the way south, in order to protect the strategic airfield at nearby Alor Star. The defenders had left their sodden positions to shelter under the dripping rubber trees, permitting fifty sword-brandishing Japanese soldiers to break through easily before they melted away down the road—"slight negligence," Colonel Masanobu Tsuji tartly reported; "we now understood the fighting capacity of the enemy." The incident confirmed his prediction in the Japanese instructional pamphlet that "while officers are Europeans, the NCO's and other ranks are almost overwhelmingly native, and consequently the sense of solidarity between officers and men is practically nil." Aided by the capture of a blood-stained map of Sitra's defenses, the Japanese advanced to capture the town the next day. Despite Percival's order to General Heath two days earlier "to hold fast," his Indian troops were fleeing down the road, leaving behind them field guns and heavy machine guns, as well as three hundred trucks and armored vehicles. Victory had cost the Japanese only twenty-seven men killed, although Tsuji had allowed for at least a thousand. Now the road south lay open and they quickly captured Alor Star airfield. This meant that Japanese aircraft could fly sorties from what they referred to as the "Churchill Aerodrome," tanking up with British fuel to drop British bombs on British positions.

Constant air attacks dislocated General Heath's efforts to regroup his forces so as to hold the road as the Japanese rolled south. On December 15, the enemy advance forced the evacuation of the garrison of Penang Island on the west Malayan coast. Defeat spread like a contagion through the units in Malaya. Time and again, British officers tried to get the Indian troops to dig in to defend the trunk road. Their positions would be remorselessly bombed by the enemy, then the Japanese would hook into the jungle to infiltrate the units from the flanks and rear. This fatal psychosis of retreat gripped General Heath, who set off on the 400-mile train journey to Singapore headquarters to press for a 100-mile retreat to Johore. Percival at first stoutly resisted. A strategic planning conference with the American, Dutch, Australian, and New Zealand representatives had decided that the Japanese must be held up for at least another month if air and sea reinforcements were to reach Singapore. Heath persisted in warning that his forces were in danger of being cut off by the Japanese thrust moving inland from Kota Bharu. Percival was supported by Major General H. G. Gordon Bennet, the terse Australian commander who wanted to launch an attack from Mersing where his troops were in place waiting to block an advance down the east coast. Heath, however, "ridiculed the idea" so remorselessly that Percival was eventually worn down.

On December 17, Heath hurried north again to supervise the withdrawal, which began inauspiciously with the hurried pullout from Penang. This cost the British face and the faith of the local population as they abandoned the Malays and Chinese to their fate. The pullback rapidly fell into near chaos as field commanders were forced to rely upon commercial telephone systems that constantly broke down, with operators primly informing spluttering brigadiers that their three minutes were up. The somber tone of the carefully censored press reports in the *Straits Times* and the increasing number of air raids on Singapore eroded the early overconfidence of the colonial administration. Consumption of liquor in bars and clubs rose, and no one now protested when hallowed cricket pitches were desecrated by swiftly dug trenches.

Churchill's growing concern about the safety of Britain's Gibraltar of the Far East became more acute as he watched with horror in his traveling map room aboard the *Duke of York* the pins marking the Japanese positions advancing down Malaya. On December 15, apparently unaware that the bastion could not be defended if Johore fell, he memoed the Chiefs of Staff: "Beware lest troops required for the ultimate defense of Singapore Island are not used or cut off in the Malay Peninsula. Nothing compares in importance to the fortress." Rough seas and the dismal news from Malaya conspired to bring down the Prime Minister's spirits. "This voyage seems very long," he complained in a signal to Anthony Eden, who had by now reached Moscow to find the Soviet dictator stonily noncommittal when it came to talk of joining the Allies in their Far Eastern war. "Great Britain is not fighting Japan alone," Stalin had pointedly reminded him: "She has allies in China, the Dutch East Indies and the United States of America."

The Grand Alliance still lacked military cohesion. There were no reinforcements that could be mustered on December 16 to prevent the Japanese landing on the north coast of Borneo at Sarawak except an "expendable battalion" of Punjabi infantry, who nevertheless managed to put up a spirited guerrilla resistance for two weeks to destroy the oil well installations. Dutch Navy submarines sank two Japanese transports and damaged a destroyer, but their efforts were no more successful than the Asiatic Fleet's submarines in preventing Japanese forces from seizing the southeasterly limb of Luzon. The *Swordfish* was the only boat to score a hit, sinking a transport off Hainan, while the Asiatic Fleet's remaining warships, including the old carrier *Langley*, retreated south to the relative sanctuary of the Java Sea. The flagship, the cruiser *Houston*, was sent to Balikpapan on Borneo's east coast; "the success of the Japanese air force over Luzon" was the reason Hart gave MacArthur in a gloomy memorandum for pulling out most of his staff and the remaining Navy seaplanes. This apparent desertion by the Navy caused a deep rift with the general, who took care to pass it on in his reports to Washington. The U.S. Joint Board, however, had decided that the thirty-three fighters left in the Philippines could not halt a major invasion.

Accepting that it would be impossible to get reinforcements through the Japanese blockade, General Marshall had diverted to Australia the convoy crossing the Pacific carrying troops and aircraft to Manila. MacArthur protested, stressing the "strategic importance" of the Philippines and calling for "the concentrated action of all resources of the Democratic Allies" to push through reinforcements. Yet by December 12, he too was admitting that "the enemy has a preponderance of air strength," by permitting General Brereton to fly the remaining B-17 bombers and most of the surviving aircraft to Port Darwin on Australia's north coast.

Still, Marshall and Secretary of War Stimson could not entirely accept that they had to abandon the islands. This was the first question the Army Chief set before Major General Dwight D. Eisenhower. The new Director of War Plans, who took over the key strategic post in the U.S. Army a week after Pearl Harbor, sensed that Marshall wanted him to agree with his view "that we could not give up the Philippines." Yet even with his own ties of three years in Manila as MacArthur's deputy, Eisenhower's sober assessment was that no reinforcements could reach him for months. He warned that this might be "longer than the garrison can hold out with any driblet assistance, if the enemy commits major forces to their reduction."

"Do your best to save them," Marshall nonetheless ordered, knowing that with the Navy so hard-pressed mounting a relief expedition to save Wake, as well as guarding Hawaii and the West Coast, the chances were extremely slim. In Manila, MacArthur lectured Admiral Hart for not doing more, but he could hardly blame him for the failure to get the desperately needed aircraft. When they had been uncrated on arrival in Brisbane it was found that their engines lacked vital solenoids, a shipping clerk's bungle that sent Stimson raging about the missing parts, "some kind of 'oid' " that reminded him of hemorrhoids.

THE FALL OF WAKE AND MANILA

Bureaucratic interference, division among senior commanders, and confusion in Washington were also taking a fatal toll of the Pacific Fleet's efforts to come to grips with the Japanese. Three carrier task forces sailed from Pearl Harbor when Admiral Kimmel received the signal relieving him of his command, "effective 3 P.M. on December 17." The move was intended as part of a major shake-up of the Navy's senior echelons by Secretary Knox to forestall public and Congressional reaction to the defeat suffered at Pearl Harbor. Admiral Stark remained as Chief of Naval Operations, but the real control of the naval war was put in the hands of the Atlantic Fleet Commander, Ernest J. King. A tough, uncompromising aviation minded admiral, King demanded and got under Executive Order 8984 sweeping authority as Commander in Chief US Fleet, with responsibility directly to the President. The admiral chosen for the critical task of rebuilding the morale of the shattered Pacific Fleet was Chester W. Nimitz. As he required some weeks to wind up his current task as Chief of the Bureau of Navigation, Vice Admiral W. S. Pye, the now dispossessed Battle Force commander, was placed in temporary control of the Fleet at Pearl Harbor.

Pye was an able strategist, an experienced seagoing officer who was put in at a critical juncture to keep the seat warm for Nimitz. It was with understandable caution that he reviewed the series of ambitious operations on which Kimmel had dispatched the three carrier task forces. Concerned that Vice Admiral Brown's Task Force 11 with the carrier *Lexington* would run into a trap by raiding the Japanese base at Jaluit in the Marshalls, he diverted the strike to Makin atoll in the Gilberts, which intelligence reported the enemy had just occupied. Vice Admiral Halsey's Task Force 8, with the *Enterprise*, was guarding the approaches to Hawaii. All was not going well for Rear Admiral Frank J. Fletcher and Task Force 14 which had the critical mission of relieving Wake. Its departure was delayed by the late arrival of the carrier *Saratoga*. Admiral Kimmel's last order before relinquishing command had been to send the tender *Tangier* on ahead with the fleet oiler the day before the *Saratoga* with three heavy cruisers and escorting destroyers sailed from Oahu, on December 16. When Admiral Fletcher finally caught up with the *Tangier*, his westerly progress across a stormy Pacific was further slowed by his insistence on frequent refueling to keep his destroyers ready for high-speed action.

On the morning of December 20, when Fletcher's Task Force 14 was more than halfway to Wake, Pye decided to recall Task Force 11 from its raiding mission to reinforce the relief expedition. That very morning, Admiral Kajioka put out from Kwajalein with his patched-up invasion force to repair his honor by taking Wake. This attempt was reinforced with a force of heavy cruisers that sailed from Truk. To assist the operation, Admiral Nagumo's returning Pearl Harbor strike force had detached two carriers whose planes next morning raided the lonely atoll. The last two Marine Wildcats put up a valiant fight, downing one Zero in the unequal battle. "This left us with no planes," Major Putnam would report, as his surviving pilots and ground crew joined the Marines dug into their sandbagged defenses ringing the atoll's shoreline.

The operational plot at Pearl Harbor had still not located the whereabouts of the Japanese striking force, but the sudden appearance of carrier planes over Wake raised Pye's fears that his two task forces might be steaming into a trap. Once again he reweighed the risks in executing his predecessor's plan, anguishing whether or not to "take a chance of the loss of a carrier group to attempt to attack the enemy forces in the vicinity of Wake." Six hundred miles to the east of Wake, Fletcher was refueling as ordered—and actually heading away from the atoll—when Pye decided that the safety of the fleet's carriers had priority over relieving the Marines. Task Force 14 was ordered to approach no closer than 200 miles, to prepare to engage enemy carriers, while the *Tangier* went in to evacuate the Marines.

Whether to attack was the question still being debated at Pearl Harbor on the morning of December 22 when Wake radioed: "ENEMY APPARENTLY LANDING." Task Force 14 was still over 400 miles away to the northeast and refueling again; Task Force 11 was twice as far away to the southwest, too distant to intervene.

In the predawn blackness, the Japanese had arrived off Wake unnoticed. This time Admiral Kajioka kept his main force anchored well outside gun range as the assault barges and patrol craft ferried in 1,000 men of the Maizuru 2nd Special Naval Landing Force through rough water and driving rain showers that concealed them until they ran aground on the reefs. The darkness was broken by the eruption of pink tracer streams. The Marine batteries sprang into action against the landing points. "The scene was too beautiful to be a battlefield," recorded a Japanese war correspondent watching the spectacle from Kajioka's cruiser *Yubari*, as the warships added their own bombardment to the pyrotechnic display. On the "thumb" of Wilkes Island, Captain Wesley M. Platt's detachment of seventy Marines succeeded in setting fire to one of the enemy boats and, with a series of rifle and grenade attacks, contained the landing. After four hours of hand-to-hand fighting, they had all but wiped out the one hundred Japanese "Marines" who had managed to get ashore.

While the Stars and Stripes still fluttered at dawn over Wilkes, an hour after daybreak on the main island of Wake, Major Devereux and his garrison of two hundred faced more than a thousand Japanese entrenched along the coral strand, their Rising Sun banners marking the beachhead to protect them from their own warships' shelling. Major Putnam's grounded flyers were still beating off the attempt to land on the southern tip of the atoll when at 5 A.M. the American headquarter's flagstaff was shot down. The flag was soon defiantly flying again from a battered watertower, but with the arrival of swarms of carrier aircraft after 7 A.M., Major Devereux saw that his position was becoming desperate and signaled: "THE ENEMY IS ON THE ISLAND ISSUE IN DOUBT." After the reply came from Pearl Harbor indicating that the nearest American war-

ships were still a day's steaming away, he took it as authorization to surrender when further resistance became hopeless.

A white bedsheet was hoisted up the watertower. Shortly after 7:30
A.M., Major Devereux, accompanied by a sergeant carrying a swab handle
to which a white rag had been attached, marched out to capitulate while
loud band music was relayed from those American loudspeakers that
survived. In the best Marine tradition, some of the outlying units refused
to surrender until their commander had made a personal tour of the island.
It was therefore well into the afternoon before Admiral Kajioka, in im-
maculate white uniform, was able to come ashore to conduct the formal
ceremony in which he renamed Wake *"Otori Shima"*—Bird Island—in the
name of Emperor Hirohito. Fifteen hundred American service and civilian
personnel were taken into captivity. Their brave defense had taken the
lives of over 800 Japanese, with American losses of 120, in what the President saluted as the "heroic and historic defense" when he announced the
award of a unit citation.

Headlines across the United States paid tribute to this fine example of
the fighting spirit of Americans, but all the rhetoric could not cover up
another defeat—and one that might have been prevented had Admiral Pye
and his subordinate commanders been more resolute in pressing ahead
with the relief operation. When the signal finally came through ordering
Task Force 14 to withdraw, talk on the bridge of the *Saratoga* became so
mutinous that Admiral Fletcher, who was not cut out for Nelsonian gestures, chose to beat a personal retreat to his cabin.

Wake's loss was to be quickly overshadowed by news of the dramatic
arrival of the British Prime Minister in the United States. He flew in to
Washington just before six o'clock on a chilly winter evening, almost the
hour that the Rising Sun was being raised over Japan's new patch of
Pacific coral half a world away. Beaming broadly, his cigar jutting from
his mouth, Churchill climbed down the steps of the aircraft that had flown
him up from Norfolk, Virginia, where the *Duke of York* had docked
earlier that afternoon. His impatience to meet Roosevelt was evident as
he strode over to where the President waited in the black limousine that
was soon speeding the pair, deep in discussion, to the White House.

The first informal talks that evening between the President and the
Prime Minister took place as messages of defeat flooded in from across the
Pacific. Not only had Wake been lost that day, but a Japanese army of
over 10,000 had advanced to within 100 miles of Manila. Less than twenty-
four hours had passed since the full-scale invasion of the Philippines had
begun, an assault that General MacArthur had been predicting only a few
months before could not get beyond the beach.

MANILA ABANDONED

It was just past midnight on the previous day, December 22, when the first of seventy-two Japanese transports, escorted by battleships and cruisers and carrying General Homma's 14th Army from their embarkation ports in Formosa and the Pescadores, dropped anchor off the gently shelving beaches of the Lingayen Gulf. The American Commander in Chief had been right about where the main blow would fall, but wrong about its timing. He had less than forty-eight hours after the submarine *Stingray* had reported the approaching armada 50 miles off the northern tip of Luzon. Within hours came news that a smaller invasion force of five transports was putting troops ashore at Davao on the southern island of Mindanao. Neither operation was seriously interfered with by the Asiatic Fleet's submarines, or by the departing B-17 bombers that were ordered to make raids before flying on to new bases in Australia.

In pitch darkness, with the aid of a heavy barrage from a large assembly of warships, the Japanese soldiers of the 48th Division began pouring ashore on three beachheads in the early hours of December 22. Rough seas again provided a greater challenge than the three divisions of Philippine infantry and the cavalry regiment of the regulars of the Filipino Army Scouts. Only the Scouts at Rosario put up resistance stiff enough to delay the assault for a few hours; at the other landing beaches the troops dropped their ancient Enfield rifles and fled in panic as the Japanese rushed their positions. All next day the tanks, men, and equipment continued to be shuttled ashore by the barges, unhindered except for a few bursts of fire. By afternoon, General Homma's advance force was moving inland to link up with the units that had landed a week earlier and were marching south from Vigan. The promised field day for the Asiatic Fleet's submarine force had failed to materialize as commanders were caught off guard in the shallow waters and only one transport was torpedoed.

On December 22—the same day it was announced that MacArthur's fourth star was being restored—he faced the shock of realizing that neither the Asiatic Fleet's submarines nor the half-trained Filipino Army could save the Philippines. Yet he was still unwilling to implement the only military option that remained: the "defeatist" but well-rehearsed ORANGE War Plan calling for a retreat to the Bataan Peninsula. With only a handful of fighters to challenge Japanese air superiority, MacArthur desperately fought to avoid the inevitable, urgently signaling the War Department for more fighters to strafe the advancing enemy columns. "Can I expect anything along that line?" he repeatedly asked, hoping that General Marshall could persuade the Navy to fight a convoy through with more troops and aircraft. When no such effort was promised, he sent a stream of dire warnings that unless succor came, the whole southwest Pacific would fall: "Counsels of timidity based upon theories of safety first will not win against such an aggressive and audacious adversary as Japan."

It took another full day of disasters on both the Luzon fronts before General MacArthur swallowed his pride and faced the stark military choice. The half-trained Filipino Army had proved hopelessly weak in the field, incapable of stopping the battle-hardened Japanese veterans from China. His North Luzon Army of 28,000 outnumbered the enemy by more than two to one, but as he toured the Lingayen front on December 23 in his Packard staff car, any remaining illusions about the fighting qualities of the Filipinos were shattered as he saw for himself how easily the Japanese were rolling up the front toward Manila. His second in command, Major General Jonathan M. Wainwright, described them as "a mob," as he vainly rushed about trying to shore up the crumbling front. "Few if any forces had been completely mobilized and all lacked training and equipment. No division or force had been assembled or trained in unit maneuvers." His staff too lacked organization and trained personnel; most of the Filipinos were without even such basic infantry equipment as steel helmets, trenching tools, and blankets. Wainwright that evening pleaded with MacArthur to be allowed to bring up the only division of American troops in order to hold the advance long enough to put into operation the retreat to Bataan.

MacArthur finally accepted the supreme danger, given his day's observations on the battlefield and the news that another landing was taking place at Lamon Bay, just 60 miles southeast of Manila. By dawn, a 7,000-strong force of the Imperial Army's 16th Division was ashore and heading out against virtually no opposition from the Philippine Army's 51st Division, which had scattered into the hills. The landing of this second part of General Homma's pincer movement on Manila brought MacArthur to a keener appreciation of the gravity of the military catastrophe facing him. That night, after forty hours of setbacks, he radioed to his commanders: "WPO [War Plan ORANGE] is in effect." Almost too late he was faced with executing the retreat to Bataan under the worst possible conditions. His 40,000-strong armies had to be withdrawn against a two-front attack, while gathering the scattered food and ammunition supplies needed to keep on fighting. Declaring Manila an open city, he prepared to evacuate his staff and family to the island fortress of Corregidor, knowing that to pull off the belated retreat was going to demand consummate generalship.

10
Standing on the Defensive

Amid the somber reports of defeat that came flooding into the White House throughout the Christmas week of 1941, seasonal cheer was provided, surprisingly, by Josef Stalin. As the President and the Prime Minister sat down with their military advisers to hammer out a common strategy for waging the global war, they could at least take comfort from the good news that the German panzers had finally been halted less than 20 miles from the snow-capped domes of the Kremlin. Like Napoleon, Hitler's dreams of conquest were broken before Moscow, where the indomitable fighting spirit of the Russians continued when arctic weather conditions had forced the Germans to retreat to ultimate defeat. "All the anti-Nazi nations, great and small, rejoiced to see the first failure of the German Blitzkrieg," Churchill recorded, noting that the "threat of invasion to our Island was removed as long as the German Armies were engaged in their life and death struggle in the East."

The Führer regarded the collapse of the Moscow offensive as a setback to be reversed by his assumption of overall command of the campaign. The significance of the defeat went almost unnoticed by the newest Axis partner as all of Tokyo was swept up in Pearl Harbor victory celebrations. Yet events in Russia were ultimately to spell defeat for Japan only days after the military leadership had committed the nation to war. The Imperial General Staff had drawn up their strategy on the assumption that a quick German victory over the Soviet Union would force Britain out of the war and oblige the United States to devote its energies to protecting its Atlantic interests at the expense of the Pacific. The irony of events was perceived by Admiral Yamamoto, Japan's new hero, who complained of the "mindless rejoicing" and "talk as though the outcome of the war was already settled." He worried about the "ability and insight" of his superiors in Tokyo. "Britain and America may have underestimated Japan, but from their point of view it's rather like having one's hand bitten by a dog one was feeding," he cautioned the

Commander in Chief of the China Area Fleet. "It seems that America, in particular, is determined before long to embark on full-scale operations."

Americans were indeed clamoring for an all-out war of vengeance against Japan; but the U.S. strategists had committed both the Army and Navy under the RAINBOW 5 Plan to concentrate on the defeat of Germany while holding a defensive line across the mid-Pacific. Britain might be safe now from invasion; yet she could still be brought to surrender because the U-boat "wolfpacks" were relentlessly gnawing at the Atlantic supply line.

On December 23, when General Sir Henry Pownall flew in to Singapore to take over command from Air Marshal Brooke-Popham, he learned that the defense plan to check the enemy invasion of Malaya along the Perak River south of the Siamese border was collapsing. The momentum of General Yamashita's well-planned and coordinated advance had carried his troops nearly a third of the way down the 400-mile peninsula and brought the Japanese control of many tin mines and rubber plantations. Sixteen hundred miles to the north, the Governor of Hong Kong called on the garrison to "hold fast for King and Empire" in a gallant but hopeless stand as the enemy burst through the island's defense lines to splinter the British positions.

Across the South China Sea in the Philippines, General Homma had landed another 10,000 soldiers at Lamon Bay, to pack an additional punch behind the southern pincer movement, now less than 60 miles from Manila. The Japanese had ignored MacArthur's proclamation making the capital an open city and the bombs were rocking the American headquarters in the Marsman Building as final steps were taken for the pullout to Bataan. The surviving patrol boats of the Asiatic Fleet had withdrawn to the shelter of the coves of Luzon's west coast, while the submarines had already been removed to the ports of Borneo and Java. Ammunition and supplies that could not be ferried across to the fortress island of Corregidor from the battered Cavite naval yard were dynamited. Luzon's four surviving fighters were flown out on Christmas Eve after General Brereton took the last American transport plane. In bidding him farewell, MacArthur entreated him: "I hope you will tell the people outside what we have done and protect my reputation as a fighter."

A few hours later the general himself was the last to board the steamer *Don Estaban* before it chugged out across the 30 miles to the tiny tadpole-shaped islet of Corregidor, which guarded the entrance to Manila Bay. Packed aboard with MacArthur's remaining staff and family entourage was President Manuel Quezon, with the senior members of his administration. Stacked in the holds below were the government's gold and silver bullion. The desperate mood of the passengers was in sharp contrast to the silver-flecked beauty of the sweeping moonlit bay; no one joined in when a lone American officer began singing the carol "Silent Night."

Far across the Pacific at Pearl Harbor few were in a mood for Christmas celebration. Admiral Nimitz had flown in by Pan Am Clipper the previous day to assume his new command. He found that morale on Oahu, already badly shaken by the attack, had fallen still lower after the failure to relieve Wake. That grim Christmas Eve had brought the extinction of the last flicker of life in the sunken hull of the battleship *West Virginia*. Five months later salvage parties would find the bodies of six men entombed in compartment A-111—the sixteen Xs chalked up on the bulkhead a mute testimony to over a fortnight of agonizing survival on emergency rations, ending the day before Christmas when life-sustaining oxygen was finally exhausted.

The gloom prevailing at the Navy Department was to be dispelled by the arrival in Washington of Admiral King to take over effective operational control of the Navy. The Commander in Chief U.S. Fleet was a staunch individualist, who quickly set a tough new tone by insisting that he was to be designated COMINCH rather than the unfortunate-sounding CINCUS. The staccato of his first official signal established the style of his new leadership. "The way to victory will be long. The going will be hard. We will do the best we can with what we've got. We must have more planes and ships at once. Then it will be our turn to strike. We will win through—in time!"

EUROPE FIRST

It was in the same resolute spirit that Admiral King joined General Marshall on the afternoon of December 23, when the American military chiefs sat down for the first time as full Allies with the British. The meeting at the White House was jointly chaired by the President and Prime Minister, to review an agenda for the most crucial planning conference of the war. Churchill had chosen "Arcadia" as an apt code name for the meeting, hoping its allusion to the pastoral tranquility of ancient Greece would be symbolic of the harmony of their joint command. It was to prove ironic, because while the President and the Prime Minister enjoyed a remarkable affinity for the Allied purpose, their military commanders did not. Unlike Stark, the architect of the "Europe First" strategy of RAINBOW 5, Admiral King was no anglophile. His prejudice against the overbearing and too-clever diplomacy of the new ally had been shaped during World War I when he had the chance to observe its workings at first hand as Chief of Staff to Atlantic Fleet Commander Henry T. Mayo, who had nursed a passionate dislike and distrust of the British. Now that he was moving to consolidate control over the U.S. Navy, King was determined that Britain was not going to dictate strategic terms that would downgrade the Pacific theater. The admiral realized that winning the war against Japan would depend primarily on naval operations, whereas the Army staff saw just as partisanly that defeating Hitler called for a final land campaign and naturally favored giving emphasis to the Atlantic. The U.S. Navy was also much more sensitive to deploying its forces to prop up Britain's threatened imperial possessions, although both shared a deep suspicion that their new ally wanted to enlist American support to shore up a tottering empire. General Marshall would later admit that there "was too much anti-British feeling on our side; more than we should have had. Our people were always ready to find Albion perfidious."

This initial hostility on the part of the U.S. Chiefs of Staff was not softened when Churchill established himself with his traveling map and communications room as the temporary headquarters of the British Empire on the second floor of the White House. His northeast suite adjoined that of the President and confidante Harry Hopkins. This gave the Prime Minister a proximity and intimacy with the President during the critical discussions that would shape Allied strategy. The gregarious Churchill enjoyed a unique advantage in running his war leadership like a family team, while the frosty personalities and dislike of White House socializing put both King and Marshall at a distance from the President.

The arrangement ideally suited the British. Churchill had come to Washington with a well-prepared brief to support continuing the "Europe First" strategy and get a resumption to the flow of Lend-Lease arms that had been interrupted after Pearl Harbor. The Prime Minister was trusting that his "tête-à-tête" conversations with the President would allow him to set "the main strategical basis for the conduct of the war," leaving the two military staffs to meet separately to fill in the details. Heading Britain's agenda was Churchill's determination to get Roosevelt to agree on a major Allied operation to push the Germans out of North Africa as an alternative response to Stalin's plea for opening up a Second Front by invading Europe.

At the opening session of the Arcadia Conference, the American military chiefs listened with ill-concealed discomfort as the Prime Minister tried to sway them to his viewpoint with the eloquent survey of British grand strategy he had used to woo the President over dinner the previous evening. In the convivial glow of late night discussion they had agreed that the defeat of Germany must take priority over the war with Japan. Now Churchill reviewed his so-called Gymnast Plan for a major offensive against Rommel in North Africa, which would be made possible with British forces released when the U.S. Army took over garrison duty in Northern Ireland. American bombers were to join in the raids against the Third Reich's industrial heartland, and what Allied re-

DEFEAT AT SEA Allied naval power in the Far East was smashed on March 1, 1942 with the loss of the ABDA fleet at the Battle of the Java Sea, when HMS *Exeter* (above) was sunk.

DEFEAT ON LAND Japan's tide of conquest rolled unstopped down Malaya (above) and on February 15, 1942 the British Command in Singapore (below) capitulated.

On April 9, 1942, American forces in Bataan surrendered to face the ordeal of the Death March (above) and on May 6, after Corregidor was overrun, General Wainwright (below) was forced to broadcast the surrender of the Philippines.

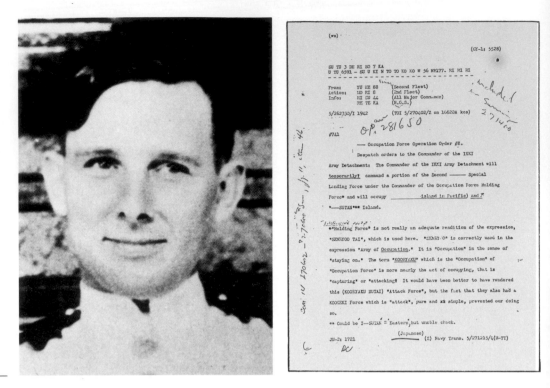

SECRET VICTORY The Doolittle Raid of April 18, 1942 (below, a B-25 takes off from the *Hornet* for Tokyo) brought a bonus of radio intelligence for Commander Rochefort (above) and the CINCPAC codebreakers.

BATTLE OF THE CORAL SEA To thwart Japan's anticipated advance south, the Pacific Fleet carrier forces on May 4 launched a four day action which sank the *Shoho* (above) and cost the *Lexington* (below).

MIDWAY—THE DECISIVE VICTORY Forewarned by radio intelligence, Admiral Nimitz sent his three carriers to disrupt Admiral Yamamoto's complex battle plan. On June 4–5, 1942 the U.S. Navy pilots (above) beat their Japanese opponents (below) into the attack. Counterstrikes

damaged the *Yorktown* (below) but American divebombers (above) sank the four Japanese carriers by nightfall.

VICTOR AND VANQUISHED The *Yorktown* foundered on June 5 (above) and the cruiser *Mikuma* (below) also sank—but Admiral Spruance had trounced Admiral Nagumo's force (insets).

sources remained would be available for guarding the Far East, where the Allies would "stand on the defensive." He explained that this meant holding Singapore for six months to control the Malay Barrier and so deny Japan access to the oil resources of the Dutch East Indies. Thus time would be won for reinforcements to reach Malaya and Burma in order to defend the overland supply route to the Chinese Nationalists.

The President, to the dismay of his own military advisers, appeared already to have accepted the British strategy. Lacking the unity of Britain's war team, the American Chiefs of Staff were ill-prepared to counter the Prime Minister's forceful exposition, but the apparent "imperial" thrust of his Mediterranean strategy moved General Marshall to express reservations. Directly after the session ended, he asked Major General Joseph Stilwell of his War Plans staff to prepare "65 reasons why we should not do Gymnast." He believed, along with General Albert C. Wedemeyer, that the British had too much influence over their Commander in Chief. "The Limeys have his head, while we have the hind tit," Stilwell complained, concerned that "Events are crowding us into ill-advised and ill-considered projects."

General Marshall was determined to prevent the United States from becoming committed to the British Mediterranean strategy as an alternative to launching a Second Front in Europe. Yet British fears that the American military leaders would give in to the great public pressure to concentrate on the Pacific War were dispelled on Christmas Eve. At the first of the sessions that day between the Chiefs of Staff in the Federal Reserve Building, the British were relieved to hear Admiral Stark reiterating the American position: "Our view remains that Germany is still the prime enemy and her defeat is the key to victory. Once Germany is defeated, the collapse of Italy and the defeat of Japan must follow." This broad agreement on sustaining the "Europe First" commitment opened the way to the more contentious process of deciding what the various operational priorities should be. It was to prove a laborious process as the debate continued for another three weeks.

Progress toward that agreement was eased by the rapport which had existed since the Atlantic Charter Conference in August between General Marshall and Field Marshal Sir John Dill. Churchill had replaced Dill as Chief of the Imperial General Staff and sent him to Washington to head the Joint Staff Mission. The friendship and mutual understanding of Dill and Marshall was to become a sheet anchor that held Anglo-American military cooperation together despite frequent storms of disagreement.

It was the Prime Minister himself who raised the biggest storm after he thought he had won Roosevelt's agreement in a late night private session on Christmas Eve to make available for the defense of Malaya the reinforcements originally destined for the Philippines and now being diverted to Australia. Enraged protest from the American generals that

MacArthur was being stripped to defend the British Empire brought a furious Secretary of War threatening resignation, and Harry Hopkins was sent to smooth ruffled sensibilities with a tactful denial. The episode convinced the British military leaders, accustomed to working under the tight direction of Churchill's War Cabinet, that the American command system was in disarray. "The whole organization belongs to the days of George Washington, who was made Commander in Chief of all the forces and just did it," Dill observed in a critique cabled to General Sir Alan Brooke. "This country has not the slightest conception of what war means, and their armed forces are more unready than it is possible to imagine."

It startled the British Chiefs of Staff when at this Christmas Day session they heard General Marshall announce his plan for establishing united war commands. Citing "human frailties" as being responsible for "nine tenths of our troubles," he urged strongly that "there must be one man in command of an entire theater—air, ground, and ships. We cannot manage by cooperation." The British Chiefs of Staff balked at the notion of appointing Supreme Allied Commanders who could not only cut across national barriers but could also put generals in charge of fleets and give admirals ultimate responsibility over soldiers. They stalled, protesting that such a far-reaching decision must be made by the Prime Minister.

Christmas Day found Churchill preoccupied with other matters. Apart from the opportunity provided by morning service at the Foundary Methodist Church to join in singing carols lustily with the President, there were precious few tidings of joy in his day. The news from beleagured Hong Kong was growing hourly bleaker. The garrison had been pushed to the extremities of the island as the Japanese seized control of the power station, and the last water supplies had been cut the day before. On Christmas Day the bombers redoubled their efforts. With his units scattered and "feeling that all was over," General Maltby reluctantly advised the Governor: "No further military resistance was possible."

White truce flags were flying by 3:30 p.m. The same evening in the grandeur of the Peninsula Hotel in Kowloon, Sir Mark Young, attired in the feathered and gold-braided splendor of a British colonial Governor, signed the formal surrender to Lieutenant General T. Saki, commanding Japan's 23rd Army. More than 1,200 British had died, a casualty rate twice that of their conquerors. This first occupation by the Japanese of a European colonial outpost was also to set a pattern of savagery, as drunken soldiers were allowed to rape and pillage the civilian population.

For all its inevitability, the fall of Hong Kong was no less keenly felt by Churchill. That night's White House Christmas dinner found him uncharacteristically silent and he excused himself early. Not only was the day's somber news weighing heavily on him, but he was troubled by the speech he was due to make the next morning to a special joint session of Congress. Many of the isolationist politicians would be actively hostile at hearing him advocate the primacy of war against Germany at the expense of retaliating in the Pacific against Japan.

The Prime Minister's state of nerves was very apparent the next day as noon approached and he paced the antechamber awaiting the call to the House. "You know, Charles, we are making history," he told his personal physician Sir Charles Wilson, who was becoming concerned at his sixty-seven-year-old patient's obviously rising stress before striding out to make the most important speech of his career.

"I cannot help reflecting," the Prime Minister observed after his opening pleasantries, "that if my father had been American and my mother British, instead of the other way around, I might have got here on my own." The delighted gale of laughter and applause won over the hearts of the assembled politicians. Next he set about winning the minds of Congress with his address, which was seen by one observer as "reading the banns" for the Anglo-American marriage. By far the warmest reception for the Prime Minister's global view of the war situation came when he turned away from emphasizing the need for defeating Germany, to condemn the attack on Pearl Harbor as "difficult to reconcile . . . with prudence and sanity. What kind of people do they think we are?" he growled. The stamping and applause erupted again as he predicted, "in the days to come," the time when "the British and American people will for their safety and the good of all, walk together in majesty, in justice and in peace." There was a final ovation before he strode from the dais, tears flooding his eyes and exchanging V-signs with Chief Justice Stone.

The banns might have been read on December 26, 1941. But hammering out the terms of the Anglo-American marriage contract was to take weeks of often heated argument between the two military teams, laboring far into the night in meetings at the Federal Reserve Building. Across town in the Mayflower Hotel, Lord Beaverbrook was ensconced with his Ministry of Supply officials. They were campaigning—in discussions with Donald M. Nelson, the Supply Priority Board head who was Roosevelt's "production czar"—to get America's industrial and armaments output doubled.

The President and the Prime Minister, meanwhile, turned their attention to drawing up a suitable declaration that would define in broad terms the Allied war aims along the lines of the principles they had enshrined in the Atlantic Charter. Churchill left the drafting of the Declaration of the "Associated Powers" to Roosevelt to make a hurried two-day visit to Ottawa and rally the Canadians with a speech in Parliament. When he arrived back in the White House on New Year's Day, the President had the "inspired idea" of substituting the "United Nations" for the "Associated Powers." The Declaration, which restated the Atlantic Charter's Four Freedoms, was signed with solemnity the next day by representatives of twenty-six nations. They included Ambassador Maxim Litvinov for the Soviet Union, who had been persuaded that "Freedom of Religion" also meant the freedom *not* to have one. "The Declaration could not by itself win battles," Churchill observed. Because of Moscow's sensibilities it made no mention of Japan, "but it set forth who we were and what we were fighting for."

The "United Nations"—in the euphonic wording of the Declaration—might now be committed to wielding a common sword to "defend life, liberty, independence and religious freedom," but the British and American Chiefs of Staff were deeply split over how the war was to be conducted and where to concentrate their limited forces. Nor did the two senior partners allow the Australians, Dutch, or Chinese to sit in on their deliberations, at which the British "kicked like bay steers" against Marshall's plan for Supreme Allied Commanders. The way to agreement was opened by Hopkins's taking Churchill aside to promise that a British general would command the Far East. General Marshall, who had already won Admiral King's support, clinched this organizational victory in a confrontation with the Prime Minister in his bedroom on December 28. After a spirited exchange over whether tank drivers could handle ships, Churchill had emerged beaming from his bath to agree that British General Archibald Wavell should head up the American-British-Dutch-Australian (ABDA) Supreme Command.

This first effort to display a united Allied military front Churchill hoped would go a long way toward stilling the fears of a nervous Australian government already fearing bombardment of its northern ports. In answer to a cable from Canberra expressing concern lest Singapore fell, the Prime Minister had responded that "we are determined to defend with our utmost tenacity" not only the fortress but "the whole front from Rangoon to Port Darwin." Convoys of troops on passage to Egypt were being diverted to the Far East, Prime Minister John Curtin was told; but with three of Australia's best divisions committed to the battle raging in North Africa, and a fourth fighting in Malaya, his cabinet was understandably alarmed that an invasion loomed if the Philippines and Singapore fell. Upset that Australian military leaders had not been invited to participate in the Arcadia Conference, and fearful that Britain would neglect her obligations, Curtin made his concerns public in the Melbourne *Herald* article of December 27. In it he rejected "the dictum that the Pacific struggle must be treated as a subordinate segment of the general conflict," and outraged Churchill with suggestions that Australia would have to call on Russia for aid as well as working out her own Pacific defense policy with the United States.

The British Prime Minister therefore had a strong political motive for wanting General Wavell to take over command of the theater. But his military advisers, who realized the impossible task of defending such a huge command area, felt that the American's might be setting him up deliberately as the fall guy. Dill argued that it would be fatal to have one of their generals responsible for the "disasters that are coming." The news of his appointment was not received with any greater enthusiasm by Wavell himself. He had already been relieved of his Middle East Command by the Prime Minister's impatience; now he cabled Dill: "I have heard of men having to hold the baby, but this is quadruplets!"

For General Wavell, a stolid campaigner given to periods of reflective silence, the ABDA Command's task of holding a 2,000-mile front line against Japan with the scattered forces of four allied nations was unnecessarily complicated by the addition of Burma. A further burden was the necessity of cooperating with Chiang Kai-shek, who was made Supreme Commander in China, Siam, and Indochina. The two generals had clashed over strategy on December 23 at a Chungking conference when the British, believing that their own troops should defend their Empire, had rejected Chinese proposals to send a force of 80,000 over the border to protect the Burma Road. Roosevelt and General Marshall both insisted that priority must be given to keeping open that vital supply line to enable China to stay in the war. Since the United States could not meet Chiang Kai-shek's persistent demands for American troops and aircraft, the President offered a $500 million loan and sent General Joseph Stilwell to become the Generalissimo's Chief of Staff, with the nominal title of Commander in Chief of U.S. Forces in China. "Such an arrangement," Roosevelt reassuringly cabled Chiang Kai-shek, "would enable your influence to be given effect in the formulation of the general strategy for the conduct of the war in all theaters."

This willingness of the President to pander to the Nationalists irritated Churchill, who protested that it "over-estimated the contribution which China could make to the general war." The Prime Minister, however, was resigned to having to humor Roosevelt and the historical rationale for what he believed was "the extraordinary influence of China on American minds." It was confirmed by a current poll showing that eight out of ten people in the United States believed the Chinese were their natural democratic allies—just about twice the number who favored Britain as their long-term partner!

BICYCLE BLITZKREIG

Satisfying Chiang's demands for a joint military campaign against the Japanese, who were already massing troops on the Thai border to threaten Burma and the vital road, was only one of the intractable problems confronting General Wavell as he tried to set up a workable structure for his ABDA Command. Sheer distance and inadequate communications militated against the Allies as he concentrated on the most pressing task: to marshal all resources to avert the military catastrophe looming in Malaya. General Henry Pownall, who became his Chief of Staff, during his tour of the front line had been appalled by the demoralized state of the Indian troops digging in for yet another attempt to block the Japanese at the Slim River, the last natural line of defense on the road to Kuala Lumpur, and the key to the southern airfields that must be held if the convoys bringing in reinforcements were to be spared heavy bombing raids. On the east Malayan coast another Japanese infantry regiment had reinforced the Imperial Guards, who had marched south to occupy the Kuantan airstrips and were halfway to Singapore.

The pell-mell retreat had to be halted if Singapore was to be held. But field commanders like Lieutenant Colonel Spencer Chapman already doubted whether their demoralized Indian soldiers had the ability to beat the Japanese in jungle fighting. "Our own front line troops at this time were equipped like Christmas trees with heavy boots, web equipment, packs, haversacks, water bottles, blankets, ground sheets and even greatcoats and respirators so that they could hardly walk, much less fight." Thanks to the foresight of Colonel Tsuji, the Imperial troops were lightly attired in tropical kit and their intensive training was now turning the jungle into an ally.

The Japanese superiority told again on January 5, 1942, when they came up against the 12th Indian Division, which had obediently set up a position to defend the road and railway crossing before the Slim River. The first attack was driven off, but during the next night probing enemy tanks circled behind the positions along a disused track. "Hooked" by dawn, the Indians were once again in headlong flight, pursued by Japanese infantry mounted on bicycles. Spencer Chapman, hidden in the thick jungle by the roadside, watched the enemy breakthrough toward the Malayan capital. "The majority were on bicycles [there were] forty or fifty riding three abreast and talking and laughing just as if they were going to a football match." Yamashita's infantry could advance up to 20 miles a day, and when the noonday heat burst the tires, his men just kept peddling on. The clattering of hundreds of wheel rims created a din that struck panic into the fleeing Indians, who believed they were being chased by tanks. Once again guns, ammunition and equipment fell into enemy hands, to be immediately turned to good use to speed the advance. Yamashita could with some confidence now order his commanders: "Depend on the enemy for rations."

On the day of the Slim River defeat, General Wavell arrived in Singapore on his way to set up the ABDA headquarters in Java. After touring the forward areas, he realized that the open terrain would speed up the Japanese advance, affording General Heath no chance to rally his disintegrating Indian divisions for another stand until they had withdrawn 100 miles to Johore Province. General Percival put down the failure of his subordinates to halt the enemy to "the utter weariness of the troops." To give them time to recover and regroup, Singapore headquarters ordered the long fallback to a defensive line along the Sungei Muar River 20 miles inside Jahore. This was the last natural obstacle before a withdrawal across the Strait to Singapore. General Gordon Bennet was instructed to reinforce the front line with a brigade of the 8th Australian Division. The rest of his forces were to be drawn up to defend the road from Mersing south to the causeway leading to the fortress island itself.

RETREAT TO BATAAN

Across the South China Sea the American and Filipino forces were also in full retreat in the Philippines. Like a caged lion General MacArthur paced his new command post deep in the Malinta Tunnel that pierced the rocky heart of the Corregidor fortress. Day and night for more than a week he studied the reports and sent directions to his field commanders, fighting to redeem his earlier failure by extricating his two army groups on Luzon from the crushing jaws of General Homma's pincer movement closing in on Manila. In a brilliantly orchestrated two-stage retreat, MacArthur succeeded in achieving a "Far Eastern Dunkirk." The key to his success was General Wainwright's inspirational leadership, and the aid of experienced American regulars. Together they rallied the ragged units of the North Luzon Force in time to check the main thrust of the Japanese attack by holding 5 temporary defensive lines and blowing up 184 bridges. General Homma's advance was slowed just long enough for General Parker to extricate the 15,000 soldiers of his South Luzon Force from the Japanese and get them safely west of Manila before Wainwright's front was swung around on the neck of the Bataan Peninsula like a giant floodgate.

The Japanese General Staff would pay tribute to this maneuver as "a great strategic move." It certainly prevented General Homma's pincers from trapping and dividing MacArthur's forces, or pressing the flanking attacks that were bringing General Yamashita his victories in Malaya.

Convinced that the Americans were in full flight, Homma mistakenly raced for Manila, neglecting to use his air superiority to wipe out the vital Calumpit Bridges 10 miles north of the city. They provided the only escape route for the retreating Filipino Army, which had battled its way past hordes of civilians whose oxcarts jammed the bridges' twin spans for days and caused a tailback of military traffic for miles.

The remaining American tanks managed to hold off a belated attempt by the Japanese to cut off the vital Calumpit crossing until early on January 1. When the last Filipino infantrymen were safely on the other side, General Wainwright gave the order to "Blow it." At 6:15 a.m. the twin spans went crashing into the torrent below. The second stage of the pullback to Bataan now began, with MacArthur's luck still holding. Like the Germans before Dunkirk, the Japanese failed to press their attack by using massive air superiority to smash the mêlée of vehicles and soldiers crowding the only two roads or to destroy the bridge at Layac. General Mashama Homma appeared more concerned with making a triumphal entry into Manila on January 2, unwisely thinking that this would mark the capitulation of the Philippines. He was to find that it would take more than the strains of the Japanese anthem "Kimigayo" or the ceremonial hauling up of the Rising Sun over the former residence of the U.S. High Commissioner to force General MacArthur to surrender.

Before the first week of 1942 had ended, some 30,000 Filipino and American soldiers were digging in behind a strong natural defense line that ran from Abucay across the Bataan Peninsula, embracing swamps and the twin volcanic peaks of Mount Natib. Some 20 miles to the rear, preparations were also being made along a fallback position across the wild Mariveles Mountains. This was the defense envisaged in the ORANGE War Plan, and with the 15,000 U.S. and 65,000 Filipino troops at his disposal, MacArthur might have expected to be able to hold off a major Japanese assault for six months or more.

But General MacArthur was now to pay a heavy penalty for his disastrous beach defense strategy. Quartermasters' reports revealed the awful truth that, while ammunition was plentiful, food was not. Less than twenty days worth of rice, thirty days of flour, and just fifty days of canned meat and fish had been gathered in the retreat. This would feed the 80,000 troops and 26,000 civilians now packed onto Bataan for less than a month. To add to their predicament, all medical supplies from antimalarial quinine to surgical dressings were short. The siege began with MacArthur ordering everyone on half-rations. This miserable allowance of less than 2,000 daily calories was to prove a starvation diet, given the rugged demands of jungle fighting in which malaria and a host of tropical diseases were soon claiming more casualties than Japanese bullets.

Across Manila Bay, Japan's 14th Army Headquarters in the captured capital was having its own share of problems. Homma had been given a tight schedule of fifty days in which to complete the conquest of the Philippines. Now, just as he appreciated the scale of the military operation confronting him, he lost his best troops. General Terauchi, Commander of Japan's Southern Army in Saigon, had decided that the speed of the advance on Singapore enabled him to bring forward the next and most important phase of operations—seizing the oil and mineral riches of the Dutch East Indies. The crack troops of the 48th Infantry Division were to spearhead the attack on Borneo and Java, leaving Homma to commit inexperienced soldiers, the 65th Infantry—the "Summer Brigade" fresh from Formosa—as a spearhead of the assault on the numerically superior American and Filipino army on Bataan.

Over-confident, and underestimating the strength of the opposition, Lieutenant General Nara sent in the Summer Brigade against the Abucay Line on January 9. His order to "pursue the enemy in column down the highway" was rendered ineffective by artillery counterattacks, while the regiment he had sent across the shoulder of Mount Natib to outflank the American defense was swallowed up in the jungle for a week. This reverse was the first military setback for Japan since the initial attack on Wake. It encouraged General MacArthur to hope that Washington would at last surely heed his repeated calls for an "American sea thrust" to bring in reinforcements from Australia.

The Asiatic Fleet's ships were now part of the ABDA Command, which had already written off the Philippines to concentrate on the defense of the Malay Barrier. The U.S. Chief of Naval Operations had told the President that there were not enough warships available to fight a convoy through the Japanese blockade. Yet Roosevelt sent a personal New Year's message to President Quezon: "I can assure you that every available vessel is bearing . . . the strength that will eventually crush the enemy and liberate your native lands." Marshall had cabled that another fifty-five fighters were on the way to join the bombers being uncrated at Brisbane and that they were doing their utmost to rush in air support; he added that the President "has seen all your messages and directs the navy to give you every possible support."

The repeated promises from Washington that help was on the way rang very hollow by the second week of January, when no ships or planes had arrived as Japanese aircraft redoubled their bombing of Corregidor. The troops dug in along the Abucay Line were showered by crude pidgin-English propaganda leaflets dropped from the skies, telling them to surrender because they were cut off and trapped. "Tokyo Rose" taunted the U.S. Pacific Fleet as MacArthur desperately begged the War Department for some planes to fly over the Philippines so as to counter the "crescendo of enemy propaganda" and the belief spreading among the hungry troops in Bataan foxholes that Washington had decided to abandon them to their fate.

In fact, that decision had already been taken. Although Marshall had radioed on New Year's Day: "Our great hope is that the rapid development of an overwhelming airpower on the Malay Barrier will cut the Japanese communications south of Borneo and permit an assault in the Southern Philippines," neither the United States nor its new allies had the ships, men, or aircraft to make good that plan. Three days later, General Eisenhower's War Plans Division finally killed any idea of fighting a relief convoy through with his report that it would be "entirely unjustifiable." Stimson recorded gloomily: "There are times when men have to die."

General MacArthur was not told of this decision, which had effectively signed the death warrant for his command and for many of his men. Instead, he was to be reassured with increasingly vague promises that everything would be done to get reinforcements through. This was the story broadcast by West Coast radio stations that was picked up on Bataan. "Help is definitely on the way. We must hold out until it arrives," MacArthur felt able to assure a group of officers on January 10 during a tour of the Abucay defenses. He returned to Corregidor optimistic enough to tell President Quezon that he "could hold Bataan and Corregidor for several months." It was the first—and last—time he went across to the front. As days and then weeks passed without the promised help arriving, it became too painful for him to face the men whom he felt he personally had let down.

VICTORY PROGRAM

The President and his military advisers might have taken the unpalatable decision that the Philippines were beyond saving, but the press and radio continued to foster the belief that General MacArthur and the gallant fighters on Bataan would be relieved by the massive counteroffensive the public was anticipating would soon be launched against Japan. Their expectations had been encouraged by the State of the Union address in which Roosevelt had unveiled the staggering production targets he was setting for the "Victory Program." It was a measure of the success of the efforts of Lord Beaverbrook and his team of experts that the President had decided effectively to double the coming year's output of aircraft ammunition and tanks. Rounding up the figures with strokes of his pen, he assured his more skeptical aides: "Oh the production people can do it if they really try." His speech to the joint session of Congress on January 6, committing American industry to the biggest armaments production effort the world had yet seen, called for 45,000 aircraft, 45,000 tanks, 20,000 antiaircraft guns, and 8,000,000 tons of new shipping in the first year alone. "These figures and similar figures for a multitude of other implements of war will give the Japanese and Nazis a little idea of just what they accomplished," Roosevelt told the astonished politicians. It was to be symbolic of the United States' total dedication to the outbuilding and outfighting of the enemy in the total war that "day and night now pervades our lives."

Confident that the Anglo-American talks had successfully swung the U.S. war production into top gear, Winston Churchill returned to Washington on January 11 from a week-long Florida vacation, to wind up the Arcadia Conference. Marshall's proposal for a Combined Anglo-American Chiefs of Staff in Washington to coordinate the military direction of the war was now quickly approved. The British half of this body was to be led by Field Marshal Dill, liaison with the newly formed U.S. Joint Chiefs of Staff. No progress, however, had been made in reconciling the conflicting demands of the operations proposed by the British and Americans, beyond agreeing to send American forces to garrison Iceland and Ireland.

The limiting factor was the shortage of shipping transport which, the planners warned, "precludes the possibility of executing one or at most two of these operations concurrently." Faced with what he termed "that harsh despotic factor of shipping," Churchill's plan for the major Gymnast landing of 90,000 British and American troops in North Africa had to be shelved, and priority given instead to maintaining the Atlantic convoys battling the U-boats with the supplies essential to keep Britain and Russia fighting. It was a time for "standing on the defensive" in the Pacific, the Prime Minister insisted. On the assumption that "fortress Singapore would hold out," he wanted resources concentrated on the ABDA defense of the Malay Barrier and the Dutch East Indies. To placate the Australian government—which was threatening to recall its three divisions in Egypt at the very time when Rommel was mounting a fresh push through Cyrenaica toward Cairo—Churchill had obtained the President's agreement to send 20,000 American soldiers across the Pacific, with the promise of another 50,000 ready to sail from the West Coast if the Japanese advance continued.

The recognition that shipping was the determining factor in deciding Anglo-American strategy resulted in a renewed effort to increase the shipbuilding capacity of the U.S. yards. It was to become the most critical battle in the great production war, which Roosevelt had announced with the establishing of the War Production Board under Donald Nelson. This former vice-president of Sears Roebuck was a bustling Missourian who with his experience on the Supply Production Board quickly established the WPB as an outfit known for getting things done. Within weeks of assuming his new post, the Board was transforming the lives of

Americans with its stream of orders banning the manufacture of three hundred consumer items from waffle irons to toothpaste tubes, beer cans, and automobiles. Henceforth the war effort had priority on metal supplies. All over the United States factories were being turned over from toymaking and toaster production to manufacturing guns and bullets.

As the U.S. industry launched into the Victory Program, a resolute mood of confidence was evident among Americans who knew that whatever initial victories Japan won through the early momentum, they would eventually be outfought and outproduced by U.S. industrial might. When he took leave of the President after a final working White House dinner on the evening of January 14, Churchill could sense "the might and will power of the American people." Arcadia had succeeded in gearing up production by the "arsenal of democracy," and unifying the Allied Command. Most important of all, the Allies were committed to the Atlantic First objective of defeating Hitler—at the expense of an improvised strategy to meet the continuing Japanese advance in the Far East.

The U-boats were already carrying the Battle of the Atlantic into the shipping lanes of the U.S. East Coast when Churchill decided to make the ocean crossing from Bermuda by BOAC flying boat. Full of the euphoria generated by Arcadia, he was anxious to waste no time getting home as reports were reaching him of a brewing political storm over his running of the war. Yet Arcadia also signaled a marked shift in the "partnership of equals." The Americans had made it plain that they would not support Britain's imperialist objectives in the Mediterranean and voiced concern at the civil unrest in India over the independence issue. The fall of Hong Kong and the ease with which Japan was gobbling up Malaya raised doubts on both sides of the Atlantic that the fabric of the British Empire could survive the war. This alarm now focused on the threat developing to Singapore, which had become both the symbol and the test of Britain's ability to defend her Empire against the Japanese.

ABDA COMMAND

The vulnerability of the Gibraltar of the Far East weighed heavily on General Wavell at his ABDA headquarters at Lembang, 600 miles away in the heart of the Dutch island of Java. Even in peacetime the task of coordinating the land, sea, and air forces of four nations would have been formidable; but Wavell, his Chief of Staff General Pownall, and Deputy Supreme Commander Lieutenant General George H. Brett of the U.S. Army Air Force, had only days to weld together a command literally under the fire of enemy attacks. Their best endeavors were frustrated by national rivalries and the vast extent of the perimeter they were being called on to defend, as much as by the rising tempo of the Japanese offensive. Air Marshal Sir Richard Peirse was nominal Air Commander, Lieutenant General Hein Ter Poorten controlled the ground forces, and Admiral Hart the collective fleet. But all were handicapped by the ABDA directive requiring their units, where possible, to operate as national entities, which left their forces widely scattered and without any previous experience of operating together. The combined forces lacked essential common codes at the very time when it was necessary to concentrate against the Japanese.

Communication problems quickly proved to be one of the principal flaws of this first attempt at inter-allied military operations. And no part of the ABDA Command suffered more than the naval staff at the port of Surabaya, on the eastern tip of Java more than 400 miles from Wavell's headquarters. With the Dutch, British, and Australian warships scattered from Singapore to the main supply base at Darwin, Admiral Hart was put in an impossible situation. On January 11, 1942, Japan finally declared war on the Royal Dutch government by launching an invasion force at the oil town of Tarakan, on Borneo's east coast, followed twenty-four hours later by a coordinated paratroop drop and naval attack on Celebes. Dutch soldiers fought back as best they could, destroying vital installations with the aid of a few aircraft and sporadic support from American B-17s ordered in by ABDA Air Command. For a week Hart battled to assemble a strong naval force, thwarted equally by poor communications and by the Dutch Naval Commander, Admiral Conrad Emile Helfrich, who was independently operating his submarines from Batavia in his role as minister of marine.

The octopus of Japanese expansion was grasping south toward the oil and mineral resources of the Netherlands East Indies and at the same time pushing exploratory tentacles north from Thailand into Burma. During the first days of January 1942 two enemy divisions were reported massing along the frontier, portending a thrust toward Rangoon. The Burmese Premier, U Saw, on his way back from discussions in London had been taken into custody by the British after Magic intercepts from the Japanese Embassy in Lisbon had revealed that he was plotting to turn his country over to the invader.

By the end of the first week in January, intelligence reported two enemy divisions massing along the border for a thrust toward Rangoon, with the objective of seizing the strategic port that fed the supply line to China. Wavell began to regret his hasty refusal of Chiang Kai-shek's troops, since he faced organizing the defense of a country more vast than France and Belgium with only the 17th Indian Division and the 1st Burma Division. Lieutenant General John Smyth, who had been sent out by the Supreme Commander with the instructions, "Look after Burma for me," was doubly handicapped. The single Indian division he found equipped and trained for desert warfare, because it had originally been intended for the Middle East. The native Burmese Division was little more than raw recruits. To add to Smyth's difficulties, Wavell had appointed Lieutenant General Hutton as his superior. Hutton had been an effective Chief of Staff in New Delhi, but was quickly found wanting by his principal field officer as "not the dynamic fighting commander which the coming events in Burma really demanded."

Hutton made the mistake of meeting the Japanese thrust by ordering his road-bound troops 200 miles south of Rangoon to defend a 400-mile jungle front. To further complicate matters, his troops were short of antimalarial drugs. Hutton knew that his men would be "suckers" for the favored "hook" tactics with which the enemy was winning in Malaya.

"The Japanese were in top gear and overdrive, the British in second gear, with no one coordinating or controlling the machine at all," was Smyth's assessment of the "nightmare campaign" he commanded in the wooded border foothills against two divisions of the Japanese 15th Army. By the third week in January, when it became plain he could not hold this advanced position, Smyth proposed withdrawing to concentrate the defense of the approaches to Rangoon along the Sittang River bridgehead. Wavell flew up to Burma on January 24 for a crisis conference. Mindful of how the retreat in Malaya had started, he agreed with Hutton that such a withdrawal was premature. Instead, they called for a series of delaying actions to be fought. Smyth believed this would only sap his division away. He was to be proved right as the Japanese over the next two weeks pushed them 100 miles back up the road from the port of Moulmein to the Sittang River.

While Wavell was in Burma insisting on the short-sighted strategy that would eventually cost him Rangoon, Admiral Hart was launching ABDA's first naval operation to block the enemy convoy his submarines had reported steaming toward the Borneo oil port of Balikpapan. It was to be dogged with the same ill fortune. His deputy, Rear-Admiral W. A. Glassford, was ordered to put out from the island of Timor with his two light cruisers and four destroyers to attack the invasion force that had already taken Balikpapan. Misfortune came early, when the cruiser U.S.S. *Boise* was forced to retire after striking an uncharted reef. Glassford's cruiser U.S.S. *Marblehead* then suffered engine trouble, forcing him to send the old "four-pipers" north up the Makassar Straits to make the attack without big gun support.

THE BATTLE OF BALIKPAPAN

The night of January 24 was moonless as the *John D. Ford* led the *Pope, Parrot*, and *Paul Jones* into the enemy anchorage, riding the phosphorescence of their 27-knot bow waves. Twelve Japanese transports lay unprotected in the anchorage because the earlier appearance of a Dutch submarine had drawn off Admiral Nishimura's destroyers on a fruitless hunt. The transports were sitting ducks, silhouetted against the blazing oil tanks ashore as the American destroyers raced in to make their attack shortly after 3 a.m. Torpedoes were fired and guns blazed. Enthusiasm prevailed over accuracy and no hits were scored. But Commander Talbot regrouped his destroyers and seized the opportunity to come in for a second attack, this time exhausting their torpedoes and leaving three transports and a patrol boat sinking. The Battle of Balikpapan was the first time the U.S. Navy had fought a surface action since Dewey had taken the Asiatic Fleet into Manila in 1898. Spirits aboard the destroyers were high as they raced to rejoin the *Marblehead* for the return to Java. However, a golden opportunity to wipe out an enemy invasion fleet had been lost: with only three transports sunk, the Japanese campaign on Borneo was not delayed by a single day.

The mood of victory at the ABDA Command was quickly overtaken next day by the news that General Percival had ordered the final retreat onto Singapore Island. The battle for Johore had been lost in just ten days. Yamashita had launched his first thrust against the 27th Australian Brigade dug in across the trunk road less than 150 miles from the Strait. Forty-eight hours earlier the second convoy of British reinforcements had docked at Singapore; there was no time to get the troops of the 18th British Division up to the front. The fifty Hurricanes that also arrived were soon airborne, but their pilots were untrained and their planes, equipped and painted for desert operations, were speedily shot out of the sky by the Japanese Zeros. The final retreat was already rolling back down Johore when troopships docked at Singapore on January 24 to unload 2,000 Australian soldiers, most of them recent recruits who had never fired a rifle.

In London, Churchill was now seriously alarmed by the collapse of the Malayan campaign. "Please let me know what would happen in the event of your being forced to withdraw to the island," he had cabled Wavell on January 15. He was shocked to be told that "little or nothing" had been done to construct defenses on the Johore side of the fortress. The Prime Minister was staggered by Wavell's revelations, noting that "the possibility of Singapore having no landward defenses no more entered my mind than that of a battleship being launched without a bottom." Anticipating that "this will be one of the greatest scandals," the Prime Minister fired off a fusillade of "Action This Day" orders to the Chiefs of Staff—who had been aware since a 1937 exercise of the fortress's vulnerability—to hasten the construction of its rearward defenses "up to the limit where picks and shovels are available . . . the city of Singapore must be converted into a citadel and defended to the death." Yet in spite of his injunction that "No surrender can be contemplated," the Prime Minister inquired of Wavell whether he should not consider putting plans in motion to transfer the freshly arrived troops to Rangoon without delay. "I regard keeping the Burma Road open as more important than the retention of Singapore."

Churchill's mind was to be quickly changed by a cable expressing alarm from the Australian Prime Minister, John Curtin: "After all the assurances we have been given, the evacuation of Singapore would be regarded as inexcusable." This left no doubt that the Canberra government was about to pull its troops out of the Middle East at a desperate juncture. There was also Washington's negative reaction to what the Prime Minister feared would be seen as "a British scuttle while the Americans fought on so stubbornly on Corregidor"—a prospect Churchill found "terrible to imagine."

Out in Singapore, the news that the Japanese advance units were less than 100 miles from the shallow Strait of Johore sent hundreds of European families to the rubble-strewn docks, trying to book passage out on the few ships still braving the enemy air and sea blockade.

On January 25, Percival was left no choice but to order the final retreat. Trainloads of civilians and truckloads of troops were jamming the causeway two days later when Wavell's headquarters were told, "we are fighting all the way, but we may be driven back into the island within a week." General Gordon Bennet noted gloomily as he withdrew with his Australian division: "The retreat complex is now here with a vengeance." Thousands of battle-weary British and Empire troops trudged across the 1,000-yard causeway to a temporary respite on Singapore Island. At dawn on February 1 the stragglers were brought up by the remnants of the 2nd Battalion of the Argyll and Sutherland Highlanders, a lone piper playing the mournful "Heilan [Highland] Laddie." At 8 a.m. the engineers were ordered to dynamite the causeway.

When the dust and smoke of the explosion settled, Singapore appeared to be again a true island, cut off by the muddy waters of the Johore Strait flowing through a wide-open gap. Yet this too, like the "fortress" itself, was symbolic. The weight of explosives had been miscalculated. Water only covered the displaced rubble to a depth of less than 4 feet— shallow enough at low tide for even the shortest Japanese soldier to wade across.

11
The Cataract of Disaster

The lightning pace of General Yamashita's advance down Johore to the Strait, which was all that now separated his army from Singapore, put renewed pressure on General Homma to revive his stalled offensive in the Philippines. Fresh troops were brought up to the Bataan front. The 25,000-strong Japanese Army was still outnumbered three to one by the defenders, but by the end of the second week in January 1942, with the help of tanks, they had driven a deep wedge into the weakest sector of the Abucay Line along the slopes of Mount Natib.

MacArthur sought to rally his troops by an Order of the Day on January 15: "Help is on the way from the United States. Thousands of troops and hundreds of planes are being dispatched. . . . We have more troops on Bataan than the Japanese have thrown against us. . . . A determined defense will defeat the enemy attack. . . . If we fight we will win: if we retreat we will be destroyed." But courage and determination were not enough to blunt the repeated Japanese assaults. When the "thousands of troops and hundreds of planes" failed to arrive, a mood of fatal resignation seeped along the front-line foxholes. Weary and hungry American soldiers chalked Vs on their helmets—for "Victim," not "Victory." Fighting around the clock their spirit was being drained away.

By day they were assaulted by relentless enemy air and ground attacks; by night the constant taunts from loudspeakers and the din of firecrackers made rest impossible. Despair was endemic, sleep was short, and the lack of food and medicine sent casualty rates soaring. The resentment of the GIs spread to the Filipinos, and was expressed in the endless verses of one of the most corrosive military dirges of World War II:

We're the Battling Bastards of Bataan
No mama, no papa, no Uncle Sam,
No aunts, no uncles, no nephews, no nieces

No rifles, no planes or artillery pieces,
                and nobody gives a damn!

MacArthur's forward defense line at Abucay began to cave in on the night of January 20, under the attack of 5,000 fresh Japanese troops who broke through the right flank over the slopes of Mount Natib. Next day, General Wainwright's left flank started to crumble under heavy air attacks. Reserves were rushed forward to shore up the collapsing front. Three days later, after General Sutherland had made a full inspection of the positions, MacArthur accepted his Chief of Staff's recommendation and ordered a withdrawal to the second line of defenses, which ran along the foothills of the Mariveles Mountains. "I have personally selected and prepared this position and it is strong," he assured General Marshall by radio. "I intend to fight it out to complete destruction."

Retreating those 20 miles under continual air attack to their fallback position brought a new mood of despair to the American and Filipino troops, who had to battle not only the Japanese but disease, widespread malaria, and night blindness brought on by the lack of Vitamin A in their starvation rations.

In the dank air of the Malinta Tunnel that now served General Mac-Arthur as home and headquarters, the mood was grim. Overhead, bombs fell thick and fast on Corregidor. No friendly planes appeared, and the radio broadcasts that were picked up from the United States, reporting how MacArthur was inflicting heavy casualties on the Japanese, rang as hollow and depressing as the constant stream of assurances from the War Department that aid was coming. But whereas the Joint Chiefs of Staff might have already abandoned a rescue effort, neither the President nor General Marshall had entirely given up hope that some way could be found. They dispatched former Secretary of War Patrick J. Hurley to Australia to organize ships to run the blockade. He was to find himself "outshipped, outplaned and outgunned" by the Japanese. For all Hurley's considerable efforts, only a few thousand tons of supplies were eventually to reach Corregidor by night, by small boats.

Nightly the sinister voice of Tokyo Rose broadcast on the radio promising General MacArthur that he would be paraded in the streets of the Japanese capital before the month was out. At the beginning of February, in a further attempt to undermine Filipino resistance, Prime Minister Tojo promised the Philippines that the nation would be recognized as independent as part of Japan's Greater Southeast Asia Co-Prosperity Sphere. Washington's failure to send reinforcements "doomed the Philippines to almost total extinction to secure a breathing space," cabled President Quezon from the Malinta Tunnel, where he lay in bed wracked by tuberculosis. He proposed a surrender engineered by a declaration of Philippine neutrality to end the pointless resistance and suffering. "You must determine whether the mission of delay would be better furthered by temporizing of Quezon or by my continued battle effort," Mac-Arthur added in his own message to the War Department on February 9. Their joint appeals landed "like a bombshell" on Stimson's desk. The President at once radioed back "emphatically deny the possibility of this government's agreement to the political aspect of President Quezon's proposal"—adding a personal "pledge of duty to you and your people" with yet more vague promises that support was on its way.

The retort from Marshall was a sharp reminder to MacArthur that there was to be no talk of surrender "so long as there remains any possibility of resistance." None of the journalists stranded on Corregidor seriously believed that the general intended to capitulate because he had already told them: "If we don't get reinforcements the end will be brutal and bloody." But Washington, anxious to prevent Quezon from making any embarrassing overtures to the Japanese, proposed that he be evacuated along with the High Commissioner, the cabinet, and MacArthur's wife. Previously the general had advised against such an attempt as too risky; but perhaps significantly it was agreed with Washington that the ailing Quezon would be taken off by submarine on February 16—the day after $0.5 million dollars had been transferred from the Philippine Treasury account with the Chase National Bank to the private account of Douglas MacArthur with the Chemical National Bank and Trust Company in New York. Such a highly unusual request had required the approval of the Roosevelt, Stimson, and the Secretary of the Interior and the exchange of cables was to be kept secret. This fortune had been Mac-Arthur's share of the $640,000 that by Quezon's executive order of January 3, 1942, was donated as "recompense and reward, however inadequate, for distinguished service" for the general, his Chief of Staff and two other officers who "forged the weapon that is now striking the blows on the field of battle."

Serving officers in the U.S. armed forces were expressly denied such golden handshakes, and if news of it had leaked out, it might well have done MacArthur's growing reputation as a national hero serious damage. It would certainly have had an explosive impact on the weary soldiers fighting the Japanese 3 miles across Manila Bay. The "Battling Bastards of Bataan" had beaten off two attempts by the enemy to leapfrog their lines by making amphibious landings. The general's reluctance to come across and visit the front was already being derided. What verses might have been added about a half-million-dollar bribe to these GIs' version of the "Battle Hymn of the Republic" can only be imagined:

Safe from all the bombers and from any sudden shock
Dugout Doug is eating of the best food on Bataan
And his troops go starving on. . . .

President Quezon was right. The Joint Chiefs of Staff in Washington had known for weeks that a return to their 1941 RAINBOW 5 war strategy of "Europe First" necessitated the loss of the Philippines. The purpose of MacArthur's stand was indeed to win a "breathing space" so as to deploy reinforcements to block Japan's southward threat and defend the East Indies and the route to Australia. On this Admiral King had been adamant when he drew a line on the map from Midway through Samoa and Fiji to Brisbane and ordered his new Pacific Fleet Commander in Chief to hold it "at all costs." Accordingly, the carrier *Yorktown* was sent out from San Diego on January 6 with troops and aircraft for the Samoa garrison. Five days later, Pago Pago was shelled by submarine, and after reports from Australian reconnaissance planes of Japanese warships massing at Truk, there was an alarm that they were coming south to break through the Pacific defense line. As it turned out they were not heading for Fiji, but intended to capture Rabaul on the Australian-administered island of New Britain at the head of the Solomon chain.

PEARL HARBOR AVENGED

That same day the *Yorktown*, escorted by the *Enterprise*'s task force, arrived to reinforce Samoa. Another convoy carrying 20,000 American troops had been dispatched post-haste for New Caledonia to garrison the New Hebrides. To counter what he now discerned as a "serious enemy threat to communications with Australia," Admiral King assumed overall command of a new ANZAC sea area, directing Nimitz to send out the heavy cruiser *Chicago* and the carrier *Lexington* when available, to join Admiral Sir John Crace's two Australian cruisers in the Coral Sea.

Nimitz saw that his fleet strength was being drained to protect the approaches to Australia even while he was short of warships to guard the west Pacific and provide escorts for the convoys between Hawaii and the West Coast. Overriding the advice of the Pacific Fleet's more conservative admirals, he intended going ahead with his scheme for bold carrier task force strikes against the enemy island bases. Then a submarine slammed a torpedo into the boiler room of the *Saratoga*, sending her limping back to the United States for dry dock repairs. With his carrier strength now cut by a quarter, Nimitz still insisted on holding to his plan to head off Japan's advance and raise the morale of the Pacific Fleet by hitting their island bases. On January 25, after the troops had been landed on Samoa, the *Enterprise* and the *Yorktown* task forces steamed north to hit Japanese bases in the Marshall and Makin islands.

For five hours, from dawn on February 1, Halsey stretched his luck with a succession of air strikes that shuttled from the *Enterprise* to strafe and bomb Kwajalein anchorage into a small scale Pearl Harbor. Transports were sunk and damaged along with shore installations in a raid that killed the Japanese commanding admiral. Thirteen American aircraft were lost and Japanese planes hit the *Enterprise* and a cruiser from enemy aircraft carriers before he gave the curt signal: "HAUL OUT WITH HALSEY." Three hundred miles to the south, *Yorktown*'s task force struck at Makin, Mili, and Jaluit. A combination of poor weather and Admiral Fletcher's lack of luck brought less significant results. Nonetheless, the press could report that the Pacific Fleet had at last taken the offensive. Headlines exaggeratedly told Americans what they had been yearning to read since December 7: "PEARL HARBOR AVENGED."

The U.S. Navy's success in hitting back at the Japanese in the central Pacific, although little more than pinpricks, was much more effective than the lackluster performance of Hart's multi-national ABDA fleet. The combined efforts by submarines and surface warships had so far only accounted for a handful of transports. Now, as Japan began moving toward Java and Sumatra, the four Allied naval forces were combined into a single squadron of eight cruisers and twenty destroyers. It was a puny force with which to challenge the Japanese battleship, cruiser, and carrier strike force that had been brought in to protect the final advance to the Dutch East Indies.

On February 1, the heavy air raids on Java's north shore had driven Admiral Hart from Surabaya to Tjilatjap on the south coast. His Fleet Commander, Rear-Admiral Karel Doorman, insisted on taking the striking force out into the Makassar Straits three days later in an abortive effort to intercept an invasion convoy heading for the southern tip of Celebes. Air attacks necessitated the U.S.S. *Marblehead* going to Ceylon for repairs; the heavy cruiser *Houston*'s rear turret was also put out of action. Then reports of a large enemy force moving south to invade Sumatra sent Doorman out once again, to brave the heavy air attacks in an effort to save Palembang. Relentless bombing runs by shore and carrier planes forced him to call off the mission after agonizing that "history would condemn him for the retirement." Palembang fell into Japanese hands on the afternoon of February 15. Within days the Australian and Dutch troops had been driven south after only partially demolishing the oilfield installations. This gave Japan control of half the reserves of the Dutch East Indies.

SINGAPORE FALLS

February 15, 1942, was a bleak day for the Allies, for it also saw the fall of Singapore. Churchill had told the Americans only a month before that the island fortress could withstand a siege of six months. It was to fall after only two weeks.

"Our task is to hold this fortress until help can come, as assuredly as it will come," General Percival's rallying Order of the Day had proclaimed on January 31 as the last soldiers were retreating across the causeway. During the next week, frequent air raids were the only manifestation of the siege as a deceptive confidence settled over the city of Singapore 14 miles south of the broken causeway. Along the mangrove swamps bordering the muddy Johore Strait, British, Australian, and Indian troops were feverishly improvising the defenses that the prewar military planners had neglected. General Yamashita and his staff watched through powerful field glasses from the picture windows of the high observation tower of the Sultan of Johore's magnificent green-tiled palace, which the retreating British had considerately omitted to raze. The vantage point allowed them to range their artillery as three hundred collapsible assault boats were brought forward and concealed in the jungle.

The Japanese were actually to underestimate by nearly 60 percent the number of defenders facing them across the Strait as they watched the British furiously throwing up strongpoints and gun emplacements. Yet, though he had 85,000 men to dig in to repel the enemy assault, General Percival was making the same error as General MacArthur in concentrating all his strength along the water's edge. Discounting the advice of General Wavell, he brought forward fresh troops of the 18th British Division along the open ground northeast of the causeway, which he believed to be the most likely assault site. The northwest shore was assigned to Gordon Bennet's Australians, who wallowed in the dense mangrove swamps to establish a defense line. The jungle prevented clear fields of fire and hampered communications between the strongpoints.

Certain that Percival had enough troops and supplies to withstand the coming Japanese assault, Governor Sir Shenton Thomas announced that Singapore would write "an epic in Imperial history." Civilians continued to hamper military preparations by insisting on written permission from "competent authority" for trenches across golf links or the cutting down of palm trees. Only when the dynamiting began at the costly new installations of the Changi naval base was the extent of the danger realized. Chinese merchants immediately stopped credit for European customers and the increasing severity of the bombing raids started fires that raged uncontrollably. Without air-raid shelters, casualties were heavy. Ditches outside the city became graves for fly-blown corpses as increasing numbers of disheveled, drunken deserters roamed the streets looting bombed-out buildings and the lines of would-be refugees trailed back from the docks. Only a few Buffalo fighters survived and the RAF command was holding them back to repel the coming assault, so no planes covered the liner *Empress of Asia* as she was bombed and sunk steaming up channel on February 5. "Singapore was burning and mutilated," one eyewitness noted: "It had the air of an abandoned city for the reason that thousands of soldiers, with no fight in them at all, were congregating on the Esplanade, Raffles Reclamation and other open spaces. They were being massacred by machine gun fire from Japanese bombers."

The final curtain on the last act of the British tragedy in Malaya went up on the evening of February 7, when General Yamashita sent the Konoye Division across the Strait to capture the island commanding the entrance to the now wrecked docks of the Changi naval base. This was a feint to throw off the defense as the Japanese began a thunderous artillery barrage that by dawn had left a pall of smoke over the blazing fuel-storage tanks shelled to prevent the flooding of the Strait with blazing oil. The barrage then systematically ranged west as the day wore on, blasting the pillboxes and defenses around the causeway.

Darkness brought Yamashita's first waves crossing the Strait, each assault boat carrying forty men and propelled by revving outboards. At 10:30 p.m. three hundred of these plywood craft were heading not for the well-defended open shore east of the causeway, but toward the mangrove swamps on the west where a weak defense was manned by the weary Australians.

General Bennet's soldiers lost their opportunity to hit the assault before it landed because no order was received by the British artillery until too late to open up or turn on the searchlights that could have illuminated the approaching armada. In a few hours over 4,000 Japanese had come ashore, infiltrating through the mangroves and the gaps in the 22nd Australian Brigade's lines. Tanks and artillery had been ferried over by raft at dawn, by which time almost half Yamashita's total force of 30,000 had successfully landed on Singapore. Overwhelmed by hordes of Japanese in bayonet charges shortly after daybreak, the Australian lines began to waver and the soldiers defending them fled in blind retreat. "They come moving at a half-trot, panic stricken," recalled one British officer. "It was pouring with rain and most of the men's feet were cut to ribbons. They'd come across rivers, through mangrove swamps, through bush and out onto the road. They'd scrapped everything that could hold them back. They'd thrown aside their rifles and ammunition. . . ."

The Japanese had routed some Australian units. Others, like the 27th Brigade defending the central area of the front around the head of the causeway, held firm all day until they were in danger of being cut off by the advance through their crumbling flank, then they too pulled back. Yamashita was so confident of victory that by evening he had descended from the Green Palace to be ferried across with his staff under heavy shellfire to direct the final attack on the causeway personally. Scrambling ashore in swamp darkness, the ubiquitous Colonel Tsuji discovered he was actually walking over bound bodies. In the early hours of February 9 the Imperial Guards, in a ferocious display of savagery, had battered their way through the final pocket of Australian resistance, slaughtering all prisoners.

At dawn the Japanese were piling through a mile-wide gap in the front toward the so-called Jurong Line, the British secondary defensive line inland along the western ridge. Thrown off-balance by the ferocity and speed of the enemy assault, the field commanders prematurely ordered another fallback. Now Percival was paying the price for committing most of his force to forward defense. Reserves were inadequate, and with no strong rear positions before the city, it was ominously clear to his worried staff by evening that it could only be a matter of time before the Japanese overran the entire island.

The fall of Singapore was just days away when General Wavell arrived by flying boat from Java on February 10, to try to stave off the impending disaster. Tempers flared and angry words were exchanged during a morning conference at Fort Canning when Wavell confronted Percival with the melodramatic directive he had received from the Prime Minister: "Battle must be fought to the bitter end. Commanders and senior officers should die with their troops. The honour of the British Empire is at stake. With the Russians fighting as they are and the Americans so stubbornly at Luzon, the whole reputation of our country is at stake."

At Gordon Bennet's forward headquarters, Wavell urged mounting a counterthrust against the advancing enemy. That it could not succeed was obvious from the number of times their talk was interrupted when they had to duck under the table to shelter from bombing attacks. Percival nonetheless issued an apologetic-sounding paraphrase of Churchill's directive before ordering a hasty counterattack. By dusk it had petered out in disastrous failure.

When the sun rose on February 11, the Japanese were in control of half the island. On the outskirts of the city limits, advance units were exchanging shots with the British across the deserted racetrack. The battle, however, was now approaching a critical stage for the Japanese. Yamashita had realized that his 30,000 men were outnumbered and that he desperately needed to bluff Singapore into a quick surrender: "I was frightened all the time that the British would discover our numerical strength and lack of supplies and force me into disastrous street fighting." He slowed the pace of his advance and sent in the bombers, unaware of just how rapidly the British will to resist was collapsing.

Colonial bureaucrats and officers propped up their dignity at the bar of the Raffles Hotel, while the streets outside were thronged with drunken deserters who had scrawled over one wall: "England for the English. Australia for the Australians, but Malaya for any son of a bitch who wants it." The smell of death mingled in the thick monsoon humidity with alcohol fumes rising from the gutters. The Governor had ordered all liquor stocks to be destroyed, anticipating the city's capture. Friday, February 13, was truly an unlucky day for Singapore—and even unluckier for the evacuees who had left in the last ship out. All but a handful of the fifty vessels that had sailed during that week carrying men, women, and children had fallen prey to the bombers and warships blockading the island. The Japanese picked up few survivors.

On that blackest of Black Fridays for the British Empire, Wavell signaled Churchill: "Fear resistance is not likely to be prolonged," before attempting to rally Percival: "Your gallant stand is serving a purpose and must be continued to the limit of endurance." That limit was reached the next morning when the Japanese severed the city's water supply. General Bennet took an independent decision not to throw away Australian lives needlessly and ordered his men to conserve their failing ammunition by firing only to defend their own perimeter. This brought the enemy storming through the weakened front to sack the Alexandria Military Hospital, barbarously bayoneting the wounded and pushing aside surgeons to smash the remaining life out of a soldier undergoing an emergency operation.

Consolidating his positions on the city's outskirts next morning, Yamashita decided the time had come to "bluff" Singapore into capitulation. "In the spirit of chivalry we have the honour of advising your surrender," began his message to Percival, in a cardboard tube gaily decked with red, white, and blue streamers that was dropped before 9 a.m. over British lines. While the staff at Fort Canning pondered over the message that Singapore "is completely isolated, and raising the fame of Great Britain by utmost exertions and heroic fighting," a cable from Wavell arrived giving Percival "discretion to cease resistance" when the fight became "pointless." Outgeneraled, outgunned, and outmaneuvered, General Percival was now outwitted. He had no way of knowing just how low enemy ammunition and supplies really were. He was more concerned with the lack of water and the threat of epidemics decimating the civilian population. A delegation of officers drove out toward the Japanese lines in a battered car, with the Union Jack flying out of one window and a white sheet flapping over the other. Yamashita, fearing a ruse to buy time, insisted that he would only deal with the Commander in Chief in person.

It was at 6 p.m. on Saturday, February 14, the hour dictated by the Japanese, that General Percival emerged with his senior officers into the still-sultry heat for the drive to the Ford Motor Company plant behind the enemy line at Bukit Timah. There General Yamashita awaited, a stocky figure in neatly pressed khaki field uniform surrounded by his staff. On hand was a phalanx of Japan's reporters and newsreel cameramen waiting to record a stage-managed surrender ceremony.

A haggard Percival arrived, his deep sense of failure betrayed by bloodshot eyes. The British in their grimy uniforms presented a sorry spectacle as they assembled across the bare wooden table. Their discomfort increased when they heard through an interpreter that this was not a discussion of surrender terms. The bullet-headed general abruptly insisted, "Yes or no?" to the capitulation document that lay before them on the table. Percival, broken though he was, was not ready for this ultimate humiliation and wanted to leave. But after consulting with his officers, he decided he must save his men and the citizens of Singapore. At ten minutes past eight, in front of the whirring movie cameras, he painfully signed the surrender document.

It had cost each side some 10,000 casualties. Japan had not only conquered the proud "City of the Lion" but had shattered the foundation of Britain's imperial power in the Far East. More suffering and death were to follow; although Yamashita had agreed that evening to spare the civilian population, in what was becoming customary Japanese behavior thousands of European women and children were rounded up and incarcerated in Changi Jail while thousands of Chinese were needlessly executed.

BURMA OR AUSTRALIA?

"GENERAL SITUATION OF PACIFIC WAR DECIDED," Tokyo newspapers announced, as the nation celebrated its biggest military victory. The government decreed that every family was to receive two bottles of beer or sake, and children a bag of candy, in celebration of the triumph of the Emperor's warriors.

For Britain it was the end of one of the bitterest weeks in World War II. Four days earlier the twin German battlecruisers *Scharnhorst* and *Gneisenau* had been allowed to escape up the Channel. Now the English faced what Churchill called "the greatest disaster and capitulation in British history." The renewed storm of criticism he encountered was relieved by an understanding message from Roosevelt with a reminder: "We must look forward constantly to the next moves that need to be made to hit the enemy."

That such Allied options were few was clear from pessimistic reports from General Wavell. The Japanese had landed on Sumatra and Bali. With only one Dutch division, the 500 miles of Java's north coast were wide open. ABDA Air Command was down to fifty-five fighters and eighty-five bombers and the naval forces of eight cruisers, twenty-two destroyers, and several submarine flotillas. The threat to Australia was increasing; while in Burma the Japanese advanced to the Sittang River. Wavell sent a cable taking stock of the bleak outlook in the Far East, which concluded: "Loss of Java, though a severe blow from every point of view, would not be fatal. Efforts should not therefore be made to reinforce Java which might compromise defence of Burma and Australia."

The dismal forecast the day after Singapore's fall left the Prime Minister wondering whether there could be any way of damming the "cataract of disaster" that was now menacing not only the great subcontinent of Australia but India as well. Churchill was at loggerheads with Prime Minister Curtin, who after the news of Singapore's fall had recalled the convoy carrying the 1st Australian Division across the Indian Ocean. "There is nothing else in the world that can save Burma," the British Prime Minister had cabled, sending his own orders redirecting the convoy to Rangoon and telling Curtin, "your greatest support in this hour of peril must be drawn from the United States." In spite of the President's commitment to send more troops, the Australian Prime Minister and his staff remained unmoved, insisting that their convoy must be turned around on February 23: "We feel a primary obligation to save Australia; not only for itself but to preserve it as a base for the development of the war against Japan."

The Australian Prime Minister's refusal to "reverse a decision we have made with the utmost care" was instrumental in sealing the fate of Burma. Rangoon had been doomed by General Hutton's refusal to give his field commander the week that he needed to pull back 40 miles across the iron railway bridge at Sittang. Instead, he insisted on General Smyth making a stand along the Bilin River; an apparent defensive line on the headquarter's maps but, as Smyth found, in the dry season "just a wet ditch in thick jungle which anyone could jump across." And the Japanese did so, "hooking" not one but both British flanks. When Smyth was finally allowed to withdraw on February 19, an orderly retreat was impossible. "We withdrew much too late, over a ghastly dirt track," recorded one of his brigadiers, irate that they "were bombed to hell by our own aircraft" because RAF headquarters in Rangoon had briefed the pilots to attack the wrong column advancing down the road to the Sittang bridge on the afternoon of February 21.

Wearily, the British officers tried to hurry the columns of trucks carrying Indian and Gurkha soldiers across the narrow spans that same night. A few of Smyth's advance units were over by dawn next day when a powerful enemy vanguard force came slicing through the jungle to cut off most of the Indian Division. The Gurkha Brigade holding the approaches to the bridge fought to break through the rear of the Japanese roadblock. All day long the thunder of the unseen battle rolled back over the river as the Indians tried to fight through. General Smyth delayed the agonizing choice of when to dynamite the bridge. At three o'clock the following morning the Japanese were closing in to rake the iron spans with machine-gun fire. The moment of decision was at hand. The Gurkhas' regimental history records the climax of the Sittang action: "The prime factor was that it must not fall into Japanese hands intact. It was becoming more and more clear that it could not be destroyed by daylight, when it would be under fire. It was doubtful even whether it could be held until daylight. To destroy it meant to sacrifice the division, but all the indications were that in any case the division could never now reach the bridge. The matter grew more urgent, the decision was taken and the bridge was blown."

When the girders of the Sittang bridge were dynamited at 5:30 a.m. on the morning of February 23, in "a series of deafening explosions followed by a blinding flash of light and a blast of red hot air," the Indian division on which the defense of Rangoon depended was cut off by the Japanese and the fast-flowing river. However, it was to take ten days for General Shoyin Ida's 15th Army engineers to drive north to build a temporary bridge 10 miles upriver. This gave the British time to demolish Rangoon's port facilities and evacuate the city. The delay saved the lives of nearly 3,000 Indian troops who broke through to the Sittang to ford the crossing by swimming on improvised rafts. Virtually all the plucky Gurkha Brigade—who could not swim—were to perish in the attempt.

The Sittang disaster was received by General Wavell with his customary imperturbability. It was evident that the vital port was already lost because the 7th British Armored Brigade and a fresh Indian division could not now reach Rangoon in time to save it. This was only one of a series of blows that was decimating his command. The Japanese invasion had beaten an Allied convoy of reinforcements to Timor on February 18; the next morning the ABDA fleet's main supply base at Darwin, 300 miles to the south on Australia's north coast, had been subjected to a repeat of Pearl Harbor by Admiral Nagumo's aircraft. The six-carrier strike force was only part of the growing concentration of enemy warships covering the wave of assaults heading south to attack the Dutch East Indies.

Admiral Hart wanted the ABDA strike force to show more offensive spirit and go out to disrupt the enemy landings, but he found he was being consistently blocked by the Dutch Admiral Helfrich, who vowed that he would not allow his ships to sail without adequate aircover. The command squabble was finally resolved when the Joint Chiefs in Washington, preferring to let the Dutch assume responsibility for the coming disaster, ordered Hart to hand over operational control to Helfrich. Assumption of the command now fired the Dutch admiral's determination to do something to save his countrymen on Java. On February 18 he ordered Admiral Doorman to attack the invasion force heading for Bali—without waiting for the heavy cruiser *Houston*, returning with her destroyers from an abortive raid on Timor, or for the British and Australian cruisers escorting convoys through the Sunda Strait 600 miles to the west.

That evening *De Ruyter* led her sister, the light cruiser *Java*, out from Tjilatjap into the tropical sunset, only to lose one of their two Dutch destroyers on the outer reef. His American escorts were to rendezvous with four more destroyers in the Bandung Strait that separated the picturesquely mountainous Bali of Java's eastern tip from the island of Lombok. Eight Dutch torpedo craft were to make up the other element of the attack. The next morning the ABDA force was still over 200 miles from Sanur Roads when the Japanese landing went in, against sporadic bombing by American B-17s. That night when Doorman's force swept into the anchorage around 10:30 p.m., what should have been a massacre of the transports was thwarted by the skillful seamanship of the Japanese. Their four destroyers won the tactical advantage by maneuvering across the T of the Allied battleline and sinking the *Piet Hein* in a fierce exchange of gunfire and torpedoes. Confusion reigned after more Japanese destroyers roared into the scrap, firing on their own ship. The chaos increased upon the arrival of the light cruiser *Tromp*, dashing up the Bandung Strait with four American destroyers. The darkness was lit up by gun flashes, tracers, and racing torpedoes which damaged one Japanese destroyer and the *Tromp* before Doorman managed to extricate his force. Not a single enemy ship had been sunk and the Dutch torpedo boats that had come racing up the Straits somehow missed both friend and foe.

The ineffective performance of the ABDA naval forces in the Bandung Strait was taken by Wavell's headquarters as an ominous indication that their seaborne forces were too disorganized to repel the expected Japanese invasion of Java. With 25,000 Dutch and 7,000 British and Australian troops on the island and less than two dozen serviceable aircraft, there was no hope of defending a 500-mile-long coastline. "I hate the idea of leaving these stout-hearted Dutchmen and will remain here and fight it out with them as long as possible," Wavell informed Churchill resignedly on February 21. Three days later, after aerial reconnaissance reported two large invasion forces heading for Java, Wavell decided the time had come to fly his staff out to Ceylon as General Brereton left on the last B-17 for Australia.

"I know that you will do everything humanly possible to prolong the battle," Churchill had cabled in a farewell message to the British soldiers and sailors who remained with the Dutch and Australian troops to make a final Allied stand on Java. The nine cruisers and eleven destroyers of the four nations' strike force were the last hope of saving any Dutch territory in the East Indies. Three more Royal Navy cruisers and destroyers were steaming toward Batavia on February 26 when they were ordered out against the large invasion convoy heading for northwest Java. Driven off by heavy air attacks, they made good their escape through the Sunda Strait to Ceylon.

THE BATTLE OF THE JAVA SEA

A second convoy was sighted heading for the eastern end of Java that afternoon. Admiral Doorman's force had barely time to refuel at Surabaya before the order came from Helfrich's Batavia headquarters: "PURSUE ATTACK UNTIL YOU HAVE DEMOLISHED JAPANESE FORCE." Signaling his multinational force: "WE WILL HAVE TO DO OUR DUTY UNTIL THE LAST MOMENT," the ships spent the night in a fruitless search. At first light they steamed back to Surabaya, escaping the Japanese aircraft which that morning had caught and sunk the venerable American carrier *Langley* as she ferried in fighters to Tjilatjap.

, When the convoy was again sighted 100 miles north of Bawean, Doorman's force set out to intercept it. There had been no time for a tactical conference, and the Dutch admiral's orders had to be translated by a U.S. Navy liaison officer aboard the *De Ruyter* and relayed by signal lamp back to the heavy cruisers H.M.S. *Exeter* and U.S.S. *Houston*. The rear was brought up by the light cruisers H.M.A.S. *Perth* and R.N.A. *Java*. Out on the column's starboard wing were three Royal Navy destroyers; its port wing was covered by two Dutch and four U.S. Navy destroyers.

Doorman's requests for spotter aircraft were rejected because every plane available had been sent out to attack the convoy. The Japanese support group was sighted by the British wing destroyers at 3:30 P.M., approaching from the northwest. This was Admiral Raizo Tanaka's light cruiser *Jintsu*, with eight destroyers. The Dutch admiral now ordered his column into battle. But without radar and spotter planes, he had no idea that there were two other enemy forces in the immediate vicinity. Seven miles west of the convoy's support group was the light cruiser *Naka*, with six destroyers, and 5 miles to the northwest still out of sight patrolled Vice-Admiral Takeo Takagi's heavy cruisers *Nachi* and *Haguro*, with four destroyers. Although Doorman's force was stronger in cruisers and therefore gunnery strength, the advantage was lost because he was steaming into action blind, while the float planes from the enemy cruisers were able to observe his every movement.

The Battle of the Java Sea, the biggest surface action since Jutland, began shortly before 4 P.M. on the afternoon of February 2, 1942. The three Japanese squadrons immediately swung onto courses that paralleled the Allied force, holding the range so that only the heavy cruiser 8-inch guns were effective. This put Doorman at the disadvantage because the damaged cruiser *Houston*'s stern turret was out of action. To even up the dueling match, the Dutch admiral sought to close the range so that he could bring his 6-inch cruiser's guns into action. He had the advantage in the smaller caliber, but as the distance decreased the Japanese launched torpedoes.

Their gunnery too proved superior. In the opening minutes, the *De Ruyter* was hit in the engine room by an 8-inch shell that failed to detonate. Then at about 4:30 another salvo from the heavy cruisers exploded in the *Exeter*'s engine room. Ablaze amidships, she was forced to haul out of line. Because she was immediately astern of the flagship and responsible for relaying orders, her movements were faithfully followed by the rest of the column, which now swung south, leaving the *De Ruyter* to race on alone. At this critical juncture a torpedo slammed into the *Kortenaer*, cutting the destroyer in two and leaving the two halves sinking.

Vital minutes were lost before Doorman hauled back to re-form his line of battle under cover of a smokescreen provided by the American destroyers. The pressure of the Japanese attack forced him to swing his column across the bow of the limping *Exeter*.

The chaos that again threatened was averted by Commander May, who in the best destroyer tradition raced out in the *Electra* to save the crippled *Exeter* by deflecting the incoming charge of the two enemy light cruisers. A Japanese destroyer was sunk before the gallant *Electra* was pummeled into immobility by hits to the engine room that left her a sitting duck for the *Jintsu*'s gunners.

The failing light of evening and the swirling smoke of battle severely hampered Doorman's judgment of the enemy movements as the *De Ruyter* signal lamps blinked: "FOLLOW ME." The Japanese had opened the range after the torpedo attacks and had already disappeared into the thick blue haze. "ENEMY RETREATING WEST WHERE IS CONVOY" Doorman frantically asked Helfrich's headquarters at 6:30 P.M. as he led his squadron around to the northeast still searching for the Japanese transports. Lacking any aerial reconnaissance, he could not know that Admiral Takagi from the flagship *Nachi* had ordered the convoy to reverse course, putting it already 30 miles out of reach and protected by the three Japanese squadrons which had now interposed themselves on a shielding southerly course.

Night fell and the darkness was punctuated at intervals by parachute flares dropped by enemy spotter planes to keep track of the Allied squadron. Occasional salvos were exchanged, eventually forcing Doorman to haul away to the northwest. He intended to shake off the Japanese planes by looping back along the coast before heading north again in search of the transports.

Doorman's move seemed to be succeeding when at 9:30 P.M. the night was rent with a fiery eruption. "I AM TORPEDOED," radioed H.M.S. *Jupiter*. The explosion that left her sinking was almost certainly caused by her striking a mine drifting from the recently laid coastal defenses; but it was the opportunity needed by the American destroyer commander to request that his four-pipers return to Surabaya because they were running low on fuel.

The Allied cruisers raced on with only a single escort, which an hour later was dropped off to pick up survivors from the hapless *Kortenaer*. The *De Ruyter* took a northerly heading, obediently followed by the three cruisers, now unescorted and wide open to enemy destroyer attack. Doorman was still searching for the enemy convoy he was determined should not reach Java when he was spotted again at 10:30 P.M. by a sharp-eyed lookout on the *Nachi*.

Admiral Takagi brought his flagship and the accompanying *Haguro* around onto a parallel northeasterly course, blocking access to the transports. He recommenced the gunnery duel, while Admiral Tanaka swung the *Jintsu*'s support group over to cover the disengaged flank. It was an unequal match because the Japanese had superiority in 8-inch guns. Their skill in night fighting quickly began to tell as orange flashes rippled back and forth. As the range closed to less than 5 miles, Tanaka's destroyers launched a salvo of torpedoes at the Allied squadron. One of the deadly "Long Lances" buried itself in *De Ruyter*'s stern. Flames engulfed the light cruiser aft, as the *Houston* and *Perth* swerved out of line, a maneuver that saved them from the fate of the *Java*, which was torpedoed a few seconds later. Her crew crowded forward to escape the blaze as the flagship's doom was signaled by a fantastic fireworks display when her signal rockets ignited. Doorman's last brave message was to signal the two remaining cruisers to withdraw without picking up survivors. The American and Australian ships raced away south on course for the sanctuary of Batavia, leaving the Japanese to preside over the pyres of the two Dutch warships. Both sank hissing into the black waters of the Java Sea, taking down Doorman and 344 of his crew.

The action that had cost the gallant Dutch admiral his life and four warships delayed by only twenty-four hours the Japanese landing on eastern Java. During that day, the *Houston* and *Perth* refueled at Batavia while 400 miles to the east the *Exeter*, escorted by the *Encounter*, limped into Surabaya to rejoin the four American destroyers. Royal Navy engineers labored to patch up damaged machinery as the dead were buried ashore. When darkness fell, the Allied naval forces prepared to make their various escapes.

That night three of the U.S. Navy four-pipers made a successful dash through the Bali Strait, evading the Japanese warships. The *John D. Pope* accompanied *Encounter* in shepherding the damaged *Exeter* westward through the dark waters of the Java Sea, ready to make a run through the Sunda Strait the following evening. The *Houston* and *Perth* had sortied, hoping to make the same trip that night to avoid enemy bombers at daybreak. They might have succeeded, but at 10:15, when they were less than 30 miles from the Strait's northern entrance, they ran slap into the Japanese invasion fleet in Bantam Bay.

Captain Waller unhesitatingly headed the *Perth*, followed by the *Houston*, past the two destroyer pickets into the bay; the Allies' big guns blazed at a crescent of some fifty anchored transports, silhouetted by their star-shells. A number of the transports were quickly ablaze and one sinking. General Hitoshi Imamura, commanding the 16th Army, was blown overboard from his headquarters ship and struggled ashore on a piece of driftwood as the night erupted in a fierce pyrotechnic display. Torpedo tracks crisscrossed wildly as the other Japanese destroyers churned back into the bay to fire blindly into the mayhem. Then four Japanese heavy cruisers arrived to block the escape of the Allied warships. They were trapped. An army observer aboard the *Houston* recorded the fight to the finish: "Enemy ships believed to be cruisers or carriers were firing at *Houston* from about 12,000 yards to seaward. Having established hitting range they were pouring fire into the ships and causing considerable damage. Destroyers operating in formations of three or four were making repeated attacks on the bows and quarters of *Houston*, using both guns and torpedoes. . . . All communications which were still operative were hopelessly overloaded with reports of damage received, of approaching torpedoes, of new enemy attacks begun, or changes in targets engaged."

Everyone aboard the two outgunned cruisers knew what the final outcome of that desperate last mêlée would be. They fought magnificently. At fifteen minutes before midnight, the *Perth* sank after four torpedoes ripped into her hull. The more heavily armored *Houston*, her decks littered with the dead and dying, was still maneuvering to avoid successive torpedo attacks. Her forward 8-inch turrets blazed away until they ran out of ammunition when three torpedoes caught her full square amidships. The battered cruiser faltered, and Captain Rooks gave the order to abandon ship. The Japanese continued raking her decks with gunfire as survivors leapt into the water. For a quarter of an hour their searchlights held the burning wreck in an icy glare. When she slid under, her tattered battle ensign was still flying. Fewer than half of the two ships' companies were to be picked up out of the tepid black water to face the dubious salvation of a Japanese prisoner of war camp.

The Dutch destroyer *Evertsen*, which had sailed from Batavia too late that evening to catch up with the cruisers, had a fortunate escape when she slipped past the battle undetected into the Sunda Strait. Then her luck deserted her as she was sunk at dawn by two enemy destroyers. News that the strait was already blocked never reached the damaged *Exeter* and her two consorts, working up to over 20 knots during the small hours of March 1. Darkness enabled *Exeter*'s Captain O. L. Gordon to steal west undetected by the Japanese warships patrolling the Java Sea. Daylight, however, betrayed his position to enemy planes. By 10 o'clock Admiral

Takagi's heavy cruisers were racing west to head off the cruiser that had escaped him thirty-six hours earlier. Another force of heavy cruisers and destroyers blocked the *Exeter*'s escape to the east.

The two faithful destroyers laid down a protective smokescreen as the *Exeter*, which had won worldwide renown for her part in the sinking of the German pocket battleship *Graf Spee*, hauled around to try to run a gauntlet of 8-inch salvos. Her engineers labored furiously with their damaged machinery to crack on every ounce of speed and for 20 miles she steamed eastward in a race against death across the Java Sea. Japanese float planes directed a rain of salvos, which straddled the *Exeter*, throwing up great waterspouts. Her own guns flashed in reply, but already her control was smashed by an early hit. Then her speed began falling away as shells smashed into her boiler room. H.M.S. *Exeter*'s career came to an end at 11:30 when Captain Gordon gave the abandon ship order and a final salvo of torpedoes sent her rolling over, under a pall of smoke and steam. The *Encounter* followed her down. The U.S.S. *Pope* managed to snatch a few more minutes of life by dodging into a thick squall—only to be dispatched by an avalanche of 8-inch shells as the fickle rainstorm lifted. Admiral Takagi's force had put the final seal on the victory won on February 27.

That morning while the final hours of the Java Sea battle were being fought out, an embarrassing scene had marked the death of the ABDA naval command. Admirals Glassford and Palliser had to inform a protesting Helfrich that they had orders to remove their surviving submarines and destroyers from his command, leaving him feeling like a raw ensign. The first Allied effort at a joint command had collapsed with its failure to prevent the Japanese from reaching their main objective—the oilfields of the Dutch East Indies. Its grim last act was to be played out in the desperate bloody engagements in the jungle, as British and Australian contingents fought alongside General Ter Poorten's men to resist the Japanese invasion. Six days later they had fought themselves to an exhausted standstill while defending Bandung, where the radio station broadcast a last sad announcement: "We are shutting down. . . . Good-bye till better times. Long live the Queen!"

BURMA AND BATAAN

March 8, 1942, was a day of double defeat for the Allies. Hours before the final surrender on Java, some 2,000 miles to the north the final trainload of British troops left Rangoon at dawn. After demolition experts had completed their destruction of dock installations, the last ships sailed from the port even as the advance units of the Japanese 33rd Division began entering the city outskirts.

General Ida mounted a triumphant victory parade through the deserted city. With Rangoon in Japan's control, the 15th Army now held the gateway to Burma. The way was open to march north to sever the strategic landline into China over which Chiang Kai-shek was rushing two armies from Chunking down to Burma to defend the vital road.

General Wavell, returning to his old headquarters in New Delhi, now took a more realistic view of Japanese military capabilities. He realized that neither the Chinese nor the recently arrived 7th British Armored Division and fresh Indian troops would be enough to hold Burma. The British Prime Minister, however, concluded otherwise, deciding, "if we could not send out an army at any rate, we could at least send a man." General Sir Harold Alexander had been dispatched to replace the ineffectual General Hutton. Churchill was counting on his reputation as a superlative military leader: "Under heavy fire men were glad to follow exactly in his footsteps." Alexander had arrived in Burma on March 8, far too late to work the kind of miracle he achieved at Dunkirk. His directive was "to hold Rangoon if possible and failing that to withdraw northward to defend upper Burma, while keeping contact with the Chinese." The first option had now vanished, leaving Alexander to issue orders for the initial stage of what would become another British retreat— a "grim race against the Japanese and approaching rains."

At the end of the first week of March 1942 the only bastion continuing to hold out against the Japanese was in the Philippines. The dogged defenders of the last few square miles of American-controlled territory on Bataan fought the bloody battle in spite of their awful privations. On the rock of Corregidor, General MacArthur directed the Filipino guerrilla resistance that was still denying the enemy control of Mindanao and the southern islands. Across the Pacific, Admiral Nimitz's raids on Japanese bases were making headlines in the United States. The *Lexington*'s pilots had beaten off heavy air attacks to strike Rabaul on February 21, and three days later Halsey's *Enterprise* task force bombed Wake Island. But these were no more than diversions as American public attention focused on the besieged soldiers in the Philippines, now completely cut off by the Japanese victories in the East Indies.

Reports of MacArthur's gallant struggle fed the mounting anti-Japanese sentiment in the United States. The demands for action against the Nisei (Americans born to immigrants from Japan) grew as they were accused of being potential spies and fifth columnists. Most were as patriotically American as any others born in the United States. But the rising current of fear on the West Coast and the evidence from the Magic intercepts the previous year of espionage organizations had been important factors in the President's decision to sign Executive Order 9066 on February 19, 1942. This emergency legislation allowed the Secretary of War to exile "any or all" persons from sensitive military areas. Couched in the broadest of terms, it enabled the military to begin rounding up 127,000 innocent Japanese-Americans, who were shipped to ten specially built camps in the Midwest—"concentration camps," so the champions of constitutional liberties charged.

Americans were still being given the impression from exaggerated headlines that MacArthur's forces in the Philippines were hitting the enemy and that it was only a matter of time before relief was forced through. The President and his Chiefs of Staff knew this was not the case, and so did certain congressmen who began pressing for the general to be brought home and deputed Supreme Commander of the U.S. Army. MacArthur himself, despairing by now of any reinforcements, was resigned to fighting to the finish alongside his men. When the American Governor of the Philippines and President Quezon were taken off Corregidor on the night of February 21 by submarine, the general's wife refused the chance to leave with her small son. Symbolically, MacArthur sent back a box containing his medals, papers, and a will.

The President had already decided that it would be politically impossible to sacrifice his distant cousin and America's popular hero. With the imminent collapse of the ABDA Command and the threat to New Guinea and Australia now alarming the Canberra government, Marshall and Roosevelt agreed on the need for the appointment of a new Supreme Allied Commander. This became more urgent with the British withdrawing to concentrate on the defense of India. The Australian Prime Minister and military leaders were having to turn increasingly to the United States. Relations between London and Canberra—already strained by the refusal to let Australian forces be diverted to the defense of Burma—were not improved when Prime Minister Curtin threatened to recall his remaining divisions from Egypt. Churchill accepted the decision of Curtin's cabinet that Australian forces would be allowed to defend the Suez Canal only if the United States would agree to send more of its Army across the Pacific, a commitment that could not be guaranteed unless the new Supreme Commander was American.

The obvious candidate was General Douglas MacArthur. That decision had already been taken on February 22 when a signal arrived in Corregidor signed by the President, Marshall, and the Secretary of War, ordering MacArthur to leave at once for Mindanao, then proceed to Melbourne "where you will assume command of all United States troops." The Australians were not told of the impending move because of the risks in getting MacArthur out. At first the general stubbornly refused to desert his staff and men, even offering to resign and reenlist as "a simple volunteer." He finally agreed to leave Corregidor only if he could pick the "psychological time." Nine days later MacArthur was still at his post in the Malinta Tunnel, gaunt and tortured as he wrestled with his pride and conscience to face breaking his pledge to die alongside his troops.

THE CATARACT OF DISASTER

Prodded by intelligence reports from Washington indicating that news of his impending escape had reached the Japanese, MacArthur at last decided to leave by PT boat on the night of March 11 rather than wait for the submarine that was on its way to take him off. At sunset that evening, with his wife and small son picking their way over the rubble of Corregidor's jetty together with seventeen members of his staff, the general embarked with his party on four PT boats. After giving his last box of cigars and two pots of shaving cream to General Wainwright, he promised as he handed over command: "If I get through to Australia you know I'll come back as soon as I can with as much as I can. In the meantime you've got to hold."

The high-speed dash began in darkness across Manila Bay, down 600 miles of choppy sea to Mindanao, in the last four PT boats in Lieutenant John D. Bulkeley's command. They dodged Japanese patrols at night and sheltered during the daylight hours on March 12 at the Cuyo Islands. It was an exhausting physical ordeal that the sixty-two-year-old general described as "a trip in a concrete mixer." Soaked, bruised, but thankful to be alive, the party arrived after thirty-five hours at the Del Monte pineapple plantation in Gayagan the next evening. That night the general's party had the first full meal they had eaten since leaving Manila two months before. Twenty-five thousand Filipinos were still holding the north of the island against the Japanese, who controlled the south of Mindanao, so only two days later a Flying Fortress was sent from Darwin to pick him up. After a bumpy five-hour flight in the B-17, MacArthur arrived in Australia to face yet another grueling four-day journey by train across the continent's desert interior. At Adelaide Station he was met for the first time by swarms of reporters to whom he made his Caesarean promise: "I came through and I shall return!"

12
Victory Disease

An air of defeat settled over Washington and London during the first months of 1942 while euphoria swept Tokyo. Each fresh Japanese victory was celebrated by long columns of flag-waving citizens trudging through the winter snow to the high gates of the Imperial Palace. The dramatic speed with which the Greater Southeast Asia Co-Prosperity Sphere was being established seemed a demonstration of the invincibility of the Imperial military forces. Their typhoon of conquest had won for Japan an extensive empire, rich in food, raw materials, and potential markets. Much of the world's rice production, most of the earth's natural rubber, three quarters of the tin reserves, and a good proportion of the vital oil resources were now available to fuel the voracious appetite of Japan's industry and the triumphant war machine it served.

Significantly, Tokyo's military-dominated government had limited strategic planning to the "First Operational Phase," which had only set a timetable for the conquest of Southeast Asia. Now that this had succeeded, in double-quick time, the pace and magnitude of their victory bred complacency and over-confidence among Japan's leaders. It would come to be called the "victory disease"; its symptoms were soon apparent in the setting of strategic objectives that fatally overreached the nation's military, industrial, and administrative resources.

The Imperial General Staff faced two fundamental problems: First, how to secure the defense of their vastly dispersed Empire and at the same time bring about a speedy peace settlement with the United States. Second, how to pacify and administer their conquered territories so as to harness the reserves of manpower and raw material to strengthen Japan's military power. "The fruits of victory are tumbling into our mouths too quickly," the Emperor Hirohito had prophetically told Marquis Kido, his Lord Privy Seal, on March 9, 1942. It was his forty-second birthday, the target date set for the completion of the First Operational Phase, and it was marked by the capture of Rangoon that day, just forty-eight hours after the last Allied troops on Java surrendered.

Defending their new and scattered Empire while they set about exploiting it to digest the economic "fruits of victory" now became the principal strategic and administrative concern of the Japanese. But lacking the colonial experience and bureaucracy of the European powers it had dispossessed, Tokyo made the mistake of using the Imperial Army to impose the same harsh military rule that had already alienated the populations of Manchuria and mainland China. Those who might have been sympathetic with Japan's proclamation that she had liberated Asia for the Asians soon encountered the iron fist of the occupying army. In Rangoon, the citizens who remained to hail their supposed "liberators" were dismayed by the arrogant attitude of the Japanese soldiers, forcing their attentions on women and "slapping the Burmese about and putting them to work hauling logs and water." The 30,000-strong "Burmese Army of Liberation" that was raised to join the fight to expel the retreating British would eventually turn against its new overlords. So, too, would revolutionary leader Achmed Sukarno, who had been released from jail to head a puppet government in Java.

In the Philippines the Executive Commission, led by "Japanophile" Jose P. Laurel (whose son was fighting alongside the Americans on Bataan), pledged obedience to General Homma. He hoped thereby to mitigate the lot of his people, but like the other puppet regimes set up by the Japanese, the "independent government" promised within the new order in Asia proved to be no more than a rubber stamp for the dictates of the Imperial Army.

It was in effect an occupation that imposed strict martial law. Rising Sun armbands had to be worn, it was compulsory to bow to Japanese soldiers, those not carrying lamps at night could be shot, all Western films and literature were banned, and the school curriculum was Japanified. This process was even extended to the calendar as 1942 became the 2062nd year after the first Japanese Emperor's accession. To stamp out all Western influence, special detachments of the army's Kempeitei (Secret Police) operated like an Oriental Gestapo to root out those who had served the old colonial administration or showed Western sympathies. Chinese populations came in for especially savage treatment because most Japanese soldiers harbored resentment for the long war against the mainland. In Singapore alone, 70,000 Chinese were summarily rounded up and interrogated; 5,000 were imprisoned, most for no other reason than that they bore tattos; and many were hideously executed as living targets for bayonet practice.

For the half-million European civilians, many of them women and children, who fell into Japanese hands in the newly conquered territories the next three years were ones of brutal imprisonment and deprivation. Many did not live long enough to reach the overcrowded jails and prison camps into which survivors were herded like cattle, often after trekking hundreds of miles through jungle tracks. The entire white population of Balikpapan had been put to the sword as punishment for the destruction of the oil installations. The British Foreign Secretary had protested the terrible atrocities suffered by the civilian population in Hong Kong, where international observers were horrified by the wanton rape and murder of young girls and even nuns. Dutch nationals suffered terribly on Java and Sumatra; in the Philippines over 3,000 American civilians were forced behind the barbed wire of St. Thomas University campus outside Manila, to live for the next three years in overcrowded squalor, short of food and medical supplies.

Japanese lack of respect for the lives of prisoners took on an extreme inhumanity when it came to military captives. Drilled in the harsh discipline of Bushido—the medieval warrior code of the Samurai, which incorporated the stern asceticism and bodily self-denial of Zen mysticism—the Imperial soldier was trained to fight to the death for his Emperor. Such sacrifice brought his family honor and himself personal salvation. His instruction manual explicitly laid down: "Bear in mind the fact that to be captured means not only that you disgrace yourself, but your parents and family will never be able to hold up their heads again. Always save the last bullet for yourself." For a Japanese soldier to be taken prisoner was far worse than death. He literally ceased to exist—his name expunged from the register of his village or town. Thus were the Japanese transformed into fanatical warriors who would rather die than surrender. This conditioning left the average soldier without any comprehension of Western ethics; he regarded all military captives as subhumans worthy only of contempt and treatment as slaves.

The 150,000 Allied prisoners of war who surrendered during the first months of 1942 experienced interminable years of slavery, starvation, disease, and death. Japan's Foreign Minister Shigenori Togo had promised that his country would observe the 1929 Geneva Convention, which set forth internationally agreed-upon treatment for prisoners of war. The Diet, however, had never ratified the treaty. In the absence of any code of conduct laid down by the Tokyo government, the handling of captives was left to the discretion of the local army commanders. They relied on a strict interpretation of Bushido rather than the Geneva Convention. Frequently short of food for their own men, the Japanese Army starved its captives in the 300 prisoner of war camps. Back-breaking labor, in flagrant contravention of the codes recognized by Western nations, was imposed on most prisoners. Many were sent underground in Manchurian coal and sulphur mines; others worked building roads and railways through thick malarial jungles, and a few were fated to become human guinea pigs in special medical experimentation camps. A wantonly high percentage of those held captive by the Japanese never survived, falling victim to starvation, epidemics, and the sadistic regime of their guard commanders—many of whom were to face trial and execution after 1945 as war criminals.

The brutality of Japan's military administration was to be matched by the clumsy efforts of the government to exploit the economies of the so-called Co-Prosperity Sphere. "There are no restrictions on us. They are enemy possessions. We can take them, do anything we want," was the basic policy laid down by the Liaison Conference held in Tokyo on March 14 between industrialists and the military. The greedy exploitation of the resources and raw materials of Southeast Asia was intended to benefit Japanese manufacturers, particularly the powerful "zaibatsu," who now sent their agents out to plunder the new territories according to the license given them under the directive headed Industry: "The southern region for the present will be a source of raw materials and a market for our manufactured products. Measures will be taken to prevent the development of industry in this area. Wages will be kept as low as possible." A Southern Region Development Bank was set up to milk all foreign assets and supervise the introduction of a new currency. Ostensibly this was the yen, but by a secret decision taken in Tokyo, it was not backed by Japan's reserves. Millions of new notes were printed, fueling the soaring inflation brought on by the army's requisitioning of all food supplies.

In a matter of months the whole of Southeast Asia was being reduced to the status of an economic colony, like Manchukuo and Korea. Wages were slashed by half on decrees from Tokyo; the traditional patterns of agriculture were overturned by arbitrarily imposed quotas on each region, cutting back rice production so as to produce more cotton for the war effort. In their hurry to loot the oil and raw material reserves of Southeast Asia, the Japanese disrupted the transportation network of the whole region. They impressed their substantial shipping fleet into serving the military and, without efficient organization, brought about a one-way traffic system intended to enrich Japan.

The normal flow of trade in the Far East was quickly disrupted. Rice was left to rot on the wharves of Rangoon while Malayans starved. "Do you stick decapitated heads up in the streets of Tokyo?" a waitress challenged a Japanese journalist in Singapore over the barbarous penalty for those caught stealing from Imperial Army grain stores. "The pompous English were replaced by the rough, vulgar Japanese," was the same journalist's sad reflection on entering the Raffles Hotel, now renamed Shonan Ryokan and exclusively serving his fellow countrymen, whose colonial domination was all the more intolerable because it was being exercised by Asians over Asians. Resentment quickly spread against their new overlords as strict rationing decreased the supply of food, bringing more malnutrition and disease to countries where these were always a burden. In the general economic decline that spread across Southeast Asia during the six months following the Japanese takeover, the peoples under the harsh reign of Tokyo's "New Order" were bitterly calling it the "Co-Poverty Sphere."

Just as the task of establishing an effective administration for Southeast Asia proved beyond a short-sighted bureaucracy and a rigid army, so too Japan's military leadership failed to resolve the strategic dilemma of how to defend the huge Pacific perimeter of its new Empire.

RIVAL STRATEGIES

Since early January there had been a fierce debate at Imperial General Headquarters over what strategy should be adopted for the "Second Operational Phase." The army staff wanted to call a halt to further expansion. The navy planners, on the other hand, encouraged by their string of successes, argued for maintaining the offensive momentum until the enemy sued for peace. Either course would impose on Japan a strategic impasse for which there could be no long-term military solution. A switch to the army's defensive policy would give the United States the time and opportunity to mobilize its vast industrial power so as to launch a massive transpacific assault. The navy still wanted to seek a decisive battle before the Americans could rebuild their fleet and so a divisive strategic tug-of-war began between the admirals on the one side and the generals on the other.

Badly infected by the "victory disease," Admiral Nagumo's Imperial Navy Staff at first put forward an ambitious proposal for the Second Operational Phase that called for the occupation of New Guinea as a springboard for the eventual invasion of Australia. The army staff was quite properly horrified at the Napoleonic scale of such an undertaking before they had even won their campaign in China. They rejected it on the grounds that they did not have the one hundred divisions available or the sea transports to supply such a massive land campaign. By the end of January 1942, the naval staff had trimmed their ambitions sufficiently to get the army's support for the first stage of their grand strategy—the occupation of New Guinea and the garrisoning of the Solomon Islands. This, they argued, was essential to secure the defense of their empire's southern perimeter against any Allied counteroffensive from Australia.

No sooner had the naval staff won Imperial General Headquarters' support for a limited southward offensive than they came under increasing pressure from the Admiral Yamamoto and his Combined Fleet staff to adopt its own more aggressive strategy directed at the mid-Pacific. Isoroku Yamamoto's views carried considerable weight in Tokyo war councils because his success at Pearl Harbor had made him a national hero.

His strategic reasoning was reflected by the Combined Fleet Chief of Staff, Rear-Admiral Matame Ugaki, who thought that: "Time would work against Japan because of the vastly superior national resources of the United States. Consequently, unless Japan quickly resumed the offensive—the sooner, the better—she would eventually become incapable of doing anything more than sitting down and waiting for the American forces to counterattack."

Accordingly, Ugaki had been ordered to initiate planning early in January for the "Seizure of Hawaii and Destruction of the American Fleet Strength." When detailed study proved that this was beyond Japan's naval resources, the Combined Fleet Staff worked up an alternative plan to launch amphibious operations against the British in Ceylon, so as to secure air superiority over the Indian Ocean as a prelude to the army's invasion of India. Britain would then be driven out of Asia by linking up with a German drive through the Middle East and the Caucasus. But Hitler rejected this vision for a combined Axis initiative. So the army staff was left to argue for the husbanding of their strength for the war in China and a possible advance against their old enemy Russia. Burma was to be the westward limit of the advance and the navy staff revised its Indian Ocean strategy into "Operation C," a raid by the carrier strike force on the Ceylon British naval base at Colombo, while cruisers attacked merchant shipping in the Bay of Bengal. Appreciating that this would offer no chance of a war-winning victory, Yamamoto continued planning for follow-up with a mid-Pacific offensive that would lure out and entrap the U.S. Fleet.

The increasing audacity of the U.S. Pacific Fleet's raids with its carrier task forces had by February 1942 brought an agreement between the Japanese generals and admirals that priority must be given to strengthening the ribbon defense of their island perimeter—particularly in the south where it was most vulnerable. However, the first stage of the advance to New Guinea was interrupted on February 20 by the raid of the *Lexington*'s task force on Rabaul.

Seized at the end of January, the fine port at the western point of New Britain was being turned into the main staging base for the southward advance. The American raids had destroyed all but three of the eighteen bombers needed to cover the assembling invasion force. Two weeks later, when the postponed operation was resumed and the convoy of transports set sail across the Bismarck Sea to establish air bases on the New Guinea coast at Lae and Salamaua, intelligence forewarned the Allies. The *Lexington* was ordered to join with the *Yorktown* task force in the Gulf of Papua to fly in long-range air strikes over the Owen Stanley Mountains to strike the Japanese beachheads. Although only two were sunk, thirteen of Vice-Admiral Shigeyoshi Inouye's eighteen transports were damaged, forcing them to return to Rabaul for repairs. The sudden appearance of so many planes caused the naval staff in Tokyo to fear that a powerful build-up of Allied naval strength was under way in the Coral Sea. They decided to postpone the next phase of the New Guinea offensive, "Operation MO" (the invasion of Port Moresby), until Admiral Nagumo's carriers returned at the end of April from Operation C in the Indian Ocean. The admirals were also more determined to put an end to the Allied freedom to operate in the Coral Sea and cut across the American supply line to Australia. This in turn necessitated expanding the navy plan in the Second Operational Phase to include the capture of New Caledonia, Fiji, and Samoa.

Tokyo had already completed the planning for this extended southward drive, which would require the full resources of the Combined Fleet, when it ran into conflict with the strategy being prepared by Admiral Yamamoto. He now wanted an advance to the mid-Pacific to capture Midway, in anticipation that this would lure the U.S. Fleet into a decisive battle. The clash between these rival strategies came to a showdown during the first week of April 1942, with a verbal duel at Tokyo's Imperial Navy Headquarters.

"The Combined Fleet's view that the seizure of Midway by threatening Hawaii would effectively undermine America's will to fight and thus pave the way to a negotiated peace" was considered "far too optimistic," by Commander Miyo, putting the case for the naval staff. He "almost tearfully" argued that the Indian Ocean operation and the need to replenish the carrier striking force would make it impossible to meet Yamamoto's June deadline for the Midway operation. He contended that his own plan would also result in a "decisive confrontation" with the Americans, because the Pacific Fleet would come charging across the ocean in response to the threat to Fiji and Samoa.

The Midway strategy was argued with equal force by Commander Watanabe, Yamamoto's staff gunnery officer and confidante. "We believe that by launching the proposed operation against Midway, we can succeed in drawing out the enemy's carrier strength and destroying it in decisive battle," he insisted. "If on the other hand, the enemy should avoid our challenge, we shall still realize an important gain by extending our defensive perimeter to Midway and the Western Aleutians." In an astute move to involve Admiral Yamamoto himself in the debate, Watanabe put a call through to the Combined Fleet flagship. He returned an answer to the staffs' contention that only their southward offensive could sever America's links with Australia. He repeated Yamamoto's counterargument that his plan for a showdown in the mid-Pacific would also "destroy the enemy's carrier force, without which the supply line could not in any case be maintained." Watanabe left the Naval Chief in no doubt that Yamamoto was expecting his strategy to be accepted or Nagumo would be faced with an embarrassing resignation.

When the army staff gave their support for the mid-Pacific strategy because it required them to provide only a small garrison force, the naval staff for the second time in a year capitulated to the Commander in Chief of the Combined Fleet. Nonetheless, they still insisted on continuing with their own South Pacific strategy at a slower pace. The end result was that the Second Operational Phase overstretched the resources of the Imperial Navy. At the risk of ignoring the fundamental dictates of naval strategy for concentrating forces, they were now committed to parceling out their fleet in three major operations. It was a fatal weakness in the Japanese strategy that the United States would be quick to discover and exploit.

PACIFIC FIRST

While the military leaders in Tokyo debated their next moves, the Allied Chiefs of Staff on both sides of the Atlantic were recasting their own strategy, which had been knocked off-balance by the success of Japan's First Operational Phase. Recognizing that the Arcadia planning was now "largely obsolescent," Churchill cabled Roosevelt for a revision of priorities and allocations because of "misfortunes that come thick and fast upon us." More tanks and aircraft were urgently required, as well as more shipping to move extra troops to the Middle East. He pleaded for "additional help to Australia" to prevent the Canberra government pulling out its remaining troops from the desert war just as Rommel was renewing his drive to the Suez Canal.

"The United States situation in the Pacific is now very grave," Roosevelt replied, following three days in "continuous conference" with the Joint Chiefs reviewing what could be done to help Britain. Though sympathetic to the magnitude of the British commitments in the Mediterranean and Indian Ocean, there were just not enough transport ships to meet all the Prime Minister's demands. In addition, America had to assume the burden of defending Australia and New Zealand against Japan. To counter the Japanese danger and respond to the Canberra government's threat to recall more troops from the Middle East, two more U.S. Army divisions were to be sent at once across the Pacific. Churchill was warned that this would mean sacrificing the U.S. troops for the build-up in Britain, as well as the curtailment of American participation in the air offensive against Germany and abandoning the British Gymnast operation in North Africa.

To meet the emergency in the Pacific, the Allied Chiefs of Staff were now, despite their Arcadia agreements, diverting troops, aircraft, and shipping *away* from the European theater. This departure from the Allied strategy agreed three months before gave Admiral King the opportunity he was looking for to press the Navy's case for beginning an immediate offensive against Japan as the only way to halt the enemy's southward advance toward Australia. The Pacific initiative reflected King's own view that the Atlantic theater had been given too much emphasis and increased his ascendency over the architect of that policy, Admiral Stark. A week later, his control over the U.S. Naval Staff would be complete when the pro-British Chief of Naval Operations was sent to London. Well before the President's order of March 12, which made COMINCH also Chief of Naval Operations, Admiral King had begun what was to develop into a vigorous campaign to modify the Stark-Marshall strategy giving priority to the war against Hitler.

At the President's emergency strategic review beginning on March 5, King's memorandum called for the immediate setting up of a forward base in the Tonga Islands. This would be the base for an offensive against Japanese-held Pacific islands before they could be fortified. He had been urging this plan on the Joint Chiefs of Staff since mid-February. It reflected his unease with the British, and his increasing doubts about the wisdom of the Arcadia "Europe First" priority. Keeping the Navy standing on the defensive in the Pacific was unpopular in Congress and the public. Polls showed that 65 percent of Americans favored an early offensive against the Japanese, while less than 25 percent supported the opening of a Second Front in Europe.

Admiral King's plan was not well received by the Army Staff. A month earlier, when he had first tried to revise the "Europe First" priority by suggesting that far more Pacific Islands should be garrisoned than originally allowed for, Marshall had suggested that such a move would represent "a change in basic strategy." The Director of War Plans, Brigadier General Dwight D. Eisenhower, insisted that strategic and logistic demands dictated the absolute necessity of concentrating in 1942 on the Atlantic theater if the Axis powers were ultimately to be defeated. In his view these demands were: "(a) Maintenance of the United Kingdom. . . . (b) Retention of Russia in the war. . . . (c) Maintenance of a position in the India-Middle East area which will prevent physical junction of the two principal enemies. . . ." This inevitably meant that the Pacific theater must remain primarily a holding operation, with it "desirable, but not essential" that a line to Australia be kept open. Eisenhower's report even went so far as to suggest that preventing a Japanese invasion of Australia was "not immediately vital to the outcome of the war."

Admiral King could not agree. The subcontinent had to be held "because of the repercussions among the non-white races of the world." He wanted the United States to restrict its contribution to the European war to supplies and munitions, and not just to keep the supply line open to Australia, but to set up strongpoints from which a step-by-step general advance could be made through the New Hebrides, Solomons, and the

Bismarck Archipelego. What King was arguing for was the redefining of American strategic priorities from the Atlantic to the Pacific—and General Eisenhower did not underestimate the formidable battle that was shaping up with the Navy. "Admiral King is an arbitrary, stubborn type with too much brain and a tendency to bullying his juniors," his diary noted; "but I think he wants to fight, which is encouraging."

The emergency sessions of the Joint Chiefs, and the President's need to reassure Churchill about the defense of Australia, by March 6 brought acceptance of the admiral's strategy, which he summed up as: "Hold Hawaii. Support Australia. Drive northwards from the New Hebrides." Although it was to be nearly six months before this "drive" began, the end of March saw the U.S. Navy establishing a forward base at Efate. Nimitz resisted King's strong advice to send the main body of the Pacific Fleet forward to the New Hebrides; but he was obliged to allow the *Yorktown* and *Lexington* to continue operating in the Coral Sea under Admiral Leary, the ANZAC area commander, and therefore under direct COMINCH control.

The War Department's apprehension that their forces would be sucked into what Secretary Stimson described as "King's creeping movement to New Caledonia" was temporarily laid to rest when the focus of the crisis was shifted from Japan by the March 7 cable from Churchill. "Everything portends an immense renewal of the German invasion of Russia in the spring and there is very little we can do to help the only country that is heavily engaged with the German armies." The Prime Minister and the President shared a concern that Stalin might be driven into a separate peace unless some effort was made in Europe to relieve the German pressure building up on the Red Army. This would be a catastrophic blow to the Allied cause, and the danger allowed General Marshall to reemphasize the priority of the war against Hitler.

After another week of debate between the Army and Navy planners over how to divide limited shipping and supply resources between the Atlantic and the Pacific strategies, the decisive meeting took place on March 16, 1942, when the Joint Chiefs of Staff sat down with the President to review their options. Three possibilities were on the table. General Arnold presented the Army Air Staff's proposal for an all-out effort to defeat Hitler in western Europe. Arguing that the collapse of Germany must ruin Japan, he advocated sending no reinforcements to the Pacific —even if this meant accepting the loss of Australia. Admiral King's proposals were, as expected, diametrically opposed. His plan called for the launching of a joint Army-Navy offensive to drive the Japanese out of Rabaul in New Britain so as to end the threat to Australia, even if this meant sacrificing reinforcements for Europe. Marshall put forward the compromise strategic plan worked out by Eisenhower. This was essentially the Atlantic strategy, with the allocation of limited forces to the

Pacific theater sufficient only to secure Australia and Hawaii. Because it was vital for available shipping to be concentrated in Britain for the Second Front that might be needed to save Russia, there was to be no early start to the Navy's major Pacific offensive.

Admiral King was outnumbered by Marshall's supporters. So "with little recorded discussion," the War Department had won. The Pacific theater was to be restricted to "current commitments." By limiting the number of aircraft they were prepared to make available to five fighter and two bomber squadrons, the generals hoped to curb any bid by the Navy in 1942 to move out from the New Hebrides to other islands. When King complained that there were not sufficient ground forces to meet Japan's threat to New Guinea, he was told he would have to rely on the Marines and the Army's Amphibious Corps, which was training on the West Coast for the "commando-style" raids advocated by the British.

The Army strategists had regained the upper hand by April 1, when the Joint Chiefs of Staff accepted General Eisenhower's outline plan for launching the Second Front in Europe by the following year. General Marshall, accompanied by Harry Hopkins, then flew to London to win British approval for their scheme to start the "Operation Bolero," the build-up of U.S. troops and equipment in Britain for a forty-eight-division Allied assault code-named "Round Up" on France during the spring of 1943. He found the Prime Minister unreceptive to the plan because Churchill believed that his strategy for a North African offensive would be a less risky way of relieving the pressure on the Russians. His Chiefs of Staff disliked the American notion that they should be on call to launch an emergency all-British cross-channel attack, optimistically christened "Sledgehammer," if the Soviet collapse was imminent. Britain's leaders did not press opposition too strongly, however, because Marshall had already let it be known that if he returned to Washington without the plan agreed on, there was a real possibility that the U.S. Navy would get its way to switch to a Pacific strategy.

Forewarned by reports from Dill of the U.S. Navy's restiveness, General Sir Alan Brooke realized that it was a "clever move" by the U.S. Army Chief of Staff to forestall King and contain MacArthur: "To counter these moves Marshall has started a European offensive plan and is going one hundred percent all out on it." He therefore urged the War Cabinet to give their broad backing to the Eisenhower plan so as to prevent the United States from switching strategic priorities. Churchill still hoped to be able "to work by influence and diplomacy" to reinstate his alternative Mediterranean schemes, but General Marshall was unaware of this when he returned to report to the President that the Army plan was now agreed on with their Ally. General Eisenhower's relief that "we are all definitely committed to one concept of fighting" was to prove premature.

The "Pacific First" lobby on Capitol Hill and in the American press was now being stirred up by the Australian government, aided by Mac-Arthur. He had arrived from the Philippines to a hero's welcome—only to discover that the Allied Army and Air Force he expected to find assembled for him to command in the campaign to defeat Japan did not yet exist. Burning to begin his crusade to recover the Philippines, he set up his headquarters in Melbourne's Menzies Hotel. He might not have an army, but he commanded enormous popularity: congressional pressure obliged the President to award him the Medal of Honor, as across the United States streets, dams, public works, children, and even a dance step were named after the general that polls showed was a military hero for most Americans. Polls also showed that Americans wanted him back in the War Department and there was talk of a draft for Republican presidential nomination. Cannily exploiting this support, MacArthur demonstrated his flare for self-promotion by holding press conferences, making speeches to the Australian Parliament, and giving radio broadcasts. His call was for "sufficient troops and sufficient material" to launch an offensive against the Japanese. For a month the disgruntled general waited—"A Hero on Ice," as *Time* magazine accurately described him—for the Joint Chiefs in Washington to resolve their strategic differences.

After he learned of the decision to sustain the "Europe First" priority, MacArthur's chagrin increased when he found out that no overall Supreme Commander was to be appointed to run the Pacific War. Like most Americans, this was the great mission he thought he had been recalled from Corregidor to undertake, but internecine rivalry between the Army and Navy had made it impossible. Admiral King refused to entertain the idea of a general dictating orders to his admirals, arguing that since naval operations would determine the course of the war against Japan, Nimitz must be the logical choice. But Nimitz was junior in rank and seniority to MacArthur.

The command of the war against Japan was to become a divided responsibility, which made Nimitz Commander in Chief of Pacific Ocean Areas, embracing New Zealand, Samoa, Fiji, west to the 160th meridian of longitude. This was the eastern boundary of General MacArthur's authority as Supreme Allied Commander Southwest Pacific Area. Sumatra, Malaya, Burma, and the Indian Ocean remained under British control. MacArthur at once saw fit to redesignate himself "Commander in Chief [to put him on a par with Nimitz] of Allied land, sea and air forces in Australia, New Guinea and the Solomons as well as the Philippines." He was to remain unshakeably convinced that "of all the faulty decisions of the war, perhaps the most inexplicable was not to unify command in the

Pacific." It fueled his already deeply held grudge against the "navy cabal" in Washington, whom he blamed for depriving him of the reinforcements in the Philippines. Now he held them responsible for denying him the Supreme Command in the Pacific. He was dismayed to find that his overall authority was to be curtailed by the Joint Chiefs' directive, which tried to avoid future contentions in the divided Pacific command by retaining a large measure of control. MacArthur was therefore obliged to report to and receive orders from General Marshall. Nimitz would receive his instructions through Admiral King, and any differences between them would be resolved by the Joint Chiefs of Staff.

MacArthur was most irked to find that he could not "command directly any national force" or direct strategy. Allied land forces in the southwest Pacific were put under the command of Australian General Thomas Blamey; COMINCH's ANZAC Naval Commander Admiral Herbert F. Leary assumed responsibility for sea operations. The Allied Air Force was initially put under General George Brett—whom MacArthur worked to replace with one of his own appointees from the "Bataan Gang" who had established his Australian headquarters. He was not immediately able to persuade General Marshall, who also insisted, over MacArthur's protests, that Wainwright should be promoted to full general to take full control over all American forces still fighting in the Philippines, including guerrillas.

THE LAST DAYS OF BATAAN

The battle for Bataan was raging on and now, as he found himself at the receiving end of General Wainwright's pleas for help, MacArthur discovered the impossibility of fighting any help through the Japanese blockade. All he could send were promises. On Corregidor, the talk of "mile-long" relief convoys that never arrived added to the bitter feeling of abandonment. Across on the front-line foxholes along the Mariveles Mountains, half-starved American and Filipino soldiers had weeks ago killed and eaten the last of their pack horses and mules. The battle against the diseases brought on by malnutrition was depleting their strength as they defended their positions against relentless enemy assault. Malaria had reached epidemic proportions on Bataan. For the scarecrow army, men were so debilitated by wasting sickness like beriberi and dysentery that just lifting a rifle became a physical ordeal.

"If the Japanese can take the Rock, they'll find me here, no matter what orders I receive," General Wainwright had told his men, trying to rally them after the news of MacArthur's escape. In the three following weeks there had been a lull in the bloody slogging march on Bataan because General Homma's offensive was also brought to a standstill by short rations and rampant malaria. Angered that MacArthur had been able to escape, Imperial General Headquarters in Tokyo assigned another division to the Philippines along with General Hattori, the Army Chief of Operations, to mount a new assault. By the end of March 1942, 15,000 Japanese soldiers and 140 artillery pieces, assisted by 80 bombers, were ready for the final attack on the last line of defense in Bataan. "There is no reason why this attack should not succeed," Homma wrote on April 2, knowing that his disgrace was certain if it did fail.

It was Good Friday on the American front line. All day Army chaplains had been passing through the positions holding field communion services. The defenders' final agony began that evening under a Japanese bombardment that reached a crescendo which reminded veterans of the horrors of the Western Front. The assault was hurled against the center of the American line held on the high ground before Mount Natib. Bombers shuttled back and forth unmolested, raining down high explosives in such quantities that by the next day the continuous deluge of fire had set the jungle ablaze. Men who had jokingly lit cigarettes on the undergrowth when it first caught light found themselves forced to flee through choking black smoke to escape being incinerated. In the confusion the Japanese were able to punch through a 3-mile wide salient. By the following afternoon the Rising Sun was being raised atop the 1,900-foot-high Mount Samat—an ominous signal to the American garrison on Corregidor that with the commanding heights over the Mariveles now in enemy control, Bataan could not hold out much longer.

"When the supply situation becomes impossible, there must be no thought to surrender. You must attack," had been MacArthur's radioed orders. Obediently, Wainwright ordered an immediate counteroffensive. His field commander on Bataan was Major General Edward P. King, a dedicated soldier whose cool military judgment rationalized that this was impossible. The Japanese had axed his front line apart, leaving neither flank with the strength or positions to muster and launch the attack. It was also impossible to prevent the Japanese from taking Mariveles, the tiny port which was now jammed with dazed American and Filipino soldiers trying to flee to the safety of Corregidor. As King reported, "in two days an army vanished into the air." Battered by the offensive, on the afternoon of April 8 he made a desperate signal: "We have no further means of organized resistance."

But Wainwright would not allow a surrender. As darkness fell and King's Mariveles headquarters was being pounded to pieces, he understood that the final hours of resistance were at hand. While the destruction of the remaining ammunition dumps began, nature herself rebelled, shaking up the cataclysmic scene with an earthquake. "The air was filled with smoke and flying debris, the din was terrific and terrifying," wrote a young Navy doctor who managed to get out on one of the boats crossing to Corregidor as a gasoline dump was dynamited, which "intensified the blast which hurled large rocks, boulders and . . . human fragments all over the area and into the sea, sinking small boats in the harbor and injuring the occupants. . . ."

At midnight, King called his staff together to tell them the situation was hopeless. To save thousands of lives, he announced that flags of truce would be put out at 6 A.M. the next morning: "I have not communicated with General Wainwright because I do not want him to assume any part of the responsibility." News reached Corregidor too late to counter the orders. By daybreak white flags of truce began appearing all over the American line. At nine o'clock the Jeep carrying Major General King bumped over the pitted ground to the Japanese headquarters at Lawao. Laying his pistol on the table before the Japanese officers, he reflected that General Lee must have felt the same awful shame when he surrendered at Appomattox on the same day in 1865.

April 9, 1942, marked the greatest defeat ever suffered by a U.S. force in the field. "No army has done so much with so little, and nothing became it more than its last hours of trial and agony," was the ringing epitaph General MacArthur delivered to a press conference. But for most of those American and Filipino soldiers who surrendered, the trial and agony were only beginning.

General Homma's headquarters had estimated that only 25,000 captives would have to be transported to the prisoner of war camps being prepared on Luzon. Faced with three times that number, Japanese logistics broke down. Not only were the truck and rail transports totally inadequate to cope with such a vast number of captives, but they had assumed that the prisoners would have their own rations. The appalling result was that already starving, ill, and exhausted men now faced the nightmare trek up the jungle trails of Bataan with little or no food to sustain them. Herded like driven cattle under the bayonets of guards, the 65 miles that the survivors completed on foot was truly to deserve its awful place in history as the "Bataan Death March." Some Japanese did show sympathy for the plight of their ragged columns of starving captives, to the extent of sharing their own meager rations, but most obeyed the callous dictates of Bushido. Stragglers would be mercilessly clubbed, those dying from disease and malnutrition were left by the wayside, and men who appeared to be succumbing were buried alive by their comrades at gunpoint.

The Japanese soldiers reserved their worst brutality for the unfortunate Filipinos. In one orgy of savagery, nearly 300 were bayoneted—they were among the more than 7,000 who never finished that terrible march. Over 60,000 survived to reach the camps, most of them no more than walking skeletons whose only relief was that the interminable march was over. For those who survived, the meager rice rations, disease, and humiliation were relentlessly to take their toll of lives behind the barbed-wire compounds for as long as the war lasted.

RETREAT FROM THE INDIAN OCEAN

On the same day that Bataan fell, the Royal Navy faced the equal humiliation of being forced to abandon the western Indian Ocean to the Japanese. In the weeks following the disastrous loss of the *Prince of Wales* and the *Repulse*, five battleships and three carriers had been rushed out to Ceylon to guard the sea approaches to India and protect the shipping routes to Burma. When the ABDA Command collapsed, Churchill insisted that one of Britain's best fighting admirals now must be sent out to take over the Eastern Fleet at Trincomalee from Admiral Layton. The man chosen was Sir James F. Somerville, who for two years had led the Royal Navy's famous Task Force F on exploits that ranged from the bombardment of the French warships at Oran to hunting the *Bismarck*. But the fleet he found awaiting him at the naval base on the northwest tip of Ceylon hardly matched up to a front-line fighting force. The five old World War I battleships, led by the *Warspite* (recently arrived from refitting in the Brooklyn Navy Yard), lacked the speed to operate effectively with the two fast modern carriers and the older *Hermes*. Eight cruisers, fifteen destroyers, and five submarines made up the Eastern Fleet—totally insufficient strength even to begin the enormous task of guarding the whole Indian Ocean from the western approaches of Australia to the Cape of Good Hope and the convoy routes to the Suez Canal and India.

Yet preparations were already under way for a big operation to pre-empt the disaster of Japan invading Madagascar, which would allow her navy to dominate the ocean and cut off both India and the Middle East as well as Britain's oil supplies from the Persian Gulf. No sooner had Somerville hoisted his flag aboard the *Warspite* on March 28 than he was handed an alarming intelligence report that appeared to make this strategic disaster a real possibility. The news was that a powerful force of Japanese carriers was steaming out into the Indian Ocean. To forestall the unthinkable, he put to sea immediately, calculating rightly that the enemy would be on its way to put the Royal Navy bases and warships at Ceylon out of action. He intended to maneuver the Japanese into a night action, when his battleships would have a gunnery superiority over a carrier strike force that could not operate its planes after dark. Three days of fruitless searching forced him to refuel at the Addu Atoll staging base in the Maldive Islands off the southern tip of India. At the same time he dispatched the small carrier *Hermes* to Trincomalee to embark her planes and two cruisers to Colombo for dockyard repairs.

Somerville's assumption that the Japanese force was still in the Indian Ocean proved a disastrous error. That same afternoon a patrolling Catalina PBY pilot reported the enemy carriers some 350 miles south of Ceylon before he was shot down by Zero fighters. Caught with his force divided and too far away to intervene, all Somerville could do was to try to cover the 600 miles to Ceylon as fast as possible.

Admiral Nagumo, lacking any information from his submarine patrols about the whereabouts of the British Fleet, had also mistakenly assumed that it must have put into the port at Colombo, where he hoped to smash it the next morning in another Pearl Harbor.

Church bells were pealing for Easter Sunday worshippers in Colombo when the approaching enemy aircraft were picked up by radar. Just before 8 o'clock the RAF Hurricanes roared off from their makeshift airfield on the race course. The first British planes to make contact, however, were a flight of Swordfish torpedo bombers on the way from Trincomalee to rejoin the *Hermes,* which had evacuated the harbor along with the two cruisers. All twelve of the lumbering biplanes were shot into the sea as the first wave of the Japanese strike flew on. At the head was Commander Fuchida's plane. "I was now sure enemy fighters were out to intercept us. To avoid them I led the whole attack force around the north of Colombo and then we dashed in on our objective. Still wet from a rain squall, the city lay glistening in the sun. No airborne fighters were visible as we came over, and the big airfield southeast of the city was also empty of planes, so it was apparent that the enemy fighters had gone south to meet us." Disappointed to find that the harbor was virtually empty of shipping, Fuchida ordered his bombers to do what they had not done at Pearl Harbor and concentrate on destroying port installations. Stiff antiaircraft fire, and some fiercely determined attacks by the RAF Hurricanes when they finally located the enemy armada, gave the Japanese carrier pilots their first taste of real opposition. Six Zeros were shot down at the cost of twenty RAF planes overwhelmed by the weight of the opposition.

Two small naval vessels were sunk and a merchantman set ablaze. This was not quite the destruction that Fuchida had hoped to inflict on the British Fleet. His planes had landed back on their carriers by midday, when float planes from the heavy cruiser *Tone* reported two cruisers to the southwest. Nagumo now launched the second strike wave, held back because Fuchida's reports indicated that there was nothing more to bomb in Colombo. Hopes rose that they had indeed trapped the British Fleet. All the eager pilots discovered were two three-funneled heavy cruisers, which writhed and twisted across the ocean trying to escape the bombs of an unequal contest. Explosions lifted the 10,000-ton *Dorsetshire* bodily out of the water, as thirty-one hits pounded her to the bottom. Twelve minutes later her sister ship *Cornwall* was set ablaze by eight bombs; she rolled over to sink shortly before 2 P.M., leaving 1,100 of their combined complement to be rescued later by British destroyers.

Somerville nearly had his chance for revenge after one of his carrier scout planes spotted Zero fighters late that afternoon some 300 miles south off Ceylon. Nagumo, unwilling to commit his carrier force to a disadvantageous night action, sped off to the east. Next day when he resumed the hunt west, he found the British did not want to do battle when the odds in daylight were against them. Playing cat and mouse by turns for the next forty hours, the two fleets never came to blows. On the afternoon of April 6, Somerville was again disposing his force to intercept a Japanese advance to the Maldives. But unknown to him, Nagumo had tired of the game and was steaming north to carry out the second objective of his Operation C—the raid on Trincomalee.

The base had been warned in time to clear the harbor of shipping that night. Next morning a hundred Japanese aircraft roared in to unload bombs, demolishing cranes, workshops, ammunition dumps, and fuel-storage tanks in "a spectacular display of fireworks" that twenty-two RAF and Fleet Air Arm fighters could do nothing to prevent. The attack was still raging when the *Hermes* and the ships that had sortied during the night prematurely decided to return. With no aircraft aboard to send up, the aged carrier was an easy target for the enemy pilots. Ten bombs sank her just before 11 A.M.; she was followed by the destroyer *Vampire*.

While Nagumo's strike force had been running rings around the Royal Navy's Eastern Fleet off Ceylon, across the ocean in the Bay of Bengal Admiral Ozawa's cruisers—the other naval component in Operation C—had sunk twenty-three merchant ships. This caused the British to suspend all shipping operations between Burma and India. The Japanese foray into the Indian Ocean had cost the Allies over 100,000 tons in losses and convinced Somerville that there was nothing for him to do but order the Eastern Fleet to retreat to the sanctuary of the African coast at Mombasa, a strategic withdrawal he would certainly not have ordered had he known that on that very same afternoon Admiral Nagumo had set course for Japan. The Japanese carrier strike force had steamed more than 50,000 miles since Pearl Harbor, piling up victories at Rabaul, Port Darwin, and Ceylon with the loss of only a dozen planes. Now Nagumo's ships needed repair, and his aircrews rest and regrouping. Only Admiral Hara's two carriers of the 5th Division were detached on the way back, to be sent to Truk to cover the final phase of the New Guinea invasion.

After this fresh round of disaster to the Royal Navy's control of the Indian Ocean, Churchill warned Roosevelt that "immense perils" were now threatening Burma and India. He proposed that the U.S. Pacific Fleet should send warships to join Somerville "to offer some menace to the Japanese." But Admiral King would not hear of such a move, and the

President replied that he could only send in more bombers to strengthen the defense of India. He gave no hint of an operation that was already under way to strike back at Japan. Intended largely as a propaganda blow to boost American morale, it would jolt the Imperial General Staff so profoundly as to change the course of the Pacific War.

13
Taking a Beating

Ever since Pearl Harbor, Roosevelt had been pressing his military planners to find a way to bomb Tokyo. Sending aircraft out on a one-way trip from China would be a suicidal mission for aircrews, though there would have been no shortage of volunteers. Not until mid-January 1942 did Admiral King's staff hit upon the scheme of launching land-based bombers from a carrier that could take them close enough to Japan's coast to continue on to the Chinese mainland. General Arnold enthusiastically supported the plan, which called for modifying the twin-engined B-25 bombers. Two dozen aircrews had spent a month rehearsing short takeoff rolls from dummy flight decks marked on runways. The mission had been given to the Army Air Force's crack pilot and one-time world air-speed record holder, Lieutenant Colonel James Doolittle.

On April 2, 1942, the newly commissioned carrier *Hornet* sailed from San Francisco with Doolittle's crews. Sixteen of the B-25s, modified with extra fuel tanks and a dummy tail gun, were carefully lashed to the flight deck. Sailing through the north Pacific storm zone to avoid detection, a rendezvous had been made between the Aleutians and Midway with Admiral Halsey's *Enterprise*. "Task Force Mike," as it was now code-named, plowed on through the heavy weather toward the launching point some 600 miles west of the coast of Kyushu. The only hitch in an otherwise smooth operation was the adding of an extra day because the planners had overlooked the International Dateline in the timetables.

On the afternoon of April 17, Task Force Mike was twenty-four hours away from launch point and still undetected. The *Hornet*'s deck crews made their final checks of the B-25s as they winched up their bombs, chalked with such messages as: "I don't want to set the world on fire, just Tokyo." That night radar picked up the outermost in the line of Japanese picket patrols. Course was altered, but shortly after 7:30 next morning one enemy craft sighted the task force and its radio alarm was picked up minutes before the vanguard cruisers sank the small auxiliary by gunfire. Doolittle and Halsey decided to go ahead at once with the attack, even at the risk that the additional 100 miles might not leave the bombers enough fuel reserves to make the Chinese mainland. They took the big gamble that although Japan's defenses would now be on the alert, they would not be anticipating a raid that day because the task force was still nearly 700 miles away.

"Launch planes to Lieutenant Col. Doolittle and gallant command. Good luck and God bless you," Halsey signaled the *Hornet* as the carrier turned into the wind shortly before 8 A.M. Klaxons were blaring as the colonel pumped the hand of Captain Mitchener before shouting to his crews, "O.K. fellas, this is it. Let's go!"

Doolittle's bomber was ready to roll—the first time he or any of his fellow pilots had attempted the tricky takeoff from a bucking carrier's flight deck. "The wind and sea were so strong that morning that green water was breaking over the carrier's ramps," Admiral Halsey would recall of those critical moments. "Jimmy led his squadron off. When his plane buzzed down the *Hornet*'s deck at 7:25 there wasn't a man topside in the Task Force who didn't help him get into the air. One pilot hung on the brink of a stall until we nearly catalogued his effects, but the last of the sixteen was airborne by 8:24, and a minute later my duty staff officer was writing in the flag log: 'Changed course and axis 90 degrees, commencing retirement from the area at 25 knots.' "

As the task force turned east, Doolittle led his B-25 Mitchell bombers west into a mission that had been described as "to bomb and fire the industrial heart of Japan." Each of his pilots had been briefed on specific military targets: steel plants, aircraft factories, and power stations. In the event that his plane was damaged, the colonel had told his men he was going to "dive in, full throttle, into any target I can find where the crash will do the most good."

Such suicidal courage was to prove unnecessary two hours later when Doolittle's bomber raced in low over Tokyo Bay. The city was at lunch and the one patrol flight he spotted had failed to raise the alarm. It was his good fortune that the silver barrage balloons which protected the capital against low-flying planes had just been winched down on completion of that morning's practice air-raid alert. Even the flight of nine fighters flying high above him had not yet spotted his dash in over the city's sprawling northern suburbs. "Continued flying low due south over the outskirts of and towards the east center of Tokyo. Pulled up to 1,200 feet, changed course to the southwest and incendiary bombed highly inflammable section," his matter-of-fact log recorded as he dropped his first high-explosive bomb. "Anti-aircraft very active, but only one near hit. Lowered away to house tops and slid over western outskirts into low haze and smoke. Turned south and out to sea."

The sirens were wailing again. In the crowded lunchtime streets and parks, eyes turned skyward as the first bombers raced in. People waved, thinking the Japanese Air Force was putting on a very realistic demonstration. It was only when explosions and smoke began rocking the capital that they knew it was for real. Monitoring Radio Tokyo, American listeners on the retreating carriers realized from the warbling sirens behind the announcer's voice that Doolittle's planes were getting through. Interned in the U.S. Embassy, Ambassador Grew, lunching with the Swiss ambassador, at first refused to believe it was "the real thing." He laid a $100 bet, which he lost when successive explosions followed over the next twenty minutes as ten more American bombers raced overhead. These had been separated from the two leaders by strong winds, but they flew in from all directions, helping to keep up the confusion that paralyzed the Japanese defenses. Simultaneously three other B-25s arrived over Nagoya, Osaka, and Kobe. The stunned fighter controllers took so long to work out where the attack was coming from that they permitted the Americans bombers to escape east out over the China Sea before a pursuit could be organized.

The fifteen attacking B-25s managed to fly on to reach the China coast. One plane, which had diverted with fuel problems, landed at Vladivostok, where its crew was promptly interned by astonished Russians. Darkness, fog, and lack of fuel ruled out any attempt to land on the Nationalists' airfields, which had been alerted to receive them. Doolittle's crews were forced to bail out, but with the aid of Chinese guerillas all but eleven airmen were eventually escorted safely behind the Nationalist lines. Three died in crash landings; eight were captured, interrogated, and tortured. Public fury had been aroused by what the *Asahi Shimbun* under the heading, "ENEMY DEVILS STRAFE SCHOOLYARD," condemned as the "inhuman, insatiable, indiscriminate bombing." The American flyers were tried and sentenced to death. Two pilots and a gunner were executed before Imperial "leniency" commuted the sentences on the others to harsh imprisonment—which only four were to survive.

The raid had done little real damage apart from wrecking ninety buildings and causing the death of fifty civilians. But as the President had foreseen, it scored a direct hit on the morale of the United States. "DOOLITTLE DO'OD IT," proclaimed the Los Angeles *Times*, and Roosevelt added a flourish of mystery by suggesting that the attack had been launched from "Shangri-La," (the secret paradise of James Hilton's novel *Lost Horizon*) to conceal the fact that a carrier had been used. The Japanese had already guessed this, but they took a week to torture it out of their captives. Meanwhile, the Combined Fleet had immediately put to sea in pursuit of the enemy force. Admiral Yamamoto, mortified that his warships had failed to prevent American bombers from violating the sacred airspace over the Imperial Palace, had retreated to his cabin in the flagship, leaving his Chief of Staff to direct the wild-goose chase. Halsey's task force easily avoided pursuing aircraft, warned by radar and navigating through the thick weather fronts. After two days the Imperial Navy abandoned the chase.

The most far-reaching impact of the Tokyo raid was the psychological effect it had on the Imperial General Staff. The generals and admirals had suffered a tremendous loss of face, and their angry over-reaction eventually brought a succession of strategic disasters. The army immediately reduced its front-line air strength on the Chinese mainland to bring back fighter groups for the defense of the home islands. But the members of the naval staff were overwhelmed with a sense of shame. Navy Chief Admiral Nagumo, who had been having second thoughts about the forthcoming Midway operation, now accepted Yamamoto's view that unless priority was given to capturing the mid-Pacific Islands to extend Japan's defensive frontier, the whole of the Imperial Navy would soon be on patrol to prevent future carrier raids on Japan. Two days after the bombing of Tokyo, the Imperial General Staff decided to give the go-ahead to the Combined Fleet to attack Midway. The operation was advanced to the first week of June, to follow hard on the scheduled landing to capture Port Moresby and the establishing of a base in the Solomon Islands. Locking the three invasion operations back to back in a tight schedule that allowed no room for any slippage was to put each at risk. But "victory disease" made the naval staff blindly confident.

The most immediate result of the Tokyo bombing was the army staff's order to the China Expeditionary Force, which sent fifty-three battalions on a punitive expedition against Nationalist-held Chekiang and Kiangsu Provinces. Seven American airmen were to die for their part in the raid, but nearly a quarter of a million Chinese peasants were slaughtered during the next few weeks. A hundred thousand Japanese soldiers rampaged across the countryside, burning, killing, and raping with a savagery that equaled the sacking of Nanking. The severity of the reprisals was a warning to the Nationalists against repeating their cooperation with the bombers. It also soured relations between Chungking and Washington since Chiang Kai-shek had not been asked to give his approval because of fears that his notoriously leaky command would betray the plan. The savagery of the Japanese reprisals was a sharp reminder to the Americans of their fanatical reaction to any assault on the sacred soil.

FIGHTING RETREAT IN BURMA

The Tokyo raid also spurred General Ida to push his 15th Army even harder in Burma to speed up its advance and sever the road over which the Nationalist Chinese were receiving their flow of Lend-Lease supplies. By April 18, 1942, the Japanese had advanced to within 200 miles of Lashio, the little town in the Shan foothills that was the starting point of the Burma Road, down which Chiang Kai-shek was now rushing from China three of his best army divisions. Led to believe that Doolittle's bombers were reinforcements for Colonel Claire Chennault's dwindling band of "Flying Tigers," the Chinese leader was understandably angry when he found that not only were no more available but the U.S. Army 10th Air Force had been sent to India to operate under Wavell's command.

The British were going to need all the support they could get to hold Burma. The attack on their shipping in the Indian Ocean had prevented reinforcements and supplies from reaching General Alexander, now facing the Japanese northward offensive. The speed with which Japan's forces were thrusting toward India encouraged an eruption of civil unrest, giving Gandhi's independence campaign a new momentum. In February, Chiang Kai-shek had flown to India to try to persuade the Mahatma to abandon his campaign in the face of the growing threat from Japan. But Gandhi, venerated as a saint by India's Hindu population, argued the necessity of exploiting the crisis to force the independence issue. "They will never voluntarily treat us as equals," he had told the Generalissimo, striking a sympathetic understanding in Chiang Kai-shek, who had often enough protested his own exclusion from the Supreme Allied War Council.

The following month Gandhi called on the all-India Congress to reject Sir Stafford Cripps's mission promising that the British would consider self-government for India after the war. "Britain must abandon her hold on India," Gandhi proclaimed, insisting that the British presence on the subcontinent was "an invitation to Japan." To the military and civil authorities in New Delhi, the continued intransigence of the India Congress leaders was a menace from within in the face of real external danger.

In the midst of this conflicting political and military turmoil in India and China arrived General Joseph Stilwell. Picked by President Roosevelt to be Chiang's Chief of Staff because his thirteen years of service in China had made him fluent in the language, this leathery warrior, with his "pick up and go" drive, proved to be an excellent fighter but a poor diplomat. He resented the timidity and corruption of the Chinese leaders, especially Chiang Kai-shek, whom he derisorily dubbed "Peanut." At the same time he became frustrated by the "do-nothing" attitude of the "Limeys," so that he was soon battling both Allied commands as well as the Japanese.

Stilwell knew from past experience that Chinese generals had little regard for the fighting qualities of their poorly fed, trained, and equipped peasant soldiers. Yet he remained convinced that good leadership could instill fighting spirit. Lectured by Chiang Kai-shek in "amateur tactics," he rejected the Generalissimo's claim that China's armies could only be committed to the attack if they held a five-to-one majority over the Japanese. Stilwell had arrived in Chungking at the most inauspicious of moments, as Rangoon's capture had panicked the Nationalists with the prospect of the supply line into Burma drying up after the loss of the port that fed it Lend-Lease material. Yet it took Stilwell over a week's argument to persuade Chiang Kai-shek to put the 5th and 6th Chinese armies under his control for the march down to defend Lashio.

Even before the fall of Rangoon had effectively sealed him off from outside help, General Alexander, who had his headquarters at the hill station of Maymyo midway between Lashio and Mandalay, was taking a pessimistic view of the military difficulties that now faced him. He had to mount a defense with ill-equipped troops who were shaken from their recent defeat. Of all the countries they had set out to conquer, the Japanese had counted on receiving the most assistance from the Burmese, who bitterly resented British rule. The "Burma Independent Army" fought alongside the Japanese, and the Buddhist monks in their saffron robes were suspected of passing intelligence to the enemy.

When Stilwell arrived on March 11, 1942, at Maymyo to set up his command post in a Baptist mission, his "anti-Limey" prejudices were aroused by the very Englishness of the colonial summer capital, with its lawns and tree-shaded red-brick mansions dominated by Flagstaff House, the Governor's residence, which now served as British military headquarters. General Alexander, the unshakeable hero of Dunkirk to whom Churchill had given the task of saving Burma, appeared to fit Stilwell's image of a haughty English Guards officer who "Looked me over as if I had just crawled out from under a rock." Among the bevy of smartly turned-out staff officers, only the newly arrived Lieutenant General William Slim impressed the hard-bitten American general as a tough fighter.

Stilwell's mistrust of the British resolve to defend Burma was increased when he heard that their strategy appeared to be directed to holding up the Japanese advance just long enough to open up a route across the Arakan Hills west into India, up which they intended to escape with the remnants of their army and the thousands of refugees. An estimated 900,000 Indians were moving north, a human tide pathetically fleeing from the hostility of the native Burmese who resented them more than the British as alien exploiters. Crowded into camps that were becoming reservoirs of smallpox and cholera, they hampered the movement of the military convoys, being already decimated by two months of attacks by Burmese villagers and marauding Dacoit bandits, as well as the Japanese.

Unlike the British commanders, who had all but resigned themselves to retreat so as to save as many soldiers as possible for the defense of India, Stilwell believed that the commitment of the Chinese armies still made it possible to hold on to upper Burma. Above all, he wanted to retain control of the strategic road to China so that he could carry out his plan to build a new extension westward from Lashio into India—a scheme the British believed was wildly unrealistic.

One thing Alexander and Stilwell could agree on was that Burma's terrain dictated their strategy in expanding the battle. The geography defied communications, except up the three great river valleys that ran north and south. The fall of Rangoon meant conceding the Japanese lower Burma, but as they fell back to defend the north of Burma and the umbilical road to China, the strategic key to the heartland of the country and to their defense was Mandalay. If the enemy succeeded in taking the ancient pagoda-filled capital and communication center, which sprawled on a bend of the upper Irrawaddy River, the British and Chinese armies would find themselves trapped between the towering mountain ranges of the Chindwins to the west and the Himalayas to the east.

When Stilwell arrived, he found the British regrouping their front at Prome on the lower Irrawaddy, 150 miles from Rangoon. He agreed that his Chinese 5th Army would advance to Toungoo on the Sittang River, to throw up a parallel defense line east to west across Burma from the Salween River. A hundred miles to the north were the oilfields on which General Alexander (using makeshift distillation plants) was depending for the fuel needed by his brigade of tanks and hundreds of vehicles. Stilwell and General Slim appreciated that the very length and weakness of their line precluded static defense; but they intended to hold their Prome-Toungoo front long enough to launch a counteroffensive. This hope was quickly dashed because Chiang Kai-shek was hesitant to commit more reinforcements to the Toungoo front, where only a single Chinese division was in place.

Then, on March 22, a two hundred bomber Japanese air strike against the airstrips in central Burma in retaliation for a raid the previous day on Rangoon, caught many planes on the ground and destroyed Allied airpower. Chennault flew out his surviving Flying Tigers to the other side of the Himalayas, while the remnants of the RAF crossed to India. Outnumbered on the ground, the Japanese now controlled the skies, further demoralizing the British forces. "Any aircraft we saw in the sky was hostile—and we were to see many," Slim recorded as the Japanese struck his lines again and again: "great wedges of silver bombers droned across the sky and one after another the cities of Burma spurted with flames and vanished into roaring holocausts."

The Japanese piled on the pressure against the weak center of the Allied line, where the one division of Chinese at Toungoo was guarding the road and rail line up the Sittang River. This 200th Division was fighting without support from the rest of the army because Chiang Kai-shek's generals were finding every excuse—from too many enemy planes to too few railcars—to delay committing their main force to the battle. "The pusillanimous bastards," Stilwell raged in his diary, frustrated that "Peanut" had, by refusing him the Vermillion Seal, enabled his subordinates to insist on appealing orders from Chungking. "I can't shoot them; I can't relieve them, and just talking to them does no good."

The failure of the Chinese generals to advance the main body of their 5th and 6th armies into the battle ended the Allies' attempt to hold their front across central Burma. Toungoo was on the verge of falling by the end of March, when Alexander ordered Slim to take pressure off the Chinese by attacking south from Prome, where the 17th Indian and Burma Division still held the line at the Irrawaddy River. The counterthrust collapsed after it had been "hooked" by the Japanese, with the loss of ten irreplaceable tanks. Now General Alexander saw there was no alternative but to abandon the whole defensive front.

April 1 saw the beginning of the month-long withdrawal, with the British pulling north from Prome up the Irrawaddy as the Chinese fell back along the Sittang from Toungoo after losing 3,000 men and most of their equipment. The retreat coincided with the driest weeks in the parched and barren hills of central Burma. Temperatures soared to 115 degrees and a desperate shortage of water plagued the Allied soldiers, who were constantly fighting rearguard actions under harassing attacks from the air. Moving troops by truck kept the British on the dusty roads and gave the enemy the advantage of infiltrating around their flanks to trap the retreating columns with roadblocks.

Progress was made agonizingly slow by the thousands of refugees straggling along by bullock cart and on foot. It was to become a nightmare ordeal for the parched and weary soldiers of Slim's command, already down to starvation rations of corned beef, rice, and hardtack biscuits so full of weevils that the men joked about their "Vitamin W." British troops were in the minority. The "Burma Corps" was made up mostly of Indians from the 17th Division, Gurkhas, and those native hill tribesmen who had remained with the Burma Division when many of their lowland countrymen deserted. It was General Slim's long service with native regiments in India that enabled him to hold his increasingly demoralized force together. Yet even he recognized the impossibility of carrying out General Alexander's scheme to join up with the Chinese forces some 100 miles north of Prome at Taunggyi, to make a stand to defend the oilfields and block the road to Mandalay.

The 40-mile-wide front that Slim and Stilwell sought to throw across the arid hill country was too thinly defended. Communications between the British and the Chinese were virtually nonexistent; getting their ally to hold a position was, as Slim observed, "like enticing a shy sparrow to perch on your windowsill." The Japanese relentlessly attacked, infiltrating through the weakly defended line to attack from the rear. By April 14, Slim was told that his front was again crumbling and that a retreat north of the oilfields was now inevitable. He gave orders for demolition of the oil installations to begin. Against a backdrop of blazing fires from the wellheads and storage tanks of the Burma Oil Company at Yenangyaung, Slim's weary soldiers resumed their retreat north, just ahead of the Japanese advance. On the night of April 16, the enemy outflanked them to cut off their escape with a roadblock. Unable to break through the strong Japanese force that had encircled them, for two days the desperate soldiers fought frantically until they escaped the trap with the help of the Chinese 38th Division. This valiant effort proved to Stilwell and the British—who awarded General Sun Li-jen an OBE—how staunchly their ally could fight when well led.

Breaking out from the Japanese encirclement at Yenangyaung cost Slim his remaining tanks, much of his artillery, and most of his transport. Now with half his command in danger of being cut off on the east bank of the Irrawaddy, he had somehow to improvise the defense of Mandalay. Its loss was foreseen by General Alexander on April 18 as he ordered Slim to keep open a line of withdrawal across the Chindwin River to the west. At the same time he wanted to give "paramount consideration" to keeping contact with the Chinese armies to the east: "They must be given no grounds for accusing the British of running away into India."

The Japanese allowed no time to put this plan into effect. While the British front was being rolled up the Irrawaddy, the other thrust of the 15th Army was battering down on the 5th Chinese Army at Pyinmana on the Sittang and another blasted the 6th Army up the slopes of the Karen Hills over the Salween River.

"We are taking a beating, I think," Stilwell recorded in his diary entry for April 16. He had been frantically trying to get Chiang Kai-shek to put pressure on his generals to reinforce the front, only to be exasperated by "Peanut's" orders insisting that his troops be given water melons to make them fight better. Those units which had arrived were so hopelessly strung out that when the main Japanese offensive developed on the night of April 20, the 55th Division of the Chinese Army was so badly smashed its survivors simply melted into the Karen Hills. "It was the God-damndest thing I ever saw," a shocked Stilwell confessed to a war correspondent.

The way was now open for the Japanese to advance up through Meiktila to Lashio to sever the Burma Road. Furious that a fresh Chinese division arrived only hours after the enemy had moved north to Taunggyi on April 24, Stilwell offered a 50,000-rupee reward to his men before personally leading them to recapture the key hill station—only to find that the Japanese had already flanked him and were racing north up the 150-mile road to Lashio with motor transport.

The Japanese had broken through the Allies' eastern front to grasp their strategic objective of cutting the Burma Road. On the western front, the British position was also being shaken apart as Slim pulled his forces back to within 100 miles of Mandalay. General Alexander held his final conference with Stilwell on April 25 as bombs fell just yards away. The British had decided they must withdraw over the Irrawaddy and head for India before their army was trapped by the Japanese thrust moving toward Mandalay. Stilwell, unwilling to give up control of at least part of the overland communications with China, chose to retreat north with the three Chinese army divisions still under his command, toward the railhead at Myitkyina. "God, if we can only get those 100,000 Chinese to India, we'll have something," he wrote, rallied by permission from Chungking to take his three armies across the border for rearming and retraining in Assam.

General Slim's ambitions were more realistic—and immediate. He had to beat the enemy advance up the Chindwin River to get his 13,000 remaining troops west across the Chin Hills onto the frontier of India.

On April 30, the Japanese advance column entered Lashio, cutting the land route into China and forcing back up into the northern mountain passes the two divisions of Chinese reinforcements on their way to defend the city. That evening saw the last of the straggling refugees and British rearguard crossing the Ava Bridge, whose broad girders spanned the wide Irrawaddy south of Mandalay. With the bomb-blasted pagodas of the city now abandoned to the enemy, it was just before midnight when Slim gave the orders to detonate the demolition charges that had been in place since the beginning of February: "With a resounding thump it was blown at 23.50 hours on April 30th and its centre span fell neatly into the river—a sad sight and a signal that we had lost Burma."

The grinding retreat lay northwest up the tortuous Chindwin Valley. Hampered by the ragged columns of refugees and by trucks that ran out of fuel, frequently breaking down on the rutted cart tracks, Slim's weary army fought stubborn rearguard actions for over 100 miles, under continuous attacks from aircraft. Reaching the Shwegyin on May 5, five days and nights of ferrying brought the thousands of troops and refugees across the Chindwin while the Gurkhas held off the Japanese vanguard. On May 10, when the enemy broke through, the final shots were exchanged as the Gurkhas withdrew into the jungle along the Kalewa River gorge. Escape now carried the exhausted army on a 90-mile trek up the steamy Kabaw Valley as the first monsoon rains began. The ground turned into mud and the malarial mosquitoes became a plague to the quinine-starved soldiers in what they named the "Valley of Death."

Finally, on May 16, Slim's advance column began straggling through the small town of Tamu in Assam Province. Twelve thousand soldiers eventually reached India to complete the longest retreat in British military history. Over 13,000 English, Indian, Burmese, and Gurkha soldiers had lost their lives in fighting the 900-mile withdrawal, which had brought the death of more than three quarters of a million refugees.

General Alexander nonetheless would be able to report that though his troops' uniforms might be ragged and their condition emaciated from the long march, more than half still carried their weapons and their fighting spirit was unbroken. This was a tribute to his imperturbable generalship and that of "Bill" Slim, whose rugged soldiering had saved the disaster from turning into a total catastrophe. Reformed and re-equipped, the troops would soon be joining the defense of India. Alexander confidently promised when he relinquished his command on May 20, 1942: "Of course we shall take Burma back; it is part of the British Empire."

While Alexander and Slim had managed a near miracle in getting most of the British Army out of Burma intact, General Stilwell's plans to bring 100,000 Chinese soldiers to the defense of India had been dogged with disaster from the start. His decision to speed the evacuation of three remaining divisions up the 250-mile railway line was frustrated when General Lo Cho-ying commandeered an engine at gunpoint to make his own escape. It crashed into an uncoming train, blocking the single track railroad. "That fat turtle egg," he raged at his Chinese deputy's bungling, as he tried in vain to get together enough trucks to move his army past the jam. One of the first American transport planes that Roosevelt had promised Chiang Kai-shek to keep open an aerial supply line had flown into Swebo airstrip as the Japanese intensified their barrage. "General Arnold sent us to rescue you, sir," the C-47's pilot reported. "Vinegar Joe" would have none of it. Instead, he set out north to try to reach Myitkyina before the enemy. But the route north was choked with the oxcarts of refugees and his vehicles kept breaking down on the rough roads.

By May 5, Stilwell, realizing that the Japanese would beat him to it, decided that he would strike out on foot for India. With 20 mules, his 114-strong party, including an American Baptist doctor and 19 Burmese nurses, set out west on May 7 to cross the Chindwin. For five days they marched through the jungle along elephant trails, eking out their half-rations with grasses and plants until they reached Homalin, and making the last part of the journey downstream on rafts. On May 13 they crossed the wide Chindwin River—just thirty-six hours ahead of the Japanese— to face the final 50-mile march up through the jungle-clad peaks into India.

On May 14, the sixty-year-old three-star general, whose indomitable willpower and lashing tongue had driven his band of stragglers over the most arduous stage of their long flight without losing a single person, finally reached Assam. Stilwell's epic feat of endurance had made him famous, but "Vinegar Joe" was under no illusions about the magnitude of the defeat the Allied cause had suffered. Of the 100,000 Chinese troops he hoped to lead out, fewer than 10,000 were eventually to reach India. "I got a hell of a beating," he told reporters at New Delhi, before flying back to Chungking to rally Chiang Kai-shek to continue the war. "We got out of Burma and it was humiliating as hell. I think we ought to find out what caused it and go back and retake it."

14
The Hidden Victory

April had been the fourth successive month of military defeat for the Allies. The only relief from what Churchill called the "cataract of disaster" that continued to flood over the Far East was the bombing of Tokyo. This had briefly cheered American spirits, but the Joint Chiefs of Staff, like the Imperial General Staff, saw it as little more than a propaganda raid. They were both to be proved wrong. In the months that followed, Doolittle's raid would prove to have initiated a chain of events through which the United States found the opportunity to dam the tide of Japanese conquest.

The bombing of Tokyo had stirred the Imperial Navy to overreact and send out nearly every warship in the Combined Fleet. This generated a vast amount of radio signal traffic, which gave the U.S. Navy the chance to win an unexpected yet crucial secret victory. Although they lacked the naval strength to match Japan's, they enjoyed an enormous advantage in the clandestine electronic war—the key to tactical supremacy in the vast reaches of the Pacific battleground. This intelligence provided the vital clues that would reveal how the "victory disease" was impelling the Japanese to disperse their overwhelming superiority in support of too many operations across too great a distance. Forewarned of the weakness in the enemy strategy, Admiral Nimitz would be able to concentrate his limited naval strength against each move in turn, and so disrupt Japan's intended advance south and west into the Pacific.

The Combined Fleet's frenzied pursuit of Admiral Halsey's retreating task force added thousands of pieces to the intelligence jigsaw that was being laboriously put together to uncover Japan's moves in her Second Operational Phase. Picked up out of the air by the listeners manning the chain of radio posts that ringed the Pacific from Alaska to Australia, the stream of ciphered messages was fed by teleprinter to the team of code-breakers working for Commander Laurence F. Safford's OP20G unit in Washington's Naval Headquarters (NEGAT) and to Lieutenant Commander Joseph Rochefort's smaller outfit working at Pearl Harbor as the Pacific Fleet Combat Intelligence Unit (HYPO).

In the five months since the war began, they had been battling night and day to penetrate the five-digit groups of the Japanese Navy's main operational code, which had been labeled JN (Japanese Navy) No. 25. Special secure "Comb" signal wavelengths were set aside from routine traffic so that Pearl Harbor, Brisbane, and Naval Intelligence in Washington could exchange a continuous flow of intercept information as they searched for patterns in messages. It was a process requiring painstaking skill and intuition on the part of the decrypting teams, multiple filing systems, and batteries of IBM tabulating machines fed with stacks of punched cards. The clues to cracking the code groups were fished from similarities and recurring patterns in the two-letter place designator codes, date-time groups, ships' and commanders' call signs, and the identifying "signature" of a Morse Code sender's fist. This information was recorded on 5 by 8 paper sheets referred to by the HYPO team as "cards," which were stored in stacks of open boxes for ready access. The first batch of important clues was assembled from the air group and ship call sign groups listed in papers salvaged from a plane that had been shot down over Pearl Harbor on December 7.

The actual process of unraveling the messages was a laborious task that relied on human ingenuity assisted by the trial-and-error processing of the IBM machines. The JN25 code, unlike the mechanically enciphered diplomatic traffic that was broken by the Purple "black boxes," was a traditional cypher generated from two code books. There was a "dictionary" volume containing columns of 45,000 randomly selected five-digit groups such as 43752 65739 14268 88221 73923. Each set was ascribed to a particular word or operational phrase in "Kana"—the phonetic version of the Japanese ideograms—into which the message was translated. Before transmission, each group was added to successive similar five-digit groups from a second book. All the groups were divisible by three, to make it easy to check for garbles; so, therefore, were their sums. Before a message was sent by Morse Code, it was prefixed by a key that referred to the page, column, and line the recipient had to look up in the second book in order to lay bare the coded message, which could then be translated by reference to the "dictionary."

The vast quantity of intercepted signal traffic that flooded in during the three days the Japanese were on their wild-goose chase was a bonanza for the codebreakers at station NEGAT in Washington and HYPO at Pearl Harbor. Not only did the tell-tale call signs betray that virtually every warship in Yamamoto's command was at sea, but because the purpose of the huge operation was known, valuable insight was provided into the meaning of many five-digit groups. This added considerably to the "dictionary" of the JN25 code that the American analysts had been compiling over the five months during which the Japanese had persisted in using the same "B" version of their cipher. To preserve security, the Tokyo Naval Staff had originally intended to replace the two code books on April 1. But they were so confident that their two-layer cipher was unbreakable that, in another manifestation of "victory disease," the changeover was postponed until May 1, and then again until June 1 because of problems in getting out the new "dictionary" book to every ship.

This allowed U.S. Naval Intelligence to become familiar enough with the JN25 B fleet code by the end of April to be routinely penetrating up to one twentieth of all intercepted messages. These, taken along with the information gleaned from the more easily broken code traffic began to produce a clearing picture of the enemy dispositions and intentions. On March 25, a signal to Air Groups containing the RZP campaign suggested that MO was the designator for Port Moresby at the tip of New Guinea and RZQ the nearby seaplane base, which was getting a lot of mentions in traffic that seemed to suggest the Japanese were moving south. This was confirmed by a vital clue deciphered from a message sent a week after the Tokyo raid, which requested 1,000 copies of documents for use in the attack plan as well as a complete map section of Australia. Three days later a message was decoded that clearly stated: "THE OBJECTIVE OF MO WILL BE FIRST TO RESTRICT THE ENEMY FLEET MOVEMENTS AND WILL BE AC-COMPLISHED BY MEANS OF ATTACKS ALONG THE NORTH COAST OF AUSTRALIA." Throughout the month as the volume of traffic focusing on Rabaul increased, it was plain that an accelerating flow of planes, shipping, and troops was building up for a southward thrust toward Australia.

A central role in building up this interpretation through codebreaking and informed guesswork to fit in the missing pieces of the intelligence puzzle was being played by Joseph J. Rochefort, who had a superlative memory for detail and a deep intuitive knowledge built up over years of studying Japanese naval operations and language. He was the leader and principal inspiration of the team of eight hand-picked cryptanalysts at Pearl Harbor's station HYPO, which had worked up a special skill in cracking the Japanese fleet code. Their unique ability won Nimitz's confidence, and he came more and more to rely on their information as his secret weapon in the most critical phase of the Pacific War.

"You don't have to be crazy—but it helps" was the notice pinned to the wall over the desk manned by Lieutenant Commander T. H. Dyer, which was permanently buried under a confusing pile of scribbled notes, intercepts, and tabulating machine printouts. Metal-rimmed spectacles perched over a neat moustache, Rochefort's chief assistant had the quizzical air of an absent-minded mathematics professor. The bizarre atmosphere in which his eight-officer team worked, with the assistance of the dispossessed musicians of the battleship *California*'s band, was typified by their chief's fondness for working in carpet slippers and a stained crimson velvet smoking jacket. "Sealed off from the rest of the world like a sub-marine," was how one member recalled the round-the-clock intensity of working against the ceaseless chatter of tabulating machines and tele-printers under harsh fluorescent lighting in the windowless basement chamber beneath Pearl Harbor's new Administration Building. The un-varying temperature of the air-conditioned environment, where the time of day lost any meaning, led to jokes that the only fresh air arrived in the pockets of visitors. These were very few because armed sentries stood guard before the single door marked simply: "Combat Intelligence Unit."

During the critical weeks of 1942, Dyer shared a twenty-four-hour duty with Rochefort, who often stayed in the chamber for days at a time, sustaining himself on a diet of sandwiches and coffee; sleeping on a cot between the IBM machines. The concentration of human and mechanical effort at HYPO was matched by that of the NEGAT team in Washington and the CAST codebreakers, attached to MacArthur's command, who were rechristened BELCONNEN when they set up new headquarters in Australia.

The combined work of these three units had already enabled the Pacific Fleet's carrier task force to carry out raids with the help of intercepted Japanese over-the-target weather reports. Radio intelligence had also led to the mining of French Frigate Shoals (reefs located between Hawaii and Midway) after the task force had located the enemy tender that had refuelled the seaplanes that raided Oahu in March. The Japanese were in for a nasty surprise if they sent another tender to that anchorage.

The output of Rochefort's team was assembled into an overall picture of Japanese naval movements by the Pacific Fleet's intelligence staff, led by Lieutenant Commander Edwin T. Layton. When Nimitz took over command he had retained this promising young officer, recognizing his talent for nosing out from day to day what the enemy would do next. This he encapsulated in the daily CINCPAC *Intelligence Bulletin*, trans-mitted in code to all ships and bases. Layton based his analysis not just on the decrypted signal traffic, but on the quantity and origination of radio traffic, in conjunction with his experience from duty tours in the Far East which provided him with a unique ability to see the Pacific from the Japanese perspective.

More than a month before the Doolittle raid set out for Tokyo, it was Layton and his staff who had pieced together the scattered clues emerging from the signal intercepts to predict a developing Japanese naval thrust toward the Bismarck Archipelago and New Guinea within days of the first operational orders being sent out by the Imperial Navy Command. It was emerging that the enemy's intention was to deploy several carriers, the South Seas Army Divisions, and the 25th Air Flotilla to launch a major offensive. "The Japanese are now in a position to strike Port Moresby and Tulagi simultaneously," the Pacific Fleet War Diary noted on April 3.

Three weeks later the NEGAT team in Washington had decyphered the orders sent to Admiral Inouye, the Japanese 4th Fleet Commander, revealing to the Americans that Operation MO would begin when the two carriers detached from Admiral Nagumo's strike force, returning from the Indian Ocean, reached the Truk base in the Marshalls.

THE SOUTHWARD THRUST

Admiral Nimitz had less than two weeks in which to concentrate his force to check the advance toward Australia when he called his staff together to plan a response. Layton reported that the landings in the New Guinea–New Britain–Solomons area were scheduled to begin on or about May 3. He predicted they would involve invasion forces of 20,000 troops, covered by several hundred land-based aircraft and a force of cruisers, in addition to the two 5th Division carriers and a new light carrier he identified as the *Ryukaku*. The enemy objective appeared to be to extend control from their New Guinea bases at Lae and Salamaua to Port Moresby at the tip of the Papuan Peninsula. This advance was to be followed by a move into the Solomons to command the Coral Sea approach to Australia and to provide an air base from which to launch an advance south to Noumea in New Caledonia and on to Fiji to threaten to sever the sea route to the United States.

Nimitz was determined to block the Japanese advance down the Solomons, which could threaten his forward base at Efate as well as a new one planned at Noumea. Like Admiral King, he saw the strategic island chain as a two-way road: a highway up which the United States could also advance to strike at Rabaul and launch the offensive against Japan's southern perimeter of island bases. The scale of the coming assault could only be deflected by the full strength of the Pacific Fleet. Lacking advanced bases and sufficient oilers to operate the seven slow battleships that had joined the Pacific Fleet after Pearl Harbor, Nimitz took the bold decision to send them back to the West Coast, to conserve fuel. He decided that the Japanese advance had to be blocked with the four carrier task forces.

Assured by Layton that "nothing appears to be heading for Hawaii yet," the Pacific Fleet Commander took an even bolder decision to leave Oahu's defense wide open by sending out all his carriers to reinforce the *Yorktown* of Admiral Fletcher's Task Force 17 in the Coral Sea. Rear Admiral Aubrey Fitch relieved Admiral Brown as commander of Task Force 11, and the *Lexington* sailed west on April 3. It would be another two weeks before Admiral Halsey—then on his way back from the Tokyo raid—could be replenished to steam west to join them. Nonetheless, Nimitz was willing to accept the risk that only the two advance carriers might have to meet the superior enemy force, telling his staff, "we should be able to accept odds in battle if necessary." He counted on the fact that his carriers loaded more aircraft and that American resourcefulness would shorten the unfavorable odds. When the plan for a naval confrontation in the Coral Sea had been completed, he flew to the West Coast to get approval from Admiral King, since sending all the Pacific Fleet's strength over 3,500 miles from Hawaii was a dramatic reversal of their post-Pearl Harbor naval strategy.

In the conference room in 12th Naval District Headquarters in San Francisco's Federal Building, King and Nimitz along with their senior staff conducted an intensive review of Pacific strategy on April 25. The prime concern was to preserve the secrecy of the radio intelligence on which their Pacific operations were now so vitally dependent if they were to succeed in hitting the enemy hard and putting the U.S. Navy on the initiative in the Pacific. King agreed that the strategic necessity of denying Japan control of the Coral Sea and the Solomons—which he saw as the starting point of his offensive—demanded the commitment of the entire Pacific Fleet's carrier strength. This was taking a very considerable risk, for with the *Wasp* and the *Ranger* in the Atlantic, Nimitz would only be left with the refitting *Saratoga* in reserve until the next year, when it was hoped that the first of the new *Essex* carriers were to be commissioned. Both admirals decided to trust to the accuracy of their intelligence.

Surprisingly, Admiral King seemed less concerned with the enormous risk they were running than with his persistent campaign to rid Pearl Harbor of "defeatists and pessimists," among whom he included Admiral Fletcher, who was due to command the task forces in the Coral Sea until Admiral Halsey arrived. A week earlier COMINCH had fired off a blistering signal querying whether Fletcher was "retiring from enemy to provision" after Task Force 17 reported that it was heading to Noumea to refuel. King, wrongly as it turned out, believed that Fletcher should have been on his way to raid Rabaul. Putting provisioning before pressing the attack against the enemy indicated a lack of aggressiveness that the Commander in Chief had made plain the previous month to Task Force 11 when he ordered Vice Admiral Wilson to delay his return to replenish at Pearl Harbor and feed his crew on hardtack if necessary. Constantly overstretched during the early months of 1942, the task forces ranging across the South Pacific were frequently reduced to a monotonous diet of beans and spaghetti, and ships' companies raffled steaks when their meat stores were nearly empty.

The southwestern Pacific was assuming such strategic importance that King agreed to appoint Vice Admiral Robert Ghormley, due to be relieved by Admiral Stark in London, to command the new area under Nimitz. However, it would be mid-May before he could cross the ocean to establish headquarters, and MacArthur was already protesting that his

Naval Commander, Admiral Leary, should be given control of all operations. The general had provoked the wrath of Churchill for persuading Prime Minister Curtin to demand at least two Royal Navy carriers and first call on reinforcements on their way out to the Middle East. Then reports circulating in the Australian newspapers about a forthcoming offensive in New Guinea, leaked by MacArthur, sent King raging to Marshall that his general was endangering the whole naval intelligence operation.

The Japanese paid little attention to the speculation in the Sidney *Morning Herald*. This was evident when Nimitz flew back to Pearl Harbor on April 28 to put Operation Plan No. 23–42 into effect and Layton reported no change discernible in Operation MO, which had now been extended to take in the phosphate islands of Ocean and Naru after Port Moresby was seized. The second occupation force had been directed to move simultaneously to a destination code-named RZ, which the HYPO team had fixed as Tulagi on Florida Island in the mid-Solomons.

The U.S. Navy's ability to martial sufficient forces to halt the Japanese advance toward Australia was now at risk because King's adoption of the opportunistic Tokyo raid strategy had made it unlikely that all Nimitz's carriers could be concentrated for a fleet action in the Coral Sea. When Admiral Halsey's replenished *Enterprise* and *Yorktown* finally sailed from Pearl Harbor on April 30, 1942, his orders were "to check further advance of the enemy into the New Guinea–Solomon area." But he knew he might not make his rendezvous with Fletcher before the Japanese attacked.

On that very day, 4,000 miles across the Pacific, two Japanese transports escorted by destroyers were already steaming across the Solomon Sea bound for Tulagi. The carriers *Zuikaku* and *Shokaku* put out from Truk to cover that landing, which was scheduled for May 3, before steaming into the Coral Sea to support Operation MO. The next day the Port Moresby invasion force of eleven transports, carrying the South Seas detachment of the Imperial Army, sailed from Rabaul with a close support of three cruisers, the small carrier *Shoho*, and Rear Admiral Goto's four heavy cruisers.

Admiral Inouye's Fourth Fleet headquarters at Truk was now committed to a tight timetable that required the completion of both operations by May 10 because the two fleet carriers had to return to rejoin the Combined Fleet for Yamamoto's June 1 Midway offensive. In the rush to execute his operation, there was no time left for the carriers to strike the airfields in north Australia so as to win air superiority over the Coral Sea. Moreover, Japanese intelligence had provided a very incomplete idea of Allied naval dispositions. They could only assume that since they believed the *Lexington* had been sunk by their submarines in January, the three carriers supposed to have taken part in raiding Tokyo must be back at Hawaii. Admiral Inouye's final prediction, as his seven units sailed to execute this complex series of operations on both sides of the Coral Sea, was: "It is not likely that powerful enemy forces are in the area." Yet his whole strategy was vitally dependent on surprise.

That essential element had already been lost when first confirmation that the Japanese plan was actually moving forward came on April 28. The Australian Coast Watching Service reported that a Japanese transport and flying boats had established an advance base at Shortland in the upper Solomons. The lookout organization had been set up during World War I to guard against German raiders; it had been revived, coordinated by officers of the Royal Australian Navy. White settlers and natives were formed into an extensive network of secret lookout radio posts in the Solomons and other islands scattered across the Bismarck Sea. A few days later they were radioing more sighting reports of the Japanese invasion force as it steamed south past New Georgia. On May 2, the fifty Australian servicemen manning the seaplane base at Tulagi were evacuated.

Unknown to the Japanese, their whole plan was laid bare during the first three days of May when most of the final operational instructions were broken, such as the one which commenced: "IF THE ENEMY STRIKING FORCE IS DETERMINED TO BE IN ———, THE MO STRIKING FORCE WILL OPERATE AS FOLLOWS PASS (NORTH NORTHEAST?) OF RX THENCE SOUTH; AT 0600 ON 5 MAY. . . ." A map of the Coral Seas area had been laid out on the makeshift operational plot at CINCPAC headquarters in Pearl Harbor. Overlaid with tracing paper and pinned to a sheet of plywood resting on two sawhorses, the staff marked in orange pencil lines the progress of the enemy naval forces. Advancing to "RZ," a track led out from Rabaul through the Solomon Sea to Florida Island. Heading south from Truk were the twin orange lines of Admiral Takagi's two carriers and Admiral Goto's heavy cruiser squadron. The predicted course of the Port Moresby invasion force wound out from Rabaul through the Louisiade Passage to the tip of Papua. Blue pencil indicated the converging American units. Heading west from Hawaii, but still nearly 2,000 miles away, was Admiral Halsey's two-carrier task force. Converging on a rendezvous marked "Point Buttercup" in the Coral Sea, some 250 miles west of the New Hebrides, was the track plotted for Admiral Fitch's *Lexington*, to join up with the *Yorktown* under Admiral Fletcher to become Combined Task Force 17. Steaming up from the east were the two Australian cruisers of Admiral Crace's force, to be reinforced by the heavy cruisers *Chicago* and *Perkins*, dispatched from Hawaii.

Admiral Inouye had no advance warning, as Operation MO began, that it had attracted such a great concentration of Allied seapower, now bearing down on the Coral Sea in an all-out bid to block Japan's southward advance. For the next six months this emerald ocean with its palm-fringed islands was to be a bloody battleground for a series of clashes that would decide the fate of the Pacific War.

THE BATTLE OF THE CORAL SEA

The first of the battles began shaping up on May 3, when the alarm flashed out from MacArthur's Melbourne headquarters that the Japanese had taken Florida Island. Admiral Nimitz was on his way back to Pearl Harbor to oversee the confrontation after a flying visit to inspect Midway's defenses. Even as it began, Japan's tightly scheduled naval operation started falling apart. Takagi's carriers, which should have been providing aircover for the invasion force, were then 500 miles to the north, refueling after being delayed by bad weather, which had prevented them from flying off fighters to reinforce Rabaul. Admiral Fletcher was still over 100 miles west from Point Buttercup when he received news that the enemy was landing at Tulagi. "This was the kind of report we had been waiting for for a month," he wrote, as he broke off his own refueling and ordered 27 knots, setting course north for the mid-Solomons. Observing strict radio silence, he dispatched a destroyer to find Admiral Fitch, whose task force was again refueling, to arrange a new rendezvous for the next day.

Dawn on May 4 brought the *Yorktown* some 100 miles southwest of Guadalcanal, undiscovered by Japanese reconnaissance seaplanes because of a wide belt of cloudy weather lying like a thick curtain across the Coral Sea. Briefed from old copies of the *National Geographic*, the carrier pilots made a series of strikes against the enemy force lying off Tulagi, smashing up the seaplanes and sending back exaggerated reports of the number of warships sunk, which led Fletcher to radio a jubilant victory report to Pearl Harbor.

Nimitz's "congratulations" proved to be premature. The so-called Battle of Tulagi would later be reassessed as "certainly disappointing in terms of ammunition expended to the results obtained." Conditions had been perfect for the American dive bombers and Wildcat fighters that had broken through the cloud front over Guadalcanal. But the pilots failed to coordinate attacks, and the fogging of their windshields as they dived from the cold air of 17,000 feet to the moist lower layer had spoiled their aim. Only one destroyer, a minelayer, and a single transport had been sunk. The surprise attack did, however, force the evacuation of the landing force. Just one small garrison was left behind when Admiral Inouye found that Takagi's carriers were too far away to lend support. The local force commander's urgent appeals for help had brought Admiral Goto's heavy cruisers, with the light carrier *Shoho*, rushing westward. He arrived that afternoon off Guadalcanal only to find that the Americans had vanished southeast into the murky weather front.

Cloaked by the heavy clouds, Fletcher rendezvoused with Admiral Crace's heavy cruisers on May 6 joining up with the *Lexington* and refueling again. The latest intelligence from Pearl Harbor indicated that the Port Moresby invasion force with two carriers providing aircover would be heading through the Louisiades next day. Fletcher accordingly set course west across the Coral Sea to lay an ambush off the Jomard Passage.

Around midday, air patrols from Port Moresby spotted Admiral Goto's force escorting a transport convoy through that same patch of sea. Ahead were the advance units of the Operation MO invasion force, on their way to establish a forward seaplane base at Deboyne Island off the tip of Papua. An oversight at MacArthur's headquarters prevented the news that a light carrier was with them from being radioed on to Task Force 11. Nor was Fletcher aware that he had been sighted that forenoon by a prowling Japanese float plane.

The report that not one, but two, enemy carriers were steaming to intercept his Port Moresby invasion fleet caused near panic at Admiral Inouye's Rabaul headquarters. Orders flashed out to the transports to check their advance while Takagi's carriers and Goto's heavy cruisers dealt with the Americans. Fortunately for Fletcher, the alarm did not reach the Japanese strike force until the afternoon. Takagi was refueling south of Guadalcanal, so by the time he got under way to close the range enough to launch an air strike, his planes ran into the thick weather front. He therefore decided to finish refueling and resume the chase at first light.

If Admiral Fletcher had known that less than 100 miles separated him from the enemy forces during that night of May 6 he might have been more hesitant at dawn when he split his task force. His battle plan had sent Admiral Crace to head west to guard the southern exit from the Louisiades, while his main force set a northerly course to blockade the entrance to the Jomard Passage. When May 7 dawned, Admiral Hara, the carrier commander of Takagi's force, decided to concentrate his resumed search for the American task force to the south. His hunch appeared rewarded just after 7:30 A.M. when scouting planes reported sighting a carrier and a cruiser. Assuming this must be the enemy's task force, a full strike was flown off the *Shokaku* and *Zuikaku*. Only after they had roared in over the two ships were the Japanese pilots dismayed to find that what had been reported as a carrier was an oil tanker, and the cruiser was nothing bigger than a destroyer. The oiler *Neosho* and her escort *Sims*, ordered by Fletcher to wait safely in the rear, now had an hour's respite as the attacking planes flew off in search of the main task force. They returned at midday to deal with the two American ships. The *Sims*'s gunners managed to fend off the first wave of attackers for a few minutes, then three groups of dive bombers simultaneously screamed down. Wrenched in half by exploding bombs, the destroyer sank in less than sixty seconds. Seven hits and an avalanche of near misses curtained the *Neosho* with fountains of water, as she was set ablaze, convincing the Japanese pilots that she was foundering. Firefighters doused the fires, however, and the oiler managed to float for four days until she was found by a rescue destroyer. The survivors of the *Sims* were to face ten terrible days clinging to life rafts, an ordeal that only sixty-eight survived.

"Much chagrin" was the Japanese reaction to the loss of six planes and the morning's strike on such insignificant targets. Fletcher had wasted his opportunity on a similar error of judgment. Two hours after dawn, when one of *Lexington*'s patrols north of the Louisiades had reported sighting two carriers and four heavy cruisers, he ordered off a full air strike against what he took to be the main enemy force. It was not until the ninety-three American aircraft were well on their way to the target that the reconnaissance flight landed back on the *Lexington* to report that it had only found two light cruisers and two gunboats. These had been magnified into a striking force through a coding error. It was too late to recall the attacking planes, which were heading away at 90 degrees from the direction of the main danger threatening Task Force 17. Fletcher's luck, however, was to hold. The Japanese float planes had glimpsed his force, but their radio signals had not been picked up by Takagi's carriers, whose own aircraft were engaged until mid-afternoon with attacking the *Sims* and the *Neosho*. The alarm had been picked up by Admiral Goto. He now stood-off the Port Moresby transport convoy safely to the north, where it could be protected by land aircover from Rabaul. Captain Ishumosuke Izawa of the *Shoho* was ordered to refuel his fighters and send out an immediate air strike against the American task force.

Less than 100 miles away to the southeast, only the weather and good fortune had saved Fletcher from being caught with most of his aircraft too far away to defend his carriers. A patrolling American bomber from the Townsville base sighted the *Shoho* through a break in the cloud cover as the deck crews were refueling her fighters. Minutes later, at 11 A.M., a pilot of the *Lexington*'s air group, led by Commander W. B. Ault, spotted the enemy task force 30 miles below his starboard wing. Diving in from 15,000 feet, Ault's attack swept aside the two Zero fighters that managed to get off the deck of the *Shoho* to intercept them. The torpedo bombers failed to score any hits, but they had the satisfaction of seeing near misses blow five Japanese aircraft overboard.

Captain Izawa now made the error of turning the *Shoho* into the wind, to try to launch his remaining planes. The reaction was understandable, but it made the carrier an easy target as she steered a steady course for those few vital minutes while the *Lexington*'s dive bombers came in. They were followed by the first group of torpedo-carrying aircraft from the *Yorktown*, summoned by radio in time to see the initial hits being scored by American planes on a Japanese carrier.

The running commentary as the attack developed was also being listened to in cramped radio rooms aboard the *Lexington* and the *Yorktown*. Cheers greeted each report of a bomb hit. Before the last of the American air groups had arrived over the battle, in a clear sky smudged with bursting antiaircraft shells from the protective ring of escorts, the *Shoho* (a recently converted freighter) was a mass of flames forward. With ninety-three American fighters and bombers piling into the assault, the outcome was never in doubt. Torpedoes smashed into her boiler rooms, bombs knocked out the last operational antiaircraft guns, below-decks passageways were heaped with the sprawling wounded whose blood mingled with the water from the firefighters' hoses. Half an hour into the attack the *Shoho*'s power died, her pumps failed, and the blazing inferno spread.

Frantic efforts to save their battered carrier were made by her six remaining Zero fighters as the *Yorktown*'s second group of torpedo bombers administered the coup de grâce. Three minutes after fresh explosions had ripped through the *Shoho*, the Emperor's picture was brought up as Izawa gave the order to abandon ship. Those who could, flung themselves overboard. Four minutes later nothing remained but a cloud of black smoke and an oily stain spreading across the Coral Sea to mark where the Imperial Navy had lost its first major warship along with nearly three quarters of her crew of nine hundred.

Then the voice of Lieutenant Commander R. E. Dixon came through the crackling static of the squawkbox of the *Yorktown:* "Scratch one flattop. Dixon to carrier, scratch one flattop." A roar went up in the radio rooms of both American carriers.

The first round of the Coral Sea battle had gone to the U.S. Navy after all but three of the American aircraft landed safely back on the *Lexington* and the *Yorktown* early that afternoon. Fletcher had recovered from a potentially disastrous start. This reinforced his desire to find the other two Japanese carriers and attack them before they jumped him. The urgency of his task was brought home by reports flashed to the flagship even as his planes were landing, that Admiral Crace's task force was under heavy air attack by Japanese land-based bombers some 60 miles south of Deboyne Island.

Skillful helmswork by the flagship H.M.A.S. *Australia* and good conning by his American, New Zealand, and Australian captains saved the squadron from all but superficial damage. Yet no sooner had he beaten off the Japanese than he watched, incredulously, as three American B-26 bombers raced in to attack. "Fortunately their bombing, in comparison with that of the Japanese formation minutes earlier, was disgraceful," Crace would report to General Brett—whose denial that any of his pilots could have made such an error was officially endorsed by MacArthur, leaving Admiral Leary to make the tactful official recommendation "to improve Army recognition of naval vessels."

The actions of May 7 had been a chronicle of errors for both sides, but it was the Japanese who had paid the penalty for their mistakes. Although they at least knew the position of their main target, Admiral Hara's air groups had spent a fruitless afternoon scouring 100 square miles of ocean without finding the American carriers in the clouds and rain squalls. By dusk they had flown so close to their quarry that Task Force 17 radars picked them up. Wildcat fighters were sent aloft to ambush a patrol of nine, and in the gloom some disoriented Japanese pilots made the mistake of attempting to land on the *Yorktown*. Eager gunners managed to shoot one into the sea as the others raced off into the darkness.

That night both the American and the Japanese commanders decided against risking their heavy cruisers in a night engagement. Fletcher's two-to-one advantage in gunpower would have been offset by lack of practice in fighting an action in the dark. Each side expected that the decisive clash between the carriers to determine the outcome of the battle must come the next day. This impending first clash between two opposing naval air groups would be an almost equal contest. The advantage would go to the air strike that managed to take its opponent by surprise. Like the great gunnery duels that had characterized the naval actions of the past, victory belonged to the warships whose guns found the enemy range fastest, to fire across the greatest number of shells before the opponent retaliated. Now for the first time, instead of guns, aircraft were the means of delivering missiles. And although the range between the opposing fleets was measured in hundreds rather than in tens of miles, the outcome would be decided on the same fundamental principle.

Tension was mounting around the CINCPAC operational plot at Pearl Harbor (May 7 in Hawaii, May 8 in the Coral Sea) as the day of battle began with the ocean suffused a gentle gray-green in the dawn light. That last hour before sunrise brought the gun crews on both opposing fleets sweeping the brightening sky as deck crews on the carriers prepared the aircraft for takeoff and the aircrews were briefed. Breakfast had been a rushed meal for Japanese and American pilots alike, as medical teams made ready supplies of surgical dressings and morphine below decks while damage control parties checked that watertight hatches were secured as the warships closed for action. *Yorktown*'s canteen issued 10,000 candy bars; aboard the Japanese warships supplies of emergency rice cakes were handed out.

It was still more than half an hour to sunrise at 5:30 A.M. when the *Lexington* headed into the westerly breeze to launch off eighteen scouting planes to search a 100-mile arc of sea to the north and west of Task Force 17.

Admiral Hara, the Japanese air commander, was much more certain than his opponent about where to direct his search as the two carriers steamed south into the weather front, also flying off a search at dawn. Counting on the thick clouds for cover, he risked sending off, in the hour before the Americans were sighted, a sixty-nine-strong striking force of torpedo and dive bombers with their fighter escorts.

Fate decreed that the searching aircraft would sight each other's target almost simultaneously. At 8:15, Lieutenant J. G. Smith, flying the most northerly leg, spotted the enemy carrier task force steaming south at 25 knots, some 175 miles northeast of the *Lexington*—only minutes before the American carrier's radio had picked up an excited Japanese report clearly indicating they too had been discovered.

Admiral Fletcher ordered his aircraft strike of eighty-seven planes into the air, then signaled to the *Lexington* that Admiral Fitch was to take over tactical command of the battle because of his greater experience in carrier operations. At the same time, he radioed to General MacArthur's headquarters giving the enemy striking force's position, course, and speed, and requesting that bombers be sent out to join in the attack.

Yorktown's thirty-nine-plane strike had set off at 9:15. An hour and three quarters later the *Shokaku* and *Zuikaku* were seen steaming on a southeasterly course some 8 miles apart, each screened by two heavy cruisers and destroyers. While the Americans spent valuable minutes forming up their attack in the heavy cumulus clouds, the *Shokaku* seized the chance to launch more fighters, and the *Zuikaku* headed into the cover of a handy squall of tropical rain.

Lieutenant Commander Joe Taylor led his torpedo squadron in to open the attack with the protection of a force of Wildcat fighters. These held off the stiff defense put up by eighteen Zeroes amid thick flak as they raced in low over the *Shokaku*'s port bow.

The American pilots, making this first attack on a well-defended enemy fleet carrier, lacked the practiced skill for coordinating their torpedo and dive bomber assault. They did not have the weight of numbers that had given them an easy victory the previous day against the light carrier *Shoho*. Torpedoes splashed into the seas too far from the target and the bombing was wild. Only two hits were scored, which started a fuel fire on the carrier's flight deck. The attack was further blunted when the *Lexington*'s air group arrived more than ten minutes later and had difficulty locating the enemy warships under the heavy cloud banks. Only fifteen bombers managed to find a target and poorly protected by six Wildcat fighters, it was easily disrupted by the Zeros, which shot down three American planes. Again their torpedo attack was abortive, as the Japanese report critically observed: "Slow torpedoes and long range. We could turn and run away from them." Only one hit was made by a dive bomber.

The American pilots, however, reported otherwise. Lieutenant Taylor had optimistically radioed after the first strike: "The area on the port side of the bow aft for about 50 to 100 feet was one mass of flames from the waterline to the flight deck. . . . When last seen, about 15 minutes after the attack, fires were burning fiercely. It is believed that this carrier was so badly damaged that it finally sank."

The *Lexington* group, thinking they had attacked the *Zuikaku*, reported that their carrier was left "settling fast." The attack had cost forty-three American planes, and although the *Shokaku* was burning forward and lost her ability to launch aircraft cover for an hour until fires were brought under control, she had not been damaged below the waterline. Over 100 of her crew were dead, but she could still carry on the battle as she withdrew northward at reduced speed.

When the American pilots began arriving back over their own carriers, they were shocked to discover that their Japanese opponents had been able to make a more effective job of their strike. In spite of radar, which gave the *Lexington*'s fighter control director warning of the enemy's approach when they were still more than 70 miles away to the northeast, only seventeen Wildcats had been put into the air, and most of them were not high enough over Task Force 17 when "the battle busted out" twenty-three minutes later, at 10:18. Half the Combat Air Patrol was too low on fuel to be sent out to intercept, and of those that were, four Wildcats failed to find the enemy, two were overwhelmed by Zero fighters, and three failed to gain enough altitude to interfere with the enemy dive-bombing attack. Fitch had also sent up twenty-three Dauntless dive bombers to augment his weak air defense force. While they proved too slow and poorly armed to perform as fighters, they did shoot down four of the sluggish Japanese torpedo bombers while losing the same number themselves.

"Bandits are closing in!" the Red Patrol leader's voice came bursting through the radio static to the *Lexington*'s fighter controller. Their iron discipline and the advantage of attacking out of the sun were in favor of the Japanese pilots as they flew on undeterred toward the carriers. One of the leading torpedo bombers racing in low toward the *Lexington* was blown apart—its crew could be seen spinning through the air—but the others came on without swerving. Employing an "anvil" technique, they executed near-perfect drops on both port and starboard quarters.

Captain Frederick C. Sherman rapped orders for the helmsman to put the rudder hard over, but at over 40,000 tons the great carrier was too slow to respond. Of the shoal of eleven torpedoes, two exploded into her port flank. "We thought we were sinking," was the reaction of Lieutenant C. M. Williams, who had come up from the coding room to the port gun platform. "It was a solid wall of water and covered the whole battery with about a foot of oil and water. Before we had time to dig ourselves out from that somebody yelled 'Dive Bombers!' This little gunner was standing on one foot, firing, holding onto his 20mm, firing up at the dive bomber and kicking the hell out of his ammunition bearer with his other foot." From below, where acrid smoke from the fires seeped up through ventilation shafts and the damaged boiler rooms, pharmacists' mates administered morphine and tannic acid jelly to men horribly burned by the blast, "skin literally dripping from their bodies."

Following the *Lexington* astern, the *Yorktown* was receiving an equal measure of attention from the enemy planes, as her remaining fighters tried to stay close and ward off the Japanese attack. The wave of torpedo bombers had attacked only from the port bow, so Captain Buckmeister had been easily able to swing his smaller carrier to avoid them. The *Yorktown*'s more responsive helm had allowed him to dodge the dive bombers more readily, taking only one 800-pound bomb near the island, which plunged through the thick flight deck, galley, and hangar decks, until it was stopped and exploded by the fourth armored deck 50 feet below. Apart from sixty-six men killed or seriously wounded, the most severe damage was suffered by the ship's soda fountain, laundry room, and Marines' quarters. The darkness and confusion below decks that resulted led engineers to think they had been badly hit and to shut down temporarily two boiler rooms.

The battle between ships and aircraft was reaching a crescendo by 11:30 A.M. Planes came hurtling in from all directions. The *Lexington*'s fighters, running out of fuel, came in to try pancake landings on the carrier's battered deck; several toppled over her sides. The whole encounter lasted scarcely thirteen minutes before the Japanese departed, jubilantly reporting that they had avenged the previous day's defeat of the *Shoho*. Admiral Hara took their reports of definitely sinking one "large carrier" and "one medium carrier" at face value. Since the *Lexington* had been presumed sunk by submarine torpedo in January, the Japanese now claimed to have sent the *Saratoga* to the bottom, along with either the *Enterprise* or the *Yorktown*. They could not immediately decide which one, but they believed their pilots had achieved the objective of dispatching both American carriers.

Yet as the smoke of battle dispersed after this first clash between rival carrier task forces, Fletcher too counted himself the clear victor. The *Lexington* had put out her fires and begun correcting her list by counter-flooding. Soon she and the *Yorktown* were working up speed and landing their planes in preparation for sending off another strike to hit the enemy.

It was 12:45 that afternoon when Captain Sherman received an optimistic call to the bridge from Lieutenant Commander Healy in the *Lexington*'s damage control center. "We've got the torpedo damage shored up, the fires out and will soon have the ship back on an even keel. But I suggest sir, that if you have to take any more torpedoes, you take them on the starboard side." Two minutes later, the great "Lady" was wrenched by a tumultuous explosion deep in her bowels. Sherman's first thought was that he had been torpedoed by a submarine, as the power went off and choking smoke filled the compartments below. The fatal bomblike blast, which sent a chain of new fires racing through the carrier's hull, would be blamed on sparks from an electric motor in the generator room, igniting fuel vapor seeping up from the bottom tanks damaged by the first torpedo hit. Firefighting parties rushed into action while for an hour the *Lexington* continued making 25 knots to land her brood of fighters.

While the *Lexington*'s crew fought a losing battle against the inferno raging deep below her flight deck, her team in fighter control was trying to bring in the final stragglers. With their coding room blasted to smithereens by a bomb, and *Yorktown*'s radar out of action, hopes of getting back Commander Ault, the leader of their dive-bombing strike, were vanishing. He and his radioman had been wounded in their attack on the *Shokaku* and now he found himself in the worst predicament for a pilot—hopelessly lost over the sea with his fuel-gauge needle quivering up against the "Empty" stop. Ault's final exchange with the *Yorktown* was stamped with a stoic heroism that was typical of the spirit of the U.S. Navy pilots:

Yorktown: Nearest land is over 200 miles away.
    Ault: We would never make it.
Yorktown: You are on your own. Good luck.
    Ault: Please relay to Lexington. We got one 1,000 lb. bomb hit on a flattop. We have both reported 2 or 3 times. Enemy fighters. Am changing course North. Let me know if you pick me up.
Yorktown: Roger. You are on your own. I will relay your message. Good luck.
    Ault: OK so long people. We've got a 1,000 lb. hit on the flat-top!

It was the last anyone ever heard of Bill Ault. Yet even as this grim tragedy was being played out over the radio net, a further series of mortal internal explosions rocked the *Lexington*. The pendant signaling "This Ship Needs Help" was run up the carrier's mainmast as the "Lady" lost way, oily black smoke curling pyrelike over her listing flight deck, mingling with clouds of white steam billowing up from the released safety valves. Life rafts were being unclipped as the wounded were brought up from below along smoke-filled passageways dimly lit by "bull's eye" emergency lamps. The destroyers *Morris* and *Hammann* nosed in upwind to come alongside the giant *Lexington* and began taking off survivors.

"Well, Ted, let's get the men off," Admiral Fitch called down to Captain Sherman at 5:07. Fitch knew that the carrier was doomed and that it would soon be impossible to walk on the decks for the heat that was scorching through from below. As they waited on the flight deck in orderly groups to drop down the 50-foot ropes to the water or onto the waiting destroyers, the men seemed sadly reluctant to leave when their turn came, unwilling to leave a dying friend.

Lieutenant Williams, who was the paymaster, wanted to rescue the hundreds of thousands of dollars in the ship's safe; one party of Bluejackets was calmly eating ice cream, which they had scooped out of a canteen in their steel helmets. Marines swarmed down the ropes, leaving their shoes neatly lined up in rows of pairs; and Wags, the captain's dog, was carefully handed down to a destroyer. Captain Sherman was the last to leave, after making a final round to see that no one remained on board alive. None of those who abandoned ship had to spend long in the pleasantly warm water.

As the rescue flotilla pulled away, dusk fell and the *Lexington*'s list increased, sending the planes still parked on deck toppling over the starboard side into the water as flames began to lick up the huge slab-sided island superstructure. When night enveloped Task Force 17, the "Lady's" death agony showed no signs of ending. Finally, at 10 P.M., Admiral Fletcher ordered the destroyer *Phelps* to end the miserable spectacle. The curtain of smoke pouring out of the *Lexington* was so dense that no one saw the finish, which came suddenly after the destroyer's torpedoes had set off a final cataclysmic explosion that sent the shattered hull to its resting place 2,400 fathoms beneath the Coral Sea.

"Congratulations on your glorious accomplishments of the last two days," Nimitz had signaled to Admiral Fletcher earlier that afternoon. But that night he took the view that the *Lexington* could have been saved, until, aware of the gloom settling over his staff in the Pearl Harbor post, he quickly added: "Remember this, we don't know anything about the enemy—how badly he's hurt. You can bet your boots he's hurt too!" Just how badly was to remain a matter of conjecture since neither the admiral nor his staff took the American pilots' claims to have sunk both Japanese carriers at face value. The loss of the *Lexington* had caused Fletcher to give up his original intention of sending his cruiser force into a night action, and on receipt of Nimitz's order not to risk his surviving carrier unduly, Task Force 17 set course to the southeast for Noumea.

Steaming through the night toward the northern Solomons, where a tanker waited to carry out urgently needed refueling, Admiral Takagi also showed no stomach for carrying on the pursuit. With the damaged *Shokaku* making for Truk at reduced speed, he was still able to operate a full strike of aircraft because serviceable planes had been transferred to the undamaged *Zuikaku*. But then neither he nor his air commander Admiral Hara saw any reason to doubt their pilots' claims that the American carriers were now safely on the bottom of the Coral Sea.

Admiral Inouye had already decided to recall the Port Moresby invasion force, postponing once again the invasion of the Papuan Peninsula until more carriers and land-based aircraft could win air superiority over the disputed sea. When Yamamoto picked up the recall signal at midnight, he angrily radioed both Admiral Goto and Admiral Takagi to reverse course to "ANNIHILATE THE ENEMY."

The following morning the *Zuikaku*'s pilots had to take off on another dawn reconnaissance patrol. For the next two days they steamed across a now sparkingly empty Coral Sea. All that remained was the postmortem on the first naval action which had been fought by opposing strikes of aircraft and in which the rival commanders never once had sight of each other's ships. The Japanese had lost 77 aircraft and 1,074 men, as well as the 12,000-ton light carrier *Shoho*. The U.S. Navy put its cost at 66 aircraft, 543 men killed, a tanker and a destroyer lost, in addition to the 42,000-ton fleet carrier *Lexington* sunk and the damage suffered by the *Yorktown*. In tonnage, the Coral Sea was clearly a tactical success for the Imperial Navy. But the number of ships sunk did not necessarily add up to a strategic victory, as the Battle of Jutland had shown in 1916. When the outcome of the naval clashes in the Coral Sea at the end of that momentous first week of May 1942 came to be weighed against how they affected the outcome of events, there can be no doubt that the United States and its Allies won a decisive victory. Admiral Fletcher's force had successfully checked the Japanese strategic plan to advance southward and dominate the Coral Sea and the approaches to Australia. For the first time since Pearl Harbor an important psychological defeat had been inflicted on the myth of Japan's naval invincibility, an event that was to result in a significant shift in the strategic balance.

Nimitz proclaimed it "a victory with decisive and far reaching consequences." Just how far-reaching he would not appreciate for another month. The loss of a light carrier and the trained aircrew was to be a small but nevertheless decisive reduction of the Combined Fleet's superiority that would seriously weaken Admiral Yamamoto's operation to seek a showdown with the Pacific Fleet at Midway.

The American press left its public in no doubt at all about who deserved the victor's laurels—but that was because the U.S. Navy carefully concealed the fact that the *Lexington* had been sunk for over four weeks. "JAPANESE REPULSED IN GREAT PACIFIC BATTLE WITH 17 TO 22 OF THEIR SHIPS SUNK OR CRIPPLED," proclaimed the normally staid *New York Times* headline for May 9. "Very Excellent News," countered the official communiqué issued by Japan's news agency, Domei, as the Coral Sea battle continued to be fought by the rival propaganda machines, with the Imperial Navy claiming they had sunk a battleship as well as two carriers.

THE END ON CORREGIDOR

The Battle of the Coral Sea was to be made to seem an even greater victory in the public's mind because it was an American success that came hard on the news that Japanese forces had finally triumphed in the Philippines. In the month since Bataan had fallen, for those 2,000 Filipino and American soldiers who at first thought themselves lucky to escape to

Corregidor, the four weeks would turn into a nightmare as the island came under the merciless pounding of Japanese artillery and bombs. For the 1,300 men of the 4th Marine Division dug in behind the beach fortifications in foxholes, it was "like living in the center of a bullseye." The rain of death continued night and day, churning up the defenses faster than they could be rebuilt, and turning "The Rock" into a landscape of rubble. The bombardment reached a crescendo on the night of April 29, when a barrage of more than 150 heavy guns thundered an awesome salute of destruction to mark the Emperor's official birthday, setting the remaining undergrowth ablaze and throwing up such a haze of dust that the sun turned blue and the mainland was obscured.

Incredibly, the next night two Navy PBY flying boats managed to land and take off again to evacuate more than fifty people, mostly female nursing staff. Conditions were becoming intolerable for the 4,000 troops crowded onto Corregidor as the tempo of the Japanese bombardment increased. Far too many were jammed into the fetid confines of the Malinta Tunnel, the only secure refuge from the enemy assault. The dust-laden heat and stench from hundreds of wounded permeated its stagnant air. Malnutrition, malaria, and dysentery sapped at the will to live and produced a nervous disorder of its own that was known as "tunnelitis." On May 3, when the submarine *Starfish* arrived in the evening to take off twenty-five more evacuees, including thirteen nurses, General Wainwright made what he knew would be his last farewell to the outside world when he told the skipper: "They will have to come and take us. . . . They will never get us any other way." He radioed MacArthur that with less than five days of fresh water, the situation was fast becoming desperate, and followed it up the next day with an appraisal intended for General Marshall: "In my opinion the enemy is capable of making an assault on Corregidor at any time."

As if responding to that cue, 16,000 shells fell on The Rock during May 4, and General Homma that night was at the port of Lamao at the tip of the Bataan Peninsula to send off the assault boats carrying more than 2,000 troops to storm the island fortress. Homma's men had not reckoned with the swift current that swept the entrance of Manila Bay. Their landings were preceded by another fierce barrage, but the assault boats missed their intended landing beaches on the island's tail by more than a mile. When they tried to come ashore, they were met with the concentrated enfilading fire from the 1st Marine Battalion, which took full advantage of the rising moon to hit back at the enemy. Fewer than six hundred Japanese troops managed to scramble over the rocky shore, where they quickly won control of the eastern end of the island to assault the hog's back of high ground that commanded the approach to the Malinta Tunnel.

"You and your devoted followers have become the symbols of our war aims and the guarantee of our victory," General Wainwright was informed by a special radio message that night from the President. It briefly rallied the spirits of the gaunt officers in the Malinta Tunnel headquarters, but communications were being rapidly severed with the outlying units, and it was followed by reports that the Japanese had overrun the Marine's battery less than 1 mile from the tunnel's sandbagged eastern entrance. There were confused reports that fresh waves of enemy troops had landed and were advancing inland with tanks.

In the heat and turmoil of his tunnel command post, it was plain that Wainwright's exhausted staff faced defeat. Valiantly, a ragged band of Marine and Navy officers who had formed up with non-coms under Major Williams mounted a last wild counterattack to recapture the key battery by the half-demolished watertower.

The gray light of dawn cast sinister flat shadows as the band crept like rats from shell crater to shell crater. With a determination born of desperation, Williams successfully launched a vicious drive that knocked the surprised Japanese from their position. It was a short-lived victory. Tanks and a pinpoint barrage of shells from the mainland had soon blasted the gallant defense apart and the advance toward the sandbagged mouth of the Malinta Tunnel moved relentlessly on.

Haunted by the anticipation of a bloody nightmare of slaughter if the Japanese blasted their way into the tunnel, which was jammed with thousands of defenseless wounded, Wainwright radioed the President, "With broken heart and head bowed in sadness but not in shame," that he must arrange a surrender. "Tell the Nips we'll cease firing at noon," he ordered his surviving field commanders, still battling on in the shell-torn dugouts. "WE MAY HAVE TO GIVE UP BY NOON WE DON'T KNOW YET THEY ARE THROWING SHELLS AT US AND WE MAY NOT BE ABLE TO STAND IT," the radio operator, Private Irving Strobing, tapped out.

At General Homma's headquarters on Bataan the first hours of daylight on May 5 brought the Japanese the anxious knowledge that they were reduced to only twenty-one landing craft. These were ferrying the last Japanese reserves into the battle raging to a bloody climax. Homma's fear that his invasion might be defeated and bring about his certain disgrace continued to mount—until just before midday, when a message arrived that the white flags of truce were now fluttering over the American positions on Corregidor. When the fighting approached the final desperate yards of the eastern mouth of the Malinta Tunnel, Wainwright knew that he must call a halt to save the lives of those inside. He ordered the surrender signal, "Execute Pontiac."

"THE JIG IS UP EVERYONE IS BAWLING LIKE A BABY," Private Strobing tapped out. "I KNOW HOW A MOUSE FEELS CAUGHT IN A TRAP WAITING FOR

THE GUYS TO COME ALONG AND FINISH IT UP." He was to sign off minutes later, sending his family address in Brooklyn with the request: "TELL MOTHER HOW YOU HEARD FROM ME."

It was not until just before four that afternoon that General Wainwright and several of his staff were ferried by the Japanese across to the mainland. They were driven to a small blue villa at Cabcaben, its porch facing out over lush mangroves to Manila Bay. There they could see that Fort Drum, the small "concrete battleship" at the tip of El Cabile Island, was still defiantly firing its 14-inch batteries.

At 5 P.M. General Homma stepped out of a Cadillac, looking determined and efficient, resplendent in a smart uniform for the benefit of the assembled Japanese cameramen. "You must be very tired and weary," he greeted the drawn and haggard Americans, as they sat down at the table set up on the porch. But his politeness soon bristled into anger when his interpreter translated Wainwright's refusal to commit his signature to the document that required him to surrender all the American forces still resisting in the Philippines. Abruptly Homma banged both fists on the table and threatened to continue the battle on Corregidor. Such an appalling thought quickly made Wainwright's staff urge their commander to reconsider, but the Japanese Commander in Chief felt insulted and directed him to return to Corregidor to make his surrender to the local commander.

General Wainwright's humiliation was completed the next day, after he was brought to Manila to sign the surrender document and read out its terms in a radio broadcast beamed throughout the Philippines. Choking back his emotion and deep personal shame, he stumbled through the Japanese dictated script ordering that all Filipino and American units obey the conditions for surrender. "Failure to fully and honestly carry them out can only have the most disastrous results. . . ." At 12:20 P.M. he stared at the microphone, unable to continue.

In Australia, MacArthur was shaken to hear that Wainwright had ordered the overall capitulation of the Philippines. Cabling Marshall that he could only assume the general was "temporarily unbalanced and his condition renders him susceptible to enemy use," he broadcast his countermanding orders, reminding General Sharp on Mindanao that the surrender had "no validity." Fighting continued for two days until one of Wainwright's staff officers was flown in by the Japanese to insist on a cease-fire. Except for guerrilla activity, the Philippines was now part of Japan's "Co-Prosperity Sphere."

The final assault on Corregidor had taken more than eight hundred American and Filipino lives and cost the Japanese in excess of three times that number. But no more than a third of the surviving remnants of the 4th Marine Division would live through the brutal captivity that was to be inflicted on them.

"Corregidor needs no comment from me," MacArthur told the press in a carefully prepared panegyric. "It has sounded its own story at the mouth of its guns. It has scrolled its own epitaph on enemy tablets. But through the bloody haze of its last reverberating shot, I shall always seem to see a vision of grim, gaunt, ghastly men, still unafraid."

This burning vision drove his personal commitment to avenge the deaths of thousands of his American and Filipino troops, and spurred MacArthur's renewed call for launching the crusade to recapture the Philippines.

15
Calculated Risks

On May 5, 1942, while the battle in the Coral Sea was moving to its climax, the towns and villages through Japan were crowded with parades. The processions of brightly painted carp banners and paper kites were celebrating the annual "Boys' Festival" in a more than usually exuberant spirit for a nation sated with military triumphs. Imperial General Headquarters in Tokyo chose the auspicious day to issue the operational directive that was to reverse the tide of victory. "By Command of His Imperial Majesty to Commander in Chief Yamamoto of the Combined Fleet," the Navy Order No. 18 began, setting out the details of "Operation MI:" "The Commander in Chief of the Combined Fleet is to cooperate with the army in the occupation of Midway and strategic points west of the Aleutians." It initiated the biggest operation ever attempted by the Imperial Navy and the strategy by which Yamamoto was hoping to bring about the "decisive naval engagement." He was confident that Japan's overwhelming naval superiority must secure a crushing victory, after which he planned to use his very great popularity to persuade Prime Minister Tojo to offer the concessions that would bring the United States to the peace table and a quick end to the Pacific War.

The very day that he received the order, Yamamoto was holding briefings and war-game rehearsals for Operation MI with his senior officers aboard the flagship, moored in the picturesque Hashirajima anchorage south of Hiroshima. For six months the Imperial Navy's main battle force, including the newly commissioned 80,000-ton monster battleship *Yamato*, had swung idly round their buoys. They were contemptuously referred to as "The Hashirajima Fleet" by carrier pilots who had seen most of the action. Now at last the admirals and captains assembled in the spacious interior of the world's greatest warship learned that the fleet would be steaming into action for an operation on the grand scale.

The task of assembling the facets of Yamamoto's complex and huge plan had been the product of many days meditation by Captain Kameto

Kuroshima, his able Chief of Operations. The result of the intensive staff work, conducted under the personal direction of the Commander in Chief, was a strategy for extending Japan's defense 2,000 miles into the mid-Pacific to threaten the lifeline to Australia. Yamamoto intended to bring the U.S. Navy to a showdown. As presented to the fleet's captains and senior officers in that four-day conference, his plan called for the execution of an intricate series of interlocking offensives involving eleven battleships, eight carriers, twenty-two cruisers, sixty-five destroyers, twenty-one submarines, and over two hundred naval aircraft. Deployed as six separate forces across the Pacific, from the Marianas to the Aleutians, the operations would be choreographed in a series of carefully synchronized movements focused on Midway. The atoll itself was to be invaded by a force of 2,000 troops on "N" Day, 72 hours after a diversionary raid on American bases in the Aleutians. The action on which the entire strategy hinged called for Admiral Nagumo's carrier strike force to soften up Midway's defenses the following day, N-2, as the invasion transports were steaming up from Saipan. Between these two widely separated assault forces, Yamamoto would be lying in wait for the U.S. Pacific Fleet to come charging west from Pearl Harbor, his submarines disposed across its line of advance to maul it before the final surface action.

The elaborate plan was not received without some criticism from the senior officers present aboard the *Yamato*. Admiral Kondo, the Second Fleet Commander, challenged the wisdom of attacking Midway, where land-based bombers could be a powerful threat to warships. Admiral Nagumo's carrier commanders were uneasy that the main battle fleet would be deployed over 300 miles away, too distant to come to their aid if needed. More potential flaws in the master plan emerged as the war games were played through in the flagship's extensive operations plot. It was apparent that there would be communications problems since the Commander in Chief would be at sea observing radio silence and the carriers were left widely exposed to attack from the northwest. But Yamamoto steadfastly refused to consider any postponement in his June 1 deadline to allow for more planning or to make major alterations to the details of his strategy. He, too, was suffering from the myopia of overconfidence. Significantly, although he had always been a leading advocate of airpower at sea, his tactical plan for the "decisive naval engagement" ultimately centered on an old-style set piece gunnery duel between the battle fleets.

It seemed that "victory disease" had taken the edge off Yamamoto's highly attuned strategic sense. He had overlooked—or chosen to ignore—the most serious flaw that ran through the very foundation on which he had constructed his grandiose plan to attack Midway and the Aleutians. By grasping for two so widely disposed objectives, he had disregarded

Captain Mahan's dictate calling for concentration of naval forces. The Combined Fleet's overwhelming superiority was to be parceled up as six forces separated by many thousands of miles of ocean. To lure his opponent into the "decisive battle," Yamamoto's strategy required that the U.S. Navy Commanders respond according to the dictates of his grand design. But given sufficient advance knowledge of Operation MI, the Americans would be able to concentrate the Pacific Fleet strength to defeat the Midway invasion, thereby upsetting the whole intricate arrangements.

History is so often accused of repetition that there was a curious double irony in Yamamoto's decision to set the first days of June for his great Midway attack. This would bring his Combined Fleet into action thirty-six years to the week after Admiral Sir John Jellicoe, with equally misplaced confidence in the German willingness to perform according to his battle strategy, had led the might of the Grand Fleet out into the North Sea for a showdown with the Kaiser's High Seas Fleet.

The Japanese admirals had intensely studied the Battle of Jutland, but they appeared to have forgotten the lesson of how the speed and confusion of modern naval actions had robbed the Royal Navy of its anticipated Second Trafalgar. The firepower and maneuverability of the dreadnought had transformed the traditional Nelsonian concept of a slogging match between two ponderously moving lines of battleships. Aircraft, which had only played a minor role in the action at Jutland in 1916, had in the intervening years brought another great revolution in naval warfare—a transformation Yamamoto himself had been instrumental in furthering. More surprising was that he ignored the lessons of the Coral Sea carrier engagements that were still being fought to their conclusions while the Operation MI conference was taking place aboard the *Yamato*. Their inconclusive outcome was a telling indictment of how the speed and destructiveness of air strikes had changed naval tactics; but astonishingly Yamamoto and his staff remained utterly unshaken in their belief that the U.S. Pacific Fleet must react as expected to their Midway gambit.

UNCOVERING JAPANESE PLANS

The secrecy that was so essential for the Japanese to pull off the centerpiece of their Second Operational Phase was to be peeled away to reveal that its main objective was not in the central, nor south Pacific area. The first clues to this had emerged in the intercepted signal traffic of March 4, 1942, when the designator mentioned as AF was identified tentatively as Midway. At the end of April, reference to the Aleutians had also been established for an operation to occur after the MO movement in the

Coral Sea. Perhaps it was a certain conviction that prompted Nimitz's May 2 flying visit to the lonely Marine garrison on Midway. But at that time what later seemed to be uncanny foresight of the enemy plan can at best have only been a hunch, because the estimates of CINCPAC Intelligence when he took off from Pearl Harbor that morning put the main offensive as continuing to develop in the Coral Sea where every available American carrier and Allied warship was being concentrated for what the Pacific Fleet Commander believed would be the showdown with the Japanese. It was not until May 4, two days after Nimitz had returned from Midway, that this estimate was being reconsidered. Rochefort's HYPO staff discovered they had mistakenly confused battleship and submarine call signs that suggested a continued movement south. That day two partially translated intercepts gave vital clues: "AS THE A FORCE AND STRIKING FORCE WILL BE IN TRUK FOR A PERIOD OF ABOUT 2 WEEKS AFTER 20 JUNE PLEASE ARRANGE FOR ——— AND DESIGNATE THE ANCHORAGES," and "THIS SHIP WILL BE UNDERGOING REPAIRS DURING THE TIME OF THE SAID OPERATION . . . THE DATE FOR COMPLETION BEING [near May 21] WILL BE UNABLE TO ACCOMPANY YOU IN THE CAMPAIGN." Taken together, these indicated that a second big operation would be rolling during the final ten days of May, *after* which the units would move to Truk. When a signal decoded the next day revealed that the Combined Fleet was asking Tokyo to "EXPEDITE DELIVERY OF FUELLING HOSE," indicating that a long-range mid-ocean operation was being planned, Commander Layton had only to look at the map to express a concern for Midway and Nimitz was ordering reinforcements to be speeded out to the island. During the action in the Coral Sea, traffic analysis failed to detect any major enemy units rushing southward to join in the battle. Significantly, on May 6 the CINCPAC assessment of the situation was: "While the Japanese offensive in SOPAC continues, it is noted that they now have sufficient force in the Central Pacific to raid in the Central and North Pacific Areas."

In the days that followed, references to AF were picked up in connection with a second "K" operation. Since the first had been an attack on Hawaii by seaplanes staged from the French Frigate Shoals, it was another pointer to Midway. On May 11, a signal to the Second Fleet directing a force to "PROCEED TO THE SAIPAN-GUAM AREA AND WAIT FOR FORTHCOMING OPERATION" was followed by another sending air groups and transport to the same area. It was evident that the focus of the Japanese concentration was being readied for a central Pacific operation of considerable scale. This was hinted at also by a four-part signal intercepted on May 16 setting out the details for a major preparatory fleet exercise. Clearly something big was afoot although its precise objective was still unclear. More clues emerged from a May 18 order to a submarine unit from Jaluit: "PLEASE CHANGE THE DIRECTIVE OF THE MOVEMENTS OF THE AF AND AO OCCUPATION FORCES . . . THE POSITIONS IN WHICH THE SUB-

MARINES MUST BE PRIOR—WILL BE 150 MILES MORE OR LESS TO THE EAST-
WARD OF AI." The CINCPAC Intelligence staff were pretty certain that
AF was Midway, AO the Aleutians, and that the submarines were to
picket Oahu, which they believed was AI.

While the jigsaw of the Combined Fleet's new offensive was being
pieced together, radio intelligence revealed that Admiral Inouye was
attempting to recover from the setback in the Coral Sea by pressing
ahead with "Operation RY" on May 17 to occupy the phosphate islands.
So on May 11, when Admiral Halsey sailed Task Force 16 into Noumea
a week too late to participate in the battle, his disappointment was alleviated by orders that he was to be ready to move to head off the invasion
of Ocean and Naru.

What CINCPAC Intelligence correctly assessed as a Japanese face-
saving operation was quite differently interpreted in Washington by
Commander Safford's OP 20 G staff in the Navy Department. Reading
it in conjunction with a signal intercepted from Admiral Nagumo asking for berth allocations for his carrier in Truk, they predicted that the
Japanese were still heading south. Had the date been deciphered, the
NEGAT report would have shown that the enemy carrier force was
intending to be at Truk *after*, not before, the "campaign." Each of the
Joint Chief's intelligence staffs was making its own inspired guesses as to
where the Japanese would jump next, based on its own pressures and
priorities. The U.S. Army Air Intelligence had convinced General Arnold
that an attack on the West Coast was imminent, making him increasingly
unwilling to send the agreed quota of new bombers to the southwest
Pacific command. General MacArthur's own BELCONNEN intelligence
team found nothing to alter his belief that Japan was planning to invade
Australia. Accordingly, he radioed impossible demands to the War Department for reinforcements, including two carriers, a thousand more
aircraft, and three divisions of troops in addition to the two already on
their way out to Sidney.

General Marshall's considered judgment was that the threat to Australia was neither so dire as MacArthur vociferously insisted nor so immediate, as King argued, to warrant prejudicing the agreement he had
just reached in Britain by diverting shipping and aircraft from the
Bolero build-up. He believed that by far the most serious peril facing the
Allies was the possibility of a Russian collapse because of Germany's
renewed drive toward the Caucasus. His refusal to meet Admiral King's
demands for more bombers and soldiers to reinforce the garrisons at New
Caledonia and Fiji sent COMINCH "jumping up and down."

"The Pacific theater must get along as best it can with the force already allocated," was the U.S. Army Chief's immovable position, cabled
to MacArthur with the assurance that "the Army and Navy air strength
is so flexibly arranged that we can strike the enemy damaging blows

ALLIED WARLEADERS Franklin D. Roosevelt and Winston Churchill relax at Marrakesh in January, 1943 after the bitter strategic debate divided their staffs at the Casablanca Conference.

FIRST STOP ON THE ROAD TO TOKYO On August 7, 1942 U.S. Marines made an easy landing (above) on Guadalcanal. The Japanese reacted by bombing the transports (below) and forced a speedy retirement of support ships.

Left without adequate supplies, General Vandegrift (above) faced a three month battle to cling onto America's hold in the Solomons as Australian Coastwatchers (below, Captain Clements and his scouts) gave warning of bombing raids and enemy convoys.

STRUGGLE OF ATTRITION General Imamura (above right) sent reinforcements to Guadalcanal by Tokyo Express convoys run by Admiral Tanaka (above center) and the cruisers of Admiral Mikawa (above left).

In the naval actions that raged around the Solomons the *Hornet* (left below) was torpedoed on September 15, and the *Wasp* (below) sunk at the Battle of Santa Cruz on October 26. Admirals Callaghan and Scott (above left, center) died in the two day action of November 12—14 that was won by the battleships of Admiral Lee (above right).

GREEN HELL IN NEW GUINEA Allied forces led by General Blamey and General Eichelberger (below left, right) by the end of 1942 won a gruelling victory in Papua after the advance over the infamous Kokoda Track (above).

STRATEGIC DEBATES The Casablanca Conference in January 1943 (above, l.–r., King, Marshall, Arnold, two staff members, Wedemeyer, Ismay, Mountbatten, Pound, Brooke, Portal). A year later at Cairo (below), Chiang Kai-shek brought the emphasis back to the Pacific.

THE FORGOTTEN WAR In 1944 Allied operations in Burma were stepped up under General Wingate (above left) and General Stilwell (above right). In May Merrill's Marauders (below) completed their 'end run' for Mytikyina.

wherever he may appear." The architect of "Europe First" was above all determined to prevent the drift toward "Pacific First" that the President appeared to be favoring when he told a meeting of the Pacific War Council at the end of April that he was "considering" dispatching another 100,000 troops and 1,000 more aircraft to Australia. Marshall—who believed that some emergency cross-Channel attack might be necessary that summer to stave-off the Red Army's defeat—warned Roosevelt that such a radical redistribution of forces would "virtually eliminate the United States from any ground participation in Europe in 1942."

The Joint Chiefs of Staff meetings through May had been divided by a renewed and frequently lively debate over strategic priorities. It had now transpired that the British Chiefs of Staff, never enthusiastic about the Sledgehammer cross-Channel attack, had become convinced that it would be impossible to execute it in 1942. Recognizing the commitment to relieve the pressure on their Russian ally by launching some attack in the West that year, they resurrected the Gymnast strategy for attacking North Africa or alternatively assaulting Norway. King accepted the "Europe First" principle but he regarded both these operations as foolhardy and of less strategic importance than the need to send every available ship, soldier, and bomber to the Pacific to stem the tide of the Japanese advance. On May 4 he put his strongly worded case in a memorandum. It warned that as Japan was now "massing strong land, sea, and air forces in the Mandates" to ward off attacks that could fall on Australia, Hawaii, or the Aleutians "with disasterous consequences," reinforcements must be sent out to the Pacific Islands "to hold what we have against any attack that the Japanese are capable of making against us."

General Marshall rejected such an open-ended commitment that could well tip the balance of Allied strategy in favor of the Pacific. He countered that it was "impossible to make every point in the island chain impregnable," and that any diversion of troops or bombers to the South Pacific must weaken the opportunity to strike against the principal Nazi power. Confronted with what appeared to be a question of upholding the Atlantic strategy at the expense of the Pacific, the President and Joint Chiefs again supported Marshall's unswerving conviction that Germany had to be defeated before Japan. Nimitz and MacArthur were told that they just had to do the best they could with the forces they already had.

The situation in the Pacific was rapidly moving to a climax when Admiral Ghormley set out to establish his command at Noumea. The Coral Sea actions had effectively cut the Pacific Fleet's carrier strength in half, leaving only Admiral Halsey's Task Force 16 and Admiral Crace's cruisers to defend the vast expanse of ocean between Hawaii and Australia. To meet the dangers, the U.S. Naval Chief signaled a request to

London on May 18: "Will Admiralty entertain request for carrier from Eastern Fleet to join up with Leary temporarily, if so move must be made at once." That King was even prepared to go begging for favors from the British was, as one of his staff observed, the true measure of the crisis. That the Admiralty refused him was a humiliation he never forgave.

In view of the U.S. Navy's earlier readiness to send battleships and a a carrier to join the Battle of the Atlantic, the Royal Navy's refusal to release even one of their three carriers then operating off the West African coast seemed nothing short of churlish. King had intended that by reinforcing the Australian cruiser force covering the Coral Sea, it could act as a diversion to any major attack that the Japanese were planning for the Pacific. It was a mistake that Churchill later regretted when he discovered just how far it had set the unforgiving Ernest J. King against the British.

The excuse that the Admiralty gave for not helping the U.S. Navy in its hour of greatest need was that its own intelligence evaluation indicated Japan was about to launch an attack on Madagascar. "Operation Ironclad" had long been planned to forestall such a strategic disaster, which could effectively shut off the Indian Ocean, denying access to India and the Persian Gulf oil.

On May 4, the British operation had finally got under way as Admiral Sir Neville Syret's force of two carriers and a battleship sailed from Durban to land two brigades of Marines at Diego-Suarez, the principal port on Madagascar. Lacking the resources for a full-scale invasion of Madagascar, which is 900 miles long, Churchill had cabled Admiral Syret reminding him that his task was not to subjugate the whole of the island but to "establish ourselves in key positions to deny it to a far-flung Japanese attack." Any chance that the Vichy Governor might capitulate to a show of force vanished, and on May 5 carrier air strikes and a bombardment by the *Ramilles'* 15-inch guns were needed to get the Marines into the port. The French refused to surrender the island and Churchill ordered Syret to halt his campaign to give the Governor "time to amend his pro-Vichy attitude." The Japanese midget submarine that penetrated Diego-Suarez three weeks later to torpedo the battleship set the seal on any hopes of an end to the impasse over Madagascar. With General Wavell calling for the Marines to reinforce the defense of India, it would not be until September that a new expedition set out to subdue the rest of the island garrisons.

After the British refused to send their carriers to Australian waters, and convinced by his COMINCH intelligence staff that the Japanese offensive was continuing in the south Pacific, Admiral King throughout the first half of May insisted on Halsey's task force remaining at Noumea. He went so far as to instruct Nimitz that it was "inadvisable" to allow the fleet's only two remaining carriers to run unnecessary risks, and even advised him to "operate one or more carrier air groups ashore" in defense of the forward island bases. CINCPAC regarded such a loss of mobility of his main strength with horror, particularly when his intelligence staff were so certain that the Japanese Navy meant to launch a major blow against the central Pacific. He could not countermand or flatly refuse King. Instead, Nimitz resorted to diplomacy and subterfuge to overcome the obstinacy of COMINCH.

On May 14, he signaled King for permission to rescind the directive keeping Task Force 16 at Noumea. On the same day, Halsey sailed north to head off the Japanese invasion force heading toward the phosphate islands. The pugnacious admiral's high hopes of a smashing victory were quickly dispelled by two messages. The first from COMINCH, passed on by CINCPAC, warned: "Operations of Task Force 16 inadvisable in forward areas beyond own shore-based air cover." The second, a personal one from Nimitz which was carefully not logged or sent to COMINCH, instructed Halsey to make sure that Task Force 16 was indeed sighted heading north before he withdrew, in compliance with King's cautious order. No doubt wondering what its purpose was, Halsey nevertheless obediently swung his course that night west toward the Solomons. The next day seaplane patrols from Tulagi spotted him continuing north, ostensibly toward Ocean and Naru. Under cover of darkness he eventually reversed course for Noumea.

The ploy was to succeed in both its objectives. HYPO intercepts confirmed that Admiral Inouye had called off the occupation of the Phosphate Islands, giving Nimitz the excuse needed to signal Halsey that evening: "DESIRE YOU PROCEED TO HAWAIIAN AREA." Within the hour a detailed justification was flashed to COMINCH outlining the latest evidence of the increasing enemy build-up. His intelligence indicated a force massing at Saipan for an operation in the mid-Pacific, and Nimitz suggested "considerable differences in estimates on the same dates" as an explanation for NEGAT's prediction of a renewed thrust to the south. "Will watch the situation closely and return Halsey to southward if imminent concentration that area," CINCPAC's report concluded, anticipating the protests from MacArthur that the Navy was leaving unguarded the approaches to Australia.

On May 17 Admiral King, after a thorough reappraisal, accepted that Japan was indeed massing forces in the central Pacific area, and agreed to the CINCPAC plan to send a cruiser force south in exchange for the carriers to thwart any renewed Japanese attack on Port Moresby. At the same time COMINCH laid down as an overriding condition that Nimitz was to "Chiefly employ strong attrition tactics and [do] not repeat NOT allow our forces to accept such decisive action as would be likely to incur heavy losses in our carriers and cruisers."

On May 18, when Admiral Halsey, still unaware of all the behind-the-scenes maneuvering, received an impatient "EXPEDITE RETURN" signal from CINCPAC, he correctly assumed that "Trouble was brewing somewhere else in the Pacific." Just how big or where the threat was directed he could only guess, but back at Pearl Harbor there was growing certainty that the "AF" designator so frequently cropping up in the intercepted Japanese orders could only mean Midway. The NEGAT team in Washington felt it might indicate Hawaii or even the West Coast, but HYPO Commander Rochefort reading back through the signals was certain of his interpretation. Then on May 20 interception of a long signal radioed out by the Combined Fleet flagship to all units contained so many references to AF that it was clearly the operational order for a battle plan. Final and definitive identification of AF was therefore vital.

While Layton and the codebreakers were laboring around the clock to decipher the Japanese operation plan, Rochefort hit upon a way to prove beyond all doubt the identity of AF. Instructions went out by submarine cable line to Midway for the garrison commander to make an emergency radio call in plain English, stating that the atoll's water-distillation plant had broken down. To maintain the deception, Admiral Bloch, the 14th Naval District Commander, immediately signaled back that a water barge was on its way with emergency supplies. The ruse worked brilliantly. Within twenty-four hours the enemy radio station on Wake was reporting that AF was apparently running short of water and orders were issued for the invasion force to take aboard extra supplies. On May 22 the "Comb" channel carried the report: "REGARDING WATER SITUATION AT AFFIRM FOX   PLAIN LANGUAGE   WAS SENT BY MIDWAY TO 14 ON SUBJECT OF FEED SITUATION FOR ANIMALS   AS STATED PREVIOUSLY AFFIRM FOX IS CONFIRMED HERE AS MIDWAY."

When Nimitz assembled the Pacific Fleet staff on May 21 to review their own order of battle, Commander Layton was able to give an accurate outline of the Japanese plan, the details of which were becoming clearer as its cipher was unraveled by the efforts of Commander Rochefort's codebreakers. There were two main elements: "Operation AL" was to attack the westernmost Aleutian Islands, supported by a two-carrier force, after raiding American bases in Alaska. "Operation AR" required the enemy's main carrier force to strike at Midway in preparation for an invasion force setting out from Saipan covered by battleships and cruisers. The first was obviously a diversionary operation; the assault on the atoll was the main objective. Deducing from the very absence of specific instructions to the Combined Fleet's main battleship force that it must be at anchor with the flagship in Hashirajima, Nimitz correctly surmised that Admiral Yamamoto intended to lead it out personally so as to pounce on the Pacific Fleet when it raced west to protect Midway. To give early warning of the U.S. approach, it was also considered probable that enemy submarines would be picketing the waters off Hawaii, in addition to those sent out to support the already-uncovered plan for a seaplane mission over Oahu.

The key pieces still missing were the precise times and dates that pinned Yamamoto's master plan together. For security this had been transmitted locked in new five-digit code. Notwithstanding, Layton was able to be certain from an overall assessment that the operation would begin in the first week of June. On this assumption Nimitz could plan his counter-strategy, which was dictated by the need to avoid a one-to-one match with the superior enemy. "We must endeavour to reduce his forces by attrition—submarine attacks, air bombing attacks on isolated units," the Pacific Fleet Commander in Chief directed, intending to use his intelligence advantage to make up for numerical inferiority so that he could concentrate his carrier strength to blunt the spearhead of the Japanese attack. In spite of the odds against him, Nimitz decided that his seven old battleships were too slow to keep up with the carriers and should remain on the West Coast. The remainder of the Pacific Fleet's heavy units would be placed under Halsey's command to aim a knockout blow against the enemy strike force when it arrived to raid Midway. Knowing that Admiral Nagumo had been deprived of two of his carriers as a result of the Coral Sea action, the additional planes carried by the larger American flattops would bring their airpower up to parity with those aboard the four Japanese carriers if the *Yorktown* could be made operational in time. Then Nimitz could count on 230 carrier planes, supported by the aircraft on the "fixed carrier" of Midway itself.

Since Nimitz's visit to the island at the beginning of May, so many reinforcements had been flown in that the Marine garrison of the 6th Defense Battalion joked about the atoll being in danger of sinking under the weight of twenty-three Navy PBY patrol seaplanes, twenty-seven Marine fighters, sixteen dive bombers, and seventeen torpedo bombers, including the Army's four B-26 Marauders, which had been joined by seventeen B-17 Fortresses that General Emmons had been persuaded to send out from Hawaii.

Concentrating so much of the Pacific Fleet against Operation AF left Nimitz few ships to spare to counter Operation AL in Aleutian waters. When Admiral Robert A. Theobald had sailed from Pearl Harbor for the icy mists of the Alaskan coast on May 21, he knew that his force of two heavy cruisers, two light cruisers, and four destroyers would not be a match for the Japanese carriers. At the same time, the seventeen Pacific Fleet submarines were dispatched as Task Force 7 to throw out a picket line around Midway. Since the American strategy, even more than the Japanese, depended on achieving the element of surprise, CINC-PAC arranged for the seaplane tender *Tangier* at Efate and the heavy

cruiser *Salt Lake City* in Australian waters to put out radio traffic simu-
lating the operations of carriers flying aircraft, so as to deceive Japanese
intelligence into believing that Halsey's force was still in the southwest
Pacific.

To ensure that his carrier was in the right place at the right time,
Nimitz had to know the precise schedule of Operation AF. But after
three days and nights of intense cryptography by the HYPO team, those
key dates still lay locked in impenetrable code. When Rochefort was
summoned to make a rare personal appearance before the Commander in
Chief on May 24, anticipating what Nimitz wanted, he began an all-night
session in a final attempt to crack the recalcitrant five-digit code. After a
supreme mental effort, by mid-morning he had solved the last links in the
puzzle. By then Rochefort realized he was late for his meeting. Making
a fast change from his smoking jacket and slippers into uniform, he appeared close to exhaustion, eyes heavily bloodshot, in front of an irritated
Nimitz. The Commander in Chief's anger evaporated when he heard
Rochefort assuring him that Dutch Harbor in the Aleutians would be attacked on June 3, one day before the assault on Midway would be
launched by the Japanese carrier striking force. This tied in with the calculations of CINCPAC intelligence staff, allowing the normally cautious
Commander Layton to predict: "They'll come in from the northwest
on a bearing 325 degrees and they will be sighted at about 175 miles
from Midway, and the time will be about 06.00 Midway time."

HIGH STAKES

On the basis of such firm predictions, Admiral King was quick to give
his approval before the return to Pearl Harbor, at noon on May 26, of
the twenty-six ship Task Force 16. As soon as the *Enterprise* and the
Hornet had berthed, Vice Admiral Halsey arrived to report to his Commander in Chief. Nimitz received a shock for which he had not been prepared when he found the normally spirited admiral reduced to exhaustion by severe dermatitis. He had counted on Halsey's proven leadership
and tactical command of carriers to lead the American forces in perhaps
the most critical naval action of the whole war.

Halsey looked upon it as "the most grievous disappointment of my
career," yet he unselfishly advised his Commander in Chief that the man
to replace him was his cruiser commander, Rear Admiral Raymond
Spruance. A methodical and quietly spoken tactician, in contrast to the
fiery "Bull" Halsey, Spruance's talent as an administrator had already
marked him out for a place on CINCPAC's staff. Nimitz appreciated that
Spruance, with his reputation for sound tactical judgement and level-
headedness, would be a good commander for what promised to be the

most crucial operation ever undertaken by the U.S. Navy. But his lack of experience as a carrier commander required that he would have to defer authority to Admiral Fletcher, who was due to make port the next day with the damaged *Yorktown*. Spruance was equally determined to rise to the demands of fighting his first sea-air battle, but he reflected a good deal less happily on his Commander in Chief's insistence that it would be his last seagoing duty for a while, as he hurried across the base to the hospital where he found Halsey smothered in ointment to calm the agonizing rash. Though incapacitated, Halsey did his best to alleviate Spruance's concern over his lack of carrier experience by assuring him this would be compensated by the full support of Task Force 16's staff officers. These were led by his Chief of Staff, Commander R. Browning, the Navy's outstanding tactician in air warfare, who had been recently credited in *Life* magazine with masterminding the raids on Japan's island bases. Spruance, however, was to find Browning disconcertingly temperamental and difficult to work with. If his own fastidiousness and frosty demeanor did not exactly help establish a warm working relationship with the assertively informal "brown shoe" aviators, Spruance's confident leadership quickly inspired their loyalty and respect.

Any apprehensions that Nimitz might have had about Spruance being the right man to command Task Force 16 were dispelled in the intense briefing sessions the following day, which were only interrupted in order to attend a parade on the flight deck to decorate members of the *Enterprise*'s crew for gallantry. "I think you'll have a chance to win yourself another medal in a few days," the Commander in Chief told one airman as he pinned on a Distinguished Flying Cross.

That afternoon, sirens and whistles and cheering sailors greeted the arrival of the *Yorktown*, which steamed slowly up harbor, trailing a 10-mile oil slick from the damage she had suffered during the Coral Sea battle. Tugs nudged the carrier through the open caisson gates of No. 1 Dry Dock. Pumps were still emptying the dock several hours later when Nimitz donned long boots to join the dockyard shipwrights surveying the vast hull. They studied the extent of the damage to those bottom plates that had been sprung open by the near misses from Japanese bombs, and decided that steel plates could be welded on to patch the hull and compartments, temporarily braced up with timbers. "We must have the ship back in three days," the Commander in Chief insisted. The *Yorktown* could not be repaired to make full speed or restored to full watertight integrity without a lengthy refit on the West Coast; but she could be patched up to allow her to operate along with Task Force 16, and her compliment of aircraft might well make the difference between defeat and victory.

Work began that night under arc lights as 1,400 dockyard workers left all other nonessential tasks to work around the clock for the next two days. A temporary blackout that evening jammed the base switch-board with complaints from angry Honolulu residents blaming the over-load on the electric arc welders. Nimitz was dealing with a more seri-ous complaint from COMINCH, who wanted Admiral Fletcher relieved because he thought he had not handled his Task Force aggressively in the Coral Sea. Convinced that King's criticism was over-hasty, Nimitz forwarded the reports of the action, with the note: "Fletcher did a fine job and exercised superior judgment."

Fletcher joined Spruance's staff and Nimitz the next day for inten-sive briefings on their battle tactics. The ten succinct pages of "Opera-tion Plan 29–42" set out the likely Japanese movements that would bring the Pacific Fleet's entire carrier strength 200 miles northeast of Midway, to "inflict maximum damage on the enemy by employing strong attri-tion tactics." By the morning of May 28, when Spruance set sail with Task Force 16, his responsibility for the safety of the two carriers was clearly emphasized by CINCPAC orders: "You will be governed by the principle of calculated risk, which you will interpret to mean the avoid-ance of exposure of your force to attack by superior enemy forces without the prospect of inflicting, as a result of such exposure, greater damage to the enemy." Normally not a Commander in Chief who told his officers how to fight their battles, Nimitz insisted on retaining his right to exercise overall command as the critical action developed.

Next day, with her hull patched by great steel plates, the *Yorktown* left dry dock. Replenishment got under way while thousands of dock-yard hands still swarmed around her damaged internal compartments, shoring up bulkheads and completing the temporary repairs. "Good Luck and Good Hunting" was the message from the Commander in Chief, who came aboard the carrier the following morning just before Task Force 17 sailed. More welcome for the *Yorktown* was Captain Buck-meister's promise that his ship really was on her final operation before a long overhaul, when the men would get their long-awaited leave, and "not just for two weeks either!"

Steaming off Oahu, the deck parties received *Yorktown*'s comple-ment of aircraft. Among the seventy-two planes safely landed that morn-ing was the squadron of seventeen torpedo bombers awaiting the arrival of the *Saratoga*, and the latest marque of Wildcat fighter, whose new fold-ing wings were so unfamiliar that manuals had to be consulted before they could be stowed in the hangar. During these operations the *York-town*'s popular executive officer was killed when an aircraft overran the arrester wire. Everyone aboard tried not to look upon it as an omen, as with her two accompanying cruisers and six escorting destroyers she set course for aptly named "Point Luck"—the designated patch of the Pacific Ocean some 350 miles north of Midway where Admiral Fletcher was scheduled to rendezvous with Spruance on June 1.

CALCULATED RISKS

The American warships were to observe strict radio silence after leaving Hawaiian waters in order to preserve the secrecy essential to the success of their mission. But on the morning of May 30, as the *Yorktown* was embarking her aircraft, the sudden increase in radio traffic had rippled out across the Pacific. It was picked up by an alert Japanese operator aboard the Combined Fleet flagship, shortly after the *Yamato* steamed out of her Hashirajima anchorage accompanied by two smaller battleships, a light carrier, a cruiser, and nine destroyers. Ahead sailed Admiral Kondo's powerful strike force of two battleships, a light carrier and cruiser, eight destroyers and four tankers, all converging on the waters off Midway to spring their own ambush.

Two days earlier, Admiral Nagumo's four carriers had sailed with their eight supply tankers, accompanied by two battleships, three cruisers, and twelve destroyers. Confidence was running high aboard the carriers on which the whole operation depended. The final rehearsal of Operation AF on the plotting tables had gone without a hitch and toasts to a great victory had been drunk in sake sent by the Emperor himself. On May 29, the 15 transports carrying the 5,000 troops to occupy Midway had sailed from Saipan with a light cruiser and 10 destroyers as close escort. Putting out that day from Guam to join them was a support force of three seaplane tenders, four heavy cruisers, and three destroyers. The Aleutians strike force of two light carriers, two heavy cruisers, two seaplane tenders, and four destroyers was already halfway across the Pacific to its objective at Dutch Harbor. On May 30, the eight transports carrying the troops to invade Kiska and Attu left Ominato, the northernmost port of Honshu, accompanied by two cruisers and six destroyers, to rendezvous with another cruiser force hovering off the bleak Kurile Islands.

On June 1, 1942, the entire strength of the Japanese Combined Fleet was at sea. Operation MI involved 145 ships whose boilers would burn more fuel than the Imperial Navy had used in the entire previous year—all directed to winning control of the tiny patch of Pacific coral sand whose 2,000 acres was less than their combined deck area. A weather front conveniently blanketed the eastward progress of those units that had sailed from Japan, adding to the general mood of anticipation aboard ship that their operation must succeed. So confident had the Japanese Army unit been that it would be in control of Midway, the men had left instructions at Saipan for their mail to be sent on to the "Island of the Rising Sun," the name chosen for the atoll.

Yet even as it began, Yamamoto's over-elaborate choreography was starting to fall out of step. Operation K, for the planned seaplane reconnaissance flight, due to take place on May 30, had to be abandoned when the submarine detailed to carry out the refueling at the French Frigate Shoals arrived to find an American minelayer at anchor. The thirteen submarines that had set out to put an iron ring around Oahu arrived on their station a day late, failing to intercept the Pacific Fleet's two task forces, which were steaming toward Midway undetected.

Yamamoto had written to Chyoko Kawai—the former geisha "Plum Dragon," who had been his intimate and mistress for eight years— "Now comes the crucial time." Of his long-anticipated decisive battle, he wrote enigmatically: "Not that I'm expecting very much of it," in marked contrast to his infectious show of confidence before his officers. So when he received the report from the *Yamato*'s communications officer that they had picked up signals apparently indicating an American carrier in Hawaiian waters, he decided that it did not warrant prejudicing the whole operation by breaking radio silence, in spite of his staff's concern that the failure of their reconnaissance flight over Pearl Harbor might now prove more serious than at first thought. Three hundred miles deeper east into the Pacific, the *Akagi*'s radio aerials were not high enough to intercept the weak signals from the *Yorktown*'s air controller, so Admiral Nagumo had no grounds for the sort of suspicions troubling Yamamoto. He continued to rely on the intelligence reports radioed out from naval staff headquarters in Tokyo. They had been completely convinced by the radio deceptions transmitted by the *Tangier* and the *Salt Lake City* into believing that the American carriers sighted two weeks before off the Solomons were still safely distant in the South Pacific. Since the *Shoho* required a three-month refit, they also assumed that it was equally unlikely any American carrier damaged in the Coral Sea battle would be at sea before then.

Good fortune and Japanese laxity gave the intelligence advantage to the Pacific Fleet until May 28, when the Japanese Combined Fleet finally switched over to their new code books. This effectively blocked the HYPO team from breaking the new fleet code for many weeks. Had the change been made only days earlier, it might have disrupted the whole of CINCPAC's carefully laid ambush. The midget submarine attacks made on the Royal Navy battleship at Madagascar on May 31, and the sinking of a ferry in Sydney Harbor that evening, might have revived the fear that Japan was, after all, heading back toward Australia and the Indian Ocean. However, too much was now known about Admiral Yamamoto's Operation MI for Nimitz to fall for this feint or for the attack next day on the coast of Alaska.

16

"Give 'Em the Works"

Fog and heavy cloud banks shrouding the barren Aleutian Islands had enabled Admiral Kurita's carriers to make a stealthy run eastward to within 200 miles of Unalaska Island by the morning of June 3, 1942. They had been undetected by the Navy PBY Catalinas that patrolled from the windswept base at Dutch Harbor. Admiral Theobald's task force of cruisers was over 400 miles away to the southeast in pursuit of his own hunch that the Japanese would not invade Kiska and Attu but Kodiak, to menace the principal Alaskan mainland ports.

Shortly after sunrise, Kurita had flown a strike off each of his carriers, headed in through soupy gray overcast toward Unalaska. Following maps that had been drawn up from charts thirty years out of date, the *Junyo*'s planes lost their way and were forced to return to refuel. The *Ryujo*'s strike had better luck, breaking through the clouds into bright sunshine almost within sight of Dutch Harbor. Not until 8 A.M. did the American radar pick up the incoming attack. This gave only a few minutes' warning before a dozen Japanese planes spitting fire came roaring in. There was no time to clear shipping or to get the PBY flying boats and a few of the Army's P-40 fighters into the air. The raid set fuel storage tanks ablaze, demolished part of the barracks and the wooden huts housing the hospital. Several PBYs were wrecked in addition to the radio station, at the cost of a single enemy plane that plunged into the icy waters of the harbor after being hit by antiaircraft gunfire. The nine Japanese dive bombers and two surviving fighters managed to get back to the *Ryujo*, where they were refueled to fly off on a second strike. However in thick cloud they lost the destroyers and submarines they had earlier sighted in Makushin Bay.

When the signals reporting the success of the Dutch Harbor raid were brought to Admiral Yamamoto's cabin aboard the *Yamato* that morning, his appetite revived for breakfast after two days of nervous stomach cramps. Far out to the east ahead of his flagship, the strike force was struggling through a fog bank so thick that Nagumo's carriers turned on their searchlights to avoid collisions. The weather front prevented any aerial reconnaissance as they approached the point where he was scheduled to swing around from a northeasterly course to the southeast for the final run in toward Midway. Lack of up-to-date intelligence on enemy movements aroused his caution. "But where is the enemy fleet?" he asked his staff repeatedly, before accepting that there was no choice in the dense fog but to permit the flagship's lowest-powered radio to transmit the change of course order. Nagumo's brief mid-morning signal caused a minor alarm when it was picked up by the *Yamato*, following some 600 miles astern. Despite Yamamoto's fears, however, it was not heard by any of the American task forces some 700 miles to the east as they steamed about "Point Luck" 200 miles northwest of Midway.

But only minutes earlier a PBY Catalina patrolling down the extreme arc of its search pattern some 700 miles west of Midway had torn aside the curtain of secrecy the Japanese believed still concealed their moves. "Do you see what I see?" Ensign Jack Reid, the flying boat's skipper, asked his co-pilot as he grabbed his binoculars. Thirty miles ahead he had sighted the transports carrying the approaching Midway Occupation Force. For two hours the Catalina tracked the convoy to confirm its course and speed before radioing: "MAIN BODY . . . BEARING 262, DISTANCE 700 MILES . . . ELEVEN SHIPS, COURSE 090, SPEED 19 KNOTS." The alarm sent the Army's B-17s roaring off the atoll's runways.

"This will clear up all the doubters now. They had just to see this to know what I told them is correct," Nimitz told Commander Layton, passing him the sighting report picked up immediately after the news of the raid on Dutch Harbor. To avoid any possible risk that it might send Fletcher's task forces chasing south to hit the transport fleet, CINCPAC radioed an urgent signal: "MAIN BODY . . . THAT IS NOT, REPEAT NOT, THE ENEMY STRIKING FORCE."

It was to be well into the afternoon of June 3 before the nineteen Flying Fortresses had rumbled west across the International Dateline into the next calendar day to reach the Japanese convoy. Hitting a slow-moving target from over 10,000 feet up was a difficult assignment for the most practiced bomb aimers in the Army Air Force, and impossible for bombardiers as unpracticed as these ex-civilians, who only months before had been taxi drivers, salesmen, and farm hands. But they were sufficiently impressed by the spectacular waterspouts thrown up by their explosives to radio back enthusiastically the sinking of several *"Normandie*-type" vessels.

Landing at Midway that afternoon, four new Navy PBY Catalina reinforcements were surprised to be ordered to load up with torpedoes and take off immediately for a second attack. It was late into the evening when the flying boats, with engines throttled right back, came swooping out of a velvet-black moonlit sky. Making a low pass over the transports, they dropped torpedoes that damaged a tanker but failed to halt the Japanese convoy's eastward march toward Midway.

The reports of these two attacks left Admiral Yamamoto in no doubt that his Midway invasion plan had been unmasked, but it did not unduly concern him or his staff. They decided it would only serve to bring the main body of the Pacific Fleet sortying out of Pearl Harbor a few hours earlier than they had originally intended. Midway was the bait in his carefully sprung trap; the advance jaw of the carrier strike force was heading for the dawn air strike on the atoll across a starlit ocean whose tranquil beauty erupted as a jittery gunner on an escorting heavy cruiser fired off at an imaginary aircraft.

On Midway itself, the tense night of June 3 passed in agonizing slowness. Marine gunners hoped they would not meet the same fate that had overtaken Wake as they tried to catch what sleep they could beside their batteries. The aircrews of the 110 planes defending the atoll dozed beside their radios, ready to scramble as the headquarters' watch, fixed on the glowing radar screen, sent invisible electromagnetic fingers into the Pacific night.

Aboard the three American carriers 300 miles to the northeast it was also a long night. Many men wrote eve-of-battle letters to loved ones. The *Yorktown* fliers broke their craps marathon at 9 P.M., just long enough to hear Lieutenant Dick Crowell tell them: "The fate of the United States now rests in the hands of two hundred and forty pilots." In the hangar decks of all three carriers the mechanics slaved through the night preparing their planes, while the galley hands turned out thousands of sandwiches for sustenance during the next day's action.

"THE SITUATION IS DEVELOPING AS EXPECTED. CARRIERS OUT MOST IMPORTANT OBJECTIVE SHOULD BE LOCATED," CINCPAC flashed in a reassuring signal to his task force commanders, reminding them: "TOMORROW MAY BE THE DAY YOU CAN GIVE THEM THE WORKS."

Pearl Harbor was on Red Alert against enemy seaplanes, and as far away as the West Coast radio stations had been silenced to prevent enemy bombers homing in on San Francisco. Standing 400 miles out to sea, a bobbing line of assorted yachts and requisitioned civilian patrol craft waited for enemy battleships to loom over the dark horizon. Sunrise had already ended the lonely night's vigil for the volunteer coastguards off California when dawn broke over the Japanese and American carrier forces.

Far across the Pacific the U.S. Navy aircrews were piped out of their bunks at 1:30 A.M. for a hearty steak and egg breakfast. Less than 300 miles away to the west, Imperial Navy pilots in their flying gear were breakfasting off trays loaded with ample dishes of rice, soybean soup, pickles, dried chestnuts, followed by a battle toast in warm sake. The two opposing forces were at the end of a giant V, 200 miles long, with its point hinged on Midway. While the American commanders had a good idea of the position of the Japanese, Admiral Nagumo, after reviewing the latest intelligence reports from Tokyo, had concluded at the final predawn briefing: "There is no evidence of an enemy task force in our vicinity." With the concurrence of Commander Genda, who was roused from the sickbay where he was recovering from pneumonia, the first strike wave was to be armed with high-explosive bombs "to attack Midway, destroy the land-based planes there and support the landing operation." This wave comprised 72 bombers and 36 fighters, leaving 126 planes in reserve, loaded with armor-piercing bombs and torpedoes. "We can then turn around, meet an enemy task force and destroy it," Nagumo assured his staff, confident they would still be left with a force of thirty-six Zero fighters to fly combat patrol over the carriers, which would steam in a tight box formation to ensure the maximum protection from the guns of his battleships and cruisers.

Believing that he had more than adequately ensured his striking force's defense against being "jumped," Nagumo now made a fatal mistake by not ordering out all ten float planes carried by his battleships and cruisers, to make a thorough dawn reconnaissance of the ocean around Midway. He might well have dispatched more than four float planes if his suspicions had been aroused, as Yamamoto's had, that an American carrier was as close as Hawaii three days earlier. Fate again intervened to reduce the effectiveness of the mission when the heavy cruiser *Tone*'s jammed catapult delayed the launching of the plane assigned the most easterly leg of the search pattern—one that in just over an hour would have taken him over the American carriers.

The gray skies over the Japanese strike force were suffused with saffron at 4:30, when the first of the 128 planes heading for Midway raced down the *Akagi* to lift off. It passed over the blood-red identification disc that had been painted at the bow end of the wooden flight deck. Watching in deep regret that an operation for appendicitis the day after the flagship sailed from Hashirajima had kept him from leading the attack was Commander Fuchida. This time the honor of leading the double Vs of the attack forming up in the brightening sky was given to Lieutenant Joichi Tomonaga, who was making his first seaborne operation at the head of *Hiryu*'s squadron of Val bombers.

THE RAID ON MIDWAY

June 4, 1942, dawned auspiciously bright and clear over the American task forces, with only a few puffy clouds floating in the sky and a gentle southeasterly trade wind. The Midway PBY Catalina patrols had taken off from the island's lagoon well before sunrise and were now fanning out across the blue expanse of ocean like the spokes of a great wheel over 1,000 miles in diameter. Admiral Fletcher was relying on their reconnaissance to pick up the disposition of the approaching enemy forces. To make doubly certain that he found the Japanese carriers before they found him, he dispatched a reconnaissance patrol to search the ocean northwest of where Layton's latest bulletin had predicted the enemy were moving in on Midway. With his strike planes bombed and fueled, the pilots donned flying gear to wait in the briefing rooms for news of the enemy's position before taking off to attack. As the minutes turned into hours, they envied the Wildcat fighter pilots who were flying the cover duties over their carriers, and the *Yorktown*'s ten Dauntless dive bomber crews, who had been out scouring the ocean since sunrise.

Flying up the leg of the same giant V from Midway, as the Japanese strike was heading down, was Lieutenant Howard Ady's PBY. An hour into his mission he sighted a seaplane closing in on him below on the opposite course, prompting his radioed "AIRCRAFT" alert. Fifteen minutes behind his plane, another Catalina flown by Lieutenant William Chase was also heading northwest up the search sector. At 5:45 A.M. he signaled: "MANY ENEMY PLANES HEADING MIDWAY BEARING 320 DEGREES DISTANT 150 MILES." Only minutes followed before Ady pushed through a cloud bank to see, just 20 miles ahead and below, "the curtain rise on the Biggest Show on Earth." It was Nagumo's striking force. Radioing "ENEMY CARRIERS," he ducked into the clouds again to dodge the fighters, later finishing the message awaited by Midway command: "TWO CARRIERS TWO BATTLESHIPS BEARING 320 DEGREES DISTANT 180 MILES COURSE 135 DEGREES SPEED 25 KNOTS."

Picked up and relayed from Midway to Pearl Harbor by cable, CINCPAC staff now could give a positive position to their main target on the operational plot. A beaming Nimitz congratulated Commander Layton: "Well, you were only five miles off."

Aboard the *Yorktown* and *Enterprise* the air staff of the two task forces were laying off courses that would bring their carriers' aircraft within striking distance of the enemy force. Unwilling to betray his presence by radioing a recall to the reconnaissance flight of Dauntlesses, Admiral Fletcher flashed by signal lamp to Spruance 8 miles astern: "PROCEED SOUTHWESTERLY AND ATTACK ENEMY CARRIERS WHEN DEFINITELY LOCATED . . . WILL FOLLOW AS SOON AS PLANES RECOVERED." Aboard the *Enterprise*, the admiral and his Chief of Staff, Browning, had been busy with chart and dividers, computing that it would take three hours more steaming at full speed in the direction of Midway to bring the enemy carriers within range of an air strike.

On the airstrip on the atoll's Eastern Island, the runways had been humming with taxiing aircraft as everything that could fly was being put into the air before the Japanese attack arrived. The PBYs lumbered off the lagoon to cruise around a safe distance to the east, while the Navy's six Avenger torpedo strike planes, followed by the four Army B-26 Marauder twin-engined bombers, led off the waves heading out to the northwest. The second wave was made up of the sixteen Marine Dauntless dive bombers, trailed by the Army's B-17 Fortresses. Last came the slow eleven Marine "Vindicator" torpedo bombers.

The island's twenty-seven Wildcat fighters and Marine Buffaloes then took off to climb to 12,000 feet, ready to swoop down on the enemy. When the din of hundreds of aero engines died, a silence descended over the atoll except for the relentless booming of the surf and the squawks of gooney birds. It was broken only by the commands relayed over loudspeakers as the Marines took cover beneath their sandbagged emplacements and steel-helmeted gun crews on the two sandy spits swung their antiaircraft batteries toward the northwest.

At 6:16 A.M. the probing radar beams at last picked up the incoming planes, still invisible 74 miles out over the horizon, as a countdown began over the loudspeaker to the opening of the antiaircraft barrage. The Japanese attack had barely time to close half that distance before Major Floyd B. Parks's Marine fighter squadron had dived into the midst of the formation of Japanese Vals and Kates escorted by protective Zeros.

Watching the swirling dogfights through field glasses, Lieutenant Colonel Ira E. Kimes, the 2nd Marine Air Wing Commander, could see with dismay that the thirty-six Zeros spectacular maneuverability once again triumphed over the obsolescent Buffaloes and Wildcats. His pilots battled valiantly as seventeen were shot down and seven planes so badly hit they would never take to the air again. While Midway's fighter defense was tied up, Lieutenant Tomonaga led his Kates in to make their bombing runs completely unopposed from 14,000 feet, scarcely troubled by the mushrooming burst of antiaircraft shells. The attack destroyed the seaplane hangar and set the oil tanks and hospital ablaze on Sand Island. On Eastern Island, they failed to carry out their objective of putting the atoll's airstrips out of operation, succeeding only in wrecking the powerhouse and the Marine command post. After twenty minutes, when the Japanese planes had exhausted their bombs, the raid ended. All but four bombers and two fighters headed back toward the carriers, as Tomonaga tersely radioed *Akagi* at 6:50 A.M.: "SECOND ATTACK NECESSARY."

MIDWAY'S PLANES ATTACK

Just ten minutes later, the need for a second strike was forcefully made when the buglers aboard the Japanese warships trumpeted out the air-raid alarm. For nearly an hour the *Akagi*'s fighter controller had been vainly trying to vector his Zeros in to shoot down the American PBYs, who adopted the "very cunning maneuver" of dodging in and out of the clouds as they radioed in the attacking flights from Midway. Without radar, Admiral Nagumo only received a late warning of the approaching enemy bombers from the *Tone*'s float plane. Additional Zero fighters raced off from the *Akagi* and at this moment, Fuchida, still weak from his operation, collapsed. Refusing to be taken to the sickbay, he was propped up on deck with a parachute to watch with astonishment as the American torpedo planes flew in low, with no fighter protection.

Lieutenant L. K. Fieberling led his six "Avenger" torpedo bombers in on a suicidal mission: "Still they kept coming in, flying low over the water. Black bursts of anti-aircraft fire blossomed all around them, but none of the raiders went down. As *Akagi*'s guns commenced firing, three Zeros braved our own fire and dove on the Americans. In a moment's time, three of the enemy were aflame and splashed into the water, raising tall columns of smoke. The three remaining planes kept bravely on and finally released their torpedoes." One was hit and crashed off the carrier's deck in a blazing fireball; the *Akagi* easily swung around to dodge the slow-running American torpedoes. Only a single Avenger survived the attack to return and report its tragic failure. They were followed by the four B-26 bombers. It was the first torpedo attack the Army pilots had ever made, and their courage in flying so low into so much fire greatly surpassed their skill. As the Japanese gunners blazed away, it was an unfamiliar experience for them to see large twin-engined planes so close they could estimate the size of the white star insignia on the wings. One bored straight into the ocean; another dropped its torpedo before passing so low over the *Akagi* that it swept away the flagship's radio aerials; a third crashed in flames before reaching the carrier.

The attack petered out at 7:15 A.M. with the Japanese gun crews congratulating themselves on their easy victory and Fuchida pondering on the courage of the American pilots. Up on the *Akagi*'s flag bridge, Admiral Nagumo was in agitated discussion with his staff making the most critical tactical decision of the battle.

The air raid on the strike force left no doubts about the need for another strike against Midway; but the ninety-three aircraft that were ready for takeoff were armed with torpedoes and armor-piercing bombs to attack warships, not runways. Taking the advice of his Air Operations Officer, Genda, Admiral Nagumo gave orders that the aircraft should be taken below to the hangars to be rearmed with high-explosive bombs.

Less than 200 miles away, their opponents were steaming down the westerly leg of the V from the Japanese carriers when news that Midway had been raided caused Spruance and Browning's air staff to reconsider their earlier decision not to launch aircraft until nine o'clock. Quick calculation revealed that the enemy carriers could be attacked while they were recovering their Midway strike, presenting a golden chance to hit them at the most vulnerable moment. Accepting the risk that the range might be just too great for his torpedo bombers to make the return flight without running out of fuel, Spruance nevertheless decided to seize this tactical advantage to launch a powerful strike first. The chances that the American task forces would be discovered were increasing by the minute as the distance between them and the Japanese narrowed. Spruance boldly ordered a strike by every bomber the *Enterprise* and the *Hornet* carried, holding back only thirty-six fighters to fly a combat patrol.

Launching operations began just before 7 A.M. with Task Force 16 turning into the southeasterly breeze. Flying off operations were therefore to take the American carriers away from the enemy force—a problem that plagued Spruance and Fletcher throughout that day's battle. It took more than an hour to get the twenty Wildcat fighters, sixty-seven Dauntless dive bombers, and twenty-nine Devastator torpedo bombers into the air. The slow takeoffs became even more painful for Spruance after the sighting of a Japanese scout plane on the horizon when less than half his strike were airborne and burning up precious fuel circling. The enemy pilot's agitated radio transmissions, picked up by the *Enterprise*, indicated he was relaying position reports to the Japanese carriers. At 7:45 Spruance gave orders for Lieutenant C. W. McClusky, leader of the dive bombers, to head off without waiting for the rest of the *Hornet*'s strike.

Following some 25 miles astern of Task Force 16's wake, Admiral Fletcher had by now decided that the *Yorktown* must launch her attack. The Midway PBY patrols had not reported sighting any other enemy carriers, but even so, he decided not to risk repeating his mistake at the Coral Sea by sending off all his planes. Half were kept in reserve as a wave of seventeen Dauntlesses, sixteen Devastators, and six Wildcats zoomed off to the west.

The American commanders by 8:30 had sent 155 aircraft out in three waves to attack the Japanese carriers. Not a single Japanese plane was yet heading to attack them. Nearly an hour had passed since Spruance's force had been spotted by the float plane from the cruiser *Tone*, which had started its reconnaissance half an hour late because of the jammed catapult. Its pilot had only then spotted Task Force 16 by chance as he was making the final dogleg of his search pattern before heading back to the cruiser to refuel.

"SHIPS APPARENTLY ENEMY SIGHTED BEARING 010 DEGREES DISTANT 240 MILES MIDWAY. COURSE 150 DEGREES, SPEED MORE THAN 30 KNOTS," the *Tone*'s plane flashed out. The alarm was rushed up to the *Akagi*'s bridge only twenty minutes after Nagumo had decided to launch a second strike on Midway. The totally unexpected news that there were U.S. Navy units less than 200 miles away hit the admiral and his staff "like a bolt out of the blue." The signal did not make it plain whether the ships included a carrier. Nagumo concluded he could not risk assuming that there was no carrier. Below decks, the flagship's hangar crews were halfway through the time-consuming task of rearming the second strike with high explosives, so orders were made to the three other carriers: "PREPARE TO CARRY OUT ATTACK ON ENEMY FLEET UNITS. LEAVE TORPEDOES ON THOSE ATTACK PLANES WHICH HAVE NOT YET CHANGED TO BOMBS."

Nagumo now desperately needed to know whether the enemy units included a carrier before making a final decision to call off the second Midway raid. "ASCERTAIN SHIP TYPES AND MAINTAIN CONTACT," was radioed to the *Tone*'s scout. Ten minutes passed without any response. Then, infuriatingly, the pilot signaled only a change in course report. Tempers rose on *Akagi*'s flag bridge.

At 8:09, the message: "ENEMY SHIPS ARE FIVE CRUISERS AND FIVE DESTROYERS," brought Nagumo only brief relief. Eleven minutes later he received the electrifying report brought up from the radio room: "ENEMY FORCE ACCOMPANIED BY WHAT APPEARS TO BE AN AIRCRAFT CARRIER BRINGING UP THE REAR." The *Tone*'s pilot was cursed for his vagueness. A fierce debate broke out between Nagumo and his staff about what to do next. In ten minutes the first of the Midway strike planes would be returning with fuel tanks low as the rearming of the second strike was nearing completion. If it was to be launched before landing-on operations, Nagumo would have to watch his first-wave planes pancaking into the sea as they ran out of fuel. But if he did not launch a strike immediately against the enemy carrier, he risked being caught by American bombs with his flight decks jammed with parked aircraft.

DISRUPTION BY MIDWAY'S TORPEDO BOMBERS

It was the worst possible predicament for a carrier commander. As he argued with his staff, trying to find a way out of the tactical dilemma, Nagumo's discomfort was heightened by the arrival of a new strike from Midway. Dive bombers led by Major Loften P. Henderson came in without fighter escort on low-gliding runs that made them easy targets for the Zeros. Half the sixteen Marine Dauntlesses were shot down, and six of the eight that managed to get back to the airstrip on Midway were so badly damaged that they never took off again. Hard on their heels, at 8:10, arrived the fifteen Flying Fortresses, which dropped their bombs from 20,000 feet through wispy clouds. A great deal of water was churned up, doing no damage—although the Army pilots would claim to have sunk two carriers.

Ten minutes later the eleven Vindicators led by Major Benjamin Norris lumbered in to deliver their torpedoes. The Zeros were so fast and the "Wind Indicators," as the Marine pilots sarcastically called their ancient planes, so tardy that the carriers easily outmaneuvered them. Instead, they concentrated their run on the battleship *Hiruna*, but none of their torpedoes connected with a Japanese warship. It was nothing short of a miracle that Norris managed to get nine of his planes back safely with their wings peppered full of bullet holes.

The tail end of the Midway air strikes might not have scored a single hit, but they had thrown Nagumo's force into the confusion of having to maneuver sharply to avoid torpedoes while the admiral and his staff tried to wrestle with their critical decision. Watching through the periscope of the submarine *Nautilus* was Lieutenant Commander Brockman, who had been on surface patrol when his radio operator picked up the first PBY Catalina report and he successfully managed to intercept the Japanese. Taking advantage of the renewed air attack to select a target, his periscope was spotted. "Ships were on all sides moving across the field at high speed and circling away to avoid the submarine's position." Nonetheless, he successfully fired one torpedo, which failed to find its battleship target, before diving at 8:25 to 125 feet to ride out a depth charge attack from the escorting destroyers.

At 8:30, with the Midway strike wave due to return, Admiral Tamon Yamaguchi of the 2nd Carrier Division was growing impatient with the hesitation aboard the flagship. The *Kaga* and *Akagi* were still loading their second-strike planes with armor-piercing bombs and torpedoes, but the *Hiryu* and the *Soryu* already had thirty-six armed dive bombers ready to take off. Their covering fighter escort had been sent aloft to meet the series of American attacks, but Yamaguchi, an aggressively brilliant tactician who was considered a future Commander in Chief, believed that any delay in making a strike against the enemy was madness. "CONSIDER IT ADVISABLE TO LAUNCH ATTACK FORCE IMMEDIATELY," he flashed from the *Hiryu*. The strike force's original box formation had now been pushed out by the air assault into a diamond shape, with Yamaguchi's carrier so far away that his signal had to be relayed to the *Akagi* by destroyer.

NAGUMO'S FATAL DECISION

On the assurance of his staff that recovery operations could be completed in half an hour, Admiral Nagumo—again with Commander Genda's acquiescence—finally decided that the first strike must be landed, refueled, and rearmed before flying off on a mission to hit the enemy force. This meant getting the second-strike planes already coming up on deck down below once more. "Here we go again," *Akagi*'s flight officer Masuda called. "This is getting to be like a quick-change contest." Elevator warning bells began clanging as the parked aircraft were struck down to the hangars to clear the flight decks for recovery. Weary crews began hauling up more trucks of bombs and torpedoes. Because the turn-around was being rushed, there were no hands or time to begin stowing the high-explosive bombs off-loaded from the second strike safely into the magazines. They were simply stacked, many still fused, in the hangars, while on deck the landings began.

"AFTER COMPLETING RECOVERY OPERATIONS WE PLAN TO CONTACT AND DESTROY ENEMY FORCE," Nagumo signaled to his carrier captains, at the same time radioing Yamamoto the dramatic news that a carrier force had been found, informing him: "WE WILL HEAD FOR IT."

Landing-on operations were completed on schedule just after nine; the decks of the Japanese carriers were a scene of feverish activity as refueling began. Hoses snaked across the decks and trolleys of bombs and ammunition wheeled out to rearm the planes. Nagumo had set a 10:30 deadline for launching a 102-plane strike, less than his full strength because he had still received no reports of there being more than a single American carrier. At the same time a fast float plane had been dispatched to confirm the reconnaissance of the *Tone*'s scout, but it had yet to reach the reported enemy force. When it did so a few minutes later, the pilot found to his dismay that his radio had packed up.

In that frantic half hour of activity following the American air and submarine attacks, Nagumo had overlooked the warning flashed twenty minutes before by one of the scouting float planes: "TEN ENEMY TORPEDO PLANES HEADING TOWARDS YOU." At 9:18, the striking force was steaming north in its diamond formation with *Hiryu* some 8 miles ahead of the *Akagi*, flanked by the *Kaga* and *Soryu*, when the outlying destroyers on the starboard screen began frantically signaling an aircraft warning and throwing up a smokescreen.

Bugles blared out aboard the flagship, signal lamps flashed: "SPEED PREPARATIONS FOR IMMEDIATE TAKEOFF," sending aircrews running across the tangle of fuel lines for their planes. Zeros began roaring off into the sky to join the air patrol already racing down on the enemy torpedo planes. "Was there any escape?" Fuchida wondered, as he lay propped up on the *Akagi*'s flight command post. "An electric thrill ran throughout the fleet as our interceptors took off amid the cheers of all who had time and opportunity to see them."

U.S. NAVY TORPEDO BOMBERS ATTACK

The *Hornet*'s squadron of fifteen torpedo planes took off with their leader, Lieutenant John C. Waldron, knowing that the chances of his men getting back were slim. Their Devastators were obsolete and slow, with tanks holding only enough fuel for a round trip of 300 miles—when they took off, the Japanese carriers were 175 miles away. "If there is only one plane left to make a final run in," Waldron, part Sioux Indian, had told his pilots, "I want that man to go in and get a hit." After losing touch with his fighter escort, he was headed out on a northerly course, following his Indian instinct rather than the flight briefing. It paid off at 9:20 when he spotted the enemy carrier force. Now some of his pilots were worrying that they were uncomfortably vulnerable without their escorts. Waldron, however, showed no hesitation in waggling his wings as the signal for his men to follow him down. "He went straight for the Japanese fleet as if he had a string tied to them," reported Ensign George Gay, who was the sole survivor after the torpedo planes fell victim to forty Zeros before they had ever reached torpedo-dropping range. Waldron was an early casualty. Gay's last sight was of his leader trying to bail out of a flaming plane.

"Their distant wings flashed in the sun," Fuchida would recall, as he watched the massacre of the torpedo planes off the *Akagi*'s starboard quarter. "Occasionally one of the specks burst into a spark of flame and trailed black smoke as it fell into the water. Our fighters were on the job, and the enemy seemed again to be without fighter protection."

Chunks were being torn out of Ensign Gay's plane by heavy antiaircraft fire as he dropped his torpedo before zooming over the carrier. "I could see the Jap Captain jumping up and down and raising hell, I could see the deck full of gas hoses and planes." With rudder controls shot away, Gay managed to pancake into the sea. Bleeding from bullet wounds, he crawled out of the waterlogged cockpit to take shelter under a seat cushion for a grandstand view of the opening round of the battle. After the Japanese had steamed off north, he inflated his yellow life raft, which kept him afloat until he was picked up the next day by a PBY.

Hard on the heels of Waldron's gallant band came the fourteen torpedo planes from the *Enterprise*, led by Commander Eugene E. Lindsey. Among the first planes to take off, almost three hours of flying had left his Devastators low on fuel and unable to wait around for the fighters to find them. The missing Wildcats were, in fact, circling 20,000 feet above awaiting Lindsey's radio call to bring them down. They never responded as Lindsey split his squadron into twos and threes to attack the *Kaga* and *Akagi*. As his planes slid down into a shallow dive, the enemy carriers were making 30 knots, showing their sterns to give their gunners and fighters more time to break up the slow-moving torpedo bombers. Lindsey and nine of his slow Devastators were shot down with no bomb hits.

The same sad fate befell Commander Lance E. Massey, who arrived about 10 A.M. with the *Yorktown*'s twelve torpedo planes. His escort of six Wildcats was overpowered by a swarm of Zeros, which shot down seven of his planes. Five closed to attack the *Soryu*, whose helmsman dodged the slow-running American torpedoes. Only two Devastators were to get back to the *Enterprise*.

Aboard the *Akagi*, Nagumo and his staff watched with relief the slaughter of the first wave of attackers. His force had won a breathing space without damage as orders went out urging the carrier deck crews to speed up completion of refueling operations. At any moment the American dive bombers might appear. The Japanese carriers' fate was now in the sweating hands of the men frantically trying to get the planes into the air and hose lines stowed before the bombs started falling. Every second was vital.

Tension was also fraying the nerves of Fletcher and Spruance, who were listening in to the radio relays on the bridges of the *Yorktown* and the *Enterprise* respectively. In the operations room at Pearl Harbor, CINCPAC staff were also eavesdropping on the static-filled aircraft control channels of their carriers. Anxiety was mounting because no positive news had come in for nearly two hours. A PBY report, relayed from Midway at 9:26, signaling the enemy invasion force 320 miles to the southwest, did not tell when the task force's air strikes would reach the Japanese carriers. The normally imperturbable Nimitz was "as frantic as I have ever seen him," before the radio crackled just before ten with the *Enterprise* air officer yelling: "ATTACK! ATTACK!"

"Wilco, as soon as I can find the bastards!" came the crisp reply. Commander Browning's angry order had been directed, not from the fighter escort for his carrier's torpedo planes but from his flight of dive bombers. For nearly two hours, Lieutenant Clarence W. McClusky had been leading thirty-seven Dauntlesses in search of a contact, unaware that the Japanese had swung around onto a more northerly course. This had inadvertently saved Nagumo from the thirty-five dive bombers sent out from the *Hornet*, which had hunted their target for over an hour before abandoning the mission to refuel at Midway. Fortunately for his country, McClusky had led his hunt north, finding the destroyer that had been left to depthcharge the *Nautilus* high-tailing northwest in what he guessed was the direction of the Japanese force. The *Enterprise* dive bombers roared down on the Japanese carriers as the two surviving *Yorktown* Devastators were being chased away from their abortive attack by Zeros.

Fortune, which had previously deserted the American torpedo bombers, now ensured that their sacrifice had not been made in vain. The three successive attacks, which had cost forty-one planes and the lives of eighty airmen, had also pulled down the Japanese fighter cover to deck level. Not even a Zero was fast enough to climb up to disrupt the tight formations of dive bombers hurtling down from 10,000 feet. Picking the two largest carriers, McClusky's Dauntlesses went into a 70-degree dive, their juddering bombsights locked on the red deck roundels of the *Akagi* and the *Kaga*, whose decks were being cleared from refueling lines and pilots scrambling for their planes.

"Hell Divers!" Fuchida recalled, as the alarm sounded at 10:24 and he looked up with horror at the American bombers looming larger by the second as he crawled for cover:

> The terrifying scream of the dive bombers reached me first, followed by the crashing of a direct hit. There was a blinding flash and then a second explosion much louder than the first. I was shaken by a weird blast of warm air. There was still another shock, but less severe, apparently a near miss. Then followed by a startling quiet as the barking guns suddenly ceased. I got up and looked at the sky. The enemy planes were already gone from sight. . . . I was horrified at the destruction that had been wrought in a matter of seconds. There was a huge hole in the flight deck just behind the midship elevator. The elevator itself, twisted like molten glass, was drooping into the hangar. Deck plates reeled in grotesque configurations. Planes stood tail up belching livid flames and jet-black smoke. Reluctant tears streamed down my cheeks as I watched the fires spread, and I was terrified at the prospect of induced explosions, which would surely doom the ship.

Bombs began detonating in the fierce heat of the pools of burning fuel, turning the *Akagi*'s flight deck into a "scene terrible to behold." Fire parties were driven back by the searing heat. The bomb which was to doom the flagship had ripped through the elevator, detonating in the hangar among the unstowed torpedoes. Bursting fireballs turned the great hangar into a roaring furnace that the extinguishing system was powerless to control. As a precaution Captain Aoki ordered the magazines flooded.

Out on the burning flagship's starboard wing, four bombs were dealing a similar fate to the *Kaga*. The first burst on her starboard quarter; the second and third wrecked the forward elevator and exploded below the island bridge, setting parked aircraft ablaze and killing the captain along with many of his senior officers. The fourth penetrated the hangar space, setting off a chain of detonations among bombs and torpedoes. Firefighters battled the engulfing tide of flame and the carrier's speed began dropping as the flight officer assumed command.

Still recovering from the attack on his flagship, Admiral Nagumo now looked out appalled to see two carriers also ablaze. The *Yorktown*'s dive bombers had made short work of the *Soryu*. Thanks to the skillful navigation of Lieutenant Commander Maxwell E. Leslie, his eighteen Dauntlesses, which had taken off over an hour after the *Enterprise*'s strike, had cut corners in their flight to arrive within minutes of McClusky's planes. Although a faulty switch had prematurely released his bomb, Leslie led his attack in notwithstanding. Guns flashed as two bombs hurled the carrier's elevator onto the bridge and set the parked planes ablaze while a third detonated in the hangar.

The rapidity of the six-minute attack paralyzed the Japanese defenses.

None of the *Yorktown*'s Dauntlesses were hit, although sixteen of Mc-Clusky's pilots were shot down by pursuing Zeros. They had, however, achieved a decisive victory. At the cost of forty-seven planes, the U.S. Navy had eliminated three quarters of the Imperial Navy's crack carrier strike force.

The *Soryu*, whose fires had by now taken uncontrollable hold, was the first to order abandon ship less than twenty minutes after the attack ended. Captain Yanagimoto supervised the ceremonial transfer of the Emperor's picture to a destroyer before seeking a warrior's death in the flames. An hour later a volunteer party of firefighters reboarded the crippled carrier and were having some success in their efforts to bring her under control when at 2 P.M. Lieutenant Commander Brockman of the *Nautilus* caught up to slam two torpedoes home. Two hours after that the American submarine surfaced to investigate the blazing hulk, which sank shortly after 7 P.M. taking down the bodies of seven hundred crew.

The *Kaga*'s acting captain was to order the ritual transfer of the Imperial portrait at 1:30 P.M., when the inferno below decks cut off the engine room. Abandon ship came at 5 P.M., and two hours later exploding fuel-storage tanks in the overheated hull sent the carrier to the bottom with eight hundred men, many trapped alive in the machinery spaces.

Nagumo's flagship managed to keep under way for twenty minutes until violent maneuvers to dodge an attack by four torpedo planes jammed the *Akagi*'s rudders. The starboard turbines went dead as she swung away from another reported attack at 10:40 A.M. Power was failing and flames were leaping up to the bridge from the blazing wreckage of aircraft as Nagumo, still in a daze, resisted the entreaties of his staff to evacuate his command to a waiting destroyer. By 10:47 the reluctant admiral was persuaded to make an undignified escape from a bridge window down a rope. Last down was Fuchida, who found the rope smoldering and the iron ladder too hot to hold, forcing him to jump and fracture both his ankles. Strapped to a bamboo stretcher, he joined the hundreds of burned and wounded who were taken across to the destroyer from the anchor deck. Evacuation was ordered at 11:30 by Captain Aoki, who remained on board to direct the desperate attempt to control the spreading conflagration. At 1 P.M. the Emperor's picture was taken off. But not until 7:30 P.M. did the captain give the final call to abandon ship, after insisting on lashing himself to a bulkhead to go down with his command. The blazing *Akagi* was still afloat at midnight when his officers reboarded to rescue their captain over his vehement protests. Four hours later on orders from Yamamoto the carrier was dispatched by a destroyer's torpedoes.

When Nagumo transferred his flag to the destroyer *Nagara* shortly before 11 A.M., he still had the undamaged *Hiryu* as well as two battleships, three cruisers, and a dozen destroyers under his command. This gave him a fighting chance to strike back at the American task forces, though it meant that the planes still aloft from the three blazing carriers would have to be ditched. "ATTACK ENEMY CARRIERS," the *Hiryu* was signaled. Nagumo's staff knew that so many aircraft could not have come from one carrier, but Captain Yamaguchi's confirmation: "ALL OUR PLANES ARE TAKING OFF NOW FOR THE PURPOSE OF DESTROYING THE ENEMY CARRIER," suggested that from his position nearly 10 miles ahead he had failed to realize this. Acting on reports from the cruiser's scouting planes, which had so far only spotted the *Yorktown*'s task force, he sent out only eighteen dive bombers and six fighters.

Conflicting and often indecipherable exchanges on the pilots' radio network had also presented a confused picture of the battle to Fletcher and Spruance. Not until the first aircraft had returned ninety minutes into the action did they finally learn of the American victory in the first round of the battle. Merely getting back to the *Enterprise* proved to be another ordeal for that carrier's pilots, when they found that their floating landing strip was not at the "Point Option." Task Force 16's air controllers had neglected to radio out an updated position, which had brought the force 60 miles to the east because of turning into the wind to launch and recover their fighters while the Dauntlesses were airborne. McClusky landed his plane with just 2 gallons of fuel left; others were not so lucky, ditching when their engines cut. Task Force 17's air control had been more diligent and Commander Leslie got all his victorious dive bombers back safely.

Mid-morning on June 4 was a time for cautious celebration for the American task forces and in the operations room at Pearl Harbor. A very different mood set in over the Combined Fleet's flagship when Nagumo's signal was received just before 11 A.M.—"FIRES RAGING ABOARD KAGA, SORYU, AKAGI RESULTING FROM ATTACKS CARRIED OUT BY ENEMY LAND-BASED AND CARRIER-BASED PLANES. WE PLAN TO HAVE HIRYU ENGAGE THE ENEMY CARRIERS, IN THE MEANTIME WE ARE RETIRING TO THE NORTH." The devastating news filled Yamamoto's staff with horror—yet their admiral showed no immediate reaction. His features, already unhealthily pallid from his stomach complaint, just seemed to tighten minutely. Faced with the prospect that his whole operation, as well as the decisive naval engagement, would slip from his grasp unless he could concentrate his scattered forces, he radioed urgent orders to the two carriers south of the Aleutians to join up with Admiral Kondo's force, now heading at utmost speed for Midway. In spite of Nagumo's message it was possible that only one American carrier was at sea. If the *Hiryu*'s aircraft could knock it out, his remaining five carriers and seven battleships might yet win a decisive victory.

THE JAPANESE ATTACK

Just before noon, the *Yorktown*'s radar picked up the *Hiryu*'s dive bombers heading in from the west when they were still nearly 50 miles away. Fletcher had guessed that one of the Japanese carriers might still be unaccounted for and had already sent out ten Dauntlesses to scout for her. This delayed the landing of the remainder of Commander Leslie's dive bombers circling overhead. Now they were ordered away to a safe distance as twelve Wildcats were sent up to meet the incoming attack. Down below, the carrier's fuel lines were flooded with carbon dioxide gas—a precaution to prevent fires and explosions spreading that had been instituted as a result of the *Yorktown*'s battle experience at the Coral Sea. By superhuman effort, engineers managed to get enough steam out of their patched-up boilers to push the carrier through the water at 30 knots.

The *Yorktown*'s fighter controllers, also recalling the lessons of the Coral Sea, managed to gain altitude to shoot down three of the escorting Zeros and six of the bombers before they began their attack. Warned that the enemy was diving in, Fletcher coolly rapped back: "Well, I've got on my tin hat. I can't do anything now." But the carrier's gunners could—and did. They knocked two more Vals out of the sky before they could release their bombs. Of the six that plummeted down, only three hit. One plane failed to pull out of its dive and disintegrated, its bomb rolling along the flight deck before it exploded, causing fires. Another bomb went through the smokestack. The backdraft of its explosion temporarily put out the burners in five of the carrier's six boilers. Steam pressure fell and the *Yorktown*'s speed began to drop as a third bomb penetrated the flight deck to pass clean through the hangar, before detonating and starting a conflagration on the armored fourth deck.

Three such hits had doomed each of the Japanese carriers; but the prompt flooding of the *Yorktown*'s magazines, the use of CO_2 gas to prevent fuel lines from igniting, and the fast work of the fire-control parties had checked the blaze in less than an hour. By 1:40 the engineers had refired the boilers and wooden planks patched the gaping hole in the flight deck. Captain Buckmeister was able to ring for 20 knots, turn his carrier into the wind, and recover the remaining dive bombers before they ran out of fuel. Because the bomb which had passed through the smokestack had destroyed the radar and subsequent fires had wiped out his communications center, Admiral Fletcher had been obliged to transfer his flag to the cruiser *Astoria*, passing over tactical command to Spruance on the *Enterprise*.

General elation greeted the valiant efforts of Captain Buckmeister's crew, who restored full air-strike capability to Task Force 17. Admiral Nagumo could not know the magnitude of his defeat: now 200 miles to the southwest of the *Yorktown,* he was leading a shattered strike force north after abandoning his three blazing carriers to the care of destroyers. After the triple blow he had suffered, the report came from the *Hiryu* that their first strike had hit and certainly sunk the American carrier, so that he believed only one remained. He still saw the chance to escape a disastrous defeat. That hope vanished shortly after 1 P.M., after the return of the aircraft that had been dispatched before the first American attack to make a full reconnaissance of the enemy units at sea off Midway. His mission negated by the radio failure, the unfortunate pilot had returned to find his carrier a blazing wreck, forcing him to land on the *Hiryu* with the bad news that he had definitely identified at least two American carriers. This was alarming enough for Admiral Yamaguchi, who was congratulating himself on having disposed of the enemy threat. It confirmed the worst fears of Admiral Nagumo, who realized that he was now facing odds of at least two to one.

YORKTOWN ABANDONED

Until the first strike aircraft returned and were refueled, Yamaguchi only had ten torpedo planes left with which to attack. They were launched at 1:30, escorted by six fighters. So vital was this mission considered by Lieutenant Tomonaga, the *Hiryu*'s senior pilot, that he insisted on leading it, though his own aircraft's damaged fuel tank would make no return trip.

An hour later, Tomonaga was nearing the end of his suicidal mission less than 50 miles from Task Force 17 when a cruiser's radar picked up the Japanese planes coming in low from the southwest. Warnings were flashed to the *Yorktown,* which had time to get four more Wildcats up to join the eight already flying cover, and they headed out to intercept. Tangling with the Zeros, they shot down one, as the Kates, dividing their attack, raced toward the *Yorktown* at masthead height from several directions. The four heavy cruisers screening the carrier tried the new tactic of shelling the sea ahead with their heavy guns to throw up a barrier of water. It proved too insubstantial to stop four determined Japanese pilots from crashing through to drop their "Long Lance" torpedoes less than 500 yards from the *Yorktown*'s bow, passing so close that the deck gunners could see the pilots shaking their fists in defiance.

Captain Buckmeister's damaged ship lacked the speed to maneuver fast enough to dodge all the torpedoes. Two plowed into the carrier's port quarter, ripping open her hull along the fuel tanks and jamming the rudder. Thousands of tons of the Pacific poured through the gash, sending the *Yorktown* heeling over in an alarming list. Damage-control parties were soon reporting that they could not handle the flooding because the temporary repairs had left the carrier far from watertight. Anticipating an imminent capsize, Buckmeister gave the order to abandon ship just before 3 P.M. Destroyers quickly secured alongside the keeling carrier to make such an efficient rescue of the survivors that no crew member was lost. Many sailors who had taken to the water were good-naturedly calling out "Taxi, Taxi," as the boats moved about in the flat calm picking them up.

While Captain Buckmeister was taking what later turned out to be a premature decision to abandon the *Yorktown,* her scouting flight of ten Dauntlesses, which had set out an hour earlier, arrived over the remnants of Nagumo's force at around 2:45 P.M. Lieutenant Wallace C. Short, in the lead, spotted the squared-off shape of a carrier far below. This sighting of the *Hiryu* some 110 miles northwest of Task Force 17 meant that the Americans had finally located the fourth carrier predicted by the pre-battle intelligence estimates.

When the news was radioed back to Task Force 16, Spruance turned the *Enterprise* to windward at 3:30 to launch off another strike of twenty-four dive bombers, including ten *Yorktown* Dauntlesses that had sought refuge while their carrier was being bombed. There were no Wildcats to spare for a fighter escort because they were held back to fly combat air patrol over the task forces. This did not unduly concern Lieutenant Wilmer E. Gallagher, who was eager for the chance to wipe out a second enemy carrier only seven hours after he had successfully attacked the *Kaga.*

THE PENULTIMATE ROUND

It was just before 5 P.M. when the new American strike arrived high over the *Hiryu,* half an hour after the carrier's five surviving torpedo planes and three fighters had landed back to attest to Lieutenant Tomonaga's posthumous triumph in supposedly sinking the *Yorktown.* Unaware that they had targeted the same carrier earlier claimed as sunk by the first Japanese strike, Yamaguchi's arithmetic showed he only had one carrier left to sink. Five dive bombers, five torpedo planes, and six fighters remained for him to reverse defeat into victory. But he decided first to feed his exhausted aircrews while fueling and rearming the planes for a strike at dusk.

A fast reconnaissance plane was ordered off at 5:03 P.M. to locate the U.S. carrier while the rest of *Hiryu*'s hungry crew were tucking into sweet rice balls. Then the lookouts in the squat bridge sang out: "ENEMY DIVE BOMBERS DIRECTLY OVERHEAD." There was not even time for the buglers to sound off the alarm before Gallagher's Dauntlesses came belting in out of the sinking sun. Deft evasive action on the helm avoided the first three bombs, but the next four tore along the deck like an explosive can opener, blasting the forward elevator into the island and starting fires in the hangars below. Minutes later the attack was over. All but three Daunt-lesses made it back to the *Enterprise* safely by dusk, to report that they had won the unique distinction of sinking two carriers on a single day.

The *Hiryu* continued to struggle on at nearly 30 knots, as all hands except the gunners turned to battle the conflagrations. Most of their fire-fighting equipment had been wiped out, and the bucket chains that were formed proved hopeless in fighting the exploding bombs and torpedoes which had been brought up to the hangar to arm the evening strike. Deck by deck the blaze spread downward, trapping the engine-room gangs in a fiery tomb. The *Hiryu* was still under way, like a floating torch, trailing a great column of smoke, when she was spotted shortly after 6 P.M. by B-17 Fortresses flown out from Midway to make another strike. For the second time that day all the Army bombs missed. As darkness fell, Mid-way's remaining Marine bombers and torpedo planes took off to make a night attack—but they failed to find the burning carrier, which had steamed much farther than anticipated before her turbines died.

It was after 1 A.M. before Admiral Yamaguchi began preparing for the ceremonial ritual that preceded the order to abandon ship, while a series of explosions roared through the blazing wreck. Wreathed in smoke, Cap-tain Kaku solemnly passed the Emperor's picture for transfer to a de-stroyer as the diminutive Admiral Yamaguchi stood on a biscuit tin to deliver an emotional farewell address. After exchanging ceremonial cups of water with his flag captain, the two led the singing of the "Kimigayo" anthem. Survivors were being taken aboard the destroyers as Yamaguchi and Kaku paused to wonder at the beauty of the moon before retiring to their cabins to commit seppuku—ritual suicide. Final orders were for a destroyer to torpedo the *Hiryu,* but she was found afloat at daybreak with seventy men still alive on board. They were taken off before the burnt-out wreck was finally dispatched at noon.

The succession of blows that had knocked out the last carrier in Ad-miral Nagumo's strike force signaled his crushing defeat. "The game is up," was the reaction of Admiral Yamamoto's yeoman at 5:30 that after-noon, as he passed to the Commander in Chief the dire message just re-ceived from the cruiser *Nagara: "Hiryu* hit by bombs and set afire." The members of the staff, their mouths shut tight, conferred for more than an hour over charts, checking off the dispositions of the remaining units. Racing down from the North Pacific, after making a second air strike against Dutch Harbor, was Admiral Kakuta with his two carriers and heavy cruisers. Up from the west, Admiral Kondo was heading toward Midway with his light carrier, two battleships, and four heavy cruisers; and from the northwest Admiral Kurita was bearing down at full speed with four heavy cruisers and three seaplane tenders. Bringing up the rear was the main force, with the mighty *Yamato,* two battleships, and a light carrier. If this formidable force could join up with Nagumo's two surviving battleships and three cruisers, Yamamoto saw a chance still to win a "decisive naval engagement." To rally his scattered forces the Commander in Chief flashed out an optimistic signal that evening: "THE ENEMY FLEET HAS BEEN PRACTICALLY DESTROYED AND IS RETIRING TO THE EASTWARD." Orders went out for the occupation of Midway to proceed as planned the next day.

THE FINAL ROUND

To Nagumo, receiving Yamamoto's 7 P.M. orders that all units were to "immediately contact and destroy the enemy force," the signal seemed hopelessly impractical in the light of the last intelligence report radioed in from the plane that had left the *Hiryu* just before the final attack, indicating that yet more enemy carriers were at sea.

"TOTAL ENEMY STRENGTH IS FIVE CARRIERS SIX HEAVY CRUISERS AND FIFTEEN DESTROYERS. THEY ARE STEAMING WESTWARD. WE ARE RETIRING TO THE NORTHWEST ESCORTING HIRYU. SPEED 18 KNOTS." This very abrupt defiance of his orders was interpreted in turn by Yamamoto's Chief of Staff Admiral Ugaki to mean that Nagumo "has no stomach for a night engagement." He knew the Americans could not possibly have five carriers at sea anywhere in the Pacific; at the most, he calculated that there could be only two operational. Yamamoto was hoping to bring whatever forces were lurking north of Midway into a battle that night, when he would have enough battleships and cruisers to win a victory that would wipe out the defeat the Imperial Navy had suffered during the day. Accordingly, he signaled to Admiral Kondo to take over tactical command and deploy his battleships and cruisers. Nagumo's force was ordered to reverse course immediately, and "participate in the night engagement."

Once again Yamamoto's plans were cast on the expectation that the enemy would fall in with his scheme. But a night engagement off Midway could only come about if the American force continued steaming eastward. In fact, Spruance for his part was well aware of the dangers of taking Task Force 16 farther west. Analysis of the Japanese radio traffic gave a strong indication that another large force was bearing in from the northwest and that the carriers that had attacked Dutch Harbor were apparently bearing down from the north to cut him off from Hawaii. Moreover, the B-17s that had attacked the *Hiryu* at dusk had reported being attacked by Zeros. These might have come from the burning carrier, or there might be a second carrier in the vicinity. Even allowing for the tactical advantage that radar would give his ships, Spruance decided that to chase Nagumo's battered force into the night could hazard the victory he and Fletcher had won. "I did not feel justified in risking a night encounter with possibly superior enemy forces," he would give as the reason for caution. "But on the other hand I did not want to be too far away from Midway the next morning. I wished to have a position from which either to follow up retreating enemy forces or break up a landing in Midway." Once he had recovered the last strike planes, the American task force withdrew east until midnight, when they reversed course to bring them back within striking distance of threatened Midway at dawn.

Although he faced later criticism for giving up the pursuit, Spruance's tactical judgment proved absolutely correct. Had he continued westward, he would certainly have run into the trap that Yamamoto set and, with his carriers unable to operate their planes at night, would have fallen easy prey to the guns of Kondo's battleships and Kurita's heavy cruisers.

After an anxious wait until midnight for word that the enemy force had been contacted, Yamamoto faced the downfall of his plan for luring the Americans into a night action. He and his staff now had to worry about the massacre that would occur if dawn caught them too near Midway's aircraft or strikes from the returning enemy carriers. The advice of some of his staff was that the atoll should be bombarded and captured as a face-saving operation; but Admiral Ugaki dismissed such an option. "Our battleships, for all their firepower, would be destroyed by enemy air and submarine attacks before we could even get close enough to use our big guns." The capture of Midway would have to be postponed. "But even if that proves impossible and we must accept defeat in this operation, we will not have lost the war. There will still be eight carriers in the Fleet, counting those which are to be completed soon. In battle as in chess, it is the fool who lets himself be led into a reckless move through desperation."

Not all his staff were prepared to accept Ugaki's hard-faced analysis. Some asked: "How are we going to apologize to His Majesty for this defeat?" Their Commander in Chief, who had maintained silent counsel, now made it clear he would swallow that most bitter of pills—"Leave that to me," Yamamoto interrupted. "I am the only one who must apologize to His Majesty."

"MIDWAY OPERATION IS CANCELED" was flashed out at midnight from the Combined Fleet flagship. By abandoning the plan, Yamamoto not only accepted defeat but also resigned himself to the fact that bringing off a war-winning naval victory against the Americans would now be more difficult to achieve.

The transports carrying the invasion force turned back for Saipan. Admirals Kondo and Kurita were ordered to join up with Nagumo and rendezvous to the northwest with the main force to return to Japan. Only the northern units were signaled to go ahead with the planned occupation of the two Aleutian Islands. A few shells from a lone Japanese submarine defiantly but harmlessly splashing into Midway's lagoon were a reminder of the Combined Fleet's awesome gunpower, which had been defeated by the U.S. Pacific Fleet's carrier aircraft without ever having had a chance to launch a salvo. The night of despair was over for Yamamoto, who promptly retired to his cabin complaining again of stomach pains. The collapse of Operation MI was to tarnish the Imperial Navy's record, its first defeat made more humiliating when two ships in Kurita's cruiser force were later involved in a collision some 90 miles northwest of Midway.

After receiving the recall signal, the four heavy cruisers of the Occupation Support Force were steaming across the Pacific at 28 knots when a lookout spotted a submarine. The leading pair swung violently to port, but the stern marker *Mogami* did not pick up the signal until too late, ramming into the *Mikuma* ahead of her. Although he had not had a chance to fire his torpedoes, the skipper of the U.S.S. *Tambor*, before crash-diving to avoid the onrushing destroyers, was delighted to see that one cruiser was aflame at the bows. The *Mogami*, one of the world's fastest and most powerful cruisers, had its bows wrecked, and *Mikuma* was badly damaged. Quick work in shoring up their damaged bulkheads enabled them to limp away at 12 knots under heavy escort.

The night of June 4 was not without its anxiety for Admiral Nimitz and his staff at Pearl Harbor. News that their task forces had knocked out and set ablaze four Japanese carriers suggested they had victory in their grasp—unless Spruance blundered into a night engagement. Nimitz was certain that he did not have to remind his commander on the spot of the risks such a battle would bring when he sent out a message that evening: "You who have participated in the Battle of Midway today have written a glorious page in our history. I am proud to be associated with you. I estimate that another day of all out effort on your part will complete the defeat of the enemy." The CINCPAC war diary noted that June 4 had seen "the start of what may be the greatest sea battle since Jutland. Its outcome, if as unfavorable to the Japs as seems indicated, will virtually end their expansion."

In Washington, the Navy Department was cautiously guarded. Their release to the press on the morning of June 5 indicated that a major naval action was going on in the Pacific, which appeared to be falling in the United States' favor. "It is too early to claim a major Japanese disaster. . . . The enemy are continuing to withdraw, but we are continuing the battle." Reading between the lines of officialese, the reporters sensed the growing assurance of the Navy that the outcome would make the biggest headlines since Pearl Harbor.

Admiral Spruance, like the CINCPAC staff, fully expected that the battle would begin afresh the next morning. At dawn the PBYs were racing off Midway's lagoon to reconnoiter the enemy units. Heavy overcast and low visibility hampered their search operations as Task Force 16 steamed at a safe distance to the northeast off the atoll while Spruance waited for news of which Japanese force to attack with an air strike. For the pilots aboard the American carriers it was a long morning of waiting, an anticlimax to the action they were anticipating. The Marines' remaining Dauntlesses and Vindicators took off soon after dawn to attack the two crippled cruisers that had been reported by the *Tambor*. The Japanese gunners put up a fierce barrage, which cost an American plane without inflicting any more damage on either the *Mogami* or the *Mikuma*. Late that afternoon, when Spruance was convinced from the morning reconnaissance that all enemy heavy units were retreating westward, he launched a strike against the cruisers. Failing to locate them, the American planes dropped their bombs wildly, leaving unscathed a lone destroyer that had been sent to *Mogami*'s assistance.

The main action for the U.S. Navy that anticlimactic day was the battle to save the *Yorktown*. She had been found at dawn still afloat by the destroyer *Hughes*, which had come alongside to investigate reports of gunfire. Two wounded sailors who had crawled up from the sickbay where they had been left for dead the previous day had been responsible for the shots. Finding that the fires were out, the *Hughes*'s skipper put a salvage party aboard and radioed for help to save the drifting carrier. When the minesweeper *Vireo* appeared, the two small vessels spent the afternoon struggling to take the huge *Yorktown* in tow, their efforts hampered by a rising sea. At dusk, the destroyer *Hammann* arrived with Captain Buckmeister and a volunteer party drawn from his crew. The fight to salvage the dead carrier and counter her flooding compartments went on all night, with the *Hammann* alongside supplying power to work the pumps.

The battle for the drifting *Yorktown* might have been won had she not been sighted the previous morning by one of the reconnaissance float planes sent out from Nagumo's retreating cruisers. The nearest Japanese submarine was radioed to sink the carrier, but because of inaccurate reports of the position, took a day and a half to find its quarry. The *Yorktown*'s list had been corrected and hopes were rising that she might be brought back to Pearl Harbor with the arrival of tugs. But the captain of Imperial Navy submarine I-168 had finally fixed the carrier in the crosswires of his attack periscope. On the afternoon of June 6, one torpedo hit the *Hammann*, breaking the destroyer in two and sinking her with heavy loss of life; others slammed into her bulky charge. For the second time in two days Buckmeister was forced to abandon ship, although he hoped to get one of the other destroyers alongside to resume salvage operations next morning. Without power to keep the pumps going, the *Yorktown* that night succumbed to the flooding, capsizing and settling deep in the Pacific. The whole saga of her dismal end—after the glorious fight she had put up at the Coral Sea and Midway—was an indelible lesson to every skipper in the U.S. Navy not to abandon ship prematurely.

While the battle was still going on to save the *Yorktown*, Admiral Spruance was planning to take advantage of perfect flying weather to resume his pursuit of the enemy, now that it was clear the Japanese had abandoned their efforts to invade Midway and were in full retreat. The old naval maxim that "A stern chase is a long one" proved to be only too true. Yamamoto had not given up all hope that he might still have a chance of victory if the American force ventured far enough west to allow the Japanese to operate in conjunction with air strikes from the planes on Wake Island. But once again Spruance had second-guessed him by sending out a strike of dive bombers west that morning to locate the two damaged cruisers, which he knew would be trying to reach the protection of the atoll's Japanese base. They located both crippled vessels at mid-morning. They were helpless targets, "as easy as shooting ducks in a barrel," one of the *Enterprise* pilots radioed in excitement as the *Mikuma* sank in a mass of flames. Badly mauled and on fire, the *Mogami* still bore a charmed life, managing to limp away and eventually reach the sanctuary of Truk.

The pictures that were taken of the two battered cruisers, smoke and flames rearing from their battered turrets, were to be dramatic proof to the American public of the smashing victory won off Midway by their Pacific Fleet. The triumph was only slightly dimmed by the news that the Japanese had landed without opposition on the most westerly Aleutian Island, Attu, to make prisoners of a handful of Aleut Eskimos and the ten members of the weather station. With the simultaneous occupation of uninhabited Kiska, this gave enemy propaganda a chance to inflate the dramatic claim that the Rising Sun was now flying over the United States' mainland. What had been originally intended as the northern outpost of a mid-Pacific defensive perimeter would prove to be a strategic liability without the possession of Midway.

The Japanese clung stubbornly to their prize. Nimitz realized that the public would be upset by the fact that the enemy was technically on American shores, and the day after the landings he ordered Task Force 16 to head north to launch strikes against the islands in an attempt to dislodge this embarrassing new outpost of Japan. Spruance was relieved next day to learn from the signal recalling him to Pearl Harbor that CINCPAC had thought better of allowing his carriers to venture where they might be ambushed by battleships and submarines in the foggy northern waters.

Yamamoto had been robbed of his last opportunity to salvage something from the defeat whose catastrophic implications for Japan were soon to become apparent. The transports returned to Saipan with the

5,000 troops wondering what disaster had befallen the "invincible" Imperial Navy. The action off Midway, which marked the beginning of the end of the Japanese Empire, cost the Imperial Navy not only its undefeated record but four carriers and a heavy cruiser, the lives of 2,200 sailors, 234 aircraft, and the best of their naval aviation. "I felt like swearing," Admiral Ugaki wrote of the defeat, which bore even more heavily on his Commander in Chief. Declaring that "It was all his responsibility, and they were not to criticize the Nagumo force," Yamamoto retired to his quarters complaining of stomach cramps, refusing to see any of his staff for three days. Aboard the *Nagato*, Admiral Nagumo wretchedly blamed himself for the disaster and had to be persuaded by his staff not to commit suicide.

A major effort to cover up the magnitude of their defeat was launched on June 10 by the naval staff in Tokyo, who feared public reaction and a severe loss of face. Heralded by the blaring strains of the navy march, the radio announcer read a communiqué that Japan had "secured supreme power in the Pacific," and that the war had been "determined by one battle" in which one Imperial Navy carrier had been sunk to two losses by the U.S. Navy, along with 120 of their planes. Lantern parades were staged in Tokyo to celebrate this new "victory" when four days later the Combined Fleet made an unheralded return to the Hashirajima anchorage. There were no comments about the absence of four carriers because they were not missed, having been continuously at sea since the war began. The survivors of the *Akagi, Kaga, Soryu*, and *Hiryu* were hustled off without leave to outlying bases in Japan and the Pacific; the wounded were landed by night and taken to sealed hospital wards, where they were denied visits by their next of kin.

The U.S. Navy was at first circumspect about its victory. On June 6, when it became clear that the Japanese were in retreat, Nimitz radioed a congratulatory signal promising that the Pacific Fleet would "continue to make the enemy realize that war is hell." His staff celebrated with the Jeroboam of champagne dressed up with admiral's stripes that General Emmons sent to CINCPAC with his compliments—and a promise never to doubt naval intelligence in the future. Nimitz magnanimously sent his car to fetch Commander Rochefort to the party, but he was so long changing from his informal attire into uniform that he arrived after the champagne had run dry. Nimitz nevertheless paid him the tribute before his whole staff: "This officer deserves a major share of the credit for the victory at Midway."

On June 7, Fleet Admiral King in Washington held his first press conference since being appointed COMINCH. He allowed that the "enemy force have taken some hard knocks." Coming from the flinty admiral, most reporters knew this meant that a sizeable triumph had been chalked up by the U.S. Navy. That same morning the Chicago *Tribune* headlined: "NAVY HAD WORD OF JAPAN PLAN TO STRIKE AT SEA." The reporter Stanley Johnson had seen an after-action dispatch from which he was able to deduce the explosive revelation that victory had been made possible by a dramatic intelligence breakthrough. The story raised a storm behind the scenes, with King charging that it endangered the entire Pacific War. The panic blew over, however, when it appeared that Tokyo's intelligence staff apparently did not read American newspapers. The lapse in security was not repeated. All officers throughout the Navy were threatened, by personal directive from COMINCH, with instant court-martial if any such leaks occurred in future.

The triumph of the American carriers at Midway was won by the tenacity and secrecy of U.S. Naval Intelligence, and by the bravery of individual pilots, as much as by the cool tactical judgments of Admirals Fletcher and Spruance and Admiral Nimitz's bold strategic calculations. It was a battle that was also helped by the Japanese's fatal "victory disease." The significance of the U.S. triumph was not lost on Admiral King, who wrote: "The Battle of Midway was the first decisive defeat suffered by the Japanese Navy in 350 years. Furthermore it put an end to the long period of Japanese offensive action, and restored the balance of naval power in the Pacific."

17

"We Must Attack! Attack! Attack!"

"Pearl Harbor has now been partially avenged," Admiral Nimitz's communiqué of June 6, 1942, announced: "Vengeance will not be complete until Japanese seapower is reduced to impotence." The public euphoria over the Midway triumph in America was in strong contrast to the bitterness developing between the Army and Navy factions as the debate between them reopened on the Joint Chiefs of Staff. Admiral King argued for keeping up the momentum against the Japanese by pressing ahead with the Pacific Fleet's offensive in the Solomons. The Australians wanted an invasion of Timor, where their soldiers along with Dutch troops were waging a guerrilla campaign; but General MacArthur wanted to marshal Allied sea and air strength for a massive assault on Rabaul. General Marshall, who regarded the Midway victory as "the closest squeak," was against launching any offensive in the Pacific because he was convinced that disaster was looming across the Atlantic.

"I must confess I view, with great concern, the Russian front," read President Roosevelt's cable to Churchill on June 6, which informed him that "our operations in the Pacific are going well" with the news of Midway. The Red Army had been defeated in the Ukraine at Kharkov and the German offensive was rolling toward the Crimea and the Caucasus. Stalin's foreign minister, Molotov, had flown to London and then Washington to get British and American commitment to a "landing on the Continent in August or September." Churchill, however, would "give no promise." His concern, like that of his military chiefs, was that a hasty cross-Channel assault in 1942 to relieve pressure on Russia would be a "sacrificial landing," and he had carefully made it conditional upon the availability of troops and transports. The Prime Minister knew that this was in fact unlikely. Britain's 8th Army had had to fall back on Tobruk after a massive defeat inflicted by Rommel that cost hundreds of tanks and thousands of casualties. Troops on their way to India were now being diverted to meet the danger to the Suez Canal. Nearly 1 million tons of merchant tonnage had been lost to the U-boat blitz still raging in American waters, and the severe shipping crisis put a viselike grip on any extension of strategic operations. Until the ambitious American "Liberty Ship" building program could mass-produce vessels faster than the enemy could sink them, priority had to be given to maintaining the Atlantic lifeline.

To resolve the crisis that was again threatening Allied strategy, Churchill proposed another conference. From his daily telephone discussions with the Prime Minister, the President was keenly aware of the impending disaster overtaking the British in the Mediterranean. The U.S. Joint Chiefs were alarmed that Roosevelt might "jump the traces" and support launching the Second Front not in Europe but in North Africa. On June 17, while Churchill's flying boat was droning across the North Atlantic, the British Chiefs of Staff's blunt memorandum advising against any such operation was being read by Roosevelt at Hyde Park. Next day, while they were still adamantly insisting to the U.S. Chiefs that there "should be no substantial landing in France this year," the Prime Minister flew down to the President's Hudson Valley estate for a personal summit, during which he sought support for his alternative Second Front strategy. On June 20, the two leaders took one of history's momentous decisions: to pool national efforts and pay whatever price was necessary to develop the atomic bomb. As Churchill recorded that the Allies "could not run the mortal risk of being outstripped in this awful sphere." Scientists working for the top-secret British Tube Alloys Project had already shown that such a terrible weapon was theoretically feasible, but only the United States, whose own scientific team was working on the problem too, had the colossal industrial and financial resources to make the bomb. Within two months the multi-billion-dollar technological effort disguised by the cover name Manhattan Engineer District, was being set up under the control of the U.S. Army with access to unlimited secret funding.

Next day the President and the Prime Minister arrived back in Washington to find the unresolved debate on the 1942 Second Front strategy overshadowed by news that the fortress of Tobruk had been captured. It was feared that the German 2nd Army might burst through the Caucasus to link up with the Afrika Corps advancing across Palestine on the Plains of Armageddon. To aid in countering Rommel's offensive, which imperiled the Middle East, the President unhesitatingly offered to send tanks, guns, and ammunition by sea. Shell fuses and medical supplies were to be flown in by a new air route across Africa. To assist the defense of Egypt, he even promised a U.S. armored division if it was needed. Forty-eight hours later, when Churchill began his long flight back across the Atlantic to take personal charge of the crisis and face another vote of censure by Parliament, the issue of the cross-Channel attack was still unresolved. However, it was already plain that the need to rush emergency convoys out to the Middle East would severely curtail major operations in both the Atlantic and the Pacific.

July would bring no respite to the hard-pressed British Army in North Africa as Rommel's panzers pressed on to El Alamein and in Russia General von Bock's Army South overran the Crimea and prepared for the drive on to Rostov and Stalingrad. The tide of German victories brought renewed fears that Japan had decided now was the time, with the Red Army on the brink of defeat, to launch an attack in Siberia. Magic intercepts of the Berlin-Tokyo circuit and the flow of traffic from Japanese consulates in South America all pointed to an imminent widening of her war effort. The President worried that this might be the final blow that would push the Soviet Union into defeat. But Washington's fears were allayed to a degree by the report of Military Intelligence Service's "Special Branch," which reviewed the evidence and concluded that the diplomatic offensive was a "plot" that had all the hallmarks of "a wily oriental mind." It soon proved accurate and was the first major contribution to the secret intelligence war made by the work of the unit established under Colonel Alfred McCormick. An outstanding member of the New York Bar, he was appointed a special assistant to the Secretary of War, with the task of recruiting a team of experts to make the kind of overall assessment and interpretation of Magic intelligence that might have saved the United States from the Pearl Harbor debacle. Drawing on some of the best legal brains under the leadership of Carter W. Clarke, who was appointed colonel in command of the Special Service Branch, they organized the critical and interpretative assessment of the mass of intelligence material along the lines established by the British teams, who were evaluating German Enigma traffic for the Ultra operation.

It was therefore ironic that the evaluation and application of intelligence had just been fumbled by the Royal Navy where the likely movements of the *Tirpitz* were concerned. Anticipation that Hitler's biggest battleship was about to attack had led to the decision to scatter the PQ-17 convoy plowing north toward Russia during the first days of July. She remained in the Norwegian fjords as the helpless merchantmen were bombed and torpedoed by the Luftwaffe and U-boats. The Admiralty decided to call off any further attempts to ship the badly needed aid to the Soviet Union. Stalin angrily protested, and the Joint Chiefs of Staff in Washington began to believe that the Red Army might only be saved from defeat by an immediate diversionary attack on France. Churchill firmly ruled out any such precipitate action in his July 8 cable to Roosevelt. His excuse that there were just no resources with which the British Army could carry out the Sledgehammer assault plan left the U.S. Army Chief of Staff "so stirred up" that he took the unusual step of presenting a joint memorandum with COMINCH that advised the President that he should insist on the British honoring their obligations or "we should turn to the Pacific and strike decisively at Japan."

The ploy to threaten Churchill with a "strategic about face" in the direction of the Allied war effort was Marshall's own idea, but fifteen years later he would suggest that "in my case it was a bluff but King wanted the alternative." However, it was immediately called by Roosevelt himself during a strained and stormy meeting in the White House on July 12, 1942. During the two-hour session with his Chiefs of Staff, the President let it be known that he was favoring sending troops to North Africa to help the British and also satisfy his own political need to get a major part of the 3 million U.S. Army troops into action before the end of the year. Marshall and King flew to London for a tough bargaining session. They found the British immovably against the Sledgehammer (cross-Channel) operations, and in a discussion that Churchill termed "strategic natural selection" they were left no choice but to agree to the Gymnast operation. Rechristened "Torch," it called for the U.S. Army to invade North Africa that autumn while the assault on the European mainland was postponed. The British agreed only to a token raid on Dieppe to placate the Russians. The Prime Minister said he would undertake a risky mission to Moscow—"like carrying a large lump of ice to the North Pole"—to explain personally to Stalin why there would be no Second Front in 1942.

Once again the crisis over Allied strategy had been resolved by the President holding firmly to his "Europe First" doctrine. The "defeat of Germany means the defeat of Japan, probably without even firing a shot," he insisted. Marshall took a less sanguine view; yet he too had held the same belief, although he resented being maneuvered by the British into committing American forces to the indirect route to Berlin via North Africa. The U.S. Army Chief had realized there was no alternative for 1942 if he was to get his divisions into the land campaign. Switching to the Pacific would have given no chance to come to grips with the Japanese in battles that would have to be fought out on tropical islands and jungle peninsulas, and he had already decided that this must primarily be an amphibious war. Admiral King was now vociferously pressing for his offensive against Japan—a campaign Congress also clamored for. Its first objective would be to hurl the Japanese out of the Aleutians.

The Joint Chiefs of Staff, however, relegated this mission to the bottom of their strategic priorities. Admiral Theobald's small task force could be relied upon to blockade and raid the strategically insignificant enemy toeholds on the bleak islands of Kiska and Attu. The Army Air Force, with the aid of the civil airlines, would then open up an air-supply route through some of the world's most hostile flying conditions, along which troops and supplies could be mustered for an eventual offensive down the

Aleutians. With Midway now secure, the strategic focus in the Pacific shifted back to New Guinea and the Solomons, where the enemy was still able to threaten Australia.

While the southwest Pacific was primarily General MacArthur's area of operations, he began his bid to win control of the entire Pacific theater by demanding a Marine division and two carrier task forces to carry out a grandly conceived offensive named "Tulsa." The operation was intended to take Rabaul in two weeks, "forcing the enemy back 700 miles to his base at Truk." King's opinion of the general as little short of megalomaniacal had been colored by Admiral Hart's unflattering and highly charged personal report on his role in bringing about the disaster in the Philippines. In any event, the autocratic admiral was not about to hand over control of the few precious carriers in the Pacific. He wanted them to play a vital role in launching his own offensive drive north up into the Solomons, which he believed could take Rabaul in a month. His insistence that such operations were of a "primarily naval and amphibious character," and therefore properly subject to the control of Admiral Nimitz, effectively prevented MacArthur from launching an offensive of any scale. The general's strident protest that this was another move by the "Navy cabal" to assume "general command of all operations in the Pacific theater" brought Marshall into a direct confrontation with the Chief of Naval Operations. For two weeks a fierce battle was fought between the Army and Navy Chiefs over who was going to run the Pacific War. A heated exchange of memoranda was fired back and forth, and King threatened to go ahead with his offensive independently of Army consent. To heal the breach, on July 26, Marshall agreed to a compromise that the Navy had proposed earlier.

A decision was reached "with great difficulty" a week later, and a directive issued on July 2, 1942, which laid down the objectives for the first stages of the limited United States offensive against Japan. Admiral Nimitz was to be in overall command of Task I, the capture of the Santa Cruz Islands as a preliminary to attacking the Japanese's mid-Solomons base at Tulagi, opposite Guadalcanal Island, by August 1. General MacArthur was to begin Task II, a parallel drive to oust the Japanese from New Guinea, preparatory to launching Task III: the invasion of New Britain and the capture of Rabaul. To avert a dispute between MacArthur and Nimitz's South Pacific Area Commander, Admiral Ghormley, the Joint Chiefs neatly shifted the CINCPAC boundary westward of Guadalcanal to bring the lower Solomons under Navy control.

The stage was now set for Task I, which had been prophetically codenamed "Operation Watchtower" in deference to King's intention that it should be the curtain raiser to the Navy's Pacific campaign. On July 3 the COMINCH staff flew to San Francisco to outline the plan to Admiral Nimitz. They found him badly shaken by a narrow brush with death when the flying boat bringing him from Pearl Harbor capsized on landing, killing the pilot. On Independence Day, the U.S. Navy brass assembled in the Federal Building to hear Rear Admiral Richmond Kelly Turner outline the operation. Fiercely outspoken, Turner was a brilliant tactician who had been head of the Navy's War Plans Division until February, when his evident partisanship had made it impossible for him to work alongside the Army planners. Then King had appointed him Commander of Amphibious Forces in the South Pacific under Admiral Ghormley, who was not at the briefing because he had been sent to Melbourne to mend the Navy's fences and secure the cooperation of MacArthur.

Optimism infused the conference. Despite the losses of two American carriers at Coral Sea and Midway, the Japanese had sacrificed their main strike force, while Nimitz could form four task forces around the *Saratoga, Enterprise, Hornet,* and *Wasp,* as well as the first of the newly commissioned class of fast battleships, the *North Carolina.* Admiral King believed that with the early capture of Rabaul, he might yet carry the naval offensive to Truk, Guam, and Saipan, smashing Japan's Pacific defense perimeter and opening up the Home Islands to attack. But his fervor was cooled by intelligence from Rochefort's HYPO team at Pearl Harbor, which by now had begun to penetrate the new version of the JN25 code, revealing that an airfield was being hurriedly constructed on Guadalcanal. Once completed, it would not only allow Japan to make a renewed bid for air superiority over the Coral Sea but also close the sea approaches to eastern Australia and threaten Fiji and Noumea.

King at once ordered a revision of Operation Watchtower, dropping the requirement for establishing advance bases in the Santa Cruz Islands. Instead, it called for simultaneous invasions of Tulagi and Guadalcanal. This new urgency caused him to reject MacArthur's call for postponing the August 1 deadline, made after his meeting with Admiral Ghormley. "Three weeks ago MacArthur stated that if he could be provided with amphibious forces and two carriers, he could push right through to Rabaul," King testily informed Marshall. "He now feels that he not only cannot undertake the extended operation, but even the Tulagi operations."

OVER THE OWEN STANLEYS

While the American strategy was focusing on the Solomons, the defeat at Midway had forced the Imperial General Staff in Tokyo to recast their Second Operational Phase objectives in the Pacific. The Combined Fleet was still very much the superior of the U.S. Pacific Fleet in battleships, cruisers, and destroyers. Notwithstanding, the loss to Nagumo's carrier force of highly trained air-striking crews, along with the four carriers, had been a serious setback to the naval staff's plans. They were obliged to abandon their Second Operational Phase assault on Samoa, through which they would have menaced Australia. Now the Japanese Army won their demand for a defensive strategy, directed at establishing interlocking air bases and fortified islands to make a secure perimeter against the launching of Allied attacks. Ocean and Naru were to be belatedly seized to secure the southern approaches to the Marshall and Gilbert islands, and priority was to be given to completing the occupation of New Guinea.

On June 12 a new directive appointed Lieutenant General Harukichi Hyakutake, the younger brother of the Emperor's Grand Chamberlain, to take command of the Imperial 17th Army Division at Rabaul. He was ordered to succeed where Admiral Inouye had repeatedly failed by executing Operation RI to win control of the Papuan Peninsula. No longer able to count on strong naval support, the army staff decided that this had to be accomplished by landings at Buna and Gona on the north coast, then marching troops across the Owen Stanley mountain trails to capture Port Moresby. Vice Admiral Gunichi Mikawa, commanding the navy's 11th Air Fleet, and the newly established 8th Fleet of cruisers and destroyers based at Rabaul, would provide air support to New Guinea and the base in Guadalcanal to secure the Solomon Islands.

The Imperial General Headquarters and General Hyakutake's staff were almost two weeks ahead of the Allies, who were also planning to seize the same strategic objectives. As a first requirement to fulfilling Task II of the U.S. Joint Chiefs' directive of July 2, General MacArthur had decided to secure the Papuan Peninsula by striking at the Japanese-held ports of Lae and Salamaua to the north by setting up an advance base and airfield at Buna. On July 10, a six-man team surveyed the coastal site at the northern end of the tortuous Kokoda Trail, which wound a precipitous 100-mile route over the Owen Stanley Mountains from Port Moresby. Planning was in full swing for "Operation Providence," to send 3,000 Australian troops over the jungle-choked mountain pass to reinforce the local militia and open an airstrip by August 10.

The Japanese, however, were swifter. The crack South Seas detachment of Major General Tomitaro Horii was already aboard transports heading for Buna and Gona as the launching base for a mountain march across Papua. On July 18, Australian reconnaissance planes reported that this transport convoy was putting out from Rabaul. There was no time now to rush Operation Providence into action. General Brett ordered his B-17 bombers out from their northern Australian base at Townsville, but operating at extreme range, the Flying Fortress bombers failed to disrupt the landings, which took Buna on July 22. Within days, 13,000 Japanese soldiers and 1,000 native bearers were able to extend their beachhead north to Gona, to begin the push south over the mountainous spine of Papua.

"WE MUST ATTACK! ATTACK! ATTACK!"

A few hundred native militiamen and an advance company of the 29th Australian Infantry were all that stood between the enemy and the strategically vital airstrip at Kokoda, 50 miles inland, up in the foothills of the Owen Stanleys. From here the mountain trail wound up over 10,000 punishing feet, crossing steep jungle-choked ravines. Neither Major Basil Morris, the Australian commander at Kokoda, nor anyone at MacArthur's headquarters realized at first that the Japanese would attempt to fight troops across such a formidable natural barrier. They had not reckoned with the determination of General Horii, who had sent up an advance party from the 41st Infantry Regiment to use its jungle-fighting skills, acquired in Malaya, to sweep through to Kokoda. Every one of the 2,000 soldiers was trained to hack his way through the undergrowth with a machete until he dropped with exhaustion; when a man fell, his place would be taken by another. Each soldier was equipped with a special shovel with holes so that mud would not stick to the blade. This soon proved an invaluable weapon in a campaign where perpetual rain and mist drenched the jungle, turning the steep trail into a slippery morass. Field and machine guns were stripped down to be carried by native bearers as the mountain trail was hacked open so that the South Seas Detachment following behind could make one of the most grueling military advances in history, over the Owen Stanley ridge and down into Port Moresby.

Too late, Lieutenant Colonel William Owen, the Australian commander, perceived that the Japanese meant to pull off the impossible. By that time his five hundred infantrymen and the Papuan Militia had retreated across the swaying suspension wire rope bridge that the natives called in pidgin English "Wairopi." Its cables had to be cut to drop it down into the raging torrents of the Kumasi River, but the enemy rapidly threw across their own bridge, and by July 29 Owen had lost his life in the pitched battle for Kokoda. Desperate counterattacks succeeded in recapturing the vital airfield for a week. When this was lost again, the only way for reinforcements to reach the defenders was along the Kokoda Trail, up which the Australians now retreated, pursued by chanting Japanese who kept up a constant deluge of mortar and rifle fire that was as persistent and demoralizing as the torrential rains.

Horii's troops bypassed the few positions the Australians managed to hold by cutting their way up jungle-covered slopes like demonic ants, to harry the head of the retreating column. Mid-August brought the Japanese over halfway to their objective as the fighting wound up to the steepest part of the trail, called aptly "The Gap." The blazing sun and thin air increased the misery of the ordeal. "The road gets gradually steeper," recorded one of Horii's soldiers; "The sun is fierce here. We make our way through a jungle where there are no roads. The jungle is beyond description. Thirst for water, stomach empty."

"Worn out by strenuous fighting and exhausting movement, and weakened by lack of food, sleep and shelter, many of them had come to a standstill," Lieutenant Colonel Ralph Honner noted of the pitiful condition of the surviving Australian troops in August, when he arrived to take command of the defense of "The Gap."

"I led one lost cause and am trying desperately not to have it two," MacArthur wrote as the Australian High Command, anticipating the loss of New Guinea and an invasion, began discussing a withdrawal to hold the "Brisbane Line." Threatening to resign as Commander in Chief unless such defeatist talk stopped at once, MacArthur deliberately moved his headquarters north to Brisbane's AMP Insurance Building, whose staff had been evacuated to Sydney. "We'll defend Australia in New Guinea," he announced, after he had moved his wife and son into the dusty town's Lennon Hotel.

The 7th Australian Division was already being shipped in to Papua. The tough soldiers, bloodied in the desert fighting in North Africa, were to face an even sterner task in Papua, where the jungle was to prove as "tenacious an enemy as the Japanese." But MacArthur was resolute. "We must attack, attack, attack!" he told the press, in a masterful theatrical address heavily larded with quotes from Plato and Lincoln. It sounded better as rhetoric than tactics, but he nevertheless received the unstinting support of General Sir Thomas Blamey. The Allied Ground Forces Commander, a former chief of the Melbourne police, had become a popular hero with his countrymen after returning from the Middle East. A successful leader of the hard-drinking, hard-fighting troops, he drew considerable support from his capable deputy, Major General George Vasey.

The arrival of General George C. Kenney to take over as Southwest Pacific Forces Air Commander from General Brett injected a needed dose of bustling aggressiveness into MacArthur's Brisbane staff. Stocky and gregarious, in contrast to the Commander in Chief, the two men quickly became good partners after an initial coolness that was broken when Kenny's brisk methods shook up the Army and Royal Australian Air Force squadrons, whose cooperation had deteriorated into a "can of worms."

Setting out on a tour of the scattered bases, Kenney was the most senior officer so far to visit New Guinea. There he shared the discomforts of Port Moresby, where lack of mosquito netting and a poor diet of canned "M&V"—canned meat and vegetables—encouraged the spread of malaria and endemic dysentery in the savage dusty heat. Kinney learned that his flyers expected to lose 30 pounds in a single duty tour. They joked about the "New Guinea Salute"—the constant gesture of brushing away swarms of black flies. The men were plagued by mosquitoes so big that the standing joke was that ground crews rushed out to refuel them at night, mistaking them for aircraft in the dark. Kenny also learned that apart from morale, MacArthur's opinion that the aircrew were a "rabble of boulevard shock troops whose contribution to the war effort was practically nil" was more than justified. Less than 50 of the command's 245 fighters were serviceable when Kenney arrived to take over, and half of the bombers were grounded for repairs because spare parts never arrived. Immediately he issued orders halting the scrapping of planes; they were to be rebuilt, "even if nothing is left but a tail wheel," from salvaged parts, and tin cans were to be beaten flat to patch up bullet holes. After a few weeks' of effective maintenance, the number of aircraft available for operations was doubled.

Kenney now set about putting them to good effect by ordering a massive raid on Rabaul. When MacArthur's egotistical Chief of Staff, General Sutherland, who was referred to as "the General's Rasputin," tried to revise the plan, Kenney stormed into Sutherland's office for a showdown. Putting a pencil dot on a large piece of blank paper on the general's tidy desk, he declared angrily: "That is what you know about airpower. The rest of the sheet is what I know about it," suggesting that if the Chief of Staff disagreed, they should go into the Supreme Commander's office next door to see "who is supposed to run this air force."

The success of the subsequent raid on Rabaul convinced MacArthur that airpower, in the form of what was to become the 5th Air Force, could play a key part in reviving his stalled campaign in New Guinea by a bombing offensive against the Japanese bases in northern Papua, as well as by harrying the enemy advance up the Owen Stanleys. At the same time, the transports were dropping supplies to the Australian soldiers laboring up the Kokoda Trail from Port Moresby.

OPERATION PESTILENCE

Across the western Pacific in New Zealand, Admiral Ghormley's staff were sweating aboard his headquarters ship *Argonne* in Auckland Harbor, trying to get Operation Watchtower launched. The five weeks they had been given proved too little time to assemble all the troops, shipping, and equipment, even though the landing force had been reduced to a single Marine division, because the 3rd Army Infantry Division, which had been undergoing amphibious training on the West Coast, was already on its way to the Atlantic ports for embarkation for North Africa. Major General Alexander Vandegrift, who confessed he "didn't even know the location of Guadalcanal," faced a tough assignment getting his 1st Marine Division assembled in New Zealand. It was "scattered over hell's half acre" when he arrived to prepare for the invasion with Admiral Turner. The Marines, who were recalled from San Francisco to New Caledonia, thought they were destined for some tropical paradise. The South Pacific command staff were not much wiser, relying on information they had gleaned from old *National Geographic* magazines and German charts of World War I vintage. Teams of intelligence officers were combing Australia to interview missionaries, sea captains, and copra planters who were familiar with the Solomons. Their reports of the malarial jungles of the island chain and its scattered dark-skinned Melanesian natives caused Vandegrift to begin referring to Watchtower as "Operation Pestilence."

Lying in the torrid latitudes just south of the equator, the double chain of islands proved far removed from the palm-fringed tropical haven the Marines were expecting. Discovered in the sixteenth century by Spanish adventurers searching for the legendary Ophir of King Solomon, Guadalcanal was one of the largest in the group. A hundred miles long by 50 miles at the widest, it was shrouded in a dense vegetation that thrived on the heavy rainfall from dense clouds trapped by a mountain backbone 8,000 feet high. Except where the lower slopes opened on meadows of razor-sharp Kunai grass, the tropical vegetation was so dense that little sunlight penetrated into the tangled undergrowth, where white cockatoos and mynah birds screeched through the green twilight. A rich variety of tropical insect life grew bloated on the rotting vegetation that sent a heavy stench of decay drifting out across the Indispensable Strait to Florida Island, where the tiny islet of Tulagi nestled in its bight.

Lacking the dense jungle and swamps of its bigger neighbors, Tulagi was one of the few islands considered healthy enough for the white settlers and administrators who managed the copra plantations and governed the Solomon's scattered territory from a one-street town of bungalows that boasted the indispensable symbol of British colonialism—a cricket pitch. Since May 5, the Rising Sun had been flying from the flagstaff where for nearly a hundred years the Union Jack had been daily raised. A garrison of 2,300 Imperial Navy "Marines" of the Special Naval Landing Force guarded the town and the two adjoining islets where Kawanshi seaplanes took off on patrol. By the beginning of July they had been joined by 1,400 men of the Imperial Navy's Airfield Construction Unit, who were ferried each morning across the sound to Guadalcanal to build the new base for the planes of the navy's 25th Air Flotilla.

The Japanese command in Rabaul waited impatiently for the airstrip to be completed so as to consolidate their hold on the Solomons. By the end of the month the construction crews had carved out a runway on Guadalcanal through the Kunai grass fields west of the mouth of the Lunga River. A rudimentary control tower and camp was being raised among the coconut palms. In Wellington, a New Zealand dock strike forced the Marines to reload their transport ships. All their supplies and equipment had been improperly loaded on the West Coast. The driving winter rains burst open many of the cardboard ration containers, leaving the quayside ankle-deep in a soggy brown mush of cornflakes and cigarette cartons.

The foul-up gave Admiral Ghormley the extra week's delay he needed before the landings to obtain detailed photo reconnaissance of the Japanese airfield and the nearby beach at Lunga Point, where most of the Marines were scheduled to come ashore. With three weeks still to go before the revised D-Day date of August 7, 1942, he issued his final Watchtower plan. Admiral Turner would be in command of the nineteen transports carrying in two combat teams of the 1st Marine Division. The transports would be escorted into the two landing areas off Tulagi and Guadalcanal by four destroyers while a force of three cruisers and six destroyers bombarded the enemy. Standing close guard over the landings would be "MacArthur's Navy"—the three Australian cruisers and five destroyers under Rear Admiral Sir Victor Crutchley, reinforced by the heavy cruiser U.S.S. *Chicago* and four Pacific Fleet destroyers. A formidable umbrella of aircover was to be provided by three of Nimitz's four carrier task forces, reinforced for the first time by the 16-inch guns of the new fast battleship *North Carolina*.

Operation Watchtower was a hastily improvised amphibious assault, which would not have stood much chance had it been going in against well-defended enemy positions. Even its commanders would derisively refer to it as "Operation Shoestring"—a name that was to prove only too accurate when its amphibious forces assembled together for dress rehearsal off Fiji on July 26. The final staff conference was treated to much table-thumping from Vandegrift and Turner, who were determined to get the invasion organized in the final forty-eight hours. The practice proved a "complete bust," and the nineteen transports set sail escorted by forty-three warships on the last day of July with the commanders praying that the old adage, "A poor rehearsal means a good first night," was not just a theatrical myth.

The opening night for the U.S. Navy's first amphibious assault of the Pacific campaign came at midnight on August 6. The shadowy columns of Admiral Turner's invasion force swung around Guadalcanal's Cape Esperance and into the dark sound, past the volcanic sentinel of Savo toward Tulagi and the islets rearing up from the ebony waters like giant whales. The Marines, who had come up on deck abandoning crap games, jitterbugging, and prayers, smelled the stench of decaying vegetation that drifted across the waters—a sickening odor they would soon come to identify as the smell of death itself. Breakfast, for those who could stomach it, was piped for 4:30 as the armada divided in two. The bombarding warships of the X-Ray Force were to glide through the still water toward Florida Island, while the Yoke Force of eleven transports and the heavy cruisers crept along the Guadalcanal shoreline toward Lunga Point.

"Everyone seemed ready to jump at the first boom of a gun, but there was little excitement," noted an American journalist, Richard Tregaskis, who at twenty-six was covering his first war assignment from the deck of one of the Tulagi-bound transports. "The thing that was happening was so unbelievable that it seemed like a dream. We were slipping through the narrow neck of water between Guadalcanal and Savo Islands; we were practically inside Tulagi Bay, almost past the Jap shore batteries, and not a shot had been fired."

Japan's intelligence had once again failed utterly to give any advance warning of the American operation about to hit the Solomons. It was not until dawn silhouetted the approaching warships that the lookouts on Tulagi awoke to their doom. A radio operator tapped out an uncertain signal to Rabaul: "LARGE FORCE OF SHIPS UNKNOWN NUMBER OR TYPES ENTERING SOUND WHAT CAN THEY BE?" Seconds later, at 6:13 A.M., the answer thundered from the eight 9-inch guns of the heavy cruiser *Quincy* leading the Y Force, which sent her first salvo crashing down east of Lunga Point, where 5,000 Japanese troops were thought to be dug into defenses. Another bombardment echoed from the X-Ray warships across the sound.

"ENEMY FORCE OVERWHELMING," the Tulagi commander radioed at 6:30. "WE WILL DEFEND OUR POSTS TO THE DEATH." It was his last message. Seconds later, shells from the warships destroyed the transmitting station. The first of the American carrier strikes roared in to join the battle, the dive bombers making flaming torches of the Japanese flying boats as they tried to scramble into the air.

"Wizard!!!—Caloo, Callay, Oh! What a Day!" Australian Coastwatcher Captain W. F. Martin Clemens recorded in his diary for the morning when he awoke to the distant rumble of guns and the appearance of RAAF Hudsons droning overhead. He was writing from a carefully camouflaged hideout deep in the jungle slopes of Guadalcanal, and the morale of his native scouts went soaring "up 500%" as Clemens tuned in to his short-wave radio to listen in rapture to the American fighter pilots' messages.

The sea and air bombardment reached an ear-splitting crescendo around seven o'clock as the transports ranged up 1,000 yards from the two assault areas. The stubby landing craft were lowered; heavy hemp nets unrolled, and the burdened Marines began scrambling down to make the tricky leap onto the bobbing decks, heaving in 4-foot swells. "Ant-like they went over the side, clinging to the rough rope nets that swayed out and in against the warm steel sides of the ships," recalled machine-gunner Private Robert H. Leckie. "They stepped on the fingers of the man below and felt their own hands squashed by the men above. Rifles clanged against helmets. Men carrying heavy machine guns or mortars ground their teeth in the agony of descending into the waiting boats with 30 and 40 pounds of steel boring into their shoulders. . . . And the boats rose and fell in the swells, now close to the ships sides, now three feet away. The men jumped, landing in clanging heaps, then crouched beneath gunwhales while the loaded boats churned to the assembly areas, forming rings and circling, finally fanning out in a broad line a few minutes before eight and speeding with hulls down and frothing wake straight for the shores of the enemy."

For all the chaos of the rehearsal, the actual landings proved to be a happy anticlimax. More Marines were injured by sharp coral heads as they waded up the dun-colored beach than by enemy bullets. The sheer weight of the bombardment had forced the enemy to take cover inland. By 8:15 the first wave of the assault was ashore on Red Beach, Tulagi, signaling: "Landing successful no opposition," as the boats churned off to bring the next companies into Blue Beach.

Colonel Merrit A. Edson, whose 2nd Raider Battalion spearheaded the attack, was in control of the small town by late morning. But that afternoon he found that the enemy had holed up in the hills at the eastern end of the small island overlooking the open cricket ground. At night the Japanese "Marines" crawled out to deliver a fierce counterattack before being beaten back. "The Nips had 200 men in dugouts and rock emplacements, with snipers scattered around," Edson reported of the fanatical resistance. It was to take another day's hand-to-hand fighting to subdue the tiny island—a portent of how tough it was going to be to defeat Japan's soldiers, who carried out literally their orders to "defend our posts to the death." "Even after we got control," Edson recounted, "machine gun nests in dugouts held up our advance for several hours. It was impossible to approach the Nip dugouts except from one direction. You had to crawl up on the cliffs and drop dynamite inside while you were under fire all the time." The Raiders were shaken by this first face-to-face lesson in the warrior code of Bushido as the Japanese held out in caves without food, water, or hope, refusing to surrender. Of nearly 2,000 defenders, only 23 were taken prisoner alive. Not one surrendered voluntarily in the three days of fighting that cost the Marines 100 dead.

Across the sound at Guadalcanal's Red Beach, 5 miles east of the partly finished airstrip at Lunga Point, the first two Marine battalions had landed without firing a single shot. The Japanese construction parties had no weapons. They fled into the jungle, abandoning their rice breakfasts, which the advancing Marines found still warm on the tables of the partially completed mess hut. The runway was three-quarters finished, the control tower was up, and the electric generator plant working. A bulldozer, construction equipment, and building materials were abandoned intact; so was what would prove to be the biggest prize of all—a small mountain of food supplies. The many tons of rice and soybeans were of less immediate interest that hot day to the thirsty Marines than hundreds of cases of Japanese beer and the refrigeration plant, which was labeled by its grateful discoverers: "TOJO ICE FACTORY—Under New Management."

The very success of the Marines' landing brought its own dangers; by noon on the first day, men and supplies were being piled up on the beaches faster than they could be moved ashore, making the landing dangerously vulnerable to air attack. However, the Japanese command at Rabaul was too taken by surprise to seize the opportunity for counterattacking. Admiral Mikawa's bombers were about to take off for another raid in support of the troops advancing across Papua, and valuable hours were lost before they could rearm with torpedoes to strike the Guadalcanal transports. His cruiser force, too, was scattered, covering convoys carrying reinforcements to Buna and the bases in the Louisiades.

In response to Admiral Yamamoto's urgent orders to repel the American landings with his sea and air forces, Mikawa boarded the *Chokai* to lead his squadron of five heavy and two light cruisers in the first bid to retake the Guadalcanal base. Racing southwest past Bougainville that evening, it became apparent to Mikawa that the force of five hundred Imperial Navy "Marines," following behind in two transports, would be hopelessly inadequate for the task. The transports were ordered to return to Rabaul. That afternoon his pilots managed to press their attack home despite the heavy fighter cover from the American carrier task forces south of the island, to sink a transport and damage a destroyer that would eventually have to be scuttled. The increasing severity of the bombing raids the next morning caused Turner to order a speeding up of unloading operations, as reports came in from Coastwatchers and air patrols that a cruiser force was bearing down on him. At 11:17 on the second day of Watchtower, Mikawa's squadron was lost. The Navy PBYs'—and Australian Hudsons' and 5th Air Force B-17s'—pilots had failed to appreciate that the Japanese were speeding along the channel that separated the outer islands of Choiseul and Santa Isabel from the sprawl of New Georgia— the most direct route to Guadalcanal, which would become known tersely as "The Slot."

The failure of the intensive air reconnaissance to locate the enemy cruisers before dusk was to open the way to a disaster. Rochefort's codebreakers at Pearl Harbor were taking two weeks to unravel the new Japanese operational cipher and CINCPAC Intelligence, which was relying on traffic analysis, could offer no indication of the force's whereabouts because it was observing radio silence. This led Admiral Turner to conclude early in the evening of August 8 that the Japanese cruisers were too far away to present a threat to his highly vulnerable transports until the next day. His more immediate worry was the decision taken by Admiral Fletcher that afternoon to pull out with his covering task force, after losing a fifth of his fighters in beating off two heavy Japanese raids. Citing his usual concern about lack of fuel and his weakened defenses, "in view of the large numbers of enemy torpedo bombers," Fletcher signaled Admiral Ghormley: "Recommend immediate withdrawal of my carriers." Without waiting for confirmation, he was withdrawing to the south and well out of range of Guadalcanal by 8 P.M. when Turner's commanders assembled on his headquarters' ship *MacCawley* (a transport whose crew fondly called her "Wacky Mac"). The humid night added to the sense of crisis as the amphibious force commander announced his stunning decision: the departure of the carrier air umbrella obliged him also to withdraw the transports and cruisers early next day. General Vandegrift protested this "running away," but Turner believed he had no option if he wanted to save his ships from being sunk by the Japanese bombers.

Harsh words were exchanged in a tense meeting that lasted until midnight. As the conference broke up and Admiral Crutchley's barge came alongside to take him to where the cruiser *Australia* lay at anchor, lightning was flickering around the dark mountain peaks of Guadalcanal. Crutchley's flagship was more than 30 miles south of the entrance to the Sound, where his four cruisers were steaming routine box patrols while two destroyers stood advanced picket guard south of Savo Island. Neither their lookouts nor radar had spotted the float plane that had been flown off by Admiral Mikawa's approaching cruisers.

THE BATTLE OF SAVO ISLAND

"May each man do his utmost," the Japanese admiral had paraphrased Nelson. His force ran at high speed toward the entrance to the Sound, high in the expectation that the Imperial Navy's expertise in night attacks would deliver them "Certain victory." Every gun was now trained silently on the distant dim silhouette of the destroyer U.S.S. *Blue*, which astonishingly reversed course after failing to spot them in the velvet blackness of the moonless night.

Mikawa had penetrated 2 miles south of Savo at 1:42 before the more alert lookouts aboard the *Patterson* signaled: "WARNING WARNING STRANGE SHIPS ENTERING HARBOR." It was another five minutes before the Japanese, without benefit of radar, realized there were two cruisers dead ahead. Swinging out to the north to cross their T, the action began with the *Chokai*'s float plane overhead dropping green-hued flares.

Searchlights blazed, illuminating H.M.A.S. *Canberra* and U.S.S. *Chicago*, caught at point-blank 3-mile range with their gun crews unprepared. Before they could get off a single salvo, the Australian cruiser was pounded into a blazing wreck at the receiving end of twenty-four shells. The *Chicago* was hit by a torpedo and charged out of the battle, mistakenly chasing one of her own destroyers north. This maneuver around Savo in two columns brought the Japanese force into a head-on collision with the second patrol of three cruisers. The sternmost, the lightly armored U.S.S. *Astoria* succumbed to repeated hits from the enemy's 8-inch armor-piercing shells. Engulfed in shellfire, the U.S.S. *Quincy* was the only Allied ship whose gun crews got into action fast enough to hit back with a few salvos, one of which damaged the *Chokai*. The odds were pitifully unequal. "Suddenly the ship shook violently, and literally leaped out of the ocean," was the graphic recollection of one survivor on board the *Quincy* as two torpedoes hit and her forward magazines blew up. "The sound of breaking glass, of steel hitting steel, the hissing of air from the compressed air lines, the explosion of countless shells and the pitiful cries of the wounded all merged into one and seemed to shout the doom of the *Quincy*." She was already sinking when the U.S.S. *Vincennes*, at the head of the column, was repeatedly hit, surviving a little longer before being blasted out of the water on both quarters as Mikawa swung his two columns north out of the Sound to regroup.

Admiral Crutchley was still racing up in the *Australia*, but his cruiser arrived on the battle scene after the half hour's action was over. With one cruiser sunk and three blazing wrecks, he could only rescue the stunned survivors. Mikawa had by now decided to abandon his original intention of going back into the Sound to sink the transports, which had only the *Australia* and a handful of destroyers to protect them. Had he seized the initiative, Operation Watchtower would have collapsed—and with it the American Solomons offensive. The Japanese admiral's decision to withdraw after winning the Battle of Savo Island saved Guadalcanal from being added to the long list of Allied disasters. Mikawa did not yet know that the American carriers had withdrawn; in fact he would not have encountered air attacks had he stayed until dawn to smash up the invasion beachhead.

The Marines were saved, but the U.S. Navy had suffered the worst sea defeat in its entire history. When the sun came up the next day over Florida Island, four cruisers and over a thousand Allied seamen lay on the mud of what would now come to be called "Ironbottom Sound." In spite of the danger, Admiral Turner carried on the unloading operations through a morning air raid until he finally decided to withdraw his surviving warships "in view of impending heavy air attacks." They took out with them the unlanded Marine Division's 1,000-man reserve, most of its heavy artillery and equipment, as well as half its food supplies.

"It is as if the Marines held Jones Beach and the rest of Long Island were loosely dominated by the enemy," the *New York Times* correspondent Hanson Baldwin summed up General Vandegrift's precarious situation. What the censor prevented both the public and the Japanese from learning was that Vandegrift's 6,000 men on Tulagi and 10,000 on Guadalcanal had been left with less than a month's rations, no heavy weapons, not a single landmine, few entrenching tools, and a few coils of barbed wire. Only one bulldozer was available to finish the airfield on which their defense was now to stand or fall.

"We have seized a strategic position," General Millard Harmon, the South Pacific Army Commander, reported to General Marshall. Then added worriedly: "Can the Marines hold it? There is considerable room for doubt!"

The American public, which was not told of the disastrous naval battle, rejoiced that the offensive against Japan had finally been launched on the distant Solomon Island with the unpronounceable name. The U.S. Navy, careful not to reveal its losses, trumpeted the simultaneous sinking of a Japanese light cruiser by submarine S-44 off New Ireland. This loss tainted Mikawa's triumph, which was still further soured when the *Chokai* steamed back to Rabaul two days later with her flags flying. Mikawa found his superiors less than satisfied with his failure to seize the chance to crush the American landing. Prime Minister Tojo now personally instructed the army to concentrate on retaking Guadalcanal. Admiral Yamamoto, recognizing they were "engaged in a desperate struggle," ordered Mikawa to "make every effort" to land reinforcements with the assistance of Admiral Kondo's Second Fleet, which he sent south to Truk along with Admiral Nagumo's strike force.

General Hyakutake, more concerned with the 17th Army's expanding offensive in New Guinea, underestimated the size of the American force preparing to defend the Solomons. He decided it could be dislodged by bringing in Colonel Kiyano Ichiki's 2,500-strong Midway occupation force, now awaiting deployment on Guam, and General Kiyotake Kawaguchi's 3,500 soldiers on Palau, assisted if necessary by a single unit of the Imperial Navy Marines. The Japanese Army and Navy commanders at Rabaul needed several weeks to ship in these troops, so it was agreed they would be landed in a makeshift, two-stage operation escorted by Rear Admiral Raizo Tanaka's destroyers. One of Japan's most promising naval commanders, Tanaka had taken part in both the Java Sea battle and Midway. Now he predicted the difficulty of "landing in the face of the enemy—to be carried out by mixed units which had no opportunity for rehearsal or even preliminary study."

"NOW LET THE BASTARDS COME!"

The Rabaul command had apparently forgotten how stubbornly the U.S. Marines had defended Corregidor and had no idea that as many as 16,000 of America's toughest fighting troops were on Tulagi and Guadalcanal. When patrols sent out to probe the jungle east and west of the Lunga beachhead revealed that the Japanese who escaped had also dug in, Vandegrift concentrated on setting up a strong defense to guard the airfield perimeter while work went ahead to complete its runway. Japan's bombers arrived every day with such clockwork regularity that 1 P.M. became known as "Tojo Time."

The raids were less of a hindrance than the torrential rainstorms, which turned the construction site into a sea of sticky black mud that bogged down the Marines' one bulldozer. Work would not have been possible without the trucks left by the enemy, and as the backbreaking task ground on, the Marines had reason to be grateful for the inadvertent Imperial generosity. They came to depend on the tons of captured rations, even though American palates did not take readily to the monotonous diet of "Fish and rice, fish and rice, fish and rice," as one Marine put it. "Sometimes the Jap diet was broken by a plate of beans, canned salmon, or a slab of beef from a Lever Brother's Cow." Unfortunately for the Marines on half-rations, the rangy cattle introduced onto the Anglo-Dutch company's copra plantations appeared about as frequently as the Navy destroyers which dashed in under cover of darkness on August 15 to ferry in more ammunition and aviation fuel.

Two days later Vandegrift was able to signal that the airstrip was finished. To clear out the Japanese positions threatening the airfield 4 miles to the west across the Matanikau River, he ordered a three-pronged attack. It ran into such strong resistance that on August 19 the Marines fell back. But the next day they were able to cheer in a flight of twelve Dauntless dive bombers. Vandegrift called it "one of the most beautiful sights of my life." They were followed on August 21 by the even more welcome arrival of fifteen fighters, which had flown in from the decks of the *Long Island*—the first of the new American escort carriers that now played a vital role in the battle by acting as the ferry to build up the "Cactus Air Force," as the Marines' planes became known after Guadalcanal's code name.

"Now let the bastards come," yelled one Marine that same day, as the Wildcat pilots jumped the regular bombing run from Rabaul, shooting down the first of eighteen Zeroes they would bag in the days ahead. Notice was served to the Japanese 11th Air Fleet that the air battle had begun for control of the skies over the island. On August 22, the first of the U.S. Army's 67th Fighter Squadron arrived, the start of a stream of reinforcements shuttled in by the *Long Island* to meet the Cactus Air Force's high attrition rate. Losses were occasioned not only by enemy planes but by night bombardments from enemy destroyers, fire from the machine guns the Japanese set up west of the airstrip, and accidents caused by frequent holes in the runways opened up after torrential downpours.

Henderson Field, as Vandegrift now christened the base—in memory of Major Lofton Henderson, who had lost his life leading Midway's Marines torpedo planes—was to become the focus of the struggle for both attackers and defenders. Three days before the airstrip became fully operational, the five hundred men of the Special Landing Force had been landed by night 10 miles east of the airstrip at Tassafaronga Point. The following evening, Tanaka's six destroyers put Colonel Ichiki and 1,000 men of his detachment ashore at Taivu, 12 miles to the west, establishing a routine when on the way back up the Sound they shelled both Tulagi and the runway.

"We have succeeded in invasion," Colonel Ichiki grandly signaled Rabaul. He decided not to wait for reinforcements or artillery but to strike out as the western claw of the pincher attack on the airstrip. Ichiki left a party of nine to man the post at Taivu and set out to win a glorious victory with his nine hundred infantrymen, who carried only a week's rations. "No enemy at all, like marching through no-man's-land," he radioed confidently two days later, but his advance through the coastal copra plantations had been reported by one of Captain Clemens's scouts. Captured, tortured, and trussed up, the gallant Jacob Vouza had chewed through his bonds and managed, despite hideous bayonet wounds, to escape to raise the alarm on August 19.

The same day, Vandegrift received confirmation of the direction that the main Japanese attack was taking when the patrols east of Henderson Field routed one of Ichiki's advance groups and found they were wearing fresh uniforms. Defenses along the evil-smelling stagnant creek that ran 4 miles east of the airstrip were strengthened with the few precious rolls of barbed wire and 37mm machine-gun posts. Marked, incorrectly, on U.S. Marine maps as the Tenaru River (it was actually the Ilu), it was no more than a thirty-yard creek with its seaward end sealed off by a sandspit, across which the Japanese would be forced to attack.

The steamy night of August 19, 1942, was made more unpleasant by the stench that assaulted the nostrils of the 1st Marine Regiment guarding the entrance to the Creek. At shortly past 1 A.M. lookout posts raised the alert that human movements could be heard over the tinny cacophony of jungle insects and frogs. "They were walking right in the edge of the surf and got tangled up in some barbed wire," according to the regimental commander, Colonel Clifton B. Cates. "They started jabbering so our bunch let go with everything they had. They immediately rushed our positions, and it was a grand mess for a few minutes. After driving them from our positions, they took refuge in the edge of the surf, underneath a three foot bank and they stayed 50 yards from our line. By that time their main force closed in and tried to advance down the narrow sand spit; naturally the slaughter was terrific."

Urged forward by sword-waving officers screaming Banzais, and throwing powerful firecrackers, Ichiki's troops charged again and again with bayonets fixed and rifles cracking, only to be lashed by American machine-gun fire. Private Leckie recalled: "Here was booming, sounding, shrieking, wailing, hissing, crashing, shaking, gibbering noise. Here was Hell!"

One Japanese officer would observe that the scene was "like a housefly's attacking a tortoise. The odds were all against it." By dawn Ichiki's force had been cut down to a few hundred survivors, reduced to taking whatever shelter they could find among the sandbanks and palm trees. Working his men around the creek, Lieutenant Colonel Leonard B. Cresswell led his battalion in an afternoon assault on the Japanese rear, supported by five light tanks that rumbled across the sandspit. "We watched those awful machines as they plunged across the spit and into the edge of the grove. It was fascinating to see them bursting among the trees, pivoting, turning, spitting sheets of yellow flame. It was like a comedy of toys, something unbelievable, to see them knocking over palm trees, which fell slowly, flushing the running figures of men from underneath their treads, following and firing at the fugitives." The tanks, whose bloody tracks Cresswell observed were "like meat grinders," decimated the Japanese.

Dusk found Ichiki with a score of survivors battling on around their blood-stained flag. The colonel knelt in the sand, committing hara-kiri as the tanks came to wipe out his pathetically futile last stand. The creek ran with gore and the sandspit was littered with the half-interred remnants of more than eight hundred enemy soldiers. The Battle of Tenaru River had been won at the cost of only thirty-five Marines killed, and was America's first victory over jungle-trained Japanese troops. It inflicted the first blow to the Imperial Army's belief in its own invincibility.

MAKIN AND THE TOKYO EXPRESS

A thousand miles north across the Pacific, in the Gilberts, a second Marine operation had also succeeded in putting another dent in Japan's military prestige. On August 17, a force of 220 men of the 2nd Raider Battalion had come silently ashore through the predawn surf of Makin atoll in rubber landing boats launched from submarines outside the reef. Trained in commando-style warfare by Colonel Evan S. Carlson, who believed in the unconventional "gung-ho"-style leadership he had observed practiced by Mao Tse-tung's guerrillas, the assault succeeded in wiping out the Japanese garrison of eighty-three. Heavy surf hindered the evacuation of the Raiders with heavy losses but the cool leadership of the President's eldest son, Major James Roosevelt, managed to get all but nine Marines back to the submarine on the second night. The confusion that attended the hit-and-run raid convinced the conservative Washington military establishment that it was "a piece of folly." Similar commando operations by the Raiders were canceled after intelligence revealed that the Japanese were hurrying reinforcements to their Pacific Island garrisons.

The Makin raid also failed to achieve its objective of diverting Japan's strength from the Solomons. The Japanese command at Rabaul now assessed, too late, that it was faced with a major operation to recover its position on Guadalcanal. Troops, ships, and planes were to be sucked into the battle as the 11th Air Fleet was flown down from Tinian, Admiral Yamamoto steamed south to Truk with the Combined Fleet, and the destroyers of Admiral Tanaka's squadron began nightly runs down "The Slot" under cover of darkness, to ferry in troop reinforcements. The Japanese soldiers called them "ant runs" and the Coastwatchers in the upper Solomons, who gave early warning of the runs, referred to them as the "Tokyo Express."

The Americans were also resorting to the same tactic of using destroyers as transports to bring in gasoline and ammunition supplies to fuel and arm the growing number of planes in the Cactus Air Force. On the night of August 22, the two supply "trains" collided in the dark waters of Iron-bottom Sound, and the U.S.S. *Blue* had to be scuttled after a torpedo hit.

A far greater naval confrontation was shaping up over the disputed waters around Guadalcanal. Decrypting of the Japanese naval messages was still lagging by more than ten days, but traffic analysis revealed a big carrier group. On August 21 CINCPAC Intelligence Summary predicted that a large Japanese striking force "although still apparently in Empire waters will definitely go south, if not already under way in that direction." Responding to this vital assessment, Nimitz ordered Ghormley to concentrate his South Pacific force off the Solomons while Admiral Fletcher was the next day ordered to send his three-carrier task force north in support. The Allied strength of thirty warships was at a one-to-two disadvantage against the fifty-eight-strong Combined Fleet, which radio intelligence warned was steaming south. However, Nagumo's strike force now only fielded 2 carriers, and their 177 planes were outnumbered by Fletcher's 259. Yamamoto had hopes that his new Operation KA might yet bring the decisive battle he had failed to achieve at Midway. But its main objective was to provide aircover for the transport convoy that was to land 1,500 Imperial Marines.

Like his earlier Midway plan, the new operation suffered from the same weaknesses of dividing the Combined Fleet to achieve too many simultaneous objectives. Yamamoto was again at sea in the flagship, plagued by the same lack of communications and intelligence during the early phase of the action. This was a critical factor in determining its outcome since his air and sea patrols had so far failed to spot the American carrier task forces patrolling the Pacific northeast of Malaita Island.

U.S. Navy PBY Catalinas, however, found the Japanese transport convoy at sea east of Bougainville Island, covered by the heavy cruiser *Tone* and the light carrier *Ryujo*. The convoy was some 100 miles ahead of Yamamoto's advance forces. Fletcher ordered an air strike launched from the *Saratoga*, but neither his carrier patrols nor the twenty-three Marine dive bombers that flew off from Henderson Field located the convoy because it had been ordered to change course to the north.

The evening of August 23 found a disappointed Fletcher, assured by a

CINCPAC intelligence bulletin that the enemy fleet carriers were still at Truk, succumbing again to his perennial concern about fuel to dispatch the *Wasp*'s task force south to rendezvous with her oilers. He was to regret his action the following morning when a PBY Catalina patrolling out from Santa Cruz Island radioed sighting a carrier and cruiser heading south some 260 miles northwest of his task force. It was still being shadowed at 11 A.M. when a four-engined Japanese flying boat appeared over the northern horizon and Fletcher, too cautious to commit an attack on a single sighting, launched only twenty-three *Enterprise* Avengers for a wide-ranging search mission.

THE BATTLE OF THE EASTERN SOLOMONS

An anxious hour of deliberation continued in the American admiral's flagship, during which the *Ryujo* sent off her strike to join the "Tojo Time" Rabaul plane raid on Guadalcanal. This succeeded in luring off the *Enterprise* search strike force, which mistakenly followed the planes rather than attacking their carriers. Radio communications were hampered for both sides by heavy static and this brought more confusion when, just before 2 P.M., another Japanese carrier force was spotted far to the north of the first sighting. After hesitating so long, Fletcher knew that an attack must now be launched at once. He "reluctantly" decided to strike at the positively identified light carrier. No sooner had the eight torpedo planes and thirty dive bombers from the *Saratoga* flown off north when reports came in from PBY Catalina and the *Enterprise*'s own scouts confirming the presence of two large Japanese carriers as part of an advance force of battleships. They were less than 200 miles to the north, putting Fletcher into the precarious situation of being jumped with few aircraft left for cover. He decided it would be suicidal to launch his fourteen remaining dive bombers and twelve torpedo planes against the main body of the enemy's fleet. Poor radio communication and undisciplined pilot chatter made it impossible to recall or redirect the first strike. All that could be done was to wait and hope that the fifty-four Wildcats retained for Combat Air Patrol would be able to protect his three carriers from the Japanese.

The Battle of the Eastern Solomons, as it was to be named by the Americans, began with Admiral Fletcher repeating the same mistake that had nearly brought him disaster four months earlier in the Coral Sea. The first round would go to the U.S. Navy because the *Ryujo* was caught refueling her fighters, which had been sent aloft to beat off an earlier attack by the 5th Air Force's B-17s. The 10,000-ton light carrier was agile enough to dodge the first wave of dive bombers, but the torpedo planes executed an "anvil" attack on both quarters. The hits sent her helplessly circling.

The fires that were to sink her four hours later engulfed the crippled carrier while her surviving planes ran out of fuel and were forced to crash into the sea or try to reach Bougainville.

When Admiral Nagumo received news of the *Ryujo*'s fate, he assumed that her sacrifice had drawn off the enemy attack from his own two carriers. An hour earlier, twenty-seven dive bombers escorted by ten Zeros had roared off the *Shokaku* and the *Zuikaku* to strike the two American carriers, which had been under surveillance by float plane scouts from his cruisers for most of the afternoon. No enemy aircraft had appeared to raid his force, so by 4 P.M. he felt confident enough to launch his reserves for a second attack wave.

Towering cumulus clouds gave the Japanese pilots cover to dodge the fifty Wildcats Fletcher had sent aloft to defend his task forces, then steaming some 10 miles apart. The *Enterprise*—protected by the new battleship *North Carolina*, two cruisers, and six destroyers—attracted the whole enemy attack. Ineffective fighter control by the flagship and the greater experience of the Zero pilots drew off the defending fighters and allowed the Japanese dive bombers to assemble in the clouds before screaming down toward the *Enterprise*, one every seven seconds, through the bursting antiaircraft shells to score three hits. Two smashed into the flight deck aft, jamming the elevator; one exploded near the island, doing no serious damage. The *North Carolina*'s stern was hit by three bombs, but the battleship's damage-control parties managed to put out the fires. The "Big E's" own firefighting teams were winning their battle against the flames, although the thick column of smoke that reared skywards from her punctured flight deck convinced the departing Japanese pilots that they had mortally wounded the great carrier.

The holes in the *Enterprise*'s deck were speedily patched with metal plates, and a quarter of an hour later, her fires extinguished, the carrier was making 24 knots and recovering her planes. Then disaster nearly overtook her as it had the *Lexington* at the Coral Sea action. Choking smoke produced a string of malfunctions in the steering-engine compartment, temporarily knocking out the crew sent to repair the machinery that controlled her rudders. Helpless and untowable, the *Enterprise* was a sitting duck; her engineers fought to restore maneuverability while the radar plotters could only apprehensively track the approaching second wave of Japanese aircraft.

Miraculously, the planes that might have won victory that afternoon for Admiral Nagumo to avenge his defeat at Midway made the mistake of changing course too soon, passing some 50 miles to the west before giving up the hunt and returning north. After sweating through this anxious thirty-eight minutes that could have cost him the battle, Fletcher regained steering control on his flagship and decided to call it a day and head south.

Just before the Japanese attack, he had sent off his task force's remaining reserve of fifteen Dauntlesses and seventeen Avengers to strike against the main enemy force. The *Enterprise*'s torpedo planes eventually returned after finding nothing to attack but a coral reef, while their thirteen dive bombers, having run low on fuel, landed on Guadalcanal, where they became welcome members of the Cactus Air Force. The puny seven-plane strike launched from the *Saratoga* had better luck. They found and attacked Admiral Kondo's Advance Force, putting the seaplane tender *Chitose* out of action before running out of fuel and ditching off San Cristobal Island.

On the morning of August 25, Yamamoto called off Operation KA. The Combined Fleet steamed back to their Truk anchorage after losing a light carrier and having failed to obtain their strategic objective. Tanaka, meanwhile, had been directed to begin landing the advance units of the Kawaguchi detachment and the reserves of the ill-fated Ichiki detachment. The "ant runs" commenced on the night of August 28. Alerted by Bougainville's Coastwatchers, the Cactus Air Force had plenty of time to find and derail the Tokyo Express that afternoon, sinking the lead destroyer, damaging two others, and forcing a retreat. It was no consolation to Tanaka to learn that Japanese bombers had sunk an American destroyer transport off Tulagi. The next night he set out again with four destroyers and managed to get several hundred reinforcements ashore at Taivu, convincing the Japanese that the fast night runs when the American aircraft were grounded were the answer to reinforcing Guadalcanal.

General Kawaguchi at first stoutly refused to consider submitting himself to "warship transportation." It was not until August 30, after Tanaka's destroyers had ferried in the final 1,000 men of the Ichiki detachment, that the stubborn army commander accepted the "ant run" for his mission. On the night of August 31 he was put ashore safely with 1,000 of his men. Expectations rode high in Rabaul that they would soon have enough strength ashore for a second attack on the airfield. That day had also brought the cheering news that Imperial Navy submarine I-26 had torpedoed and sunk an American carrier off the southern Solomons.

Admiral Ghormley suffered this setback to his hopes of keeping a carrier stationed south of Guadalcanal to ferry in planes to Henderson Field, although it was not quite the victory trumpeted by the Tokyo press. The stoutly built hull of the *Saratoga* had absorbed her second torpedo that year with minimal damage, but like the January hit, it had shaken her vulnerable turbo-electric propulsion machinery, sending her back across the Pacific for another spell in dry dock.

MILNE BAY AND PORT MORESBY HELD

The loss, albeit temporary, of the carrier was an indication of the rising price the U.S. Navy was having to pay to maintain its position in the Solomons. The cost to the Japanese strategic plans was even higher. In the three weeks since the Marines had landed on Guadalcanal and Tulagi, what had at first seemed an easy task of dislodging them to restore Imperial prestige had become a major operation, drawing troops, aircraft, and ships away from the Japanese offensive on New Guinea. When the army staff at Imperial General Headquarters decided on August 31 to designate the recapture of Guadalcanal as a main objective, General Hyakutake and his staff on Rabaul were ordered to cut back the 17th Army's drive in Papua at the very time when their two-pronged thrust on Port Moresby was stalling.

The thrust that had been launched across the wild Owen Stanley range was making steady progress as General Horii's five battalions leap-frogged each other in the exhausting battle across "The Gap." Colonel Honner's brawny 39th Australian Division was fighting an equally debilitating retreat, with the added disadvantage of having their backs to the wall-like jungle slopes. When the Japanese cracked Honner's defensive position at Isaruva by striking out through the trailless rain forest to outflank it, it seemed that nothing could stop them from breaking through The Gap where the Kokoda Trail (or Track) reared over the cloud-hung crest of Papua's mountain spine. Once over the top, they would be less than 50 miles from their objective, with the advantage of momentum to carry them down to Port Moresby.

Only small parties of reinforcements from the 7th Australian Division could be spared to make the laborious five-day hike up the Kokoda Trail, since the main units were retained to forestall a Japanese attack which intelligence had revealed was being mounted against the port of Milne Bay. When MacArthur got wind of Hyakutake's Operation RE—as the Japanese commander had designated the second claw of his Papuan pincer movement—the 18th Australian Infantry Brigade was rushed in by air along with 1,300 American troops, to protect the three key airfields that the Royal Australian Air Force and the 5th Air Force needed as staging bases to carry on the bombing of Rabaul.

While the opposing fleets were hesitantly locking horns in the eastern Solomons on August 25, two cruisers and five destroyers of the Imperial Navy were escorting the transports of the RE invasion force toward Rabi Island at the northern tip of Milne Bay. Their approach was concealed by thick rain squalls until the afternoon of the 25th, when Australian fighters and bombers sortied to attack the convoy, sinking one minesweeper and damaging a transport. This did not prevent 1,200 Special Naval Landing

Force Marines being put ashore that evening. The Rabaul command had underestimated the opposition, but they had continuing bad weather on their side, which hampered Allied air attacks, permitting the Japanese to land reinforcements and light tanks bringing their total strength up to over 2,000. The Allied commander at Milne Bay, Major General Cyril A. Clowes, had been reinforced with the 18th Australian Infantry Brigade, two Royal Australian Air Force Fighter Squadrons, and 1,300 American soldiers. The Japanese were outnumbered ten to one, and only succeeded in overrunning one outlying Australian unit as the men pushed through the dark in pouring rain toward the heavily defended airfield and their assault faltered when their tanks bogged down in swampy ground.

In the three-day battle that followed, the defenders' strength was decisive. The Japanese repeatedly failed in suicidal frontal assaults to make any dent in the Australian positions. Supported by aircraft, the Allied counterattacks steadily drove the invaders back onto the beaches. Urgent appeals for reinforcements from Rabaul were ignored because of General Hyakutake's instructions from Tokyo to give priority to Guadalcanal.

"TRY AND GET THEM OUT," the Rabaul command signaled to the destroyers on September 5, as Operation RE was abandoned. Only 600 Japanese troops escaped from a debacle at Milne Bay that had cost them over 2,000 casualties—a defeat made worse when a 5th Air Force B-17 sank one of the rescue destroyers. "The enemy fell into the trap with disastrous results for him," General MacArthur's communiqué reported after his first victory. It was also the first time that such an amphibious assault by Japanese forces had been crushed. At the same time, his cable to General Marshall blamed the delays holding up the New Guinea offensive on the failure of General Blamey to "energize" the attacks on the enemy advance over the Kokoda Trail. MacArthur indicated that he was "not yet convinced of the efficiency of the Australian units." Now that the Japanese thrust to Milne Bay was repulsed, MacArthur could safely devote his main force of the 7th Australian Division to the battle for the Kokoda Trail.

General Horii's battalions had broken through The Gap on September 5 and were fighting their way down toward Port Moresby, but the incredible effort of their ordeal was beginning to tell. Their strength was sapped by the jungle and disease, and the 65-mile-long Japanese supply line was under increasing attack from the air, which destroyed the bridge at Wairopi. On Imita Ridge, just 30 miles from Port Moresby, Horii's advance was finally halted on September 17 by fresh Australian troops after the Japanese had captured the last village of Ioribaiwa.

"How can we fight against this?" one officer complained, as the Japanese encountered a stiff defense and their rice, medicine, and ammunition ran low. Illness and starvation threatened. Tantalized, they could see the searchlights of their objective sweeping the sky. General Horii was stubbornly determined not to give up. "The Detachment will stay here and firmly hold its position in order to perfect its organization and replenish its fighting strength. We will strike a hammer blow at the stronghold of Port Moresby," he ordered. But there were no reinforcements coming to provide those hammer blows. The 17th Army reserves were being sent to Guadalcanal. On September 18 came the order to fall back on Buna. A nightmare retreat began for General Horii and his men that few would survive. Papua had been saved by the tenacious valor of the Australian fighting soldiers, the 5th Air Force, and the jungle itself.

18

"Everybody Hopes That We Can Hold On"

"This is the toughest war of all time," President Roosevelt told the nation in a solemn broadcast on September 7, 1942. Americans might have been spared the devastation of bombing, but they felt the privations of a war economy that had deprived them of new cars and made unobtainable a host of household items from toothpaste to electrical goods, as factories were ordered to save metal and turn over to arms production. Japan's conquest of the Malayan rubber plantations had resulted in a shortage of tires that kept cars off the roads more effectively than gasoline rationing. Sugar supplies were restricted by points; coffee and meat would soon follow.

For the first time since the beginning of the Depression, the drafting of men along with the expansion of industrial effort to turn the United States into the "arsenal of democracy" had eliminated unemployment and caused inflation. "Overall stabilization of prices, wages, salaries and profits is necessary to the continued increasing production of tanks, ships and guns," Roosevelt warned. Congress, with Democratic power on the wane before the critical mid-term elections that November, was dragging its feet on the bill that would give the President draconian powers over the economy to fix prices and salaries. Tax hikes and controls were essential, he cautioned. Americans were "not doing enough" at home to support their men fighting at the front. Now they had to pay the price for waging a global war which he estimated "will cost this nation nearly one hundred million dollars by the end of 1943."

After the broadcast, Roosevelt upstaged the bickering politicians on Capitol Hill by making a secret but nonetheless well-publicized coast-to-coast tour of the key industrial plants. His purpose was to make the nation aware just how staggering the cost of financing the war was. Publicity was given to the $65-million new Ford-built bomber plant at Willow Run and the West Coast shipyards of Henry J. Kaiser, who was lionized by the press as one of the most successful of the new breed of entrepreneurs and whose "Liberty Ship" matched the demands of the global conflict.

"EVERYBODY HOPES THAT WE CAN HOLD ON"

Others had failed, but "Old Man Kaiser" succeeded in getting millions of dollars of contracts and all the steel he needed from Washington's "arsenal of bureaucracy" to turn out 10,000-ton standardized vessels using prefabricated production line techniques just as Detroit had mass-produced cars. Employing thousands of "Rosie the Riveters," his yards stitched together prefabricated sections around the clock, cutting the time needed to build a vessel from over six months at the beginning of the year, to less than three by May, to an average of four weeks by September. In a spectacular stunt, the record was established that fall when the *Robert E. Peary* was launched with paint still wet in an incredible four days, fifteen hours, after keel laying (a record that has never been broken).

The war against the U-boats was finally being won that fall by what Henry Kaiser termed the "miracle of God and the Genius of the Free American worker." In September for the first time tonnage built exceeded that sunk by enemy action. The shipping crisis, which had been the principal limiting factor in Allied strategic planning, now began to ease month by month. The pressure was reduced only slowly in 1942 because of the huge demands for transports to carry the Operation Torch landings to North Africa, to supply the Bolero build-up in Britain, and to restart the Arctic convoys to sustain the Red Army as it made its stand at Stalingrad. These operations had all been curtailed when emergency convoys of Sherman tanks and ammunition were sent around the Cape of Good Hope to Egypt to provide the new British 8th Army Commander, General Bernard Montgomery, with more punch for his offensive against Rommel's front at El Alamein.

The Combined Chiefs of Staff had to juggle all these priorities against the Pacific, where additional shipping was also urgently needed just to keep supplies and reinforcements moving across the ocean to sustain the Marines' precarious hold on Guadalcanal and support General MacArthur's expanding New Guinea operations. Despite continued calls for more aircraft and ships for the South Pacific, the Joint Chiefs in Washington had told MacArthur and King that they could not expect so much as an additional gun or plane or a single transport vessel that might weaken the overriding demands of the October Torch invasion of North Africa.

AIRLIFT TO CHINA

China and India rated even lower on the Allied scale of strategic priorities in 1942. The B-24 Liberator bombers promised to Chiang Kai-shek had been diverted to the Middle East, and General Wavell had been similarly deprived of a British division originally allocated to defend the frontiers of India. The monsoon season had brought four months respite in operations in Burma, where the 15th Imperial Army had moved north up to the border with Assam when it had been halted by the weather. This had prevented the Japanese from exploiting the rising civil unrest in India. British troops had to be withdrawn from the front to control spreading riots and bombings as the Congress Party's nonviolent campaign for independence degenerated into bloodshed after the jailing of Gandhi, Nehru, and hundreds of their supporters. Japan encouraged the subversive propaganda of the "Free India Movement" directed by Subhas Chandra Bose, the breakaway Congress Party leader. Bose had found Tokyo far more helpful than Berlin, where he had fled in 1940 to get Hitler's backing. Recruiting 5,000 soldiers from among the more than 40,000 captured in Malaya, he established his so-called Indian National Army, which was shipped back to Rangoon to fight alongside the Japanese in Burma.

Internal problems were also distracting Chiang Kai-shek's army from the fighting against Japan. An unofficial truce settled over the front in eastern China as more Nationalist troops were sent north to prepare for a renewed move against Chiang's Chinese Communist allies. Unwilling to fuel another civil war, and facing a shortage of military supplies, Washington steadfastly refused to meet the Generalissimo's repeated calls for more Lend-Lease supplies. Less than half the 100 transport planes that Roosevelt had originally promised when the Burma Road was cut were flying "The Hump" route into China by the fall, delivering only one tenth of the intended 5,000 monthly tons of military material. Supplies were piling up on the docksides at Karachi and Bombay, partly because of delays in transporting them 1,500 miles across the overworked Indian railway system. The worst bottleneck was the old single track line that wound up from Bengal. Built to serve the tea plantations of Assam, it was justifiably cursed as the "Toonerville Trolley." Material bound for China was then trucked to the dusty airstrips of the Brahmaputra Valley in northeastern India. Here it was loaded onto the rugged C-47 twin-engined Dakotas and the larger four-engined C-54 Commandos, which took off east over the Naga Hills to make the 500-mile flight across the Himalayas into China.

"The Hump" was the name that the American pilots of China National Airlines, who had originally pioneered the route, gave the run, which was now also flown by the crews of Army Air Command. One of the most arduous flights in the world, it negotiated the 15,000-foot mountain range where planes flew near their performance ceiling and men needed oxygen. Turbulent winds tossed aircraft like leaves, thick clouds made navigation a hit-or-miss affair, and the rugged peaks and lurking Japanese fighters over Burma rendered each trip a test of nerve, courage, and physical flying ability. Ammunition, spare parts, and vital fuel had to be flown in to keep the Flying Tigers airborne. Claire Chennault had found that Washington still paid little heed to his repeated requests for these essential supplies, even after he was commissioned a brigadier general in July, when the

China Air Task Force—as his outfit was officially designated—became part of the U.S. Army 10th Air Force. Instead of raiding the Japanese, his handful of bombers had to be kept operating over The Hump just to ferry in enough fuel and spare parts to keep his fighters aloft.

General Stilwell, the American forces' commander in China, spent a summer of increasing frustration as he shuttled back and forth over The Hump between New Delhi and Chungking, trying to get General Wavell and Chiang Kai-shek to agree with his scheme to launch a joint offensive during the coming dry season. The offensive's goal was to reopen a route from Ledo in Assam across northern Burma to restore the strategic China overland supply line. In Stilwell's view, the British were proving infuriatingly slow in providing the promised arms and training facilities for the 8,000 Chinese troops in India. The Generalissimo, with more concern for the Communists than the Japanese, hesitated to release the twenty Nationalist Army divisions that Stilwell needed to support his offensive from the east.

Chiang was growing more impatient with the President's failure to step up Lend-Lease aid. No more than fifty of the promised one hundred transport planes had arrived by July, and when Chennault was deprived of additional bombers in favor of the British, Chiang fired off a petulant ultimatum to Roosevelt in the form of a "request" for the U.S. commitment to China to be reaffirmed by meeting three essential demands. These were: sending three U.S. Army divisions to launch the campaign to reopen the Burma Road; five hundred combat planes to defend Chungking; and enough transport aircraft to meet his "minimum requirement" of 5,000 tons of supplies over The Hump each month. If these conditions were not met, Chiang threatened "liquidation of the China theater" and "other adjustments."

Unwilling and unable to meet such preposterous demands, which would hazard operations in every other theater of war, the President temporized. Soothingly, he assured Chungking that they would be investigated. Stilwell, who was facing an attempt to oust him by General Chennault with the support of Madame Chiang, made no secret in his reports to Washington of his view that the Generalissimo's demands were unrealistic and that much of the Lend-Lease aid was being pocketed by corrupt officials when not directed by Chiang into his anti-Communist build-up. He was also dismayed that Marshall's cool reactions indicated he could count on no support from the Joint Chiefs of Staff in pushing the British into a Burma offensive.

BURMA OFFENSIVES

General Wavell and his staff, in their palatial New Delhi headquarters, talked grandly about a proposed "Anakim" operation. This called for amphibious landings to retake Rangoon, and sending the Chinese troops in India to launch an offensive with the British into Burma, while the Nationalist Army marched down from China. As long as the plan remained no more than a series of erudite staff papers, Stilwell was convinced "the bastards will sabotage the scheme." Not until late August 1942 did his Chinese soldiers get a training base in India. Stilwell's expectations for Wavell's operation fell through when Wavell informed him there could be no amphibious assault that year because the landing craft and Royal Marine Division were being sent to Madagascar to renew operations against the Vichy garrisons. The only British offensive that could be mounted was a limited drive down Burma's Arakan coast—which the American general dismissed as "a joke."

Wavell felt obliged to make a British contribution to the war against Japan. He launched the thrust against the occupiers of Burma on September 21, when the 14th Indian Army Division struck south from Chittagong accompanied by a British infantry brigade. Japanese resistance at first proved light, but the soldiers from the dry plains of the Punjab made slow progress down the swampy coast, their advance impeded by the dense mangrove swamps and tidal creeks that punctuated the rice paddies. Supplied by a motley fleet of sampans, a landing craft, and a couple of ancient paddle steamers, the force took nearly a month to advance the less than 100 miles required to reach the neck of the Mayu Peninsula. Its southernmost tip was to be the springboard for launching an amphibious assault against the strategic port of Akyab. When the RAF failed to win air superiority, the Arakan campaign began faltering in October, as the Japanese brought up more troops to stiffen their defense.

The British Burma operation was neither making sufficient progress nor on the scale Chiang Kai-shek had anticipated. He therefore used it as the excuse not to commit any Chinese armies to a simultaneous offensive in the north. Stilwell protested, but the Generalissimo complained that he had yet to receive a reply to his three demands.

The arrival that month of former Republican presidential candidate Wendell Willkie, acting as Roosevelt's roving morale-boosting ambassador, was a further complication. He spoke out too forcefully against Washington's neglect of the Nationalist cause, and acted as a go-between in General Chennault's bid to depose Stilwell. Willkie carried back to the President the aviator's overblown promise that if he was given control of the theater and 150 combat aircraft at once, he could "accomplish the downfall of Japan . . . probably within six months." It was scorned by

General Marshall as "not bad strategy, just nonsense." Roosevelt therefore reiterated his support for Stilwell in his letter of October 14, formally reassuring Chiang Kai-shek that the United States was committed to China, but could not meet all his demands at once because of the pressures in the other theaters. He promised more combat planes as soon as they could be spared, and agreed to ensure that one hundred transports were flying to The Hump by the end of 1942. This concession was enough to persuade Chiang tentatively to support Stilwell's scheme to launch his drive from Ledo in Assam to join up with the northern end of the Burma Road as soon as the Chinese troops in India had finished training. He also promised Stilwell twenty divisions of Nationalist soldiers if the British launched their full Anakim offensive.

There were real doubts that this would ever come off, as Stilwell learned from his November trip to New Delhi, where he found General Wavell intensely worried with the lack of progress in the Arakan. Without landing craft and naval support to carry the soldiers across from the Mayu Peninsula to the island port of Akyab, the whole operation appeared to be degenerating into an improvised shambles. The Torch invasion of North Africa had the overriding call on Allied resources, and material originally destined for China was being diverted in a renewed attempt to send aid to the struggling Soviet forces. Anything left over was sent to reinforce the critical battles in Guadalcanal and New Guinea. Stilwell's angry protest to the Washington War Department elicited only General Marshall's "sympathize with your reaction"—but no more aircraft or materiel. "Peanut and I are on a raft with only one sandwich between us and the rescue ship is heading away" was how "Vinegar Joe" despairingly summed up his miserable situation in a letter to his wife.

CRISIS IN THE SOLOMONS

The Pacific theater was also suffering from the Allied commitment to the North African invasion. General MacArthur had warned repeatedly since August of the "disastrous outcome" if the Allies failed to match the reinforcements Japan was rushing to its southern perimeter after the failure to take Port Moresby. Admiral King called for more aircraft in the Solomons "regardless of interference with commitments in the Eastern Atlantic," but the Joint Chiefs stood firm behind General Marshall's refusal to endanger Operation Torch by sending an additional ship or plane to the Pacific. The Americans lost what Admiral Turner had termed "a golden opportunity, not to be missed" to send to Guadalcanal air and ground reinforcements after the first enemy counteroffensive had been smashed at the beginning of September.

Instead, it was the Japanese who were bringing in reinforcements in their nightly runs down The Slot, which ferried in General Kawaguchi's 3,000-strong detachment. The only additional strength that General Vandergrift received was a noncombatant naval construction battalion. The first unit of CBs to see active duty in the front line soon earned their popular name of "Seabees." Armed with picks, hammers, shovels, and wrenches, they were destined to play as vital a role in the battle for Guadalcanal as the Marines with their rifles, machine guns, and grenades. The CBs had been established less than nine months before, the brainchild of Admiral Ben Moreell, then Chief of the Navy's Bureau of Yards and Docks. He recruited teams from the civil engineering industry to provide the skilled manpower for construction of the docks, roads, and airstrips that were going to play such an important part in the Pacific War. The Seabees' battle honors began with their arrival on Guadalcanal on September 1, when they came in with two bulldozers and construction equipment. They were soon filling the bomb craters and shell holes with which the Japanese bombers and warships daily tried to put Henderson Field out of action.

Over sixty dive bombers and fighters now operated from the airstrip on an island where natural forces were as great an obstacle to sustaining the defense as the Japanese. The field, subjected to torrential downpours, was alternately transformed from "a bowl of black dust which fouled up airplane engines" to "a quagmire of black mud which made takeoff resemble nothing more than a fly trying to rise from a runway of molasses."

Keeping the airstrip open so that the American planes could operate was as crucial to the mounting pace of the battle for Guadalcanal as the Marines defending their positions around the airfield perimeter. On September 3, General Roy S. Geiger arrived to assume command of 1st Marine Aircraft Wing (as the "Cactus Air Force" had now been designated after the American code name for Guadalcanal). His task was to see that the U.S. Navy retained control of the approaches to the island in the daylight hours, so that supplies, ammunition, and the vital gasoline could be brought in by converted destroyer transports and the occasional freighter. As dusk fell every evening, control of the disputed waters of Ironbottom Sound passed to the Japanese destroyers of the Tokyo Express, which sped down The Slot to carry on their troop build-up. The question of who dominated the black night-time waters of the Sound was settled, at least temporarily, on September 5 when the Japanese destroyers sank two U.S. Navy destroyer transports that had just ferried the 1st Raider Battalion across from Tulagi.

Three nights later, General Vandegrift wisely waited until just before dawn to land Colonel Edson's Raider Battalion at Tasimboko to disrupt the enemy build-up that had been reported by Major Clemens's native scouts. The Japanese supply base was raided successfully, but too late. General Kawaguchi had already set off along the same westward trek through the coconut groves down which Colonel Ichiki and his 1,000 men had marched to their death at the Tenaru River battle three weeks before.

General Kawaguchi, with less justification, suffered from the same fatal over-confidence, which led him to believe that with three times the force of the failed first offensive, he could capture the American positions by September 13. He had devised what he thought was a foolproof three-pronged assault plan. His detachment would divide east of the Ilu (Tenaru) River; the main body would smash into the rear of the Marines' defense perimeter, while his secondary force drove against the airfield from the west, and a contingent of Imperial Navy Marines landed at Lunga Point to coordinate an attack on the other side of Henderson Field.

Thanks to continuous surveillance by Clemens's scouts, General Vandegrift was forewarned of Kawaguchi's movements. So when Edson's Raiders returned from the Tasimboko operation, they were sent forward to establish advance defenses along the ridge of high ground that stood clear of the jungle overlooking the rear of the perimeter.

THE BATTLE OF "BLOODY RIDGE"

The Raiders were well placed in their foxholes, with machine-gun posts covering the ridge on September 12, when the first wave of Kawaguchi's troops came screaming out of the jungle in front of them just after 9 P.M., in an attack that was timed to coincide with the arrival of supporting fire from destroyers on the Sound. "It was a combined sea and land attack, with Japanese naval units standing off the coast and lobbing shells directly over the ridge and into the jungle beyond in the general direction of Colonel Edson's outfit," was how Colonel William McKennon described it. From his battalion's position covering the Lunga River flank of the airfield he saw the opening night's battle for what came to be called "Bloody Ridge."

The Marines holding the front line knew that with the Japanese withdrawal into the jungle at dawn the night attack "had been but a prelude." They made only a limited counterattack, which merely flushed a few snipers out of the trees. As the sun went down that evening the stirrings of new activity could be heard over the chorus of jungle insects and the screech of cockatoos. Ordered to move forward because "the situation up front was threatening," McKennon advanced toward the ridge. His outfit, which had had no sleep for nearly two days, stumbled, groping their way forward to new positions in the dark. The crunch of mortar shells heralded the beginning of that night's assault. Suddenly the jungle came alive with Japanese yelling obscenities and Banzais and hurling firecrackers. This was a "special brand of terrorism," as the colonel described it. "The sky and the jungle were blazing with fireworks and a hellish bedlam of howls." Firecrackers, a cheap imitation of machine guns, exploded in front of, in, and behind their positions. Parachute flares that burned brightly for an instant, bobbed along, then went out, lighted the scene intermittently. From the jungle below came the rhythmic accompaniment of the slapping of gun butts and the chant: "U.S. MARINES BE DEAD TOMORROW. U.S. MARINES BE DEAD TOMORROW."

The chanting became "a mad religious rite," which heralded a series of frenzied Banzai charges through the pouring rain, as the darkness was broken by the flashes of gunfire and the eerie green glare of the Japanese flares. For a time Edson's battalion, holding out on the top of Bloody Ridge, was cut off, until McKennon's men drove back assaults with machine guns. "When one wave was mowed down—and I mean mowed down—another followed it into death."

The suicidal Banzai charges succeeded by their sheer weight and remorselessness in forcing Edson to pull back his line to within 1,000 yards of the end of the runway by dawn, as the bodies piled up in front of them littering the ridge like human chaff. But Kawaguchi ran out of live bodies before the Marines ran out of live ammunition to keep their red-hot machine guns blasting away. By first light, Marine fighters took off to strafe the enemy regrouping in the jungle behind the ridge. The Japanese flank attacks were no more successful in penetrating the American perimeter than the mad frontal assault.

The sun that rose up over Henderson Field that morning was not the Imperial emblem of Japan that General Kawaguchi had intended. His pride shattered, he could now only order a retreat through the jungle, leaving behind over six hundred dead. His confidence that they would be breakfasting on American supplies that day had caused him to leave most of his food stocks at Tasimboko. The demoralized Japanese soldiers faced a week-long trek through the hostile jungle with starvation rations which, added to battle fatigue and disease, would increase the casualty rate of his detachment to more than 50 percent. The Marines had won their second victory on Bloody Ridge at the cost of only forty killed—a small enough price to pay for smashing the second Japanese attempt to retake Guadalcanal.

When the news of their humiliating defeat reached the 17th Army Headquarters at Rabaul, General Hyakutake's staff officers were reduced to foot-stamping fury. Admiral Yamamoto was inclined to agree with his staff prediction that nothing short of a full divisional assault could retake Guadalcanal. The Second Fleet, supported by Admiral Nagumo's carriers, was having no better luck searching east and south of the island for American convoys. They had been bombed by B-17s but had not sighted a single American vessel. But that morning one of their submarines did have more success, sighting a large American convoy west of the New Hebrides.

THE END OF U.S.S. WASP

The six transports carrying the 7th Marine Division had put out from Espiritu Santo escorted by two carriers and a battleship under orders from Admiral Ghormley to fight their way through to reinforce Guadalcanal. The spanking breeze whipped the long Pacific swells into crested waves which concealed the attack periscope as the skipper of Imperial Navy submarine I-15 maneuvered into position. Then, just before 2:30 A.M., he sent two torpedoes racing into the starboard flank of the *Wasp* as she steamed to windward to land her Combat Fighter Patrol for refueling.

A conflagration erupted below decks. Fueled by the open gasoline lines and the failure of the fire mains, which hampered efforts to control the blaze, thick black smoke billowed over the sparkling ocean. Five miles away from the stricken carrier, her sister ship *Hornet* and the battleship *North Carolina* were already being lined up in the cross wires of the periscope of a second submarine. I-19's commander could hardly believe his good fortune at having so easily penetrated the escort screen. The torpedo tracks were sighted minutes before 3 P.M., in good time for the *Hornet* to take evasive action, but a 30-foot gash was ripped in the port side of the *North Carolina* with a chance hit smashing into the *O'Brien*. The crippled destroyer was to founder in rough weather as she limped back across the Pacific; the battleship was able to steam slowly back to Pearl Harbor for dry docking.

Less than half an hour after being hit, the *Wasp* had become a floating inferno after a magazine explosion tore out her vitals, wrecking the bridge and killing everyone on its port side. Shortly after three o'clock she was abandoned, after twenty-four planes had managed to take off before the flames licked over her flight deck. Over two hundred of her crew had perished before she was dispatched to the bottom at 9 P.M., still blazing furiously, by a torpedo from her attendant destroyer.

Japan had chalked up a victory at sea that day against the one won by the Marines on the island. It might have been fatal to American chances of holding Guadalcanal, since Admiral Ghormley now had only a single carrier task force to fight reinforcements through. Admiral Turner, his amphibious force commander, stoutly insisted that his convoy must press on —and luck proved to be on their side. Bad weather grounded the enemy reconnaissance planes and bombers at Rabaul and, much to Yamamoto's fury, the Second Fleet failed to intercept. Four days later the convoy arrived safely in Ironbottom Sound where the transports were anchored off Lunga Point. Uninterrupted by air raids, they unloaded the 7th Division along with its 147 vehicles, 1,000 tons of rations, and 400 drums of aviation gasoline. General Vandegrift could now count on over 19,000 Marines, with the 1,000 men and 50 planes of the 1st Marine Air Wing to join the

Cactus Air Force to defend Guadalcanal. His efforts to extend the beach-head perimeter, however, ran into fierce resistance from what was estimated to be a force of around 5,000 Japanese dug in 6 miles on either side of the airfield.

The Solomon's campaign settled into a battle of attrition. At their September conference in San Francisco, King and Nimitz calculated that the advantage was passing to the U.S. Navy, which had to press the struggle regardless of cost. The battle now hinged on whether the Marines could hang on long enough for the Pacific Fleet to win the slogging match at sea. When the question was put by a correspondent of the *New York Times*, General Vandegrift considered for a moment, then firmly stated: "Hell, yes, why not?"

A similar tempered optimism prevailed among the Japanese on Rabaul. General Hyakutake announced that he would personally take charge of the next effort to recover Guadalcanal. He made a start to prepare for a fresh operation by sending in heavy artillery to support Lieutenant General Masai Maruyama's "Sendai" Division, whose troops were assembling on Shortland Island in preparation for embarkation on six fast transports that would put them ashore on the night of October 14, so that the fresh offensive could begin a week later. His plan called for air and bombardment support from the Combined Fleet, but Hyakutake found that the admirals were understandably hesitant to expose their carriers and battleships to possible retaliation by American land-based planes. He raged that he would go ahead without their help, before turning to the ubiquitous Colonel Tsuji, the army staff's troubleshooter, who had just arrived from Tokyo.

Tsuji flew to Truk on September 24 to plead the case with Admiral Yamamoto. "Our supply has been cut off for more than a month. Officers and men have to dig for grass roots, scrape moss and pick buds from the trees and drink water to survive," he told the admiral bluntly, sparing no details of the ordeal suffered by the men under Kawaguchi, who was now "thinner than Gandhi himself." The ascetic colonel had been mortally offended by the "high living" aboard the flagship, which was deservedly known as "The Yamato Hotel," and his account apparently moved Yamamoto to give tearful promise: "I'll give you cover, even if I have to bring the *Yamato* alongside Guadalcanal myself."

Yamamoto certainly had no intention of letting the world's largest battleship end up among the mounting pile of wrecks littering Ironbottom Sound, but he signed a memorandum which Tsuji took back to General Hyakutake promising that the Combined Fleet's cruisers would be sent in to knock out the American airstrip on the eve of the new assault and that his carriers and battleships would be sent to guard against any more enemy convoys reaching Guadalcanal. At least one of the 17th Army staff on Rabaul cautioned that they now had "no chance of winning the war of attrition even with the naval support." However, General Hyakutake, abetted by the fanatical Colonel Tsuji, was once again underestimating the strength of the American position as they prepared an all-out attempt to retake the island.

Proof of the United States' determination to hold on to Guadalcanal was given at the end of September, when Admiral Nimitz set off on a tour of the South Pacific by four-engined Coronado flying boat. General Arnold joined him for a conference with Admiral Ghormley at Noumea, and they were both concerned to find eight transports waiting still loaded in the New Caledonia harbor. They were equally disturbed that Ghormley had no plans to rush in the U.S. Army division still on the island. On September 29, Nimitz courageously flew by B-17 bomber to Guadalcanal to decorate the Marines and rally General Vandegrift. He was confident that as long as they held the airfield and were not waylaid by diversionary tactics, they could win the battle. Promising to send in more planes and troops at once, his very presence there overnight sharing the humidity, mosquitoes, and meager rations did almost as much to stiffen the morale of the garrison. Flying back to Noumea, he insisted that Ghormley immediately send in the 164th Infantry Regiment, a 3,000-strong National Guard unit of brawny lumberjacks and strapping Minnesota farm hands who had adopted the title of the "Americal" Division because they had been lazing inactively for so many months on New Caledonia.

The convoy was to be escorted by the *Hornet*'s task force, which had been strengthened by the new fast battleship *Washington*. The Americal Division was embarked on transports led by Admiral Turner's command ship *MacCawley*. On October 9, 1942, this powerful force sailed to batter its way through to Guadalcanal. Sent ahead to patrol the approaches to the Sound off Lunga Point, where the troops were scheduled to go ashore on October 13, was Rear Admiral Norman Scott's Task Force 64, made up of four cruisers and six destroyers, whose orders directed them to "search for and destroy enemy ships and landing craft."

The American and Japanese reinforcement operations, unknown to each other, were piling in for a collision in the dark waters of Ironbottom Sound. Every night the "Rat Express," as it was called by the Imperial Army, was ferrying in 150 troops on each destroyer while float planes from Admiral Mikawa's covering heavy cruisers—dubbed "Washing Machine Charlies" by the Marines—dropped fragmentation bombs. Warnings by the Coastwatchers sent the dive bombers of the Cactus Air Force out to try to derail these Tokyo Expresses as they raced each afternoon up The Slot. On October 8, they had successfully forced that day's run to retreat. But the following afternoon they failed to stop a transport and five destroyers from getting through to land General Hyakutake and his staff with a sizeable force at Tassafaronga.

The following afternoon, October 9, Admiral Scott arrived in Ironbottom Sound, anticipating taking his task force into action against the enemy destroyers. However, he retired after aerial reconnaissance failed to locate any Japanese naval movements that afternoon in The Slot. The Tokyo Express was not running that day since Admiral Mikawa was gathering his force for the big run on the night of October 11. His arrival would be preceded by Admiral Goto's bombardment force of three heavy and light cruisers; and he had been assured by the 11th Air Fleet Commander that the airstrip would be put out of action by his bombers. Over sixty Japanese planes had raided Guadalcanal that day, but most of their bombs fell ineffectively on the jungle and ten planes were lost at the cost of two aircraft to the Cactus Air Force. At the same time, patrolling B-17s spotted the tell-tale white-tipped tracks of the powerful enemy squadron slicing through The Slot, so by late that afternoon Admiral Scott had ordered his task force to work up to its maximum speed of 29 knots to reach the waters off Savo Island before the estimated time of enemy arrival there at midnight.

THE BATTLE OF CAPE ESPERANCE

It was a typically oppressive Guadalcanal night, dripping with humidity, quivering with lightning discharges in the clouds over the island's peaks. Scott, recently promoted to flag rank, was determined to seize the chance to avenge the U.S. Navy's defeat at the Battle of Savo Island. He had left nothing to chance and was following a carefully rehearsed tactical plan: his flagship *San Francisco* was leading the cruisers in the center of his battle column, with three destroyers in the van and two bringing up the rear. He had hoped to catapult off his four Kingfisher scout planes to find the enemy because of the poor performance of radar in confined waters, but two crashed on takeoff and the surviving pair proved ineffective. One almost alerted Admiral Goto to the trap he was steaming toward as they buzzed low over the Japanese cruisers, which were sweeping the water ahead with their searchlights to decoy any enemy naval forces away from the destroyer transports.

Ten minutes before eleven, the American spotter planes radioed that the enemy warships were approaching from the northwest, heading for the passage between Savo Island and Cape Esperance. Scott was heading north, yet he managed, with parade-ground precision, to execute the tricky maneuver that brought his column right around to head off the Japanese, who were making for the southern entrance into the Sound. He found he had succeeded in bringing his battle line across the head of the enemy—crossing the T—so that every one of his guns could be brought to bear. His destroyers were racing hard to take up their position in the van as his radars probed the closing range and all guns pointed into the silent darkness. At 11:46 the cruiser *Helena*, with the advantage of the latest radar, opened fire first. The American battle line erupted into action, blinding the onrushing enemy with starshells and well-placed salvos.

Surprise was complete and utter. Admiral Goto believed that his ships were firing at their own transports. He never lived to appreciate his error because *Aoba*'s bridge was smashed seconds later by a shell and the mortally wounded admiral was heard muttering over and over, "Stupid bastards!" before he expired.

The confusion was not exclusively Japanese. A minute after the *San Francisco* had opened fire Scott, too, became convinced they were firing at their own destroyers in the darkness. He ordered a cease-fire to check the identification lights of the targets. The four-minute halt in the action gave the stunned Japanese captains just enough time to take measures to rectify their predicament, with two cruisers already set ablaze. They were turning about as the American line reopened fire and the *San Francisco* blasted an unfortunate enemy destroyer out of the water with her first salvo. The cruiser *Furataka* was being hit repeatedly and was falling behind the general retreat as Scott swung around to the northwest in pursuit.

At midnight, when Scott again called for a halt in the firing so that his line could re-form, the Japanese seized the opportunity to hit back at the *Boise* after an inadvertent searchlight flipped on to draw a well-aimed salvo crashing through her forward turret. She was saved from disaster only by her thin hull, which allowed water to flood into the magazines before they could explode, and by the quick action of the *Salt Lake City*'s captain, who swung his heavy cruiser out of line to cover the crippled *Boise*. As they made off into the dark, the Japanese launched torpedoes at their pursuers. Only twenty minutes after the action had begun so fiercely, it sputtered out when Scott ordered his column onto a southwesterly course.

"Providence abandoned us," was the official Japanese explanation for the crushing defeat at Cape Esperance. They had suffered their first defeat ever in a night action, losing a cruiser and a destroyer, with another heavy cruiser badly damaged. Scott, in spite of confused communications that had nearly cost him the battle, had brought the U.S. Navy a welcome Columbus Day victory that wiped out its earlier defeat.

One American cruiser and two destroyers had been badly mauled; the destroyer *Duncan* proved to be too battered to salvage and was run aground. The Americans had driven off the bombardment force, but they had not disrupted the Japanese destroyers, which took advantage of the battle to race in and land their detachments of troops and four heavy artillery pieces before stealing out of Ironbottom Sound undiscovered. Then in the small hours of October 12, the Japanese made the mistake of sending back destroyers to search for survivors. Two were caught and sunk the next morning by Marine dive bombers and torpedo planes.

The evening of October 12 saw the arrival of the first four PT boats under tow by American destroyers. The establishment of a base at Tulagi marked the beginning of the U.S. Navy's determined effort to deny the enemy undisputed night-time control over the waters around Guadalcanal. They were followed next morning by the arrival of Admiral Turner's transports, which quickly disgorged the 3,000 troops of the Americal Division. The Japanese had arranged a warm welcome that night, when the first U.S. Army soldiers on Guadalcanal would receive such a terrible baptism of fire that they would look back on the horror as the worst of their whole long ordeal.

That afternoon, the beginning of Japan's biggest offensive drive to re-capture the island was heralded by two heavy air raids, which destroyed grounded planes, set ablaze 5,000 gallons of aviation fuel, and rendered temporarily inoperable the main runway as well as the auxiliary fighter strip just completed. The Seabees now went into around-the-clock action, battling to fill in the craters faster than the bombs and the long-range mortars the Marines nicknamed "Pistol Petes" could tear them up. But the damage wrought so far was insignificant compared with that done by the thunderous barrage which erupted at midnight. The air was filled with a noise like screeching railroad cars as man-size projectiles came crashing down, causing small earthquakes as they plowed up the ground in fountains of red fire.

The battleships *Kongo* and *Haruna* had arrived as Yamamoto had promised, to lend their mighty support by lobbing in 14-inch shells from 10 miles out in Ironbottom Sound. The four PT boats from Tulagi raced out, but could only snap helplessly like terriers as the destroyers kept them at bay. "The ensuing scene baffled description as the fires and explosions from the 36cm shells hit the airfield, setting off enemy planes and fuel dumps and ammunition storage places," recorded Admiral Tanaka, whose light cruiser and destroyers added their punier shells to the raging bombardment of Henderson Field. "The scene was topped off by flare bombs from our observation planes flying over the field, the whole spectacle making the Tyogoku fireworks seem like mere child's play."

The rain of destruction was watched with equal satisfaction by General Hyakutake at his field headquarters less than 20 miles away, to the east of the American positions. When Admiral Kurita called a halt to the bombardment shortly after 2:30 A.M., he had all but succeeded in his aim of cutting the Cactus Air Force to pieces. Out of ninety planes, only six bombers and five fighters were left operational. The steel matting on the runways had been shredded like cardboard. Miraculously, only forty-one men had been killed, but the Marines and the newly arrived Army "doggies" had been badly shaken. By early afternoon the Seabee gangs had repaired "Fighter One" and the surviving planes were able to take off to raid that afternoon's Tokyo Express, whose six destroyers nonetheless pressed on to land their 1,000 troops that night as cruisers resumed the bombardment. General Geiger's pilots had to siphon the last drop of fuel from damaged aircraft to keep the remaining ones flying. Defying air raids, C-47s flew in from Espiritu Santo with more drums of the vital fuel, which was put to effective use on October 15 in wrecking three enemy transports from which General Maruyama's 2nd Division was defiantly disembarking by daylight.

General Hyakutake had marshaled over 20,000 troops and 100 artillery pieces, as well as a company of light tanks, ready for the final assault. It was due to begin in a week when his forces were in place around the American positions. General Vandegrift was now alarmed that sustained heavy bombardment would shatter his defense. After two more nights of destruction, he sent off an urgent signal on October 15 addressed to Admiral Turner, Admiral Ghormley, and Admiral Nimitz: "Situation demands two urgent and immediate steps. Take and maintain control of sea area adjacent to Cactus to prevent further enemy bombardments such as this force has taken for the last three nights. Reinforcement of ground forces by at least one division in order that extensive operations may be taken to destroy hostile force now on Cactus."

"It now appears that we are unable to control the sea in the Guadalcanal area," was the sober assessment of Nimitz and his staff at Pearl Harbor. "Thus our supply of the positions will only be done at great expense to us. The situation is not hopeless but it is certainly critical."

Yamamoto had concentrated the four battleships, five carriers, ten cruisers, and twenty-nine destroyers of his Second and Third fleets under overall command of Admiral Kondo to blockade the approaches to the Solomons. On the morning of October 15, his carrier aircraft had jumped a supply convoy 75 miles from Guadalcanal, turning back the transports and sinking a destroyer and a tug. Each C-47 transport could only fly in enough fuel to keep twelve Wildcats aloft for less than an hour; as a desperate measure, 9,000 gallons of gasoline and 10 tons of badly needed bombs were brought in by submarine. The next morning, October 16, a lone seaplane tender arrived to discharge her cargo of precious aviation spirit before being bombed onto the beach at Tulagi. The American carriers approached to within 60 miles to fly in fighter reinforcements for the Cactus Air Force without being discovered by Admiral Nagumo's strike force. On the night of October 16/17 two U.S. Navy destroyers slipped into the Sound for a quick counter-bombardment of the Japanese positions building up west of the airfield, successfully evading Admiral Mikawa's cruisers, which were carrying out another night's shelling of Henderson Field.

A FIGHTING CHANCE

"Everybody hopes that we can hold on," Secretary of the Navy Knox told reporters with cautious optimism as the struggle for Guadalcanal raged on to a climax. The battle of material attrition in the Solomons was, as Admiral King anticipated, drawing in the Japanese ships, men, and aircraft at a rate they could not afford to continue for much longer. It was precisely the kind of campaign Imperial General Staff had planned to avoid because it reduced their ability to fortify their Pacific defensive perimeter. To meet the approaching crisis, Marshall and Arnold agreed with King's proposal that Nimitz should be given the authority to reinforce the Solomons with aircraft drawn from other Pacific bases without prior reference from the Joint Chiefs of Staff. Bombers were ordered west from Hawaii where the Army's 25th Regiment was put on standby for transportation to Guadalcanal.

It was evident to CINCPAC headquarters at Pearl Harbor that Admiral Ghormley was faltering under the pressure of the exhausting campaign and that a fresh man was needed to take over. Nimitz's staff believed the pugnacious Halsey was the best choice, and after reflecting they agreed that the changeover should be made without delay.

Admiral Halsey, now recovered from his illness, was on his way across the Pacific to a liaison with General MacArthur. "You will take command of the South Pacific area and South Pacific forces immediately," was the message awaiting him on October 18 when his Coronado flying boat docked at Noumea. "Jesus Christ and General Jackson! This is the hottest potato they ever handed me," was his first reaction. "This is a tough job they've given you," was Ghormley's sympathetic reaction to the man who was to replace him in the most demanding assignment in the whole Allied command. Halsey knew that he lacked ships, men, and supplies. "Europe was Washington's darling, the South Pacific was only a stepchild," he was later to write of the way his repeated requests for reinforcements were turned down.

The news that America's grizzled fighting admiral was taking charge of their battle brought a wave of elation to the Marine defenders of Guadalcanal—"One minute we were too limp with malaria to crawl from our foxholes, the next we were whooping it up like kids." General Vandegrift was now more optimistic when he flew two days later to Noumea for a crisis staff conference. "I can hold," he promised, "but I've got to have more active support than I've been getting." Supplies would have to be fought through, but Admiral Halsey faced a major problem of strength now that his naval strength had been reduced to Scott's cruisers, the battleship *Washington*'s task group, and the *Hornet* task force. The situation, he felt, was "almost hopeless," until on October 23 the *Enterprise* task force, with the new battleship *South Dakota*, steamed into Noumea. "Now we had a fighting chance!"

October 1942 was a pivotal point in the war as Allied fortunes hung in the balance not only in the Pacific but in North Africa and Russia. The crisis aroused fresh controversy over strategy at the meetings of the Joint Chiefs in Washington. Stalin was pressing for more fighters and ammunition to bolster the Red Army's attempt to hold the shattered rubble of Stalingrad, but the British were committed to the forthcoming offensive in Egypt and only ten freighters were available to sail individually, to try to break through the German blockade of Murmansk. The Americans could spare no ships because the Torch invasion's commander, General Eisenhower, had been given another division and at his request the landing had been postponed a week, to November 8.

From Brisbane, General MacArthur was again warning of the dangers to Australia if New Guinea and Guadalcanal were captured. He demanded that the "entire resources of the United States be diverted temporarily to meet the critical situation." General Arnold, who had just returned from the fact-finding tour of the South Pacific commands, reported that in his opinion MacArthur was "battle weary" and should be relieved. It led to the half-serious suggestion in the War Department that the four-star general could do more good in Moscow as a substitute for Lend-Lease because he had made no secret of his conviction that the war could only be won by concentrating an all-out effort in Europe through Russia.

Reacting to the mounting "anxiety about the southwest Pacific," the President directed the Joint Chiefs on October 24 to "make sure that every possible weapon gets through to that area to hold Guadalcanal." Fighters were being rushed out from Hawaii and MacArthur was ordered by General Marshall to get every bomber that had the range into the skies over the Solomons to bomb Japanese positions—even at the expense of New Guinea.

THE ASSAULT ON HENDERSON FIELD

The besieged Marines on Guadalcanal were already battling back attempts by the Japanese to push across the Matanikau River 4 miles to the west of the airfield perimeter with the support of light tanks. Those probing thrusts, as General Tadashi Sumiyoshi positioned his 3,000-strong force and artillery, were an important element in the plan prepared by Colonel Tsuji to draw off American strength from the southern perimeter below Bloody Ridge, where General Hyakutake was to make the main attack. The latter had already prepared the details of the surrender ceremony, which had been set for October 22, but his schedule was falling behind because the jungle was defeating the best efforts of General Maruyama's

5,000 soldiers to get themselves and their heavy guns into position. "X Night," as it had been designated, was postponed until October 23, and Colonel Tsuji hurried forward to hustle the front-line commanders. He found it necessary to call for another twenty-four-hour postponement.

This brought an impatient signal from Admiral Yamamoto at Truk. His two blockading fleets off the Solomons were running low on fuel. He warned that a further delay would prevent them from arriving as planned on the morning after the airfield had been put out of action, to "apprehend [sic] and annihilate" the American positions with a massive bombardment.

By an oversight, the Rabaul command failed to pass on this second postponement to General Sumiyoshi's headquarters. His tanks went ahead with their planned attack a day early, pushing across the Matanikau sandspits supported by yelling infantry on the night of October 23. The Marines had been anticipating such a thrust and had brought up 37mm antitank guns, which quickly smashed through the light armor of eight of the tanks. The last one was sent spinning into the surf when a well-placed grenade knocked it off its track. General Sumiyoshi was sick with a bout of malaria, but his officers pressed the frontal assault, which turned into a series of suicidal charges mowed down by the American mortar and machine-gun fire.

General Hyakutake's elaborate battle plan was now totally blunted. It had already been weakened because Maruyama's force was reaching the point of physical exhaustion, hacking a path through the rain-sodden jungle to line up its artillery on nonexistent American positions (Tsuji's tactical preparations had been made on the basis of a captured map that was long out of date).

Awaiting accurate information as to where the Japanese would concentrate their main attack, General Vandegrift on October 24 received news from the native scouts of "many rice fires" along the Lunga River 2 miles south of Bloody Ridge. That afternoon a Japanese officer was spotted studying the southern perimeter through field glasses. The forward defenses were alerted. Lieutenant Colonel Lewis Puller's 1st Battalion had cut fields of fire for their machine guns out across the Kunai grass clearing, where they hung the barbed-wire perimeter with shell fragments that would warn them of intruders approaching in the dark. This trick was learned by "Chesty" Puller, a barrel-chested Marine, during the "banana wars" he had fought in Nicaragua. He was leaving nothing to chance; neither was the regiment of newly arrived Americal Infantry Division, dug in to his rear and spoiling for a fight.

Large oily drops of rain were falling from a pitch-black night around 9:30 that evening when the Japanese began slithering on their bellies up the ridge. Their approach would have been invisible but for the jangling on the barbed-wire perimeter. A Marine in an outpost foxhole reported in an alarmed whisper through the field telephone: "Colonel, there are about three thousand Japs between you and me." Puller ordered his posts to hold fire. More than an hour passed as vague shadows dipped and bobbed forward through the Kunai grass. Then cries in high-pitched English rent the darkness: "Blood for the Emperor! Marine you die!" A gutsy voice yelled back: "To hell with your goddamned Emperor! Blood for Franklin and Eleanor!" followed by a choice barrage of Marine obscenity. "Commence firing," Puller bellowed. The sticky night was rent by flashes and streams of bullets.

The first Japanese wave was caught off-balance by the ferocity of the fire, which was intensified because the Americal regiment in the rear was equipped with new semi-automatic rifles. Sheets of rain added to the confusion as the enemy came forward, slipping in the mud and sliding into the pits torn up by the cascading mortar fire. Small units of frantically screaming Japanese hurled grenades, advancing into the American lines in successive waves. Most were cut down by machine-gun fire; those who managed to penetrate the front line were dealt with in bitter hand-to-hand fighting as the Army platoons came forward to assist the Marines. One machine-gunner fired 26,000 rounds before daybreak, when General Maruyama was forced to call off the attack. He left more than 1,000 dead on the no-man's-land in front of Puller's firmly held front line.

The first assaults had failed for the same reasons that had defeated Ichiki and Kawaguchi's earlier attacks: the Japanese had not yet appreciated that the "bamboo spear" tactics of the Banzai charges were no match for the concentrated fire of American machine guns and mortars. In the uproar of that night's battle, a lookout had mistaken one of the green flares for the prearranged signal that the advance parties had broken through to the airfield. Maruyama had at once ordered the good news passed to Hyakutake's field command post, who in turned flashed out the "BANZAI" signal to inform Rabaul that the assault on the airfield had succeeded.

Admiral Mikawa's cruiser force was well down The Slot, ready for the radio order that now sent them racing into Ironbottom Sound to seize control of the waters as part of the plan. In what was later admitted to be a "pitiful example of a lack of cooperation between the Army and Navy," he was not recalled after the Rabaul army headquarters learned a few hours later that the victory signal was premature. So when the Japanese naval squadron steamed into Ironbottom Sound at first light to attack a convoy of fuel barges, it was the torrential downpour and not Maruyama's occupation of Henderson Field that prevented the Marines' bombers from taking off. Three Wildcat fighters did get aloft, to strafe the enemy destroyers; but it was not until noon, when the warships were engaging the battery at Lunga Point in a fierce artillery duel, that the airstrip had dried out enough to permit the main body of the Cactus Air Force to join the battle. Maruyama was forced to retreat, pursued by dive bombers that badly damaged the cruiser *Yura*, which was beached and later sunk that afternoon by B-17 bombers from Espiritu Santo.

The raiders from Rabaul also made the mistake of assuming that American air strength had been knocked out, enabling General Geiger's fighters to score a record bag of twenty-two kills. Five more were downed by antiaircraft fire, but only three Cactus Air Force Wildcats were lost. However, October 25 was not a total American victory. The liner *President Coolidge* steamed into a minefield on her way into Espirito Santo Harbor. Although all but two of the Army infantry division destined to reinforce Guadalcanal were picked up, they lost all their stores and equipment.

On Guadalcanal, the American troops spent the long hours of what they called "Dugout Sunday" reinforcing their front and eating lustily, to keep up their strength for the second assault they knew would be made that night. Mortar shells from the "Pistol Petes" thudded into the airfield with depressing ten-minute regularity, sending the Seabee squads out with bulldozers so that the fighters could be kept flying to disrupt the air raids. "Chesty" Puller was finally persuaded to yield to the attentions of a medical corpsman, to treat his shrapnel wounds. "Take that damned label and paste it back on a bottle," he angrily bellowed when the tag was being written out for his evacuation to the field hospital. "I remain in command here!"

Bandaged up, Colonel Puller was in the front line again that night when the Japanese began repeating their suicidal frontal charges against his newly strengthened machine-gun positions behind the wire of Bloody Ridge. When Puller later interrogated a captive to find out why they had mindlessly repeated their attacks instead of probing for a weaker sector of the line, the enemy soldier protested that the assault had been so meticulously planned that there could be no question of deviating from the strict orders of General Hyakutake.

This typical Japanese inflexibility was to cost them the action, which by midnight had degenerated into a "blitz that became a hand-to-hand battle" for many forward American units. Sergeant Mitchell Page led a countercharge, picking up his heavy machine gun like an automatic, with ammunition belt tossed over his shoulder. "A colonel dropped dead about four feet in front of me with his yellow belly full of good American lead. In the meantime the skirmish line came over the nose, whooping like a bunch of wild Indians. We reached the edge of the clearing where the jungle began and there was nothing left to holler or to shoot at."

Littering the torn-up ground in front of Puller's lines were another 1,000 Japanese dead. The only attack that got anywhere near the airfield was on the western perimeter along the Matanikau River, where an enemy detachment under Colonel Oka had circled around to launch an assault from the lower slopes of Mount Austen. It had some success. The

Japanese took front-line Marine foxholes and machine-gun posts in the early hours of October 26, before they were dislodged by a scratch force of the 2nd Marine Battalion, made up of signalmen, messmen, and one cook!

Well before first light that morning, General Maruyama was forced to concede defeat. After two nights of some of the fiercest fighting the Pacific War would ever see, the Sendai Division was spent. A third of its strength had been cut to ribbons and half of its officers lost. The Stars and Stripes was again hauled defiantly over Henderson Field, while the exhausted Japanese began their five-day trek back through the hostile jungle, sending the casualty rate to over 50 percent in what had been an extremely costly defeat.

"They failed because I underestimated the enemy's fighting power," Colonel Tsuji brokenly admitted to General Hyakutake, before reporting to Imperial General Headquarters that he deserved "the sentence of a thousand deaths." General Kawaguchi, shattered by the two successive defeats, also blamed Tsuji but shouldered equal responsibility for the debacle, "feeling as if my intestines had been cut out." General Hyakutake, however, with over 15,000 troops still on the island, was convinced that another division must turn the balance in his favor. He signaled Rabaul to begin ferrying in by destroyer the 12,000 men of the 38th Division. The battle of attrition had to be pressed to a victory.

19

The Fork in the Road to Victory

The focus of the struggle being waged for Guadalcanal now shifted to the sea. A gigantic game of hide-and-seek was being played out between the rival fleets, which on the night of October 25 had brought them within air strike range of one another in the Pacific east of the Solomons. Admiral Kondo's Second Fleet had received a signal from Yamamoto indicating that the main offensive against the airfield would be made that evening: "Accordingly there is a great likelihood that the enemy fleet will appear in the area northwest of the Solomons and the Combined Fleet will destroy it on the 26th." From the security of the anchorage in Truk, the Commander in Chief was getting mightily impatient with an over-cautious Admiral Nagumo, who had spent the week hauling north in retreat every time his strike force was spotted by American air patrols. Yamamoto ordered that an engagement must be pressed, "regardless of weather and enemy planes." Out at sea that night the fleet was attacked by U.S. Navy flying boats carrying torpedoes. Already shaken by the "Banzai" signal confusion, Kondo and Nagumo decided to retreat again, anticipating that dawn would bring out the American bombers from Espiritu Santo.

Unknown to Admiral Kondo, less than 200 miles then separated his most southerly battleship force from powerful American units racing northward. That night *Hornet*'s aircraft ranged on the moonlit flight deck ready for an immediate takeoff. The PBY "Black Cats'" attack report had, however, not been picked up by Admiral Thomas C. Kinkaid. His Task Force 16, with *Enterprise* and the battleship *South Dakota*, had been dispatched by Halsey to reinforce Admiral George D. Murray's Task Force 17, and dawn ended a frustrating night of waiting for the carrier's aircrews, smoking and chatting nervously in the ready rooms. It also brought an impatient "ATTACK REPEAT ATTACK" signal from Halsey, who could not fathom why Kinkaid had not yet launched his air strike.

THE BATTLE OF SANTA CRUZ ISLAND

When the sun rose at 5:23 A.M. on October 26, 1942, Admiral Kinkaid and his staff aboard the *Enterprise* were still at a loss to know where the enemy force was they were supposed to attack. However, in response to the urgent signal from Halsey, they launched off sixteen Dauntlesses, armed with 500-pound bombs, to search the Pacific to the northwest. It was a prudent decision. An hour later, Kinkaid had received the message from Halsey at Espiritu Santo giving the approximate position and course of the Japanese Fleet when his dive bombers spotted Kondo's advance force of battleships. They pressed north in search of bigger prey. At 6:50 A.M. came the radio report that they had sighted three carriers.

Dodging into a convenient cloud bank to escape the swarm of Zeros that climbed up to intercept, Lieutenant Commander James R. Leed formed up his patrol and raced down on the light carrier. Two of their bombs tore a 50-foot crater in the aft end of the *Zuiho*'s flight deck. Unable to land aircraft, the Japanese captain launched his remaining planes and, his ship blazing astern, returned northward.

Aboard the flag bridge of the heavy carrier *Shokaku*, the departure of the *Zuiho* was taken stoically by Admiral Nagumo, who had been radioed by his own scouting patrols that they had finally found the American task force they had been hunting for five days. When a signal, "LARGE ENEMY UNIT SIGHTED, ONE CARRIER, FIVE OTHER VESSELS," had been received at 7:00 A.M., he at once ordered the launching of a sixty-plane strike. Half an hour later they roared south without spotting the *Hornet*'s twenty-nine-plane strike heading north to attack their carriers. The nineteen aircraft following from the *Enterprise*, however, did draw off the Zero pilots, who left their torpedo planes and dive bombers to join in an aerial scrap that held this American strike down 100 miles from its target. The *Hornet*'s second strike of twenty-three planes skirted the aerial battle to fly north unmolested.

Kinkaid's force was steaming off Santa Cruz Island when radar warnings brought the *South Dakota* closing up with two cruisers and eight destroyers, to provide a strong screen of antiaircraft fire around the *Enterprise*. Ten miles astern, Task Force 16's four cruisers and seven destroyers gathered their protective ring formation around the *Hornet*. The carrier fighter controllers were inexperienced, so when the Japanese bombers were sighted as they came streaking in low over the horizon just before 9 A.M., the thirty-eight Wildcats of the Combat Air Patrol were circling the task forces too tightly to have a chance to break up the strike before it closed. Task Force 17 sought the protection of a fortuitous rain squall, leaving the less well defended *Hornet* to become the main target for the Val dive bombers, which came hurtling down from 17,000 feet through the bursting antiaircraft shells.

The first damage was inflicted by the Japanese leader's suicide crash as he plunged his burning machine through the carrier's flight deck and the two bombs detonated, setting the hangar ablaze. Then the Kate torpedo bombers raced in at masthead height astern, scoring two hits that wrecked the carrier's engine rooms, while three more bombs crashed through the forward deck, jamming the elevator and exploding deep in her hull. The ten-minute attack left the *Hornet* ablaze and dead in the water under a rising column of smoke. Fire parties fought the flames as destroyers came alongside to try to get the cripple under tow.

At the same time, 200 miles to the north, the savaged *Hornet*'s first strike was extracting an "eye for an eye" as Lieutenant "Gus" Widhelm bored his Dauntlesses down on the *Shokaku,* and his fighter escort tangled with the covering Zeros. Nagumo was shaken by the impact of six 1,000-pound bombs ripping open the flagship's flight deck. The dive bombers had not coordinated their attack with the torpedo-carrying Avengers, which were successfully beaten off when they came in minutes later. The heavy carrier therefore escaped, unable to fly her aircraft but able to steam with her hull and machinery undamaged. The *Hornet*'s second strike missed the carriers altogether, scoring only a single hit on a cruiser. The *Enterprise*'s pilots had been so badly shaken up by their scrap that when they did eventually arrive, their attack on one battleship was ineffective.

Again Admiral Nagumo found he had to order his staff to transfer his flag to a cruiser in the midst of the battle. This time his situation was more favorable than at Midway; the heavy carrier *Zuikaku* was still fully operational and her planes, together with those of the light carrier *Junyo,* ahead with Admiral Kondo's battleship force, had already set out to strike the Americans. He knew from the reports of undisciplined radio chatter by the American pilots that he was only dealing with two carriers—and one, his own pilots reported, was now out of action. All depended on the success of the second sixty-four-plane strike that Nagumo had ordered off an hour earlier.

Admiral Kinkaid was not in a healthy situation. Having done what he could, he was awaiting the return of his own strikes while refueling his Combat Air Patrol for the next action. Shortly after 10 A.M., the *South Dakota* flashed a warning that her radar had picked up the approach of the second enemy strike, coming in from 50 miles away to the northwest.

The *Enterprise* was the main target for the Kate bombers, which alternated high- and low-level attacks without waiting for the torpedo-carrying Vals. This gave the U.S. Navy fighter controllers a chance to vector out the Wildcats, which shot down ten enemy planes. Five of those that broke through the Combat Air Patrol were smashed by the task force's newly fitted Bofors guns, the most effective antiaircraft weapons of World War II. Two bombs did hit the carrier; one plummeted through the fo'c'sle overhang into the sea, and the other exploded and jammed the forward elevator. Near misses off the starboard side had sprung hull plates, causing an oil tank leak and also jumping a turbine from its bed. The "Big E" still had enough power to avoid the torpedo attack that developed a few minutes later when a suicidal Val pilot caused the only damage by crashing his plane into an escorting destroyer.

There were less than forty minutes between the second and third Japanese strikes, during which the aircraft of both American carriers gathered to protect the *Enterprise*. Then, at one minute past eleven, the *South Dakota* warned that another attack was coming. The twenty-nine planes that had flown off the *Junyo* were mauled by the Wildcats, and the heavy barrage downed ten of the attackers. Kinkaid's flagship escaped with only another near miss, and the *South Dakota* took a hit on a forward turret, while the cruiser *San Juan* received a bomb which jammed her rudder.

Just in time, the *Enterprise* beat off the enemy planes, to turn into the wind and begin the task of recovering her circling aircraft before their tanks ran dry. With the damaged elevator, the carrier could not accommodate the crippled *Hornet*'s planes. These were refueled and sent on to Espiritu Santo. The two task forces then retired south, leaving the cruiser *Northampton* and her destroyers to try to tow the listing *Hornet*, her fires by now extinguished.

The Japanese had lost over one hundred planes, but Nagumo had no intention of letting the Americans escape. Sufficient aircraft had been recovered and refueled by the two surviving carriers to launch a fourth-wave strike shortly after 1 P.M. An hour later, those from the *Zuikaku* discovered the *Hornet* under tow. A torpedo slammed into the cripple, while her gunners beat off the dive bombers. With the engine room rapidly flooding, there was a scramble topsides as her list increased. The second abandon ship order was passed to the party of volunteers who had come aboard to fight the fires. Destroyers were picking up the survivors when the ten Kates sent out from the *Junyo* to find the second American carrier mistakenly spent their bombs on the badly listing cripple, leaving her ablaze once again. The departing American destroyers fired torpedoes into the wreck, but the coup de grâce was left to Admiral Kondo's advance forces. They came upon the *Hornet*, still burning furiously, at 11 P.M. as they charged south intending to smash the American task force with their four battleships.

The spectacle of the fiery warship sinking beneath the Pacific would have been relished even more by the Japanese had they known that the carrier was the very one that had launched the bombers which violated the sacred airspace over the Imperial Palace in April. Although he had not achieved the decisive annihilation that Yamamoto called for, Admiral Kondo had won a tactical victory and partial revenge for Midway. At the time, his triumph seemed much greater because Nagumo's pilots had inflated their success into the sinking of four American carriers and three battleships—reports the navy staff in Tokyo were only too delighted to take at face value. An Imperial Rescript was posted and a cheering victory parade marched through Tokyo to the Palace gates.

HANGING ON

The Battle of Santa Cruz had in fact been a tactical defeat for the United States. It had cost the Americans one precious carrier for the two that were now on their way back to repair in Japan, although the Japanese had lost a hundred planes to the U.S. Navy's seventy-four. The action left Admiral Halsey in the unenviable predicament of having only a damaged carrier and a battleship to keep open the sea supply line to the besieged Marines.

"The General Situation at Guadalcanal is not unfavorable," the CINCPAC war diary concluded after the battle, which Nimitz and his staff regarded as a standoff. The strategic position as seen from Pearl Harbor was brighter than it appeared to Halsey, because the Combined Fleet could not afford to go on losing skilled aircrew. Action reports were already revealing that there was a noticeable falling off in the tenacity with which the enemy planes were pressing their attacks. The Battle of Santa Cruz had also shown that the Bofors gun was an effective weapon against aircraft, as well as demonstrating the need for improved tactical control by the fighter directors aboard the carriers. The Pacific Fleet could only grow stronger, while the Combined Fleet was getting progressively weaker.

The Japanese land, sea, and air forces were plainly losing the battle of attrition against Guadalcanal. Most significant of all was the temporary retreat of the Combined Fleet to Truk for replenishment, which gave Halsey the opportunity he badly needed to rush in reinforcements to the Marines. The Cactus Air Force had been reduced by enemy raids to its lowest point of twenty-nine operational planes on the morning after the Santa Cruz action. But while Halsey's air commander, Captain Marc A. Mitscher, still controlled the skies east of the Solomons, more dive bombers and fighters could be ferried in. Additional bombers were diverted from Australia and long-range patrols by torpedo-carrying PBY flying boats stepped up to give warning of any new approach by the enemy. Every transport that could be mobilized was dispatched with gasoline, ammunition, and food supplies. On October 30, the first of these arrived to land the M-2 "Long Tom" 155mm howitzers that General Vandegrift so desperately needed to outrange and outshoot the Japanese "Pistol Petes."

The destroyers of the Tokyo Express were also rushing Japan's reinforcements every night. The Marines, with the aid of heavy artillery and assisted by destroyer bombardment, now were able to push their perimeter west across the Matanikau River as well as east to eliminate a new Japanese beachhead at Koli. The accelerating pace of the build-up by both sides inevitably brought more clashes. On November 7, the Cactus Air Force demonstrated its still powerful punch by shooting up an eleven-strong Express in The Slot before it was attacked that night again by the PT boats from Tulagi. It was trying to land the first wave of the 38th Division at Tassafaronga. Next morning Halsey himself flew in to Henderson Field to promise reinforcements and deliver his headline-catching formula for winning the battle and the war: "Kill Japs, kill Japs and keep on killing Japs!"

This injunction was taken to heart that night by the PT boats putting out from Tulagi to battle against another incoming Tokyo Express. On the other side of the world, General Eisenhower's troops were wading ashore on the coast of North Africa. During the four days that the first American beachhead across the Atlantic was being established on the shores of Casablanca, two convoys carrying a total of 6,000 men were rushed in to reinforce Guadalcanal because HYPO cryptanalysts at Pacific Fleet Intelligence had uncovered another massive Japanese effort to take the island, to be launched on November 13. The main strength of the Imperial Army's 38th Division was intending to come ashore covered by air and sea bombardment, supported by the big guns and planes of the Combined Fleet.

To meet this challenge posed by "two carriers, four battleships, five heavy cruisers and about thirty destroyers," Halsey had available only Admiral Scott's force of a cruiser and four destroyers escorting the three transports due to arrive off Lunga Point on November 11. Admiral Kelly Turner's cruiser and three destroyers covering his four transports had rendezvoused that same day with Rear Admiral Daniel J. Callaghan's support group of three cruisers and five destroyers, which was to reach the beachhead the next morning. The only heavy force that could be mustered was too far away to be of immediate assistance. The damaged *South Dakota* and the battleship *Washington* of Rear Admiral Willis Lee's Task Force 64, with four destroyers, were at Noumea while repairs were rushed to patch up the *Enterprise*. The carrier put to sea with Task Force 16's three cruisers and six destroyers on November 11, while welders were still working on the damaged bows of Kinkaid's flagship.

Her forward elevator was left just as the bombs had jammed it at deck level. "We didn't dare test it. If we had and lowered it and been unable to raise it again, she would have been useless."

The battleships and carrier were some 700 miles southeast of Guadalcanal that morning, off New Caledonia, when Scott's convoy anchored off Lunga Point to begin unloading. Operations were hampered by raids from the Japanese carriers already back within striking distance off the Solomons. They were joined by the bombers from Rabaul. Little damage resulted, although the disembarcation of troops was halted. That evening, Scott's cruisers joined up with Callaghan's to sweep up Indispensable Strait with orders to intercept the Tokyo Express. But it was not being run that night, and daylight forced the cruisers back to guard the arrival of Turner's convoy. As the soldiers worked feverishly to get ashore with their supplies, word was received from Coastwatchers at Buin on Bougainville Island, that another massive Japanese air raid was flying down The Slot. Shortly after one o'clock that afternoon, offloading was halted to get the transports under way. The massed torpedo bomber attack was beaten off by the warships' heavy antiaircraft fire and the Marine Wilcats that raced off from Henderson Field. Only superficial damage was inflicted on a destroyer and the *San Francisco*.

Late afternoon saw all but the last 10 percent of supplies landed before Admiral Turner up-anchored again. The convoy was shepherded south before Callaghan's force left to steam back into Ironbottom Sound and face the Japanese warships which scouting B-17s had reported were heading for Guadalcanal. It was the most powerful assault yet. Admiral Kondo had dispatched two battleships under Vice Admiral Hiroaki Abe to wipe out the American airstrip that night. He intended to clear the way for an unmolested landing next morning of the new division of troops, whose eleven fast transports had sailed that evening from Shortlands escorted by Admiral Tanaka's twelve destroyers.

Prowling PBY Black Cats kept track of the biggest Tokyo Express ever to come thundering down The Slot. Admiral Callaghan knew he would be outnumbered, but he was never to know just how great were the overwhelming odds faced by his five cruisers and eight destroyers as he steamed out to patrol the waters off Savo Island to meet the enemy.

THE NAVAL BATTLE OF GUADALCANAL—CRUISER ACTION

The night, November 12, 1942, was sweltering hot. A starlit sky without a moon was no ally to Callaghan because he had failed to order his force of four destroyers far enough ahead of Admiral Scott, who led the column in the light cruiser *Atlanta*. Callaghan's flagship, *San Francisco*, followed with her sister, the heavy cruiser *Portland;* the two light cruisers *Helena* and *Juneau* with four destroyers brought up the rear of the American battle line. "Uncle Dan"—as Callaghan was popularly known from his benign clerical appearance and black eyebrows offset by white hair—was a man of deep religious conviction. He would now have to trust his god of battles because there was no time to draw up a tactical plan.

Not until 1:30 A.M. did the *Helena*'s powerful new radar set pick up a contact 18 miles to the northwest of Savo. Then a series of conflicting reports and confused maneuvers cost Callaghan the advantage as he wasted valuable minutes trying to determine which heading his column should take to cross the enemy's T. Admiral Abe, whose battleships were advancing protected by a protective V of nine destroyers spearheaded by a light cruiser, was also thrown into confusion by an "Enemy Sighted" report. This had been made when a matter of minutes later his two scouting destroyers found that they were heading into the American line as it swung round to the north. The Japanese had delayed their approach, waiting for a thick rain squall to clear, while their gunners loaded up with high-explosive shells in preparation for the bombardment of the airfield.

Urgent orders now ran out on the battleships to switch to armor-piercing projectiles. The operation would take nearly a quarter of an hour as hoists and turrets were unloaded and reloaded. These minutes Callaghan might have used to win a tactical advantage for his weaker force, but he gave no order to open fire until 1:51 P.M., when the decision was made for him after a searchlight on the *Hiei* came stabbing through the dark onto the *Atlanta*.

"COMMENCE FIRING! COUNTER ILLUMINATE!" Scott's flagship ordered. The 5-inch guns blasted out the offending light—but not fast enough. Two miles across the black water, the first salvo from the enemy battleship came crashing into the light cruiser. The *Atlanta*'s bridge was wiped out, killing all but one officer. Scott met his death just as the orders came from the *San Francisco* astern, "Odd ships commence firing to starboard, even ships to port." The American column was now plowing into the enemy advance, taking them between the battleships on one flank and the cruiser and destroyers on the other.

The dark waters erupted in a series of brilliant yellow and vermilion flashes as the engagement broke up into individual battles between ships at point-blank range. The churning tracks of torpedoes sliced across in a furious mêlée that was fought out between the racing packs of destroyers as the American column convulsed, then broke. The burning *Atlanta* was stopped dead by two torpedoes. The *Cushing* rushed in to save her, hurling her torpedoes at the *Hiei*. Caught in the battleship's searchlight, the destroyer was pounded into a fiery wreck as her partner, the *Laffey*, whose own gallant attack also failed to connect, was blasted to pieces by two 14-inch salvos.

The puny shells of the American destroyers and cruisers bounced off the thick armor of the Japanese battlewagons, which were nonetheless being stung. The fires started in their upperworks by hits made at point-blank range forced Admiral Abe to retreat because the sheer ferocity of the attack made him uncertain about the size of the force confronting him.

The blind confusion of the opening minutes of the action forced Callaghan to call for a temporary cease-fire so that his cruisers could sort out their targets. "We want the big ones," he bellowed. "Get the big ones first!" It was to be his last command. The Japanese also used the break to recover, and they were now hauling around into the battle again. Searchlights snared the *San Francisco*. A full broadside from the *Kirishima* came crashing through the cruiser's superstructure, destroying the bridge with all hands. Following astern, the *Portland* took a torpedo that ripped open her stern plates and turned them into an impromptu rudder that made her circle wildly, while her gunners continued to blast the *Hiei* with 8-inch shells. The *Juneau* was put out of action when a torpedo exploded in her engine room. Another torpedo sliced the destroyer *Barton* into two sinking halves. Her partner *Monssen* rashly switched on a searchlight and was promptly pounded into a burning wreck.

Just twenty-four minutes after the action began, the rumble of gunfire died away over Ironbottom Sound. Admiral Abe had decided to retire. Although he had lost only two destroyers, his flagship's upperworks were blazing from hits by the American cruisers and his steering gear was failing. Caution overcame the purpose of his mission because he worried that the approach of daylight would bring heavy American air strikes.

An uncanny stillness closed over the Sound, which was fitfully illuminated with the flickering pyres of American warships as the gray light revealed waters blackened with oil, floating with bodies and debris of battle. The *Atlanta* had sunk after her crew had managed to run her aground. Least damaged, the *Helena* was leading the crippled *San Francisco* and battered *Juneau*, escorted by three surviving destroyers, southward into Indispensable Strait on course for the sanctuary of Espiritu Santo. The *Juneau* had just cleared the channel at 11 A.M. when she was hit by a torpedo fired by Japanese submarine I-26. She was blown skyward "with all the fury of an erupting volcano." The survivors sped on south without attempting a rescue for fear of more attacks, and all but a few of her seven hundred hands went down with the light cruiser or succumbed to the sharks. (Mr. and Mrs. Thomas Sullivan of Waterloo, Iowa, lost five sons. As a result, the Navy issued regulations forbidding relatives from serving on the same ship.)

Nearly 1,000 U.S. Navy personnel, including the two admirals, had given their lives in what Admiral King was to describe as "one of the most furious sea battles ever fought." The first Battle of Guadalcanal on the night of November 12, 1942, was a tactical defeat for the Pacific Fleet. But the Japanese battleships had been driven off before they could carry out their bombardment. The outcome would lead to a strategic victory for the United States in the hard-fought struggle for Guadalcanal.

Admiral Abe's failure to put Henderson Field out of operation was to rob him of any claim to the victor's laurels the next morning. Rudderless, and crippled by worsening machinery breakdowns, the *Hiei* was caught at first light limping north of Savo by the torpedo planes and dive bombers of the Cactus Air Force. Combined Fleet Headquarters ordered that the *Kirishima* take her still-smoking sister battleship in tow, but Abe had sent her to escape as a light cruiser stood by trying to fend off the air attacks. By mid-morning the dive bombers from the *Enterprise* had arrived, and their bombs were blasting into the battleship when B-17s from Espiritu Santo flew in to join the attack. At 4 P.M. Abe finally abandoned the *Hiei* after the Emperor's picture was safely aboard the *Yūkaze*. He ordered his burning flagship scuttled—an action for which an infuriated Yamamoto deemed him unworthy of any further command.

The *Kirishima* evaded the air attacks to rejoin Admiral Kondo's two fleets cruising off the eastern Solomons. The collapse of Abe's mission forced the Rabaul command to recall Admiral Tanaka's troop convoy to Shortlands for a twenty-four-hour postponement. Admiral Mikawa's heavy cruisers were sent down The Slot to carry out the bombardment where the battleships had failed. Except for the small force at Tulagi, no American warships were at hand to block them, and not even frantic attacks by the Tulagi PT boats stopped the three heavy cruisers from firing 1,000 rounds onto Henderson Field. Had these been 14-inch shells, instead of 8-inch, the devastation would have been total, since that night's bombardment wrecked eighteen of General Geiger's planes and gave the Seabees a tough task filling in all the runway craters. Nonetheless, their backbreaking efforts by sun-up on November 14 enabled the Marine pilots to fly off in their Avengers.

COUNTERPUNCHES

An intensive search of The Slot commenced at first light for the invasion convoy that the Americans knew from the Coastwatchers and radio intelligence was already heading down for Guadalcanal. It was mid-morning on November 14 before Tanaka's destroyer-escorted transports were sighted, 150 miles northwest of their destination.

Admiral Mikawa's cruisers were 10 miles ahead, steaming south again after retiring from their night's bombardment, when at 10 A.M. they became targets for the Marine dive bombers and torpedo planes. The strike from *Enterprise* arrived to sink the *Kinugasa* and set the *Isuzu* ablaze swiftly. The *Maya* was damaged, as well as Mikawa's flagship *Chokai;* before noon, he ordered a retreat.

The American aircraft now concentrated their attack against the invasion convoy as Tanaka's destroyers zigzagged trying to fend off the successive waves with antiaircraft fire. That morning and afternoon became a nightmare for the Japanese on the transports. Flying Fortresses alternated high-level bombing with successive strikes from the *Enterprise*. Admiral Tanaka was to describe how "the general effect is indelible in my mind, of bombs wobbling down from high flying B-17s, of carrier bombers roaring towards targets as though to plunge full into the water, releasing bombs and pulling out barely in time; each miss sending up towering columns of mist and spray; every hit raising clouds of smoke and fire as transports burst into flame and take the sickening list that spells their doom. Attackers depart, smoke screens lift and reveal the tragic scene of men jumping overboard from burning, sinking ships. Ships regrouped each time the enemy withdrew, but precious time was wasted and the advance delayed."

Tanaka's hellish day continued right through to dusk when, half an hour before sunset, another twenty-one-plane strike set one of his remaining five transports ablaze. Rescue work was interrupted by the arrival of the last three-bomber attack as the sun was sinking. Darkness found the Japanese still doggedly pressing on toward Guadalcanal with their invasion force now cut down to four transports and three destroyers.

Tanaka himself concluded that "prospects looked poor for the operation," but Admiral Yamamoto signaled orders that the landing must go in that night. He directed Admiral Kondo to go in to put the airfield out of action with a bombardment by his remaining battleship and five cruisers.

BATTLESHIP ACTION

The last round in the three-day naval battle began with fears rising in Washington that the Marines might, after all, be forced to evacuate Guadalcanal. Halsey's entire hopes of stopping the Japanese rested on two battleships of Task Force 64, which he ordered to block the enemy advance.

Admiral Willis Lee, whose sobriquet was "Ching," was "one of the best brains in the Navy," and an expert on radar, well qualified to tackle what he appreciated would be a difficult night action in the confined waters off Savo Island. He had made a careful tactical plan, which called for fighting in the more open waters off Cape Esperance. That evening, as his two great battleships steamed north across Ironbottom Sound, their magnetic compasses spun as they passed over the sunken warships. The offshore breeze, usually heavy with the stench of decay, was strangely redolent with the sweet scent of honeysuckle. It was taken as a good omen by the crews of the topsides, as the moon dipped below the craggy outline of Cape Esperance in the last hour of October 14. The two battleships, preceded by their four scouting destroyers, patrolled on a southeasterly course past Savo Island after they had signaled to the Tulagi PT boat patrol: "STAND ASIDE, I'M COMING THROUGH. THIS IS CHING LEE." Kondo's battleships had been spotted by a submarine and PBY patrols making for Guadalcanal. They were some 150 miles away to the north at 4 P.M., so Lee was anticipating their appearance around 11 P.M. Sure enough, the *Washington*'s radar plot picked up four groups of warships as the predicted hour of battle approached. The nearest was 9 miles off.

This was the light cruiser *Sendai*, scouting ahead of the battleship force Kondo was intending to sweep into the Sound on either side of the dark sentinel of Savo. Lee hauled around onto a westerly course to put a T across the Japanese advance, allowing the range to close before opening fire at 11:17 P.M. The lookouts in the Japanese van had mistaken the lean battleships' silhouettes for two cruisers until the mountainous waterspouts thrown up by the salvos of 16-inch shells sent the hapless *Sendai* racing around in retreat under cover of heavy smoke.

A fierce scrap then broke out, with the enemy destroyers sweeping around the other side of Savo. Against the theatrical glare of bursting starshells, the two destroyer advance forces battled it out, with the Japanese quickly proving superior in shellfire and torpedoes. Two of Lee's leading destroyers were sent rapidly to the bottom and the bows were lopped off a third; but only one of Kondo's destroyers was left sinking.

Swerving to avoid the wreckage as they tossed out life rafts to the survivors, Lee's battleships (reduced to a single escort) now raced into the channel between Savo and Cape Esperance. At this critical juncture of the battle an electrical fault tripped the *South Dakota*'s generators and her powerless turrets fell silent. The *Washington* swept on, piling salvo after salvo into a light cruiser, but losing contact with the *South Dakota*, whose engineers fought to restore the vital electricity.

The American battleships now emerged from behind the shelter of Savo to run full-tilt for the 14-inch guns of the *Kirishima* and her two heavy cruisers and destroyers. When the *South Dakota*'s turrets reopened fire, she was illuminated by searchlights to draw the fire of Kondo's main force and her masts were swept away as heavy shells battered her upperworks, setting many fires burning.

The *Washington* had moved on ahead undetected, but Lee's well-drilled radar operators found the enemy range, saving the *South Dakota* when nine well-placed 16-inch salvos at 5-mile range sent the *Kirishima* staggering out of line, her pagoda-like superstructure in shambles and her rudders jammed. Circling helplessly, her captain struggled to steer with the main engines as her steam pressure began falling.

Admiral Kondo's flagship, the heavy cruiser *Atago*, was already flashing out the signal for a withdrawal as she hauled off to the north. Lee pressed on in pursuit for 7 miles while the Japanese steamed for the Santa Isabel Channel, until renewed torpedo attacks launched by the enemy destroyers against his unescorted battleship sent him back to rejoin the *South Dakota* whose crew was extinguishing the last of her superstructure

Four destroyers were still hovering around the blazing wreck of the *Kirishima* northwest of Savo after 3 A.M. when her captain abandoned the battleship, ordering her sunk by torpedoes rather than suffer the ignominious fate that had overtaken the *Hiei*. Kondo had lost his battle. But Admiral Tanaka lived up to his sobriquet as "the tenacious" by slipping his destroyers and surviving transports into the Sound while the action was at its peak. Arriving off Tassafaronga beachhead undetected just before dawn, he obtained Kondo's approval for the desperate measures he judged would now be needed to get the troops ashore under anticipated air attacks. "Run aground and unload troops," he ordered the captains of the four transports, before hauling back up the Sound at full speed to put as much distance between his destroyers and the airfield as possible.

At dawn, the Cactus Air Force Avengers took off to shuttle-bomb the beached transports with fragmentation devices the Marines dubbed "Molotov breadbaskets." The Japanese soldiers were bombed and strafed as they came swarming down the ropes into the surf. The attack set the stranded transports ablaze, destroying all the supplies and equipment of the several thousand soldiers of the 38th Division who managed to struggle ashore.

The massive Japanese effort to reinforce General Hyakutake had all but failed. Only 10 tons of supplies and 2,000 fresh troops were eventually landed, at the tremendous cost of scores of aircraft, two battleships, a heavy cruiser, three destroyers, and eleven transports sunk. Admiral Yamamoto now decided that the Combined Fleet could no longer afford such attrition to support the army campaign. The Tokyo Express continued to run, but it could only keep a trickle of reinforcements and supplies flowing in to sustain the 32,000 soldiers on what the Japanese were already referring to as the "Island of Death."

The naval battles of November 13, 14, and 15 marked the decisive turning point. "The last large-scale effort to reinforce Guadalcanal had ended," commented Admiral Tanaka, who "felt a heavy responsibility" for the failure. One Japanese officer whose papers were later captured foresaw that "the success or failure in re-capturing Guadalcanal Island, and the vital naval battle related to it, is the fork in the road which leads to victory for them or for us."

Admiral Halsey agreed. "Unobstructed the enemy would have driven south, or cut our supply lines to New Zealand or Australia and enveloped them," he wrote of the decisive naval actions that ended in Admiral Kondo's retreat in the small hours of November 15, 1942. "Until then he had been advancing at his will. From then on he retreated at ours." The news that Guadalcanal had been saved was greeted with wild celebration in the United States, and nowhere more enthusiastically than in New Jersey, Halsey's native state, where the church bells pealed on November 20, the day named in his honor. Admiral King recommended that the President award the South Pacific Commander a fourth

men under his command. The greatest compliment in his eyes came from General Vandegrift, who congratulated the Navy in a signal that said it all: "THE MEN OF CACTUS LIFT THEIR BATTERED HELMETS IN DEEPEST ADMIRATION."

20

"The End of the Beginning"

The successes in the three-day naval battles off Guadalcanal crowned a glorious fortnight of Allied victories that would make the first two weeks of November 1942 the turning point of World War II. The advantage began moving from the Axis to the Allies on November 3, when General Montgomery's ten-day tank and artillery offensive at El Alamein finally broke through Rommel's front line, rolling the Afrika Corps into a headlong retreat that saved the Middle East. Five days later, the Torch landings had brought American soldiers into the European war in Morocco, opening the way to the ultimate defeat of the Axis in North Africa. On November 13, British 8th Army tanks recaptured Tobruk, and a week later the ferocious battle for Stalingrad was reaching its terrible climax as the German troops, who had fought their way through the city's ruins to within a block of the Volga River, were being forced back by a mounting Red Army offensive.

"During the past two weeks we have had a great deal of good news, and it would seem that a turning point in this war has at last been reached," President Roosevelt declared in a New York speech on November 17. "There is no time now for anything but fighting to win," he was careful to remind Americans, echoing Winston Churchill's eloquently guarded optimism in London: "Now, this is not the end, it is not even the beginning of the end. But it is, perhaps, the end of the beginning."

The beginning of the end for the Japanese in New Guinea, too, followed hard on the victories in the Solomons campaign, with the launching on November 17 of a drive by American and Australian troops along the north Papuan Coast from Milne Bay toward the enemy bases at Buna and Gona.

MacArthur had planned the offensive to reinforce the punishing advance of the Australian troops up the Kokoda Trail, which was driving the Japanese back mile by bloody mile. Since the last week of September, the indefatigable General Horii had been fighting a slow and extremely costly withdrawal. His South Seas Detachment was becoming steadily more exhausted, yet it managed a series of determined stands that were reinforced by fresh troops who had come up the trail from Buna. On October 21, they had set up a strongpoint in improvised log and earth bunkers on the heights above Eora Creek. For a week the Japanese had held out against the 16th Australian Infantry, whose dismantled artillery pieces had been dragged by mule trains and many hundred native bearers up and over the Kokoda Trail from Port Moresby.

"The Bloody Track" was the subject of more richly foul oaths than the enemy. "The Wet"—as the Australian infantry graphically called the rainy season—now settled in with a vengeance, making the steaming jungle-occupied slopes even more of a hell. It was not unusual for an inch of torrential rain to fall in five minutes, turning the winding pathway into a knee-deep morass of black mud. Soldiers' boots rotted and fell to pieces in a week. The damp made the miseries of malaria even more intolerable. Painful jungle sores erupted on exposed flesh of arms and legs; swarms of insects joined the mosquitoes which bit day and night. Food was always scarce because the supplies the 5th Air Force planes parachuted in daily—"biscuit tin drops," in the Aussie slang—landed wide of their positions and had to be retrieved from the jungle, where Japanese suicide squads and the wounded had been left behind to snipe at the enemy.

"The insect life, from scorpions to butterflies, is impressive," recorded an Australian journalist, George H. Johnson, in his graphic account of the rigors of what he called the toughest fighting in the world:

Only for a time though. You eventually reach a stage when flora and fauna, and even the Japs, gradually lose interest. Your mental processes allow you to be conscious of only one thing—"The Track," or more usually, "The Bloody Track." You listen to your legs creaking and stare at the ground and think of the next stretch of mud, and you wonder if the hills will ever end. Up one almost perpendicular mountain face more than 2,000 steps have been cut out of the mud and built up with felled saplings inside which the packed earth has long since become black glue. Each step is two feet high. You slip on one in three. There are no resting places. Climbing it is the supreme agony of mind and spirit. The troops, with fine irony, have christened it "The Golden Staircase"!

Life changes as you push up the track. Standards of living deteriorate, sometimes below normally accepted standards even of primitive existence. Thoughts become somber, humor takes on a grim, almost macabre quality. When men reach the nadir of mental and physical agony there are times when sickness or injury and even death seem like things to be welcomed. Near Efogi, on a slimy section of the track that reeks with the stench of death, the remains of an enemy soldier lie on a crude stretcher, abandoned by the Japanese retreat. The flesh has gone from his bones, and a white bony claw sticks out of a ragged uniform sleeve, stretching across the track. Every Australian who passes, plodding up the muddy rise that leads to the pass, grasps the skeleton's grisly hand, shakes it fervently and says, "Good on you, sport!" before wearily moving on.

The Japanese were blasted out of their defenses before Kokoda itself on October 28, enabling the Australians to advance and capture its airfield. Horii's exhausted troops prepared for a last stand at Oivi in the foothills above the Kumusi River.

General MacArthur, who had moved his advance headquarters to Port Moresby on November 8, was becoming impatient with the slow pace of the advance. General Blamey took the brunt of his complaints that "progress on the Trail is NOT satisfactory. The tactical handling of the troops is faulty." The Australian Army Commander responded by putting Major General G. Vasey in command of the operation; "Bloody George," as he was popularly known after his favorite expletive, flew in to get the 7th Australian Division moving more rapidly toward Buna.

Executing a flanking movement through the jungle, Vasey turned the enemy's favorite tactic against them. On November 10, he dislodged the Japanese troops from their last bitterly defended strongholds and sent them fleeing to the Kumusi River. The wooden bridge they had built in August had been destroyed by bombing, so they were forced to ferry 1,200 men across the raging currents in collapsible boats. The South Seas Detachment was reduced to a wretched band of half-starved men, many wearing blankets and discarded rice bags because their uniforms had rotted away. They were barefoot, many hobbling along on sticks; hair matted, bearded, and with the wild staring expressions of exhausted defeat. One Japanese newsman was appalled at their condition: "The soldiers had eaten anything to appease hunger—young shoots of trees, roots of grass, even cakes of earth. These things had injured their stomachs so badly that when they were brought into the field hospital they could no longer digest any food. Many of them vomited blood and died." General Horii did not live to see the full horrors of defeat. Crossing the lower Kumusi, he was drowned when the current overturned his improvised log raft.

"An ignominious death," General MacArthur commented sourly, as he issued a new plan on November 14 to speed up the Papuan operations. The 126th and 128th regiments of the U.S. Army's 32nd Infantry Division were to be airlifted over the Owen Stanleys to join the advance on Buna, while Vasey's Australians concentrated on taking Gona. More American troops were making painfully slow progress by another mountain trail 30 miles to the south of the Kokoda Trail, while 5th Air Force control of the skies allowed more troops and supplies to be shipped by barge along the treacherous coastal waters to Cape Nelson.

Intelligence estimates had some 5,000 Japanese troops garrisoning the two New Guinea ports. However, by mid-November, after their failure to retake Guadalcanal, the Imperial General Staff once again began sending in reinforcements to hold these bases. With General Hyakutake stranded on Guadalcanal, the Rabaul command was put in the hands of General Hitoshi Imamura, the conqueror of the Dutch East Indies. After an emotional audience with the Emperor in which he gave his solemn pledge to retake Guadalcanal, Imamura flew to Rabaul on November 22. He had been promised additional troops from the Japanese Army in China. Anticipating the coming American offensive, he sent 2,000 troops in a convoy of reinforcements across the Bismarck Sea to Buna just in time to dig in before the offensive that turned the tiny port into the pivotal battle in the struggle for Papua.

"BLOODY BUNA"

General Edwin F. Harding now led the regiments of the U.S. Army's 32nd Infantry Division in a multi-headed thrust through the swamp, jungle, and Kunai grass toward Buna. He was to regret openly stating his belief that the operation would be "easy pickings." The exhausting 85 percent humidity and 90-degree heat of the rainy season sapped the strength of his forces. Dysentery, deadly scrub typhus, fever, and jungle rot were bringing high casualty rates before the fighting began in earnest. The appalling conditions were taking their toll of the Australians to the north, whose progress in the final 20 miles to Gona was even slower. Harding very nearly lost his life when Japanese planes shot up the barge convoy that was ferrying him, along with his staff and more supplies, up the coast. When his advance stalled 10 miles south of Buna, he confessed he was facing "a catastrophe of the first magnitude."

Feuding again broke out with the Australians to the north over who should get the only available regiment of artillery; neither had the heavy mortars that were needed to deal with the surprisingly resistant Japanese fortifications. Improvising with tree trunks, steel, concrete, and earth, the enemy had dug a network of bunkers, machine-gun nests, and interconnecting tunnels to defend their beachheads. After two weeks of hammering, neither Vasey's nor Harding's troops had been able to advance more than a few hundred yards. For the green National Guardsmen of the 32nd Division, the stubborn resistance and bloody hand-to-hand combat eroded morale, already low from disease, the swampy terrain, and the appalling heat.

General MacArthur had no personal notion of the terrible conditions under which his troops were fighting at the front. Commuting the 1,500 miles in his personal B-17 Flying Fortress between the Brisbane Hotel and the elegant white bungalow of the former Government House in Port Moresby which he shared with General Kenney, the Supreme Commander was growing ferociously impatient. He was even oblivious to the squalor of Port Moresby, where nurses had frequently to turn aside from soldiers showering in the open or wandering about neglectfully naked. Reporters caught occasional glimpses of MacArthur through the frangipani bushes. He would be pacing the veranda "in a pink silk dressing gown with a black dragon on the back," or leafing through dispatches while he munched on one of the crisp heads of lettuce specially flown in for him by the crate.

On November 22 the general's temper was vented on Harding in a dispatch ordering him to take Buna at once "regardless of cost." Obediently, the attack was launched against the fortified enemy positions referred to as "The Triangle." When a frontal assault was driven back, Harding tried a flanking movement, which came to grief in the swamps where the GIs sank to their waists in leech-infested slime and became sitting ducks for the Japanese gunners. Still MacArthur's orders piled on the pressure. On November 30, Harding's northernmost units at last managed to penetrate the outskirts of Buna itself. "Machine gun tracers lit the entire sky and our own rifle fire made a solid sheet of flame," recalled Lieutenant Robert H. Odell, a 126th Infantry platoon leader of that nightmare assault: "Everywhere men cursed, shouted and screamed. Order followed order. Brave men led and others followed. Cowards crouched in the grass, frightened out of their skins." With superhuman courage and effort, sufficient men pressed on by sheer determination to seize the outlying enemy foxholes. The sheer impregnability of the Japanese rear bunkers defied anything but the heaviest mortar fire, stalling any further advance.

Casualty rates were now rocketing to alarming proportions. As well as the wounded and those suffering from tropical diseases, General Kenney told MacArthur, his transports were "bringing back loads of shell-shocked troops." The deteriorating fighting spirit of the American soldiers was a "bitter pill" for him to swallow, particularly after General Blamey insisted that rather than bringing in more units of the inexperienced 41st American Division (training on the mainland), Australian soldiers "who knew they would fight" should be sent to support Harding. MacArthur, furious that "he was being gloated over by the Australian High Command," summoned Lieutenant General Robert L. Eichelberger, recently promoted from the 41st Division to his I Corps Commander. He ordered Eichelberger to take over the 32nd Division and to fire any officer who did not show fighting spirit. His parting words were: "Go out there, Bob, and take Buna—or don't come back alive."

On December 1, Eichelberger flew to the 32nd Division headquarters set up at the Dunropa Plantation 2 miles south of Buna. He was to find that the reports of collapsing morale had not been exaggerated and that "a very pallid siege was being waged" to capture Buna. "In any stalemate it was obvious that the Japanese would win, for they were living among the coconut palms along the coast on sandy soil, while our men lived in swamps." When he toured the lines shortly after three in the afternoon, he was appalled to find that the men had not had anything to eat since the previous day and no hot food in ten days. Command communications were on the verge of disintegrating. "There was no front line discipline of any kind," he noted despairingly. "There was never any idea of the men going forward." When it was suggested to the soldiers that they should fire at the palm trees where enemy snipers were concealed, he was told, "Don't fire! They won't shoot at us if we don't shoot at them."

Eichelberger had no choice but to exercise the authority that Mac-Arthur had given him to relieve Harding and his staff officers. "I stopped all fighting and it took two days to effect the unscrambling of the units and an orderly chain of command." The timely arrival of a supply convoy bringing the Bren gun carriers and howitzers needed to blast apart the Japanese bunkers absorbed most of the explosive impact and the Bren gun The Urbana Force was to drive for Buna itself, while the Warren Force would break through the heavily fortified positions on the Dunropa flank in the south.

The renewed American assault began on December 5, supported by heavy raids from the 5th Air Force. But the sand mounds covering the Japanese bunkers absorbed most of the explosive impact and the Bren gun carriers bogged down in the mud. Eichelberger now realized it was going to take days of hand-to-hand fighting to force the enemy out. After a week of bloody battles, progress was measured in a few depressing yards into the outer line of defenses. Eichelberger rallied his men to spur their efforts, touring the front-line foxholes at total disregard of his own safety.

VICTORY AT GONA AND BUNA

While the Americans were battering away at Buna, 10 miles to the north the Australians were encountering the same stubborn defense from the enemy's fortified positions surrounding Gona. The combat, in stinking swamps, mainly involved bayonet charges, which were graphically reported by one Australian private: "It was the wildest, maddest, bloodiest fighting I have ever seen. Grenades were bursting among the Japs as we stabbed down at them with our bayonets from the parapets above. Some of our fellows were actually rolling on the sand with Japs locked against them in wrestling grips. It was all over within a few minutes. A few of the Japs had escaped, but the bodies of thirty were tangled among their captured guns."

After a whole week of battling against fanatical opposition—"Those bastards fight to the last. They keep fighting until your bayonet sinks into them"—the 25th Brigade of the 7th Australian Division had been cut to under a third of its original strength by heavy casualties. The 21st Brigade moved up to the front line. By December 8, General Vasey was planning to shift the stalled attack south to Sanananda between Gona and Buna. Then that morning his artillery reinforcements set to work with delayed-action fuses on the mortar shells that finally blasted apart the fortified dugouts at the Gona Mission. This was the breakthrough needed to rally the Australian soldiers in a last effort to overwhelm the defenses of the village. One by one the bunkers and foxholes were taken that night in bloody hand-to-hand combat. At first light the next day, the signal: "GONAS GONE," was radioed to MacArthur. Ten more days of hard fighting were needed to flush out the last enemy defenders. Many Japanese held on to the end, donning gasmasks to fight against the stench of the putrefying bodies that they had piled up to add to the defenses of their bunkers.

The fall of Gona was followed by MacArthur with a stream of messages to Eichelberger, goading him to capture Buna. One sent on December 13 told him to strike because "time is working desperately against us"; it actually arrived a few hours after the fall of the Japanese positions. The breakthrough had been made at last after a week of ferocious fighting, to hold a salient down the Buna beach which had been driven into the Japanese defenses by Sergeant Herman Bottscher and twelve volunteers. A native of Landesberg, near Berlin, who could barely speak English, Bottscher had fought for the Republicans in the Spanish Civil War before emigrating to enlist in the U.S. Army. Hundreds of Japanese tried through the night and the next day to dislodge the thirteen Americans as Bottscher repeatedly crawled out to destroy their machine-gun pits with grenades. The attack that led to Buna's capture was launched from his grimly defended position. It was supported by four tanks, which stormed the defenses of The Triangle on the village's other flank.

There was another month of bitter fighting before the Australians and Americans had finally cleared the area between Buna and Gona of the last Japanese positions. More than 7,000 enemy soldiers were thought to be defending nearby Sanananda, which would not be taken until mid-January. It therefore came as something of a surprise to Generals Vasey and Eichelberger when on January 8, 1943, they learned that MacArthur had issued an official communiqué announcing: "The Papuan Campaign is in its closing phase." It was nearly two weeks before the last enemy soldier had been winkled out of the bunkers at the Buna Mission, where it was horrifically obvious that some of the starving soldiers had resorted to cannabalism during their stubborn defense.

The fanatical last-ditch resistance in Papua chilled both soldiers and the generals. Kenney, in his report to General Arnold, warned: "there are hundreds of Buna's ahead of us," predicting that the awful cost in "time, effort, blood and money" to defeat the Japanese "may run to proportions beyond all conception."

ENERGY, PERSISTENCE, AND COURAGE

If the Joint Chiefs in the comfort of Washington offices needed any confirmation of the Japanese determination to hang on to their positions, then Guadalcanal was providing another lesson of just how difficult it was going to be to defeat them militarily. Although the naval battles of mid-November had ended any large-scale attempt to reinforce the troops on the island, the Tokyo army and navy staff still sought more shipping to get men and supplies in.

Appreciating that they could not risk losing any more transports to American air attacks, the naval command at Rabaul found a solution in ingenius improvisation. On the night of November 30, seven of Admiral Tanaka's destroyers were approaching the entrance to Ironbottom Sound, towing behind them drums packed with food, ammunition, and medical supplies. Just before 11:30 P.M. they collided with a strong force of five American cruisers and six destroyers off Tassafaronga Point. Cutting their tows adrift, the Japanese captains fought the Battle of Tassafaronga against overwhelming odds that proved the Imperial Navy had not yet lost its edge when it came to night actions. In twenty minutes their well-aimed guns and torpedoes had badly damaged three cruisers and left the *Northampton* sinking for the loss of only one of Tanaka's destroyers.

It was a superb display of fighting seamanship, which Admiral Nimitz acknowledged showed "energy, persistence, and courage." In the coming weeks the steadily growing force of PT boats at Tulagi sortied to meet and derail the Tokyo Expresses that continued to run the gauntlet of the American daylight raids as the destroyers sped down The Slot. The anchorage at Shortland, which was the terminal for Tanaka's operations, came under increasingly heavy attack through December, and losses in damaged ships and stores mounted. Still the Rabaul command did not give up.

On Guadalcanal, sustained by only a trickle of supplies, starvation sent the disease rates soaring among the Japanese troops. General Vandegrift was preparing to move westward toward the high ground around Mount

Austen to the southwest of Henderson Field. The Cactus Air Force had grown to almost two hundred aircraft by the first week in December, when the Marines got the good news that they were to be relieved after their ordeal of over fourteen weeks. "If the surface Navy continues to perform as they have since Admiral Halsey took over, then this place is safe for democracy," wrote General Vandegrift three days before he handed over command of forces on Guadalcanal to General Alexander M. Patch, on December 9. The 2nd Marine Division was landed with the units of the 35th Infantry Division as Vandegrift and his men were taken aboard. Paying tribute to the "unbelievable achievement of his Marines," the general did not in any way understate the truth when he told them: "It may well be that this modest operation begun four months ago today has, through your efforts, been successful in thwarting the large aims of our enemy in the Pacific."

It was a year exactly to the day since Pearl Harbor, and it was going to take another two months of bitter fighting for General Patch and his men to secure Mount Austen with mortars and bayonets, dragging the remaining Japanese physically out of their foxholes, trenches, and caves. But it was General Vandegrift's Marines and the Army "doggies" from North Dakota and Minnesota in the 126th Infantry who deserved the Guadalcanal battle honors. Tanaka's Tokyo Express continued running throughout January until the Tokyo General Staff at last accepted defeat. General Hyakutake's December 23 request to launch a final suicide assault on the American positions was refused, in spite of his repeated pleas to be allowed "honorable death rather than to die of hunger in our own dugouts."

It was the end of December before Imperial General Headquarters in Tokyo realized that they could not muster the soldiers or the naval resources to continue the war of attrition on Guadalcanal. Japan had suffered her most staggering military defeat: over 40,000 troops sent in to fight on the "Island of Death"; nearly 23,000 were never to leave it. Those who died of disease and starvation far outnumbered the actual battle casualties. The campaign had been no less of a catastrophe for the Imperial Navy and Admiral Yamamoto. The Combined Fleet had lost two battleships, three cruisers, twelve destroyers, sixteen transports, in addition to many hundreds of planes. "There is no question that Japan's doom was sealed with the closing struggle for Guadalcanal," Admiral Tanaka was to conclude. "Just as it betokened the military character and strength of her opponent, so it presaged Japan's weakness and lack of planning that would spell her military defeat."

Japan had lost far more in the great campaign of attrition than just Guadalcanal Island. As the Imperial General Staff were forced to adopt a strategy of retreat, the ability of their forces to hold their inner defensive perimeter deteriorated because so much of their strength had been spent.

"THE END OF THE BEGINNING"

The epitaph had been written in the fine brush strokes of Admiral Yama-moto himself, in characters composed during the closing hours of 1942: "How splendid the first stage of our operation was! But how unsuccess-fully we have fought since the defeat of Midway."

21
"Combined Deadlock"

"Our withdrawal from Guadalcanal is regrettable," the Emperor admonished General Sugiyama at an audience on the last day of 1942. The Army Chief of Staff had come to the Palace to obtain Hirohito's formal approval of the reluctant decision of Imperial General Headquarters to effect Japan's first military retreat. The reality was concealed from the public while the truth of Admiral Yamamoto's 1940 prediction that Japan could have its way for six months but after that would be a hostage to fortune haunted Japan's leaders. Forced onto the defensive, they were discovering that reinforcing the threatened island outposts on their perimeter was draining the reserves of manpower, aircraft, and shipping. Workers might labor night and day in Japan's aircraft-manufacturing plants and shipyards, but they were fighting a losing campaign to outproduce the huge industrial capability of the United States. There could be no way, moreover, to replace the thousands of highly trained naval aviators who had been lost in the great carrier battles at Coral Sea, Midway, and the actions of Guadalcanal. The spear of Japan's military superiority had been blunted by the end of 1942.

In contrast to the gloom of the previous December, Allied spirits had been rallied by the turning tide of war. Christmas 1942 was the brightest for the British in three years, with news that the Germans in North Africa were being squeezed between the Allied armies, and that the Russians were closing the ring on Stalingrad. "The Axis knew that they must win the war in 1942 or lose everything" Roosevelt began his State of the Union address on January 6. He announced a dramatic increase in America's war production and brought Congress to its feet with his declaration: "I suspect Hitler and Tojo will find it difficult to explain to the German and Japanese people just why it is that 'decadent and inefficient democracy' can produce such phenomenal quantities of weapons, munition and equipment—and fighting men!"

Two days later the President left Washington by train, ostensibly for a Florida vacation, but actually to board a Pan Am flying boat at Miami. He and his aide Hopkins traveled as "Mr. P. and Mr. Q." on the long haul around South America, to cross the Atlantic and fly up the African coast to Casablanca where the Combined Chiefs of Staff were already holding preliminary meetings in an attempt to resolve the differences in strategy that were once again threatening to split the Allied command.

Allied success had brought a strategic impasse over how to proceed with the war. Stalin was demanding that the Anglo-American promise must be kept to open the Second Front in Europe. The British Chiefs of Staff, facing the U-boat attacks on the Atlantic supply line, wanted to put off the invasion of France for another year and take advantage of their successes in North Africa to widen the Mediterranean offensive to Italy. To strike what he would term the "soft underbelly" of the Axis might be Churchill's preferred strategy, but he was aware that it was strongly opposed by the American military leaders. The British feared that Admiral King might swing the Joint Chiefs away from the "Europe First" commitment if he succeeded in expanding the Solomons campaign into a larger Pacific offensive.

To break the "combined deadlock," the Prime Minister had cabled the President, "the only satisfactory way of coming to the vital and strategic conclusions the military situation requires is for you and me to meet personally with Stalin." Exchanges followed between London, Washington, and Moscow, trying to reach an agreement on a suitable time and location. Roosevelt's preference was for Morocco, "a comfortable oasis to the raft at Tilsit," but unlike the Emperor Alexander in his meeting with Napoleon in 1807, Stalin would have no truck with a ceremonial summit. He wanted a Second Front, but realized that he was not likely to get it in 1943. Churchill cabled Roosevelt that "he [Stalin] thought he might just as well get that (news of no second front in 1943) by post as verbally," after the Soviet leader had excused himself because the Stalingrad front was "so hot that it is impossible for me to absent myself for even a single day."

DISAGREEMENT AT CASABLANCA

The Joint Chiefs were as firm as the Russians in their collective determination that the British must not be allowed to slip out of their undertaking to launch a cross-Channel assault. They had set out for the Symbol Conference, as it was termed, leaving a firmly worded position paper for the President to digest on his long flight. Yet when they arrived at the heavily guarded white villa at Anfa, overlooking the glistening sea and red roofs of Casablanca, they found that the British Chiefs of Staff had brought a large planning staff, piles of memoranda, and a communications ship in continuous touch with London. They had the advantage in their bid to push their strategy on the Americans, who were outnumbered because Admiral Leahy, their chairman, had fallen ill in Miami, so they arrived with a minimum of aide-memoires and only two staff planning officers.

The U.S. Joint Chiefs lacked both the unity and the committee teamwork of their allies when they sat down at a highly polished mahogany table in the Anfa Hotel conference room on January 14, 1943. "To make a fruitless assault before the time is ripe would be disastrous to ourselves, of no assistance to Russia and devastating to the whole of occupied Europe," the British commanders argued, in a position paper which set out a detailed case as to why an invasion of France was impractical during the coming year. Instead, it cogently proposed the rationale for extending the North African campaign to Sicily and then Italy, to knock Germany's principal Axis partner out of the war. Before leaving London, Churchill had carefully briefed his team on tactics and the need for patience—"the dripping of water on a stone"—to concentrate on winning over General Marshall while the Prime Minister worked on the President.

Admiral King and General Marshall were united in opposing any major expansion of the Mediterranean offensive, believing it to be tainted by imperial designs. What they failed to appreciate was that the British reluctance for a frontal assault on Hitler's Fortress Europe was in fact rooted in the historical experience of an island nation, which traditionally had husbanded its limited military resources to hit an enemy at its most vulnerable point. The difference was one of basic philosophy. American generals like Marshall had been schooled in continental military strategy, which emphasized quick victory by frontal assaults employing massive armies. Marshall wanted to get the Allied forces ashore in France so as to take the most direct and fastest road to Berlin. "Every diversion or side issue from the main plot was a suction pump," he argued, draining off resources from the effort to defeat Germany. The U.S. Army Chief pointedly reminded the opening Symbol session that for many Americans that "main plot" was not Europe but the struggle against Japan.

The bitter struggle being waged for the Solomons and New Guinea showed that the Allies could not "allow the Japanese any pause." The division of arms and materiel between the Atlantic and Pacific theaters, he proposed, must now be adjusted accordingly, doubling the commitment of men, planes, and shipping from 15 percent to 30 percent to fight the Japanese in the coming year. The vigorous support Marshall received from Admiral King convinced some of the British delegation that the U.S. Navy Chief looked on the European war as "just a great nuisance that kept him from waging his Pacific war undisturbed." Nonetheless, King did agree on the one strategic issue on which both sides were united: that every priority must be given to defeating the U-boats. "The shortage of shipping was a stranglehold on all offensive operations," British

Chief of the Imperial General Staff, General Sir Alan Brooke, reminded the conference. "Unless we can effectively combat the U-boat menace, we might not be able to win the war."

The sessions over the next four days were taken up in debating grand strategy and tempers frequently reached breaking point. The staff officers would be asked to leave as the Chiefs continued the wrangling in private sessions. General Sir Alan Brooke, of whom one aide commented "cannot make his brain move slowly enough for his speech," allowed his Irish temper to show in the verbal exchanges with King, who was "always on the lookout for slights or attempts to put something over on him." The admiral proved an intransigent champion of the Pacific strategy. Although he never actually said it of himself, it was widely held that on being appointed COMINCH he commented: "When the going gets rough, they call in the sons of bitches." Dill and Marshall often had to cool tempers while they patiently searched for a compromise. The President and the Prime Minister were careful to stay out of the arguments. Marshall's team met the British resistance to a cross-Channel attack by refusing to make any concessions to widening the Mediterranean offensive. This was countered by General Brooke, who maintained that the near disaster of that summer's Dieppe raid proved any invasion of France on a large enough scale to succeed could not be mounted for at least another year.

The U.S. Navy's plan to launch a major drive in the Pacific against the Marshalls and the Carolines was met with an equally stubborn refusal by the British, since it was estimated that it would draw off 1 million men and hundreds of aircraft, besides the 1.5 million tons of shipping needed to support it across the vast ocean distance. This, they contended, was tantamount to reversing the "Europe First" Allied strategy because it "cannot but adversely reflect on the defeat of Germany." The British argued that any widening of the Pacific offensive must leave General Wavell without landing craft needed to launch their long-awaited Anakim operation to recapture Rangoon. King, in a surprise move, spiked this by volunteering to supply all the boats necessary. When the British refused the firm commitment to a launching date in 1943 for the Burma offensive that Chiang Kai-shek was demanding, Marshall reminded them bluntly that if it could not be done, "a situation might arise in the Pacific at any time that would necessitate the United States regretfully withdrawing from commitments in the European theater."

Over a dinner on the third evening, just as everyone was beginning to despair of reaching agreement, the good food and best French wine mellowed the discussion. It continued over cigars and cognac until well past midnight, by which time enough gentlemanly concessions had been made for both sides to reach an "agreement in principle." The British would accept an extension of the Pacific offensive, in return for the Americans accepting the invasion of Sicily. Another "very heated" debate took place on the morning of January 18, before the damage was repaired after lunch by a subtly worded British compromise that Pacific operations "must be kept within such limits as will not in the opinion of the Combined Chiefs of Staff, prejudice the capacity of the United Nations to take any opportunity that may present itself for the decisive defeat of Germany in 1943."

That very afternoon at 5 P.M. the President and the Prime Minister joined with their Chiefs of Staff to endorse the agreed order of Allied strategic priorities for 1943. Immediate efforts were to be concentrated on the Battle of the Atlantic, since "defeat of the U-boats remains the first charge on resources." Second, "Russia must be sustained by the greatest volume of supplies." Third, the Bolero build-up in Britain was to continue for a full-scale invasion of France by 1944. (As a concession, the British had agreed to leave open the possibility of a small-scale cross-Channel attack in case it was needed to relieve pressure on Russia.) Fourth, the bomber offensive against Germany was to be stepped up. Fifth, planning was to begin for the invasion of Sicily following the Axis defeat in North Africa. Sixth, subject to the limitations of the compromise wording, operations in the Pacific were to be extended from securing New Guinea and the Solomons to include the recapture of the Aleutians and an offensive against Japanese bases in the Caroline and Marshall islands. Last, the British reluctantly agreed to plan for the Anakim offensive in Burma by November 1943.

This was not the "blueprint for how to set about winning the war" that both Allied teams had expected Symbol to draw up because many key strategic issues were still left unresolved. The conference, however, satisfied the British that priority would be given to defeating the U-boats, which were putting such a stranglehold on Allied shipping. Brooke noted: "We had got practically all we hoped to get when we came here." The U.S. Joint Chiefs were less happy with the outcome of Casablanca, with General Wedemeyer taking the extreme view: "We lost our shirts." Not quite an accurate assessment because King at last had got his Central Pacific offensive. General Marshall, however, was concerned that America had been committed another step deeper into the Mediterranean whereas the British had yet to be nailed to a firm commitment to either the Second Front or launching the Burma offensive that Washington believed would be necessary to keep China in the war.

Churchill and Roosevelt were able to take comfort that their military Chiefs were at least agreed on basic strategy. On the final day at Casablanca, the Allied leaders gathered for reporters in the tropical splendor of the Anfa garden to put on a euphoric appearance of unity as they predicted that the drive had now begun toward Berlin and Tokyo. In a gesture intended to impress the absent Stalin, Roosevelt also announced that "their only terms would be unconditional surrender"—a commitment that Churchill was later to regret.

The President and the Prime Minister had plenty to congratulate themselves about the next day: news came that MacArthur had finally crushed the last Japanese strongholds on the Papuan Peninsula and the Red Army was in the final stages of encircling a hundred thousand-strong German army at Stalingrad. Had they then also known that Japan's troops were finally evacuating Guadalcanal their dinner that evening would have been even more of a celebration.

JAPAN ON THE RETREAT

On January 14, 1943, Imperial General Headquarters had issued the orders to the Rabaul command for Operation KE, the withdrawal of General Hyakutake's starving and exhausted troops, then being battered west across the Matanikau River into the jungle by General Patch's fresh troops and artillery. That same night, Admiral Tanaka's force set out with nineteen destroyers, speeding up The Slot to begin the evacuation by landing a party of the Special Navy Landing Force to act as a rearguard. American radio intelligence failed to discover the reason for the new nightly series of runs by the Tokyo Express. Halsey, worried that a fresh offensive was brewing, stripped the aircraft from his three new escort carriers to reinforce the Cactus Air Force. Destroyers had already been sent up The Slot ten days earlier to bombard the Japanese Munda Airfield on New Georgia. The Tulagi PT boats were now racing into battle each evening. Then the heavy cruiser *Chicago* was sunk by torpedo planes. Six days later, Japanese radio deception ploys convinced CINCPAC Intelligence to predict that the Combined Fleet units were moving south from Truk to resume the offensive in the Solomons. Reports of air reconnaissance appeared to confirm this. Halsey signaled his commanders to prepare for the "final supreme effort."

General Patch's westward push along Guadalcanal's north shore had by now trapped General Hyakutake's force, and another American battalion landed to make a pincer movement from Cape Esperance. All the U.S. Navy surface units in the South Pacific were steaming south of the Solomons awaiting the call to strike the new enemy invasion fleet. It never came. The Tokyo Express was given the opportunity on three clear nights during the first week of February 1943 to ferry out General Hyakutake and over 10,000 of his surviving troops. Pushing past the PT boats and air attacks, the final run down The Slot was made on the night of February 7, exactly six months to the day since the first Americans had landed on the island.

Next morning, Patch's 161st Army Division united some 12 miles from Tassafaronga Point. Their pincer snapped shut on a few enemy snipers, a litter of abandoned weapons, and wrecked landing barges at the tiny village of Tenebro. It was a welcome anticlimax to a long and bitterly fought campaign. Patch signaled triumphantly: "ORGANIZED RESISTANCE ON GUADALCANAL HAS CEASED." Halsey good-humoredly responded: "WHEN I SENT A PATCH TO ACT AS A TAILOR FOR GUADALCANAL, I DID NOT EXPECT HIM TO REMOVE THE ENEMY'S PANTS SO QUICKLY. THANKS AND CONGRATULATIONS."

"The dead of Bataan will rest easier tonight," General MacArthur had observed approvingly two weeks earlier, on January 21, after news came that the final pocket of resistance between Gona and Buna had been crushed. The fall of the stronghold at Sanananda marked the end of the Papuan campaign and the completion of Stage I—six months behind schedule—of the Joint Chiefs of Staff directive of July 1942. This, however, did not prevent the Southwest Pacific Command from issuing an exultant communiqué claiming that victory had been won with a "low expenditure of life and resources." In fact, the campaign cost 1,600 lives, making it one of the most expensive of the entire Pacific War for the number of troops involved. MacArthur's bombastic press statements, referring to "Allied Forces" or "American troops" but hardly ever to the Australians, who had borne the brunt of the jungle fighting in the savage campaign, inspired a many-versed lampoon which ended: "So bet your shoes that all the news/ That last great Judgment Day/ Will go to press in nothing less/ Than DOUG'S COMMUNIQUE."

MacArthur was now to assume overall command under the Joint Chiefs' directive for the next stage of the drive to Rabaul, by advancing up the coast of New Guinea to the Huon Peninsula ports and undertaking operations against the northern Solomons. This he intended to be the first step toward assuming supreme command of the war against Japan.

"Give enough thought to your plans so that Lae and Salamaua do not become another Guadalcanal," the Emperor had cautioned General Sugiyama. Accordingly, the 17th Army Command in Rabaul had dispatched an additional force of 3,000 troops to hack their way inland from the ports toward the Australian airstrip at Wau. They discovered that MacArthur had anticipated the move by reinforcing the field's defense with a brigade of Australian troops flown in from Port Moresby. Their attack had been halted on January 29, just 400 yards from the end of the runway. Within a week the Japanese supplies were running out, but the Australians were being supplied by the C-47 transports of the 5th Air Force. A week later they had built up enough strength to break out, and the counteroffensive drove the would-be occupiers back in a retreat through the jungle to Lae.

At his headquarters in Rabaul, General Imamura perceived the defeat at Wau as presenting a serious threat to his bases in New Guinea. At once a force of 6,000 men was embarked on eight transports escorted by eight destroyers to sail for Lae and Salamaua. The convoy put to sea at midnight on the last day of February, after Imamura's meterologists assured him that several days of thick weather would conceal their approach from enemy aircraft. Allied reconnaissance had revealed the ship movements to Rabaul's Simpson Harbor, and General Kenney ordered over two hundred bombers to bases in Papua to attack the transports.

THE BATTLE OF THE BISMARCK SEA

The weather proved a fickle ally for the Japanese. On February 1, when the heavy clouds began breaking up, a patrol of 5th Air Force B-25s spotted the convoy hugging the coastline of New Britain. The skies were clear the next day as wave after wave of heavy bombers roared down. The Japanese sailors manning the machine guns on the transports were stunned when the large twin-engined bombers came roaring in at them from masthead height. It was the first demonstration of the "skip-bombing" technique that had been perfected by the 5th Air Force. It proved deadly as the Mitchell bombers sent their bombs skimming like stones across a pond to crash into the hulls of ships with the impact and accuracy of torpedoes. Eight transports, along with four destroyers, were sunk, all but wiping the convoy out by nightfall. In addition, more than sixty Japanese planes sent out to protect the transports were blasted from the sky at the cost of only four American fighters. Darkness brought continuing slaughter as the lifeboats carrying General Hatazo Aidichi and his surviving troops were attacked by PT boat flotillas from Milne Bay. Fewer than 2,000 of his men were rescued, along with the general himself, by the four surviving Japanese destroyers. Only a hundred managed to make their way across the Dampier Strait by raft and lifeboat to land eventually on New Guinea.

The Battle of the Bismarck Sea was a major victory for the Allies. It ended any major effort by Japan to send reinforcements from New Britain to their garrisons in New Guinea; these were now cut off except for night destroyer and barge runs.

"A merciful providence guarded us in this great victory," declared another of MacArthur's effusive communiqués, as he renewed demands for Washington to provide him with 5 more divisions, 1,800 aircraft, and naval forces, including carriers. He wanted to set in motion his ambitious plan, code named "Elkton," for a five-stage advance up New Guinea and across to Rabaul in conjunction with the drive up the Solomons due to be launched from Guadalcanal. But because of the decisions taken at Casablanca, it was impossible for Marshall to commit forces on such a scale. Admiral King, concerned that Halsey's command would now be subject to MacArthur's authority, opposed what he saw as a plot to siphon off the warships and troops required to launch his mid-Pacific drive. General Wedemeyer was dispatched as Marshall's emissary to explain to the Commander in Chief South West Pacific that he would have to trim back his ambitious Elkton plan.

MacArthur reacted with a stormy lecture, in which he poured scorn on the "Navy cabal" he was convinced was depriving him of the forces needed to win the war within the year. Then he cabled Marshall that his New Guinea campaign was "temporarily suspended for lack of resources." But Halsey was already taking the next move to gain the Solomons. On February 21, he pushed his South Pacific Command area to its designated Northern limit by sending out a force from Guadalcanal to set up an air base on Banika in the Russell Islands, 50 miles to the north of Henderson Field. This operation encountered no opposition.

To get the war against Japan moving again, MacArthur, Nimitz, and Halsey were ordered to send their representatives to Washington for a "Pacific Military Conference" to resolve the conflicting strategic demands on limited resources. However, when they assembled under the auspices of the Joint Chiefs of Staff on March 12, 1943, they were soon caught up in a bitter stalemate. Marshall was dismayed to find that General Sutherland, on MacArthur's instructions, had demanded yet more military strength. This could only be at the expense of Nimitz's command, so King steadfastly refused to give way. Locked as they were into their Symbol agreement to limit the Pacific offensive, the Joint Chiefs decided to cut back on their earlier set of objectives. But Roosevelt intervened decisively to order Marshall to send aircraft to the Pacific before North Africa and MacArthur was directed to modify his Elkton plan. Rabaul was dropped, as an objective for 1943; preparations were to be made for the "ultimate seizure of the Bismarck Archipelago" with an advance to Lae, Salamaua, Finschhafen, and Madang on New Guinea. Halsey was restricted to advancing up the Solomons "to include the southern portion of Bougainville." At the same time King was defeated in his effort to get Admiral Nimitz appointed Supreme Commander of all Pacific naval operations. An uneasy compromise was reached whereby CINCPAC would have final authority over the movement of Allied warships, but only those units not already assigned to specific operations under the control of General MacArthur's command.

The rivalry over whether the southwest Pacific or Central Pacific should be the area of the main offensive against Japan was settled by the compromise of this divided relationship. MacArthur interpreted the Joint Chiefs' decision to mean that he had now been given control of a significant part of the U.S. Navy's fleet; he came to regard as his own Halsey's battleships, carriers, and cruisers. Along with his earlier force of 400 aircraft and 7 Marine and Army divisions, MacArthur regarded it as an important addition to his own 15 Australian and American divisions and the 1,200-strong 5th Air Force. All told, it certainly constituted the most powerful Allied force in the Pacific, which MacArthur's staff now prepared to direct against the 90,000 troops and 400 aircraft that the Japanese were estimated to have in place to defend Rabaul, protected by its advance defense bases in New Guinea and the upper Solomons.

The dispute between the U.S. Army and Navy and consequent revision of plans meant that it was to be nearly three months before the Allied offensive began moving forward again. During this time it was the 5th Air Force and the Marine fighters on Guadalcanal who kept the Japanese garrisons effectively blockaded, hammering away at their bases. So during the first half of 1943 the British forces in Burma were the only Allied troops actively engaged in fighting the enemy on the ground.

PAYING FOR MISTAKES

The Arakan offensive by the end of 1942 had been grounded in the swampy Mayu Peninsula, where the 14th Indian Army was trying to launch itself on an amphibious attack on the port of Akyab. Lacking landing craft, a makeshift flotilla of three paddlesteamers, five motor launches, and a handful of invasion boats had been assembled to ferry the troops across the heavily defended channel. Fortunately for the Indian soldiers, this rag-tag invasion was destined never to put sail.

The Japanese commander of the Imperial Army's 55th Division had got ahead of the British to advance his battle-hardened veterans into place at the tip of the peninsula. By the end of January 1943 they had effectively blocked General Lloyd's advance 5 miles short of Bonbaik, the scheduled port of embarkation. The second prong of the British thrust had been halted across the estuary of the Mayu River at Rathedaung, forcing postponement of the whole operation for the next four weeks as the British force tried unsuccessfully to break through the unyielding defenders.

At the end of February, General Wavell's staff at the New Delhi headquarters decided the Arakan expedition must be abandoned. But Churchill would not hear of it. Keenly aware that the Americans had made Burma a test of faith in Anakim at Casablanca, he was convinced that another retreat would damage the morale of the Indian Army beyond repair. A reluctant Wavell was told to continue the attack against what the Prime Minister insisted was "numerically insignificant enemy opposition."

General Slim, then training the Indian Army XIV Corps, was sent into the Arakan on a trouble-shooting mission. He at once saw that General Lloyd had made the same tactical errors of keeping to the roads and depending on frontal assaults as had brought about the previous year's defeat. Slim's advice was not heeded in time and by early April the Japanese had infiltrated their forces through the swamps and thick jungle of the Mayu Peninsula to attack the rear of the British line. When Slim was sent back to take command in mid-month, he found that it was too late to save a campaign already collapsing. In what was to become a reprise of the previous year, he began the unenviable task of fighting a retreat back up the Arakan coast to Chittagong. His division was steadily shot to pieces, leaving the bodies of 2,500 of its soldiers rotting in the jungle.

In London, the Prime Minister fumed at the ease with which the Japanese had won another victory against superior British forces. "In war you have to pay for your mistakes," Slim philosophically summed up the first Arakan campaign. When he returned to New Delhi headquarters, he found Wavell and his staff deep in despondency. The defeat confirmed Wavell's belief that mounting any large-scale operation in the Burma jungle was futile, and hardened his already jaundiced view of the Anakim strategy that his staff were preparing. The fresh British disaster froze the already cool relations with Chiang Kai-shek, who continued to withhold assistance from Stilwell's Ledo Road campaign. It was therefore more in desperation than with the hope of achieving any great military success, beyond a symbolic effort to keep the fight going against the Japanese, that Wavell approved launching a limited guerrilla campaign in Burma in the spring of 1943.

"Long Range Penetration" was the exalted title that Brigadier Orde Wingate had chosen to describe operations which had so impressed Wavell during his tenure of command in North Africa. Wingate had brought about the surrender of a 20,000-strong Italian Army in Ethiopia by applying principles he learned from the Jewish insurgents in Palestine. Wingate, like the legendary Lawrence of Arabia (to whom he was distantly related) was cast in the mold of an inspirational and unorthodox guerrilla leader, whose bearing was as unconventional as his tactics. His beard and preference for topee and stained battledress infuriated the Sandhurst-instilled standards of the British generals. Wavell had rescued him from a mental breakdown and brought him to India, where he had been put in charge of training a force of 3,000 British, Gurkha, and Burmese soldiers in guerrilla warfare. This force was created to operate behind the Japanese lines as an element of the Anakim plan.

The 77th Indian Brigade—as it was originally designated—had for months been undergoing a rigorous training program of jungle warfare. Driven by Wingate's fanatical, almost hypnotic style of leadership, his men were subjected to an irresistible combination of bombast and zeal, interspersed with quotations from the Bible and Greek philosophers. His brigade adopted the name "Chindits" from the stone lions that guarded Burmese shrines. They had perfected the ability to operate as a self-sufficient fighting unit in the monsoon-drenched jungle, relying only on their mule trains and air drops for supplies. Now the British failure in the Arakan gave Wingate the chance to persuade Wavell to test his "Long Range Penetration" tactics against the Japanese, even though the stalled coastal offensive had already, by February, led the British commander to curtail major operations into Burma in 1943.

On February 8, the Chindits and their mules, armed with an inspiring order of the day by Wingate, set out from Imphal, the main British base in Assam. Crossing the Burmese border in a two-column thrust over the Chindwin River, the force set out to disrupt the enemy's communications by cutting the strategic road and rail links that ran north from Mandalay to Myitkyina. By the first week of March, Wingate's forces were succeeding in their mission, destroying bridges and blowing up the railway—cutting one 30-mile stretch of track in thirty places. They then vanished back into the rain forest, where they were kept supplied by air. "If they stay in the jungle, they will starve," Lieutenant General Renya Mutaguchi predicted, but the Japanese 15th Army Commander would soon be forced to send out two divisions to protect his lines of communication.

Had Wingate stayed within the shelter of the "green hell" where his men had learned to live and operate, his initial success might have sustained the two columns of guerrillas. But he was determined to push ahead with a bold scheme to cross the broad Irrawaddy River and rendezvous with his southern force. This proved the undoing of the first Chindit campaign. Once over the river, Wingate's men found they were without protective cover on the hot, dusty plain, which was intersected by roads crawling with Japanese patrols. Advancing beyond the range of air drops, the Chindits were caught with only a few mortars and machine guns to fend off increasing attacks. The following weeks became a nightmareish ordeal as they fought thirst, disease, and hunger, in addition to an enemy unwilling to pursue them into the jungle but now able to harry their columns in the open country. Most of the mules had been eaten to keep the soldiers alive, when on March 24 Wingate received orders to give up his attempt to make the rendezvous point in the Kachin Hills.

To get his brigade back across the heavily patrolled Irrawaddy, where the Japanese were gathering their forces to cut off his retreat, Wingate divided his force into many small units that were to infiltrate back through the enemy lines. Many never made it, and one group marched east to safety in China. For those who got over the Irrawaddy, like his own unit, which hid up for a week before crossing the river, the 150-mile trek back through the jungle to the Chindwin was a supreme test of endurance. They survived only by eating plants, monkeys, and snakes.

"As a military operation the raid had been an expensive failure," Slim concluded, as fewer than two hundred Chindits finally struggled back across the Assam border. This, however, did not prevent the British press from making Wingate a hero—dubbing him "Clive of Burma." The Prime Minister was also mightily impressed with the Chindits' boldness, extolling their leader as "a man of genius and audacity." Wingate was promptly recalled to London to discuss future offensives, and the possibility of making him the commander of a Burma Army. This idea of Churchill's was no doubt intended to impress the Americans with Britain's offensive spirit, but it was fiercely resisted by his generals. They were adamant that for all the publicity, Wingate had actually secured "little tangible return for the losses." What disruption the Chindits had done to enemy communications "was repaired in a few days and it had no immediate effect on Japanese dispositions and plans." Their assessment proved correct; not a single Japanese soldier had been brought back from the Pacific to defend Burma. The Chindits' failure turned Wavell's doubts over the advisability of Anakim into outright resistance.

DEATH RAILWAY

Wingate's campaign in north Burma had, however, caused the Imperial General Staff in Tokyo to hasten the construction of the strategic rail link between Bangkok and Rangoon, over which they could rush in reinforcements overland. This brought additional misery and death to the thousands of Allied prisoners of war who had been slaving since the previous autumn to push the single track line through some of the most hostile terrain over which any railroad had ever been constructed. Painfully slow progress was made in building the embankments and cuttings to carry the track over malarial swamp, through jungle-hung ravines, and across swift-flowing streams.

The Siam-Burma rail link was a huge undertaking that demanded matching reserves of labor. There was no shortage of that because Prime Minister Tojo had decreed in May a "no work, no food" policy for the 300,000 Allied prisoners of war. Japan had conveniently failed to ratify the Hague Convention, which forbade the employment of military captives on industrial work, so the crowded camps in Singapore, the Philippines, and Java were looked on as a captive pool of workers. Thousands of the inmates had already been transported to the mines of Korea or to work on the construction of airfields but the railway line was to be the worst ordeal for the slave laborers—who were to be "paid," on Prime Minister Tojo's orders, a nominal 3 to 30 cents a day, depending on rank.

The Burma railway line had been begun in October 1942 by 3,000 Australian prisoners, shipped in to Moulmein after they had finished building the new airfields in Siam. From the port they were taken by railcars to Thanbyuzayat where the line ran into the jungle. Here they began the herculean labor, under savage Japanese guards, of hacking the railroad through the dense rain forest with spades, axes, and only the occasional help of elephants to drag away the monstrous teak trunks. Within weeks British prisoners were being taken into Siam to begin toiling on the other end of the line. Hundreds of thousands of tons of earth were scraped and carried, basket load by backbreaking basket load, to make a log-reinforced embankment that would carry the roadbed over the malarial swamps. By the end of the year, more than 10,000 prisoners were laboring under sadistic taskmasters drawn from the Kwantung Army, whose whips and bayonets brutally translated the engineers' blueprints into two opposed tracks that moved to a meeting in the dense jungle at an agonizing pace. Inadequate rice rations, mosquitoes, and parasitic diseases further drained the strength of the weakened prisoners of war.

The British thrusts into Burma in the spring of 1943 brought fresh orders from Tokyo to advance the completion date for the railway from December to August. More than half the track remained to be pushed through. Conditions for the Allied prisoners, already bad, now became intolerable. Their ranks were swollen by the arrival of 60,000 more prisoners and 300,000 native laborers. They worked through the night by the fitful light of hand-powered generators, in shifts that were extended to sixteen punishing hours. Epidemics of cholera swept the camps, increasing the death rate, which was already soaring from overwork, starvation, and malaria. Not until the late summer, when the line was again falling behind its punishing schedule, did Tokyo send in the most rudimentary medical supplies. Three months late, in November 1943, the "railway of death" was opened. Every one of its 250 miles had cost the lives of 400 men to move the 150 million cubic feet of earth and build over 9 miles of bridges. Yet the very labor of building it generated a fanatical pride in some of the captured British officers who, despite the fact that 13,000 Allied prisoners of war and an estimated 90,000 native workers had died, would struggle for the rest of the war to keep the line open, their misplaced enthusiasm immortalized in the fictional *Bridge on the River Kwai.*

22
Trying to Run Two Wars at Once

While yet another defeat of arms was inflicted on the British in Burma, a victory was being won in the secret war of intelligence that was to have a profound long-term impact on the struggle against Japan. For over a year, Allied cryptanalysts had been waging a battle to break into the Imperial Army ciphers with little success, because (unlike the Navy traffic) messages were scrambled before encoding and transmission. Then, during March 1943, the first successes were finally achieved by the Army codebreakers at the Wireless Experimental Center established in New Delhi to monitor Imperial Army signals from Burma. The penetration of the supply orders of the so-called water transport code system proved to be the key to the main operational cipher. With the rapid expansion of personnel, most of the processors were women drawn from WAC enlistees. The British and U.S. armies set up an Ultra system to provide field commanders with accurate preemptive intelligence of the enemy ground forces throughout the Pacific theater. Within six months this had achieved such proficiency that, according to a secret American assessment, from August 1943 "every movement of a Japanese Division was discovered either while it was still in transit or very shortly after it reached its final destination."

It was one of those ironies of war that this breakthrough—which was to hasten the collapse of Japan's military power in Southeast Asia—happened to come during the very month when the advantage in the secret war swung to the Germans in the Battle of the Atlantic. The U-boat Enigma codes had been revised, temporarily blinding the Admiralty's tracking operations. Convoy after convoy fell prey to massive "wolfpack" attacks as March 1943 brought the worst Allied merchantmen losses of the war.

Churchill was forced to inform Roosevelt: "there will not be sufficient shipping to implement in full the decisions taken at Casablanca." As a result, orders went out to theater commanders to cut "to the bone" their supply requirements. Stalin was told the bad news that the Russian convoys might have to be once more suspended. The Foreign Secretary Anthony Eden was sent by the Prime Minister to Washington. His difficult mission was to explain the "extreme gravity" of the crisis and warn the Americans that "the British Chiefs of Staff see little prospect of Anakim and much less Bolero, unless from now onwards a good deal more shipping than is now in sight can be provided for Indian and United Kingdom theatres."

For a few weeks, the prospect that the U-boats were on the verge of winning the long and bitter Atlantic struggle loomed very real and menacing over the Prime Minister. He would later confess that: "The only thing that ever really frightened me during the war was the U-boat peril." The drain on shipping resources, however, was to be felt most severely in the Pacific, because it was exacerbated by the enormous distances in that theater. "IS IT IN THE REALM OF PRACTICABILITY OF MATERIALS AND SUPPLIES?" read the eye-catching notice that Admiral Nimitz had hung on the wall over his desk to remind himself and his staff of the constraints they were living under as they labored to put together the Navy's great Pacific offensive. Impatient signals from COMINCH urged them to speed up the attack on the Marshalls. But the launching of the operation had to be postponed until the autumn when more shipping and the new carriers then commissioning arrived to reinforce the fleet. Meanwhile everything available was being concentrated in the South Pacific to revive the temporarily halted offensive against the Japanese in New Guinea and the Solomons. But one task was slated for immediate execution as a matter of urgent U.S. national prestige: the two Aleutian islands seized by Japan had to be recaptured.

Replanting the Stars and Stripes on Kiska and Attu was the first mission for the Pacific Fleet in 1943. The Army reluctantly assisted in January by occupying neighboring Amchitka. From its airstrip, bombers flew the 60 miles to raid Kiska whenever the Arctic fogs and gales permitted. In response, the Imperial High Command issued a directive on February 5 "to hold the western Aleutians at all costs." When reconnaissance flights revealed that the Japanese were building an airstrip on Kiska, Admiral Kinkaid, the victor of the naval Battle of Guadalcanal and now Northern Pacific Commander, stepped up the blockade.

THE BATTLE OF THE KOMANDORSKI ISLANDS

On February 18, Admiral Charlie H. McMorris's cruiser task force set out to bombard Attu, intercepting and sinking two transports that were sneaking in supplies and ammunition. The enemy's Fifth Fleet, based in the Kurile Islands north of Japan, was ordered to fight the next convoy through. U.S. Navy radio intelligence failed to reveal that Admiral Boshiro Hosagoya's entire strength of four cruisers and four destroyers set out a month later to escort a two-transport convoy to reinforce Attu.

On March 26 off the Komandorski Islands, when McMorris's task force ran into the convoys just after sunrise on an unusually bright and clear morning, he was surprised to find himself outnumbered two to one. The Japanese could have had the advantage in the four-hour running gunnery duel if Admiral Hosagaya had not been over-cautious in protecting the transports. The American admiral nicknamed "Socrates," employed intelligence to drive off the enemy and extricate his force from potential disaster—in spite of the hits putting the heavy cruiser *Salt Lake City* out of the action. The Japanese reinforcements never reached their destination; nor did two destroyers that attempted to run in supplies two weeks later. The arctic outposts of the Rising Sun were now cut off by McMorris's small fleet. By the end of the month the American invasion forces were sailing north from San Francisco.

The ill-fated decision by the Imperial General Command to cling on to Kiska and Attu was taken in the midst of a fierce strategic debate between the army and navy staffs about how best to secure New Guinea and their key base at Rabaul against the renewed Allied offensive. The navy wanted to concentrate forces on the Solomons, because if those islands fell, New Britain would be defenseless. The army, however, insisted on giving priority to New Guinea. Its pressure triumphed over military logic on March 25, when the "Army-Naval Central Agreement" was communicated to General Imamura at Rabaul and Admiral Yamamoto at Truk. This directed that reinforcements be sent to Lae and Salamaua after Allied airpower had been defeated. The onus of clearing the skies of the 5th Air Force planes was placed on the Imperial Navy, since it had the largest reserves of fighters and bombers. Yamamoto's staff obediently put together "Operation I-GO," which called for stripping Truk and the carriers of aircraft to reinforce the 11th Air Fleet, enabling it to launch a series of massive strikes against the American air bases in the lower Solomons and the Papuan Peninsula.

Admiral Yamamoto himself flew to Rabaul on April 3 to supervise his "I-GO" strategy, due to begin the following morning to coincide with his birthday. Bad weather and squalls, however, kept the planes grounded for three days until April 7, when the Commander in Chief, immaculately attired in white dress uniform, watched the first of two hundred fighters and bombers take off from the Rabaul airstrip southeast for Guadalcanal, to launch the biggest air raid since Pearl Harbor. The strike, which sank a destroyer, a tanker, and a corvette, cost many planes. Yamamoto was deceived by his pilots' exaggerated reports of many more American warships sunk. Three more strikes over the next four days were directed against the Allied bases in New Guinea. The 11th Air Fleet briefing rooms rang to the cheers of returning pilots as they filed reports claiming to have sunk a cruiser and twenty-five transports, in addition to putting airstrips out of action and shooting down two hundred planes.

YAMAMOTO'S DEATH WARRANT

Admiral Yamamoto, even allowing for his pilots' enthusiasm, concluded that his "I-GO" offensive must be succeeding. He decided to make a personal tour of the airfields to spur his aircrews on to greater efforts. It was to prove a fatal mistake. Pearl Harbor radio intelligence picked up his signal and decrypted it. "Our old friend Yamamoto," Commander Layton commented to Admiral Nimitz on the afternoon of April 14, passing him a Japanese signal intercepted from "CinC Southeastern Air Fleet" to an addressee believed to be the commander of the garrison at Ballale on Bougainville. It had been almost completely deciphered and began: "ON 16 APRIL CINC COMBINED FLEET WILL VISIT RYZ, R⎯ AND RXP IN ACCORDANCE WITH THE FOLLOWING SCHEDULE:

    1. DEPART RR AT 0600 IN A MEDIUM ATTACK PLANE ESCORTED BY 6 FIGHTERS ARRIVE RXZ AT 0800. PROCEED BY MINESWEEPER TO R⎯ ARRIVING AT 0840

    2. AT EACH OF THE ABOVE PLACES THE COMMANDER IN CHIEF WILL MAKE A TOUR OF INSPECTION AND AT ⎯⎯ HE WILL VISIT THE SICK AND WOUNDED BUT CURRENT OPERATIONS SHOULD CONTINUE."

After studying his map and tracing the itinerary that would take Yamamoto on a round trip by air and sea to Ballele, Shortlands, and Buin, Nimitz concluded that the first leg would bring the Imperial Navy's premier admiral just within range of fighters from Henderson Field. Here was a tempting chance to eliminate the sole man other than the Emperor whose death would be a tremendous blow to Japanese morale.

"Do we try to get him?" he wondered aloud. Layton had no doubt.

"You know," he would recall telling his admiral, "it would be just as if they shot you down. There isn't anyone to replace you."

Nimitz decided to pass the vital information on to Halsey, cautioning him on the need to devise an operation that would also protect the secrecy of the intelligence. "IF FORCES YOU COMMAND HAVE THE CAPABILITY TO SHOOT DOWN YAMAMOTO AND STAFF, YOU ARE HEREBY AUTHORIZED TO INITIATE PRELIMINARY PLANNING," CINCPAC's order ran. Nimitz also sought approval from Washington. The President agreed; so did the Secretary of the Navy, after he had taken the advice of leading churchmen on the morality of killing enemy leaders. On April 15, 1943, Nimitz signaled the go-ahead for "Operation Vengeance" with a "GOOD LUCK AND GOOD HUNTING."

On Henderson Field, Major John Mitchell's squadron of P-38 Lightnings was fitted with belly tanks to give them additional range and the pilots, sworn to secrecy, were briefed on the aerial ambush to be executed over the islands of the upper Solomons.

Just after sunrise the next morning Yamamoto, wearing a dark green uniform, boarded a Mitsubishi "I"-type twin-engined bomber, accompanied by his secretary. The admiral's insistence on punctuality was a legend throughout the fleet. When his plane took off precisely at 6 A.M., followed by another carrying his Chief of Staff, Admiral Ugaki noted approvingly that they were right on schedule, unaware that seventeen American pilots of the P-38s then flying toward Bougainville were also counting on Yamamoto's being on time. An hour and a half later, as the two bombers and their escort Zeros were skirting Buin's coastal jungle at 6,000 feet, Yamamoto's pilot passed back a slip of paper which the admiral held in white-gloved hands. It read: "Expect to arrive Ballale 07.45."

Seconds later his staff realized something was amiss when one of the escorting fighters veered off to starboard to intercept planes that had been spotted 1,600 feet below. At the same instant Mitchell yelled on the intercom: "Bogey's eleven o'clock high." The American pilots pulled the switches, releasing their fuel-drop tanks, as they raced after the two bombers that had separated while diving to tree-top height in a bid to escape.

Eight P-38s engaged the Japanese fighters while the rest of the squadron split after both bombers. They had been briefed to expect only one and Mitchell had no idea which contained their prize quarry. Cannonfire quickly sent one Mitsubishi crashing through the jungle canopy in flames while the other, its wing torn off, pancaked into the sea.

Admiral Ugaki struggled ashore after his bomber sank, but the Commander in Chief's luck had finally run out—he lay dead in the wreckage under the gash torn in the trees. A party of soldiers stationed at the village of Aku were already hacking their way through to the wreck. Next day they found the crashed bomber with the admiral strapped in his seat, his body unblemished except for neat maroon holes that had been left by a bullet that passed through his jaw and came out at the temple. If the soldiers had not found his diary and the collection of poems by the Emperor Meiji, they would still have known at once it was Yamamoto, for the gloved left hand that gripped his sword had its index and middle fingers missing.

"POP GOES THE WEASEL"—the prearranged signal indicating that Operation Vengeance had been a success—was flashed out from Guadalcanal that afternoon after Mitchell's fighters had all returned safely to celebrate a secret triumph. The victory signal was brought into Halsey while he was in conference with Admiral Richmond Kelly Turner, who immediately "whooped and applauded." "What's good about it?" Halsey demanded, "I'd hoped to lead that scoundrel up Pennsylvania Avenue in chains, with the rest of you kicking him where it would do the most good."

The elimination of Admiral Yamamoto was another victory made possible by American intelligence, and a heavy blow to Japan, delivered a year to the very day after Tokyo had been shocked by Doolittle's bombers. Yet for more than a month his death was kept secret from the Japanese, only publicly announced at the end of May, when Yamamoto's ashes were brought home by the battleship *Musashi* to be paraded through Tokyo in a national day of mourning. The death of Admiral Yamamoto hit the Imperial Navy as severely as if one of its superbattleships had been sunk—a loss that was all the more keenly felt because they had been robbed of their leading naval strategist. Admiral Mineichi Koga, Yamamoto's own nominee, was appointed to succeed him, but the new Commander in Chief of the Combined Fleet lacked his predecessor's strategic genius and implemented a very conservative policy. He soon learned that the apparent success of the I-GO plan was as exaggerated as its pilots' reports. U.S. 5th Air Force bombers and the American planes from the lower Solomons' airfields, supposedly wiped out, pressed on with their raids without let-up.

The continuing Allied domination of the air over the Bismarck Sea made it all but impossible for General Imamura to carry out the reinforcements of the army's garrisons in New Guinea except by Tokyo Express destroyer runs and barges slipping down the coast under cover of darkness or thick weather. Fighters and antiaircraft fire had taken a disastrous toll of the Japanese carrier pilots; the surviving pilots and planes flew back to rejoin their ships at Truk before the end of April.

The conviction that the Allies had won another important victory was an important contribution to the harmony that resulted at the first meeting, on April 15, 1943, between Admiral Halsey and General MacArthur at the Southwest Pacific Commander's Brisbane headquarters. This harmony had been achieved despite their staffs' fears of a clash of strong personalities, as well as Halsey's apprehension that the divided responsibility to Nimitz and MacArthur would make it difficult to carry out a joint offensive. The general, however, would record: "[I] liked him [Halsey] from the moment we met," considering that he was entirely free of "the bugaboo of many sailors, the fear of losing ships." If the admiral's pugnaciousness was the quality that MacArthur had taken to his heart, Halsey was equally impressed with the general's eloquent presence. "Five minutes after I reported, I felt as if we were lifelong friends," he later wrote. "We had our arguments, but they always ended pleasantly."

The three days of intensive planning sessions proved that MacArthur and Halsey could indeed work as an effective team, much to the relief of the Joint Chiefs in Washington. Now they were able to draw up the blueprint for a final version of the Elkton offensive for 1943, which was to be known as "Cartwheel."

The plan called for no less than thirteen amphibious landings to be made step by step in the Solomons and New Guinea through to December of 1943. Each command was to provide support for the other's operations. Originally set for May 15, the first round would begin with MacArthur's forces occupying Woodlark and Kiriwina as forward bases in the Trobriands off Papua. Simultaneously Halsey's Marines would advance up the next rung of the Solomons by invading New Georgia. Two months later the New Guinea offensive would move forward to take Lae and Salamaua before securing Madang and the Huon Peninsula, while the Solomons' advance reached to Shortland and Buin on southern Bougainville. Then it was anticipated that MacArthur's forces would be able to make the jump from the Huon Peninsula across to New Britain, while Halsey moved to occupy the whole of Bougainville, making Rabaul the focus of a two-pronged assault by early 1944.

ATTU AND KISKA RETAKEN

The initial Cartwheel landings had originally been planned to coincide with the offensive assault on the Japanese-held Aleutian Islands at the end of the first week of May, but shortages of shipping and landing craft forced MacArthur to postpone the opening moves for another month. The third major American amphibious assault of World War II therefore was launched against Attu Island. The transports carrying the 11,000 troops of the U.S. Army 7th Infantry Division had assembled by the end of April under the shelter of bleak, snow-capped mountains at Cold Bay on the westernmost tip of Alaska. Rear Admiral Francis W. Rockwell, commanding the operation, had decided that by taking the more distant Attu first, he would effectively isolate and neutralize the garrison in Kiska. His twenty-nine-strong invasion fleet included the battleship *Idaho*, the reconstructed *Pennsylvania*, and the *Nevada*, which would have their first opportunity to hit back against the enemy that had so crippled them at Pearl Harbor.

Aleutian fogs delayed the sailing of Rockwell's invasion forces until May 4. Five days later, as they approached Attu, giving Kiska a wide berth, reports of high surf on the landing beaches forced another postponement until May 11. That morning, sweeping banks of heavy mist concealed the invasion force's approach as it was guided in by the submarines *Narwhal* and *Nautilus*. Observing the Arctic mariners' rule not to approach closer to the treacherous black reefs than the barking distance of a sea lion, the transports anchored while the battleships delivered a radar-controlled bombardment of the enemy main base and airstrip at Holtz Bay. It was estimated that several thousand troops would be opposing them, but the initial landing force went in against very light opposition on beaches to the north and south of the Bay.

Ignoring the leaflets inviting them to surrender that were dropped along with bombs from the escort carrier *Nassau*, Colonel Yamakazi's men fought a stubborn rearguard action by retreating to the cul-de-sac of Chichagof Harbor. The muskeg terrain of semi-frozen mud bogged down the American armored vehicles. Frequent blankets of fog hampered the bombardment from the supporting warships. After a week's bitter battle, General Brown's men had not broken through to Chichagof Harbor as planned. Outnumbered five to one, the Japanese had dug themselves into the hillside; they would sell their lives dearly.

Admiral Koga was racing north from Truk with the Combined Fleet and the heavy cruisers of the Northern Pacific Fleet were halfway across the Pacific from their base in the Kuriles, when Imperial General Headquarters decided to call off a relief operation that would draw the navy's strength thousands of miles away from the main strategic perimeter. The only help Yamakazi received were the glimpses of a "Betty" bomber that made an ineffective attack on the U.S. Fleet on May 21.

A week later Yamakazi was running out of food and supplies. In the early hours of May 29, he ordered a last desperate assault. Two hours before daybreak, the Japanese soldiers came screaming down from their positions on the ridge to make the largest Banzai charge of the war. More than 1,000 men, yelling: "Japanese drink blood like wine!" hurled themselves repeatedly against the amazed Americans holding the front line. The battle raged on through the following day with Yamakazi's soldiers mown down by murderous fire. The last desperate assault of the survivors took place at dawn on May 30, leaving a grisly tideline of corpses on the slopes above Chichagof Harbor. If the Americans needed any explanation of the Bushido-inspired fanaticism of their enemy, they found it on one of the bodies; a soldier had written before his final charge: "I will become a deity with a smile in the heavy fog. I am only waiting for the day of death." Only 28 prisoners were taken out of 2,500. Retaking Attu had cost over 1,000 American dead.

The news that a lonely outpost of the United States had been restored brought rejoicing across America. The Tokyo government also announced a celebration for the national heroes who had given "tremendous stimulant to the fighting spirit of our nation." Imperial General Headquarters had by now decided to evacuate indefensible Kiska, but a first attempt to break the American blockade and get the garrison off by submarine failed. The Imperial Navy decided to try repeating their Guadalcanal evacuation operation. Taking advantage of heavy fog, two cruisers and six destroyers arrived two months later, on July 28, and in less than an hour had embarked nearly 5,000 men to spirit them back to the Kuriles completely undetected. Three weeks after that, when 35,000 American troops stormed ashore onto the barren muskeg, they were astonished to find that the only signs of the "enemy" were four abandoned mongrel dogs.

The restoration of the Stars and Stripes over Attu brought a renewed call in the United States for more resources to be concentrated on the Pacific War. The clamor reached General MacArthur, whose candidacy for the next year's presidential election was being canvassed on Capitol Hill. He was careful to stay aloof from the political fray, but allowed his outspoken view on the need to pursue the war against Japan vigorously to be communicated to the journalists at his Brisbane headquarters. Admiral King offered his own strong opinions about the need to step up the naval war in the Pacific—and his sentiments also reached the carefully attuned ears of the politicians on Capitol Hill.

The reports of a growing American lobby to redirect their war effort into a Pacific-oriented strategy caused worry in London, where the recapture of a barren scrap of arctic tundra had seemed insignificant to Allied global strategy when set against the North African campaign, on the brink of defeating the quarter of a million Axis troops surrounded in Tunis. By May 1943 it was becoming evident that the tide had finally turned in the Battle of the Atlantic, with the U-boats retreating from the convoy routes. The British were determined to press their advantage in the Mediterranean, and the Americans, while they had reluctantly agreed to the invasion of Sicily, now found that Churchill wanted to develop an ambitious strategy involving Italy and even the Balkans.

The Prime Minister had called for another review of Allied grand strategy. General Alan Brooke concluded: "We are just about where we were before Casablanca. Their hearts are really in the Pacific and we are trying to run two wars at once." Churchill, in a cable to FDR, claimed it was most necessary "for them to settle Husky and future as well as Anakim. . . ." Separately he told presidential aide Harry Hopkins: "I am conscious of serious divergences beneath the surface which, if not adjusted, will lead to grave difficulties and feeble action in the summer and autumn."

23

"Keep 'Em Dying!"

For the third time in less than a year, the British war leaders crossed the Atlantic. They made the voyage in the hastily restored luxury suites of the *Queen Mary*, while thousands of German and Italian prisoners of war were quartered under heavy guard on the decks below. As the great liner plowed unescorted westward, zigzagging across the ocean too fast for any U-boat to catch her, the Prime Minister conducted a series of briefing sessions in his map-hung state room, to prepare for the Trident Conference. Its purpose, he reassured Stalin by cable in mid-voyage, was "to settle exploitation in Europe after Sicily, and also to discourage bias toward the Pacific, and further deal with the problem of the Indian Ocean and the offensive against Japan."

In her drab gray wartime camouflage as one of the Allies' "Monster" troopships, the *Queen Mary*'s familiar outline was hidden in mist and drizzle on May 11, 1943, when she steamed into New York Harbor to disembark the Prime Minister's party by launch to the Hoboken Piers, where a special train waited to rush them to Washington. "I do not look forward to these meetings; in fact I hate the thought of them," General Brooke noted in his diary, seeing an ominous sign in the gloomy weather. He was forewarned that they were facing a difficult mission to persuade the American military leaders to defer the Second Front and press on with the invasion of Italy after the landing in Sicily. General Wavell had also been brought along to present the case for abandoning the Anakim offensive after Churchill had decided that instead of mounting operations in Burma, which he compared to "munching a porcupine quill by quill," the Allied effort in Southeast Asia should be switched to amphibious assaults on Sumatra and Malaya.

The Joint Chiefs had resolved, for their part, not to be trapped at a tactical disadvantage by the British as they had been at Casablanca. Detailed staff plans had been prepared, and the President briefed on the urgent need to "pin down the British" both to the invasion of France and the Burma offensive, which Chiang Kai-shek had now set as his price for keeping China in the war.

The first session began at the White House on May 12, only hours after the news had been received of the surrender of a quarter of a million Axis troops at Tunis. This victory was used by Churchill to promote the Mediterranean strategy, calling for immediate landings in Sicily with a full-scale invasion of Italy to "cause a chill of loneliness to the German people." Roosevelt reacted coolly to the proposal. He had been persuaded by Marshall that any widening of the Mediterranean war must drain resources from the main thrust against Germany. Nor would he agree to the Prime Minister's call to abandon Anakim in favor of what Roosevelt termed "nibbling at the piecrust" of the Japanese Empire. Having stuck to the letter of the brief he had been given by the Joint Chiefs, the President left with Churchill for the retreat in Maryland's Catoctin Mountain, then known as Shangri-La (later to be called Camp David). Here they enjoyed a renewal of convivial discussions while the Combined Chiefs of Staff argued through two wearying days in Washington.

Confident that the President was now firmly of the same mind, Marshall held out for a cross-Channel attack and no extension of the attack on Italy beyond the agreed landing in Sicily. General Stilwell disputed General Wavell's opinion of how the war should be pursued against Japan. The discussions became a "tangled mass of confusion" when General Chennault joined the fray to press his case for concentrating on an air war from China. Admiral King was determined that the British should be committed to an assault on France in 1944 and he threatened that the United States would withdraw from the Mediterranean in accordance with his view that "we ought to convert our forces into the Pacific." Even Marshall now agreed that this might have to be done, "unless the British Chiefs propose to do something effectual in Europe."

The strategic arm-twisting had its effect on General Alan Brooke, who concluded that "the swing toward the Pacific is stronger than ever, and before long they will be urging that we should defeat Japan first." This time it took more than a convivial dinner to heal the breach between the Allies. The Prime Minister, on Brooke's advice, tentatively accepted that May 1, 1944, would be the date for invading Europe, but could not reach any agreement on whether or not to invade Italy. It was decided to review strategy again after the landing on Sicily to determine the move "best calculated to eliminate Italy from the war and contain the maximum number of German forces."

The British Chiefs of Staff also had no choice but to accept the American strategy as set out in the Joint Chiefs' memorandum entitled "Strategic Plan for the Defeat of Japan." This called for: (1) A submarine blockade of Japan's oil-shipping route to the East Indies; (2) sustained aerial bomb-

ing of Japan as soon as bases in China and the Pacific had been won; and
(3) invasion of the home islands. When it came to the Far East, the Prime
Minister failed to convert the President to his Sumatra/Malaya strategy—
but insisted the British would not "undertake something foolish to placate
the Chinese" in Burma. The Trident Agreement therefore called for "continuance of administrative operations in India for the eventual launching
of an overseas operation the size of Anakim." The general issue was to be
a continual thorn in the side of the Anglo-American partnership.

In his speech to Congress on May 19, the British Prime Minister had
talked movingly of his deep feelings for "tortured China," promising
Chiang Kai-shek "everything humanly possible." Yet he clashed violently
with Foreign Minister T. V. Soong and refused to go to meet Madame
Chiang in New York after she had haughtily refused to come to Wash-
ington to meet him. Reviewing the final Trident draft memorandum on
May 24, the Prime Minister for the first time realized that the British
Chiefs had conceded nearly every point to the Americans. In a fit of pique
he threatened not to accept it, driving Brooke to exasperation until
Churchill was finally persuaded that his refusal would reduce Allied planning to chaos and endanger the "Europe First" strategy. When he left
Washington by air, he was still hoping to win over General Marshall, who
was to accompany him on the flight to North Africa to see General Eisenhower. He did not have much opportunity. The U.S. Army Chief of Staff
passed most of the long air journey resolving with his tactful pen the difficult message the President and the Prime Minister had left him to draft,
breaking the news to Stalin that there was to be no Second Front until
1944.

The Trident Conference in Washington forced the Prime Minister and
the British Chiefs of Staff to recognize for the first time, that the United
States would henceforth dictate strategy in the Pacific and was now in a
position to dominate the Atlantic strategy. Britain had become the junior
partner in the Alliance. Although Churchill was to sustain a relentless fight
to pursue his Mediterranean schemes, his nation's strength was ebbing after
nearly four years of exhausting war and its Chiefs of Staff were never
again to be able to impose their strategic direction as they had done at
Casablanca.

None of the U.S. Joint Chiefs savored their Trident victory as much
as Admiral King. He realized that the British had tacitly relinquished their
share of the joint direction of the Pacific War. He was free now to expand
the offensive. As soon as the conference ended, he flew to San Francisco
to discuss the planning of mid-Pacific operations with Admiral Nimitz.
King approved giving Admiral Spruance, the victor of Midway, overall
command of the island campaign, with General Holland Smith of the
Marine Corps as his amphibious commander. Task Force 50, a new striking

fleet, was being assembled at Pearl Harbor as the *Essex*—the first of nine 27,000-ton new fast carriers—arrived to spearhead the U.S. Navy's drive across the Pacific.

On June 18, 1943, after Nimitz and General Smith returned to Hawaii having carried out an inspection tour of naval bases in the South Pacific, a directive came from the Joint Chiefs to begin operations against the Marshall Islands on November 15. The first assault was to be launched by the 1st and 2nd Marine divisions. This provoked protests from MacArthur —a response no doubt anticipated by Admiral King, who was growing impatient with the general's delay in launching his Cartwheel operations. The 1st Marine Division, which had stubbornly held Guadalcanal during the first four months of the Solomon campaign, was retraining in Australia. MacArthur complained, with some justification, that its removal from his command, together with two of his bomber groups, would "in my opinion collapse the offensive effort in the Southwest Pacific Area." His cable left General Marshall in no doubt that MacArthur regarded his front as the "main effort" against Japan and the proposed operations in the Marshalls as no more than "a diversionary attack."

"From the broad strategic viewpoint I am convinced that the best course of offensive action in the Pacific is a movement from Australia through New Guinea to Mindanao," MacArthur insisted. However, Marshall's reply carefully avoided endorsing the general's call for recognition of the supremacy of his proposed crusade through the Philippines. He did allow MacArthur to retain the 1st Marines; King had exchanged them for the 27th Army Division, then training for amphibious operations at Oahu.

The new flare-up in MacArthur's private war with the U.S. Navy had precisely the impact King intended. The general and Admiral Halsey agreed on June 30 as the date when their Operation Cartwheel would begin rolling. Halsey was soon to be preempted when reports reached Noumea from Coastwatchers on Bougainville that the Japanese were moving in strength into southern New Georgia. Australian Captain Donald G. Kennedy had been running one of the most valuable observation posts hidden in the jungle at Segi Point, some 45 miles west of Munda Point. Here the Japanese had been racing to complete an airfield camouflaged from reconnaissance planes by draping jungle vegetation over wires hung across the perimeter trees. Kennedy's scouts had constantly monitored the progress of the airstrip, which if completed might endanger the forthcoming Allied operation to take the island. The scouts had also rescued downed American pilots and harried enemy patrols. The information that the Japanese had sent out a force to raid Segi Point, as well as stepped up work on the airstrip, forced Halsey to send in the 4th Marine Raider Battalion ten days before his scheduled "L-Day" for "Operation Toenails," the landings on Rendova Island across the channel from Munda Point.

NEW GEORGIA LANDINGS

Before the main operation began, Colonel Michael S. Currin's Raiders were put ashore by destroyers on June 20 at the Segi station. The next day two infantry companies went in to hold the position, while the Raiders struck out westward on June 27 by rubber boats to make a landing to take the small port of Viru for a PT boat base. Their attack was to coincide with a seaborne assault force due to come in on "L-Day" itself.

The New Georgia jungle, clinging to the damp hill slopes, proved to be denser, wetter, and far more resistant to military operations than anything encountered on Guadalcanal, where it was broken up by fields of Kunai grass. The conditions that the Americans were going to have to contend with in New Georgia were graphically recalled by Sergeant Anthony P. Coulis, whose P Company hacked for twelve exhausting hours to advance 7 miles, under constant enemy sniper fire:

"We alternately crawled up and tobogganed down greasy ridges. We forded numerous jungle streams and swam three of them. The repeated torture of plunging into icy streams; the chopping away of endless underbrush and foliage; the continuous drizzle of rain; the days without hot food or drink; the mosquitoes tormenting us at night. It was sheer physical torture; the racking struggle of overtired muscles and empty bellies against the viciousness of the jungle itself. How I ever lived through that day I'll never know. That night we didn't even stand guard. We plunged into the brush next to the trail and fell asleep with a prayer for protection on our lips."

The agonizingly slow pace of the advance next day was made more unbearable for the Raiders because they had now fallen twenty-four hours behind schedule. They pressed on to Viru knowing that the American landing craft and destroyers would already be putting men ashore there in an attack that was threatening to become a total shambles. Eventually, the assault drove the Japanese garrison back into the jungle—where they fell upon the advancing Raiders who were all but dead beat. By a superhuman effort Currin's Marines rallied sufficient strength to fight a four-hour battle that was to be recalled as "one of the most vicious in the New Georgian campaign."

The Japanese then pulled back to Munda Point where a garrison was entrenched in heavily fortified positions to repel any attempt to take the airstrip. The defenders were counting on the assistance of several hundred aircraft from Rabaul to hurl back any attack, but they were to be taken by surprise on June 30 when the American transports arrived in the channel 6 miles away. The flotillas of American landing craft churned in to overwhelm the small garrison holding tiny Rendova Island. The assault was carried out by 6,000 troops of the U.S. Army's 43rd Infantry Division under the command of Major General John Hester, who came ashore in spite of heavy Japanese air raids. Admiral Turner's command ship *McCawley* was hit in three heavy air strikes that were broken up by fighters from Guadalcanal which shot down over forty enemy bombers. The same morning another American group was landing unopposed on Vangunu Island off New Georgia's southern tip.

The American toehold was now firmly on the next rung up the island ladder, as 400 miles to the east across the Solomon Sea General Mac-Arthur's first Cartwheel objectives were secured on Kiriwina and Wood-lark, the two largest Trobriand Islands off the Papuan Peninsula. Some 300 miles further north up the New Guinea coast, the American 41st Division made a landing at Nassau Bay and began moving inland to join up with the 3rd Australian Division, which still held the Wau airstrip. The Japanese concluded, just as MacArthur intended they should, that nearby Salamaua was now threatened with imminent attack. Prevented by Allied control of the skies from sending another reinforcement convoy, General Imamura ordered units out of Lae to march the 20 miles south and reinforce the garrison at Salamaua. By so doing, he fell for MacArthur's ploy, "to siphon off enemy strength from his Lae defenses and lure his troops and supplies southward."

The Solomons campaign moved ahead to plant the first Americans on New Georgia proper on July 2, when Hester's landing craft ferried his main force across the channel from Rendova to come ashore unopposed 5 miles south of the strong enemy defenses guarding the Munda airstrip. That same day another regiment of the 43rd Division and a Marine Raider Battalion landed at Rice Inlet to the north to begin a march south through the jungle, to bottle up the enemy in the narrow neck of New Georgia.

After closing for two days, the jaws of the American pincer were jammed apart by tough Japanese resistance that proved too great for the untested New England National Guardsmen of the 43rd Division. The troops had only a few weeks of jungle-fighting training and found every night an unnerving hell. Constant taunts, firecrackers, and feint attacks made sleep impossible as the soldiers crouched in their damp foxholes, jumpily firing off bullets at slithering snakes, land crabs, and even rotting logs that gave off an evil green phosphorescence. "Combat neurosis" was soon proving more of a problem for the front-line medical units than battle wounds.

Major General Nabor Sasaki, the resourceful Japanese commander at Munda, had stopped the advance of superior American forces at the outer defensive perimeter his troops had constructed around the airfield. Their defense was a veritable fortress; gun emplacements and strongpoints had been dug 5 feet down into the coral, then piled high with logs and earth and skillfully camouflaged. At first, Rabaul headquarters overruled Sasaki's requests to launch a counteroffensive directed at recapturing Rendova. Then Imamura decided to send in reinforcements by destroyer to strengthen their garrison at Vila on Kolombangara Island, 6 miles north of Vila.

The first run of a new Tokyo Express, assigned to land 4,000 troops on the night of July 5, encountered Rear Admiral W. L. Ainsworth's task force of three light cruisers and four destroyers on its way back from bombarding the port. The *Strong* was torpedoed at extreme range before the Americans realized they were heading into a running skirmish in the early hours of the next morning. The American's superior gunnery radar enabled their force to sink one of the troop-carrying Japanese destroyers and to drive another aground for the loss of his light cruiser *Helena*. Only nine hundred soldiers were landed at Vila. However, the derailing of that night's Tokyo Express did not prevent another attempt on July 13, but once again Ainsworth blocked its advance, sinking the light cruiser *Jintsu* for the loss of the destroyers *Gwyn* and heavy damage to the New Zealand cruiser *Leander*.

The rising tempo of the naval engagements and the crawling pace of General Hester's advance toward Munda convinced Admiral Halsey that "Toenails" was in danger of faltering through poor leadership. He moved decisively to correct it, in order to forestall the development of another Guadalcanal. On July 15, he sent the tough General Oscar W. Griswold, the Army XV Corps Commander, to New Georgia. Hester was relieved without more ado, replaced by Guadalcanal veteran Major General John H. Hodge. Halsey wrote many years later, "the smoke of charred reputations still makes me cough."

To crack what Hodge labeled the "Munda Nut"—the heavy enemy fortifications around the base's airfield—he called for reinforcements, including tanks and artillery, as well as an increase in the naval and air bombardment. The New Georgia offensive was resumed on July 25, but the jungle mud and the fanaticism with which General Sasaki's troops defended their positions ensured that the American crawl toward the airstrip was slow and bloody. The defenders had to be pried out of each of their cleverly camouflaged pillboxes with tanks and flamethrowers. Taking apart the fortress, strongpoint by strongpoint, was a battle that dragged on for ten grim days of hand-to-hand fighting.

By August 1, the American advance patrols had reached the edge of the airstrip. Four days more slogging and they surged into Munda over the dead and dying bodies of its expiring defenders. Sasaki pulled out his survivors, spiriting them through the jungle before crossing the sound to Kolombangara Island, where another equally strong defensive system was being dug.

"Our ground forces today wrested Munda from the Japs and present it to you as sole owner," Griswold triumphantly signaled Halsey. "Keep 'em dying," came the admiral's characteristically abrupt reply. A week later the first Marine fighters were operating from the Munda strip, which had been hurriedly expanded by the Seabees to accommodate the bigger American planes. At the end of the month, after the enemy had finally been cleared from New Georgia, Halsey reckoned the cost. It was much heavier than anticipated; originally he had thought that Operation Toenails would require 15,000 troops to crush an estimated 9,000 Japanese on the island. It had actually taken more than three times that number and had cost 1,136 dead.

To continue the American advance up the Solomons, Halsey had to take Kolombangara, where General Sasaki was entrenched for an even more protracted defense, with 10,000 troops defending the island's airstrip. The Japanese were also managing to run Tokyo Expresses in spite of disruptions by U.S. Navy PT boat squadrons that had been moved up to a forward base on Rendova. On the night of August 1, PT-109 was among a force of fifteen sent out to attack a reinforcement convoy. One of the destroyers escorting the Japanese troop barges sliced through the boat, commanded by a future President of the United States. Lieutenant John F. Kennedy would recall the instant of impact when he was slammed against his frail cockpit: "This is what it feels like to be killed." He managed to free himself and then save a fellow crewman in a four-hour swim across the dark waters of Blackett Strait to Plum Pudding Island. He and his ten surviving crew would later be picked up, thanks to the vigilance of Coastwatchers on nearby Kolombangara. Five nights later, six American destroyers had a greater success off Vella Lavella Island, north of Kolombangara, when they intercepted another Tokyo Express rushing more troops in to General Sasaki. Three Japanese destroyers and the soldiers jamming their narrow decks were sent to the bottom in the first action fought by American destroyers free to maneuver in a night action, unencumbered by the need to cover light cruisers. The engagement proved that given the chance, their captains had every bit as much élan in a night battle as the well-practiced Japanese destroyer crews.

Concerned that his part of the Cartwheel operations had now fallen nearly a month behind schedule, Halsey was "wary of another slugging match"; yet he knew this would be inevitable if he proceeded according to plan, carrying out landings on the heavily defended Kolombangara. At Nimitz's urging, he decided to adopt Admiral Kinkaid's Aleutian campaign and "jump over the enemy's strong points, blockade them and leave them to starve." Halsey and his staff took a momentous decision: "Next above Kolombangara is Vella Lavella, thirty-five miles nearer the Shortlands and Kahili. According to coastwatchers, its garrison numbered not more than 250, and its shoreline would offer at least one airstrip."

PT boat reconnaissance parties confirmed that indeed there were few Japanese on Vella Lavella, so at dawn on August 15, 1943, landing craft carried in the 25th U.S. Army Division. "Operation Goodtime" lived up to its name. The only resistance encountered was from the survivors of the Tokyo Express, which had been hit so decisively nine days earlier. The American leapfrogging move took the Japanese command at Rabaul completely by surprise. General Sasaki and his strong garrison found they had been effectively isolated. General Imamura ordered a counter-landing, but the Americans established themselves so quickly and in such strength that he eventually called it off, anticipating it would be "like pouring water on a hot stone." The Americans had now advanced two more rungs up the Solomons and proved a new strategy to speed up MacArthur's drive for the Philippines.

In the six weeks that it had taken the U.S. forces to fight their way only 200 miles up the Solomons, the end of July 1943, on the other side of the globe, saw a successful "Operation Husky" land two Allied armies on Sicily. General Montgomery and General Patton had then driven the British and U.S. forces through to the Straits of Messina. Fearing an imminent Allied crossing to the mainland, the Fascist Grand Council had ousted Mussolini on July 26—a move that allowed Churchill to insist on an immediate invasion as the next step, "best calculated to eliminate Italy from the war."

The U.S. Secretary of War, Stimson, who had just returned from London, was convinced that the British were only paying "lip tribute" to a cross-Channel assault; he reminded the President that they were pledged to Stalin to open a "real Second Front." The Soviet leader, he warned, would not be fooled by "pinprick warfare." Churchill once more prevailed on the President to agree to another summit to review the strategic options. Stalin's refusal to attend, with his increasingly sharp reminders of the Anglo-American pledge to invade France, was emphasized by the U.S. Joint Chiefs' eve-of-conference report, which stipulated that the British "must not be allowed to get out of doing Overlord"—the code name chosen for the assault on Hitler's vaunted "Festung [Fortress] Europa."

QUADRANT STRATEGY

Sailing from the Clyde on August 5, once again on the *Queen Mary*, Churchill spent the greater part of the voyage drilling his military advisers in the tactics to be followed at the Quadrant Conference, which was to take place in Quebec. His aim was to persuade the Americans of the wisdom of attacking Italy as part of his "soft underbelly" Mediterranean strategy, which now extended to the Balkans. This, and his hope of making Norway an alternative to France, disturbed the British Chiefs of Staff, who were also less than enthusiastic about the Prime Minister's insistence on bringing along newly promoted Brigadier Orde Wingate. The Prime

Minister hoped that the Chindit plan for an ambitious "Long Range Penetration" strategy in Burma might be substituted for the Anakim offensive
and paired with his pet scheme for a "Far Eastern Torch"—the amphibious
assault on Sumatra and Malaya designated "Operation Culverin."

General Alan Brooke had been warned to "expect a very difficult time."
He knew how the Prime Minister's schemes would upset the Americans,
who were determined, as General Dill had cabled from Washington, "to
carry on with preparations for re-entry into France and for a Burma campaign at the expense of the elimination of Italy." Notwithstanding Brooke's
advice, as soon as the *Queen Mary* docked at Halifax, Churchill flew off
for a forty-eight-hour "tête-à-tête" with Roosevelt at his Hyde Park
estate. If he had hopes of winning the President over before joining with
the Combined Chiefs, they were to be dashed when he found that for all
his formidable powers of persuasion and the deep "special relationship"
between them, Roosevelt stuck by the brief he had been given by his Joint
Chiefs. They had decided that a U.S. Army general and not Brooke should
be in charge of the invasion of France, although the British would be
allowed to nominate their man to Supreme Allied Command in Southeast
Asia. On only one vital issue did Churchill manage to win over Roosevelt
against his military advisers, and that was the crucial one of restoring the
British scientists to a full interchange of information on the atomic bomb
project. The U.S. Army, in charge of the by now mammoth Manhattan
Engineer District, had recommended that the secrets of the industrial
and technological processes being developed in the laboratories at Los
Alamos in New Mexico must remain an American asset.

The sharing of knowledge on how to construct the fission weapon was
to be a far-reaching concession to Britain. It was endorsed at the Quadrant
Conference, which got under way on August 14, 1943, at the Château
Frontenac, the great Gothic hotel overlooking the St. Lawrence. That the
Joint Chiefs were "determined to make their ideas prevail by all means
at their disposal" was made obvious to General Sir Alan Brooke when
Marshall insisted on setting an agreed, firm date for Overlord after rejecting the British case for invading Italy. The Americans wanted Allied
forces in the Mediterranean to be used to launch a simultaneous landing in
the South of France, to coincide with the main cross-Channel attack. For
three days the arguments raged on, with Churchill's men insisting that
their commitment to Overlord did not exclude the possibility of making
amphibious landings to capture Rome and knock Hitler's chief European
ally out of the war.

Admiral King was determined that not another warship or landing
craft was going to be sent to the Mediterranean at the expense of his mid-
Pacific offensive, and he articulated his opposition in what one British
officer termed "very undiplomatic language." Everyone appreciated that
because "Uncle Ernie" controlled over 90 percent of the available landing

craft, he would be able to dictate which amphibious assaults had priority. Not until August 17, when the new government in Rome put out its first peace feelers, did the U.S. Joint Chiefs soften their attitude toward the British strategy for occupying Italy before a million Germans crossed the Alps to make the "soft underbelly" firm. Nonetheless, their agreement directed that "available resources will be distributed and deployed with the main object of ensuring the success of Overlord."

The British in turn were nailed down to launching the Second Front in Europe before the Quadrant Conference turned to discussing the war against Japan. The British had already conceded that the Americans were running the action in the Pacific and were only concerned about limiting the diversion of shipping from the Atlantic. The victory over the U-boats that spring had seen King ordering a steady procession of U.S. Navy warships into the Pacific to join the Fifth Fleet for the November offensive against the outer perimeter of the Japanese island bases. King was also accused of hoarding the reserves of Allied landing craft. This had become such a bone of contention by August 19 that when shots rang out, the staff officers, who had been sent to wait outside the conference room, jumped up in alarm at the prospect of their Chiefs shooting out their differences. It turned out to be Admiral Mountbatten, the British Chief of Combined Operations, proving with his revolver the toughness of Pykrete—sawdust-bonded ice which its inventor claimed would make practical huge floating airfields in the Atlantic.

All the vociferous discussion in the open and closed sessions at Quadrant did not allow the Combined Chiefs of Staff to make much headway in resolving a strategy to recapture Burma and to bring China fully into the war. General Sir Claude Auchinleck, who had become the new British Army Commander in India after General Wavell was made Viceroy, was, if anything, more strongly opposed to Anakim now because of the shortage of landing craft and naval resources. Nor did Churchill's Culverin plan to seize air bases on Sumatra from which to bomb Singapore and Rangoon find favor with Americans. They saw it as another attempt by Britain to regain her old imperial possessions rather than assisting the defeat of Japan with the reopening of the strategic overland route through Burma. Chiang Kai-shek had made this the condition for committing his Nationalist Army to the war. The Prime Minister proposed as an alternative Wingate's plan for "Long Range Penetration," which the Chindit leader himself expounded brilliantly to the conference. General Arnold agreed to provide air support, and Marshall was sufficiently impressed that within six months the U.S. Army had formed its own 5307th Composite Unit to specialize in the same guerrilla tactics.

Yet if no real strategic agreement was reached on the newly designated Southeast Asia theater, the appointment of Admiral Lord Louis Mountbatten as Allied Supreme Commander at least raised the hopes that the brilliant young cousin of King George VI might have a better chance of resolving them. He had proved his flair as a naval war hero and his talent for innovative organization as Chief of Combined Operations, which laid down much of the basic planning for Overlord. Now he was going to need all his charm and ability to win American and Chinese cooperation to get the war finally moving against Japan in an area that had been plagued by a lack of resources and constant inter-Allied bickering. The Quadrant Conference specified that his main effort must be toward re-opening the Burma Road. To assist Mountbatten, General Wedemeyer was appointed his deputy. In addition, the irascible Stilwell was to retain his position as Chiang Kai-shek's nominal Chief of Staff and commander of all American forces in China.

24
Crippling Blows

While the Quadrant Conference in Quebec had deferred a final decision on specific strategic operations in Southeast Asia, there had been no dispute over the Pacific. The Combined Chiefs of Staff had endorsed Admiral Nimitz's revised plan for launching the drive against the Japanese outer defense perimeter of islands by attacking the Gilberts, which were within range of American bombers in the Ellice Islands bases, before assaulting the more heavily defended Marshalls and Carolines. In advance of the conference, General MacArthur had also submitted his post-Cartwheel strategy, entitled "Reno II," for the capture of Rabaul early in 1944, to provide a naval base for amphibious operations north against the New Guinea coast and on up to the Philippines. He counted on having the full support of the Pacific Fleet; but Admiral King had other ideas.

The conference at Quebec did not resolve the conflicts between the U.S. Army and Navy plans for a strategic advance on Japan. Significantly, while MacArthur had approval for his post-Cartwheel strategy in New Guinea, the Admiralties, and the Bismarcks, the Joint Chiefs had made no mention of his proposal to invade Mindanao. Moreover, they specified that "Rabaul is to be neutralized rather than captured," enshrining the bypassing strategy, and thereby depriving the South West Pacific Command of the naval base it needed to launch its invasion of the Philippines.

When he received the orders, MacArthur perceived them as another move by Admiral King to curtail his drive toward Manila in favor of the Navy's central Pacific thrust. His suspicions were not allayed by Marshall's equivocal assurance that no decision had yet been taken as to which stepping stone would be next on the road to Tokyo. "It appears that the next logical step for the SWPA Forces is the seizure of Mindanao. However, it may be found practicable to make this effort through the Bonins." The U.S. Army Chief indicated that a final decision would depend on the rate of progress of MacArthur's advance up the coast of New Guinea.

THE BATTLE FOR LAE AND SALAMAUA

August 1943 saw the 5th Air Force hammering hard at the Japanese bases on the New Guinea coast to prevent attempts to send in reinforcements. From their new airstrips in the Trobriands, American and Australian airmen flew "barge-hunting" patrols over the Bismarck Sea, scouring the coasts of New Guinea's Huon Peninsula and the waters off New Britain for the motorized launches that were being employed to ferry troops into Lae, Salamaua, and Finschhafen. Over 150 barges were sunk, forcing the further reduction in the strength of the garrison at Lae as more soldiers were sent overland to reinforce Salamaua. With the aid of Ultra intelligence MacArthur could follow just how well his plan to persuade the Rabaul command that this was his next target for attack was working. To provide increased protection from the air, two hundred planes had been gathered at the Japanese base of Wewak on the New Guinea coast some 300 miles north of the twin ports that guarded the Huon Peninsula. General Kenney staged a massive surprise raid by the 5th Air Force, which caught the enemy air fleet on the ground. To the Japanese, August 17, 1943, was "The Black Day" after their air strength in New Guinea had been all but wiped out. "It was a crippling blow at an opportune moment," MacArthur recorded, doubtless remembering his own painful experiences on the opening morning of the Pacific War, when his Philippine Air Force suffered the same fate. "Nothing is so helpless as an airplane on the ground," he observed.

With less than half a dozen planes left to defend the port, the main obstacle to the capture of the now weakly garrisoned Lae had been removed. The Allied assault went in on the morning of September 4, protected from marauding Japanese planes (flown in from Rabaul) by a helpful fog. The 41st U.S. Army Division and the battle-hardened veterans of El Alamein in the 9th Australian Division landed 20 miles east of Lae. Encountering no real resistance, they pushed rapidly toward the port the following morning.

The next blow in the assault was delivered by the U.S. 503rd Parachute Regiment, which jumped in to take Nadzab, some 15 miles up the Markham River. MacArthur had insisted on flying in his personal B-17, appropriately named *Bataan*, to watch the impressive spectacle of the ninety-six C-47 transport planes delivering the first big aerial assault of the Pacific War. Ignoring Kenney's concern that "some five-dollar-a-month Jap aviator might shoot a hole through you," the four-star general's only worry was that he might get airsick and "disgrace myself in front of the kids."

The Commander in Chief was not airsick and was able to supervise the drop in which "Everything went like clockwork." In two days his paratroopers had captured the airstrip at Nadzab and planes were flying off to blast Lae. On September 19, the American and Australian forces began closing the ring around the port. Three days before Salamaua was to fall, the Japanese command tried to remedy their mistake by recalling the thousands of troops who now made a forced march back to defend Lae. It was too late. Lae was taken six days later, forcing over 9,000 enemy soldiers to take the only escape route open—the arduous trek over the mountains to New Guinea's north coast.

As his offensive picked up momentum, MacArthur stepped up the pace by bringing forward the launching of the next phase of Cartwheel, the assault on the port of Finschhafen at the tip of the Huon Peninsula. On September 22, the 22nd Infantry Battalion of the 9th Australian Division came ashore. What they had anticipated would be light resistance by a few hundred defenders turned out to be a powerful counterattack by more than 5,000 Japanese. All the fighting skills of the veteran Australian troops were needed to capture the port by October 2, when reinforcements were brought in to hold it after reports were received that the entire Japanese 20th Division was on the march down the northern New Guinea coast.

The lightning speed of the Allied advance, which had brought them control of the Huon Peninsula and a jumping-off base to invade New Britain, thoroughly alarmed the Japanese command in Rabaul, at the other end of the island. Their garrison on Bougainville the last of the Solomons some 300 miles to the southeast, was all that now stood between the main Japanese base in the South Pacific and the other wing of the American advance. Imperial General Headquarters now reversed themselves once more by ordering Imamura to switch all his reserves to holding Bougainville as the final island bastion.

The Combined Fleet was directed to help, but Admiral Koga was preparing to meet the threat of the American offensive against the central Pacific perimeter of islands and had already moved the main body of the fleet forward to Eniwetok from Truk. Now he was to repeat Yamamoto's earlier strategic error by ordering a large part of his carrier-based air strength back to Rabaul. Logistics and distance ensured that they would arrive too late to prevent the initial American landings on Bougainville. When they did join the battle, many aircraft would be cut down in a fruitless sacrifice that deprived Japan of still more of its carrier-borne striking power.

The 150-mile-long fiddle-shaped island of Bougainville was the largest of the Solomons and the final rung in the strategic ladder up which Halsey's forces had been climbing to neutralize Rabaul. This time Halsey knew that there could be no bypassing and that it was going to be a tough assignment. Natural features on the jungle-clad mountain peaks, two of which were active volcanoes, favored the defenders: there were only narrow beaches on which to land the large forces that would be needed to wrest the island from an estimated 35,000 enemy troops. The Japanese had stationed the crack 6th Imperial Division (which had terrorized Nanking) on Bougainville to protect its six airfields, four at Buin on the southern coast and two more at Buka and Bonin in the north. This was ample indication that they meant to hold on. After the American occupation of nearby Vella Lavella Island, destroyers had intercepted one of the night express runs, but had lost the *Chevalier* in the scrap with Japanese destroyers escorting in twenty barges of troops.

The completion of Operation Cartwheel was set for December 1943, as Halsey and his planners searched for a plan to establish a foothold on Bougainville that would neutralize the enemy airfields without the lengthy slogging battle of attrition that would result from a direct assault on Buin or Buka. The decision was made to land on a lightly defended stretch of coast, build an airfield, and hold it. Coastwatchers' intelligence, confirmed by reconnaissance, showed that the only suitable assault beaches were in the vicinity of Empress Augusta Bay on the southern waist of the Bougainville "fiddle." The disadvantage was that the only level land around Cape Torokina was swampy and unsuitable for an airstrip. After a long debate on just how difficult it would be for the Seabees to build the airstrip there, Halsey announced abruptly: "It's Torokina. Now get on your horses!"

THE BOUGAINVILLE LANDING

"Cherryblossom" was the romantic name the admiral perversely chose for a singularly unromantic operation. He set November 1 as "L-Day." Preparations began ominously, with the 3rd Marine Corps Commander mysteriously falling to his death from the third-floor window of the Noumea officers' quarters. General Vandegrift, then en route to Washington, was urgently recalled to take control of the critical opening phase of the operation, in which the Marines would land, followed by the 37th U.S. Army Division of Major General Robert S. Beightler, whose men had seen action on New Georgia.

As part of the plan to conceal the destination of the main assault, there were to be no bombardments of Empress Augusta Bay and the planes and warships would blast away at Buin and Buka. A feint would then be made toward Shortland, while the 8th New Zealand Division would be landed simultaneously on the nearby Treasury Islands to open up an advance airstrip. In another move aimed at hurling the Japanese defenses off-balance, a battalion of the 2nd Marines would be put ashore on the northern tip of Choiseul Island for a week's extended raiding operation before withdrawing. Cherryblossom was portrayed by General Geiger—who was slated to take over from Vandegrift once the landings had been made—as a "series of short right jabs to throw the enemy off-balance and to conceal the real power of our left hook to his midriff at Empress Augusta Bay."

The "right jabs" were landed in the predawn grayness of October 27. The desired impact was achieved and the Japanese began rushing thousands of troops in to reinforce Choiseul, leaving the New Zealanders to begin building the Treasury airstrip. Four days later, Rear Admiral A. S. "Tip" Merrill took his four light cruisers and eight destroyers in to shell Buka and Bonin on the night of October 31, before dashing south around Bougainville to make a daylight bombardment of Shortland. The strikes from the *Saratoga* and the new light carrier *Princeton* simultaneously delivered a second pounding to the airstrips in the north as Marine aircraft flew up from Henderson Field to hammer Buin.

The heavy air strikes were repeated the next morning when Cherryblossom's "left hook" was delivered by the 3rd Marine Division, which spearheaded the assault against Empress Augusta Bay. The Japanese were caught completely by surprise. This was fortunate, because the beach turned out to be enfiladed by eighteen well-camouflaged pillboxes, which fully manned could have wrecked the landing, already badly disorganized in the heavy surf. The only enemy position to threaten the Marines was destroyed by Sergeant Robert A. Owens, who led a grenade-throwing charge up the beach that won him a posthumous Medal of Honor. The other positions were quickly overcome after a series of sharp engagements that cleared the beachhead for the landing craft to ferry in the main body.

Many of them might not have lived to see the dawn, and Cherryblossom could well have become a catastrophic disaster for the Americans, if the powerful Japanese counterattacking force dispatched that morning from Rabaul had reached the beachhead. More than 1,000 troops escorted by 2 heavy cruisers, 2 light cruisers, and 6 destroyers were bearing down on Empress Augusta Bay from the north during the final hours of October 28. At midnight, they were less than 50 miles away from the beach where American troops were crouching in shallow foxholes under pouring rain.

All that stood between the Americans and disaster was Admiral Merrill's Task Force 39, which was guarding the transports now standing off the Bay. Coastwatchers had raised the alarm, sending Merrill's outnumbered and outgunned task force of four light cruisers and eight destroyers racing north to intercept the three columns of Japanese warships.

Just after 1:30 A.M., when his flagship *Montpelier* picked up the enemy on her radar, Merrill turned to send his destroyers ahead to make a torpedo attack. Relying on radar to range their guns, the four U.S. cruisers opened up on the leading cruiser. At 1:50 A.M., a curtain of shells smashing onto the *Sendai* blew her into the black sky in an eruption of flames. The destruction of his cruiser and the very swiftness with which the U.S. destroyers delivered their attacks plunged Admiral Omori's force into confusion. Two of his destroyers collided, one later sank, and it was more than twenty minutes before his heavy cruisers could open fire—and then only very briefly. The concentrated radar-controlled gunnery of the weaker American force had so unnerved the Japanese that they were beaten off in a northerly retreat. Merrill's masterly night fighting in the battle had saved the Bougainville landings.

To avenge such a stinging defeat, Admiral Koga decided to send in heavy units of the Combined Fleet to cover a reinforcement convoy. Three days later, Halsey's command received alarming aerial reconnaissance reports indicating that six more heavy cruisers had joined Admiral Omori's force in Rabaul's Simpson Harbor. "This was the most desperate emergency that confronted me in my entire term as COMSOPAC," Halsey was to admit. Merrill's task force, replenishing in Purvis Bay, was now too distant and too badly outnumbered to stop such a powerful enemy force from charging in to devastate the beachhead at Empress Augusta Bay. All the U.S. Navy heavy cruisers had been recalled to the Fifth Fleet at Pearl Harbor. Halsey would be taking an enormous risk if he sent in his two carriers, *Saratoga* and *Independence*, without adequate surface escorts; but the admiral knew that he had to smash the Japanese force assembling in Rabaul.

CARRIER RAIDS ON RABAUL

"Cherryblossom's success—perhaps the success of the South Pacific war, hung on it being stopped," Halsey was to record of the decision to risk his two carriers. "I sincerely expected both air groups to be cut to pieces and both carriers stricken, if not lost (I tried not to remember my son Bill was aboard one of them), but we could not let the men at Tokorina be wiped out while we stood by and wrung our hands." His Chief of Staff could not help noticing that his admiral "looked 150 years old" as he announced, after a period of silence, "Let 'em go."

It was a bold gamble, but heavy weather on November 5 shrouded the ninety-six-plane strike that roared off Rear Admiral Frederick C. Sherman's two-carrier task force that morning. The U.S. Navy pilots braved the heavy antiaircraft fire that filled the sky with brown explosions over Simpson Harbor, plunging into the attack on the anchored warships. The one hundred carrier aircraft assembled on the island from the Combined Fleet were slow to get up to intercept and twenty-five were shot down in the first raid, which succeeded in damaging six cruisers and four destroyers for only ten American aircraft lost. Rabaul became the prime target for every B-17 in General Kenney's 5th Air Force. Believing that the U.S. carriers' task forces must be operating with formidable protection, and unwilling to risk his heavy cruisers, a cautious Koga recalled them to the safety of Truk without even ordering out a search-and-strike mission.

Nimitz had already dispatched three of his new carriers and three light cruisers west across the Pacific in response to Halsey's pleas to meet the emergency. On November 11, their aircraft joined those from the *Saratoga* and the *Independence* to make the biggest air strike ever delivered by the U.S. Navy. Its five air groups Halsey figured "ought to change the name from Rabaul to rubble." But his pilots found, much to their disappointment, that all the heavy warships had fled. So had most of the enemy's aircraft; only a destroyer and four Zeros were left to be destroyed. The massive air strikes had already produced a turning point in Japan's strategy. One of her senior naval staff officers was to admit later: "Two factors radically changed our plans. The first was the serious damage received by several Second Fleet cruisers at Rabaul by carrier air attack on November 5, 1943. . . . The second was the intensified air war in the Solomons. . . ."

If the Combined Fleet, by withdrawing its heavy force and aircraft after the Rabaul raids, was accepting its defeat in the Solomons campaign, General Hyakutake, the Japanese land commander on Bougainville, was not. Determined to avoid the "mortification" of a second Guadalcanal, he nonetheless made the mistake of delaying the launch of his main overland counterattack against the American beachhead. He was convinced that its purpose, like the Choiseul raid, was a diversion to draw off his garrisons from the airfields. Hyakutake had no idea that the Seabees were taking on the impossible task of turning a swamp into an airfield, so, before he made the first major effort to dislodge them, the Marines were given plenty of time to stake out a defensive perimeter 1 mile deep and 5 miles long. The main body of the 37th Infantry Division was landed on November 8, and by the end of those first critical weeks nearly 34,000 troops were dug into defensive positions. The Seabees toiled ahead, draining the swamps to begin the construction of the badly needed airstrip.

In the three weeks before Hyakutake's men began hacking their way overland through the dense jungle, the Japanese advance patrols were held off by the Marines who probed the terrain overlooking the beachhead to establish strong defensive positions. A platoon of the 21st Marines made a vital contribution by capturing the 400-foot ridge that dominated the rear of Empress Augusta Bay. Lieutenant Steve Cibik left an account of his patrol that gives a vivid picture of the demands of fighting in the Bougainville jungle:

> We were a veteran company, with Guadalcanal behind us, and we thought we knew jungle. But here on Bougainville we were battling a jungle such as we had never dreamed of. For nineteen days we struggled in miasmal swamps, fought vines that wrapped themselves about our necks like whips, birds that dived at us like screaming Stukas, bats whose wings whirred like falling artillery shells, and snakes and lizards and insects without name or number. For nineteen days we attacked this natural enemy with our machetes and knives, hacking our way through almost solid barricades of vegetation run riot.
>
> It rained daily from noon to dusk—fierce pounding tropical rains. If we had been lucky to hit fairly dry ground we slept in foxholes, six or eight inches deep. During the night water seeped through the earth. We invariably woke drenched.

On the nineteenth day in the jungle, Cibik's company stumbled on a ridge that rose almost invisibly concealed in the dense undergrowth. Crawling up vines for ladders, they came upon a Japanese observation position:

> I walked to the edge of the ridge and almost gasped. What a view of Bougainville! We were on a thumb of earth 500 feet high, an oasis in a sea of mist-covered jungle, the only high ground for miles around. . . . From here we could spot Jap positions and direct our artillery fire; from here, we could drive down into the valley, engaging the Japs while our main forces fought their way across the river. On the other hand, were the Japanese in control of the ridge, the tables would be turned. This ridge could be the key to success or failure in this phase of the Battle of Bougainville.

With a determination born of this knowledge, Cibik and his fifty-one-man patrol held the ridge against every enemy effort to regain it. Living on emergency K rations and with only eleven belts of machine-gun ammunition and three hand grenades apiece, they fought off the Japanese until November 23. Then their troops got safely across the river below and their company was finally relieved.

The Americans were able to establish their Bougainville beachhead long before Hyakutake's forces made their drive across the island. He was still anticipating that a U.S. force would land to capture the Buka airstrip, by now being rendered useless by constant air attacks. On November 25, a Tokyo Express of destroyers began ferrying in more troops to reinforce Buka before evacuating the now redundant aviation personnel. American air patrols spotted the five Japanese warships on their run that evening, and Captain Arleigh Burke's five destroyers raced to Cape St. George when the enemy steamed out of Buka into the narrow channel.

In the resulting action, Burke once again proved that U.S. Navy destroyer captains could outfight the Imperial Navy. Three destroyers were sent to the bottom by American torpedoes and gunfire, the others were chased almost all the way back to Rabaul. It was an ignominous end to the last Tokyo Express, and the last surface naval action that the Pacific War would see for over nine months.

Two weeks later, after the Seabees' monumental construction effort, General Geiger's hold on Bougainville was assured when the airstrip became operational. It would still take a further two weeks before the Japanese artillery on the aptly named Helzapoppin Ridge above Tokorina Point was finally dislodged, by which time General Hyakutake had fought his troops through the island's dense vegetation. He found many planes and two U.S. Army divisions well prepared to blast his soldiers back into the jungle. Although the battles would rage sporadically into the next spring, the Japanese on Bougainville had effectively been neutralized as Cartwheel came full circle by the end of 1943.

25
Cracking the
Japanese Shell

The U.S. Navy's long-awaited offensive in the central Pacific was set in motion ten days after the Marines came ashore on Bougainville. "Operation Galvanic" commenced on November 11, 1943, with the sailing of sixteen transports carrying the 2nd Marine Division from their New Hebrides staging base at Efate, accompanied by a powerful bombardment force of three battleships, five escort carriers, and five cruisers escorted by twenty-one destroyers. Its destination was a Pacific island code-named Helen. It was not until the convoy was seventy-two hours out to sea that Rear Admiral Harry W. Hill, the Southern Force Commander, announced their objective: "Just six days from today at 0830 we're going to hit Tarawa Atoll in the Gilbert Islands. We're going to land on this island at the end of the atoll; the natives call it Betio. Before we land on the place, we're going to pound it with naval shell fire and dive bombers. We're going to steamroller that place until hell wouldn't have it."

The romantic-sounding name meant little to the 18,000 Marines. They whiled away the long hot days aboard the crowded transports by sunbathing, playing in marathon poker games, honing bayonets, or just penning wistful letters home. During the seven months that they had spent recuperating in New Zealand after their ordeal on Guadalcanal, one private had devised an ingenious code to let his sweetheart in the United States know where he was going next. "My dearest Violet" meant he would be on his way to Truk, while "My darling Violet" indicated Rabaul; but he had never heard of Tarawa and had to resort to the single word "Precious," meaning that he was at sea.

A hundred miles to the north of Tarawa was Makin Atoll, the target for the northern Galvanic force; 6,700 soldiers of the 27th U.S. Army Division were aboard 6 transports escorted by 4 battleships, 3 escort carriers, and 4 cruisers. Their nine-day voyage through balmy mid-Pacific winter trade winds encouraged high spirits and made the Crossing the Line ceremonies even more boisterous than usual—a welcome break from the endless assault briefings.

There could be no real rest for anyone except Admiral Spruance, the new U.S. Fifth Fleet Commander in overall charge of Galvanic. Because the actual execution of his assault was in the hands of his tactical commanders, the victor of Midway found plenty of time to pace the decks of his flag cruiser *Indianapolis*, clad in a pair of Hawaiian shorts and acquiring a deep suntan. The landing phase of the two assaults was the responsibility of the Fifth Fleet Amphibious Commander, Admiral Turner. His transports and landing craft would be supported by the greatest carrier strike yet marshaled. It was covered by Task Force 50—comprising four of the new *Essex* Class fast carriers, five light carriers, and the venerable *Saratoga* and *Lexington*—under the command of Rear Admiral Charles Pownall, who could also count on six battleships, three heavy and five light cruisers, three antiaircraft cruisers, and twenty-one destroyers. Spruance's Fifth Fleet carrier task groups were now powerful enough to guard both Galvanic forces against any attack by the Combined Fleet, and the planes and guns were scheduled to soften up the Japanese positions on Tarawa and Makin. The two carriers that Nimitz had detached to assist Halsey's emergency blitz on Rabaul were also heading north, detouring to strike at the enemy bases on the phosphate island of Naru, some 350 miles southwest of Tarawa, before joining in the pre-landing bombardment of the atoll.

The U.S. Pacific Fleet was now moving into overwhelming numerical dominance. The crisis of the previous year, when a lack of carriers and battleships had threatened the U.S. Navy's ability to hold on to Guadalcanal, was being replaced by a new problem: how to supply and fuel the huge fleets operating over the distances of the Pacific. More than two hundred warships would be involved in Galvanic. To keep them at sea and fighting for three weeks thousands of miles from the fleet base in Pearl Harbor required a logistics and support operation on a scale never before attempted by any navy in history.

The Service Force Pacific Fleet had been created under Vice Admiral William Calhoun, who had assembled an armada of transports, repair and supply vessels, and a collection of 300-foot concrete oil barges. He had established a floating naval base at Funafuti Lagoon in the Ellice Islands. Everything that the Fifth Fleet would need to sustain its 200 ships and 20,000 men, from bandages to bombs, strawberry ice cream to spare aircraft parts, was ready and waiting. The thirteen fleet oilers, the flotilla of minesweepers and repair vessels, were only the beginning of a massive naval housekeeping operation that was to grow as the Fifth Fleet expanded. Spruance was later to pay tribute to Calhoun: "There was nothing the Fleet wanted that 'Uncle Bill' couldn't get."

The mammoth logistical support operation finally made possible an execution of the ORANGE strategy for a grand fleet sweep across the central Pacific. It was not until the fall of 1943 that prodigious feats of shipbuilding in the United States yards turned out the warships and hundreds of new Liberty and Victory freighters that would enable the fleet to move across the central Pacific. Only when the U-boats had been defeated and the tide of battle decisively turned in the Atlantic theater could the Combined Chiefs of Staff have taken the decision at the Quebec Conference to divert to Nimitz's command the shipping he required for such strategy. The Quadrant directive, which initiated the first stage of the ORANGE War Plan to punch through the outer crust of Japan's Pacific Island defense, left uncertain whether the thrust would continue through to the Philippines, to support MacArthur's intended advance on Tokyo. The U.S. Joint Chiefs had originally hoped that an eastward drive by the Chinese Nationalists would free Hong Kong or Shanghai's port facilities for use as the final base of operations. But the British reluctance to embark on a major offensive in Burma to open up the overland supply route that Chiang Kai-shek would need to support such a drive forced the American Joint planning staff after Quebec to begin considering Formosa, with Okinawa or Manila as alternative springboards from which to mount the invasion of Japan.

The CINCPAC staff at Pearl Harbor was concerned with the more immediate problems of how to break through the outer shell of the Japanese Pacific defense perimeter, while COMINCH wanted the Marshalls taken by December 1943. Nimitz was a careful strategist, who saw the need to minimize the risk of launching his untried amphibious forces against such heavily fortified enemy bases out of range of aircover. Drawing on the lessons of the Solomon campaign, the CINCPAC plan proposed making the Gilberts the first stepping stone to the more strongly defended Marshalls. The Gilberts would be just within striking distance of bombers flying from the Funafuti base in the Ellice Islands some 700 miles to the south, as well as the airstrips on Howland and Baker islands the same distance to the west. In another crucial modification of King's original directive, Admiral Spruance and General Holland Smith, the ground forces commander, had convinced COMINCH that it would take more than a division of Marines to scale the precipitous cliffs of the island of Naru. Makin Atoll which was also closer to Tarawa, was substituted as an easier subsidiary target for the final Galvanic plan.

After "Carlson's Raiders" had made their commando-type attack on Makin fifteen months before, the Japanese had strengthened the defenses on Butaritari, the largest atoll of the group. Yet its fortifications were light compared to the bastion that had been constructed at Betio, the two-mile-long musket-shaped patch of coral sand that commanded the Tarawa Atoll. British-made 8-inch artillery taken from Singapore had been incorporated into a twenty-five-gun battery that covered the approaches. Fourteen tanks had also been dug in to cover the beaches with overlapping zones of fire; they augmented a chain of over one hundred pillboxes, machine-gun posts, bunkers reinforced with concrete, and mounds of sand antiblast barriers piled up behind coconut-palm trunks: Tarawa had been made the formidable bastion in the Japanese Empire's outer defense barrier. Imperial General Headquarters' "New Operation Plan," issued in September, ordered the fortified islands of the Gilberts and Marshalls to hold up any American advance while an inner line of fortress islands was constructed from Timor, through New Guinea, and up the Caroline and Mariana islands to Iwo Jima and Japan. The 4,500 Japanese troops on Betio were exhorted by their commander, Admiral Maichi Shibasaki, to "withstand assault by a million men for a hundred years."

The Americans were counting on massive naval and air bombardment to flatten the Japanese defenses before a single Marine or soldier came ashore onto the narrow coral beaches. The amphibious assault phase of Galvanic had been planned in often stormy sessions by Admiral Turner, the Fifth Amphibious Force Commander, and General Holland Smith. "Terrible Turner's" driving pace had been an important element in turning the tide on Guadalcanal, and he was now matched with equally relentless "Howlin' Mad" Smith—the only general in the Marine Corps "who could shout louder than any admiral." They were "plain ornery" fighters, whose rough-riding military expertise was the foundation on which victory in the Navy's island-hopping campaign would be built.

Operation Galvanic marked a phase of the Pacific campaign that required the application of new amphibious warfare techniques. The "Atoll War," as it came to be known, appeared to offer tactical advantages over the difficult jungle fighting required in the Solomons. Bombardment was expected to reduce the defenses on the small islands, which could then be invaded with a concentrated force without the risk of enemy air attacks or flanking movements. The first wave of assault troops, at General Holland Smith's insistence, was to be ferried in with flotillas of amphibious vehicles called "Amphtracs"—so far used only experimentally in the Solomons and in the Torch landings in North Africa. Armed with a machine gun, these 25-foot-long craft carried twenty soldiers protected from small arms fire. Their tracks and propellers enabled them to swim in and crawl over the coral reefs that could rip the bottom out of conventional craft. The "Amphtracs" added considerably to the rising mood of confidence among the Marines under General Julian Smith and the New York National Guardsmen under Major General Ralph C. Smith, as they received last-minute briefings aboard the two transport convoys steaming toward Tarawa and Makin.

"We will not neutralize; we will not destroy; we will obliterate the defenses on Betio," promised Admiral Kingman F. Howard, the naval bombardment force commander for Taiwan. To counter the impression that there would be little left for his men to do but step ashore, General Julian Smith felt obliged to add: "Gentlemen, remember one thing. When the Marines meet the enemy at bayonet point, the only armor a Marine will have will be his khaki shirt."

On November 19, as the equatorial sun burned down, the officers and men aboard the American ships anticipated an easy victory the next day. They were not at all worried when they were sighted by three Japanese planes patrolling from Tarawa. There could be no doubt about the timing and destination of such a large invasion as the alarm flashed out to Kwajalein and Truk. The Imperial General Staff's original plan to defend the Gilberts had depended on long-range bomber strikes from Rabaul and a sortie by the Combined Fleet, but this was now unrealistic as a result of the destruction of so many aircraft during operations against the American landings on Bougainville.

Only a few hundred troops were holding Makin. However, at Tarawa Admiral Shibasaki could count on a strong garrison to beat off the impending attack. "Defend to the last man," the admiral ordered his 4,000 hand-picked Imperial Marines of the Sasebo 7th Special Naval Landing Force who, along with several hundred Korean laborers, were exhorted to "destroy the enemy at the waters' edge." His forces were concentrated on the seaward side of Betio because this appeared the most likely direction from which the Americans would land during the phase of the erratic neap tides, which were exposing nearly half a mile of concrete-like coral flats in the lagoon. Shibasaki could not know that the invaders were relying on charts from the previous century, and that Admiral Turner had decided to take a long gamble that the "dodging tides"— which could remain in or out for a whole day—would be in his favor.

STORMING TARAWA

That night, as the two forces of Operation Galvanic approached Tarawa and Makin, the restless troops were making their final preparations in the sweltering heat below decks. Disaster almost overtook the submarine *Nautilus* when she was attacked by her own forces as an enemy after she surfaced in order to ferry in a detachment of Marines who were assigned the task of capturing the nearby atoll of Abemama.

The blare of buglers sounding reveille began November 20 for the 2nd Division Marines. After tumbling out of their cramped bunk stacks, many had no time to shave; the men quickly ate their steak and egg breakfast, struggled into their heavy uniforms, and checked their weapons and kit, which included ammunition clips, grenades, two canteens of water, and K rations. The transports rang to the clatter of heavy boots as

UNCOMMON VALOR The shattering ordeal of storming Japan's fanatically defended island defense is expressed by the features of a battle-weary Marine on Peleliu.

RETURN TO THE PHILIPPINES On July 26, the President (above, with MacArthur and Leahy seated, Nimitz pointing) accepted the Philippine invasion plan. On October 22, 1944 MacArthur (below) led his forces ashore on Leyte.

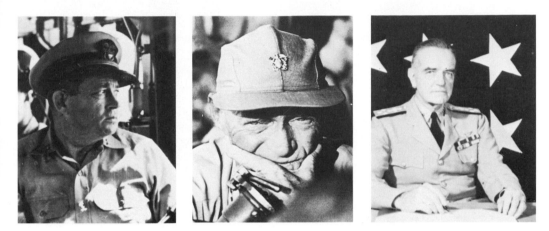

THE BATTLE OF LEYTE GULF The Third Fleet of Admiral Halsey (above right) was supreme in the three day fight which began on October 23 and which was dominated by the fast carriers of Admiral Mitscher (above center). Admiral Sprague's (above left) escort carriers halted the charge of Japanese battleships (below, the *Gambier Bay* surrounded by salvoes).

DEATH THROES OF A NAVY The hybrid battleship *Ise* attacked (above) in the closing round of the Leyte Gulf battle. Japan's merchant marine had been decimated in 1944 by U.S. submarines (below USS *Seawolf* sinking a Maru.)

the Marines struggled up through narrow hatches to assemble expectantly at their boat stations.

At 3:30 A.M. the men of the first wave, in the bargelike LSTs, began clambering aboard the Amphtracs. On the transports, assault boats and landing craft were made ready for lowering. An hour later, when the Armada reached the assembly point 5 miles north of Betio off the entrance to the reef, the minesweepers steamed through to clear a channel. They were followed by two destroyers to give close fire support to the first Amphtrac waves, which were to come ashore on the red beaches on either side of a 700-foot pier that reached out across the coral shallows.

In the dark, bosuns' pipes trilled as the water around the transports churned with circling assault craft. These were joined by the Amphtracs splashing into the water through the yawning bow doors of the LSTs. A Japanese searchlight probed tentatively, and at 4:41 A.M. a single red starshell arched into the sky over the atoll. Then the darkness closed in again for half an hour until the first gray light filtered over the eastern horizon. At 5:10 the battleship *Maryland* catapulted off her spotter plane. The Japanese took the flash of the catapult's discharge as the signal to commence firing. They were answered by the mighty broadsides of the three American battleships, five cruisers, and seven destroyers. For over half an hour the 3-mile-long patch of coral erupted in flames and explosions.

"The sun rose now in a brilliant display of red. There was only one planet and it was Mars—bright and significant," recalled Captain Carl H. Jones, the *Maryland*'s skipper. Smoke poured up from the island to mix with the mist that was lifting over the island. The Japanese batteries had not been silenced when the naval bombardment halted on schedule at 5:45 A.M. in anticipation of the arrival of the first air strike. But twenty minutes passed and the carrier planes had not arrived. The careful timing of the assault was thrown out because the transports had to up-anchor and move out of range of increasingly accurate enemy fire. When the carrier aircraft finally struck, just after six, their seven-minute attack was too short and the bombs failed to penetrate the heavily protected fortifications. The naval barrage recommenced, systematically raking the island for two and a half hours. Watching the bombardment from his position aboard the Fifth Fleet flagship, *Indianapolis*, Spruance's Chief of Staff, Captain Charles J. Moore, was impressed: "Fires were burning everywhere. The coconut trees were blasted and burned and it seemed that no living soul could be on the island . . . the troops approached the beach and it looked like the whole affair would be a walkover."

The amphibious assault, which was moving in across the 6 miles of lagoon, had fallen still further behind schedule because stiff headwinds added to the delays at the assembly point. H Hour, the deadline for the first wave to land, had to be postponed twice. It was 8:55 A.M. before the control vessel signaled the leading Amphtracs to go in. They were still fifteen minutes out from the beaches.

At this moment the bombardment was halted, allowing the Japanese to make use of a vital quarter hour to redirect their gunfire. They also shifted forces across to the lagoon shore. American Hellcat dive bombers from the carriers caused only slight interference.

"They'll go in standing up. There aren't fifty Japs left alive on that island," remarked the officer on the bridge of the *Ashland*. The U.S. Navy's first dock landing ship nosed her way into the lagoon and released her flotilla of landing craft, which made up the fourth wave. She carried amphibious tanks as well. The interior of her hull was a floating harbor for such small craft. The lagoon waters ahead were being lashed by a storm of shellfire and machine-gun bullets as the ninety-three Amphtracs bearing the first three waves, commanded by Colonel David M. Shoup, began churning their way in at 4 knots. Their advance was "like a nightmarish turtle race." Slow though the clumsy craft were, their tracks enabled them to crawl over the coral flats which began half a mile from the beach. Turner had lost his gamble with the tide, however. The landing craft carrying in the next waves of reinforcements could not approach the shore. Only the hippo-like Amphtracs were able to plow ashore, where they encountered heavy enemy fire. Disaster threatened as Japanese shells began knocking out the Amphtracs; others lost their tracks on clumps of coral. Private N. M. Baird was manning the machine gun of one, which led the assault into Red 1 Beach to the right of the pier. "We were 100 yards in now and the enemy fire was awful damn intense and getting worse. They were knocking boats out left and right. A tractor'd get hit, stop and burst into flames, with men jumping out like torches.

"The bullets were pouring at us like sheet rain." Baird's Amphtrac, hit by a shell, came to a halt. Its eleven survivors were forced to scramble the last 30 yards to shore. Like hundreds of others, they made for the only shelter available from the murderous fire, a 4-foot log wall along the high-tide line.

"Come on men," Lieutenant Colonel Herbert R. Amey, Jr., was heard to yell on Red 2 Sector: "We're going to take the beach. Those bastards can't stop us." Then, cut down by a bullet, he fell into the litter of bodies and dead fish already staining the shallows crimson. On the adjacent Red 3 Beach, Colonel Shoup battled in through chest-deep water, and used the pilings of the pier for cover. Heavy artillery and tanks were needed to knock out the Japanese pillboxes, but the landing craft carrying the tanks and guns could not get over the coral barrier. Only eleven tanks had so far managed to crawl into the shallows where they were destroyed by mortar fire as seawater stalled their motors. The wounded tank force commander dragged himself out of his turret and clung to a

CRACKING THE JAPANESE SHELL

pile of bodies. Because the radio sets succumbed to the salt water, ninety minutes of murderous confusion passed before Colonel Shoup managed to find one set still in operation and called desperately for "ALL POSSIBLE FIRE SUPPORT."

Only the destroyers *Ringgold* and *Dashiel* were available to give covering fire from the lagoon. The follow-up landing craft were still halted by the exposed reef. The surviving Amphtracs, attempting to ferry in the fourth wave, attracted so many salvos that it was impossible for them to reach shore. The hapless Marines were deposited in chest-deep water and subjected to the ordeal of a half-mile struggle to shore. They waded and swam through the shallows, which were lashed by Japanese bullets and mortars. Robert Sherrod, covering Tarawa on assignment for *Time* magazine, came in with that wave. "We had seven hundred yards to walk slowly into that machine gun fire, looming into large targets as we rose onto higher ground. I was scared as I had never been scared before." He found temporary salvation at the pier, where he crouched behind wooden piles with hundreds of others. Eventually, he reached the beach by following one of the few bulldozers that had managed to crawl in: its large metal blade made a welcome shield against the bullets, which clanged and ricocheted off into the water.

By noon on Tarawa the casualties had passed the 20 percent mark. Less than 1,500 Marines of the first assault were ashore and clinging to a few yards of beach below the log wall. At the farthest end of the Red Sector, a pair of Sherman tanks had begun to push a flanking attack into Green Beach at the butt end of the Betio Island musket. Lieutenant William D. Hawkins led his platoon of snipers in behind an Amphtrac which scaled the wall and knocked out a strategically placed machine-gun nest. Another company pushed 100 feet inland by destroying pillboxes with sticks of dynamite and flamethrowers. The naval bombardment hammered into the seaward side of the island only a few hundred yards ahead of the American positions. It prevented Shibasaki from rallying his forces for a coordinated drive to hurl the attack back into the lagoon. But the extremely precarious position of Shoup's men was apparent from his midday message: "WE NEED HELP. SITUATION BAD." It was sent from the colonel's command post set up on the sheltered side of a Japanese bunker, whose occupants were still trapped inside.

Communications problems on board the *Maryland* were still preventing General Julian Smith and Admiral Hill from forming a clear understanding of the battle. They realized—from Shoup's desperate signals and reports that more than a hundred landing craft were jamming up the lagoon—that the landings were running into serious trouble. At 1:30 P.M. they requested Admiral Turner's approval to release the reserves; their message was accompanied by the ominous report: "STILL ENCOUNTERING STRONG RESISTANCE . . . ISSUE IN DOUBT."

The message, its conclusion deliberately echoing the last signal made by the doomed Marine garrison that had defended Wake two years before, both puzzled and concerned Admiral Nimitz at Pacific Fleet Headquarters in Pearl Harbor. Aboard the battleship *Pennsylvania*, standing off Makin Atoll, tension was increasing in the 5th Amphibious Force operations room as Admiral Turner and General Smith conducted a crisis consultation with their staff before agreeing to the release of the Corps reserves. They had anticipated that the northern Galvanic assault would be exposed to the greatest risk from the Combined Fleet, but as it had turned out, the amphibious force commanders now found they were out of touch with the disaster developing 85 miles south on Tarawa.

Turner's uneasiness was increasing because the Makin landings themselves had fallen far behind schedule. The opposition on Butaritari Island was weak, but the admiral insisted that the bombardment be sustained longer than planned because he saw that Japanese batteries had managed to continue firing. The transports had approached to within a mile of the shore before the assault craft went in at 8:30 A.M. An operation that should have been a walkover also suffered from the same freak low tides as had disrupted the landing. The first Amphtracs crawled in over the coral shelf against relatively light resistance, then came the follow-up waves aboard landing craft that could not reach shore. General Ralph C. Smith's assault had to rely on Amphtrac shuttles to land his soldiers and were hampered by the inefficiency and poor combat effectiveness of the 27th Division. "Frankly they were jittery before starting and they stayed jittery," Admiral Turner later reported of the Army division's poor showing, which he put down to "the inexperience and lack of moral fiber of the officers and noncommissioned officers." The assault at Makin Atoll was to grind on at a much slower pace than anticipated, but its problems paled in comparison to the disaster looming over Tarawa. By the end of the afternoon, Turner was able to radio to Spruance: "ADVANCING. NO OPPOSITION."

The very opposite was true at Tarawa as the bloody landings pressed on through the afternoon. The tide refused to rise and the incoming battalions were still fighting their way in through the shallows encountering murderous fire. The narrow island had been subjected to heavy strafing and bombing from carrier planes until dusk, when an appropriately blood-red sun sank over a lagoon choked with corpses and the smoking wreckage of tanks and Amphtracs. "At no time during the day have tide conditions permitted any boats to land on the beach," Admiral Hill signaled to the 5th Amphibious Force Commander. "No artillery or supplies yet landed." He reported casualties of almost 1,500, nearly one third of the estimated 5,000 Marines who were then ashore.

Admiral Turner's command ship was standing off Makin that evening when he was given the grim assessment that the fate of the Tarawa operation hung in the balance. His concern sharply increased a few minutes later when news came in that the light carrier *Independence* had been forced to retire under tow after being badly damaged during a raid at sunset by sixteen Japanese bombers.

At dusk on Betio the Japanese fire slackened enough for the first U.S. landing craft to approach the end of the pier and put ashore the first artillery pieces and desperately needed plasma and medical supplies for the wounded awaiting evacuation from the beach. Throughout the night the medical teams worked furiously to save lives, while the Marines dug into shallow foxholes along the 1,000 yards of beach they had managed to take by sunset. Admiral Shibasaki intended to make use of the dark to infiltrate and encircle the American positions, but shattered communications made a coordinated counterattack impractical. Suicide parties instead were sent out to take up sniping positions on the pier and in the wrecked craft out on the reef.

At dawn the next morning, when the landing craft began ferrying in the reserve combat teams, the tide was still too low to float the craft over the reef. The ramps came down and disgorged the men into the coral shallows. The enemy snipers in the litter of wrecked craft added their bullets to the fire from the pillboxes ashore. During the five hours of landings on the second day, the Marine casualties reached a higher rate than that sustained on the first morning. Ashore, Colonel Shoup still had not enough artillery or tanks to puncture the enemy defenses. He was running dangerously low on water, rations, medical supplies, and ammunition, while Japanese strongpoints kept firing and resisting the rain of bombs and naval shells. Progress inland was slight. Blazing wreckage continued to pile up in the shallows and corpses yielded a sickly stench under the fiery sun.

The capricious tide that had played such havoc with the American landings finally rose around noon. Five destroyers closed the shore, plastering the enemy pillboxes and batteries with accurate fire just as the first landing craft scraped over the outer reef of coral heads. Now troops could storm the beach throughout the afternoon. With the support of more tanks and artillery, Shoup's forces advanced across the narrow waist of the island and cut the Japanese defense in two. "CASUALTIES MANY. PERCENTAGE DEAD NOT KNOWN. COMBAT EFFICIENCY: WE ARE WINNING!" the colonel optimistically radioed by the end of the afternoon, as his tanks began driving against the pillboxes on either flank.

Heavy fire continued from Japanese positions through the night. Cut off in his massive command bunker on the center of Betio, Admiral Shibasaki the next morning radioed a final message: "OUR WEAPONS HAVE BEEN DESTROYED AND FROM NOW ON EVERYONE IS ATTEMPTING A FINAL CHARGE. MAY JAPAN EXIST FOR TEN THOUSAND YEARS." One by one his remaining pillboxes were pounded into silence by tanks, TNT charges, and flamethrowers. Shibasaki was to be incinerated along with three hundred men when Marine bulldozers sealed the entrances to the two-story blockhouse with sand, then gasoline was pumped down the ventilation shaft and ignited by a grenade. Some Japanese strongpoints held out until the following afternoon, when Admiral Hill transmitted the signal that Betio was "SECURED."

In the seventy-five hours and forty-five minutes that it took to secure Betio, "the bitterest fighting in the history of the Marine Corps" was encountered, according to official records. The battle had transformed the narrow patch of coral sand into a savage landscape of broken palms, bomb craters, and the charred ruins of blockhouses. Dazed chaplains were directing bulldozers in the gruesome work of digging mass graves. Only a single Japanese officer, 16 enlisted men, and 129 Korean laborers were captured alive. Days later, thirst-crazed enemy soldiers were still emerging from the rubble to make fanatical suicide attacks. It had taken over 18,000 American Marines not the one day planned but three days to secure Betio at a cost of 1,300 dead.

"MAKIN TAKEN"

Operation Galvanic was not an auspicious start to the Navy's Pacific drive against Japan. Capturing even weakly defended Makin had taken the 27th Army Division nearly the same amount of time. When General Ralph Smith signaled at 10:30 A.M. on the morning of November 23, 1943, "MAKIN TAKEN," his losses of 64 killed and 150 wounded were light compared to the slaughter on Tarawa, but his assault forces had overwhelmingly outnumbered the defenders' soldiers.

On November 24, the number of casualties for the Makin assault escalated when the Japanese submarine I-75 torpedoed the *Lipscombe Bay*. The escort carrier disintegrated in a sheet of flame and took down with her more than six hundred crewmen. During the succeeding days the American forces, aided by natives, fanned out along the necklace of adjoining islets at Tarawa and Makin to mop up the isolated Japanese outposts, and the landing of the Marine raiding party from the damaged *Nautilus* brought an easy victory at Abemama Atoll. The overall cost of Galvanic had been alarmingly high—and not just in lives and equipment. Even the hard-bitten General Holland Smith was visibly shocked when he arrived to inspect the 291 acres of wrecked fortifications. "I don't see how they ever took Tarawa. It's the most completely defended island I ever saw," he observed, deeply moved at the condition of the Marines. "I passed boys who had lived yesterday a thousand times and looked older than their fathers. Dirty, unshaven, with gaunt almost sightless eyes, they had survived the ordeal, but it had chilled their souls. They found it hard to believe they were actually alive. There were no smiles on these ancient youthful faces; only passive relief among the dead." Three days after the bloody ordeal was over, Nimitz himself insisted on flying in, and found the slaughter and devastation comparable to the Battle of Ypres, the campaign that raged for weeks in World War I.

The American public was also to be shocked at the heavy cost of capturing this single Japanese-held island after reports leaked out in the press despite the wartime censorship. The appalling casualty rates worried Admiral Turner. Within the week he had carefully reviewed the operation in a report that was flown to Nimitz at Pearl Harbor. "Lessons Learned at Tarawa" concluded that the tides had been an important factor in bringing about the near disaster of the Galvanic assaults on both atolls. This was attributed to the failure of reconnaissance and the need for more accurate and sustained bombardment before similar landings could be sent in against other heavily fortified Japanese atolls such as Kwajalein in the Marshalls. In response to the report and the terrible impressions he gathered during his visit to Betio, Nimitz had replicas of the Japanese pillboxes and sand-covered bunkers built on an outlying Hawaiian island. After bombardment tests, it was found that the most effective way of destroying such fortifications was not by close-range shelling with flat trajectory, but by distant, plunging salvos. Better-waterproofed radios were devised, and the need was recognized for faster organization of the assault phases as well as more amphibious craft and tank landing ships. Galvanic was to teach the Americans a costly but nonetheless vital lesson on how to win the "Atoll War."

26
Common Fronts

On November 23, 1943, the day the U.S. Navy secured its first island stepping stone on the path to Tokyo, half a world away, the British, American, and Chinese war leaders were gathering at the palatial Mena House Hotel near Cairo. The Sextant Conference marked the fourth time that year that the President, Prime Minister, and their Combined Chiefs of Staff had met to resolve the strategic differences that were again threatening to disrupt the higher command of the war. A month earlier, an unprecedented meeting of all their foreign ministers in Moscow had finally cleared the way to holding a full Allied summit with the Russians at Tehran.

The President, who had been trying to arrange such a meeting for over a year, was particularly encouraged to hear from his Secretary of State, Cordell Hull, that Stalin had let it be known he was considering joining the war against Japan. Churchill, however, was deeply apprehensive that the Soviet leader was seeking a trade-off to obtain American backing for the launching of the Second Front and to give the Red Army a free hand in eastern Europe and the Balkans. The Prime Minister insisted on a preliminary Anglo-American discussion of what he saw as "very grave defects" in their strategic plans for 1944.

Churchill had arrived at Cairo suffering from a heavy cold that was later to develop into pneumonia. His ill humor was increased considerably when he found that the President had invited Chiang Kai-shek to participate for the first time as an equal partner in the Cairo talks. Roosevelt intended both to spur the Nationalist leader to fight the Japanese and to put pressure on Britain finally to launch a major offensive in Burma. The British leaders had quite a different purpose. Churchill was hoping to use the meetings to make the Americans sufficiently "Mediterranean-minded" to agree to his strategic plan for the theater. He wanted an invasion of the Balkans to preempt the Russians and the commitment of more Allied forces to the Italian campaign. This was in danger of becoming a grueling slogging match after the Germans had marched down to occupy Rome when the government of Marshal Badoglio had formally surrendered on September 3. A week later the Panzers had all but hurled the U.S. Army back into the sea when it landed at Salerno.

The British came prepared to argue for the postponement of the agreed invasion of France, although they knew this could lead to serious difficulties with the Americans and the possibility of an open breach with the Russians. Churchill found the Cairo meetings locked in the intractable issues of China, due to the President's insistence on giving priority to a theater in which operations were, the Prime Minister maintained, "lengthy, complicated and minor." "All hope of persuading Chiang and his wife to go and see the Pyramids and enjoy themselves till we returned from Tehran fell to the ground," he acidly recorded, "with the result that Chinese business occupied the first instead of the last place at Cairo."

Churchill's view of China was quintessentially Victorian, British, and imperialistic. He failed to appreciate that Roosevelt's effort to establish Chiang Kai-shek as one of the "Big Four" followed the United States' traditional policy and insistence that China must be encouraged and supported to become a world power. As a result, the British were pressed by both Chiang Kai-shek and Roosevelt to reopen the overland supply route in Burma rather than launch a series of major Allied amphibious offensives to drive the Japanese out of Malaya and the Dutch East Indies. The American rationale had been clearly set out in a memorandum which General Stilwell had circulated to the Joint Chiefs of Staff before the conference. In it he asked: "Why should American boys die to recreate the colonial empires of the British and their Dutch and French satellites?" It revived the old U.S. hostility toward Britain's supposed imperial ambitions, and the Joint Chiefs gave weight to it in their decision that Allied operations must, if possible, be restricted to Burma, because "by concentrating our Asiatic efforts and operations in and from China, we keep to a minimum our involvement in colonial imperialism."

The American military leaders therefore gave their vigorous support to the Burma offensive outlined in the first plenary session at Cairo by Lord Louis Mountbatten. The Supreme Allied Commander of Southeast Asia had transformed the earlier Anakim plans into a campaign to open up the overland route in upper Burma in 1944. Stilwell's three divisions would drive east from Ledo, while the Nationalist armies advanced down west from Chungking and the British forces relaunched their thrust down the Arakan coast. The offensive through the jungles of upper Burma, aptly code-named "Tarzan," would be supported by "Operation Buccaneer," whose purpose would be to sever the Japanese line to Rangoon by amphibious landings on the Andaman Islands off Burma's south coast. But Chiang Kai-shek's repeated vacillation over just when and where he would be able to commit his armies drove his Anglo-American allies "absolutely mad." Before he would agree to participate, he laid down extensive conditions, demanding more aircraft and Hump supplies as well as seeking to dictate the scale of British operations in Burma. Churchill and his Chiefs of Staff adamantly refused to be pinned down to an offensive to which they were still fundamentally opposed. They were unaware that the President had already privately promised the Generalissimo that Operation Buccaneer would go ahead.

The American military leadership became exasperated with their principal Ally after the first afternoon session. General Alan Brooke tried to shift the strategy with his suggestion that the Buccaneer amphibious forces could be better used in making landings in the eastern Mediterranean. Across the table this was taken as an attempt to widen the scope of operations in a theater in which the Joint Chiefs were only reluctantly fighting at all and another attempt by the British to wriggle out from their commitment to Overlord. A major argument broke out. "Brooke got nasty and King got good and sore," Stilwell's partisan account noted, "everyone throwing his cards on the table face up." The dispute came to a head the next day when Churchill proposed his pet scheme for an invasion of Rhodes and a Balkan landing for "keeping the Mediterranean ablaze." Marshall exploded in anger: "God forbid I should try to dictate, but not one American soldier is going to die on that beach." The violence of the normally mild U.S. Army Chief's reaction visibly stunned the Prime Minister. Realizing the strength of American opposition, he tactfully gave up his attempt to push through his Mediterranean strategy.

After three days of exhausting debate, the Allied grand strategy was still undecided. Chiang Kai-shek left by air for Chungking. China had been at last admitted to big power status and Chiang—the beneficiary of the first part of the Sextant talks—had been promised the return of Japanese-conquered territory in the Cairo Declaration. He had obtained the President's assurance of more supplies as well as a unilateral promise of a major Burma offensive in 1944.

TEHRAN AND THE RUSSIANS

The deep rift in Anglo-American war plans had been no more than papered over by November 27, when the two teams embarked in the fleet of bombers that were to take them on the arduous flight to the Eureka Summit with the Russians. The momentous first meeting with the Soviet leader took place in the heavily guarded British and Soviet legations which adjoined one another in Tehran, the Persian capital. To avoid the risk of sabotage on the long drive from the American legation, and to get acquainted with Stalin, Roosevelt accepted the offer of taking up residence in the Russian compound. Churchill's fears that his old friend was putting himself too much in the Russian leader's pocket increased when he found that the President was deliberately avoiding him at meetings and formal dinners.

Despite the massive circular oak table which had been built so that no one group should be given apparent precedence, the British soon found that they were indeed in a minority of one at the first plenipotentiary session. Roosevelt—assuming the presiding role as the youngest leader present —allowed Churchill to open with another of his masterful oratorical reviews of global strategy, in which he laid heavy emphasis on the Mediterranean. "Now let us get down to business," Stalin brusquely announced through his interpreter. The speed and incisiveness with which the Russian leader proceeded to do so was in sharp contrast to his resplendent appearance in a mustard drab uniform heavy with gold braid. To Marshall's immense satisfaction, the Soviet leader was emphatically in favor of giving Overlord priority over all Allied plans for the coming year. Rejecting again Churchill's advocacy of the "soft underbelly" Mediterranean strategy, he insisted that the Italian campaign had to be limited and rejected any Balkan adventure, which pleased the U.S. Joint Chiefs but roused the deepest suspicions of the Prime Minister.

Stalin's skill in exploiting Anglo-American differences allowed the Russians to dominate the Tehran Conference. He had recognized that the U.S. delegation, and particularly the President, were not only anxious to accommodate their prickly ally but would gladly exploit the opportunity to end the British efforts to launch a peripheral Mediterranean offensive. Only over the relative insignificance of China did the Russian leader support Churchill. Effusively praising the U.S. Navy's recent success in the Pacific, Stalin promised that once Germany was defeated, he would join the war against Japan. "Then by our common front we shall win," he confidently predicted, and by doing so successfully deflated Chiang Kai-shek's importance to the alliance.

On November 30, Stalin's persistent demands finally forced Churchill to make an irrevocable commitment to launch the Overlord invasion of France by May 1944. At that night's dinner, ostensibly to celebrate the British leader's sixty-ninth birthday, the vodka toasts continued into the small hours. The conviviality evaporated the next day at the political sessions, at which the President was unable, despite his best efforts, to extract any future commitments from the Soviet leader on the future of eastern Europe or the United Nations. As he flew back to resume the Cairo talks, Churchill was in a black depression, convinced of the need to "do something with these bloody Russians."

STRATEGIC REVERSAL AT CAIRO

The Prime Minister's pessimism appeared only too well founded when the Anglo-American staff reopened their Cairo talks to work out implications of the far-reaching strategic decisions taken at Tehran. The British Chief of Staffs' earlier bid to get the Buccaneer operation called off in favor of extending the Mediterranean offensive to the Aegean had finally been killed by Stalin. As an alternative strategy, they reluctantly agreed to the "Anvil" landings in southern France in addition to Overlord, but argued that the extra landing craft this would demand ruled out a major amphibious operation in the Far East. Churchill could now seize upon this contention to persuade the President that Stalin's commitment to join the war had reduced the importance of involving the Chinese actively against Japan, and so had removed the need for a major Burma campaign. Marshall, on the other hand, countered with the wider implications. "If Buccaneer was canceled, then the Generalissimo would not allow the Chinese forces to take part in Tarzan. There would be no campaign in Upper Burma and this would have its repercussions in the Pacific," he warned, having obtained radio confirmation from Mountbatten in New Delhi that this would indeed be Chungking's reaction. Still, the British argued, the allocation of forces required by Buccaneer would endanger the success of the invasion of France.

"I've been as stubborn as a mule for four days, but we can't get anywhere," the President told a disconsolate General Stilwell on the evening of December 5, when he explained that he could not let the conference end in a deadlock. For the first and only time during the war, Roosevelt decisively overruled his Chief of Staff. The President's abrupt "Buccaneer is off" announcement, which delighted the British, was seen as another "Limey plot" by "Vinegar Joe." His thrust into Burma by the three Chinese divisions he had been training in India was already crossing the Chindwin to begin the campaign to recapture Myitkyina and reopen the overland route to China. Stilwell was determined to press on with the offensive, although he realized that Roosevelt's reneging on his earlier promise to Chiang Kai-shek would mean that he could now expect no assistance from the Nationalist Army.

The reaction from Chungking was predictable. Chiang had been provided with the excuse he wanted to avoid reopening the major land conflict with the Japanese. This suited his long-term intentions of continuing the unofficial truce with the Imperial forces occupying China's eastern provinces, because as long as his Nationalist Army was avoiding the main struggle, it could build up its strength with American equipment for the day when Chiang had to settle old scores by moving to suppress Mao Tsetung's Communist forces, entrenched in the hills of Yenan. His corrupt generals and bureaucrats could also be kept content as they grew rich from the black market. Most of the profits came from diverted Lend-Lease supplies being flown in over The Hump at the cost of so many lives and transport planes that the route was now being referred to by its regular pilots as the "Aluminum Trail."

The Nationalist regime had little inclination to take on the Japanese since the corruption and astronomic inflation were destroying what remained of China's fragile economy. Chiang astutely used the President's about-face as an excuse to demand a billion-dollar loan—the price that America now had to pay to keep him in the war. He also insisted that Lend-Lease supplies be increased to 10,000 tons a month, and still more aircraft be sent to General Chennault, whose 14th Air Force was keeping up a token fight against the Japanese.

Chiang Kai-shek had boasted after the Cairo Summit that there was nothing the President would refuse him. However, he did not know that China's transient big power status had already been compromised by the secret agreement made by America and Britain with Stalin at Tehran. Roosevelt took a tougher line after Treasury Secretary Morgenthau flatly refused to propose the new billion-dollar loan to Congress because the Chungking regime was rapidly exhausting its capital of goodwill.

Although the Tehran Summit had finally resolved the major strategic debate between the Allies over which route to take to Berlin, the Combined Chiefs of Staff were still unable to decide which road they were going to take to Tokyo. After the U.S. Navy had taken the Gilberts in November, the Joint Chiefs' planners had reported "operations in the Central Pacific promise a more rapid advance to Japan." With the support of General Arnold, who wanted bases for his strategic bombers within range of Tokyo, King persuaded Marshall to agree to commit the weight of American forces behind his offensive. But at the same time it was politically impossible to abandon MacArthur's drive up through the southwest Pacific toward the Philippines. This resulted in the decision to continue with both offensives and a directive that "The advance along the New Guinea–Netherlands–East Indies–Philippines axis will proceed concurrently with operations for the recapture of the Mandated Islands. A strategic bombing force will be established in Guam, Tinian and Saipan for the strategic bombing of Japan proper."

The Army planners were now putting great store by their new B-29. The four engined "Superfortress" bombers, with 141-foot wingspan and 2,200-horsepower engines, could deliver 4 tons of bombs over a range of 3,500 miles. The B-29 had been plagued with technical problems when first introduced the previous year. Despite the setbacks, General Arnold saw great strategic possibilities for the bomber, which was so powerfully armed that it could defend itself from fighters. The Superfortress, he promised, might save the United States from having to make an extremely costly invasion of the enemy's home islands. The bombing campaign against Japan was to be staged from India and from specially built forward airstrips north of Chungking, until the U.S. Navy campaign had advanced to the Marianas and secured closer bases for the aerial assault on Tokyo. Such was the Allied confidence in the effectiveness of strategic bombing that the Sextant directive concluded: "Invasion of the principle Japanese islands may not be necessary and the defeat of Japan may be accomplished by sea and air blockade and intensive bombardment from progressive advanced bases."

Ardent convert to the potential of airpower though General Mac-Arthur had become as a result of the efforts of General Kenney's 5th Air Force in the advance through New Guinea, he had yet to be convinced that bombing would make an invasion of Japan unnecessary. Retaking the Philippines was an essential part of his "Reno III" strategy and his personal crusade. However, the Joint Chiefs had specifically withheld endorsement of it. MacArthur's frustration was rising when General Sutherland reported back from Cairo that the Joint Chiefs appeared to be favoring that the more direct route to Tokyo be opened up by the Navy's advance through the central Pacific to establish a base on Formosa or even the Chinese mainland.

To reassure his difficult Supreme Commander Southwest Pacific, General Marshall decided to make the arduous flight home around the world, stopping off at Brisbane. General MacArthur's first reaction was that he should avoid a "somewhat embarrassing" confrontation by absenting himself to lead the scheduled landing of Allied troops on Arawe, which was to begin the drive against Rabaul on New Britain. Nonetheless, he decided to take the opportunity of imposing his view of Pacific strategy on Marshall, whom he found to his surprise both understanding and insistent that the Joint Chiefs had not taken any final decision on which route to take to Tokyo. MacArthur was therefore encouraged to hear the President's radio broadcast on Christmas Eve, promising that the Army Chief of Staff's recent meeting in Australia "will spell plenty of bad news for the Japs in the not too distant future."

NEW BRITAIN AND NEW GUINEA

The New Britain and New Guinea promise was fulfilled two days later, on December 26, when "Operation Dexterity" began. The transports carrying the 1st Marine Division crossed the Dampier Strait to anchor off Cape Gloucester. Landing craft carrying the veterans of Guadalcanal churned ashore in a two-pronged assault to capture the airfield on the westernmost tip of New Britain. Their Marine commander, General William H. Hubertus, had risked MacArthur's wrath at the eleventh hour by insisting on replanning the assault to eliminate a paratroop drop. It was a change in the plan that saved the whole operation as once again the Japanese defense capability had been underestimated. The American P-38 fighters of the supporting 5th Air Force beat off the enemy planes that swarmed in from Rabaul 300 miles to the east on the other end of the island, but the Marines found that what were marked as "Damp Flats" on their maps were actually "damp up to your neck." Fighting for three days through deep swamps in which men were actually killed by sodden branches falling from rotting trees, the Marines had a tough battle to capture the airstrip. Another three weeks of hand-to-hand combat were needed to clear more than 10,000 enemy troops from the thick jungle where 16 inches of rain fell in a single day. Conditions in the "green hell" of New Britain proved infinitely more severe than any encountered in the Solomons. Yet they continued to battle their way to victory with less than three hundred dead in what was to prove the last jungle campaign fought by a Marine division in World War II. In a tribute to the endurance of the veterans, of whom their historian wrote: "Nothing was ever too bad for the 1st Marine Division."

The Cape Gloucester base on the tip of New Britain effectively bottled up the 135,000 Japanese troops at Rabaul. The dense jungle-swathed mountain ridges of the interior were impassable; they could not get out by sea because the American fighters from New Gloucester dominated the air. While the Marines were going ashore in New Britain, across on the New Guinea side of the 100-mile Vitiaz Strait, General Vasey's 7th Australian Division was already hacking its way from Lae up the jungle-choked valleys of the Finisterre Range. Their aim was to break through to the north coast of the Huon Peninsula and cut off the Japanese troops who had escaped over that punishing route when the port was seized the previous September.

The arduous battle along the ravines and precipitous Finisterre ridges developed into a repetition of the struggle they had waged before, along the Owen Stanleys. For two weeks the Australian soldiers waged bloody hand-to-hand combat to win control of the 6,000-foot pass that snaked its way over what they aptly named "Shaggy Peak."

The Australians were still battling over the Finisterre peaks when MacArthur put into operation the next stage of his plan to prevent the Japanese troops on the Huon Peninsula from retreating north toward Madang to reinforce General Hatazo Adachi's 10,000-strong garrison. On January 2, 1944, two battalions of the U.S. Army's 32nd Division were landed near the port of Saidor to act as a roadblock. Adachi was a resourceful commander, who had no intention of seeing a large part of his army trapped between the American anvil and the advancing Australian hammer. Taking a submarine to come ashore behind the Japanese held line at Sio, he directed the final stages of the retreat over the Finisterre passes and orga-

nized the escape of 14,000 soldiers inland along the coastal jungle. Thousands more moved out by barge just before the Allied pincer snapped shut,
but a third of the Japanese in the jungle would die of hunger and disease
during the 100-mile trek.

Aided by captured enemy code books, which enabled his radio intelligence team to piece together General Adachi's intentions, MacArthur
planned to rapidly roll up the Japanese front along the north New Guinea
coast by making widely separated amphibious landings to seize weak garrisons. This would isolate and neutralize those bases, like Madang, that the
enemy was concentrating on holding. Admiral Nimitz was exploiting this
same intelligence advantage as he planned the next stage of the Navy's
campaign in the central Pacific.

ASSAULT ON THE MARSHALLS

"Well, gentlemen, our next objective will be Kwajalein," Nimitz announced to the conference he had called in Pearl Harbor on December 14
to put the finishing touches to Operation Flintlock, the plan for assaulting the principal Japanese positions in the Marshall Islands. The senior
commanders of the Fifth Fleet were visibly upset. After the horrors of
Tarawa, it had been decided to capture the weakly defended outer atolls
before assaulting the main bases at Kwajalein and Eniwetok. Then
COMINCH radio intelligence had revealed that this was precisely what
the Japanese were anticipating. Troops were being drawn from the inner
islands to reinforce the garrisons on Wotje and Maloelap. These were now
slated to be attacked by bombers from the American airstrips on Makin
and Tarawa, while the assault struck right to the heart of the Marshalls
with landings on Roi-Namur and Kwajalein. The capture of these islands
at opposite corners of the 50-mile-wide triangular Kwajalein atoll chain
that enclosed the world's biggest lagoon would be followed up immediately with an assault on Eniwetok.

The CINCPAC Flintlock plan to leapfrog the eastern Marshalls won
Admiral King's blessing at a conference held in San Francisco on January
3, 1944, at which he also urged Nimitz to press on with the advance to
the Marianas. This in turn met the Joint Chiefs' need to obtain bases
within Superfortress bombing range of Tokyo and to cut off the air and
sea supply routes to the Carolines. It rendered unnecessary the capture of
Truk, which had long been boasted of as the Imperial Navy's "Gibraltar
of the Pacific." Admiral Halsey, who was at the meeting, got approval to
bypass the heavily defended base of Kavieng in New Ireland and complete
his Solomons campaign to neutralize Rabaul by capturing bases in the undefended Green Islands off Bougainville. The strategy of bypassing the
enemy strongpoints relied heavily on the Fifth Fleet's rapidly increasing

carrier force, which could make wide-ranging strikes to neutralize the Japanese bases that were cut off.

These Navy decisions exacerbated the argument between the Pacific and the Southwest Pacific commands over which should control the final offensive against Japan. The Joint Chiefs' directive to Nimitz to make a priority of neutralizing Truk and bypassing Kavieng was interpreted by MacArthur as a downgrading of his campaign. He wanted to take Rabaul as a base from which the Fifth Fleet could operate in support of his intended assault on the Philippines. Once more he reacted with bitter criticism of the "Navy Cabal" for what he saw as its plot to prevent him taking control of the Pacific War. "These frontal attacks by the Navy, as at Tarawa, are tragic and unnecessary massacres of American lives," MacArthur told General Osborn, the Secretary of War's emissary, whom he charged with presenting his case to the President. "The Navy fails to understand the strategy of the Pacific," he insisted, promising that if he was given overall command of the war against Japan it could be over in little more than a year.

MacArthur's argument met with a stony reception from the Joint Chiefs of Staff, who were not yet prepared to commit themselves to a single road to Tokyo. But the powerful advocacy of Generals Kenney and Sutherland for a single advance up through the Philippines, which they made at the conference Nimitz had called at Pearl Harbor on January 27, appeared to persuade CINCPAC. Studies by his staff had already indicated that the planned attacks on the Marianas to take heavily defended Guam, Tinian, and Saipan might prove even bloodier operations than Tarawa. After the Seventh Fleet's commander, Admiral Kinkaid, confirmed the general naval opinion that "any talk of the Marianas leaves me cold," Nimitz agreed to support efforts to revise the Joint Chiefs' directive and MacArthur's call for a single line of advance strategy.

"If you come with me, I'll make you a greater man than Nelson ever dreamed of being!" the Southwest Pacific Commander in Chief enthusiastically promised Halsey, confident that his scheme would be accepted. MacArthur believed he was going to be assigned "a big piece of the fleet." However, the admiral, who had just returned from Washington, knew that King would never agree to relinquish control of his carrier task forces. He replied that he was "flattered, but in no position to commit myself." Halsey's judgment was right. When the proposal to bypass the Marianas and concentrate on the Philippine strategy reached Washington, it received the vehement opposition of Admiral King, who termed it "absurd." He was supported by General Arnold, who wanted the islands taken as a main base from which his B-29 bombers could blitz Japan.

While the battle of words was raging in Washington over the Pacific strategy, Operation Flintlock proceeded. After two postponements, D-Day had been finally set for the last day of January 1944. Full account had been taken of the lessons of Tarawa, and two target islands on either side of the Kwajalein lagoon were blasted by battleships for three days while the land-based bombers from Tarawa and Makin were knocking out the air-strips on Jaluit and Mili. Wotje and Maloelap were raided by two of Spruance's four carrier task groups, while the others concentrated their strikes on Kwajalein.

Admiral Kelly Turner was again in overall command of amphibious operations. Tactical control of the Kwajalein Southern Force was under Major General Charles H. Corlett's 7th Infantry Division, the veterans of the Attu landing. Rear-Admiral Richard L. Conolly commanded the Northern Force of the newly formed 4th Marine Division, which was as-signed the task of taking the twin islets of Roi-Namur on the other corner of the 50-mile lagoon. Admiral Hill was in charge of the assault on Majuro Atoll, which was expected to be speedily accomplished by one battalion of the Army 27th Division. Then transports carrying two Marine bat-talions and regiment corps reserves were to steam on to Eniwetok, once Kwajalein had been secured.

Admiral Spruance was in overall tactical command of the Fifth Fleet and one of the most extensive naval operations ever mounted. With 375 ships at his disposal, 700 carrier-based and 475 land-based aircraft, his mis-sion was to get the 53,000 assault troops ashore on the three islands, each separated by over 300 miles of open Pacific. In addition to its role of neutralizing the outlying enemy islands, Admiral Mitscher's Task Force 58 (consisting of twelve carriers, eight fast battleships, six cruisers, and thirty-six destroyers) had to be ready to meet and destroy the Japanese main fleet should it venture out from its base at Truk. It was a mighty armada that gathered in Pearl Harbor before setting out on January 22, 1944, as sailors joked that it was possible to walk across an anchorage paved with steel.

The "Big Blue Fleet" nonetheless made its way successfully across the Pacific to carry out the complex objectives of Operation Flintlock's pre-cisely timed schedule. Carrier- and land-based bombers destroyed every Japanese plane in the Marshalls, and the landings proceeded with a clock-work precision that was a tribute to the detailed planning effort.

At 9:50 A.M. on January 31, Admiral Hill signaled that the undefended Majuro Atoll was captured. After a three-day air and sea bombardment, Kwajalein Island some 230 miles to the northwest that morning "looked as if it had been picked up to 20,000 feet and then dropped." Although nearly 5,000 of the defenders had somehow managed to survive the most concentrated pounding of the entire atoll war, the American carrier strikes at H Hour left them too dislocated to offer any real resistance to the waves of Amphtracs that brought in the 4th Marines on their first assault under fire. The overwhelming weight of the assault was not enough to force a surrender from the fanatical Japanese; four days of fierce skirmishing passed before the hub of the Empire's defenses in the Marshalls had finally fallen.

Across the lagoon, the defenders of Roi and Namur had proved less resilient to the battering they had received from Admiral Conolly's warships on the day before the assault. Thanks to "Close-in" Conolly, as he thenceforth became known, the U.S. infantrymen overran the two islands and the narrow causeway that joined them in little more than forty-eight hours. Mopping-up operations began along the ninety-seven islets that comprised the world's largest atoll. Major General "Howlin' Mad" Smith positively showered praise on the Navy, whose bombardment had been so effective that the Americans had lost just 400 men in subduing a Japanese garrison of over 8,000. Admiral Turner was to remark after the war, "Maybe we had too many men and too many ships for the job, but I prefer to do things that way. It saved us a lot of lives."

The quick success of the first stages of Operation Flintlock made it possible for Spruance to accept Nimitz's suggestion to put the second stage into effect without bringing the Fifth Fleet back to Pearl Harbor. They now had the advantage of captured up-to-date charts of all the Japanese bases. On February 14, 1944, Admiral Turner and his commanders assembled aboard the *Rocky Mount*, the new amphibious force headquarters ship, to make the final plans for the assault on Eniwetok 360 miles to the northwest. Admiral Mitscher's task force was sent to hit Truk, some 800 miles west, in order to neutralize Japan's mid-Pacific fortress in the Carolines. This raid would be a prelude to the landings on Eniwetok, set for February 18. To the disappointment of the American pilots who roared in over Truk's fine anchorage on February 17, there were no signs of the heavy units of the Imperial Navy. Admiral Koga had fled to the relative safety of the Palaus only days earlier when the Fifth Fleet was reported off the Marshalls. In two days and one night of continuous raids at Truk, the Americans destroyed 275 enemy planes and over 200,000 tons of auxiliary vessels. The Truk raid removed any need for an invasion of the Caroline Islands before the U.S. Navy made its strike against the Marianas and Japan's inner defense perimeter.

While Truk was being finished off as an effective naval base, Admiral Turner's forces were attacking the Eniwetok atoll. The combined reserve force of Marines and the 27th Infantry Division took Engebi Island in one day, and Japanese documents captured there indicated, contrary to American intelligence, that a strong garrison was installed across the lagoon on Parry and Eniwetok islands. This discovery brought a hurried revision of the next day's assaults. Instead of the simultaneous landings by light units, the full reserves were brought up to land in strength on each island successively, after another heavy naval bombardment. The New York National Guardsmen of the 27th Infantry Division, however, required two and a half days to subdue Eniwetok, while the Marines succeeded in crushing all resistance on nearby Parry in less than a day.

The American sledgehammer assault on the Marshalls had smashed the outer layer of Japan's defensive perimeter and opened the way for a 1,000-mile advance to the Marianas. Truk—the Gibraltar of the Pacific— was neutralized, and the other Japanese garrisons in the outlying islands cut off. Imperial General Headquarters, which had intended that lengthy battles would slow up the Americans as they fought their way through the island barriers, were shocked by the speed with which the assault had come crashing through the Gilberts and the Marshalls. There was now alarm in Tokyo that the inner line of fortress islands running up from New Guinea through the Palaus and the Marianas would stand up no better to the growing might of the U.S. forces. The American carrier strikes on Guam, Saipan, and Tinian in the third week of February robbed the defenders of over two hundred more aircraft. "The Marshalls really cracked the Japanese shell," Admiral "Close-in" Conolly would accurately assess: "It broke the crust of their defenses on a scale that could be exploited at once. It gave them no time adequately to fortify their inner defensive line that ran through the Marianas."

The shock of defeat revived the old rivalry between the Imperial Army and Navy staffs as they argued how best to defend the Empire. Yamamoto's dream of the "decisive naval engagement" that would decide the Pacific War, and which had led him to disaster at Midway, died hard among his successors. The Combined Fleet, because of new carrier construction, was still a powerful force to be reckoned with—but it was hardly the "Greater East Asia Annihilation Fleet" that Prime Minister Tojo assured the nation would be able to wipe out its opponent and guard Japan. The tremendous expansion of the U.S. Pacific Fleet in the previous year had given it an overwhelming superiority. Yet the naval staff was still convinced that they could lure the U.S. Fifth Fleet to a showdown battle by using their island bases as "unsinkable carriers" from which to strike at the American task forces when they penetrated the inner defensive perimeter.

The Imperial Army Staff countered by arguing that since the navy had failed to guard the outer perimeter of the islands, their plan could not hold the Marianas, Carolines, and Palaus, which Tojo had designated as "the last defense line." Some of the generals even went so far as to suggest a withdrawal to concentrate on defending the Philippines and Formosa, where the decisive battle could be fought on land.

In an effort to resolve the strategic deadlock as well as to impose his own authority on the military leadership, Prime Minister Tojo used the raids on Truk as a pretext to sack the Navy Chief of Staff, Admiral Nagumo. Tojo replaced him with the pliant Admiral Shigetaro Shimada, and also fired General Sugiyama to take over himself as Chief of Staff of the Army. This was a major step toward the assumption by the Prime Minister of an executive dictatorship, although government propaganda insisted the changes were a result of "direct Imperial guidance."

The American breakthrough to Truk had indeed shaken the very foundations of Japan's Empire. Bombs and shells might not yet be falling on the home islands, but the sinking of so many merchant ships during the American carrier raids on the Carolines dramatically increased the effect of the U.S. submarine campaign, which by the spring of 1944 was interdicting the maritime lifelines of the Empire.

THE SILENT WAR

Japan had begun the war with more than 6 million tons of merchant shipping. This capacity might have proved just sufficient to meet the demands of moving cargo throughout the scattered island Empire as well as carrying the burden of military supply. But too little attention had been given by the Tokyo government, until too late, to setting up the kind of efficient shipping-control organization that helped Britain win the Battle of the Atlantic against the German U-boat campaign. The army had requisitioned large numbers of merchantmen as freighters sailing from Japan when they might have utilized other vessels that frequently made the trip south from Japan in ballast to bring back the plunder of the Co-Prosperity Sphere. The Imperial Navy, which had been reared in the same aggressive thinking as the Royal Navy, was to make the same mistakes in relegating antisubmarine forces and tactics to a low priority. The British had learned a sharp lesson in World War I and remembered it only just in time in World War II. In spite of the devastating success of their Axis partners' undersea warfare, however, the Imperial Navy was to remain fatally blind to the need for convoying and escort tactics.

The United States immediately after Pearl Harbor had declared a policy of unrestrictd submarine warfare in the Pacific. It produced limited results at first because of defective torpedoes and a lack of aggressiveness on the part of the American commanders. Misapplied use of radio intelligence was at first to send the Pacific Fleet submarines chasing over the ocean after the enemy's big warships instead of concentrating on blockading Japan's main shipping routes. In the first six months the U.S. submarines sank only thirty-five Japanese merchant ships, less than ace German U-boats managed to sink in a single Atlantic patrol. Such poor performance was reflected in the Tokyo Naval Staff's response in setting up in Formosa the "First Convoy Escort Fleet," whose over-age officers were matched by the few ancient destroyers they were assigned. Their ineffectiveness was not important, for in the whole of 1942 the Japanese lost less than 700,000 tons of shipping to all Allied submarine activity, while the Germans were sinking that much nearly every month in the Atlantic. That year Japan's shipyards turned out over 1 million tons of new capacity, more than enough to keep pace with the attrition.

Not until the end of that disastrous first year was the American submarine campaign shaken up. Rear Admiral Charles A. Lockwood was promoted from leading the flotillas stationed at Brisbane to become Commander Submarines Pacific Fleet. Recalled from his attaché's post in London, where he had a chance to study at first hand the reports of the U-boat assault on Britain's shipping lifelines, Lockwood had initially commanded the flotillas operating from Australian bases. There he soon became convinced that the poor performance of his boats, which time and again failed to sink warships or disrupt the poorly protected transport convoys during the invasion of the Dutch East Indies, must be caused by a combination of defective torpedoes and lack of aggression by his captains. Experiments proved that the technical cause of the problem was the standard American Mark XVII torpedo's faulty depth-keeping mechanism, which unless adjusted would cause the torpedo to pass harmlessly below the keel of the target warship. Orders were sent to compensate for the inaccurate settings, but the first months of 1943 brought no greater successes.

That year Lockwood systematically replaced almost a third of the captains. When the younger, aggressive commanders' sinking rates were still not commensurate with the number of hits they claimed, it became obvious that their torpedoes were still badly defective. After Lockwood had ordered an exhaustive series of tests at Hawaii in which torpedoes were fired at cliff targets, it was found that their magnetic and contact-detonating pistols were hopelessly unreliable.

"If the Bureau of Ordnance can't provide us with torpedoes that will hit and explode, or with a gun larger than a peashooter," he blasted at a Washington conference early that year, "then, for God's sake get the Bureau of Ships to design a boathook with which we can rip the plates off the target's sides." In spite of such caustic words and constant prodding, it was to be September 1943 before the first of the new Mark XVIII torpedoes arrived for use by his Pacific submarines—and many more months before their teething troubles were finally engineered out.

Just under 1.5 million tons of Japanese merchant ships had been sent to the bottom in 1943, but their shipyards had succeeded in providing a net gain in tankers. The beginning of 1944 saw the American submarine campaign at last begin to gain effect. Lockwood—borrowing Admiral Doenitz's U-boat tactics—organized wolfpacks of submarines directed by radio intelligence against convoys off the Luzon Straits, through which many of the enemy shipping lanes funneled. The Pearl Harbor flotillas were sent to operate from the forward bases at Midway and then from the captured atolls. Success rates began to climb sharply both for the Pacific Fleet boats and those of MacArthur's naval commander, whose flotillas were reorganized at Brisbane by Rear Admiral James Fife, Jr.

Radio intelligence and code breaking played an increasingly important part in concentrating the American submarine patrols against Japan's diminishing merchant fleet. The enemy convoy signals and position reports would be sifted by the Fleet Radio Unit, Pacific Fleet (FRUPAC) team led by Commander W. J. Holmes at Pearl Harbor and a daily report radioed out at noon. As the Japanese losses mounted, the Tokyo Naval Staff were trying to step up antisubmarine measures. The previous fall they had established the "Grand Escort Command" under Admiral Koshiro at Okinawa. He had been assigned a handful of escort carriers, an air group, and destroyers, but without adequate training in sonar detection and escort work, his convoy protection force was too little and too late.

The Japanese lacked the weapons, escorts, and training to provide more than token cover to the convoys, which multiplied through the spring of 1944 as troops and supplies were rushed to the threatened island perimeter. Assembling the merchantmen into poorly protected and ill-disciplined gaggles only made success easier for the American submarine skippers. In January 1944 294,902 tons of Japanese shipping were sunk—the highest monthly total of the war, and a clear warning to Tokyo that the assault against both their island defense and convoys was accelerating. That month saw a triumphant series of successes for Nimitz, arousing MacArthur's concern that unless his Southwest Pacific Command stepped up the pace of its campaign, he would be forced to take second place to the Fifth Fleet in the final drive on Japan.

In a dramatic bid to speed up the New Guinea campaign, MacArthur brought forward the date for his planned landing in the Admiralties by a full month. Aerial reconnaissance had confirmed what his staff had already guessed from eavesdropping on the radio traffic between Japanese garrisons: that the Los Negros Island base was weakly defended. Located strategically just 200 miles off the New Guinea coast and nestled off the eastern tip of Manus, largest of the Admiralties, was one of the finest anchorages in the South Pacific. Here, MacArthur had decided, was the base he needed from which the Fifth Fleet could be staged to support an 800-mile leapfrog up the New Guinea coast to Hollandia.

ASSAULT ON THE ADMIRALTY ISLANDS

The Los Negros landing was reset for February 29, 1944. Preparations were rushed in four days for what MacArthur carefully described as a "reconnaissance in force." The crew of the flagship U.S.S. *Phoenix* was rounded up from the bars of Brisbane at two hours' notice on February 24 before the cruiser steamed north; seventy-two hours later, General Mac-Arthur himself came aboard at Milne Bay as the small convoy plowed north through the Vitiaz Strait under heavy aircover. The next day reports from a landing party of scouts that, after all, Los Negros was "lousy with Japs," sent apprehension racing among the force of 1,000 men of the U.S. 1st Cavalry Division. MacArthur nonetheless decided to go ahead with the operation, though he was ready to pull the troops out if things went badly wrong.

Luck was with the Americans on the morning of February 29. By attacking from the rear of the island rather than through the great harbor, the cavalrymen under cover of bombarding warships took the Japanese defenders off-balance. Early that same afternoon they seized control of the airstrip after suffering only four casualties. Despite a torrential downpour, MacArthur insisted on going ashore, oblivious to the dangers of snipers and the thick mud. While congratulating his soldiers, he chanced on two recently killed Japanese. "That's the way I like to see them," he snapped, to the delight of the men with him.

Stout fighting was now called for. The cavalrymen clung to their positions for the forty-eight hours it took reinforcements to arrive and turn the "reconnaissance in force" into a seven-day battle that was finally to win the Americans control of Los Negros. A week later, a large force crossed the harbor to land on Manus. After another ten days of fighting, the main enemy base in the Admiralties was safely in the hands of the U.S. Army. MacArthur's initiative won praise from the Joint Chiefs and the press as a master stroke; even Admiral King termed it a "brilliant maneuver." Realizing that he was now outflanked if the Americans leapfrogged back to the New Guinea coast, General Adachi, who had been gathering his forces at Madang for a final showdown, sent his weary troops to begin the grim 150-mile trek north along the coastal jungle to Wewak in order to avoid being cut off.

Unintentionally, MacArthur's "brilliant maneuver" precipitated an open clash with the Navy. Nimitz proposed that the Pacific Command area should now be extended west to include the Admiralties so that the Seabees could expand the base facilities to accommodate the Fifth Fleet. Angrily protesting that this would be an unjustifiable reflection on his "personal honor," MacArthur implied that he would resign when he wrote to Marshall demanding "an early opportunity to present the case to the Secretary of War and the President." The internecine conflict was averted by an agreement that Halsey's South Pacific Command should establish the base on Los Negros. The Joint Chiefs decided that the time was ripe to settle the underlying dispute, which centered on whether the main thrust toward Japan was to be developed north or south of Truk. Admiral Nimitz and General MacArthur were therefore summoned to Washington to present their alternative plans on March 2, 1944.

Issuing his usual regrets about being unable to leave his command, MacArthur sent his Chief of Staff. General Sutherland forthrightly insisted on the merits of the advance up New Guinea, followed up with the invasion of Mindanao in November as the quickest way of establishing a jumping-off point in the Philippines for the invasion of Japan. This conflicted with the strategy planned by King who favored taking Formosa and ports on the China coast and saw no virtues in staging from the Philippines. The Joint Chiefs had so far avoided making any final commitment which would open up a rift between the Army and the Navy strategies. So while MacArthur's Chief of Staff pressed the case for Luzon, Nimitz carefully avoided taking open issue, but nonetheless insisted that any Philippines operation must be dovetailed into his schedule, which called for taking Truk in June, the Marianas in September and the Palaus in November. His alternative plan for speeding up the advance was to bypass Truk in June, to land in the Marianas, and then move into Palau by way of Yap Island. In either case he pointed out that the simultaneous invasion of the lower Philippines envisaged by MacArthur could assist his campaign by dividing and drawing off the Japanese forces. However, he was careful to explain that his advance might be delayed into the typhoon season if the Fifth Fleet—whose aircover was to play a major role in both operations—was required to support MacArthur's proposed assaults on New Ireland as well as the Hollandia landing. It was therefore agreed that the Kavieng operation would be eliminated because, by capturing Emirau Island 70 miles to the north of New Ireland's tip from where Halsey's forces would just as effectively be able to isolate the Japanese at Rabaul.

On March 12, 1944, the Joint Chiefs issued their directive for the next round of operations. The SWPA Hollandia landings were approved for April 15, with the Fifth Fleet operating in support. The CINCPAC invasion of the Marianas was set for June 15, to be followed by the assault on the Palaus on September 15. Truk was to be bypassed; accordingly, by October 1944 the Fifth Fleet would sail in support of MacArthur's invasion of Mindanao. While still carefully deferring a decision about which direction to take after that move, the Joint Chiefs directed Nimitz to plan for the invasion of Formosa on February 15, 1945, and MacArthur to prepare for the landings on Luzon in the same month. The wording of their communiqué, which gave precedence to Formosa over Luzon, naturally did not meet with MacArthur's pleasure. Once again the Joint Chiefs had failed to concentrate everything on his axis of attack, although he would at least begin the liberation of part of the Philippines and could now count on the support of the Fifth Fleet.

While strategy was being argued out in Washington, military crisis for a time threatened to disrupt the final moves in the Solomons' campaign. For three months General Hyakutake's soldiers had been laboring in the jungle interior of Bougainville to manhandle their heavy artillery across the island and make an all-out assault on the American positions.

"There can be no rest until our bastard foes are battered and bowed in shame," General Hyakutake, told his 15,000 weary troops on March 9. Hoping to avenge his defeat on Guadalcanal he rallied them for their assault on the enemy base at Empress Augusta Bay. The "bright red blood" that he urged his men to spill to add "yet more luster to the badge of the 6th Division" was to be mainly their own. Since December 1943 when the Marines had been replaced by three army divisions, the Americans had been afforded plenty of time to strengthen their defensive perimeter, and to construct a third airstrip to secure their hold on Bougainville. The repeated Japanese efforts to break through the American positions over the following two weeks resulted in bloody combat, which cost the lives of more than 1,000 Americans. Hyakutake suffered a second crushing defeat before finally calling off his troops after half their strength had been wiped out. A week before the Japanese gave up their efforts to dislodge the U.S. Army from Empress Augusta Bay and Bougainville, the eighteen-month Solomon campaign ended when on March 20, 1944, Americans secured Emirau Island off New Ireland. The Japanese garrisons surviving in the Solomons and Rabaul were now firmly contained.

27

The Common Cause

The American strategy for Southeast Asia called for restricting the Allied war effort to the Burma theater. Their attempt to avoid being dragged into a British campaign to recover colonial possessions, however, was only partially successful. Stalin's promise to join the final round against Japan allowed Churchill to argue his way out of a major land campaign and Chiang Kai-shek to renege on committing his Nationalist Army. The Joint Chiefs of Staff could appreciate by early 1944 the accuracy of Stilwell's assessment that the wily Generalissimo welcomed this chance to let the Americans win the war. Meanwhile, Chiang prepared for a showdown with Mao Tse-tung's Communists over the control of postwar China.

By January 1944, the Joint Chiefs had abandoned their optimistic position that the Nationalists might yet be persuaded into launching an eastern offensive that would open up Hong Kong or Shanghai as the port from which the final stage of the assault on Japan could be staged. Notwithstanding, they persisted with the plan for establishing air bases in China from which the Superfortresses could mount what the Joint Chiefs termed "an overwhelming bomber offensive preparatory to a final invasion."

Construction of the extra-long runways needed by the B-29 bombers had been scheduled to begin in the Chengtu district some 200 miles north of Chungking in mid-January. Orders came from Chiang Kai-shek that work was to be held up until Washington agreed to meet his price of $800 million for the four airfields. Treasury Secretary Morgenthau's angry response to such an extortionate demand was "tell them to go and jump in the Yangtze." The cost of financing a theater that had yet to produce any significant returns was becoming prohibitive. The administration balked at Chiang's additional requests for more bombers for General Chennault and for assurances that the gasoline and supplies flown at great cost over The Hump would be increased to over 10,000 tons a month. The haggling with the Chinese continued through the middle of March before construction of the great 9,000-foot runways was begun by half a million Szechuan peasants. This laborer army toiled for over two months, using primitive tools, their bare hands, bamboo baskets, and battalions of squeaking wheelbarrows which the superstitious coolies refused to grease because they believed the noise kept the devils away.

General Chennault had rashly promised the year before to win the war against Japan from the air. Now he chafed against orders from Washington which forbade his B-24 bombers to strike Formosa and Tokyo before the Superfortresses. The "Liberators" of his 14th Air Force had been sinking hundreds of tons of enemy shipping off the China coast and along the Yangtze. The thirty Chinese divisions, however, held a semi-official truce with the occupying Japanese. Because the Imperial General Staff was reluctant to draw upon the more than 1 million troops in China to reinforce the island perimeter, the high command decided at the beginning of 1944 that the time had come to restart the eight-year-old campaign and subdue China once and for all.

The army commanders in Burma relayed warnings to Tokyo that during the dry season the British would renew their coastal offensive and repeat the effort the previous year to mount long-range thrusts into the country to dislocate communications. The Japanese generals wanted only a limited campaign to forestall this threat, but Subhas Chandra Bose, the Indian Nationalist leader, had called for a "March on Delhi" in December 1943 at Japan's "Southeast Asia Conference," attended by representatives of all the puppet governments. Prime Minister Tojo used the occasion to announce the establishment of "a new order on a basis of wealth and happiness for all," and promised independent status to the Philippines.

Bose was also told that he would lead an India "liberated" by the Japanese Army. In January 1944, Tokyo gave the Burma army commander, General Masakazu Kawabe, authority to launch, "at the opportune time," a limited offensive that was intended primarily to counter the threat of growing Allied airpower and to secure his northern front by seizing the British bases in Assam. It was hardly the great crusade of liberation Bose had called for, but the Indian National Army was shipped in to take part in the campaign. Tojo anticipated that a year of intense civil unrest and a disastrous famine had made the brightest jewel in the British Empire vulnerable to invasion. He assured Bose that the final goal was "to exercise political control of India."

Allied Ultra intelligence intercepted from Japanese Army traffic had revealed the impending build-up coming in Burma even before the first troop trains began rolling along the "Death Railway" from Thailand. This accelerated the launching of General Stilwell's drive into Upper Burma. While he was still in Cairo, his two American-trained Chinese divisions had crossed the Chindwin only to be halted in the matted green valley of the Tanai River by General Tanaka's 18th Division, crack troops whose jungle fighting ability had been honed in fighting the Malayan campaign and capturing Rangoon. "If the bastards will only fight, we can make a dent in the Japs," Stilwell had recorded of his Chinese. He had at last obtained Chiang's vermilion seal, which gave him ultimate control over three divisions. Stilwell aimed to drive down the jungle-choked Mogaung Valley. His troops would be followed by road construction gangs, which would open a 200-mile overland route to the Myitkyina railhead. He expected that Chiang's armies would meanwhile have pressed west to reopen the supply line to China. But the British abandoned plans for their Buccaneer offensive after the Tehran Conference and as a consequence Chungking refused to take part. Stilwell was left feeling that his plan was "wishful thinking."

"We have to go in through a rat hole and dig the hole as we go," he had told his men. Hacking through the jungle allowed only slow progress —often less than half a mile a day. The troops depended on and made heavy demands on the U.S. 10th Air Force, whose transports kept the force supplied by air drops. Soon an open confrontation came about between Stilwell and the Southeast Asian Command. Supreme Allied Commander Lord Louis Montbatten who had, like his British staff, already made no secret that he regarded the whole scheme to reopen the overland supply route to China as hopelessly ambitious. The British SEAC staff, convinced that Stilwell would soon be stalled, intended to allocate as few resources as possible to him. They then found that the American was adept at using his multiple authorities—as Commander in Chief of U.S. Military Forces in China and Chief of Staff to the Supreme Allied Commander in China—to work his will on the SEAC command. What vexed Mountbatten's staff even more was the way he chose to fly off into his jungle "rat hole" in Mid-December to get his offensive moving again.

ALLIED ADVANCE IN UPPER BURMA

"Vinegar Joe" knew he could be most effective up in the front line inspiring his soldiers, rather than at headquarters, where his lack of tact and persuasion worked against him in struggles with the SEAC staff. His irascilibility was highly effective in rallying the Chinese troops, who were impressed by a general's presence in the thick of action. They affectionately referred to him as "hsien sheng"—the old gentleman. (In New Delhi, he was less reverently referred to as "the best three-star company commander in the U.S. Army.") Stilwell's success in reviving his campaign was directly attributable to his inspirational leadership and the loyalty of the American-trained General Sun Li-jen.

By the beginning of 1944, the New China Army, as Stilwell named his command, had broken through into the Hukawng Valley. He then flew by DC-3 Dakota out of a jungle airstrip to New Delhi for a "walla-walla" with Mountbatten. Forty-eight hours later he was back at the front, after having agreed to submit to the authority of General Slim, the one British general (now the 14th Army Commander) who had won his respect. In return Stilwell had arranged to have the U.S. Army's 5307th Composite Unit put under his command for the campaign.

Modeled and trained by Colonel Frank D. Merrill along the lines of the Chindits, the 5307th had rejected their official nomenclature as sounding "disgustingly like a street address in Los Angeles" in favor of "Merrill's Marauders." The 3,000-strong unit had been recruited in a War Department appeal for volunteers for "particularly hazardous and self-sacrificing operations." Many were veterans from the Solomons or New Guinea, and all had acquired a reputation for toughness during their three months of jungle combat training with Brigadier Wingate's guerrilla units. Originally, they had been trained to fight alongside the Chindits for the Buccaneer drive through upper Burma. Now that this had been abandoned after the Sextant decision, Mountbatten agreed, over Wingate's protests, that Stilwell should deploy the Marauders in flanking hooks ahead of his advance. By the end of February, when the three Chinese divisions were expected to have reached the head of the Hukawng, the Chindits would be sent in to penetrate some 150 miles to the south at Indaw in order to cut the Japanese rail and road supply lines.

Stilwell made slow progress throughout January on the first 20 miles of the Ledo Road to China. A single company of light tanks was sent down this muddy track in response to his repeated pleas for reinforcements. The reaction from Chungking and New Delhi left Stilwell convinced that he was very much "out on a limb." At the end of the month, when he was summoned back to a SEAC staff conference, he was appalled to find that the British were preparing to lop off that limb entirely. Mountbatten called for the halting of all operations in upper Burma as part of his revised "Axiom" plan for concentrating on amphibious assaults on Rangoon and Singapore. According to Stilwell's uninhibited diary, the SEAC staff had pitched their case with "fancy charts, false figures and dirty intentions," and contended that the war would be over in the more than two years it would take to push the Ledo Road through. In response, Stilwell dispatched his deputy, General Hayden Boatner, to Washington to forestall Mountbatten's presentation of Axiom to the American military leaders.

The U.S. Joint Chiefs of Staff were to reject the revised SEAC strategy for the very reasons that Churchill had approved it. Boatner had been diligent in executing his mission and persuading Marshall and the President that the SEAC strategy was primarily directed at restoring Britain's colonial possessions at China's expense. "General Stilwell is confident that his Chinese American Force can seize Myitkyina by the end of this dry season, and once there can hold it," Roosevelt had pointedly cabled Churchill on February 24, 1944. "I realize this imposes a most difficult task, but feel with your energetic encouragement, Mountbatten's commanders are capable of overcoming the many difficulties involved." The Prime Minister failed to persuade the President of this, but in a final effort to avoid being "sidetracked and entangled in Burma," he pointed out that the British were already giving what he considered "vigorous support" to Stilwell by their renewed drive down the Arakan. This had been launched at the beginning of January 1944 by the 5th and 7th Indian Army divisions accompanied by the 81st West African Division of Nigerian troops.

Heavy air support from the RAF enabled the British XV Corps Commander, General A. F. P. Christison, to move much faster down the Burma coast than his predecessor. By the end of the month the British passed the halfway point down the Mayu Peninsula toward the jumping-off point for an amphibious assault on the strategic port of Akyab. The slight Japanese resistance was part of General Renya Mutaguchi's strategy. The commander of the Japanese 15th Army, who had been in charge of the regiment of the Kwantung Army that had sparked off the Marco Polo Bridge incident in 1937, had a keen eye for military advantage. He was only waiting for the "opportune time" when the British forces were hanging down the Burma coast like a ripe bunch of grapes before launching his "Ha-Go" offensive to cut the stem of their supply line.

In February 3, 1944, Lieutenant General T. Hanaya, who was advancing north with the 56th Division, was ordered to make a series of four hooking assaults to slice across the rear of Christison's advance. Within days he had severed the British supply line and cut off the 7th Indian Division. The 14th Army Commander, General William Slim, with forewarning of the enemy dispositions given by Ultra intelligence, had made his plans to deal with the old tactic of hooking his force's line of communication. The encircled advance divisions were sent radio orders to stand firm. They were to be supplied by air to become "an anvil against which the reserve division was to advance to hammer the Japanese rear."

At Mountbatten's direction, American transport planes were temporarily diverted from The Hump to join the daily RAF shuttle. For two weeks they parachuted in everything from rice to ammunition as the 16th Indian Division marched south. Because Slim had foreseen that the Japanese supply lines were also over-extended and could not be relieved by air drops, the surrounded British divisions kept attacking while the relief column fought its way south, forcing the Nagkayeduk Pass on February 23. By then the sustained blows had cost the Ha-Go offensive both its momentum and 3,000 casualties; Hanaya was forced to retreat. This first defeat of an Imperial Army front-line division on the Asian mainland by an Allied force of Indian, Nigerian, and Gurkha soldiers was a tremendous boost to British morale and validated SEAC's belief in the capabilities of aerial supply.

Five hundred miles to the northeast Merrill's Marauders, at the same time, were pushing through the punishing jungles in upper Burma. They pushed way ahead of Stilwell's front down the Hukawng Valley to put up a roadblock in the Japanese rear at Walawbum. It had taken all of Merrill's skills as a "born leader" to drive his men forward 60 miles in less than eight days. He then found that General Tanaka, anticipating the hooking tactic, had turned his main force against the Marauders. For five more days and nights the Japanese hammered attacks on the outnumbered Americans, who beat off repeated bayonet charges with machine guns. One of Merrill's units was cut off on a hilltop for forty-eight hours without food and water, but fanatical Banzaiing soldiers could not break through its defenses. Stilwell's two divisions arrived to relieve the unit on March 5.

To the general's fury, his Chinese subordinates—who had been trained always to leave an escape route for a cornered enemy—allowed Tanaka to slip away. Walawbum was nonetheless the first important victory for the New China Army, which had inflicted thousands of casualties and a telling defeat on one of the Imperial Army's finest divisions. "Plenty of dead Japs, horses and junk," Stilwell recorded of a personal visit and inspection by the Supreme Commander. Mountbatten had flown in with an escort of sixteen Spitfires: "Louis much impressed. Doesn't like corpses. Left at 9:00."

THE CHINDITS GO IN

The second stage of the New China Army's campaign now began, with more cooperation from New Delhi. SEAC sent a brigade of Chindits down the partly finished road from Ledo. Simultaneously, 9,000 men and 1,300 mules of two other brigades were ferried in by gliders and transports to landing strips hacked out of the jungle in the Indaw area by the recently organized American Air Commando, commanded by Colonel Phillip Cochrane. "All our columns are inserted into the enemy's guts," Wingate signaled on the execution of the first part of his operation, which had been facilitated by the accurate knowledge of the whereabouts of Japanese forces from radio intelligence. Now he struck out to cut off the railway, which served as both supply line and a potential avenue of retreat for General Tanaka's 18th Division.

When the Chindit airlift was in its final stages on March 8, the Japanese came rolling toward the British divisions on the frontier. "The Army had now reached a state of invincibility, and the day when the Rising Sun shall proclaim our definite victory in India is not far off," General Mutaguchi had proclaimed. He launched his long-awaited "U-Go" offensive, which sent the 33rd, 15th, and 31st divisions of the Imperial Army crashing across into Assam, with the 7,000 soldiers of Bose's Indian National Army in support. Believing that the retreating "Ha-Go" operation had drawn off two divisions from the British forces defending the border front, Mutaguchi now proclaimed a "March on India." But he had gambled and undertaken his offensive with less than a month's supplies. He estimated that he would need only a month to reach and take the British Assam base at Imphal. It was to prove the fatal mistake in the U-Go campaign.

Ultra intercepts had provided General Slim's 14th Army Headquarters accurate intelligence about the scale and direction of the Japanese movements. Slim had therefore confidently approved his IV Corps Commander's tactical plan for leaving three divisions of his force in their forward positions over the Assam frontier. Slim intended to withdraw them and entice the Japanese north onto the Imphal Plain. There the British superiority in tanks and aircraft would have a decisive advantage in the final battle. As it turned out Lieutenant General A. P. Scoones and his troops were trapped by the remarkable speed of the Japanese advance. In just ten days, the 17th Indian Division was encircled 100 miles south of Imphal by the Japanese 33rd Division, while the 28th Indian Division at the center of the front was being flanked by Mutaguchi's 15th Division.

IMPHAL AND THE BATTLE FOR KOHIMA

Once more Mountbatten called upon the American Hump and RAF transports to meet the crisis. In a spectacular feat of military logistics, the entire 5th Indian Division with its mules and artillery was airlifted 400 miles up from the Arakan. But no sooner had these reinforcements secured the rear of General Scoones's divisions to prevent encirclement than a catastrophic threat menaced the entire Burma front. By March 5, General Sato's lightning advance through the Assam Highlands had placed his forces across the vital road at Kohima, a small town 5,000 feet up in the hills just 50 miles northeast of Imphal.

Only a single battalion of the West Kent Rifle Brigade had managed to climb into Kohima with a unit of the native Assam Regiment before the 20,000-strong Japanese division completed its encirclement of the force on the Kohima hilltop. Disaster now threatened the Allies in Burma during the second week of April 1944, because Dimapur was wide open to attack. Less than 50 miles up the road, the railhead on the "Toonerville Trolley" not only formed the strategic supply line for both Slim and Stilwell's front in Burma but also fed supplies to The Hump airlift into China. The small town was virtually ungarrisoned, yet it was packed with stores and ammunition and could have been taken by a small Japanese force. Its loss would strike a paralyzing blow that might have brought defeat to the Allies in Southeast Asia.

General Mutaguchi saw that golden opportunity and at once ordered General Sato to commit his main force and capture Dimapur to win a massive victory. But angry exchanges between Mutaguchi and General Kawabe in Rangoon caused Mutaguchi to rescind the order. The Imperial Army's overall commander in Burma had decided that Mutaguchi was overreaching his authority. He stated categorically that Dimapur was "not within the strategic objectives of the 15th Army."

The inflexible judgment was to cost the Japanese the U-Go campaign. The chance of a quick victory vanished and supplies began to run low. The strategically less significant objective to which the 31st Division was now committed continued to elude General Sato. Over the next two weeks the perimeter around Kohima was squeezed tighter and tighter, yet the five hundred men in the garrison received ammunition and food to enable them to resist the siege. On April 18, when the Japanese won control of a ridge above the defenders and began raining shells down, the soldiers still holding out in the ruins of the town made preparations for a final stand. They were saved that day by the timely arrival of the 161st Indian Army Regiment, which was spearheading the relief column of XXXIII Corps that Slim had rushed up to save Dimapur. "The ground everywhere was ploughed up with shellfire and human remains lay rotting as the battle raged over them," Major John Nettlefield recorded. "Flies swarmed everywhere and multiplied with incredible speed. Men retched as they dug in." The additional strength along with air drops, and the bombing of the Japanese positions enabled the garrison to hang on. The epic battle of endurance was sustained while a brigade of Chindits advanced through the thick jungle toward the Chindwin to cut the enemy supply lines. "Long Range Penetration" was to play a vital role in saving Kohima, although Wingate did not live to see it through. He was killed when his plane crashed in the rugged hills west of Imphal on March 24, 1944.

"Within a bright flame was extinguished," wrote Winston Churchill. He mourned the loss of the eccentric military genius who had blazed the way back for the Allies in Burma. Wingate died at the very moment when the techniques of aerial supply that he had pioneered were being effectively used to check the Japanese offensive. Not only Kohima was being kept alive by such means; British divisions supplied by air 50 miles to the south were turning the tide of battle on the Imphal Plain. To meet the Japanese offensive, some 12,000 troops and 18,000 tons of supplies had been flown into action in just eight weeks to reinforce General Scoones. "There was always a Japanese thrust somewhere that had to be met and destroyed," Slim would write of the relentless actions that pressed back and forth for the next months.

Aerial supply drops were allowing Stilwell to advance up the Mogaung Valley. Yet every time he sent the Marauders ahead, they failed to hold up the retreating enemy division long enough for the following Chinese divisions to inflict a decisive defeat. One of these "left-hook" movements stranded a battalion of Merrill's men for two weeks on a hilltop before a relief column fought its way through the encirclement. Tanaka managed to withdraw before Stilwell's main force arrived in strength. After the death of Wingate, Chindit operations came directly under the American general's control, and he deployed the additional forces in an all-out effort to cut off Tanaka's supply lines.

By the first week in April 1944, when the New China Army was preparing to attack Tanaka's base at Kamaing midway down the Mogaung Valley, Stilwell's own supply line was threatened by the Japanese thrust toward Dimapur. He responded by offering to send back a Chinese division to aid the 14th Army. Urgent pleas were relayed to Chiang Kai-shek to send his Nationalist Army down into eastern Burma. When Chungking failed to respond to the Allied campaign's most desperate crisis, Roosevelt intervened; he cabled a stern request to Chiang to bring his men into the fight. "If they are not to be used in the common cause," the President said of the Nationalist Army, "our most strenuous efforts to fly in equipment and furnish instructional personnel have not been justified." This was a clear threat to halt Lend-Lease aid unless the Nationalist Army speedily marched into Burma. Chiang realized that he could not stall this time and had to respond; without the aid of the United States, his regime would collapse.

There was no formal reply, but within ten days an army of 72,000 Chinese began the 150-mile march down through the foothills of Yunnan toward the Salween River and the eastern frontier of Burma. Then, seventy-two hours later, the Japanese responded—as if on cue—with an attack. This conflict shattered the unspoken truce which for two years had reigned over the ground war in China's eastern provinces. The Imperial General Staff had ordered the "Ichi-Go" offensive with twin objectives. After securing their hold on the Yangtze and Yellow rivers communication lines, they would launch the divisions of the Expeditionary Army south and west into Huan and Kwangsi provinces in order to capture the airfields from which General Chennault's B-25s were mounting increasingly heavy attacks on Japanese coastal and river shipping. The Japanese offensives in both Burma and China had caught the Nationalists in a closing vise. Chiang Kai-shek was committed to concentrating on opening the overland supply route through Burma in order to sustain his armies in a two-front war.

END RUN FOR MYITKYINA

Although spurred by the news from Chungking that "the Japanese had finally forced 'Peanut' into action to save himself," Stilwell was concerned by the ominous build-up of heavy clouds which indicated an early start to the 1944 monsoon season. Accordingly, he decided to gamble on capturing Myitkyina before the heavy rains. The strategic railhead was over 100 miles southeast from where his forces were "still plugging away down the rathole" in the Mogaung. They now faced increasing opposition from the enemy, who were digging in midway down the valley to defend Kamboung. Stilwell's plan called for the Marauders to make an end run for Myitkyina, which would require a forced march through thick jungle and over the 6,000-foot Kumon Range. Meanwhile, his New China Army would tie down the 18th Division in the Mogaung jungle.

There was little reason for believing that the gamble would succeed. Merrill was hospitalized because of a heart attack suffered after an exhausting campaign which had taken a 50 percent casualty toll of the Marauders. Stilwell's proposal was received with disbelief by the SEAC command, who decided it was "unsound and should not be attempted." Mountbatten was still working to turn the Southeast Asian campaign away from Burma and toward an amphibious strategy. He pointedly shifted his headquarters from New Delhi to Kandy to be near the Ceylon base of the Royal Navy's Eastern Fleet.

Warned by Ultra reports of Japanese preparations to launch into a major new offensive in China that might threaten the bomber bases being constructed at Chengtu, the Joint Chiefs approved Stilwell's appropriately named "Operation End Run." It was launched on April 28, after Colonel Merrill discharged himself from the hospital. He then rallied his 1,400 survivors for a final supreme effort in which they were reinforced by two Chinese regiments and a band of OSS-trained guerrillas from the Kachin Hills.

"The die is cast and it's sink or swim," Stilwell noted in his diary, as he made the bid to reach Myitkyina. Then, only three days after the Marauders had set out on their forced march, the monsoon rains began early. The increasing downpour made for precarious travel up slithery mountain trails, and reduced the Marauders often to crawling on hands and knees to get over the lofty Kumon Pass. They had to abandon their mules and most of their supplies in the process. The conditions took a heavy toll of the battle-weary Americans as dysentery and typhus added to the soaring incidence of malaria. Still Merrill kept them driving forward with fanatical determination. On May 15 as they were descending toward their destination, he signaled hopefully: "WE HAVE A FAIR CHANCE." Stilwell sent back the bluff encouragement: "ROLL ON IN AND SWING ON 'EM!"

The following afternoon the Marauders' deputy commander, Colonel Charles N. Hunter, brought his assault group to within striking distance of the key airfield. The field lay only 4 miles from Myitkyina and was apparently only lightly guarded by the unsuspecting Japanese. "In the ring," Hunter signaled just before 11 A.M. the next morning, some twenty minutes after the attack began. By 3:30 that afternoon his "MER-CHANT OF VENICE" signal indicated that the airstrip was captured. DC-3 transports were already taking off from the Assam airstrips to ferry in supplies before dark.

"Will this burn up the Limeys?" Stilwell jubilantly recorded that day when Mountbatten radioed congratulations "on a feat which will live in military history." But he was soon cursing the British again. Because they had moved in antiaircraft guns to defend the airstrip before sending the troop gliders, the reinforcements arrived too late to attack Myitkyina itself before the Japanese had rushed more soldiers up the railroad. Since the monsoon threatened the airlift, the first priority had to be supplying the force of 3,000 holding the airfield. A hundred miles to the northeast the rain also bogged down Stilwell's main force advancing on Kamaing against heavy opposition. "Mud, mud, mud, typhus, malaria, dysentery, exhaustion, rotting feet, body sores," he complained. "If we are so badly off, what about the Japs?" Tanaka was in fact becoming more desperate. The Chindits had repeatedly cut his supply lines to the south and his urgent calls for reinforcements to help hold the Mogaung were never answered.

VICTORIES IN UPPER BURMA

The other Japanese commands in Burma were reeling from Allied pressure on all fronts. By mid-May, the 56th Division holding the China flank along the Salween River had been attacked by twelve Nationalist divisions. On the other side of Burma on the Imphal Plain, General Mutaguchi's U-Go offensive had been stalled by the shortage of supplies. Air drops and ground reinforcement had enabled Scoone's forces to break out of the Japanese 15th Army's encirclement to join up with heavy air and tank support. Slim's XXXIII Corps was pressing through the Kohima roadblock. Mutaguchi stubbornly persisted in the hope that he could apply enough pressure for his three divisions to smash through the four British ones holding the center of the front.

"CONTINUE IN THE TASK TILL ALL AMMUNITION IS EXPENDED," his 15th Army Headquarters had ordered by radio to his field commanders. "IF YOUR HANDS ARE BROKEN, USE YOUR TEETH. IF THERE IS NO BREATH LEFT IN YOUR BODY, FIGHT WITH YOUR SPIRIT. LACK OF WEAPONS IS NO EXCUSE." Lack of food rather than ammunition made it impossible to respond to the exhortations. Mutaguchi replaced the generals commanding the 33rd and 15th divisions, but could bring his forces no closer to a breakthrough.

By the end of May, General Sato's 31st Division was in desperate straits. It had suffered 7,000 casualties as it was being pressed to withdraw from Kohima. "Since leaving the Chindwin we have not received one bullet from you nor a grain of rice," he testily reminded Mutaguchi while again demanding supplies. When none came, he signaled that he was retreating, and brushed off a threatened court-martial.

"He has lost the battle for me," the 15th Army Commander raged, forgetting how his own decision to provide no more than four weeks' supplies was responsible. The crazed Mutaguchi ordered a fresh attempt to break through at Imphal. He soon found though that Sato's failure to hold the road at Kohima had allowed Slim's XXXIII Corps reserve to break through and reopen the line of reinforcement to the main battle area at Imphal. For a few more weeks the Japanese desperately pressed their attack forward despite soaring casualties, air attacks, and a famine so severe that the Japanese soldiers were obliged to exist on grass and slugs to keep alive. Weeks later the entire U-Go offensive was reduced to abject retreat.

CHINESE DEFEATS

Although the Japanese campaign in Burma was stalled, their Ichi-Go offensive made rapid progress after it began on April 18. General Shun-roku Hata's 12th Army took only three weeks to complete the first phase by routing 300,000 Chinese soldiers in Honan to secure the central section of the Peking-Hankow railroad. From Canton in the far south, the 23rd Army was pushing west in order to join up with the Japanese forces occupying French Indochina. The 14th Air Force and the Chinese Air Force's combined efforts could not check the offensive. General Chennault's defeat was a bitter one, since he had persistently promised both Chungking and Washington that his pilots could defend China. "He tries to duck the consequences of having sold the wrong bill of goods, and put the blame on those who pointed out the danger long ago and tried to apply the remedy," Stilwell reported. Mutual recrimination between the two generals flared; Chennault blamed his compatriot for "not sending a single bullet to any Chinese armies not under his direct supervision," and consequently, causing the collapse of the Nationalist Army in Honan.

The failure of Chiang Kai-shek's Nationalist troops to make an effective ground defense against the advancing Japanese, together with what Stilwell considered the lackluster performance of the 72,000 Chinese slowly fighting their way into Burma, prompted Stilwell to send a long critique to General Marshall at the end of May. In it he warned of the danger to the B-29 airfields, and proposed that the Joint Chiefs must make a decision either to pull out altogether or put in an American army. As he saw it, "ultimately the Japs must be fought on the mainland of Asia." That such a strategy now ran completely counter to Washington's policy was evident in Marshall's response. He asserted that Japan had to be defeated "without undertaking a major campaign against her on the mainland of Asia," and that henceforth Stilwell's primary task must be to protect the new bomber bases. By the end of May 1944, the Joint Chiefs of Staff had finally and realistically written off the China theater. It would play only a peripheral role in the final phase of the war against Japan.

28
Decisive Battles

The revival of Japanese land campaigns on the Asian mainland during the spring of 1944, when the Empire's Pacific frontier was being assaulted both at its center and on its southern flank, was to prove ultimately disastrous. The responsibility was General Hideki Tojo's. Virtual military dictator since assuming direct control of the army after February's American breakthrough in the Marshalls, the Prime Minister had thereby committed Japan to a two-front war. The Burma and China offensives now absorbed much of the Imperial Army's strength, which might otherwise have been available for garrisoning the inner defense perimeter. Only seventeen divisions could therefore be sent to defend the Empire's 4,000-mile arc of supposedly interlocking bases stretching from Timor, off the coast of northern Australia, along Dutch New Guinea, through the Philippines and up the Palau, Marianas, and Bonin islands, to Japan herself. Tojo had decreed that these bastions must be held, not only to guarantee the continuing flow of oil from the Dutch East Indies but to form the first line of defense against an invasion on the home soil.

The task of defending such an extended line across so much water inevitably placed an impossible burden on the Imperial Navy. Although the Combined Fleet was still powerful, the U.S. Pacific Fleet's superiority in capital ships was assuming overwhelming proportions. The U.S. Navy had proved in the Marshalls that it was the master of the mass amphibious assault. In response to this threat, the Japanese Combined Fleet's role was now primarily defensive. The naval staff had redesignated its main force as the First Mobile Fleet and restricted its operations to areas where it could be protected by island-based planes, in order to compensate for American carrier-borne air superiority.

However, Commander in Chief Admiral Koga was not yet ready to abandon Yamamoto's aggressive strategy. Koga and his staff had devised a new "Operation Z," a plan for luring the U.S. Fifth Fleet into the Philippine Sea. Once within range of the Imperial Navy's island-based aircraft, the American force would be depleted by air attack before a surface action.

Driven west from its Truk anchorage by the Fifth Fleet raid on February 17, 1944, Koga's force had sought temporary shelter at Palau while he looked for a suitable base from which to launch Operation Z. Tawitawi, an island in the Sulu Archipelago off the western Philippines, was chosen because of its proximity to the Borneo oil wells whose high-grade crude could be burned directly in the warships' boilers. Then, on March 8, Koga was flying to his new headquarters when his plane was lost in a severe storm. His Chief of Staff, Admiral Fukidome, was forced to ditch off Cebu, where he was fished out of the water by Filipino guerrillas, who also picked up his floating briefcase containing a mass of secret documents including the important Operation Z battle plan. This priceless intelligence was passed on from Cebu via MacArthur's command to the CINCPAC staff at Pearl Harbor. The new Commander in Chief, Admiral Soemu Toyoda, was to make no radical changes in his predecessor's strategy, except that his "A-Go" plan shifted the area in which the decisive battle would be fought to the waters off the Palaus, which were believed to be the next U.S. Navy objective. A hundred planes of the 1st Air Fleet were now sent south to be within striking range to sink "at least a third of the enemy's task force units" before the First Mobile Fleet engaged the balance. There would have been few Japanese warships left to fight if the First Mobile Fleet had not been moved west from its anchorage only days before March 29, when the American carrier task forces raided the Palau bases, destroying 150 planes and 17 auxiliary vessels and tankers. Much to Admiral Mitscher's disappointment, Koga had already sent his fleet to Singapore's Lingga Roads where it was out of reach of air strikes.

Following the Palau raid, the Fifth Fleet's fast carrier task forces refueled at Majuro Atoll before steaming south to the Admiralties to support MacArthur's ambitious 600-mile leapfrog up the New Guinea coast to Hollandia. This operation was to be launched at April 13. After Ultra intelligence revealed that Japan's 18th Army was concentrating at Wewak to repel the next Allied landing, every effort was made by U.S. forces to confirm General Adachi's expectations, including abandoning rubber boats to give the appearance of reconnaissance parties having landed on that sector of shore.

THE HOLLANDIA LANDING

On April 22, when the bombarding warships and flotillas of landing craft came looming through the morning mists off Hollandia, the Japanese headquarters staff in the former Dutch administrative capital were completely surprised to find Americans "already in the harbor with their battleships and transports." Most of the 11,000 base personnel fled into the hills in response to what was only one assault in a massive triple-pronged attack. While the 41st Division was storming ashore unopposed near Hollandia, the 24th Division was making a second landing 22 miles to the west at Tanahmerah Bay, and a regiment of the 41st Division was securing Aitape 120 miles to the east.

"The operation throws a loop of envelopment around the Eighteenth Army dispersed along the coast of New Guinea," MacArthur announced in a triumphant communiqué. The spectacular victory was won without having to call upon Mitscher's Task Force 58 for support because General Kenney's 5th Air Force had wiped out all but a score of the Japanese planes on the New Guinea coast. The next day, MacArthur decided to strike again to sustain the momentum of his leapfrogging advance. On May 17, the "Tornado Task Force," made up of the 163rd Regimental Combat Team, was put ashore 125 miles west of Hollandia to seize the enemy airstrips inland from Maffin Bay, while another force sought to capture the large airfield that covered most of Wakde Island.

The spectacular pace and brilliant execution of MacArthur's spring advance up the northern coast of New Guinea owed as much to the remarkable efficiency of the U.S. Army's Ultra intelligence as it did to his generalship. Accurate estimates of the garrison strengths had enabled him to attack only the weakest points in the southern flank of Japan's defense perimeter, and accurate reports—frequently within hours—allowed him to keep ahead of the enemy's countermoves. As the secret official report of the Army Intelligence Division put it, "never has a commander gone into battle as did the Allied Commander Southwest Pacific, knowing so much about the enemy."

LEAPFROGGING TO THE VOGELKOP

Yet it was typical of MacArthur that his impatience to wrap up the campaign by exploiting what he predicted to be "the amazing weakness" of the defense at Biak Island meant that the assault almost ended in a bloody reverse. He had preferred to believe his own intelligence estimate that there were fewer than 3,000 Japanese in the garrison although Ultra indicated that the island was held by over 7,000 troops.

The Hurricane Task Force was assigned to take Biak on May 27, 1944. After a heavy sea and air bombardment by planes flying from the new base at Wakde, the American infantry landed. They were confronted by jungle-clad hills honeycombed with caves that were put to good defensive use by the Japanese, who let the invaders get ashore before they began putting up a strong resistance. So deceptively easily had the initial landings progressed that the SWPA Command released a premature communiqué proclaiming "the practical end of the New Guinea campaign" even as the Japanese soldiers emerged from their caves and put up a stiff fight. The American assault was stalled by next day just beyond the beachhead, but MacArthur officially insisted the enemy was "collapsing" and two days later "mopping up" was under way. The reality was closer to a stalemate; yet he would not send in reinforcements. "The progress at Biak is unsatisfactory," he angrily announced to his staff. To have done so would have revealed that his assault was in difficulties, and this would have been a setback for his reputation in the very week when the Allied press was celebrating General Eisenhower's triumph in Normandy.

The American attack on Biak was seen at Admiral Toyoda's Combined Fleet Headquarters on Tawitawi as a direct threat to his "A-Go" strategy, since its airfield was essential to maintaining air superiority over the waters south of the Palaus. Attempts were made on June 3 to send south a convoy of reinforcements to Biak, before it was turned back by Allied bombers. Four days later, after an attempt at mounting a "Tokyo Express" destroyer run was chased off by Admiral Crutchley's cruiser force, Toyoda decided to send in his biggest units and ordered his two superbattleships to bombard the enemy beachhead.

On June 13, Admiral Ugaki's force with the mighty *Yamato* and *Musashi* was racing southward at full speed when their mission was called off after news came from Saipan that the island was undergoing a fierce bombardment. To the consternation of the Imperial Navy Staff, the Americans had clearly decided to make the Marianas and not the Palaus their next objective. Toyoda was forced to recast his A-Go plans for bringing about the decisive engagement in the Philippine Sea. The First Mobile Fleet made ready to sail from Tawitawi, and Admiral Ugaki was ordered to join it with his battleships.

ASSAULT ON THE MARIANAS

The Pacific Fleet's attack relieved MacArthur from his justified fear that he was faced with another Guadalcanal. It took another eight weeks to crush the unreinforced Japanese resistance on Biak. "Operation Forager" was the name Nimitz had chosen for the Marianas campaign; its objectives were to seize Saipan and nearby Tinian and recapture Guam. On June 15, the biggest assault of the Pacific War was to begin with Admiral Mitscher's fast carriers delivering a two hundred bomber strike against the airfields in the Marianas. The fields were left in smoking ruins; over one hundred of the planes that Toyoda was counting on to implement his A-Go plans were destroyed. Operation Forager's 535 ships and the 127,571 troops assigned to the American assault in the Marianas made it not only the largest force yet assembled for any naval operation but also the instrument of a new phase of the war. "We are through with flat atolls now. We learned to pulverize atolls, but now we are up against mountains and caves where Japs can dig in. A week from now there will be a lot of dead Marines," General Holland Smith told one of the final briefing conferences to be held aboard the 5th Amphibious Force command ship U.S.S. *Rocky Mount* before the great armada sailed from Eniwetok. The switch from pursuing the "Atoll War" to attacking the large fortified Japanese bases of the inner defense line had taken three months of intensive planning. Admiral Kelly Turner and General Holland Smith were in charge of the Northern Attack Force which consisted of the 2nd and 4th Marine divisions and was to land on Saipan on June 15 and secure it before taking nearby Tinian. Rear Admiral Conolly and Marine Major General Roy S. Geiger were in command of the Southern Attack Force, scheduled to hit Guam three days later, with Major General Ralph S. Smith and the 27th Army Division as their floating reserve.

Special consideration had been given to the need for a very heavy bombardment of Saipan which, intelligence predicted, was held by a powerful garrison of over 20,000 Japanese, equipped with heavy artillery and entrenched in massive fortifications. Intensive bombing raids would reinforce bombardment by the massed guns of Admiral Lee's seven fast battleships. Unfortunately, Task Force 58's gunners were not practiced in the methodical bombardment techniques needed to take out static gun emplacements and blockhouses, so many defenses were still intact when the older battleships arrived next day to begin the systematic reduction of the fortifications. This was to be a bitter irony for Admiral Nagumo, now relegated to command Saipan's tiny naval flotilla, for he found himself on the receiving end of shells fired by three of the battleships his airmen had sunk at Pearl Harbor. During the bombardment, the swimmers of the U.S. Navy underwater demolition searched the reefs off the landing beaches for obstacles and mines. There were none. The transfer of Imperial Army units from China to man Japan's inner island defense line had been carefully monitored by U.S. Army Intelligence, and Ultra reports had told CINCPAC that the Marianas were taking second priority to the Palaus. Not only were the beach defenses not yet in place in the Saipan shallows, but many Japanese civilians were still on the island awaiting evacuation.

D-DAY ON SAIPAN

"We're ready for you," Tokyo Rose had tauntingly broadcast on the evening of June 14. But General Yoshitsugu Saito's 43rd Division, concentrating its main strength on the west coast of the island, was quite unprepared for the magnitude of the assault that hit them next morning as

DECISIVE BATTLES

the bombardment rose to a hellish crescendo. A phalanx of six hundred Amphtracs came churning toward the shore as H-Hour approached. Marine Sergeant David Dempsey would later set down a vivid personal account of what happened as the amphibious tractor carrying his platoon splashed down the ramp-bowed landing craft:

> Nosed out a hundred yards or so from the ship and rendezvoused waiting for the waves to form. Ahead, the control boat bobbed just seaward of the reef, bedecked with signal flags that would send us across the line of departure. Idling there, we had a grandstand seat for the show our warships were putting on as a curtain raiser to the landing. We watched shells bite into the coral sand and shred the palm trees that lined the shore. After an hour the fire was lifted and dive bombers went in on the final strike. They wheeled in formation over our heads, peeled off and plummeted savagely down, dropping bombs a few hundred feet from the ground. As they began their climb, explosions threw bursts of fire, rubble and talcum-fine dust into the air and in a few minutes the beach was obscured. Ahead the first assault wave—cannon bearing amphibious tanks—lined up along the line of departure, like nervous horses.
>
> We looked at each other, and our glances formed a common pool of anxiety. I was conscious of a tightening in my stomach and I knew if I had been alone I would have been afraid. Half an hour was to elapse before we hit the beach. Some of the boys tried to read a little paper bound "Navy Expendable." One man was seasick and lowered himself to the deck and vomited. . . . In a few minutes our tractor grumbled up onto the reef, lurching tipsily we crawled over it, giving us the feeling, for the moment, that we were very naked and exposed.

Like hordes of armored water beetles, the Amphtracs rolled up onto the eight landing beaches which made up the four-mile long assault front, while rockets screamed down from Avengers operating from escort carriers offshore and delivering a carefully timed final pounding of the enemy's positions. Somehow Japanese artillery managed to keep firing, but the momentum of the assault was such that in less than twenty minutes more than 8,000 Marines were ashore and digging into the beach. Throughout the day the defenders held out from behind the airstrip, supported by firepower from batteries on high ground marked on the Marine maps as Hill 500 and from the slopes of Mount Tapotchau, the volcanic peak which commanded the heights above the main town of Garapan.

The continual Japanese shelling prevented any deep penetration, although by late afternoon more than 20,000 Marines and their artillery were ashore, ready to begin the drive inland the next day. General Saito sent a signal to Tokyo announcing he was launching a counterattack to "Annihilate the enemy at one swoop."

At 3 A.M. the following morning, thirty-six light tanks, then a thousand soldiers, led by officers brandishing swords and yelling Banzais, came clanking and yelling down the slopes of Hill 500 to drive the Marines into the sea. Destroyers delivered accurate shellfire that smashed up the assault. After nearly three quarters of his force was cut down, Saito called the attempt off. He returned to his headquarters, demoralized but nonetheless determined to hold out on the slopes of Mount Tapotchau until the Imperial Navy's planes and warships had smashed their way through the American Fleet to win a decisive victory and relieve Saipan.

"The Japanese are coming after us," Admiral Spruance told his naval and amphibious force commanders at a conference aboard his flagship *Indianapolis* on the afternoon of June 16. Submarines patrolling off the Philippines had radioed reports that two large naval forces were debouching through the San Bernadino and Surigao Straits. Assuming that they would certainly be heading toward the Marianas to smash up his beachheads, Spruance postponed the assault on Guam and ordered the transports carrying the 27th Division to lie a safe distance to the west. Offloading operations were speeded up the next day on Saipan. To forestall Japanese air attacks, Mitscher was sent north with Task Force 58. Two of his carrier task groups were to blast the airstrips on Guam and Rota, while the other two made a fast run north to strike the Volcano Island and Bonin bases to stop planes from being flown down from Japan to join the fight.

Next day on Saipan the Marines battled on against heavy opposition toward Garapan and the main airfield at Aslito in the north. The amphibious force weighed anchor at dusk and Admiral Spruance sailed his flagship to join Admiral Lee's six battleships to rendezvous with the returning Task Force 58. "OUR AIR WILL FIRST KNOCK OUT ENEMY CARRIERS," the Fifth Fleet Commander specified in his radioed battle orders, before giving the tactical command to Admiral Mitscher. "THEN WILL ATTACK ENEMY BATTLESHIPS AND CRUISERS. . . . LEE'S BATTLE LINE WILL DESTROY ENEMY FLEET . . . ACTION AGAINST A RETREATING ENEMY MUST BE PUSHED VIGOROUSLY BY ALL HANDS TO COMPLETE DESTRUCTION OF HIS FLEET."

"This operation has immense bearing on the fate of the Empire," warned Admiral Toyoda's message that same evening to the Mobile Fleet as it steamed northeast across the Pacific toward Saipan. "It is hoped that the force will exert their utmost to achieve as magnificent result as in Tsushima." Primarily a careful tactician, the new Commander in Chief had decided not to make the mistake of cutting himself off from communications by going to sea to fight the battle as Yamamoto had done at Midway. Toyoda had flown back to Tokyo to direct operations from the big plot at the Naval Headquarters because he knew he would have to position all his forces precisely if he was going to make the A-Go strategic plan a success.

Upon receiving the Commander in Chief's signal, Admiral Ozawa aboard the *Taiho*, Japan's newest and biggest carrier, must have reflected that the mighty American Fifth Fleet he was challenging to a decisive battle hardly bore comparison with the coal-burning pre-dreadnoughts of the Russian Czar's Baltic Fleet, which had steamed halfway around the world to face annihilation at Tsushima thirty-nine years earlier.

The 106 warships of Admiral Spruance's fleet were disposed across the ocean in the form of a 35-mile letter F; the 15 carriers of his four task groups formed its points and Admiral Lee's 7 battleship task force its middle bar. The Fifth Fleet's carrier-borne air strength of nearly 900 planes outnumbered by two to one the 430 planes on the First Mobile Fleet's nine carriers. Toyoda hoped that land-based aircraft would even up the odds. In accordance with the Imperial Navy preference for multiple-unit battle plans, Admiral Kurita was leading a vanguard force that included three light carriers to decoy the American attack, while 100 miles astern, Ozawa's main force of six carriers and five battleships were disposed to deliver the main blow.

Radio direction findings established that the Japanese force was some 600 miles west of Guam on the evening of June 17, heading straight for the patrol line of six American submarines. They were signaled a "SHOOT FIRST AND REPORT LATER" warning that night by CINCPAC. No new intelligence had been received after Spruance decided that his principal task was to guard the American beachheads. This restricted his freedom of operations to a 300-mile radius of Saipan, a considerable disadvantage for Mitscher's carriers because his more heavily armored planes had shorter ranges. The Japanese fighters and bombers had no armor protection for the pilots and the consequent saving in weight gave Ozawa almost a 100-mile advantage in striking range. Japan's planes, whose performance had outclassed the Americans during the first years of the war, were now inferior to those of the U.S. Navy—Hellcat fighters could outshoot and outfly the Zeros. The heavily armed Avenger had proved superior to Japanese strike aircraft in successfully attacking warships with either bombs or torpedoes.

THE BATTLE OF THE PHILIPPINE SEA

All through the day on June 18 the two rival fleets stalked one another across the Philippine Sea west of the Marianas like blind boxers uncertain of the whereabouts of their opponent. The Americans were wary of the Imperial Navy's longer reach, and the Japanese were determined not to submit to the Fifth Fleet's heavier punch. Not until dawn the next day, when Ozawa broke radio silence to signal the launching of a patrol that would refuel at Guam, was Spruance alerted to the actual position of his opponents. He was steaming some 200 miles west of Saipan. Over 300 miles separated the American and Japanese fleets, too great a range for the U.S. Navy's strike aircraft to attack.

Ozawa had assumed that, as provided for in his battle plan, he could count on the support of 500 land-based planes ranged within striking distance of the Fifth Fleet. However, Admiral Kurita, commanding the 1st Air Fleet, had dispersed his planes between Yap and the Palaus in expectation of diversionary raids. Now he compounded his mistake by untruthfully signaling that his planes were already inflicting heavy damage on the American warships.

The exact reverse was the case. Mitscher's carrier task groups, after picking up the flight of Japanese planes heading toward Guam shortly after sun-up, had sent Hellcats and Avengers racing in to attack at 7:30 A.M. Thus began the Battle of the Philippine Sea in which so many Japanese were to be shot down in one day that the American pilots would call it "The Great Marianas Turkey Shoot." The aircrews were returning from their first kills that morning over Guam when, shortly before 10 A.M., the American radar plots picked up an air strike heading in toward Task Force 58, steaming 150 miles west of the island. The Fifth Fleet's "F" formation reversed course eastward and headed into the wind. Swarms of Hellcats rose from the carriers. The battleships with batteries of anti-aircraft guns bristling skyward were in the van to draw the enemy attack. Over a year had passed since the last carrier action had been fought off Guadalcanal and the Americans had used that time to improve their planes and to perfect the tactical coordination of integrated air and sea fighting. Well-rehearsed fighter controllers now operated with new radar plots to direct the pilots aloft, disposing and vectoring the squadrons against the enemy with cool deliberation. The excited radio exchanges between pilots, which had previously jammed and confused the radio controllers, had been replaced by a crisp pattern of standardized orders and responses to and from fighter wing pilots in well-rehearsed combat maneuvers.

Pitted against them were Japanese pilots lacking the training, experience, and discipline, but not the fanatical courage, that had made Yamamoto's aircrews such a formidable striking force in the first year of the war. By 1944 most Combined Fleet pilots were no match for the skilled Fifth Fleet veterans, as was quickly and brutally demonstrated in the first Japanese attack on the morning of June 19. Hellcats shot down half the attacking force even before it got within shooting distance of the fleet's guns; the few Japanese planes that did break through the Combat Air Patrol and head for the battleships were met with such deadly antiaircraft fire that only one plane scored a bomb hit on the *South Dakota*. No serious damage resulted. Of the seventy attackers, only twenty-eight escaped destruction.

The first strike was headed to a spectacular defeat when Ozawa launched his second attack of 130 aircraft at 9 A.M. Ten minutes later, just after the last aircraft had roared off the *Taiho*'s huge flight deck, the largest carrier in the Imperial Navy shuddered from a torpedo hit. The First Mobile Fleet had encountered the American submarine picket line. Commander J. W. Blanchard had the good fortune to line up the large carrier in the cross wires of the U.S.S. *Albacore*'s attack periscope and had fired two torpedoes before going deep to escape depth charges. The two dull crumps picked up on hydrophones told him that they had exploded. Only one had hit because the other had been detonated by a Zero pilot's suicide dive as it streaked toward its target. This sacrifice had temporarily saved the flagship. Her forward elevator had been jammed by the first torpedo explosion. Thousands of tons of water poured through the hole in her starboard bow. When he found that his giant carrier could still make 26 knots, Ozawa praised the heroism of the dead pilot, thanked his luck and the *Taiho*'s diligent damage-control parties, and ordered the launching of a third strike. No one on the bridge realized that deadly gasoline fumes were building up in the sealed-off compartments and creating a time bomb deep within her hull.

The second Japanese strike turned into a bigger "turkey shoot" than the first; only 31 of its 130 fighters, torpedo planes, and bombers escaped. The third strike—launched an hour after the *Taiho*'s torpedoing—failed even to find the Fifth Fleet. American fighters were vectored onto it by radar and added another ten to their mounting score. At 11:30 A.M. Ozawa sent off a fourth wave of eighty-two aircraft, forty-nine of which chased off after what proved to be a false sighting south of Guam. Directed to refuel on the island, the fourth wave became victims of another American strike as they came in to land. Those pilots who located one of the American task groups fared no better.

Aboard the *Indianapolis*, Spruance was pacing his flag plot, fretting that the Japanese were still out of reach of his aircraft. His irritation was increased by his staff's insistence on smoking to relieve the mounting tension. Ozawa had now spent his attacks without damaging a single American carrier, and he had lost half his air strength. The greater part of the five hundred planes of the First Air Fleet was too far away to join the battle. The A-Go plan was a shambles. He was reflecting on his lost opportunity when at 12:22 P.M. four successive explosions hurled the *Shokaku* out of line. The heavy carrier had been hit by a fan of torpedoes fired by Captain Herman Gossler of the U.S.S. *Cavella*. For the next three hours the Battle of the Philippine Sea belonged to Admiral Lockwood's submariners as the flames engulfing the *Shokaku* reached her magazines around 3 P.M. and tore apart the veteran of the Pearl Harbor raid in a gigantic explosion. At 3:20 the *Taiho*'s decks were heaved up and her sides blown out by a fiery blast. The seeping gasoline vapors had ignited with titanic power. The Japanese paid the penalty for using the volatile

Borneo crude for fuel—its fumes contributed to a blaze so fierce that the rescue destroyers found it all but impossible to take off survivors. Protesting that he would go down with his ship, Admiral Ozawa was nevertheless persuaded by his staff to bring the Emperor's portrait aboard one of the rescue ships. Then a second explosion sent the *Taiho*'s searing hull below the waves, along with 1,650 of her crew.

That night the First Mobile Fleet had still not been sighted by the Fifth Fleet's wide-ranging air patrols. Ozawa, with a hundred aircraft still left aboard his surviving carriers, was misled by continuing reports from Admiral Kurita that the 1st Air Fleet was flying reinforcements into Guam in an all-out bid to salvage a victory.

It was not until a garbled sighting report was received at 3:40 the following afternoon, June 20, that Admiral Spruance's commanders finally knew the Japanese Fleet was some 250 miles to the northwest and at last within range of their planes. Spruance decided to risk an attack, although his pilots would have to grope their way back and land after dark. Two hundred and sixteen American aircraft were airborne in ten minutes and heading out into the sun. Ozawa had been conducting a leisurely refueling operation while awaiting the chance to renew his attack when his radio staff reported picking up transmissions from an enemy aircraft. Realizing he had been spotted, Ozawa stopped refueling and ordered the First Mobile Fleet to withdraw to the northwest in the hope of avoiding any strike in the dusk.

When the leading American planes caught up with the Japanese, they were at the extreme edge of their fuel range and the sun was already half-hidden by the rim of the western horizon. With no time to coordinate an attack, most pilots dived on whatever ships they caught zigzagging below on the darkening ocean. The light carrier *Hiyo* was hit by two torpedoes and sank; *Zuikaku* and *Junyo* suffered heavy damage; three tankers were sent down and two heavy cruisers badly hit. Of the eighty Japanese aircraft that had managed to take off before the blow fell, sixty-five were shot down. Twenty American planes were lost while making the attack, and nearly half of those that set off on the long return flight in the gathering gloom never reached their carriers. Spruance ordered the Fifth Fleet's searchlights on to assist the returning flyers making the hazardous night landings, which began around 8 P.M. Many aircraft ran out of fuel and were forced to pancake in the sea. The night rescue operation held up Spruance's pursuit of the Japanese. Not until the next day was the chase resumed. The enemy had time to show a clean pair of heels and the Fifth Fleet abandoned the hunt that evening.

"The enemy had escaped," Admiral Mitscher recorded with regret in his battle report. "He had been badly hurt by one aggressive carrier strike at the one time when he was within range. His fleet was not sunk." Spruance's own disappointment was that his decision to give priority to guarding the Saipan invasion force had denied him the opportunity to inflict an annihilating defeat. His critics would maintain that he had lost a great opportunity through his over-cautious conduct in the battle. Events, however, were soon to prove that the victory Spruance had won in the Battle of the Philippine Sea was one of the most complete of the whole Pacific War.

The Combined Fleet's A-Go strategy to lure the U.S. Fleet into a decisive engagement had failed due to lack of support from land-based aircraft. The Combined Fleet had lost a third of its surviving carriers and all but thirty-six of its aircraft. Highly trained aircrew replacements needed to combat the skilled U.S. Navy squadrons were no longer available. Although on paper the surviving Japanese battleships and carriers were still formidable, they comprised an enfeebled fleet. The fact that the naval war in the Pacific was all but over was attested to by Admiral Ozawa, who wanted to resign. Assuming full responsibility for the disastrous defeat, Toyoda refused to accept Ozawa's resignation. He was ordered to sail the First Mobile Fleet back to Okinawa.

The prospect of defeat was hanging heavily over the now isolated General Saito. Realizing that his garrison's last hope of reinforcement was gone, he resolved to extract a heavy price for Saipan, issuing orders for a suicidal defense to the last bullet. Pushing steadily up from the south, the three American divisions encountered increasing resistance as the enemy was compressed into the northern third of the island by the first week of July. Impatient with the slowing down of the advance, General Holland Smith had stormed ashore to take personal command and relieved Major General Ralph S. Smith of his command of the 27th Infantry Division. The division's plodding battle performance had been an irritant to "Howlin' Mad" Smith ever since its lackluster showing on Makin. His decision was to kindle a fierce inter-service row which was due, in part, to the difference between the thrusting advance of the Marines and the more conservative tactics favored by the U.S. Army.

SUICIDAL DEFENSE

The Japanese, from the advantage of their positions on the hills and slopes of Mount Tapotchau, were able to fight a stubborn rearguard action although outnumbered nearly four to one. The heavy losses suffered by the Marine battalion that stormed up the valley to take a well-fortified enemy position on Hill 500 were compared to those of the Light Brigade after its charge at Balaclava. By July 6, the American pressure was becoming intolerable for the Japanese holed up in the northern corner of Saipan. That night General Saito sent a final message to Tokyo, blaming his predicament on the lack of reinforcement by air. He concluded: "We deeply apologize to the Emperor that we cannot do better." After issuing a final order to his surviving troops that before they died each would take "Seven lives to repay our country," he committed ritual seppuku. Admiral Nagumo prepared to end his life with a pistol.

After spending the night fortifying themselves with sake, the surviving Japanese soldiers carried out their dead general's last command at dawn. Yelling Banzaiis, wave after wave hurled themselves against the 27th Infantry Division lines at Tanapag Harbor. It reminded Major Ed McCarthy of the cattle stampedes at the movies. "The camera is in a hole in the ground and you see the herd coming and then leap up and over you and are gone. Only the Japs just kept coming and coming. I didn't think they would ever stop."

Defying machine-gun fire, officers led the suicidal charges brandishing swords, while others advanced with only knives and sticks. Even the wounded joined the attack, hobbling on crutches. The sheer force and ferocity of the greatest Banzai charge ever made by the Imperial Army carried the screaming human tide over the mounds of bodies that piled up and through the American front line. Ultimately it spent its force against scratch platoons of hurriedly rounded up cooks, typists, and base personnel.

Bulldozers had to be brought up the next morning to bury more than 4,000 enemy corpses in a mass grave. The battle for Saipan was now over, but the slaughter was not. Thousands of Japanese civilians, with army survivors, had taken refuge in the caves of the island's rocky northern promontory. Conditioned to believe that the Americans would kill them, they refused to give themselves up in spite of appeals in Japanese broadcast through loudspeakers. On July 9, an appalling mass suicide took place at the Morubi Bluffs. American soldiers watched disbelievingly as women and children hurled themselves from the 800-foot cliffs, soldiers pulled the pins on their own grenades, and mothers with infants-in-arms struggled across the rocks into the sea rather than let themselves be captured.

This terrible self-destruction brought the total loss of life during the struggle for Saipan to over 50,000. The United States lost 3,000 men who, along with the 13,000 casualties suffered by General Holland Smith's units, made the battle the most costly operation the United States had fought in the Pacific.

TAKING TINIAN AND GUAM

Yet the sacrifice, when measured against the strategic advantage gained, was not considered an excessive price to pay for securing a base that would bring Tokyo within range of B-29 bombers. As the Seabee construction teams arrived to begin extending the island's runways, the delayed second and third stages of Operation Forager swung into action. Four miles due south of Saipan lay the flat rolling sugar-cane fields of Tinian. After only two weeks to recover from the exhausting battle for Saipan, units of the two Marine divisions were landed on Tinian's northern beaches on July 24. Heavy air strikes and naval bombardments had softened up its defenses, and a feint landing to the south had drawn off most of the 10,000 Japanese troops. Inside a week the Marines had won control of Tinian with only four hundred casualties, in what General Smith was to call "the perfect amphibious operation of the Pacific War."

Recapturing Guam 130 miles to the southwest, where for over two years the Rising Sun had flown in place of the Stars and Stripes over the Governor's Mansion at Agana, was reckoned to be a much tougher operation. The former American outpost was the biggest of the Marianas, a rugged island 30 miles long with a mountainous spine that made for ideal defense. Guam had no broad landing beaches on which a massive frontal assault could come ashore. The Army's 77th Infantry Division had been shipped out from Oahu to join the 3rd Marine Division in a forked attack. "My aim is to get the troops ashore standing up," Admiral Conolly had promised the Southern Force Commander, General Geiger. "You tell me what you want done to accomplish this and we'll do it." Conolly's battleships began lobbing their shells onto Guam's strongpoints on July 8. The bombardment rumbled on for nearly two weeks—the longest of the entire Pacific War. "On this island, no matter where one goes, the shells follow," one Japanese soldier recorded in his diary.

Early on the morning of July 21, 1944, the Guadalcanal veterans stormed ashore at the Agat beach, to find a "Welcome Marines" notice left for the 3rd Division by the Navy underwater demolition teams. Five miles to the north, the 77th Infantry was landing at the other side of Apra Harbor. Both forces came under unwelcoming heavy fire from the Japanese artillery positions that had survived the intensive bombardment. It was to take five days of heavy combat for the two forces to link up and lock most of the island's defenders into the narrow appendage of the Orote Peninsula. The Japanese tried to make their own amphibious assault to effect a breakout. When this failed, they resorted to trying a frontal charge which had to be mounted through a swamp against the 3rd Marine Division. By now familiar with the futile Japanese tactic of last resort, the Americans held firm through a tropical downpour as the alcohol-crazed enemy, sounding "like New Year's Eve in the zoo," hurled themselves vainly into the machine-gun fire. The assault collapsed. Yet for days the attempt to drive the Marines back into the sea was pressed with ferocity by the Japanese, until most of their strength had been wiped out in suicidal attacks.

Inland, the fighting against the defenders sheltering in cliff positions and hillside caves dragged on. Two weeks later, on August 10, the end of organized resistance came when General Obata made his final stand after radioing Tokyo: "THE HOLDING OF GUAM HAS BECOME HOPELESS. I WILL ENGAGE THE ENEMY IN THE LAST BATTLE TOMORROW." Over 3,500 Japanese and 1,500 Americans died. Mopping up operations against isolated pockets of continuing enemy resistance were still going on in 1945, and the last enemy soldier did not give himself up until 1972.

29
Moral Obligations

"Hell is on us!" one of the Emperor's advisers exclaimed on June 15, 1944, on hearing the news that Saipan was under attack. The next eight weeks, as the American forces battled to subdue the island bases in the Marianas, was indeed to bring a hellish series of military disasters on Hirohito's generals and admirals.

That very afternoon B-29s of the U.S. Army's 20th Air Force took off from the Chinese airfields to make their first raid on the southern home island of Kyushu. The target was Yawata, Japan's steel center; the bombs fell wide, causing slight damage to the Imperial Iron and Steelworks, but heavy civilian casualties. A week later came the news of the Combined Fleet's disastrous defeat in the Battle of the Philippine Sea. Then, on July 8, the 15th Army in Burma was ordered to give up its futile struggle to break through the British front at Imphal. General Mutaguchi's U-Go campaign had collapsed and with it the "March to India." The advancing soldiers of the British 14th Army discovered a message scrawled on a wall by the retreating enemy: "British too many guns, tanks and troops. Japanese going, but back in six months." General Slim, who had now won "the first decisive battle of the Burma campaign," intended otherwise. He ordered a full pursuit of General Mutaguchi's emaciated and demoralized troops; but it was soon bogged down to a snail's pace in the monsoon mud for the next four months.

Each of the defeats was a severe blow to Prime Minister Tojo's war leadership. He faced a growing revolt among his cabinet and the increasing hostility of the Emperor's advisers, who were seeking the opportunity to cut his near-dictatorial powers. Three days after acknowledging the disastrous outcome of operations in Burma, Tojo went to the Palace to submit his resignation. Accepting the advice of the Jushin Council, Hirohito appointed General Kaniaki Koiso Prime Minister. The stolid former military governor of Korea was considered a moderate. The complexion of Japan's new government was emphasized by the appointment of the benign ex-Prime Minister, Admiral Yonai, as his deputy and the reinstatement of General Sugiyama, whom Tojo had supplanted, as army minister and Chief of Staff. A Supreme War Council was established in response to the Emperor's desire as expressed to his new Prime Minister: "You will need to collaborate to put an end to the war in Asia and I recommend you not to antagonize the Russians."

The pressures on Japan to seek some face-saving peace were heavy. The navy minister had been warned by Admiral Toyoda that the probability of the Combined Fleet being able to survive until the end of the year "would be very difficult," although its survival was essential to prevent the Empire's defense from collapsing and bringing the invasion of Japan. But with the Allies insisting on nothing less than humiliating unconditional surrender, even the moderates in the cabinet dared not think of proposing peace feelers. This would have been impossible in the summer of 1944, not least because the Imperial Army at last appeared on the way to winning its eight-year war against China and Japan's giving up her hold on the mainland would be insisted on by the United States. No member of the cabinet would yet dare support any measure that would even appear to deny the generals the prize for which over a million soldiers had died, no matter how many more lives had to be sacrificed to defend the Empire's crumbling Pacific perimeter.

RETREAT IN CHINA, ADVANCE IN BURMA

The China Occupation Army's Ichi-Go offensive, which now assumed an increasingly important role in Japan's war strategy, was entering its second phase by June. The push west into Hunan was advancing toward the capture of the airfields from which Chennault's 14th Air Force was putting up the only real opposition to the Japanese offensive. The American raid on Yawata had spurred this drive, although the B-29 bases at Chengtu were, thanks to Stilwell's foresight, still safely 600 miles behind the approaching front line. The safety of General Chennault's bases, as well as the continued survival of the Nationalist regime, was in doubt. On June 18, 1944, the Japanese captured Changsha, which lay just 400 miles east of the Yangtze city of Chungking, where Chiang Kai-shek's government now faced the peril of serious famine because of the loss of China's southern rice bowl. The advance pressed on another 100 miles, to invest Hengyang and its nearby airfield. The siege was temporarily lifted when the Japanese withdrew, only to renew their attack with four fresh divisions. The city fell on August 8, after Chiang Kai-shek petulantly cut off support for the 10th Chinese Army whose commander, he suspected, was plotting against him. Stilwell refused to allocate more gasoline and ammunition to Chennault's relief efforts because it "would be a waste of effort."

While the Japanese armies in China were biting deep into the shrinking Nationalist territory, 800 miles west across the foothills of the Himalayas, the two-month Allied siege of Myitkyina ended on August 3, 1944, with the ritual suicide of the Japanese general commanding the 18th Army. His surviving troops retreated down the Irrawaddy toward Mandalay. Stilwell had finally achieved success after a campaign of eleven months, but it had brought over 18,000 casualties, making it as costly as the bloodiest of the Pacific battles. The capture of the strategic communications center of upper Burma meant that the aerial leg of The Hump route into China could be shortened and the monthly tonnage of supplies flown to the Nationalist armies doubled at a critical time. Some 100 miles to the south, twelve divisions blocked the eastern thrust of the Allied pincer movement, which was pushing its way around to Lashio to achieve the reopening of the Burma Road. The British had now no choice but to support the campaign that was approaching its goal. "It is clear, now that Stilwell has led us down to Myitkyina," General Brooke recorded, "we shall have to go on fighting in Burma."

This hard-won victory brought Stilwell promotion to full general and orders to leave the front for SEAC headquarters in Kandy. But the President advised Chiang Kai-shek to put Stilwell, as the one man "who had the ability, the force and the determination to offset the disaster which threatens China," in control of all his armies. Roosevelt, launching his campaign for a fourth presidential term, was eager to show that he was not neglecting America's support of China. He had sent Vice President Henry Wallace on a mission in June to try to persuade Chiang Kai-shek and Mao Tse-tung to patch up their quarrel and unite their forces under the unified command of the American general who had achieved a spectacular success leading Chinese soldiers. But Chiang Kai-shek was still backing Chennault, and was no more prepared to let the President foist Stilwell upon him than he was to reach an accommodation with his Communist foes. Adept at the art of stalling to get his way, Chiang was not as worried as Washington by the Japanese advance into his southern provinces, whose dissident warlords had always been a source of problems for the Nationalists. He agreed to receive the President's special emissary, General Patrick Hurley, who arrived in August via Moscow with Donald Nelson. He was charged with the nearly impossible mission of persuading the Nationalist leader to agree to a reconciliation with the Chinese Communists. The former Secretary of War failed to produce either agreement or a common military strategy to meet the Japanese threat.

In Washington, the Joint Chiefs were taking a much more sanguine view of China's military potential than the President, as they prepared their strategy for the final defeat of Japan. The capture of the Marianas reduced the usefulness of the Chengtu bomber bases because Saipan's airfields were nearer Tokyo and safer from the threat of Japanese attack.

After Marshall had returned in mid-June from a tour of the rapidly advancing Allied front in France, he sent General MacArthur and Admiral Nimitz a directive asking them to consider "possibilities of expediting the Pacific Campaign." He outlined the Joint Chiefs' plans for lines of advance for an invasion of Japan, and invited their "views and recommendations."

MacArthur interpreted the repeated references to Formosa and the lack of any mention of his planned November assault on Mindanao as a threat to his promised crusade. "It is my most earnest conviction that the proposal to bypass the Philippines and launch an attack across the Pacific directly on Formosa is unsound," he replied to Marshall on June 18, requesting an "opportunity of personally proceeding to Washington to present my views." Nimitz's response to the Joint Chiefs' request was also cautious. He too believed that to make an assault on Formosa without first taking the Palaus or the Philippines could expose the attacking forces to too great a risk. Of all Nimitz's commanders, only Admiral Halsey was positively in favor of making the next landing on Luzon and then thrusting directly to Japan by way of Okinawa Island in the Ryukus.

"We must be careful not to allow our personal feelings and Philippine political considerations to override our great objective, which is the early conclusion of the war with Japan," General Marshall cautioned MacArthur. At the same time, his reply soothingly reminded MacArthur that "bypassing" was not "synonymous with abandonment." Disregarding the implied rebuff as well as the semantics, MacArthur sent his "Musketeer" blueprint for the invasion of the Philippines to Washington in July. Musketeer was supported by Nimitz's insistence that the old ORANGE Plan bases would be essential for the final move north. The apparent agreement of the two Pacific commanders was a powerful factor in persuading the Joint Chiefs to drop their plan to bypass the Philippines. The President was concerned about the political damage he might suffer in the coming election by appearing to abandon the Filipinos. Such a decision, MacArthur intimated to Marshall would lead to his resignation. Nor was it an idle threat since MacArthur had earlier that year been seriously considered as a presidential candidate by a group of Republican senators. His status as a popular hero and the constant attention of the press, together with his widely known opposition to the New Deal philosophy, had made him the focus of anti-Roosevelt feeling. A silent candidate in the early primaries, MacArthur had been running respectably until a political storm was raised by a letter in which he appeared openly critical of the President, bringing his formal declaration that he was "not a candidate" because it would be "detrimental to the war effort."

Roosevelt was relieved to have been rid of a potential political rival, but MacArthur had demonstrated how large was his constituency of popular support among Americans. The general was therefore inclined to dismiss as "purely political" the June summons from the White House to meet with the President and Admiral Nimitz at Pearl Harbor. He regarded it as an attempt by Roosevelt to be seen playing the role of an active Commander in Chief before the election. The Joint Chiefs of Staff, who were not invited to attend, were apprehensive about the pressures that would be put on the President to intervene personally in the rivalry between MacArthur and Nimitz. Making a tour of the Pacific bases just before Roosevelt set out for Hawaii, Admiral King impressed on Nimitz his own view that Formosa was a more suitable strategic base for launching the final assault on Japan than the Philippines. He also expressed concern over the growing British effort to get involved in the final advance and his desire to keep the Royal Navy well east of the Philippines. It had been rumored that Churchill was going to make a bid to regain colonial possessions in the Far East by extending Mountbatten's authority into the Southwest Pacific Command.

On the long flight from Brisbane, MacArthur paced the *Bataan*, holding forth about the "humiliation of forcing me to leave my command to fly to Honolulu for a political picture taking junket." After ignoring earlier requests, he had finally been ordered by General Marshall to be in Hawaii to meet the President on July 26. He had never left his Pacific command and was now being called away at another moment of crisis, during the terminal stage of the New Guinea campaign. The resourceful General Adachi, whose 20,000 troops had been leapfrogged at Wewak, had now marched his men 100 miles through the coastal jungle to launch an attack on the American base at Aitape. The U.S. 6th Army Commander had sent out the 43rd Infantry Division to repulse a flanking move at the Driniumor River, but it took three weeks of some of the fiercest fighting in the whole New Guinea campaign to hurl back the attempt by the Japanese 18th Army to break through. The attack was pressed so hard that for a time it threatened to postpone the final move in the New Guinea campaign: the landing of the Typhoon Force to secure Mar and Sansapor. Once Allied soldiers were safely ashore on these two points on the head of New Guinea's Vogelkop Peninsula by July 20, MacArthur's attention was focused on the need to capture Halmahera Island by September 15, to put a final stepping stone in position for the invasion of the southern Philippines.

For MacArthur, the hard-fought New Guinea campaign, which had been won by his brilliantly executed strategy, was now all but over. Once General Adachi had been dealt with, MacArthur decreed that the isolated enemy garrisons "represent no menace to current or future operations." The task of "mopping up" was to be passed over to General Vasey and his Australian divisions, as they moved in to replace the American-held bases along the coast. Not surprisingly, many of the Japanese garrisons proved more aggressive than MacArthur had anticipated. In the months ahead resentment grew in the Australian High Command, as the mopping up turned into a thankless ordeal of unpublicized jungle fighting while the withdrawn American forces went on to win the final battles of the Pacific War.

General MacArthur's cavalier treatment of the Australian forces, without whom he would have lost the Papuan campaign, was equalled by his disdain for the President. On July 26, his B-17 had landed at Honolulu a full hour before the heavy cruiser *Baltimore*, carrying Roosevelt's party, docked. But he did not join Admiral Nimitz and the formal welcoming party on the pier. The general's absence was underscored by his delayed arrival in a conspicuous motorcade; MacArthur was informally attired in his flying jacket.

STRATEGIC CHOICES

The President, however, was determined to carry off the incident affably, despite the fears of Admiral Leahy, his Chief of Staff, that it might sour the atmosphere of an already difficult conference. The mood of cordiality lasted through dinner that evening in the luxurious Officers' Club villa, with balconies opening out onto the magnificent sweep of Waikiki Beach. Then Roosevelt adjourned to a map-hung room and told MacArthur and Nimitz that the purpose of their meeting was "to determine the next phase of the Pacific War."

The President used a bamboo stick to jab at the maps while Nimitz presented his carefully prepared case, bringing out charts and statistics to show the advantages of using Formosa as a main base for the final operations against Japan. He was careful to acknowledge that the neutralization of the enemy air bases in the Philippines was an essential precondition, but he did not insist that the invasion of the entire archipelago was necessary. MacArthur decided to "go it alone" and rely on his own eloquence to persuade the President that the United States was under a "moral obligation" to liberate 17 million Filipinos before assaulting Japan. He argued that this would provide a much larger jumping-off base. Bypassing most of the Philippines would, in his view, be military and politically disastrous: "American public opinion will condemn you, Mr. President. And it would be justified."

Discussions continued through the next morning with the President trying to establish the extent to which the two commanders differed over the role that the Philippines would play in their strategies for the final assault on Japan. Before attending a formal luncheon, Roosevelt insisted on making a motor tour of the Oahu bases. In the course of the drive, in which the admiral and the general were sandwiched in the open limousine on either side of the President, Nimitz knew from the congenial conversation between the general and the President that MacArthur had won all his points. The Commander in Chief Southwest Pacific was in no doubt about his victory. "We've sold it," he announced that afternoon, as soon as the *Bataan* had taken off from Hickham Field on the first leg of the return flight to Australia. When he reached Brisbane, he assured his staff that "the President has accepted my recommendations and approved the Philippines plan."

The Joint Chiefs still had to endorse MacArthur's strategy. It took another month of debate before Admiral King reluctantly agreed to an assault on Luzon because a Philippines invasion demanded fewer troops than an assault on the Japanese defense on the rugged coast of Formosa. Yet on his return to the United States, Roosevelt gave a radio broadcast in which he simply announced "complete accord with my old friend General MacArthur." This was a clear signal to the Americans, as well as the Japanese, that the promised return of the U.S. Army to Manila was not going to be long delayed. Some shrewd White House observers saw the hand of the master politician, who had now arranged it so that the invasion of the Philippines would be timed to grab the headlines during the final stage of the presidential election campaign.

On September 8, the Joint Chiefs issued the directive to the Southwest Pacific Command setting December 20 as the date for landings on Leyte. On that same day American carrier aircraft were hammering Yap and the Palau Islands in the Philippine Sea. Under Nimitz's policy of "changing drivers" to rotate command, three days later the Fifth Fleet was to become the Third Fleet when the battleship *New Jersey* arrived flying the flag of Admiral Halsey. He proceeded to carry out a systematic series of air strikes against the Philippines. After receiving the reports from the task group pilots, who had been raiding Mindanao and the airfields on Luzon, he came to the conclusion that a great opportunity was opening up to exploit the surprising weakness of the Japanese defense.

On September 12 Halsey signaled Nimitz, enthusiastically reporting that it appeared virtually all the enemy air strength on the islands had been wiped out, there was "no shipping left to sink," and the "enemy's non-aggressive attitude" was "unbelievable and fantastic." He concluded that the Philippines' defenses must be "wide open" and he urged that assembling for the Third Fleet's upcoming assault on the Palau Islands be switched to a full-scale invasion of Leyte in the Philippines.

The planned landings on Peleliu were just a week away. Nimitz and his CINCPAC planners were reluctant to call off the assault on the main Japanese base in the Palaus; they believed that the island was a necessary staging point for future operations north against Japan or south to the Philippines. Nonetheless they accepted the possibility that Halsey's proposed advancing of the Leyte assault might well shorten the Pacific War by months. Nimitz signaled the Joint Chiefs in Washington accordingly, offering the 24th Army Division, then embarking at Pearl Harbor for the attack on Yap, for assignment together with the Third Fleet to an invasion of Leyte as soon as a pullback from the Palau campaign was completed.

OCTAGON STRATEGY

The American military leaders were gathered at Quebec for the Octagon Conference with the British; from there, Marshall radioed the proposed change timetable to MacArthur. He was at sea, accompanying the landing forces that were to assault Morotai Island off Halmahera, and so observing strict radio silence. General Sutherland, his Chief of Staff, was in no doubt that his superior must agree to the proposal. Sutherland signaled back from Brisbane: "SUBJECT TO COMPLETION OF ARRANGEMENTS WITH NIMITZ, WE SHALL EXECUTE LEYTE OPERATION ON OCTOBER 20."

The Southwest Pacific Command message was brought into the Château Frontenac dining room where the Joint Chiefs were being lavishly entertained by the Canadian General Staff. The U.S. Army and Navy Chiefs excused themselves from the table for a brief conversation. Marshall would recall that it was "not a difficult decision to make." Within ninety minutes a coded "go-ahead" signal was flashed back across the Pacific. By the time MacArthur had returned to his advance headquarters at Hollandia, he found to his immense delight that the Joint Chiefs had ordered him to go ahead with preparations to invade Luzon, a decision which he realized ended any chance of pursuing the alternative strategy to invade Formosa. The Philippines—just as the old ORANGE War Plan had intended—were to be the major base for the final operations against Japan, with Okinawa or Iwo Jima as intermediate jumping-off points.

The decision to accelerate the pace of the Pacific War now meant that the Combined Chiefs of Staff could dramatically shorten the projected timetable for the defeat of Japan to a year or eighteen months after the end of hostilities against Germany. At Quebec, the most optimistic were predicting a German surrender by Christmas. This contributed to what Churchill called the "blaze of friendship" between the Allied partners; "everything we had touched had turned to gold." After more than three years of wrangling and rescheduling, the invasion of France had succeeded; Paris had been liberated and General Eisenhower's forces were across the Seine, while the Allied troops who had come ashore in the Anvil landings in the South of France drove north to Lyons. In Italy, the Germans had been pushed back from Rome to Florence, and the Red Army's front had advanced to Warsaw.

The prospect of a German collapse, bringing the Russians into the war against Japan by the end of the year, brought a new sense of urgency to the British over operations in the Southeast Asia theater. "We had to regain on the field of battle our rightful possessions in the Far East," Churchill had resolved, in spite of the President's resistance to deploying American forces to restore former European colonial possessions. Recognizing Roosevelt's dilemma, the Prime Minister proposed that the U.S. Army send two divisions through Burma to China in order to release British forces to execute Mountbatten's scheme for a series of amphibious assaults on first Rangoon and then Sumatra and Malaya.

It was also part of the Prime Minister's plan that the Royal Navy should act alongside the U.S. Fleet, to show the postwar world that the Pacific was not an American lake. Admiral King had already vetoed this scheme in the Joint Chiefs of Staff's meetings, on the grounds that their ally lacked adequate logistical support for long range operations. The very idea of the British now wanting a larger or at least more visible role in a war they had for three years done their best to keep a low Allied priority was anathema to the admiral. Churchill, however, insisted on pressing his offer at the final plenipotentiary session in Quebec. King indicated that the matter was "under study." Offended, the Prime Minister urged still more firmly: "The offer of the British Fleet has been made. Is it accepted?" Anxious to avoid a bitter clash, Roosevelt, exercising his authority as Commander in Chief, accepted, leaving his Chief of Naval Operations scowling.

In the second week of September 1944, while the British and American war leaders deliberated on the problems of ending the war, American forces on the other side of the world were making two more thrusts against Japan. Following the Octagon decision to speed up the Pacific War timetable, both proved unnecessary. But the substitution of Leyte for Mindanao came forty-eight hours too late for MacArthur to call off the September 15 landings of the 31st Infantry Division on Morotai Island to secure control of north Molucca Sea. Nimitz refused to cancel the Palau offensive.

Steaming midway between the two assaults, the fast carriers of Admiral Halsey's Task Force 38 were covering both Allied landings. He realized that "Operation Stalemate" was redundant. But because Nimitz had canceled the attack on Yap, he decided that occupying Ulithi, Angaur, and Peleliu was required as additional insurance for successful operations against the Philippines and Japan.

Ulithi, the easternmost atoll of the Carolines, was valuable for its deepwater anchorage. It was assaulted on September 22, and, because it was undefended, fell into American control in a matter of minutes. L-Day on Angaur was September 17. In three days the soldiers of the 81st Infantry Division had most of the island under control. Five miles to the north lay Peleliu itself; but its capture would take the 1st Marine Division nearly eight weeks of rugged fighting before they could claim victory.

The Japanese had given the Palaus priority over the Marianas in their spring efforts to toughen up their inner defense perimeter. Peleliu, with its towering limestone ridges, was a natural fortress. Artillery batteries, machine-gun nests, and blockhouses had been dug into the soft rock through which miners had excavated interconnecting tunnels, many too deep to be reached by the bombs and shells of the bombardment that began on September 12. The garrison of over 5,000, with as many construction troops, had taken refuge in their bastion confident that they had enough reserves of ammunition and supplies in the deep caves to resist a long siege.

BLOODY PELELIU

"Victory depends on our recent battle lessons, especially those of Saipan," General Inoue told his garrison. "The Americans rely solely upon material power. If we can repulse them with material power, it will shock them beyond imagination." However, he was not able to test his theory since he was off the island on an inspection tour when the attack began. His men had been well drilled in the systematic tactics of defense; the wild Banzai charges had been discarded in favor of fighting to hold each cave and every bluff. Using the terrain and their extensive fortifications, the Japanese intended that the Americans would pay a heavy price for Peleliu.

On September 15, the carrier strikes roared overhead to deliver their pre-assault rocket attacks while the 1st Marine Divisions' Amphtracs headed toward the landing beaches at the southern tip of the island. The landing force was met by heavy artillery fire from the enemy's well-protected gun emplacements. Hardest hit of all was General Rupertus's left flank, where Japanese beachhead pillboxes that had not been revealed by aerial reconnaissance photographs opened up from a rocky promontory at point-blank range. It took thirty hours for Captain George Hunt's company to neutralize them in savage hand-to-hand combat that left him with only a third of his force. The burning wrecks of Amphtracs caught in the enfilading fire and mangled corpses spewed out across the shallows created a scene of bloody carnage reminiscent of Tarawa.

The beachhead was under heavy Japanese fire all day. The same afternoon, the defenders launched the first of a series of tank counterthrusts across the northern perimeter of the airfield ahead of the Marine line. They broke through briefly before reserves were rushed up to plug the gap. Dusk found General Rupertus less than halfway to his assigned L-Day objectives; his 1st Marine Division had taken over 1,000 casualties, 20 percent of whom were dead. The Stalemate plan allowed two days for

ARBITERS OF SEAPOWER One of the mighty task forces of carriers and battleships that by 1945 had won for the U.S. Navy the undisputed mastery over the Pacific.

AN ALTAR OF PEACE The Japanese delegation arrives aboard the USS *Missouri* on September 2, 1945 for the formal surrender ceremony.

capturing the entire island. But true to its unfortunate name, this was only the beginning of an operation that would drag on for almost two months. The bloody, grinding warfare was to reach a savagery the 1st Marines had not encountered even in their long struggle on Guadalcanal. The main cause of their ordeal was the rugged and well-defended terrain of the Umurbrogol Hills, which were honeycombed with caves and enemy strongpoints.

Spearheading the grueling assault was Colonel "Chesty" Puller's 1st Regiment, whose task was well described by Private Russell Davis:

> Clawing and crawling up the cliff went platoons that were no more than squads, and companies that were no more than large platoons. . . . From the base of the cliffs we could pick out each man and follow him until he got hit, went to the ground or climbed to the top. Not many made the top. As they toiled, caves, gulleys and holes opened up and the Japanese dashed out to roll grenades down on them, and sometimes to lock, body to body, in desperate wrestling matches. Knives and bayonets flashed on the hillside. I saw one man straighten and lunge to kick something that attacked his legs like a mad dog. He reached and heaved, a Japanese soldier came end over end down the hill. The machine gunners yelled encouragement.

The remorseless attack on the hills during the first week of the Peleliu battle cost Colonel Puller's regiment a third of its strength. The 5th Regiment had also suffered heavy casualties while securing the airfield, and the 7th Regiment lost almost as many men crushing the Japanese in the south of the island. General Geiger, the ground forces commander for the whole operation, fearing that Stalemate was becoming just that, brought in the infantrymen, who had taken nearby Angaur, to join in the battle to clear the enemy position in the Umurbrogol Hills. Flame-throwers were modified to enable them to penetrate 50 feet and incinerate the enemy in the deep tunnels.

Cave by cave, ridge by ridge, the advance inched north as the Japanese were blasted and burned out of their positions. One large cavern was found to contain more than 1,000 dead, and 10,000 enemy soldiers were estimated to have died by November 25, when the resistance finally ended. The Japanese garrison commander radioed "ALL IS OVER ON PELELIU" before taking his own life. Two thousand American soldiers and Marines had died; many times that number had been wounded. It had taken 1,589 rounds of heavy and light ammunition to kill *each* enemy defender of Peleliu. Such grisly statistics were attributed by the field commanders as much to the terrain as to the well-drilled defenders. It was one of the tragedies of war that the slaughter was unnecessary. Peleliu had ceased to be a vital objective to the Americans long before the first Marine died on the island. However, as the naval bombardment force commander Admiral J. B. Oldendorf observed: "If military leaders were gifted with the same accuracy of foresight that they are with hindsight, undoubtedly the assault and capture of the Palaus would never have been attempted."

A month before one of the bitterest island battles of the Pacific ended, the operation which had made Stalemate unnecessary was set in motion as General MacArthur sailed with his invasion armada to fulfill his promise to return to the Philippines.

30

"The Flowers of Death"

"All of Admiral Mitscher's carriers have been sunk tonight—INSTANTLY!" Tokyo Rose gloated over the airwaves on the evening of October 15, 1944. Americans on the Pacific bases who regularly tuned in for the dance music that Mrs. Iva Ikuko D'Aquino made a feature of her propaganda broadcasts jeered heartily at such a preposterous claim. Yet the Japanese public awoke the next day to the news that its "Wild Eagle" naval pilots had won a "Second Pearl Harbor" in the waters off Formosa. The Emperor announced a public victory holiday, the first in over two years.

The American Third Fleet's Commander in Chief had forced Japan to invent a face-saving triumph after his carriers delivered yet another catastrophic hammering. On October 10, Halsey had begun a series of strikes on Okinawa and the adjoining Ryukyu Islands air bases to "destroy enemy naval and air forces threatening the Philippine area." Two days later, after refueling, the Third Fleet's 1,000 carrier fighters and bombers launched a fresh round of raids on Formosa. They were joined by one hundred Superfortresses of the Army's 20th Air Force staging through the Chengtu bases. The Imperial Navy's 6th Air Fleet was ordered aloft into the battle. Most of Admiral Fukudome's flyers were green trainees whose combat experience was limited to film simulators (employed to save fuel). Over five hundred were shot down like "so many eggs thrown against the stone wall of indomitable enemy formations," as Fukudome sorrowfully reported. Halsey, by contrast, lost only seventy-nine planes, although one of his cruisers and a carrier had been hit when a thirty-bomber enemy strike surprised the Third Fleet task groups after dark on October 14. Obviously mistaking their own flaming crashes as ships hit, the surviving Japanese pilots returned to claim a spectacular victory, which Fukudome inflated in his reports to Tokyo before sending out another one hundred-plane strike the next day to pursue the retreating Americans.

"Third Fleet's sunken and damaged ships have been salvaged and are retiring towards the enemy," Halsey, tongue-in-cheek, signaled to Pearl Harbor. He was hoping that the Japanese would send out their Mobile Fleet to attack the damaged carrier *Franklin* and the crippled heavy cruiser *Canberra*, both under tow and being very deliberately trailed behind the Third Fleet as "Combait Division 1." Disappointed that the Imperial Navy did not take the bait, Halsey set course south to cover the invasion of Leyte as MacArthur's transport armada sailed from the New Guinea ports. He was now more determined than ever to carry out his intention "to completely annihilate the Jap Fleet if the opportunity offers."

The naval staff in Tokyo were also waiting for the next assault. They were again intending to concentrate their remaining air- and naval power in a last all-out effort to smash the Third Fleet. This was to be the Japanese Navy's role in the Shō-Gō "Victory Operation"—a strategy that had been devised by Imperial General Headquarters to protect the inner defense line of the Empire. Four plans had been prepared for each "theater of decisive battle," depending on whether the Americans assaulted the Philippines, Formosa, the Kuriles, or Honshu itself. Alerted by diplomatic sources in Moscow, early in October Tokyo had put Field Marshal Count Hisaichi Terauchi's Manila headquarters of the Southern Army on alert to implement Shō-1. Yet even without the leaks from the Kremlin, the Philippines appeared to be the most likely next target for the Allied offensive, an obvious move north after their victory in New Guinea.

A quarter of a million troops were already in the Philippines as reinforcements were rushed south to strengthen the garrison on Mindanao, closest to the Molucca island of Morotai, which had just been seized by MacArthur's forces. Terauchi was counting on the help of the 6th Air Fleet to smash the enemy beachheads before they could get established, although his 14th Army Commander, Lieutenant General Shigenori Kuroda, had argued for a proper defense in depth, constantly warning: "Words will not sink American ships." For his criticism he was replaced by General Tomoyuki Yamashita, the "Lion of Malaya," who had been languishing in Manchuria after his spectacular victory over the British two years earlier because General Tojo had seen him as a potential rival.

Yet as the Shō-1 strategy was being prepared to defend the Philippines, it was fatally disrupted by the Third Fleet's raids, which had triggered the premature implementation of the Shō-2 plan to defend Formosa. Many of the aircraft which were used in Formosa's defense were intended to be used to defend the Philippines as well. This air force had now lost half of its strength before the real decisive battle was joined.

It was not until October 17 that Imperial General Headquarters finally knew for certain from which direction the Americans would attack. Early that morning an urgent alarm had been received from their 16th Army Command, that an enemy force was approaching Leyte. U.S. Navy minesweepers had been spotted sweeping the mouth of the landlocked gulf while Ranger battalions made a series of landings to capture the small islands guarding its entrance.

The army staff learned for the first time that the navy was intending to commit every surviving warship to the battle. Admiral Toyoda argued that a supreme gamble was necessary as this was the "last chance to destroy the enemy, who enjoys the luxury of material resources." The generals feared that another defeat would leave the fleet too weak to protect the home islands. Shō-1 was submitted for the Emperor's approval only after Admiral Nakazawa, the Chief of Naval Operations and principal architect of the strategy, had pleaded tearfully for the Combined Fleet to be given an opportunity to win a decisive victory or "bloom as the flowers of death."

That afternoon the coded radio signals flashed out from Tokyo's army and navy commands to put Shō-1 into operation. Toyoda appreciated well enough that with only half of the planned air fleet at his disposal the odds were against him, but he was counting on luck and improvisation to pull off his plan to use the Combined Fleet's surviving carriers as bait to lure off the main strengths of the Third Fleet long enough to send his battleships in to destroy the American landings.

When Admiral Takijiro Onishi arrived in Manila on October 17 to assume command of the Air Fleet's coming battle, he was horrified to find that there were fewer than one hundred operational planes in the entire Philippines. This was hardly enough airpower to carry out the orders he had been given to "hit the enemy carriers and keep them neutralized for at least a week." He therefore concluded he had no choice but to implement the plan for sending Special Attack Groups to make suicide strikes as "the only way of assuring our meager strength will be effective to a maximum degree, and that is for our bomb-laden fighter planes to crash dive into the decks of the enemy carriers." The relatively unskilled pilots who had volunteered to make one-way flights to death assumed the title of Kamikaze—after the Divine Wind that scattered the Mongol invasion fleet in 1281.

Six centuries later the fate of Japan in the Shō-1 decisive battle again rested on the hand of providence as the rival forces headed for the waters off the eastern Philippines. The Imperial Navy could muster 7 battleships, 4 carriers, 2 hybrid battleship carriers, 20 cruisers, and 29 destroyers, supported by 150 naval aircraft for this decisive engagement. Against them was pitted an overwhelming American force of 12 battleships, 32 carriers, 23 cruisers, 100 destroyers, and a massive air umbrella of almost 1,400 planes. The truly massive scale of the combined forces MacArthur commanded for the Leyte landing rivaled those which had taken part in the Allied invasion of Normandy four months earlier. The Third Fleet was to provide distant cover for the Armada of 430 transports, which were steaming north with the 174,000 men of General Walter Krueger's Sixth Army escorted and to be given fire support by Kinkaid's Seventh Fleet.

LANDING ON LEYTE

MacArthur had set October 20, 1944, as "A-Day" to avoid confusion with "D-Day," which the public now associated with the June 6 landings in France. His command ship, the heavy cruiser *Nashville*, was still two days steaming south of Leyte when Rear Admiral Oldendorf brought his bombardment force of six old battleships into the thirty-mile-wide Leyte Gulf and began the systematic reduction of enemy shore positions, supported by the bombs and rockets of American carrier planes.

The night of October 19 was coal black as the *Nashville* led the huge armada toward the mouth of island-locked Leyte Gulf before heaving to until dawn. General MacArthur—conscious of sharing the "universal sameness in the emotions of men"—read inspirational passages from the Bible before turning in. He slept soundly, confident that a ton of high explosives had been put ashore for each of his soldiers who would be landing next day.

A deadly rain of shells and bombs was raining down on the beachhead at sunrise as the *Nashville* steamed up the Gulf and anchored 2 miles from the beachhead. Her own guns were blasting away, adding to the spectacle MacArthur watched from the flag bridge:

> Landings are explosive once the shooting begins, and now thousands of guns were throwing their shells with a roar that was incessant and deafening. Rocket vapor trails criss-crossed the sky and black, ugly ominous pillars of smoke began to rise. High overhead, swarms of airplanes darted into the maelstrom. And across what would have ordinarily been a glinting, untroubled blue sea, the black dots of the landing craft churned towards the beaches.
>
> From my vantage point, I had a clear view of everything that took place. Troops were going ashore at Red Beach near Palo, at San Jose on White Beach and at the southern tip of Leyte on tiny Pansom Island. On the north, under Major General Franklin C. Sibert, the X Corps, made up of the 1st Cavalry and the 24th Infantry Divisions; to the south XXIV Corps under Major General John Hodge, consisting of the 7th and 96th Infantry Divisions. In overall command of the troops was Lieutenant General Walter Krueger of the Sixth Army.

The simultaneous assault by MacArthur's four divisions was plowing ashore on a 10-mile wide front against almost no enemy resistance. The few strongpoints had already been blasted out of existence, thanks to the careful reporting by the Philippine guerrillas, who had been in constant radio communication as the invasion armada approached. The beachhead was secured so rapidly that shortly after 1 P.M. that afternoon an impatient MacArthur, in a freshly pressed uniform, with a corncob pipe and aviator glasses, ordered a landing craft to carry him and President Osmeña to Red Beach for a dramatically staged arrival. The boatload of VIPs and press was caught in a traffic jam of vessels making for a makeshift sand-pier that had been especially bulldozed into the shallows. A harassed beachmaster, oblivious to the party of brass aboard, directed it away with a surly bellow of "Let 'em walk." This accounts, possibly, for the fierce expression the general wore as he strode through knee-deep water up to the beach. Accompanying cameramen photographed for posterity the first of numerous walks ashore that showed the world the general had finally fulfilled his promise.

"People of the Philippines, I have returned!" MacArthur broadcast at 2 P.M. from a battery of microphones set up on the beach by the Signal Corps in front of two remaining palm trees on which the Stars and Stripes flew alongside the Commonwealth flag. "Rally to me! Let the indomitable spirit of Bataan and Corregidor lead on!" the general ended an emotion-packed address to the Filipinos; his aides noticed that the speech left him trembling and visibly moved.

"A-Day" had been a brilliant triumph for MacArthur. By evening the Americans had command of a 17-mile front, with light casualties. The only serious enemy counterattack came with the appearance of a handful of torpedo bombers that had succeeded in dodging the fighters and anti-aircraft fire to score a hit on the heavy cruiser *Honolulu*. The drive inland toward Tacloban now began against patchy resistance as the Japanese intended to make their stand in the hills behind the island's capital. Fighting was still raging 2 miles from the city on October 23, when MacArthur insisted on the attendance of his senior commanders on the steps of the shattered Tacloban Municipal Building for a formal ceremony marking the restoration of President Osmeña's civil government in the Philippines. While Americans and Filipinos were celebrating the unexpectedly rapid progress of their first effort to liberate the Philippines, Japan's Shō-1 plan was rolling toward the invasion beaches.

THE BATTLE OF LEYTE GULF

At 7 A.M. on the morning of October 22, the Combined Fleet's line of battleships steamed out of Brunei, thick black clouds streaming from their smokestacks as the boiler-room mechanics struggled to readjust the burners to consume thick crude oil after the ships' 600-mile voyage from Singapore. In the mists off the north Borneo coast, ranks were split shortly before midday. Admiral Kurita, with five battleships, set course north through the treacherous Palawan reefs, heading toward Leyte Gulf through the San Bernardino Strait. Admiral Shogi Nishimura headed west to the Sulu Sea, with a two battleship force that was to be reinforced by three heavy cruisers steaming down from Hashirijama against the invasion beachhead.

Recently changed Japanese naval codes, deception, and strict radio silence had kept CINCPAC Intelligence from a full appreciation of the Sho-1 plan. So by next evening, Kurita was able to congratulate himself on having negotiated the reefs with the world's two biggest warships. He was unaware that he had been sighted by two hostile submarines. Confused at first by so many radar echoes, the skippers of the U.S.S. *Darter* and *Dace* patrolling the Palawan Passage mistook the Japanese as an approaching rain squall. Once they had established that it really was a battle fleet, they maneuvered on the surface to get into position for a dawn ambush.

Shortly after 5 A.M., the submarines slid below. Raising their periscopes cautiously in the oily calm, the two American captains waited for the zigzagging warships to materialize against the gray horizon. The executive officer of the *Dace*, Lieutenant Commander R. C. Benitez, felt the increasing tension in the submarine as the torpedo crews stood by their tubes for the order to fire: "The Japanese as unwilling and unsuspecting participants, propelled themselves on the stage and were promptly greeted by a salvo of torpedoes from the *Darter* on the port flank. A series of rapid explosions indicated to all in the *Dace* that the *Darter* had made a successful attack.

" 'It looks like the Fourth of July out there,' exclaimed the Captain. 'One is burning,' he continued. 'The Japs are milling and firing all over the place. What a show! What a show!' It must have been a grand show. Those of us unable to see what was happening. . . . 'Here they come,' said the Old Man. 'Stand by for a set up. Bearing, Mark! Range! Mark! Down 'scope! Angle on the bows ten port.' . . . With the Captain's words, 'Let the first two go by, they are only heavy cruisers,' we began to fire. We fired six torpedoes from the forward tubes. Almost immediately they began to strike home—one—two—three—four explosions. Four hits out of six torpedoes fired!"

As she went deep to avoid the depth charge attacks from escorting destroyers, the *Darter* picked up loud noises like "crackling cellophane," which first gave rise to fears that *Dace* was breaking up in the counterattack. It was, in fact, the heavy cruiser *Maya* sinking after being blasted apart by the *Dace*'s torpedoes. The *Darter*'s tin fish had slammed into the flank of the heavy cruiser *Atago*. Kurita's flagship was quickly engulfed in flames and the admiral and his staff had to save themselves by jumping overboard. Rescued by destroyer, Kurita transferred his command to the mighty *Yamato;* the involuntary dunking he received aggravated the slow recovery he was making from a bout of dengue fever. Now he was dismayed to find that another of his heavy cruisers, the *Takao*, had taken two torpedoes astern and was endeavoring to limp back to Brunei escorted by one destroyer, as others made a furious counterattack.

Depth charges came thundering down on the two submarines: "The Japs were very mad and we were very scared," Benitez recorded. But the counterattack was more savage than systematic. After some bad shaking up, the *Dace* and the *Darter* were able to creep out of range. When they surfaced to make their sinking reports, only the crippled cruiser was in sight. They were working into position to finish her off when their triumph was dented as the *Darter* ran aground on an uncharted section of the Palawan Reef. The *Dace*'s captain abandoned the chase to rescue the crew of his sister submarine, which was helplessly stranded and under attack by Japanese dive bombers.

What was to develop into the greatest naval clash in history had begun with the first round going decisively to the Americans. For the loss of a submarine, they had unmasked the main Japanese striking force and stripped it of three heavy cruisers. The odds were stacking up against the Shō-1. Nonetheless, Kurita, with his battleships intact, was plowing on in the spirit of desperation that characterized the whole operation. Knowing that he could expect little or no aircover because the Japanese land planes would be sent against the American carriers, he could hardly have been encouraged when he was passed a signal that had been received during the submarine attack, from Combined Fleet Headquarters: "IT IS VERY PROBABLE THAT THE ENEMY FORCE IS AWARE OF THE FACT THAT WE HAVE CONCENTRATED OUR FORCES," followed by Toyoda's blunt order: "EXECUTE ORIGINAL PLAN."

Patrol planes from the American carriers were already heading for the position radioed by the *Darter*. At 7:46 they were signaling that they had sighted the enemy battleship force rounding the southern tip of Mindoro. In the dimly lit plot of the *New Jersey*, Halsey was making his dispositions to fight the "tremendous battle" that was now looming. He recalled his Task Group 38.1, which had been detached the previous day to refuel at Ulithi, and sent orders to his three other groups, which were ranged along 300 miles of the eastern approaches to the Philippines launching air strikes, to make for a rendezvous point to reform Task Force 38's mighty battle formation. Marshaling his forces on the VHF Talk Between Ship's (TBS) network, Halsey spoke over the hissing loudspeakers in a hundred warships, his unmistakeable gravely voice bellowing, "Strike! Repeat! Strike! Good luck!"

Barely half an hour after air patrols sighted Kurita's force making for the San Bernardino Strait, the radio circuits were crackling again with news that another group of battleships had been spotted 300 miles to the south. Little guesswork was needed to determine that they were the second arm of the enemy effort to attack Leyte and would be swinging around up through the Surigao Straits. Admiral Davison's Task Group 38.4 was ordered to launch a second wave of strikes against them since his carriers were nearest to Leyte.

The glowing lucite panel of the *New Jersey*'s main battle plot was now marked with all the Japanese dispositions except for the enemy carriers. This was a considerable worry for Halsey since his dawn patrols had failed to reach far enough north to find Admiral Ozawa, who was waiting to be discovered as the "bait" being dangled some 200 miles off Luzon, to lure the Third Fleet away from Leyte Gulf. Halsey could not know that the flight decks of the four carriers and two hybrid battleships were empty of all but a handful of planes because the rest had been sent to the 1st Air Fleet on the Philippines. He fretted all day that, unless he found the Japanese carriers, they would jump his fleet.

The Third Fleet staff aboard the *New Jersey* anxiously waited for the air strikes to reach the enemy battleships. Patrols scoured the Pacific for the missing enemy carriers. The hunt was in full swing when the Japanese found the northernmost of Halsey's units. Shortly after 9 A.M., Admiral Frederick Sherman's Task Group 3 came under heavy attack by the first waves of enemy aircraft from the Luzon airfields. Combat Air Patrols, directed from the carrier *Essex*, broke up their formations, but the heavy barrage of antiaircraft fire did not stop a Japanese Kamikaze bomber from punching through to hit the *Princeton* squarely on the flight deck. Its 100-pound bomb plowed through the hangar, setting off a tumultuous blaze that blew her stern off when it reached down into the bomb magazines an hour later. Alongside, to assist in the firefighting, the cruiser *Birmingham* was caught up in the detonation, which blasted her superstructure, killing two hundred crewmen. The *Princeton* remained a floating inferno throughout the afternoon until she was dispatched in a mighty terminal explosion by American torpedoes that evening.

ACTION IN THE SIBUYAN SEA

The Japanese were only briefly to hold the lead in round two of the burgeoning sea and air confrontation. Shortly after the Kamikaze had mortally wounded the *Princeton*, the first strike wave of Task Force 38's aircraft came hurtling down on Kurita's force at 10:30 A.M. as it steamed at 18 knots across the island-locked Sibuyan Sea between Mindoro and Luzon. For the first time American pilots saw the immense size of Japan's vaunted superbattleships, as the *Musashi* and the *Yamato* maneuvered at high speed, with all the ponderous agility of a pair of elephants, trying to dodge the attack from 120 aircraft. A heavy barrage of flak was hurled skyward, but the twenty-four leading Avengers from the *Cabot* and the

Intrepid plunged unscathed through it to deliver two bombs and a torpedo, which vanished into the vast bulk of the *Musashi* forward. Even more stoutly constructed than her sister ship, "The Palace" was believed to be unsinkable by most of her crew. She plowed on with barely a shudder. Her attendant heavy cruiser *Myoko*, lacking the protection of 400mm armor plate, was hit and sent limping back to Brunei badly damaged.

Noon brought the second wave of American air strikes. Again the sky over the Japanese battleships puffed pink and purple with bursting antiaircraft shells. Three more torpedoes crumped into the *Musashi*. Still "The Palace" hurtled on, an elephant brushing off an attack by hornets. Without air protection, Kurita was becoming alarmed about how long his ships could take sustained punishment. At 1:15 he anxiously radioed Ozawa: "WE ARE BEING SUBJECTED TO REPEATED ENEMY CARRIER BASED AIR ATTACK. ADVISE IMMEDIATELY OF CONTACT AND ATTACKS MADE BY YOU ON THE ENEMY." His hopes that the American carriers must soon be put out of action were dashed when, fifteen minutes later, a third strike roared in. Like hunters driven by a primeval instinct, the aerial assault concentrated attacks on the *Musashi*. The battleship's damage-control parties were laboring frantically to deal with the damage when the next torpedoes hit "The Palace." The combined blows were beginning to have a cumulative effect as the great warship began losing speed.

The *Yamato* was now hit by two bombs and took on a temporary list; the battleship *Nagato* had lost a turret and one of her boiler rooms, and two destroyers had been put out of action. Kurita radioed urgently: "REQUEST LAND-BASED AIR FORCE AND MOBILE FORCE TO MAKE PROMPT ATTACK ON ENEMY CARRIER FORCE ESTIMATED IN SIBUYAN SEA."

The call for help that went out from the *Yamato* went unanswered. Recognizing the desperate position he was now in without aircover, Kurita gave orders for the experimental "Sanshikidon" shells to be loaded up in the battleship's mighty 18-inch guns. These were designed to hurl aloft fragmentation bombs to blast low-flying aircraft to pieces. He had hesitated to use them because they wrecked the main armaments' barrels, whose primary purpose was bombardment. Lookouts reported another sixty-five-plane strike approaching, and when they had closed, the earthquake blast of the world's biggest naval weapons jolted the battleships far more than the hits they had sustained.

The thunderous "Sanshikidon" failed to stop the American planes, which sent seven torpedoes thudding into the *Musashi*'s port quarter even as bombs blasted her pagoda-like bridge tower, killing many officers and wounding her captain. Any other warship would have foundered under such blows, but the battered superdreadnought still managed to make 6 knots. She was listing badly at 3:20 P.M. when another strike of planes arrived. After taking seventeen bombs and nineteen torpedoes, her fo'c'sle was now awash and Kurita ordered the *Musashi* to retire. An hour later, when reports of uncontrolled flooding made it plain that she would never reach port, he radioed: "GO FORWARD OR BACKWARD AT TOP SPEED AND GROUND ON NEAREST ISLAND TO BECOME LAND BATTERY." This ignominious fate the world's greatest warship avoided when, as dusk was falling, the mighty *Musashi* heeled over. Her giant screws turned briefly against the reddening sky as she slipped vertically beneath the waves of the Sibuyan Sea with all the grace of a sinking skyscraper.

Kurita's four remaining battleships held course eastward until 4 P.M., when he accepted his staff's advice that without air support they would merely make themselves "meat for the enemy" and ordered his force to retire to Combined Fleet Headquarters. However, when no further American air strikes appeared, Kurita thought better of retreating. Gambling on being able to make a night-time dash through the San Bernardino Strait to bring him off the coast of Leyte the following morning, by which time Admiral Ozawa should have lured off the Third Fleet carriers to the north, he ordered his force to reverse course and resume their original plan.

HALSEY IS LURED NORTH

The last report Halsey was given indicated that the badly mauled battleships were in full retreat west before 4:40 P.M. when he received the news he had been awaiting all day—scouting planes spotted the Japanese carriers 190 miles west of Luzon's Cape Engaño. The Commander in Chief of the Third Fleet was convinced he "had all the pieces of the puzzle." No doubt recalling how Admiral Spruance had been criticized for being too defensively minded during the Battle of the Philippine Sea, he decided to seize the chance to win a Nelsonian annihilation of the surviving Japanese carriers.

"CENTRAL FORCE HEAVILY DAMAGED ACCORDING TO STRIKE REPORT," Halsey Signaled CINCPAC at 7:05 P.M. "AM PROCEEDING NORTH WITH THREE GROUPS TO ATTACK CARRIER FORCE AT DAWN." "Bull" Halsey was taking the bait, just as Toyoda had predicted. He was unaware that the enemy carriers were planeless and only a lure. After his pilots had turned back the main force of enemy battleships it seemed to him "childish" to stay guarding the San Bernardino Strait. Even if the Japanese did try a break through to the beachhead, he believed Admiral Kinkaid would be able to fend them off with the assistance of the carriers of the Third Fleet's Task Group 38.1 due to return next day.

In the welter of signals passing back and forth that afternoon, both Kinkaid and Nimitz had wrongly assumed that Halsey would cover the San Bernardino Strait by leaving at least one force of carriers to guard the exit. This confusion had arisen as a result of a signal to the Third Fleet from the flagship just before 3:30 P.M. indicating that four battleships "WILL BE FORMED AS TASK FORCE 34 UNDER VICE ADMIRAL LEE COMMANDER BATTLE LINE. TASK FORCE 34 WILL ENGAGE DECISIVELY AT LONG RANGES." That this was only a preparatory order was not clear unless they had also picked up a second short-wave radio clarification from Halsey that Lee's force "WILL BE FORMED WHEN DIRECTED BY ME." But when he radioed his commander, "WE GO NORTH AND PUT THOSE JAP CARRIERS DOWN FOR KEEPS," there appeared no need to divide his fleet and leave Task Force 34 behind.

THE NIGHT ACTION IN SURIGAO STRAIT

If Kurita succeeded in making his breakthrough to join up with Nishimura heading for the Surigao Strait that night, his six battleships and ten heavy cruisers could easily overwhelm Kinkaid's six old battleships and three heavy cruisers protecting the vulnerable invasion beachhead. Throughout the day, Nishimura's southern force had steamed on through sporadic air attacks which had only hit the *Fuso*, wiping out her seaplanes. Passing between Negros and Mindanao, by nightfall he was less than 150 miles from the Strait, which debouched right into the mouth of Leyte Gulf. So close was he to his objective that Nishimura raced on through the dark without waiting or radioing Admiral Shima's heavy cruisers, who were left to catch him from 50 miles astern.

"Prepare for a night engagement," Kinkaid ordered Admiral Oldendorf that evening, anticipating that the second group of Japanese battleships would try to force the Surigao Passage in the small hours of the next morning. The bombardment force commander had made a careful disposition of his forces, with his six battlewagons and eight cruisers ranged in a double line of battle blocking the 16-mile wide exit to the Strait. Ahead in the narrow waters were twenty-eight destroyers, and the first line of defense was the thirty-nine "Expendable" PT boats, which had been sent to station themselves in the shadows of the islands off the southern entrance to the Strait.

The night hung thick, black, and moonless over a glassy calm, which mirrored the occasional lightning flash revealing the jagged northern shore of Mindoro. Gunfire flashes erupted shortly after 10 P.M. when the warships leading Nishimura's column came under attack from the first group of PT boats. They raced out from the dark shoreline to launch their torpedoes before speeding back again. No hits were made and for the next two hours the Japanese squadron plowed on at 20 knots.

The Japanese radar sets were cluttered by the multiple echoes from the nearby islands and failed to resolve the two lines of American destroyers which Cerberus-like were guarding the Surigao Strait. Turbines racing and their phosphorescent bow waves streaming, the first group raced within torpedo range of the enemy battleships without being sighted. The pace and excitement of the night action was recalled by Lieutenant Leonard R. Hudson, an officer on the *Remey*, which led Destroyer Squadron 54 in along the eastern shore of the Strait.

"The Captain radioed to the ships astern 'FOLLOW ME.' Then came the rapid orders 'STAND BY TO FIRE TORPEDOES! FIRE TORPEDOES! TORPEDOES AWAY!' About the time we fired our torpedoes the Jap radar picked us up. . . . They quickly turned on their searchlights and they were right on target. I felt like my picture was being taken with a giant flashbulb camera.

"We were so close that they shot over us with their AA guns. They shot in front of us; behind us and straddled us, but we got out without a scratch, and so did all the ships of Desron 54."

For all their dash, the first two flanking destroyer attacks failed to score any hits, and it was not until the 24th Division came charging to meet the Japanese battle line head-on that well-aimed torpedoes began hitting targets. The three leading Japanese destroyers were hit and one sunk. Then just past 2 A.M. the *Fuso* collected two torpedoes which set her ablaze. With a terrifying suddenness her magazines exploded, cleaving the battleship in half, leaving two burning wrecks that both the Americans and Admiral Nishimura, plowing on ahead, mistook for separate ships. "ENEMY DESTROYERS AND TORPEDO BOATS IN NORTH MOUTH OF SURIGAO STRAIT," the admiral signaled at 2:30. "TWO OF OUR DESTROYERS TORPEDOED AND DRIFTING. YAMASHIRO HAS ONE TORPEDO HIT, NOT HANDICAPPED IN ABILITY TO FIGHT."

Another American torpedo cut the *Yamashiro*'s speed down to 5 knots; still Nishimura stumbled on, accompanied only by a single destroyer and the heavy cruiser *Mogami*. When his shattered force reached the mouth of the Strait, the Japanese admiral suffered the terrible blow of finding that the T of his line had been capped by the blazing arc of gunfire from the American battleships and cruisers.

It was a supreme moment in the career of a naval commander, and Admiral Oldendorf aboard the cruiser *Louisville* relished his dominating position: "Upon giving the orders to 'open fire' it seemed as if every ship in the flank forces and the battle line opened up at once, and there was a semi-circle of fire which landed squarely on one point, which was the leading battleship. The semicircle of fire so confused the Japanese that they did not know what target to shoot at. I remember seeing one or two salvos start toward my flagship but in the excitement of the occasion, I forgot to look where they landed."

Those on the flag bridge of the *Yamashira* were left in no such doubt as salvo after salvo of 15-inch shells crashed down. With three turrets out of action and her superstructure a blazing shambles, the battleship still moved forward as though impelled by the blind determination of the now dead Nishimura's last command: "YOU ARE TO PROCEED AND ATTACK ALL SHIPS."

Shortly after 3 A.M. the blazing wreck turned turtle and sank. The *Mogami* was also badly ablaze and hauled around to flee up the Strait, plowing into the *Nachi*, which was bringing Admiral Shima's force into the battle. He promptly turned about and made good his escape, but the *Mogami* was sunk the next morning when Oldendorf's pursuing cruisers caught her.

The battle that wiped out the Japanese southern force was raging through the dark hours in Surigao Strait while 200 miles to the north, Kurita's northern force was threading its way through the San Bernadino Strait. As early as 9:30 P.M. the previous evening scouting patrols had spotted that the Japanese force had turned east again and signaled to Halsey that the enemy battleships were clearly heading for the now unguarded Strait. The report confirmed Admiral Lee's suspicions that Task Force 34 might indeed be rushing north after a decoy. The battle force commander had radioed his concern to the flagship, only to receive a curt "Roger" in reply to his query whether such a possibility had been considered. Doubts were also being expressed by Task Force 34's staff, in spite of Admiral Mitscher's decision to turn in early because "Admiral Halsey is in command now." He was woken with reports from PBY Black Cat flying boat patrols that the navigation lights were burning in the islands marking the San Bernadino Strait. After confirming that the flagship had indeed received the message, he went back to sleep. Admiral Halsey was not going to pass up a great victory just to "protect the Seventh Fleet." He gave it no more thought after 2 A.M. when a night patrol from the *Independence* sighted the enemy carriers. "We have them!" he exclaimed, and ordered full speed and all planes prepared for a dawn strike.

After Admiral Kinkaid commanding the Seventh Fleet received the news that Oldendorf's battleships had wiped out the Japanese southern force around 4 A.M., his attention had turned to the other enemy squadron. He had not picked up or been relayed the earlier reports from Task Force 34's night patrols, which would have warned him that Kurita had reversed course. His own PBY Black Cats had not found the enemy squadron, but it had occurred to him that they could be making a run through to the Philippine Sea. "IS TASK FORCE 34 GUARDING SAN BERNARDINO STRAIT?" he radioed to the *New Jersey*, just after 5 A.M. He would wait more than two hours for a response because of a signal snarl-up on the *New Jersey.*

THE ORDEAL OF THE ESCORT CARRIERS

After their drubbing the previous day, hopes began rising throughout the night aboard Kurita's warships. Leaving the Strait at 4 A.M., he was plowing south as fast as the damaged *Yamato* could steam, hardly daring to speculate why he had not been spotted. The sighting of the American patrol plane at 7 A.M. on October 25, followed by reports that lookouts had sighted masts 16 miles up over the horizon ahead, led Kurita to assume they must be one of the Third Fleet's carrier task group. If this was all that now stood between his battleships and the Leyte Gulf invasion transports, he saw the chance for his big guns to polish them off while his antiaircraft gunners held off the enemy planes. "BY HEAVEN-SENT OPPORTUNITY WE ARE DASHING TO ATTACK ENEMY CARRIERS," he signaled Combined Fleet Headquarters. "OUR FIRST OBJECTIVE IS TO DESTROY THE FLIGHT DECKS AND THEN THE TASK FORCE."

At 7:15 A.M., minutes after Kinkaid had eventually received the Third Fleet Commander's terse "NEGATIVE" to his 5 A.M. query, his worst fears were suddenly confirmed by a stream of urgent signals from the northernmost group of his escort carriers, which had just set off on their dawn antisubmarine patrols off the coast of Samar Island less than 100 miles away from the Leyte beachhead.

"ENEMY SURFACE FORCE OF 4 BATTLESHIPS, 7 CRUISERS AND 11 DESTROYERS SIGHTED TWENTY KNOTS TO THE NORTHWEST," flashed Ensign Hans Jensen, whose Avenger was armed with depth charges for attacking submarines, not enemy warships. "Tell the pilot to check his identification," the commander of the Taffy 3 escort carrier group, Rear Admiral Clifton A. Sprague, told his signals officer, assuming his greenhorn pilot must be mistaken. "IDENTIFICATION OF ENEMY FORCE CONFIRMED. SHIPS HAVE PAGODA MASTS," was the message that came flashing back.

"Ziggy" Sprague, a bluff, level-headed officer, realized he was "on a spot." His six small carriers and their six destroyers were all that now stood between the enemy battleships and the invasion beachhead. He could count on the planes from the Taffy 2 and 3 groups further to the south, but the "Jeep Carriers'" 14 knots top speed was too slow to escape. Their thin hulls would not give much protection to the explosive stores of gasoline, bombs, and torpedoes. "Tomato Cans," the sailors called them; the Navy classified them CVEs and the joke about their being "Combustible, Vulnerable and Expendable" now seemed only too accurate.

The early morning haze magnified the appearance of Taffy 3 to the lookouts on the advancing battleships so Kurita was never to realize just what a glittering chance heaven had actually sent him, because he thought he was up against five to seven big fleet carriers escorted by the same number of cruisers. He also made the second mistake of not concentrating his force into a single battle line before giving the order to "open fire with front turrets," which left each ship to fight on her own.

After radioing Kinkaid of the danger threatening the beachhead where the transports were still unloading, Admiral Sprague took the courageous decision to hurl his puny force against the Japanese, knowing that there would be little chance of surviving more than "a quarter of an hour" against such odds, but he calculated: "If we can get this task force to attack us, we can delay its descent on Leyte until help comes, though obviously the end will come sooner for us."

Sprague's apparently sacrificial tactic was to work out far better than he could have dared expect. "Out of the fog loomed his big battlewagons —pagoda masts and all—and opened fire with their 14- and 16-inch guns at 25,000 yards. He had committed his whole task force to attack us. Wicked salvos straddled the U.S.S. *White Plains* and then colored geysers began to spurt among all the other carriers from projectiles loaded with dye to facilitate the spotting of gunfire. In various shades of pink, green, red, yellow, and purple, they splashed with a horrid beauty."

"They're shooting at us in technicolor," yelled one astonished seaman aboard the *Fanshaw Bay*, in disbelief as the escort carrier worked up to full speed, dodging the bright dye-stained fountains of water that the Japanese used for ranging and seeking the shelter of the destroyer-laid smokescreens. Intermittent rain squalls helped Taffy 3 to launch off all remaining aircraft, but since it had never been intended that the "Jeep Carriers" should take battleships, the carriers had no armor-piercing bombs. Their Avengers were loaded up with torpedoes, and when these ran out they were replaced with depth charges and antipersonnel bombs. The latter were deadly against submarines and soldiers but did little more than rattle the steel sides and gunshields of the enemy warships.

The Japanese peppered the sky with bursting antiaircraft fire while their main armament blazed away, hurling salvo after salvo across the 15 miles that separated them from the American escort carriers. The Taffy 3 pilots were joined within ten minutes of the battle's beginning by the planes flying up from the other escort groups to sustain a continual aerial bombardment.

The increasing number of planes coming in to attack reinforced Kurita's belief that he was indeed grappling with a big Third Fleet Task Group. His battleships and cruisers struggled to keep an accurate range on the carriers, but were constantly being frustrated by the need to change helm to avoid the air attacks—a confusion that increased as the first destroyer attack developed a quarter of an hour after the battle had begun.

Led by the *Johnston*, Taffy 3's three destroyers charged to within 10,000 yards of the line of four Japanese heavy cruisers. Their 5-inch guns were no match for the storm of heavy caliber shells, which threw up mountainous walls of water on either quarter. One of their torpedoes blew the bows off the *Kumano*, forcing the heavy cruiser to drop out of the battle along with the *Suzaya*, which had been hit by bombs. Then a salvo of 14-inch shells hit the *Johnston*. "It was like a puppy being smacked by a fire truck," one of her officers recalled, but a handy rain squall sheltered the stricken destroyer just long enough for her engine-room gangs to repair the damage and get her under way again. She rejoined the action with her 5-inch guns under manual operation. The *Hoel*, all but her forward turrets wrecked, came dashing with the *Heerman* to take on the Japanese battleships. Their torpedoes failed to connect, but turning to avoid them, the heavy cruiser *Haguro* caught a shell in her rudder, which took her out of action, as the *Yamato* broke off firing to outrun the streaking tracks. This maneuver took the flagship so far astern of the engagement that Kurita was never able to regain tactical control of his force as the confusion and smoke disrupted his battle line.

During the hour when the Japanese admiral believed his battleships were locked with the Third Fleet carriers, Task Force 38 was actually some 300 miles due north. Halsey sent off air strikes against Admiral Ozawa's decoy force, looking forward by noon to the "prospect of blasting the cripples that our planes were setting up for us." At 8:30 A.M., half an hour before the first wave of aircraft made contact with the Mobile Fleet, he was handed a priority signal from Kinkaid: "URGENTLY NEED FAST BATTLESHIPS LEYTE GULF AT ONCE." Oldendorf had reported that his six battleships were running low on ammunition after their night engagement. The Seventh Fleet Commander knew he needed more firepower to defend the beachhead, anticipating the Japanese battleships must break through the line of escort carriers and come crashing down to bombard Leyte Gulf.

THE ACTION OFF CAPE ENGAÑO

"There was nothing I could do," Halsey would write, "except become angrier." His fast battleships and carrier aircraft were already too distant to get into the battle soon enough to rescue either the escort carriers or the beachhead. All he was able to do was send a signal to McCain's Task Group 38.1 to hasten their return. He was, in any case, preoccupied with the reports coming in from the aircraft launching the first wave of strikes against the Japanese force he had been chasing all through the night.

Ozawa's two hybrid battleships and four carriers had retained only thirteen planes to put up a token defense. At 8 A.M. all the antiaircraft guns in the Mobile Fleet began blasting shells skyward as they came under aerial siege from 130 American aircraft. A well-coordinated series of dive-bombing and torpedo plane attacks came in from all around the compass, focusing on the *Zuikaku*. The big flight deck of the only survivor from Pearl Harbor erupted with bomb hits and a torpedo cut her speed in the opening minutes of the assault. Her crew tried defending their ship by firing rockets with lines attached, to snag the racing American dive bombers, but it was a futile defense. At the end of an hour's constant attack, she was ablaze and badly listing. The two hybrid battleships were also taking hits as another wave of 170 aircraft arrived to jump the force of three surviving light carriers. The *Chitose* was soon dead in the water with her two sister light carriers and their escorts suffering a heavy beating.

"WHAT WE NEED IS A BUGLER"

When Ozawa finally transferred his flag from the burning *Zuikaku* to a light cruiser around 9 that morning, the Mobile Fleet had been scattered over more than 30 miles of the Philippine Sea, 200 miles west of Cape Engaño. His battle had already been lost, but he had no way of knowing whether his sacrificial mission had been successful or not.

Kurita, to the south, had not picked up Ozawa's "UNDER ATTACK" signals, so he was still under the impression that the fleet carriers were barring his way to Leyte Gulf. Sprague was finding that his Jeep Carriers' thin hulls were, to his amazement, actually working in his favor. His own flagship *Fanshaw Bay* had been hit six times and was still operational because the Japanese shells, fused to detonate against heavy armor, were passing through without exploding. This was not, however, enough to save the *Gambier Bay*. After being hit in the engine room and losing speed, she became a sitting target before she sank under a smoky pyre at 8:20 A.M. Twenty minutes later, Sprague saw that the Japanese cruisers were advancing to flank him. He was left with only the destroyer escorts to hurl into the battle. "SMALL BOYS LAUNCH TORPEDO ATTACK," he signaled, and they raced out, joined by the three badly battered destroyers. Out of torpedoes, Commander Amos T. Hathaway of the *Heerman* recorded: "Anything we could do from now on would have to be mostly bluff." He told his deck officer, "Buck, what we need is a bugler!"

For the second time that morning the American destroyers charged into the enemy gunfire, dodging wildly to avoid the salvos. A ride of death was ended for the *Heerman* when she took a heavy shell forward, flooding her fo'c'sle and spreading a brown mess from a damaged provisions locker all over her deck, to mingle with the blood of her wounded. Hathaway would manage to save his ship by flooding the magazines, but the other two destroyers were not so fortunate. The *Hoel*'s port engine room was wrecked by a shell. Stopped dead in the water, she was quickly pounded beneath the waves. The gallant *Johnston* suffered the same end; her crews valiantly carried on firing until the water rose over the gun mounts. The heroic charge of the destroyers allowed the smaller destroyer escorts to race in and deliver their torpedoes. The attack succeeded in turning the Japanese cruisers away from the carriers, but left the destroyer *Samuel B. Roberts* an "inert mass of battered metal."

The aircraft from the three Taffy groups were by now, in the words of one Avenger pilot, "hitting the Jap ships with everything in the armory —including the doorknobs." When their bombs and torpedoes ran out, they refueled and came back to make dummy runs. They had already taken a heavy toll of Kurita's heavy cruisers. The bowless *Kumano* was limping back toward the Strait when the *Chikuma* and *Chokai* sustained crippling bomb hits. Their crews were soon taken off by destroyers prior to scuttling. Kurita decided shortly after 9 A.M. to try to regain tactical control of his scattered force, signaling them to break off the action and "come north with me 20 knots."

"Goddamnit, boy, they're getting away!" Sprague heard one of the signalmen yell on the *Fanshaw Bay* at 9:25. "I could not believe my eyes, but it looked as if the whole Japanese fleet was indeed retiring. However it took a whole series of reports from circling planes to convince me. And I still could not get the fact to soak into my battle-numbed brain. At best, I had expected to be swimming by this time."

BATTLE OF BULL'S RUN

Three hundred miles to the north, Ozawa's surviving warships were also in deep trouble. The second air strike from Task Force 38 had reached the dispersed units of the Mobile Strike force to discover that the carrier *Chitose* was sinking. While the relentless air attack continued, Admiral Ozawa evacuated his staff from the *Zuikaku*. Only some 60 miles now separated him from Admiral Lee's battleships, which were thundering down on the hapless decoy fleet. Anticipation of a total victory was running high in the *New Jersey* flag plot where Halsey was looking to gunnery action that would finish off the might of the Imperial Navy.

His hopes were to come crashing down at 10 A.M. when he was handed another signal from Kinkaid. "WHERE IS LEE?"—a note of desperate urgency given special emphasis because the Seventh Fleet Commander had deliberately transmitted it in plain English. Halsey's astonishment that Kinkaid's own carriers and battleships could apparently not deal with a battered Japanese task force turned to anger a few minutes later when he was handed a signal from Nimitz. It was unprecedented for the Commander in Chief Pacific to give tactical instructions. His request: "WHERE

IS REPEAT WHERE IS TASK FORCE 34?" was unintentionally given the tone of a rebuke because the enciphering officer at Hawaii had "padded" the transmission for coding purposes with a suffix "THE WORLD WONDERS," which in the circumstances appeared so much like a part of the signal that the decoding officer on the *New Jersey* had handed it down in this form. The implied criticism stunned the Third Fleet Commander "as if I had been struck in the face. I snatched off my cap, threw it on the deck and shouted something that I am ashamed to remember." Choking with anger, he brooded with his staff for nearly an hour before deciding reluctantly to order Lee to take his battleship task force to Kinkaid's assistance. At five minutes before 11 A.M., the *New Jersey* was hauling around onto a southerly course. Halsey would write bitterly: "I turned my back on the opportunity I had dreamed of since my days as a cadet. For me one of the biggest battles of the war was off, and what has been called the 'Battle of Bull's Run' was on."

The surviving Japanese warships were left to Mitscher's three carrier task groups. Through the rest of the morning and afternoon, four more waves of American carrier aircraft hammered away at Ozawa's scattered force as it fled north. The *Zuikaku* was sunk shortly after 2 P.M.; an hour later the *Zuiho* went down, to be followed at 5 P.M. by the *Chiyoda*. The victory was to fall short of the annihilation Halsey hoped for because the two hybrid battleships managed to escape, along with two cruisers and six destroyers. Despite criticism for leaving the San Bernardino Strait unguarded, Halsey remained convinced to his dying day that his "real mistake was in turning my fleet around" because he knew that his dash to the south would never be able to reach Kinkaid in time.

It took more than two hours for Kurita to gather together his force and set off again south toward Leyte Gulf shortly after midday. During that time Sprague's Taffy 3 survivors were congratulating themselves on their seemingly miraculous escape when ten minutes before eleven the five remaining "baby flat-tops" were attacked by Kamikazes.

KAMIKAZE ATTACK

Five Zeros with bombs strapped to their wings were led in under radar by Lieutenant Yukio Seki, who hauled his suicide squadron up to 1,000 feet to bring them screaming down on the carriers. Antiaircraft guns blazed away but did not deter what the American sailors were soon calling the "devil divers." Sprague's flagship was lucky and the *Fanshaw Bay*'s gunners hit the two planes, whose pilots were making the carrier their target. A third, misjudging his aim, glanced off the *Kitun Bay*'s deck before exploding; but a fifth Zero, which veered away from the *White Plains* at the last moment, plunged squarely through the deck of the *St. Lo*. The Jeep

Carrier had stood up to the Japanese battleships that morning, but now a succession of explosions sent her to the bottom within half an hour. After being frustrated by two days of bad weather, Seki's Shikishima Unit of the Special Attack Corps had vindicated Admiral Onishi's scheme to harness "an enthusiasm that flames naturally in the hearts of youthful men" for suicide attacks. Earlier, the first Kamikaze from another group had crashed into the deck of the *Santee* of the Taffy 1 group.

The ordeal of Taffy 3 was not yet over. An hour later the aircraft and guns of the elated but by now very battle-weary force were in action again, beating off another Japanese air attack, which left the *Kalinin Bay* crippled by a bomb that plummeted down her smoke stack. Sprague's carriers had survived by what he attributed to "the very definite partiality of Almighty God." He would now know that morning just how great that partiality had been. After regrouping his battleships, Kurita was heading south again toward Leyte Gulf for a renewed clash with the escort carriers. Then at 12:35 he had turned back to "engage in decisive battle" another carrier force to the north, which had been mistakenly reported by shore-based aircraft. He searched for it in vain throughout the afternoon until he came under attack from carrier planes. This time it was a Third Fleet Task Group, as Admiral McCain finally arrived to join the battle. With his force running low on fuel, a weary and dispirited Kurita that evening finally abandoned his mission and returned to the San Bernardino Strait. "I did not know," he would later confess, "that Admiral Halsey had taken his fleet to the north. I moved only with the knowledge that I was able to acquire with my own eyes and did not realize how close I was to victory."

The Battle of Leyte Gulf, which sputtered to a fitful close on the evening of October 25, 1944, marked the end of the Imperial Navy's Sho strategy. By smashing its desperate "Banzai Charge," the U.S. Navy had ended the challenge to its naval supremacy in the Pacific. The three-day action was the greatest naval engagement in history. Like the Battle of Jutland of 1916, which had ended the Kaiser's naval challenge, controversy was to rage about the way the battle had been fought. Halsey would be censured for his failure to guard the San Bernardino Strait and in turn would blame "rotten" communications that cost him an annihilating victory.

The punishing defeat at Leyte all but wiped out the Imperial Navy. The sinking of four carriers, three battleships, six cruisers, and twelve of its destroyers, as well as the loss of many hundreds of planes, had reduced its handful of surviving warships to an impotent rump of a fleet that could neither protect itself from air attack nor effectively guard the sea approaches to Japan. More than 10,000 airmen and sailors were dead, at the cost of less than 3,000 American lives lost in a light carrier, 2 escort carriers, and 3 destroyers, which had been sunk along with less than 200 aircraft. Once again the U.S. Navy's airpower had proved the decisive factor. It was ironic—but appropriate—that the final great battle in the Pacific War should see the last duel between battleships. In the twenty-eight years that had elapsed since Jutland, the carrier-borne aircraft had become the decisive naval weapon; the Battle of Leyte Gulf was to confirm once again that the dreadnought battleship had seen a final hour of glorious combat.

While the Imperial Navy's desperate bid to disrupt the invasion was foundering, General Terauchi, overruling Yamashita, was pouring in heavy reinforcements to Leyte. General Makino's 10,000 troops were falling back west and north into the mountains as the American forces fanned out across the coastal plain. He was expecting airpower to provide the main punch of the counteroffensive. The days following the great naval battles did see the planes from bases all over the inner islands being flown down to Luzon to join the Battle for the Philippines.

The bombing and strafing attacks were successful in stalling the American advance. For the first time since the early days of the Papuan campaign, MacArthur found himself fighting without the benefit of close air support for his ground forces. Typhoon storms had interrupted the long-range patrols being flown at extreme range from the 5th Air Force advanced base at Morotai. Army engineers found that even with tons of steel matting, laying out airstrips on Leyte's swampy east coast was like "metal laid on a Jello mold." The Marines had only 150 planes operational at the end of the first week, and attrition rates soared alarmingly because of the heavy enemy bombing and the poor landing strips. MacArthur was to be constantly reminded by daily raids that singled out his field headquarters that Japan controlled the air over the island. The attacks became increasingly heavy despite the success of antiaircraft gunners in shooting down enemy planes at the rate of over a hundred a week. The necessity for Kinkaid to withdraw his force of Taffy escort carriers after their heavy battering found MacArthur having to plead with Nimitz for replacements. On November 10, it was agreed to postpone the Third Fleet's next strike mission against Japan so that Halsey could bring his carrier groups to support the ground troops and protect the convoys now being scheduled to bring in a flow of reserves. A crack Marine squadron of night fighters was also to be transferred from the Palaus to shore up the defense against air raids being flown by the Japanese from airfields in Luzon and Mindoro.

STALEMATE ON LEYTE

While the battle raged for control of the skies over the Philippines during November, the struggle for the strategic northern cusp of Leyte bogged down in a stalemate as the reinforcing Japanese divisions came ashore to dig in on the high ground commanding Carigara Bay. For more than a month, the troops of General Sibert's 24th Infantry Division hammered away at the line of pillboxes and dugouts that the enemy had set up along a natural defense line the Americans dubbed "Breakneck Ridge." It guarded the northern part of Leyte and, as long as it held, Yamashita's reinforcement convoys could land their troops at the sheltered port of Ormoc some 25 miles to the south, on the other side of the island's central mountain range. It was here that the main battle for Leyte was fought out after General Krueger's plan to send his corps south around the range to take Ormoc from the rear was blocked by heavy enemy forces defending the west coast route up Highway 2. Tanks and artillery were concentrated in the slogging match against Breakneck Ridge as rain and mud transformed the battle into a campaign reminiscent of the Western Front in World War I.

A grim battle of attrition was being waged which the Japanese began losing, as Yamashita had predicted, after November 11 when a massive air strike by the planes of the Third Fleet all but wiped out a convoy bringing in 10,000 more Japanese troops. Field Marshal Terauchi ordered 1,000 planes to Luzon to cover another transport convoy as he launched a desperate operation to drop suicide squads of paratroopers to seize the five American airfields around Tacloban. Operation WA, as it was designated, was intended to "annihilate the enemy's air power," but it was doomed because of poor timing and lack of coordination. General Makino's 16th Division was supposed to descend from the hills in a simultaneous thrust, but the Japanese paratroopers only succeeded in briefly capturing the airstrip at Buri. They held it for three days before, cut off and unreinforced, they were overwhelmed.

During the third week in November 1944, the sheer weight of the American artillery began to punch through the Japanese line on Breakneck Ridge. MacArthur was obliged to postpone the scheduled invasion of Luzon by ten days, releasing the troops of the 77th Division, which on December 7 were landed near Ormoc on the west coast to drive a wedge between the Japanese rear positions. The assault 4 miles south of the port, beat by only hours Terauchi's convoy of reinforcements. The transports were beaten back out to sea in heavy attacks by the covering Marine fighters and bombers from Tacloban. Kamikazes nonetheless managed to penetrate the defenses and sink two American destroyers while the infantrymen were put ashore with little opposition. In three days American tanks had broken through into Ormoc. The envelopment of the now cut-off Japanese forces fighting in the northern part of the island began.

While the Battle for Leyte was reaching its climax, MacArthur opened the preparatory moves for the postponed assault on Luzon by setting December 15 for landings on Mindoro to secure its strategically located airfields. The specially formed Visayan Task Force was given the task of neutralizing the Japanese garrison of 1,500. The worst opposition they encountered was from Kamikaze fliers during the three-day voyage from Leyte Gulf, an attack which damaged one of the escorting carriers. Within five days they had won control of the island airfields for less than five hundred killed, and Marine pilots flew in to strike the enemy forces holding out in northern Leyte.

The new air bases would prove essential four days later when a typhoon of terrific intensity struck the Third Fleet. It cost the lives of eight hundred sailors when three destroyers capsized and sank at the height of the storms. Mountainous seas wrecked two hundred aircraft and damaged seven other warships so badly that Halsey was forced to withdraw to Ulithi for repairs. However, the two months during which his pilots had been providing badly needed air support for MacArthur's forces had broken the enemy defense over Leyte. General Suzuki was now cut off in the central Philippines with only 27,000 troops and without hope of relief.

The advancing columns of the U.S. 7th Army Division had joined up with the 77th Division 10 miles north of Ormoc at Libongao to encircle and divide the Japanese forces remaining on the island. By December 27, 1944, MacArthur was confident of the final outcome, announcing: "General Yamashita has sustained the greatest defeat in the annals of the Japanese Army." His communiqué claiming that the "Leyte-Samar campaign can now be regarded as closed except for minor mopping up" proved to be four months premature.

The Battle for Leyte, which had already claimed 3,000 American and 56,000 Japanese lives, was to continue through April 1944. The U.S. Eighth Army was brought in for the task of "mopping up"—an arduous series of operations which their official historian was to describe as "bitter, rugged, fighting—physically the most terrible we were ever to know."

Leyte was to take another 1,000 American lives and many times that number of Japanese, who stubbornly refused to surrender. The heavier than anticipated enemy ground and air strength that had been committed to the island's defense put back MacArthur's schedule for retaking the Philippines by a month and forced the deployment of an entire division of his reserves. The closer the American forces approached to Japan, the stiffer the resistance became. It was an ominous lesson that was not lost on the Southwest Pacific Commander as final plans were made for the landing on Luzon, set for January 19, 1945.

31

"A Determined
Fighting Spirit"

While the American advance thrust through the Palaus and the Philippines during the fall of 1944, on the Asian mainland the Japanese Army was victorious as the Ichi-Go offensive rolled forward. Lingling had fallen in September as the 11th Army pushed south to Kweilin. The Chinese Nationalist forces melted away, the deserting soldiers joining the human tide as a mass panic seized millions of peasants. Kweilin fell on November 10, 1944, when General Chennault lost the 14th Air Force's main base. Chiang Kai-shek's hold on southern China was slipping, and his Nationalist regime was close to military and economic destruction.

Concern in Washington mounted as the Americans increased pressure on the Southeast Asia Command to send troops from Burma into China, a move that was resisted by General Slim. After crushing the Ha-Go offensive, his six divisions of the British 14th Army were preparing for a post-monsoon drive down through central Burma with the October arrival of the dry season.

The new Japanese commander of the 15th Army, General S. Katura, who had replaced the disgraced General Mutaguchi, found that he had only just over 21,000 troops in the three shattered divisions to hold the central front against an estimated 200,000 in the six British divisions. General Kimura's Burma army had to defend the entire country, with the three divisions of Lieutenant General Honda's 33rd Army holding the northeast against Stilwell's New China Army, and Chiang Kai-shek's divisions battling their way across the Salween while the two divisions of the 28th Army were holding the coast approaches to Rangoon. Kimura's response to the gathering Allied offensive was to plan for a stage-by-stage withdrawal by the 15th Army to protect the crucial oilfields, while General Honda launched a counteroffensive in the east against the Chinese. The Japanese 56th Division counterattacked the Nationalist front so effectively that by the end of September they had been driven back up the Yunnan passes to Tengchung. Alarm grew in Chungking that the terminus of The Hump supply operation at Kunming would soon be endangered. As the Japanese vise squeezed both his fronts, Chiang Kai-shek demanded that Stilwell and his divisions come to the rescue. The New China Army was then advancing south from Myitkyina with the objective of taking Lashio, and the American general adamantly refused to abandon his drive to reopen the Burma Road.

"The crazy little bastard would sabotage the whole damn project—men, money, material, time and sweat we have put into it for two and a half years," Stilwell raged in his diary after Chiang had threatened to relieve him of his command. In more formal language he dashed off a cable to General Marshall on September 15 warning him: "The jig is up in China. We are getting out of Kweilin now, and will have to get out of Luchow as soon as the Japs appear there." Blaming Chiang Kai-shek for the coming disaster, he believed the only chance to save China was to take over command for the Nationalist armies to organize the defense of Chungking. The President, who had lost all patience with the Generalissimo, sent him a cable that read like an ultimatum, insisting that his Chief of Staff must "command all forces in China." Stilwell barely concealed his delight as he handed the message directly to Chiang Kai-shek, against the advice of envoy Patrick Hurley and the U.S. ambassador.

"The harpoon hit the little bugger in the solar plexus and went right through him," but Stilwell's pleasure was to be short-lived. Chiang fired off his own response to the President, protesting that the Nationalist Army would mutiny if an American was out in command, and demanding Stilwell's immediate recall because he had "no intention of cooperating with me." Roosevelt was inclined to agree with Marshall and support Stilwell's assessment that the Nationalists were fighting a lost cause. But he was unwilling to alienate the powerful China lobby in the United States before the upcoming presidential election. After receiving Hurley's report that the two men were "incompatible" and that if he backed Stilwell, "you will lose Chiang and possibly you will lose China too," Roosevelt decided to recall the irascible general.

The news that "Vinegar Joe" would be leaving the troubled Southeast Asia theater brought almost as much relief to Mountbatten's headquarters in Kandy as it did to Chungking. Stilwell's deputy, General Sultan, was appointed to assume field command of the ground troops, and General Wedemeyer was to leave SEAC headquarters to assume the role of Chiang's Chief of Staff. The simultaneous resignation of the American Ambassador signaled the end of Washington's efforts to take a firm line on getting an American commander to take over the Chinese Nationalist armies. The rambunctious Hurley was appointed envoy, with instructions to work for a political reconciliation between Mao Tse-tung and Chiang Kai-shek. Like most Presidents since the turn of the century, Roosevelt was wedded firmly to the belief in America's mission on the

Asian mainland, convinced that "despite a temporary weakness . . . 450,-000,000 Chinese would someday become united and modernized and would be the most important factor in the Far East." However, the threat of Russian expansionism into China became apparent after Churchill's October mission to Moscow. The Prime Minister feared Stalin meant to communize eastern Europe and Roosevelt was also beginning to see that when the Red Army entered the war against Japan, the Soviet territorial designs might encompass China.

"If the Russians go in, will they ever go out?" Roosevelt had demanded of Ambassador Averell Harriman in Moscow. Hurley in Chungking was less apprehensive, however, having taken at face value Molotov's assurances that the Soviets were not supporting Mao Tse-tung and that "the Chinese Communists are not in fact communists." In this naive spirit the former Rough Rider flew to Yenan in November and greeted the Communist leader, whom he called "Moose Dung," with ebullient Chocktaw Indian cries. Their talks resulted in a five-point plan "for the immediate defeat of Japan and the reconstruction of China" under a coalition government that would bring the 3 million-strong Communist Army to the aid of Chungking. But Chiang Kai-shek, who regarded Mao Tse-tung as a bigger menace to his regime than the Japanese, refused to cooperate in the discussions, accusing Hurley of being sold a Communist "Bill of Goods." Dismayed but undaunted, the ambassador worked to modify the proposals, only to find it was the Communists who believed they had been betrayed. Both sides continued professing that they were "anxious for a settlement" but no mutually acceptable terms were forthcoming in spite of Hurley's repeated efforts.

In November 1944, once Roosevelt had been reelected to a fourth term, the intractable Chinese puzzle receded in the face of Soviet territorial demands in eastern Europe, which were becoming obvious as the victorious Red Army advanced. The President had already decided to wait until the summit conference at Yalta early in 1945, when he hoped his personal charm would persuade Stalin to support bringing the Communists into a united China. At the same time Roosevelt suspected that the British and French were sabotaging the grand design for a unified postwar China, because both countries wanted to see a continuation of the Chinese weakness they had exploited successfully for more than a century so they could recover territorial possessions on the mainland that were now occupied by the Japanese.

General Wedemeyer faced a tough challenge when he arrived in Chungking in October 1944, determined to use his considerable talents for diplomacy to soothe the passions inflamed by the abrasive Stilwell. He had decided on "a honey instead of vinegar policy." He locked up his predecessor's files, and professed respect for Chiang Kai-shek, who he believed was doing his best to deal with an impossible military and political situation with only a corrupt bureaucracy to fall back on. A planner by temperament, Wedemeyer was soon drafting an ambitious scheme to reorganize and reequip the Nationalist Army, to transform it into a potent fighting force. To put his "Plan Alpha" into operation, he would need the supplies and arms that could only be brought in if the Burma Road was reopened. But that campaign was being threatened by the string of disasters facing the Nationalist armies. Chiang had assured him that besieged Kweilin would hold; it fell within two weeks as the 23rd Japanese Army was marching north from Canton to Kunming. The Nationalist divisions that had shown themselves able to defeat the Japanese were those of the New China Army. Wedemeyer now decided that they must be airlifted in to save Chiang Kai-shek's regime.

Mountbatten and Slim both argued against the crippling of the Allied drive in Burma that must result; but Wedemeyer, backed by the Joint Chiefs, decided that the threat to Chungking was the greater danger. A huge airlift got under way early in December to ferry an entire division of General Sultan's forces over The Hump. By the end of 1944, some 25,000 Chinese troops were in place to defend an advance against the Nationalist capital. However, the threat was already diminished because it had not been in Imperial General Headquarters' plan to advance up the Yangtze as far as Chungking. Accordingly, General Yasuji Okamura pulled back his 11th Army to consolidate control of the railway line to Hanoi when it was still more than 300 miles south of the threatened city.

Meeting the threatened Japanese offensive, as well as coping with the urgent need for more supplies to begin Plan Alpha and supporting the B-29 bomber bases and 14th Air Force, was proving beyond the capacity of The Hump airlift. So until the final drive could be made to reopen the overland route into China, Wedemeyer's December report strongly urged the Joint Chiefs to halt the 20th Bombardment Group's operations from Chengtu. With some justification he argued that the strategic success of "Operation Matterhorn" was falling far short of General Arnold's expectations.

THE STRATEGIC BOMBING OF JAPAN

In the fall of 1944, the B-29 force had been ranging out to bomb the oil-fields at Palembang and Sumatra as well as raiding Japan and Formosa in support of the Third Fleet. Some successes had been realized, but the damage that the Superfortresses had inflicted was in no way commensurate with the colossal effort needed to support the operations. It required six round trips over The Hump by each of the giant four-engined bombers just to haul in enough fuel and bombs for a single mission. Technical problems plagued the B-29s in the monsoon humidity. The poorly disci-

plined attacks had barely begun to be rectified after General Curtis Le-
May was appointed to take over command of the 20th Bombardment
Group in September. At thirty-eight, LeMay was the brightest tactician
as well as the youngest two-star general in the Army Air Force. He had
been responsible for devising the tight formation bombing by B-17s that
had brought great initial success during the daylight raids over Germany.
Now he was equally determined to prove that his theory of strategic
bombing could be made to work against Japan; but, in his own words,
the B-29 was the "buggiest airplane that ever came down the pike." Only
after weeks of rigorous training and technical work could the 20th Bombardment Group mount a hundred-plane raid on the Okayama Aircraft
Assembly Works on Formosa as a prelude to the Philippine landings. The
following months saw the B-29s flying in support of Chennault's 14th Air
Force and, in December, gutting Japanese-held Hankow with firebombs.

By January 1945, General Arnold had finally come around to accepting Wedemeyer's suggestion. He recommended to the Joint Chiefs,
whose direct responsibility the strategic bombers were, that the 20th
Bombardment Group should be transferred to the Marianas, where the
21st's Superfortresses were already flying operations against Japan.

Logistics and distance had worked against the B-29's operations from
China, but operating from the huge runways being bulldozed across the
flat sugar-cane fields of Tinian would cut the flying distance to Tokyo in
half. On the last day of October 1944, the first Superfortress—appropriately named "Tokyo Rose"—made the first high-level reconnaissance
mission over the Japanese capital. During the following week, the practice missions dropped hundreds of tons of high explosives on the airfields
of Iwo Jima, to keep down its fighters. Then, on November 24, a battery
of press cameramen recorded the awe-inspiring sight of 111 B-29s taking
off to make the first mass raid on Tokyo.

Led by Brigadier General Emmett "Rosie" O'Donnell, commanding
"Dauntless Dotty," the Superfortresses rumbled north over the 1,500
miles of ocean with the intention of obliterating the Masashima Aircraft
Works north of Tokyo. Bad weather and thick overcast hindered the
attack, which was delivered with the aid of radar from 30,000 feet.
Fewer than fifty bombs actually hit the target, but because of the great
height at which they operated, only one B-29 fell victim to over a hundred Zeros which tried to claw their way up to intercept them. Three days
later the second raid proved equally ineffective when the target was concealed by a heavy cloud cover. The new round of air attacks on Tokyo
did bring a bonus for the American submarines stationed off the Japanese
coast to pick up aircrews who ditched in the sea. The superbattleship
Shinano, sister ship of the ill-fated *Musashi*, was undergoing conversion
to a monster 60,000-ton aircraft carrier. Still unfinished, she was being

towed out of the Tokyo yards to a more remote harbor where work could be completed when, on November 29, she was spotted by the *Archerfish* and sent to the bottom with a salvo of torpedoes.

The arrival of the heavy bombers in the skies over Japan was a new ordeal for the dense populations living in the crowded Tokyo suburbs. It was a bitter end to a dismal year of increasing privation and shortages, appalling losses due to the American submarine campaign, and the approaching tide of military defeat in the Pacific perimeter. High-level precision bombing by radar had proved a dismal failure against industrial plants and factories, but the hundreds of tons of explosives that rained down on the closely packed urban areas of the Japanese cities brought a huge toll of death and destruction. Two years after people had discounted the Doolittle bombing attack, precautions by the government and the public were now being carried out with a sense of deep urgency.

Primitive trench shelters had been dug in backyards and along the flowerbeds that lined the middle of main roads. In common with other features of Japan's wartime life, ritual morale-building and propaganda assumed an important role, with civilians swearing the "air defense oath of certain victory." Fire drills were carried out to the blare of martial music, and to make up for the lack of fighter defenses, great reliance was placed on searchlights and antiaircraft guns though it was obvious that the B-29s were carrying out their attacks by radar far above the maximum range of antiaircraft shells. When Imperial General Headquarters belatedly issued its overall air-raid plan and instructions for a nationwide blackout, only an inadequate force of professional firefighting services remained. The burden of dealing with the attacks fell on the volunteers drawn from the community councils and neighborhood associations. The sirens now wailed so often that people began to "listen to the silence." The evacuation of schoolchildren to the countryside was under way by the beginning of 1945. With typical Japanese practicality, the authorities decreed that the older children should assist in the farms and makeshift factories that were springing up in rural areas.

In the fall of 1944 hundreds of thousands of sunflowers had been distributed by government decree, in a pathetic effort to brighten up the increasingly drab life of Japan's citizens, who were soon to find that bombing had put them in the front line of the war. Flowers were more plentiful than food and clothing; food was strictly regulated by a points system, and the fabric used to make what new clothes were available was so poor that people preferred to wear dirty garments rather than risk their disintegration in the wash.

Food was becoming scarcer as heavy shipping losses cut into imports. Priority in rice rations was given to the 3 million soldiers being posted back to defend the home islands. They received a scant 400 grams a day, while civilians had to make do with 100 less. Only pumpkins were plentiful. Dogs had long ago disappeared from the city streets to satisfy the craving for meat and, although outlawed, the Black Market flourished in cities like Tokyo, where workers relied on it to supply half their fish and vegetable requirements. Sugar and soap had all but disappeared; to save rubber and leather, people had taken to wearing the traditional clogs.

Winter arrived, with charcoal and wood for cooking and heating stoves in such desperately short supply that whole libraries were sold for fuel. Neighborhood Associations, which had become a mainstay of the civilian war organization, scoured the bombed-out homes and buildings for scraps of combustible material. Unable to survive government regulation and the worsening shortages, Geisha houses, bars, and restaurants had been forced to close. Only movie houses, showing suitably patriotic propaganda films on a curtailed schedule remained an escape from the wartime drudgery. The winter of despondency deepened as the weather grew colder, the news from the battlefronts became bleaker, and the bombing raids intensified. The semi-official notice headed "HAPPY NEW YEAR" posted by the Community Council of the Tokyo suburb of Nakanoku was typical in its excess of fighting spirit and minimal cheer: "In the face of warnings that the war situation is growing more severe, let's greet the New Year with faith in inevitable victory and a determined fighting spirit, so that this year will be a fight to the finish."

American air and sea blockades were depriving Japan of the oil and raw materials needed to produce new planes to replace those lost in futile air defense and by enemy bombing. Over 3 million tons of shipping had been sunk in 1944, more than the total of the two previous years. Now less than 2 million tons of carrying capacity, besides tankers, survived. By dint of prodigious tanker construction, the shipyards had kept pace with the losses, but tankers became the priority target for the U.S. submarines locking the home islands in an undersea blockade of steel. In October, the sixty-eight U.S. boats on patrol had sunk over 300,000 tons; the next month, they were joined by an increasing number of Royal Navy submarines.

Most ships flying the Rising Sun ensign were now restricted to short voyages across the Sea of Japan, in which they could make passage by night and take shelter in coastal ports by day. Cut off from the strategic oil supply in the East Indies by the end of 1944, the Japanese government desperately launched a crash program to distill aviation fuel from potatoes so that their fighters could be kept in the air to defend the home islands. Aluminum stocks to make new planes were diminishing as the smelting plants ran out of the bauxite ore, and steel output plummeted as iron ore and coke supplies could not be shipped from the Asian mainland. The Imperial Navy was paying the price for neglecting antisubmarine defenses;

those warships that survived the Leyte Gulf battles had to stay in their home ports because tankers could not get oil to Japan. When they did venture out, they faced a high risk of destruction from lurking U.S. Navy submarines, who took a heavy toll of the remaining warships. On December 9, the carrier *Junyo* was torpedoed and sunk; then, ten days later, the new carrier *Unryu* followed her down.

The opening hours of 1945 began with a heavy air raid on Tokyo and were an ominous foretaste of what was in store for Japan. The crump of falling bombs could be felt through the night in the Emperor's underground bunker beneath the Imperial Palace library, as Hirohito closely questioned the Prime Minister on the setbacks suffered at Leyte. He hardly needed to stress the urgency of more effective measures to deal with the increasing air raids.

Their deliberations about the likely course of the war and how to sue for peace might have taken an even more urgent tone had they been aware of the contents of the top-secret report that landed on General Marshall's desk that week. Dated December 29, 1944, it was from General Groves, who commanded the Manhattan Project—the massive commitment of American scientific and technological skills to develop the atomic bomb. Millions of dollars had been poured into a project so confidential that only a few key aides besides the President himself and the Joint Chiefs of Staff were aware of its existence. The combined efforts of the most brilliant scientific and engineering talents were behind the massive industrial plants that had been built in remote areas of the United States. Groves could now give an optimistic prediction that within half a year the results of all the efforts would give birth to a weapon that would unleash the most destructive power in history.

"The first bomb, without previous full scale test, which we do not believe will be necessary, should be ready about August 1, 1945," Groves was able to assure Marshall. Hand-picked aircrews of the 509th Composite Group were already beginning training at an isolated air base at Wendover in the Utah desert under Colonel Paul W. Tibbets, as the first pieces of the costly uranium weapon began arriving under heavy guard at the Los Alamos laboratories in New Mexico for assembly into the atomic bomb.

According to a secret memorandum drawn up by Churchill and Roosevelt, the preliminary decision to use the atomic bomb, if the Japanese did not surrender, had already been taken. The prospect of another year of war hung heavily on the President, whose cardiovascular system was showing signs of failing. Only his personal physician knew how fast Roosevelt's health was deteriorating, but the ravages of illness were clearly evident in FDR's countenance, and those who lived in the White House could not help noticing it. Aware that his physical strength was waning, the President drew on his unquenchable spirit to push harder to achieve the great goals he had set for the postwar world. At his fourth inauguration, Roosevelt knew he had to secure these goals if his design for a permanent peace through the United Nations was to be set in place before the Grand Allied Alliance splintered from its differences. The omens were not good. The optimism about an early defeat of Germany had vanished on the night of December 15 when panzer divisions came crashing through the Ardennes Forest in a last-ditch counteroffensive. The German offensive had been halted by Christmas Eve, but with the Russian tanks then within 200 miles of Berlin, it was clear that the Red Army would win the race to the capital of the Third Reich. This would leave the Red Army occupying much of central Europe and raised the prospect of a Communist takeover which alarmed the western Allies.

The President believed only his personal efforts could resolve the crisis that was threatening to break up the wartime Alliance to secure Russian backing for the United Nations at the forthcoming Yalta Summit. "This organization must be the fulfillment of the promise for which men have fought and died in the war," he stated in his State of the Union message. "It must be made the justification for all the sacrifices made—of all the dreadful misery that the world has endured."

That misery, as the President well knew, still had a long course to run. As his address was being read out to Congress, American naval forces were gathering for the invasion of Luzon. On January 2, Admiral Oldendorf's battleships had left Leyte to carry out the preliminary bombardment of the landing beaches. Their passage north through the Sulu Sea ran a gauntlet of Japanese Kamikaze attacks that sank an escort carrier and a destroyer and damaged a dozen more ships before the invasion force had even reached the waters off the Lingayen Gulf. On January 7, 1945, as the battleships began shelling the shore installations, the U.S. Navy suffered its worst losses since the Battle of Savo when suicide pilots put two battleships out of action and damaged cruisers and destroyers, as well as sinking three minesweepers.

Halsey's carriers, which were providing cover from a distance after making their first foray into the China Sea to raid Japanese air bases on Hong Kong and Formosa, were hampered by bad weather. Their planes were kept deckbound while the Kamikazes exploited the cloud cover to hurl themselves down into the Seventh Fleet and cause a total of over 2,000 casualties. Oldendorf's battleships beat off their attackers and carried out a three-day bombardment of the invasion beaches before the transports carrying the U.S. 6th Army arrived at the assembly points in the Lingayen Gulf.

MACARTHUR INVADES LUZON

General Yamashita had long been preparing for what he knew would be the decisive battle, confidently telling reporters from Japan: "I shall write a brilliant history of the Greater Southeast Asia Co-Prosperity Sphere in the Philippines."

Yamashita, with more than a quarter of a million troops and plenty of supplies and ammunition at his disposal, was ready with a well-planned defense in depth. Rather than waste his tanks and soldiers in an all-out effort to hurl the invaders back into the sea, he drew the lesson from MacArthur's failure three years earlier and concentrated his forces in three powerful groups inland. His intention was to let the Americans get ashore, then encircle and crush them. More than half of Yamashita's strength of some 152,000 men was disposed as the Shobo Group in the northern sector of Luzon; 30,000 soldiers of the Kembu Group were formed up in the south and west of Lingayen to guard the airfields, and 80,000 men of the Shembu Group stood ready to defend Manila and Luzon's pendulous southeastern peninsula. "The Philippines have an extensive area and we can fight to our heart's content," the burly Yamashita predicted confidently.

Over a thousand ships were crowding off Luzon's northwestern coast on the morning of January 8 as the sun rose. Opposition was light to nonexistent when the landing craft swarmed in. At Lingayen, Major General Oscar Griswold's XIV Corps, made up of the 37th and 40th Infantry divisions, established itself 17 miles north across the Bay from where Major General Inis P. Swift's I Corps of the 6th and 43rd Infantry Division landed. By evening more than 50,000 American troops and their equipment were safely ashore and linking up to form a continuous beachhead 4 miles deep. MacArthur had again repeated his walk ashore for the benefit of the cameramen and a cheering crowd of Filipinos. Setting off to tour the front, he issued another of his momentous communiqués: "The decisive battle for the liberation of the Philippines and the control of the Southwest Pacific is at hand." Now he assigned to Griswold's XIV Corps the mission of pushing south to liberate Manila, letting Swift's I Corps secure his flank and rear from enemy attack.

The build-up and drive inland met little opposition during the first week. Not until the Americans reached the Japanese lines along the Agno River 25 miles south of the beachhead did the advance falter. Yamashita had disposed his Kembu force to defend the zone around the large air base of Clark Field. A week of fierce fighting was pressed before Griswold's divisions punched their way through to Tarlac to drive the retreating Japanese up into the Zambalese Mountains.

This delay in the planned schedule brought directions from an impatient MacArthur. Claiming he "knew every wrinkle of the topography," he urged that flying columns be sent on to make a lightning advance to Manila. But General Krueger, the U.S. 6th Army Commander, was more cautious. Swift's I Corps had by now slammed up against the main body of Yamashita's Shobo Group and engaged in fierce tank battles around San Manuel. For a day it seemed likely that the Japanese might break through across the advancing Griswold's rear. MacArthur rushed up to the front to take personal charge, "steadying the ranks." He ordered the 25th and 32nd division reserves to give Krueger's northern forces the necessary drive to push Yamashita out of his headquarters at Baguio into the central mountain plateau where he could no longer threaten the advance across the north Luzon Plain.

MacArthur repeatedly issued orders reminding his field commander of the urgency of pressing on to liberate Manila. He was echoed by his Chief of Staff, General Sutherland, who went so far as to suggest that Krueger should be "sent home" so that he could take over the 6th Army. Nevertheless, by the end of January progress was being made against heavy enemy opposition, in spite of MacArthur's petulant reminder that the infantry was displaying a "noticeable lack of drive." Swift's division in the north was pushing across through San Jose to cut off the Shobo Group in the northern bulge of Luzon, while Griswold's advance units had pushed down the highway to within 13 miles of Manila.

To accelerate the Luzon campaign, MacArthur ordered in more reserves. On January 29, the 38th Division landed at San Antonio north of Bataan with orders to secure the peninsula where, almost three years before, the American forces had begun their bitter retreat toward Corregidor. Two days later, the main body of the 11th Airborne Division came ashore south of Manila Bay, backed up on February 3 by air drops of the remaining paratroop units who sealed off the capital. The American advance into the city from the north was also halted by stiff opposition in the outskirts. With three divisions now encircling Manila, MacArthur wanted the city taken quickly as a symbol of his commitment to rid the Philippines of the hated Japanese.

On January 29, a force of Filipino guerrillas and Rangers had broken through the lines at San Jose to free five hundred Americans from a prison camp. Spurred on by the news, MacArthur next day sent the rousing signal to the commander of the newly arrived 27th Infantry Division and the 1st U.S. Cavalry: "GO TO MANILA. GO AROUND THE NIPS, BOUNCE OFF THE NIPS, BUT GET TO MANILA." Though he was still nearly 70 miles from the city, Brigadier General William Chase responded to the clarion call by forming two flying columns of tanks and vehicles and setting off down the road, telling war reporters: "The rest of the Division will be coming along after us and we'll let them worry about what we leave behind."

Dashing south down Highway 5 at 30 miles an hour, the columns took the Japanese by surprise by racing across the river bridges before they could be dynamited. On the evening of February 3 they burst past the astonished guards ringing the Santo Thomas University campus, which the Japanese had made a prison, to release 5,000 American civilian captives. An ebullient MacArthur now began preparing for a triumphal victory parade through the streets of Manila. But next day when the first units of the 37th Division at last reached the northern outskirts, they found that the capital was being heavily defended.

THE BATTLE FOR MANILA

The fanatical Rear Admiral Sanji Iwabachi had discounted Yamashita's order making Manila an open city. He commanded the naval garrison of 17,000, whom he had ordered to fight to the death alongside the 4,000 army soldiers who also found themselves trapped. A four-day initial battle left much of northern Manila in flames as the American tanks and artillery spearheaded the push through to the Pasig River, which divided the city and marked the boundary of the old Spanish metropolis with the stately public buildings that had given the title "Pearl of the Orient" to the Philippines' capital. To the southeast, help from the 11th Airborne Division was still being barred by the Japanese roadblock holding the southern outskirts.

The Battle of Manila was to be fought with a savagery that made nonsense of MacArthur's February 7 communiqué proclaiming that "our forces are rapidly clearing Manila," and predicting that the "complete destruction" of the enemy was "imminent." Churchill and Roosevelt had cabled their congratulations, but they were premature. Concern for the 700,000 Filipino citizens led MacArthur to forbid the use of aircraft to bomb the enemy strongpoints, so artillery had to be brought up to blast the Japanese out building by building. The hub of Iwabachi's defense lay in the old walled town of Intramuros, south of the river, where the battlements and thick stone walls stood up too well against the American pounding with shells and mortars.

"Day and night the shelling goes on," *Time* magazine correspondent W. P. Gray reported, as the Pacific War's only major battle for a city ground relentlessly on. "How many hundreds or thousands of civilians have already died by fire or shellfire outside Intramuros, nobody knows. Hundreds of city blocks are burned and flattened. Many unburned buildings are pocked or shattered by gunfire." The civilian population suffered horribly. Over 100,000 Filipinos died from the heavy bombardment and the butchery and indiscriminate rape by increasingly desperate Japanese troops.

The battle for Manila was in its second week when the airborne troops of the 503rd U.S. Infantry were parachuted onto Corregidor on February 16 to crush a garrison estimated to be less than 1,000 strong. They found there were more than 5,000 entrenched Japanese, who were able to wage a strong defense from the security of the Malinta Tunnel. MacArthur was concerned that a fanatical enemy might hold out for four months as the Americans had managed three years earlier. He was relieved on the night of February 21 when the Japanese plan to blast their way out went dramatically wrong and tons of TNT ignited prematurely. Five days later, the detonations of another ammunition dump caved in a large section of the tunnel and forced the survivors out into the open, where they put up a bitter fight that cost the U.S. paratroops a heavy 25 percent casualty rate before they were able to wipe out the Japanese almost to a man.

On March 2, MacArthur made a symbolic return to Corregidor, as he had left in the dark days of 1942, by PT boat. At the solitary flagstaff still standing in front of the shattered main barracks building, he ordered the 34th Infantry Division commander: "Have your troops hoist the colors to its peak and let no enemy ever haul them down!"

It was the beginning of a triumphant twenty-four hours for MacArthur. The next day the last pocket of organized enemy resistance in the Intramuros citadel was blasted out of the Finance Building by American howitzers. The personal satisfaction at having fulfilled his three-year-old pledge was dimmed only by the destruction of over three quarters of Manila, at the heavy cost of 25,000 American casualties and the lives of nearly five times that number of its Filipino inhabitants. With the "Pearl of the Orient" in ruins, MacArthur abandoned his victory parade. Only the Malacana Palace, in which President Osmeña had been formally installed a week before, had survived the savage destruction.

More than 100,000 Japanese troops were still holding out in the northern mountains of north Luzon. The campaign against Yamashita's carefully waged resistance would go right on until the end of the war. But on February 19, MacArthur had launched the first of the operations to liberate the outlying islands, and troops from the 8th Army began landing on Palawan. This ran counter both to his original plan and to directives from the Joint Chiefs, who intended to leave operations in the bypassed islands to the Filipino guerrilla forces. The bloody destruction the Japanese had forced on Manila, however, had so hardened MacArthur's determination that he decided to use the full weight of the forces at his disposal to liberate the Philippines as fast as possible, island by island.

REVITALIZING THE CBI EFFORT

General MacArthur's forces were advancing toward Manila as the first overland supply convoy for nearly three years rolled along the reopened Burma road into China. On January 12 the trucks set out from Ledo and crawled up the tortuous mountain passes toward Kunming. They were followed at a slower pace by gangs of the U.S. Army Corps of Engineers who were hampered by the rugged terrain, landslides, and sabotage by Japanese-paid guerrillas as they built a pipeline. Anticipation that Chiang Kai-shek's armies would soon be connected to an artery of oil pulsing into China, as well as a greatly increased flow of ammunition and supplies, raised General Wedemeyer's hopes that his Alpha Plan for reequipping them could soon be fulfilled. He was already ready with "Plan Beta" for an offensive thrust that would drive through the Japanese occupying eastern China to the coast.

In Burma, General Slim's 14th Army was rolling south as General Christison's XV Corps advanced, pushing the 28th Japanese Army down the Arakan coast toward Rangoon. This time the third British attempt to capture the strategic island port of Akyab succeeded, when the Royal Marine Commandos landed on January 12, 1945, under covering fire from the battleships of their Far East Fleet. The British had now secured a base from which the 14th Army could be supplied for the long advance down the valleys of central Burma. With the beginning of the dry season in November, Slim had sent five of his six divisions across the Chindwin on a series of Bailey bridges. This was the first stage of his offensive called "Capital," the objective being to subject the Japanese 15th Army to a crushing defeat on the Swebo Plain.

General Kimura, the Japanese Army Commander, was a shrewd artilleryman from Imperial General Headquarters who showed no inclination to allow his dwindling force of less than 20,000 to be trapped by British tanks and aircraft on the western bank of the Irrawaddy. He had withdrawn across its muddy expanse to form a new defensive line around Mandalay. There he reckoned his inferior strength would be compensated for by the natural obstacle of the broad, fast-flowing water if the British divisions tried to make a mass crossing under his guns.

In mid-December, after it became clear that the Japanese had slipped out of his noose, Slim improvised a master stroke. Initiating his "Extended Capital Plan," the IVth Corps started south on a 200-mile march down the west bank of the Irrawaddy. They would cross at Pakokku and make a quick end run to seize the road and rail center of Meiktila, some 500 miles below the ancient Burmese capital. General Sir Frank Misservy's force would thereby cut off Kimura's line of retreat and become the anvil against which his 15th Army could be crushed when

General Stopford's XXIII Corps made their frontal assault across the river. Simultaneously, Chiang Kai-shek's armies were expected to advance down the Salween in coordination with Mountbatten's long-planned amphibious landing to recapture Rangoon. The four Allied offensives would effectively box in and trap Japan's army in Burma before the new monsoons began.

COMPROMISE AT YALTA

"No more let us falter from Malta to Yalta. Let nobody alter," the Prime Minister had humorously cabled Roosevelt before FDR set out to cross the Atlantic in the heavy cruiser *Quincy* three days after his fourth inauguration ceremony on January 20, 1945. "I have things which must be done," he confided to his favorite daughter Anna, asking her to accompany him to the Argonaut Conference and help support him on what he considered his great mission to chart the peace strategy now that the military forces of Germany and Japan were crumbling.

Roosevelt's hope of reaching a global accommodation with the Allied partners suffered its first setback at Malta. Preliminary talks with the British, code-named "Cricket," proved to be not remotely in the spirit of the gentlemanly game. The sharpest division came when the American military leaders refused to accede to Churchill's demands for General Eisenhower to be ordered to push through to Berlin in a bid to strengthen the western Allies bargaining position to counter a Soviet takeover of Europe. The old divisions stemming from British intentions to recover their colonial possessions caused problems at the February 2 Combined Chiefs of Staff meeting. The Americans were less than unreserved in their support of the British scheme for a quick campaign to drive the Japanese out of Burma, before pushing forward to liberate French Indochina. Sensing that such an offensive was intended to restore the European dominance in Southeast Asia, the U.S. Joint Chiefs put forward General Wedemeyer's Beta Plan for the Nationalist Army to advance to open up a port on the Chinese coast.

The American strategic policy had again taken an "about-turn." Influenced by the President's particular aversion to allowing France to regain Indochina, General Marshall proposed that the Japanese-occupied territories in Malaya and the Netherlands East Indies should be bypassed in favor of concentrating Allied resources and British troops in China. Churchill was politely cool, leaving it to the British Chiefs of Staff to oppose the scheme as impractical. Mountbatten was adamant that SEAC's long-planned and oft-postponed amphibious offensive could not be prejudiced by the diversion of supplies to Chiang Kai-shek.

On the morning of February 5, 1945, the Big Three sat down with their advisers in the czarist splendor of the Livadia Palace overlooking the Black Sea at Yalta for the first plenary session of the Argonaut Summit. The formal speeches concealed deep rifts in the Alliance, yet divided though the British and Americans were over policy in the Far East, Roosevelt and Churchill were firmly united in their determination to prevent Russia from dominating central Europe.

Yalta found Stalin at the height of his powers, alert, persuasive, even humorous. Roosevelt, on the other hand, was visibly declining; there were times during the talks when his jaw drooped and he appeared distant from the discussion. Cordell Hull's recently appointed successor as Secretary of State, Edward Stettinius, was left to carry a burden for which he lacked the experience. This put Churchill at a further disadvantage when the Russians stated their terms for joining the Pacific War. Stalin demanded the return of all the territory the Czar had lost as a result of the peace treaty President Theodore Roosevelt had engineered to end the 1905 Russo-Japanese conflict. It was a price that the U.S. Joint Chiefs were willing to meet. Until the atomic bomb had been proved, they were planning for an eventual invasion of Japan that could cost the lives of up to half a million American soldiers. The horrific casualty toll might be considerably reduced if the Soviets attacked the Japanese in Manchuria and permitted American planes and warships to operate from bases in Vladivostok and the Kamchatka Peninsula.

The President, too, still believed he could obtain Stalin's support for his goal of uniting the Chinese Nationalists and Communists with a "real estate deal" that would return to Russian control the Kurile Islands and the southern half of Sakhalin, recognize Outer Mongolia as a Soviet Socialist Republic, and restore—according to the secret accord drafted at Yalta—the "former rights of Russia violated by the treacherous attack of Japan in 1904."

The accord had to remain secret because the Nationalists were not to be told of the deal until just prior to Russia's declaration of war on Japan. Roosevelt was confident he would have no trouble getting Chiang Kai-shek's agreement, because Stalin had given his assurance that he would work to persuade the Communists to unite with the Nationalists. The President trusted the Soviet leader far more than his Joint Chiefs of Staff. They warned FDR that it would be putting too much on Stalin's word to rely on his carrying out his promises in China. They were just as unhappy about accepting bland Russian guarantees that a "liberated" Poland would be allowed to determine her own form of government in return for a tacit understanding that the Soviets would have a free hand in determining the fate of the Balkans and eastern Europe. It was all uncomfortably reminiscent of the old "spheres of influence" diplomacy that the European powers had employed in dealing with China at the beginning of the century.

Nonetheless, Churchill, much against his own conviction and the advice of his Foreign Secretary, Anthony Eden, was finally swayed by Roosevelt's determination to believe Stalin: "noblesse oblige, he won't try to annex anything and will agree to work with me for a world of democracy and world peace." With profound misgivings, the Prime Minister signed the secret protocols, because he felt that to do otherwise would irrevocably damage his "special relationship" with the President and end all chance of American cooperation in recovering Britain's Far Eastern empire. Roosevelt left the Yalta Conference believing he had scored a personal triumph in securing cooperation among the Big Three powers. Had he noticed Stalin surreptitiously watering his vodka during the endless rounds of toasts at the final dinner in the Livadia Palace on February 10, he might well have had his doubts about having set his hopes for postwar Europe and Asia so firmly on the Soviet leader.

Roosevelt's sense of triumph quickly faded into a deep physical and mental exhaustion during the long voyage back to the United States, which was intensified after Hopkins succumbed to another bout of stomach illness, and a sudden stroke killed his aide and close confidante Major General Edwin M. Watson, whom everyone in presidential circles called "Pa." This double blow of personal tragedy to a visibly failing President was soon to be followed by reports from Poland indicating that the Red Army, despite Stalin's pledges at Yalta, was taking steps to establish a Communist regime. Within five weeks of returning to Washington and delivering a glowing report to Congress on the Argonaut summit, on March 29 the President finally took his doctor's orders and boarded the train south to his Warm Springs retreat in Georgia, for a vacation to recover his rapidly fading strength. It was the last time Franklin Delano Roosevelt saw the White House.

32

Uncommon Valor

"WE HAVE DRIVEN THE ENEMY OFF THE SEA AND BACK TO HIS INNER DEFENSES. SUPERLATIVELY WELL DONE." Admiral Halsey signaled to his ships on January 26, 1945. The mighty U.S. Third Fleet was at anchor in Ulithi Atoll, replenishing after operations in support of the Philippines' invasions. During three months the world's greatest naval force had sunk a greater tonnage of enemy warships than any other fleet in history. Now it was about to become the Fifth Fleet again, as Halsey transferred command to Admiral Spruance for operations to establish advance bases in the Bonin and Ryukyu Islands for the invasion of Japan.

The assault on Iwo Jima, which lay midway between Tokyo and the Marianas, had been delayed by nearly a month because the fleet had been providing aircover for the invasions in the Philippines. Admiral Nimitz had moved his forward headquarters to Guam as the rivalry for the Southwest Pacific Command revived when MacArthur sought to retain the old battleships of the bombardment fleet to assist in the campaign to liberate the southern Philippines.

The internecine fight between the U.S. Army and Navy resurfaced as a complicating factor was added by the Royal Navy. Admiral Sir Bruce Frazer had been appointed Commander in Chief of the British Pacific Fleet of four fleet carriers, two battleships, five cruisers, and fifteen destroyers. This deceptively mild-mannered sailor with twinkling eyes and ruddy cheeks was a tactful diplomat who faced the difficult task of carrying out his role as the U.S. Navy's junior partner. The "fleet" the Prime Minister hoped would reestablish the Union Jack in the Pacific was less than the size of an American task force. It was commanded by Admiral Sir Bernard Rawlings who could only muster logistical support to keep his ships at sea for a maximum of 20 days. So to avoid unnecessary problems, Nimitz assigned Rawlings to operate as an independent task group under Spruance's overall control.

The arrival of the British warships in the main theater to give a useful additional punch to the final round of the war against Japan was a political concession to Churchill that Roosevelt had insisted on over strong objections by Admiral King. As far as the other Joint Chiefs of Staff were concerned, its contribution was relatively insignificant compared with the strategic bombing offensive which they hoped might hasten the end of the conflict and eliminate the need for actual invasion of the Japanese home islands. The results of the Superfortress raids, however, had been disappointing.

"This outfit has been getting a hell of a lot of publicity without having really accomplished a hell of a lot in bombing results," General Curtis LeMay told his new command's press officer after he had been sent by General Arnold to improve the proficiency of the 21st Bombardment Group. Bad weather and high winds over the target areas of Honshu were given as the reason for the Superfortress's failure to achieve the promised results in the three months since October 1944 when they had begun raiding Japan. Another factor was the increasing number of enemy fighters that swarmed up from Iwo Jima to disrupt the tight formations of big bombers as they passed over the island, whose radars also served to give Tokyo early warning of approaching raids. One of LeMay's first tasks was to neutralize the enemy fighters on Iwo Jima, which he also regarded as a potentially useful refueling and emergency landing strip for crippled bombers halfway to Japan. "Without Iwo Jima I couldn't bomb Japan effectively," he told Spruance at a conference aboard the *Indianapolis* at Saipan on January 28, 1945, as the admiral was en route to assume command of the Fifth Fleet.

"That took a load off my mind," Spruance recorded, relieved that there would be some justification for the heavy cost that he anticipated paying to capture the 8-square-mile chunk of volcanic ash and tufa that was his first operational objective. The island of Iwo Jima, shaped like a pork chop, was barely 5 by 2.5 miles in all, but the most recent photo reconnaissance had shown that the Japanese were building a third airfield on the island.

Three Marine divisions had rehearsed for the Iwo Jima assault operation, which had been masterminded by Admiral Kelly Turner and General Holland Smith. The Marine commander, anticipating a possible 20,000 casualties, was predicting it would be "the toughest place we have had to take." The task was assigned to veterans of the 4th Marine Division under Major Clifton B. Cates, and the men of the 5th, a new division under Major Keller E. Rockey, with the battle-hardened 3rd Division in reserve. Unit commanders had briefed their men on the exacting task ahead, with the aid of foam rubber models of the island that pinpointed the many enemy pillboxes, gun emplacements, and blockhouses visible from the aerial photographs. What, however, was invisible was the extensive network of underground trenches and tunnels that they anticipated riddled the volcanic peak, making Iwo Jima the modern equivalent of a medieval castle. The island's heavily fortified "keep" was the 500-foot Mount Suribachi, which bristled with gun and mortar positions and dominated the black volcanic sand of the only landing beach on the southern shore of the island. More than two hundred emplacements and twenty-one blockhouses had been picked out in photographs, guarding the hinterland where the shore rose up in a series of 15-foot ridges that had been formed when underwater cataclysms had thrust Iwo Jima out of the ocean. On the northern plateau were the airfields, defended by lines of interconnecting trenches and strongpoints dug into the soft tufa.

The fortress had been constructed under the capable direction of Lieutenant General Tadamichi Kuribayashi, a thoroughgoing professional soldier who had been chief of the Imperial Guard and now commanded a mixed army and navy garrison that included 20,000 veterans of the crack Special Naval Landing Force. Tokyo Rose boasted that Iwo Jima's defenders were "packed full of fighting spirit." As the American aerial bombardment stepped up, Kuribayashi's men had taken cover in their deep tunnels on Mount Suribachi; they fortified themselves with a series of "Courageous Battle Vows" as they waited for the Americans to land. They had learned from the defense of Peleliu and were not going to waste their strength fighting on the beaches. Kuribayashi's battle plan called for "a gradual depletion of the enemy's attack forces, and even if the situation gets out of hand, defend a corner of the island to the death."

General Smith, convinced that taking Iwo Jima was going to be awesomely difficult, wanted ten days of continuous naval bombardment to take out the gun positions that had not been reduced in the preceding six weeks of almost daily bombing by American aircraft. But Nimitz had not yet succeeded in obtaining the return of the six battleships attached to MacArthur's Seventh Fleet, nor could he increase the availability of the Fifth Fleet because Spruance was scheduled to make a series of strikes on the Tokyo airfields to prevent Kamikazes being flown south. Not even the mighty U.S. Fifth Fleet could carry fuel and extra ammunition for more than three days' sustained shelling of shore positions. So a reluctant Curtis LeMay was ordered to add his B-29s' firepower to that of the Air Force B-24s from Saipan and hit the island from the air.

By the second week of February 1945, a quarter of a million U.S. Marines, soldiers, sailors, and airmen were poised to take Iwo Jima from its 20,000 defenders. More than nine hundred ships made up the two great invasion fleets preparing to sail northward from the assembly areas at Saipan and Ulithi. The sixteen carriers and eight fast battleships of Admiral Mitscher's Task Force 58, with their flock of escorting cruisers and destroyers, set out ahead of the amphibious and bombardment forces to deliver the first blows of the operation against the Japanese coast. Accompanying them in the *Indianapolis*, Spruance decided that the planned air strikes on Tokyo must go ahead on February 16 in spite of thick weather over the target. The Japanese capital was bombed, and over three hundred planes were destroyed on the surrounding airfields.

IWO JIMA

"1,200 PLANES OF THE U.S. FLEET ATTACK TOKYO AS SHIPS AND FLYERS BOMBARD IWO ISLE," the headlines of the *New York Times* proclaimed the following morning, when Mitscher's fast battleships and the *Indianapolis* were by now steaming south at full speed to join Rear Admiral Blandy's bombardment force, which had already begun its deadly contribution. Heavy rain and mist, however, combined with fierce antiaircraft fire, rendered the first day's shelling ineffective; only 17 of the 750 targets assigned to the big guns of the warships had been dealt with. The next day, Landing Craft equipped with batteries provided covering for the underwater demolition teams who swam in to clear the beachhead. The Craft drew fire from well-concealed batteries whose commanders thought the assault must be starting. Nine of the twelve support craft were damaged, as well as the cruiser *Pensacola*.

"At dawn on D-Day the waters of Iwo Jima looked like New York harbor on a busy day," wrote eyewitness John P. Marquand of *Harper's* magazine, who had been with the bombardment force and recorded the invasion armada's arrival.

The transports were there with three divisions of Marines—a semicircle of gray shipping seven miles out. Inside that gray arc of sea, turned choppy by the unsettled weather, was dotted by an alphabet soup of ships.

There were fleets of LST's filled with amphibious tanks and 'alligators'; there were LSM's; there were smaller LCTs and packs of LCI's gathering about the kill. The ring of ships was drawing tighter. Small boats were moving out bearing flags to mark the rallying points from which the landing waves would leave. It looked like a Hollywood production, except that it was a three billion, not a three million dollar extravaganza. There must have been as many as eight hundred ships at Iwo Jima, not counting the small boats being lowered.

At nine o'clock exactly the first assault wave was due to hit the beach, but before that Iwo Jima was due to receive its final polishing. Its eight square miles were waiting to take everything we could pour into them and they must have already received a heavier weight of fire than any navy in the world had previously concentrated upon so small an area.

The contorted island appeared "like a sea monster with the little dead volcano for the head, and the beach area for the neck and all the rest of its scrubby, brown cliffs for the body." Iwo Jima seemed to writhe under the pounding of heavy shells and bombs that threw up a great gray dust cloud, hiding the landing beach from the observers aboard the 5th Amphibious Force flagship, *El Dorado*. Admiral Turner had recovered from the bout of overwork and nervous exhaustion to be present and see his plan running like clockwork. Secretary of the Navy Forrestal, a former naval officer, was also aboard to thrill to the sight of such concentrated naval power. A refreshing northerly breeze sent puffy little clouds chasing across an azure sky as Turner gave his by now famous order: "LAND THE LANDING FORCE!" Waves of landing craft and Amphtracs churned in toward the beaches, but when they landed the discipline vanished as their tracks failed to get a grip in the powdery sand. The advance stalled just above the water's edge; it was disrupted by the shells and mortar bombs that came plunging down from the slopes of Mount Suribachi, twinkling with gunfire like a deadly Christmas tree.

The Japanese defenders had clearly survived the 20,000 rounds of heavy naval shells and the thousands of tons of bombs. They emerged from their caves and poured round after round down onto the 9,000 Marines coming ashore in the first wave. The defenders seemed oblivious to American bombing and shelling.

"All right, be ready to bail out of here goddamn fast," Colonel Thomas Wornham ordered his 27th Marine Regiment, as their Amphtracs reared through the churned-up shallows toward Red Beach. Minutes later, *New Yorker* reporter John Lardner was lying prone, squeezing his body against the hot black sand like the hundreds packing in on either side of him, who at least had the comfort of being able to fire their rifles back at the Japanese. "When you stopped running or slogging, you became conscious of the whine and bang of mortar shells dropping and bursting near you. All up and down Red Beaches One and Two, men were lying in trenches like ours, listening to shells and digging or pressing their bodies closer into the sand around them. We were legitimately pinned down for about forty minutes."

Other units made better progress. Aided by tanks, B Company of the 28th Marine Regiment blasted their way across the 1,000-yard wide "bone end" of the Iwo Jima pork chop in less than ninety minutes, to encircle the base of Mount Suribachi. Now, to their right, the 27th Regiment finally began pushing inland toward the perimeter defenses of the No. 1 airfield.

"There were live Japs near enough," recorded Lardner, "for whenever the Navy's Grumman fighter planes dived at a point just to our right near the airfield, they drew machine gun fire. Looking around, I had the leisure for the first time to think what a miserable piece of real estate Iwo Jima is . . . no water, few birds, no butterflies, no discernable animal life—

nothing but sands and clay, hump-backed hills, stunted trees, knife-edge Kunai grass in which mites who carry scrub typhus live, and a steady, dry dusty wind."

The regiments of the 4th Marine Division, which had come in on the left flank of the beachhead, had the cover of their Amphtracs to help them over those first vital yards inland from the shore. For the men of the 5th Division, in action for the first time, their advance under heavy fire was blocked by the succession of 15-foot sand ridges, which made it "like trying to fight in a bin of loose wheat." By midday they had made little progress inland, although wrecked and overturned Amphtracs littering the sandbanks afforded shelter at least from the thundering Japanese barrage.

Sergeant T. Grady Gallant of the 25th Marine Regiment left an indelible record of the horrors of that murderous morning, during which *Life* correspondent Robert Sherrod reported the "smell of burning flesh was heavy in some areas" and the men of the 5th Division retched as they clawed and fought their way up the shifting black lava dunes:

> It was quite impossible to dig a hole. The gravel was too slippery, too shifting and powder light, too formless; it was dry as quicksand that sucked at anything touching it, filling every hole as soon as it was formed. Shells arrived one after another, sighing at their work. slamming great metal doors, venting smoke, crashing and flinging bits and parts over the heads of men. The shells beat against the beach. Gravel patterned over the silent, strangely motionless bodies of the wounded, who lay on their backs facing the sky.
>
> As the shells burst, as they crashed and shrieked, one of the wounded rose from his stretcher. He rose slowly, bending at the waist. His head was bare and his arms were straight and rigid at his side. . . . He sat this way—taut, stiff and straining every muscle of his body. He sat, mouth open, stretched at the sides . . . and screamed . . . and screamed . . . and screamed . . . and screamed. 'Oh my God! My God . . . Good God Almighty!' the corporal sobbed into the dirt.

At 11 A.M. Turner signaled Nimitz: "EIGHT BATTALIONS SUPPORTED BY TANKS LANDED BY 10:20. LITTLE OPPOSITION WAS MET INITIALLY THOUGH SOME MORTAR AND ARTILLERY FIRE AT LST'S AND OTHER BOATS. MORTAR FIRE AND ARTILLERY FIRE DEVELOPED ON ALL BEACHES . . . REGIMENTAL RESERVES BEING LANDED. PERSONNEL CASUALTIES LIGHT." This message gave the CINCPAC staff the impression that all was going according to plan, raised hopes at Guam that the island could be taken in the scheduled four days. The dust-shrouded beach had concealed the awfulness of the assault from the *El Dorado*, but it was apparent to the Marines who continued to come ashore throughout the D-Day afternoon. Thirty thousand Marines had been landed by nightfall, yet the beachhead was still under intensive fire and was far shallower than planned. The 2,000 casualties sustained that day were an ominous indication by the end of February 19 that capturing Iwo Jima was going to demand a bitter struggle.

In anticipation of a counterattack that first night, the American warships fired starshells continuously, turning the hours of darkness into pallid day. General Kuribayashi's men attempted no suicidal "Banzai" charges. They knew only too well the strength of their position and remained in their fortified positions firing shells and mortar bombs as the Marines tried to push across the coverless terrain.

Next day it was obvious to General Smith that Iwo Jima would only be taken yard by yard. The remorseless pattern of the battle was set as the Navy sent fire-control parties ashore to coordinate the spotter planes flying overhead with the bombardment of the warships against the enemy pillboxes and gun emplacements on Mount Suribachi. Because of Iwo Jima's distance from Japanese airfields, Spruance's carriers supplying the vital air support were to be spared the numerous Kamikaze attacks that had plagued the landings in the Philippines. The one attack that did, however, develop on February 21 damaged the *Saratoga* and the escort carrier *Bismarck Sea*.

Ashore on the bleak lava dunes of the island, the Marines fought their way painfully toward the two airfields on Iwo's "waist." On its extremity, Colonel Liversedge's 28th Marine Regiment was closing in toward the lower slopes of encircled Mount Suribachi at the rate of 400 yards a day. Spearheading the attack were three combat teams who used flamethrowers, grenades, and stachel charges to burn, blast, and bomb the Japanese out of their pillboxes and caves. By February 23, they had reached the base of the sinister volcanic peak, its steep brown sides crumbling and smoking under the relentless impact of exploding bombs and shells. The effects of the sheer weight of the bombardment being hurled against Mount Suribachi were recorded in a Japanese soldier's diary. "Today we annihilate those who have landed," he had confidently written on D-Day. But on the morning of February 23, before he was killed, he asked: "There are no reinforcements for us—are we not losing the battle?"

That night as a steady drizzle turned the brown volcanic ash to slippery mud, Liversedge led his men in an attack against sword-swinging Japanese officers in an attempt to win control of the lower slopes of the peak. "At dawn we climb. We keep on climbing till we reach the top of that stinking mountain," he announced.

At sunrise on February 24, a forty-man combat patrol under Lieutenant Harold G. Schirer began battling their way up the gutted slopes, using bayonets and grenades to blast to the top of the crater shortly after 10:30 A.M. On a length of pipe they ran up a small Stars and Stripes, after first disposing of an enraged Japanese officer who had emerged from his dugout to make a desperate attempt to cut down the flag with his sword.

The unmistakable red, white, and blue banner, fluttering defiantly over the peak from which enemy guns were still firing, was spotted from the landing craft carrying General Smith's party in to inspect the beachhead. It was a moment of great emotion, summed up in Secretary Forrestal's comment: "The raising of the flag on Suribachi means a Marine Corps for the next five hundred years." Like *Washington Crossing the Delaware*, it was to become an immortal image of American history, popularized by the photograph taken some four hours later by Joe Rosenthal of the Associated Press, when Shirer's men restaged the original flag-raising with a larger Stars and Stripes that had been sent up the mountain from LST-779.

The capture of Mount Suribachi now gave the Americans control of the southern third of Iwo Jima. General Erskine landed that day along with the 3rd Marine Division, because the five days of fighting had already cost over 6,000 American casualties, 1,600 of whom were killed. The formidable lines of Japanese pillboxes and bunkers still guarded the approaches to the northern plateau where Kuribayashi exhorted his men with a final order: "We shall infiltrate into the midst of the enemy and annihilate them. We shall grasp bombs, charge the enemy tanks and destroy them. With every salvo we will, without fail, kill the enemy. Each man will make it his duty to kill ten of the enemy before dying!"

General Smith had predicted a maximum of ten days to secure Iwo Jima. He was now to face a steady attrition that would test every sinew of the U.S. Marine Corps' proud fighting traditions. As a lieutenant recorded in the 4th Division's official history: "It takes courage for officers to send their men ahead, when many they've known since the division came into existence are already gone. It takes courage to crawl ahead, 100 yards a day, and get up the next morning, count losses and do it again. But that's the only way it can be done."

While the Japanese were being slowly ground down yard by yard in the north, the Seabee construction teams were working to repair the airstrip in the south. By the first week of March it was in operation. The Stinson Sentinel spotter planes that the Marines' dubbed "Maytag Messerschmitts" were now able to take over in directing the artillery fire as the first B-29 came in to land after being damaged in a raid over Japan.

At the end of that week major cracks at last began to be made in Kuribayashi's stubbornly defended lines, after General Erskine had been given permission to mount a bold night attack. At 5 A.M. on March 7, a battalion of the 3rd Marines forged ahead on a compass bearing to capture one of the key fortified hills that stood between the American lines and the sea. Two days later they had fought their way through, dividing the Japanese defense lines by splitting Iwo Jima lengthwise. As confirmation of their feat, General Erskine was sent a canteen of seawater tagged: "For inspection not consumption."

The breakthrough opened up Kuribayashi's still effective defense to flanking attacks, which within a week had chopped his lines up into isolated pockets of resistance. These held out fanatically until March 21—a full week after Iwo Jima had been declared "secure." On that day Kuribayashi signaled Tokyo from his massive command bunker that resistance was continuing: "WE HAVE NOT EATEN OR DRUNK FOR FIVE DAYS. BUT OUR FIGHTING SPIRIT IS STILL HIGH." The Emperor promoted him to a full general, and Japanese newspapers cited his gallant defense as an inspiration to all citizens; but it was only to be another three days before the command bunker was forced by artillery and flamethrowers and a last radio message flashed out: "ALL OFFICERS AND MEN ON CHICHI JIMA FAREWELL."

Only 216 Japanese were taken alive out of a garrison of 20,000 in the six-week battle for Iwo Jima that had seen the fiercest fighting so far in the Pacific War. It cost the U.S. Marines 25,000 wounded and 6,000 dead, an appalling casualty rate of 1.25 to 1 that was the highest in the history of the Corps. Admiral Nimitz delivered the appropriately ringing tribute on the greatest amphibious assault in history: "Among the Americans who served on Iwo Island, uncommon valor was a common virtue."

General Kuribayashi achieved a posthumous triumph as Japan's war hero. While his men may not have taken ten American lives for each Japanese in their ferocious defense, the high price they had extracted for the few square miles of volcanic ash served as an awful indication to the United States of the terrible cost that would be paid to invade Japan. On the home islands, children and women were being drilled with bamboo spears to defend their sacred soil. Even while the bloody struggle on Iwo Jima was raging into its third week, the battle was brought to Japan's cities when B-29s flew in to make the first wave of firebomb raids.

FIRESTORM OVER TOKYO

After his aircrews in their eighth attempt had failed to knock out Tokyo's Masashima Aircraft Works, on March 4 General Curtis LeMay concluded that, in spite of his intensified training program, the high-level precision bombing offensive against military and industrial targets was a failure. In three months, twenty-two missions had been flown in which less than half the planes had reached their targets. The B-29 was now becoming vulnerable to fighters that could climb up to 30,000 feet, and LeMay was aware that a critical assessment had been circulated to the Joint Chiefs claiming—correctly, as it turned out after the war—that "Japan's production capacity has not yet been fundamentally weakened."

Pondering the 21st Bombardment Group's dismal record and knowing that it was for the strategic bombing campaign's primary benefit that hundreds of Marines were daily sacrificing their lives to capture Iwo Jima, LeMay took only forty-eight hours to decide to "throw away the book" and abandon precision bombing in favor of incendiary raids. Even for the outspoken general, who was known for his innovative tactics, it was the biggest gamble of his career. "I could have been wrong," he was later to reflect, aware that inconclusive results had been reported by the pilots of Superfortresses who had dropped incendiaries in earlier attacks on Kobe. This time LeMay decided that every plane would be loaded with fire-bombs instead of high explosives, and that they would make the raid after dark at low level because he had reasoned "from a study of photographic intelligence that Japan was poorly prepared for a low altitude night attack. She had little in the way of radar equipment or anti-aircraft guns. I wanted to take advantage of her weakness, and to exploit it for all it was worth."

On March 9, Army Air Force crews assembled in the Quonset huts on Tinian and Saipan for a mission briefing. Their apprehension at being told they would be making the first low-level attack that night on Tokyo was replaced by shocked disbelief when they heard that their aircraft were to be stripped of all guns except for the tail turret. The weight saved by the dismantling and the gunners left behind, in addition to the saving in fuel by not having to form joint uptight formations or climb to 30,000 feet, enabled each Superfortress to increase its bomb load by 65 percent, to over 7 tons.

Speed and surprise were to be the Superfortresses' new defense; but the discomfort of the crews was not alleviated by the advice that, if they were shot down, they should make for the sea before bailing out. This would give them at least a chance of being picked up by U.S. rescue submarines. Now that their principal targets were the citizens of Japan, they could expect "the roughest sort of treatment," and were warned: "If you are shot down, try and get picked up by the Japanese military as quickly as possible. The civilians will kill you outright."

If the risks facing the American Superfortress crews were going to be greater, the actual demands of their new mission were much less. Instead of having to drop bombs with pinpoint accuracy from an altitude of over 5 miles, each B-29 would release 500-pound clusters of M-69 canisters to carpet-bomb a densely packed urban area from less than 10,000 feet.

"You're going to deliver the biggest firecracker the Japanese have ever seen," LeMay told his units in the briefing for what he billed as "Operation Meeting House." Only a few hours earlier, General Arnold had given final approval to raid the downtown Tokyo suburb of Shitamachi. More than three quarters of a million people, mostly the poor and low-paid workers, were estimated to be living and working in lathe and clapboard wooden frame buildings that sprawled out along the eastern bank of the Sumida River. Obviously the highly inflammable construction of this densely packed area, where less than 3 feet separated adjoining two-story buildings, made Shitamachi an ideal target on which to test the effects of firebombing. LeMay had long talked about setting ablaze the "paper cities" of Japan. The strategic military justification for a raid that would incinerate thousands of civilians was provided by the decentralized nature of Japanese industrial production; light industrial production was believed to be under way twenty-four hours a day in tiny machine shops under the roofs of Shitamachi. Destroying these so-called "shadow factories," many of them small family concerns that employed less than thirty people, would disrupt the flow of pre-fabricated war material to the larger assembly plants, such as the aircraft factories on the outskirts of Tokyo.

The high-level Superfortress raids had already shown that Japan's anti-aircraft and firefighting defenses had not been equipped to deal with any kind of raid on urban areas, even though the American bombers had been regularly penetrating Japan's airspace for many months. Apart from regulation foxhole-type dugout shelters in backyards and a drum of water and paper bags of sand kept at the ready in every home, the civilian urban population had no real protection. There were just over 8,000 trained firemen and 2,000 auxiliaries, with 1,117 vehicles, to cover an urban area of 213 square miles housing millions of people. Hoses were pitifully short, firetrucks were restricted to only two hours' worth of gasoline, and the pressure in the municipal water mains was sustained by electrically driven pumps which failed when power lines were cut. Some firebreaks had been driven through the crowded streets of the Shitamachi district, but because of protests by the inhabitants (packed in at an incredible density of over 100,000 to the square mile), these were not extensive and often ended in cul-de-sacs. Even with adequate fire appliances, the Japanese were handicapped by their training, which relied on ritual rather than science; the brigade's standard bearer often threw himself into the flames to spur on his colleagues.

What meager defenses Tokyo possessed were in any case hopelessly inadequate to deal with the massive scale of the raid on the night of March 9. Over three hundred B-29s were loaded up with more than 2,000 tons of firebombs, sufficient to set alight a large section of the Japanese capital.

At 5:34 P.M. a green signal flare arcing into the evening sky over Guam sent the first Superfortress trundling down the runway. For over two hours the sustained rumbling continued over the airfields on Tinian and Saipan as the stream of four-engined B-29s roared up into the skies and headed north along the route to Tokyo their pilots had christened the "Hirohito Highway."

Midway to the target, the American pilots, apprehensive about making their first low-level attack on the Japanese capital, could look down on Iwo Jima as a friendly haven to run for if they were hit by enemy gunfire. Apart from a few scattered clouds, the night was unusually clear as the blacked-out Honshu coastline appeared on the navigators' radar screens, and the crews began donning their protective flak jackets and helmets.

"The darkest hour is just before the dawn," was the homily with which the NHK announcer on Tokyo Radio had chosen to close the day's broadcasting, after forecasting fine spring weather for the next morning's Armed Forces Day parade. The sirens had already wailed out long before the Pathfinder B-29s came roaring in over the capital's suburbs at 500 feet at 12:15 A.M. and spread foot-long sticks of napalm over the Shitamachi district. Before the surprised enemy air defenses could aim the first searchlight at the attackers in the dark sky, the two leading bombers sped away at 300 miles an hour, leaving behind a 10-mile swathe of burning buildings. "BOMBING TARGET VISUALLY. LARGE FIRES OBSERVED. FLAK MODERATE FIGHTER OPPOSITION NIL," their pilots radioed as ten more Pathfinders flew in to add to the flames.

The falling incendiaries made a spectacular show for Vichy French correspondent Robert Guillain, who was observing the raid from the Yamata residential district, safely on the high ground west of Shimada:

> Bright flashes illumine the sky's shadows, Christmas trees blossoming with flame in the depths of night, then hurtling downward in zigzagging bouquets of flame, whistling as they fall. Barely fifteen minutes after the beginning of the attack, the fire whipped up by the wind starts to rake through the depths of the wooden city.
>
> Once more, luckily (or rather due to the methodical plans of the American command) my district is not directly hit. An immense dawn brought forth by the bombs has been rising above the center of the city. Now the dawn is apparently winning the battle—the green light chases away the darkness, and here and there a B-29 appears in the sky. For the first time they are flying at low or medium altitude at varying levels. Among the oblique columns of smoke which are starting to rise from the city, one can see their long metal wings, razor sharp, shining harshly in the reflected glow of the flames, casting black silhouettes on the fiery sky, reappearing, golden, in a distant stretch of the sky, or like blue meteors in the gleam of the searchlights whose compasses open and shut on the horizon. . . . The Japanese people in the gardens near mine are all outside, or at the mouth of their holes, and I hear their cries of admiration (how typically Japanese!) at this grandiose, almost theatrical, spectacle.

The awesome drama would continue for three more hours, as wave after wave of bombers flew in to dump tons of incendiaries into a conflagration that was transforming the 4- by 3-mile area of Shitamachi, the most densely populated urban district on earth, into a giant bonfire. Attempts to fight the holocaust had to be abandoned after the blaze spread out of control in the first half hour of the attack. The inferno was fanned by a stiff 30-knot wind, which carried red-hot cinders to ignite nearby streets and alleys choked with thousands of fleeing people.

"Fire winds with burning particles ran up and down the streets. I watched people, adults and children, running for their lives, dashing madly about like rats. The flames raced after them like living things, striking them down. They died by the hundreds right in front of me," recorded a factory worker, Hidezo Tsuchikura, who survived on a school roof by immersing himself, his wife, and his two children in a water tank. "The whole spectacle with its blinding lights and thundering noise reminded me of the paintings of purgatory—a real inferno out of the depths of hell itself." Tsuchikura's family was more fortunate than most of their fellow citizens, who packed into temples and buildings for shelter only to be incinerated in the suffocating heat or boiled alive in the pools and rivers in the parks, which became cauldrons that killed thousands trying to find relief in any available patch of water.

The inferno of flame and searing gases that destroyed much of Shitamachi boiled up to temperatures that surpassed the white-hot firestorms that Allied raids had loosed on Hamburg and Dresden. The fierce winds blowing across Tokyo that night prevented a sustained firestorm from developing, but it fed oxygen into the blaze to generate a more intense heat. The fire at ground level superheated air that reached 1,800 degrees F. Metal melted while people and the many wooden buildings spontaneously ignited.

Long after the antiaircraft fire had died away, the great B-29s flying over the volcano of crimson and yellow flames were often tossed thousands of feet up into the sky by swirling gasses. "Gusts from the inferno were so powerful," reported a U.S. Air Force sergeant, "that men were rattled around inside the ships like dice in a cup. Floor boards were uprooted. All loose equipment was hurled about like sharpnel." In one of these wild plunges, a B-29 was flipped over onto its back, looping the loop as its pilot struggled to regain altitude. Some bomber pilots lost control of their machines, which plunged into the funeral pyre that drove great gusts of blood-red mist heavenward, fouling windshields and filling the planes with the sickly stench of burning flesh—sending the retching aircrews grabbing for their oxygen masks.

On the streets below, firemen and police could not control either the advancing flames or the fleeing mass of terrified humanity. Many people were in such a blind panic that they rushed on oblivious of direction or unaware that their bundles of salvaged belongings or clothes were aflame. Dr. Shigenori Kubota headed the only military rescue unit in Tokyo; his nine doctors and eleven nurses arrived in the outskirts of Shitamachi shortly before dawn. They faced an overwhelming scene of suffering and devastation. The fire still roared and the bridges across the river were jammed with fleeing survivors. "In the black Sumida River countless bodies were floating, clothed bodies, naked bodies, all black as charcoal. It was unreal. These were dead people, but you couldn't tell whether they were men or women. You couldn't even tell if the objects floating by were arms or legs or pieces of burnt wood."

The night-time winds had died away by dawn, when the inferno burned itself out. A chilly spring morning revealed the horrible extent of the devastation. A large section of eastern Tokyo had been obliterated; 60 percent of the city's commercial heart had been destroyed; a quarter of a million buildings, houses, shops, and factories had vanished. A million people were homeless and fleeing to the countryside in a state of shocked panic, having lost everything but their lives. Official U.S. estimates put the death toll at 80,000; it is more likely that 100,000 civilians had perished in the holocaust of March 9, 1945, which consumed 16 square miles of Tokyo.

At his Guam headquarters that morning, General Curtis LeMay received with considerable satisfaction the debriefing reports of his bomber groups. No fewer than twenty-one flag pins marking supposed industrial plants in the Shitamachi district were removed from his map of strategic targets around the Japanese capital. Only fourteen B-29s had failed to return, and five of their crews had been saved—a lower casualty rate than the last high-level bombing raid. No one was in any doubt that many thousands of enemy civilians had died as a result of the awesome firebombing of Tokyo, but by the spring of 1945 reports of the fanatical savagery with which the Japanese fought had hardened Allied servicemen to the view that such a fate was deserved by any and all of the Emperor's subjects. By a single deadly night's raid, LeMay had given new confidence to the advocates of strategic bombing. The terror firebombing of Japan's cities appeared to be the means of delivering the final blow to her war effort, thereby making an invasion unnecessary and saving the lives of hundreds of thousands of American troops.

Less than twenty-four hours after they had returned from setting 40 percent of Tokyo ablaze, the three hundred B-29s were airborne again, their navigators setting course north to Nagoya. That night they attempted to kindle a 3-square-mile triangular area at the heart of this industrial city. Its more modern buildings and better firefighting service managed to contain the conflagration, but the tons of incendiaries caused widespread destruction, enabling more markers to be removed from LeMay's target map. His next objective was Osaka. On the night of March 14, 9 square miles of this port and center of Japan's heavy industry were razed, in a raid that wiped out factories, steelworks, and docks. Three days later, similar treatment was meted out to the port of Kobe. The 21st Air Force was then sent back to destroy what remained after their earlier raid on Nagoya. After this operation, stocks of incendiary bombs were running so low that many Superfortresses were loaded again with high explosives.

The five firebombing missions were judged a brilliant success by General Arnold. As a result of LeMay's new strategy, the costly B-29 strategic bombing program was finally proving its worth. In less than two weeks, for the expenditure of 10,000 tons of incendiaries, the core had been burned out of nearly 29 square miles of Japan's main industrial centers. The Superfortress crews, in spite of their initial fears, had brought about this enormous devastation for a loss rate of less than 1 percent. In Washington, the Army Air Force strategists were soon expanding B-29 operations to aerial mine-laying in Japanese waters. The Joint Chiefs hoped that by stepping up the frequency and weight of the strategic bombing effort, the invasion blueprints they were drawing up with such pessimistic forecasts of casualties might yet be made redundant.

33
Floating Chrysanthemums

The Joint Chiefs of Staff had decided by the end of 1944 that the 60-mile-long island of Okinawa, rather than Formosa or the Philippines, would be the springboard for the final invasion of Japan, if that undertaking should eventually prove necessary. The biggest and most southerly island of the Ryukyu chain was some 400 miles from the Japanese home island of Kyushu. It had been visited by a small squadron of four U.S. frigates in 1853 while it was still the Independent Kingdom of Okinawa. Now, in March 1945, Admiral Spruance was preparing to retrace the same route to Tokyo with 1,500 warships. The Fifth Fleet was to provide the main strength of the mightiest naval force the world had ever seen, to escort the 1,200 ships in the invasion armada under the command of Admiral Turner. So vast was the operation that the forces were staged and assembled across the breadth of the Pacific, from the West Coast to Hawaii, the Marianas, Leyte, Espiritu Santo, and Guadalcanal.

For the first time, the team that had masterminded the amphibious assault planning begun in September 1944 was not to be the one that would guide the final U.S. Pacific invasion. The War Department insisted that Lieutenant General Simon Bolivar Buckner should displace General Holland Smith for the shore command of the mixed force of Marines and the newly designated U.S. 10th Army. The Okinawa assault would be carried out by the 3rd Marine Corps under Major General Roy S. Geiger; it included the 1st Division that had taken Eniwetok, Guam, and Saipan. They would come ashore alongside the XIVth Army Corps, consisting of the 7th and 96 Infantry divisions fresh from the Leyte operation. Two Marine divisions that had taken Tarawa and Saipan made up the reserve, along with the 27th Army Infantry Division, which had stormed the beaches of the Marshalls and Saipan.

The 154,000 Americans, all battle-hardened, were considered by the planners of "Operation Iceberg" to be more than enough to overwhelm the estimated 70,000 Japanese on Okinawa. Before the two great armadas set sail from their bases for the western Pacific rendezvous, the defenses on their target island were being systematically pounded by General Curtis LeMay's Superfortresses, in response to the Joint Chiefs' order to interrupt their firebombing raids on Japan and support the invasion. The costly lesson of Iwo Jima, as well as aerial reconnaissance, had shown that the enemy must be blasted out of the strong defense line they were constructing across the southern waist of the island. However, not for the first time the U.S. intelligence had badly underestimated the strength of the 100,000 soldiers of the 32nd Japanese Army who were digging in on Okinawa.

Lieutenant General Mitsuru Ushijima would have been even better prepared for a siege if Tokyo had not delayed his plan to concentrate his forces in the rugged south of Okinawa, where feverish work was erecting lines for a powerful defense. Only 3,500 men of the Special Naval Landing Force were positioned to put up a token resistance on the limb of the Motobu Peninsula in the northern half of Okinawa. Applying the sound tactical judgment that he could not stop the Americans landing on the wide beaches below Hagushi, and realizing that the relatively flat terrain of the northern two thirds of Okinawa would favor their overwhelming superiority in tanks and aircraft, Ushijima decided to make his stand among the hills and valleys of the south. Here he was assembling the heaviest concentration of Japanese artillery of the war to support his mortar companies and tanks, dug in on a series of defiles. Like the Regents of Okinawa, who for centuries had maintained the island's independence by defending it from invasion, he centered his defensive lines around the ancient walls of the castle at Shuri, a bastion that dominated the 6-mile-wide neck of the southern third of the island.

Ushijima's battle plan was to let the invasion "land in full" and press inland until it had been "lured into a position where he cannot receive cover and support from naval gunfire and aerial bombardment, we must patiently and prudently hold our fire. Then leaping into action we shall destroy the enemy."

The Japanese strategy of tying down the assault force on land would also force the Americans to keep their fleet off Okinawa to give air support, thus making it a target for the Kamikazes. "The brave, ruddy faced warriors with white silken scarves tied about their heads, at peace in their favorite planes, would dash spiritedly out to the attack," Ushijima told his men. "The skies are slowly brightening!" There would be no such sacrificial tactics on the ground. "Do not depend on your spirits overcoming the enemy. Devise combat methods based on mathematical precision; then think about your spirit power."

American military intelligence might have miscalculated the reception the Japanese were planning for them on Okinawa, but not the danger from the Kamikaze aircraft, which were now within easy range of the Kyushu airfields. Ten days before L-Day, Spruance, aboard his flagship *Indianapolis*, joined up with Admiral Mitscher's Task Force 58 to lead his sixteen fast carriers and escorting battleships, cruisers, and destroyers in a series of massive raids on the airfields on Kyushu and the naval base at Kure on Honshu, hoping to trap the remnants of the Imperial Navy. What was left of the First Mobile Fleet had evacuated the harbor before the air strike arrived. Several small naval vessels were sunk and over four hundred Japanese planes destroyed during the two days that Spruance's Fifth Fleet task groups ranged along the Honshu coast. Camouflage and dispersal enabled many Kamikaze planes to survive, to keep up a steady procession of one-way sorties against the American carriers. The new *Wasp* and the *Enterprise* were both hit on the morning of March 19, 1945, the same day that a suicide plane dived out of the overcast to smash through the flight deck and badly damage the heavy carrier *Franklin*.

Task Force 58's aircraft had successfully reduced many enemy airfields to rubble, but the damage to the three big carriers was a serious blow to Spruance, now deprived of their planes on the eve of the biggest Pacific operation. It was a loss that was to be partly compensated for by the arrival of the five smaller Royal Navy carriers. Admiral Rawlings's squadron was designated Task Force 57: the British contribution to the Okinawa invasion was to fly strikes against the southern Ryukyu Islands, while Spruance re-formed the carriers and fast battleships of Task Force 58 into three task groups to cover Turner's invasion fleet.

A colossal military plan, Operation Iceberg was mounted on a scale that matched the previous year's Allied landing in Normandy. The first phase, on March 26, went smoothly as units of the 77th Infantry Division were put ashore at Kerama Retto to secure the island's anchorage as an emergency repair and replenishment base for the Fifth Fleet. They quickly installed long-range guns, which could shell the southern tip of Okinawa 10 miles to the northwest. Air strikes and bombardment of the enemy positions from the sea had already been under way for four days by Vice Admiral Morton Deyo's battleships and Admiral Blandy's escort carriers. Two days before the invasion armada was due to arrive for "L-Day," the frogmen of the Navy's demolition teams were sent in under the barrage to clear the extensive obstacles that the Japanese had planted in the shallows around telephone poles strewn with barbed wire and mines. Equipped only with flippers and goggles, and towing ropes to which blocks of Tetrytol explosives were fixed—each one vulnerable to explosion by a sniper's bullet—a vital role in the invasion was played by the cool dedication of men like Edward T. Higgins, who swam in to the beach:

FLOATING CHRYSANTHEMUMS

Over our heads the fire support drummed a thunderous tattoo. The little LCI (G's) lay close behind us, their 20 and 40 mm quads and .50 machine guns pumping in perfect rhythm as they fired scant feet above our heads at the beach. Behind them the destroyers worked back and forth across their grid patterns, slamming three and five inch shells in arithmetical patterns into the jungle above the shore line. Beyond the destroyers were the cruisers and battlewagons salvoing their six, eight and sixteen inch guns in great bursts of fire that made their land targets jump and shiver, erupting in clouds of dust and debris.

When the swimming teams had been all picked up without a single casualty, the "prima cord" was fired; the succession of explosions blasted the tangle of barbed wire and poles free. But so densely had the obstacles been planted in the shallows that a second effort by the swimming teams was required to clear the way to the beach.

At dawn on April 1, Easter Sunday, the climactic roar of another naval bombardment signaled the arrival of H-Hour, as 1,300 American transport vessels and warships maneuvered into position off the west coast of Okinawa. The five-division assault went in to a 5-mile arc of the Haguushi beachhead in response to Admiral Turner's signal: "LAND THE LANDING FORCE." The Amphtracs charged toward a shoreline that was erupting for the hundredth time to heavy shells, and the aircraft delivered bombs and rockets.

It had been taken for granted that the opposition would be ferocious, and extra medical teams were going in with the first waves to deal with casualties that were expected to be far greater than on Iwo Jima. Three days had been allowed for the advance inland to capture the two nearest airfields. It came as a surprise and immense relief to the soldiers going in with the first wave when their Amphtracs eased up the beach unopposed shortly after 8:30 A.M. It might have been a peacetime exercise. Within two hours, the leading Marine units had advanced inland to take control of the airfields.

Remembering that it was after all April Fool's Day, the question ashore and afloat was: "Where are the Japs?" It did not seem possible that the divisionary landing engineered by the 2nd Marine Division on the eastern side of the island could have so successfully drawn off all the defenders. "PRACTICALLY NO FIRE AGAINST BOATS. NONE AGAINST SHIPS. CONSIDERABLE NUMBER OF TANKS AND ARTILLERY LANDED. REGIMENTAL RESERVE NOW LANDING," Turner radioed Nimitz at midday, concluding his message with the line: "TROOPS ADVANCING INLAND STANDING UP." By evening, the U.S. Navy's most successful amphibious operation of the entire war was nearly complete; 60,000 men were ashore, along with most of their tanks, artillery, and supplies.

When General LeMay heard the good news, he immediately requested that CINCPAC allow the B-29 force to resume strategic bombing of

Japanese cities. Ever cautious, Nimitz called for more strikes against the enemy airfields in Kyushu, because over seven hundred planes, half of them Kamikazes, had swarmed out that morning to assault the invasion fleet. One suicide plane struck Spruance's flagship, sending the *Indianapolis* limping to the emergency anchorage at Kerama Retto for repairs. Kamikazes had also struck the Royal Navy warships as Task Force 57 patrolled some 300 miles to the south of Okinawa. The deck landing officer of one of the British carriers reported: "The Jap aircraft came straight for the *Indefatigable* from five or six thousand feet and passed over her to the starboard. It then pulled straight up and looped over the top to come down vertically into the ship. I imagine the pilot intended to down the funnel, but missed and hit the flight deck."

The tough armored flight decks of the British carriers proved able to resist penetration by the 500-pound bomb strapped to the Zero. Just the previous week, three of Mitscher's wooden-decked carriers had been put out of action. But this first Royal Navy encounter with the Japanese "Hell Divers" left only a 3-inch dent in the heavy steel deck, although eight ratings were killed by the blast. Off Okinawa the Fifth Fleet had fared far worse. Over two hundred Japanese planes had been shot down by fighters and antiaircraft fire, yet Kamikazes had got through to sink three destroyers, an LST, and two ammunition transports, and had damaged many other ships.

That evening while the soldiers and Marines ashore celebrated their easy victory, the welders' torches flared as repair gangs at Kerama Retto labored to make good the damaged warships. Spruance now received reports from a submarine picket stationed off the southern approaches to Japan's Inland Sea that the superbattleship *Yamato*, in company with a light cruiser and a force of destroyers, had broken out through the Bungo Strait and was obviously heading south for Okinawa.

STRATEGY OF DESPERATION

The Combined Fleet was ordered out on its own suicide mission by Admiral Toyoda, who signaled: "THE FATE OF OUR EMPIRE TRULY RESTS ON THIS ONE ACTION." There would be no second chance because there was sufficient fuel left for the Imperial Navy's last battle squadron to make only one sortie. The mighty *Yamato* was to blast her way through the American invasion fleet, sinking as many transports as possible before running ashore, where her 2,000 crew members would join in the defense of the island. "Fight gloriously to the death and completely destroy the enemy fleet," Vice Admiral Seichi Ito was ordered, as he set sail on the biggest Kamikaze attack mission of all.

A thrill ran through the crews of the Fifth Fleet when, in the small hours of April 2, the battleship captains received Spruance's signal to be ready for a surface action. But the opportunity for a last great naval gunnery duel between these floating titans was to be lost even before Admiral Deyo had weighed anchor the next morning. Carrier planes from the *Enterprise*'s task group sighted Ito's force steaming south. Shortly after midday on April 3, the massive air strike Mitscher had launched swept out of a rain squall to catch the *Yamato* some 175 miles south of Kyushu. For two hours, successive waves of bombers and torpedo planes streaked down over the hapless warships. It was a massacre, reminiscent of the one inflicted by the Japanese on the *Prince of Wales* and the *Repulse* off the coast of Singapore three years earlier. The Japanese were now on the receiving end as the great battleship and her escorts fought back with every gun that could be elevated skywards while maneuvering frantically to dodge the bombs and torpedoes. The odds were against them. At 2:17 P.M. the *Yamato*, holed by scores of hits, finally keeled over and sank. A 1,000 foot column of black smoke rose up, hanging pall-like over the final resting place of the greatest dreadnought ever built. She went down accompanied by her escorting light cruiser to the depths of the South China Sea. The graves were shared with over 2,000 men of the Imperial Navy; only four destroyers escaped to rescue a handful of survivors who sadly reported the news of Admiral Ito's last desperate mission.

"I MAY BE CRAZY BUT IT LOOKS LIKE THE JAPS HAVE QUIT THE WAR AT LEAST IN THIS SECTION," Admiral Turner radioed to CINCPAC headquarters that afternoon. "DELETE ALL AFTER CRAZY," Nimitz signaled back, knowing from Ultra estimates that the garrison on Okinawa was only waiting for the Americans to push inland. The *Yamato*'s Kamikaze mission had been doomed to failure, but the "Divine Wind" of the Special Attack Force pilots was being felt as their planes damaged the *Enterprise*, hit a battleship, and crippled two of the destroyers that formed a radar picket line to give early warning of enemy planes approaching Okinawa.

Ashore, the pattern of the enemy's defensive strategy was finally being revealed to General Buckner. After cutting across the narrow waist of the island, the two Marine divisions had pushed north across the rolling wheat fields of the Okinawan farmers. For a week they met no real opposition; then at 12 miles from the beachhead they ran into the lines thrown up by the troops of the Special Naval Landing Force holed up in the Motobu Peninsula. It took only two days for Major General J. R. Hodge's Army Corps advancing south to come up against the first line of strongpoints that Ushijima had built to defend his southern stronghold.

The American advance slowed as enemy resistance intensified, and it came to a halt when the Japanese made their first determined stand under intense artillery fire to maintain their fortified line along the Kazuku Ridge. Heavy rain turned the ground to mud, which bogged down the

American tanks in a slogging match that began on April 12. That same day saw another major air assault on the invasion fleet by more than four hundred Japanese planes covering another run by the Kamikazes. The radar pickets again took the brunt of the attack, which included the first deployment of a new Japanese suicide weapon, the "Baka," a piloted bomb that sank the *Mannert L. Abele*. The towering superstructures of the American battleships were an easy target for the "Sons of Heaven." Damage began to pile up on the Fifth Fleet's battlewagons.

A great and unanticipated blow struck the Americans the next day, Friday, April 13. Just after dawn, a radio message was relayed to the fleet that the United States Commander in Chief had died of a cerebral hemorrhage at his Warm Springs vacation home in Georgia. "President Roosevelt is dead," the loudspeakers in 2,000 ships blared out. From the smallest LCI to the biggest battleship, the news was greeted with respectful moments of silence. Many of the young soldiers and sailors had grown up knowing no other man in the White House. They were visibly moved by the loss of the leader who had come to personify America and the cause they were fighting for.

A few days later, leaflets boldly entitled *The American Tragedy* were showered down on the soldiers embroiled in the grinding struggle for Kazuku Ridge. "The dreadful loss that led your late leader to death will make orphans on this island. The Japanese Special Assault Corps will sink your vessels to the last destroyer. You will witness it realized in the near future." The crude Japanese propaganda heralded a fresh all-out effort by Ushijima to make his threat a reality when he launched a two-day counteroffensive against the American front. It collapsed in bloody failure and cost him 5,000 casualties when by April 14, the battle for the strategic ridge had settled into a grim stalemate. The only consolation for an increasingly concerned General Buckner was the news that 30 miles to the north, the 4th Marines had finally broken through into the Motobu Peninsula.

On April 16, the Imperial General Headquarters launched a third massive air assault. From the fields of Kyushu and Formosa the Kamikaze pilots took off—after an elaborate ritual of toasts and prayers—escorted by Zero fighters and Judy and Betty bombers, whose crews were flying on the same deadly mission to sink American ships. The *Kikusui*—"Floating Chrysanthemums"—concentrated their attacks on destroyers. Unlike the battleships and carriers, the numerous small ships could not be so easily protected by the swarms of American fighters. The destroyer *Laffey* alone was made a target of twenty-two Kamikaze attacks; six hit her and reduced her upperworks to a smoldering wreck. Somehow, the crew managed to fight their battered ship to survival. The carrier *Intrepid* was also damaged, as well as a hospital ship and two transports, and another transport and an ammunition ship were sunk.

"THE SKILL AND EFFECTIVENESS OF THE ENEMY SUICIDE AIR ATTACKS AND THE RATE OF LOSS AND DAMAGE TO SHIPS ARE SUCH THAT ALL AVAILABLE MEANS SHOULD BE EMPLOYED TO PREVENT FURTHER ATTACKS," Spruance signaled Nimitz, urging him to send the 20th Air Force to put the Kyushu and Formosa airfields out of action before the Fifth Fleet suffered any more losses. Curtis LeMay protested to General Arnold the delay in letting his planes resume the firebombing of Japanese cities. Admiral King, in his bluntest manner, let it be known that if the Army Air Force was unwilling to continue supporting the Navy off Okinawa, he would withdraw his ships from the support of the Army fighting ashore.

THE PACIFIC SUPPLY LINE

This was no idle threat, since by 1945 the Pacific front was being sustained by the Navy and a waterborne supply operation that was one of the organizational miracles of the war. The greatest sea and air offensive of all time involved fourteen hundred ships backed by almost a quarter million fighting men who were relying on a floating conveyor belt of transport ships to ferry everything from the last bolt, clip of ammunition, pint of ice cream, gallon of oil and high explosive shell across the ocean from the United States. Just to feed the men ashore and afloat was a massive logistical exercise dependant on delivering 25,000 tons of fresh and frozen food a month across the Pacific along with twice that amount of dried comestibles—from flour to biscuits.

Over three years of war, this immense supply operation had grown steadily. Its starting point was the wharves and warehouses of the West Coast feeding the hundreds of cargo ships and tankers that sailed from Portland, San Francisco, and San Diego. By 1945 Hawaii had been turned into a gigantic oil and supply depot. From here Vice Admiral John Henry Towers, CINCPAC deputy commander, masterminded a logistics effort that fed bases in the south and central Pacific. The ports like Nouméa, Espiritu Santo, and Wellington which had been the staging ports that had fed supplies to sustain the Solomons and New Guinea offensives had now been replaced by great floating supply bases constructed by the SeaBee engineers in the sheltered lagoons of Eniwetok, Kwajalein and Ulithi atolls. A massive shuttle operation started from fleets of storage barges, carrying everything from canteens to bunkering fuel, were moored in the island lagoons, and freighters would load supplies from them and proceed direct to a beachhead at Okinawa.

In the days before computer and Xerox machines, keeping this monumental supply chain operating required thousands of tons of paperwork and an army of clerks. Inevitably there were snarl-ups and the brunt of administrative failure would be borne by the men of the merchant marine who were the vital links in the whole operation. Often freighters would ride at anchor at Ulithi for weeks before they were able to discharge their cargoes; discontent among the crewmen, who had often been at sea for months on end, reached near-mutinous levels. The panic wrought in January 1945, when Japanese midget submarines broke into the huge anchorage and torpedoed two ships, was regarded by many seamen as welcome relief to the monotonous routine. Legend has it that one Liberty ship skipper has sailed round the anchorage for six months vainly trying to deliver his cargo of barbed wire. Only after he had steamed back to the United States was he told that his destination should have been Naples. Long after the war ended, it is recorded that a whole flotilla of PT boats was still on the dockside of a south Pacific port where it had been off-loaded by a freighter captain who had been unable to find anyone to accept them.

On the whole, this incredible logistics system worked well, thanks largely to the silent endurance of the unsung heros of the Pacific War—the men of the U.S. Merchant Marine. Many had come to the theater after surviving a year or more's voyages through the U-boat infested waters of the Atlantic. They were to find Japanese submarines less numerous, but the menace of sudden death was nonetheless very real when a torpedo struck swiftly and suddenly. On December 20, 1941, the tanker *Emidio* had become the first merchant victim of the Pacific war when she was torpedoed by Imperial Navy submarine I-58 within sight of the coastline off Crescent City, California. Yet, after the initial months of convoying, it was realized that the Japanese undersea campaign was not as menacing as the German effort and most ships made the voyage westward individually, although those going from Australian and New Hebredian ports to the forward bases in New Guinea and the Solomons were escorted. Even in their most successful period, between 1942 and 1943, Japanese submarines only managed to sink little more than a hundred thousand tons of merchant shipping in the entire Pacific. But those crews whose ships did fall victim faced enemy savagery that often led to lifeboats being machine gunned. Of the forty-three man crew of the SS *Donerail*, which was carrying sugar and pineapple from New Zealand to Fiji, only twenty-four were left alive in bullet-riddled lifeboats early in 1943—and of these only sixteen survived a terrible thirty-eight day ordeal drifting across the Pacific until they were rescued by a Japanese ship and taken to captivity on Tarawa. Even though the home stretch between Honolulu and San Francisco was considered relatively free of danger, as late as October 1944, the Liberty ship *John A. Johnson* was sunk by a Japanese submarine whose laughing crew fired machine guns and pistols at her lifeboats. Only seventeen crew members managed to cling onto a makeshift raft until rescue came after they were spotted by a Pan Am pilot.

All merchant seamen braved the common dangers, yet for the majority the real threat was the monotony of the long Pacific haul, which averaged a month's continual steaming in each direction. The vastness of the ocean was measured in tedious routine of "four hours on, eight hours off" watchkeeping as their Liberty ship churned endlessly on, making at best less than 300 miles a day. The bane of a seaman's job, "chipping and painting" were the only relief for a restless crew while the volunteers in the Navy's Armed Guard prayed for the appearance of a Zero to give them some target practice for their guns. In strict accordance with U.S. Navy practice, all American merchant ships were dry. This did not stop ingenious efforts to smuggle on liquor and the bosun was always the most popular man on ship. He had access to the only legal booze aboard—the 100 proof alcohol used to top off the compass. Sheer thirst, not the fierce heat of the tropical sun, accounted for the remarkable increase in the rate at which binnacles dried out during a Pacific crossing. The pure alcohol was much superior to the alternative home-made brews, such as the one that involved fermenting bread with vanilla extract.

The heat and humidity of the long voyage dampened the ardor of many young volunteer seamen. Seeking the better pay and freedom offered by the Merchant service as an alternative to the draft, after rigorous boot-camp training the new breed of wartime deck officers sailing west for the first time under the Golden Gate Bridge cast themselves as "instant heros" following in the romantic footsteps of Melville. Such visions evaporated by the time they reached Sydney or Brisbane a month later. In the first year of the war, although the Australians welcomed the American sailors and GI's "like the Fifth Cavalry coming to save them from the Japanese," life on the far side of the ocean was provincial and stuffy. The government restricted the availability of liquor in the bars, and long waits were common for beer and ice cream. Worst of all, the dance halls were stuffy and women were accustomed to the old-fashioned style of dancing at arms length. Such were the impressions of one former merchant seaman whose wheezing old "rustbucket" of a freighter staged through the north Queensland ports of Townsville and Cairns ferrying supplies to General MacArthur's forces in New Guinea. "Like South Dakota by the sea" was his memory of these dusty townships in which armies of GI's swamped the local population with an invasion of lusty American youth that rationed girls at one for every two thousand men.

The welcome given to the Yanks by Australia's women caused resentment among the returning men of the Australian Divisions who had been fighting in North Africa. During the first year of the war there were many legendary "Battles of Sydney" when the short but tough Desert Rats came to blows with Americans in barroom brawls "that made John Wayne fights look like high school picnics."

The flood of American servicemen pouring through Australia reached a peak before the invasion of the Philippines, most of them making the Pacific crossing in conditions that resembled slave ships. "You wouldn't even treat sardines that way" was the recollection of one deck officer of the Army Transport Service Liberty troop ships. These hurriedly converted merchant ships, often modified by little more than the installation of trough latrines and field kitchens, were the means by which many GI's made the voyage out from the West Coast. Upwards of 900 men were crammed aboard, some sleeping on bare decks and others packed in holds which, in the fierce tropical heat, reeked of sweat, urine and vomit. "Passage on a Liberty ship," one general stated, "serves well in preparation for the hardships ahead." The troops who had to endure this privation had a saying, "You spend a couple of weeks in the troop compartment of a Liberty ship and you'll fight anyone to come ashore."

Many of the merchant seamen agreed with them. During the final year of the war there was often little chance for the crews to get a run ashore; freighters and tankers often spent months shuttling between the beachheads of Leyte, Luzon, Iwo Jima, and Okinawa. It was in these final great assaults that the civilians of the U.S. Merchant Marine saw their biggest share of action as the Japanese Kamikaze planes concentrated on transport ships. In the last six months forty-four freighters were lost or badly damaged. During the Okinawa campaign one Liberty ship, the *Wilton R. Davies* was attacked by suicide aircraft no fewer than seventy-two times as her crew struggled to offload the cargo of supplies—including 2,500 homing pigeons for the Army Signal Corps. Over a hundred Japanese planes were shot down during the same period by the gunners of the Armed Guard. General MacArthur noted, in recognition of the contribution that the merchant marine made to the Pacific War: "They brought us our lifeblood and they paid for it with their own. "I saw them bombed off the Philippines and in New Guinea ports. When it was humanly possible, when their ships were not blown out from under them by bombs or torpedoes, they delivered their cargoes to us who needed them so badly. In war it is performance that counts."

THE BATTLE FOR THE SHURI LINE

After two weeks, the performance of the Army was faltering and the battle for Okinawa appeared to be becoming another Guadalcanal—war of attrition on land and at sea. Increasingly concerned about the threat to his transport and supply ships, Admiral Turner's notoriously fierce temper was directed at the Army commander, whom he urged make another amphibious assault behind the enemy lines on the southern promontory of the island in order to break the stalemate. Buckner was a characteristically cautious Army general, whose preference was for winning battles by methodical frontal advances rather than by the swift and more risky flanking movements favored by the U.S. Marine Corps. But he had, in any event, decided to attempt to break the stalemate that still locked his southern front. On April 18, he ordered his Corps commander to launch a powerful drive against the right flank, in a maneuver intended to bypass the strong central fortifications of the Japanese front.

"It is going to be really tough," General Hodge had warned. "There are 65,000 to 70,000 Japanese holed up in the south end of the island, and I see no way to get them out except to blast them out yard by yard." The failure of his offensive, after nearly a week, to make any dent in the defense confirmed his pessimism. The fanaticism with which the enemy soldiers rushed in to bolster any weakness that developed in their positions led one 96th Division officer to the exasperating conclusion: "You cannot bypass a Jap, because a Jap does not know when he is by-passed." The emotional effect of rising casualty rates was beginning to tell on the Americans. The 27th Infantry, which had suffered over 3,000 wounded since landing, had to be pulled out and the 1st Marine Division brought in to replace it.

The growing seriousness of the Kamikaze raids and the deadlock on the ground brought Admiral Nimitz himself to Okinawa on April 23, 1945. He found inter-service rivalry threatening the unity of his subordinate commander because of the increasing friction being generated by Buckner's reluctance to adopt the Marine plan to break through by mounting an amphibious attack behind the enemy lines. Impatient for a breakthrough that would release the Fifth Fleet, which was being forced to stand guard off the island and endure the Kamikaze attacks, Nimitz was inclined to support the Marines, and resented Buckner's insistence that the Navy could not interfere in the ground battle. "Yes, but ground though it may be," Nimitz stonily told the general, "I'm losing a ship and a half a day. So if this line isn't moving in five days, we'll get someone here to move it so we can all get out from under these stupid air attacks."

But even as the wrangling was going on at 10th Army Headquarters, the American troops were at last beginning to break through the outer crust of the defensive line. The next days saw the Japanese falling back just over a mile to another line of pillboxes and hills loaded with gun emplacements. It was evident that a round had been both won and lost as a still deadlier phase opened up in the battle for Okinawa. General Ushijima was now calling on his men to defend to the death their principal defense line, anchored on the ancient fortress of Shuri Castle, where his headquarters had been dug into tunnels 100 feet below its battlements.

In April as the bloody attrition ground on in Okinawa, fears were growing in Washington that this was just a sample of the price that would have to be paid by a September invasion of the home islands, for which plans were now prepared by the Joint Chiefs. It was precisely the mood that Tokyo wanted to encourage. To enable the civilian population to meet the danger of assault by the American forces now just over 300 miles from their sacred shore, the government propaganda machine was hard at work inculcating the military spirit. Children were drilled with bamboo staves, factory workers practiced lunging with bamboo spears, farmers were taught how to turn their implements into spears. Teenage girls were to be armed with carpenters' awls and shown how to use them as lethal weapons, "to guard their honor like samurai," with the instructions: "If you don't kill at least one enemy soldier, you don't deserve to die!"

THE STRUGGLE FOR PEACE IN TOKYO

The firebombing of their cities had enraged the Japanese population, and propaganda had directed this anger against the Americans so that the will of the whole nation to fight to the death if necessary had been stiffened. Yet at the same time the will of the government was faltering, undermined by a growing number of civilian leaders who began to suggest the hitherto unspeakable possibility that continuing the military struggle was hopeless. Japanese confidence was being further shaken by the news of the impending defeat of their Axis partner in Europe as the Allies crossed the Rhine and the Red Army surrounded Berlin.

Unofficial soundings were made to the Russians for proposing a face-saving alternative to the Allies' repeated demand for unconditional surrender. These demands had precluded any real chance for the success of tentative peace feelers, put out in March through Widav Bagge, the Swedish Minister to Japan. But Prime Minister Kuniaki Koiso, secretly pursuing a peace initiative with Moscow, was undercut by Stalin who, five days after the Americans landed on Okinawa, let it be known the Soviet government would not be renewing the Non-Aggression Pact with Japan. Imperial General Headquarters believed that the Soviet attack would not come until the three months' grace period laid down by the terms of the pact had expired. The preponderance of hard-line militarists on the Supreme War Council made any open discussion of peace negotiations quite impractical, yet the peace faction in the government was gaining strength even as the army and navy supporters insisted on a fight to the finish. Most influential of the conciliators at the Imperial Palace was Marquis Kido. He had secretly submitted a memorandum to the throne saying: "Regrettable though it is, I believe Japan has already lost the war." His report advised the Emperor that, "although they cannot win," the military faction would "fight to the death."

Floundering in an impossible situation, Prime Minister Koiso decided he now had no choice but to tender his resignation after Moscow's refusal to renew the neutrality pact appeared to rule out Russia's help in obtaining a negotiated peace. The task of advising the Emperor on a successor who could survive the contending factions fell once again on the Jushin Council. This body of former ministers itself reflected the bitter internal struggle. It took a long, stormy session before they agreed to nominate the seventy-eight-year-old president of their Council as the only possible choice. Baron Kantoro Suzuki had impeccable credentials: as an admiral and hero of the Russo-Japanese War, he was acceptable to the militarists, and the peace faction respected his sagacious level-headedness. His age, deafness, and continued pain from the 1926 assassin's bullet still lodged above his heart made him a reluctant candidate. Marquis Kido had to appeal to his sense of duty "to make a firm decision to save the nation" before he finally bowed to the Emperor's wishes.

Yet for even such a respected figure to have made direct proposals for a negotiated peace treaty would have been to invite assassination by military hotheads. The aged Suzuki became Japan's third wartime Prime Minister, determined to play what he called *"Haragei"*—the stomach game—a strategy prevalent in Japanese political circles which meant publicly stating support for one position while actually working for the opposite end. "We have no alternative but to fight," he announced in his first public statement released to the press. But the return of Shigenori Togo as foreign minister was intended to be a signal to the Allies that he favored peace. "As to diplomacy you shall have a free hand," the new Prime Minister assured Togo; his efforts toward peace would not be wrecked by the opposition of the military.

The significance of the reshuffle in the Tokyo government during the middle of April 1945 did not make the intended impact on the Allies, whose own foreign ministers were on the way to San Francisco for the ceremonies marking the opening session of the first United Nations meeting. Both the Western leaders and the Russians wondered how the new President of the United States would measure up to his awesome responsibilities. Americans wondered too, doubting that anyone could replace Franklin D. Roosevelt, let alone a former habadashery owner, farmer, and three-term senator from Kansas City. Vice President Harry S Truman had his own doubts. When he was informed of the President's death, he groaned: "I'm not big enough for the job."

Extensively read on the wars of the past and something of an expert on Hannibal, Truman was ill-prepared to assume the role of Commander in Chief of the most powerful military machine in history. During his first two weeks in office, extensive briefings had put him in touch with the vast complexity of the United States' war effort. However, he was quite unprepared when on April 25, 1945, the Secretary of War arrived to brief him on "a highly secret matter" he had so far kept from the new President for fear of putting too heavy a burden on him too soon.

34

The Awful Way

At San Francisco on April 25, 1945, the delegates of fifty-one nations were preparing for the opening session of the United Nations, which Franklin D. Roosevelt had seen as the main hope for securing the peace of the world, when the terrible implications of another great scheme initiated by the late President confronted his successor. Accompanied by General Groves, the head of the Manhattan Engineer District, Stimson arrived that afternoon in the Oval Office to report that the United States was less than four months from testing the first plutonium atomic bomb. Truman was told that the United States would then possess "the most terrible weapon ever known in human history, one bomb could destroy a whole city."

The momentous decision now facing the President was whether to go ahead to develop and then use nuclear weapons. Two billion dollars had already been invested on the war's most expensive project. Truman, as the former chairman of a committee probing the rumors of arms contract waste, knew that whatever the moral issues involved, neither the Congress nor the public would forgive him if he abandoned the project or hesitated to use the bomb. If it worked, it would save the lives of hundreds of thousands of American soldiers. Accordingly, he gave instructions to proceed to a test as fast as possible, and told Stimson to set up an ad hoc Interim Committee to advise him on whether or not actually to use the atomic bomb. "I am going to have to make a decision which no man in history has ever had to make," he told an aide after the meeting was over, without revealing what had been discussed. "I'll make the decision, but it is terrifying to think about what I will have to decide."

There was little doubt that the seven members of the administration that Stimson picked for the Interim Committee were primarily concerned with advising the President not on the moral niceties of whether the atomic bomb should be used, but rather how and when. The same views were reflected by the Joint Chiefs, who, until they had proof that the superbomb worked, were proceeding with the plans to invade Japan, even as their planners were increasing the estimates of anticipated military casualties as a result of events on Okinawa. General MacArthur was pressing his claim to be appointed overall Supreme Commander in the Pacific for the assault on Japan, openly criticizing the "awful way" in which Nimitz was sacrificing thousands of American lives to capture the whole of an island when he only needed its airfields. Still the Joint Chiefs found it impossible to make such a neat resolution of the old Army versus Navy confrontation on the Pacific commands. Their directive of April 3, 1945—which set November as the target date for the Operation Olympic landing on Kyushu, and December for the Coronet assault on Honshu—once again compromised by making MacArthur overall commander with control of all Army air and ground forces while Nimitz remained in command of all seagoing elements.

Having failed to win overall command of the final phase of the Pacific War, MacArthur was already acting as a law unto himself in the Philippines. In accordance with his decision that Yamashita's forces in northern Luzon "should be driven into the mountains, contained and weakened, and our main effort devoted to areas where greater power may be applied," General Krueger's 6th Army had been stripped of three divisions, which were transferred to General Eichelberger's 8th Army for the "Victor Campaign" to liberate all the Philippine islands. It took over a month for Yamashita to be driven out of the area around Baguio where his 100,000 soldiers menaced the dams holding Manila's water supply. It took another two months of fierce fighting in north Luzon before Krueger's army finally broke through the Balete Pass to force the Japanese to withdraw into the eastern Sierra Madre Mountains, where Yamashita would continue his resistance until the end of the war.

General MacArthur appreciated that there was little glory to be won in mopping-up operations when, without waiting for formal approval by the Combined Chiefs of Staff, he launched his Victor plan. In double-quick time landings were made on Palawan in February, followed the next month with assaults on Mindoro, Sulu, Negros, and Panay, before Debu and Tawitawi saw the arrival of General Eichelberger's forces in April. They were relatively small-scale operations compared to the campaign to retake the second-largest Philippine island of Mindanao. This began when the first American troops came ashore in April. More landings took place through July to deal with the strong resistance put up by 20,000 troops of General Suzuki's 35th Army.

The new Philippine operations brought strong protests from Australia that MacArthur had apparently unilaterally decided to abandon the Allied strategy of bypassing Japanese-held islands whose liberation was not vital. General Blamey was irritated that his men had been left the chore of mopping up the enemy garrisons fighting it out in New Guinea, New

Britain, and Bougainville, while the Americans got on with the highly publicized task of winning the war. After attending a conference in Manila on March 13, 1945, he concluded that his Commander in Chief's difference in policy "between the Philippines and the rest of the Southwest Pacific area is based on political rather than military grounds." He added to the storm brewing up in the Canberra Parliament and in the Australian press by charging that Anzac troops were being left to complete the U.S. Army's unfinished campaign in New Guinea, calling it a "colossal waste of manpower, material and money."

To still the criticism, MacArthur had proposed using the Australian division in an April assault on the Borneo oilfields; but the Combined Chiefs of Staff at Yalta turned it down. The Americans were still trying not to get involved in strategically unnecessary operations that were directed at restoring the British and Dutch to their colonial possessions. Prodded by Roosevelt before he died, the Joint Chiefs had reluctantly given their approval to MacArthur's using the 1st Australian Corps as part of his "Oboe" operations, which called for landings on the Borneo coast at Tarakan in May; the capture of the oil installations at Brunei and Balikpapan in June; and an expansion of operations by July and August to Java and Sumatra.

MacArthur had justified his Oboe offensive as essential to the process of cutting Japan off from her strategic oil and raw material supplies. Yet by the spring of 1945, the U.S. air and submarine blockade had already accomplished this. Thus there remained little doubt that the Netherlands East Indies operations were merely a sideshow intended to keep MacArthur's forces fighting while he waited the arrival of the U.S. Army divisions from Europe and the call to lead the autumn offensive against Japan.

TO MANDALAY AND RANGOON

That Japan's Empire's defenses were now a shaky facade, to be smashed wherever and whenever the Allies chose, was being brilliantly demonstrated in Burma, where General Slim's "Extended Capital" pincer movement was closing in on the Japanese 15th Army. During the last week of February 1945, his 20th Indian and 2nd British divisions began crossing the 1,000-yard wide Irrawaddy by improvised raft, pontoon, and boat west of the old town of Ava and the vital communications center of Mandalay, which General Katura had made the center of his defense on the east bank of the river. While General Stopford's 23rd Corps was absorbing the brunt of the Japanese counterattack, General Misservy was ferrying the 7th Indian Division across the Irrawaddy some 70 miles

to the south and joining the rest of the IVth Corps, which had successfully crossed at two points lower down the river, North of Mandalay, the
British 19th Division had already established bridgeheads for the push
south. East of the Irrawaddy, General Honda was falling back as the remnants of his 33rd Army were being driven out of northern Burma by the
combined punch of the 6th Division of the New China Army, the American "Mars Force," and the Nationalist Chinese 11th Army, which had
finally succeeded in driving the 56th Japanese Division down the Salween
Valley.

The first week of March 1945 began on the Burma fronts with the
British 4th Corps' tanks successfully completing their 60-mile dash to
Meiktila, making Honda's withdrawal of Mandalay inevitable. At Ava,
the soldiers of the British 2nd Division found themselves locked in a
fierce battle that raged around the ancient Buddhist pagodas. When
Slim learned from Ultra that Mandalay was being held by only a token
force, he diverted the 20th Indian Division south and sent in the RAF to
bomb the city. The remaining Japanese garrison had managed to survive
the bombardment, sheltering behind the battlements of Fort Duffering,
which commanded the high ground. Not until March 20 could the Indian
troops of the 19th Division hold their triumphant march into Mandalay,
after three weeks of intense hand-to-hand fighting.

Airpower and accurate intelligence had been the decisive factors in
making Slim's Extended Capital operations work. Now, with the remnants of the Japanese 15th and 33rd armies pulling back down central
Burma, Slim meant to exploit his advantage and secure the whole of
Burma before the monsoon. There would be less than a month before the
rainy season closed in, but with sufficient transport of aircraft provided
by Mountbatten to keep five divisions supplied by air, he decided to
make a dash for Rangoon. To make the 350-mile run southward and reach
the strategic port before the rains made the roads impassable, he needed
to advance at a punishing 10 miles a day—a pace that could only be
achieved by bypassing any strong pockets of enemy resistance.

The gamble, if it succeeded, could advance the Allied victory in
Burma by many weeks. Slim toured his units surrounding the Japanese
south of Meiktila, urging his tank commanders, who were to spearhead
the drive, to do everything humanly possible to keep their battered vehicles going until they reached the coast. The advance was planned as a
division-by-division leapfrogging operation, with Stopford's XXIIIrd
Corps moving down the Irrawaddy to the railhead at Prome, pacing
Misservy's IVth Corps, which would set off south down the main road link
following the Sittang Valley. Because these units were supplied only by
air, each would be making the dash with a slimmed-down force of two
motorized infantry divisions, led by an armored brigade. Troops would

be on half-rations so that more ammunition could be loaded into their trucks. To join in the final attack on Rangoon, Mountbatten ordered the 26th Indian Division, which had captured Ramree Island, to prepare to go in on an amphibious assault covered by the Navy as part of "Operation Dracula," which involved the Royal Navy Eastern Fleet bombarding the Japanese bases in the Andaman Islands off the south Burma coast.

The race against the rains and the still powerful formations of retreating Japanese troops commenced at the beginning of the second week of April. Within seven days Misservy's force had reached Pegu, to begin crossing the river by the Bailey bridge just 50 miles north of Rangoon.

Then the monsoon, as Slim feared it might, began two weeks early. Heavy rain made the rivers flood and the advance became mired down, but Operation Dracula was already rolling. The British 15th Corps invasion convoys had sailed down the Arakan coast, preceded by Gurkha paratroops dropped at dawn on May 1 at Elephant Point to clear the approaches to Rangoon for the landing craft. Royal Navy destroyers had intercepted a Japanese transport heading out of the port the previous night. It was plain that the enemy was evacuating. Aircraft flying over the Rangoon jail, which housed British prisoners, reported that "JAPS GONE" and "EXTRACT DIGIT" had been painted on its roof by the understandably impatient inmates.

The amphibious force landed at Rangoon on May 2, south of the port, to begin pushing up through sodden rice paddies. Its spearhead broke into the undefended· city the next morning, released the prisoners, and was welcomed as liberators by the Burmese. Within a week all three British forces had joined up. Except for mopping-up operations against the Japanese trapped in the center of the country who were trying to march toward Siam, the Burma campaign was over. Churchill radioed "heartfelt congratulations" to Mountbatten's SEAC headquarters. "In spite of diminution and disappointment you and your men have done all and more than your directive required." It was a welcome tribute to the success of General Slim and the brilliant offensive he had waged with his 14th Army. Through three terrible years of fighting under impossible conditions, his soldiers had cynically thought of themselves as the "forgotten army," waging a war to which the British had been reluctant to commit resources sufficient for victory.

HOLDING CHINA AND ADVANCING TO BORNEO

The final stages of the Burma campaign had been executed without the help of the Chinese forces. By the end of March 1945, the 80,000 men of the Japanese Army in China had resumed their offensive against the Nationalist positions to relieve the pressure on their troops in Burma. The Japanese drive toward the airfields around Chihkiang, less than 200 miles from Chungking, panicked Chiang Kai-shek into recalling his 11th Army Group, which had taken Lashio, and demanding the support of American planes then supplying Slim's advance. Under pressure from Churchill, Marshall had agreed that Slim would have the use of the aircraft until June. Even without the airlifting in of supporting troops, General Wedemeyer's American-trained "Alpha Force" of the Nationalist Army managed to hold the Japanese offensive, with the assistance of Chennault's 14th Air Force.

It was a significant reversal of fortune for Chiang Kai-shek and a boost to Wedermeyer's hopes of launching a thrust toward the coast to regain control of southern China. Yet already a more significant tide was running farther north, where the well-drilled cadres of Mao Tse-tung's Peoples Army beat off Japanese attacks in the Hunan-Hupeh front in March. Their success renewed Washington's fears about the possibility of civil war between the rival Chinese armies if agreement was not speedily reached between the regimes in Yenan and Chungking. Wedermeyer and Hurley flew to Washington for urgent consultations after receiving Chiang's blunt refusal to consider sharing power with the Communists. An ailing Roosevelt could offer no hope of a solution beyond relying on Stalin to keep his word. The Russians did not carry out their Yalta promise and Churchill dismissed the idea of a united China as "the great American illusion." Stalin ignored Roosevelt's appeals to use his influence to persuade Mao Tse-tung to reach an accommodation with Chiang. By May 1945, the Chinese Communists were demonstrating a formidable military capability by driving south of Nanking across the Yangtze with the ultimate objective of reaching Shanghai. This move anticipated American landings on the mainland and was intended to divide China in two before the Nationalists recovered enough strength to push the Japanese north.

The capture of Rangoon, which signaled the beginning of the end for the Japanese forces now bottled up in Burma, came two days after MacArthur launched the first of his Oboe landings to drive out the enemy occupiers of Borneo. After a massive bombardment by the warships of the U.S. Seventh Fleet and a series of heavy raids by the 13th Air Force, the landing went in through a forest of steel obstacles in the shallows on the island of Tarakan off Borneo's northeastern coast. The soldiers of Australia's veteran 7th Division, accompanied by a token force of Dutch troops, had a tough battle to establish a beachhead. It was hardly a great triumph for the Australians, whose first major amphibious operation of the war was a pyrrhic victory on an island of wrecked oil installations, where the airfields could no longer support Borneo operations because they had been devastated by American bombers.

BREAKTHROUGH ON OKINAWA

The Tarakan landings took place while, 2,000 miles to the north, the Japanese were attempting to pull off an amphibious assault as part of a renewed counteroffensive on Okinawa. General Buckner's forces had been able only to inch forward against the heavy defense and shelling of the Shuri Line. Now Ushijima tried to burst out with an attack that was timed for May 3, 1945, to coincide with the heaviest air assault the Imperial Navy Kamikazes had yet launched against the Fifth Fleet—whose planes were still playing a critical role in the American operation. Two destroyers and two LSMs were sunk and many warships damaged, with heavy casualties. The Kamikazes were followed by bombers raiding the rear of General Buckner's lines that night, as cover for the Japanese barges setting out up the coast to make simultaneous landings of troops on either side of Okinawa behind the American lines.

Ushijima's ground forces had no better luck than the amphibious teams, which were smashed by destroyers and artillery. Under a long barrage they briefly pushed through the American lines to push one Marine battalion off a strategic hill position. Most of the Japanese tanks had been knocked out early in the assault; with no heavy weapons or armor to support them, the counteroffensive's bulge in the front collapsed within twenty-four hours.

The counteroffensive was exhausted by May 8, when the waters off Okinawa shook to a thunderous roar as every American warship fired three rounds into the Japanese positions to salute the end of the war against Germany. Hitler had shot himself in the Führerbunker on April 30, just forty-eight hours before the Red Army completed the capture of Berlin. Within five days Admiral Karl Doenitz, his chosen successor as Führer, was forced to accept an unconditional cease-fire.

On May 11, the Japanese marked their survival as the only member of the Axis Pack by launching another Kamikaze raid against the warships crowding off Okinawa. Destroyer pickets and the carrier *Bunker Hill* were put out of action. Ashore, the momentum of the American advance was gathering as one after another the fortified hill positions— incongruously dubbed Sugar Loaf, Chocolate Drop, and Flattop, by the battling GIs—were captured or subdued. Ushijima's right flank was being bent back on Shuri Castle, which by May 21 was invested on three sides. Soaking rains then stalled the American tanks in thick mud as a furious battle raged. Dogged American persistence forced Ushijima to begin withdrawing to his rearward defense line. On May 25, the "Floating Chrysanthemums" again flew across from Japan for another mass assault, damaging more ships and killing more Navy men. They were preceded by the appearance of a new suicide effort as five fully loaded bombers crashed into the Okinawa airstrips, setting parked planes and fuel tanks ablaze.

Two days later, in the midst of another heavy air attack, Admiral Halsey arrived in the *New Jersey* to exchange command of the naval forces with Admiral Spruance. It was now the Third Fleet that reported yet more damage from the relentless enemy air assault. On Okinawa, General Buckner received reports that the enemy's Shuri front was finally breaking. On the last day of May the Marines were scrambling over the battered remains of the medieval castle. Its long defense had cost the Japanese an estimated 60,000 men, a carnage that had also taken a toll of nearly 6,000 U.S. soldiers and Marines.

"It's all over now bar the cleaning up of pockets of resistance," General Buckner hopefully announced that May 31, as the Marines broke through to capture Shuri Castle, assuming that after the heavy slaughter the enemy's defense would crumble like the ancient ramparts. He was soon to find that he could not have been more wrong. Ushijima had pulled back only 6 miles to a rugged coral escarpment, an imposing natural barrier between two hills that had been cunningly pierced by tunnels and gun emplacements. Here he determined to make his final stand to hold the southernmost tip of the island for as long as any of his men survived.

PEACE MOVES

Fired by the defiant messages reaching them during the month-long death throes of the Okinawa defenders, Imperial General Headquarters was so blinded by the "last-stand" mentality that they ignored two efforts at negotiating peace which had opened up during May. The first was initiated by Commander Yoshijiro Fujimara, who had escaped from Berlin to Switzerland. In his capacity as naval attaché and with the assistance of Dr. Friederich Hack, a German with extensive business contacts in Tokyo, the two men had opened unofficial discussions with Allen Dulles, the OSS Chief in Berne. The burgeoning espionage and intelligence network of the Office of Strategic Services that had been created by Roosevelt's confidante, Colonel "Wild Bill" Donovan, had already been instrumental in achieving the surrender of German forces in northern Italy.

On May 8, 1945, the day of the German surrender, Fujimara had begun the tricky task of persuading his superiors on the naval staff to take the peace feelers seriously by radioing that the initial approach had come from the Americans. Simultaneously, the Office of War Information in Washington sponsored a series of Japanese radio broadcasts by Captain Elias Zacharias, in which he hoped by subtle propaganda to encourage the opening of a dialogue. Close monitoring by Magic of the Berne-Tokyo circuit indicated that the Navy Chief of Staff was not reacting to Fujimara's increasingly direct suggestions, which culminated in his relaying the proposal on May 20 that a senior admiral would be guaranteed a safe flight to Switzerland to begin preliminary discussions with an American official who had direct access to the President. Allen Dulles had flown to Washington for consultations with Truman, when Tokyo's long-awaited response was finally intercepted. From the warning that the attaché was to beware "some enemy ruse," it was evident that the Japanese Naval Staff were not willing to pursue what was described as an American "stratagem."

As if on cue to orchestrate Japan's plight, the Superfortress bombers had returned to make new firebombing tours of the homeland. General LeMay was now so confident that his accompanying fighters would be able to smash Japan's aerial defenses that on May 14 he sent the B-29s to raid Nagoya by daylight. They burned out 3 square miles of the city and returned on following nights to smash the docks and industrial areas. Raids by five hundred bombers on the nights of May 23 and 25 laid waste another 16 square miles of Tokyo, although the 21st Air Force pilots had been carefully ordered not to bomb near the Imperial Palace "since the Emperor of Japan is not at present a liability and may later become an asset."

Tokyo Radio transmitters survived to continue broadcasting a futile exhortation to those citizens who had not fled to the countryside, to stand resolute:

Why should we be afraid of air raids?
The big sky is protected by iron defenses.
For young and old it is time to stand up;
We are loaded with the honor of defending the homeland.
Come on, enemy planes! Come on many times!

Devastated Tokyo had already been removed by LeMay from his list of targets, but there were plenty of other Japanese cities left. Four nights later, he responded to the challenge by sending his planes to raid Yokohama. The raid left all but 15 percent of Japan's major port in smoking ruins. Reports of such devastation being wrought by the Superfortresses suggested to LeMay and the Joint Chiefs that it must now be only a matter of weeks or a month at the most before the Japanese government would accept unconditional surrender rather than continue to endure the raids that were burning out its cities and industries.

The destruction was indeed causing concern to Suzuki's cabinet. Before the resumption of the firebombing, the Prime Minister had set up a planning board of military and civilian experts to assess how much damage they could take and still go on fighting. The report was bleaker than even the most die-hard militarist in his cabinet had anticipated. Hardest hit were the heavy industries that were essential to sustain the faltering war machine. Steel production had dropped to less than two thirds of the official minimum quotas, aircraft production had fallen to a third because of aluminum shortages; less than 1 million tons of shipping remained, all of it was blockaded due to coastal operations by the Allied aircraft and submarines. Internal railway and road transport was on the verge of collapse from bombing. The lack of fuel led to desperate efforts to produce synthetic gasoline from pine resin to keep on sending up the Kamikazes.

The Supreme War Council was facing the reality of military defeat, yet surrender was inconceivable to the military leaders as long as they had their 3 million-strong army and over 9,000 planes with pilots willing to seek immortality as Kamikazes in defense of the homeland. When Germany capitulated, Prime Minister Suzuki was still hopeful of negotiating a face-saving peace through the neutral Soviet government, allowing Japan to retain at least a part of her Empire. Foreign Minister Togo argued that this was unrealistic and that they should attempt to negotiate directly with the United States. The failure to open negotiations through the OSS channels in Switzerland led to the rejection of his advice in favor of resuming approaches through Moscow.

Togo warned that Stalin's price would be "much beyond our imagination," including territory in Manchuria and Port Arthur. Former Premier Hirota Koki was appointed to open discussions with the Russian ambassador. General Anami, the war minister, was making his own plans to "prosecute the war to the bitter end" by organizing a volunteer citizen's army. Bowing to the pressure of the militarists, Suzuki continued playing the "stomach game" by accepting the army plan endorsed by the Emperor at the beginning of June.

The inspiration for the militarists in the cabinet and the fanatical masses of Japanese civilians drilling with pitchforks, carpenters' tools, and bamboo spears was provided by the Okinawa garrison, which had fought the American invaders for three months and still refused to surrender. Reduced to less than 40,000, Ushijima's force was defiantly battling on from the caves in the hills ringing the Oruku Peninsula. More Kamikaze attacks had been sent against the American carriers, but the Fifth Fleet aircraft continued to send bombs and rockets thundering relentlessly into the enemy positions. Buckner concentrated his artillery fire on their key positions on a hill called "The Big Apple." When it was captured, Ushijima's remaining soldiers were squeezed back into the last few square miles at the tip of the island.

The final stages of the battle for Okinawa began on June 17, 1945, as the Americans pushed forward with their specially developed flame-throwing tanks, which hosed napalm into the deep Japanese redoubts.

General Buckner was killed next day by flying coral thrown up by an enemy shell that landed as he was touring the front. Four days later, Ushijima's surviving forces had been chopped up into three isolated groups. Tokyo ordered another massive Kamikaze strike—it was too late to affect the outcome. That day a final radio message was flashed from Ushijima's headquarters deep in the caves of Hill 89: "OUR STRATEGY TACTICS AND METHODS WERE ALL UTILIZED TO THE UTMOST." In the tunnels, medical orderlies were injecting the wounded with lethal doses of morphine. At 4 A.M. the next morning, after a haircut and a final round of toasts in scotch whisky, Ushijima sat down on a mat at the mouth of a cave less than 50 feet from the American positions and committed seppuko with his dagger. His aides decapitated the body.

That same day, June 22, 1945, U.S. 10th Army Headquarters at last radioed a communiqué announcing that Okinawa was secure. Mopping-up operations were to continue for another month, but Admiral Nimitz formally declared Operation Iceberg ended on July 2. There was not much celebration of a victory that had involved the bloodiest slaughter of the entire Pacific war. Over 107,539 Japanese soldiers had died in battle and 27,769 were entombed in caves. Only 10,755 prisoners were taken and an estimated 75,000 Okinawan civilians had become casualties. The land battle had cost the Americans over 7,374 dead and 31,807 wounded. At sea, the Japanese had lost 16 warships and over 800 planes, many of them Kamikazes. The 34 ships sunk by the Japanese suicide pilots—the 763 carrier planes lost, and the 4,907 American sailors killed— were the heaviest casualties inflicted by the Imperial Navy on the U.S. Navy in any battle of the entire war. In recognition of this, Churchill cabled Truman on June 22 that the epic struggle for Okinawa would go down as "among the most intense and famous of military history."

35

The Miracle of Deliverance

The awful cost of capturing the small island of Okinawa forced the President and the Joint Chiefs of Staff to find a means of bringing about the surrender of Japan without the planned autumn invasions, whose potential cost in American lives was now being revised at over the million mark. The champions of strategic bombing, led by General Arnold, were still hoping that the holocaust raids might force the Tokyo government to accept an unconditional surrender. Although this option was already fading, the unofficial peace feelers continued to be put out through neutral channels. The alternative means of shocking the Japanese into a surrender was the use of the atomic bomb, but a test had yet to be conducted that would convince the American military leaders they could take this gamble. Any failure of a new weapon dropped over Japan was likely to prolong the war.

Dropping the atomic bomb on military objectives "such as large naval bases" or "manufacturing areas" was considered at the May 29 meeting between General Marshall and the Secretary of War. The U.S. Army Chief was then in favor of making arrangements for a demonstration by warning the Japanese to evacuate all such designated target zones before selecting one of them. Marshall emphasized the need to "keep our record of warning clear" to "offset by such warning the opprobrium which might follow from an ill-considered employment of such force." He also revealed that the Army operational planners were investigating alternative ways to deal with the kind of "fanatical but hopeless" defense that had inflicted such heavy casualties on Okinawa and which would confront the invasion of the home islands. He proposed saturating areas with mustard gas while American forces "just stand off." But he recognized that public opinion had to be considered, although he himself believed "the character of the weapon was no less humane than phosphorous and flame throwers and need not be used against dense populations of civilians." Yet it was to turn out that both the warning as well as the alternative of chemical warfare were abandoned as being insufficient to bring about the final surrender of Japan. This decision was reached in Washington during the next month.

General Groves reported to the President's Interim Committee that the Manhattan Project scientists and engineers were confident a fantastic power would be released by the weapon they were creating. Dr. J. Robert Oppenheimer's team of physicists, who had designed the atomic bomb at the Los Alamos laboratories, predicted that the device, based on explosively combining two pieces of highly fissionable Uranium-235, would create the "critical mass" necessary for an uncontrolled chain reaction and generate an explosive force of many thousand tons of TNT. Almost all of this extremely precious metal, which the United States had extracted and refined at a cost exceeding $4 million, had been carefully machined into the two units that would be fired together inside the 10-foot-long, 28-inch-diameter hardened steel casing that the engineers who built it had dubbed "Little Boy."

This one bomb, even if it worked, would not be enough to end the war. The Los Alamos scientists had therefore devised a second nuclear bomb, in which the even more highly fissionable plutonium (which had been bred from uranium in the Hanford, Washington, atomic piles) would be implosively compressed into the critical mass needed to set off the chain reaction by the sequential firing of the spherical explosive "lens." This more sophisticated weapon was being assembled to be fired in the remote New Mexico desert at Alamogordo, 190 miles from the Los Alamos laboratories where scientists and engineers were racing to meet the July 1945 deadline.

If the "Trinity" test proved successful, then two atomic bombs would be available for use against Japan by August. These would be delivered by the B-29s of Colonel Paul Tibbets's Special 509th Unit, whose pilots were flying south from their base on Tinian in the stripped-down Superfortresses to practice dropping 1,000-pound bombs and much bigger mysteriously sand-filled, orange-painted containers they called "Pumpkins" on the bypassed Japanese islands of the Carolines.

On June 18, 1945, while the fighting on Okinawa was reaching its climax, the President of the United States met with his advisers to make a major strategic decision governing the future course of the war. He had already promised Congress that America's policy for bringing about the unconditional surrender of Japan called for "using ships, aircraft, armor, artillery and all other material in massive concentrations. We have the men, the materiel, the skill, the leadership, the fortitude to achieve total victory." On June 1, the same day Truman sent this message to Capitol Hill, he received the report of the Interim Committee containing the unanimous recommendation that the atomic bomb be used as soon as possible to hasten the end of the Pacific War.

Secretary of War Stimson's ad hoc committee had taken the widest possible soundings commensurate with security in reaching this momentous conclusion. The Joint Chiefs had decided that, although bombing and blockade might eventually starve the Japanese into unconditional surrender, the stubborn fanaticism with which the enemy had fought every Pacific battle to the bitter end would make this an arduously long process.

There was no alternative but to commit the United States to an invasion, even though Okinawa had now made the grim specter of 1 million casualties very real. Marshall's opinion that "the bomb would be a wonderful weapon as a protection and preparation for landings" prevailed. Some atomic scientists involved with the Manhattan Project were already beginning to have doubts about the genie of technological destruction their work had uncorked. The great Danish theoretical physicist Niels Bohr had tried to warn Churchill; and another émigré, James Franck, chairman of a committee on the bomb's "Social and Political Implications," had drawn up a closely argued report which had been sent to the Secretary of War on June 11. Emphasizing the limitless destructive power of nuclear weapons and the problems of international control, the report warned that "the advisability of an early use of nuclear bombs against Japan becomes even more doubtful—quite independently of any humanitarian considerations" because, as the committee argued, it would "precipitate the race for armaments and prejudice the possibility of reaching an international agreement on the future control of such weapons."

The possibility of arranging a demonstration of the atomic bomb's awesome power that would impress the Japanese was discussed as an alternative. This option was discounted by the Interim Committee, which included Dr. Oppenheimer. "We can see no acceptable alternative to its direct military use," they had reported. "We can propose no technical demonstration likely to bring an end to the war." Their considered advice to the President was that the atomic bomb was "to be used against the enemy as soon as it could be done."

The unanimous opinion of his advisers that the bomb should be used could hardly have been neglected by the President at that crucial strategy meeting which took place in the White House on June 18, 1945. "As I understand it," Truman summed up, "the Joint Chiefs of Staff, after weighing all the possibilities of the situation and considering all the alternative plans, are still of the unanimous opinion that the Kyushu invasion is the best solution in the circumstances." Stimson concurred that an invasion was the only way to bring about Japan's unconditional surrender unless, as he put it, "something" could be done "to influence them." Only Admiral Leahy suggested that this "something" might be to soften the unconditional surrender demand. "Why not drop the atomic bomb?" asked the Assistant Secretary of War, John McCloy, who called the invasion scheme, with its staggering casualty rate predictions, "fantastic."

Since it was not yet certain whether the bomb would actually work,

Truman, appreciating that the unconditional surrender policy was now an article of faith for the Congress and the public, resignedly endorsed the Kyushu invasion plan, with the hope that the Army and Navy Chiefs could find "some way" of avoiding being dragged into another Okinawa "from one end of Japan to the other." Although there was therefore never any formal decision actually taken to use the nuclear weapon, the President, by his very decision not to interfere with the train of events, cleared the way for dropping the atomic bomb. "Independently," as he later claimed, he had come to the same conclusion as the Interim Committee that it would enable America to administer the "tremendous shock" he felt would be necessary to "extract a genuine surrender from the Emperor and his advisers."

If moral issues had been weighed only lightly in the minds of the President, the Prime Minister, and the Secretary of War, whose "mature consideration" had counted most in the by now irreversible momentum toward actually dropping the bomb, it must be seen in the context of a war in which the enemy was regarded as guilty of unparalleled slaughter and atrocities. Faced with the overriding desire to bring about a quick end to the fighting, President Truman rested his decision on the simple but bloody arithmetic of death, calculating that the bomb "would save many times the number of lives, both American and Japanese, than it would cost."

"MASTER CARD" AT POTSDAM

There was another important factor in his calculations, one that Secretary of War Stimson drew his attention to when he referred to the nuclear weapon as "the master card" that the United States could play at the forthcoming Allied summit. Truman's foreign affairs adviser and his representative on the Interim Committee, James F. Byrnes, clearly saw that the possession of such an awesome weapon must greatly enhance the power of the United States in bargaining with the Russians. Now the Secretary of State designate saw the bomb as a counter to the Red Army's occupation of much of eastern Europe. He had advised the President that it "might well put us in a position to dictate our own terms at the end of the war." The Soviets were already moving fast, despite the Yalta agreements, to ensure that Communist regimes would come to power in Poland and in the other countries they had "liberated" from Naziism.

Churchill recognized the danger of Russia's territorial ambitions. On May 6, he cabled for an urgent summit meeting to "come to an understanding with Russia, or see where we are with her, before we weaken our armies mortally or retire to the zones of occupation." Stalin's hand could only grow stronger when the Americans began withdrawing their troops to the Pacific, leaving the exhausted and militarily over-extended British facing the monolithic Soviet presence in Europe.

The ailing Harry Hopkins flew on a final mission to Moscow to persuade Stalin to agree to another Big Three summit in July. He reported that the Russians still were ready to honor their Yalta pledges over Polish elections and the United Nations, and to come into the war against Japan by August. Stalin was also favorable to American plans to revive the "Open Door" policy for postwar China, promising assistance in persuading the Communists in the north to unite under the Nationalist government in the south. This brought some relief to the State Department, which had been receiving alarming reports that a civil war on the mainland would break out if Mao Tse-tung's army began driving south to the coast. Such events would make things difficult, for the President had yet to secure Chiang Kai-shek's approval of the secret protocols that Roosevelt had signed at Yalta ceding control of the Manchurian railways and Port Arthur to the Russians.

Washington's confidence in Soviet intentions, however, was soon to evaporate again in June as Allied troops were withdrawing to their designated boundaries in Europe. There were now fewer cards in the United States' hands for the forthcoming summit. At Stalin's insistence, the Big Three were due to assemble at Potsdam for the aptly named Terminal Conference as Truman and his advisers became increasingly anxious about delaying the meeting until the atomic bomb had been tested and they could sit down at the conference table to play their "master card."

On July 6, 1945, when the President boarded the heavy cruiser *Augusta* for the Atlantic crossing to Antwerp, he had been assured by General Groves that by the time Truman arrived at his destination the plutonium "Fat Man" bomb being assembled in a round-the-clock effort by his team of scientists and engineers would have been detonated. When the presidential plane, the *Sacred Cow*, flew Truman into Berlin's Templehof Airport from Belgium on July 16, the countdown for the first atom bomb explosion was already under way. When he returned to No. 2 Kaiserstrasse after meeting Churchill and touring the rubble of Berlin, the President was handed a top-secret cable: "Diagnosis not yet complete but results seem satisfactory and already exceed expectations."

It was the positive news that Truman and the Joint Chiefs of Staff had been waiting to receive. The code message, from General Groves, told them that the world's first atomic explosion had taken place. At precisely 5:43 that morning the sunrise over the Alamogordo hills had been preempted by man. As the general's official report prosaically described it: "For a brief period there was a lightning effect within a radius of 20 miles equal to several suns at midday; a huge ball mushroomed and rose to a height of over ten thousand feet before it dimmed."

The news that the United States now commanded such power boosted

Truman's confidence in his first approach to Stalin at a private lunch meeting the next day, before the first plenary session to be held that afternoon. When he took the chair at their first meeting in the ornate Cecilienhof Palace at Potsdam, which had been the country estate of Crown Prince Wilhelm, Churchill immediately noted the change in the President, who "generally bossed about the whole meeting." He took a firm line with Stalin about the need to establish democratic governments in a Soviet-liberated Europe. After the session, the British Prime Minister learned the reason why.

It was contained in General Groves's eyewitness report of the previous day's nuclear explosion. When Churchill had read a copy of the confidential memorandum handed him by the Secretary of War, he quickly grasped its immense import: "Stimson, what was gunpowder? Trivial. What was electricity? Meaningless. This atomic bomb is the second coming in wrath!" He realized, as he later wrote, that the Americans now had the instrument with which to end the slaughter in the Pacific; it seemed, "after all our toils and perils, a miracle of deliverance."

The news from Alamogordo had also changed the Americans' minds about the need for Russian help in winning the war against Japan. Although, as Marshall advised, Stalin would have his own reasons for going ahead with the invasion of Manchuria, it was no longer a prime concern of the President's diplomacy as the conference settled into long wrangling sessions about German reparations and the control of eastern Europe.

Deliberately, Truman withheld any hint to Stalin that the United States had an atomic bomb, until the afternoon of July 24 when the meeting was breaking up. With studied casualness he went up to the Soviet interpreter, Pavlov. "Will you tell the generalissimo that we have perfected a very powerful explosive which we are going to use against the Japanese and we think it will end the war." Jealously guarding America's secret, he had carefully avoided mentioning that it was an atomic bomb; nor did he seek Russia's cooperation in setting up an international control system for nuclear weapons that would avoid another postwar arms race.

It would probably not have made any difference if he had been frank, for by now both sides were becoming openly suspicious of each other's intentions. Stalin's cursory reply, that he hoped the President "would make good use of it against Japan," concealed the fact that he also knew about the bomb. Soviet intelligence had penetrated the tight security of the Manhattan Project to acquire the information they needed to develop their own bomb, as well as to follow the progress of the American effort.

The Russians were less than frank, too, about the extent of the Japanese efforts then under way to bring about a negotiated peace.

AN IMPOSSIBLE SITUATION

Impatient at the tortuous pace with which peace negotiations were being conducted while Japan's cities continued to go up in flames, the Emperor intervened again with the suggestion that Prince Konoye should be dispatched at once to Moscow as his special representative.

On July 11, Sato received the news in an "extremely urgent" instruction "to sound out the extent to which it is possible to make use of Russia with regard to ending the war." Foreign Minister Togo was pessimistic about the Konoye mission's chance of success, telling the Supreme War Council: "A peace treaty by negotiation is something that cannot win the support of the Soviet Union." His opinion was to be confirmed by Sato's quick response the same day: "I firmly believe that any attempt to reach rapprochement with the Soviet Union at this time when our war situation is so grave, is bound to end in failure and disappointment." As he predicted, the Soviet Foreign Ministry refused to receive the Konoye mission because the terms of the Emperor's peace proposal "could not be clarified."

Stalin only hinted at the intensive activity behind scenes that was focusing on Moscow during the Potsdam discussions. But Magic intercepts kept the British and Americans in hour-by-hour touch with the Soviet stalling as the Japanese diplomats became increasingly frantic. On July 21, the Japanese ambassador in Stockholm reminded the Foreign Ministry in Tokyo of Japan's "impossible situation" and advised immediate peace negotiations; but efforts to open these up through Swedish intermediaries proved unsuccessful. On July 22, the British and American Joint Chiefs read with great interest a surprisingly forceful forecast from Sato that the Americans intended to use their B-29 bombers to set ablaze the rice crop as soon as the paddy fields were drained for harvesting in November. "If we lose this autumn's rice harvest, we will be confronted with absolute famine and will be unable to continue the war," he reported, urging the cabinet to "lay down our arms to save the state and its people." The foreign minister's blunt response was equally significant in shaping the climax of events: "Even if war drags on and it becomes clear that it will entail much more bloodshed, if the enemy demands unconditional surrender, the whole country, as one man, will pit itself against him in accordance with the Imperial will."

When it came to the issue of unconditional surrender, it appeared to the Allies meeting at Potsdam that even Japanese diplomats were now immovable. Sato was instructed that preservation of the throne must be a precondition, with the implication that anything less would amount to a surrender that Tokyo repeatedly told him would be "unacceptable." From these intercepts, hardliners among the presidential advisers, led by Secretary of State James F. Byrnes, had understandably taken the exchanges at face value to mean that the peace faction in Tokyo, and the weakest section of the cabinet was still far from bringing about the consensus necessary to compromise over the surrender terms.

Joseph Grew, the former ambassador to Japan, had advised Truman before he set out for Potsdam that some assurance about the Emperor's future position would immeasurably strengthen the hand of those Japanese cabinet members favoring a quick end to the war. A powerful sentiment now prevailed in Congress, with the American press and the public that "Hirohito must go." So much wartime propaganda had emphasized how Hirohito was responsible for the atrocities committed in the Emperor's name. Intelligence sources had also suggested that Japan's peace efforts in Moscow might be part of a plot to spread dissension among the Allies.

The Joint Chiefs themselves advised that any concessions to the unconditional surrender demand might be taken as a sign that American resolve had been weakened by their soldiers' ordeal on Okinawa. There was also some fear that it could cost them a serious loss of face with the Russians during the critical Potsdam bargaining sessions. By the third week of July, the President and his closest advisers had come to accept that the dropping of the atomic bomb was inevitable. As General Groves saw it, "his decision was one of noninterference—basically a decision not to upset the existing plans."

On July 24, the President approved the Joint Chiefs' order to General Carl A. Spaatz, who had flown back to Washington from Europe to take command of the Strategic Air Forces for the impending invasion of Japan. It began: "The twentieth Air Force will deliver its first special bomb as soon as weather will permit visual bombing after about August 3, 1945 on one of the targets: Hiroshima, Kokura, Niigata and Nagasaki." The committee of military men and scientists that had been set up to select the cities to be attacked had carefully chosen those so far spared from fire-bombing, so that the impact of the nuclear weapon would be even more dramatic. The historic city of Kyoto, filled with ancient shrines, had been a prime target which the generals argued for; the destruction of its ancient shrines was seen as a highly symbolic blow to the Japanese. But Stimson had overruled them twice, because he did not want another Dresden on the Allies' conscience.

On July 25, 1945, "Tooey" Spaatz started out on his four-day flight to Guam carrying the fateful presidential order. That same day the heavy cruiser *Indianapolis* put out to sea from Tinian after making a high-speed dash across the Pacific to deliver the lead buckets containing the charges of precious Uranium-235 and the 15-foot crates containing the firing gun and case for the "Little Boy" bomb. The former Fifth Fleet flagship had been selected for the mission because she happened to be at San Francisco completing repairs after the Kamikaze attack off Okinawa. Her new captain, Butler McVay, was given strict orders that the mysterious cargo was to be guarded night and day. He was not told the nature of their contents, but he knew they were vitally important from his instructions: "If she goes down, save the cargo at all costs, in a lifeboat if necessary. And every day you save on your voyage will cut the length of the war by just as much."

Relieved that his mission was discharged safely, McVay set sail from Saipan for Leyte. The *Indianapolis* never made port again. She was torpedoed by the Japanese submarine I-58 in the small hours of July 30. It was a tiny yet significant revenge that the Imperial Navy sank the last major warship lost in World War II. Her rapid sinking meant no SOS was sent and by oversight the cruiser was not reported missing for three days. In a tragedy that could have been averted, only 316 of McVay's crew of over 1,000 survived one of the worst sea disasters for the U.S. Navy.

As the engineers at Tinian began the delicate task of assembling the "Little Boy" uranium bomb, in Britain a general election had brought a new Allied leader to the Potsdam conference table. Denied "the power to shape the future" by the ballot box, Churchill was ousted as Prime Minister by the landslide victory of the Labour Party, led by his deputy in the coalition cabinet, Clement Attlee.

One of Churchill's final acts at the conference had been to sign what was to be called the "Potsdam Declaration." Initialed by Britain, China, and the United States, but not Russia, it was a thirteen-point appeal to end the war that was at once broadcast to Tokyo. "There are no alternatives. We shall brook no delay," ran the document addressed to the Emperor and his ministers. It closely followed the Cairo Declaration in restricting Japanese sovereignty to her home islands and promising that stern justice would be meted out to her so-called war criminals in the military leadership. "We call upon the Government of Japan to proclaim now the unconditional surrender of all Japan's armed forces and to provide proper and adequate assurances of their good faith in such action." With an ominous but not specific allusion to the atomic bomb, it concluded: "The alternative for Japan is prompt and utter destruction."

Since it lacked any reference to the Emperor's future and only reiterated the demand for unconditional surrender, the Declaration gave the peace faction in Tokyo little reinforcement. "The proclamation in my opinion is just a repeat of the Cairo Declaration and the Government therefore does not consider it of great importance," Prime Minister Suzuki commented, intending, as he put it, to "mokusatsu" the appeal; translated literally, this meant "kill with silence"—the Japanese equivalent of "no comment." But the aged Baron's not entirely negative position was taken as an outright rejection.

"JAPAN OFFICIALLY TURNS DOWN ALLIED SURRENDER TERMS ULTIMATUM," ran the *New York Times* headline on the morning of July 30, 1945. And that was certainly the impression of the Allied leaders at Potsdam when the newly elected British Prime Minister arrived to support the President in the arguments against the Russian demands for the $2 billion of German reparations that had been promised him at Yalta.

"There was no alternative now," was Truman's comment as, half a world away, he knew that events would be moving toward their terrible conclusion in the Pacific. General Spaatz had arrived at Guam on July 29 to brief LeMay and Tibbets with the orders to drop the bomb that was being assembled. The plutonium and explosive components for the "Fat Man" bomb were being flown in by separate transports from the United States. General Grove's schedule called for two nuclear weapons to be ready for dropping by the beginning of August, and two more plutonium bombs to be assembled for use two weeks later. That very day, Tibbets's crews had completed the final phase of the training by dropping 10,000-pound, orange-painted blockbuster bombs on Japanese targets.

During the last week of July, Admiral Halsey's task groups were ranging at will off the enemy coast, launching a series of massive air strikes against cities, port installations, and the surviving warships of the Imperial Navy that still floated, locked up in harbors. "The Third Fleet's job is to hit the Empire hard and often," the admiral had recently said in a War Bond broadcast, growling that his only regret was that "our ships don't have wheels, so that when we drive the Japs from the coast, we can chase them inland." On July 24, American bombs, rockets, and torpedoes from the Third Fleet's planes had rained down on the Kure Naval Base where, according to Halsey, "Jap warships went to die." By sunset four days later he was able to report with satisfaction that the Imperial Navy had "ceased to exist." Of the five carriers still afloat, all were damaged beyond operations and only a single crippled battleship, the *Nagato*, survived above water; almost all cruisers and destroyers had been sunk. As he was to observe with relish: "The Commander in Chief of the Combined Japanese Fleet could reach his cabin in his flagship, the light cruiser *Oyodo*, only in a diving suit."

While the American carrier task groups were hammering Kure, Halsey had assigned the Royal Navy Task Force 37 a separate target at Osaka, where there were no major warships, to "forestall a possible postwar claim by Britain that she had delivered even a part of the blow that demolished the Japanese Fleet." The British were not to be denied. On July 31, Royal Navy midget submarines of the X-craft type that had crippled the *Tirpitz* stole into Singapore Harbor to lay charges that exploded and disabled the Japanese heavy cruiser *Takao*.

It was another significant triumph for Mountbatten, as Southeast Asia Command readied itself to extend the campaign south from Burma into Malaya. In the Philippines, the U.S. 6th Army had driven the remnants of

Yamashita's army into the Sierre Madre Mountains on the east of the island, while the 8th Army campaign on Mindanao had entered its final stages with what would be the last landing of the Pacific War on July 12, when the GIs came ashore to battle against the enemy holed up in the southern extremity of this sprawling island. In Borneo, the Australians had captured Brunei on June 10, and on July 1 had landed to take Balik-papan on the east coast.

While the Allied forces continued steadily to hack away pieces of Japan's overseas Empire, the American strategic bombers blasted the cities on the home islands. By the end of July, General LeMay's Superfortress fleet was nearly 1,000 strong and had left a trail of fiery destruction over 100 square miles of Japan's urban areas, destroying homes along with military installations and shops with factories. More than 100,000 civilians had died and with their deaths came the increasing fanaticism of the survivors. "Day by day Japan was turned into a furnace," wrote former Foreign Minister Shigemitsu; "the clarion call was accepted. If the Emperor ordained it, they would leap into the flames."

Prime Minister Suzuki, after rejecting the Potsdam Declaration, was still counting on Stalin's help to negotiate some peace initiative that could halt the terrible rain of destruction from the skies. Yet he seemed oblivious to the intelligence reports reaching Imperial General Headquarters from the Kwantung Army command, which indicated that Russian troops and tanks were massing to attack on the borders of Manchuria. More in hope than conviction, Foreign Minister Togo radioed Sato in Moscow: "Further efforts to be exerted to somehow make the Soviet Union enthusiastic over special envoy," concluding with a desperate reminder: "Loss of one day relative to the present matter may result in a thousand years of regret."

Japanese procrastination, Russian dissembling, and American war-weariness had already led to the conditions under which the United States was ready to drop the atomic bomb. Stimson, back in Washington on July 30, cabled the President (then in the last stages of the Potsdam Summit) for his final approval for the first targets and the wording of the announcement that would be released after the detonation. In longhand, Truman drafted his answer for transmission: "Suggestion approved. Release when ready but not sooner than August 2." This was the day the presidential plane was scheduled to fly him from Berlin to Plymouth in England, to lunch with King George VI, before boarding the heavy cruiser *Augusta* for the voyage home.

DROPPING THE BOMB

At their Tinian base, Colonel Tibbets and the crew of his B-29, named the *Enola Gay* after his mother, were waiting to fly their momentous mission along with the crews of the two B-29s carrying the War Department observers and the cameras that would record for posterity the most powerful single blow ever delivered by man. Perfect conditions were required for the highly precise bombing run over the target. The weather forecasts for August 2 and for the next three days were bad. On August 5, the meterologists predicted that skies would be clear at dawn over the target cities, and B-29 weather scouts were sent off to fly over each one to report conditions.

At 2:45 A.M. on August 6, 1945, Colonel Tibbets eased the Superfortress's stick back as the huge bomber roared down the Tinian airstrip and lifted off into the night. Bright lights glinted along the B-29s silver, sausage-shaped fuselage, which carried the "Little Boy" whose blue steel casing was daubed with rude messages to the Emperor and, reputedly, a pin-up of Rita Hayworth. The B-29 was well beyond safe takeoff weight and the bomb was unarmed at takeoff for fear that a crash would blow the island and its hundreds of aircraft out of the Pacific. The tricky task of assembling the explosive detonator was undertaken in the air by U.S. Navy Captain William Parsons.

Accompanied by two escorting B-29s, Special Bombing Mission 13 droned north along the Hirohito Highway to an as yet undecided final target city on Honshu. The red lights in the cockpit indicating that the bomb was now live had been glowing for over two hours when Iwo Jima slipped by in the polished black ocean below as the B-29 flew on autopilot.

At 7:42 came the coded message from the Hiroshima weather scout: "CLOUD COVER LESS THAN THREE TENTHS AT ALL ALTITUDES. ADVICE: BOMB PRIMARY." The city had been selected for doom by the fickle forces of nature. "It's Hiroshima," Tibbets told the twelve men aboard on their intercom. Enola Gay was now at 26,000 feet and climbing at a shade less than 200 miles an hour. For the first time, his crew was told that they were about to deliver an entirely new type of bomb of staggering destructive power.

At 8:05 Enola Gay was coming in at 30,800 feet, followed by the observer planes, and less than 50 miles from Hiroshima. Major Thomas Ferebee, the bombardier, took up position in the plexiglass nose to fix the crosswire of his sight on the city's T-shaped Aioi Bridge.

Down below in the teeming city, nearly one third of a million people were starting another day's work for the nation's faltering war effort. Few even heard or noticed the planes flying in so high from the east. Leaflets had been dropped by the Americans two days before warning them to evacuate the city before a forthcoming heavy attack. The Superfortress flying as weather scout had set air-raid sirens wailing at dawn, but three quarters of an hour earlier the "All Clear" had sounded. Those who did look up paid little attention on seeing only three aircraft.

"On glasses," Tibbets ordered at 8:14, as all but three of the twelve aboard pulled on their heavy polaroid goggles. Through the shimmering haze, Ferebee made out the bridge and locked the cross hairs of his bomb-sight. The final fifteen seconds to dropping were automatic. At seventeen seconds past 8:15, the bomb bay doors opened and "Little Boy" plum-meted free, wobbling a bit until it picked up speed.

The supersonic scream it generated was never to reach the ears of people on the ground. At precisely 1,800 feet, the barometric pressure device triggered the detonating mechanism. In split milliseconds a brief flash had become an engulfing ball of light and destructive energy.

"My God!" was the startled reaction of one of the *Enola Gay* crew members, heard by Tibbets in his headphones as he turned the bomber away to the right from the dropping zone, in a steep power dive.

"Suddenly a glaring whitish pink light appeared in the sky accompanied by an unnatural tremor that was followed almost immediately by a wave of suffocating heat and wind that swept everything away in its path," was how one observer recorded that moment of detonation. The fireball blos-somed to a temperature thousands of degrees hotter than the surface of the sun, melting granite and imprinting the shadows of people and objects on the ground and the walls of what few buildings survived the "Pika" of the nuclear reaction flash and the "Don" of the thunderous shockwave that instantaneously flattened the center of Hiroshima.

"Within a few seconds the thousands of people in the streets and the gardens of the center of town were scorched by a wave of searing heat. Many were killed instantly, others lay writhing on the ground, screaming in agony from the intolerable pains of their burns. Everything standing upright in the way of the blast, walls, houses, factories and other buildings, was annihilated and the debris spun round in a whirling wind and was carried up into the air."

"There was the mushroom cloud growing up, and we watched it blos-som," Tibbets recorded, after the *Enola Gay* had reared in the blast. "And down below it the thing reminded me more of a boiling pot of tar than any other description I can give it. It was black and boiling underneath with a steam haze on top of it."

A Japanese journalist's account recorded the turmoil raging below that ugly cloud. "Beyond the zone of utter death in which nothing remained alive, houses collapsed in a swirl of bricks and girders. Up to about three miles from the center of the explosion, lightly built houses were flattened as though they had been built of cardboard. Those who were inside were either killed or managed to extricate themselves by some miracle, found themselves surrounded by fire. And the few who succeeded in making their way to safety generally died about twenty days later from the de-layed effects of the deadly gamma rays."

Half an hour after the explosion, through a clear, cloudless sky, a mysterious drizzle began to fall on the survivors. Those not dying or in agony from their terrible burns began to fear that the black drops of rain contained some more deadly poison. Ten square miles of Hiroshima had been obliterated and more than 130,000 people had perished in those few interminable minutes of hell, which also cost the lives of American prisoners of war held in Hiroshima Castle.

Colonel Tibbets circled three times high over the devastated city while the *Enola Gay*'s radio operator sent the radio message back to Tinian: "CLEAR CUT. SUCCESSFUL IN ALL RESPECTS. VISIBLE EFFECTS GREATER THAN ALAMOGORDO. CONDITIONS NORMAL IN AIRPLANE FOLLOWING DELIVERY. PROCEEDING TO BASE."

At Spaatz's Guam headquarters the news was greeted with elation. At Los Alamos the men who had built the bomb clapped one another on the backs. "This is the greatest thing in history," Truman exclaimed when he was brought the message, "HIROSHIMA BOMBED," while lunching with sailors aboard the *Augusta* in mid-Atlantic.

"It is an atomic bomb," announced the prepared White House release. "It is harnessing the fundamental power of the universe. The force from which the sun draws its power has been loosed against those who brought war to the Far East." The Japanese had been given a shocking example of American power in a detonation estimated at 20 thousand tons of TNT, and a terrible warning: "If they do not now accept our terms, they may expect a rain of ruin from the air, the like of which has never been seen on this earth." To avoid panic, the Japanese people were told nothing about nuclear weapons, and even the Prime Minister at first refused to believe the reports that a single bomb had caused so much destruction.

No response came from Tokyo to the President's warning. But in Moscow, Ambassador Sato made another appeal to the Soviet Foreign Ministry to act while cabling Tokyo, "Situation becoming acute." The following afternoon he was finally summoned to the Kremlin. But the answer he received was not the one expected. Foreign Minister Molotov coldly read him the Russian declaration of war on Japan.

That night Major Charles W. Sweeny took off from Tinian piloting the Superfortress named *Bock's Car* after its usual pilot, Captain Frederick C. Bock, who had traded aircraft with him for the mission. Slung in the B-29s hull was the second of America's nuclear weapons, the "Fat Man" plutonium bomb which scientists expected might prove more powerful than the uranium bomb dropped three days earlier. His mission was not to run so smoothly. There were technical snags in getting the device armed, and the weather reports were bad that night as *Bock's Car* thundered toward its primary target at Kokura, the site of a huge army arsenal. Thick clouds blanketed the city at dawn, and Sweeny determined to try his alternative dropping zone over Nagasaki. With his reserve tanks not functioning by the time he arrived over the city shortly before 11 A.M., he decided to ignore orders and bomb by radar. Then his bombardier sighted a hole in the overcast.

The detonation of the "Fat Man" plutonium bomb generated a fireball of destruction that annihilated 35,000 people and flattened the center of the city, but the extent of the damage was contained because of the shielding effect of the surrounding hills.

Hours before this second thunderclap of nuclear destruction was unleashed over the Japanese homeland, the Emperor's soldiers defending the Manchurian frontiers had been subjected to a massive artillery bombardment, which heralded a dawn offensive by hundreds of Red Army tanks and aircraft that swamped their positions like a tidal wave. Yet even the Russian attack, overwhelming though it was, did not break the stalemate between the militarists and the peace faction in the Japanese cabinet. They argued late into the evening, gripped by a paralysis of inaction and fear. Shortly before midnight they adjourned for a meeting of the Supreme War Council with the Emperor presiding. The foreign minister's case was that they had no choice but to accept the Potsdam Declaration. This was opposed by War Minister Anami, who would not accept that the Imperial Army could ever surrender, pleading that they must fight to the end, to "find life in death."

"We have been discussing this matter for many hours without reaching a conclusion," Admiral Suzuki wearily announced at last, maintaining as he had throughout an apparent position of neutrality. "The situation is indeed serious, but not a moment has been spent in vain. We have no precedent—and I find it difficult to do—but with the greatest reverence I must now ask the Emperor to express his wishes."

The August night heat made the atmosphere of the Imperial air-raid shelter under the Obunko Library oppressive, but the Prime Minister's startling appeal chilled the Supreme War Council members. The war minister at once protested this unprecedented break with the constitution. The Emperor's role was to assent, not advise his ministers. Hirohito seized the chance he had been provided. His piping, almost expressionless voice denounced the futility of "prolongation of bloodshed and cruelty." The terms of Potsdam, calling for the disarming of the services and the punishment of the war leaders, were "unbearable," he agreed. "Nevertheless the time has come when we must bear the unbearable."

36
"This Is the Payoff"

The Emperor had broken the deadlock. Now the Supreme War Council had to accept unconditional surrender. The next morning a full Imperial Conference was summoned to decide to agree to the Potsdam Declaration, "with the understanding that the said declaration does not compromise any demand which prejudices the prerogatives of His Majesty as sovereign ruler." Cables to this effect were sent out to Japan's legations in neutral countries.

Washington's reaction was swift. The President and his advisers favored acceptance, agreeing that their response must make some reference to clarify the Emperor's position without going the whole way to meet Japan's proviso. The British agreed; alone of the Allied powers, the Russians were skeptical. Stalin wanted his army to advance as deeply as possible into Manchuria before the cease-fire.

"This is a peace warning," Admiral Nimitz signaled to the Pacific Command on August 14, 1945, as the Allied response was broadcast by radio to Japan and through diplomatic channels in Switzerland. "From the moment of surrender," Tokyo was told, "the authority of the Emperor and the Japanese government shall be subject to the Supreme Commander of Allied powers." At the same time, General Spaatz was ordered to have the third atomic bomb ready to drop if a satisfactory response was not received. Instead of the bombs, LeMay sent his Superfortresses to drop leaflets on the enemy capital that day announcing Japan's acceptance of the Potsdam Declaration.

The Allied response brought more angry division in the Japanese cabinet as to whether the divine nature of the Emperor could permit him to submit to mere mortal authority. This issue of religious semantics was settled when it was pointed out that in pre-Meiji times the throne had been "subject" to the power of the Shōguns. His Majesty's firm decision to accept the Allied terms for terminating the war was relayed to the world by a radio announcement broadcast by the government Domei news agency just before 3 P.M. that afternoon: "It is learned that an imperial message accepting the Potsdam Proclamation is forthcoming soon." While the world waited, throughout Japan and her commands in Southeast Asia stunned officers were notified that they would be expected to comply immediately with the Emperor's call next morning to lay down their arms. It was considered too risky an ordeal for the God-Emperor to make his first broadcast on such a momentous occasion live. Station technicians from NHK radio were summoned to the Imperial Palace that evening to set up their recording equipment. When Hirohito was finally ushered into place before the microphones it was nearly midnight; everyone present was painfully embarrassed. Unhappy with his first read-through of the short speech, the Emperor insisted on making two more recordings before retiring to his underground sleeping quarters. The fragile black shellac discs that contained the fate of Japan's disintegrating empire were taken away by Yohiro Tokugawa, the court chamberlain. He locked them in his wall safe for the night.

It was to prove a justified precaution. The trauma of defeat had proved too much for a group of headstrong army staff officers. Under the leadership of Major Keni Hatanaka, they were already taking the first steps in a plot to dispose of the Imperial advisers who had been instrumental in engineering the surrender. Their intention was to isolate the Emperor, in the belief that he could be persuaded to change his mind before the speech was broadcast next day. For several hours they had been trying to talk the Imperial Guards' commander into joining their coup. But General Takeshi Mori proved a reluctant conspirator, and at 2 A.M., with time running out, he was shot by an impatient Hatanaka and his aide decapitated. Salvaging the general's personal seal from his blood-spattered office, the conspirators employed it to forge orders that were sent to Eastern Army Headquarters calling for help in occupying the Palace. Another band of rebel soldiers headed for the Prime Minister's residence. They arrived minutes after the aged Suzuki had been hustled away by car. Frustrated by their victim's escape, the would-be assassins set fire to the building.

Hatanaka's men had no more success as they stormed through the buildings in the Imperial Palace grounds searching for the crucial recording. By dawn their coup had collapsed; Eastern Army Headquarters forces failed to join the insurrection. When General Anami received word of its failure, he promptly committed ritual suicide. The war minister had sympathized with the plotters, but had not thrown in his lot with them although he had led the opposition to the peace in the Supreme War Council.

Anami intended the gesture of his death as symbolic atonement to the Emperor for the army's failure to win the war. His body was being prepared for cremation at 11 A.M. when the entire nation of Japan was summoned to the radio. Millions bowed in reverence before their sets as a reedy, monotone voice they had never heard before delivered the shocking news of defeat: "We have ordered our Government to communicate with the Governments of the United States, Great Britain and the Soviet Union that our Empire accepts the provisions of the Joint Declaration." With leaden understatement the Emperor explained to his people that this was now essential because the "war situation has developed not necessarily to our advantage," and the "enemy has begun to employ a new and cruel bomb, the power of which is indeed incalculable." Japan was acceding to the Potsdam demands since "to continue to fight . . . would not only result in an ultimate collapse and obliteration of the Japanese nation, but would lead to the extinction of human civilization." He concluded with an apology of "deep regret to the Allied nations of Southeast Asia who have consistently co-operated with the Empire towards emancipation of East Asia."

Not once was the word "surrender" used in the Emperor's speech. Saving face was never more necessary to the Japanese nation than in the hour of defeat. Tears of agonized disbelief were shed by civilians in Japan and by soldiers still guarding the defenses of a crumbling empire on the Pacific Islands and the Asian mainland. A vast throng gathered in front of the Imperial Palace. In the outpouring of national sorrow, the crowd paid little heed to the zealous army officers who chose to commit suicide rather than accept the shame of their country's first military defeat in over two and a half thousand years.

August 15, 1945, was a joyful day of celebration for the British and American forces.

Admiral Halsey bellowed an uninhibited "Yippee!" when he was handed the terse signal, SUSPEND AIR ATTACK OPERATIONS, shortly after six that morning. The mighty Third Fleet was off the coast of Japan when the battleship *Missouri* blasted a minute-long victory salute on her siren. The chorus was taken up by every ship as the flag signal "Well Done" was run up the great battlewagon's mainmast. Halsey recalled the air strikes that had just been launched from his carriers. Typically distrustful of the Japanese, he kept a strong air patrol aloft with orders to "investigate and shoot down all snoopers—not vindictively but in a friendly sort of way."

To the south of the main fleet, the Royal Navy Task Group was given the news by Admiral Rawlings's "Cease hostilities against Japan" signal flapping from the halyards of the battleship *King George V*. Cheering seamen were soon crowding the superstructure, tossing their steel helmets overboard—premature exuberance that some would regret only hours later when a lone Judy bomber suddenly flew in to drop near misses alongside the carrier *Implacable*. Fighters shot the intruder down, then raced off on a radar contact that proved to be flights of Kamikazes. Like Admiral Ugaki, who had taken off on a last suicidal mission that afternoon, these pilots were faithfully obeying the Emperor's orders to cease hostile acts. The astonished Fleet Air Arm gunners kept their fingers on the trigger buttons as they watched Japanese planes circling before crashing into the sea.

That morning at his Guam headquarters, Nimitz had accepted the terse signal from Admiral King ordering the end of hostilities with only a delighted smile while some of his staff literally jumped for joy. It was also characteristic of this self-effacing admiral, who had been one of the principal architects of Pacific victory, that in the congratulatory signal he sent out that afternoon, he reminded the men under his command that now the war was over, "the use of insulting epithets in connection with the Japanese as a race or individuals does not now become the officers of the United States Navy."

Nimitz's great task was almost over; but General MacArthur's was only just beginning. "IN ACCORDANCE WITH AGREEMENT AMONG THE GOVERNMENTS OF THE UNITED STATES, CHINESE REPUBLIC, UNITED KINGDOM AND UNION OF SOVIET SOCIALIST REPUBLICS," President Truman had signaled him, "YOU ARE HEREBY DESIGNATED AS THE SUPREME ALLIED COMMANDER FOR THE ALLIED POWERS." It was the appointment that MacArthur had aspired to, argued for, and sought since the outbreak of the war, so it was not without an awareness of the irony of the situation that he read that his task was "to require and receive from the duly authorized representatives of the Japanese Emperor and Japanese Government and the Japanese Imperial General Headquarters the signed instrument of surrender." At last in command of the largest assemblage of fighting power in history, MacArthur replied triumphantly to the White House: "The entire eastern world is inexpressibly thrilled and stirred by the termination of the war."

The presidential press conference that morning had set off a wave of celebration across the United States. Times Square, New York, was soon packed with crowds cheering as sailors and soldiers embraced any pretty girl in sight. It was a scene of wild celebration that was to be repeated across the country. The rejoicing and revelry continued into the morning of the next day. Police were under strict orders to intervene only if the national exuberance got out of control.

For the many thousands of emaciated Allied prisoners of war, it was a day of particular humiliation and suffering as they were forced to endure the angry resentment of their guards. For some American airmen who had recently bailed out over Kyushu it was a day of death. In a squalid act of vengeance, sixteen were to be hacked to pieces by officers of the Western Headquarters Command. Little attention was paid to the cease-fire by the Red Army forces, which continued driving down through Manchuria to the 38th parallel on the Korean peninsula.

Stalin was determined to avenge Russia's humiliation in 1905, and even proposed Soviet participation in the occupation of Japan. The move was rejected by Truman, but it was only too evident that the chances of the

Kremlin carrying out its promised role as mediator in bringing a lasting peace to China were dim; Mao Tse-tung's and Chiang Kai-shek's forces began girding for the decisive power struggle that would open as soon as the Japanese started to withdraw from the mainland. Bringing about the orderly evacuation of 3 million armed Japanese from the huge areas still under their control was the first task facing the new Supreme Commander Allied Powers (SCAP). MacArthur's staff began establishing the authority of SCAP with the controversial order to the British, Dutch, and French that their forces would not be allowed to move in to retake their former possessions until the formal surrender of Japan had been accepted. This allowed several weeks for communist and nationalist groups in Java and Indochina to consolidate their forces in order to continue battling against the Japanese occupiers, whose services the old colonial powers would find themselves temporarily obliged to rely on to maintain law and order.

In Japan herself, sporadic insurrections flickered on against the government's authority. Prime Minister Suzuki, his peace mission accomplished, had stepped down in favor of a caretaker cabinet under the Emperor's uncle, Prince Higashi Kuni. Senior members of the Imperial family were sent out bearing Hirohito's orders to ensure that the scattered army commanders were personally reminded of their sacred duty to obey the throne, regardless of their personal preference for seeking a warrior's death by continuing the conflict.

On August 19, sixteen delegates nominated by Japan's military leaders flew to Manila in two planes emblazoned, at MacArthur's order, with identifying green crosses on their wings and tails. They arrived to prepare the wording of the Imperial rescript of surrender required by the Potsdam Declaration. The priority of the first stage of the American occupation was to provide for the humanitarian care of all the Allied captives. The Flying Fortresses were sent aloft again; this time, instead of bombing missions, they dropped food and medical supplies over the Japanese prison camps in Thailand and northern China.

RETURN TO TOKYO BAY

After a week's delay caused by a typhoon and renewed civil unrest, the first American soldiers to set foot on Japanese soil flew into the Atsugi airfield near Yokusuka on August 28. That same day, the flagship of the Third Fleet steamed into Tokyo Bay. It was not quite the spectacular arrival with guns thundering that Admiral Halsey had promised. There was not even the crash of saluting cannonades that had enlivened his visit as an ensign with the Great White Fleet thirty-eight years earlier. Although the Third Fleet had grown too big for all its warships to gather under the shadow of Japan's sacred Mount Fuji, it was one of the most formidable displays of naval power ever assembled in one anchorage. The gray silhouettes of battleships, carriers, cruisers, destroyers, and landing ships reaching into the distance was a telling reminder of the might of the United States that had brought about Japan's crushing defeat. The Royal Navy was represented by the *Duke of York*, flying the flag of Admiral Bruce Frazer, Commander of the British Far East Fleet. That afternoon the Commander of the U.S. Pacific Fleet himself flew in by seaplane to break out his flag aboard the battleship *South Dakota*.

Nimitz derived some satisfaction from the knowledge that he had arrived before the Supreme Allied Commander. When he had been told that MacArthur was to accept the surrender of Japan, he had allowed a rare display of anger to surface; this, Nimitz growled, would appear to give the Army credit for winning the Pacific War. He had resolved not to attend the ceremony; the situation was saved when Secretary of the Navy Forrestal persuaded the President that it would be appropriate for the documents to be signed aboard a battleship named after the President's home state—and that it was only fitting that the Pacific Fleet Commander in Chief should sign for the United States.

The next day Marines were landed to occupy the Yokosuka naval base as the 11th Airborne Division flew in to take over the adjoining airfield where rows of Japanese aircraft had earlier been forcefully shorn of their propellers to disuade mutinous Kamikaze pilots from any last-minute gestures of immortality. American bands were playing at 2:19 when the gleaming C-54 transport named *Bataan* taxied in. MacArthur appeared in the rear doorway wearing the battered cap and sunglasses, and chewing the corncob pipe that had become his wartime trademark. With all the solemnity of an actor consciously taking center stage, he stepped deliberately down the stairway and, as the photographers blazed away, greeted General Eichelberger: "Bob! This is the Payoff."

In what must certainly have been one of the most incongruous military triumphs in history, MacArthur's motorcade, headed by a red fire engine, took two hours to make the short trip to Yokohama because the battered vehicles provided by the Japanese were fired by charcoal and repeatedly broke down. Along the route the American generals were puzzled that the soldiers lining the road turned their backs to the procession. They were informed that this was a mark of respect normally reserved for the Emperor. The Allied command established temporary headquarters in the Grand Hotel—one of the few undamaged buildings still standing in Tokyo's port city. The next evening there was an emotional reunion over dinner when General Wainwright and General Percival arrived. Emaciated and ill, they had been flown from a prison camp at Mukden to be present at the surrender ceremony.

"AN ALTAR OF PEACE"

The morning of September 2, 1945, was heavy with overcast as destroyers began ferrying Allied generals and admirals out to the *Missouri* along with press representatives of the world, including Japan. It was just eight years short of a century since Commodore Perry had arrived to open up the West's door to Japan. With a fine sense of history, Admiral Halsey had arranged for the very Stars and Stripes flown by Perry's flagship in 1853 to be flown out to Japan from the U.S. Naval Academy Museum. It was now prominently displayed on the quarterdeck bulkhead above the baize-covered table on which the formal surrender documents were to be signed. The battleship's upperworks were crowded with seamen as below, on deck, the uniformed representatives of the naval and army staffs of nine Allied powers jockeyed for position, anticipating their places in the photographic record of a historic event.

The destroyer with the Japanese delegation aboard stood off at a respectful distance until the one carrying the Supreme Commander's party drew alongside the great battleship. As MacArthur was piped over the side, the *Missouri*'s mainmast presented the unusual sight of a general's red flag flying alongside the blue one of Admiral Nimitz—a reminder of their equal rank in the Pacific Command.

There were no such salutes for the Japanese coming aboard as defeated enemies suing for peace. General Yoshijiro Umezu represented the Imperial General Headquarters, and the painfully frail Mamoru Shigemitsu was to sign for the government. Even climbing the steep companion ladder proved an ordeal for the foreign minister, who had lost a leg many years before in an assassination attempt. Tapping his way into position with a cane, he was a pathetic symbol, in his silk hat and frock coat amid a sea of military uniforms, of Japan's defeated civilian population.

When the Allied leaders had taken their places, the band struck up the Star-Spangled Banner. After the chaplain's invocation, MacArthur stood before the array of microphones and with practiced skill delivered a briefly eloquent address that concluded: "It is my earnest hope, and indeed the hope of all mankind, that from this solemn occasion a better world shall emerge out of the blood and carnage of the past—a world dedicated to the dignity of man and the fulfillment of his most cherished wish for freedom, tolerance and justice."

"This narrow quarterdeck was now transformed into an altar of peace" was how a member of the Japanese delegation recalled the scene that followed, as his country's representatives were called on to sign the surrender document. Then the Supreme Commander drew out his signature, letter by letter, and handed the separate pens to General Wainwright, General Percival, and members of his staff. Admiral Nimitz signed for the

United States. He was followed by General Hsu Yung-chang of China, Admiral Bruce Frazer for Britain, Lieutenant General Kuzma Dereyanko for the Soviet Union, General Thomas Blamey for Australia, and then the representatives of Canada, France, the Netherlands and New Zealand.

"Let us pray that peace be now restored to the world and that God will preserve it always," MacArthur intoned, before announcing: "These proceedings are now closed." The perfect timing of his performance, which brought the sun bursting out of the clouds just as the first waves of 1,900 Allied aircraft came roaring overhead, was almost destroyed when the departing Japanese discovered an irregularity in the document. The Canadian delegate and those who followed him had signed in the wrong places, and General Sutherland had to make some rapid corrections.

Japan's delegates, no longer enemies, were saluted off the quarterdeck. In a gesture to their new status, Nimitz had issued instruction to the destroyer carrying the Japanese that they were to be offered hospitality in the form of coffee and cigarettes. The Allied Commanders adjourned to coffee and doughnuts—because the U.S. Navy was "dry," there could be no champagne toasts.

It would, in any case, have been inappropriate. As General MacArthur was already broadcasting in a worldwide radio hook-up: "Today the guns are silent. A great tragedy has ended. . . ."

A SPIRITUAL TRANSFORMATION

When the final curtain fell on the slaughter and destruction of World War II on that September morning, it was peculiarly fitting that it should have been effected in a ceremony conducted by an American general aboard a U.S. Navy battleship in Tokyo Bay. It was after all just less than ninety-three years since the same waters had echoed to the thunder of gunfire of an American naval squadron knocking on Japan's door. The Superfortress bombers rumbling over the *Missouri*'s great 16-inch guns were testimony to the terrifying advances in the destructive capability of weapons since 1853, when Commodore Perry's cannonfire had awed the Japanese. Less than a century later, General MacArthur was calling on the people of the world to bring about "a spiritual recrudescence and improvement of human character" to avert the danger of nuclear war: "It must be of the spirit if we are to save the flesh."

Guns might speak many times louder than in Perry's day and bombs might now erase whole cities from the face of the earth, but the American mission had remained steadfast. "God's purpose" had been Perry's justification for setting out across the Pacific "to bring a singular and isolated people into the family of nations." The nineteenth-century apostles of expansionism believed that the United States was destined to become "the master organiser of the world" because their nation was above all others "divinely commissioned to be, in a peculiar sense, his brother's keeper." Impelled by the commercial and moral impulses of America's first century of nationhood, successive U.S. administrations sought to sustain a "manifest destiny" to control the Pacific against the growing Japanese challenge by establishing an international moral commitment to the "Open Door." When these treaties had failed, the belated efforts to enforce them through a policy of threats and economic sanctions had turned the ocean into an arena of war. The mobilization of vastly superior industrial and military potential had not only crushed Japan by 1945 but transformed the world's greatest ocean into an "American lake" and sphere of influence, thus fulfilling the prophesies of Captain Mahan and Theodore Roosevelt.

A longtime student of Asian affairs, molded by the same Republican political tradition that had aroused the call for pursuing manifest destiny, General Douglas MacArthur's avowed mission was nothing less than "a spiritual transformation of Japan" by establishing "peaceful and responsible government"—by which he meant government on the American model. That he would successfully complete this staggering task was to be his greatest contribution to history.

When the SCAP headquarters was set up in Tokyo in the autumn of 1945, MacArthur was faced with administering a nation shattered as much by the trauma of defeat as the destruction of war. Half the cities were in ruins, a third of all industry wiped out, and a population of 70 million on the brink of starvation even before the 6 million soldiers and civilians overseas began arriving home. The burden of the American Army of occupation was eased, however, because after so many years of totalitarian rule, the Japanese accepted the transition from one military authority to another. On a surprisingly loose rein from Washington, MacArthur became the virtual ruler of Japan, with a free hand to supervise the writing and implementation of a new constitution. Adopted in 1947, it retained the Emperor as a constitutional monarch and reestablished the primacy of the Diet. Its provisions freed the Japanese from many traditional restraints and enfranchised women for the first time. It also provided for the breaking up of the "zaibatsu" industrial combines that dominated the economy. Although Japan was not to achieve full sovereignty until the 1951 San Francisco Peace Treaty was signed, the process of national revival and reconstruction was quickly under way. The Japanese people demonstrated the same remarkable ability to embrace Western ideas, methods, and style as had followed the Meiji reforms. By the end of the first decade after the war, a new state would have emerged: demilitarized, democratized, and—with a national passion for baseball and Hollywood films—Americanized.

As American forces began occupying Japan, Britain celebrated her hour of triumph in the Far East on September 12 when Lord Louis Mountbatten, as Supreme Allied Commander, accepted the surrender of all enemy forces in Southeast Asia in Singapore. The Union Jack was proudly flying again before the imperial porticos of Government House. But like the Japanese soldiers who were temporarily relied on to maintain law and order because of Britain's overstretched resources, the restoration of power was transitory. The defeats of the spring of 1942 had abolished the mystique of European supremacy on which colonialism had been founded. Exhausted by war, and dependent on the United States for financial aid, the British Socialist government possessed neither the will nor the forces to combat the rising tide of nationalism that was sweeping the East. In 1947, Britain lightened the "White Man's Burden" by granting independence to the separate Hindu and Muslim states of India and Pakistan within the Commonwealth. Burma became a free nation outside the British "family of nations" the following year. The remainder of her sprawling possessions in the Far East, with the exception of prosperous Hong Kong, were made into the Federation of Malaya, which remained dependent on British forces to combat Communist terrorists until 1957, when the Malay States were granted independence as part of the Commonwealth.

The French and the Dutch—lacking both the wisdom and the flexible interpretation of postwar colonial policy shown by the British—tried to crush the Nationalist forces that had been carrying on a guerrilla war against the Japanese occupiers of their territories. The Indonesian Republic had already been declared in 1945 by Sukarno, but it would take four years of fighting before the government in The Hague was to recognize it as a sovereign state. Ho Chi Minh's Communist guerrillas had relied on American support in their long struggle against the Japanese occupiers and the Vichy colonial authorities who cooperated with them. At the end of the war, the United States backed the restoration of colonial power by General de Gaulle's government. But guerrilla war in Indochina would continue until 1954, when after a series of spectacular defeats culminating in the Battle of Diem Bien Phu, France effectively withdrew. The United States, under President Eisenhower and Secretary of State Dulles, refrained from signing the Geneva accords that effectively created North and South Vietnam. But the elaborate defense pact of SEATO proved to be worthless when the United States next elected to contain Communist expansion in Asia and took the fatal role of intervention on South Vietnam's behalf.

Independence came to the Philippines, on schedule, in 1946; it enabled the United States to avoid the confrontation with nationalism that marked the twilight of Western colonialism in the Far East. The American commitment to Japan, and the enormous task of providing the economic foundation for European reconstruction, made it impossible for the Truman administration to become deeply involved in the struggle to control China. The withdrawal of Japanese occupying forces from the mainland and Stalin's backing of the Chinese Communists in spite of his Yalta pledge rendered American attempts to mediate an agreement between Mao Tse-tung and Chiang Kai-shek futile. As the confrontation between the two rival regimes flared into war during 1946, the Nationalists—as they had always done—relied on the United States for arms and finance. But it was a war for the hearts and minds of the Chinese, in which Mao's incorruptible peasant army could call on immense human reserves and moral support. By 1949, Chiang Kai-shek had fled the mainland with the remains of his defeated army and set up the so-called Republic of China on Taiwan, leaving the victorious People's Army in control of the mainland.

The establishment of a Communist regime in Peking was seen in the United States as another victory for Russia in a new global confrontation challenging the Western democracies no less menacingly than Nazi Germany had done a decade before. The main threat was perceived to be in Europe, as eastern Europe fell totally under Soviet domination. When Moscow closed land routes to Berlin, American forces launched a massive airlift to keep the Western sectors of the city free. The alarming news that the Soviets had tested their own atomic bomb (in August 1949) was followed in June 1950 by the Communist regime of North Korea crossing the 38th parallel. This marked the northern border of the South Korean state, which had been established by American occupation forces as an independent republic. MacArthur's tenure as "Shōgun" of Japan was ended by the urgent demands of what became a U.N.-sanctioned "police action." The Cold War became a hot one in the Far East. General MacArthur took command and, after a brilliantly executed amphibious assault at Inchon, by the end of the year had driven the North Koreans back to the Yalu River that marked North Korea's frontier with China. Mao Tse-tung reacted by sending the People's Army into battle. The Communist counteroffensive reached Seoul, the South Korean capital, before the United Nations forces, in a month of heavy fighting, pushed the Communists back to the 38th parallel. In April, President Truman fired MacArthur for threatening to defy his authority and launch a general anti-Communist crusade on the Asian mainland. After two years of negotiation, an uneasy truce was established along the border between the two states.

The war brought not only the departure of MacArthur, who for fourteen years had been a dominating force in shaping U.S. policy in the Far East, but also a new status for Japan. No longer a defeated enemy to be punished by occupation, her sovereignty was restored and, along with South Korea, she became an important bastion of American influence in the continuing global struggle against the threat of communism. A model capitalist state, Japan thrived on the relaxation of attempts to dismantle the industrial combines. The spectacular rise in Japan's trade in the sixties sent her national economic growth soaring. During the agonized years of U.S. military intervention to prevent a Communist takeover of South

Vietnam, Japanese public and government opinion took on an increasingly independent posture—an independence tempered by a keen Japanese appreciation that their well-being was dependent upon imported oil and a huge volume of American trade. Ironically, Japan's spectacular rise to become the third-greatest industrial power in the world was largely due to her manufacturers' ability to exploit the "Open Door" for the consumers of the richest nation on earth—the United States.

This irony is perhaps the most important lesson to be drawn for the future as the vision of a potentially vast "China market" is being revived on both sides of the Pacific through the decision of a post-Mao regime in Peking to begin reopening its doors to the West. Once again China and America share apparent interests and a precarious friendship—and Russia looks uneasily at the massive nation and population of the Middle Kingdom that marks her eastern border. This, perhaps, will determine the terrible questions of "when" and "why" for the next Pacific confrontation.

An After-
Action Report

In the rational light of historical perspective, it is evident how the Japanese military operation that began in Manchuria in 1931 initiated a chain of events that ultimately brought about World War II. The deeper America became involved in her "undeclared war" aiding the British fight against Nazi Germany, the greater became Hitler's pressure on Japan to make a diversionary attack in the Far East. The Japanese leaders, particularly the naval staff, feared that this would force them into a David and Goliath clash with the overwhelming industrial potential of the United States. As Admiral Yamamoto succinctly put it in 1941, "Japan cannot vanquish the United States. Therefore we should not fight the United States."

Neither Japan nor the United States wanted a Pacific war, but its outbreak became almost inevitable in the summer of 1941 with the German invasion of the Soviet Union. The then apparent likelihood of a swift Russian defeat, which would give Hitler dominance over Eurasia, was anticipated by the Japanese and they planned to jump into the conflict in 1942—unless steps were taken by America and Britain to constrain Japan militarily. With Britain temporarily relieved of the threat of invasion, the Anglo-American strategy was revised in August 1941 to make a stand against further Japanese expansion. Oil supplies for Japan were cut off by the U.S. embargo and, to prevent the seizure of alternative supplies in the Dutch East Indies, planes, tanks, and troops were rushed out to the Philippines. The threat of strategic bombing raids and a powerful British fleet operating between Singapore and Manila were the principal components of a deterrent to Japanese action that was to be in place by the spring of 1942.

It proved to be a strategic miscalculation both in timing and reality. Japan wanted to establish her New Order in Asia and negotiate with America for a resumption of oil supplies and a settlement of the Sino-Japanese War on terms that required a compromise of the "Open Door" doctrine. The United States was not prepared to compromise, but hoped to spin out diplomacy long enough for the deterrent force to be built up in the Philippines. Tokyo's time and patience was running out faster than Washington's. When a compromise became impossible, the Japanese decided they had to risk war or accept the effective crippling of their economy and military capability. As Prime Minister Tojo put it, "sometimes a man has to jump with his eyes closed from the temple of Kiyomoto into the ravine below."

If embarking on Pacific War was an "act of suicide" for Japan, so too was the way it ended. By the summer of 1945 accurate intelligence was providing the United States with very clear evidence that Japan was already finished as a military power. Yet given the stubborn Japanese national character and the determination not to repeat the mistakes of World War I, which had been followed by Germany's rapid revival, the Allies were adamant—they would accept nothing less than the unconditional surrender set forth in the Potsdam Declaration.

The Japanese could not just be allowed to submit; they had be seen to accept total defeat. The fanaticism with which the warriors of Bushido had sought death rather than submission all the way from the jungles of Guadalcanal to the caves of Okinawa had led the Americans to believe that the Japanese nation could not be made to accept the reality of their defeat until administered a profound shock. It was this rationale and the unstoppable momentum built up behind the Manhattan Project, and arguably President Truman's need to demonstrate the U.S. military dominance at a time when he was confronting the Soviet Union over the future of Europe, that made the dropping of the atomic bomb the inevitable and terrible conclusion to the Pacific War.

If the debate over the final act continues to try to discover why not just one, but two, nuclear devices were detonated in the summer skies over Japan in 1945, the controversy over how the United States was caught off guard in the opening hours of the war has been raging ever since the bombs fell on Pearl Harbor on December 7, 1941. Seven wartime investigations—one presidential and three each by the Army and Navy—tried to apportion blame for the catastrophe. Their thousands of pages of evidence were included in the staggering thirty-nine volumes of testimony of the Joint Committee of Investigation set up by Congress in September 1945. For nine months it labored, like the service investigations, to discover and establish where individual culpability lay. Among the members of the panel of inquisitors were those who suspected that the late Franklin D. Roosevelt might well be proved guilty of complicity or duplicity in engineering the events at Pearl Harbor in order to overcome the isolationists and get America into war. A rigorous examination of every link in the chain of military and executive command reaching into the White House was conducted in both secret and open sessions. Testimony was given by the surviving participants. But although harsh questioning of leading witnesses revealed how human error and failures had contributed to the tragedy that befell the Pacific Fleet, these appeared sins of omission rather than a conspiracy of commission. No "smoking gun" was uncovered in the 15,000 pages of testimony. The committee's divided report made it all too clear that the burden of responsibility was a collective one, arising from a shared disbelief that the Japanese would make a strategically "illogical" attack on Pearl Harbor.

Since 1946, more than a dozen books have reopened what is perhaps the most popularly fascinating aspect of the whole of World War II. Several had sought to exonerate Admiral Kimmel and General Short, who were made scapegoats for the disaster and removed by their military supervisors, who in turn bore perhaps a greater burden of blame. Revisionist historians in the early fifties—principally Charles Callan Tansill in *Back Door to War: The Roosevelt Foreign Policy, 1933–1941* and Robert A. Theobald in *The Final Secret of Pearl Harbor: The Washington Contribution to the Japanese Attack*—put forward (as their titles suggest) the thesis that Roosevelt deliberately provoked or concealed warnings of the impending attack so that America would have a "causus belli" for joining Britain's struggle against Hitler. Others have convicted him by ex-post facto analysis. The dangers of such "Monday morning quarterbacking" are repeatedly emphasized by Roberta Wohlstetter, whose *Pearl Harbor: Warning and Decision* provides the most credible explanation and detailed account (so far) of just how the United States was surprised on that December morning in 1941. Her masterly interpretation of the evidence available to the Joint Committee of Congress in 1946 comes to the important conclusion that "relevant signals so clearly audible after the event, will be partially obscured before the event by surrounding noise. . . ."

Professor Wohlstetter's thesis has been widely accepted as the definitive version of the events leading up to Pearl Harbor. But it is nearly twenty years since it was first published, and much of its crucial intelligence data is carefully based on the censored Magic documents released in 1945 at a time when some very distinguished senior American commanders and politicians still in power were particularly anxious to protect their reputations. All but a few of the leading wartime figures are now dead, which is perhaps not unconnected with the decision of the National Security Agency (NSA) in recent years to begin releasing what has become a veritable mountain of intelligence intercepts, summaries, and analyses. Packed in marching rows of anonymous gray cardboard boxes on the thirteenth-floor stack rooms of the National Archives, the tightly bound Xerox copies of original microfilm records contain the day-to-day records of the secret intelligence battles that were being won and lost by American codebreakers and agents, years before the first shell was fired or the first bomb dropped in World War II.

OTHER GENTLEMEN'S MAIL

Considering that Secretary of State Stimson had insisted less than a decade earlier that "Gentlemen do not read each other's mail," the proficiency with which the U.S. radio intelligence experts had overcome such moral strictures by 1940 is nothing short of amazing. The material is composed of a quarter of a million pages of hitherto classified material, ranging from "Black Chamber" reports to Japanese and German signal translations and intelligence summaries covering World War II. Such is the range of new evidence open to inspection by the summer of 1981. Much more is still awaiting declassification, ironically a task almost as time-consuming as that undertaken by the original codebreaking teams. Each document has to be scanned by officials of the National Security Agency, who delete what is still considered to be sensitive information.

Leafing through the day-by-day Magic intercepts of Japan's diplomatic traffic to and from her overseas embassies and consulates, it is not hard to understand the problems faced by the harassed seven-man staff of Lieutenant Commander Kramer in the Navy OP 20 G unit and Colonel William Friedman's equally small team in the Army Signal Intelligence Service. They had to process some 10,528 pages of messages intercepted through the end of 1941. This averaged slightly over 200 a week, in fact more during the hectic diplomatic activity in the weeks preceding Pearl Harbor. At the same time, additional units were adding German and Russian decoded foreign traffic to the volume of information that Commander Safford was assessing for the Navy and Colonel Otis Sadtler for Army Intelligence. On top of this, there is evidence—though still scanty in the material released so far by the NSA—that the Americans were reading the British diplomatic and military ciphers with as much facility, not to mention interest, as they were monitoring the Axis traffic!

It is now easy to see how the principal cause of the breakdown in American military intelligence during the period before Pearl Harbor was that it was grossly overloaded and unable to carry out an adequate evaluation procedure. The lessons learned brought about a rapid expansion in 1942 in both services' cryptanalysis, translation, and assessment teams. Personnel training took time, but such was the proficiency achieved by the naval units that within six months they had laid the groundwork for the Midway victory. The Army succeeded in cracking the Japanese Army ciphers by the following spring, and both services contributed to the establishment of units that monitored the German Enigma traffic using the British-supplied decrypting machines. The measure of the Allied victories in the battles fought and won by their codebreakers is the sheer volume of material now piling up along the shelves in London's Public Record Office and the National Archives in Washington. The highlights of the role of Ultra—as both Britain and the United States labeled their most secret intelligence—played in the war are now known, with the Battle of Britain, Midway, the Battle of the Atlantic, El Alamein, D-Day, and New Guinea perhaps the most spectacular achievements. But it will take years for historians to sift patiently through the records that have now become available to reveal the fascinating details of just how significant a contribution intelligence actually played in the overall perspective of the Atlantic and Pacific theaters—and just how much of the credit that has until now been given to the most successful military commanders should in fact go to Ultra.

The sheer volume and breadth of the intelligence material, only recently released, carefully scrutinized, and where necessary censored though it is, is sufficient indication that it must inevitably provide a freshening insight into such "hot" topics as Pearl Harbor which have been given nearly forty years to cool off! Indeed, it is intriguing to discover amongst the new material a memorandum of June 1944 entitled "The Need for New Legislation Against Unauthorized Disclosure of Communication Intelligence Activities." Recalling the damage done by Herbert O. Yardley's 1931 revelations of his codebreaking work with the Army "Black Chamber" and citing the Japanese suspicions of April and May 1941 that their diplomatic cipher was being read, and pointing out what might have been the consequences of the press leak that Midway was won because the Pacific Fleet had uncovered the enemy battle plan, the report's recommendation for legislation proposing harsh penalties for illegal disclosure and steps to ensure that the wartime intelligence operations would *never* be declassified. Magic would certainly not have been revealed in 1945 had it not been for the need to protect prominent U.S. military leaders from the charges of the Congressional Investigation Committee. Despite the obvious temptation there must have been for certain British figures to reveal their great wartime Enigma operation's success, word of honor and the Official Secrets Act blocked its revelation until 1974.

One valid argument for keeping such revelations under wraps for so long was that for many of the tension-filled Cold War years, machine ciphers were employed in the principal diplomatic and military channels of supposedly secure communications. Neither Britain nor the United States wished to give the Russians too much information about the extent to which their intelligence services had become highly skilled at cracking such codes. Although the subsequent revolution in electronics had provided cryptologists with the powerful new tools of computers and satellites for enciphering and transmitting communications, it has also provided codebreakers with the same facilities for collecting and penetrating radio traffic.

The reading of other gentlemen's mail—in the literal sense—along with espionage, analysis of media, and the reports from diplomatic attachés, is another ingredient of the broad spectrum of information on which governments base their actions. But the paramount role of radio intelligence was established by World War II. Whether the decrypting of eavesdropping is carried out by a clattering electro-mechanical Purple machine, as it was then, or by the silent stacks of microchips in powerful IBM computers today, the vital information ends up in the same form: a "hard copy" printout requiring evaluation and action by human decisionmakers. Well-informed and skilled analysis is required to weigh the significance of information received against other evidence and determine what response (if any) is appropriate. It was this part of the process that failed the United States in the final weeks before December 7, 1941—and for all the increased sophistication in transmitting and collecting information, the critical procedure of analysing the data remains much the same today. Then the decisionmakers had days to consider and react; today, intercontinental ballistic missiles move many thousand times faster than carrier strike forces and have reduced the reaction time to minutes, if not seconds. It is this tremendous compression of the human response period that has made the prospects of a "nuclear Pearl Harbor" scenario so alarming.

Evaluation is the most important part of the whole operation of an intelligence system, so it is not surprising that the material most heavily censored before reaching the archives are the daily Magic summaries. Beginning only after December 1941, these daily reports show how the Army and Navy Intelligence officers carried out the analytical process, because it is possible to compare them to the raw intelligence intercepts from which their assessments were made. These too have been carefully censored, with all references to the original Japanese cipher in which they were transmitted carefully blanked out on the copies lodged in the archives. Often unit commands, ship names, and the location of the two-letter place designator code are wiped out—although the reason for such fastidiousness is hard to understand because it is well enough known by now that AF was Midway.

By reading through the 130,401 pages of the translations of the Japanese naval messages, it is possible to follow the day-by-day progress of the Pacific War as it was seen through the eyes of the officers who made the strategic decisions on which victory was won. From this source we can now establish some new details of fact that cut through the embroidery of myth surrounding the Battle of Midway. Documents captured from an enemy plane downed in the Pearl Harbor attack provided the first clues to penetrating the Japanese Navy's operational code; an intercept of April 17, 1942, requesting maps of Australia was a vital clue in uncovering the Coral Sea offensive; a May 5 order for fueling hose from the Combined Fleet was a pointer toward a shift in operations to the mid-Pacific; and the famous "water signal" sent out from Midway on May 22 referred to supposedly thirsty animals. It is now clear to what extent American Naval

Intelligence was blinded by the Japanese code change of May 28, just before the decisive action that put the U.S. Navy on the offensive; how the slow penetration of the new operational cipher contributed to the defeat at the Battle of Savo Island three months later; and how the Japanese became more wily at radio deception. It is also more than a little awesome to turn up the original April 13, 1943, signal intercept that was Admiral Yamamoto's death warrant and to discover just how precisely timed the American plan had to be, since most of his inspection trip was to be made by minesweeper.

So, too, a detailed examination of the thousands of pages of Japanese Army intercepts will throw new light on the later stages of the Burma campaign and show why General MacArthur in New Guinea and the Philippines was better informed about the enemy dispositions than any other military leader in history. The intercepts of the Japanese diplomatic messages during the summer of 1945—when they have been pieced together and the intriguing gaps that exist in them bridged by careful reconstruction—will reveal the full story of why the peace effort that might have changed the course of history came to nothing. Other fascinating sidelights on the war will be explored, such as why U.S. Army Intelligence in the autumn of 1943 dismissed Magic reports of Axis subversion in India as "the product of British 'hocus pocus.' "

CENSORSHIP AND SUBVERSION

Many of the new insights provided by this radio intelligence data came from its immediacy and the cryptic penciled marginal notes (a number blanked out subsequently) that along with the date/time indicators show when it was received and when and by whom is was translated. Such information is essential to the proper evaluation of intelligence data's importance and *how* a particular signal decisively influenced the march of events. This is often not easy to establish because it would appear that the main purpose of the National Security Agency's censoring of the documents is to conceal as much as possible of the evaluation process. This is particularly evident in the case of the Magic summaries. But it is hard to understand, for example, why in the May 11, 1942, naval intelligence report of the estimated whereabouts of the Japanese carriers the whole of paragraph (c) dealing with the main enemy striking force has been blanked out.

Heavy-handed censorship (sometimes whole pages have been obliterated, leaving only an index number) invites speculation that the missing information must have been vitally important in 1941 if it was considered so sensitive forty years later that it was concealed with masking tape in the copying process. Just as Commander Layton explained to the Pearl

Harbor Inquiry that his suspicions would immediately have been aroused by the Japanese carriers' continued radio silence *if* the carriers had been addressed by any signals in the weeks preceding the attack, so the glaring gaps in the Magic records provide very important intelligence for the historian. Because of the sheer volume of material and duplication of channels through which information was communicated to the President, Department of State, and Joint Chiefs of Staff, detective research can often turn up clues to the missing evidence that have slipped by the censors' hand.

The Magic intercepts of the 1941 Japanese diplomatic traffic, now available for the first time in sequential entirety—albeit with extensive deletions —give a fascinating indication of how the officially neutral United States, and particularly Washington, had become the focus of conspiracy and espionage. Within the Roosevelt administration's most intimate circles it appears there were some who, consciously or unconsciously, were considered valuable sources of intelligence by Tokyo and Berlin. Who were the mysterious "J---- and W----" that the Japanese ambassador reported were reliable informants because they "are in touch with the President and his wife"? Who were the recipients of the half million yen that the Washington Embassy spymaster Terasaki received in May "for the development of intelligence"? Equally intriguing is the possibility that after Terasaki had identified his Brown University Classmates, W--- of the State Department's European Section and Senator G---, as sources in a report intercepted on May 19, they were used to "plant" information on the head of Japanese espionage in the United States. Terasaki's messages to Tokyo also revealed how he was cultivating "very influential Negro leaders" in hopes of directing racial discontent "to stall the program the U.S. plans for national defense and the economy, as well as for sabotage." It is possible to speculate that Roosevelt's decision to intern the Nisei population in midwestern camps was based on the evidence that these Magic diplomatic intercepts gave of Terasaki's extensive network of informants among "our second generation workers in airplane plants."

Even more revealing are the volumes of intercepts of the reports made from Washington and Berlin by the Japanese military attachés. Only made available to public inspection for the first time in the spring of 1981, these communications provide a fascinating record of the details of the intelligence picture seen from the Japanese and German point of view. Although it is clear that the signals were not being decoded on a day-to-day basis until 1943, the intercepts made during 1940 and 1941 were recorded then and ultimately decrypted during 1944 and 1945. So the information they contain was *not* known to American intelligence in the crucial period leading up to Pearl Harbor. The evidence they afford opens up a new perspective for historical re-assessment.

The attaché's reports clearly show the extent to which Tokyo had advance evidence of Hitler's plan to attack Russia in the summer of 1941.

In addition, the Japanese were informed by the Germans—through a leak from inside Churchill's cabinet—of the British government's decision to virtually abandon the Far East. These communications reveal the extent to which Berlin was pressuring Tokyo to join the war against Russia and Britain: the Germans revealed details of the Red Army's defenses along the Siberian frontier and documented American reluctance to go to war to defend British or Dutch territorial positions in the Far East. It is also clear how reluctant Tokyo was, throughout 1941, to contemplate war with the United States. The Japanese were suspicious of German motives. On September 21, 1941, the Vice Chief of the Imperial General Staff asked his Army attaché in Washington to "make [a] discreet investigation of the German attaché's real opinions" after a report had been passed on from Berlin to Tokyo claiming that "the American government will probably have no desire to pull chestnuts out of the fire for Russia" and that Roosevelt was resorting to "bluff and bluster" to make "a great show of naval and air strength" when the U.S. Fleet was too weak to fight a war in the Far East. Other attaché reports from Manila and Bangkok show how closely the Japanese were keeping track of the British and American build-up in the autumn of 1941; how the defense of Malaya was being undermined by a propaganda campaign against Indian Army troops (masterminded in Tokyo by Subhas Chandra Bose) and the extent to which Royal Navy and RAF radio traffic was being read.

One of the most astonishing documents to come to light so far among the attaché's reports is an intercept dated December 12, 1940. Transmitted by the Japanese naval attaché in Berlin to the Chief of the Third Section, Naval Staff, Tokyo, the translation (*which was not made until August 19, 1945*) reads: "I have received from the GERMAN Navy minutes of a meeting of the BRITISH War Cabinet held on 15 August this year dealing with operations against JAPAN." It outlines the main points of the British War Cabinet's decision that day that Britain was "not in a position to resort to war" if Japan attacked French Indo-China or Siam: that "HONG KONG would be abandoned" because "the existing situation would not allow BRITAIN to send her fleet to the FAR EAST."

The signal is remarkably similar to the wording of the pessimistic July 31 report of the British Chiefs of Staff entitled: "The Situation in the Far East in the Event of a Japanese Intervention Against Us" which was discussed by the War Cabinet during the first two weeks of August 1940. The absence of other such leaks suggests that it was not the result of a German "mole" at work in the upper reaches of Whitehall but that it had been leaked to Berlin via Moscow. Soviet agent Donald Maclean was at the time back from Paris working in the Foreign Office and could have had access to one of the seventy-two copies.

It certainly suited Stalin's purposes at the close of 1940 to deflect Japan from another northern adventure into an attack south against the vulnerable British possessions. The receipt of this prize intelligence clearly shaped Tokyo's diplomatic strategy in 1941 and explains the Japanese efforts to drive a wedge between Britain and her potentially powerful ally with the clandestine Washington peace mission that spring.

The communications from the Japanese Embassy in Washington also provide some fascinating insights into contacts maintained with the anti-Roosevelt isolationist lobby. Again and again Lindbergh's name (curiously *not* excised like those of his associates on the America First Committee) crops up in the intercepts. On July 8, he was quoted as the reliable source that "peace talks will bud in July and blossom in autumn" between Britain and Germany. Four months later he and Colonel McCormick, owner of the isolationist Chicago *Tribune,* were reported to be preparing to impeach the President. They were apparently plotting the sensational revelation that "Roosevelt planned the elimination of Chamberlain and the advent of the Churchill cabinet." Their "evidence" was obviously provided by Axis sources since it involved information supposedly obtained by Virgil [sic] Kent, a former clerk in the American Embassy in London. He had been passing on to the Germans contents of cables that Winston Churchill had sent to Roosevelt, before his espionage activity was uncovered in 1940.

The extent to which American isolationists were prepared to join Axis machinations was a measure of just how bitterly they and the Roosevelt administration were carrying on a domestic political fight. British undercover agents, with the unofficial blessing of the White House, were operating along with the FBI to expose such conspiracies at the risk of violating American constitutional rights. The machinations of both sides stirred the normally conspiratorial Washington scene into something of a Byzantine frenzy. It was an unhealthy climate in which to conduct negotiations, particularly those that required cool and temperate discussion during the last effort by Japan to reach an accommodation with the United States. It is therefore all the more surprising to find that a Magic intercept of November 10 reports to the Tokyo Foreign Ministry that "a certain cabinet member" had confidentially warned: "The American government has very reliable reports that Japan will be on the move soon," and that the Japanese had already decided that the new proposals, timed to coincide with the arrival of Saburo Kurusu, "wouldn't have any effect on the situation." As the Japanese ambassador emphasized in his verbatim account of the meeting with the informant: "Well, our boss, the President, believes those reports and so does the Secretary of State."

There is every indication that a month before the attack on Pearl Harbor, it was the United States that had decided to bring about the rupture of discussions and was about to prepare for the worst. There is now evidence for believing that President Roosevelt was not only expecting war but possibly knew exactly when it would break out. Clues have come to light in the recently opened archival documents on both sides of the

Atlantic that suggest that after the third week in November 1941, the British and American governments had not only decided that war with Japan was inevitable—but they knew the attack would hit Malaya and the Philippines.

38

Pearl Harbor—
Warning or Decision?

On October 15, 1941, President Roosevelt was well aware that his refusal to attend a summit meeting with the Japanese Prime Minister (without prior concessions from Tokyo) might rupture negotiations. That day he cabled his concern to Churchill, whom he always called "The Former Naval Person": "The Jap situation is definitely worse and I think they are headed north—however in spite of this, you and I have two months of respite in the Far East." His prediction reflected the current consensus of military intelligence in both Washington and London that "the Japs will advance on Vladivostok and the Maritime Provinces the minute Soviet disintegration appears imminent." Russia's situation was not expected to grow critical until the German advance threatened Moscow sometime in December. "Japan would not advance southward except possibly into Thailand," was the October estimate reaching the War Department from London, "because of the danger of becoming embroiled with the United States and Britain, especially in view of the first stand taken by the United States."

That stand was made on the confidence of America's steadily increasing military power in the Philippines. Some Army planners were already looking at the islands as much more than a base for a deterrent to Japan or the "key and base point" of a strong defense line that could check any southward advance. On October 8, the Secretary of War had been advised that more B-17 bombers, more fighters and dive bombers should be rushed out across the Pacific to form "strong offensive air forces." The ultimate objective of boxing in the Japanese with the threat of an aerial blockade and strategic bombing looked fine on the maps, and Stimson enthusiastically seized on the report's conclusion that "air and ground forces now available or scheduled for dispatch to the Philippines have changed the entire picture in the Asiatic area." The big bombers had not only provided the Army with the means to defend the islands but also the weapon with which to threaten Japan if the Russians could be persuaded to lend bases in Vladivostok. Not since Theodore Roosevelt sent out the Great White Fleet had the United States had the chance to wave such a potent "big stick"—or so it seemed to the Secretary of War. He was more than ready to take the risk that setting "frontiers" at the enemy's boundaries might invite attack.

The War Department's October "Strategic Estimate" indicated that "a strong stand may result in Japanese capitulation." Even if a conflict developed, the U.S. Army was confident of a quick victory, which guaranteed certain other advantages: "If our position does result in hostilities, American popular support will be reflected in greatly accelerated industrial production that may not only insure the liquidation of our Pacific problem, but may benefit the United States assistance to Great Britain and Russia in the European theater." An assumption which plainly shows the extent to which American military intelligence dangerously underestimated the potential enemy, the ultimate hubris was the suggestion that an easily defeated Japan's 6 million tons of merchant shipping "could be used to excellent advantage in the European theater."

The Naval Staff on the Joint Board were not quite so smitten with the Army planners' vision that fleets of Philippines-based bombers would smash an invasion force before it landed or that the Russians would be agreeable to B-17s flying out from Vladivostok to set the cities of Japan ablaze. It would take many months to ship out planes and troops in sufficient numbers to give the deterrent strategy offensive as well as defensive credibility. The Navy's fears were very real that Japan might make a preemptive strike; then the news came on October 16 that the Konoye government had fallen. A crisis meeting in the White House that afternoon prompted Admiral Stark to send out a war alert. All naval commands were warned of a "grave situation" and the "strong possibility of the Japanese attacking Russia." Since the U.S. and Great Britain "are held responsible by Japan for her present desperate situation there is also a possibility that Japan may attack these two powers."

Alarm rose sharply in Washington with the news of General Tojo's appointment as Prime Minister, on the assumption that, as a militarist, his cabinet would be pro-German and bent on war. The crisis began to ease after Ambassador Grew reported that Tokyo intended to continue negotiations and Tojo made a conciliatory speech on October 19 offering "to promote amicable relations with friendly powers." So as preparations were made for another round of the diplomatic game, both Britain and the United States stepped up efforts to rush reinforcements to the Far East.

THE IMPERFECT THREAT

After a heated War Cabinet meeting on October 20, Churchill finally persuaded the Admiralty, against its better judgment, to order the *Prince of Wales,* accompanied by a new carrier, to the Indian Ocean where the force was to join up with the battlecruiser *Repulse* en route to Singapore. The next day, Stimson briefed the President in the most enthusiastic terms on the Army's bomber plan, which he described as "A strategic opportunity of the utmost importance. . . . Our whole strategic possibilities [sic] of the past twenty years have been revolutionized. . . . From being impotent to influence events in that area, we suddenly find ourselves vested with the possibility of great effective power. Indeed we hardly yet realize our opportunities." His breathless memorandum pointed out that one possibility being explored was getting Soviet cooperation for using Vladivostok as "the base of a northern pincer movement of American influence and power," through which the B-17 bombers could be ferried to the Far East and also bomb Japan. "The control over the western Pacific which it would open could hardly fail to have immense powers of warning to Japan as well as of assurance to Russia." Merely the threat of bombing, Stimson predicted, "might well remove Japan from the Axis powers."

The War Plans Division on November 3 advised Stimson "the principal objective in the Far East is to keep Japan out of war." More time was essential for the reinforcement of the Philippines to escalate the deterrent strategy into an offensive posture. But the Secretary of War already knew that it would take until April for MacArthur to recruit and train more than 100,000 Filipinos who were going to be needed (in addition to the 17,000 Army troops awaiting ships to transport them to join the 18,000 American soldiers already in the Philippines). So far there were only nine of the vaunted heavy bombers on Luzon airfields, and another twenty-six were to be flown out by November. But even with the planned increase in B-17 production rate from 12 to 40 a month by February 1942, Stimson's own notes reveal that he appreciated that it would take until April to establish even a relatively small force of 128 Fortresses. "Yet even this imperfect threat," he assured Roosevelt, "if not promptly called by the Japanese, bids fair to stop Japan's march to the south and secure the safety of Singapore, with all the revolutionary consequences of such action."

As the Japanese reopened diplomatic negotiations (and Imperial General Headquarters set a deadline for progress to be made in a matter of weeks), the American government was determined *not* to compromise but to spin out the talks for as long as possible. Stimson, with unwarranted optimism, had informed the Secretary of State on October 6 that "we need three months to secure our position." But as the plan to reinforce the

Philippines grew more ambitious, the War Department was to give Mac-Arthur until April 1942 to complete the buildup.

It would therefore appear that the diplomatic timetables of Washington and Tokyo were running hopelessly out of step. This was evident on November 5, two days before Ambassador Nomura reopened negotiations with Japan's "A" proposal, when a joint memorandum from Marshall and Stark cautioned the President that Germany was the prime enemy of the United States. They warned that at least six months would be needed to establish the bombing force and adequate reserves of troops in the Philippines. Yet Roosevelt and Hull both decided to gamble on dragging out the talks—while Prime Minister Tojo had been given a November 25 deadline for achieving some rapprochement that would restore the flow of oil supplies and lead to a settlement with the Chinese Nationalists. Tokyo's impatience was conveyed both by Ambassador Grew's reports to Washington and the instructions to Ambassador Nomura from Tokyo. The Magic intercepts ring with frequent and urgent references: "our people are growing impatient" (November 2); "the situation does not permit of delays" (November 4); "it is absolutely necessary that all arrangements for the signing of this agreement [the last Japanese diplomatic proposals before the outbreak of hostilities, known as Proposals A and B] be completed by the 25th of this month" (November 5); "we are on the last lap of these negotiations" (November 6); "no further delays" (November 11); "the crisis is fast approaching" (November 15); "the transfer of troops from southern French Indo-China to the northern part is an important concession we would venture to make for the sake of speeding up the agreement" (November 19); and "in view of the extremely critical situation, [we can] only hope most earnestly for a speedy settlement" (November 24).

Only hours away from the November 25 "absolutely immoveable" deadline that Tokyo had imposed, the President and Secretary of State must have known they were running out of time. The Magic intercepts contained references to Japanese preparations for evacuating their embassy officials by sea and air, as well as instructions for destroying secret documents and codes. On November 7, Ambassador Nomura had presented the Tojo Cabinet's proposal for a comprehensive settlement. Magic had already provided Hull and the President with its substance and, although the President agreed it was totally unacceptable, the Secretary of State had been instructed to "strain every nerve to satisfy and keep on good relations." The American government knew of the "B" proposal for a short-term accommodation and that the special envoy Kurusu was on his way from Tokyo to assist in its presentation a week later.

"CONSIDERABLE CONCESSIONS"

When the Japanese ambassador came to the White House on November 10 and claimed that the latest proposal represented "considerable concessions," he stressed his government's desire for a rapid response. Roosevelt patiently explained that "Nations must think one hundred years ahead." The next day Bishop Walsh arrived at the State Department to advocate another memorandum of accommodation. This was dismissed by Stanley Hornbeck as "naive." "The fate of the Empire hangs by a slender thread," Tokyo warned Nomura on November 17, when he was told to "please fight harder." That day the President had delayed his trip to the Warm Springs retreat in order to attend another meeting with Nomura and the special envoy, who had just arrived in Washington. Kurusu expressed his concern that the Pacific "was like a powder keg," but Roosevelt and Hull seemed more concerned with getting Japan to abandon her Tripartite Pact connections. "There is no last word between friends," the President reminded them.

However, in the course of the discussion, the two Japanese envoys believed that they detected a new note of accommodation in the American position, and dutifully reported to Tokyo: "it seems very clear that they are of a mind to bring about a compromise after making sure of our peaceful intentions." Their conclusion was that this American receptivity was due to "the attention . . . the United States has turned more and more than ever toward the Atlantic of late." They were correct. The torpedoing of two U.S. Navy destroyers within two weeks of one another at the end of October had prompted the President to challenge the isolationists and press for three important amendments to ease the restrictions of the Neutrality Act. The change in the law to allow U.S. merchantships to be armed and sail to British ports had passed by a slim vote but only after the President had gone on the radio and revealed what he claimed was a secret Nazi occupation plan for South America. A British delegation had arrived in Washington on November 9 to negotiate the purchase of some of the heavy bombers that were now being sent to the Far East.

This was yet another reminder to the President and his military chiefs of just how ill-prepared the United States was to engage in a Pacific conflict at that time. "We have sweated blood to endeavor to divide adequately our forces for a two-ocean war," Admiral Stark had written on November 15 in reply to Admiral's Kimmel's insistence that "more consideration be given to the needs of the Pacific Fleet." Two days earlier, John Hay Whitney, Donovan's representative, had cabled from London a brief summary from Churchill of the need for the United States intervention:

(1) every week sooner we come in will reduce the war by one month.
(2) order of choice:
    (a) United States without Japan
    (b) United States and Japan both in war
    (c) neither at war
    (d) Japan without America (this possibility unthinkable).

So it is clear that just a week before Japan's November 25 deadline, American diplomacy and military strategy were being pulled apart by conflicting forces. Against stiff isolationist opposition, the President had nudged the United States nearer to Britain and closer to the brink of open hostilities with Germany, making it imperative to avoid a showdown in the Pacific. The Philippines deterrent was incomplete and the strategic bomber threat would not become effective for months. Yet because of the Tripartite Pact a preemptive move by the United States against German or Japanese forces would set ablaze a two-ocean war. This was not the worst that Churchill could imagine, but it was for Roosevelt and his military Chiefs. These were the pressures that, for the first time in two decades, forced U.S. foreign policy toward Japan to soften into an accommodation.

During the November 17 discussions in the White House (before the presentation of Tokyo's B proposal) Kurusu had on his own initiative suggested the President might give his government more time by coming to a temporary arrangement: "if the Japanese were now to withdraw their troops from Indochina, could the United States ease their economic pressure to the point of sending small quantities of rice and oil . . . ?" That night Hull told the British minister in Washington that the idea was "attractive enough to warrant its being tried at least." The rationale for the President and the State Department to do everything to avoid being embroiled in a Pacific War was set out that same day in a memorandum from Treasury Secretary Morgenthau, entitled "An Approach to the Problem of Eliminating Tension with Japan and Insuring the Defeat of Germany." Drawn up by his principal aide, Harry Dexter White, the memo set out the terms for securing a permanent peace in the Pacific that would allow the United States to shift its fleet to the Atlantic. It called for the immediate withdrawal of Japanese troops from Indochina and the Manchurian border, and a phased pullout from China, in return for the United States lifting the oil and trade embargo.

The President also revived his earlier idea of offering Japan a six-month truce—"some oil and rice now—more later"—provided no more troops were sent to Indochina; peace talks began with the Chinese Nationalists; and, perhaps most significantly, "Japan (were) to agree not to invoke (the) tripartite pact even if (the) US gets into European war." Tokyo had rejected Kurusu's suggestion of an independent policy, fearing it would only lead to delay or breakdown. He was instructed to submit the B proposal on November 20. Nevertheless, both Hull and Roosevelt wanted to seize the opportunity and "made a desperate effort to get something worked out." The State Department officials worked on drafts of a modus vivendi that would not be regarded as appeasement, but which came close to the conditions set out by Japan's proposal B which offered a withdrawal of their troops to northern Indochina and no further "armed advancement." In return the United States was to restore commercial relations and "a required quantity of oil," as well as suspending aid to the Nationalists in order to get peace talks under way.

"A FAIR PROPOSITION"

The final draft of the American modus vivendi, which set a 25,000 limit on Japanese troops that could remain in northern Indochina for the three months for which the temporary accommodation was to run, was deliberately vague about whether or not aid to the Nationalists would be stopped. But it did make some positive proposals: the Philippines would be a site for peace talks and the United States would unfreeze Japan's assets and revert to trade control, which would have meant enough oil supplies for civilian purposes but not enough for aviation fuel.

The two "modus vivendi" positions were not irreconcilably apart. Significantly, the United States appeared ready to buy three more months of peace in the Pacific with a limited relaxation of the embargo and some encouragement on the Chinese to negotiate with Japan. The possibility, at least, had been opened, if the two governments wished to continue diplomacy. Tokyo certainly seemed to be making favorable indications. On November 22, Nomura was told that the deadline had been extended by four more days, until the 29th; "after that things are automatically going to happen."

It was this pronouncement that was the cause for Roosevelt's pessimistic tone two days later, when he cabled Churchill: "This seems to me to be a fair proposition, but its acceptance or rejection is really a matter of internal Japanese politics. I am not very hopeful and we must all be ready for trouble, possibly soon." The same day, November 24, Hull discussed the proposal with the British, Dutch, Chinese, and Australian ambassadors. The final American draft modus vivendi was cabled to Chiang Kai-shek's government, accompanied by a ten-point proposal that incorporated the Morgenthau memorandum clearly restating the stiff conditions to be met by any permanent settlement. These included Japan's recognition of the Nationalist regime and evacuation of all forces from China, as well as withdrawal from the Tripartite Pact.

Six months of fruitless negotiations and the long list of Japanese perfidies that he liked to rehearse had left the elderly Secretary of State far from certain about either the wisdom or the probability of reaching even a temporary accommodation. Yet he was aware of the pressing need for obtaining more time to consolidate the United States's military position and strategy. This weighed less with the State Department hardliners, and particularly Stanley Hornbeck, who feared that any deal with Tokyo would weaken Chiang Kai-shek. Hornbeck would complain that the Navy "had asked for six months last February and that the Secretary, through his negotiations, had got them six months. Now they wanted three more." Playing for time meant appeasing Japan to some degree—and the danger of American involvement in a Far Eastern Munich. In any case, Japan's trustworthiness in observing any accommodation of the modus vivendi appeared to be questioned by the November 24 cable to Nomura from Tokyo. It stiffened the conditions of the B proposal: "our demand for a cessation of aid to Chiang (the acquisitions of Netherlands-East Indian goods and at the same time the supply of American petroleum to Japan as well) is the most essential condition."

The Secretary of State's concern about the fragile point the negotiations had reached that day were conveyed in his meeting with the Chief of Naval Operations. After this meeting, Stark flashed out another alert to all commands in the Pacific: "Chances of favorable outcome with Japan is [sic] very doubtful. This situation coupled with statements of Japanese governments and movements of their naval and military forces indicate in our opinion that a surprise aggressive movement in any direction including an attack on Philippines or Guam is a possibility. Chief of Staff has seen this dispatch and concurs and requests action addresses to inform Senior Army Officer in their area. Utmost secrecy necessary in order not to complicate an already tense situation or precipitate Japanese action."

It was against this background of tension and uncertainty that the President held his weekly meeting of the War Council on the morning of November 25. Before the conference, Hull took care to show the text of the American modus vivendi to the Secretaries of War and the Navy. They approved. "It adequately protected all our interests" Stimson recorded; although he did not give much hope of Japanese acceptance, he approved of the three months time that it would buy the Army to complete the Philippine build-up. The discussions went on unusually long into the lunch hour. Europe and the Atlantic war, normally the main topic, was hardly touched on at all by the President, who was preoccupied with the Pacific. He was clearly worried about the deadline coming up in five days' time, and the possibility of a surprise assault coming as early as two days later—the time that it would take to launch an assault on the Philippines from Formosa. According to Stimson's diary, Roosevelt said: "the Japanese are notorious for attacking without warning and the question was what we should do? The question was how we should maneuver them into the position of firing the first shot without allowing too much danger to ourselves." It was, as the Secretary of War recorded, "a difficult question." If the United States fired first, Japan would be able to invoke the terms of the Tripartite Pact and the United States would be hurled into the two-front war that it was so anxious to avoid.

One of the significant conclusions to be drawn from that morning meeting was that the American leaders were now coming to a consensus, given the latest intelligence evidence that Japan was not going north but preparing to strike southward. This is evident from Stark's letter, dashed off to Kimmel that afternoon, warning the Pacific Fleet Commander that the President, Hull, and he had agreed they would not be taken aback "over a Japanese surprise attack. From many angles an attack on the Philippines would be the most embarrassing thing that could happen to us. . . ." The most important outcome of that War Council was that the United States would continue negotiations, and that the modus vivendi arrangement offered the chance of a few more months in which measures could be completed to ensure that there would be no "embarrassment" if the Philippines were attacked.

The President and the Secretary of State were awaiting the reaction of the British and Chinese before putting their proposals for a three-month temporary accommodation to the Japanese envoys. Churchill's response was clearly a deciding factor, since it might have been anticipated that Chiang Kai-shek would disapprove of any attempt to treat with his enemy. The Prime Minister was in favor—quite strongly, so it appears from a November 23 minute to Anthony Eden: "Our major interest is: no further encroachments and no war, as we have already enough of this latter. . . . I must say I should feel pleased if I read that an American-Japanese agreement had been made by which we were able to be no worse off three months hence in the Far East than we are now." Churchill's overriding concern was, like Roosevelt's, to build up forces to deter Japan, and he was no doubt thinking about the *Prince of Wales* and *Repulse* steaming across the Indian Ocean to Singapore without the promised aircover. The carrier that should have accompanied them had run aground in the West Indies and plans were already being made to send out a replacement as well as more battleships so that, by the end of March 1942, a sizable fleet would be ready to defend Malaya.

Yet, the Prime Minister sent only a cautious reply to the President. Dispatched before he retired on November 25—as Churchill was careful to point out in his memoirs, although it was sent out in the early hours of the next day, it arrived in Washington by breakfast time on November 26—it said: "Of course it is for you to handle this business and we certainly do not want an additional war. There is only one point that disquiets us. What about Chiang Kai-shek? Is he not having a very thin diet?"

While Churchill intended to express approval of the American effort to reach an accommodation with Japan, Chiang protested loudly and furiously through every available channel of communication. Hull was deeply affronted when he heard of "numerous hysterical cables to different cabinet officers and high officials in the Government, other than the State Department and sometimes even ignoring the President, intruding into a delicate situation with no idea of what the facts are." The Generalissimo was adamant in his demands that the United States "announce that if the withdrawal of the Japanese Armies from China is not settled, the question of the embargo or freezing could not be considered." On the evening of November 25, he had met the Chinese ambassador to counter the rumors that Chiang's American friends were spreading word to the press of an impending "appeasement." Hu-shih was told firmly: "our proposals would relieve the menace of Japan in Indochina to the whole Pacific area, including Singapore, the Netherlands East Indies, Australia and also the United States, with the Philippines and the rubber and tin trade routes." The Secretary of State's blunt manner gave no hint that he would be dissuaded from at least trying for an accommodation just because of Chiang's virulent objections, ones that took no account of the larger issues at stake. Hull stressed the ninety-day time limit and insisted that "the limited amount of more or less inferior oil products that we might let Japan have during that period would not to any appreciable extent increase Japanese war and naval preparations." Hull warned, "we can cancel this proposal, but it must be with the understanding that we are not to be charged with failure to send our fleet into the area near Indochina and into Japanese waters, if by chance Japan makes a military drive southward." This chiding reflected his annoyance after the previous day's meeting when the ambassadors clearly expected the United States "to be ready to move in a military way and take the lead in defending the entire area." His predecessor had ruled this out when the Japanese moved their troops out into Manchuria in 1931, and Hull himself had repeatedly argued against direct involvement as the war in China widened. By the last month of 1941, with the United States on the brink of war with Germany, it was neither his nor the President's policy to precipitate a Pacific conflict.

Hull, and clearly Roosevelt, were on the evening of November 25 therefore quite determined to go ahead with trying to buy time by reaching a modus vivendi. There was opposition on the part of Henry Morgenthau, who had been stirred up by some harsh words from T. V. Soong, Chiang Kai-shek's brother-in-law. Interior Secretary Ickes would also have been arguing against any relaxation of the "iron firmness" he believed was the only policy Japan respected. Significantly, he was not told about the modus vivendi until later—when he went on record as saying he would have resigned and charged the President with appeasement. The State Department hardline officials, led by the redoubtable Hornbeck, made no secret of their disapproval. There were obvious dangers in the

United States being forced to reverse a quarter century of uncompromising policy to make a deal that would ultimately prove as conciliatory as the 1917 Lansing-Ishii Accord. Roosevelt and Hull were certainly aware of the tough voice of Tokyo, since they were eavesdropping through Magic intercepts.

"A PRETTY SWEEPING INDICTMENT OF U.S. POLICY"

In spite of the pessimism being expressed in Washington—carefully emphasized in all the official accounts—that it would have been impossible to reach a temporary accommodation with Japan in November 1941, it was the United States which unilaterally decided to abandon the search for a modus vivendi. According to a confidential British Foreign Office report "the President and Mr. Hull were . . . fully conscious of what they were doing." They had been repeatedly warned by Ambassador Joseph Grew that Japan was being pushed into a diplomatic impasse from which war was the only exit. This was certainly the opinion of Sir Robert Craigie, His Majesty's Ambassador in Tokyo at the time, whose report, filed after his repatriation, caused Sir Alexander Cadogan, Permanent Under Secretary at the Foreign Office to observe that it was "a pretty sweeping indictment of U.S. policy." "I consider," Craigie wrote in his controversial memorandum, "that had it been possible to reach a compromise with Japan in December 1941 involving the withdrawal of Japanese troops from South Indo-China, war with Japan would not have been inevitable."

It was a view which echoed the cables and reports of the United States ambassador in Tokyo, but Churchill found such opinions offensive and tried to suppress Craigie's report when it was finally circulated in September 1943. "It is a very strange document and one which should be kept most scrupulously secret" the Prime Minister noted, obviously fearing the damage it might do to Anglo-American relations by suggesting that Roosevelt might in any way be responsible for precipitating the outbreak of war. "A more one sided and pro-Japanese account of what occurred I have hardly ever read . . . ." He also writes of the breach with Japan as if it were an unmitigated disaster. ". . . It was [in fact] a blessing that Japan attacked the United States and thus brought America wholeheartedly into the war."

Whether such an accommodation would have worked out in practice is less important than the fact that it was the United States which decided to abandon the modus vivendi—thereby making a Pacific war inevitable.

Even more intriguing is precisely what happened between the evening of November 25, when Cordell Hull was (to judge from all the available evidence), clearly intent on presenting the American version of the modus vivendi to the Japanese at 10 A.M., and the following morning. Then, on the 26th, in a telephone conversation with the Secretary of War, he announced that he had "about made up his mind" not to pass on the truce proposal, "but to kick the whole thing over—to tell them he has no other proposition at all."

In the light of subsequent events, this decision proved to have been one of the most momentous in America's history. Yet, if we are to believe the version authorized for posterity by those involved, it would appear to have been taken as an angry reaction to the discovery of Japan's duplicity. Just what that piece of evidence was which prompted so violent a reversal in the minds of the President and his Secretary of State that they decided to jeopardize the entire U.S. military strategy by effectively breaking off diplomacy, has always been the subject of speculation.

New evidence has come to light that now casts doubt on the accepted explanations given by the Secretary of State and the Secretary of War, both of whom were instrumental in bringing about a decision that made the Pearl Harbor attack inevitable.

Interestingly enough, both their versions differ significantly in emphasis. Cordell Hull, in his "Memoirs," suggests that what prompted his reconsideration was the cable that came in during the night from Churchill: "the Prime Minister wondered whether the Generalissimo was not getting 'rather meagre rations' under the modus vivendi. China, he said, was the cause of his being anxious and the Chinese collapse would hugely augment our common danger. After talking this over with the State Department, I came to the conclusion that we should cancel out the modus vivendi. Instead we should present the Japanese solely the ten-point proposal for a general settlement, to which the modus vivendi would have been in the nature of an introduction." As the other main factors shaping his decision, Hull cites American public opinion; the violent opposition of the Chinese; the "either unfavorable or lukewarm" reaction of other interested governments, and the "slight prospect of Japan's agreeing to the modus vivendi."

In his own memoirs, Churchill's account specifically tried to play down any part that he may have had in influencing the decision. "I understood the dangers attending the thought 'the British are trying to drag us into war.' I therefore placed the issue where it belonged, namely in the President's hands," he wrote in 1950. He also insisted: "We had not heard up to this moment of the 'Ten Point Note' which not only met our wishes and those of the associated governments, but indeed went beyond anything for which we had ventured to ask." It is also interesting that he claimed the British government had to rely on the Americans sending Magic intercepts, which "were repeated to us, but there was an inevitable delay—sometimes of two or three days—before we got them. We did not know therefore at any given moment all that the President or Mr. Hull knew. I make no complaint about this."

Just how much the President knew on the morning of November 26 when Henry Morgenthau came into his bedroom is a matter of great speculation. Plainly, Roosevelt had just received some news which had shaken him because "He had not touched his coffee. He had some kippered herring which he had just begun to eat when Cordell Hull called up. He was talking to Hull and trying to eat his food at the same time, but by the time he finished his conversation his food was cold and he didn't touch it." Roosevelt had apparently promised Hull that he would see the Chinese ambassador and T. V. Soong to "quiet them down."

Henry Stimson's diary implies that it was his telephone call that morning which caused the President's consternation. The Secretary of War recounts how the previous afternoon, on returning to his office after the War Council meeting, he had found a message waiting for him from the head of Military Intelligence, G-2, Division. In his diary it is recorded that "five divisions have come down from Shantung and Shansi to Shanghai and there they had embarked on ships—30, 40 or 50 ships—and have been sighted south of Formosa. I at once called up Hull and told him about it and sent copies to him and to the President of the message from G-2."

The President was supposed not to have received his copy, but the next morning when Stimson telephoned him to inquire "whether he had received the paper which I had sent him over last night about the Japanese having started a new expedition from Shanghai down toward Indochina. He fairly blew up—jumped up into the air, so to speak, and said he hadn't seen it and that that changed the whole situation because it was evidence of bad faith on the part of the Japanese that while they were negotiating for an entire truce—an entire withdrawal—they should be sending this expedition down there to Indochina. I told him that it was a fact that had come to me through G-2 and through the Navy Secret Service and I at once got another copy of the paper I had sent last night and sent it over to him by special messenger."

What is very puzzling about this account (which labels the evidence of Japanese duplicity so specifically) is how such an important document *failed to reach the White House.* What had happened to the messenger on his way to the White House the previous afternoon? Had the presidential staff mislaid a communication of supposedly urgent nature? If the document, as Stimson would have us believe, contained such dramatic news, why had he not reached the President at once on the telephone? The answer may be found in Hull's reaction to his phone call that afternoon. Stimson does not record that the Secretary of State "fairly blew up"— yet Hull's Tennessee explosiveness was well known and he, far more than Roosevelt, had lost patience with the Japanese. On the contrary, his account of that evening makes no mention of receiving such startling news of Japan's duplicity, news that would have made him more sympathetic to the pleadings of the Chinese ambassador.

KICKING THE WHOLE THING OVER

That Roosevelt had received some explosive piece of intelligence by the morning of November 26 is beyond doubt. It was certainly damning enough to cause Hull to "kick the whole thing over" as far as the modus vivendi policy was concerned—a decision he clearly would not have made without the President's consent, however severely his conscience had been pricked by Churchill to heed Chiang Kai-shek's protests.

It is now possible to conclude, with some certainty, that it was not Stimson's report that proved crucial. That "missing" document has been recovered from the recently declassified Confidential File of the Secretary of War. Dated November 25, the MEMORANDUM FOR THE PRESIDENT, subject: *Japanese Convoy Movement towards Indo-China* refers to a "convoy of from ten to thirty ships," which had assembled "near the mouth of the Yangtse River below Shanghai." It carried a force estimated at 50,000 Japanese troops. Stimson made quite clear that: "The officers concerned, in the Military intelligence Division, feel that unless we receive other information, this is more or less a normal movement, that is, the logical follow-up of their previous notification to the Vichy Government."

Reporting a "more or less normal movement" that had been anticipated from Magic intercepts to Vichy six weeks before was not exactly the sort of exposure of Japanese duplicity to cause even the moralistic Hull to leap about—and certainly not the supremely self-possessed Franklin D. Roosevelt. What Stimson's diary claims was something of a bombshell proves, on examination, to be little more than a damp squib. Nor does the summary estimate by the British Joint Intelligence Committee, which evidently accompanied the message to the White House, contain any startling revelations. In fact, it was the official copy of the British code radiogram which Army Intelligence had intercepted as it was transmitted from London four days earlier. A copy of the decrypt (of the intercepted British secret message!) was sent to the Secretary of State twenty-four hours earlier with the heading: "In order that the source may be protected do not reveal to the British that you have received the following information." In this instance, the gentlemen in the War Department could take comfort from their advance reading of "other gentlemen's mail." Up to November 18, the consensus of Britain's intelligence on Tokyo's intentions was: "Japan will make last effort at agreement with U.S.A. Decision whether or not to take aggressive action involving major powers would follow failure of conversations." Its conclusions were that, "if such decision is taken Thailand will be first probable objective involving least risk of major conflict. . . . Action against Russia likely to be deferred until position of Russia in Far East is seriously weakened. . . . Operation in China will continue in absence of general agreement with U.S.A. . . . Early attack on Burma Road is unlikely. . . ."

It must have been very reassuring reading for the Secretary of War and relieved the Secretary of State's fears that continuing negotiations would threaten the Chinese. Just what the President's reactions were can only be surmised—for the two documents certainly did *not* get lost before reaching Roosevelt's office. They were returned to the War Department on November 27 by Major General Edwin M. Watson, the President's confidential aide and secretary, whose covering note was decidedly cryptic:

> Dear Mr. Secretary,
> I am sending herewith the English estimate and the original of your report sent to the President Tuesday afternoon.
> We found this in due course in the inside pocket of a very distinguished gentleman
> I am, Very sincerely yours, [signed] "Pa" Watson.

It is difficult to believe Stimson's story that his top-secret communication, referring to the closely guarded Magic and containing intercepted British intelligence, did not reach its addressee—particularly since it was returned by the President's most trusted aide, the man who ran his private office in the White House. The logical deduction can therefore be made that the "very distinguished gentleman" was none other than Franklin D. Roosevelt himself.

The suspicion is further justified because the original, and the curious note, are not filed with Stimson's official White House communications. By chance or design, they were buried amid a voluminous mass of general correspondence relating to the Philippines. However, in chronological order among the Secretary of War's exchanges with the President, is a carbon copy of the second letter. Dated November 26, it informs Roosevelt that he is being herewith sent "another memo about the Japanese movement to the south from Shanghai" along with the British estimate. Stimson is careful to note for the record, "This is highly abbreviated from the original verbal information." In comparing the two memorandums, it is intriguing to note that he has attempted to add to the implied urgency of the second with the new line, "Later reports indicate that this movement is already under way and ships have been seen south of Formosa." Yet in the scribbled notes the Secretary of War obviously made after phoning military intelligence that morning, he has clearly written "no new direct reports of Captains at sea—since the five ships Capt. last reported from Shanghai."

Moreover the correspondence of November 26 is filed with its routing stamp "ORIGINAL BY HAND Sgt. Quick (written in) with the delivery time of 12:20 carefully added. At the top of this copy is the penciled remark, "For complete file (?) see White House."

This then raises the question of why it was necessary to make the claim that the President had not received the *original* report dated November 25 with its none-too-startling revelations that the Japanese were carrying out predicted operations? That it was returned the day after Stimson's telephone call and duplicate note conveying the same information—news that supposedly was dramatic enough to precipitate the abandoning of any further attempt to reach an agreement with the Japanese—suggests that it might have served as convenient camouflage. Clearly, if the Secretary of War's version of that day's events were to stand up, two copies of the letter could not remain on the presidential files. That Stimson considered the documents particularly significant is confirmed by the fact that they were squirreled away among his Philippines folders, in the most confidential file of documents. Yet only his "official" diary version of how Roosevelt "blew up" was made public at the time of the 1946 Congressional Report on Pearl Harbor.

This points to the conclusion that a plausible cover story was set up between the President and the Secretary of War to conceal the real nature and origin of the information that landed on the presidential breakfast tray that morning. Since Stimson's account is so specifically tied to circumstance surrounding the supposed nondelivery of a specifically identified report, it suggests that even less weight was given to other intelligence that had come in through Army and Navy channels and might have indicated Japan's intentions. A Magic intercept of November 25 suggested that an invasion of Thailand was in the offing; the same day what appeared to be a troop convoy was reported assembling in southern Taiwan, and the day before a Dutch submarine spotted an expeditionary force steaming for the Palau Islands.

It does not seem credible that either Stimson's message or the overall intelligence picture as it stood on the morning of November 26, 1941, were sufficient stimuli to prompt the President's dramatic reaction. Hours earlier, the Pearl Harbor strike force had sailed from its secret rendezvous point in the Kuriles but, since it was observing strict radio silence, its opening move in Japan's war plan could not have been—and was not—discovered by American radio listening posts. What evidence was available showed a continuing southward movement of Japanese forces, but at a pace predictable enough not to upset the U.S. military analysts unduly. This was indicated by the interpretation of the Dutch submarine report via London: "no clear indications as to the direction or strength of such movement and the situation must be watched."

Indeed, one of the central objectives of the two modus vivendi proposals was to check any further southward advance by Japan. So whatever persuaded the President and his Secretary of State to "kick the whole thing over" must have been serious enough to convince them that there was no chance of avoiding a collision. If they concluded that morning that war was inevitable—and would soon break out—it is possible to understand why they decided to abandon any effort to negotiate a three-month accommodation, one that would certainly raise a charge of appeasement which would weaken and even discredit the administration when Japan launched her attack.

It is, therefore, logical to infer that whatever reached the President that morning was some kind of a positive war warning. It follows that it must have been quite specific, absolutely believable and from a trusted source that reached him through *an entirely confidential channel*. The clue that possibly points to the likely source and channel is to be found in the account of William Stephenson, then head of Britain's secret intelligence network in the United States. The President's son, Colonel James Roosevelt, brought him the news that an attempt to reach a modus vivendi was being abandoned. "Japanese negotiations off," Stephenson in turn cabled Churchill next day, adding: "Services expect action within two weeks."

Roosevelt trusted his son to act as the go-between with Stephenson, the man Churchill called "Intrepid." He acted as the channel of communication between the Prime Minister and President in the exchange of super-secret information that could not be carried on through the usual channels. That he routed what appears to be a reply via Stephenson, supposedly because the British ambassador in Washington was on a trip to Virginia, suggests that whatever war warning the President received on the morning of November 26, it almost certainly came from Churchill.

"SPECIFIC EVIDENCE"

There are *no* indications in the published accounts, or the Prime Minister's papers so far made available, that he must have been the source of a warning. There is only Churchill's own account, in which he appears to go to very detailed lengths to disclaim that even his cable sent the night before was intended to influence the U.S. decision. He also goes out of his way to deny that the British had up to date information on the Japanese, even at a time when they were decoding the Tokyo diplomatic traffic with their own Magic machines and, it would seem from the British official history, having more success than the Americans in penetrating the Imperial Navy operational code.

What is intriguing is Churchill's elaborate attempt to distance himself from the American decision. Curiosity leads to suspicion when one considers how intimately connected were the two nations' deterrent strategies against Japan, especially since the Atlantic-Charter meeting in August 1941. Moreover, that suspicion grows stronger on examination of the Prime Minister's papers in the Public Records Office. In the PREM 3 file, which contains Churchill's most secret wartime intelligence briefs, the 252 group dealing with the Japanese situation in 1941 is open, with one very intriguing omission. Section 5, dealing with events through November, is marked with official finality as "closed for 75 years."

Does the still-sealed group of papers in London conceal the details of the war warning passed on by the Prime Minister to the President two weeks before Pearl Harbor? In light of the new evidence, which must cast doubt on Stimson's account as well as the official version of why the United States so dramatically and unexpectedly reversed its policy toward Japan on the morning of November 26, 1941, there is good reason to believe that it does. That some war warning *was* received in the White House that day was certainly believed by Admiral Kimmel. Whether he was told this or not is unclear; but in the course of the U.S. Navy's Court of Inquiry in the summer of 1944, he certainly tried to establish the existence of such a warning. On July 29, the day's record of Admiral Stark's testimony reveals that the former Pacific Fleet Commander made strenuous efforts to "ask enough questions to ascertain the specific information he was being denied."

"Do you recall whether on or about 26 November you received information from the Office of Naval Intelligence that they had specific evidence of Japan's intention to wage an offensive war against both Britain and the United States?" Kimmel asked Stark in the inquiry. Stark declined to answer, claiming this was a State secret, and the judge advocate objected that the question went beyond the scope of direct examination. The court upheld that the matter was privileged information and, significantly, no confirmation or denial was made.

The fact that Admiral Kimmel was the first to suggest publicly that a specific war warning was received on November 26 is highly significant. Just what that war warning can have been is not yet clear, but Stimson's "lost" memorandum must raise serious doubts about the hitherto accepted version which offers as explanations the Shanghai convoy report as well as Hull's uneasy conscience over ignoring the objections of Chiang Kai-shek and Churchill's lukewarm reaction to the modus vivendi. However, it is possible, with the support of new evidence, to conclude that whatever form the warning took, it must have been seen as irrefutable proof of an impending attack. Unless information was leaked by a trustworthy source close to the Japanese cabinet, court, or military commands—which is conceivable but unlikely because the Imperial Conference that took the irrevocable decision to begin hostilities did not meet until December 1—the only other intelligence credible enough to convince military analysts in London and Washington could only have come from precise details of the war plan itself.

Indeed, this would appear to be the most likely source since Japanese Army and Navy operational orders were distributed during the first week of November. It is evident from the military attachés' communications that these plans were given wide circulation and that key embassies, such as the one in Bangkok, were sent copies. By the third week in November, therefore, the number of personnel who knew all or part of Japan's great military secret were multiplied several thousandfold: the Navy Operation Order No. 1 had a circulation of 700. Whether disaffected Japanese leaked or agents of foreign powers obtained all or only part of the war plan is a matter for speculation. So, too, is the route by which the vital information reached London. The Dutch, as well as the British, maintained an extensive intelligence network in the Far East, one centered on their wide-ranging commercial interests. Submarines of the Royal Dutch Navy were keeping Japanese shipping under surveillance. Nor is it beyond the realm of possibility that Soviet agents might have been involved. It was less than a month after Sorge's spy ring had been exposed, the network that had provided Stalin with the intelligence confirming Japan's decision to strike to the south. This intelligence enabled him to withdraw Siberian divisions of the Red Army and redeploy them to defend Moscow before the final German offensive.

According to the records, no detailed plan of the Pearl Harbor Attack—Operation Z—survived the Japanese destruction program at the end of the war. However, one complete version of Yamamoto's first operation order was captured from the cruiser *Nachi* in 1944, and we can see that it was circulated by the Pearl Harbor section:

COMBINED FLEET TOP SECRET OPERATION ORDER 1

Flagship NAGATO, SAEKI BAY 5 Nov 1941

YAMAMOTO, Isoruku

145 of 700 Copies

Commander in Chief
Combined Fleet.

Combined Fleet Operations in the War Against the UNITED STATES GREAT BRITAIN *and the* NETHERLANDS *will be conducted in accordance with the Separate Volume.*

The fifty-four page document which, from the notes, is evidently translated from an original amended on November 17, sets out the objectives, logistics, and communication procedures for the takeover of South-east Asia:

> The Empire is expecting war to break out with the UNITED STATES GREAT BRITAIN and the NETHERLANDS. When the decision is made to complete over-all preparations for operations, orders will be issued establishing the ap-proximate date (Y Day) for commencement of operations and announcing "First Preparations for War". . . .

Included is COMBINED FLEET TOP SECRET OPERATION ORDER 2, issued the same day stating "Y Day will be 8 December." Japan's naval war plan suc-cinctly set forth the main objectives as follows:

1. In the east the American Fleet will be destroyed and American lines of operation and supply lines to the ORIENT will be cut.
2. In the West, British Malaya will be occupied and British supply lines to the ORIENT, as well as to the BURMA ROAD will be cut.
3. Enemy forces in the ORIENT will be destroyed, bases of operation seized, and areas with natural resources will be occupied.
4. Strategic areas will be seized and developed; defenses will be strengthened in order to establish a durable base for operations.

The document then specifically outlines the forces committed to and the operational plans for the capture and occupation of Malaya, the Philippines, the Netherlands East Indies and Burma, as well as seizure of the American outposts on Guam and Wake. What is most telling is that the only references to Hawaii are in an organizational table detailing the objectives of what is described as the "Striking Force" which "Will prepare to make suitable moves against the American Fleet in accordance with the enemy situation" after sailing from Tankan Bay in the Kuriles. Beneath this entry the objective of the "Advance Expeditionary Force" attached to the 6th Fleet is specified. Clearly submarines are to be posi-tioned so that they "Will observe and attack American Fleet in Hawaii area. Will make a surprise attack on the channel leading into Pearl Harbor . . . Until the *end of the surprise attack on Hawaii by Striking Force (X plus 3)* [author's italics] the Advance Expeditionary Force will be under the command of the Striking Force Commander."

Apart from the submarine operations, it will be noted that there are *no* references to a full scale attack on Pearl Harbor—only the broad indica-tions that the Striking Force would deal with the American Fleet. So if all or part of Yamamoto's Secret Operation Order No. 1 had been in British or American hands by November 26, it would have provided unambiguous proof that Japan was preparing to strike, as anticipated, in Malaya and the Philippines. But it does not explicitly outline the extent to which an attack on Pearl Harbor was the cornerstone of the Combined Fleet's battle plan. So far no original of this document in Japanese has been found among the records, nor any indication of the date on which this translated operational order (copy No. 145) reached American hands. While this in no way proves that it *was* in fact the War Warning received on November 26, its existence and the lack of any clear picture of the degree of threat to Hawaii in it, fits the hypothesis that its contents could well have been the evidence of Japanese treachery that so shook the President that morning.

What and precisely how much the British knew must be entirely guess-work until more evidence comes to light, but it seems that Churchill must certainly have been able to pass on to Roosevelt that Japan's attack was timed for the end of the first week in December. This would have been easily confirmed from the Magic-revealed deadline of November 29, and the rate at which striking forces could move from Indochina and Taiwan to hit the Malay Peninsula and the Philippines. A process of strategic deduction would reveal these as the first objectives to be taken before the conquest of the Netherlands East Indies. Whether the secret evidence which reached the White House by November 26 indicated that Pearl Harbor was included in Japan's grand strategy requires a far bolder leap in the deductive process than to make the case that Roosevelt must have known at least the date of the war plan's launch.

Like a chess player who suddenly realizes that he is only a move away from checkmate, the President must have been shocked to discover that the Anglo-American deterrent strategy against Japan had collapsed. The only escape from war was surrender to diplomatic blackmail. This was unthinkable. With Japan coiling to attack in less than two weeks, there was no time, even if men and equipment had been ready, to rush rein-forcements out to the other side of the Pacific. It would be three months before enough bombers were in place in the Philippines to threaten the Japanese homeland. Any use of the fleet for a preemptive attack presented too great a risk and would have divided the nation, because the isolationists could charge that Roosevelt had engineered it to get into the war with Germany.

WAR WARNINGS

The first blow *had* to be struck by the Japanese; all that the President and his military chiefs could do was to prepare to meet it and, in what-ever time remained, get every available bomber out to strengthen the Philippines. These were the two urgent matters that occupied the Chief of Staff's conference on the morning of November 26, with General Marshall reporting that the Japanese "will soon cut loose" and that, although he was less certain, "the President and Mr. Hull anticipate a possible assault on the Philippines." They had now to decide what instructions to give in anticipation of the breakdown of negotiations that "would not necessarily mean a declaration of war." There is another hint in the verbatim record of that crisis meeting that Marshall must have been privy to the secret war warning that the President restricted to his key advisers: "We know a great deal that the Japanese are not aware that we know, and we are familiar with their plans to a certain extent. . . ." The extent plainly indicated the immediate threat to the Philippines because Marshall insisted that General MacArthur "prior to a state of war" be "directed" (not merely "desired") by a communiqué to "take such reconnaissance and other measures as you deem necessary. These matters left to your judgment." It is recorded that this was intended to give MacArthur the discretion to "attack threatening convoys" and begin flights over Japanese territory, even if his planes were shot at. "I would say do that," Marshall told General Arnold, after learning that B-24 bombers were on twenty-four-hour standby on the West Coast to fly out via Midway and Wake to carry out reconnaissance of the Gilberts and Marshalls.

Their most pressing concern was providing immediate protection for the forty-eight additional B-17s ready to make the long haul across the Pacific. The decision was taken to ask the Navy to ship out fighter squadrons to Wake and Midway because it would take too long to get Army squadrons transported by sea. The very fact that Marshall was prepared to accept "there will be nothing left at Hawaii until replacements arrive" seems to indicate that his information about Japan's war plan did *not* include the Pearl Harbor attack. The Chief of Staff concluded that once the forty-eight Fortresses were in the Philippines, "we will be over the hump." His confidence rested not only on the bombers but on the convoy carrying more fighters and troops, at that moment passing Guam en route to Manila.

That afternoon the Secretary of State met with the Japanese envoys and presented *only* the ten-point proposals without the modus vivendi. Kurusu read this stiff restatement of American principle and decided that "his Government would be likely to throw up its hands." The President, anticipating Tokyo's reaction, sent a warning to the U.S. High Commissioner in the Philippines that he was expecting an "early aggressive movement of some character," that the islands were under threat, and that he considered it possible "that this next Japanese aggression might cause an outbreak of hostilities between the United States and Japan."

The following day the President was to receive Tokyo's ambassadors, who hoped to make a final try to reach the modus vivendi. That morning the Secretary of State made it quite plain to Stimson that there was no hope: "I have washed my hands of it and it is now in the hands of you and Knox—the Army and the Navy." Hornbeck, who had evidently *not* been told of the war warning, submitted a memorandum to Hull that day predicting 5:1 odds against Japan going to war before December 15; 3:1 by January 15; and even odds of hostilities by March 1942—he later regretted his "wishful thinking and gratuitous predictions." Military Intelligence Division that day reported: "it is evident that the Japanese have completed plans for further aggressive moves in South Eastern Asia" but as yet had not decided whether any attack would develop against Thailand first or Malaya, the Philippines or the Dutch East Indies.

The belief that there was a chance that Japan might yet hesitate caused Marshall and Stark jointly to advise the President in a memorandum of November 27 that "Precipitance of military action on our part should be avoided as long as consistent with national policy." They pointed out that transports evacuating Marines from Shanghai were heading for Manila, that another Army convoy was in the vicinity of Guam, and 21,000 more troops were due to sail from the United States in the first week of December. They stressed the important part that MacArthur's forces could play in blocking a Japanese advance and stressed how important it was for "this troop reinforcement to reach the Philippines before hostilities commence." Since they considered the most likely next move by Japan was an invasion of Thailand, they urged the President to get British and Dutch agreement to issue a warning to Tokyo before taking military countermeasures.

A discussion that morning of the situation with Roosevelt on the telephone was enough to convince Stark that Admiral Kimmel's state of readiness at Pearl Harbor should be stepped up. "I suggested and he approved the idea that we would send him [Kimmel] the final alert; namely that he should be on the qui vive for any attack." The signal that was sent out commenced: "THIS DISPATCH IS CONSIDERED TO BE A WAR WARNING. NEGOTIATIONS WITH JAPAN TOWARDS STABILIZATION OF CONDITIONS IN THE PACIFIC HAVE CEASED. . . ." But Kimmel assumed that Hawaii was under no direct threat because the Chief of Naval Operations had appended the latest intelligence estimate that "PHILIPPINES, THAI OR KRA PENINSULA OR POSSIBLY BORNEO" were probably the Japanese objectives.

The dispatch ultimately radioed to MacArthur ended with the reconnaissance instructions agreed to by Marshall the previous day. Negotiations had been broken off and he was warned: "UNPREDICTABLE BUT HOSTILE ACTION AT ANY MOMENT." The Japanese were to be allowed to commit the first act but this "SHOULD NOT REPEAT SHOULD NOT, BE CONSTRUED AS RESTRICTING THE SUCCESSFUL DEFENSE OF THE PHILIPPINES." MacArthur's reaction was to order the four groups of B-17s to be flown to Mindanao where they would be out of range of Formosa-based bombers. Because of their superior range the B-17s were able to hit back in accordance with MacArthur's war plan orders to raid "Japanese forces and installations within tactical operating radius of available bases." His air commander, General Brereton, would eventually send half the force of heavy bombers south, because he was apparently concerned that the arrival of the next forty-eight Fortresses would overtax the facilities of the only two airfields from which they could operate.

The War Department, in response to MacArthur's request, was already sending out the target maps for a strategic bombing offensive against Japan, but no agreement had yet been reached with the Russians over the use of bases in Vladivostok. Six days earlier, Marshall's idea for "general incendiary attacks to burn up the wood and paper structure of the densely populated Japanese cities" had been dashed by a report from General Lawrence K. Kuter. One of the brightest of the Army Air Force staff, he had pointed out that even with the 160 to 170 heavy bombers that were expected to be out in the Philippines by the following April, they were hardly a "strong air force" with which to destroy 600 industrial objectives. He reminded the Chief of Staff: "In the 'victory program' some 8,000 bombers are set up as the requirement for the positive assurance of destroying of 154 industrial objectives."

"The very clearest idea existed in General MacArthur's mind as to what needed to be done. The fact remains, however, that there was neither equipment nor money nor manpower organized and available for the immediate implementation of the program." This was General Brereton's on-the-spot assessment of the inadequate state of the Philippine defense in the third week of November. The hopelessness of the dreams of generals in Washington (of mounting an air offensive against Japan) was evident as soon as Brereton arrived in Manila to find the airfield inadequate and "no spare parts for P-40s nor was there so much as an extra nut or washer for a Flying Fortress." There was a running feud between MacArthur and the Asiatic Fleet Commander, Admiral Hart, who feared that the Army Command "was going far beyond its war plans." Hart wanted control of any air operations launched against a Japanese invasion fleet at sea. MacArthur found this "entirely objectionable": he denied that the bombers would be operating in support of Navy since, as he tartly put in his November 7 reply, "the term 'Fleet' cannot be applied to two cruisers and the division of destroyers that comprise the surface elements of your command."

Stark had to intervene directly with Marshall to restore cooperation between the two commands as the threat of Japanese assault increased. From the Secretary of War's decision, on November 22, to get the President's approval to ferry out mustard-gas shells from Hawaii, it was evident that the desperate unreadiness of the Philippine defenses was becoming clear to the War Department. The Chief of Naval Operations had not been understating the situation when he told Admiral Kimmel on

November 25: "From many angles an attack on the Philippines would be the most embarrassing thing that could happen to us."

The imminent assault by Japanese forces was uppermost in Churchill's mind in his November 30 cable suggesting that the President send a message to the Emperor stating: "any further Japanese aggression would compel you to place the gravest issues before Congress." Roosevelt rejected the appeal—for the moment—but Hull and the State Department were hard at work drafting a speach to be ready for the President in three days. It was salted with references comparing Japan to Nazi Germany, and promises to do their part in the efforts that "free countries in Europe and Asia are making to defend themselves against Hitlerism." The President was to tell Congress: "I have full confidence that it is within our capacity to withstand any attack which anyone may make upon us because of our pursuit of that course. As Commander in Chief I have given appropriate orders to our Forces in the Far East."

The President already knew he would never have to deliver the address. Contents of the Magic intercepts made it abundantly plain that Japan was moving toward belligerency at an accelerating pace. The exchanges between Berlin and Tokyo provided the clearest warning. On November 27, Roosevelt had told the two Japanese envoys: "We are prepared to continue to be patient"; yet next day their ambassador to Germany was told by Tokyo: "the negotiations will be de facto ruptured in two or three days." He was so informed on November 30, and instructed to warn Hitler: "there is extreme danger that war may suddenly break out between the Anglo-Saxon nations and Japan through some clash of arms, and that the time of the breaking out of this war may come quicker than anyone dreams." The Washington envoys were repeatedly told not to abandon negotiations, but it was evident that Japanese forces were on the move southward and that strenuous efforts were under way to ensure that the Germans honored their Tripartite Pact obligations to Japan, even if she struck the first blow. Instructions were being sent out from Tokyo to the embassies that would be affected to destroy their codes and arrange for the evacuation of personnel. Japanese officials from all over the United States and Canada were being told to book passage on a liner that would be sailing from the West Coast during the first week of December.

ROOSEVELT'S TRIP WIRE

The Magic intercepts were, by November 30, giving the Secretary of State sufficient cause for alarm for him to advise the President to cut short his Thanksgiving trip to Warm Springs. Returning to the White

House by midday on December 1, Roosevelt held a crisis meeting with the War Council. News had come in that the Japanese were deep in conference with the Thai government in Bangkok and seeking to clear the way for their march into Malaya. It is evident from Stimson's diary that the concern in Washington was still how to maneuver Japan into firing the first shot. The President was worried that an attack on Malaya would make it difficult to carry out his secret commitment to Churchill if the Japanese did not simultaneously strike the Philippines. He therefore gave instructions to Admiral Stark to see that the Navy established what was, in effect, a trip wire across the South China Sea.

"THE PRESIDENT DIRECTS THAT THE FOLLOWING BE DONE AS SOON AS POSSIBLE AND WITHIN TWO DAYS IF POSSIBLE AFTER RECEIPT OF THIS DISPATCH," the Chief of Naval Operations radioed Admiral Hart in Manila that afternoon. Hart was ordered to "CHARTER THREE SMALL VESSELS FOR QUOTE DEFENSIVE INFORMATION PATROL UNQUOTE X MINIMUM REQUIREMENTS TO ESTABLISH IDENTITY AS UNITED STATES MEN OF WAR ARE COMMAND BY A NAVAL OFFICER AND TO MOUNT A SMALL MACHINE GUN WOULD SUFFICE X FILIPINO CREWS MAY BE EMPLOYED WITH MINIMUM NUMBER NAVAL RATINGS TO ACCOMPLISH PURPOSE WHICH IS TO OBSERVE AND REPORT BY RADIO JAPANESE MOVEMENTS IN WEST CHINA SEA AND GULF OF SIAM . . ."

Reconnaissance was hardly the purpose of this curious mission, since Admiral Hart, on his own initiative, had been sending out Navy PBY patrol planes to overfly the Japanese invasion fleet building up at Camranh Bay five days before he had received the November 30 order confirming the operation. It had been specifically approved by the President. Stark told Hart that the Navy aircraft "MUST NOT APPROACH SO AS TO APPEAR TO BE ATTACKING BUT MUST DEFEND THEMSELVES IF ATTACKED." Furthermore Roosevelt was specific about the positions to be taken up by this picket line of expendable vessels, one of which, he proposed, would be the Asiatic Fleet's official yacht. On December 3, Admiral Hart sadly watched the ancient *Isabel* steam out into Manila Bay, anticipating that he would never see his "holiday flagship" again. Two days later, after the Japanese patrol planes had spotted the boat less than twenty-two miles from the coast of Indo-China, Hart decided to recall the *Isabel* after it had become plain that the Imperial Navy was not going to take the bait. Back in the Cavite naval base two schooners, the *Lanikai* and the *Molly Moore* were being readied for the sacrificial mission. Equipped with a cannon and First World War machine guns, the ship had a radio that could not transmit and a Filipino crew that delighted in the chance to wear U.S. Navy uniforms. Lieutenant Kemp Tolley, her commander, was putting to sea on the morning the news came that the Japanese had attacked Pearl Harbor.

Although the trip wire was never actually in place, Roosevelt was confident enough after issuing the order on December 1, that any repetition of the *Panay* incident involving these naval vessels flying the Stars and Stripes would give him a *causis belli*. That day he advised the British Ambassador that "we should all be in it together" if the Japanese made a move across the China Sea to invade Malaya, and two days later he assured Halifax that this really did mean "armed support."

Forty-eight hours later it appeared that the President might be called upon to fulfill that promise sooner than anticipated and before the trip wire had been activated. On December 5, the Dutch High Command in Java became so alarmed at the bold incursions of the Japanese air force over their islands that they called for the implementation of the secret A2 section of the Rainbow 5 War Plan which would have required the Americans to join in offensive air operations from the Philippines. The Australian War Council met in emergency session in response, the British Chiefs of Staff in London were alerted, and the alarm prompted a late-evening call by Halifax on Hull to tell him "the time has come for immediate cooperation in the Dutch East Indies." Whatever assurances he received were flashed to London before they were radioed to Singapore next day in time for Admiral Phillips to pass them on after flying down to his conference with General MacArthur in Manila. The existence of the secret American undertaking to go to the aid of the British and Dutch came as a surprise to Admiral Hart. "LEARN FROM SINGAPORE WE HAVE ASSURED BRITAIN ARMED SUPPORT UNDER THREE OR FOUR EVENTUALITIES." He radioed Washington complaining, "HAVE RECEIVED NO CORRESPONDING INSTRUCTIONS FROM YOU."

EAST WIND RAIN

The United States commitment to her future allies in the Far East is evidence of the extent to which Washington's attention was focussed on the Philippines and Malaya during the final week before war broke out. Whatever warnings of the coming attack were received, there appears to be no evidence indicating that Hawaii was in peril. None of the Magic signals decoded had given any special indication that Pearl Harbor was the subject of particular interest to the Japanese—any more interest, that is, than the regular reports from Manila, the Canal Zone, and the West Coast. Pacific Fleet Naval Intelligence did *not* have a machine for decoding Purple, so it was not possible for Kimmel's staff to keep in touch with the diplomatic traffic. Since July, when security had been tightened on Magic, to the first week of December, the only insight into this important source of intelligence had been the bits and pieces of information that Stark had conveyed in his correspondence to the Pacific Fleet commander. However, Stark was later to testify that he had "enquired on two or three occasions as to whether or not Kimmel could read certain dispatches when they came up and which we were interpreting . . . *and I was told he could.*" [author's italics]

This apparent confusion in Washington over who was receiving what Magic intelligence was to matter a great deal, because the important clues in Japan's particular attention to shipping movements at Pearl Harbor was contained in the messages sent out by Consul Kita from Honolulu. Until the last few days before the attack, these were transmitted in the J19 code, not Purple. While J19 presented the American codebreakers with no great difficulty in decrypting, it could only be read in Washington where the personnel were under pressure to work on the more important ciphers. Consequently, its translation was generally delayed, often for weeks. A September 24 instruction from Tokyo to Honolulu to divide Pearl Harbor into five alphabetically designated sections and comply in their weekly report was decoded on October 9, marked by Commander Kramer with an asterisk as worthy of attention, *but not passed on to the Pacific Fleet.* Similarly, the November 15 signal from Tokyo requesting a twice-weekly report and stressing the need for "extreme secrecy" was not relayed to Pearl Harbor when it was finally decoded on December 3. Two days later the November 18 request from Tokyo for specific area reports stayed in the file in Washington because it did not seem significant.

Had these three messages been passed on to Commander Layton, the Pacific Fleet intelligence officer, they might have made a very different impression to a man on the spot. Had Layton and Commander Rochefort's codebreakers been aware of the unusual amount of detail Tokyo was requesting, as well as the doubling of the reports from the consulate in Honolulu, they might well have given priority to decoding the signals made by the local agent after December 2. On that day Kita, in accordance with his instructions, destroyed all but the lowest grade codebooks, and from then on transmitted his reports in PAK2 cipher, which Rochefort's team could read with ease. Their suspicions would most certainly have been aroused by Tokyo's consecutive requests (on December 4 and 5) for detailed ships in-harbor reports—and even more so by Kita's long reply on December 6, specifying the lack of antiaircraft balloons, the absence of torpedo net protection for the battleships, and the prophetic observation that "there is considerable opportunity left to take advantage of a surprise attack." This intelligence might also have made them take more heed of the local FBI reports of suspicious overseas telephone conversations (between a local dentist and a person in Japan), which could have referred to a weather report and the burning of papers by the consular staff.

These last-minute signals went unheeded, even though three intercepts were sent to Pearl Harbor in the first week of December—and this might have been considered unusual by the Pacific Fleet intelligence staff. The first, intercepted on November 29 from the Japanese consulate in Bangkok, was sent in connection with an invasion ruse designed to lure British troops across the border and provide justification for the Imperial Army to attack. It appears to have confirmed Kimmel's belief that the main theater of enemy operations was across the Pacific. He was anticipating no more than possible sabotage because, the day after the war alert received from the Chief of Naval Operations on November 27, Stark had relayed the Army warning signal that ordered a sabotage alert. On December 3, Kimmel received the most important warning he was to get after Stark's signal, that war was imminent: "Highly reliable information has been received that categoric and urgent instructions were sent yesterday to Japanese Consulates . . . burn and destroy ciphers." It was confirmed by another Magic intercept the next day—and so apparently it came as no surprise to the Navy to hear from the local FBI three days later that Japan's consul and his staff were furiously burning large quantities of paper.

The only other Magic report to be sent to Kimmel would later assume major significance because of the congressional hearings. This was the "winds execute" message, which was transmitted on November 19 in the J19 cipher. As this code had a low priority for translation, it was not sent out with the Magic intercepts until November 26. It established word codes for broadcasting, "in case of emergency (danger of cutting off our diplomatic relations and the cutting off of international communications)." There were actually two sets of word codes, but the first group, referring to weather, which were to be repeated twice during the forecasts in the Tokyo Radio shortwave broadcasts, were the ones that caused much excitement. HIGASHI NO KAZEAME—EAST WIND—RAIN—was to indicate that Japanese-American relations were in danger; KITA NO KAZE KUMORI—NORTH WIND CLOUDY—meant Russo-Japanese relations were threatened; and NISHI NO KAZE HARE—WEST WIND CLEAR—meant relations between Britain and Japan were in danger.

Translation of the "winds execute" instructions created great excitement in American intelligence because the receipt of any one of the three code forecasts was assumed to be an indication that war was imminent. The "kana" forecasts were distributed printed on cards and Japanese broadcasts were monitored round the clock. Teletype traffic into the naval intelligence centers from the listening posts soared with reports that one or other message had been received. The importance of the so-called "winds execute" messages is not so much in their intrinsic value as in *the* war warning—there were many others intercepted in the final week of Magic decodes before the Japanese attack—but in the issue that East Wind Rain became during the subsequent investigations. The dispute over whether or not a genuine message had been received and why it was not sent out to the Pacific commands revealed a deep division among the naval staff in Washington, exacerbated by the efforts of Rear Admiral

R. K. Turner's War Plans Division to restrict Captain T. S. Wilkinson's Office of Naval Intelligence to a purely collecting function. Astride the factions was Admiral Leigh Noyes, who as Director of Communications claimed that he had to do justice and cooperate with both points of view. "Terrible" Turner had been insisting, with the acquiescence of Stark, on his right to censor and control intelligence communications.

Admiral Noyes was responsible for failing to pass on to Admiral Kimmel the October 9 Army decode which revealed that the Japanese had ordered their Honolulu consulate to divide up the base when making detailed reports. This so-called "bomb plot message" was interpreted by Military Intelligence as evidence of sabotage preparations. But on December 3, it was Turner who insisted, with Stark's approval, on modifying the two-and-a-half page briefing memorandum that the Navy's Far Eastern expert Captain A. H. McCollum wanted sent to the Pacific Fleet Commander. The memo would put Kimmel completely in the picture as to what was going on with the negotiations and what to expect, but, as McCollum testified, the War Plans Division had "so amended the dispatch as to make it worthless." It was therefore never sent. But that same day Wilkinson was persuaded to send on the Magic evidence that the Japanese embassies and consulates had been given orders to destroy their codes. It was followed by a second warning, initiated by Safford, that deliberately mentioned "WASHINGTON ALSO DIRECTED TO DESTROY PURPLE." This caused Kimmel to ask in surprise "What is Purple?"

It is painfully apparent that the division in the upper reaches of the U.S. Navy in Washington increased as the crisis with Japan reached its climax. What was to become a *cause célèbre* of the Senate Hearings—the dispute over the East Wind Rain message—was at the center of a controversy which still rages on. From recently released documents it is interesting to note that the issue was being raised while the war was still going on and before the first full-scale investigations began.

The man at the center of the dispute was Commander Safford who began his long campaign to prove that the "winds execute" warning had indeed been received by sending a confidential letter on December 22, 1943, to Captain Alwyn Kramer, who was then at Pearl Harbor. Guardedly he indicated that he was "phrasing my questions very carefully, in the event that my letter might fall into unauthorized hands." Safford asked his former subordinate in Op 20 G to reply to a long string of questions about what messages he remembered seeing and who he showed them to on the eve of the Japanese attack. After a favorable response from "Kramersan," he followed up in January 1944, with another letter setting up a code-system for future communications between them. "I can see the hand of providence," he wrote congratulating Kramer on his recent appointment to the CINCPAC staff. He suggested that when a suitable opportunity presented itself "take Admiral Halsey into [your] confidence" and followed with a significant paragraph:

> Be prudent and patient. I am just beginning to get things line [sic] up on this end. No one in Opnav can be trusted. Premature action will only tip off the people who framed Adm. Kimmel and Gen. Short, and will also get Safford and Kramer in very serious trouble. Yet we must have the backing, the rank, and the prestige afforded by Adm. Halsey. Tell Halsey that I knew Adm. Kimmel was a scapegoat from the start, but I did not suspect that he was the victim of a frameup until about 15 November 1943, could not confirm it until 2 December 1943, and did not have absolute proof until about 18 Jan 1944. Capt. Safford has overwhelming proof of the guilt of Opnav and the Gen. Staff, plus a list of fifteen reliable witnesses.

Just what that "overwhelming proof" was he would never be able to exploit because Safford never managed to get the backing of powerful flag officers in order to fight his case through the various inquiries in which pressure was put on junior officers by those with a vested interest in protecting their reputations. But it is plain that he was convinced that what was later claimed to be a "false" weather report picked up by the Maryland listening station at 4:30 EST on the morning of December 4, 1941, in morse code and sent to Op 20 G by teletype a few minutes later included the "winds execute" "Higashi no kazeame." This was the East Wind Rain message that indicated war with the United States was imminent. He wrote Kramer that although it was "not sent in the manner prescribed" and subsequently caused confusion with the watch officer, he had been greeted that morning on arrival at his office with the words "Here it is!"

FACT OR FRAMEUP?

Kramer had certainly believed in 1941, that he had seen a "Japan British, Japan U.S." signal, but, by the time of the Senate hearings in 1946, he had revised his memory, only conceding that it had come in on the morning of December 7, after the news of Pearl Harbor. Notwithstanding, Safford remained unshaken in his conviction that he had, on the morning of the 4th or 5th, personally taken the East Wind Rain warning up to Admiral Noyes. He was supported by the testimony of Colonel William Friedman before Brigadier General W. Clarke, who presided over the Army's official investigation in 1945. Although Friedman was relying on what he had been told by Safford he was convinced "there was no question in his mind of the transmission of the Winds message." That some signal created a stir in Military Intelligence that morning was testified to by Friedman's evidence that Colonel Sadtler, his close friend for twenty years, had told him that he was in the office of General Sherman Miles, head of Military Intelligence, when Admiral Noyes telephoned the news that "It's in!"

The mystery deepens because, according to Friedman and others, when Colonel Rufus S. Bratton wanted to confirm the message's authenticity, Admiral Noyes was evasive and vague. As a result the warning "BREAK IN RELATIONS BETWEEN JAPAN AND THE UNITED STATES MAY BE EXPECTED WITH THE NEXT 24 OR 48 HOURS. TAKE ALL NECESSARY STEPS TO ENSURE THAT THERE WILL BE NO REPETITION OF PORT ARTHUR" was never sent by Bratton to General Short on Oahu. Although the Clarke inquiry found otherwise, testimony was given that all copies of the winds message received that morning—whether false or genuine—were destroyed on the express orders of General Marshall.

The controversy over whether or not a genuine "EAST WIND RAIN" signal *had* been picked up around December 4 became a major focus at the hearings. Both Admiral Kimmel and General Short gave testimony that suggested they would have stepped up their alerts had they received the "winds" message. They had apparently assumed, incorrectly, that it was *the* Japanese war warning. In fact, the "winds" codes were never intended, even by the Tokyo Foreign Ministry to be more than a preliminary alert and had, in any case, been superseded as far as American intelligence was concerned by the December 3 Magic intercept that directed Japanese embassies in North America and Britain to destroy their codes and Purple machines.

Nonetheless, the "winds" message assumes a significance not just because Kimmel claimed that his level of alert might have been raised had he received it, but because of the dispute within Naval Intelligence over whether or not it had actually been picked up. It is yet another element in the whole Pearl Harbor story that has added to the mystery—and which has recently been given a further twist by fresh testimony. This is in the form of testimony given to the National Security Agency in 1977 by Ralph T. Briggs, a retired Navy chief warrant officer. He was on duty at the Cheltenham, Maryland, radio listening post on December 4, 1941. He claims that he was the one who actually picked up the HIGASHI NO KAZE AME weather report and, aware of its importance, had it put on the teletype to Op 20 G in Washington "right away." He made out two carbon copies and a log sheet entry.

In 1946, at the time of the congressional investigation into Pearl Harbor, Safford, according to Briggs, contacted him after looking up the microfilm logs because he could find no record of the signal itself. As told to Briggs, Safford claimed that the watch officer at Op 20 G had at once taken the message to Kramer, and then both took it to Admiral Noyes, who telephoned its contents to Admiral Turner, Chief of Naval War Plans Division, and to Colonel Otis K. Sadtler, of Army Military Intelligence. He was also certain that it had been seen by the Chief of Naval Operations. Right after this, all copies of the signal apparently mysteriously disappeared. What makes the incident more significant is not only that Briggs was ordered *not* to testify in support of Safford at the hearings, but that in 1960, when he was officer in charge of World War II communications intelligence in the Navy archives, he hunted extensively through volumes of signals but could not locate the EAST WIND RAIN signal or any copies. However, in May 1960 he found his original signal log sheet of December 2, 1941, *dated two days earlier* than he maintained in his account, and against it is noted: "all transmissions intercepted by me between 0560 thru 1300 on the above date are missing from these files & . . . these intercepts contained the 'winds message.' "

There is therefore still no hard proof that such a message was ever received, but there is the testimony of other persons—the operator who is convinced that he received the signal, to suggest that yet another piece of the complex jigsaw puzzle of Pearl Harbor has still to be found. Even if the "winds" message had been passed on to Kimmel, it might not have prevented the catastrophe. But if it indeed was received and if the EAST WIND RAIN signal "went missing," it indicates the lengths to which the most senior naval officers in Washington might have been prepared to go to cover up what could be construed as a fatal omission in not passing on vital intelligence.

CRYING WOLF

If the disaster that befell the Pacific Fleet was contributed to by the failure of Naval Intelligence in Washington to pass on vital information, a large measure of the responsibility also rests with the local commanders for their failure to mount an effective alert. In their defense it can be seen that their level of response was conditioned to the succession of warnings they had received since June 1940 that Japan was about to attack. None of the alerts, including the one flashed out on November 27, had in any way indicated that Hawaii was under threat—in fact, by its specific listing of possible enemy strikes on the other side of the Pacific, it created a false sense of security. Not only was the last alert a case of "crying wolf" once too often, but Admiral Kimmel and General Short were told that the wolf was snapping at Thailand, Malaya, Guam, and the Philippines.

There was no reason to doubt the intelligence emanating from Washington. Since August 1941, the United States Pacific defense frontier had been moved westward 5,000 miles by the decision that reversed twenty years of strategic planning: the U.S. would defend the Philippines. Reinforcements had been streaming across the Pacific to General MacArthur and the air defense of Oahu was being sacrificed to protect the route out to Luzon. On November 28, the carrier *Enterprise* sailed for Wake, to be followed on December 5 by the *Lexington* bound for Midway, both on ferry missions to bolster the fighter strength of the island stepping stones so that the forty-eight B-17s waiting on the West Coast could be flown safely to the Philippines. Even before Marshall's concern that the B-17s might be attacked had been raised by Magic intercepts of Japanese attention to the route the bombers were taking, Admiral Kimmel had decided to send out more Marine P-40s. On the morning of December 7 it was, therefore, ironic that the imminent arrival of the first flight of B-17s should have caused the Army Headquarters at Fort Shafter to dismiss the reports of two excited radar operators that a large flight of aircraft was approaching Oahu. This was the last of many ignored warnings indicating Pearl Harbor was a prize target for enemy attack.

When the Japanese fleet code was changed on December 1 for the second time, Rochefort's intelligence report had warned: "The fact that service calls lasted only a month indicates an additional progressive step in preparing for active operations on a large scale." This in itself might have been an indication that the coming offensive could reach beyond the western Pacific area. But Commander Layton was unable to penetrate the Imperial Navy's fleet code and had to rely solely on traffic analysis, so he deduced that the nearest Japanese carrier was in the Marshalls. He assumed from the lack of *any* signal traffic that most of the Combined Fleet was in home waters, communicating by low-powered radio or at anchorages where it was linked to navy headquarters by land lines. If the carrier groups had been signaled by Tokyo and still maintained radio silence, he testified, his suspicions that they were at sea would have been immediately aroused—"the fact that they were never addressed, not even once, led me to the belief that they were in the same situation as the carrier divisions were in July 1941 when the Japanese had a task force go down with their ultimatum into French Indochina."

It is another irony of the events leading up to December 7, 1941, that the Pearl Harbor strike force steamed unseen through seas empty of American shipping because the October crisis had cleared the sea lanes of the northern Pacific; traffic to and from the Philippines and Guam had been re-routed to the *south* as a safety measure. That there were no aircraft sent out to patrol the northern approaches to Hawaii was the ultimate failure that made catastrophe inevitable. Two Pacific Fleet war games exercises had provided dramatic proof that the way to launch a successful strike against the United States' supposedly impregnable Pacific fortress was via its unguarded back door. Only nine months before Japan repeated the demonstration for real, the March 1941 report of the Naval Air Patrol Commander, Admiral Patrick Bellinger, and General F. L. Martin, commanding the Hawaiian Army Air Force, revealed that the route was still wide open. Their estimate emphasized the dangers of a dawn strike by enemy carriers and recommended a round-the-compass seaward patrol deep into the Pacific. Their scenario, which read like a duplicate of Admiral Yamamoto's Pearl Harbor attack plan, was again echoed by an August 1941 report from a group of air officers in Hawaii which General Short forwarded to General Arnold in Washington. It pointed out that the 35 B-17s then in the Hawaiian Islands were "entirely inadequate" and that at least 180 heavy bombers were needed. "The Army Air Force units are at present not charged with the reconnaissance mission for the defense of Oahu," their report stated, emphasizing the approach of a Japanese striking force of six carriers to within 300 miles and predicting: "The early morning attack is, therefore, the best plan of action open to the enemy."

The Navy was responsible, under its joint agreement with the Army, for long-range aerial reconnaissance. But it had been decided, because of the shortage of aircraft and the need for training the Philippine Air Force crews on the six remaining B-17s, that long-range air patrols would be sent out only if an attack seemed imminent. It is an indication of the relatively low level of the state of alert on Oahu that on the morning of December 7, Admiral Bellinger concluded that from the information at his disposal there was no need to carry out long-range reconnaissance. Even if he had done so, the chances are that there were too few Fortresses to carry out an effective patrol sweep around the compass that could have found the Japanese in time to forestall the attack.

THE MACARTHUR ENIGMA

The stripping of the Hawaiian Army Air Command of all but a half-dozen of its long-range bombers was yet another example of just how far the U.S. Pacific defense rested on the Philippines by December 1941. After the war, General MacArthur would maintain how inadequate this strategy proved when he recalled the final days before his confrontation with the might of Japan: "I prepared my meager forces, to counter as best I might, the attack that I knew was coming from the north, swiftly, fiercely and without warning."

This is in marked contrast to his bombastic report to the War Department of the tremendous potential of his Commonwealth Army which, earlier in 1941, had been one of the main factors in bringing about the reversal of twenty years of American strategic policy not to send reinforcements for a Philippine defense. By mid-November, MacArthur had half of all the U.S. heavy bombers and a sixth of the fighter strength. He was prodding Washington to speed up preparations for a strategic bombing offensive against the Japanese home islands and, even allowing for his "window dressing" to entice the British, his confidence was unbounded at the December 5 meeting with Admiral Sir Tom Phillips, who had flown to Manila from Singapore to discuss mutual strategy in the face of an impending Japanese assault.

"Nothing would please me better than if they would give me three months and then attack here," MacArthur maintained, outlining the accelerating pace at which reinforcements, aircraft, and tanks were arriving from the United States. Until then his plan was "in the nature of an improvisation," but he had "every confidence that we can defend this place" with a force which he put at 125,000 men. It is interesting to note that MacArthur himself commented on Washington's "sudden reverse of policy regarding the arming of the Philippines." Now he presented himself as a second Churchill—"I have three great defensive lines, the first is on the shore, the second is on the shore, the third is on the shore"—to emphasize his strategy. "We intend to fight to the destruction on the shore lines." With his 112 tanks, he believed, he had "nothing to fear at all" when it came to hurling a Japanese invasion force back into the waves, because their generals had "utterly failed" in the use of armor to win any "outstanding successes in their four years in China."

MacArthur also claimed that his propaganda had confused the Japanese, who would invade with inferior forces. "I don't believe he knows we have so completely built up," he assured the British, dismissing the press stories of poor morale in his forces. In fact, as both the general and the Japanese knew, the reports were only too accurate. MacArthur should have been aware from Magic intercepts that the local consulate had been accurately reporting the details of what limited build-up had taken place as the bombers and American troops landed. Naturally, MacArthur made much of his B-17s, which he called "the best in the world." They were his "ace unit" and what he termed "the finished product for operations in the case of necessity."

Admiral Phillips was evidently impressed. He reported that the British situation was much the same as the American, that with four more battleships and possibly a carrier expected early in the new year, the longer the Japanese attack was delayed the better. "Clearly, until you have a fleet you can't do much except act on the defensive and it is quite clear that to stick your head out where the enemy is with a very inferior force would be foolish," the admiral observed, just four days before he was to demonstrate the truth of his words. That Phillips was not a man for standing on the defensive is clear from the records of this conference, at which he was primarily concerned with arranging to base the prospective fleet (which he hoped ultimately to command) not at Singapore—"not much of a base when you think of offensive measures"—*but in Manila*. This met with both Hart's and MacArthur's approval, and it was agreed that the Philippine fighter defenses were more than adequate to protect a British fleet. "We should look on this as a base," Phillips declared enthusiastically, picturing Manila as a Far Eastern Scapa Flow from which the Royal Navy battleships would steam out to challenge the Japanese Fleet in the China Sea. Such flights of fancy were to be abruptly terminated next afternoon when RAF reports of a Japanese force in the Gulf of Siam sent Admiral Phillips flying back to Singapore "to be there when the war starts."

Considering how much emphasis MacArthur had placed on his "ace unit" of heavy bombers, it is little short of astonishing that he had allowed no reconnaissance to be made of the Japanese forces assembling in Taiwan. That had been the intention of the carefully worded war alert which he had received from Washington; and Japan had been sending her planes snooping over airfields where half the American heavy bomber force was based as of December 1. Two days later, there was another brazen intrusion over the coast. "They've got all they need now," observed Colonel Harold H. George, the commander of the Philippine Air Force interceptor squadrons, who had been forbidden to fire the first shot. "The next time they won't play. They'll come in without knocking!"

"Our Air Force in the Philippines, containing many antiquated models, were hardly more than a token force with insufficient equipment, incompleted airfields and inadequate maintenance. They were hopelessly outnumbered and never had a chance of winning. They were completly overwhelmed by the enemy's superior forces"—so General MacArthur maintained after the war, in an apologia for his humiliating defeat. Yet the contemporary record shows that he was presenting himself as another Churchill—and he certainly had better odds for success in meeting the Japanese air assault than the RAF had in the Battle of Britain. Half the enemy air strength based in Taiwan, the Army Air Group's eighty-one bombers and seventy-two short-range fighters, could not even operate south of Baguio, the Philippine summer capital over 100 miles north of Clark Field that was the principal American base. Moreover, the 86 Zero fighters which were to escort the 11th Navy Air Fleet's 108 bombers could only reach Manila by reducing engine revolutions; they also had no fuel reserve for aerial dogfights.

The Philippine Air Force fielded 107 P-40 "Warhawk" fighters, which, though not a match for the Zero in performance, certainly had the advantage, like the RAF during the Battle of Britain, of being able to operate over their own bases. They also had just enough range to fly to Taiwan and back to cover raiding operations by the thirty-five heavy bombers. In addition, MacArthur had sixty-eight older fighters and thirty-nine obsolescent bombers as back up. The Japanese knew, like the Germans in 1940, that they had to win air superiority before they could launch a successful invasion. An officer of the 11th Air Fleet is on record as saying that their greatest fear was that "the American planes would take refuge in the southern areas, making the campaign very difficult."

It is all the more astonishing, given the confidence of both General MacArthur and the War Department, that airpower was to be the backbone of the Philippines' defense, to see how easily the Japanese smashed more than half the American aircraft on the ground during their first attack. There had been over *nine* hours warning since the Pearl Harbor attack, and these were wasted, apparently because MacArthur was in a state of shock that temporarily paralyzed his command. The evidence shows that General Brereton repeatedly tried to get permission to send the B-17s to raid the enemy airfields in the south of Taiwan—where, as fate would have it, the Japanese planes were fogbound and wide open to attack. Lack of reconnaissance was the excuse given at the time by General Sutherland, MacArthur's overbearing Chief of Staff, who supposedly refused to let even a photo-mission be sent off first thing on that fateful morning. Lack of target reconnaissance was the main reason MacArthur gave for his reluctance to send off his bombers that morning. Yet this hardly squares with both Marshall's November 27 instruction to begin overflying Japanese territory and a Magic intercept of December 3 from Tokyo to Washington protesting that "on 20th last month a U.S. plane made a reconnaissance flight over Garaspi in southern Formosa." Had Brereton been able to get through to his Commander in Chief earlier, he might have persuaded MacArthur to change his mind about letting the Japanese strike the first blow—after all, he had been given explicit orders by Marshall that such a stance must not prejudice the Philippine defense. In any event, the least that such a review of options might have produced was an evacuation of the remaining heavy bombers to Mindanao.

Yet with all the inevitability of a Greek tragedy, the paralysis and indecision that gripped the Philippine command caused not just the bombers but also the fighters to be caught on the ground and become the sacrificial victims of the Japanese attack at midday. "If I had been caught with my planes on the ground," observed one high-ranking American general after the war, "I could never again have looked my fellow officers squarely in the eye." A navigator of the Philippine Air Force, Lieutenant Edgar D. Whitcomb, put it more bluntly: "Our generals and leaders committed one of the greatest errors possible to military men—that of letting themselves be taken by surprise."

UNANSWERED QUESTIONS

On the evening of December 7, Edward R. Murrow kept a supper invitation with the President. "Maybe you think it didn't surprise us?" a weary Roosevelt remarked cryptically in the small hours of the next day. The broadcaster would recall how Roosevelt's anger still boiled that so many American planes had been destroyed "on the ground, by God, on the ground!" He foresaw that the destruction of so much of the Philippine Air Force presaged the loss of the islands. America's deterrent had been exposed as an empty threat that had been crushed by Japan's first blow. The fall of the Philippines would prove to be a catastrophe of incalculably greater magnitude than Pearl Harbor—the mortal blow to the strategic defense of the Far East. Yet there was never any inquiry to establish why the battle for the Philippines had effectively been lost on the first day of the Pacific War.

If the swift disaster that had overtaken the Philippines was caused by a local command failure as much as by strategic miscalculation in Washington, the Pacific Fleet battleships had been lost through an over-complacent command, which had received less than adequate intelligence on the Japanese and put on the alert too many times. Since August 1941, the focus of U.S. military attention and reinforcements had shifted to the Philippines. This had weakened the Hawaiian air defenses but, by a paradox of fate, was to save the U.S. Navy's two carriers, which subsequently played an indispensable role in holding the American defense line in the Pacific.

The Japanese were able to make their surprise attack on Pearl Harbor because of a breakdown in communications within the service organizations in Washington and the U.S. failure to transmit the complete intelligence situation to the Hawaiian command. On November 28, after Admiral Stark had radioed the Pacific Fleet to "be prepared" to carry out its offensive move to the Marshalls in the event of hostilities, he assumed that Admiral Kimmel would see from Magic intercepts how war was becoming inevitable and would act on his initiative. "Nobody in ONI, nobody in G-2 knew that any major element of the Fleet was in Pearl Harbor on Sunday morning of 7th December. We had all thought they had gone to sea . . . because that was part of the war plan and they had been given a war warning," was how Colonel Rufus S. Bratton of U.S. Army Intelligence testified to the general opinion in the service departments in Washington. Even had he known that the fleet was still in Pearl Harbor, the head of Naval Intelligence, Captain T. S. Wilkinson, believed that "an approaching force would be detected before it could get into attack range."

If the service Chiefs made the tragic mistake of assuming that the Pacific

Fleet was at a high state of readiness and could sortie in the event that a Japanese strike force was discovered closing on Oahu; then it follows that the President must also have been of the same opinion. Even if Roosevelt had been provided, as there is evidence to suggest, with twelve days' advance warning that Japan was going to war, it is impossible to accept that he would knowingly have conspired in the loss of 2,353 American lives, 19 ships, and 150 aircraft to ensure that the nation entered the war united in moral outrage. It is even less conceivable that Marshall and Stark would have countenanced such a sacrifice. Moreover, the continued withdrawal of aircraft from Hawaiian defense to the Philippines is another indication that, whatever the prior warning was, it did not include details of the strike against Pearl Harbor.

The most obvious pointers to the Pacific Fleet as a target for Japan's opening attacks lay locked in the Magic intercepts of the communications to and from their Honolulu consulate—and fate decreed that these were not decoded until the afternoon of December 7. Had Washington had firm evidence that an attack on Pearl Harbor was imminent, it may be assumed that a warning would have been passed on at once to the Hawaiian commanders. This is evident from Marshall; and others' reactions to the 1 P.M. deadline for the delivery of the final Japanese reply to the State Department. It had been received and decoded in Washington shortly after 5 A.M. on the fateful day; but because the Chief of Staff was out on a longer than usual Sunday morning horseback ride, he could not take any action until he arrived at his office around eleven thirty. A final warning was sent out to the Pacific commands, but fate again intervened to prevent it reaching Pearl Harbor in time because Marshall had casually rejected the Chief of Naval Operations' offer to transmit it; Marshall had *not* been informed that Army communications to Fort Shafter were temporarily out of commission.

This unfortunate chain of fortuitous events, as well as the general's extended absence from his desk that critical morning, have frequently been made important issues in the controversy that still rages about how the catastrophe at Pearl Harbor came about. The much more intriguing questions still to be answered concern such issues as: Why did the FBI not take more notice of the Popov report of August 1941? What became of the confidential book of military plans that Kilsoo Haan, the front man for a Korean espionage group, stole from Japanese naval officers staying in a Los Angeles hotel? And who placed the cryptic December 7 warning in the November 26 issue of *The New Yorker* magazine. "Achtung, Warning, Alerte!" headlined a drawing of a bunker with figures playing a dice game called the Deadly Double under a double-headed German Eagle emblem. "We hope you'll never have to spend a long winter's night in an air raid shelter, but we were just thinking . . . it's only common sense to be prepared" ran the strange copy on page eighty-six. Yet even more intriguing is the small box ad on page 100 showing two dice, with a XX and the numbers on other faces arranged so that they appear to spell out "0" hour for a "double cross" on the 7th day of the 12th month at the 5th hour out of 24. After the Pearl Harbor attack the FBI investigated this curious coincidence. They discovered that the suspicious advertisements for the non-existent game made by a Monarch Trading Company (a dummy corporation) had been placed by a white caucasian male who had delivered the printing plates and paid in cash. Still more curious was the fact that the man they identified as the suspect apparently met a sudden death a few weeks later under circumstances that were typical of the way British secret agents had disposed of Nazi operatives in New York. Was *The New Yorker* warning genuine and were the Germans responsible for trying to raise the alarm? The fascination of the Pearl Harbor story lies in questions like these that still remain to be answered.

Intriguing pieces of evidence continue to surface that suggest that Washington knew—or ought to have known—of the impending attack in the mid-Pacific. A recently released diary of the Dutch army commander in Java indicates that a Japanese army signal was intercepted which apparently revealed that Hawaii, as well as Malaya and the Philippines, was a target for Japan's first strike. But there is no hard evidence that the warning was indeed specific enough or that it reached the President and his military chiefs five days before Pearl Harbor.

The same reservations must apply to revived speculation regarding the mysterious signals picked up by the Matson lines S.S. *Lurline* during her passage in the first days of December to Honolulu from San Francisco. The affair was debated at the Congressional Hearings in 1946 and has been given additional credibility by the recent testimony of a former naval radio operator who claims that bearings made at the time by the U.S. Navy listening posts on the West Coast put the source of the signals northwest of Oahu. Subsequently it appears the records were destroyed as part of the cover-up by senior naval staff in Washington who did not want to be accused of ignoring, what seems with hindsight, to be very clear warnings of the attack on Pearl Harbor. Yet even if bearings were taken that indicated that a Japanese vessel was in the mid-Pacific within a thousand miles of Hawaii, the Americans had not broken the naval codes. Thus, there could have been no way of telling whether the radio messages emanated from a liner, a scouting submarine or a striking force. Before December 7, 1941 it would certainly not have been taken as an indication of the presence of "the missing carriers" because U.S. naval intelligence did not believe the Japanese carriers were missing. They had been duped by the transfer of the carriers' call signs to destroyers into believing that the Combined Fleet's carrier force was in the waters of the Western Pacific.

Whether the British were similarly taken in is perhaps a more important question to be asked in the light of new evidence provided in the hitherto secret American archives. None of Britain's intercepted Japanese radio messages has yet been released—yet the U.S. records show that from April 1941 the Purple decoding machine at Bletchley Park was spewing out decrypted diplomatic traffic. We still do not know how Britain's eaves-dropping compared with Washington's Magic because none of it has been released. Still more significant are the hints given in the official history of British wartime intelligence which states that from September 1939 the Royal Navy cryptanalysts had been able to penetrate Japan's Fleet cypher—the operational code traffic that defied the Americans until after Pearl Harbor. Moreover, we know that not only was there a massive British signals intelligence operation mounted in Singapore, but the Far Eastern Combined Bureau of the three services was continuously evaluat-ing Japan's war preparations.

If the British had indeed been reading the Japanese Fleet codes for two years, they might have accumulated the necessary interpretative skills, and therefore not have been blacked-out for long by the two cypher changes that Tokyo ordered in November. Also we now have a number of the Combined Fleet orders sent out in the first week of December that the U.S. Navy captured during the war. If the British had been reading these, together with the ships-in-harbor reports from Honolulu that were being relayed out to the Strike Force from Tokyo, it must have been apparent in London that a Japanese attack force was heading for Hawaii on December 5 even as the main weight of the assault uncoiled, as anticipated, against Malaya and the Philippines.

Had these suspicions been well-founded, then it is unlikely that Churchill would not have been informed. Yet there is no evidence to sug-gest that in the final days before Pearl Harbor was attacked the Prime Minister passed a warning to Roosevelt. It requires a callous reading of the President's character to suggest that he would not have acted on such intelligence. At the very least he would have ensured an alert was passed to Hawaii to begin round-the-compass air patrols deep into the Pacific.

If Churchill was indeed forewarned, it might explain his extreme touch-iness over the subject of the Pearl Harbor attack and his repeated denials that Britain was privvy to Japan's diplomatic communications. It would also explain the continued reluctance of the British government to release so far any of their Japanese Ultra intelligence files—and why key reports dealing with Japan in the Prime Minister's records have been removed and remain closed for seventy-five years.

It is not inconceivable that the final secret of Pearl Harbor still remains locked in the secret British records. The fascination of the subject is that for every answer new questions arise. One of the most curious is raised by recent testimony of a former U.S. Navy intelligence officer which was released only last year.

Captain George W. Linn, a former officer on the wartime staff of Naval Intelligence, added yet another twist to the enigma with the testimony provided thirty-nine years later of a most curious request that was made to the Op 20 G staff only a matter of hours after the Japanese planes had struck:

> Early in the afternoon GZ came into the watch office and motioned me to one side. I was floored when he asked if we could encrypt a message in the Purple System for transmission. This was a requirement I had never considered and [I] had to do some fast thinking before saying we could, but that it would be a very slow process. Next, I can remember saying something along the following lines (probably needlessly) "I hope that whatever this message is supposed to accomplish is of the highest importance. Ultimately the Japanese will discover our ruse and certainly will re-evaluate all of their crypto-systems, including military. Years of work will go down the drain and we may not be reading Japanese traffic for months or years." GZ nodded and left, saying he would let me know. Although I cannot recall it, he must have returned sometime and said it was off. I sensed it was not GZ's idea; it came from higher up. I did not question GZ about it then or later. I doubt that he would have told me—I had no need to know.

To learn of Lieutenant-Commander Kramer's curious request, which "came from higher up," is as startling today as it must have been for Linn. What was the purpose of sending a signal to the Japanese *after* war had broken out—could it have been an attempt to cover up the intelligence record? We may never know, since the man who made the request is now dead. But, had the ploy been tried and the enemy discovered the extent to which the Americans had penetrated their most secret channels of communication, a timely revision of their codes might have deprived the U.S. Navy of the intelligence that made their victory at Midway possible—and the whole course of the Pacifice War might have been altered.

APPENDIX A

THE RAID ON PEARL HARBOR December 7, 1941

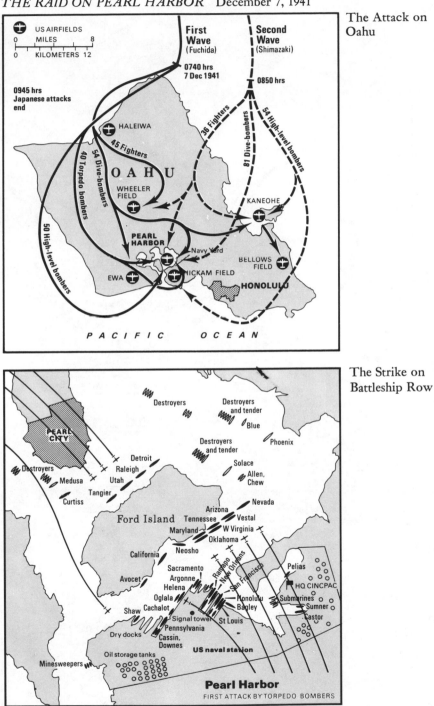

The Attack on Oahu

The Strike on Battleship Row

JAPAN INVADES THE PHILIPPINES December, 1941–May, 1942

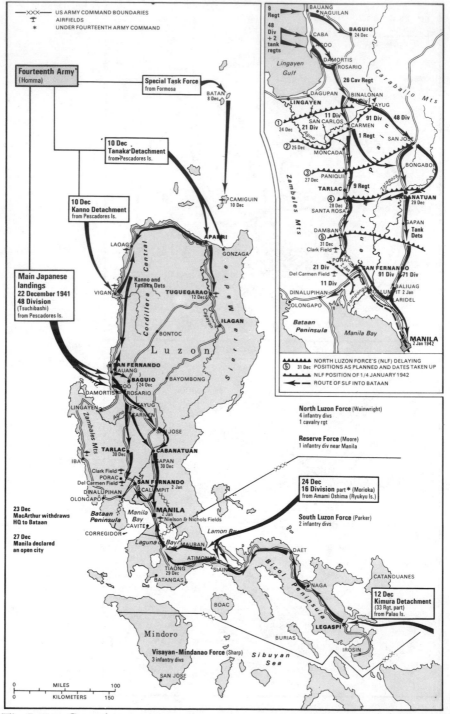

Legend:
- ——×××—— US ARMY COMMAND BOUNDARIES
- ✈ AIRFIELDS
- ✱ UNDER FOURTEENTH ARMY COMMAND

Fourteenth Army * (Homma)

Special Task Force from Formosa · BATAN 8 Dec.

10 Dec Tanaka Detachment from Pescadores Is.

10 Dec Kanno Detachment from Pescadores Is.

Main Japanese landings 22 December 1941 48 Division (Tsuchibashi) from Pescadores Is.

CAMIGUIN 10 Dec

LAOAG · APARRI · GONZAGA

Kanno and Tanaka Dets · VIGAN · TUGUEGARAO 12 Dec · ILAGAN

Cordillera Central · BONTOC · Luzon · Sierra Madre · Cagayan

SAN FERNANDO · SAUANG · BAGUIO 24 Dec · BAYOMBONG

DAMORTIS · ROSARIO · CABA · AGOO · BAYOMBONG

LINGAYEN · AGNO · CAYUG · CARMEN · SAN JOSE

Zambales Mts · IBA · TARLAC 30 Dec · CABANATUAN · GAPAN 30 Dec

Clark Field · PORAC · Del Carmen Field · SAN FERNANDO 2 Jan · CALUMPIT

DINALUPIHAN · OLONGAPO

23 Dec MacArthur withdraws HQ to Bataan

27 Dec Manila declared an open city

Bataan Peninsula · CORREGIDOR · Manila Bay · CAVITE · MANILA 2 Jan · Nielson & Nichols Fields

Laguna de Bay · MAUBAN · Lamon Bay · DAET

ATIMONAN · SIAIN · Bicol Peninsula · NAGA · CATANDUANES

TIAONG 29 Dec · BATANGAS · BOAC · BURIAS · IROSIN · LEGASPI

12 Dec Kimura Detachment (33 Rgt. part) from Palau Is.

Mindoro · Sibuyan Sea

Visayan-Mindanao Force (Sharp) 3 infantry divs · SAN JOSE

Inset map (upper right):

9 Regt · BAUANG · NAGUILAN · BAGUIO 24 Dec

48 Div + 2 tank regts · CABA · AGOO · DAMORTIS · ROSARIO

Lingayen Gulf · 26 Cav Regt · Caraballo Mts

DAGUPAN · BINALONAN · LINGAYEN · 1 Div · AYUG

① 24 Dec · 11 Div · SAN CARLOS · 91 Div · 48 Div

② 25 Dec · 21 Div · CARMEN · 1 Regt · SAN JOSE

Agno · MONCADA · BONGABON

③ 27 Dec · PANIQUI · 9 Regt · CABANATUAN 29 Dec · TARLAC

④ 28 Dec · SANTA ROSA · GAPAN Tank Dets

⑤ 31 Dec · DAMBAN · Clark Field · PORAC · SAN FERNANDO · 91 Div · 71 Div

21 Div · Del Carmen Field · 11 Div · BALIUAG · CALUMPIT 2 Jan · MARIDEL

DINALUPIHAN · Pampanga · OLONGAPO

Bataan Peninsula · Manila Bay · MANILA 2 Jan 1942

▲▲▲▲ NORTH LUZON FORCE'S (NLF) DELAYING
⑤ 31 Dec POSITIONS AS PLANNED AND DATES TAKEN UP
— · — NLF POSITION OF 1/4 JANUARY 1942
←— ROUTE OF SLF INTO BATAAN

North Luzon Force (Wainwright) 4 infantry divs 1 cavalry rgt

Reserve Force (Moore) 1 infantry div near Manila

24 Dec 16 Division part ✱ (Morioka) from Amami Oshima (Ryukyu Is.)

South Luzon Force (Parker) 2 infantry divs

Scale:
MILES 0 — 100
KILOMETERS 0 — 150

The Luzon Campaign

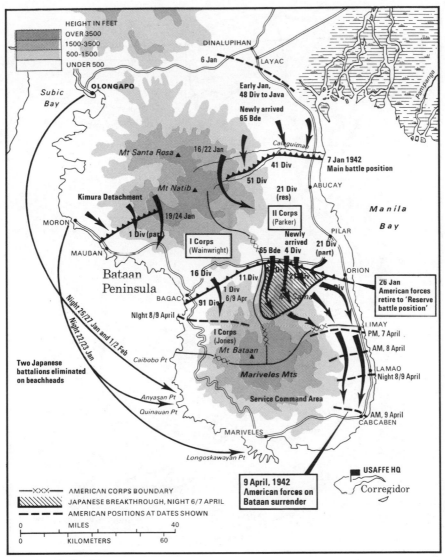

The Battle for Bataan

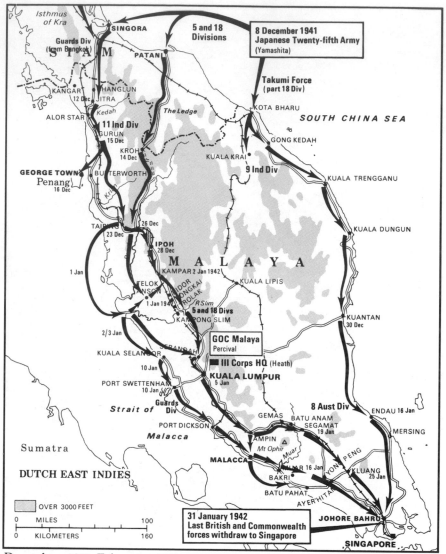

December, 1941–February, 1942

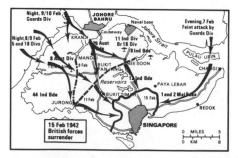

THE JAPANESE CONQUEST OF BURMA February–May, 1942

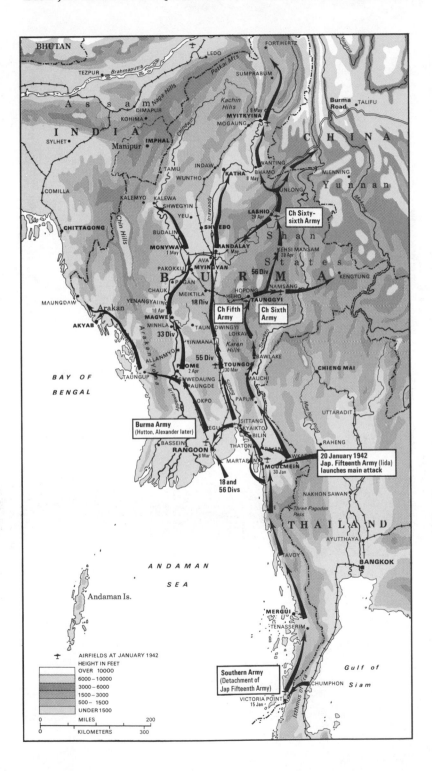

THE BATTLE OF THE CORAL SEA   May 3–7, 1942

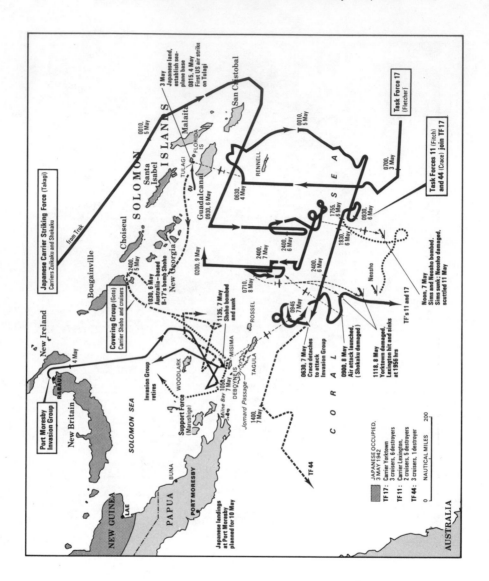

THE BATTLE OF MIDWAY   June 3–5, 1942

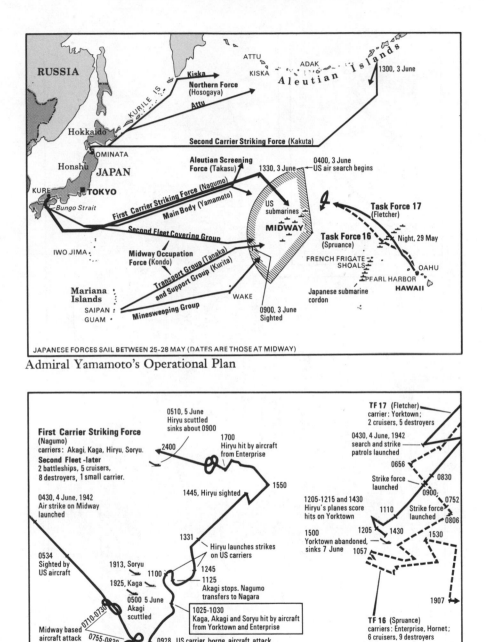

Admiral Yamamoto's Operational Plan

The U.S. Pacific Fleet's Victory

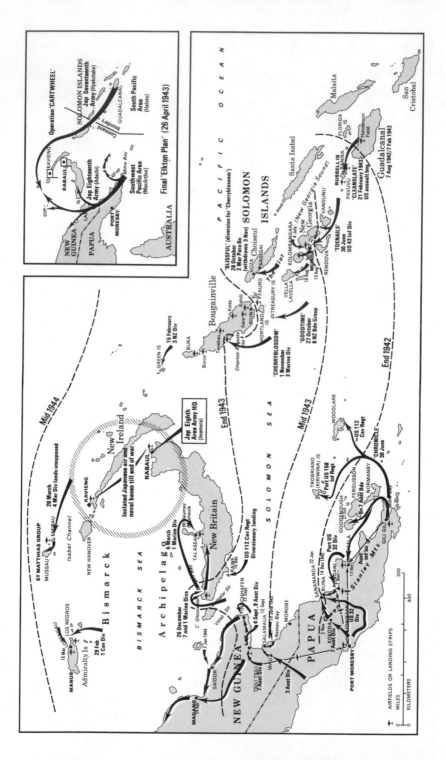

THE STRUGGLE FOR GUADALCANAL   August, 1942–January, 1943

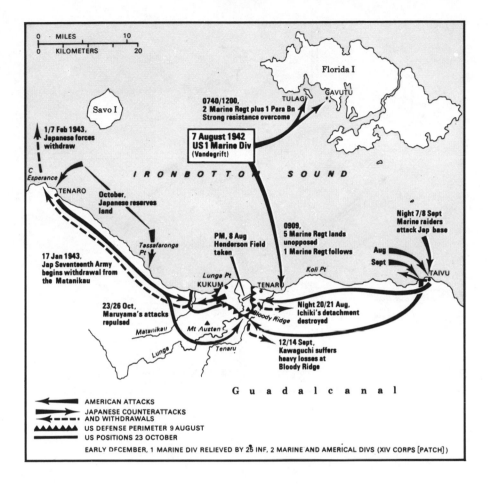

MILES 0 — 10
KILOMETERS 0 — 20

Florida I

GAVUTU
TULAGI

0740/1200,
2 Marine Regt plus 1 Para Bn
Strong resistance overcome

Savo I

7 August 1942
US 1 Marine Div
(Vandegrift)

1/7 Feb 1943.
Japanese forces
withdraw

C
Esperance   I R O N B O T T O M   S O U N D

TENARO

October,
Japanese reserves
land

Night 7/8 Sept
Marine raiders
attack Jap base

0909,
5 Marine Regt lands
unopposed
1 Marine Regt follows

PM, 8 Aug
Henderson Field
taken

Aug
Sept

17 Jan 1943.
Jap Seventeenth Army
begins withdrawal from
the Matanikau

Tassafaronga
Pt

Koli Pt

TAIVU

Lunga Pt
KUKUM

TENARU

23/26 Oct,
Maruyama's attacks
repulsed

Bloody Ridge

Night 20/21 Aug,
Ichiki's detachment
destroyed

Matanikau   Mt Austen

Lunga   Tenaru

12/14 Sept,
Kawaguchi suffers
heavy losses at
Bloody Ridge

G u a d a l c a n a l

◄——— AMERICAN ATTACKS
►——— JAPANESE COUNTERATTACKS
- - - ► AND WITHDRAWALS
▲▲▲▲▲ US DEFENSE PERIMETER 9 AUGUST
———— US POSITIONS 23 OCTOBER

EARLY DECEMBER, 1 MARINE DIV RELIEVED BY 25 INF, 2 MARINE AND AMERICAL DIVS (XIV CORPS [PATCH])

NEW GUINEA CAMPAIGNS 1943-1944

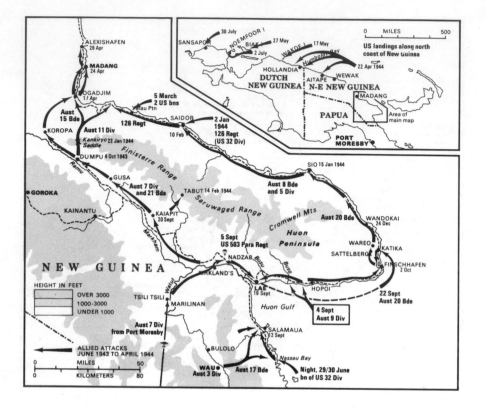

ALEXISHAFEN
26 Apr

MADANG
24 Apr

OGADJIM
1 Apr

5 March
2 US bns
Yalau Ptn

Aust
15 Bde

Aust 11 Div

126 Regt

SAIDOR

2 Jan
1944
126 Regt
(US 32 Div)

KOROPA

Kankiryo 22 Jan 1944
Saddle

10 Feb

DUMPU 4 Oct 1943

Finisterre Range

Ramu

GUSA

Aust 7 Div
and 21 Bde

TABUT 14 Feb 1944

SIO 15 Jan 1944

Aust 8 Bde
and 5 Div

GOROKA

KAINANTU

Saruwaged Range

KAIAPIT
20 Sept

Cromwell Mts

WANDOKAI
24 Dec

Aust 20 Bde

Markham

5 Sept
US 503 Para Regt

Huon
Peninsula

WAREO

SATTELBERG

KATIKA

NEW GUINEA

NADZAB

Busu

Buso

FINSCHHAFEN
2 Oct

HEIGHT IN FEET

OVER 3000
1000-3000
UNDER 1000

KIRKLAND'S

Watut

LAE
16 Sept

HOPOI

22 Sept
Aust 20 Bde

TSILI TSILI

MARILINAN

Huon Gulf

4 Sept
Aust 9 Div

ALLIED ATTACKS
JUNE 1943 TO APRIL 1944

Aust 7 Div
from Port Moresby

SALAMAUA
12 Sept

MILES 50

BULOLO

Nassau Bay

KILOMETERS 80

WAU
Aust 3 Div

Aust 17 Bde

Night, 29/30 June
bn of US 32 Div

30 July

SANSAPOR

NOEMFOOR I

2 July

BIAK 27 May

WAKDE I 17 May

Humboldt Bay

US landings along north
coast of New Guinea

MILES 500

22 Apr 1944

HOLLANDIA

AITAPE

WEWAK

**DUTCH
NEW GUINEA**

N-E NEW GUINEA

MADANG

PAPUA

Area of
main map

**PORT
MORESBY**

THE BATTLE OF THE PHILIPPINE SEA   June 13–16, 1944

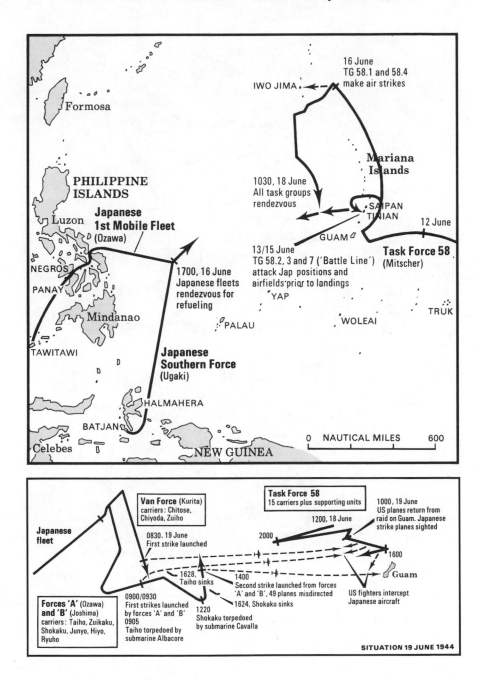

SITUATION 19 JUNE 1944

THE ALLIED ADVANCE IN BURMA 1944–1945

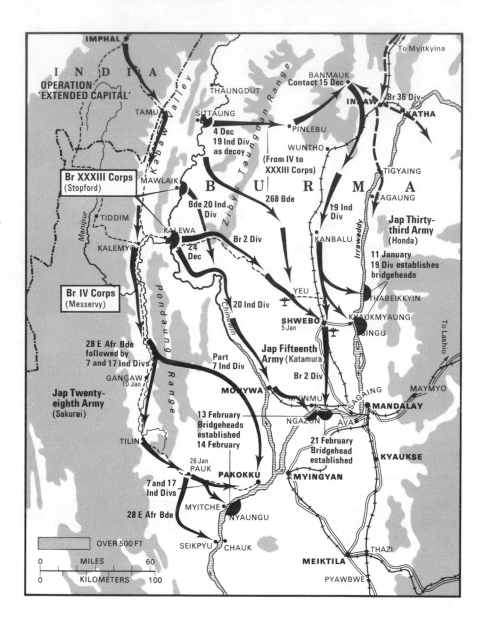

IMPHAL

I N D I A

OPERATION 'EXTENDED CAPITAL'

To Myitkyina

BANMAUK
Contact 15 Dec ●

Br 36 Div

THAUNGDUT

INDAW ● KATHA

Kabaw Valley

TAMU

SITTAUNG

PINLEBU

4 Dec
19 Ind Div
as decoy

WUNTHO

Ziby Taungdan Range

(From IV to
XXXIII Corps)

TIGYAING

Br XXXIII Corps
(Stopford)

MAWLAIK

B U R M A

TAGAUNG

Bde 20 Ind
Div

268 Bde

↑9 Ind
Div

**Jap Thirty-
third Army**
(Honda)

Manipur

TIDDIM

Chindwin

KALEWA

Br 2 Div

KANBALU

Irrawaddy

11 January
19 Div establishes
bridgeheads

KALEMYO

24
Dec

YEU

Br IV Corps
(Messervy)

Pondaung Range

20 Ind Div

THABEIKKYIN

SHWEBO
5 Jan

KYAUKMYAUNG

SINGU

28 E Afr Bde
followed by
7 and 17 Ind Divs

Part
7 Ind Div

**Jap Fifteenth
Army** (Katamura

Br 2 Div

To Lashio

GANGAW
10 Jan

**Jap Twenty-
eighth Army**
(Sakurai)

MONYWA

MYINMU

SAGAING

MAYMYO

MANDALAY

TILIN

13 February
Bridgeheads
established
14 February

NGAZUN

AVA

21 February
Bridgehead
established

KYAUKSE

26 Jan
PAUK

7 and 17
Ind Divs

PAKOKKU

MYINGYAN

28 E Afr Bde

MYITCHE

NYAUNGU

OVER 500 FT

SEIKPYU CHAUK

THAZI

MEIKTILA

0   MILES   60

PYAWBWE

0   KILOMETERS   100

OPERATIONS IN CHINA 1937–1945

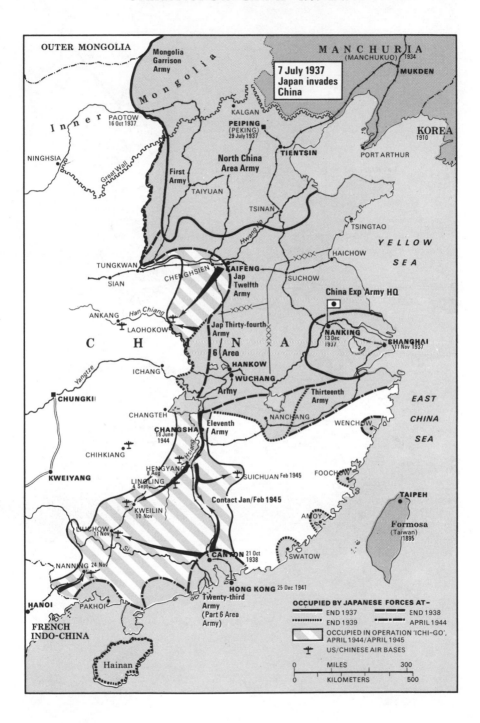

OUTER MONGOLIA

Mongolia Garrison Army

MANCHURIA (MANCHUKUO) 1934

7 July 1937 Japan invades China

MUKDEN

Inner Mongolia

KALGAN

PAOTOW 16 Oct 1937

PEIPING (PEKING) 29 July 1937

KOREA 1910

PORT ARTHUR

NINGHSIA

Great Wall

TIENTSIN

First Army

North China Area Army

TAIYUAN

Hwang Ho

TSINAN

TSINGTAO

YELLOW SEA

HAICHOW

TUNGKWAN

CHENGHSIEN

KAIFENG

Jap Twelfth Army

SUCHOW

SIAN

Han Chiang

ANKANG

LAOHOKOW

Jap Thirty-fourth Army

China Exp Army HQ

C H   N   A

6 Area

NANKING 13 Dec 1937

SHANGHAI 11 Nov 1937

Yangtze

ICHANG

HANKOW

WUCHANG

Army

Thirteenth Army

EAST CHINA SEA

CHUNGKI

CHANGTEH

NANCHANG

WENCHOW

CHANGSHA 18 June 1944

Eleventh Army

CHIHKIANG

KWEIYANG

HENGYANG 8 Aug

SUICHUAN Feb 1945

FOOCHOW

LINGLING 4 Sept

TAIPEH

KWEILIN 10 Nov

Contact Jan/Feb 1945

AMOY

Formosa (Taiwan) 1895

LIUCHOW 11 Nov

Si

CANTON 21 Oct 1938

SWATOW

NANNING 24 Nov

Twenty-third Army (Part 6 Area Army)

HONG KONG 25 Dec 1941

HANOI

PAKHOI

FRENCH INDO-CHINA

Hainan

OCCUPIED BY JAPANESE FORCES AT–

———— END 1937 — ·· — END 1938

·········· END 1939 — · — APRIL 1944

OCCUPIED IN OPERATION 'ICHI-GO', APRIL 1944/APRIL 1945

✈ US/CHINESE AIR BASES

0   MILES   300

0   KILOMETERS   500

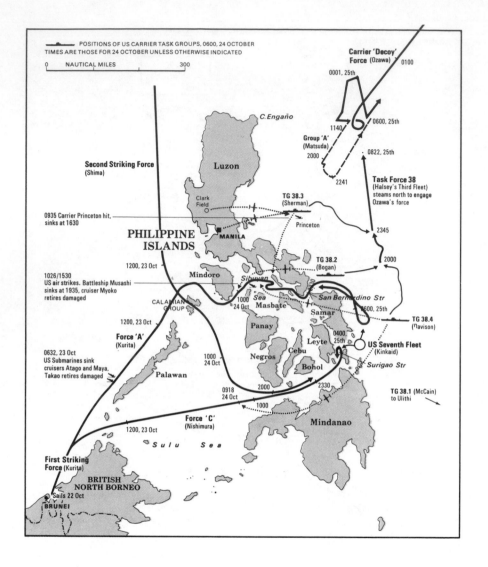

U.S. FORCES INVADE LEYTE October–December, 1944

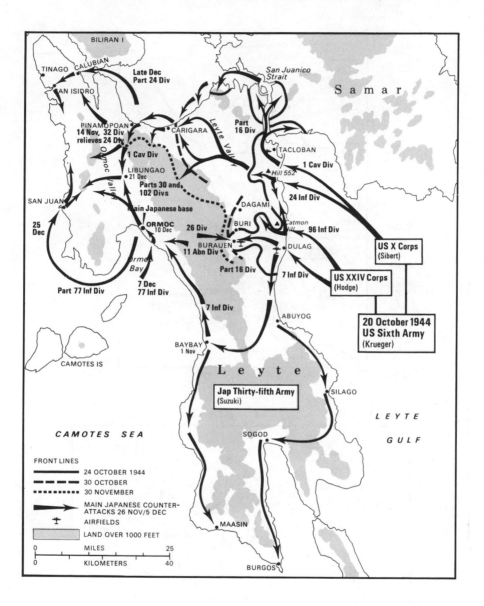

BILIRAN I

TINAGO CALUBIAN

SAN ISIDRO

Late Dec
Part 24 Div

San Juanico
Strait

S a m a r

PINAMOPOAN
14 Nov, 32 Div
relieves 24 Div

CARIGARA

Part
16 Div

Leyte Valley

1 Cav Div

TACLOBAN

1 Cav Div

Hill 552

LIBUNGAO
• 21 Dec

Parts 30 and
102 Divs

Main Japanese base

24 Inf Div

DAGAMI

SAN JUAN

25
Dec

ORMOC
10 Dec

26 Div

BURI

Catmon
Hill

96 Inf Div

Ormoc Valley

BURAUEN
11 Abn Div

DULAG

US X Corps
(Sibert)

Ormoc
Bay

Part 16 Div

7 Inf Div

US XXIV Corps
(Hodge)

Part 77 Inf Div

7 Dec
77 Inf Div

7 Inf Div

ABUYOG

20 October 1944
US Sixth Army
(Krueger)

BAYBAY
1 Nov

CAMOTES IS

L e y t e

SILAGO

Jap Thirty-fifth Army
(Suzuki)

L E Y T E

G U L F

CAMOTES SEA

SOGOD

MAASIN

BURGOS

FRONT LINES

———————— 24 OCTOBER 1944
– – – – – – – 30 OCTOBER
• • • • • • • • 30 NOVEMBER

➤ MAIN JAPANESE COUNTER-
ATTACKS 26 NOV/5 DEC
✈ AIRFIELDS
▨ LAND OVER 1000 FEET

0 _____ MILES _____ 25
0 _____ KILOMETERS _____ 40

THE STRUGGLE FOR OKINAWA April–June, 1945

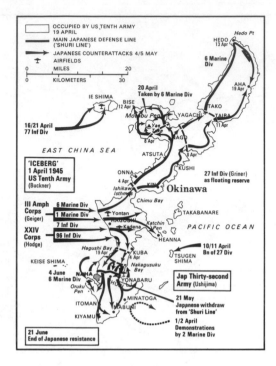

SECURING THE PHILIPPINES February–June, 1945

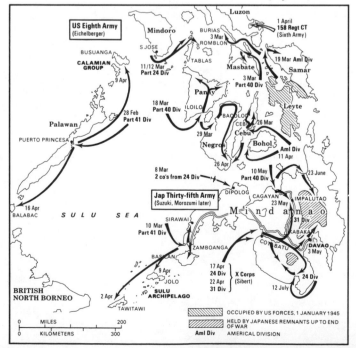

APPENDIX B

SELECTED STATISTICAL INFORMATION   Sources: Official Histories

1. *TOTAL ARMED FORCES OF COMBATANT POWERS AND CASUALTY RATES*

	Peak Services Strength	Casualties (Dead and Wounded) World Wide	Pacific Casualties (As Percentage of Total)
United States	12,364,000	1,073,000	27.6%
Britain	4,683,000	755,000	11.9%
India	2,150,000	100,000	84.6%
Australia and New Zealand	837,000	101,000	29.7%
China	5,000,000	3,086,000	100%
Japan	6,095,000	1,435,000	100%

2. *JAPANESE BOMBING RAID CASUALTIES*   *Official Estimates*

Tokyo March 9–10, 1945 (Incendiary Bombs)	83,973
Hiroshima August 6, 1945 (Atomic Bomb)	70,000
Nagasaki August 8, 1945 (Atomic Bomb)	20,000

3. *MAJOR WARSHIP LOSSES IN THE PACIFIC THEATER 1941–1945*

U.S. Navy: 2 Battleships; 5 Aircraft Carriers; 6 Escort Carriers; 10 Cruisers.
Royal Navy, Commonwealth and Dutch Navies: 1 Battleship; 1 Battlecruiser; 1 Aircraft Carrier; 6 Cruisers.
Japanese Navy: 10 Battleships; 15 Aircraft Carriers; 5 Escort Carriers; 36 Cruisers.

4. *JAPANESE MERCHANT MARINE*

Ships sunk by Allied action: 2,346—totaling 8,618,109 tons

5. *COMPARATIVE DIVISIONAL STRENGTH OF GROUND FORCES*

U.S. Army Infantry Division = 14,000 men (Fighting and support personnel)
U.S. Marine Division = 17,000 men (Fighting and support personnel)
British Infantry Division = 18,000 men (Fighting and support personnel)
Chinese Infantry Division = 12,000 men (Strength varied widely)
Japanese Infantry Division = 18,000 men (Fighting and support personnel)

6. COMPARISON PERFORMANCE OF PRINCIPAL COMBAT AIRCRAFT TYPES IN PACIFIC

	In Service	Speed (mph)	Ceiling (feet)	Range (miles)	Armament
a. Fighters					
Mitsubishi Zero-Sen "Zeke" or "Zero"	1941	360	39,370	1,000	3 x 13.2mm cannon
F4F "Wildcat"	1941	318	35,000	900	4 x .50 cal
F4U "Corsair"	1942	415	37,000	1,015	6 x .50 cal
F6F "Hellcat"	1943	376	37,500	1,090	6 x .50 cal
b. Dive Bombers					
Aichi D3A "Val"	1941	281	31,750	1,131	380 lb bombload
Yokosuka D4Y "Judy"	1943	360	34,500	749	680 lb bombload
SBD "Dauntless"	1941	252	24,300	985	1,000 lb bombload
SB2C "Helldiver"	1943	281	24,100	1,100	1,000 lb bombload
c. Torpedo Bombers					
Nakajima B5N2 "Kate"	1941	235	27,100	1,237	21" Torpedo
TBD 1 "Devastator"	1941	207	24,100	985	21" Torpedo
TBF 1 "Avenger"	1942	259	23,000	1,000	21" Torpedo
d. Level Bombers					
Mitsubishi 7KI "Sally"	1941	294	30,500	1,635	2,000 lb bombload
Mitsubishi GM "Betty"	1941	283	30,000	2,200	2,000 lb bombload
B-25 "Mitchell"	1941	275	24,000	1,500	4,000 lb bombload
B-17 "Flying Fortress"	1941	317	35,000	2,000	6,000 lb bombload
B-24 "Liberator"	1941	290	28,000	2,200	5,000 lb bombload
B-29 "Superfortress"	1944	357	36,000	3,250	10,000 lb bombload

Notes

Abbreviations used in the Notes:

CINCPAC   Commander in Chief, Pacific

COS   Chief of Staff

JCS   Joint Chiefs of Staff

N.A.   National Archives, Washington, D.C.

OPD   Records of the War Department Operations Division, National Archives

PHH   Hearings Before the Joint Committee on the Investigation of the Pearl Harbor Attack, 39 volumes, 79th United States Congress, Washington, D.C.

PRFRUS   *Papers Relating to the Foreign Relations of the United States*, GPO, Washington, D.C.

PRO   Public Records Office, London

SRDG   Intercepts of German Diplomatic Messages, 1940–1941, National Archives

SRDJ   Intercepts of Japanese Diplomatic Messages, 1941–1945, National Archives

SRH   National Security Agency, Naval Intelligence History

USAF   United States Asiatic Fleet

WDCSA   War Department, Chief of Staff of the Army, Washington, D.C.

WPD   War Plans Division, War Department, Washington, D.C.

CHAPTER 1 *THE WHITE MAN'S BURDEN*

Page

4   "AIR RAID PEARL HARBOR . . ." Robert Sherwood, *Roosevelt and Hopkins: An Intimate History* (New York: Harper and Row, 1948), p. 431.

5   "to see the United . . ." Howard K. Beale, *Theodore Roosevelt and the Rise of America to World Power* (Baltimore: Johns Hopkins Univ. Press, 1956), p. 81.

5   "Did you ever see . . ." Robert A. Hart, *The Great White Fleet* (Boston: Little, Brown, 1965), p. 58.

5   "might get the 'Big Head' . . ." Beale, *op. cit.*, p. 234.

6   "entangling alliances" Thomas Jefferson, Inaugural address, 1801.

7   "commerce of the East . . ." Richard Van Alstyne, *The United States in East Asia* (London: Thames and Hudson, 1973), p. 21.

8   "Our commerce must be . . ." Thomas Jefferson, Letter to John Hay, 1785, quoted in William A. Williams, *The Tragedy of American Diplomacy* (Cleveland: World, 1959).

8   "a breeder of wars . . ." Richard O'Connor, *Pacific Destiny* (Boston: Little,

Brown, 1969), from Jefferson to Gallatin, Aug. 15, 1808, Jefferson Papers, Library of Congress.

8   "handful of fir-built . . ." Nathan Miller, *The U.S. Navy* (Annapolis, Md.: U.S. Naval Institute Press, 1977), p. 85, from *The Times* of London.

9   "windows on the Orient" Thomas J. McCormick, *The China Market* (New York: Quadrangle, 1967), p. 15.

9   "the harvest which ripens . . ." Milton Plesur, *America's Outward Thrust* (Dekalb,

Page

Ill.: Northern Illinois Univ. Press, 1971), p. 198.

10 "insults to a mighty"
O'Connor, *op. cit.*, p. 58.

10 "your people pounded . . ."
Ibid.

11 "the sole emporium . . ."
Ibid., p. 81.

12 "Our duty—our vocation . . ."
Ronald Hyam, *Britain's Imperial Century, 1815–1914* (New York: Harper and Row, 1976), p. 49.

12 "Philanthropy plus 5%"
C. J. Lowe, *The Reluctant Imperialists* Vol. I, *British Foreign Policy 1878–1902* (London: Routledge, 1967), p. 3.

12 "self-exiled heralds of God"
Herman Melville, *Typee* (New York: Harcourt, Brace, 1920), p. 287.

12 "poised between barbarism . . ."
Ibid., p. 288.

12 "Niagara of souls . . ."
Rev. Hudson Taylor, 1894, quoted in Williams, *op. cit.*

14 "weak and semi-barbarous . . ."
Samuel E. Morison, *Old Bruin: Commodore Matthew C. Perry* (Boston: Little, Brown, 1969), p. 417.

14 "friendship, commerce . . ."
Millard Fillmore, *Papers* (Buffalo: Buffalo Hist. Soc., 1907), p. 395.

14 "God's purpose . . ."
Morison, *op. cit.*, p. 417.

15 "friendly mediators"
Charles E. Neu, *The Troubled Encounter: The U.S. and Japan* (New York: John Wiley, 1969), p. 12.

15 "the constitution, laws . . ."
O'Connor, *op. cit.*, p. 148.

16 "ineffable folly."
Ibid., p. 156.

17 "War is not fighting . . ."
Alfred T. Mahan, *From Sail to Steam* (New York, 1907), p. 277.

17 "We may hold all . . ."
Hyam, *op. cit.*, p. 98. For statistical information on Britain's economic retardation, see *ibid.*, p. 99.

18 "We are brothers in the same . . ."
Ibid., p. 204.

18 "advance agent . . ."
O'Connor, *op. cit.*, p. 232.

18 "trustee under God . . ."
Ibid., p. 283.

18 "mighty workshop of . . ."
McCormick, *op. cit.*, p. 15.

18 "Whether they will or no . . ."
Richard W. Van Alstyne, *Missionaries, Chinese and Diplomats* (Princeton: Princeton Univ. Press, 1958), p. 18.

21 "OFFENSIVE OPERATIONS . . ."
O'Connor, *op. cit.*, p. 264.

21 "If only old Dewey . . ."
Bernard Bailyn, et. al. *The Great Republic* (Boston: Little, Brown, 1977), p. 990.

21 "to fulfill our destinies . . ."
Ibid., p. 992.

22 "would help our work."
Beale, *op. cit.*, p. 140.

22 "take up the White Man's . . ."
Angus Wilson, *The Strange Ride of Rudyard Kipling* (New York: Viking, 1978), p. 204.

22 "Rather poor poetry . . ."
J. Stewart, *Rudyard Kipling* (London, 1966), noted in Hyam, *op. cit.*, p. 396.

22 "our inland sea"
Beale, *op. cit.*, pp. 164–165; cf. Brooks Adams, *America's Economic Supremacy* (New York: Macmillan, 1900).

22 "American factories . . ."
Williams, *op. cit.*, p. 23.

23 "Our capacity to produce . . ."
New York Bankers Association Journal, August 1898, p. 143.

23 "East Asia is the prize . . ."
McCormick, *op. cit.*, p. 15.

23 "Not prepared to undertake . . ."
Lowe, *op. cit.*, p. 1.

23 "Even the anti-imperialists . . ."
Williams, *op. cit.*, p. 23.

23 "noblest of causes . . ."
Beale, *op. cit.*, p. 142.

24 "industrializing the Monroe . . ."
Williams, *op. cit.*, p. 30.

25 "a sound argument for . . ."
Selborne Memo, Sept. 4, 1901, Public Records Office, London (cited hereafter as PRO), CAB 37/58/87.

25 "great civilized nation"
Beale, *op. cit.*, p. 234.

25 "Japan is never likely . . ."
Ibid., pp. 237–238.

26 "come to love Japan . . ."
Neu, *op. cit.*, p. 43.

26 "The larger interests . . ."
Beale, *op. cit.*, p. 131.

26 "of all the power . . ."
Richard D. Challener, *Admirals, Generals and American Foreign Policy, 1898–1914* (Princeton: Princeton Univ. Press, 1973), p. 101.

27 "idiots of the California . . ."
Beale, *op. cit.*, p. 284.

27 "Your cruise is . . ."
Hart, *op. cit.*, p. 51.

27 "the greatest enterprise . . ."
New York Herald, Dec. 31, 1907.

28 "Champagne festivities . . ."
Hart, *op. cit.*, p. 89.

28 "If we had known . . ."
William F. Halsey and Joseph J. Bryan III, *Admiral Halsey's Story* (New York: Whittlesey House, 1947), p. 13.

28 "the independence and . . ."
Papers Relating to the Foreign Relations of the United States, 1908–1912, Vol. I (Washington, D.C.: GPO, 1912), p. 108.

28 "powerful force . . ."
Hart, *op. cit.*, p. 239.

28 "Never again will they . . ."
Ibid., p. 297.

CHAPTER 2
SCRAPS OF PAPER

Page

30 "the American dollar . . ."
Beale, *op. cit.*, p. 287.

31 "The Great Game of Empire"
Van Alstyne, *The U.S. in East Asia*, p. 9.

31 "the American investor . . ."
Williams, *op. cit.*, p. 50.

32 "Japan's dominion of Asia . . ."
William Manchester, *American Caesar* (Boston: Little, Brown, 1978), p. 169.

32 "If we had a fleet . . ."
William Reynolds Braisted, *The U.S. Navy in the Pacific,*

Page

1909–1922 (Austin, Tex.: Univ. of Texas Press, 1960), Vol. II, p. 115.

33 "Germany shall not be . . ." Bailyn, et al., *op. cit.*, p. 1008.

33 "champions of the sovereign . . ." Arthur S. Link, *The Struggle for Neutrality* (Princeton: Princeton Univ. Press, 1960), p. 294.

33 "incomparably the greatest . . ." Harold and Margaret Sprout, *The Rise of American Naval Power, 1776–1918* (Princeton: Princeton Univ. Press, 1966), p. 334.

33 "the world must be mad . . ." Williams, *op. cit.*, p. 47.

33 "yet another pious accord . . ." *Papers Relating to the Foreign Policy of the United States, 1917*, Vol. IV (Washington, D.C.: GPO, 1935), p. 264.

34 "Prussian militarism" Neu, *op. cit.*, p. 98.

34 "China should not . . ." *Papers Relating to the Foreign Relations of the United States, 1919: Paris Peace Conference,* Vol. V (Washington, D.C.: GPO, 1935), p. 316.

34 "the most eminent . . ." *New York Times*, March 6, 1921.

35 "protect our interest . . ." U.S. Navy General Board Report, 1916.

35 "We should be up . . ." William Roger Louis, *British Strategy in the Far East, 1919– 1939* (New York: Oxford Univ. Press, 1971), p. 53.

35 "no more fatal policy" *Ibid.*, from Minutes of Committee for Imperial Defense, Dec. 14, 1921–PRO, CAB 23.

36 "We had to kill, lay out . . ." Bunker Davies, *The Billy Mitchell Affair* (New York: Random House, 1967), p. 101.

36 "attending a funeral . . ." *Ibid.*, p. 108.

37 "The battleship is still . . ." *Ibid.*, p. 111.

37 "We are seeking . . ." Williams, *op. cit.*, p. 91.

37 "competition in naval . . ." Harold and Margaret Sprout, *Toward a New Order of Seapower, 1918–1922*

(Princeton: Princeton Univ. Press, 1940), p. 155.

37 "Mr. Secretary Hughes . . ." A. C. Repington, *After the War* (London: Constable, 1922), p. 433.

38 "to maintain our close . . ." Stephen Roskill, *British Naval Policy Between the Wars* (London: Collins, 1968), Vol. I, p. 301.

39 "the modern riddle of . . ." Lionel Wigmore, *The Japanese Imperial Thrust* (Canberra, Aust.: Australian War Memorial, 1957), pp. 2–3.

40 "the sovereignty, the . . ." *Papers Relating to the Foreign Relations of the United States, 1922*, Vol. I (Washington, D.C.: GPO, 1934), pp. 278– 279.

40 "the greatest step . . ." Neu, *op. cit.*, p. 115.

40 "An international kiss" Bailyn, et al., *op. cit.*, p. 1161.

40 "Achilles heel" Beale, *op. cit.*, p. 25.

41 "era of good feeeling" Neu, *op. cit.*, p. 115.

41 "Everywhere I go . . ." *Ibid.*, p. 117.

43 "the spurning of an . . ." Bradford A. Lea, *Britain and the Sino-Japanese War, 1937– 1939* (Stanford, Calif.: Stanford Univ. Press, 1973), p. 5.

44 "GUARD AGAINST IMPETUOUS . . ." John Toland, *The Rising Sun* (New York: Random House, 1970), p. 8.

44 "If we lie down . . ." Henry L. Stimson, *On Active Service in Peace and War* (New York: Harper and Row, 1957), p. 233.

44 "more of a warrior . . ." Elting E. Morison, *A Study of the Life and Times of Henry L. Stimson* (Boston: Little, Brown, 1960), p. 382.

44 "solely moral instruments" William S. Myers, *The Foreign Policies of Herbert Hoover, 1929–1933* (New York: Scribner's, 1940), p. 156.

44 "Non-recognition might not . . ."

Meyers, *op. cit.*, p. 233.

45 "to put the situation . . ." Neu, *op. cit.*, p. 139.

45 "to encourage China . . ." Meyers, *op. cit.*, p. 249.

45 "will of the people of the world" *Ibid.*, p. 259.

46 "It would be the height of . . ." Louis, *op. cit.*, p. 211.

47 "The military themselves . . ." D. Borg and S. Okamoto, *Pearl Harbor as History* (New York: Columbia Univ. Press, 197), p. 32.

47 "uphold the sanctity . . ." *Ibid.*, p. 32.

47 "deepest sympathy" Robert Dallek, *Franklin D. Roosevelt and American Foreign Policy, 1932–1945* (New York: Oxford Univ. Press, 1977), p. 496.

48 "gracefully and gradually perhaps . . ." Borg and Okamoto, *op. cit.*, p. 33.

48 "insist and continue to insist . . ." *Ibid.*

48 "we should speak softly . . ." Borg and Okamoto, *op. cit.*, p. 35.

48 "because the United States . . ." *Papers Relating to the Foreign Relations of the United States, 1933*, Vol. II (Washington, D.C.: GPO, 1949), pp. 483– 484.

49 "spectacular rise . . . available." Tuleja, *op. cit.*, p. 99.

50 "a reign of law and order . . ." Cordell Hull, *Memoirs* (New York: Macmillan, 1948), p. 503.

50 "many of the old . . ." B. Nixon, ed., *F. D. Roosevelt and Foreign Affairs, 1931– 1937* (Cambridge, Mass.: Harvard Univ. Press, 1969), pp. 152–156.

50 "To hell with Europe" Dallek, *op. cit.*, p. 95.

52 "blinded by faith . . ." Borg and Okamoto, *op. cit.*, p. 68.

52 "demonstrated impotency . . ." *Ibid.*, p. 68.

52 "China's sovereign rights . . ." James B. Crowley, *Modern*

Page

East Asia (New York: Harcourt Brace World, 1970), p. 253.

52 "crush the Chinese . . ." Toland, *op. cit.*, p. 51.

53 "bandit nations" S. I. Rosenmann, ed., *The Public Papers and Addresses of F. D. R.*, (1937) (New York: 1938–50), p. 149.

53 "moral thunderbolts" *Papers Relating to the Foreign Relations of the United States, 1937*, Vol. III, p. 508.

CHAPTER 3
FOREIGN WARS

Page

55 "Peaceful below us . . ." *U.S. Naval Institute Proceedings*, June 1953, pp. 587 ff.; cf. Masatake Okumiya, *How the Panay Was Sunk.*

55 "They're letting go . . ." Hamilton Danby Perry, *The Panay Incident—Prelude to Pearl Harbor* (New York: Macmillan, 1969), p. 68.

56 "the Imperial Way . . ." Toland, *op. cit.*, p. 55.

56 "wild half-insane . . ." Hull, *op. cit.*, p. 599; cf. *Papers Relating to the Foreign Relations of the United States and Japan, 1931–1941*, cited hereafter as *PRFRUS, Japan*, Vol. I (Washington, D.C.: GPO, 1949), p. 520.

56 "naval war of strangulation . . ." Borg and Okamoto, *op. cit.*, p. 212.

56 "the utterance of . . ." PRO, Doc Foreign Office (FO) 3/1/2091 (1937—report of Sir Ronald Lindsay).

57 "he could not imagine . . ." PRO, CAB 1, October 1936.

57 "hold his hand . . ." Keith Feiling, *The Life of Neville Chamberlain* (London: Macmillan, 1946).

57 "seriously handicapped . . ." Lea, *op. cit.*, p. 171.

57 "adequate fleet" *Ibid.*

58 "the security of . . ." Paul M. Kennedy, *The Rise of British Naval Mastery* (New York: Scribner's, 1976), p. 292.

58 "unsound in general" Maurice Matloff and Edwin M. Snell, *Strategic Planning for Coalition Warfare* (Washington, D.C.: Office of the Chief of Military History, 1953), p. 3.

59 "We in the Americas . . ." Rosenmann, ed., *op. cit.* (1937), pp. 491–494.

59 "for the sake of humanity" *Ibid.*

59 "Liberate Asia from Imperialism" Thomas R. Havens, *Valley of Darkness* (New York: Norton, 1978), p. 12.

60 "conduct contrary . . ." *Ibid.*

61 "new order in East . . ." *Ibid.*, p. 26.

62 "would not abdicate . . ." Lea, *op. cit.*, p. 171.

62 "any Japanese threat . . ." *Ibid.*, p. 172.

62 "What Britain calls . . ." Roger J. Bell, *Unequal Allies* (Melbourne, Aust.: Melbourne Univ. Press, 1977), p. 12.

62 "must depend on our . . ." Paul M. Kennedy, *The Rise and Fall of British Naval Mastery* (New York: Scribner's, 1976), p. 292.

62 "the British lion . . ." Tuleja, *op. cit.*, p. 184.

63 "could damage Major . . ." Matloff and Snell, *op. cit.*, p. 6.

63 "contrary to a reasoned . . ." *Ibid.*, J. P. C. Study cited.

64 "violation of the letter . . ." Matloff and Snell, *op. cit.*, pp. 7–8.

64 "securing control . . ." *Ibid.*

64 "without further preparation" PRFRUS, 1949, p. 204.

65 "cool and unreliable" Frank W. Ikle, *German-Japanese Relations, 1935–1940* (New York: Bookman Associates, 1956), p. 102.

65 "little worms" *Ibid.*, p. 133.

65 "companion piece . . ." *Ibid.*

66 "complicated and inscrutable . . ." David Bergamini, *Japan's Imperial Conspiracy* (New York: Morrow, 1971), p. 744.

66 "keep war from . . ." Rosenmann, ed., *op. cit.* (1939), pp. 464–478.

66 "even a neutral . . ." *Ibid.*

67 "keep in touch . . ." John Costello and Terry Hughes, *The Battle of the Atlantic* (New York: Dial, 1977), p. 14.

68 "the tendency is . . ." Borg and Okamoto, *op. cit.*, p. 43.

68 "there is a vast . . ." *Ibid.*

68 "blood. toil, tears . . ." Winston S. Churchill, *The Second World War*, Vol. I: *The Gathering Storm* (Boston: Houghton Mifflin, 1950, paperback edn.), p. 25.

68 "to keep the Japanese . . ." F. L. Lowenheim, *Roosevelt and Churchill—Their Secret Wartime Correspondence* (New York: Dutton, 1975), p. 95.

69 "because of the deterrent . . ." Tuleja, *op. cit.*, p. 193.

69 "IMMEDIATELY ALERT . . ." Roberta Wohlsetter, *Pearl Harbor: Warning and Decision* (Stanford, Calif.: Stanford Univ. Press, 1962), p. 91.

69 "Main Principles for Coping . . ." Bergamini, *op. cit.*, p. 754.

70 "Positive arrangements . . ." *Ibid.*

70 "like inviting a robber . . ." *Saionji-Harada Memoirs*, cited in U.S. Army Special Report and Bergamini *op. cit.*, p. 753.

71 "some straight acting . . ." Dallek, *op. cit.*, p. 242.

71 "we must not push . . ." *Ibid.*, p. 242.

71 "with all political . . ." Nobutake Ike, ed., *Japan's*

Page

Decision for War—Records
of the 1941 Policy
Conferences (Stanford,
Calif.: Stanford Univ. Press,
1967), p. 13.

71 "it is the best way to . . ."
Toland, *op. cit.*, p. 13.

72 "The United States cannot . . ."
Bell, *op. cit.*, p. 16.

72 "any specific guarantee . . ."
Ibid.

72 "An act of war . . ."
Dallek, *op. cit.*, p. 247.

72 "I give you one more . . ."
Sherwood, *op. cit.*, p. 191.

CHAPTER 4
EUROPE FIRST

Page

73 "I believe the United . . ."
James A. Herzog, *Closing the
Open Door* (Annapolis, Md.:
U.S. Naval Institute Press,
1973), p. 223, Appendix A,
Memorandum.

74 "The support of the . . ."
Matloff and Snell, *op. cit.*,
p. 22.

74 "Advisory Committee on
Uranium"
Martin J. Sherwin, *A World
Destroyed* (New York:
Knopf, 1973), pp. 3–34.

74 "stripped to the bone"
Winston S. Churchill, *The
Second World War*, Vol. II:
Their Finest Hour (Boston:
Houghton Mifflin, 1950), pp.
475–482.

74 "get rid of this . . ."
Rosenmann, ed., *op. cit.*
(1940), pp. 604–615.

75 "Since Germany is the . . ."
Matloff and Snell, *op. cit.*,
p. 43.

75 "Singapore is the key . . ."
Ibid., p. 34.

75 "a strategic error . . ."
Ibid., p. 37.

75 "the retention of Singapore . . ."
Ibid., p. 38.

76 "Many drifting straws . . ."
Lowenheim, *op. cit.*, p. 129,
Feb. 15, 1941.

76 "wipe out England's . . ."
National Archives (N.A.)
(Washington, D.C.), Record
Group 457, SRDJ Series.

77 "It was the old question . . ."
N.A. RG 80, "Pearl Harbor
Liaison Office," Copies of
Stimson Diary entries.

77 "popping up her and . . ."
Herzog, *op. cit.*, p. 153; cf.
*Hearings Before the Joint
Committee on the
Investigation of the Pearl
Harbor Attack* (cited
hereafter as PHH), 79th
Congress of the U.S. (39 vols.,
Washington, D.C.: GPO,
1946), p. 2163.

77 "the question of our . . ."
Ibid.

77 "If we lose in the . . ."
N.A. RG. 165, WDCSA,
Chiefs of Staff Conferences,
April 16, 1941.

77 "we cannot win this . . ."
Wayne S. Cole, *C. A.
Lindbergh and the Battle
Against American
Intervention* (New York:
Harcourt, Brace, 1974),
p. 189.

78 "broad and ambitious . . ."
Borg and Okamoto, *op. cit.*,
p. 47.

79 "Must we dance to . . ."
R. J. C. Butow, *John Doe
Associates* (Stanford, Calif.:
Stanford Univ. Press, 1974),
p. 68.

79 "crooked as a bundle . . ."
Ibid., p. 69.

79 "much less accommodating . . ."
Hull, *op. cit.*, pp. 982–984.

80 "Now that Japan and . . ."
Toland, *op. cit.*, p. 75

81 "as the only way to . . ."
M. Carver, ed., *The War
Lords* (Boston: Little, Brown,
1976), p. 396.

81 "to reach superhuman . . ."
Ibid.

81 "Anyone who has seen . . ."
Borg and Okamoto, *op. cit.*,
p. 237.

81 "At this stage . . ."
Hiroyuki Agawa, *The
Reluctant Admiral* (Tokyo:
Kodansha, 1979), p. 189.

82 "If we are ordered . . ."
Ibid., p. 191.

82 "Yogeki Sakusen"
Borg and Okamoto, *op. cit.*,
p. 235.

82 "It makes me wonder . . ."
Agawa, *op. cit.*, p. 219.

83 "Success would not be . . ."
Ibid., p. 227.

83 "the outcome must . . ."
Ibid., p. 228.

83 "Highest priority . . ."
PHH, part 33, p. 1283.

85 "gentlemen do not read . . ."
Ladislas Farago, *The Broken
Seal* (New York: Random
House, 1967), p. 54.

88 "It is necessary . . ."
National Archives, Record
Group 457, *Japanese-German
Diplomatic Messages 1940–
1941*, MAGIC Intercepts
SRDJ Series (cited hereafter
as N.A. SRDJ), March 1941.

88 "violently anti-Axis . . ."
Ibid.

88 "unlimited national emergency"
Rosenmann, ed., *op. cit.*
(1941), p. 95.

89 "to ensure the delivery . . ."
Ibid.

CHAPTER 5
A SINISTER TWILIGHT

Page

90 "We are resolved to . . ."
Winston S. Churchill, *The
Second World War*, Vol. III:
The Great Alliance (Boston:
Houghton Mifflin, 1953,
paperback edn.), p. 314.

91 "Germany is confident . . ."
N.A. RG 457, SRDJ Series,
NC3-457-80-2; April 1941.

91 "some Japanese leaders . . ."
PRFRUS, Japan, Vol. II,
p. 481.

91 "Japan is preparing for all . . ."
N.A. RG 457, SRDJ Series.

92 "we Japanese are not . . ."
Ibid.

92 "Japan is so occupied . . ."
James M. Burns, *Roosevelt:
The Soldier of Freedom,
1940–1945* (New York:
Harcourt Brace Jovanovich,
1970), p. 107.

Page

92 "I think it will interest . . ."
Ibid.

92 "I simply have not got . . ."
Ibid.

92 "Outline of National Policies"
Nobutake Ike, *Decision for
War—Records of 1941
Foreign Policy Conferences*
(Stanford, Calif.: Stanford
Univ. Press, 1967), pp. 77–90.

93 "further a more obvious . . ."
PRFRUS, *Japan*, Vol. II, p.
485.

94 "was still unwilling . . ."
Harold L. Ickes, *The Secret
Diary of Harold L. Ickes*, Vol.
III (New York: Simon and
Schuster, 1954), p. 558.

94 "the most drastic blow . . ."
Cited in Toland, *op. cit.*,
p. 99.

94 "vicious circle . . ."
Grew, *op. cit.*, p. 109.

94 "immediate steps to . . ."
N.A. RG 457, SRDJ Series.

95 "broad principles . . ."
Dallek, *op. cit.*, p. 282.

95 "We are now trying . . ."
National Archives
(Washington, D.C.) Record
Group 18–337, Army–Air
Force Notes, Staff
Conference, Aug. 11–12, 1941.

95 "gravely concerned . . ."
J. R. M. Butler, *Grand
Strategy*, Vol. II: *Sept. 1939–
June 1941* (London: H.M.
Stationery Office, 1957),
p. 493.

96 "any further encroachments . . ."
PRFRUS, *Japan*, 1941, Vol.
VI (Washington, D.C.: GPO,
1949), pp. 354–356.

96 "re-embark on a program . . ."
Ibid.

97 "The whole of the . . ."
Churchill, *op. cit.*, Vol. II

97 "Unit 82 Strike Plan South"
Masanobu Tsuji, *Singapore—
The Japanese Version*
(Sydney, Aust.: Ure, Smith,
1960), pp. 11–13.

98 "If we commence . . ."
Ibid.

98 "The presence of the . . ."
Agawa. *op. cit.*, p. 232.

99 "Unless it is carried . . ."
Ibid.

99 "the employment of . . ."
Wohlsetter, *op. cit.*, p. 23.

99 "A declaration of war . . ."
Ibid., p. 23.

99 "enemy carriers . . ."
F. C. Pogue, *George C.
Marshall* (New York: Viking,
1973), Vol. II, p. 173.

99 "U.S. forces in the . . ."
Ibid., p. 178.

99 "From 1922 until late 1940 . . ."
National Archives
(Washington, D.C.: War
Department, War Plans
Division, cited hereafter as
N.A. WPD), pp. 3251–3255.

100 "which might result . . ."
Pogue, *op. cit.*, Vol. II, p. 178.

100 "just what Germany . . ."
Ibid.

100 "The project would greatly . . ."
N.A. RG 165, WPD, pp.
3251–3281. Letter from
MacArthur to Marshall, Feb.
8, 1941.

101 "all practical steps . . ."
Ibid.

102 "The present attitude of . . ."
N.A. RG 165, WPD, pp.
3251–3255

103 "to get back into . . ."
N.A. RG 107, Sec. of War
Safe File, Philippines—Memo,
Oct. 21, 1941, to the President.

103 "The present deterrents . . ."
N.A. RG 165, WPD, pp.
3251–3255.

104 "Experience has shown . . ."
Ibid.

104 "a tremendously strong . . ."
N.A. RG 165, WPD, pp.
3251–3281.

104 "too negativistic"
D. Clayton James, *The Years
of MacArthur*, Vol. I:
1880–1941 (Boston: Houghton
Mifflin, 1975), p. 595.

104 "has changed the whole
picture . . ."
N.A. RG 165, Oct. 8, 1941.
Memo WPD 325/60.

105 "Lewis, you're as welcome
as . . ."
Lewis Brereton, *The Brereton
Diaries* (New York: Morrow,
1946), p. 19.

105 "the greatest concentration . . ."
Morton, *op. cit.*, p. 69.

105 "general incendiary attacks . . ."
National Archives
(Washington, D.C.) RG 165,
Army COS Project Decimal

File, War Department, Chief
of Staff of the Army (cited
hereafter as WDCSA),
1381–12–4–41.

106 "to halt Japan's march
south . . ."
N.A. RG 107, Sec. of War
Safe File, Philippines—*op. cit.*

106 "formidable, fast . . ."
Public Records Office (PRO),
London, PREM 3, 163/2.
Memo to First Lord of the
Admiralty, Aug. 29, 1941.

107 "More guns than currants . . ."
A. Percival, *The War in
Malaya* (London: Eyre and
Spotteswoode, 1949), p. 47.

107 "in most places not . . ."
Stanley L. Falk, *70 Days to
Singapore* (Princeton:
Princeton Univ. Press, 1975),
p. 37.

108 "Let England have . . ."
Richard Hough, *The Death
of a Battleship* (New York:
Macmillan, 1963), p. 153.

108 "discourage the chaps . . ."
J. Leasor, *Singapore: The
Battle That Changed the
World.* pp. 32–33.

108 "you can take it from me . . ."
Ibid.

108 "The idea of trying . . ."
Churchill, Vol. II *op. cit.*,
Memo to Gen Ismay 10 Sept.
1940.

109 "floating coffins"
Roskill, *Churchill and the
Admirals*, Vol. II, p. 197.

109 "The most economical . . ."
PRO, PREM 3, 183/2.

109 "bombers were no match . . ."
Roskill, *op. cit.*, Vol. II, p. 199.

109 "The firmer your attitude . . ."
Lowenheim, *op. cit.*, p. 163.

109 "Deterrent to Japan."
Churchill, *op. cit.*, Vol. III,
p. 163.

110 "each separately . . ."
Martin Middlebrook,
Battleship (London: Allen
Lane, 1977), p. 68.

110 "Consideration of . . ."
N.A. WPD, pp. 3251–3260.
Memo from Grew to Sec. of
War, Oct. 8, 1941.

111 "Things cannot be . . ."
Toland, *op. cit.*, pp. 108–109.

Page

111 "Although I feel . . ."
   Ibid.

111 "For the self-defense . . ."
   Ibid.

CHAPTER 6
NATIONAL HARA-KIRI

Page

112 "The purposes of war . . ."
   Ike, *op. cit.*, pp. 133–163.

112 "operation in the . . ."
   Ibid.

113 "All the seas . . ."
   Ibid.

113 "the least possible delay"
   Joseph C. Grew, *Ten Years in Japan* (New York: Simon and Schuster, 1944), p. 367.

113 "we are all but . . ."
   Pearl Harbor Hearings (PHH), part 5, p. 2292.

113 "will probably lead . . ."
   Grew, *Ten Years in Japan*, pp. 436–442.

115 "petition the Emperor . . ."
   Butow, *op. cit.*, pp. 301–302.

115 "go back to blank . . ."
   Ibid., p. 301.

116 "BEST INTELLIGENCE . . ."
   PHH, part 14, p. 1402.

116 "the situation is urgent . . ."
   Butow, *op. cit.*, p. 301.

116 "the firmer your attitude . . ."
   Lowenheim, *op. cit.*, p. 163.

116 "The most dangerous enemy"
   N.A. RG 165, WPD, 4-389-29, Serial B0012, p. 195.

116 "all-out do-or-die"
   Grew, *Ten Years in Japan*, p. 442.

117 "strain every nerve"
   Dallek, *op. cit.*, p. 305.

117 "continuing efforts . . ."
   Lowenheim, *op. cit.*, p. 163.

118 "nations must think . . ."
   PRFRUS, *Japan*, Vol. II, p. 589.

118 "not entirely unreceptive"
   MAGIC, PHH, part 1, p. 107.

118 "Fate of the Empire . . ."
   MAGIC, PHH, part 12, p. 1371.

119 "After that things . . ."
   Ibid., part 1, p. 165.

119 "critical and virtually . . ."
   N.A. Record Group 80, Pearl Harbor Liaison Office. Copies of Stimson Diary entries (cited hereafter as Stimson Diary).

119 "we must all prepare . . ."
   Lowenheim, *op. cit.*, p. 165.

119 "SURPRISE AND AGGRESSIVE . . ."
   PHH, part 14, p. 1406.

119 "in case negotiations . . ."
   M. Fuchida, *U.S. Naval Institute Proceedings*, Sept. 1952, "I Led the Air Attack on Pearl Harbor" (Annapolis) p. 990.

119 "evidence of bad faith . . ."
   PHH, part 2, p. 5434.

119 "on a monthly basis . . ."
   Ibid., pp. 1113–1115.

120 "withdrawal of all . . ."
   Ibid.

120 "This is an ultimatum . . ."
   Butow, *op. cit.*, p. 343.

120 "the Japanese government . . ."
   PHH, part 5, p. 2089.

120 "washed his hands of it . . ."
   Ibid., part 2, p. 5434.

120 "If the current negotiations . . ."
   Ibid., part 14, p. 1083.

120 "NEGOTIATIONS . . ."
   Ibid., p. 1407.

120 "MEASURES SHOULD BE . . ."
   Ibid.

120 "THIS DISPATCH IS TO BE . . ."
   Ibid.

121 "SHOULD HOSTILITIES OCCUR . . ."
   Ibid.

121 "If the British fought . . ."
   Stimson Diary, Nov. 25, 1941.

121 "Should Japan become engaged . . ."
   N.A. RG 457, SRDJ Series. Berlin–Tokyo, Nov. 29, 1941.

121 "that any further act . . ."
   Lowenheim, *op. cit.*, p. 168.

121 "to disconcert the Japanese . . ."
   PRO, ADM 199/1149.

122 "Matters have reached the point . . ."
   Ike, *op. cit.*, pp. 262–283.

122 "we should all be in it . . ."
   PRO, Foreign Office I13136/86/23.

122 "Do you mean to say . . ."
   PHH, part 14, p. 1408.

122 "I would hope they . . ."
   Ibid.

122 "highly reliable information . . ."
   Ibid., part 10, p. 4882.

122 "as relations between Japan . . ."
   Ibid., part 12, p. 262.

123 "against Japanese movements . . ."
   PRO, ADM 199/1149.

123 "the most probable . . ."
   PHH, part 14, p. 1377.

123 "It is not possible . . ."
   Arthur Bryant, *The Turn of the Tide*, Vol. I (New York: Doubleday, 1957), p. 225. Diary entry of Gen. Sir Alan Brooke.

124 "THE RISE OR FALL OF THE . . ."
   Fuchida, *op. cit.*, p. 944.

124 "now would be a good . . ."
   PHH, part 12, pp. 268–270.

124 "FOR THE SAKE OF HUMANITY . . ."
   Joseph P. Lash, *Roosevelt and Churchill: The Partnership That Saved the West* (New York: Norton, 1976), p. 486.

124 "This son of man . . ."
   Ibid.

124 "This means war . . ."
   Ibid., p. 487.

124 "no reason for alerting . . ."
   PHH, part 12, p. 238.

125 "It can wait . . ."
   Edward Van Der Rhoer, *Deadly Magic* (New York: Scribner's, 1978), p. 64.

126 "ALL CARRIERS . . ."
   PHH, part 12, p. 270.

126 "unless other intelligence . . ."
   Ibid., p. 3455.

126 "the strongest fortress . . ."
   Pogue, *op. cit.*, Vol. II, p. 173.

127 "the best entertainment . . ."
   Manchester, *op. cit.*, p. 203.

127 "READ THIS AND THE WAR . . ."
   Tsuji, *op. cit.*, pp. 295–300.

127 "a hundred million Asians . . ."
   Ibid.

127 "what fools to think . . ."
   Ibid.

128 "it is my sole wish . . ."
   Toland, *op. cit.*, p. 233.

CHAPTER 7
A DATE THAT WILL LIVE IN INFAMY

Page

129 "The Japanese government . . ."
   PHH, part 12, p. 245.

Page

129 "In my flying togs . . ."
Fuchida, *op. cit.*, p. 443.

130 "URGENT VERY IMPORTANT . . ."
PHH, part 12, p. 248.

130 "an attack on an American . . ."
PHH, part 2, p. 942.

131 "JUST WHAT SIGNIFICANCE . . ."
Pogue, *op. cit.*, Vol. II, p. 229.

131 "something hanging in . . ."
Stimson Diary, Dec. 7, 1941.

131 "someone's opened fire . . ."
James Leasor, *Singapore: The Battle That Changed the*

World (New York: Dial, 1968), pp. 166–167.

131 "Well, I suppose you'll . . ."
Ibid.

132 "WE HAVE ATTACKED . . ."
PHH, part 23, p. 1033.

133 "something completely out . . ."
Ibid., part 27, p. 520.

133 "Don't worry about it."
Ibid.

133 "Ally with us . . ."
Tsuji, *op. cit.*, pp. 84–85.

133 "is suspended . . ."
Ibid.

134 "All of a sudden the clouds . . ."
Fuchida, *op. cit.*, p. 949.

134 "Notify all planes . . ."
Ibid.

135 "I was in the bunk . . ."
U.S. Navy Operational Archives (Washington, D.C., cited hereafter as USNOA), CINCPAC Serial 0479. Report of Japanese Raid on Pearl Harbor, Vols. I–III.

135 "Suddenly I noticed planes . . ."
Ibid.

135 "AIR RAID PEARL HARBOR . . ."
Ibid.

135 "saw waterspouts rising . . ."
Ibid.

135 "As I went up . . ."
Ibid.

136 "During all this time . . ."
Ibid.

136 "Just about then . . ."
Ibid.

136 "As I reached . . ."
Ibid.

136 "Dark grey bursts . . ."
Fuchida, *op. cit.*, p. 948.

136 "About two minutes later . . ."
USNOA CINCPAC Serial 0479.

137 "Shortly after I had . . ."
Ibid.

137 "Four bombs in perfect . . ."
Fuchida, *op. cit.*, p. 949.

138 "This can't be true . . ."
Samuel Eliot Morison, *History of United States Naval Operations in World War II*, Vol. III: *The Rising Sun in the Pacific* (Boston: Little, Brown, 1948), p. 10.

138 "to receive their reply . . ."
Hull, *op. cit.*, p. 1096.

138 "in all my fifty . . ."
Ibid.

138 "Scoundrels and . . ."
Toland, *op. cit.*, p. 257.

138 "He could look through . . ."
Walter Karig and Welbourn Kelly, *Battle Report*, Vol. I: *Pearl Harbor to Coral Sea* (New York: Farrar Rinehart, 1944), p. 79.

138 "Damn it, those are . . ."
Toland, *op. cit.*, p. 249.

138 "Don't shoot! . . ."
Walter Lord, *Day of Infamy* (New York: Holt, 1957), p. 129.

140 "A warm feeling . . ."
Fuchida, *op. cit.*, p. 951.

141 "Mr. President, what's . . ."
Churchill, *op. cit.*, Vol. III, p. 510.

141 "Pearl Harbor . . ."
Manchester, *op. cit.*, p. 205.

142 "my order were explicit . . ."
James, *op. cit.*, Vol. II, p. 10.

142 "that the Philippines . . ."
Ibid.

142 "he had not the slightest . . ."
Ibid.

142 "Before we're through . . ."
Morison, Vol. III, *Rising Sun*, p. 212.

143 "To remain within range . . ."
Fuchida, *op. cit.*, p. 952.

143 "The Army and Navy divisions . . ."
Toland, *op. cit.*, p. 260.

143 "To annihilate this enemy . . ."
Ibid., p. 261.

143 "our tails are up in . . ."
Manchester, *op. cit.*, p. 209.

144 "The pilots in every one . . ."
Robert D. Heinl, *Soldiers of the Sea* (Annapolis, Md.: U.S. Naval Institute, 1962), p. 326.

145 "If Clark Field . . ."
Manchester, *op. cit.*, p. 209.

145 "It was obvious to me . . ."
Lash, *op. cit.*, p. 488, as quoted by Frances Perkins, Columbia Oral History Project.

145 "send out a mission . . ."
Manchester, *op. cit.*, p. 210.

145 "at the earliest . . ."
Ibid., p. 211.

145 "Here comes the navy . . ."
Ibid.

146 "how in the hell . . ."
James, *op. cit.*, Vol. II, p. 6.

146 "ON ASSUMPTION . . ."
PRO, ADM 199/1149.

147 "Reconnaissance 100 . . . 10th December . . ."
Ibid.

147 "We are ready . . ."
S. Woodburn Kirby, et al., *The Surrender of Japan* (London: HMSO, 1969), p. 525.

147 "I'm not sure Pulford . . ."
PRO, ADM 199/1149.

148 "FIGHTER PROTECTION . . ."
Ibid.

148 "Well . . . we must get . . ."
Ibid.

148 "Being saturated and . . ."
Churchill, *op. cit.*, Vol. III, p. 512.

CHAPTER 8
DIRECT SHOCKS

Page

149 "So we had won . . ."
Churchill, *op. cit.*, Vol. III, p. 511.

149 "Yesterday, Dec. 7"
Burns, *op. cit.*, p .165.

149 "from such an . . ."
New York Times, Dec. 8, 1941.

150 "We can whip them . . ."
Ibid.

151 "no doubt that they . . ."
Los Angeles Times, Dec. 8, 1941.

151 "The British Empire . . ."
Churchill, *op. cit*, Vol. III, p. 511.

Page

151 "Oh, that's the way . . ."
Bryant, *op. cit.*, Vol. I, p. 198.

151 "Your coming here . . ."
PRO, PREM 4 127/129

151 "Consider themselves . . ."
Rosenmann, ed., *op. cit.*
(1941), pp. 516–530.

151 "to the most . . ."
Ibid.

151 "half-judaized . . ."
William L. Shirer, *The Rise
and Fall of the Third Reich*
(New York: Simon and
Schuster, 1959), p. 1174.

152 "within 24 hours the U.S. . . ."
Ibid., p. 1173.

152 "JAPANESE LANDING . . ."
PRO, ADM 199/1149.

152 "Whatever we meet . . ."
Hough, *op. cit.*, p. 171.

154 "THEY COULD ATTACK YOU . . ."
PRO, ADM 199/1149.

154 "JAPANESE LANDING NORTH . . ."
Ibid.

154 "the only key weapon . . ."
Churchill, *op. cit.*, Vol. III,
p. 519.

154 "to knit the English-
speaking . . ."
Ibid.

154 "as the hour was late . . ."
Ibid.

155 "ALL'S QUIET AS A WET . . ."
PRO, ADM 199/1149.

156 "SIGHTED ENEMY
BATTLESHIPS . . ."
Ibid.

156 "Look at those yellow . . ."
John Toland, *But Not in
Shame* (London: A. Gibb and
Phillips, 1961), p. 99.

157 "WE HAVE DODGED . . ."
PRO, ADM 199/1149.

158 "You've put up a good
show . . ."
Hough, *op. cit.*, p. 199.

158 "We have finished our task . . ."
Middlebrook, *op. cit.*, p. 257.

159 "During that hour . . ."
Ibid., p. 279.

159 "I hope you don't blame . . ."
Toland, *But Not in Shame*,
p. 96.

159 "In all the war . . ."
Churchill, *op. cit.*, Vol. II, p.
522.

159 "It means that . . ."
Bryant, *op. cit.*, Vol. I, p. 226.

CHAPTER 9

*THE SOMBER
PANORAMA*

Page

161 "expected to have . . ."
Heinl, *op. cit.*, p. 327.

161 "Both shells entered . . ."
Ibid.

161 "Knock it off . . ."
Ibid., p. 328.

162 "fiercely counter-attacked . . ."
P. S. Dull, *Imperial Japanese
Navy* (Annapolis, Md.: U.S.
Naval Institute Press, 1979),
p. 25.

162 "additional attacks in . . ."
Edwin P. Hoyt, *How They
Won the War in the Pacific*
(New York: Weybright and
Talley, 1970), p. 9.

162 "retrieve our initial . . ."
Morison, *op. cit.*, Vol. III,
Rising Sun, p. 220.

163 "Russian declaration . . ."
Churchill, *op. cit.*, Vol. III,
p. 529.

163 "the stubborn defense . . ."
Ibid., p. 534.

163 "You must look . . ."
Ibid., p. 536.

164 "The eyes of the Empire . . ."
Compton MacKenzie, *Easter
Epic* (London: Chatto and
Windus, 1951), Vol. II, p. 258.

165 "slight negligence . . ."
Tsuji, *op. cit.*, pp. 129–130.

166 "ridiculed the idea . . ."
Kirby, et al., *op. cit.*, p. 216.

166 "Beware lest troops . . ."
Churchill, *op. cit.*, Vol. VIII,
p. 538.

166 "This voyage seems very long"
Ibid., p. 532.

166 "Great Britain is not . . ."
Churchill, *op. cit.*, Vol. II,
p. 556.

167 "the success of the . . ."
United States Asiatic Fleet
(USAF), War Diary, Dec.
15, 1941.

167 "strategic importance . . ."
James, *op. cit.*, Vol. II, p. 22.

167 "that we could not give . . ."
N.A. RG 80, Stimson Diary,
Dec. 14, 1941.

167 "longer than the garrison . . ."
Pogue, *op. cit.*, Vol. II, p. 239.

167 "Do your best to save . . ."
Ibid.

167 "some kind of 'oid' . . ."
Ibid., p. 241.

168 "effective 3 P.M. Dec. 17 . . ."
Hoyt, *op. cit.*, p. 15.

168 "This left us with . . ."
Heinl, *op. cit.*, p. 332.

169 "take a chance . . ."
Hoyt, *op. cit.*, pp. 20–21.

169 "ENEMY APPARENTLY LANDING"
Heinl, *op. cit.*, p. 332.

169 "The scene was too . . ."
Ibid.

169 "THE ENEMY IS ON THE . . ."
Ibid.

170 "heroic and historic defense"
Ibid., p. 335.

171 "Can I expect anything along
that line?"
Manchester, *op. cit.*, p. 217.

172 "Counsels of timidity . . ."
James, *op. cit.*, Vol. II, p. 22.

172 "Few if any forces . . ."
Ibid., p. 25.

172 "WPO is in effect."
Manchester, *op. cit.*, p. 217.

CHAPTER 10

*STANDING ON THE
DEFENSIVE*

Page

173 "All nations"
Churchill, *op. cit.*, Vol. III.

174 "hold fast for king . . ."
Kirby, et al., *op. cit.*, p. 23.

174 "I hope you will tell . . ."
Brereton, *op. cit.*, p. 62.

175 "The way to victory . . ."
Morison, *op. cit.*, Vol. III,
Rising Sun, p. 255.

176 "was too much anti- . . ."
Pogue, *op. cit.*, Vol. II, p. 264.

176 "the main strategical . . ."
Churchill, *op. cit.*, Vol. VIII,
p. 544.

177 "65 reasons why we . . ."
Theodore H. White, ed., *The
Stilwell Papers* (New York:
Sloane, 1948), p. 16.

177 "The limeys have his head . . ."
Ibid., p. 25.

Page

177 "Our view remains that . . ."
N.A. RG 165, Minutes of
"Arcadia" Meetings, ABC 337,
Dec. 24, 1941, and Jan. 14,
1942.

178 "The whole organization . . ."
Bryant, *op. cit.*, Vol. I, p. 239.

178 "human frailties . . ."
Pogue, *op. cit.*, Vol. II, p. 276.

178 "feeling that all was . . ."
Kirby, et al., *op. cit.*, p. 157.

179 "You know, Charles . . ."
Lord Moran, *Churchill: The
Struggle for Survival* (Boston:
Houghton Mifflin, 1966),
p. 16.

179 "I cannot help reflecting . . ."
Henry H. Adams, *1942—The
Year That Doomed the Axis*
(New York: McKay, 1967),
p. 54.

179 "difficult to reconcile . . ."
Churchill, *op. cit.*, Vol. VIII,
p. 566.

179 "inspired idea . . ."
Ibid., p. 574.

180 "The Declaration could not . . ."
Ibid., p. 575.

180 "kicked like bay steers"
Pogue, *op. cit.*, Vol. II, p. 278.

181 "disasters that are coming"
Bryant, *op. cit.*, Vol. I, p. 335.

181 "I have heard . . ."
Carver, *op. cit.*, p. 224.

181 "Such an arrangement . . ."
Dallek, *op. cit.*, p. 328.

181 "over-estimated the . . ."
Ibid., p. 328.

181 "the extraordinary . . ."
Ibid.

182 "Our own front-line . . ."
Leasor, *op. cit.*, pp. 195–197.

182 "The majority were on . . ."
Ibid.

183 "Depend on the enemy . . ."
Ibid.

183 "the utter weariness . . ."
Ibid.

183 "a great strategic move."
James, *op. cit.*, Vol. II, p. 36.

185 "pursue the enemy in
column . . ."
Toland, *But Not in Shame*,
p. 298.

185 "American sea thrust"
N.A. RG 165, WDCSA 381,
MacArthur to Marshall, Feb.
4, 1942.

185 "I can assure that . . ."
Manchester, *op. cit.*, p. 239.

185 "President has seen . . ."
N.A. RG 165, WDCSA 381,
Marshall to MacArthur, Feb.
8, 1942.

185 "crescendo of enemy . . ."
Manchester, *op. cit.*, p. 238.

186 "Our great hope is . . ."
Ibid., p. 239.

186 "entirely unjustifiable"
Ibid., p. 241.

186 "There are times when . . ."
Ibid.

186 "Help is definitely . . ."
Ibid., p. 240.

186 "could hold Bataan and . . ."
Ibid.

186 "Oh, the production . . ."
Sherwood, *op. cit.*, p. 474.

187 "These figures and similar . . .'
Ibid.

187 "preclude the possibility . . ."
N.A. RG 165, Minutes,
"Arcadia" Meetings, ABC
337, Dec. 24, 1941.

187 "the limitation of shipping . . ."
Churchill, *op. cit.*, Vol. VIII,
p. 91.

187 "standing on the defensive"
N.A. RG 165, Minutes of
"Arcadia" Meetings, ABC
337,

188 "the might and will power . . ."
Ibid., p. 593.

189 "Look after Burma for me . . ."
Smyth, *Leadership in War*
(New York: St. Martin's
Press, 1974), pp. 123–194.

190 "not the dynamic fighting . . ."
Ibid.

190 "The Japanese were in . . ."
Ibid.

191 "Please let me know . . ."
Churchill, *op. cit.*, Vol. IV,
p. 42.

191 "the possibility of . . ."
Ibid., p. 43.

191 "this will be one . . ."
Ibid., p. 44.

192 "up to the limit . . ."
Ibid., p. 45.

192 "I regard keeping . . ."
Ibid., p. 47.

192 "After all the assurances . . ."
Ibid., p. 51.

192 "a British scuttle while . . ."
Ibid., p. 52.

192 "we are fighting all . . ."
Arthur Swinson, *Defeat in
Malaya* (New York: 1970).

p. 177.

192 "The retreat complex . . ."
Leasor, *op. cit.*, p. 198.

CHAPTER 11
*THE CATARACT
OF DISASTER*

Page

193 "HELP IS ON THE WAY . . ."
Hanson Baldwin, *Battles Lost
and Won—The Rock* (New
York: Harper and Row,
1948), p. 130.

193 "were the Battling Bastards . . ."
Douglas MacArthur,
Reminiscences (New York:
McGraw-Hill, 1964), p. 133.

194 "I have personally selected . . ."
James, *op. cit.*, Vol. II, p. 66.

194 "outshipped, outplaned . . ."
Pogue, *op. cit.*, Vol. II, p. 246.

194 "doomed the Philippines . . ."
Stimson, *On Active Service*,
p. 398.

194 "You must determine . . ."
James, *op. cit.*, Vol. II, p. 75.

195 "pledge of duty . . ."
Ibid., p. 96.

195 "so long as there . . ."
Pogue, *op. cit.*, Vol. II, p. 248.

195 "If we don't get . . ."
Manchester, *op. cit.*, p. 248.

195 "Battle Hymn of the Republic"
Baldwin, *op. cit.*, p .422.

196 "at all costs."
Morison, *op. cit.*, Vol. III,
Rising Sun, p. 257.

196 "serious enemy threat . . ."
Ibid.

197 "HAUL OUT WITH HALSEY"
Ibid., p. 264.

197 "History would condemn
him . . ."
Ibid., p. 310 (From Kroese,
The Dutch Navy at War,
p. 57).

198 "Our task is to hold . . ."
Kate Cafrey, *Out in the
Midday Sun* (New York:
Stein and Day, 1973), p. 144.

198 "an epic in Imperial history"
Ibid., p. 149.

198 "Singapore was burning . . ."

Page

Leasor, *op. cit.*, p. 211.

199 "They came moving at . . ."
Kenneth Attwill, *Fortress*
(New York: Doubleday,
1960), p. 175.

200 "Battle must be fought . . ."
Churchill, *op. cit.*, Vol. IV,
p. 87.

200 "I was frightened all . . ."
Swinson, *op. cit.*, p. 197.

200 "ENGLAND FOR THE ENGLISH . . ."
Toland, *The Rising Sun*, p.
313.

201 "FEAR RESISTANCE IS NOT . . ."
Churchill, *op. cit.*, Vol. IV,
p. 91.

201 "your gallant stand . . ."
Ibid.

201 "In the spirit of chivalry . . ."
Toland, *The Rising Sun*, p.
313.

201 "discretion to cease resistance,"
Churchill, *op. cit.*, Vol. IV,
p. 264.

202 "Yes or no?"
Toland, *The Rising Sun*, p.
316.

202 "GENERAL SITUATION OF . . ."
Ibid., p. 317.

202 "The greatest disaster and . . ."
Lowenheim, *op. cit.*, p. 184.

202 "We must look forward . . ."
Churchill, *op. cit.*, Vol. IV,
p. 93.

203 "Loss of Java . . ."
Ibid., p. 121.

203 "cataract of disaster"
Ibid., p. 125.

203 "There is nothing else . . ."
Churchill, *op. cit.*, Vol. IV,
p. 142.

203 "We feel a primary . . ."
Ibid.

203 "reverse a decision . . ."
Ibid.

203 "just a wet ditch . . ."
Smyth, *Before the Dawn*
(London: Cassell, 1957), pp.
160–167.

203 "We withdrew much too . . ."
Ibid.

204 "The prime factor . . ."
Ibid., pp. 178–193.

204 "a series of deafening . . ."
Ibid.

205 "I hate the idea . . ."
Churchill, *op. cit.*, Vol. IV,
p. 125.

205 "I know that you will . . ."
Ibid., p. 127.

205 "YOU MUST CONTINUE
ATTACKS . . ."
Churchill, *op. cit.*, Vol. VI,
p. 128.

206 "We will have to do . . ."
Morison, *op. cit.*, Vol. III,
Rising Sun, p. 337.

207 "FOLLOW ME"
Ibid., p. 353.

207 "ENEMY RETREATING WEST . . ."
Ibid.

207 "I AM TORPEDOED"
Ibid., p. 356.

209 "Enemy ships believed to . . ."
Ibid., p. 368.

210 "We are shutting down . . ."
Toland, *The Rising Sun*, p.
325.

211 "if we could not send out . . ."
Churchill, *op. cit.*, Vol. IV,
p. 144.

211 "Under heavy fire men . . ."
Ibid., p. 144.

211 "to hold Rangoon . . ."
Ibid., p. 145.

211 "grim racc against . . ."
Ibid., p. 147.

212 "where you will assume . . ."
Pogue, *op. cit.*, Vol. II, p. 251.

212 "a simple volunteer"
James, *op. cit.*, Vol. II, p. 98.

212 "psychological time"
Manchester, *op. cit.*, p. 256.

213 "If I get through . . ."
James, *op. cit.*, Vol. II, p. 101.

213 "a trip in a concrete mixer"
Manchester, *op. cit.*, p. 271.

213 "I came through and . . ."
Ibid.

CHAPTER 12
VICTORY DISEASE

Page

214 "the victory disease"
Fuchida and Okumiya, *op.
cit.*, p. 245.

215 "The fruits of victory . . ."
Bergamini, *op. cit.*, p. 951
(from Kido's *Diary*, pp.
940–950).

215 "slapping the Burmese . . ."
Saburo Ienaga, *The Pacific
War* (New York: Pantheon,
1968), p. 174.

216 "Bear in mind the fact . . ."
Ibid., p. 150.

217 "There are no restrictions . . ."
Ibid., p. 155.

217 "The southern region for . . ."
Ibid.

217 "Do you stick decapitated . . ."
Ibid., p. 173.

217 "The pompous English . . ."
Ibid.

219 "Time would work against . . ."
Fuchida and Okumiya, *op.
cit.*, p. 50.

219 "Seizure of Hawaii and . . ."
Ibid.

220 "The Combined Fleet's . . ."
Ibid., p. 59.

220 "decisive confrontation"
Ibid.

220 "We believe that by . . ."
Ibid., p. 60.

220 "destroy the enemy's
carrier . . ."
Ibid.

221 "misfortunes that come . . ."
Lowenheim, *op. cit.*, p. 185.

221 "The United States
situation . . ."
Ibid., p. 187.

222 "a change in basic strategy"
Matloff and Snell, *op. cit.*,
p. 155.

222 "(a) Maintenance of . . ."
Ibid., p. 158.

222 "desirable, but not essential"
Ibid.

222 "not immediately vital . . ."
Ibid.

222 "because of the
repercussions . . ."
Ernest J. King and Walter
Muir Whitehill, *Fleet Admiral
King: A Naval Record* (New
York: Norton, 1952), p. 382.

222 "set up 'strong points' . . ."
Ibid.

223 "Admiral King is an . . ."
New York Times, Sept. 18,
1979.

223 "Hold Hawaii. Support . . ."
John B. Lundstrom, *The First
South Pacific Campaign*
(Annapolis, Md.: U.S. Naval
Institute Press, 1976), p. 52.

223 "King's creeping movement . . ."
Ibid., p. 54.

223 "Everything portends . . ."

Page

Lowenheim, *op. cit.*, p. 187.

224 "with little recorded discussion"
Matloff and Snell, *op. cit.*,
p. 161.

224 "current commitments."
Ibid.

224 "clever move"
Bryant, *op. cit.*, Vol. I, pp.
288–289.

224 "To counter these moves . . ."
Ibid.

224 "to work by influence . . ."
Churchill, *op. cit.*, Vol. IV,
p. 319.

225 "we are all definitely . . ."
Pogue, *op. cit.*, Vol. II, p. 319.

225 "Sufficient troops and . . ."
Manchester, *op. cit.*, p. 282.

225 "A Hero on Ice"
Ibid.

226 "Of all the faulty . . ."
James, *op. cit.*, Vol. II, p. 123.

226 "If the Japanese can . . ."
Baldwin, *op. cit.*, p. 134.

226 "There is no reason why . . ."
Toland, *The Rising Sun*, p.
329.

227 "WHEN THE SUPPLY
SITUATION . . ."
Baldwin, *op. cit.*, p. 136.

227 "in two days an army . . ."
Ibid., p. 137.

227 "We have no further . . ."
Ibid.

227 "The air was filled with . . ."
Ibid., pp. 136–137.

228 "I have not communicated . . ."
James, *op. cit.*, Vol. II, p. 147.

228 "No army has done so
much . . ."
Ibid.

230 "I was now sure enemy . . ."
Fuchida and Okumiya, *op.
cit.*, p. 41.

230 "a spectacular display of . . ."
Ibid., p. 44.

231 "immense perils"
Churchill, *op. cit.*, Vol. IV,
p. 159.

231 "to offer some menace . . ."
Ibid.

CHAPTER 13
TAKING A BEATING

Page

233 "I don't want to set . . ."
Carroll V. Glines, *Doolittle's
Tokyo Raiders* (Princeton:
Van Nostrand, 1964), pp.
100–111.

234 "Launch planes to Col. . . ."
Ibid.

234 "O.K. fellas, this is . . ."
Ibid.

234 "The wind and sea were so . . ."
Ibid.

234 "Jimmy led his squadron
off . . ."
Halsey and Halsey, *op. cit.*
p. 98.

234 "Changed course and axis . . ."
Glines, *op. cit.*, pp. 128–130.

234 "to bomb and fire the . . ."
Ibid.

234 "dive in, full throttle . . ."
Ibid.

234 "continued flying low . . ."
Ibid.

234 "Anti-aircraft very active . . ."
Ibid.

235 "the real thing"
Ibid.

237 "They will never voluntarily
treat . . ."
Barbara Tuchman, *Stilwell
and the American Experience
in China* (New York:
Macmillan, 1971), p. 331.

237 "Britain must abandon . . ."
Churchill, *op. cit.*, Vol. IV,
p. 191.

238 "amateur tactics"
Tuchman, *op. cit.*, p. 341.

238 "Looked me over as . . ."
Ibid., p. 347.

239 "Any aircraft we saw . . ."
Viscount Slim, *Defeat into
Victory* (New York: McKay,
1961), p. 59.

240 "The pusilanimous bastards"
Tuchman, *op. cit.*, p. 355.

240 "I can't shoot them . . ."
Ibid., p. 356.

240 "like enticing a shy sparrow . . ."
Slim, *op. cit.*, p. 64.

241 "They must be given no
grounds . . ."
Ibid., p. 91.

241 "We are about to take a
beating . . ."
Tuchman, *op. cit.*, p. 366.

241 "It was the God-damnest . . ."
Ibid., p. 369.

242 "God, if we can only . . ."
Ibid., p. 372.

242 "With a resounding thump . . ."
Slim, *op. cit.*, p. 92.

243 "Of course we shall take . . ."
Tuchman, *op. cit.*, p. 374.

243 "That fat turtle egg"
Ibid., p. 373.

243 "General Arnold sent us . . ."
Tuchman, *op. cit.*, p. 374.

244 "I got a hell of a beating"
Ibid., p. 385.

CHAPTER 14
THE HIDDEN VICTORY

Page

245 "cataract of disaster"
Churchill, *op. cit.*, Vol. IV,
p. 125.

245 "The objective & mo"
N.A. RG 457–SRN March
28, 1942.

247 "YOU DON'T HAVE TO BE . . ."
W. J. Holmes, *Double-Edged
Secrets* (Annapolis, Md.:
U.S. Naval Institute Press,
1979), p. 54.

248 "Sealed off from the rest . . ."
Ibid., p. 56.

248 "The Japanese are now in a . . ."
U.S. Naval Operational
Archives (USNOA), Captain
Steele's Running Estimate and
Summary, 1941–42. CINCPAC
Files, April 3, 1942 (cited
hereafter as the *Greybook*).

249 "nothing appears to be
heading . . ."
Ibid., April 22, 1942.

250 "we should be able . . ."
Ibid.

250 "defeatists and pessimists"
King and Whitehill, *op. cit.*,
p. 376.

251 "to check further advance . . ."
Halsey and Bryan, *op. cit.*

252 "it is not likely that . . ."
Lundstrom, *op. cit.*, p. 72.

Page

252 "IF THE ENEMY STRIKING . . ."
N.A. RG 457, SRN Intercepts.

253 "This was the kind of . . ."
Lundstrom, *op. cit.*, p. 102.

254 "certainly disappointing in . . ."
E. B. Potter, *Nimitz*
(Annapolis, Md.: U.S. Naval
Institute Press, 1976), p. 70.

255 "much chargin"
Morison, *op. cit.*, Vol. IV,
Coral Sea, p. 37.

256 "Scratch one flattop . . ."
Ibid., p. 42.

256 "Fortunately their bombing . . ."
James, *op. cit.*, Vol. II, p. 161.

256 "to improve Army
recognition . . ."
Ibid.

258 "slow torpedoes and long . . ."
Morison, *op. cit.*, Vol. IV,
Coral Sea, p. 51.

258 "The area on the port side . . ."
Hoyt, *op. cit.*, p. 86.

259 "the battle busted out"
Morison, *op. cit.*, Vol. IV,
Coral Sea, p. 53.

259 "Bandits are closing in!"
Hoyt, *op. cit.*, p. 97.

259 "We thought we were . . ."
Ibid., p. 121.

259 "skin literally dripping . . ."
Ibid., p. 120.

260 "We're got the torpedo . . ."
Ibid., p. 127.

261 "*Yourktown:* Nearest land . . ."
Ibid., p. 150.

262 "Well, Ted, let's get . . ."
Ibid., p. 162.

262 "Congratulations on your . . ."
Potter, *op. cit.*, p. 75.

262 "Remember this, we don't
know . . ."
Ibid., p. 76.

262 "ANNIIHILATE THE ENEMY."
Lundstrom, *op. cit.*, p. 113.

263 "a victory with decisive . . ."
Potter, *op. cit.*, p. 77.

263 "JAPANESE REPULSED IN
GREAT . . ."
New York Times, May 9,
1941.

263 "Very excellent news"
Toland, *The Rising Sun*, p.
371.

264 "like living in the center . . ."
Baldwin, *op. cit.*, p. 139.

264 "They will have to come . . ."
Ibid., p. 142.

264 "SITUATION HERE IS FAST . . ."
Toland, *The Rising Sun*, p.
356.

264 "In my opinion the enemy . . ."
Ibid.

265 "You and your devoted . . ."
Baldwin, *op. cit.*, p. 145.

265 "WITH BROKEN HEART . . ."
James, *op. cit.*, Vol. II, p. 1448.

265 "Tell the Nips we'll . . ."
Baldwin, *op. cit.*, p. 148.

265 "WE MAY HAVE TO GIVE . . ."
Ibid.

265 "THE JIG IS UP . . ."
Ibid., p. 149.

266 "You must be very . . ."
Toland, *The Rising Sun*, p.
358.

266 "Failure to fully . . ."
Ibid., p. 361.

266 "is temporarily unbalanced . . ."
James, *op. cit.*, Vol. II, p. 149.

267 "Corregidor needs no
comment . . ."
Ibid., p. 148.

CHAPTER 15
CALCULATED RISKS

Page

268 "By Command of His
Imperial . . ."
Agawa, *op. cit.*, p. 304.

268 "The Hashirajima Fleet"
Ibid., p. 301.

269 "decisive naval engagement"
Fuchida and Okumiya, *op.
cit.*, p. 78.

269 "Second Trafalgar"
John Costello and Terry
Hughes, *Jutland 1916* (New
York: Holt, Rinehart and
Winston, 1977), p. 236.

271 "As the A Force . . ."
N.A. RG 457, SRN Intercepts,
May 4, 1942.

271 "Expedite delivery fueling . . ."
N.A. SRH 036, *Radio
Intelligence in World War II.*

271 "PROCEED TO GUAM . . ."
Ibid.

271 "PLEASE CHANGE THE
DIRECTIVE . . ."
Ibid.

272 "jumping up and down"
Lundstrom, *op. cit.*, p. 131.

272 "The Pacific theater must . . ."
Ibid., p. 168.

272 "virtually eliminate the . . ."
Ibid., p. 131.

273 "massing strong land . . ."
Matloff and Snell, *op. cit.*, p.
212.

274 "WILL ADMIRALTY . . ."
U.S. NOA COMINCH Signal
Log May 18, 1942.

274 "impossible to make every . . ."
Ibid.

274 "establish ourselves in key . . ."
Churchill, *op. cit.*, Vol. IV,
p. 201.

274 "time to amend his . . ."
Ibid., p. 206.

274 "inadvisable"
Lundstrom, *op. cit.*, p. 154.

275 "operate one or more . . ."
Ibid., p. 152.

275 "OPERATIONS OF TASK FORCE
16 . . ."
Ibid., p. 154.

275 "DESIRE YOU PROCEED TO . . ."
Ibid., p. 161.

275 "Considerable differences
in . . ."
Greybook, May 17, 1942.

275 "Will watch the situation . . ."
Ibid.

275 "Chiefly employ strong . . ."
Ibid.

276 "EXPEDITE RETURN"
Lundstrom, *op. cit.*, p. 161.

276 "regarding water situation . . ."
U.S. ONA, CINCPAC Signal
Confidential Log.

276 "Trouble was brewing . . ."
Halsey and Halsey, *op. cit.*,
p. 75.

277 "We must endeavor to . . ."
Greybook, May 21, 1942.

277 "They'll come in from . . ."
Potter, *op. cit.*, p. 83.

278 "the most grievous . . ."
Ibid., p. 84.

279 "I think you'll have a . . ."
Ibid., p. 85.

279 "We must have the ship . . ."
Ibid.

280 "Fletcher did a fine . . ."
Ibid., p. 86.

280 "inflict maximum damage
on . . ."
Morison, *op. cit., Coral Sea*,
Vol. IV, p. 84.

280 "You will be governed by . . ."

Page

Thomas B. Buell, *The Quiet Warrior* (Boston: Little, Brown, 1974), pp. 12–14.

280 "Good Luck and Good Hunting"
Potter, *op. cit.*, p. 87.

280 "not just for two weeks either"
Ibid.

282 "Now comes the crucial time"
Agawa, *op. cit.*, p. 310.

CHAPTER 16
GIVE THEM THE WORKS

Page

284 "But where is the enemy fleet?"
Fuchida and Okumiya, *op. cit.*, p. 127.

284 "Do you see what I see?"
Morison, *op. cit.*, Vol. IV, *Coral Sea*, p. 98.

284 "Main Body . . . bearing 262 . . ."
Potter, *op. cit.*, p. 91.

284 "This will clear up . . ."
Ibid., p. 92.

284 "MAIN BODY . . . THAT IS NOT . . ."
Ibid.

285 "The fate of the United . . ."
Stanley Johnson, *The Queen of the Flattops* (New York, 1965). p. 89.

285 "THE SITUATION IS DEVELOPING . . ."
Potter, *op. cit.*, p. 92.

286 "There is no evidence . . ."
Fuchida and Okumiya, *op. cit.*, p. 144.

286 "to attack Midway . . ."
Ibid.

286 "We can then turn . . ."
Ibid.

287 "MANY ENEMY PLANES . . ."
Morison, *op. cit.*, Vol. IV, *Coral Sea*, p. 63.

287 "the curtain rise on . . ."
Ibid., p. 103.

287 "ENEMY CARRIERS . . . 25 KNOTS."
Potter, *op. cit.*, p. 93.

287 "Well, you were only . . ."
Ibid.

287 "PROCEED SOUTHWESTERLY . . ."
Morison, *op. cit.*, Vol. IV,

Coral Sea, p. 103.

288 "SECOND ATTACK NECESSARY"
Fuchida and Okumiya, *op. cit.*, p. 136.

289 "very cunning maneuver"
Ibid., p. 158.

289 "Still they kept coming . . ."
Ibid., p. 160.

290 "SHIPS APPARENTLY ENEMY . . ."
Ibid., p. 165.

290 "like a bolt out . . ."
Ibid.

291 "PREPARE TO CARRY OUT . . ."
Morison, *op. cit.*, Vol. IV, *Coral Sea*, p. 107.

291 "ASCERTAIN SHIP TYPES . . ."
Ibid.

291 "ENEMY SHIPS ARE FIVE . . ."
Ibid.

291 "ENEMY FORCE ACCOMPANIED . . ."
Ibid.

292 "Ships were on all sides . . ."
Ibid., p. 112.

292 "CONSIDER IT ADVISABLE . . ."
Fuchida and Okumiya, *op. cit.*, p. 170.

293 "Here we go again"
Ibid., p. 171.

293 "AFTER COMPLETING RECOVERY . . ."
Ibid.

29 "TEN ENEMY TORPEDO PLANES . . ."
Ibid., p. 175.

293 "SPEED PREPARATIONS FOR . . ."
Ibid., p. 174.

293 "An electric thrill . . ."
Ibid., p. 175.

293 "If there is only one . . ."
Toland, *The Rising Sun*, p. 382.

294 "He went straight for the . . ."
Life magazine, Aug. 31, 1942, pp. 78–80.

294 "Their distant wings . . ."
Fuchida and Okumiya, *op. cit.*, p. 175.

294 "I could see the Jap Captain . . ."
Life magazine, *op. cit.*, p. 78.

295 "as frantic as I have . . ."
Potter, *op. cit.*, p. 95.

295 "Wilco, as soon as I can . . ."
Morison, *op. cit.*, Vol. IV, *Coral Sea*, p. 122.

296 "The terrifying scream of the . . ."
Fuchida and Okumiya, *op. cit.*, p. 177.

296 "scene terrible to behold."
Ibid., p. 179.

298 "ATTACK ENEMY CARRIERS . . ."
Morison, *op. cit.*, Vol. IV, *Coral Sea*, p. 132.

298 "ALL OUR PLANES ARE TAKING . . ."
Ibid.

298 "FIRES RAGING ABOARD KAGA . . ."
Toland, *The Rising Sun*, p. 386.

299 "Well, I've got on . . ."
Morison, *op. cit.*, Vol. IV, *Coral Sea*, p. 133.

299 "ENEMY DIVE BOMBERS . . ."
Fuchida and Okumiya, *op. cit.*, p. 196.

302 "The game is up"
Morison, *op. cit.*, Vol. IV, *Coral Sea*, p. 138.

302 "HIRYU HIT BY BOMBS . . ."
Fuchida and Okumiya, *op. cit.*, p. 213.

303 "THE ENEMY FLEET HAS BEEN . . ."
Fuchida and Okumiya, *op. cit.*, p. 213.

303 "IMMEDIATELY CONTACT AND . . ."
Ibid.

303 "TOTAL ENEMY STRENGTH IS . . ."
Ibid.

303 "has no stomach for a night engagement"
Ibid., p. 214.

303 "REVERSE COURSE IMMEDIATELY . . ."
Ibid.

303 "I did not feel justified . . ."
Morison, *op. cit.*, Vol. IV, *Coral Sea*, p. 142.

304 "Our battleships, for all their . . ."
Fuchida and Okumiya, *op. cit.*, p. 216.

304 "But even if that proves . . ."
Ibid.

304 "Leave that to me . . ."
Ibid., p. 217.

304 "MIDWAY OPERATION IS CANCELLED"
Ibid., p. 218.

305 "YOU WHO HAVE PARTICIPATED . . ."
Potter, *op. cit.*, p. 99.

305 "the start of what may be . . ."
Greybook, June 4, 1942.

305 "It is too early to claim . . ."
Morison, *op. cit.*, Vol. IV, *Coral Sea*, p. 143.

307 "stern chase is a long one"
Ibid., p. 149.

308 "I felt like swearing"
Morison, *op. cit.*, Vol. IV, *Coral Sea*, p. 158.

Page

308 "It was all his responsibility . . ."
Agawa, *op. cit.*, p. 321.

308 "CONTINUE TO MAKE THE
ENEMY . . ."
Potter, *op. cit.*, p. 101.

308 "This officer deserves a major
share . . ."
Ibid.

309 "NAVY HAD WORD OF JAPAN . . ."
Buell, *op. cit.* (King), p. 203.

309 "The Battle of Midway was
the . . ."
King and Whitehill, *op. cit.*

CHAPTER 17
*WE MUST ATTACK,
ATTACK, ATTACK!*

Page

310 "Pearl Harbor has now
been . . ."
Potter, *op. cit.*, p. 107.

310 "the closes squeak"
Pogue, *op. cit.*, Vol. II, p. 325.

310 "landing on the Continent . . ."
Matloff and Snell, *op. cit.*, p.
233.

310 "give no promise."
Churchill, *op. cit.*, Vol. IV,
p. 297.

310 "sacrificial landing."
Pogue, *op. cit.*, Vol. II, p. 327.

311 "should be no substantial . . ."
Bryant, *op. cit.*, Vol. I, p. 327.

311 "could not run the mortal . . ."
Churchill, *op. cit.*, Vol. IV,
p. 330.

312 "so stirred up"
Pogue, *op. cit.*, Vol. II, p. 340.

313 "We should turn to the . . ."
Ibid.

313 "strategic natural selection"
Churchill, *op. cit.*, Vol. IV,
p. 300.

313 "like carrying ice to the North
Pole"
Ibid., p. 394.

313 "defeat of Germany means . . ."
Burns, *op. cit.*, Vol. II, p. 243.

314 "forcing the enemy back . . ."
James, *op. cit.*, Vol. II, p. 186.

314 "primarily naval and
amphibious . . ."
Pogue, *op. cit.*, Vol. II, p. 379.

314 "general command of all
operations . . ."
Ibid., p. 380.

314 "with great difficulty"
Ibid., p. 381.

315 "Three weeks ago . . ."
Potter, *op. cit.*, p. 179.

317 "Worn out by strenuous . . ."
Rafael Steinberg, *Island
Fighting* (Chicago: Time–Life
Books, 1970), p. 50.

317 "The road gets gradually . . ."
Ibid., p. 51.

318 "I led one lost cause . . ."
James, *op. cit.*, Vol. II, p. 193.

318 "We'll defend Australia . . ."
Manchester, *op. cit.*, p. 298.

318 "tenacious an enemy as . . ."
Ibid., p. 299.

318 "We must attack . . ."
Ibid., p. 298.

318 "can of worms"
George C. Kenney, *General
Kenney Reports* (New York:
Duell, Slone & Pierce, 1949),
p. 41.

318 "rabble of boulevard shock . . ."
James, *op. cit.*, Vol. II, p. 198.

319 "even if nothing is left . . ."
Kenney, *op. cit.*, p. 43.

319 "the General's Rasputin"
Manchester, *op. cit.*, p. 301.

319 "That is what you know . . ."
Kenney, *op. cit.*, pp. 52–53.

319 "didn't even know the
location . . ."
S. E. Smith, ed., *U.S. Marine
Corps in World War Two*
(New York: Random House,
1969), p. 147.

319 "scattered over hell's . . ."
Ibid.

321 "complete bust"
Heinl, *op. cit.*, p. 347.

321 "Everyone seemed ready to . . ."
Richard Tregaskis,
Guadalcanal Diary (New
York: Random House, 1943),
p. 34.

322 "The thing that was
happening . . ."
Ibid., p. 33.

322 "LARGE FORCE OF SHIPS . . ."
Toland, *The Rising Sun*, p.
402.

322 "ENEMY FORCES OVERWHELMING"
Ibid.

322 "Wizard!!! Caloo, Callay . . ."
Smith, ed., *op. cit.*, p. 168.

322 "Ant-like they went over . . ."

Ibid., p. 163.

323 "landing successful . . ."
Ibid., p. 165.

323 "The Nips had 200 men . . ."
Ibid.

324 "in view of the large . . ."
Samuel Eliot Morison, Vol. V,
The Struggle for Guadalcanal
(Boston: Little, Brown, 1948),
p. 27.

325 "running away"
Toland, *The Rising Sun*, p.
408.

325 "MAY EACH MAN DO HIS UTMOST"
Morison, *op. cit.*, Vol. V,
Guadalcanal, p. 22.

325 "Certain victory"
Ibid.

325 "WARNING WARNING STRANGE . . ."
Morison, *op. cit.*, Vol. V,
Guadalcanal, p. 37.

326 "Suddenly the ship shook . . ."
Smith, ed., *op. cit.*, p. 177.

326 "in view of impending
heavy . . ."
Morison, *op. cit.*, Vol. V,
Guadalcanal, p. 39.

326 "It is as if the Marines . . ."
Heinl, *op. cit.*, p. 353.

326 "We have seized a strategic . . ."
Ibid.

327 "engaged in a desperate
struggle . . ."
Morison, *op. cit.*, Vol. V,
Guadalcanal, p. 61.

327 "make every effort"
Ibid.

327 "landing in the face of . . ."
R. Tanaka, *Japan's Losing
Struggle for Guadalcanal*
(Annapolis, Md.: U.S. Naval
Institute Proceedings, 1956),
p. 690.

328 "Fish and rice, fish . . ."
Heinl, *op. cit.*, p. 354.

328 "one of the most beautiful . . ."
Steinberg, *op. cit.*, p. 29.

328 "Now let the bastards come"
Ibid.

329 "WE HAVE SUCCEEDED IN INVASION"
Toland, *The Rising Sun*, p.
416.

329 "NO ENEMY AT ALL . . ."
Ibid.

329 "They were walking right
in . . ."
Heinl, *op. cit.*, p. 356.

329 "They started jabbering so . . ."
Ibid.

329 "Here was booming,

Page

sounding . . ."
Smith, ed., *op. cit.*, p. 218.

329 "like a housefly's attacking . . ."
Tanaka, *op. cit.*, p. 691.

330 "We watched those awful . . ."
Smith, ed., *op. cit.*, p. 234.

330 "like meat grinders"
Ibid.

331 "a piece of folly"
Heinl, *op. cit.*, p. 357.

331 "although still in Empire . . ."
CINCPAC, Greybook, *op. cit.*,
Aug. 21, 1942.

334 "warship transportation"
Tanaka, *op. cit.*, p. 695.

336 "TRY AND GET THEM OUT"
James, *op. cit.*, Vol. II, p. 205.

336 "The enemy fell into the . . ."
Ibid., p. 208.

336 "not yet convinced of the . . ."
Ibid.

336 "How can we fight against this?"
Steinberg, *op. cit.*, p. 51.

336 "The Detachment will stay
here . . ."
Ibid.

CHAPTER 18
*EVERYBODY HOPES
WE CAN HANG ON*

Page

338 "This is the toughest war . . ."
Rosenmann, ed., *op. cit.*
(1942), p. 368.

338 "Overall stabilization of
prices . . ."
Ibid.

338 "will cost this nation . . ."
Ibid.

339 "miracle of God and the
genius . . ."
Hughes and Costello, *op. cit.*,
p. 209.

341 "liquidation of the China
theater"
Tuchman, *op. cit.*, p. 401.

341 "other arrangements"
Ibid.

342 "the bastards will sabotage . . ."
Ibid., p. 417.

342 "accomplish the downfall
of . . ."
Ibid., p. 431.

343 "sympathize with your reaction"
Ibid., p. 442.

343 "Peanut and I are on a raft . . ."
Ibid.

343 "disastrous outcome . . ."
Pogue, *op. cit.*, Vol. II, p. 386.

343 "regardless of interference
with . . ."
Ibid., p. 387.

343 "a golden opportunity, not . . ."
Morison, *op. cit.*, Vol. V,
Guadalcanal, p. 115.

344 "a bowl of black dust which . . ."
Heinl, *op. cit.*, p. 360.

344 "a quagmire of black mud . . ."
Ibid.

345 "It was a combined sea and . . ."
Smith, ed., *op. cit.*, p. 260.

345 "had been but a prelude"
Ibid., p. 261.

345 "the situation up front is . . ."
Ibid., pp. 260–265.

345 "special brand of terrorism"
Ibid.

345 "The sky and the jungle . . ."
Ibid.

346 "U.S. MARINES BE DEAD
TOMORROW."
Ibid.

346 "a mad religious rite"
Ibid.

346 "When one wave was
mowed . . ."
Ibid.

348 "Hell, yes, why not?"
Toland, *The Rising Sun*,
p. 439.

348 "Our supply has been cut
off . . ."
Ibid., p. 491.

348 "thinner than Gandhi himself."
Ibid.

348 "I'll give you cover . . ."
Ibid.

348 "no chance of winning the . . ."
Jack Coggins, *The Campaign
for Guadalcanal* (New York:
Doubleday, 1972), p. 93.

349 "search for and destroy . . ."
Morison, *op. cit.*, Vol. V,
Guadalcanal, p. 149.

351 "Stupid Bastards!"
Coggins, *op. cit.*, p. 93.

351 "Providence abandoned us"
Morison, *op. cit.*, Vol. V,
Guadalcanal, p. 171.

352 "The ensuing scene baffled . . ."
Tanaka, *op. cit.*, p. 815.

352 "The scene was topped off . . ."
Ibid.

353 "SITUATION DEMANDS TWO
URGENT . . ."
Toland, *The Rising Sun*,
p. 452.

353 "It now appears that we are
unable . . ."
Morison, *op. cit.*, Vol. V,
Guadalcanal, p. 178.

354 "Everybody hopes that we can
hold on"
Ibid.

354 "YOU WILL TAKE COMMAND OF
THE . . ."
James M. Merrill, *A Sailor's
Admiral* (New York:
Crowell, 1976), p. 51.

354 "Jesus Christ and General
Jackson . . ."
Ibid.

354 "This is a tough job . . ."
Ibid.

354 "Europe was Washington's . . ."
Halsey and Halsey, *op. cit.*,
p. 113.

354 "One minute we were too
limp . . ."
Ibid., p. 116.

354 "I can hold . . ."
Smith, ed., *op. cit.*, p. 315.

355 "Now we had a fighting
chance."
Halsey and Halsey, *op. cit.*,
p. 120.

355 "entire resources of the
United . . ."
Pogue, *op. cit.*, Vol. II, p. 392.

355 "battle weary"
Ibid., p. 389.

355 "anxiety about the southwest
Pacific . . ."
Ibid., p. 393.

356 "apprehend and annihilate"
Morison, *op. cit.*, Vol. V,
Guadalcanal, p. 199.

357 "Colonel, there are about . . ."
Smith, ed., *op. cit.* (Burke
Davis), p. 320.

357 "Blood for the Emperor!"
Ibid.

357 "To hell with your
goddamned . . ."
Ibid.

357 "pitiful example of a lack . . ."
Tanaka, *op. cit.*, p. 817.

358 "Take that damned label . . ."
Frank Hough, *The Island
War* (Philadelphia:

Page

Lippincott), p. 189.

358 "blitz that became a . . ."
Smith, ed., *op. cit.*, pp. 329–340.

358 "A colonel dropped dead about . . ."
Ibid.

359 "This failed because I underestimated . . ."
Toland, *The Rising Sun*, p. 468.

359 "the sentence of a thousand deaths"
Ibid.

359 "feeling as if my intestines . . ."
Ibid., p. 469.

CHAPTER 19
*THE FORK IN THE
ROAD TO VICTORY*

Page

360 "Accordingly there is a great . . ."
Morison, *op. cit.*, Vol. V, *Guadalcanal*, p. 203.

360 "regardless of weather and . . ."
Ibid., p. 203.

360 "ATTACK REPEAT ATTACK"
Ibid., p. 204.

361 "LARGE ENEMY UNIT SIGHTED . . ."
Ibid., p. 209.

364 "The general situation at Guadalcanal . . ."
Ibid., p. 224.

365 "Kill Japs, kill Japs . . ."
Potter, *op. cit.*, p. 204.

365 "two carriers, four battleships . . ."
Halsey and Bryan, *op. cit.*, p. 124.

366 "We didn't dare test it . . ."
Ibid., p. 125.

367 "COMMENCE FIRING. COUNTER ILLUMINATE."
Morison, *op. cit.*, Vol. V, *Guadalcanal*, p. 242.

367 "ODD SHIPS COMMENCE . . ."
Ibid., p. 243.

368 "We want the big ones . . ."
Coggins, *op. cit.*, p. 134.

368 "with all the fury . . ."
Ibid., p. 141.

368 "one of the most furious . . ."
Ernest J. King, *Fleet Admiral*

King: A Naval Record (New York: Norton, 1952), p. 211.

370 "the general effect is indelible . . ."
Tanaka, *op. cit.*, p. 822.

370 "prospects looked poor for . . ."
Ibid., p. 823.

370 "one of the best brains . . ."
Morison, *op. cit.*, Vol. V, *Guadalcanal*, p. 270.

371 "STAND ASIDE. COMING THROUGH . . ."
Ibid., p. 273.

372 "RUN AGROUND AND UNLOAD TROOPS"
Tanaka, *op. cit.*, p. 824.

372 "The last large-scale effort . . ."
Ibid.

372 "felt a heavy responsibility"
Ibid.

372 "the success or failure in . . ."
Morison, *op. cit.*, Vol. V, *Guadalcanal*, p. 287.

373 "Unobstructed, the enemy . . ."
Halsey and Bryan, *op. cit.*, p. 132.

373 "Until then he had been . . ."
Ibid., p. 131.

373 "THE MEN OF CACTUS LIFT THEIR . . ."
Potter, *op. cit.*, p. 206.

CHAPTER 20
*THE END OF THE
BEGINNING*

Page

374 "During the past two weeks . . ."
Rosenmann, ed., *op. cit.* (1947), p. 656.

374 "There is no time now for . . ."
Ibid.

374 "Now, this is not the end . . ."
Ibid.

375 "The insect life, from scorpions . . ."
George H. Johnston, *The Toughest Fights in the World* (New York: Duell, Sloan, Pearce, 1943), p. 99.

375 "Only for a time though . . ."
Ibid.

375 "Progress on the trail is not . . ."
James, *op. cit.*, Vol. II, p. 236.

376 "The soldiers had eaten anything . . ."
Sezo Okada, *Lost Troops*, Australian War Memorial, as quoted in Lida Mayo, *Bloody Buna* (New York: Doubleday, 1974), pp. 98–99.

376 "An ignominious death . . ."
Manchester, *op. cit.*, p. 304.

377 "easy pickings"
James, *op. cit.*, Vol. II, p. 240.

378 "a catastrophe of the first . . ."
Ibid.

378 "in a pink silk dressing gown . . ."
George H. Johnston, *Pacific Partner* (New York: Duell, Sloan & Pearce, 1944), p. 93.

378 "regardless of cost."
James, *op. cit.*, Vol. II, p. 241.

378 "Machine gun tracers lit the . . ."
Steinberg, *op. cit.*, p. 53.

378 "Everywhere men cursed . . ."
Ibid.

378 "a bitter pill"
James, *op. cit.*, Vol. II, p. 243.

378 "bringing back loads of . . ."
Kenney, *op. cit.*, p. 157.

378 "who knew they would fight"
James, *op. cit.*, Vol. II, p. 243.

378 "he was being gloated over by . . ."
Ibid., p. 244.

378 "Go out there, Bob . . ."
Ibid.

379 "a very pallid siege was . . ."
Ibid., p. 261.

379 "In any stalemate it was . . ."
Ibid., p. 261.

379 "There was no front . . ."
Ibid.

379 "There was never any idea . . ."
Ibid.

379 "Don't fire. They won't . . ."
Ibid.

379 "I stopped all fighting . . ."
Ibid.

379 "It was the wildest, maddest . . ."
George H. Johnston, *New Guinea Diary* (London: Gollanez, 1944), p. 45.

380 "Those bastards fight to the . . ."
Ibid.

380 "GONAS GONE"
Mayo, *op. cit.*, p. 149.

Page

380 "time is working desperately . . ."
James, *op. cit.*, Vol. II, p. 268.

380 "The Papuan campaign is in . . ."
Ibid., p. 271.

381 "there are hundreds of Buna's . . ."
Toland, *The Rising Sun*, p. 487.

381 "time, effort, blood and money . . ."
Ibid.

382 "If the surface Navy continues . . ."
Heinl, *op. cit.*, p. 374.

382 "unbelievable achievement of his Marines"
Smith, *op. cit.*, ed., p. 359.

382 "It may well be that this . . ."
Ibid.

382 "honorable death rather than die . . ."
Toland, *The Rising Sun*, p. 489.

382 "There is no question that Japan's . . ."
Tanaka, *op. cit.*, p. 831.

382 "Just as it betokened . . ."
Ibid.

383 "How splendid the first stage . . ."
Toland, *The Rising Sun*, p. 486.

CHAPTER 21
COMBINED DEADLOCK

Page

384 "Our withdrawal from Guadalcanal . . ."
Bergamini, *op. cit.*, p. 1010.

384 "The Axis knew that they must win . . ."
Adams, *op. cit.*, p. 491.

384 "I suspect Hitler and Tojo . . ."
Ibid.

385 "combined deadlock . . ."
Lowenheim, *op. cit.*, p. 290.

385 "a comfortable oasis to the . . ."
Ibid.

385 "he thought he might just as well . . ."
Dallek, *op. cit.*, p. 369.

385 "so hot that it is impossible . . ."
Ibid., p. 368.

386 "To make a fruitless assault . . ."
Churchill, *op. cit.*, Vol. IV, p. 671.

386 "the dripping of water on . . ."
Bryant, *op. cit.*, Vol. I, p. 445.

386 "Every diversion or side issue . . ."
Pogue, *op. cit.*, Vol. III, p. 22.

386 "allow the Japanese and pause."
Ibid.

386 "just a great nuisance that kept . . ."
Bryant, *op. cit.*, Vol. I, p. 446.

386 "The shortage of shipping was . . ."
Ibid., p. 451.

387 "Unless we can effectively combat . . ."
Ibid., p. 450.

387 "cannot make his brain move . . ."
Ibid., p. 451.

387 "always on the lookout for . . ."
Ibid., p. 445.

387 "cannot but adversely affect . . ."
Pogue, *op. cit.*, Vol. III, p. 27.

387 "a situation might arise in the . . ."
Pogue, *op. cit.*, Vol. III, p. 26.

387 "must be kept within such limits . . ."
Bryant, *op. cit.*, Vol. I, p. 450.

388 "defeat of the U-boats remains . . ."
Churchill, *op. cit.*, Vol. V, p. 60.

388 "Russia must be sustained . . ."
Ibid., p. 61.

388 "blueprint for how to set about . . ."
Bryant, *op. cit.*, Vol. I, p. 439.

388 "We had got practically all . . ."
Ibid. p. 454.

388 "We even lost our shirts"
Eddie Bauer, *The History of World War II* (New York: Galahad, 1979), p. 332.

389 "Their only terms would be . . ."
Pogue, *op. cit.*, Vol. III, p. 33.

389 "final supreme effort."
Halsey and Bryan, *op. cit.*, p. 147.

390 "ORGANIZED RESISTANCE ON . . ."
Merrill, *op. cit.*, p. 82.

390 "WHEN I SENT A PATCH . . ."
Ibid.

390 "The dead of Bataan will rest . . ."

James, *op. cit.*, Vol. II, p. 279.

390 "low expenditure of life and . . ."
Ibid.

390 "So bet your shoes that all . . ."
Ibid.

390 "Give enough thought to your . . ."
Toland, *The Rising Sun*, p. 486.

391 "A merciful providence guarded us . . ."
James, *op. cit.*, Vol. III, p. 295.

392 "temporarily suspended for lack . . ."
Ibid., p. 309.

392 "ultimate seizure of the . . ."
Ibid., p. 310.

392 "to include the southern portion . . ."
Ibid.

393 "numerically insignificant enemy opposition"
Bauer, *op. cit.*, p. 620.

394 "In war you have to pay . . ."
Slim, *op. cit.*, p. 162.

395 "If they stay in the jungle . . ."
Ian Moser, *China—Burma—India* (Chicago: Time-Life Books, 1978), p. 98.

395 "As a military operation the raid . . ."
Slim, *op. cit.*, pp. 162–163.

396 "a man of genius and audacity"
Churchill, Vol. V, *op. cit.*, p. 567.

396 "little tangible return for the losses."
Slim, *op. cit.*, p. 163.

396 "was repaired in a few days . . ."
Ibid.

CHAPTER 22
TRYING TO RUN TWO WARS AT ONCE

Page

398 "every movement of a Japanese . . ."
N. A. RG 457–SRH, History of U.S. Army Ultra Intelligence.

398 "there will not be sufficient . . ."
Lowenstein, *op. cit.*, p. 322.

Page

399 "the British Chief of Staff sees . . ."
Ibid.

399 "IS IT IN THE REALM OF . . ."
Potter, *op. cit.* p. 221.

401 "Our old friend Yamamoto"
Potter, *op. cit.*, p. 233.

401 "The Commander in Chief Combined . . ."
N.A. SRNA CF Signal, April 14, 1943.

401 "Do we try to get him?"
Potter, *op. cit.*, p. 233.

401 "Lou know . . ."
Ibid.

401 "If the forces you command . . ."
Ibid.

401 "Good Luck and Good Hunting"
Ibid., p. 237.

401 "Expect to arrive Ballalle 07.45."
N.A. RG 457, SRNA Series, Japanese Naval Intercepts, April, 1943.

402 "Bogey's eleven o'clock high."
Toland, *The Rising Sun*, p. 501.

402 "Pop goes the weasel"
Potter, *op. cit.*, p. 234.

402 "whooped and applauded."
Toland, *The Rising Sun*, p. 502.

402 "What's good about it?"
Ibid.

403 "I liked him from the moment . . ."
James, *op. cit.*, Vol. II, p. 315.

403 "Five minutes after I reported . . ."
Ibid.

405 "Japanese drink blood like wine"
Morison, *op. cit.*, Vol. VII, p. 50.

405 "I will become a deity . . ."
Ibid.

405 "tremendous stimulant to the fighting . . ."
Ibid.

406 "We are just about where . . ."
Bryant, *op. cit.*, Vol. I, p. 493.

406 "most necessary"
Lowenheim, *op. cit.*, p. 325.

406 "I am conscious of serious . . ."
Dallek, *op. cit.*, p. 393.

CHAPTER 23
"KEEP 'EM DYING"

Page

407 "to settle exploitation . . ."
Churchill, *op. cit.*, Vol. IV, p. 686.

407 "I do not look forward to . . ."
Bryant, *op. cit.*, Vol. I, p. 500.

407 "munching a porcupine quill by quill"
Ibid., p. 499.

407 "pin down the British"
Pogue, *op. cit.*, Vol. III, p. 196.

408 "cause a chill of loneliness"
PRFRUS, Washington and Quebec, 1943, pp. 24–33.

408 "tangled mass of confusion"
Bryant, *op. cit.*, Vol. I, p. 505.

408 "we ought to convert . . ."
Pogue, *op. cit.*, Vol. III, p. 201.

408 "Unless the British Chiefs propose . . ."
Ibid.

408 "the swing toward the Pacific . . ."
Bryant, *op. cit.*, Vol. I, p. 507.

408 "best calculated to eliminate . . ."
Ibid., p. 516.

409 "undertake something foolish . . ."
PRFRUS, Washington and Quebec, 1943, pp. 121–123.

409 "continuance of administrative . . ."
Pogue, *op. cit.*, Vol. III, p. 211.

409 "everything humanly possible."
PRFRUS, Washington and Quebec, 1943, p. 135.

410 "in my opinion collapse the . . ."
James, *op. cit.*, Vol. II, p. 318.

410 "main effort"
Ibid., p. 319.

410 "a diversionary attack"
Ibid.

410 "From the broad strategic viewpoint . . ."
Ibid.

411 "We alternately crawled up . . ."
Sgt. Collis, in Smith, ed., *op. cit.*, p. 387.

411 "one of the most vicious in . . ."
Ibid., p. 389.

412 "to siphon off enemy strength . . ."
James, *op. cit.*, Vol. II, p. 323.

413 "the smoke of charred reputations . . ."

Halsey and Halsey, *op. cit.*, p. 161.

413 "OUR GROUND FORCES TODAY . . ."
Ibid., p. 164.

413 "KEEP 'EM DYING"
Ibid., p. 165.

414 "This is what it feels . . ."
Steinberg, *op. cit.*, p. 83.

414 "wary of another slugging match"
Halsey and Halsey, *op. cit.*, p. 170.

414 "jump over the enemy's . . ."
Ibid., p. 171.

414 "Next above Kolombangara . . ."
Ibid.

414 "like pouring water on a hot stone"
Ibid.

414 "best calculated to eliminate . . ."
Bryant, *op. cit.*, Vol. I, p. 516.

415 "lip tribute"
Stimson, *On Active Service*, p. 438.

416 "expect a very difficult time."
Bryant, *op. cit.*, Vol. I, p. 569.

416 "to carry on with preparations . . ."
Ibid.

416 "determined to make their ideas . . ."
Ibid., p. 571.

416 "determined to make their
Pogue, *op. cit.*, Vol. III, p. 243.

417 "available resources will be . . ."
PRFRUS, Washington and Quebec, 1943, p. 527.

CHAPTER 24
CRIPPLING BLOWS

Page

419 "Rabaul is to be neutralized . . ."
James, *op. cit.*, Vol. II, p. 331.

419 "It appears that the next logical step for South West Pacific Forces"
Ibid., p. 334.

420 "It was a crippling blow . . ."
Ibid., p. 325.

420 "Nothing is so helpless . . ."
Ibid.

Page

420 "Some five-dollar-a-month Jap
aviator . . ."
Kenney, *op. cit.*, p. 289.

420 "disgrace myself in front . . ."
Ibid.

420 "Everything went like
clockwork"
James, *op. cit.*, Vol. II, p. 327.

422 "It's Torokina. Now get on
your horse!"
Halsey and Halsey, *op. cit.*,
p. 174.

423 "series of short right jabs . . ."
Heinl, *op. cit.*, p. 380.

424 "This was the most desperate
emergency . . ."
Halsey and Halsey, *op. cit.*,
pp. 180–181.

424 "Cherryblossom's success—
perhaps . . ."
Ibid., p. 181.

424 "I sincerely expected both
air . . ."
Ibid.

424 "looked 150 years old"
Ibid.

424 "Let 'er go."
Ibid.

425 "ought to change the name . . ."
Ibid., p. 183.

425 "Two factors radically changed
our . . ."
Ibid., p. 184.

426 "We were a veteran
company . . ."
Smith, ed., *op. cit.* (Cibik),
pp. 439–460.

426 "I walked to the edge of . . ."
Ibid.

CHAPTER 25
CRACKING THE
JAPANESE SHELL

Page

428 "Just six days from today . . ."
Smith, ed., *op. cit.*, p. 501.

429 "My dearest Violet"
Smith, ed., *op. cit.*, p. 556.

429 "There was nothing the Fleet
wanted . . .
Samuel Eliot Morison,
*History of United States
Naval Operation in World*

War II, Vol. VII, *Aleutians,
Gilberts and Marshalls*, p. 103.

431 "withstand assault by a million
men . . ."
Ibid.

431 "who could shout louder than
any admiral"
Heinl, *op. cit.*, p. 406.

431 "We will not neutralize . . ."
Ibid., p. 410.

432 "Gentlemen, remember one
thing . . ."
Ibid.

432 "Defend to the last man"
Baldwin, *op. cit.*, p. 241.

432 "destroy the enemy at the
water's edge."
Ibid.

433 "The sun rose now in a
brilliant . . ."
Ibid., p. 242.

433 "Fires were burning
everywhere . . ."
Buell, *op. cit.*, p. 198.

434 "They'll go in standing up . . ."
Morison, *op. cit.*, Vol. VII,
Gilberts and Marshalls, p. 198.

434 "like a nightmarish turtle race."
Smith, ed., *op. cit.* (Shoup),
p. 507.

434 "We were 100 yards in now . . ."
Morison, *op. cit.*, Vol. VII,
Gilberts and Marshalls, p. 103.

434 "The bullets were pouring at
us . . ."
Ibid.

434 "Come on men . . . We're
going to take . . ."
Baldwin, *op. cit.*, p. 244.

434 "ALL POSSIBLE FIRE SUPPORT."
Morison, *op. cit.*, Vol. VII,
Gilberts and Marshalls, p. 160.

435 "We had seven hundred yards
to walk . . ."
Smith, ed., *op. cit.* (Sherrod),
p. 702.

435 "WE NEED HELP. SITUATION BAD."
Morison, *op. cit.*, Vol. VII,
Gilberts and Marshalls, p. 166.

435 "STILL ENCOUNTERING STRONG
RESISTANCE . . ."
Ibid.

436 "Frankly they were jittery
before starting . . ."
Ibid.

436 "the inexperience and lack of
morale . . ."
Holland Smith, *op. cit.*, p. 125.

436 "ADVANCING. NO OPPOSITION."
Potter, *op. cit.*, p. 257.

436 "AT NO TIME DURING THE
DAY . . ."
Ibid., p. 258.

436 "NO ARTILLERY OR SUPPLIES YET
LANDED."
Ibid.

437 "CASUALTIES MANY. PERCENTAGE
DEAD . . ."
Heinl, *op. cit.*, p. 413.

473 "OUR WEAPONS HAVE BEEN
DESTROYED . . ."
Morison, *op. cit.*, Vol. VII,
Gilberts and Marchalls, p. 173.

438 "SECURED."
Ibid.

438 "MAKIN TAKEN"
Ibid.

438 "I don't see how they ever
took . . ."
Holland M. Smith, *Coral and
Brass* (New York: Scribner's,
1949), p. 109.

438 "I passed boys who had
lived . . ."
Ibid.

CHAPTER 26
COMMON FRONTS

Page

440 "very grave defects"
*Conferences at Cairo and
Tehran, 1943–44* (cited
hereafter as *PRFRUS, Cairo-
Tehran*) *Papers Relating to
Foreign Relation of the
United States*, pp. 23–25.

440 "lengthy, complicated, and
minor."
Churchill, *op. cit.*, Vol. V,
p. 279.

441 "All hope of persuading
Chiang . . ."
Ibid.

441 "why should American boys
die . . ."
PRFRUS, Cairo-Tehran,
p. 354.

441 "by concentrating our Asiatic
efforts . . ."
Ibid., pp. 371–372.

442 "absolutely mad"
Ibid., pp. 242–243.

442 "Brooke got nasty and King . . ."
Pogue, *op. cit.*, Vol. III, p. 305.

Page

442 "keeping the Mediterranean
ablaze."
PRFRUS, Cairo-Tehran,
p. 301.

442 "God forbid I should try to
dictate . . ."
Pogue, *op. cit.,* Vol. III, p. 307.

443 "Now let us get down to
business"
Ibid., p. 310.

443 "we shall be able by our
common front to win"
Burns, *op. cit.,* Vol. II, p. 408.

443 "do something with these
bloody Russians"
Lord Moran, *Churchill:
Taken from the Diaries of
Lord Moran* (Boston: Little,
Brown, 1966), p. 150.

444 "If Buccaneer was canceled,
then . . ."
Pogue, *op. cit.,* Vol. III, p. 317.

444 "I've been stubborn as a
mule . . ."
Stilwell, *op. cit.,* p. 251.

445 "operations in the Central
Pacific . . ."
James, *op. cit.,* Vol. II, p. 365.

445 "The advance along the New
Guniea . . ."
Ibid.

446 "invasion of the principal
Japanese . . ."
Ibid., p. 368.

446 "will spell plenty of bad
news . . ."
Ibid., p. 372.

447 "damp up to your neck."
Heinl, *op. cit.,* p. 391.

447 "Nothing was ever too bad
for . . ."
Ibid., p. 396.

448 "Well, gentlemen, our next
objective . . ."
Potter, *op. cit.,* p. 265.

449 "These frontal attacks by the
Navy . . ."
Pogue, *op. cit.,* Vol. III, p. 440.

449 "The Navy fails to
understand . . ."
Ibid.

449 "any talk of the Marianas leaves
me cold"
Potter, *op. cit.,* p. 281.

449 "If you come with me . . ."
Halsey and Bryan, *op. cit.,*
p. 186.

449 "a big piece of the fleet."
Ibid.

449 "flattered, but in no
position . . ."
Ibid.

450 "looked as if it had been
picked . . ."
Holland Smith, *op. cit.,* p. 144.

451 "Maybe we had too many . . ."
Ibid.

452 "The Marshalls really
cracked . . ."
Morison, *op. cit.,* Vol. VII, p.
332.

452 "It broke the crust of their . . ."
Ibid.

453 "direct Imperial guidance."
Bergamini, *op. cit.,* p. 1064.

454 "If the Bureau of Ordinance
can't . . ."
Clay Blair, Jr., *Silent Victory*
(Philadelphia: Lippincott,
1975), p. 403.

455 "reconnaissance in force."
James, *op. cit.,* Vol. II, p. 382.

456 "lousy with Japs"
Ibid.

456 "That's the way I like to see . . ."
Ibid., p. 383.

456 "brilliant maneuver."
Ibid., p. 387.

456 "an early opportunity to
present . . ."
Ibid., p. 389.

458 "There can be no rest . . ."
Morison, *op. cit.,* Vol. VI, p.
301.

458 "yet more luster to the
badge . . ."
Ibid.

CHAPTER 27
THE COMMON CAUSE

Page

459 "an overwhelming bomber
offensive . . ."
PRFRUS, Cairo-Tehran,
pp. 779–781.

459 "tell them to go and jump in the
Yangtze."
J. Morton Blum, ed., *From
the Morgenthau Diaries*
(Boston: Little, Brown, 1967),
p. 116.

460 "a new order on a basis of
wealth . . ."
Bergamini, *op. cit.,* p. 1053.

460 "at the opportune time"
Ibid.

460 "to exercise political control of
India."
Ibid.

461 "If the bastards will only
fight . . ."
Stilwell, *op. cit.,* p. 266.

461 "wishful thinking"
Ibid.

461 "We have to go in through a
rat hole . . ."
Ibid., p. 261.

461 "the best three-star company
commander . . ."
Moser, *op. cit.,* p. 120.

461 "disgustingly like a street
address . . ."
Charlton C. Ogburn, Jr., *The
Marauders* (New York:
Harper and Row, 1959), p. 61.

462 "particularly hazardous and . . ."
Ibid.

462 "out on a limb."
Stilwell, *op. cit.,* p. 277.

462 "fancy charts, false figures and
dirty intentions"
Ibid., p. 279.

463 "General Stilwell is confident
that . . ."
Lowenheim, *op. cit.,* pp. 454–
455.

463 "I realize this imposes . . ."
Ibid.

463 "sidetracked and entangled in
Burma . . ."
Churchill, *op. cit.,* Vol. V,
p. 480.

463 "vigorous support"
Churchill, Cable, Feb. 25, 1944,
to FDR.

464 "an anvil against which the
reserves . . ."
Slim, *op. cit.,* pp. 246–253.

464 "plenty of dead Japs, horses and
Junk"
Stilwell, *op. cit.,* p. 282.

464 "Louis much impressed . . ."
Ibid.

464 "ALL OUR COLUMNS ARE
INSERTED . . ."
Christopher Sykes, *Orde
Wingate* (New York: World,
1959), p. 522.

465 "The Army had now reached a

Page

state . . ."
Moser, *op. cit.*, p. 148.

466 "not within the strategic
objectives . . ."
Ibid., p. 150.

466 "The ground everywhere was
ploughed . . ." *Ibid.*, p. 152.

466 "Flies swarmed everywhere . . ."
Ibid.

466 "With him a bright flame was
extinguished"
Churchill, *op. cit.*, Vol. V,
p. 485.

467 "There was always a Japanese
thrust . . ."
Slim, *op. cit.*, p. 41.

467 "If they are not to be used . . ."
Dallek, *op. cit.*, p. 488.

468 "still plugging away down the
rat-hole"
Stilwell, *op. cit.*, p. 289.

468 "unsound and should not be
attempted."
Ibid.

468 "The die is cast and it's sink or
swim"
Ibid., p. 291.

469 "we have a fair chance"
Ogburn, *op. cit.*, pp. 241–243.

469 "ROLL ON IN AND SWING ON 'EM."
Stilwell, *op. cit.*, p. 295.

469 "IN THE RING"
Ogburn, *op. cit.*, p. 243.

469 "WILL THIS BURN UP THE
LIMEYS?"
Stilwell, *op. cit.*, p. 296.

469 "on a fear which will live . . ."
Ogburn, *op. cit.*, p. 243.

469 "mud, mud, mud, typhus,
malaria . . ."
Stilwell, *op. cit.*, p. 300.

469 "If we are so badly off . . ."
Ibid.

470 "CONTINUE IN THE TASK
TILL . . ."
Moser, *op. cit.*, p. 156.

470 "IF YOUR HANDS ARE BROKEN . . ."
Ibid.

470 "SINCE LEAVING THE
CHINDWIN . . ."
Ibid.

470 "He has lost the battle for me"
Ibid.

471 "He tries to duck the
consequences . . ."
Charles Romanus and Riley
Sunderland, *Stilwell's Mission*

to China (Washington, D.C.:
Dept. of the Army Historical
Division, 1956), p. 366.

471 "not sending a single bullet . . ."
Ibid., p. 367.

471 "ultimately the Japs must be
fought . . ."
Romanus and Sunderland, *op.
cit.*, pp. 363–364.

CHAPTER 28
DECISIVE BATTLES

Page

471 "without undertaking a major
campaign . . ."
Ibid.

473 "already in the harbor with . . ."
James, *op. cit.*, Vol. II, p. 448.

474 "The operation throws a
loop . . ."
Ibid., p. 449.

474 "the practical end of the New
Guinea campaign"
Ibid., p. 459.

475 "mopping up was proceeding"
Ibid.

475 "The progress at Biak is
unsatisfactory"
Ibid., p. 460.

476 "We are through with flat
atolls . . ."
Holland Smith, *op. cit.*, p. 162.

477 "We're ready for you"
Toland, *The Rising Sun*,
p. 555.

477 "Nosed out a hundred yards or
so . . ."
Smith, ed., *op. cit.* (Sgt.
D. Dempsey), pp. 578–579.

477 "ANNIHILATE THE ENEMY AT ONE
SWOOP"
Toland, *The Rising Sun*,
p. 558.

478 "The Japanese are coming after
us"
Buell, *op. cit.* (Spruance),
p. 262.

478 "OUR AIR WILL FIRST KNOCK
OUT . . ."
Ibid., p. 264.

478 "THEN WILL ATTACK ENEMY
BATTLESHIPS . . ."
Ibid.

478 "THIS OPERATION HAS IMMENSE
BEARING . . ."
Morison, *op. cit.*, Vol. VIII,
New Guinea, p. 232.

478 "IT IS HOPED THAT THE FORCE . . ."
Ibid.

479 "SHOOT FIRST AND REPORT LATER"
Potter, *op. cit.*, p. 299.

483 "The enemy had escaped"
Buell, *op. cit.* (Spruance),
p. 277.

483 "He had been badly hurt . . ."
Ibid.

483 "Please deeply apologize to
the . . ."
Toland, *The Rising Sun*,
p. 576.

484 "Seven lives to repay our
country"
Ibid., p. 582.

484 "The camera is in a hole . . ."
Ibid., p. 584.

485 "the perfect amphibious
operation . . ."
Holland Smith, *op. cit.*, p. 201.

485 "My aim is to get the troops . . ."
Heinl, *op. cit.*, p. 445.

485 "You tell me what you want
done . . ."
Ibid.

485 "On this island, no matter
where . . ."
Ibid.

485 "sounding like a New Year's
Eve in the zoo"
Heinl, *op. cit.*, p. 459.

486 "THE HOLDING OF GUAM HAS
BECOME . . ."
Ibid.

CHAPTER 29
MORAL OBLIGATIONS

Page

487 "BRITISH TOO MANY GUNS,
TANKS . . ."
Moser, *op. cit.*, p. 157.

487 "the first decisive battle of the
Burma campaign"
Slim, *op. cit.*, p. 346.

488 "You will need to
collaborate . . ."
Bauer, *op. cit.*, p. 443.

Page

488 "would be very difficult"
Ibid.

488 "would be a waste of effort."
Romanus and Sunderland, *op. cit.*, p. 403.

489 "It is clear, now that Stilwell . . ."
Fred Eldridge, *Wrath in Burma* (New York: Doubleday, 1966), p. 289.

489 "who had the ability, the force . . ."
Tuchman, *op. cit.*, p. 601.

490 "views and recommendations."
James, *op. cit.*, Vol. II, p. 522.

490 "It is my most earnest conviction . . ."
Ibid., pp. 522–523.

490 "We must be careful not to allow . . ."
Ibid., p. 525.

490 "bypassing . . . synonymous with abandonment."
Ibid.

490 "not a candidate . . . detrimental to the war effort"
Ibid., p. 438.

491 "purely political"
Ibid., p. 527.

491 "humiliation of forcing me to leave . . ."
Ibid.

491 "represent no menace to current . . ."
Ibid., p. 464.

492 "to determine the next phase . . ."
Ibid., p. 530.

492 "go it alone"
Ibid.

492 "moral obligation"
Ibid.

492 "American public opinion will . . ."
Potter, *op. cit.*, p. 318.

493 "We've sold it"
Ibid., p. 319.

493 "the President has accepted my . . ."
James, *op. cit.*, Vol. II, p. 534.

493 "complete accord with my old friend . . ."
Ibid., p. 535.

493 "no shipping left to sink"
Potter, *op. cit.*, p. 323.

493 "enemy's non-aggressive attitude . . ."
Ibid.

494 "Subject to completion of arrangements . . ."
James, *op. cit.*, Vol. II, p. 539.

494 "not a difficult decision to make."
Potter, *op. cit.*, p. 323.

494 "blaze of friendship"
Churchill, *op. cit.*, Vol. VI, p. 133.

494 "everything we had touched . . ."
Ibid., p. 128.

495 "We had to regain on the field . . ."
Ibid., p. 123.

495 "The offer of the British Fleet has . . ."
Ibid., p. 132.

496 "Victory depends on our recent . . ."
Steinberg, *op. cit.*, p. 176.

496 "The Americans rely solely . . ."
Ibid.

497 "Clawing and crawling up the cliff . . ."
Smith, ed., *op. cit.* (R. Davis), pp. 674–675.

497 "If military leaders were gifted . . ."
Heinl, *op. cit.*, p. 473.

CHAPTER 30
THE FLOWERS OF DEATH

Page

499 "All of Admiral Mitscher's . . ."
Halsey and Bryan, *op. cit.*, p. 210.

499 "destroy enemy naval and air forces . . ."
Potter, *op. cit.*, p. 325.

499 "so many eggs thrown against the stone . . ."
Toland, *The Rising Sun*, p. 607.

499 "THIRD FLEET'S SUNKEN AND DAMAGED . . ."
Potter, *op. cit.*, p. 328.

500 "to completely annihilate the Jap . . ."
Halsey and Bryan, *op. cit.*, p. 207.

500 "Words will not sink American ships."
Toland, *The Rising Sun*, p. 602.

500 "last chance to destroy the enemy . . ."
Baldwin, *op. cit.* (Leyte), p. 289.

501 "bloom as the flowers of death."
Toland, *The Rising Sun*, p. 610.

501 "hit the enemy carriers and keep them . . ."
Baldwin, *op. cit.* (Leyte), p. 291.

501 "the only way of assuring our meager . . ."
Ibid.

502 "universal sameness in the emotions of men"
MacArthur, *op. cit.*, pp. 214–215.

502 "Landings are explosive once the shooting . . ."
Ibid.

503 "Let 'em walk."
James, *op. cit.*, Vol. II, p. 555.

503 "People of the Philippines . . ."
Ibid., p. 557.

503 "Rally to me . . ."
Ibid.

504 "The Japanese as unwilling and . . ."
Smith, ed., *op. cit.* (Benitez), pp. 846–848.

504 "It looks like the Fourth of July . . ."
Ibid.

504 "Here they come . . ."
Ibid.

505 "The Japs were very mad and . . ."
Ibid.

505 "IT IS VERY PROBABLE THAT THE . . ."
Toland, *The Rising Sun*, p. 620.

505 "tremendous battle"
Halsey and Bryan, *op. cit.*, p. 210.

505 "STRIKE! REPEAT! STRIKE! GOOD LUCK!"
Ibid., p. 214.

507 "WE ARE BEING SUBJECTED TO REPEATED . . ."
Toland, *The Rising Sun*, p. 623.

Page

507 "REQUEST LAND-BASED AIR
FORCE . . ."
Ibid., p. 624.

508 "GO FORWARD OR BACKWARD AT
TOP . . ."
Ibid., p. 626.

508 "meat for the enemy"
Ibid.

508 "had all the pieces of the puzzle"
Halsey and Bryan, *op. cit.*,
p. 216.

508 "CENTRAL FORCE HEAVILY
DAMAGED . . ."
Baldwin, *op. cit.* (Leyte), p.
297.

509 "WILL BE FORMED AS TASK
FORCE 34 . . ."
Ibid.

509 "WILL BE FORMED WHEN DIRECTED
BY ME."
Ibid.

509 "WE GO NORTH AND PUT THOSE
JAP . . ."
Edwin P. Hoyt, *The Battle of
Leyte Gulf* (New York:
Weybright and Talley, 1972),
pp. 145–164.

509 "PREPARE FOR A NIGHT
ENGAGEMENT"
Ibid.

510 "The Captain radioed to the
ships . . ."
Ibid., pp. 194–201.

510 "ENEMY DESTROYERS AND TORPEDO
BOATS . . ."
Ibid.

510 "Upon giving orders to 'open
fire' . . ."
Ibid., pp. 260–263.

511 "YOU ARE TO PROCEED AND ATTACK
ALL SHIPS"
Baldwin, *op. cit.* (Leyte),
p. 298.

511 "Admiral Halsey is in command
now."
Ibid.

511 "protect the Seventh Fleet."
Morison, *op. cit.*, Vol. XII,
Leyte, p. 219.

511 "We have them!"
Halsey and Bryan, *op. cit.*,
p. 218.

511 "Is Task Force 34 guarding
San . . ."
Hoyt, *Leyte Gulf*, p. 263.

512 "BY HEAVEN-SENT OPPORTUNITY
WE ARE DASHING . . ."
Toland, *The Rising Sun*, p.
638.

512 "OUR FIRST OBJECTIVE IS TO
DESTROY . . ."
Ibid.

512 "ENEMY SURFACE FORCE OF 4 . . ."
Smith, ed., *op. cit.* (Sprague),
pp. 864–868.

512 "Tell the pilot to check . . ."
Ibid.

512 "IDENTIFICATION OF ENEMY
FORCE . . ."
Ibid.

513 "open fire with front turrets"
Ibid.

513 "If we can get this task
force . . ."
Ibid.

513 "Out of the fog loomed . . ."
Ibid.

513 "They're shooting at us in
technicolor . . ."
Ibid.

514 "It was like a puppy being
smacked . . ."
Morison, *op. cit.*, Vol. XII,
Leyte, p. 257.

514 "prospect of blasting the
cripples . . ."
Halsey and Bryan, *op. cit.*,
p. 218.

514 "URGENTLY NEED FAST
BATTLESHIPS . . ."
Ibid., p. 219.

514 "There was nothing else I
could do . . ."
Ibid., p. 220.

515 "SMALL BOYS LAUNCH TORPEDO
ATTACK"
Baldwin, *op. cit.*, p. 304.

515 "Anything we could do from
now . . ."
Ibid.

516 "inert mass of battered metal."
Ibid.

516 "hitting the Jap ships with
everything . . ."
Ibid.

516 "COME NORTH WITH ME 20
KNOTS."
Dull, *op. cit.*, p. 326.

516 "Goddamnit, boy, they're
getting away."
Smith, ed., *op. cit.* (Sprague),
p. 871.

516 "I could not believe my
eyes . . ."
Ibid. (Sprague), p. 871.

516 "WHERE IS LEE?"
Halsey and Bryan, *op. cit.*,
p. 220.

517 "WHERE IS REPEAT WHERE IS . . ."
Ibid.

517 "THE WORLD WONDERS"
Ibid.

517 "as if I had been struck . . ."
Ibid.

517 "I turned my back on the
opportunity . . ."
Ibid., p. 221.

517 "real mistake was in turning my
fleet around"
Ibid., p. 226.

518 "an enthusiasm that flames
naturally . . ."
Toland, *The Rising Sun*, p.
643.

518 "the very definite partiality of
Almighty God"
Baldwin, *op. cit.* (Leyte),
p. 307.

518 "engage in decisive battle"
Toland, *The Rising Sun*, p.
645.

518 "I did not know . . . that
Admiral Halsey . . ."
Hoyt, *Leyte Gulf*, p. 263.

519 "metal laid on a Jello mold."
Bauer, *op. cit.*, p. 528.

520 "annihilate the enemy's air
power"
James, *op. cit.*, Vol. II, p. 579.

520 "General Yamashita has
sustained . . ."
James, *op. cit.*, Vol. II, p. 602.

521 "Leyte-Samar campaign can
now be . . ."
Ibid.

521 "bitter, rugged fighting—
physically . . ."
Ibid.

CHAPTER 31
A DETERMINED FIGHTING SPIRIT

Page

523 "The crazy little bastard
would . . ."
Stillwell, *op. cit.*, p. 330.

523 "The jig is up in China . . ."
Ibid.

523 "must command all forces in
China."
Tuchman, *op. cit.*, p. 629.

Page

523 "The harpoon hit the little
bugger . . ."
Stilwell, *op. cit.*, p. 333.

523 "no intention of cooperating
with me."
Romanus and Sunderland, *op.
cit.*, pp. 452–453.

523 "you will lose Chiang and
possibly . . ."
Tuchman, *op. cit.*, p. 640.

524 "despite a temporary
weakness . . ."
Dallek, *op. cit.*, p. 501.

524 "If the Russians go in, will . . ."
Averill Harriman, *Special
Envoy, 1941–1946* (New
York: Random House, 1975),
pp. 370–371.

524 "the Chinese communists are
not . . ."
Dallek, *op. cit.*, p. 499.

524 "for the immediate defeat of
Japan . . ."
James, *op. cit.*, Vol. II, p. 588.

524 Communist "Bill of Goods"
Albert C. Wedemeyer,
General Wedemeyer Reports
(New York: Henry Holt,
1958), p. 311.

524 "anxious for a settlement"
Ibid.

524 "a honey instead of vinegar
policy"
Ibid., p. 305.

527 "air defense oath of certain
victory."
Havens, *op. cit.*, p. 137.

527 "listen to the silence."
Ibid., p. 161.

528 "In the face of warnings that
the war . . ."
Ibid., p. 151.

529 "The first bomb, without
previous . . ."
Burns, *op. cit.* (MacGregor),
Vol. II, p. 558.

530 "This organization must be
the . . ."
Rosenmann, ed., *op. cit.*,
(1944–45), pp. 511–514.

531 "I shall write a brilliant
history . . ."
Manchester, *op. cit.*, p. 406.

531 "The Philippines have an
extensive . . ."
Ibid.

531 "The decisive battle for the
liberation . . ."
James, *op. cit.*, Vol. II, p. 622.

532 "knew every wrinkle of the
topography"
Manchester, *op. cit.*, p. 410.

532 "noticeable lack of drive."
James, *op. cit.*, Vol. II, p. 628.

532 "GO TO MANILA . . . GO
AROUND . . ."
Ibid., p. 632.

532 "The rest of the Division . . ."
Steinberg, *op. cit.*, p. 114.

534 "Have your troops hoist the
colors . . ."
James, *op. cit.*, Vol. II, p. 652.

536 "No more let us falter from . . ."
Churchill, *op. cit.*, Vol. VI,
p. 291.

537 "former rights of Russian . . ."
Smith, ed., *op. cit.*, p. 321.

537 "noblesse oblige, he won't
try . . ."
Bauer, *op. cit.*, p. 591.

CHAPTER 32
UNCOMMON VALOR

Page

539 "WE HAVE DRIVEN THE ENEMY
OFF . . ."
Potter, *op. cit.*, p. 352.

540 "This outfit has been getting a
hell . . ."
Heinl, *op. cit.*, p. 479.

540 "WITHOUT IWO JIMA . . ."
Buell, *op. cit.* (Spruance), p.
324.

540 "That took a load off my mind"
Ibid.

540 "the toughest place we have had
to take"
Potter, *op. cit.*, p. 358.

541 "a gradual depletion of the
enemy's . . ."
Smith, ed., *op. cit.*, p. 711.

542 "1,200 PLANES OF THE U.S.
FLEET . . ."
Potter, *op. cit.*, p. 362 (*New
York Times*, Feb. 17, 1945).

542 "At dawn on D-Day the
waters . . ."
John P. Marquand, *Thirty
Years* (Boston: Little, Brown,
1954), p. 201.

542 "like a sea monster . . ."
Ibid.

543 "All right, be ready to bail
out . . ."
Smith, ed., *op. cit.* (Lardner),
p. 725.

543 "When you stopped
running . . ."
Ibid., p. 726.

543 "There were live Japs near . . ."
Ibid., p. 728.

544 "like trying to fight in a bin of
loose wheat"
Heinl, *op. cit.*, p. 486.

544 "smell of burning flesh . . ."
Robert Sherrod, *On to
Westward* (New York: Sloan
and Pearce, 1945), p. 180.

544 "It was quite impossible to
dig . . ."
Smith, ed., *op. cit.* (Gallant),
pp. 728–733.

544 "EIGHT BATTALIONS
SUPPORTED . . ."
Potter, *op. cit.*, p. 362.

545 "Today we annihilate those
who . . ."
Smith, ed., *op. cit.*, p. 791.

545 "There are no
reinforcements . . ."
Ibid., p. 791.

545 "At dawn we climb . . ."
Ibid., p. 792.

546 "The raising of the flag . . ."
Holland Smith, *op. cit.*, p. 261.

546 "We shall infiltrate into . . ."
Smith, ed., *op. cit.*,

546 "It takes courage for
officers . . ."
Heinl, *op. cit.*, p. 490.

546 "For inspection not
consumption."
Ibid.

547 "WE HAVE NOT EATEN OR
DRUNK . . ."
Heinl, *op. cit.*, p. 441.

547 "ALL OFFICERS AND MEN ON
CHICHI JIMA FAREWELL."
Ibid.

547 "Among the Americans who
served . . ."
Potter, *op. cit.*, p. 367.

547 "Japan's production
capacity . . ."
Martin Caidin, *A Torch to
the Enemy* (New York:
1960), p. 71.

547 "throw away the book"
Wesley Frank Craven and
James Lea Cate, eds., *The*

Page

Army Air Forces in World War II (Chicago: Univ. of Chicago Press, 1948), Vol. IV: *The Pacific, Guadalcanal to Saipan*, pp. 143–144.

548 "I could have been wrong"
      Ibid.

548 "from a study of photographic . . ."
      Ibid.

548 "the roughest sort of treatment"
      Caidin, *op. cit.*, p. 79.

548 "If you are shot down . . ."
      Ibid.

548 "You're going to deliver . . ."
      Gordon Thomas and Max Morgan Witts, *Enola Gay* (New York: Stein & Day, 1977), p. 97.

549 "The darkest hour is just before . . ."
      Havens, *op. cit.*, p. 178.

550 "BOMBING TARGET VISUALLY . . ."
      Caidin, *op. cit.*, p. 111.

550 "Bright flashes illumine . . ."
      Robert Guillain, *Le Peuple Japonais et la Guerre* (Paris: Juillard, 1947), pp. 198–211.

550 "Fire winds with burning particles . . ."
      Caidin, *op. cit.*, p. 141.

551 "The whole spectacle . . ."
      Ibid.

551 "Gusts from the inferno . . ."
      Ibid., p. 119.

551 "In the Black Sumida river . . ."
      Havens, *op. cit.*, p. 179.

CHAPTER 33
FLOATING CHRYSANTHEMUMS

Page

555 "lured into a position . . ."
      Heinl, *op. cit.*, p. 494.

555 "The brave, ruddy faced warriors . . ."
      Smith, ed., *op. cit.*, pp. 859–860.

557 "Over our heads the fire . . ."
      Smith, ed., *op. cit.* (Edward T. Higgins), p. 938.

557 "LAND THE LANDING FORCE"
      Morison, *op. cit.*, Vol. XIV, *Victory in the Pacific*, p. 147.

557 "PRACTICALLY NO FIRE AGAINST BOATS . . ."
      Potter, *op. cit.*, p .369.

558 "The Jap aircraft came straight . . ."
      John Winston, *The Forgotten Fleet* (New York: Coward, McCann, 1969), p. 121.

558 "THE FATE OF OUR EMPIRE . . ."
      Toland, *The Rising Sun*, p. 778.

558 "FIGHT GLORIOUSLY TO THE DEATH . . ."
      Ibid.

559 "I MAY BE CRAZY BUT . . ."
      Potter, *op. cit.*, p. 372.

559 "DELETE ALL AFTER CRAZY"
      Ibid.

560 "The dreadful loss that led . . ."
      Toland, *The Rising Sun*, p. 793.

560 "THE SKILL AND EFFECTIVENESS OF . . ."
      Baldwin, *op. cit.*, p. 376.

562 *SS Emidio; Donerail; John A. Johnson*
      John Gorley Bunker, *Liberty Ships—The Ugly Duckling of World War II* (Annapolis, Md.: U.S. Naval Institute Press, 1972), pp. 139, 155, 156.

563 "like the Fifth Cavalry . . ."
      Interviews with former U.S. merchant seamen.

563 "like South Dakota by sea . . ."
      Ibid.

563 "that made John Wayne fights . . ."
      Ibid.

564 "Passage on a Liberty ship . . ."
      Bunker, *op. cit.*, p. 142.

565 "It is going to be . . . yard by yard."
      Bauer, *op. cit.*, p. 642.

565 "You cannot bypass a Jap . . ."
      Ibid.

565 "Yes, but ground though . . . air attacks."
      Potter, *op. cit.*, p. 775.

566 "to guard their honor like samurai"
      Havens, *op. cit.*, p. 190.

566 "if you don't kill at least one . . ."
      Ibid.

566 "Regrettable though it is . . ."
      Toland, *The Rising Sun*, pp. 767–768.

566 "although they cannot win . . . fight to the death"
      Ibid.

567 "to make a firm decision to save the nation"
      Quincy Howe, *Ashes of Victory* (New York: Simon and Schuster, 1972), p. 396.

567 "We have no alternative but to fight"
      Ibid., p. 397.

567 "As to diplomacy you shall . . ."
      Toland, *The Rising Sun*, p. 788.

567 "I'm not big enough for the job"
      Robert J. Donovan, *Conflict and Crisis* (New York: Norton, 1977), p. 15.

567 "a highly secret matter"
      Thomas and Witts, *op. cit.*, p. 123.

CHAPTER 34
THE AWFUL WAY

Page

568 "the most terrible weapon ever . . ."
      Donovan, *op. cit.*, p. 46.

568 "I am going to have to make . . ."
      Ibid., p. 49.

568 "I'll make the decision . . ."
      Ibid.

569 "should be driven into the . . ."
      James, *op. cit.*, Vol. II, p. 670.

570 "between the Philippines and the rest . . ."
      Ibid., p. 703.

570 "colossal waste of manpower . . ."
      Ibid.

572 "JAPS GONE . . . EXTRACT DIGIT"
      Bauer, *op. cit.*, p. 636.

572 "heartfelt congratulations . . . required."
      Churchill, *op. cit.*, Vol. VI, pp. 530–531.

573 "the great American illusion"
      Ibid.

575 "It's all over now bar . . ."
      Toland, *The Rising Sun*, p. 812.

576 "since the Emperor of Japan is

Page

not . . ."
Ibid., p. 837.

576 "Why should we be afraid . . ."
Ibid.

577 "much beyond our imagination"
Ibid., p. 840.

577 "prosecute the war to the bitter end"
Ibid., p. 842.

578 "OUR STRATEGY, TACTICS AND METHODS . . ."
Bauer, *op. cit.*, p. 645.

578 "among the most intense and famous . . ."
Churchill, *op. cit.*, Vol. VI, p. 535.

CHAPTER 35
THE MIRACLE OF DELIVERANCE

Page

579 "manufacturing areas . . ."
N.A. RG 165. Minutes of Meeting U.S. Army Chief of Staff, May 29, 1945.

579 "character of the weapon . . ."
Ibid.

580 "using ships, aircraft, armor . . ."
Donovan, *op. cit.*, p. 65.

581 "the bomb would be a wonderful . . ."
Daniel Lilienthal, *The Atomic Energy Years* (New York: Harper and Row, 1964), p. 198.

581 "the advisability of an early . . ."
Barton J. Bernstein, ed., *The Atomic Bomb: The Critical Issues,* (Boston: Little, Brown, 1976), pp. 25–26.

581 "precipitate the race for armaments . . ."
Ibid.

581 "We can see no acceptable alternative . . ."
Barton J. Bernstein and Allen J. Materson, eds., *The Truman Administration* (New York: Harper and Row, 1966), p. 15.

581 "We can propose no technical . . ."
Ibid.

581 "to be used against the enemy . . ."
Ibid.

581 "As I understand it . . ."
Howe, *op. cit.*, p. 400.

581 "something could be done to influence them."
Ibid.

581 "Why not drop the atomic bomb . . . fantastic."
Howe, *op. cit.*, p. 401.

582 "some way . . . from one end of Japan to another."
PFPRUS, Potsdam, 1945, Vol. I, p. 903.

582 "Independently . . . surrender from the Emperor and his advisers."
Ibid.

582 "would save many times the number . . ."
Martin J. Sherwin, *A World Destroyed* (New York: Knopf, 1973), p. 194.

582 "might well put us in a position . . ."
Ibid.

582 "come to an understanding with Russia . . ."
Donovan, *op. cit.*, p. 52.

583 "DIAGNOSIS NOT YET COMPLETE . . ."
Toland, *The Rising Sun,* p. 863.

583 "For a brief period there was . . ."
Groves, *op. cit.*, pp. 433–434.

584 "generally bossed about the whole meeting."
Churchill, *op. cit.*, Vol. VI, p. 544.

584 "Stimson, what was gunpowder? . . ."
Stimson and Bundy, *op. cit.*, p. 634.

584 "after all our toils and perils a miracle . . ."
Ibid., p. 639.

584 "Will you tell the generalissimo . . ."
Donovan, *op. cit.*, p. 93.

584 "would make good use of it against Japan"
Ibid.

585 "is extremely anxious to terminate the war."
Toland, *The Rising Sun,* p. 853.

585 "A peace treaty by

negotiation . . ."
Ibid.

586 "his decision was one of . . ."
Leslie R. Groves, *Now It Can Be Told* (New York: Harper and Row, 1962), p. 265.

586 "The twentieth Air Force will . . ."
Thomas and Witts, *op. cit.*, p. 206.

587 "If she goes down, save the cargo . . ."
Ibid., p. 176.

587 "the power to shape the future"
Churchill, *op. cit.*, Vol. VI, p. 577.

587 "There are no alternatives . . ."
Hans Adolph Jacobsen, *World War II—Selected Documents with Commentary* (Oxford: Clio, 1979), p. 345.

587 "We call upon the Government of . . ."
Ibid.

587 "The alternative for Japan is . . ."
Ibid.

587 "The proclamation in my opinion . . ."
Toland, *The Rising Sun,* p. 872.

587 "JAPAN OFFICIALLY TURNS DOWN ALLIED . . ."
Donovan, *op. cit.*, p. 95.

588 "There was no alternative now"
Ibid.

588 "The Third Fleet's job is to hit . . ."
Merrill, *op. cit.*, p. 232.

588 "that our ships don't have wheels . . ."
Halsey and Bryan, *op. cit.*, p. 266.

588 "Jap warships went to die."
Ibid.

588 "ceased to exist."
Ibid.

588 "The Commander in Chief of . . ."
Ibid.

588 "forestall a possible postwar . . ."
Ibid.

589 "Day by day Japan was turned into a furnace"
Bauer, *op. cit.*, p. 650.

589 "the clarion call was accepted . . ."
Ibid.

589 "Suggestion approved. Release okayed"
Donovan, *op. cit.*, p. 96.

Page

589 "FURTHER EFFORTS TO BE
EXERTED . . ."
Craig, *op. cit.*, p. 72.

590 "CLOUD COVER LESS THAN THREE
TENTHS . . ."
Thomas and Witts, *op. cit.*,
p. 252.

590 "It's Hiroshima"
Ibid.

591 "On glasses!"
Ibid., p. 255.

591 "My God!"
Ibid.

591 "Suddenly a glaring
whitish . . ."
C. L. Sulzberger, et al., eds.,
World War II (New York:
American Heritage, 1966),
p. 616.

591 "Within a few seconds the
thousands . . ."
Ibid.

591 "There was the mushroom
cloud . . ."
Ibid.

591 "Beyond the zone of utter
death . . ."
Ibid.

592 "CLEAR CUT. SUCCESSFUL IN
ALL . . ."
Thomas and Witts, *op. cit.*,
p. 266.

592 "This is the greatest thing in
history"
Donovan, *op. cit.*, p. 96.

592 "It is an atomic bomb . . . Far
East."
Ibid.

592 "If they do not now accept . . ."
Potter, *op. cit.*, p. 387.

592 "SITUATION BECOMING ACUTE"
Craig, *op. cit.*, pp. 72–95.

592 "We have been discussing . . ."
Ibid.

593 "Nevertheless the time . . ."
Ibid.

CHAPTER 36
THIS IS THE PAYOFF

594 "With the understanding . . ."
Craig, *op. cit.*, p. 95.

594 "THIS IS A PEACE WARNING"
Potter, *op. cit.*, p. 388.

594 "From the moment of
surrender . . ."
Craig, *op. cit.*, p. 145.

595 "IT IS LEARNED THAT AN
IMPERIAL . . ."
Ibid., p. 177.

596 "We have ordered our
Government . . ."
Ibid., pp. 210–212.

596 "war situation has developed
not . . ."
Ibid.

596 "to continue to fight . . ."
Ibid.

596 "deep regret to the Allied
nations . . ."
Ibid.

596 "Yippee "
Potter, *op .cit.*, p. 389.

596 "INVESTIGATE AND SHOOT
DOWN . . ."
Ibid., p. 390.

596 "CEASE HOSTILITIES AGAINST
JAPAN"
Winston, *op. cit.*, p. 345.

597 "the use of insulting
epithets . . ."
Potter, *op. cit.*, p. 390.

597 "In accordance with the
agreement . . ."
James, *op. cit.*, Vol. II, p. 776.

597 "you are hereby designated . . ."
Ibid.

597 "to require and receive
from . . ."
Ibid.

597 "The entire eastern world is . . ."
Ibid., p. 777.

599 "Bob! This is the Payoff."
Ibid., p. 785.

600 "It is my earnest hope . . ."
Ibid., p. 789.

600 "This narrow quarterdeck was
now . . ."
Ibid., p. 790.

601 "Let us pray that peace . . ."
Ibid., p. 791.

601 "Today the guns are silent . . ."
Ibid.

601 "It must be of the spirit . . ."
Ibid.

601 "to bring a singular and
isolated . . ."
Morison, *Old Bruin*, p. 417.

602 "the master organiser of the
world"
Josiah Strong, *Our Country*
(New York, 1885), p. 209.

602 "divinely commissioned to
be . . ."
Ibid.

602 "a spiritual reformation of
Japan"

Neu, *op. cit.*, p. 205.

602 "Peaceful and responsible
government"
Ibid., p. 204.

CHAPTER 37
AN AFTER-ACTION
REPORT

Page

606 "Japan cannot . . ."
Carver, ed., *op. cit.*, p. 397.

607 "Sometimes a man . . ."
Toland, *op. cit.*, p. 128.

608 "relevant signals so clearly
audible . . ."
Wohlstetter, *op. cit.*, p. 397.

609 "Gentlemen do not read other
gentlemen's mail"
Farago, *op. cit.*, p. 56.

610 "*The Need for New
Legislation* . . ."
N.A. RG 457, Records of the
National Security Agency,
SRH 016.

612 "the product of British 'hocus
pocus' "
N.A. RG 457, SRH, 062.

613 "are in touch with the President
and his wife"
N.A. RG 457, SRDJ Series,
Washington–Tokyo, May 19,
1941.

613 "for the development of . . ."
Ibid.

613 "very influential Negro leaders"
N.A. RG 457, SRDJ Series,
Washington–Tokyo, May 9,
1941.

613 "to stall the program the
U.S. . . ."
N.A. RG 457, SRDJ Series,
Washington–Tokyo, July 4,
1941.

613 "our second generation workers
in airplane plants"
N.A. RG 457, SRDJ Series,
Washington–Tokyo, May 9,
1941.

614 "make a discreet
investigation . . ."
N.A. RG 457, SRDJ Series,
Tokyo to Washington, Sept.
21, 1941.

Page

614 "the American government will . . ."
Ibid.

614 "I have received from the German . . ."
N.A. RG 457, SRNA 0020, Berlin to Tokyo, Dec. 12, 1940.

615 "that peace talks will bud in July and blossom in autumn"
N.A. RG 457, SRDJ Series, Washington–Tokyo, July 8, 1941.

615 "Roosevelt planned the elimination . . ."
N.A. RG 457, SRDJ Series, Washington–Tokyo, Nov. 6, 1941.

615 "a certain Cabinet member"
N.A. RG 457, SRDJ Series, Washington–Tokyo, Nov. 10, 1941.

615 "The American government has very . . ."
Ibid.

615 "wouldn't have any effect on the situation"
Ibid.

615 "Well, our boss the President . . ."
Ibid.

CHAPTER 38
PEARL HARBOR— WARNING OR DECISION?

Page

617 "The Jap situation is definitely . . ."
Lowenheim, *op. cit.*, p. 162.

617 "the Japs will advance on Vladivostok . . ."
PHH, part 16, p. 2140.

617 "Japan would not advance southward . . ."
N.A. RG 165, WPD 3251– 3260.

617 "key and base point"
Ibid.

617 "strong offensive air forces"
Ibid.

617 "air and ground forces now available . . ."
Ibid.

618 "a strong stand may result in Japanese capitulation."

N.A. RG 165, OPD Exec. File, Enc. 8, WPD Strategic Guide.

618 "If our position does result . . ."
Ibid.

618 "grave situation . . . strong possibility"
Ibid.

618 "Since the U.S. and Great Britain . . ."
PHH, part 14, p. 1402.

618 "In view of these possibilities . . ."
Ibid.

618 "to promote amicable relations with friendly powers"
PRFRUS, *Japan, 1941*, Vol. II, pp. 692–698.

619 "A strategic opportunity of the . . ."
N.A. RG 107, Stimson, White House File, Oct. 21, 1941.

619 "the base of a northern pincer . . ."
Ibid.

619 "The control over the western Pacific . . ."
Ibid.

619 "It might well remove Japan from the Axis powers."
Ibid.

619 "Yet even this . . . of such action."
Ibid.

620 "our people are growing impatient"
N.A. RG 457, SRDJ, MAGIC Intercepts Oct.–Nov. 1941.

620 "the situation does not permit of delays"
Ibid.

620 "it is absolutely necessary . . ."
Ibid.

620 "we are on the last lap . . ."
Ibid.

620 "no further delays"
Ibid.

620 "the crisis is fast approaching"
Ibid.

620 "the transfer of troops from . . ."
Ibid.

620 "in view of the extremely critical . . ."
Ibid.

620 "strain every nerve to satisfy . . ."
Ibid.

621 "Nations must think one hundred years ahead"
PRFRUS, *Japan*, Vol. VII, p. 589.

621 "The fate of the Empire hangs by a slender thread"
N.A. RG 457, SRDJ Series.

621 "please fight harder"
Ibid.

621 "was like a powder keg"
Ibid.

621 "There is no last word between friends"
PRFRUS, *Japan*, Vol. II, p. 560.

621 "it seems very clear that they are . . ."
N.A. RG 457, SRDJ Series, Washington–Tokyo, Nov. 18–19, 1941.

621 "We have sweat blood to endeavor . . ."
PHH, part 16.

621 "more consideration be given to the needs of the Pacific Fleet"
Ibid.

621 "every week sooner we come . . ."
Lash, *op. cit.*, p. 464.

622 "attractive enough to warrant . . ."
PRO, Foreign Office 12475 86/23.

622 "some oil and rice now—more later"
PRFRUS 1941, Vol. IV, p. 626.

622 "Japan to agree not to invoke . . ."
Ibid.

623 "made a desperate effort to get something worked out"
PHH, part 2, p. 554.

623 "a required quantity of oil"
PRFRUS, *1941*, Vol. II, p. 755f.

623 "after that things are automatically going to happen"
N.A. RG 457, SRDJ Series, Washington–Tokyo, Nov. 29, 1941.

623 "This seems to be . . ."
Lowenheim, *op. cit.*, p. 166.

624 "had asked for six months last February . . ."
Lash, *op. cit.*, p. 472.
A. Berle and T. Jacobs, eds., *Navigating the Rapids* (New York: Harcourt, Brace, 1966), p. 338.

624 "our demand for a cessation of aid . . ."
N.A. RG 457, SRDJ Series, Washington–Tokyo, Nov. 29, 1941.

Page

624 "CHANCES OF FAVORABLE OUTCOME
WITH . . ."
PHH, part 14, p. 1405.

624 "It adequately safeguarded all
our interests"
N.A. RG 80, Pearl Harbor
Liaison Office, Copies of
Stimson Diary entries.

624 "the Japanese are notorious for
attacking . . ."
Ibid.

624 "a difficult question"
Ibid.

625 "over a Japanese surprise
attack . . ."
PHH, part 9, p. 1103.

625 "Our major interest is . . ."
PRO, Foreign Office 12813/
86/23

625 "Of course it is for you . . ."
Churchill, *op. cit.*, Vol. III,
p. 503.

625 "announce that if the
withdrawal . . ."
PHH, part 14, p. 1168.

626 "numerous hysterical"
PHH, part 14, p. 1494.

626 "our proposals would relieve
the . . ."
Ibid.

626 "we can cancel this
proposal . . ."
Ibid.

626 "to be ready to move in . . ."
PHH, part 14, p. 1145.

626 "about made up his mind"
PHH, part 11, p. 5434.

627 "the President and Mr.
Hull . . ."
PRO, Foreign Office 371 file
35957. See Christopher
Thorne, *Allies of a Kind*
(New York: Oxford Univ.
Press, 1979), pp. 74–75, and
Richard Graigie, *Behind the
Mask* (London, 1946).

627 "a pretty sweeping
indictment . . ."
Ibid.

627 "It is a very strange
document . . ."
Ibid.

628 "but to kick the whole
thing . . ."
Ibid.

628 "the Prime Minister wondered
whether . . ."
Churchill, *op. cit.*, Vol. III,
p. 503.

628 "either unfavorable or
lukewarm"
Ibid.

628 "slight prospect of Japan's
agreeing to the modus vivendi"
Ibid.

628 "I understood the dangers
attending . . ."
Churchill, *op. cit.*, Vol. III,
p. 502.

628 "We had not heard . . ."
Ibid., p. 503.

628 "were repeated to us, but there
was . . ."
Ibid., p. 504.

629 "He had not touched his
coffee . . ."
Blum, ed., *op. cit.*, pp. 415–416.

629 "quiet them down."
Ibid.

629 "five divisions have come
down . . ."
PHH, part 11, p. 5433f.

629 "whether he had received the
paper . . ."
Ibid., p. 5434.

629 "fairly blew up"
Ibid.

630 "convoy of from ten to thirty
ships"
Ibid.

630 "near the mouth of the Yangtse
River below Shanghai"
N.A. RG 107, Sec. of War
Safe File, Philippines Sector.

630 "The officers concerned, in
the . . ."
Ibid.

630 "more or less normal movement"
Ibid.

630 "In order that the source . . ."
N.A. RG 80, Pearl Harbor
Liaison Office, Sec. of State's
Testimony.

630 "Japan will make last effort
at . . ."
Ibid.

631 "if such decision is taken . . ."
Ibid.

631 "Dear Mr. Secretary . . ."
Ibid.

631 "another Memo about the
Japanese . . ."
N.A. RG 107, Stimson Safe
File, White House
Correspondence, June 26,
1940–Dec. 31, 1941.

631 "This is a highly

abbreviated . . ."
Ibid.

631 "Later reports indicate . . ."
Ibid.

632 "no new direct reports . . ."
Ibid.

632 "Original by hand . . ."
Ibid.

633 "no clear indications as to
the . . ."
Ibid.

634 "ask enough questions to
ascertain . . ."
PHH, part 11, page 732.

634 "Do you recall whether on or
about . . ."
Ibid.

635 "Combined Fleet Operation
Order . . ."
N.A. RG 80, Pearl Harbor
Liaison Office, CNO
Documents, Box 36.

635 "The Empire is expecting
war . . ."
Ibid.

635 "Y Day will be 8 December"
Ibid.

635 "1. In the east the American
Fleet"
Ibid.

635 "Will prepare to make suitable
moves . . ."
Ibid.

635 "Japanese negotiations off . . .
Services expect action within
two weeks"
Lash, *op. cit.*, p. 473.

637 "will soon cut loose"
N.A. RG 165, Army Chief of
Staff Project Decimal File—
Philippines—WDC SA/38.

638 "the President and Mr. Hull
anticipate . . ."
Ibid.

638 "would not necessarily mean a
declaration of war"
Ibid.

638 "We know a great deal
that . . ."
Ibid.

638 "directed . . . left to your
judgment."
Ibid.

638 "attack threatening convoys"
Ibid.

638 "I would so do that"
Ibid.

Page

638 "there will be nothing left
at . . ."
Ibid.

638 "we will be over the hump."
Ibid.

638 "his Government would be
likely . . ."
PRFRUS, Japan, Vol. II,
p. 770.

638 "early aggressive movement of
some character"
PHH, part 11, p. 5214.

638 "that this next Japanese
aggression . . ."
Ibid.

638 "I have washed my hands
of it . . ."
PHH, part 14, p. 1494f.

639 "wishful thinking and gratuitous
predictions"
PHH, part 5, p. 2089.

639 "it is evident that the
Japanese . . ."
PHH, part 14, p. 1368.

639 "Precipitance of military
action . . ."
Ibid., p. 1083.

639 "this troop reinforcement to
reach . . ."
Ibid.

639 "I suggested and he approved
the idea . . ."
Ibid.

639 "THIS DISPATCH IS CONSIDERED
TO BE . . ."
Ibid., pp. 1046–1047.

639 "PHILIPPINES, THAI OR KRA
PENINSULA . . ."
Ibid.

639 "UNPREDICTABLE BUT HOSTILE
ACTION AT ANY MOMENT"
Ibid.

639 "SHOULD NOT REPEAT SHOULD
NOT . . ."
Ibid.

639 "Japanese forces and
installations . . ."
Morton, *op. cit.*, p. 67.

640 "general incendiary attacks to
burn up . . ."
Army RG 165 COS Project
Decimal File, Memo, Nov. 21,
1941, WDCSA 381.

640 "The very clearest idea
existed . . ."
Brereton, *op. cit.*, pp. 24–25.

640 "no spare parts for P-40s . . ."
Ibid.

640 "was going far beyond its war

plans."
USNOA, Asiatic Fleet,
Admiral Hart, War Diary,
Sept. 15, 1941.

640 "entirely objectionable"
Ibid., Memo, Nov. 7, 1941,
"Control of Air Operations
Over Water," from Gen.
MacArthur.

640 "the term 'Fleet' cannot be
applied . . ."
Ibid.

641 "the most embarrassing thing
that . . ."
PHH, part 16, p. 2224.

641 "any further Japanese
aggression . . ."
Lowenheim, *op. cit.*, p. 167.

641 "free countries in Europe and
Asia . . ."
N.A. Sec. of State's Files,
30-page draft of speech dated
Dec. 3, 1941.

641 "I have full confidence that
it is . . ."
Ibid.

641 "We are prepared to continue
patient"
PRFRUS, Japan, Vol. II,
pp. 770–772.

641 "the negotiation will be de
facto . . ."
N.A. RG 457, SRDJ Series,
Tokyo–Berlin, Nov. 30, 1941.

641 "there is extreme danger that
war . . ."
Ibid.

642 "THE PRESIDENT DIRECTS . . ."
Kemp Tolley, *Cruise of the
Lanikai* (Annapolis, Md.: U.S.
Naval Institute Press, 1973),
p. 265. Signal reproduced.

642 "MUST NOT APPROACH SO
AS TO . . ."
Ibid., p. 266.

643 "the time has come for
immediate . . ."
Ibid., p. 65.

643 "LEARN FROM SINGAPORE . . ."
Ibid., p. 57.

643 "WASHINGTON ALSO DIRECTED TO
DESTROY . . ."
PHH, part 6, p. 2764.

643 "What is Purple?"
Ibid.

643 "enquired on two or three
occasions . . ."
PHH, part 5, p. 2175.

644 "extreme secrecy"
Ibid., part 12, p. 262.

644 "Here is considerable
opportunity"
Ibid., pp. 268–270.

645 "HIGHLY RELIABLE INFORMATION
HAS BEEN . . ."
Ibid., p. 249.

645 "IN CASE OF EMERGENCY . . ."
Ibid., p. 154.

646 "so amended . . ."
PHH part 8, p. 3388.

646 "I can see the hand of
Providence"
N.A. RG 80, Pearl Harbor
Liaison Office. Copies of
correspondence between
Safford and Kramer.

647 "Be prudent and patient. I am
just . . ."
Ibid.

647 "not sent in the manner
prescribed . . ."
Ibid.

647 "It's in"
PHH, part 1, p. 79.

648 "BREAK IN RELATIONS BETWEEN
JAPAN . . ."
PHH, part 1, p. 80.

648 "sudden reverse of policy . . ."
USNOA, Asiatic Fleet, Hart
Records. Minutes of meeting,
Dec. 6.

649 "all transmissions
intercepted . . ."
N.A. RG 457, SRH 051,
Interview with Ralph T.
Briggs, June 13, 1977.

650 "The fact that service calls
lasted . . ."
PHH, part 10, p. 4838.

650 "the fact that they were never
addressed . . ."
Ibid.

651 "entirely inadequate"
N.A. RG 18 (U.S. Army Air
Force), Central Decimal File
337, Memo, Aug. 20, 1941, to
General Arnold from U.S.
Air Center Hawaii.

651 "The Army Air Force units are
at present . . ."
Ibid.

651 "The early morning attack
is . . ."
Ibid.

651 "I prepared my meager
forces . . ."
MacArthur, *op. cit.*, p. 111.

652 "Nothing would please me
better . . ."

Page

USNOA, Asiatic Fleet,
Report of Conferences, Dec.
6, 1941.

652 "in the nature of . . . defend
this place"
Ibid.

653 "They've got all they need now"
Brereton, *op. cit.*, p. 35.

653 "The next time they won't
play . . ."
Ibid.

653 "Our Air Force in the
Philippines . . ."
James, *op. cit.*, Vol. II, p. 12.

654 "the American planes would
take refuge . . ."
U.S. Strategic Bombing
Survey, Gen. Shimoda,

*Japanese Naval Air
Operations in the Philippines
Invasion*, p. 7.

654 "on 20th last month a U.S.
plane . . ."
N.A. RG 457, SRDJ Series,
Tokyo–Washington, Dec. 3,
1941.

655 "Maybe you think it didn't
surprise us . . ."
A. Kendrick, *Prime Time—
Edward R. Murrow* (Boston:
Little, Brown, 1969), p. 239.

655 "If I had been caught with my
planes . . . squarely in the eye."
Claire Chennault, *Way of a*

Fighter (New York, 1949),
p. 124.

655 "our generals and leaders
committed one . . ."
Edgar D. Whitcomb, *Escape
from Corregidor* (Chicago:
Univ. of Chicago Press, 1958),
p. 23.

655 "on the ground, by God, on the
ground"
Kendrick, *op. cit.*, p. 239.

656 "Achtung, Werning Aleute!"
New Yorker, Nov. 22, 1941,
p. 86.

656 "double cross"
Ibid., p. 100.

656 "Early in the afternoon . . ."
N.A. RG 457, SRH 51

Bibliography

OFFICIAL HISTORIES

U.S. Dept. of the Army. Office of Military History. *United States Army in World War II Series.*

Australia in the War of 1939–1945. Canberra, Australian War Memorial, 1952–1968. Series.

History of the Second World War: United Kingdom Military Series.

Butler, James R. M. *Grand Strategy,* Vol. II, *September 1939–June 1941* (London, 1957). Vol. III, *June 1941–August 1942* (London, 1964).

Craven, Wesley F. and James L. Cate, eds. *The Army Air Forces in World War II* (Chicago, 1948–58). Vol. 1, *Plans and Early Operations, January 1939 to August 1942* (1948). Vol. 4, *The Pacific: Guadalcanal to Saipan, August 1942 to July 1944* (1950). Vol. 5, *The Pacific: Matterhorn to Nagasaki, June 1944 to August 1945* (1953).

Dexter, David. *The New Guinea Offensives* (Canberra, 1961).

Gill, George H. *Royal Australian Navy, 1939–1942* (Canberra, 1957).

Gillison, Douglas. *Royal Australian Navy, 1942–1945* (Canberra, 1968).

Kirby, Stanley Woodburn, et al., *The War Against Japan.* Vol. 2 (London, 1958). Vol. 3 (London, 1961). Vol. 4 (London, 1965). Vol. 5 (London, 1969).

Leighton, Richard M. *Global Logistics and Strategy: 1940–1943* (Washington, D.C., 1955).

Long, Gavin M. *The Final Campaigns* (Canberra, 1963).

McCarthy, Dudley. *Southwest Pacific Area—First Year: Kokoda to Wau* (Canberra, 1959).

Matloff, Maurice and Edwin M. Snell. *Strategic Planning for Coalition Warfare: 1941–1942* (Washington, D.C., 1953).

Matloff, Maurice. *Strategic Planning for Coalition Warfare: 1943–1944* (Washington, D.C., 1959).

Miller, John. *Cartwheel: The Reduction of Rabaul* (Washington, D.C., 1959).

Milner, Samuel. *Victory in Papua* (Washington, D.C., 1957).

Morison, Samuel Eliot. *History of the United States Naval Operations in World War II* (Boston, 1947–62).

Vol. 3, *The Rising Sun in the Pacific, 1931–April 1942* (1948). Vol. 4, *Coral Sea, Midway, Submarine Actions, May 1942–August 1942* (1949). Vol. 6, *Breaking the Bismarck's Barrier, July 22, 1942–May 1, 1944* (1950). Vol. 8, *New Guinea and the Marianas, March 1944–August 1944* (1953). Vol. 12, *Leyte, June 1944–January 1945* (1958). Vol. 13, *The Liberation of the Philippines: Luzon, Mindanao, the Visayas, 1944–1945* (1959). Vol. 14, *Victory in the Pacific, 1945* (1960).

Morton, Louis. *The Fall of the Philippines* (Washington, D.C., 1953).

————. *Strategy and Command: The First Two Years* (Washington, D.C., 1962).

Odgers, George. *Air War Against Japan, 1943–1945* (Canberra, 1957).

Roskill, S. W. *The War at Sea*, Vols. 1–3 (London, 1954–61).

Smith, Robert R. *Triumph in the Philippines* (Washington, D.C., 1963).

Stauffer, Alvin P. *The Quartermaster Corps: Operations in the War Against Japan* (Washington, D.C., 1956).

Walker, Allan S. *The Island Campaigns* (Canberra, 1957).

OTHER SOURCES CONSULTED

Adams, Brooks. *America's Economic Supremacy* (New York, 1900).

Adams, Henry H. *1942: The Year That Doomed the Axis* (New York, 1967).

Adler, S. *The Isolationist Impulse* (New York, 1960).

Agawa, Hiroyuki. *The Reluctant Admiral: Yamamoto and the Imperial Navy* (New York, 1979).

Allen, H. C. *Great Britain and the United States* (London, 1954).

Allen, L. *Singapore, 1941–1942* (London, 1977).

Anders, L. *The Ledo Road* (Norman, Okla., 1965).

Arnold, H. H. *Global Mission* (New York, 1949).

Avon, Lord. *Memoirs: The Reckoning* (London, 1965).

Bailey, Ronald H. *The Home Front, USA* (Alexandria, Va., 1977).

Bailyn, Bernard, et al. *The Great Republic* (Boston, 1977).

Baldwin, Hanson Weightman. *Battles Lost and Won: Great Campaigns of World War II* (New York, 1966).

Barber, Nöel. *A Sinister Twilight: The Fall of Singapore* (Boston, 1968).

Bauer, Eddy. *The History of World War II* (London, 1979).

Beale, Howard Kennedy. *Theodore Roosevelt and the Rise of America to World Power* (Baltimore, 1956).

Beard, Charles A. *American Foreign Policy in the Making, 1932–1940* (New Haven, Conn., 1948).

Beitzell, R. *The Uneasy Alliance: America, Britain and Russia, 1941–1943* (New York, 1972).

Bell, Roger John. *Unequal Allies: Australian-American Relations and the Pacific War* (Carlton, Victoria, 1977).

Beloff, M. *Imperial Sunset*, Vol. 1 (London, 1969).

Belote, James H. and William M. Belote. *Titans of the Seas: The De-*

velopment and Operations of Japanese and American Carrier Task Forces During World War ll (New York, 1975).

Bergamini, David. Japan's Imperial Conspiracy (New York, 1971).

Berle, B. and T. Jacobs, eds. Navigating the Rapids: From the Papers of Adolf A. Berle (New York, 1973).

Bernstein, Barton J. and Allen J. Materson, eds. The Truman Administration: A Documentary History (New York, 1966).

Birkenhead, Lord. Halifax (London, 1965).

Bishop, James Alonzo. FDR's Last Year: April 1944–April 1945 (New York, 1974).

Blair, Clay. Silent Victory: The U.S. Submarine War Against Japan (Philadelphia, 1975).

Blum, J. M. From the Morgenthau Diaries: Years of War, 1941–45 (Boston, 1967).

———. Roosevelt and Morgenthau (Boston, 1970).

———. The Price of Vision: The Diary of Henry A. Wallace, 1942–1946 (Boston, 1973).

Bond, B., ed. Chief of Staff: The Diaries of Lt. General Sir Henry Pownall, Vol. 2 (London, 1974).

Borg, Dorothy and Shumpei Okamoto, eds. Pearl Harbor as History: Japanese-American Relations, 1931–1941 (New York, 1973).

Borg, D. The United States and the Far Eastern Crisis of 1933–1938 (Cambridge, Mass., 1964).

Boyle, J. H. China and Japan at War. 1937–1945 (Stanford, 1972).

Braisted, William Reynolds. The United States Navy in the Pacific 1897–1909, Vol. I (Austin, 1958).

Brereton, Lewis Hyde. The Brereton Diaries: The War in the Air in the Pacific, Middle East and Europe, 3 October 1941–8 May 1945 (New York, 1946).

———. The Turn of the Tide, 1939–1943: A study Based on the Diaries and Autobiographical Notes of Field Marshall, the Viscount Alanbrooke (London, 1957).

Bryant, Arthur. Triumph in the West, 1943–1946 (London, 1959).

Buell, Thomas B. The Quiet Warrior: A Biography of Admiral Raymond A. Spruance (Boston, 1974).

Buhite, R. D. Patrick Hurley and American Foreign Policy (Ithaca, N.Y., 1973).

Bunker, John Gorley. Liberty Ships: The Ugly Ducklings of World War II (Annapolis, 1972).

Burns, James MacGregor. Roosevelt: The Soldier of Freedom (New York, 1970).

———. Roosevelt: The Soldier of Freedom, 1940–1945 (London, 1971).

Butow, Robert Joseph Charles. The John Doe Associates: Backdoor Diplomacy for Peace, 1941 (Stanford, 1974).

———. Tojo and the Coming of War (Princeton, 1961).

———. Japan's Decision to Surrender (Stanford, 1954).

Cadogan, Alexander. The Diaries of Sir A. Cadogan, O.M., 1938–1945 (New York, 1972).

Caidin, Martin. Flying Forts (New York, 1968).

———. A Torch to the Enemy: The Fire Raid on Tokyo (New York, 1960).

Calvocoressi, P. and G. Wint. *Total War* (London, 1972).

Carver, Michael, ed. *The War Lords: Military Commanders of the Twentieth Century* (Boston, 1976).

Cave Brown, Anthony and Charles B. MacDonald. *The Secret History of the Atomic Bomb* (New York, 1977).

Challener, Richard D. *Admirals, Generals, and American Foreign Policy, 1898–1914* (Princeton, 1973).

Chapman, F. S. *The Jungle Is Neutral* (London, 1949).

Chennault, C. L. *Way of a Fighter* (New York, 1949).

Churchill, Winston Leonard Spencer. *The Second World War*. Vols. I–VI (Boston, 1948–53). *The Gathering Storm, Vol. I. Their Finest Hour, Vol. II. The Grand Alliance, Vol. III. The Hinge of Fate, Vol. IV. Closing the Ring, Vol. V. Triumph and Tragedy, Vol. VI.*

Clark, Ronald William. *The Man Who Broke Purple: The Life of the World's Greatest Cryptologist, Colonel William F. Friedman* (London, 1977).

Cline, Ray S. *Washington Command Post: The Operation Division*, in the series *United States Army in World War II* (Washington, D.C., 1951).

Coffey, Thomas M. *Imperial Tragedy: Japan in World War II, the First Days and the Last* (New York, 1970).

Caffrey, Kate. *Out in the Midday Sun: Singapore 1941–45* (New York, 1973).

Coggins, Jack. *The Campaign for Guadalcanal: A Battle That Made History* (Garden City, N.Y., 1972).

Cole, Wayne S. *Charles A. Lindbergh and the Battle Against American Intervention in World War II* (New York, 1974).

Collier, Basil. *The War in the Far East, 1941–1945* (New York, 1969).

Collis, M. *First and Last in Burma* (London, 1956).

Connell, J. *Wavell, Scholar and Soldier: To June 1941* (London, 1964).

Corson, William R. *The Armies of Ignorance: The Rise of the American Intelligence Empire* (New York, 1977).

Costello, John and Terry Hughes. *Jutland, 1916* (New York, 1977).

Craigie, Sir Robert Leslie. *Behind the Japanese Mask* (London, 1945).

Crowley, James B., ed. *Modern East Asia: Essays in Interpretation* (New York, 1970).

Dallek, Robert. *Franklin D. Roosevelt and American Foreign Policy, 1932–1945* (New York, 1979).

Davis, George Thomas. *A Navy Second to None: The Development of Modern American Naval Policy* (Westport, Conn., 1971).

Davis, Kenneth Sydney. *Experience of War: The United States in World War II* (New York, 1965).

Deane, J. R. *The Strange Alliance* (London, 1947).

Dilks, D., ed. *The Diaries of Sir Alexander Cadogan* (London, 1971).

Donovan, Robert J. *Conflict and Crisis: The Presidency of Harry S. Truman, 1945–1948* (New York, 1977).

Dull, Paul S. *A Battle History of the Imperial Japanese Navy, 1941–1945* (Annapolis, 1978).

BIBLIOGRAPHY

Edmonds, Walter D. *They Fought With What They Had* (Boston, 1951).

Eichelberger, R. L. *Our Jungle Road to Tokyo* (New York, 1950).

Eldridge, F. *Wrath in Burma* (New York, 1946).

Esthus, Raymond A. *Theodore Roosevelt and Japan* (Seattle, 1966).

Falk, Stanley Lawrence. *Seventy Days to Singapore* (New York, 1975).

Faragó, Ladislas. *The Broken Seal: The Story of Operation Magic and the Pearl Harbor Disaster* (New York, 1967).

Feiling, Keith. *The Life of Neville Chamberlain* (London, 1946).

Feis, H. *Between War and Peace* (Princeton, 1950).

———. *The China Tangle* (Princeton, 1972).

———. *Churchill, Roosevelt and Stalin* (Princeton, 1967).

———. *Japan Subdued* (Princeton, 1961).

———. *The Road to Pearl Harbor* (Princeton, 1971).

Fest, Joachim C. *Hitler* (New York, 1974).

Fillmore, Millard. *Millard Fillmore Papers: Buffalo Historical Society Publications*, Vols. 10–11 (Buffalo, 1907).

Fleet, Eric A. *The Coastwatchers* (New York, 1979).

Freidel, F. *Franklin D. Roosevelt: The Apprenticeship* (Boston, 1952).

———. *Franklin D. Roosevelt: The Ordeal* (Boston, 1954).

———. *Franklin D. Roosevelt: The Triumph* (Boston, 1956).

Fuchida, Mitsuo and Masatake Okumiya. *Midway: The Battle That Doomed Japan* (Annapolis, 1955).

Garfield, Brian Wynne. *The Thousand-Mile War: World War II in Alaska and the Aleutians* (Garden City, N.Y., 1969).

Gilbert, Martin. *Winston S. Churchill.* Vol. V: *1922–1939, The Prophet of Truth* (Boston, 1977).

Glines, Carroll V. *The United States Air Force* (New York, 1973).

———. *Doolittle's Tokyo Raiders* (Princeton, 1964).

Gowing, M. *Britain and Atomic Energy, 1939–1945* (London, 1964).

Greenfield, Kent Roberts. *American Strategy in World War II* (Baltimore, 1963).

Grenfell, Russell. *Main Fleet to Singapore* (London, 1951).

Grenville, John Ashley Soames and George B. Young. *Politics, Strategy, and American Diplomacy: Studies in Foreign Policy, 1873–1917* (New Haven, Conn., 1966).

Grew, Joseph Clark. *Ten Years in Japan* (New York, 1944).

———. *Turbulent Era: A Diplomatic Record of Forty Years, 1904–1945* (Boston, 1952).

Groves, Leslie R. *Now It Can Be Told: The Story of the Manhattan Project* (New York, 1962).

Guillain, Robert. *Le Peuple Japonais et la Guerre: Choses Vues, 1939–1946* (Paris, 1947).

Hall, W. H. D. *North American Supply* (London, 1955).

Halsey, William F. and Joseph J. Bryan III. *Admiral Halsey's Story* (New York, 1947).

Harriman, Averell and Elie Abel. *Special Envoy to Churchill and Stalin, 1941–1946* (New York, 1975).

Hart, Robert A. *The Great White Fleet* (Boston, 1965).

Hassett, W. D. *Off the Record with F.D.R.* (New Brunswick, N.J., 1958).

Havens, Thomas R. *Valley of Darkness: The Japanese People and World War II* (New York, 1978).

Hearings Before the Joint Committee on the Investigation of the Pearl Harbor Attack. 39 vols. (Washington, D.C., 1946).

Heinl, Robert Debs. *Soldiers of the Sea: The U.S. Marine Corps, 1775–1962* (Annapolis, 1962).

Herzog, James H. *Closing the Open Door: American-Japanese Diplomatic Negotiations, 1936–1941* (Annapolis, 1973).

Hicken, Victor. *The American Fighting Man* (New York, 1969).

Hinsley, Francis Harry, et al. *British Intelligence in the Second World War: Its Influence on Strategy and Operations* (New York, 1979).

Holmes, Graeme M. *Britain and America—A Comparative Economic History, 1850–1939* (Newton Abbot, England, 1976).

Holmes, Wilfred Jay. *Double-Edged Secrets: U.S. Naval Intelligence Operations in the Pacific During World War II* (Annapolis, 1979).

Hough, Frank Olney. *The Island War: The U.S. Marine Corps in the Pacific* (Philadelphia, 1947).

Hough, Richard. *The Death of the Battleship* (New York, 1963).

Howe, Quincy. *Ashes of Victory: World War II and Its Aftermath* (New York, 1972).

Hoyt, Edwin Palmer. *The Battle of Leyte Gulf: The Death Knell of the Japanese Fleet* (New York, 1972).

———. *Blue Skies and Blood: The Battle of the Coral Sea* (New York, 1975).

———. *How They Won the War in the Pacific* (New York, 1970).

———. *The Lonely Ships: The Life and Death of the U.S. Asiatic Fleet* (New York, 1976).

Hughes, Terry and John Costello. *The Battle of the Atlantic* (London, 1977).

Hull, Cordell. *The Memoirs of Cordell Hull* (New York, 1948).

Hyam, Ronald. *Britain's Imperial Century, 1815–1914* (New York, 1976).

Hyde, H. M. *The Quiet Canadian* (London, 1962).

Ickes, Harold L. *The Secret Diary of Harold L. Ickes.* Vol. 3, *The Lowering Clouds* (New York, 1954).

Ienaga, Saburo. *The Pacific War: World War II and the Japanese, 1931–1945* (New York, 1978).

Ike, Nobutaka, ed. *Japan's Decision for War: Records of the 1941 Policy Conferences* (Stanford, 1967).

Ikle, Frank William. *German-Japanese Relations, 1936–1940* (New York, 1956).

Ind, Allison. *Bataan, the Judgment Seat: The Saga of the Philippine Command of the United States Army Air Force, May 1941 to May 1942* (New York, 1944).

Inoguchi, Rikihei, Tadashi Nakajima and Roger Pineau. *The Divine*

Wind: Japan's Kamikaze Force in World War II (Westport, Conn., 1978).

Iriye, A. *Across the Pacific* (New York, 1967).

———. *Pacific Estrangement* (Cambridge, Mass., 1971).

Ismay, Lord. *Memoirs* (London, 1960).

Israel, F. L., ed. *The War Diary of Breckenridge Long* (Lincoln, Nebr., 1966).

Jablonski, Edward. *Flying Fortress: The Illustrated Biography of the B-17s and the Men Who Flew Them* (New York, 1965).

Jacobsen, Hans Adolf. *World War II: Policy and Strategy* (Santa Barbara, Calif., 1979).

James, Dorris Clayton. *The Years of MacArthur* (Boston, 1970–75). Vol. 2.

Johnston, George Henry. *New Guinea Diary* (London, 1944).

———. *Pacific Partner* (New York, 1944).

———. *The Toughest Fighting in the World* (New York, 1943).

Jones, Francis Clifford. *Japan's New Order in East Asia: Its Rise and Fall, 1937–1945* (London, 1954).

Jungk, Robert. *Brighter Than A Thousand Suns: A Personal History of the Atomic Scientists* (New York, 1958).

Kahn, David. *The Codebreakers: The Story of Secret Writing* (London, 1967).

Karig, Walter and Welbourn Kelly. *Battle Report: Pearl Harbor to Coral Sea* (New York, 1944).

Kato, Masuo. *The Lost War* (New York, 1946).

Kemp, Tolley. *The Cruise of the Lanikai* (Annapolis, 1973).

Kennan, George F. *American Diplomacy, 1900–1950* (Chicago, 1951).

———. *Memoirs, 1925–1950* (London, 1968).

Kennedy, Paul M. *The Rise and Fall of British Naval Mastery* (New York, 1976).

Kenney, George Churchill. *General Kinney Reports: A Personal History of the Pacific War* (New York, 1949).

Kimball, W., ed. *Franklin D. Roosevelt and the World Crisis, 1937–1945* (Lexington, Mass., 1973).

———, ed. *The Most Unsordid Act* (Baltimore, 1969).

Kimmel, Husband E. *Admiral Kimmel's Story* (Chicago, 1955).

King, Ernest J. and Walter Muir Whitehill. *Fleet Admiral King: A Naval Record* (New York, 1952).

Kirby, S. W. *Singapore: The Chain of Disaster* (London, 1971).

Kubek, A. *How the Far East Was Lost* (Chicago, 1953).

Land, Emory Scott. *Winning the War with Ships* (New York, 1958).

Langer, William L. and Everett S. Gleason. *The Challenge to Isolation* (New York, 1952).

———. *The Undeclared War, 1940–41* (New York, 1953).

Lash, Joseph P. *Roosevelt and Churchill, 1939–1941* (New York, 1976).

Lea, Bradford A. *Britain and the Sino-Japanese War: 1937–1939* (Stanford, 1973).

Leahy, W. D. *I Was Here* (London, 1950).

Lewin, Ronald. *Churchill as Warlord* (London, 1973).

———. *Ultra Goes to War: The First Account of World War II's Greatest Secret Based on Official Documents* (New York, 1978).

———. *Slim: The Standardbearer* (London, 1976).

Lilienthal, David Eli. *The Journals of David E. Lilienthal*. Vol. 2, *The Atomic Energy Years* (New York, 1964).

Lingeman, R. *Don't You Know There's a War On?* (New York, 1970).

Link, Arthur Stanley. *Wilson*. Vol. 3, *The Struggle for Neutrality, 1914–1915* (Princeton, 1960).

Lippmann, W. *United States War Aims* (London, 1944).

Livingston, Jon, ed. *The Japan Reader*. Vol. I, *Imperial Japan, 1800–1945* (New York, 1973).

Lord, Walter. *Day of Infamy* (New York, 1957).

———. *Incredible Victory* (New York, 1967).

———. *Lonely Vigil: Coastwatchers of the Solomons* (New York, 1977).

Louis, William Roger. *British Strategy in the Far East, 1919–1939* (Oxford, 1971).

Lowe, Cedric James. *The Reluctant Imperialists*. Vol. I, *British Foreign Policy, 1878–1902* (London, 1967).

Lowe, P. *Great Britain and Japan, 1911–1915* (London, 1969).

———. *Great Britain and the Origins of the Pacific War* (Oxford, 1977).

Lowenheim, F. L., ed. *Roosevelt and Churchill: Their Secret Wartime Correspondence* (New York, 1975).

Lundstrom, John B. *The First South Pacific Campaign* (Annapolis, 1976.)

MacArthur, Douglas. *Reminiscences* (New York, 1964).

McCormick, Thomas Joseph. *The China Market* (Chicago, 1967).

MacKenzie, Compton. *Eastern Epic* (London, 1951).

Macmillan, H. *The Blast of War, 1939–1945* (London, 1967).

Mahan, Alfred Thayer. *From Sail to Steam: Recollections of Naval Life* (New York, 1907).

———. *The Interest of America in Sea Power, Present and Future* (Boston, 1898).

Manchester, William Raymond. *American Caesar: Douglas MacArthur, 1880–1964* (Boston, 1978).

———. *Goodbye Darkness: A Memoir of the Pacific War* (Boston, 1980).

Mashbir, Sidney Forrester. *I Was an American Spy* (New York, 1953)

Maxwell, N. *India's China War* (London, 1970).

Mayo, Lida. *Bloody Buna* (Garden City, N.Y., 1974).

Mellnik, Stephen Michael. *Philippine Diary, 1939–1945* (New York, 1969).

Melville, Herman. *Typee: A Romance of the South Seas* (New York, 1920).

Merrill, James M. *A Sailor's Admiral: A Biography of William F. Halsey* (New York, 1976).

Middlebrook, Martin. *Battleship: The Loss of the Prince Wales and the Repulse* (London, 1977).

Miles, M. E. *A Different Kind of War* (New York, 1967).

Millar, Thomas Bruce. *Australia in Peace and War: External Relations, 1788–1977* (New York, 1978).

Miller, Nathan. *The U.S. Navy* (New York, 1977).

Millis, W., ed. *The Forrestal Diaries* (London, 1952).

Millis, Walter. *This Is Pearl!* (New York, 1947).

Moon, P., ed. *Wavell: The Viceroy's Journal* (London, 1973).

Moran, Lord. *Winston Churchill: The Struggle for Survival, 1940–1965* (London, 1966).

Morison, Elting Elmore. *Turmoil and Tradition: A Study of the Life and Times of Henry L. Stimson* (Boston, 1960).

Morison, Samuel Eliot. *Old Bruin: Commodore Matthew C. Perry, 1794–1858* (Boston, 1960).

Morton, L. *Strategy and Command: The First Two Years* (Washington, D.C., 1962).

Moser, Don. *China, Burma, India* (Alexandria, Va., 1978).

Mosley, Leonard O. *Hirohito, Emperor of Japan* (Englewood Cliffs, N.J., 1966).

Myers, William Starr. *The Foreign Policies of Herbert Hoover, 1929–1933* (New York, 1940).

Neu, Charles E. *The Troubled Encounter: The United States and Japan* (New York, 1975).

Nixon, Edgar B., ed. *Franklin D. Roosevelt and Foreign Affairs* (Cambridge, 1969).

O'Connor, Richard. *Pacific Destiny: An Informal History of the U.S. in the Far East, 1776–1968* (Boston, 1969).

Ogburn, Charlton. *The Marauders* (New York, 1959).

Okumiya, Masatake and Jiro Horikoshi with Martin Caidin. *Zero* (New York, 1956).

Pacific Rivals: A Japanese View of Japanese-American Relations, by the Staff of the Asahi Shimbun (New York, 1972).

Parish, Thomas D., ed. *The Simon and Schuster Encyclopedia of World War II* (New York, 1978).

Peers, W., and D. Brelis. *Behind the Burma Road* (London, 1964).

Percival, Arthur Ernest. *The War in Malaya* (London, 1949).

Perry, Hamilton Darby. *The Panay Incident: Prelude to Pearl Harbor* (New York, 1969).

Plesur, Milton. *America's Outward Thrust: Approaches to Foreign Affairs, 1865–1890* (DeKalb, 1971).

Pogue, Forrest C. *George C. Marshall: Ordeal and Hope, 1939–1942* (New York, 1966).

———. *George C. Marshall: Organizer of Victory, 1943–1945* (New York, 1973).

Popov, Dusko. *Spy/Counterspy: The Autobiography of Dusko Popov* (New York, 1974).

Potter, Elmer Belmont. *Nimitz* (Annapolis, 1976).

Potter, E. B. and Chester W. Nimitz. *Triumph in the Pacific* (New Jersey, 1963).

Rauch, Basil. *Roosevelt, From Munich to Pearl Harbor: A Study in the Creation of a Foreign Policy* (New York, 1975).

Reischauer, Edwin Oldfather. *The Japanese* (Cambridge, 1977).

Repington, Charles à Court. *After the War* (Boston, 1922).

Reynolds, Clark G. *Command of the Sea* (New York, 1974).

———. *The Fast Carriers: The Forging of an Air Navy* (New York, 1968).

Romanus, Charles F. and Riley Sunderland. *Stilwell's Mission to China* (Washington, D.C., 1953).

———. *Stilwell's Command Problems* (Washington, D.C., 1956).

———. *Time Runs Out in C.B.I.* (Washington, D.C., 1959).

Roosevelt, Keimet. *War Report of the Office of Strategic Services* (New York, 1976).

Rosenman, S. I. *Working with Roosevelt* (London, 1952).

Roskill, S. W. *British Naval Policy Between the Wars*, Vol. 1 (London, 1968). Vol. 2 (London, 1976).

Sawyer, Leonard Arthur and W. H. Mitchell. *The Liberty Ships: The History of the·"Emergency" Type Cargo Ships Constructed in the U.S. During World War II* (Cambridge, Mass., 1970).

Schram, S. *Mao Tse-tung* (London, 1967).

Seth, Ronald. *Secret Servants: A History of Japanese Espionage* (New York, 1957).

Sherrod, Robert L. *On to Westward: War in the Central Pacific* (New York, 1945).

Sherrod, Robert. *Tarawa: The Story of a Battle* (New York, 1975).

Sherwin, Martin J. *A World Destroyed: The Atomic Bomb and the Grand Alliance* (New York, 1975).

Sherwood, Robert. *Roosevelt and Hopkins: An Intimate History* (New York, 1948).

Shigemitsu, Mamoru. *Japan and Her Destiny* (London, 1958).

Shirer, William Lawrence. *The Rise and Fall of the Third Reich: A History of Nazi Germany* (New York, 1960).

Shiroyama, Saburo. *War Criminal: The Life and Death of Hirota Koki* (New York, 1977).

———. *Defeat into Victory* (New York, 1961).

Smedley, A. *Battle Hymn of China* (London, 1943).

Smith, G. *American Diplomacy During the Second World War* (New York, 1965).

Smith, Holland McTyerie. *Coral and Brass* (New York, 1949).

Smith, Stanley E., ed. *The United States Navy in World War II* (New York, 1966).

———. *The United States Marine Corps in World War II* (New York, 1969).

Sprout, Harold H. and Margaret Sprout. *Toward a New Order of Sea Power: American Naval Policy and the World Scene, 1918–1922* (Princeton, 1940).

———. *The Rise of American Naval Power, 1776–1918* (Princeton, 1966).

Steinberg, Rafael. *Island Fighting* (Alexandria, Va., 1979).

———. *Return to the Philippines* (Alexandria, Va., 1979).

Stettinius, E. R. *Roosevelt and the Russians* (London, 1950).

Stevenson, William. *A Man Called Intrepid: The Secret War* (New York, 1977).

Stimson, Henry Lewis and McGeorge Bundy. *On Active Service in Peace and War* (New York, 1948).

Strong, Josiah. *Our Country: Its Possible Future and Its Present Crisis* (New York, 1885).

Sulzberger, Cyrus Leo, et al., eds. *The American Heritage Picture History of World War II* (New York, 1966).

Swinson, A. J. *Defeat in Malaya* (New York, 1970).

Sykes, Christopher. *Orde Wingate* (London, 1959).

Tanaka, R. *Japan's Losing Struggle for Guadalcanal* (Annapolis, 1956).

Tansill, Charles C. *Back Door to War: The Roosevelt Foreign Policy, 1933–1941* (Chicago, 1952).

Theobald, Robert A. *The Final Secret of Pearl Harbor* (New York, 1954).

Thomas, Gordon and Max Morgen Witts. *Enola Gay* (New York, 1977).

Thompson, R. W., ed. *Churchill and Morton* (London, 1976).

Thorne, Christopher. *Allies of a Kind —The United States, Britain and the War Against Japan, 1941–1945* (Oxford, 1978).

Togo, Shigenori. *The Cause of Japan* (New York, 1956).

Toland, John. *But Not in Shame: The Six Months after Pearl Harbor* (London, 1961).

———. *The Rising Sun: The Decline and Fall of the Japanese Empire, 1936–1945* (New York, 1970).

Tolischus, Otto D. *Tokyo Record* (New York, 1943).

Trask, David F. *Captains & Cabinets —Anglo-American Relations, 1917–1919* (Missouri, MO., 1972).

Tregaskis, Richard William. *Guadalcanal Diary* (New York, 1943).

Truman, H. S. *Years of Decisions, 1945* (London, 1955).

Tsuji, Masanobu. *Singapore: The Japanese Version* (Sydney, 1960).

Tuchman, Barbara. *Stilwell and the American Experience in China, 1911–1945* (New York, 1970).

Tugwell, R. *In Search of Roosevelt* (Cambridge, Mass., 1972).

Tuleja, Thaddeus V. *Statesmen and Admirals: Quest for a Far Eastern Naval Policy* (New York, 1963).

Underbrink, Robert L. *Destination Corregidor* (Annapolis, 1971).

United States Strategic Bombing Survey: Interrogations of Japanese Officials, Vols. I and II (Washington, D.C., 1946). *Japanese Air Power* (Washington, D.C., 1946). *Japanese Military and Naval Intelligence Division* (Washington, D.C., 1946) *Summary Report* (Washington, D.C., 1946).

Van Alstyne, Richard. *Missionaries, Chinese and Diplomats* (Princeton, 1958).

———. *The United States in East Asia* (New York, 1973).

Van Der Rhoer, Edward. *Deadly Magic: A Personal Account of Communication Intelligence in World War II in the Pacific* (New York, 1978).

Varg, P. *Missionaries, Chinese and Diplomats* (Princeton, 1958).

———. *The Making of a Myth: The United States and China, 1897–1912* (East Lansing, Mich., 1968).

Waller, George Macgregor. *Pearl Harbor: Roosevelt and the Coming of the War* (Boston, 1953).

Wallin, Homer Norman. *Pearl Harbor: Why, How, Fleet Salvage and*

Final Appraisal (Washington, D.C., 1968).

Wedemeyer, A. C. *Wedemeyer Reports!* (New York, 1958).

Welles, S. *A Time for Decision* (London, 1947).

Wheeler, G. C. *Prelude to Pearl Harbor* (Columbia, Mo., 1963).

Wheeler, Keith. *The Road to Tokyo* (Alexandria, Va., 1979).

Wheeler-Bennett, J., ed. *Action This Day: Working with Churchill* (London, 1968).

White, Theodore H., ed. *The Stilwell Papers* (New York, 1948).

———, and A. Jacoby. *Thunder Out of China* (London, 1947).

Wigmore, Lionel. *The Japanese Imperial Thrust* (Canberra, 1957).

Williams, William Appleman. *The Tragedy of American Diplomacy* (Cleveland, 1959).

Willoughby, C. A. *Shanghai Conspiracy* (New York, 1952).

Wilson, Angus. *The Strange Ride of Rudyard Kipling: His Life and Works* (New York, 1977).

Wilson, Charles. *Diaries* (Boston, 1966).

Wint, G. *The British in Asia* (New York, 1954).

Winterbotham, F. W. *The Ultra Secret* (London, 1954).

Winton, John. *The Forgotten Fleet: The British Navy in the Pacific 1944–1945* (New York, 1969).

———. *War in the Pacific: Pearl Harbor to Tokyo Bay* (London, 1978).

Wohlstetter, Roberta. *Pearl Harbor: Warning and Decision* (Stanford, 1962).

Woodward, L. *British Foreign Policy in the Second World War* (single vol., London, 1962).

Zich, Arthur. *The Rising Sun* (Alexandria, Va., 1977).

Index

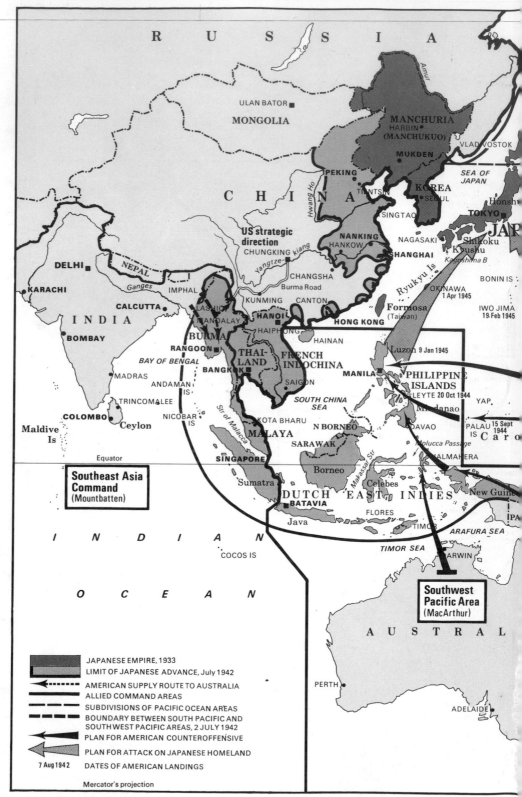

THE PACIFIC WAR—1942–45 The Allied Offensives